GENERAL HISTORY OF AFRICA · IV

Africa from the Twelfth to the Sixteenth Century

Unesco General History of Africa

Volume I	Methodology and African Prehistory (Editor J. Ki-Zerbo)
Volume II	Ancient Civilizations of Africa (Editor G. Mokhtar)
Volume III	Africa from the Seventh to Eleventh Century (Editor M. El Fasi)
Volume IV	Africa from the Twelfth to Sixteenth Century (Editor D. T. Niane)
Volume V	Africa from the Sixteenth to Eighteenth Century (Editor B. A. Ogot)
Volume VI	The Nineteenth Century until 1880 (Editor J. F. A. Ajayi)
Volume VII	Africa under Colonial Rule, 1880–1935 (Editor A. A. Boahen)
Volume VIII	Africa since 1935 (Editor A. A. Mazrui)

UNESCO International Scientific Committee for the Drafting of a General History of Africa

GENERAL HISTORY OF AFRICA · IV

Africa from the Twelfth to the Sixteenth Century

EDITOR D.T. NIANE

HEINEMANN · CALIFORNIA · UNESCO

First published 1984 by the
United Nations Educational, Scientific
and Cultural Organization,
7 Place de Fontenoy, 75700 Paris

and

Heinemann Educational Books Ltd
22 Bedford Square, London WC1B 3HH
P.M.B. 5205, Ibadan P.O. Box 45314, Nairobi
EDINBURGH MELBOURNE AUCKLAND
HONG KONG SINGAPORE KUALA LUMPUR
NEW DELHI KINGSTON PORT OF SPAIN

First published 1984
in the United States of America by the
University of California Press
2120 Berkeley Way, Berkeley
California 94720, United States of America

Heinemann Educational Books ISBN 0 435 94810 5

Unesco ISBN 92-3-101-710-1
University of California Press ISBN 0-520-03915-7

Filmset in 11 pt Monophoto Ehrhardt by
Northumberland Press Ltd, Gateshead, Tyne and Wear
Printed and bound in Great Britain by
Richard Clay (The Chaucer Press) Ltd, Bungay, Suffolk

Contents

List of figures

List of plates

Acknowledgements for plates

Arbey, J. L., 2.1, 2.2, 2.4, 2.5, 4.3
Bazin, J., 7.1
Bedaux, R. M. A., *Tellem*, 1977, 6.8–6.10
Bernheim, M. and Bernheim, E./Agence Rapho, *Afrique, continent méconnu*, Sélection du Reader's Digest, Paris, 1979, 18.3
Bibliothèque Nationale, Paris, 7.3, 12.1, 26.1
British Museum, London, 12.9–12.15
Cairo, A life story of one thousand years (969–1969), 15.4
Camps, G., *Berbères, aux marges de l'histoire*, ed. des Hespérides, 1980, 5.1
Connah, G., *The Archaeology of Benin*, 1975, 14.2
Dapper, O., *Description of Africa*, 1668, Amsterdam, 12.6–12.8
de Grunne, B., *Terres cuites anciennes de L'Ouest Africain*, Publications d'Histoire, de l'Art et d'Archéologie de l'Université Catholique de Louvain, 22, 1980, 6.11–6.16
Department of Information, Zimbabwe, cover page, 21.5
Devisse, J., 2.3, 3.1, 3.2
de Maret, P., Musée Royal de l'Afrique Centrale, 22.2–22.4
Fagan, B. M., 21.1, 21.6
Filipowiak, W., *Etudes archéologiques sur la capitale médiévale du Mali*, National Museum, Stettin, 1979, 6.6, 6.7
Forman, W., Forman, B. and Dark, P., *Benin art*, Hamlyn, London, 1960, 14.3, 14.4
Garlake, P. S., *Great Zimbabwe*, London, Thames and Hudson, 1973, 21.2–21.4
Gerster, G./Agence Rapho, *Afrique, continent méconnu*, Sélection du Reader's Digest, Paris, 1979, 17.1
Haberland, E., Frobenius Institute, 17.2–17.4
Held, André, 14.15
IFAN, from M. M. Viré, Stèles funéraires musulmanes soudano-sahariennes, *BIFAN*, 21, serie B, no. 3–4, 1959, 8.1, 8.2
IMRS, 6.1
Institut d'Histoire, d'Art et d'Archéologie Africains, Abidjan, 13.1–13.5
Jansen, Gérard, Institute of Anthropobiology, State University, Utrecht, from *Palaeohistoria*, 20, 1978, 6.1–6.5
Ly, Madina, 7.2
Michalowski, K., *Faras, fouilles polonaises*, Warsaw, University of Warsaw, 1962, 16.1, 16.2
Musée de l'homme, Paris (MH 02.28.1–28.4), 12.2–12.5
Musée Royal de l'Afrique Centrale, 22.1, 22.5
Nantet, B., 5.2
Nigeria, its archaeology and early history, London, Thames and Hudson, 1978, 14.1
Rambeloarison, from a drawing by J. P. Domenichini, 24.3
Royal Library (reference no. BN/GE AA 2004), 1.1
Shaw, T., *Igbo-Ukwu, an account of archaeology in eastern Nigeria*, 1970, 14.5–14.14
Unesco, Dominique Roger, 4.1, 4.2
Unesco/New York Graphic Society, *Ethiopia: illuminated manuscripts*, New York, 1961, 17.5–17.7
Unwin, S., 18.1, 18.2, 18.4–18.7
Vérin, P., 24.2

Werner Forman Archive, William Fagg, *Afro-Portuguese ivories*, London, 1970, 12.6–12.8
Werner Forman Archive, W. Forman, B. Forman and P. Dark, *Benin art*, London, 1960, 14.4
Wiet, G. and Hautecoeur, L., *Les Mosquées du Caire*, Paris, 1932, 15.1–15.3
Zimbabwe, Department of Information, Harare (cover)

Preface

AMADOU-MAHTAR M'BOW
Director-General of Unesco

For a long time, all kinds of myths and prejudices concealed the true history of Africa from the world at large. African societies were looked upon as societies that could have no history. In spite of important work done by such pioneers as Leo Frobenius, Maurice Delafosse and Arturo Labriola, as early as the first decades of this century, a great many non-African experts could not rid themselves of certain preconceptions and argued that the lack of written sources and documents made it impossible to engage in any scientific study of such societies.

Although the *Iliad* and *Odyssey* were rightly regarded as essential sources for the history of ancient Greece, African oral tradition, the collective memory of peoples which holds the thread of many events marking their lives, was rejected as worthless. In writing the history of a large part of Africa, the only sources used were from outside the continent, and the final product gave a picture not so much of the paths actually taken by the African peoples as of those that the authors thought they must have taken. Since the European Middle Ages were often used as a yardstick, modes of production, social relations and political institutions were visualized only by reference to the European past.

In fact, there was a refusal to see Africans as the creators of original cultures which flowered and survived over the centuries in patterns of their own making and which historians are unable to grasp unless they forgo their prejudices and rethink their approach.

Furthermore, the continent of Africa was hardly ever looked upon as a historical entity. On the contrary, emphasis was laid on everything likely to lend credence to the idea that a split had existed, from time immemorial, between a 'white Africa' and a 'black Africa', each unaware of the other's existence. The Sahara was often presented as an impenetrable space preventing any intermingling of ethnic groups and peoples or any exchange of goods, beliefs, customs and ideas between the societies that had grown up on either side of the desert. Hermetic frontiers were drawn between the civilizations of Ancient Egypt and Nubia and those of the peoples south of the Sahara.

It is true that the history of Africa north of the Sahara has been more closely linked with that of the Mediterranean basin than has the history of sub-Saharan Africa, but it is now widely recognized that the various civilizations of the African continent, for all their differing languages and cultures, represent, to a greater or lesser degree, the historical offshoots of a set of peoples and societies united by bonds centuries old.

Another phenomenon which did great disservice to the objective study of the African past was the appearance, with the slave trade and colonization, of racial stereotypes which bred contempt and lack of understanding and became so deep-rooted that they distorted even the basic concepts of historiography. From the time when the notions of 'white' and 'black' were used as generic labels by the colonialists, who were regarded as superior, the colonized Africans had to struggle against both economic and psychological enslavement. Africans were identifiable by the colour of their skin, they had become a kind of merchandise, they were earmarked for hard labour and eventually, in the minds of those dominating them, they came to symbolize an imaginary and allegedly inferior *Negro* race. This pattern of spurious identification relegated the history of the African peoples in many minds to the rank of ethno-history, in which appreciation of the historical and cultural facts was bound to be warped.

The situation has changed significantly since the end of the Second World War and in particular since the African countries became independent and began to take an active part in the life of the international community and in the mutual exchanges that are its *raison d'être*. An increasing number of historians has endeavoured to tackle the study of Africa with a more rigorous, objective and open-minded outlook by using – with all due precautions – actual African sources. In exercising their right to take the historical initiative, Africans themselves have felt a deep-seated need to re-establish the historical authenticity of their societies on solid foundations.

In this context, the importance of the eight-volume *General History of Africa*, which Unesco is publishing, speaks for itself.

The experts from many countries working on this project began by laying down the theoretical and methodological basis for the *History*. They have been at pains to call in question the over-simplifications arising from a linear and restrictive conception of world history and to re-establish the true facts wherever necessary and possible. They have endeavoured to highlight the historical data that give a clearer picture of the evolution of the different peoples of Africa in their specific socio-cultural setting.

To tackle this huge task, made all the more complex and difficult by the vast range of sources and the fact that documents were widely scattered, Unesco has had to proceed by stages. The first stage, from 1965 to 1969, was devoted to gathering documentation and planning the work. Operational assignments were conducted in the field and included campaigns to collect oral traditions, the creation of regional documentation centres for oral traditions, the collection of unpublished manuscripts in

Arabic and Ajami (African languages written in Arabic script), the compilation of archival inventories and the preparation of a *Guide to the Sources of the History of Africa*, culled from the archives and libraries of the countries of Europe and later published in nine volumes. In addition, meetings were organized to enable experts from Africa and other continents to discuss questions of methodology and lay down the broad lines for the project after careful examination of the available sources.

The second stage, which lasted from 1969 to 1971, was devoted to shaping the *History* and linking its different parts. The purpose of the international meetings of experts held in Paris in 1969 and Addis Ababa in 1970 was to study and define the problems involved in drafting and publishing the *History*: presentation in eight volumes, the principal edition in English, French and Arabic, translation into African languages such as Kiswahili, Hausa, Fulani, Yoruba or Lingala, prospective versions in German, Russian, Portuguese, Spanish and Chinese, as well as abridged editions designed for a wide African and international public.

The third stage has involved actual drafting and publication. This began with the appointment of the 39-member International Scientific Committee, two-thirds African and one-third non-African, which assumes intellectual responsibility for the *History*.

The method used is interdisciplinary and is based on a multi-faceted approach and a wide variety of sources. The first among these is archaeology, which holds many of the keys to the history of African cultures and civilizations. Thanks to archaeology, it is now acknowledged that Africa was very probably the cradle of mankind and the scene – in the neolithic period – of one of the first technological revolutions in history. Archaeology has also shown that Egypt was the setting for one of the most brilliant ancient civilizations of the world. But another very important source is oral tradition, which, after being long despised, has now emerged as an invaluable instrument for discovering the history of Africa, making it possible to follow the movements of its different peoples in both space and time, to understand the African vision of the world from the inside and to grasp the original features of the values on which the cultures and institutions of the continent are based.

We are indebted to the International Scientific Committee in charge of this *General History of Africa*, and to its Rapporteur and the editors and authors of the various volumes and chapters, for having shed a new light on the African past in its authentic and all-encompassing form and for having avoided any dogmatism in the study of essential issues. Among these issues we might cite: the slave trade, that 'endlessly bleeding wound', which was responsible for one of the cruellest mass deportations in the history of mankind, which sapped the African continent of its life-blood while contributing significantly to the economic and commercial expansion of Europe; colonization, with all the effects it had on population, economics, psychology and culture; relations between Africa south of the Sahara and the Arab world; and, finally, the process of decolonization and nation-building which mobilized the intelligence and passion of people still alive and sometimes still active today. All these issues have been broached with a concern for honesty and rigour which is not the least of the *History*'s merits. By taking stock of our knowledge of Africa, putting forward a variety of view-points on African cultures and offering a new reading of history, the *History* has the signal advantage of showing up the light and shade and of openly portraying the differences of opinion that may exist between scholars.

By demonstrating the inadequacy of the methodological approaches which have long been used in research on Africa, this *History* calls for a new and careful study of the twofold problem areas of historiography and cultural identity, which are united by links of reciprocity. Like any historical work of value, the *History* paves the way for a great deal of further research on a variety of topics.

It is for this reason that the International Scientific Committee, in close collaboration with Unesco, decided to embark on additional studies in an attempt to go deeper into a number of issues which will permit a clearer understanding of certain aspects of the African past. The findings being published in the series 'Unesco Studies and Documents – General History of Africa' will prove a useful supplement to the *History*, as will the works planned on aspects of national or subregional history.

The *General History* sheds light both on the historical unity of Africa and also its relations with the other continents, particularly the Americas and the Caribbean. For a long time, the creative manifestations of the descendants of Africans in the Americas were lumped together by some historians as a heterogeneous collection of *Africanisms*. Needless to say, this is not the attitude of the authors of the *History*, in which the resistance of the slaves shipped to America, the constant and massive participation of the descendants of Africans in the struggles for the initial independence of America and in national liberation movements, are rightly perceived for what they were: vigorous assertions of identity, which helped forge the universal concept of mankind. Although the phenomenon may vary in different places, it is now quite clear that ways of feeling, thinking, dreaming and acting in certain nations of the western hemisphere have been marked by their African heritage. The cultural inheritance of Africa is visible every-where, from the southern United States to northern Brazil, across the Caribbean and on the Pacific seaboard. In certain places it even underpins the cultural identity of some of the most important elements of the population.

The *History* also clearly brings out Africa's relations with southern Asia across the Indian Ocean and the African contributions to other civilizations through mutual exchanges.

I am convinced that the efforts of the peoples of Africa to conquer or strengthen their independence, secure their development and assert their cultural characteristics, must be rooted in historical awareness renewed, keenly felt and taken up by each succeeding generation.

My own background, the experience I gained as a teacher and as chairman, from the early days of independence, of the first commission set up to reform history and geography curricula in some of the countries of West and Central Africa, taught me how necessary it was for the education of young people and for the information of the public at large to have a history book produced by scholars with inside knowledge of the problems and hopes of Africa and with the ability to apprehend the continent in its entirety.

For all these reasons, Unesco's goal will be to ensure that this *General History of Africa* is widely disseminated in a large number of languages and is used as a basis for producing children's books, school textbooks and radio and television programmes. Young people, whether schoolchildren or students, and adults in Africa and elsewhere will thus be able to form a truer picture of the African continent's past and the factors that explain it, as well as a fairer understanding of its cultural heritage and its contribution to the general progress of mankind. The *History* should thus contribute to improved international cooperation and stronger solidarity among peoples in their aspirations to justice, progress and peace. This is, at least, my most cherished hope.

It remains for me to express my deep gratitude to the members of the International Scientific Committee, the Rapporteur, the different volume editors, the authors and all those who have collaborated in this tremendous undertaking. The work they have accomplished and the contribution they have made plainly go to show how people from different backgrounds but all imbued with the same spirit of goodwill and enthusiasm in the service of universal truth can, within the international framework provided by Unesco, bring to fruition a project of considerable scientific and cultural import. My thanks also go to the organizations and governments whose generosity has made it possible for Unesco to publish this *History* in different languages and thus ensure that it will have the worldwide impact it deserves and thereby serve the international community as a whole.

Description of the Project

B. A. OGOT

President, International Scientific Committee for the Drafting of a General History of Africa

The General Conference of Unesco at its 16th Session instructed the Director-General to undertake the drafting of a *General History of Africa*. The enormous task of implementing the project was entrusted to an International Scientific Committee which was established by the Executive Board in 1970. This Committee under the Statutes adopted by the Executive Board of Unesco in 1971, is composed of thirty-nine members (two-thirds of whom are African and one-third non-African) serving in their personal capacity and appointed by the Director-General of Unesco for the duration of the Committee's mandate.

The first task of the Committee was to define the principal characteristics of the work. These were defined at the first session of the Committee as follows:

(a) Although aiming at the highest possible scientific level, the history does not seek to be exhaustive and is a work of synthesis avoiding dogmatism. In many respects, it is a statement of problems showing the present state of knowledge and the main trends in research, and it does not hesitate to show divergencies of views where these exist. In this way, it prepares the ground for future work.
(b) Africa is considered in this work as a totality. The aim is to show the historical relationships between the various parts of the continent, too frequently subdivided in works published to date. Africa's historical connections with the other continents receive due attention, these connections being analysed in terms of mutual exchanges and multilateral influences, bringing out, in its appropriate light, Africa's contribution to the history of mankind.
(c) *The General History of Africa* is, in particular, a history of ideas and civilizations, societies and institutions. It is based on a wide variety of sources, including oral tradition and art forms.
(d) The *History* is viewed essentially from the inside. Although a scholarly work, it is also, in large measure, a faithful reflection of the way in which African authors view their own civilization. While prepared in an international framework and drawing to the full on the present stock of scientific knowledge, it should also be a vitally important element in the recognition

of the African heritage and should bring out the factors making for unity in the continent. This effort to view things from within is the novel feature of the project and should, in addition to its scientific quality, give it great topical significance. By showing the true face of Africa, the *History* could, in an era absorbed in economic and technical struggles, offer a particular conception of human values.

The Committee has decided to present the work covering over three million years of African history in eight volumes, each containing about eight hundred pages of text with illustrations, photographs, maps and line drawings.

A chief editor, assisted if necessary by one or two co-editors, is responsible for the preparation of each volume. The editors are elected by the Committee either from among its members or from outside by a two-thirds majority. They are responsible for preparing the volumes in accordance with the decisions and plans adopted by the Committee. On scientific matters, they are accountable to the Committee or, between two sessions of the Committee, to its Bureau for the contents of the volumes, the final version of the texts, the illustrations and, in general, for all scientific and technical aspects of the *History*. The Bureau ultimately approves the final manuscript. When it considers the manuscript ready for publication, it transmits it to the Director-General of Unesco. Thus the Committee, or the Bureau between Committee sessions, remains fully in charge of the project.

Each volume consists of some thirty chapters. Each chapter is the work of a principal author assisted, if necessary, by one or two collaborators. The authors are selected by the Committee on the basis of their *curricula vitae*. Preference is given to African authors, provided they have requisite qualifications. Special effort is also made to ensure, as far as possible, that all regions of the continent, as well as other regions having historical or cultural ties with Africa, are equitably represented among the authors.

When the editor of a volume has approved texts of chapters, they are then sent to all members of the Committee for criticism. In addition, the text of the volume editor is submitted for examination to a Reading Committee, set up within the International Scientific Committee on the basis of the members' fields of competence. The Reading Committee analyses the chapters from the standpoint of both substance and form. The Bureau then gives final approval to the manuscripts.

Such a seemingly long and involved procedure has proved necessary, since it provides the best possible guarantee of the scientific objectivity of the *General History of Africa*. There have, in fact, been instances when the Bureau has rejected manuscripts or insisted on major revisions or even reassigned the drafting of a chapter to another author. Occasionally, specialists in a particular period of history or in a particular question are consulted to put the finishing touches to a volume.

The work will be published first in a hard-cover edition in English, French and Arabic, and later in paperback editions in the same languages. An abridged version in English and French will serve as a basis for translation into African languages. The Committee has chosen Kiswahili and Hausa as the first African languages into which the work will be translated.

Also, every effort will be made to ensure publication of the *General History of Africa* in other languages of wide international currency such as Chinese, Portuguese, Russian, German, Italian, Spanish, Japanese, etc.

It is thus evident that this is a gigantic task which constitutes an immense challenge to African historians and to the scholarly community at large, as well as to Unesco under whose auspices the work is being done. For the writing of a continental history of Africa, covering the last three million years, using the highest canons of scholarship and involving, as it must do, scholars drawn from diverse countries, cultures, ideologies and historical traditions, is surely a complex undertaking. It constitutes a continental, international and interdisciplinary project of great proportions.

In conclusion, I would like to underline the significance of this work for Africa and for the world. At a time when the peoples of Africa are striving towards unity and greater cooperation in shaping their individual destinies, a proper understanding of Africa's past, with an awareness of common ties among Africans and between Africa and other continents, should not only be a major contribution towards mutual understanding among the people of the earth, but also a source of knowledge of a cultural heritage that belongs to all mankind.

Note on Chronology

It has been agreed to adopt the following method for writing dates. With regard to prehistory, dates may be written in two different ways.

One way is by reference to the present era, that is, dates BP (before present), the reference year being +1950; all dates are negative in relation to +1950.

The other way is by reference to the beginning of the Christian era. Dates are represented in relation to the Christian era by a simple + or − sign before the date. When referring to centuries, the terms BC and AD are replaced by 'before the Christian era' and 'of the Christian era'.

Some examples are as follows:

(i) 2300 BP = −350
(ii) 2900 BC = −2900
AD 1800 = +1800
(iii) 5th century BC = 5th century before the Christian era
3rd century AD = 3rd century of the Christian era

1 Introduction

D. T. NIANE

The present volume covers the history of Africa from the twelfth to the sixteenth century. The more traditional method of dividing the period under consideration into smaller time units seems scarcely relevant here: how can one date or one century have the same importance for a whole continent? In fact, one is led to ask whether it is really meaningful to treat the history of Africa in terms of such a period of time.

Although the problem of subdivision remains, the proposed period does in fact present a certain unity, and from more than one point of view it constitutes a crucial phase in the historical evolution of the continent as a whole. Indeed it was a very special period, in which Africa developed its original culture and assimilated outside influences while retaining its own individuality. In the preceding volume, drawing on Arabic texts, Africa was shown to emerge from obscurity with the Muslim discovery of the rich Sudan to the south of the Sahara; this area was dominated by the Soninke, whose king, or *Kaya Maghan*, controlled all the western regions of the Sudan from the Niger Bend to the Senegal estuary. This vast empire, described in all its glory by al-Bakrī, was not the only large political grouping of the time. Contemporary with it were the Songhay empire and further east, as far as Lake Chad, the countries and kingdoms of Kanem-Bornu.

Written records concerning Africa south of the Sahara become more abundant after the end of the eleventh century, and especially from the end of the thirteenth to the end of the fourteenth century. From the middle of the fifteenth century we are able to fill the gap with the aid of Portuguese sources, which tell us a good deal about the then-flourishing coastal kingdoms of West Africa – further proof that the absence of written records means virtually nothing. The Gulf of Guinea and the Congo estuary were great centres of civilization. Several major themes characterize the history of this period.

First, there was the triumph of Islam over a large part of the continent, propagated both by soldiers and by merchants. The Muslims proved to be excellent traders and came to dominate the commercial world, helping to foster progress in science, philosophy and technology wherever they settled. As far as Africa is concerned, the essential fact is that Africa imparted its own stamp on Islam both in the north and in the vast Sudan region south of the Sahara. We may recall that in the eleventh century the Almoravids, setting out from the Senegal estuary with armies which included large forces of Negroes from Takrūr, conquered parts of the Maghrib and of the Iberian peninsula and restored *sunna*, a strict Muslim orthodoxy, throughout western Islam.

Between 1050 and 1080 the Almoravids warred against the Ghana empire, which finally collapsed in 1076. There then began a sombre period of struggle for supremacy amongst the provinces of the empire. 1076 is an important date in the history both of the Maghrib and the Sudan, but at the time the fall of Koumbi Ṣāleḥ (the capital of Ghana) passed almost unnoticed because the trade in gold went on practically uninterrupted. In fact the gold trade probably increased, because certain vassal kingdoms of Ghana, namely Takrūr and Manding, which were rich in gold, together with Gao, an ancient kingdom on the eastern branch of the Niger – all of them long ago converted to Islam – continued their active trade with the Berber Arabs.

On the other side, merchants from Arabia and the Persian Gulf opened up the eastern coasts of Africa, from the Horn to Madagascar, to inter-continental trade. The rich trading settlements of Sofala, Kilwa and Mogadishu became Africa's outlets to the Indian Ocean. From Egypt, Islam advanced towards Nubia, the eastern Sudan. But here it came up against strong resistance from the old Coptic Christian kingdoms, where the stubborn determination of the Nubians temporarily halted the march of Islam along the Nile. However, from the direction of the Red Sea, and chiefly from the Horn of Africa, Islam penetrated into the interior and fostered the establishment of Muslim states encircling the Christians. The struggle between the two religions was bitter in this region, with Ethiopia embodying the resistance to Islam from the twelfth to the fifteenth century. At the end of the fifteenth and the beginning of the sixteenth century the Neguses profited from a new Christian force represented by the Portuguese.

In Chapter 17 below, Professor Tamrat emphasizes the particularly African form of Christianity which then prevailed in Ethiopia, with its no less original art and the characteristic style of its churches. King Lalibela (*c*.1181–*c*.1221), known as 'Saint Louis of Ethiopia', founded a new capital which he called 'New Jerusalem'; the pious ruler intended it as a place of pilgrimage for his subjects, since Ethiopia was cut off from the patriarchate of Alexandria and the cradle of Christianity. Monasteries sprang up all over the high plateaux of Ethiopia, and in the silence of these lofty and almost impregnable fastnesses the monks wrote the history of the kings and planned reform. In the middle of the fifteenth century Ethiopian Christianity was at its height, preserving and giving Christian form to early, pre-Christian, African religious practices. The ancient

Cushitic influence survived in festivals, dances, songs and animal sacrifices. Here, again, the African personality asserted itself, for the Christianity of Nubia and Ethiopia, like African Islam, took a completely African form.

Along the coast, from the Horn to Madagascar, an original Muslim African civilization developed around the Muslim trading settlements: the Swahili civilization. It found expression in a language of the same name, which retained the Bantu structure with many Arabic loan-words, and it was to spread all over East Africa from the coast to the great lakes, and thence gradually to the River Congo. Thus did the influence of Islam make itself felt, directly or indirectly, throughout the region.

People have often wanted to know the reasons for Islam's rapid success, not only in Africa but also elsewhere. It has to be remembered that the way of life of the nomads of Arabia was not very different from that of the Berbers and *fallāḥīn* of North Africa. In the Sudan, apart from the warlike episode of the Almoravids, Islam spread slowly and peacefully in the interior. There were no established clergy or missionaries as in the Christian West. Islam, a religion of cities and courts, did not destroy the traditional structures. Neither the kings of the Sudan nor the sultans of East Africa went to war with the purpose of converting their people. Trade was the main consideration and Islam showed enough flexibility to ask no more of the conquered peoples than that they pay taxes; thus each was able to preserve its own personality.

The second main theme of this period is closely linked to Islam and its spread. It is the amazing extension of trade relations, cultural exchanges and human contacts. From the Indus to Gibraltar, from the Red Sea to Madagascar, from North Africa to the sub-Saharan regions, men and goods circulated so freely that Robert Cornevin, writing of the economic unity of the Muslim world and African Islam's political independence of Baghdad, has said:

> In the modern world, tormented by frontiers, where one needs a passport and a visa every time one moves, it is hard to imagine this unity. Throughout the Middle Ages the Muslim pilgrim or merchant, wherever he went, from the Indus to Spain or the Sudan, found everywhere the same language, the same way of life and also the same religion, for the Kharijite and Shīʿite heresies seem to have been political rather than specifically religious.

From the twelfth to the sixteenth century, Africa became a crossroads of international trade, exercising an extraordinary attraction on the rest of the world. In Chapter 26 below, J. Devisse demonstrates eloquently that it was the Indian Ocean rather than the Mediterranean which became a kind of *mare islamicum*, until China's predominance began, based on navigation by dhows.

Inter-regional relations were equally developed. Immense caravans, some numbering as many as 6000 or even 12 000 camels, crossed the Sahara from north to south, carrying provisions and goods of all kinds. Between the savannahs of the Sudan and the forest regions farther south, from Casamance to the Gulf of Guinea, there grew a busy traffic almost unknown to the Arabs, for whom, outside the area of Gao and Mali which they knew, there was nothing but desert. Nowadays archaeology, toponymy and linguistics help us to a better understanding of the age-old relations between the savannah and the forest. South of the Equator there was no Muslim influence, but inter-regional exchanges took place on a considerable scale, owing to movements of population and to frequent contacts that occurred at markets and fairs.

The fundamental cultural unity of the African continent may be explained by the exchanges that took place between regions during this period. New food crops were introduced, mainly from the Indian Ocean, and techniques were transmitted from one region to another. In order to bring out the originality of Africa south of the Sudan, a region less well known to the Arabs and all other foreigners, the authors of Chapters 19–23 below have stressed the economic, social and political life of the areas from the great lakes to the rivers Congo, Zambezi and Limpopo, vast stretches almost uninfluenced by Islam. After the upper Nile valley, from Aswan to the sources of the river, the southern part of Africa comes in for special mention, and we shall return to this. In addition to gold, Africa exported worked and unworked ivory across the Indian Ocean to Arabia and India. The flourishing crafts of the Sudan and the rich agriculture of the Niger valley also contributed to trade across the Sahara: cereals, slippers, skins and cotton goods were exported to the north; and the royal courts at Niani and Gao, towns like Timbuktu, and the Hausa cities of Kano and Katsina imported mainly luxury goods such as silks, brocades and richly ornamented weapons.

The Sudan also exported slaves for use in the courts of the Maghrib and Egypt – women for the harems and men for the sultan's ceremonial guard. It should be noted that Sudanese pilgrims also purchased slaves in Cairo, especially those skilled in the arts, including musicians. Some authors have given exaggeratedly high figures for the number of slaves exported to Arab countries from the Sudan and the east coast. But however many black slaves there were in Iraq, Morocco or the Maghrib in general, it must be emphasized that there is no comparison between the slave trade in the period with which we are concerned and that trade which was set up by Europeans on the Atlantic coasts of Africa, after the discovery of the New World, to supply labour for the American sugar and cotton plantations. Volumes V and VI will concentrate on this 'haemorrhage' called the slave trade.

Finally, a third theme to emphasize is the development throughout Africa of kingdoms and empires between the twelfth and sixteenth centuries. For many years, colonial historians and researchers sought to give credence to the idea that states developed south of the Sahara as a result of Arab influence. Although such influence is unquestioned in the Sudan–Sahel area – but even there several kingdoms emerged before Islam was introduced into the region – it must be acknowledged that states such as the kingdom of the Kongo, Zimbabwe and Monomotapa owed little or nothing to the influence of Islam. Obviously, the urban life of the Maghrib and Sudan–Sahel is better known, thanks to written Arab accounts.

Trading towns bordered both sides of the Sahara, and a dynamic class of merchants and men of letters created a lively economic and cultural life in Jenne, Niani, Gao, Timbuktu and Walata in the western Sudan. North of the Sahara were Sijilmasa, Tuat, Wargla, Marrakesh, Fez and Cairo. In the central Sudan, in Kanem-Bornu and the Hausa cities such as Zaria, Katsina and Kano, there was a cultural and economic life no less intense. This was influenced by the Wangara, people who, like the Hausa, specialized in trade. On the east coast of Africa, Arab–Persian colonies which had settled in the ports during the ninth and tenth centuries made Mombasa, and especially Sofala and Madagascar, active trade centres in constant communication with India and China.

At the same time, on the political level, the Sudan had its own institutions and social structures which the superficial Islam of the courts left untouched. The Berbers adopted Arab ways very slowly. Arabic was a means of communication among men of letters close to the mosques and among some wealthy merchants in the towns of the Sudan, but there was

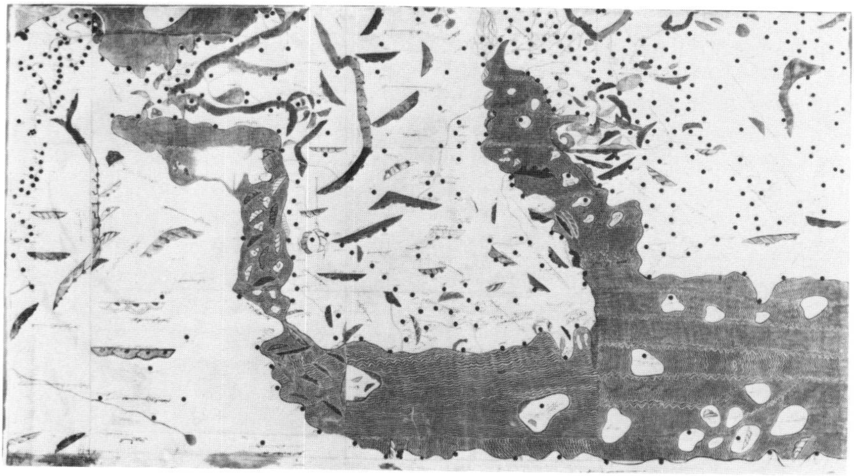

PLATE 1.1 *Al-Idrīsī's map of the world (12th century of the Christian era). The map includes Egypt, Arabia and Iran; the east coast of Africa can be seen at the bottom right-hand corner of the map. Al-Idrīsī's map is based on the cartographic conception put forward earlier by Ptolemy (The original is kept in the manuscript room housing the map collections of the Royal Library, under reference No BN/GE AA 2004.)*

no Arabization. Even in the Maghrib, where Arabization followed on the heels of the imposition of Islam, the Berber substratum remained very much alive and the Berber language is still used even today in the mountainous areas. Egypt became the cultural centre of the Muslim world, displacing Baghdad, Damascus and the towns of Arabia, which could no longer claim the prestige of the pilgrimage. Since the tenth and eleventh centuries, the Maghrib and western Andalusia had been important centres for the diffusion of science and philosophy to Europe. They played a large part in preparing Europe for a scientific and cultural renaissance.

Southern Italy was touched by this Muslim influence, for it was at the court of the Christian king, Roger of Sicily, that al-Idrīsī produced his famous *Geography* in 1154, bringing together all the knowledge then available on the countries of the world. Al-Idrīsī's book was a great step forward; thanks to his work, Italy discovered Africa and their businessmen thenceforward took an interest in this eldorado. But Europe's hour had not yet come.

On the political level, after the Almoravid episode, which brought gold from the Sudan to Spain, the Muslims rapidly lost their momentum and their empire declined from the beginning of the twelfth century. King Alfonso VI of Castile recaptured the rich city of Toledo from the Muslims. In 1086 Ibn Tā<u>sh</u>fīn briefly rekindled the torch of the Almoravids, and led a Muslim army, which included a large body of men from Takrūr, to a dazzling victory over the Christians at Zallaca, where the black warriors of the Almoravids distinguished themselves. In Africa itself, in the Sudan and the Maghrib, the eleventh century ended with the disintegration of Almoravid power. The rivalries between the *ḳaba'il*[1] of the Maghrib and the Sahara, and the resistance of the Ghana provinces after the death of Abū Bakr in Tagant in 1087, put an end to the efforts of the Almoravids in sub-Saharan Africa.

So for northern Africa the twelfth century opened with the Almoravids in retreat on several fronts. King Roger II of the 'Two Sicilies' ventured as far as the African coast and imposed tribute on certain ports which harboured the Barbary pirates. But such temerity was cut short by the Muslim revival under the Almohads in the twelfth century. Further east, in Egypt, the revival came about under the Ayyubids, and more particularly under the Mamluks in the thirteenth and fourteenth centuries. The Christians were at this time intensifying their crusading movement in the Middle East, but Egypt under the Mamluk dynasty put a stop to the European drive; the Crusaders were obliged to take refuge in 'kraks' or fortresses and they lost control of Jerusalem. While Egypt was thus containing the Christian peril in the thirteenth and fourteenth centuries, its schools were flourishing and giving a special brilliance to Muslim civil-

1. *Ḳabīla* (pl. *ḳaba'il*): 'a large agnatic group, the members of which claim to be descended from one common ancestor' and who may 'jointly own an area of grazing land'. *Encyclopaedia of Islam*, new edn, Vol. 4, pp. 334–5. In this volume the plural is given as *ḳabīla*s.

ization. This was also the era of expansion and the apogee of the kingdoms and empires of the Sudan, to which we must now turn our attention.

In Chapters 6–10 below, black African experts have studied the rise of the states of Mali, Songhay and Kanem-Bornu and the kingdoms of Mossi and Dagomba within the Niger Bend. The study of the institutions of Mali and the kingdom of Mossi, for example, reveals their common basis in African tradition. Islam, the state religion of Mali and Gao, fostered the rise of a literate class. Ever since the Ghana empire, the Wangara (Soninke and Malinke), specialists in trade, had stimulated the economic life of the area, organizing caravans bound for the southern forests, from which they brought back kola nuts, gold, palm oil, ivory and valuable timber in exchange for smoked fish, cotton goods and articles made of copper.

The Muslim emperors of Mali developed their relations with Egypt at the expense of the Maghrib. In the fourteenth century the empire was at its height, but little is known of the twelfth century. Fortunately al-Idrīsī, partly relying on information supplied by al-Bakrī, tells us of the existence of the kingdoms of Takrūr, Do, Mali and Gao. The traditions of Manding, Wagadu and Takrūr still show us today how bitter the struggle for supremacy was between the successor provinces after the breakup of the Ghana empire.

We now know, through the study of oral traditions, that between the fall of Ghana and the rise of Mali there was an interlude under the domination of the Soso, a Soninke–Mandingo splinter group who had rebelled against Islam and who for a time imposed unity on the provinces once governed by the *kaya maghan*. With the thirteenth century the rise of the kingdom of Mali began. The great conqueror Sundiata Keita defeated Sumaguru, king of the Soso, at the famous battle of Kirina in 1235, and founded the new Mandingo empire. Sundiata, faithful to the traditions of his ancestors who had been converted to Islam in 1050, restored relations with black and Arab traders and men of letters. From 1230 to 1255 he established institutions which for hundreds of years were to influence the empires and kingdoms which followed one another in the western Sudan. The Sahara was once more crossed by pilgrims; the great traffic across the desert resumed.

Merchants and black pilgrims met in the streets of Cairo. Black embassies were set up in the cities of the Maghrib. Cultural and economic relations with the Muslim world were particularly strengthened in the fourteenth century, in the reigns of the flamboyant Mansa Mūsā I and Mansa Sulaymān. In central Sudan, Kanem and Bornu maintained still closer relations with Egypt and Libya. Arab sources, local written records and oral traditions combine once more to throw light on the fourteenth century in the Sudan. This is an appropriate place to mention certain Arab writers – historians, geographers, travellers and court secretaries – who have left us an excellent body of documentation on Africa, particularly concerning the fourteenth century.

The greatest historian of the Middle Ages, Ibn Khaldūn (1332–1406), came from the Maghrib. He was involved in the political life of his time, not only in the courts of Fez and Tunis but also in Andalusia. After various misfortunes he retired to a castle to write. His monumental *Kitāb al-ʿIbār* (*Universal History* including the section translated as 'History of the Berbers') is the most detailed socio-historical study of the Maghrib ever written, and one of its volumes contains some celebrated passages on the empire of Mali. It is to Ibn Khaldūn that we owe the list of kings of the thirteenth and fourteenth centuries, until 1390. His *Muḳaddima* – the *Prolegomena* or introduction to the *History* – is a major work in its own right; it laid the foundations of sociology and defined the principles of a scientific and objective history based on the critical appraisal of sources.

Ibn Baṭṭūṭa, a veritable globe-trotter of the fourteenth century, wrote accounts of China, the east coast of Africa, and a report of a journey to Mali which are still model ethnological studies. Nothing escaped his attention – ways of life, food problems, modes of government, popular customs – all are treated with authority and accuracy. It is Ibn Baṭṭūṭa who provides us with our fullest information on the coast of East Africa, inter-regional trade in Africa, and the importance of trade in the Indian Ocean. Of the Maldive Islands he wrote:

> The currency here is the cowrie. It is a creature they gather from the sea. They put it in pits, and the flesh disappears, leaving only white bone ... They trade through the medium of these cowries, on the basis of four *bustu* to one dinar. Sometimes the value sinks to twelve *bustu* to one dinar. They sell them to the people of Bangala [Bengal] in exchange for rice. The cowrie is also the currency used by the people of Bilad Bangala ... It is also the coinage used by the 'Sudan' [black men] in their own country. I have seen it sold at Malli [Niani, in the empire of Mali] and Gugu [Gao, capital of Songhay] at 1150 to one gold dinar.

During this period the cowrie shell was the currency of most of the kingdoms of the Sudan. The fact that they are only found in the Maldive Islands shows how highly developed was the circulation of men and goods in Africa and the Indian Ocean.

A third author who gives us accurate information based on carefully sifted documentation is Ibn Faḍl Allāh al-ʿUmarī, secretary to the Mamluk court between 1340 and 1348. The kings of the Sudan at that time maintained consulates in Cairo to assist the hundreds of pilgrims on their way to Mecca. Al-ʿUmarī had part of the royal archives at his disposal, and also sought information both from the citizens of Cairo who had met the kings of the Sudan as they passed through, and from the travellers from the Sudan themselves. His 'Description of Africa excepting Egypt' is one of the chief sources for the history of medieval Africa. Finally there is Leo Africanus, guest of the Pope, who visited the Sudan twice at the beginning of the sixteenth century. His descriptions of western and central Sudan are very important for us and concern the era when history shifted in the favour of the 'white caravels'. By the end of the sixteenth century the decline was complete and the towns of the Sudan slowly withered away.

Five centuries later, in 1914, Koumbi Ṣāleḥ (Ghana) was identified and excavated. Awdaghust, the famous trading town between Koumbi and Sijilmasa, has for the last ten years drawn archaeologists to its site, and Professors J. Devisse and S. Robert have found several levels of human occupation there. Treasures have also been discovered which prove that Aouker was indeed the 'Land of Gold'. Further south, at Niani, the capital of Mali, a city built of beaten earth bricks, the tumuli are being excavated and sifted; year by year the medieval city, capital of Sundiata and of Mansa Mūsā I, yields up its secrets. Archaeology increasingly proves itself to be an indispensable science for extracting from the soil of Africa evidence more eloquent than either texts or tradition.

Now we must turn to that part of Africa unknown to Islam. As we have already said, the absence of written evidence means nothing; the equatorial, central and southern regions of Africa offer an excellent illustration of this fact, with their stone monuments reminiscent of the kingdoms of ancient Egypt. These Cyclopean constructions, far inland, these Zimbabwes and Mapungubwes, can be counted by the dozen. These fortified towns and giant stairways built by the Bantu people show how far certain techniques were developed without the use of writing. There is no need to dwell on all the theories that have been put forward concerning the builders of these stone monuments, for it goes without saying that colonialists could not accept the idea that the ancestors of the Shona or the Matabele were responsible for such staggering creations. Nor were colonialist historians willing to admit that black men were able to build in stone. In his book, *Africa before the White Men*, Basil Davidson's title for chapter IX, on central and southern Africa, is 'The builders of the south'. In it he offers a new vision of the problems of African history, returning to Africa its just due, the moral benefit of the work of its ancestors.

The Portuguese, coming up the east coast of Africa after rounding the Cape of Good Hope, had heard in Sofala of a powerful empire inland. They even entered into contact with some natives who came to the coast regularly to trade with the Arabs. The earliest Portuguese records speak of the kingdom of Benametapa. Da Goes gives one of the first descriptions of the stone monuments now familiar to everyone through pictures:

> In the middle of this country is a fortress built of large and heavy stones both within and without ... a very curious construction and well built, for it is said no mortar can be seen holding the stones together. In other parts of the said plain are other fortresses built in the same manner, in each of which the king has captains. The King of Benametapa lives in great style, and is served with great deference, on bended knee.[2]

De Barros adds: 'the natives of this country call all these edifices "Symbaoe", which in their tongue means "court", because thus may be denoted any place where Benametapa may be, and they say all the other dwellings of the king bear this name because they are royal property'.[3] This is reminiscent of 'Madugu', the name given to the residences of the rulers of Mali.

Today, thanks to the work of many researchers, central and southern Africa are better known. The joint efforts of linguists, archaeologists and anthropologists have already thrown much light on these buildings and their creators. Zimbabwe and Mwene Mutapa (the Benametapa of the Portuguese and the modern Monomotapa) were powerful kingdoms which reached their greatest heights between the eleventh and fourteenth centuries, and were thus contemporary with the empires of Ghana and Mali in the north. The power of these kingdoms was based on a strong social and political organization. Like the *kaya maghan*, the Mwene Mutapa (this was the royal title) had a monopoly of gold, and like his contemporary in the Sudan he was 'lord of metals'.[4] These regions, which today correspond to parts of Mozambique, Zimbabwe, Zambia and Malawi, were lands rich in copper, gold and iron. According to Davidson, 'thousands of ancient mines have been discovered, perhaps as many as 60 000 or 70 000'.

Chronology still presents problems, but what is certain is that although Zimbabwe and Mwene Mutapa were still great powers when the Portuguese came, decadence had already set in, and was to be accelerated by the rapacity and depredations of the Portuguese and the other Europeans who came after them. The people of these lands practised terraced farming and had developed a flourishing agriculture. It is becoming more and more clear that the different ethnic groups and local cultures all stemmed from the same Bantu origin. In one sense, ethnology did history a disservice in regarding each ethnic group as a distinct race; but fortunately linguistics permits us to rehabilitate the picture. All the tiny groups that were born out of the turmoil of four centuries of slave-trading and man-hunting are part of the same Bantu world. The Bantu superimposed themselves on earlier populations and drove pygmy and other non-Negroid groups towards the inhospitable forests and the deserts. Excavation is proceeding in Zambia; the young republic of Zimbabwe offers a very promising field of research. In the Transvaal and other areas of South Africa, vestiges still exist of brilliant civilizations which arose before the twelfth century.

After their first attribution of Zimbabwe and Mwene Mutapa to the Phoenicians, thus renewing the gilded legend of the 'Land of Ophir', researchers have come round to a more objective view. Most of them now

2. Translated from D. da Goes, French trans. n.d.

3. J. de Barros, Eng. trans. 1937.

4. For certain authors, the meaning of Mwene Mutapa is 'master pillager'; for others, it is 'lord of metals'.

recognize that outside influences were non-existent. David Randall-MacIver, an Egyptologist who visited Southern Rhodesia (Zimbabwe), has declared that the monuments are of African origin. Scientific archaeology finds expression when he writes:

> There is no trace of any oriental or European style of any period whatever ... the character of the dwellings enclosed in the stone ruins and forming an integral part of them is unmistakably African ... The arts and techniques exemplified in the objects found in the houses are typically African, except when they are clearly medieval or post-medieval imports.

These words were written in 1905 but the archaeological evidence failed to discourage the advocates of the 'Ophir' theory. A quarter of a century later, however, Dr Gertrude Caton-Thompson wrote an account of the culture of Zimbabwe in which, according to Basil Davidson, she confirmed with crystal clarity and with great archaeological intuition what MacIver had said before her. Dr Caton-Thompson, whose book was based on rigorous archaeological investigation, wrote: 'A study of all the existing evidence, from every sector, has not been able to produce a single article which does not accord with the claims of Bantu origin and medieval date.'[5] In Chapter 21 of the present volume, working from archaeological data, Professor Fagan has shown that Zimbabwe and the other civilizations of the south developed well before the sixteenth century and were almost completely sheltered from outside influences, or at least that the latter had no substantial effect on their genesis.

We can easily imagine the grandiloquent account we should have had from an Arab pen, if geographers and travellers had visited Zimbabwe and the kingdom of the 'lord of the metals', as they did Ghana and Mali. They might have written: 'Great Zimbabwe and its stone enclosures rise up as enigmatic as the pyramids, bearing witness to the strength and cohesion of the institutions that ruled over the men who raised these monuments to the glory of their kings, and of their gods.'

The surprise and wonder of the Portuguese sailors when they reached the 'Ethiopia of the west' (modern West Africa) began at the estuary of the Senegal river. It was in Senegambia that they came into contact with the mansas of Mali and established relations with the kings of Wolof. Aboard their caravels in the river estuaries, these emulators of the Muslims inquired about the sources of gold. The first thing that struck them was the country's political and administrative organization, its prosperity and the abundance of its wealth. The further south they sailed, the more conscious they were of their own poverty and their greed increased, diminishing their sense of superiority which they derived from their Christian faith.

In Chapters 12–14 we see the state of affairs on the Atlantic coast of

5. G. Caton-Thompson, 1931.

Upper Guinea and in the Gulf of Guinea; in other words, in Senegambia and the Niger delta. Although our knowledge is still meagre, we know that the forests were not an environment hostile to human settlement, as so many Africanists have maintained; a vast field for research has been opened to the investigations of historians and archaeologists. The cities of Benin and the lovely Yoruba sculptures developed in this forest environment. The heads of brass, the bas-reliefs in the palaces and many of the works of art which are today found in the British Museum and the museums of Berlin and Brussels were attributed to hypothetical non-Africans, until good sense prevailed and placed those pieces in their social and cultural context, recognizing that their only begetters were the native populations themselves. Today the connection is well established between the earthenware of the brilliant Nok civilization (500 years before the Christian era) and the Benin bronzes of the tenth to fifteenth centuries of the Christian era. But what floods of ink were spilled to defraud Africa of its past, what crimes committed to strip it of its artistic masterpieces!

This brief survey has shown that there were many kinds of African states. The clan or lineage was the rudimentary form of state; their members recognized a common ancestor and they lived under an elected chief or patriarch, whose essential function was to ensure a fair distribution of group wealth. He was both father–provider and father–judge. The clan inhabited a clearly defined territory or else it had an area in which to roam, if its members were nomadic herdsmen. In the deserts (the Sahara) or the forests they occupied larger or smaller territories; they often established symbiotic relations with more sedentary peoples with whom they exchanged the fruits of their labours. The clan chief did not have discretionary power, but when the group's income rose the chief benefited from the surplus and no longer had to work with his hands; he became the judge in disputes that arose over the sharing out of land.

The kingdom grouped together several clans. Frequently, the king was the head of the dominant clan, for example, the Keita clan, founders of the Mali empire in the thirteenth century. The king was assisted by a council whose members were dependent upon him for sustenance; the kingdom occupied a fairly extensive territory, although each clan retained its land-holding customs and particular religious rites. What was important was the allegiance owed to the king, which was expressed by the payment of taxes (often in kind). Although he was a political ruler, the king usually retained the religious attributes of the clan chief; he was sacred. This 'sacred' quality was clearest in the cases of the king of the Kongo, the ruler of Monomotapa and the emperor of Mali: their subjects swore oaths in their name.

In theory, those rulers whom we call 'emperors', although they did not control vast areas of land, at least ruled over kings who had a fair degree of autonomy. The Almohad empire, for example, covered a good part of the Maghrib; the sultan, who came from a *ḳabīla* or clan, had under him other sultans who in their turn had authority over clan chiefs or shaykhs. The emperor or mansa of Mali had twelve provinces, including two kingdoms, under his authority. Whether king or emperor, the sovereign was always assisted by a council; in general, this body was a moderating influence because a 'constitution' or 'custom' always circumscribed power.

We have already mentioned the city-states which, in point of fact, were kingdoms reduced to the scale of a city and its immediately surrounding territory; the Hausa cities or the Yoruba cities of Benin were the most typical examples. Here, too, institutional structures were complex; officials and aristocrats made up the king's court. The Hausa cities recognized a mother city, Daura; for the Yoruba, it was Ife which fulfilled this role. The tie that bound these often warring states was their common culture.

We have therefore banished from our vocabulary such terms as 'segmented' or 'stateless' societies, words dear to the researchers and historians of a certain period. We have banished also such terms as 'tribe', 'Hamitic' and 'fetishist'. In certain parts of Africa, the word 'tribe' has acquired pejorative connotations. Since independence, social and political conflicts have been called 'tribal wars', with the implication of 'wars among savages'. The word 'tribalism' was created to fit these circumstances. Originally, a tribe was the name for a socio-cultural group; today, as applied to Africa, it means a 'primitive' or 'backward' unit. The word 'fetishism' has a no less derogatory sense; it is used to describe traditional African religion and has become synonymous with 'charlatanism' or 'the religion of savages', if one can call African observances a religion. 'Animism', as a description of the traditional religion of Africa, also carries a negative charge. Rather than fetishism or animism, we will speak of the traditional religion of Africa.

The word 'Hamitic' has a long history. It was used to describe certain white pastoral peoples, so-called 'bearers of civilization'. These presumed pastoralists, whose reality or historical existence has never been demonstrated, are supposed to have wandered hither and thither through the continent, bringing culture and civilization to black agriculturalists. Strangely enough, the origin of the word is Ham (the biblical ancestor of the blacks). How this word came to designate a white people is an intriguing mystery. It is, in fact, one of the greatest historical mystifications. Colonial historians held that herdsmen were superior to tillers of the soil, which has no basis in fact. It is sad that colonialism, by exacerbating the rivalries between clans and between agricultural and pastoral peoples, left a veritable powder ḳeg in Rwanda and Burundi on the eve of independence, in the form of the struggles between the Tutsi and the Bahutu. The persecutions and bloody episodes of 1962–3 must be laid at the door of the Belgian colonialists who had fanned the flames of discord for more than half a century between the clans of their 'colonies', between 'Hamitic' stock-raisers and 'black' cultivators.

The way to decolonize history is precisely to knock down these false theories and all the prejudice raised by colonialism in order to establish the system of domination and exploitation and to justify a policy of intervention. These pseudo-scientific theories are still to be found in many works and even in our school textbooks. It is important here to bring some precision to history.

2 The unification of the Maghrib under the Almohads

O. SAIDI

The Almohad period, from the middle of the twelfth century to the middle of the thirteenth, marks the high point of attempts to unify the Maghrib, and even the whole Muslim West. The Almohad attempt at unification, which later powers tried vainly to restore, completely transcended that of the preceding Almoravids. It stemmed from a religious 'reform' led by the famous Mahdī of the Almohads, Ibn Tūmart; it rested on a well-organized 'community', the *Muwaḥḥidūn* ('unitarians') and it developed into a total political enterprise. The venture was led by the rulers of a dynasty, the Mu'minids, founded by one of Ibn Tūmart's earliest and most distinguished companions.

This unification venture was far from having only religious and political motives and objectives; it was also influenced by economic considerations, imperatives and constraints. The two essential elements were, on the one hand, control of the various great trans-Saharan trade routes (or at least of their northern outlets) and, on the other, the integration of the various economic growth points of the Maghrib and the Muslim West, by extending the former Almoravid domain to the Maghrib and Ifrīḳiya.

The religious situation in the Maghrib and the Almohad quest

Orthodoxy and Islam

In the middle of the eleventh century, the esoteric, Batinite Sh̲ī'ite, proselytizing drive, or *Da'wa*, was still powerful, despite the political decline of the Fatimids in Egypt;[1] the movement towards unification, which had begun long before – at least from the Mu'tazilite set-back in the middle of the ninth century – was slow, and the community remained fragmented.

Various approaches can be distinguished in the quest for unification, which had not yet achieved a doctrinal synthesis. One was ascetic purifica-

1. See A. Laroui, 1970, p. 163.

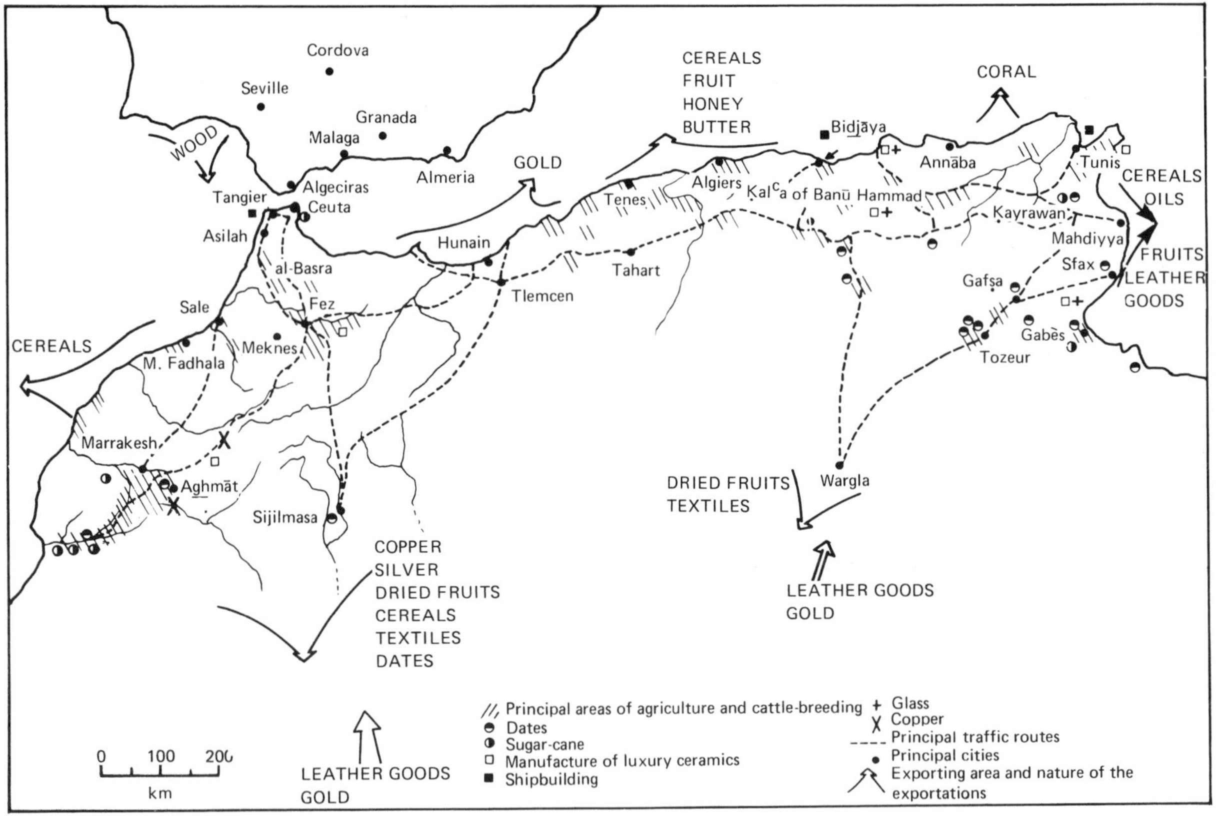

FIG. 2.1 *The Maghrib during the 12th century – economic activities (J. Devisse, based on originals by O. Saidi and C. Vanacker)*

tion, based on the study of Sunnī tradition and *ḥadīth*, which was capable of falling into the excesses of Ṣūfism; another was the codification of the law, which often declined into formalism and a quasi-mechanical ritualism; and a third, the deepening and refinement of the theological propositions of the Ashʿarite synthesis.[2]

These approaches – in opposition to Shīʾism and *falsafa* (philosophy) – and these partial, if not personal, attempts at a synthesis were notable, as we shall see, for a real effort at the unification of the community over a long period of time, to an extent that was inversely proportional to the political fragmentation of Islam. It is in the light of these developments that we must examine the situation of Islam and of orthodoxy, not only in the Maghrib but also in the whole of the Muslim West.[3]

Islam had very great difficulty in establishing its sway and achieving unity in the Maghrib.[4] There it met the strongest and the most tenacious resistance, which soon took the form of the Khāridjite 'heresy', characterized by a mixture of anarchy and egalitarianism, which was particularly attractive to nomadic and rural societies. In its ideas and organizational forms this heresy drew on ethnic traditions, and profited from the particular ways in which Islamic sovereignty was then exercised to establish itself among the Berbers, amongst whom its preachers attacked both the hereditary principle in the succession to the caliphate and the primacy of any given tribe, even that of the Prophet.[5]

Khāridjism in the Maghrib was not always a strictly doctrinal attitude; it also served as an ideological cover for all kinds of opposition; the term sometimes denoted attitudes marked by great negligence in the observance of religious duties, and in certain cases even the negation of Islam. In addition, it is important to remember the long survival of Berber customary law, which continued, sometimes running counter to Islamic law, until the Almoravid Yūsuf b. Tāshfīn.

In spite of the immense efforts of the Umayyads in Spain, the Idrisids and even the Fatimids to spread Islam, it was not until the time of the Almoravids and the Almohads that the major corruptions of Islam began to disappear, including the more obvious forms of Berber dissidence which generally overlay socio-economic attitudes that have not yet been adequately investigated.

Another characteristic of Islam in the Maghrib, which prevails there to this day, was the adoption of Mālikism. The disciples of Mālik b. Anas,

2. For al-Ashʿarī (born 873–4, died 935–6 of the Christian era) see *Encyclopaedia of Islam*, new edn, Vol. 1, pp. 694–5.

3. It is clear that Ibn Tūmart's opposition to the religious position of the Maghrib is a practical illustration of that position itself and of the attitude of the Muslim West towards the different Islamic schools of religious thought.

4. Cf. especially I. Goldziher, 1887; M. Talbi, 1966, pp. 17–21.

5. On the success of these propositions and the recalcitrant attitude of the Berbers, see Talbi, op. cit., p. 19.

such as Ibn al-Ḳāsim, propagated and consolidated his doctrine in the Maghrib through local devotees.[6] Ḳayrawān soon became a focal point of Mālikism and provided a line of doctors of the law, including Imam Saḥnūn (776–854 of the Christian era), a zealous propagandist of the school of Ibn al-Ḳāsim, who often succeeded in identifying with the mass of the people, especially against the Fatimid Shī'ite offensive of the tenth century.[7]

Whereas the foundations of the religious law – the Koran and *ḥadīth*s – occupied a smaller and smaller place, the manuals of *furū*ʿ (treatises of applied jurisprudence) became the principal authority in the practice of law. This tendency sometimes even resulted in scorn for the study of the *ḥadīth*s, as can be seen in the teaching of a great scholar and *ḳāḍī* of Cordova, al-Asbagh Ibn Khalīl.[8] The few timid attempts at dissent – such as that of Baḳī b. Makhlad[9] – came to nothing in the face of the impregnable fortress formed by the 'guild' of Mālikite jurists, who were often wealthy landowners.

The situation was also characterized by the lack of interest on the part of the jurists, or *fuḳahā*', in the spiritualist dogmas then prevailing in the East.[10] They claimed to keep to the literal 'truth' of the word of God, eschewing all interpretation, which in their view could only be a source of corruption. This attitude involved some difficulties, not to say contradictions, in particular as regards the attributes of God; that was why these Mālikite *fuḳahā*' were accused of being 'anthropomorphists' or *ḥashwiyya*, concerned only with externals, adhering slavishly to applied jurisprudence and making the salvation of believers dependent on the external observance of legal requirements, yet allowing no place for the inner religious life.

Therefore no attempt at renewal or deeper inquiry came to anything, and the exclusive, oppressive domination of the Mālikites isolated the few supporters of the contemplative, inquiring approach that had eventually triumphed in the East. This ultra-conservatism provoked extreme reactions in the name of free thought and even gave rise to a sort of universal religion, leading to a kind of parallelism which precluded all attempts at synthesis.[11] In particular, the speculative Ashʿarite theology, whose purpose was to find a middle way between the intellectual spiritualism of the Muʿtazilites on the one hand and anthropomorphist literalism on the other, was sadly lacking in the Maghrib. Even philosophers such as Ibn Rushd encouraged

6. Ibn al-Ḳāsim, who died in Cairo in 806 of the Christian era, produced *al-Mudawwana*, the major work of the Mālikite rite, apart from the famous book by the Imam, Mālik b. Anas himself, the *Kitāb al-Muwaṭṭa*' ('The Smoothed Path').

7. See H. Monès, 1962, Vol. 1, pp. 197–220.

8. On Mālikism in Andalusia, see I. Goldziher, 1903.

9. On this Cordovan apologist, see *Encyclopaedia of Islam*, new edn, Vol. 1, pp. 956–7.

10. *Faḳīh* (pl. *fuḳahā*') originally denoted a learned man, but it became a technical term for a specialist in the science of religious law (*Encyclopaedia of Islam*, new edn. Vol. 2, p. 756).

11. ibid., Vol. 3, pp. 868–72, under Ibn Masarra.

this parallelism in the Muslim West, because they declared that the mass of believers were impervious to speculative thought and accused the Ash'arites of upsetting the beliefs of simple people. Thus objectively they were serving the interests of the Mālikites, who showed a surprising tolerance towards them.

In conclusion, Islamic orthodoxy in the Maghrib and Andalusia (al-Andalus) in the time of Ibn Tūmart was primarily concerned with laying down rules; this left no room for anxiety or mystery. Religion became a matter of forethought, calculation and 'capitalization'; it represented the triumph of ritual, reduced to the monotonous repetition of certain rites in order to ensure one's reward. It is not surprising that several great minds, such as al-Ghazālī and Ibn Ḥazm, should have regarded this form of Islam as nothing but a matter of ritual and rule-making, in danger of losing the true faith.[12] Al-Ghazālī, in particular, in his famous work *Iḥyā' 'ulūm al-dīn* ('The revival of religious learning') violently attacked this type of *fuḳahā'*, reproaching them with monopolizing religion and using it to live on the fat of the land through the administration of pious foundations and the property of orphans. He also reproached them with their casuistry in justifying the actions of the temporal power, to which they displayed a servility unworthy of true men of religion. He rejected their dry, sterile formalism in favour of a return to the use of the 'life-giving waters', the springs of the Koran and the *sunna*. This is why al-Ghazālī was the object of violent hostility on the part of the Mālikite *fuḳahā'*, who went so far as to accuse him of having rejected the true faith because of his Ash'arite dogmas and his mystical tendencies.

Ibn Tūmart's education

Ibn Tūmart's destiny, like his person, is surrounded with legends, mysteries and imaginary events. In fact we know very little about the man.[13] He is supposed to have been born about 1075 in the Anti-Atlas mountains of present-day Morocco, at Īgīllīz-n-Hargha. His father belonged to the Hargha *ḳabīla*:[14] his mother to the Masakkāla; both were branches of the Maṣmūda, a group known today as the Shlūḥ. The ideological requirements of his preaching, and of his Mahdist claims, caused him to give himself (or to arrange the fabrication of) an Arabic name and a Sharifian ancestry, with several Berber interpolations in this genealogical fiction.[15]

Certainly he must have come from a relatively well-off background, for

12. A. Merad, 1960–1, p. 379.

13. See *Encyclopaedia of Islam*, new edn, Vol. 3, pp. 958–60.

14. On the problems posed by this Berber *ḳabīla*, see E. Lévi-Provençal, 1928b, p. 55; R. Montagne, 1930, p. 64. Cf. also the excellent restatement in *Encyclopaedia of Islam*, new edn, Vol. 3, p. 207.

15. The same thing happened to his father, Tūmart Ibn Ugallid, who became 'Abd Allah.

his father bore the title of Amghar, denoting the headman of a village or *ḳabīla* in southern Morocco; and he himself was able to pursue his studies and make a long journey to the East to complete them. His family, if Ibn 'Khaldūn is to be believed, was distinguished by its piety;[16] and he himself earned the appellation of *asafu* ('torch') by virtue of his assiduity in study and in prayer.

In 1107 Ibn Tūmart set out on a long journey to complete his education. There are many versions of the route, stages and scope of this journey, which has given rise to considerable controversy.[17] What is certain is that, contrary to Tūmart's hagiography, he did not meet the great mystic imam, al-Ghazālī, nor receive his instruction;[18] still less is there any evidence that he was given by him the mission of reforming the law in the Maghrib and destroying the power of the Almoravids there.[19] In fact, the invocation of al-Ghazālī's name and prestige came much later. His name appears as the starting-point of Ibn Tūmart's career only when the animosity nurtured by Maghrib theology towards the system of the great imam of the East had subsided.[20]

Ibn Tūmart's career can be divided into several stages. He was successively: the censor of morals; the theologian who asserted himself at Marrakesh; the head of a new school at Aghmāt; and the leader of a communal party and a candidate for power, solidly entrenched at Tīnmallal, high up in the mountains.

In Ifrīḳiya, Ibn Tūmart seems to have begun by impressing people with his learning and piety; during his many long halts, more and more numerous and attentive audiences gathered round him. In the course of his westward march, the stop at Bidjāya (now Bougie) – the brilliant and prosperous capital of the Hammadids, where morals were particularly free – marked the high point of Ibn Tūmart's activities as a custodian of morals. Warned of the real dangers he was running, he went to Mallāla, on the outskirts of Bidjāya, where he seems to have spent a long period in study and contemplation.

This stage is of great importance for its later political significance, for it was at Mallāla that Ibn Tūmart met his future successor, 'Abd al-Mu'min b. 'Alī b. 'Alwī b. Ya'lā al-Kūmī Abū Muḥammad, then on an educational journey to the East.[21] He was persuaded to abandon it, and stayed with

16. Ibn Khaldūn, French transl. 1852–6, Vol. 2, p. 163.

17. See, for example, Ibn al-Ḳaṭṭān, ed. M. A. Makkī, n.d. (1964?), p. 4; Ibn Ḳunfudh, 1968 edn, p. 100.

18. See Ibn al-Athīr, 1876–91 edn, Vol. 10, pp. 400–7, for a denial of the meeting; and especially A. Huici Miranda, 1949, Vol. 14, pp. 342–5.

19. See Ibn al-Ḳaṭṭān, op. cit. 14–18; Le Tourneau, 1969, p. 79, citing *al-Ḥulal al-Mawshiyya*.

20. See Goldziher, 1903.

21. For 'Abd al-Mu'min and his country, see *Encyclopaedia of Islam*, new edn, Vol. 1, pp. 78–80.

Ibn Tūmart. This meeting has been surrounded with legend and mysterious symbolism, but it may be noted that after this meeting Ibn Tūmart was no longer a lone figure; his westward march seems to have become more organized, and his entourage grew larger and larger. Improvised instruction and discussion sessions were succeeded by organized meetings at the houses of men of religion. Ibn Tūmart began to gather information on the far Maghrib, and perhaps had already received emissaries. At each stop he made contacts.[22]

Going from Sale (Sala') to Marrakesh Ibn Tūmart refused to pay the toll; and in the Almoravid capital the famous debate took place with the court *fuḳahā'* in the presence of the Almoravid amir, 'Alī Ibn Yūsuf, in which Ibn Tūmart's adversaries, who dominated the ruler, were reduced to silence by his performance.

Ibn Tūmart's criticism went beyond the theological field, and hence became dangerous. This led the vizier Mālik Ibn Wuhayb to advise that he be done away with; but another court personality, Yintān b. 'Umar, took him under his protection and persuaded him to flee the capital. He then withdrew to Aghmāt;[23] there a new and decisive phase in his career began, in which he entered into open rebellion against the Almoravids, refusing to go to Marrakesh when the amir ordered him to do so.

From then on Ibn Tūmart was preoccupied with the effective establishment and organization of the Almohad movement, whose political purpose – the overthrow of the Almoravid regime – was to become clearer day by day. Gradually Ibn Tūmart found himself in the position of spiritual head of larger and larger forces, united at this stage more by anti-Almoravid tribal feeling than by a concern for the purity of the law or strict Muslím observance.

Ibn Tūmart's Almohad reforms

The principles, ideas and formulations of Ibn Tūmart's reforms in the fields of morality, theological dogma and law seem to have gradually taken shape in his mind during his educational journey in the East, on his way back to the outermost parts of the Maghrib, and also in contacts with his companions, whose number was growing and with whom he eventually settled in his native country.[24]

22. A map of Ibn Tūmart's itinerary would be very interesting on several counts, especially if compared with that of 'Abd al-Mu'min's victorious eastward march in later years.

23. On Aghmāt, see *Encyclopaedia of Islam*, new edn, Vol. 1, pp. 250–1; J. Devisse, 1972, pp. 63, 66 and 70.

24. 515 H/1121: Īgīllīz, his native village, where he installed himself in a cave, thereafter proclaimed *al-Ghār al-muḳaddas* (a sacred cave); 517 H/1123: Tīnmallal, in the upper valley of the Nfis, about 75 km south-west of Marrakesh.

The first point of course concerned the *tawḥīd* (the affirmation of the uniqueness of God), which according to Ibn Tūmart, is 'the affirmation of one God and the denial of all that is not He: divinity, associate, saint or idol'.[25] Basing himself on various *ḥadīth*s, Ibn Tūmart asserted that knowledge of the *tawḥīd* is the primary obligation, for three reasons: it is one of the foundations of religion; it is the most important of obligations; and it is the religion of both the earliest and the latest prophets.

The Almohads were believers in the one God, al-Muwaḥḥid – whence they derived their name, al-Muwaḥḥidūn, which was later corrupted to Almohads – and preached a mysticism that showed the influence of al-Ghazālī. It was in fact a return to the original sources of Islam, in opposition to the more legalistic Almoravids, who were more drawn to the study of texts than to the unadorned law. The Almohads were marked by moral austerity and a sobriety which was generally approved by the Berbers, countryfolk little drawn to luxury. It is worth noting that the Mahdī preached in the Berber language; he even drafted short treatises in his mother tongue. At the political level, he relied on the advice of a council of notables, in Berber style, and remained faithful to the rules of the Shlūḥ *ḳabīla*.

Ibn Tūmart espoused the ideas of the Muʿtazilites, who made Allah a pure spirit; he commended the allegorical interpretation of certain verses of the Koran described as ambiguous, in which material or human terms or phrases are used, particularly in relation to the attributes of God. These terms and phrases should not be made to conform to the limitations of human reason, and an allegorical interpretation should be adopted, which excluded *tashbīh* (comparison) and *taklīf* (modality).[26] This was one of the essential points in his condemnation of the Almoravids.[27] He described them as infidels because they were guilty in particular of *tadjsīm* (anthropomorphism). On this point Ibn Tūmart held an extremist position, which led inevitably to excommunication, for he applied the principle that those in power are responsible for the conduct of their subjects, and thus made the Almoravids principally responsible for the anthropomorphism current in the Maghrib. He therefore proclaimed that a *djihād* (holy war) must be waged against them. This led to the most extreme Ashʿarite and Muʿtazilite positions.

As a consequence of his *tawḥīd*, Ibn Tūmart denied the very existence of the attributes of God, and violently attacked those whom he called *mushrikūn* ('associationists'), or those who gave attributes to God. Thus he made a stand both against the Ashʿarites, who held that God has eternal

25. Ibn Tūmart, French transl. 1903, p. 271.

26. See Ibn Tūmart's letter to the Almohad community, translated by E. Lévi-Provençal, op. cit., p. 78, in which he warns his followers against the tendency to circumscribe God with limits and directions, which leads to making God a creature; anyone who reaches that point is like someone who worships an idol.

27. See R. Bourouiba, 1973, p. 145.

attributes inherent in His essence, and against the traditionalists, who held that these attributes were distinct from His essence.

In Ibn Tūmart's view the epithets given to God, *al-asmā' al-ḥusnā* (the most beautiful names), are qualities which are there only to confirm the absolute uniqueness of God. The creator is thus necessarily living, knowing, powerful, endowed with will, and all this without anyone comprehending the modality of it.[28]

Having demonstrated the oneness of God, Ibn Tūmart emphasized the eternity of God; He is the creator, and nothing can precede Him. God is thus the first, having no beginning, and the last, having no end.[29] He also strongly emphasized God's omnipotence, which is nevertheless qualified by the fact that God does not demand of creatures what is beyond their capabilities; in that, Ibn Tūmart was fairly close to the Mu'tazilites. On the concept of the prophetic mission, Ibn Tūmart adopted the point of view of the Sunnites, who recognized the truthfulness of God's messenger by extraordinary signs, the *āyāt*. On a problem as crucial as that of predestination, which could have had – and had had – political implications, Ibn Tūmart diverged from the Mu'tazilite duality of God's omnipotence and justice and, despite his affirmation of the divine wisdom, he asserted predestination.

There was one component of Ibn Tūmart's doctrine that differed sharply from the Sunnite position: this was belief in the Mahdī (the impeccable guide), who is guided by God. The traditions about the Mahdī go back to the Prophet, to whom *ḥadīth*s were attributed announcing the coming of the restorer and redeemer, who would be of the family of the Prophet. For the Sunnīs, the Mahdī was to appear only the day before the end of the world, to restore and implement the true religion. For the Shī'ites, there was a hidden imam who was to reappear and govern in person by divine right. Among the mass of the people, belief in the Mahdī was widespread, for he symbolized justice. This expectation was witnessed by Ibn Khaldūn as late as the fourteenth century, at Massa in the Sūs.[30]

Ibn Tūmart placed his own mission as imam immediately after the death of 'Alī in +661. It was therefore obligatory to obey him blindly as regards religion and the things of this world, to copy him in all his actions, to accept his decisions and to refer to him in all things. To obey the Mahdī was to obey God and His Prophet, for the simple reason that the Mahdī was the one who knew God and His Prophet best. For some people, Ibn Tūmart's announcement that he was the Mahdī was the logical outcome of his vocation to extol good and forbid evil. For others, it simply meant that he was using local traditions and beliefs, which he had patched up with Islamic references, invoking *ḥadīth*s which were probably apocryphal

28. Ibn Tūmart, loc. cit., p. 235.
29. ibid., p. 232.
30. Ibn Khaldūn, French transl. 1863–8, Vol. 2, p. 200.

and which foretold an exceptional role for the people of the Maghrib.[31] The two approaches are not necessarily inconsistent. However, it must be stressed that the creed of Mahdism suspended, as it were, those aspects of Almohad doctrine which could have stimulated deeper theological inquiry to enrich the superficial, formalistic Islam of the time.

On the subject of individual judgement, Ibn Tūmart adopted the same position as the Ẓāhirites: he rejected it as a source of error. In reply to the implicit objection concerning the *shahāda* (testimony), he added that this was not an *aṣl* (absolute principle), but merely an indication of relative worth.[32]

Thus for Ibn Tūmart the sources which must be used to establish the laws of religion were the Koran, the *sunna* and, in certain circumstances, consensus and reasoning by analogy. For the *ḥadīth*s, he gave preference to the people of Madina, and this is further proof of Ibn Tūmart's concern to stick to the sources closest to the Prophet. We cannot agree with Goldziher when he explains Ibn Tūmart's concern for Madina tradition and practice by his desire not to offend the Mālikite school.[33] As regards *idjmā*ʿ (consensus), Ibn Tūmart limited it to the companions of the Prophet. As regards *ḳiyās* (analogy), his position was cautious; he certainly condemned *al-ḳiyās aḳli* (speculative analogy).

Having set out the sources of Muslim law, the *fiḳh*, Ibn Tūmart advocated their direct use, and condemned the exclusive use of treatises of *furū*ʿ (the applied branch of jurisprudence). This was an opportunity for him to attack the Almoravid doctors, who were guilty in his eyes of neglecting and abandoning the traditions and even sometimes of ending up with a positive scorn for the *ḥadīth*s.

For Ibn Tūmart, the *fiḳh* needed to be amended and enriched, for *idjtihād* did not end with Mālik and the other leaders of schools; and anybody versed in the science of *uṣūl al-fiḳh* (foundations, sources of the law) could himself derive the law from the sources. Ibn Tūmart condemned membership of a legal school (*madhhab*), for, he said, variety of opinions on a single question is absurd. By the same token, he stressed, like the Ẓāhirites, the impossibility of confining the application of an order to particular cases when it was expressed in general terms.

The organization of the Almohad movement: a party of propaganda, indoctrination and battle

It was probably from the time he withdrew to Aghmāt that Ibn Tūmart found himself increasingly at the centre of a movement which was hence-

31. For example, Ṣāliḥ, the prophet of the Barghwāṭa, and Ḥā-Mīm, the prophet of the Rif. On the subject of Ṣāliḥ, see the *Encyclopaedia of Islam*, new edn, Vol. 1, pp. 1043–4, and also 1st edn, Vol. 4, pt 1, p. 113. For Ḥā-Mīm, see ibid., new edn, Vol. 3, pp. 134–5.

32. Goldziher, 1903, p. 46.

33. ibid., p. 50.

PLATE 2.1 *The Ḳibla, or eastern wall, of the mosque at Tīnmallal (Morocco). As the first major oratory of the Almohad community, the mosque is an example of the architectural and decorative austerity that the Almohads wanted to impose*

PLATE 2.2 *The inner courtyard of the mosque at Tīnmallal*

forth to grow in order to achieve not only religious but political objectives, involving the peoples of the Atlas. It was in this context that the idea of proclaiming himself the Mahdī probably took form in Ibn Tūmart's mind. As soon as he arrived in Īgīllīz in + 1121, he was at pains to reproduce the behaviour of the Prophet, in particular by settling himself in a cave, and so prepared people's minds for the coming of the Mahdī, who would be none other than himself. Thus he had himself proclaimed the Mahdī by ten of his companions including 'Abd al-Mu'min, which is reminiscent of *al-'As͟hara al-Mubas͟hs͟hara* (the ten to whom Paradise was promised).[34] The proclamation took place under a tree, just like the *bay'a* at al-Riḍwān. Ibn Tūmart's campaigns, like the Prophet's, were called *mag͟hāzī*, his withdrawal to Tīnmallal was called a *hid͟jra* (hegira) and the people of that place, the *Ahl Tīnmallal*, were likened to the Anṣār.

After this initial organization, skirmishes and surprise attacks won for Ibn Tūmart the greater part of the Anti-Atlas and the Sūs, and all the *ḳabīla*s of the Maṣmūda were ready to support him.

However, Almoravid pressure was growing stronger and stronger, and Ibn Tūmart judged it wiser to withdraw to a more easily defended position. So in 1123 he 'emigrated' to Tīnmallal. His settling in this place seems to have been accompanied by violence: the *Ahl Tīnmallal* of the Almohad hierarchy appear to have been a heterogeneous group, which suggests that the former inhabitants were liquidated and replaced by a mixed group of Almohad supporters. Following this, the Almohad movement took advantage of the difficulties the Almoravids were encountering in Spain, and of the hostility shown towards them by the mountain *ḳabīla*s, to expand and consolidate. However, there were many internal dissensions in the Almohad ranks and the Maṣmūda, fragmented into small groups, were not prepared to let themselves be incorporated into a wider federation.

From the outset, the partisan structure of the movement was reflected in the workings of the state, and for this reason a study of the partisan organization can be a profitable way of elucidating the bases, aims and key features of the Almohad edifice.

The 'ten' were distinguished by learning, organizing ability and the spirit of sacrifice; they had all been Ibn Tūmart's companions before his proclamation as Mahdī, except for Abū Ḥafṣ 'Umar Ibn Yaḥyā al-Hintātī, who had been co-opted after the *tawḥīd* from the Hintāta, a large group of *ḳabīlas*, of which he was one of the leading chiefs.[35] The group, incidentally, contained not a single member of the Harg͟ha.

The constitution of the 'fifty' (*Ahl al-K͟hamsīn*) was brought into effect progressively. The fifty represented the Almohad *ḳabīla*s, which formed

34. *Encyclopaedia of Islam*, new edn, Vol. 1, p. 693.

35. Ibn 'Id͟hārī al-Marrākus͟hī, 1949 edn, p. 188; see also *Encyclopaedia of Islam*, new edn, Vol. 1, p. 87. Ibn Abī Zar', Latin transl. 1843, p. 113; see also *Encyclopaedia of Islam*, new edn, Vol. 3, pp. 694–5. Ibn al-Ḳaṭṭān, op. cit., p. 87; A. Huici Miranda, 1956b, Vol. 1, p. 103.

the basis of the movement and rallied to it at different times; the Haskura, for example, only joined the movement in the reign of ʿAbd al-Muʾmin.[36] This leads us to suppose that this council must have been in embryo form at Īgīllīz and begun to take its functional form at Tīnmallal.[37] Some *ḳabīlas* must have been represented on it before joining it collectively.

The *ṭalaba* group seems to have been earlier than the other two. Al-Marrākushī tells us that Ibn Tūmart – before his proclamation as Mahdī – used to send men whose spirit he admired to rally the tribes to his cause.[38] These *ṭalaba* were thus the propagandists of the movement; their activities were of course to continue after the proclamation of Ibn Tūmart.[39] Each of these bodies had a specific role, which helps us to have a clearer idea of them.

The ten – Ahl al-Djamāʿa

The fact that the sources give this council two names, speaking both of the *ashara* ('the ten') and of the *Ahl al-Djamāʿa* (literally the 'people of the community'), makes it difficult for us to know whether the name refers to the body itself or to the number of its members, which varies according to the source. Al-Baydhaḳ, for example, calls them only *Ahl al-Djamāʿa*. Elsewhere, figures of seven, ten and twelve are given; this makes us think that the number ten was given to the council out of analogy with the companions of the Prophet. The actual number and the composition must have fluctuated, either by dismissals such as that of al-Faḳīh al-Ifrīḳi, or by replacements. Some authors also mention individuals who belonged both to the ten and to the *Ahl al-Dar* (the 'people of the house' or privy council of the Mahdī), which implies a certain flexibility and a functional interchange between the two bodies.[40]

The order in which the members of the council of ten are listed varies, again according to the source, and scarcely helps us to understand their relative importance and roles. The majority of sources put ʿAbd al-Muʾmin at the head of the list, perhaps because he had succeeded the Mahdī. Some authors, however, put first either ʿAbd al-Waḥīd Ash-Sharḳī or the famous al-Bashir al-Wansharisi, principal architect of the famous *tamyīz* of 1128–9, who, if he had not been killed at the battle of al-Buḥayra, would have seemed best placed to succeed Ibn Tūmart.[41] The members of the council of ten, or *Ahl al-Djamāʿa*, were in a way the Mahdī's ministers; these were

36. E. Lévi-Provençal, 1928a, pp. 35–6, 28 and 76; Ibn al-Ḳaṭṭān, op. cit., pp. 28 and 92–3; Ibn Khaldūn, French transl. 1956, Vol. 6, p. 476.

37. Huici Miranda, 1956b, Vol. 1, p. 103.

38. Ibn ʿIdhārī al-Marrākushī, loc. cit., p. 187.

39. Lévi-Provençal 1928a, p. 132; Ibn al-Ḳaṭṭān, op. cit., pp. 84–93.

40. See Lévi-Provençal, 1928a, pp. 34–6 and *passim*; Ibn ʿIdhārī al-Marrākushī, loc. cit., pp. 188 and 337; Ibn al-Ḳaṭṭān, op. cit., pp. 28, 30, 74, 76 and 97; Ibn Abī Zarʿ, loc. cit., p. 113.

41. I. U. A. Musa, 1969, p. 59; Huici Miranda, 1956b, Vol. 1, p. 101; Ibn al-Ḳaṭṭān, op. cit., pp. 102–3.

trustworthy men, whom he consulted on important questions and charged with the execution of great decisions. Among them, al-Bas͟hīr was often, and ʿAbd al-Muʾmin, ʿUmar Asnad͟j and Mūsā Ibn Tamara were sometimes, given military commands. Others were secretaries, *ḳāḍī*s and so on.[42]

The council of fifty – Ahl al-K͟hamsīn

Then came the consultative councils, the most important of which seems to have been the council of fifty (*Ahl al-K͟hamsīn*). The number fifty seems to be a point of departure on which most sources agree, but there are other sources which put the number variously at seventy and seven.[43] We have explained above how this council represented the *ḳabīla*s which had joined; the process of joining suggests a fluidity in the number of members which would explain the different figures found in the sources.[44] The seven mentioned by some sources were probably only a limb of the council of fifty, on which they may have represented the three most important *ḳabīla*s, viz. the Harg͟ha, the *Ahl Tīnmallal* and the Hintāta. As for the figure of seventy, it could have been the result of a combination of the council of fifty and another Almohad body.[45]

The dominant groups on the council were the *Ahl Tīnmallal* – a mixed group – the Harg͟ha, the Mahdī's *ḳabīla* and the D͟janfīsa; the first were allied to the Hintāta from the earliest days of the movement.[46] The fifty were described as the people he consulted and whose advice he sought (*aṣḥāb mas͟hwaratihi*).[47]

The ṭalaba

This word, whose origin the sources do not give, seems to be an Almohad invention. Even in the Mahdī's lifetime there were a great many *ṭalaba*s. In 1121 he sent many of them to the Sūs – 1500 of them, according to Ibn Abī Zarʿ al-Fāsī – which suggests that these envoys were disciples of Ibn Tūmart's whom he apparently instructed and trained during the discussion and disputation sessions which he constantly encouraged on the way back to Morocco. His stay in Marrakesh gained him still more disciples, and his teaching at Īgīllīz, for about a year before his proclamation as Mahdī, must have consolidated this body of disciples.[48]

42. Ibn al-Ḳaṭṭān, op. cit., pp. 74, 81 and 117; *al-Ḥulal al-Maws͟hiyya*, French transl. 1936, p. 88; Lévi-Provençal, 1928a, pp. 75 and 33; Ibn ʿId͟hārī al-Marrākus͟hī, loc. cit., p. 338.

43. Ibn al-Ḳaṭṭān, op. cit., pp. 28–32.

44. In AH 524/ + 1130, more than ten people were added to the council of fifty, after the purge; Lévi-Provençal, 1928b, p. 35.

45. It was either the fifty plus the *Ahl al-D͟jamāʿa*, or the fifty plus the *Ahl al-Dar*; see J. F. P. Hopkins, 1958, p. 90.

46. Mūsā, op. cit., Vol. 23, p. 63.

47. Ibn al-Ḳaṭṭān, op. cit., pp. 75 and 81; Ibn Abī Zarʿ, loc. cit., p. 114.

48. Ibn ʿId͟hārī al-Marrākus͟hī, in Huici Miranda, 1965, Vol. 3, p. 18; Ibn al-Ḳaṭṭān, op. cit., pp. 87 and 93; Lévi-Provençal, 1928b, p. 132; Ibn Abī Zarʿ, loc. cit., p. 113; al-Salāwī, 1894, Vol. 2.

Al-ḳāffa

This was the mass of the Almohads. They did not remain unorganized, either, for Ibn Tūmart made the *ḳabīla* both a political and a religious entity. He put a *naḳīb* at the head of every ten people, and held frequent parades (*ʿarḍ*).[49] Each category of Almohad had a rank (*rutba*) and, according to Ibn al-Ḳaṭṭān, there were fourteen of these.[50]

These forms of organization allowed intensive and often effective indoctrination, whose twofold purpose seems to have been to inculcate in the Almohads a feeling of exclusivity and an attitude of systematic, violent hostility towards non-Almohads. This dual attitude was to ensure perfect obedience, as produced by the system of education. The latter was based on three elements: the ideas of Ibn Tūmart, the sources and approaches to knowledge that he had authorized, and the methods of acquiring knowledge that he had laid down.

Ibn Tūmart's ideas cannot be reduced to any other doctrine already worked out. They were distinguished by a subtle doctrinal eclecticism which seems to have fostered among the Almohads the feeling of being different, united and even isolated in this difference, in the true faith, as compared to all other Muslims. Ibn Tūmart's doctrine was a total break with the practices adopted by the Mālikīs. The Almohads had to be distinguished from others even by their dress, and they had to leave places where men did not uphold the divine unity and join their brethren in the true faith.[51]

All this was tirelessly taught by Ibn Tūmart, in the form first of lectures and then of treatises with lengthy commentaries. He was at pains to link knowledge and action (*ʿilm* and *ʿamal*), using Arabic and Berber and adapting his training methods to different levels of understanding.[52] These methods of training were characterized by often excessive severity, which ensured such blind obedience that an Almohad – if so ordered – could go to the point of executing his father, brother or son. This severity often took the form of purges, which were sometimes veritable massacres.[53]

Almohad organization did not remain immutable. After Ibn Tūmart's death, the *Ahl al-Djamāʿa* and the *Ahl al-Khamsīn* are mentioned only on the occasion of the *bayʿa* (the oath of allegiance) to ʿAbd al-Muʾmin, which suggests that the latter suppressed the two councils. In fact, Ibn Tūmart died after the crushing defeat of al-Buḥayra, and the problem of his succession seems to have shaken Almohad unity. ʿAbd al-Muʾmin, who seems to have found himself very isolated, must have thought it wiser

49. Ibn al-Ḳaṭṭān, op. cit., p. 27; *al-Ḥulal al-Mawshiyya*, op. cit., p. 89, which says that the *naḳīb* was also called *mizwār*.

50. Ibn al-Ḳaṭṭān, op. cit.

51. Ibn Tūmart, loc. cit., pp. 258–64, 266–7, 290 and 296; Ibn al-Ḳaṭṭān, op. cit., pp. 42, 46 and 85.

52. Ibn ʿIdhārī al-Marrākushī, loc. cit., pp. 188 and 191; Ibn Abī Zarʿ, Latin transl. 1843–6, pp. 114 and 118–19; Ibn al-Ḳaṭṭān, op. cit., pp. 24, 29 and 103.

53. Mūsā, op. cit., pp. 71–2.

PLATE 2.3 *The minaret of the unfinished Ḥasan Mosque at Rabat; a good example of Almohad surface decorative sculpture*

to collaborate with individuals on the two councils rather than using the councils as such.[54] This would explain the appearance of the Almohad council of shaykhs, which seems to have replaced the two councils, *Ahl al-Djamā'a* and *Akl al-Khamsīn*. This tactical regrouping seems to have been the cause of the unrest among the Almohad dignitaries which broke out in the revolt of Ibn Malwiya in 1133.[55]

The shaykhs are known to have played an increasingly important role; they tended to constitute a power parallel to that of the caliphs, which led Caliph al-Nāṣir to deal a heavy blow to their prestige on the eve of the battle of Las Navas de Tolosa; this was probably the cause of that serious defeat.[56] The weakening of the Almohad caliphate must have given them fresh power; they then formed a sort of caste, whose pressure became intolerable to Caliph al-Ma'mūn, and he eventually suppressed the creed of the Mahdī.

Among the shaykhs, the descendants of members of the *Ahl al-Djamā'a* and the *Ahl al-Khamsīn* were the most numerous, according to Ibn Khaldūn, particularly the Ḥintata and the people of Tīnmallal; by contrast, the Hargha seem not to have provided any influential shaykhs.[57] This was perhaps the cause of the revolt by the Mahdī's two brothers. The council of shaykhs seems to have been a structure designed to broaden the base of the Almohad movement, for it served as a model for the organization of newly recruited sectors. Thus we see the appearance of the council of Arab shaykhs and that of the Andalusian shaykhs of Djund, whose role, however, was pre-eminently military.[58]

The corps of the *ṭalaba* was the object of particular attention by 'Abd al-Mu'min. Their role as propagandists remained very important after the taking of Marrakesh, as shown by the official letters, notably the one sent by 'Abd al-Mu'min to the *ṭalaba* of Andalusia in A.H. 543/1148 of the Christian era. However, they acquired other responsibilities, and were active in various spheres: education, teaching, administration and the army. Admittedly, it was their particular duty 'to enjoin the good and to forbid the evil', but with the growth of the empire they seem increasingly to have fulfilled the role of political and 'ideological' commissars, above all in the armed forces, and more particularly the navy.[59]

54. Huici Miranda, 1956b, Vol. 1, p. 102.

55. Ibn 'Idhārī al-Marrākushī, ed. Lévi-Provençal, n.d., Vol. 3, pp. 240–1; Ibn Abī Zar', loc. cit., p. 169.

56. Ibn 'Idhārī al-Marrākushī, loc. cit., Vol. 3, p. 85; Ibn Ṣāḥib al-Ṣalāt, 1964 edn, pp. 148, 324 and 399–400; see also *Encyclopaedia of Islam*, new edn, Vol. 3, p. 924. Ibn al-Athīr, 1851–76 edn, Vol. 11, p. 186.

57. Ibn Khaldūn, 1956–9 edn, Vol. 6, pp. 534, 542, 545–6.

58. Ibn Ṣāḥib al-Ṣalāt, loc. cit., pp. 218 and 399–400; Ibn 'Idhārī al-Marrākushī, loc. cit., Vol. 3, p. 85; Ibn al-Ḳaṭṭān, op. cit., p. 226.

59. See the text of the letter in Ibn al-Ḳaṭṭān, op. cit., pp. 155 ff.; E. Lévi-Provençal, 1941a, p. 6, on the commission of the *ṭalaba* to supervise the construction of the city of Djabal al-Fatḥ; Ibn 'Idhārī al-Marrākushī, loc. cit., Vol. 4, pp. 43–4, on the administrative

The sectarian attitude of the Almohads was admittedly maintained for a long time, but it seems to have been felt very early as a factor leading to political isolation; this explains al-Ma'mūn's abandonment of the dogma of Mahdism.[60]

Unification of the Maghrib by the Almohad/Mu'minid caliphs

The Almohad movement had led to the creation of a party whose political goal became increasingly clear: the establishment of a new power to implement Ibn Tūmart's reform. The Almoravids became very conscious of this. The beginnings of the confrontation were marked by three events of great importance. The Almoravids failed against Aghmat; the Almohads won their first victory at Kik in 1122, and at once set out to capture Marrakesh. They besieged it for forty days, but the Almoravid cavalry crushed them at the battle of al-Buḥayra in 1128, which was a disaster for the Almohads: al-Bashir al-Wanharisi, one of Ibn Tūmart's most prominent companions, lost his life there, and 'Abd al-Mu'min, who was seriously wounded, had great trouble in bringing the remnants of the Almohad contingents back to Tīnmallal.[61]

It was in these difficult circumstances that Ibn Tūmart died, in 524/+1130; the arrangement of the succession and the accession of 'Abd al-Mu'min in 527/+1133 gave rise to problems. Ibn Tūmart was buried at Tīnmallal and, if Leo Africanus is to be believed, his tomb was still venerated there five centuries later.

Period of 'Abd al-Mu'min Ibn 'Alī and the foundation of the empire (1133–63)

The Almohad movement no doubt experienced a rather long period of crisis following Ibn Tūmart's death, although we know very little about it. 'Abd al-Mu'min's accession has been variously explained. The 'tribalist' explanations seem too superficial; and Jean Devisse is right in seeing at the heart of the problem 'Abd al-Mu'min's position alongside Ibn Tūmart and his role in the movement after the meeting at Mallāla.[62] In this sense his accession,

---

role of the *ṭalaba* at Gafṣa after the Almohads had reconquered the city in AH 583/+1187; Lévi-Provençal, 1928a, p. 215.

60. Musa, op. cit., p. 23; Ibn 'Idhārī al-Marrākushī, op. cit., Vol. 3, pp. 85, 263–6 and 291–2; Ibn Khaldūn, 1956–9 edn, Vol. 6, pp. 630–7; Ibn Abī Zar', loc. cit., pp. 167–8.

61. On the battle of Kik, see Lévi-Provençal, 1928a, pp. 122 ff. On the battle of al-Buḥayra, see *Encyclopaedia of Islam*, new edn. Vol. 3, p. 959, where the date is given as 524/1130; *al-Ḥulal al-Mawshiyya*, loc. cit., p. 94; Lévi-Provençal, 1925, Fragment 4; Ibn al-Athīr, French transl. 1876–91, Vol. 10, p. 407, and French transl. 1901, p. 536.

62. J. Devisse, review of R. Le Tourneau, 1969.

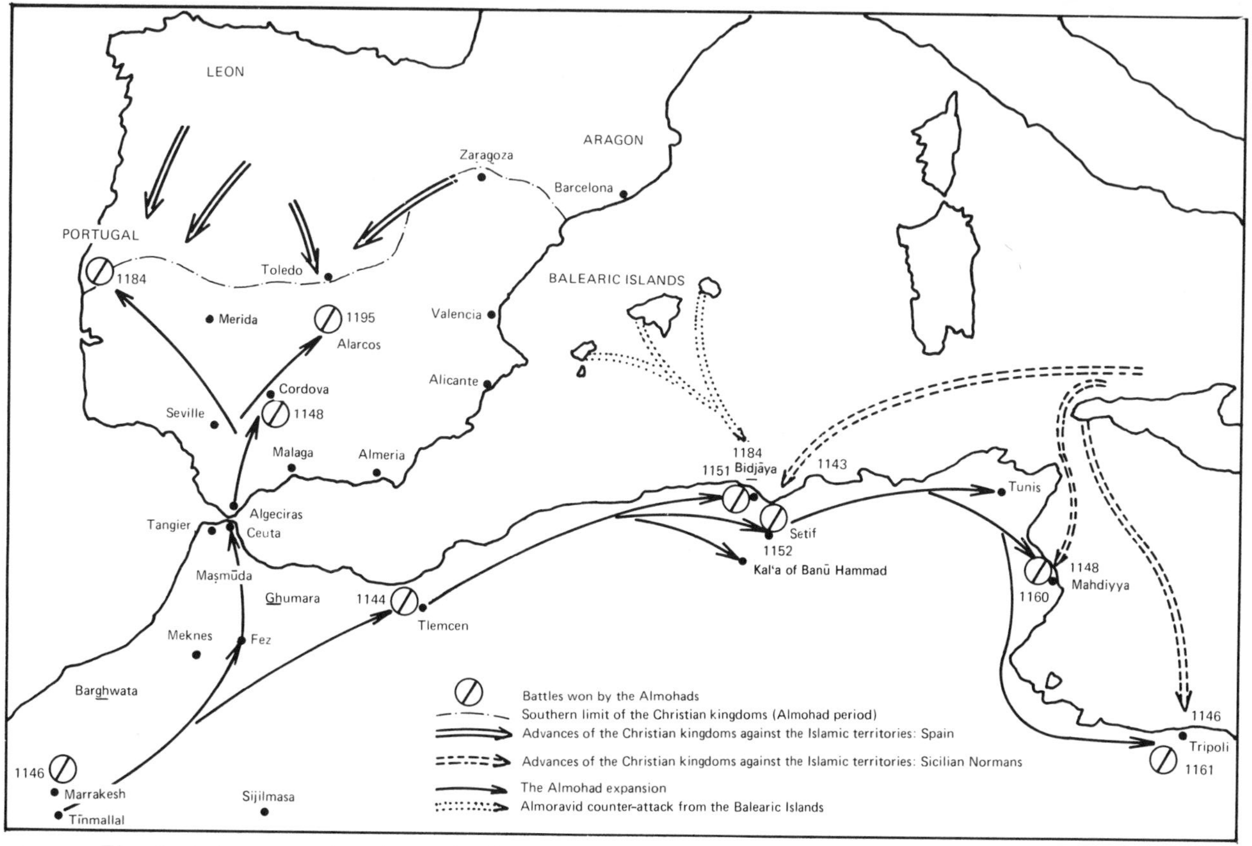

FIG. 2.2 *The Almohad reconquest (based on original by O. Saidi)*

in which another companion, Abū Ḥafṣ ʿUmar al-Hintātī, seems to have played a predominant role, must be seen as an event transcending the local messianism, and probably reflecting a plan devised by ʿAbd al-Muʾmin himself. Was he realizing a dream, dimly perceived since Mallāla, of a Maghrib reunified in the strict observance of Islam? Or was he acting as an empire builder in his own and his family's interests? Or (as seems most probable) had he conceived a plan to reconcile the two?

During a long reign of thirty years ʿAbd al-Muʾmin, who was 35 years old at the time of his accession, was to demonstrate his outstanding qualities as a good general, an energetic leader of a still heterogeneous coalition and a statesman. These qualities were essential if he was to carry out successfully his twofold purpose of a *dj̲ihād* against the Almoravids and the organization and consolidation of the Almohad movement, whose aim in turn was to bring about the submission, subjugation and pacification of the Maghrib and the consolidation of political power.

This task, which turned out to be long and difficult, was carried out methodically in several stages, following a very precise strategy which combined both military and economic aspects.[63] We do not here propose to go into details, or even to enumerate all the episodes, but merely to highlight the key stages.

The conquest of Morocco

The first objective was to gain possession of Morocco; this took place in two phases. Drawing a lesson from the crushing defeat at al-Buḥayra, ʿAbd al-Muʾmin decided to avoid the plains, where the Almoravid cavalry had the advantage, and set out to subjugate the Berber mountains in order to secure both their trade routes and their mineral wealth.[64] Winning over many *ḳabīla*s in the Atlas, he subdued the Sūs, and the Wādī Darʿa (Draa);[65] these were areas essential to the Almoravid arrangements for the very lucrative trade with sub-Saharan Africa. He made them into a strong base for attack – and for withdrawal in case of need. Thus the Almohads could contemplate attacking the line of fortresses encircling the High Atlas to the north and barring the way to the plains and the capital.

Leaving the plains, the Almohad army followed the route along the ridges, moving north-east in a manoeuvre designed to isolate the Almoravid heartland. They took the Middle Atlas and the Tāfīlālet oases during the years 1040–1.[66] Debouching into northern Morocco, they used the D̲jebala mountains as a base to take the fortresses in the Tāzā area. From this position of strength ʿAbd al-Muʾmin set out to win over the sub-Mediterranean *ḳabīla*s in the area, and ended up entering his own village

63. ibid.
64. See B. Rosenberger, 1970.
65. The opinion of Le Tourneau, op. cit., p. 52, that ʿAbd al-Muʾmin lacked severity, seems to need considerable qualification.
66. Laroui, op. cit., p. 168; cf. *Encyclopaedia of Islam*, new edn, Vol. 1, p. 78.

PLATE 2.4 *Gate of the Ḳaṣaba des Oudaïas, built at Rabat by the Almohads facing the city of Sale, to stand sentinel over the yet unsubdued territories of Morocco's Atlantic coast (general view)*

PLATE 2.5 *Gate of the Ḳaṣaba des Oudaïas at Rabat (detail). Decoration on the monumental Almohad gateway, as found in a number of Spanish and Moroccan cities*

of Tagra in triumph. Thus the Almoravid dispositions were outflanked and the strategy of encirclement succeeded. Recent research leads us to believe that this route was not only of military value but also had an economic objective, namely the mountain mines, the sinews of war.[67]

From now on ʿAbd al-Muʾmin, at the head of already sizeable forces and no doubt possessing large resources, thought himself strong enough to go over to the offensive on the plain and face the Almoravids there. Conditions were very favourable to this initiative. In 1143 the succession to ʿAlī Ibn Yūsuf Ibn Tāshfīn caused dissension between the chiefs Lamtūna and Masufa, the pillars of the Almoravid regime. In 1145 the death of the Catalan, Reverter (al-Ruburṭayr), leader of the Almoravids' Christian militia, robbed them of one of their cleverest and most devoted generals. Finally, the balance was tilted in favour of the Almohads when the *tawḥid* of the Zenāta rallied to their cause. They took Tlemcen and forced the Almoravid amir Tāshfīn Ibn ʿAlī to withdraw to Oran, where he died after a fall from a horse.

By this date the whole of the Atlas as far as the Rif had been subjugated, the Mediterranean coast subdued and the western part of the central Maghrib taken. The Almohad pincer movement gripped the Almoravid territory, where power was more and more disorganized. ʿAbd al-Muʾmin set out to organize his new conquests on the basis of the political system of the Almohad community. The Almohad conquests had not been easy, and the new caliph had to show extreme severity to withstand revolts and conspiracies.[68]

The new caliph did not command unanimous support among the Almohads, whose homogeneity seems to have been less than perfect at the time; there were some who opposed the new leader and others who toyed with the idea of going back to the old freedom. In the event, two Almohads, Ibn Mālwiyya, former shaykh of *ahl al-Djamāʿa*, representing the Janfisa, and ʿAbd al-ʿAziz Ibn Karman al-Harghi, of Ibn Tūmart's own *ḳabīla*, rebelled, but without really threatening the new leadership. The Almohads also had to face many revolts and resistance movements during the conquest itself, the most important being those led by an individual known by the nickname of *Maṣbūgh al-Yādayn* ('the man with stained hands') in the Adjarsi (Guercif) Fez area, by Abū Yaʿla of the *ḳabīla* of the Izmasin (the Ṣanhaja) and by Sāʿid of the Ghayyāta in the Tāzā area.

Despite these movements, the Almohads had managed to set up a military power which validated the precise commercial axis then in the process of development between the Sudan and the Mediterranean in eastern Morocco. From then on, continuing revolts in the Sūs and from Ceuta to Agadir (Aghadīr) – areas that had become economically unimportant –

67. B. Rosenberger, 1964, p. 73.
68. A. Merad, 1957, pp. 114 ff.

could hardly be a real threat;[69] especially since the Almohads, absorbed in an enormous undertaking, going from victory to victory and amassing booty upon booty, remained firmly united around ʿAbd al-Muʾmin. He remained faithful to the Mahdī's doctrine, countenanced no innovations, and kept around him the famous shaykhs who guarded the interests of the Almohads and hence guaranteed their loyalty.

However, the importance of the change can be gauged by the way it was carried out and the reactions of the people concerned. The Almohad successes were usually bloody; during the conquest there were no lightning strokes, no easy victories, and no large towns that did not have to be taken by storm. Almoravid society seemed to have relatively resilient structures.[70] According to the author of the *ḳirṭaṣ* and Abū ʿAbd Allāh Muḥammad b. Abi ʾl-Maʿāli Ibn Sammāk, the author of the *Ḥulal*, the Almoravid period was one of peace and prosperity; the people certainly did not regard the Almoravids as ungodly princes, and accepted Mālikism.[71] The Almohads could not therefore be regarded – outside the Maṣmūda mountains – as liberators, except by malcontents anxious to escape, if only temporarily, from the demands of the tax collector. Most towns, which were admittedly growth points, resisted the assaults of the Almohads and it took them fifteen years to subdue the whole of Morocco. Hence we should not be surprised by the frequent revolts which followed the taking of Marrakesh by ʿAbd al-Muʾmin, encouraged as they were by popular participation and doubtless inspired by motives far more decisive than religious devotion to Mālikism. More probably, they expressed the reaction of a society radically challenged by an 'exclusivist' community imposing its power by means of a merciless war.

The conquest of the central Maghrib

Once his position had been solidly re-established in the far Maghrib, ʿAbd al-Muʾmin reckoned that he could extend his conquests beyond the frontiers of the Almoravid possessions to the rest of the Maghrib. But before embarking on this project the caliph was obliged to intervene in Andalusia, where the people could no longer tolerate the authority of the Almoravids and where the Castilian danger was becoming more and more threatening. Already, during the siege of Marrakesh, the caliph had received an Andalusian delegation after certain towns came over to his side, such as Jerez in 1144. He then sent an expeditionary force, including two of the Mahdī's brothers, ʿAbd al-ʿAziz and ʿIsa Amghar.[72] Other defections followed, the most important being Seville and Cordova; but the eastern

69. Devisse, op. cit.

70. See al-Idrīsī, 1866 edn, p. 8, on Aghmāt, Fez and Zarkashi.

71. Ibn Abī Zarʿ, loc. cit., p. 108; *al-Ḥulal al-Mawshiyya*, loc. cit., 115–16.

72. On the initial foothold of the Almohads on the Iberian peninsula, see *Encyclopaedia of Islam*, new edn, Vol. 1, p. 79. On the details of the expeditionary force, see Ibn Khaldūn, French transl. 1852–6, Vol. 2, pp. 183–8.

provinces remained cautious towards the Almohads. That was why it did not occur to ʿAbd al-Muʾmin in 1150, when he received delegates from Andalusia who had come to take an oath of allegiance to him, to involve himself at once in the affairs of the peninsula: he was looking first and foremost towards the east. It is hard not to think that at this point in the mid-twelfth century the first Almohad caliph was probably formulating some clear ideas on political strategy: above all, to secure a solid base by unifying the Maghrib, and then to launch out across the Straits.

In Ifrīḳiya there was also a Christian threat. The power of the Sanhajan dynasties of Ḳayrawān and Bid̲j̲āya was being undermined at its foundations by a new territorial organization in Ifrīḳiya and the central Maghrib, to the advantage of the Sanhajan and Arab principalities in the hinterland, whilst the Normans, led by King Roger II of Sicily, were gaining a foothold in the main ports on the coasts of Ifrīḳiya. An Almohad expedition into Ifrīḳiya could therefore be justified, especially since it invoked the duty of *d̲j̲ihād*. After two years of preparation ʿAbd al-Muʾmin made his way to Ceuta, and it might have been thought that he intended to cross to Spain. But from there, pretending to return to Marrakesh, he took the road east at the beginning of the summer of 1152, and by forced marches reached the central Maghrib.[73]

He first seized Algiers, and then made himself master of Bid̲j̲āya without great difficulty. Then he sent a detachment under the command of his son ʿAbd-Allah to occupy the old Hammadid capital, the *Ḳalʿa*, which they took by main force and sacked, putting the inhabitants to the sword. Constantine, where the Hammadid prince, Yaḥya Ibn ʿAbd al-ʿAziz, had sought refuge, was handed over by the Hammadid ruler's vizier, and from there an expedition was sent against the Beduin of the Constantine area. During these operations a certain Abū Ḳasaba launched a raid on Bid̲j̲āya with the Banū Zaldawīw, which looked very much like a commando operation to assassinate the caliph. Following this the repression was very harsh, and ʿAbd al-Muʾmin dispersed the Sanhaja, the Luwata and the Kutama, who had joined them.[74]

The fate of the central Maghrib was in the course of transformation, and this alerted the Arabs, who were allies or clients of the defeated

73. On the central Maghrib and Ifrīḳiya from about the middle of the sixth to the twelfth century of the Christian era, see H. R. Idris, 1962, Vol. 1, ch. 6, pp. 303 ff. and 363 ff. On the Almohad conquest of the central Maghrib, see a good summary in J. Brignon, *et al.*, 1967, p. 112.

In the central Maghrib, the last Hammadids of Bid̲j̲āya, al-Mansūr, al-ʿAziz and Yāḥya, had established a *modus vivendi* with the Hilalians, the new masters of the plateaux, had developed both trade and piracy, taking advantage of the difficulties of their Zirid cousins at Māhdiyya, and had got a real recovery under way. See Laroui, op. cit., p. 168.

74. See Lévi-Provençal (ed.), 1928a, text, p. 115; French transl., pp. 189–90; Ibn al-At̲h̲īr, French Transl. 1901, p. 504.

Sanhaja dynasty. Just when ʿAbd al-Muʾmin was starting on his way back to the far Maghrib, they rushed to the aid of Bidjāya. Driven back by the Almohads, they were then drawn on as far as the plain of Setif, where in 1153, after three days of heroic resistance, they were defeated and despoiled of their possessions, women and children. The organization, strength and discipline of the battle-hardened Almohad army was more than a match for their mettle and mobility. The battle caused a sensation, and marked a new phase in the fortunes of the new Almohad power.

The conquering Almohad caliph, who had a reputation for severity and indeed cruelty, showed a surprising 'generosity' towards the defeated Arabs whose coalition he had broken. Did he aim to impress them by a show of strength and then to win them to his cause by overwhelming them with his clemency? This seems probable, if we take into account the importance of the Arab factor in the central Maghrib and Ifrīḳiya, and the caliph's need to broaden the Berber–Almohad base of his regime in proportion to his growing empire. He may also already have been thinking of using the Arabs, in the name of the *djihād*, in Andalusia; appeals for help from that region were growing in number in the face of the increasingly dangerous Christian threat. Following these events, the caliph preferred not to venture beyond the Constantine area; he left governors and garrisons in the central Maghrib and set out for the far Maghrib.

Consolidation of Muʾminid power

We have already said that ʿAbd al-Muʾmin's accession to the caliphate was far from meeting with unanimous approval. Only his energy and vigour and the signs he had continually given of his qualities could have restrained the opposition, however muted, which existed within the Almohad ranks. His victories, which increased the chances that his power would endure, must have sharpened the impatience of the opposition; and it came out into the open under the impetus of Mahdī Ibn Tūmart's own relatives among the Hargha and the people of Tīnmallal, but without involving other Almohad *ḳabīla*. ʿAbd al-Muʾmin had the rebels killed and he disgraced the Ait Amghar, Ibn Tūmart's family, sending them away to Fez under house arrest. After this crisis he went on a sort of pilgrimage to Tīnmallal, where he distributed gifts and had the mosque, the Mahdī's sanctuary, enlarged, to make people forget the recent bloody events and at the same time to pave the way for his own dynasty. In 1156–7, encamped at Sale, he managed first to get his eldest son Muḥammad recognized as heir presumptive, and then to appoint his other sons as governors of the chief cities of the empire, with the title of *sayyid*.[75]

These steps were made possible by the support of the new imperial forces, the Hilal Arabs and the *ḳabīla*s of the east, particularly the Sanhaja,

75. Merad, 1957, pp. 135 ff.; Lévi-Provençal, 1941b, pp. 34–7; and Ibn al-Athīr, French transl. 1901, p. 581, whose chronology agrees with the official letters.

and could be put into effect as a result of the agreement of the famous Almohad shaykh al-Ajall ('the eminent') Abū Ḥafs 'Umar al-Hintātī. Once these operations had been carried out the caliph, in order to calm the people, lost no time in informing the Almohad 'colonies' of the various provinces that each Mu'minid *sayyid* would be accompanied by an Almohad shaykh as lieutenant – a vizier, admittedly, but also an adviser. 'Abd al-Mu'min's conquests and victories had crushed the dignitaries of earlier times, and the approval of the Atlas chiefs was not so much a matter of loyal adherence as a sign of weakness. These actions by the caliph provoked the rebellion of several *ḳabīlas*, especially in the south-east.[76]

The Gazūla gave a great welcome to the famous Yaḥya al-Sahrawi, the former Almoravid governor of Fez and former leader of the Ceuta revolt, which caused unrest on the borders of the Sūs. The Lamuta, the Hashtuka and the Lamtuna also rebelled. Yet these tribes were marginal to Almohad policies: their rebellion was therefore probably due to the excesses of the Mu'minid governors.[77] More generally, these movements seem to have marked a phase in the development of the new regime during which Mu'minid power was apparently trying to find its balance.

These revolts, as a whole, were of little importance in comparison with another event which was, in its future consequences, much more significant: the revolt of the Mahdī's two brothers, 'Isa and 'Abd al-'Aziz, who set up a conspiracy in Marrakesh that nearly succeeded. The caliph returned to his capital by forced marches and, in the investigation that followed, documents were discovered that revealed the names of 300 conspirators, including five leading merchants of Marrakesh. They were handed over to the wrath of the population.

After these testing times, 'Abd al-Mu'min seems once and for all to have become the head of an empire rather than of a community of believers, and a sort of coolness developed between him and the leaders of the Almohad movement. After the defeat of the Ait Amghar conspiracy, al-Baydhaḳ reports that he called together the people of Marrakesh and told them: 'I now know that apart from you I have neither brothers nor clients.'[78] A sincere and bitter admission, or a piece of demagogy? One thing seems certain, namely that henceforth 'Abd al-Mu'min gave his policy a new direction: he stopped relying exclusively on the ruling 'clan', the Maṣmūda aristocracy, and tried to enlarge his power base to include other *ḳabīlas*, particularly those of the Hilal Arabs and the central Maghrib. 'Abd al-Mu'min gradually began to free himself from Ibn Tūmart's concept of the community, based on clan and sect, and to promote a genuinely imperial policy, taking account of all levels of this society in the new empire.

76. Merad, 1957, p. 146.

77. Lévi-Provençal, 1928a, quotes 'Abd al-Mu'min as telling Abū Ḥafṣ, whom he sent to put down these rebellions, 'The camel has reared up in spite of her load.' (Text p. 177, French transl. p. 193).

78. ibid., text p. 119, French transl., pp. 198–9.

The conquest of Ifrīḳiya[79]

In 1156 Mu'minid power was solidly established and all opposition and disputes had died down.[80] 'Abd al-Mu'min could then undertake the second eastern campaign, at the end of which he was for the first time to unify the Maghrib under one single authority. He took particular care over preparations for this campaign, and it was only in 1159 that he resolved to march eastwards. The Zirid al-Ḥassan Ibn 'Alī, who had taken refuge with him, continually urged him on, and the people of Ifrīḳiya made repeated appeals for help against the activities of the Christians.

Leaving Abū Ḥafṣ as his lieutenant in Morocco, the caliph set off from Sale in the spring of 1159 at the head of a considerable force, while an impressive fleet steered a parallel course towards the east.[81] Six months later the Almohad army arrived before Tunis, which was taken after a blockade.[82] Then it was the turn of Mahdiyya, which had been in the hands of the Christian Normans for twelve years, to be besieged and taken after seven months of effort, including a blockade and other strong measures. The caliph's son, 'Abd-Allah, took Gabès and Gafṣa. Meanwhile Sfax and Tripoli fell into the hands of the Almohads. The hinterland of Ifrīḳiya, caught in a pincer movement between the attacks of the fleet against the coast and the breaches made by the cavalry in the south, was eventually subdued. Thus in Ifrīḳiya the small principalities which had shared the spoils of the Zirid kingdom had disappeared, the Normans had been dislodged from their positions on the coast and the Maghrib found itself united.

Preparations for the intervention in Andalusia, and the end of 'Abd al-Mu'min's reign[83]

Meanwhile the situation in Andalusia was increasingly disquieting. One of the greatest Andalusian lords, Ibn Mardanī<u>sh</u>, had revolted against Almohad authority and threatened the whole of the eastern part; the last representative of the Almoravid dynasty, Ibn <u>Gh</u>āniya, was carrying out

79. On the conquest of Ifrīḳiya by 'Abd al-Mu'min, see Idris, op. cit., Vol. 1, pp. 384 ff.

80. Official Letter no. 17 tells us of a pilgrimage by 'Abd al-Mu'min, a sort of tour of inspection by the caliph and his entourage. He went to Īgīllīz and then to Tīnmallal, and during this journey received delegations from many *ḳabīla*s, both those who had been loyal from the start and those who had been conquered after a more chequered past, who now assured him of their loyalty. He exhorted the people to strengthen their devotion to Almohad doctrine. Returning to Marrakesh on the 28th of Ramaḍān 552 (4 November 1157), he was able to celebrate the 'Id al-Fiṭr (feast at the end of the fast) as a festival of Mu'minid peace in the far Maghrib. See Merad, 1957, p. 154.

81. For details of the number of troops as given by different sources, see Merad, 1957, pp. 154–5.

82. For details, see 'Inān, 1964, Vol. 1, pp. 289–302.

83. ibid., pp. 304–411, for details of developments in Spain.

anti-Almohad agitation; and the Christians were continually pressing their advantage by making more and more incursions against northern Andalusia.[84]

Once he was back in Morocco, ʿAbd al-Muʾmin began to prepare for his intervention in Spain. He sent reinforcements, including Arab contingents, which carried the day both at Badajoz and Béja. He went to Marrakesh, where he received many *ḳumiyya* from among his taxpayers, apparently to form his personal bodyguard; and in 1163 he set off for Sale to direct a great expedition to Spain. However, he died there suddenly before he could carry out his plan. He was taken to Tīnmallal, where he was buried near the tomb of the Mahdī, Ibn Tūmart.

There is no need to dwell on ʿAbd al-Muʾmin's qualities as military leader and strategist; the important thing is that he carried out the conquest methodically, showing great qualities of organization and a sure knowledge of the country and of military science. However, the most striking fact is that ʿAbd al-Muʾmin's policy of conquest included economic objectives. Thus he cut off the Atlantic coast of Morocco – which the Almoravids had been the first to link with the Sahara on a grand scale – from its contacts with Africa, and secured control of an axis from Darʿa (Draa) to Oran, which was henceforth to be the caravan route bringing gold and produce from western Sudan.

The caliph also had to look both northwards and eastwards, for the Mediterranean was vital to the Maghrib, especially as Christendom was going over to the offensive on all fronts. Here we already glimpse the difficulty that lay ahead for the Almohad unitarian enterprise; it was to become virtually impossible to hold both Andalusia and Ifrīḳiya at the same time.

The Maghrib, however, acquired political unity under ʿAbd al-Muʾmin, in addition to its already long-standing economic and cultural unity. Breaking with Almoravid tradition, which had been inspired by Hispano-ʿUmayyad organization, he set up an administrative system for the whole area which took account both of the political constraints resulting from the size of the empire and also of his wish to spare the feelings of his entourage, who were by origin Almohad Berbers. Many of the rules of this system survive in the organization of the Ma<u>kh</u>zen of modern Morocco. When the Almohads turned to the Andalusians – or to men of the Maghrib trained in Andalusia – they were meeting a technical necessity for the administrative framework, while at the same time serving both their political purposes – expressed in the duality between the Muʾminid *sayyid* and the Almohad <u>sh</u>ay<u>kh</u> – and also their ideological purposes, represented by the *ṭalaba* and the *ḥuffaẓ*, the real 'political commissars' of the regime.

84. On Ibn Mardanī<u>sh</u> and Ibn <u>Gh</u>āniya, see *Encyclopaedia of Islam*, new edn, Vol. 3, pp. 864–5 and Vol. 2, pp. 1007–8.

This organization, which was far more differentiated than that of the Almoravids, was financed by a new tax system. It is said that on his return from Ifrīḳiya in 555/1160, ʿAbd al-Muʾmin caused a survey to be made of the whole of the Maghrib, from Barḳa in Tripolitania to Nul in southern Morocco;[85] one-third was deducted for mountains and unproductive land, and the rest was made liable to the *kharādj* (land tax), payable in cash or in kind. ʿAbd al-Muʾmin's land register was the first to be set up since Roman times; this gives an idea of the considerable resources at this caliph's disposal. He made all the inhabitants pay the *kharādj*, thus putting them on a level with non-Muslims because they were not – except for the Almohad community – true *muwaḥḥidūn*. The Hilalians had probably instituted a similar tax in the eastern Maghrib, and ʿAbd al-Muʾmin had only to make it universal, using the Hilalians themselves to collect it. Only the lands of the Almohads were not liable to the *kharādj*; thus the central Maghrib and Ifrīḳiya were regarded as conquered territory. Unity was therefore turned to the victor's advantage. The unification of the Maghrib was made more difficult by this, especially since Almohad ideology, despite ʿAbd al-Muʾmin's modifications, remained too sectarian to achieve 'a calming of minds'.[86]

ʿAbd al-Muʾmin seems nevertheless to have relied more on his army and navy than on a policy of genuine unification, despite the enlargement of the original Maṣmūda nucleus. Because of their tax system and sound currency, the Almohads were able to maintain a large army and navy; but the Almohad army, renowned for its organization, discipline and fighting qualities, was never unified, and this was to prove a weak point which became more and more serious.

One other feature of ʿAbd al-Muʾmin's reign is worth mentioning, although it is hard to assess within the limits of the present study; this is what is often called the 'deportation' of the Hilalians. The transfer of the Beduins was a response to too many motives and had too many varied consequences for us to sum it up in one word, as did the late Le Tourneau, who described it as a 'calamity' – no doubt carried away by the prejudices of the all-too-recent French colonial period.[87]

The period of stability and balance

Abū Yaʿḳūb Yūsuf (1163–84)

ʿAbd al-Muʾmin was succeeded not by the heir presumptive, Muḥammad, designated in 1154, but by another of his sons, Abū Yaʿḳūb Yūsuf, who did not take the title of caliph, *Amīr al-Muʾminīn*, until 1168. Thus there was a succession crisis, which probably lay behind the unrest that erupted

85. Ibn Abī Zarʿ, loc. cit., text p. 129, French transl., p. 174.
86. Laroui, op. cit., pp. 171–2.
87. Le Tourneau, op. cit., p. 59.

in northern Morocco among the Ghumara, between Ceuta and al-Ḳaṣr al-Kabīr. Their unrest spread to their Sanhaja and Awraba neighbours, and succeeded in giving them a leader who seems to have struck a coinage. Reading the *Ḳirṭaṣ*, one gains the impression that the unrest perhaps arose because the new caliph disbanded the army mustered by ʿAbd al-Muʾmin for the Andalusian expedition. Official Letter no. 24, however, gives a religious explanation for this revolt, which was led by a certain Sabaʿ Ibn Managhfād and lasted two years.[88] The Mālikite resistance in the Ceuta region, at the prompting of the famous Ḳādī ʿIyāḍ, may give this explanation a certain plausibility.

In any case the rising was a very serious one and the new caliph himself had to lead a campaign against the rebels in 1166–7, in the company of his two brothers, ʿUmar and ʿUthmān. According to Ibn al-Athīr, the caliph's victory ended in a massacre.[89] It gave him an opportunity to take the title of *Amīr al-Muʾminīn*; and to round off his campaign he gave his own brother the governorship of Ceuta, with the task of watching over the Rif.

THE ANDALUSIAN CAMPAIGN

The caliph sent his two brothers, ʿUmar and ʿUthmān, ahead of him. They managed to defeat Ibn Mardanīsh and his Christian mercenaries in 1165; but the capital, Murcia, held out against them, and the principality was to return to its independence for five more years. Meanwhile, serious threats were beginning to be identified in Portugal to the west. Giraldo Sempavor, Alfonso Henriques's famous captain, seized several positions in 1165, and then came with his king to besiege Badajoz, which owed its salvation only to the intervention of the Almohads' ally, Ferdinand II of Leon.

While this was happening, the threat of Ibn Mardanīsh in the east was removed almost without cost to the Almohads. At loggerheads with his father-in-law and lieutenant, Ibn Hamushk (the Hemochico of the Christian chronicles), Ibn Mardanīsh was deserted by most of his followers and died in 1172, grief-stricken to see his efforts come to nothing. The members of his family rallied to the Almohads, and became valued advisers. In 1172–3 the failure of the siege of Huete (Wabdha), the newly repopulated centre which constituted a threat to Cuenca and the Levantine border, revealed the weaknesses of the Almohad army and commissariat, and also the caliph's lack of energy. The mere approach of the Castilian army was sufficient to raise the siege, and the Almohads fell back on Murcia, where the army was disbanded. In 1181–2 the caliph entered Marrakesh with his army, and was joined there by Arab contingents from Ifrīḳiya led by the Arab shaykh, Abū Sirḥan Masʿud Ibn Sulṭan.

88. See *Encyclopedie d'Islam*, new edn, Vol. 2, p. 1121; A. Merad, 1962, Vol. 20, p. 409 and notes; Ibn Abī Zarʿ, loc. cit., text pp. 137–8, French transl., pp. 295–6.

89. See ʿInān, 1964, Vol. 2, pp. 23 ff.; *Encyclopaedia of Islam*, new edn, Vol. 1, pp. 160–1.

Abū Yūsuf Ya'ḳūb al-Manṣūr (1184–99)

Prince Abū Yūsuf Ya'ḳūb al-Manṣūr does not seem to have been designated as heir presumptive. When the choice of the Almohads fell on him there was some contention – from his brother 'Umar, governor of Murcia, among others. However, he must have established himself quite quickly, for he is known to us for his qualities of dynamism and gallantry. He had also been his father's vizier and close associate, and had thus been initiated into affairs of state.[90] Nevertheless, the beginning of the reign was marked by difficulties not unconnected with the growth of unrest in the central Maghrib and Ifrīḳiya, provoked this time by hostile agents, the Banū Ghāniya, who were determined to challenge the Almohad order.

THE BANŪ GHĀNIYA IN THE CENTRAL MAGHRIB

This family took its name from the Almoravid Princess Ghāniya, who was given in marriage by the Almoravid Sultan Yūsuf Ibn Tashfīn to 'Alī Ibn Yūsuf al-Masufi. He had two sons by her, Yaḥyā and Muḥammad.[91]

The two brothers played an important part during the Almoravid period, particularly in Spain. Muḥammad was governor of the Balearics at the time of the collapse of the Almoravids; he turned them into a place of refuge, proclaimed himself independent there and made the islands a base to which many supporters of the defeated dynasty withdrew. His son, Isḥāḳ, continued his policy and made the little kingdom prosper through piracy. Isḥāḳ's son, Muḥammad, was inclined to recognize Almohad suzerainty, but his brothers deposed him in favour of another brother, 'Alī, and then decided to wage a ruthless war against the Almohads to stop them seizing the islands.[92] They resolved soon afterwards to carry the war into the Maghrib, mainly for reasons of trade. This was not a simple rebellion, but almost a political struggle which was to have profound repercussions for the people of the Maghrib and heavy consequences for the Almohad enterprise. It was 'Alī, known as 'Alī Ibn Ghāniya, who took up the battle under pressure from his entourage of implacable Almohads.

The new caliph, Ya'ḳūb, came to power in conditions that could hardly be called splendid. The Hammadid Sanhaja of Bidjāya had not lost all hope of regaining power. The Majorcan Almohads took the opportunity offered by favourable conditions to bring off an audacious coup, which resulted in the capture of Bidjāya on 12 November 1184.[93] They then undertook, on their own account, to reconstitute the Hammadid kingdom.

90. On the reign of this prince, see *Encyclopaedia of Islam*, new edn, Vol. 1, pp. 165–6; Merad, 1962; Ibn 'Idhārī al-Marrākushī, loc. cit., text pp. 189 and 192, French transl. pp. 226 and 229; Lévi-Provençal, 1941a, No. 27, pp. 158–62; the latter rules out any decision on the part of Caliph Abū Ya'ḳūb Yūsuf.

91. See *Encyclopaedia of Islam*, new edn, Vol. 2, p. 1007; A. Bel, 1903.

92. See 'Inān, op. cit., Vol. 1, pp. 148, 305 ff. and especially 314–15, and Vol. 2, pp. 144 ff.; *Encyclopaedia of Islam*, new edn, Vol. 2, p. 1007; Merad, 1962, p. 422 n. 9.

93. Huici Miranda gives the date 19 Ṣafar 581 (22 May 1185).

The success of this unexpected attack, achieved with very modest forces – a detachment of 20 units, a troop of 200 cavalry and 4000 infantrymen – demonstrated the fragility of Almohad power, exposed as it was to numerous attacks. This must have facilitated the Majorcan operation that drove out the Almohad governor, who withdrew to Tlemcen.

Given this impetus, ʿAlī Ibn G͟hāniya, assisted by the Arabs Riyaḥ, At͟hbad͟j and D͟jud͟hām, left his brother Yaḥyā at Bid͟jāya and marched westwards to cut off the central Maghrib from the Almohad authority. He succeeded in occupying Algiers, Mūzaya and the west, although he feared an encounter with the people of the Tlemcen area, who supported the Almohads. Then he returned eastwards, took Ḳalʿa and fell upon Constantine, which offered fierce resistance. The approach of the Almohad caliph caused him to withdraw and, in the end, to flee. This first Almoravid venture did not last long, but caused a considerable stir. With some reason the author of the *Muʾd͟jib* saw it as the first obvious blow against the Maṣmūd empire, whose effects were still palpable at the time he was writing (1224–5).[94]

The Majorcan roused and mobilized all the anti-Almohad forces, which no doubt found in him the leader of whom they had been dreaming. Ibn K͟haldūn, for example, describes the great zeal with which the Arabs supported the Majorcan.[95] Another factor was the obvious inertia of the Almohad central government; it took six months to react, which was enough to disturb the peoples least inclined to challenge Almohad authority.

Ibn G͟hāniya had taken advantage of the difficulties at the beginning of the reign; but when the new caliph returned from Seville, he took special care over the preparations for his counter-stroke. From Ceuta he launched a combined expedition by sea and land aimed at Algiers. The Almohad operation succeeded in reoccupying the ground lost; but the army commander, Sayyid Abū Zayd, nephew of the caliph, made the serious mistake of supposing that Ibn G͟hāniya, fleeing deep into the south towards Moab, had been put out of harm's way. In fact he had taken refuge with his brothers in Ifrīḳiya, and was to acquire new strength there and return to the fray refreshed.

THE BANŪ G͟HĀNIYA IN IFRĪḲIYA

With their fleet lost and their bridgehead at Bid͟jāya recaptured by the Almohads, the Banū G͟hāniya were to change the style of their anti-Almohad war. It became a sort of guerrilla war, using the desert, where the inhabitants were in a state of perpetual dissidence, as a base for withdrawal and regrouping. ʿAlī Ibn G͟hāniya went back to the D͟jarīd and, with the help of the local Arabs, took Gafṣa. With Tozeur holding out against him, he

94. See Merad, 1962, p. 424; ʿInān, op. cit., Vol. 2, pp. 148 ff. and 156–8 for the situation in the Balearics during Ibn G͟hāniya's action in the Maghrib; for the *Muʾd͟jib*, see Ibn ʿId͟hārī al-Marrākus͟hī, loc. cit., p. 230.

95. Ibn K͟haldūn, 1852–6 edn; Merad, 1962, pp. 427 ff.

decided to join forces with the Armenian Ḳarāḳūsh, a freedman of a nephew of the Ayyubid Salaḥ al-Din (Saladin), who held the Tripoli area with a force of Turcomans from Ghuzz. On his way Ibn Ghāniya rallied the Lamtuna and Masufa Berbers and won the support of the Banū Salaym Arabs.[96] His position being considerably strengthened thereby, he took a step that revealed the true extent of his political ambitions: he sent his oath of allegiance to the Abbasid Caliph al-Nāṣir, from whom he obtained support and the promise of help. The Abbasid, if Ibn Khaldūn is to be believed, urged Saladin to favour the alliance between Ḳarāḳūsh and Ibn Ghāniya:[97] this co-operation soon bore fruit. The Armenian made Gabès his main base, and the Majorcan occupied the whole of the Djarīd, thus producing a homogeneous domain in the south-west of Tunisia.

From these positions the threat of the two allies continually overhung the whole of Ifrīḳiya; their raids reached Cape Bon, and only Tunis and Mahdiyya escaped their activities.[98] Action by the imperial government became essential.

ABŪ YŪSUF YAʿḲŪB'S INTERVENTION IN IFRĪḲIYA

Despite the hesitation and disquiet within the Mu'minid family itself, the Caliph Abū Yūsuf Yaʿḳūb decided to lead an expedition to the east in person.[99] At the head of 20 000 horsemen, he set off for Tunis in December 1186. When Ibn Ghāniya heard the news, he disengaged his troops and withdrew to Djarīd. Pursued by an Almohad force of 6000 horsemen, he led them on into his own area, and only engaged them at ʿUmra, near Gafṣa, where on 24 June 1187 he inflicted a heavy defeat on them. The caliph himself took part in the operations; he marched on Ḳayrawān, and cut off Ibn Ghāniya's retreat from Gafṣa. Ibn Ghāniya was then beaten at al-Ḥamma on 14 October 1187; his troops were annihilated, but he himself, although wounded, managed to 'vanish' into the desert; the caliph made the mistake of not having him pursued. Yaʿḳūb turned against Ḳarāḳūsh, took his base (Gabès) on 15 October 1187, and captured both his treasure and his family, but spared his life.

Following these victories, the caliph set out to re-establish Almohad authority in these troubled areas. He carried out a mopping-up operation throughout the Djarīd, the rich basin that supplied the enemy's forces. He seized Nafzawa (Tozeur), Takyus and Naftī. He retook Gafṣa after a hard siege and punished the Almoravid officials severely, but showed clemency towards the Ghuzz, whom he apparently wanted to make an élite corps in his army.

96. Some sections of the Banū Sulaym refused to leave their own areas in Tripolitania and Cyrenaica, despite the warnings of Caliph Yūsuf; see Lévi-Provençal, 1941a, no. 26, p. 156.

97. See Ibn Khaldūn, 1852–6 edn, pp. 93–4.

98. Ibn al-Athīr, loc. cit., pp. 607–8.

99. Merad, 1962, Vol. 2, pp. 432 ff.

The Almoravid forces had been annihilated, their bases demolished and their allies dispersed. The whole of southern Tunisia was once more under Almohad authority. After the end of his campaign Abū Yūsuf Ya'ḳūb proceeded to the great 'deportation' of the Djudhām, Riyaḥ and 'Āṣim groups, who were mostly settled in the Tāmasnā, an area virtually emptied of its inhabitants, the famous Barghawāṭa, following the Almoravid conquest and the various repressive Almohad expeditions.[100] The Arab element in Morocco was thus substantially strengthened.

Events were to show that Ifrīḳiya was far from having been pacified. Yaḥyā Ibn Ghāniya, who succeeded his brother 'Alī, was to rebuild the anti-Almohad coalition with unusual energy and skill. He carried on the war against the Almohad empire for about half a century, delivering swingeing blows to its power. He undermined its eastern province, causing it enormous difficulties, and thus greatly helped to weaken it.

THE REAPPEARANCE OF THE BANŪ GHĀNIYA IN IFRĪḲIYA AND THE CENTRAL MAGHRIB

The new leader of the Banū Ghāniya, Yaḥyā, rebuilt his forces, renewed the alliance with Ḳarāḳūsh and took up his former activities. Avoiding Ifrīḳiya, where the nomad Arab element had been weakened by the great deportation of 1187–8, he concentrated his attacks on the central Maghrib. Was he trying by these tactics to reach the coast and re-establish contact with Majorca?[101] In any case his attacks against Constantine failed, and he withdrew to the south to link up with Ḳarāḳūsh, with whom his relations were to become increasingly difficult.

Meanwhile Ḳarāḳūsh abandoned his tactical alliance with the Almohads.[102] With the help of a Riyahid Arab chief, Mas'ūd al-Bult, he re-established his former domain, which stretched from Tripoli to Gabès.[103] Yaḥyā made himself master of Biskra, and once again, with his ally, controlled the whole of the interior of Tunisia. In 1195 a dispute broke out between the two allies and, owing to the intervention of a fleet sent from the Balearics by his brother 'Abdallah, Yaḥyā drove Ḳarāḳūsh back into the Djabal Nafūsa. Thus he became master of a vast territory extending unbroken from Tripolitania to the Djarīd.

In addition, a crisis had arisen in the Almohad ranks, weakening their positions in Ifrīḳiya still further. In 1198 an Almohad officer, Muḥammad Ibn 'Abd al-Karim al-Raghraghi, who was very popular in his native town of Mahdiyya, which he was defending against the incursions of the nomads, quarrelled with the Almohad governor of Tunis and proclaimed himself

100. Lévi-Provençal, 1941a, nos 31, 32, p. 218, and 33 (from Manzil Abī Sa'id, near Mahdiyya, dated 10 Rabi' II), p. 584; 1941b, pp. 63–4.

101. See Bel, op. cit., p. 89.

102. Probably as a result of the failure of Saladin's embassy to Ya'ḳūb al-Manṣūr in 586 (*c.* + 1194); see 'Inān, op. cit., pp. 181–6.

103. G. Marçais, 1913, pp. 203–4.

independent, even taking the title of al-Mutawakkil.[104] His venture came to nothing, but his death opened up great possibilities for Yaḥyā, who in two years of campaigning devastated the country and made himself master of Bedja, Biskra, Tebessa, Ḳayrawān and Annāba.

The Almohad governor of Tunis finally surrendered; an attack by the Khāridjites in the Djabal Nafūsa came just at the right moment to strengthen the position of Ibn Ghāniya, who was now master of the whole eastern half of the Maghrib, and at the height of his power.

THE AL-ARAK (ALARCOS) CAMPAIGN AND THE END OF YAʿḲŪB'S REIGN

These serious events in the east coincided with equally serious difficulties in Spain.[105] The Almohad dilemma – the impossibility of operating on both fronts – reared its head in an acute form. How did Yaʿḳūb face up to events? The sources are contradictory; but we may note that from 1194 the caliph seems to have resigned himself to virtually abandoning Ifrīḳiya to its fate in order to concentrate on the affairs of Spain.[106]

The truce of 1190 with the Castilians was about to expire and Alfonso VIII was approaching the Seville area. The caliph once more crossed the Straits, and on 18 July 1195 he won the famous battle of al-Arak (Alarcos) against the Castilians. This victory earned him the title of *al-manṣūr billah* ('the victor through God's will'). In the following year the caliph launched a campaign of devastation which took him to the walls of Madrid, aided in particular by the disagreements that had arisen between Castile, Navarre and Léon. However, these operations were only raids, with no future; the caliph must have realized this, for he hastened to accept the offers of a truce from Castile, which had allied itself with Aragon against Léon.

Caliph Yaʿḳūb left Seville for Morocco in March 1198. On his arrival, weakened by sickness, he had his son Muḥammad proclaimed heir presumptive, and entered upon a period of meditation, so we are told, which lasted until his death in January 1199.

Abū ʿAbd Allah Muḥammad al-Nāṣir (1199–1214)

Muḥammad al-Nāṣir's accession took place without problems (although the author of the *Ḳirṭas* mentions a revolt in Ghūmara country in 596/ *c.* + 1204).[107] However, he inherited a situation which was far from healthy, although Morocco was apparently experiencing a period of peace and prosperity. In Spain the balance of power had not changed, and in Ifrīḳiya Ibn Ghāniya reigned as absolute master after the surrender of the governor of Tunis.

The new caliph gave priority to Ifrīḳiya, sending bodies of troops there

104. For details, see Merad, 1962, p. 440.
105. For details, see 'Inān, op. cit., Vol. 2, pp. 196 ff.
106. See Merad, 1962, p. 443; Ibn al-Athīr, loc. cit., p. 613.
107. Ibn Abī Zarʿ, loc. cit., p. 153.

to try to contain Ibn Ghāniya. But the latter extended his possessions further and further west, installed his own governors and had prayers said in the name of the 'Abbasid' caliph, according to Ibn Khaldūn.

Even so the caliph could not mount a large-scale operation in the east because of a simultaneous revolt in the Sūs and among the Gazula, which was led by one Abū Ḳasaba, who claimed to be the expected *ḳaḥṭani*; it thwarted the Almohads in Morocco, where they were embattled in the very name of Mahdism. A major campaign was needed to put it down, with the special help of the Ghuzz contingents of the army. The caliph bitterly reproached the peoples of the area that Abū Ḳasaba's movement should have been able to reach such proportions there, of all regions, the one which was the cradle of the Almohad movement.[108]

This shows how different these late twelfth-century Almohads were from the 'knights of the faith' and the unitarian reformers of the early days. Apathy and weariness were spreading among them, and this was the most serious danger to a movement which was showing many signs of running out of steam. This defeatist attitude showed more clearly when it came to the question of the attitude to be adopted towards Ibn Ghāniya. Of all the caliph's advisers, only Abū Muḥammad 'Abd al-Waḥid, son of the famous shaykh Abū Ḥafṣ 'Umar, opposed the idea of making peace with the Almoravid, and advocated an expedition to drive him out of Ifrīḳiya once and for all.[109] Thus signs of defeatism, auguring the failure of the imperial idea, were beginning to appear even among the caliph's entourage. However, in a burst of energy Caliph Muḥammad al-Nāṣir resolved to launch a great offensive against Ibn Ghāniya.

AL-NĀṢIR'S OFFENSIVE AGAINST THE BANŪ GHĀNIYA AND THE REORGANIZATION OF ALMOHAD POWER IN IFRĪḲIYA

Al-Nāṣir's offensive was distinguished by a new strategy: he began by reducing the Almoravid refuge in the Balearics, and stormed Majorca in December 1203, thus robbing the Banū Ghāniya of a naval – and, even more, a commercial – base, from which they had been maintaining close links with Aragon, Genoa and Pisa, all hostile to the Almohads.[110] The Almoravid positions in Ifrīḳiya, however, became stronger and stronger, and on 15 December 1203 they took Tunis. The caliph then took the field; at his approach Ibn Ghāniya fled into the interior, leaving his family and treasure at Mahdiyya for safe-keeping.[111] He reached Gafṣa, one of his most secure strongholds. An Almohad landing led to the capture of Tunis, and this was followed by a great massacre;[112] then the Almohad forces

108. See 'Inān, op. cit. Vol. 2, p. 656; Merad, 1962, pp. 448–9; Ibn 'Idhārī al-Marrākushī, loc. cit., p. 276.

109. Ibn Khaldūn, French transl. 1852–6, Vol. 2, pp. 220–1.

110. On the capture of Majorca, see Lévi-Provençal, 1941a.

111. For details of these campaigns, see 'Inān, op. cit., Vol. 2, pp. 257–70.

112. Ibn Khaldūn, French transl. 1852–6, Vol. 2, pp. 221–2 and 286–7.

were deployed in two directions. The caliph marched on Mahdiyya, and shaykh Abū Muḥammad set out in pursuit of Ibn Ghāniya.

Mahdiyya was taken after a long and difficult siege. Its governor, ʿAlī Ibn Ghazi, nephew of Ibn Ghāniya, finally surrendered and joined the Almohads on 11 January 1206. The caliph then returned to Tunis to spend a year there reorganizing the province, whose reconquest and pacification were entrusted to his brother, Abū Isḥāḳ. The latter subdued the Maṭmaṭa and the Nafūsa, and pursued Ibn Ghāniya (who had meanwhile been defeated by the Hafsid Abū Muḥammad at Tadjra, near Gabès, and robbed of all his wealth) as far as the Barḳa area, but did not succeed in capturing him.

On the sensible, though possibly self-interested, advice of his chief lieutenants, the caliph decided to appoint to the governorship of Ifrīḳiya, an important and difficult office, the victor of Tadjra, the Hintāta shaykh Abū Muḥammad ʿAbd al-Waḥid, son of Abū Ḥafṣ ʿUmar. As a 'grandee of the empire' he accepted this delicate mission, which took him away from the central power, only on his sovereign's insistence and on conditions which made him to all intents and purposes a kind of viceroy.[113] This wise measure constituted yet another admission of the failure of the Almohads' imperial endeavour.

In May 1207 the caliph again set out for Morocco. Ibn Ghāniya reappeared and, with the support of many Arabs (Riyaḥ, Sulaym and Dawawida), tried to cut the road; but his forces were crushed in the plain of Chelif. He then fell back, following the edge of the desert, and reappeared in southern Ifrīḳiya; but the new governor, who had won over large sections of the Sulaymids, marched against him and overwhelmed him in Wadi Shabrou, near Tebessa, in 1208.

Ibn Ghāniya went deep into the desert and reappeared in the west. He pushed as far as Tāfīlālet, captured and sacked Sijilmasa and defeated and killed the governor of Tlemcen. During this campaign he had devastated the whole of the central Maghrib, of which Ibn Khaldūn was to write in the fourteenth century, 'Not one fire still burns there, and cockcrow is heard no more'.[114]

ʿAbd al-Waḥid, the new governor of Ifrīḳiya, intercepted Ibn Ghāniya on his way back from this campaign of devastation, defeated him and robbed him of all his booty near the Chelif. The Majorcan withdrew into Tripolitania with his allies and there prepared to try his luck for the last time against ʿAbd al-Waḥid; but the latter crushed him in 1209–10 at the foot of the Djabal Nafūsa with a very numerous force of Arabs – Riyaḥ, ʿAwf, Dabbab, Dawawida and some Zenāta. Ifrīḳiya was to enjoy at least ten years of peace, owing to the energy of its new governor.[115] Ibn

113. R. Brunschvig, 1940, p. 13.

114. See *Encyclopaedia of Islam*, new edn, Vol. 2, pp. 1007–8.

115. Merad, 1962, Vol. 2, pp. 454 ff.; ʿInān, op. cit., Vol. 2, pp. 271–6; Ibn Khaldūn, French transl. 1852–6, Vol. 2, pp. 290–1.

Ghāniya went still further south into the Waddān, where he rid himself of his old ally and rival, Ḳarāḳūsh; he had him killed and took his place in 1212. Ibn Ghāniya was finally to be captured in 1233 by ʿAbd al-Waḥid's successor.

The stormy epic of the Banū Ghāniya lasted more than half a century. Its remarkable combination of an island and maritime background with a nomad Saharan element is highly reminiscent of the beginnings of the Almoravid epic. Various views have been expressed about it. Georges Marçais, for example, being more concerned with effects than with essential causes, saw in it only an extension of what he called the Hilal 'catastrophe' and 'accused' the Majorcans of spreading the Arab 'scourge' to the central Maghrib.[116] Today, however, the Hilalian problem has been studied more dispassionately; researchers and historians have abandoned the tendentious theory of the Beduin as the scourge of civilization.

Nevertheless, this venture cannot be reduced to a mere agitation or an ordinary rebellion without political objectives. It was a remarkably persistent struggle against the Mu'minid dynasty, and even more against the Almohad system. In short, it was a power struggle waged by the Banū Ghāniya in an endeavour to present themselves as an alternative to the Almohad order. The perseverance, endurance and steadfastness of their struggle shows that the Banū Ghāniya campaign sprang from deep-rooted motives and served a cause to which they must have been profoundly devoted. Politics and ideology no doubt had an important place among the essential motives of this struggle, for it united all those in opposition to the Almohads: fallen former dynasties, Mālikites, supporters of the Abbasid caliphate in Baghdad, nomad Arab *ḳabīla*s, and Berbers in Tripolitania anxious to escape from their mountain isolation. A study of these opponents and their role in the 'Majorcan epic' is certainly needed.

Two aspects may help us at least to glimpse some very probable economic reasons for the Majorcans' relative success. The first is that Majorca constituted a naval, trading and diplomatic base, whose fall presaged the end of the Banū Ghāniya. The second concerns the geopolitical sphere of influence of the Banū Ghāniya. In the Maghrib, this consisted essentially of an area from the Waddān and south-eastern Tripolitania in the east to the former Khāridjite settlements of the southern central Maghrib in the west. This long horizontal strip, capable of extension to the south and sometimes also to the north, comprised rich oases and dissident peoples; above all, it was the outlet of the great traditional trans-Saharan routes, whose importance has been emphasized in more than one chapter of the present volume. Trans-Saharan trade was of major economic importance in the Maghrib.

Thus the struggle of the Banū Ghāniya may well have been designed to regain the heritage of the Fatimids, the Zirids and the Almoravids in

116. Marçais, 1913; cf. *Encyclopaedia of Islam*, new edn, Vol. 2, pp. 1007–8.

the crucial realm of trade. Almohad power, by contrast, despite the attraction of Spain, seems to have remained essentially on an east–west axis, aligned with the Tell and Lower Tell. We may therefore hazard the guess that the Almohad enterprise took shape in a period less prosperous than that which saw the birth and development of the Almoravid epic: the Almohads, confronted with the success of the *reconquista* in the north, always seem to have lacked the commercial and strategic depth of the rich Sudan, whose gold breathed life into the Mediterranean economy.

THE DEFEAT OF AL-ʿIḲĀB (LAS NAVAS DE TOLOSA) AND THE END OF AL-NĀṢIR'S REIGN[117]

The battle of Alarcos in 1195 had sounded an alarm for the Christians. They lost little time in forgetting their differences, reorganizing themselves, and resuming their anti-Almohad activities, despite the truce and the protests of al-Nāṣir. In 1200, Alfonso VIII of Castile threatened the Murcia area, and in 1210 Pedro II of Léon inflicted widespread destruction on the Valencia area. These operations were symptomatic of a new situation on the Christian side. Under the impetus of the famous bishop of Toledo, Rodrigo Jimenez de Rada, the reconquest was to become a real crusade, silencing the disagreements among the Christians and receiving support from the whole of Europe. The bishop of Toledo's campaign was crowned with success when Pope Innocent III agreed to declare a crusade.

Unfortunately for the Almohads, their ranks were lacking in strength and unity. One of al-Nāṣir's first measures, when he crossed the Straits, was to embark on a purge of the army, which entailed the execution of several senior officers. It was thus not surprising that on 16 July 1212 the Almohads suffered the severe defeat of Las Navas de Tolosa, which soon turned into a disastrous rout.

The Christians clearly exaggerated the size of their victory. A Spanish scholar, Ambrosio Huici Miranda, has reduced it to its true proportions by pointing out that it did not lead to the collapse of the Muslim positions in Spain.[118] It was nevertheless valuable as a symbol. It was, after all, the first major victory by the united Christians over the Muslims of Spain and the Maghrib, led by their caliph in person; it caused quite a sensation, for it was not just an Almohad army that had been defeated, but the Almohad empire, with its caliph in command.

On the Muslim side, the defeat, in addition to its military aspect, demonstrated the fragility of the Almohad system. More than a military set-back, it was both a political defeat for a regime that was approaching crisis and a failure by a military machine that had lost its fighting spirit. Admittedly, the Almohad empire was to have a few more brilliant years, but Las Navas de Tolosa was the undeniable symptom of the beginning of the disinte-

117. For details, see ʿInān, op. cit., Vol. 2, pp. 282–326.
118. Huici Miranda, 1956a, pp. 219–37, and 1956b, Vol. 2, pp. 428–9.

gration of the regime. It is perhaps significant also that the Muslim West showed no reaction nor shock after the defeat; indeed, there was an attitude of passivity and almost of indifference, exemplified by the caliph himself, who hastily returned to Marrakesh and sank into a depression which lasted until his death in 1213, curiously reminiscent of his father's attitude in 1198.

The break-up of the Almohad empire and the disintegration of the Almohad system

Al-Nāṣir's successor, Yūsuf al-Muntaṣir or al-Mustanṣir, was a young boy whose enthronement by the Almohad leaders was hedged around with conditions limiting his powers. He undertook not to keep Almohad contingents in enemy territory for long, and not to delay paying their wages. Affairs of state then underwent a distinct deterioration.[119]

The reign was relatively untroubled, however, despite the appearance among the Sanhaja and then among the Gazula of two individuals claiming descent from the Fatimids and the Mahdīs. The calm was to last until 1218, when the Banū Marīn made their first appearance on the outskirts of Fez. This peace was deceptive, however. In fact, the Christian danger was becoming more and more of a threat. Meanwhile the Banū Ghāniya were stirring again and the Banū Marīn, hitherto held back beyond the Saharan borders of the empire, were penetrating right to the heart of the far Maghrib, first between Tāzā and Meknes and then in the Fez area.[120] In addition, as regards the internal working of the regime, the viziers were beginning to have exorbitant powers and to take over the actual authority of the state.

We can therefore say that al-Mustanṣir's reign was an interval of deceptive calm, a waiting period; the various new protagonists were soon to show themselves and hasten the end of the empire. After al-Mustanṣir's death in 1224 events moved swiftly and there began a long period of confusion, a slow agony.[121] Two of the rulers of this period stood out for their obvious energy: al-Ma'mūn (1227–32) and his son, al-Sa'īd (1242–8). But their attempts at recovery were doomed to failure, because the forces making for disunity had become too strong.[122]

The most serious of these pressures was perhaps the military weakness.

119. Merad, 1962, Vol. 2, pp. 459–60; Ibn Khaldūn, French transl. 1852–6, Vol. 2, p. 227; Ibn Abī Zar', loc. cit., text p. 161, French transl. pp. 186–7.

120. The position of the Banū Marīn in the high plains of Figuig, where they did not recognize Almohad authority, is only one of several indicators showing that Almohad power no longer extended beyond the Tell in the central Maghrib; see Le Tourneau, op. cit., pp. 90–1.

121. See Huici Miranda, 1956b, Vol. 2, pp. 451 ff., and 1954.

122. Cf. Chapter 4 below.

The conquering Almohad army of the past had been superseded by a heterogeneous force, which was unable to hold its multiple fronts and ended by giving way to the pressure of what was becoming a western crusade.[123] After this military collapse, other weaknesses appeared, in particular the Almohads' inability to take the lead doctrinally and the muted hostility between the Mu'minids and the Almohad shaykhs. From 1224 onwards the latter were to try to regain power, and in particular to avenge themselves on the viziers, such as Ibn Djāmiʿ; but, lacking leaders and objectives, their attempts were derisory and only added to the confusion. The collection of taxes and the pillage organized by a court with ever-growing needs ended by alienating the shaykhs, who presented themselves as defenders of the people.

On al-Mustanṣir's death the Almohad shaykhs proclaimed an old man as caliph; he was then opposed by the Andalusian 'Levant', where a brother of al-Nāṣir, al-Adil, was proclaimed successor and succeeded in establishing himself. But by means of intrigue, in particular with the Christians, they managed to get al-Adil assassinated in 1227; this brought about the rebellion of several *ḳabīla*s, including the Khult. Thus began a period of internecine strife, in which the Christians and the Arab *ḳabīla*s were to play an ever-increasing role.

Abu-'l-ʿalā Idrīs, who had assumed the title of al-Ma'mūn as caliph at Seville in 1227, made an agreement with Ferdinand III, king of Castile, which allowed the caliph, in exchange for giving up some fortresses in Andalusia, to recruit a Christian militia; he used this to overcome his rival, Yaḥyā Ibn al-Nāṣir, who had been proclaimed caliph at Marrakesh and was supported by Tīnmallal and the Hintāta.

In 1230 al-Ma'mūn was master of the whole empire. He then took two very revealing steps. The first was the adoption of a policy of tolerance and understanding towards the Christians; the second, which was even more significant, was a solemn renunciation of Almohad doctrine, including the principle of the Mahdī and his infallibility.[124] This latter measure caused much controversy, and received extremely varied explanations and interpretations. Was it a move against the Almohad aristocracy, or a gesture of goodwill towards the Mālikites? Whichever it was, al-Ma'mūn seems to have taken an essentially opportunist decision, which in fact had the effect of undermining his own dynasty by robbing it of all legitimacy.[125]

From 1230 onwards he was condemned to rely on Christian mercenaries in return for increasingly substantial concessions, which were to be the origin of Christian trade in Morocco and of privileges granted to the Hilālī

123. From the time of al-Mustanṣir, and perhaps earlier, the Almohads had begun to use Christian militia in Morocco to defend their regime. See C.-E Dufourcq, 1968, p. 41.

124. ibid., p. 43.

125. Before he died in 1232, al-Ma'mūn had time to restore the Almohad orthodoxy and the pre-eminence of the Mahdī Ibn Tūmart, under pressure from the Almohad shaykhs. See Brunschvig, op. cit., Vol. 1, p. 22, n. 4.

Arabs who collected taxes. In 1232 he died in the valley of the Wādī Oum al-Rabiʿ, marching against his rival, Yaḥyā, who had retaken Marrakesh.

Al-Maʾmūn's son, al-Rās͟hid, won the succession, as a result of the astuteness of his mother Habbada – a slave of Christian origin – and the energy of the Christian leader of the militia. He was only 14 years old, however, and his reign ushered in a period of anarchy and factional struggles from which the Christian powers sought to gain as great an advantage as possible, particularly in Morocco's Mediterranean ports.[126] Until his death in December 1242, al-Rās͟hid had to fight against his rival Yaḥyā, who was always quick to flee into the Atlas and come down again, and against the Banū Marīn.

It was his young half-brother al-Saʿīd, son of al-Maʾmūn and a black slave, who succeeded him. He pursued the same policy, and was harassed by the Banū Marīn and the Abd al-Wadids from Tlemcen. His death in 1248 marked the beginning of a long period of difficulty, which lasted until 1269, when the Banū Marīn conquered Marrakesh. From 1269 to 1275 an Almohad 'power' was maintained at Tīnmallal. There is an odd symbolism about this return to the starting-point.

The Almohad agony thus went on for more than half a century, its area of control continually shrinking under the blows of numerous external enemies and increasingly strong centrifugal forces. First, Ifrīḳiya broke away from the empire, following the long and stubborn resistance of Yaḥyā Ibn G͟hāniya, who had thwarted all imperial operations in the east.[127] Abū Zakariyyā, son of the Hafsid, ʿAbd al-Waḥid, took power in 1228, captured Ibn G͟hāniya in 1233 and then, using the pretext of the reshuffle that followed al-Maʾmūn's death, proclaimed his independence; he even put in a claim to the office of caliph.

The breaking away and then the loss of Spain followed a pattern that had become familiar since the beginning of the eleventh century. Authority was dispersed among Almohad governors, who gave way to Andalusians, who in turn appealed for help to the Christian kings and after a time submitted to them.[128] The example, moreover, came from above, for the various claimants to the caliphate often sought support from the Christians. This situation opened the way to the descendants of the former local dynasties, Banū Hūd and Banū Mardanīs͟h, who set up amirates that were inevitably to become vassals of the Christian rulers. In 1230 Almohad power disappeared from the peninsula, and was replaced either by the remote and tenuous 'Abbasid' suzerainty or by that of the Hafsids of Ifrīḳiya. The Muslim cities of Andalusia then began, one by one, to fall under the domination of the kings of Castile (Cordova in 1236) or Aragon (Valencia in 1238).

126. Dufourcq, op. cit., pp. 54–5.

127. Brunschvig, op. cit., Vol. 1, pp. 18–23.

128. This disintegration of unity and the interference of Christians in the internal politics of the Muslim West foretold the end of Muslim dominance in the Mediterranean area.

3 The spread of civilization in the Maghrib and its impact on western civilization

M. TALBI

The century of the Almohads

The apogee

It is hard to decide just when a civilization reaches its peak, when its influence is greatest. For the Maghrib, was it under the Aghlabids in the ninth century, when the armed might of Ifrīḳiya threatened Rome and ruled the Mediterranean? Or in the tenth, when the Fatimids made Mahdiyya the seat of a caliphate which rivalled that of Baghdad? Or should we opt for the Almohad era (1147–1269), when for the first time, under a local, authentically Berber dynasty, a vast empire was united which extended from Tripoli to Seville? We have to recognize that there were several peaks, and among all those peaks that of the twelfth century was certainly not the least.

And Spain? It had certainly fallen from the political greatness it had known of old under ʿAbd al-Raḥmān II (912–61) or under the 'reign' of the dictator, al-Manṣūr b. Abī ʿAmir, the redoubtable Almanzor of the Christian chronicles. But the case of Spain and the Maghrib was comparable with that of Greece and Rome: Spain conquered its uncouth Berber conquerors, Almoravid or Almohad, twice over, and by giving them the age-old treasures of its artistic and cultural traditions made them into builders of a civilization. So from the twelfth century onwards, the civilization of the Muslim West was a fusion of the culture of Spain and the Maghrib, even more than it had been in the past.

It was a civilization built in part – although how great a part is difficult to say – by blacks who came from the regions south of the Sahara. They were to be found in large numbers in Morocco and throughout the whole of the Maghrib. Intermarriage, against which there was no prejudice whatsoever, was common and naturally had some biocultural influence, the nature of which, however, is difficult to determine with any degree of certainty or accuracy.[1] There were also blacks to be found in Spain,

1. See R. Brunschvig, 1940, Vol. 2, 1947, p. 158.

principally in Seville and Granada. As slaves for a time, or as free men, they played a considerable role in the army and the economy, and they also brought with them certain customs of their native country.[2] Some of them, such as Jean Latin, a university professor in Spain, attained the highest levels of the intellectual world and gave a stronger African flavour to the Spanish Maghrib.

Art and architecture

In the period that we are interested in, this civilization was centred in the western half of the Maghrib. Ḳayrawān had declined greatly and Ifrīḳiya had lost its primacy. We should note that the century of the Almohads was also that of the Almoravids (1061–1147). Apart from the religious aspects, which do not concern us here, there was no break between the two dynasties as regards their civilization.[3] Almohad art, in particular, was merely the flowering culmination of processes which had been developed or introduced from Spain under the Almoravids.

The Almoravids were great builders. Few vestiges remain of their civil architecture, more exposed to the fury of men and the ravages of time and weather. Of the palaces they erected at Marrakesh and Tagrart, nothing is left; of their fortresses, very little; nor do we know much about their public engineering works, in particular their irrigation. But some of the finest religious monuments are still there for us to admire. The most characteristic of those extant today are in Algeria. The Great Mosque of Marrakesh, unfortunately, disappeared under the tidal wave of Almohadism. At Fez, the mosque of al-Ḳarawiyyīn is not entirely Almoravid, but a building of the mid-ninth century, altered and enlarged. On the other hand, the Great Mosque at Algiers, built around 1096, is a genuinely Almoravid foundation which has not suffered unduly from the alterations made in the fourteenth century and again during the Turkish period. There is also the mosque of Nedroma. But the most beautiful building is undeniably the Great Mosque of Tlemcen, an imposing monument measuring 50 m by 60 m, begun about 1082 and completed in 1136. It united the vigour and majesty of the Saharans with the refinement and delicacy of Andalusian art. Marçais writes: 'There is no need to emphasize the importance of the Great Mosque of Tlemcen. The peculiarities of its design, and still more the juxtaposition, even the close association, of the Andalusian ribbed dome with the Iranian-inspired corbels [projections] in the form of *muḳarnas* [stalactites] . . . give it an eminent place among Muslim works.'[4]

Almoravid art was continued and fruitfully developed in Almohad art, which through the majesty of its proportions, the balance of its volume and the richness of its ornament added a greater nobility and grace. This

2. See Chapter 26 below.
3. See Chapters 2 and 5 in this volume.
4. G. Marçais, 1954, p. 196.

was the peak of western Muslim art. The jewel of this art is *Djāmiʿ al-Kutubiyyīn*, the Mosque of the Booksellers at Marrakesh, one of the loveliest creations of Islam, built like the mosque of Tīnmallal by the founder of the dynasty, ʿAbd al-Muʾmin b. ʾAli (1130–63). Its six-storey minaret, with halls variously vaulted, rises more than 67 m from the ground. Five stalactite domes, 'which may be considered a culmination of the history of the *muḳarnas*', adorn the transverse nave.[5] Here, even more than at Tlemcen, there are lobate or scalloped arches enriched with decorative motifs; they span the seventeen naves and seven bays, endlessly intersecting and giving a sense of amplitude and spaciousness. ʿAbd al-Muʾmin's son and successor, Abū Yaʿḳūb Yūsuf (1163–84) was responsible for the building of the Great Mosque of Seville, another jewel of Almohad art. This was replaced by a cathedral after the *reconquista*, and today all that is left is its minaret, the famous Giralda, completed by Abū Yūsuf Yaʿḳūb al-Manṣūr (1184–99) and crowned since the sixteenth century with a Christian lantern.

The most grandiose monument, the mosque of Ḥasan, begun at Rabat by al-Manṣūr, remains unfinished. But we can still admire the forest of columns, rising over an area of 183 m by 139 m, and the imposing minaret, the famous Ḥasan tower, which soars majestically from the centre of the façade. The mosque of the Marrakesh *ḳaṣaba* (casbah), also founded by al-Manṣūr, has been too fundamentally altered in later times to give a faithful reflection of Almohad art.

With the Almohads as with the Almoravids, and for the same reasons, less civil architecture has been preserved. Nothing is left either of their palaces or of the great hospital with which they endowed their capital. At Rabat, founded by al-Manṣūr, two of the gates of the ancient cob wall, which extended for over 5 km, are still preserved: Bāb al-Ruwāḥ (or Bāb er-Ruāḥ) and Bāb Oudāya. Other Almohad works include the *ḳaṣaba* of Baṭalyaws (Badajoz), the al-Ḳalʿa of Guadaira – a citadel built 15 km from Seville – and the celebrated twelve-sided Tower of Gold which overlooked the ships on the Guadalquivir. Finally, we may remark that in Almohad art majesty and force are accompanied by an airy lightness of ornamentation and iridescent colours, especially due to the use of polychrome faience (*zallīdj*). It was an art of maturity, strength and grandeur.

Literature

The twelfth century was also notable for brilliant literary activity. The initial reservations of the Almoravids and Almohads concerning poets and profane works in general soon dissolved under the hot sun of Spain. The princes of both dynasties lived up to the tradition that an Arab sovereign should also be an interested and enlightened patron. They encouraged culture and gave their patronage to men of letters.

5. Brunschvig, op. cit., p. 237.

Here, too, the western part of the Spanish Maghrib held the place of honour. Ifrīḳiya did not make much of a showing. Almost the only writer to be mentioned during this period is Ibn Ḥamdīs (*c.* 1055–1133), who was a genuine poet with a widespread reputation – and he was born in Sicily. As a youth he had to leave 'his Sicilian fatherland', which had been conquered by the Normans, and ever afterwards he dwelt on his memories of it with an engaging nostalgia. After a short stay at the court of al-Muʿtamid ʿala ʾllāh (more properly called Muḥammad b. ʿAbbād al-Muʿtadid) at Seville, he spent the greater part of his life in Ifrīḳiya.

The Muses were cultivated more successfully in the far Maghrib and above all in Spain. Among the more talented practitioners of the art were Ibn ʿAbdūn (who died at Evora in 1134); Ibn al-Zaḳḳāḳ al-Balanṣī (d. *c.* 1133); Ibn Baḳī (d. 1150), who spent his life journeying back and forth between Spain and Morocco and whose muwa<u>shsh</u>aḥ (a genre in which he excelled) ended in a *<u>Kh</u>ar<u>dj</u>a* in the Romance tongue; Abū Baḥr Safwān b. Idrīs (d. 1222); Abu ʾl-Ḥasan ʿAbī b. Ḥarīḳ (d. 1225); Muḥammad b. Idrīs Mar<u>dj</u> al-Ḳul (d. 1236); Ibn Diḥya, who left Spain, travelled all through the Maghrib, living for a while in Tunis, and died in Cairo; Ibn Sahl (d. 1251), a native of Seville, of Jewish origin and great poetic sensibility, who entered the service of the Governor of Ceuta after his native city fell to Ferdinand III (1248); and Abu ʾl-Muṭarrif b. ʿAmīra (d. *c.* 1258), who was born at Valencia, served the last Almohads in various cities of Morocco and ended his life in the service of the Hafsids of Tunis.

In this constellation two stars shone with particular brilliance: Ibn <u>Kh</u>afā<u>dj</u>a (1058–1139), uncle of the Ibn al-Zaḳḳāḳ mentioned earlier, and above all Ibn Ḳuzmān (b. after 1086, d. 1160). The former, without quite being a court poet (he came from a well-to-do family from Alcira, in the province of Valencia), did the conventional thing and eulogized the important men of the day, among them the Almoravid prince Abū Isḥāḳ Ibrāhīm b. Tā<u>sh</u>fīn. But it is mainly as an inimitable poet of nature that Ibn <u>Kh</u>afā<u>dj</u>a has come down to posterity. In his sensuous and romantic verse he sings of the joy of living, the water of rivers and ponds, gardens and flowers, fruits and the pleasures of existence. He was called al-<u>Dj</u>annān (the gardener) and there is no anthology old or new that does not offer a selection of his poems. He is one of the classic Arabic poets.

Ibn Ḳuzmān was the undisputed 'prince of popular poetry' (*imām al-za<u>dj</u><u>dj</u>ālīn*), a poetry which eschews learned diction for racy expression in colloquial Hispano-Arabic. Tall and extremely ugly, with a red beard and little squinting eyes, Ibn Ḳuzmān led a roistering, dissolute, licentious life, drinking hard and careless of the sexual taboos against adultery (*zānī*) and homosexuality (*lawwāt*). Always in need of money, he wandered from town to town, inside Spain, in search of generous patrons and love affairs. He naturally knew what it was like to be in prison, and escaped death by flogging only through the intervention of an Almoravid dignitary, Muḥammad b. Sīr. Impecunious, inspired, ribald, he reminds one, right up to his repentance – which was probably sincere, with the onset of old age – of the untypical destiny of Abū Nuwās or François Villon. His *zadjal*, mostly dedicated to his protectors, are ballads of a sort, either very short (three stanzas) or very long (forty-two stanzas), in which he breaks with classical prosody to create new metres and vary the rhyme-scheme. The dedicated poems end in a kind of panegyrical envoy, which is very commonplace in workmanship. It is in the undedicated *zadjal*, all in praise of love and wine, and in the 'banter' which introduces the dedicated pieces that the poet's art blossoms forth. There he gives free play to his inspiration, and we have lively, telling burlesque sketches of his contemporaries. He catches them 'live' in their tipsy quarrels, their cuckolds' annoyances, and other equally comical scenes of everyday existence. He describes songs and dances, he adores civilized nature – the nature of the gardens and pools where pretty bathers display themselves. He is coarse, but rarely obscene. In short, he has a genuinely popular vein of art, served by a rare gift of observation and an unflagging gusto. The convention which he set, and of which he was a past master, was continued by his compatriot Madghalīs and was imitated long afterwards, even in the East.

There is no living literature without critics and anthologists. Ibn Bassām (d. 1148), who dabbled in verse himself on occasion, was above all eager to defend and illustrate the literature of his Spanish homeland. National pride, in opposition to the wanted superiority of the East, spurred him on to compile his *Dhakhīra*, a vast and intelligent anthology which is now our best source for literary activity in Spain in the eleventh and the early twelfth centuries. To his fellow countryman Ibn Bashkuwāl (1101–83), son of Pascual, we owe the *Kitāb al-Ṣila fī ta'rīkh a'immat al-Andalus* (completed in 1139), which was conceived as a continuation of the *Ta'rīkh* of Ibn al-Faraḍī (who was killed in 1013) and contained the biographies of 1400 celebrities of Islamic Spain.

Philology was represented by two eminent specialists. Ibn Khayr al-Ishbīlī (1108–79) gives us information about the books which were taught in his day in his *fahrasa* or catalogue. The even more important Ibn Maḍā' al-Kurtubī (1119–95), whose work preceded by several centuries the present-day proponents of simplification, made a close criticism of Arabic grammar and denounced its excessive and pointless complications, in his *Kitāb al-Radd 'alā 'l-nuḥāt*.[6]

It is impossible to list all the good historians and geographers of the period here; but one geographer should be mentioned, 'perhaps the greatest of the Islamic world'.[7] Al-Idrīsī (1099–*c.* 1166) lived at the court of King Roger II of Sicily and his work is now in the process of scholarly editing in Italy.[8]

6. An edition was published in Cairo in 1947.
7. A. Mieli, 1966, p. 198.
8. Al-Idrīsī, 1970 Latin edn; T. Lewicki, 1966, may also be consulted on the scientific qualities of al-Idrīsī's work.

Philosophy, medicine and science

The Almohad century was one in which philosophy, in particular, was represented by a whole galaxy of illustrious names: Ibn Bādjdja (or Avempace, d. 1139); Abū Bakr, also known as Ibn Ṭufayl or al-Andalusī, and to contemporary Christians as Abubacer – he died in 1185; Ibn Rushd (Averroes, 1126–98); and the Adalusian Jew, Ibn Maymūn (Moses Maimonides, 1135–1204). With the exception of the last-named, who emigrated to Egypt before 1166, all these philosophers served the Almohads and, despite some temporary reverses of fortune, enjoyed their protection and their financial support. In addition to their prowess in philosophy, they all acquired a good knowledge of the religious disciplines; and they all to some extent studied various practical sciences: mathematics, astronomy, botany and especially medicine. Furthermore, as is shown by the Latin deformation of their names, they were all adopted by the Christian Middle Ages, a period long nourished by their thought.

We cannot linger on each man. Let us therefore stop and consider the brightest star of this whole constellation, Ibn Rushd the Cordovan, famous in the medieval West as Averroes. Ibn Rushd was not only a philosopher but a *faḳīh* (a specialist in religious law) and Abū Ya'ḳūb Yūsuf made him *ḳādī* of Seville. He made astronomical observations and wrote a medical book, *Kitāb al-Kulliyyāt*. The decisive event in his career occurred around 1169, when his friend Ibn Ṭufayl presented him to Caliph Abū Ya'ḳūb Yūsuf, who was passionately interested in philosophy and complained about the obscurities in Aristotle's works. At the caliph's invitation Ibn Rushd undertook a commentary, and he has come down to posterity as the inspired interpreter and successor of the great philosopher of antiquity.

Despite the caliph's encouragement and protection, the voice of Ibn Rushd was stifled by intolerance. He was condemned by the theologians and knew exile and disgrace. His works were burned. They have therefore come down to us only partly in Arabic. Most of his writings have been transmitted in Latin or Hebrew translation. Besides the *Commentaries*, special mention should be made of the *Faṣl al-Maḳāl* ('The Positive Treatise'), in which he tries to resolve the difficult and eternal conflict of faith and reason, and the *Tahāfut al-Tahāfut* ('The Incoherence of Incoherence'), a closely researched point-by-point refutation of the *Tahāfut al-Falāsifa* ('The Incoherence of the Philosophers') of al-Ghazālī (1058–1111), the greatest theologian of orthodox Islam.

Ibn Rushd's ideas and contribution have been variously judged. His originality has been disputed. Stress has been placed on the duplicity which led him to conceal his atheistic materialism – reserved for the élite – behind a curtain of orthodox discourse intended for the vulgar. In point of fact, for all the many works that have been devoted to it, the last word has not yet been said about Ibn Rushd's thought: far from it. No one has yet explored it in its entirety or thoroughly followed its development through the Arabic, Latin and Hebrew texts in which it is expressed. Of course Ibn Rus͟hd, like all the philosophers of the Middle Ages, owes a great deal to Aristotle. But we must not forget that his thought was formed in contact with a whole current of Arab philosophy, and often by way of reaction against that current. Moreover, we must be careful not to separate Ibn Rus͟hd the theologian from Ibn Rus͟hd the philosopher, as is sometimes done, rather arbitrarily. In my opinion the sincerity of his faith – naturally enlightened, therefore suspect – is beyond doubt. With respect to Aristotle he was undeniably a commentator of genius, 'the greatest commentator on philosophy that history has known', according to A. Badawī.[9] But he was likewise, and just as indubitably, a rich, profound and original thinker. It does not matter that some have found this originality mainly in the *Faṣl al-Maḳāl* and others in the *Tahāfut*. That only emphasizes the richness and flexibility of the thought – the author being as much at ease in theology or *fiḳh* (*Faṣl al-Maḳāl*) as in pure philosophy (*Tahāfut*). His genius provided the swan song of western Muslim philosophy.

The Almohad century also boasted eminent scientists. We must mention some of them only briefly: the physicians Abu 'l-ʿAlāʾ Zuhr b. ʿAbd al-Malik b. Muḥammad (Aboali, to western scholars), and his son Abū Marwān (Avenzoar, *c.* 1092/5–1161); the scientists Ibn al-Rūmiya, al-ʿAs͟hs͟hāb ('the herbalist') (d. 1239) and Ibn al-Bayṭār ('the veterinary surgeon') (d. 1248); and, above all, the three mathematical astronomers, D͟jābir b. Aflaḥ, al-Biṭrūd͟ja and al-Zarḳālī, all of the twelfth century.

The last gleams of light before the dusk

The empire founded by ʿAbd al-Muʾmin did not survive the disaster suffered at Las Navas de Tolosa (1212). Exhausted by foreign wars and corroded from within, it gave way to four independent kingdoms, one in Spain and three in the Maghrib (see Chapter 4, pp. 79–95 below).

Granada

As a result of the influence of Romanticism, the little kingdom of Granada, the precious casket of the jewel of the Alhambra, has been regarded as the pinnacle of medieval Muslim civilization. This is, of course, a very exaggerated judgement. Granada was perhaps the pinnacle of luxury and of a certain refinement. But in fact, as H. Terrasse points out, 'in every respect this little kingdom was merely a diminished and belated reflection of the caliphate of Cordova'.[10]

The Nasrids of Granada left many civil and military monuments, the most spectacular of which is the Alhambra. This gives a visitor the im-

9. A. R. Badawī, 1972, Vol. 2, p. 869.
10. H. Terrasse, 1958, p. 203.

PLATE 3.1 *The Alhambra of Granada: a room adjoining the Court of the Lions, 14th-century decorative sculpture*

pression of having been dictated by the most exuberant fancy. Twin pairs of doors and windows, rows of stone-laced arches surmounting slender marble columns, bays of light and patches of shade, galleries and corridors – the aim of the whole conception seems to have been to manipulate the effects of contrast adroitly, to astonish at every turn, and to break up the monotony of enclosed spaces by means of subtle, confusing perspectives. But this fanciful disorderliness is only apparent. Seen from outside, discovered from above, the monument is astonishing for the balance of its forms and the harmonious distribution of its volume. But what charms most, what makes the initial appeal and leaves the deepest impression, is the richness and unequalled sumptuousness of the decoration (see Plate 3.1.). There are no new inventions, rather a skilful use of the expertise and experience of the artists of the Spanish Maghrib and a perfect mastery of technique. Stalactite domes, ceilings of painted wood, sculptures on stucco, panels and frescos, a symphony of discreet or deliberately aggressive colours – everything combines to create an atmosphere of tranquil opulence and languidly sensuous reverie. The art of Granada hates empty solitude. The walls are covered with a tracery of floral, epigraphic or geometric motifs. An abstract, allegorical art, it leaves an impression of space, of infinity. The lines stretch out, flee in all directions, check themselves, spring up again, and cross in a wild dance that never ends. For generations their subtle music, often written to the words of Ibn Zamraḳ, has enchanted even the most unprepared visitors. It is a magical art; but also, it must be said, an art lacking in vigour. It was the last song of a civilization that was becoming enclosed in its own meanderings, the cosy cocoon of its dreams, and no longer had the strength to renew itself or meet life face to face.

Under the Nasrids, culture had this same physiognomy. It continued and prolonged the past and in certain fields might seem fairly brilliant. But there was a decline in philosophy, which no longer had worthy representatives. Science as a whole was either marking time or losing ground. To be fair, one should mention the physician, Ibn Khātima (who died in 1369), and the mathematician, al-Ḳalaṣādī (1412–86).

In literature, Granada retained a certain distinction to the end. The kingdom never lacked philologists, poets and polished stylists who could turn out the highly wrought, refined prose which was so esteemed by the cultivated public. Theirs was the art which covers the walls of the Alhambra. The most typical of them was known as Ibn al-Khāṭīb Lisān al-Dīn (1313–75), who was the greatest humanist of his time and who is still considered a great classical Arabic writer. His friend Ibn Khaldūn regarded him as 'a veritable prodigy in prose and in verse, in science and in letters'.[11] Secretary and vizier of the Nasrids, he attained the highest honours and distinguished himself in every branch of learning: poetry, anthology, letter-writing of various sorts, travel narratives, history, mysticism and medicine. He produced at least sixty works. He was particularly outstanding for the magic of his style and the matchless virtuosity of his language. But this virtuoso magician had a wretched end. Falsely accused of heresy by powerful personages – among them his protégé the poet, Ibn Zamraḳ, who succeeded him as vizier – he was summarily strangled in a dark dungeon in Fez and his body was burnt. The art of his successor was no less fascinating and his end no less tragic. Ibn Zamraḳ (b. 1333) was another verbal magician in verse and prose, but was assassinated in the end by order of the amir, some time after 1393. His *dīwān* (poetry) has not come down to us. But some of his poems, 'transfigured into hieroglyphic beauties, into refined calligraphy with scrolls and ornaments', still adorn the walls of the Alhambra.[12] There is no better expression of the subtle interplay between Nasrid art and literature.

Granada was a civilization that ended in learned verbal and architectural arabesques, exquisite and already antiquated, like so many museum pieces. How could Granada possibly listen to Ibn al-Hudhayl (d. after 1392), who tried in vain to rouse the country from its dreams, extolling the manly virtues of the art of horsemanship?

The heirs of the Almohads in the Maghrib

In other respects, a loss of vitality was apparent in every field in the Muslim West. The history of the Maghrib under the Marinids, the Abd

11. Ibn Khaldūn, French transl., 1956–9.
12. E. Garcia-Gomez, cited by H. Terrasse, op. cit., p. 211.

al-Wadids and the Hafsids – that is, up to the last decades of the sixteenth century – is simply that of a slow ossification. This is not the place to trace the history of that sluggishness leading to decadence, a significant phenomenon which has not yet been sufficiently studied.

However, one thing is certain: whereas the Christian West was undergoing a real demographic explosion, the Muslim West was becoming depopulated. This decline was evident from the middle of the eleventh century and appears to have reached its low point in the middle of the fourteenth. Ibn Khaldūn observed the phenomenon and rightly viewed it as one of the decisive factors in the decline and fall of civilizations. Agriculture, especially arboriculture, diminished. Nomadism spread. Cities and villages disappeared or became depopulated. Ḳayrawān, which had had hundreds of thousands of inhabitants in the ninth and tenth centuries, was now a small town. Leo Africanus says of Bidjāya (Bougie) that the town had only 8000 households and could easily have sheltered 24 000.[13]

Studies in demographic history are essential, if we are to understand this era. Meanwhile, by extrapolation, we can estimate that the population of the Maghrib had fallen by two-thirds. Why was this? Plagues – which are not only causes, but also effects – do not entirely explain it. In any case the acute drop in population in the Maghrib explains better than events, which are surely only epiphenomena, the constantly growing imbalance between the north shores of the Mediterranean – where, as Ibn Khaldūn noted, the Renaissance was dawning[14] – and the south, where the dusk has been kept steadily thickening right up to the contemporary *Nahḍa*, accompanied (fortuitously?) by a demographic explosion that is still going on.

In architecture, Andalusian – that is, Granadan – influences continued in the Maghrib, particularly in Morocco and western Algeria; this was less manifest in Ifrīḳiya, where relatively few Hafsid monuments are preserved. The great builders of the time were the Marinids. It is impossible to mention all they did; let us merely note that the thirteenth century was marked by the appearance of a new type of monument: the medersa, a college of higher education borrowed from the East. The plan was usually rather simple: an inner courtyard with a fountain in the centre, surrounded by balconies with rooms for the students leading off them. On one side was a large room furnished with a *miḥrāb*, serving as both classroom and oratory. All the Maghrib capitals and many other large towns had their medersa. The most monumental of them is the Abū ʿInāniyya of Fez (1350–7). Another new type of building to appear was the *zāwiya*, which served as the hall of a confraternity and the burial sanctuary of its founding saint. Post-Almohad art in the Maghrib can be considered the art of maturity. It represents a certain classicism. Its technique is perfect, but no

13. Leo Africanus, French transl. 1956, Vol. 2, p. 361.
14. Ibn Khaldūn, French transl. 1956–9, pp. 700 and 866.

progress is made. It is an art that has become rigidly fixed, and therefore presages decadence.

Culture presented the same features. Ibn Khaldūn noted with his usual perspicacity that in the Maghrib of his day 'the progress of learning had totally stagnated'; and he added later, in his chapter on the rational sciences, that these in particular 'had practically disappeared and were scarcely cultivated any longer except by a few rare individuals who incurred the censure of orthodox doctors'.[15] He attributed this depressing situation to the decline of civilization and the decrease in population (*tanāḳuṣ al-ʿUmrān*).

The Moroccan Ibn al-Bannā' (1256–1321) was the last mathematician of merit, and the Ifrīḳiyan, Ibn al-Kammād, the last astronomer. For philosophy, we may mention al-Ābilī (1282–1356) of Tlemcen, whose main achievement was to have contributed to the education of Ibn Khaldūn. Descriptive geography in the form of travel narratives (*riḥla*) found a master in the Moroccan, Ibn Baṭṭūṭa (1304–*c.* 1377), who visited India, China and Africa, and far excelled his emulators and contemporaries, al-ʿAbdarī, Khālid al-Balawī and al-Tīdjanī. We cannot list all the historians, among whom Ibn Khaldūn (1332–1406) stands out, nor all the hagiographers, biographers and anthologists.

Poets and prose writers were not lacking, but despite some successful work the period we are considering here was marked by decadence. Writers naturally went on composing *ḳaṣīda*, panegyrics of increasing pomposity which seem all the more ridiculous today in that they were grotesquely at odds with the realities of that time. Poets also wrote *rithā*, shedding crocodile tears over important men or, more rarely, inspired by a genuine grief.[16] They took great delight in the descriptive genre. They loved to evoke the ephemeral beauty of a lily or an almond flower, and to sigh with the *naʿūra* (the water wheel). They sang of mystical love. But they sang also of wine and let themselves be lulled by the equivocal charm of erotic poetry, in which the silhouette of the mistress is often confused with that of the young Adonis.

All these had long been standard themes, and they were handled without originality. The poets wrote 'antique verse' without any 'new thinkers'. Their strength was sapped, but the craftsmanship was still perfect. What people savoured was the delicacy of the performing artist, the dexterity of the juggler. They liked to pick and choose among hackneyed productions which they readily took to be masterpieces so long as the shape was perfect. It was the literature of a refined class which took refuge in the aroma, the atmosphere of the past; a literature in which verse and artistic prose – often mingled in tender epistles – were so many finely carved trinkets. Their graceful design irresistibly recalls the fragile, graceful arabesques

15. ibid., pp. 789 and 866.

16. *Rithā* refers to an elegiac genre. The word *marthiya* is more generally used to describe this sad and mournful genre, which was often written in an artificial, conventional style.

adorning palaces and bourgeois houses. They were stiff and decadent forms, to be sure, but none the less they revealed a real culture, that of the urban bourgeoisie. Perhaps there had never been such a love of books and libraries. Education, including the education of women, was relatively widespread, and people adored music, in which Andalusian influence – the *mālūf* – was certainly already predominant. Leo Africanus wrote of Tedelles (Dellys), 'the people are pleasant and lead a merry life. They are nearly all good lute-players and harpists.' Later he adds, 'The men of Bidjāya are agreeable. They like to enjoy themselves. They can all make music and dance, the lords especially.'[17] These were the last rays of a civilization whose sun was setting.

The impact of the Maghrib on western civilization

In spite of the inevitable conflicts and divergent destinies, material and cultural exchanges between the Muslim and the Christian West had never been interrupted. To give a balanced picture, I shall first briefly outline the specific features of the material exchanges, confining myself to Spain – the principal platform, as we shall see, for the cultural interchange, which is considered at greater length.

Material exchanges

Trade with Spain, as with the rest of Europe, was governed by treatise which fixed procedures and regulated the establishment of personal businesses. Under these treaties the Iberians, among whom rivalry was not unknown, controlled a whole chain of *funduḳ*s in all the large ports of the Maghrib and even in the interior, for example at Tlemcen and Marrakesh. These *funduḳ*s, at once inns (with chapels, ovens, restaurants and so on), depots and business offices, were usually run by consuls who represented their co-religionists in dealing with the local authorities.

The men of the Maghrib were less dynamic – a fact that must be emphasized – and did not have the support of a comparable organization in the Christian countries. In maritime transport, too, their role was negligible. The bourgeoisie accepted commercial development, making a certain amount of profit, without really becoming an integral part of it. There was no spirit of enterprise, no stimulation of home production for export. Profits, which generally took the form of fees paid by the foreigners, went mostly to assist the state treasuries.[18]

There was also an imbalance in the products exchanged. In principle, there was no limitation on imports on either side. But exports were controlled: quotas were established for certain foodstuffs such as grain, and

17. Leo Africanus, loc. cit., Vol. 2, pp. 352 and 361.
18. On trade with Europe and the Christian control of the high seas, see Chapter 26 below.

there were export bans, more or less obeyed, on strategic materials such as arms, iron and wood. The Iberians exported to the Maghrib metals, wood, ironmongery, spices purchased in the East, dyestuffs, wine, paper and especially textiles of all kinds. They imported wool, skins, dates, carpets, other craft products and wax – the town of Bougie (Bidjāya) gave its name to the French language as a word for wax candle, and *bougie* passed from French into English, where it still exists as a rare word. The kingdom of Aragon often demanded a rebate on the duties paid by its merchants and in various ways took particular pains to keep control of the Barcelona–Majorca–Tlemcen–Sijilmasa trade route, one of the roads which led to the gold of the Sudan.[19]

At a disadvantage on the plane of material exchange, the Maghrib was a large exporter of a product that was non-material – its cultural heritage, which it could no longer properly appreciate or use in a fruitful way. The Christian West discovered with enthusiasm that this was of priceless value; and its Renaissance was thereby stimulated and developed in every field.

Cultural exchanges

The Maghrib had a dual role. It served as an intermediary, as the channel through which all the values of Muslim Arab civilization necessarily had to pass to be introduced into the West; it also exported its own cultural legacy. I shall confine myself here to this second aspect of the question, which has seldom been given sufficient emphasis.

Atmosphere and motivation

The transfer to the Christian West of cultural values developed in the Muslim West was encouraged, especially in the twelfth and thirteenth centuries, by the great tolerance that prevailed. Only after the fall of Granada (in 1492) did this atmosphere begin to suffer the serious deterioration which was to end in the Inquisition and the expulsion in 1609 of the Moriscos (Muslims who had remained in Granada under Christian rule). There were two reasons for openness to those values; disinterested sympathy and spiritual strategy. King Roger II of Sicily (1105–54) attracted a circle of Arab scholars as a matter of personal taste. His practice was continued and expanded under Frederick II (1197–1250), who conceived a deep admiration for Muslim thought. In Spain, 'Peter I of Aragon (1094–1104) signed his letters in Arabic and struck Muslim-type coins.'[20] But there were also tactical considerations. Dominicans and Franciscans, in particular, dreamed of spiritual conquests. From this era dates the study of the Arabic language and of Muslim thought, with the tactical aim – which

19. For a general picture of Aragon's activity in the Maghrib, see C.-E. Dufourcq, 1966, p. 664.

20. Dufourcq, op. cit., p. 23.

did not necessarily preclude generosity – of supporting missionary efforts. This spirit, which has never totally disappeared, was perhaps best symbolized by Ramon Lull (1235–1315), one of the most striking figures of the Spanish Middle Ages. All his life he sought a 'dialogue' with the Muslims. He wrote treatises in Arabic and preached in Morocco, at Tunis and at Bidjāya, at the risk of life and liberty.

But although Lull preferred philosophy as the means for saving the Muslims from their infidelity, he continually urged a revival of the crusades upon Pope Celestine V in 1294, Boniface VIII in 1295, Philippe le Bel in 1298 and Clement V in 1302. At the Council of Vienna in 1311 he proposed not only the foundation of colleges for the study of Arabic but also the creation of a military order to crush Islam. In this double crusade, the study of Arabic was only one weapon among others. The man who perhaps did more than any other to forge the weapon did not know that posterity would see him as a 'Christian *ṣufī*' Because of his receptivity to the influence of Ibn al-ʿArabī (1165–1240), the greatest mystic of Spanish Islam. Thus tactics and disinterested sympathy converged to provide favourable conditions for the impact of Muslim Arab civilization on a Christian West which was, so to speak, vibrant with all the frenetic energy, enthusiasm and appetites of adolescence.

The Studia Arabica

The contribution of this civilization made its way along two routes: by way of Sicily and Italy or, far more important, by way of Spain and southern France. Contrary to an opinion once very widespread, the crusades played only a very secondary role.

The first school from which Arab science began to spread by way of Italy seems to have been that of Salerno. Its foundation is attributed to Constantine the African (Constantinus Africanus), a doctor and businessman born at Tunis *c.* 1015. Converted from Islam to Christianity, he ended his life (1087) as abbot of the monastery of Monte Cassino. But it was from Palermo in particular that the Arab influence was exerted in the most fruitful way, as a result of the encouragement of Frederick II (1197–1250), his natural son Manfred (1258–66) and the early Angevins. In Sicily, this was the golden age of translations from Arabic into Latin, the age of the astrologer Theodore, of John and Moses of Palermo and, above all, of the Scotsman Michael Scot (d. 1235), all in the entourage of Frederick II. To their number we should add Faradj b. Salim of Agrigento, a Jewish writer, who put his pen at the service of Charles of Anjou (1264–82).

In Spain, the movement which began in tenth-century Catalonia at the famous monastery of Ripoli is still not well understood. The monk Gilbert, who took part in the 971 mission to al-Ḥakam II of Cordova and later became Pope Sylvester II (999–1003), studied at that monastery. But few details of the movement are available until the first quarter of the twelfth century. It was Barcelona that first took the lead in translation. In the first rank of the Barcelona group were Plato Tiburtinus and the Andalusian Jew, Abraham Bar-Hiyyā (d. *c.* 1136), better known as Savasorda (Ṣāḥib al-Shurṭa). They collaborated on translations of several works of astrology and astronomy, including the important tables drawn up by the oriental scholar, al-Battānī (Albategni or Albatenius, who died in 929).

Then Toledo came to the fore and eclipsed the other centres with its brilliance. Scholars were attracted from every corner of Europe: England, France, Germany, Italy and Dalmatia. In the fertilization of western Christian culture by Muslim Arab culture, Toledo played exactly the same role as ninth-century Baghdad had played with respect to the Hellenic heritage; Alfonso X the Wise (1252–84) was the exact counterpart of al-Ma'mūn (813–33), who dreamed of Aristotle. We can distinguish two major periods in the activity of the school of Toledo. The first was inspired by Archbishop Raymond (1125–52) and the second by another archbishop, Rodrigo Jimenez de Rada (1170–1247). Jews and Mozarabs (Christian Spaniards who lived under Muslim rule) served as guides and teachers of Arabic, especially at the beginning. Translations often went through several stages, the Arabic having to be put into Hebrew or Castilian before the final Latin form was produced, so that some errors were inevitable.

Among the translators of the earlier period were the archdeacon of Segovia, Dominicus Gondisalvius (d. 1181), who was one of the most important philosophers of the Spanish Middle Ages, profoundly influenced by the Arab peripatetic tradition. His collaborator was Jean d'Espagne Abendaud (d. 1166), a Jewish convert to Christianity. But the foremost figure was unquestionably Gerard of Cremona, the Lombard (1114–87). He learned Arabic under the Mozarab, Galippus (Ghālib) and quickly acquired an adequate knowledge of the language, which he put to the service of his tireless zeal for translating. We owe to him translations of no fewer than seventy works. Two Englishmen should also be mentioned – Adelard of Bath and Robert of Ketton; the latter made the first Latin translation of the Koran (finished in 1143) for Peter the Venerable, the Cluny reformer (1092–1156). To these should be added Hermann of Dalmatia.

The second period of the Toledo school was dominated by two translators: Michael Scot and Hermann of Germany. Toledo's enormous success was contagious. *Studia Arabica* multiplied. In 1236 the preaching friars, meeting in Paris, recommended that Arabic be studied wherever Christians were in contact with Muslims. In 1250 Ibn Rashīḳ of Murcia admiringly described the monastery of that still Muslim city, where he had met monks (certainly Dominicans) who were perfectly conversant with Arabic and with the Koran. At the same date the *Studium Arabicum* of Tunis, founded by Dominicans on the recommendation of the king of Aragon, James I the Conqueror (1213–76), was in full swing. It received, along with seven other preaching friars, Ramon Martini (1230–86), author of the *Pugio Fidei adversus Mauros et Judaeos* ('The Dagger of Faith directed against Muslims and Jews'). Ramon Martini's perfect mastery of Arabic is demonstrated by the Arabic–Latin dictionary attributed to him.[21] In 1256 there was also a school at Seville, founded at the instance of Alfonso X and run by Egidio de Tabaldis and Pietro de Reggio. Arnold of Villanova (d. 1312) was its last great figure. In 1269 Alfonso X entrusted the direction of the school in Murcia – which had been conquered in 1266 – to a Muslim philosopher of the region, al-Rakūtī, but transferred it to Seville in 1280. In 1276, at Majorca, the Franciscan Ramon Lull founded the famous Miramar College, where thirteen minor friars took up the study of Arabic before going forth to evangelize the lands of Islam. Eventually, on Lull's proposal at the Council of Vienna (1311), *Studia Arabica* were opened at Oxford, Paris, Salamanca, Rome and Bologna, where Leo Africanus (*c.* 1489–*c.* 1550) was still teaching in the sixteenth century.

In southern France, special attention should be called to the activity of a Jewish family from Granada, the Tibbonids. In particular, we owe many translations from Arabic into Hebrew to Yehuda Ibn Tibbon, who died at Lunel in 1190, and his son Shmuel b. Yehuda, who died at Marseilles in 1232. The grandsons carried on the family tradition for some time afterwards.

Translations of works from Andalusia and the Maghrib and their impact

PHILOSOPHY

Although the current of direct transmission was never totally interrupted, it is certain that the heritage of ancient thought was really *discovered*, *appreciated* and *understood* by the Christian Middle Ages only through the Muslim Arab philosophers, among whom those of Andalusia and the Maghrib hold a very honourable place.

We have no Latin version of Ibn Bādjdja (Latinized as Avempace); only Hebrew versions have come down to us, among them that of the *Tadbīr al-Mutawaḥḥid* ('The Rule or Regime of the Solitary'), produced by Moses of Narbonne in the mid-fourteenth century.[22] The same is true of Ibn Ṭufayl, known as Abubacer. His *Ḥayy b. Yaḳẓān*, translated into Hebrew at an indeterminate date, was commented on by Moses of Narbonne, in the same language, in 1349. The first known Latin translation, produced by Pococke under the title *Philosophus Autodidactus*, dates from 1671. But it is certain that Ibn Bādjdja and Abū Bakr b. Ṭufayl al-Ḳaysīr, were well known in the Latin Middle Ages under their Latin names.

21. The dictionary was republished in Paris in the nineteenth century and in Spanish in 1961.

22. Solomon Munk published a French rendering of the Hebrew translation in 1859.

The grand master, however, was indisputably Ibn Rus̲h̲d (Averroes). His works were widely translated – to the point that they have mostly come down to us only in a Latin or a Hebrew version – and passionately discussed. In the crowd of his translators the figure of Michael Scot stands out. This Scotsman may be regarded as the pioneer in the dissemination of Averroism. Hermann of Germany (who died in 1272) has a special place by his side. They both formed part of the entourage of Frederick II and had worked at Toledo. The efforts of the Tibbonids of Provence in spreading Averroism among the Jews should also be mentioned. Averroes' works had such success that there were several versions of the *Commentaries* in existence as early as the thirteenth century.

In the Latin Middle Ages, Ibn Rus̲h̲d, al-G̲h̲azālī's adversary and author of the *Tahāfut* (translated under the title of *Destructio destructionis*), naturally appeared as the champion of rationalism and anti-dogmatism. Consequently the Christian West divided into two camps: Averroists and anti-Averroists. Averroes' most fervent partisan was Siger de Brabant at the University of Paris. But theses regarded as Averroist, asserting *inter alia* the eternity of the world and denying the immortality of the individual soul, could not fail to mobilize the defenders of the Church. Albertus Magnus (1206–80), St Thomas Aquinas (1225–74) and Ramon Lull (*c.* 1235–1315) conducted a particularly vigorous offensive. But Averroism still continued to exert its seductive attraction. In 1277 it had to be condemned officially. Excommunicated and imprisoned, Siger met a tragic end around 1281. That the condemnations were due to an error in interpretation mattered little. Jules Romains has shown us in *Donogoo* how fertile error can be. Averroes caused a great mental ferment. He made people think, whether they were adherents or in reaction.

One sure sign of Averroes' success and of the passions he aroused is that he became a subject for painters, who used him as the very symbol of disbelief. At Pisa, Andrea Orcagna gives him a choice situation beside Muḥammad and the Antichrist in the hell that adorns the Campo Santo; and in the church of Santa Caterina, in a painting by Francesco Traini executed around 1340, we see him upside down at the feet of St Thomas. Yet, by one of those ironies and reverses of fortune, it was precisely over his supposed victor that Ibn Rus̲h̲d had his greatest triumph. 'St Thomas was at once the most serious adversary the Averroist doctrine encountered and, we can say without paradox, the Great Commentator's chief disciple', wrote Ernest Renan. This judgement has been confirmed by Asín Palacios and Jose Maria Casciaro, who published the *Theological Averroism* of St Thomas Aquinas, which includes no fewer than 503 quotations from the great philosopher. Expurgated, or better understood, Ibn Rus̲h̲d triumphed yet again in the fourteenth century; John of Baconthorpe (d. 1346), Provincial of the English Carmelites, was called the 'prince of the Averroists of his time'. And in 1473, when Louis XI reorganized the teaching of philosophy, he recommended the doctrine of 'Aristotle and his commentator Averroes, long recognized as wholesome and sure'.[23] But it was at the University of Padua that Averroism had its most brilliant and enduring effects. Its last great disciple there was Cesare Cremonini (d. 1631) and the tradition did not die out completely until the eighteenth century.

SCIENCE

In the Middle Ages philosophers were often medical doctors as well. The Christian West therefore welcomed the medical works of Ibn Rus͟hd. In 1255 his *Kitāb al-Kulliyyāt* ('The Book of Generalities') was translated as *Colliget* by Bonacossa, a Jew, at Padua. The best works of the representatives of the famous medical school of Ḳayrawān – Isḥāḳ b. 'Imrān (d. 893), Isḥāḳ b. Sulaymān al-Isrā'īlī (d. 932) and Ibn al-D̲jazzār (d. *c.* 1004) – had already been translated in the eleventh century by Constantinus Africanus and used in teaching at Salerno. Isḥāḳ al-Isrā'īlī's medical works continued in high favour until the end of the sixteenth century. They were published at Lyons in 1575 as *Omnia opera Ysaac*. The *Zād al-Musāfir* ('Traveller's Viaticum') of Ibn al-D̲jazzār enjoyed no less success. Besides the Latin version, there were translations in Greek and Hebrew. The *Kitāb al-Ta'rīf* of the Andalusian al-Zahrāwī (Abu 'l-Ḳāsim K̲h̲alat, known as Abulcasis, 936–1013), partially translated by Gerard of Cremona as *Alsaharavius* or *Açaravius*, enjoyed great renown throughout the Middle Ages, especially on the subject of surgery. Finally, Paravicius' Latin version of Abū Marwān Ibn Zuhr's *Taysīr* (written between 1121 and 1162) came out in Venice in 1280. Although it was the *Canon of Medicine* by Avicenna (Ibn Sīnā, of Persian origin) that was the Bible of all medieval doctors, the works mentioned above, with a smaller circulation and less authority, nevertheless made a large and effective contribution to the progress of medical studies in the Christian West. Medieval pharmacology owes to the Andalusian Ibn Wāfid (Abenguefith, 988–1074) one of its basic works, translated by Gerard of Cremona as *Liber Albenquefith philosophi de virtutibus medicinarum et ciborum.*

The contribution of Andalusia and the Maghrib to the spread of mathematical and astronomical science in the Christian West was no less important. Adelard of Bath translated the *Astronomical Tables* of Maslama al-Mad̲jrītī, which had been drawn up around the year 1000, following the work of Muḥammad b. Mūsā al-K̲h̲^{w}ārizmī (d. 844). In 1254 Yehuda ben Moshe made a Castilian translation of the vast astrological encyclopaedia of the Ifrīḳiyan Ibn Abī 'l-Rid̲jāl (d. after 1037), the *Kitāb al-Bāri fī-aḥkām al-Nud̲jūm*. On the basis of the Castilian text, there were two Latin versions, three Hebrew, and one each in Portuguese, French and English, which shows the enormous success of the work. Gerard of Cremona translated the *Tables* of al-Zarḳālī (Azarquiel) – which were presented to medieval Europe under the title of the *Tablas Toledanos* – and the *Iṣlāḥ*

23. E. Renan, 3rd edn, 1866, pp. 236 and 317.

al-Madjistī ('Reform of the Almagest') of Djābir b. Aflaḥ (Geber). The *Treatise on Astronomy* (*Kitāb fī 'l-Hay'a*) of al-Biṭrūdjī (Alpetragius) was translated into Latin by Michael Scot and into Hebrew by Moshe Ibn Tibbon in 1259. On the basis of the latter version, Kalonimos ben David produced in 1528 a new Latin translation which was printed in Venice in 1531, a sign of the book's continuing success. Finally, we should note Leonardo of Pisa (b. *c.* 1175), a mathematician of genius; he lived for a long while at Bidjāya, where his father was an attorney, and he owed much, especially in algebra, to the influence of the Arabs, whose numerical system he introduced into Europe.

LANGUAGE, LETTERS AND ART

The problem of the influence of literature in Arabic on medieval Europe has been much discussed, and often with heat. Take the poetry of the troubadours, which flowered in the twelfth and thirteenth centuries and which was so new in its form of rhythmic, rhymed stanzas, its psychological climate and its themes of courtly love; was it Arab in origin? According to Anglade it was not: 'Content and form alike, it was created by the Troubadours.' However, according to Ribera and, above all, Menéndez Pidal, one of the greatest specialists in Romance literature, it was.[24] No one denies that there are striking resemblances between the muwashshaḥ or *zadjal* of Muslim Spain (a genre in which, as we have seen, Ibn Ḳuzmān was a past master) and the poetry of Languedoc, represented by Guillaume IX of Poitiers. Moreover, contacts between Christians and Muslims were not rare and were sometimes close, especially in Spain. Why should there not have been an influence, under the circumstances? But some contemporary specialists like Le Gentil still demur; thus the debate continues.

Another debate now seems to be closed, albeit one which caused a great deal of ink to flow, on the subject of Dante's *Divine Comedy*. Asín Palacios, in *La escatologia musulmana en la Divina Commedia*, an analysis which may be considered a model of its kind, pointed to undeniable Muslim Arab influences in the *Commedia*. Not everyone accepted his views. The missing link which was needed to make them definitely convincing was found in a version of the *Mi'rādj*, a popular tale of Muḥammad's ascension to heaven, which had a great vogue in Muslim Spain. This was translated into Castilian for Alfonso X, and on the basis of that version, now lost, the Italian Buonaventura of Sienna made one translation in Latin, *Liber scalae Machometi*, and another translation in Old French, the *Livre de l'Eschiele Mahomet*. It has now been established, by Cerulli among others, that Dante knew the *Mi'rādj* – which, of course, in no way detracts from his genius.[25] The only question for discussion now is the *extent* of Muslim influence on the *Divine Comedy*. It may be added that medieval Europe

24. R. Menéndez Pidal, 1941.
25. E. Cerulli, 1949.

PLATE 3.2 *The cloister at Soria: an example of the Islamic influence on Christian art in Spain*

was also influenced by the Arabic literature of moral philosophy, which was widespread in Spain and was popularized by Petrus Alfonsi, among others, in the *Disciplina clericalis* he composed for Alfonso I of Aragon (1104–34), a work which had a sustained success up to modern times.

This long intimacy between the Muslim West and the Christian West, between Europe and Arabic-speaking Africa, left many traces in European languages. Words like algebra, logarithm, zenith, nadir, azimuth, alembic, alcohol, cipher, tariff, syrup, sugar and hundreds of other terms from the vocabulary of mathematics, astronomy, medicine, chemistry, botany and daily life are of Arabic origin: in Spanish, such words number about 4000.

Influences are also perceptible in art; not only in *Mudéjar* art, that 'autumnal flower' of Hispano-Moorish architecture, as Marçais puts it, but also in Romanesque art (see Plate 3.2). Since the second aspect was pointed out in analyses by Mâle, other studies have made it even clearer.[26] Finally, as Rodinson has shown, even the cooking of medieval Europe owed something to the culinary art of the Arabs.

Conclusion

Owing to the two cultural bridges linking Africa to Europe across the Mediterranean – Sicily and especially Spain – material and cultural exchanges between the two worlds, the two continents, were never interrupted. In the twelfth century the flame of African culture blazed up in

26. Marçais, op. cit.; E, Mâle, 1923.

Andalusia and the Maghrib for the last time before its light, ever more flickering, was extinguished in the darkness of decadence. Demographic collapse, engendering economic stagnation, retardation or regression, brought cultural atrophy. Forms had become lifeless. It was at this point that the heritage accumulated on the northern borders of Africa and in Muslim Spain was acquired by Europe, which, in full demographic explosion, enthusiastically discovered its priceless cultural and tactical value. It was a powerful stimulant of the Renaissance in Europe.

Today the Maghrib and the whole of Africa, in their turn, are undergoing the influence of western civilization. They are therefore experiencing a certain crisis, a certain struggle of conscience, opposing authenticity and modernism. What will the outcome be?

4 The disintegration of political unity in the Maghrib

I. HRBEK

The downfall of the Almohads

The battle at Las Navas de Tolosa (Arabic, *al-ʿIḳāb*) in 1212, at which the Almohad army was defeated by the combined forces of the Spanish Christian kingdoms, is generally acknowledged as being the starting-point of the decline of the Almohad empire. Even so, its downfall did not come about suddenly, nor was it a long-drawn-out process; disintegration started in the aftermath of the battle, at first slowly and then with increasing speed and intensity. The territory actually under the control of the Almohad rulers became progressively smaller: the pattern started in the east (Ifrīḳiya) and in al-Andalus (Andalusia or Muslim Spain), later spreading to the central Maghrib (Tlemcen) and on to Morocco, before culminating in the conquest of southern Morocco – the last remnant of the Almohad state – by the Marinids in 1269. When we look at the deeper causes of the decline of this powerful dynasty, we can discern several, some of which are closely related, whereas others are at first sight less so.

Although many Almohad rulers attempted to improve communications in the empire by building roads, its sheer size – it embraced both Andalusia and the whole of the Maghrib – made efficient central administration very difficult, and the geographical eccentricity of the capital, Marrakesh, further compounded the existing difficulties.

The fighting at both extremes of the empire, in Ifrīḳiya and in Spain, strained its resources to the full; a struggle had to be waged not only against external enemies but also against a great many uprisings and revolts fomented by nomad Arabs, the Banū Ghāniya, a variety of Berber groups and even by townspeople. The Almohad army lost its original fighting spirit as the dynasty progressively recruited more and more mercenaries of Arab, Zenāta and even Christian origin. The Almohad aristocracy was intent on retaining its privileges and looked upon all non-Almohad Muslims as infidels; many of these lost the title to their lands and became subject to a heavy tax burden. This cleavage between the subject masses and the narrowly based ruling class was the source of many revolts and uprisings in the Maghrib and Andalusia. The Almohad aristocracy itself was divided into two mutually hostile groups: on the one side were the descendants of ʿAbd al-Muʾmin, known as *sayyid*s, who were supported by their own *ḳabīla*, the Lumiya (a branch of the Zenāta) and by some Arabs, while on the other stood the Maṣmūda Almohads, who were both the headmen and leaders of various branches, as well as the religious shaykhs. Relations were also strained between these shaykhs and the Andalusian bureaucracy, which did not share the Almohads' beliefs and was loyal only to the caliph.

The succession of weak caliphs following the death of al-Nāṣir (1199–1213) also contributed to the decline of the dynasty, which was itself torn by internal strife. The rivalry between the Almohad shaykhs and the dynasty was brought out into the open in 1230, when a brother of Abū Yūsuf Yaʿḳūb, al-Maʾmūn, came over from Spain with Christian cavalry supplied by the king of Castile, defeated the reigning caliph and the Almohad shaykhs and proclaimed himself *Amīr al-Muʾminīn*. Until his death in 1232, he led an intensive campaign against the religious shaykhs and even went so far as to repudiate openly the Almohad doctrine and thereby deprive his own dynasty of its religious legitimacy. Although his successor, al-Rashīd (1232–42), attempted to overcome internal dissension by restoring the doctrine of the Mahdī and reaching agreement with the shaykhs, it was already too late and, since the empire was unable to recover from anarchy, it disintegrated. The dynasty lingered on and continued to occupy a steadily diminishing territory in Morocco until 1269, when the last Almohad caliph, al-Wāthiḳ (1266–9) was deposed by the Marinids.

The threefold partition of the Maghrib

The downfall of the Almohad empire set back the Maghrib to the stage it had reached before the rise of the Fatimids.[1] There emerged three independent and often mutually hostile states, weakened by dynastic strife and revolt from within, and later increasingly threatened by attacks from external Christian enemies.[2] The three territories formed the bases for what, at later periods, were to become the states of Tunisia, Algeria and Morocco; each of them developed in a different way, although they had several features in common.

As the society of the post-Almohad Maghrib is described in detail in the next chapter, we shall merely touch on the most general characteristics of the political and social structure of these states. Each of them was ruled by a dynasty that had originally been Berber but had become profoundly Arabized, supported by *makhzan ḳabīla*s.[3] Their control extended virtually only to the towns and plains with settled populations. The mountain regions

1. Cf. Volume III, Chapter 10.
2. See Chapter 3 above.
3. *Makhzan* originally meant treasury, but came to be used for the official system of government in Morocco. *Encyclopaedia of Islam*, 1st edn, Vol. 3, pp. 166–71.

and extensive steppe-like plains were occupied by Berber hill-settlers and/or Arab nomads, who were ready at any time to raid the outer fringes of the *makhzan* territory. The extent to which the ruler's writ was obeyed depended on his effective power or ability. The rulers of two of these dynasties, the Hafsids and the Marinids, aspired at different times to the title of caliph, since that was the only means of securing at least spiritual recognition by their turbulent subjects, but the response to their claims was confined to their own territories. Apart from the short-lived recognition of the Hafsid, al-Mustanṣir, in the mid-thirteenth century by the *sharīf*s of Mecca and the Mamluks in Egypt, these western 'caliphs' were incapable of competing with the shadow Abbasid caliphate of Cairo in the bid to win universal acceptance for their claims.

Another common factor in the post-Almohad period was the struggle against the growing pressure exerted on the entire Maghrib by the Christian states, chiefly those of the Iberian peninsula, but also to a lesser degree by Italy, Sicily and France. This combination of military, political and economic pressure was the outcome of the changing balance of power between the western European and the Islamic Mediterranean countries. The three Maghrib states endeavoured to find ways of responding to the new and aggressive thrust of the Christians; although they suffered many minor losses and were unable to save Granada, the final remnant of Muslim Spain, from falling into the hands of the Christians, they generally succeeded in preserving their heritage. However, the whole of the Maghrib, or at least its eastern parts, might well have shared the fate of Granada in the sixteenth century, had it not been for the emergence of a new Muslim power, in the shape of the Ottoman empire, which at the decisive juncture restored the balance of power in the Mediterranean. It should not be forgotten, of course, that at the same time the Iberian states, Portugal and Spain, were becoming increasingly involved in their overseas enterprises and that this absorbed the bulk of their attention and human resources.

Three dynasties succeeded the Almohads, sharing out the Maghrib between them and continuing in power for the greater part of the period under discussion. These were the Hafsids (1228–1574) with their centre in Tunis; the Abd al-Wadids or Zayyanids (1235–1554) at Tlemcen; and the Marinids in Morocco (*c.* 1250–1472) (see Fig. 4.1). We shall first outline the main events in the history of these three dynasties and then turn to the crucial issues of North African history as a whole.

The Hafsids

The eponymous ancestor of the Hafsid dynasty was the celebrated companion of Mahdī Ibn Tūmart, Shaykh Ḥafṣ Ibn 'Umar of the Hintāta Berbers, who made a significant contribution to the splendour of the Almohad empire. His son, 'Abd al-Wāḥid Ibn Abī Ḥafṣ, effectively governed Ifrīḳiya from 1207 to 1221 with almost autonomous powers and

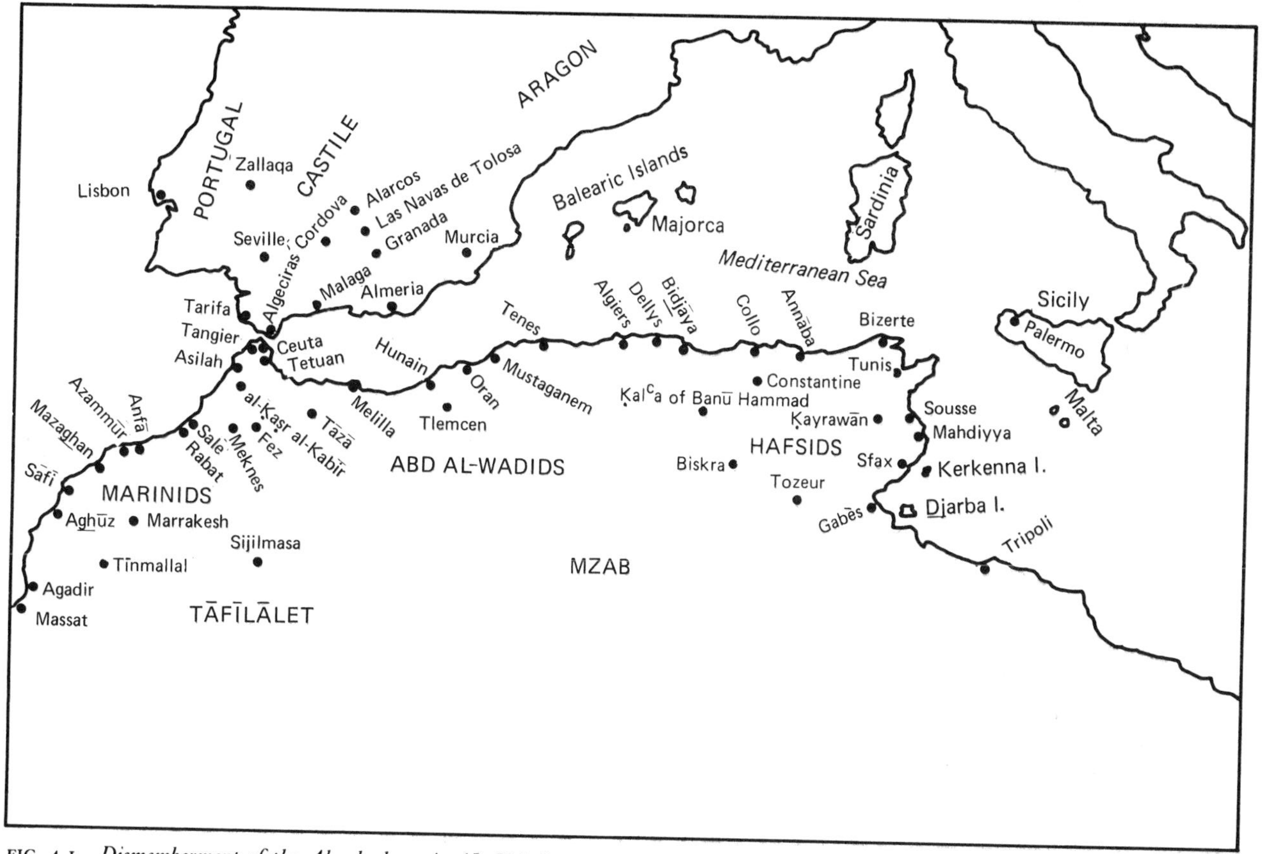

FIG. 4.1 *Dismemberment of the Almohad empire (I. Hrbek)*

thereby laid the foundations for its future independence. In 1228 Abū Zakariyyā', son of 'Abd al-Wāḥid, who had distinguished himself in the struggle against the Banū Ghāniya, the last representatives of the Almoravids in Ifrīḳiya, subsequently became governor. On the pretext of defending the true teaching and spirit of the Almohad movement – this was at the time when the Almohad caliph, al-Ma'mūn, had repudiated the doctrine[4] – Abū Zakariyyā' omitted the name of the caliph from the Friday *khuṭba* (the sermon given by the *khaṭib*, or spokesman) and in 1229 he assumed the title of independent amir. Seven years later, his full sovereignty was affirmed by the inclusion of his own name in the *khuṭba*.

Although he had cast off the political authority of the Almohad caliphs, Abū Zakariyyā' had not renounced the Almohad doctrine; on the contrary, he justified his seizure of power as a means of rekindling the true Almohad orthodoxy. In this regard, he was partially successful and found himself acknowledged as rightful caliph in various centres in Morocco and in Andalusia. By 1234, he had put a final end to the Banū Ghāniya uprising in the southern part of Ifrīḳiya. In his victorious campaigns to the west he successively seized Constantine, Bidjāya (Bougie) and Algiers, while in the east the entire coast of Tripolitania was subjugated. He accordingly brought together what was to become the Hafsid territory. Even the founder of the Abd al-Wadid dynasty, Yaghmurāsan b. Zayyān, submitted to his rule, and both the Marinids and Nasrids in Granada acknowledged his suzerainty.

The establishment of peace and security was followed by rapid economic growth, and the capital, Tunis, was again frequented by foreign merchants from Provence, Catalonia and the Italian republics. Relations with Sicily became friendly, but in 1239 the Hafsid ruler began to pay tribute to the Emperor Frederick II in return for the right to engage in maritime trade and for the freedom to import Sicilian wheat.

When Abū Zakariyyā' died in 1249, he left to his son and successor, Abū 'Abd Allāh Muḥammad al-Mustanṣir (1249–77), a prosperous and secure state, whose hegemony in North Africa went unchallenged. The rule of al-Mustanṣir was never seriously jeopardized by plots and rebellions, although it was disturbed from time to time by the rivalry between Almohad shaykhs and Andalusian refugees and immigrants, who constituted a political élite wielding considerable influence. In 1253 he assumed the title of *Amīr al-Mu'minīn* and was recognized as caliph by the *sharīf*s of Mecca in 1259 and a year later even by the Mamluks of Egypt. His recognition in the East did not last for long, however; it came about only in the special circumstances that, in 1258, the last Abbasid caliph in Baghdad had been killed by the Mongols and the caliphate was still vacant. However, in 1261 the Mamluk sultan, Baybars, installed a puppet Abbasid caliph at Cairo and, from that time until 1517, the entire Muslim East recognized only that caliphal line. Even so, the short-lived caliphate of al-Mustanṣir

4. See Chapter 2, p. 55 above.

bears witness to the considerable prestige of the Hafsids in the Islamic world, where their state was regarded as being one of the most stable and powerful.

A few years later, al-Mustanṣir was able to enhance his reputation in the Muslim world through the outcome of the crusade led by St Louis of France against Tunis in 1270. The true causes of that belated crusade are not entirely clear and there have been many different interpretations.[5] It has been suggested that the prosperity of Ifrīḳiya was a source of temptation to the French or that, as recounted by Ibn Khaldūn, some Provençal merchants encouraged the expedition because they had failed to recover the money they had lent to the Tunisians. Louis himself believed that al-Mustanṣir wished to become a Christian and hoped also to make Ifrīḳiya the springboard for a further campaign against Egypt. The expedition was badly prepared, and even Charles of Anjou, king of Sicily and brother of Louis, was informed about it only at the last moment. The crusaders landed in Carthage, but within a few weeks an epidemic broke out in their camp; the king himself fell victim to it.

Charles of Anjou quickly concluded peace, since he was in no way interested in the crusade and was anxious to reopen friendly commercial relations with the Hafsid state. Al-Mustanṣir, who had initially proclaimed the *djihād* (holy war) and had assembled contingents from various towns and from among the Arab nomads, was as ready as Charles to terminate the unfortunate affair, the more so as his nomad allies had started to withdraw towards their winter pastures in the south. The peace treaty was a compromise and the Hafsid caliph agreed to continue paying tribute to Sicily, along with taxes on the import of wheat; he also promised to expel from Ifrīḳiya the last members of the Hohenstaufen dynasty, who had fled to African territory after their overthrow by Charles of Anjou. One rather unexpected result of this last crusade was that trade was resumed on a larger scale than before.

The Hafsid empire reached its first apogee in the reigns of Abū Zakariyyā' and al-Mustanṣir. Its supremacy was recognized all over the Maghrib; its authority extended as far as Muslim Spain in the west and the Ḥidjāz in the east; all the European states of the western Mediterranean had to take account of its power; and the Spanish and Italian rulers eagerly sought alliances with it.

After al-Mustanṣir's death there was an anticlimax. For almost a century the Hafsid empire was the scene of recurrent internal disputes between the members of the ruling dynasty, and it was shaken by Arab revolts and by the dissidence of various towns and even of entire regions. This was especially notable in Bidjāya and Constantine, which repeatedly set up independent principalities under rival members of the dynasty. In periods of weak central government, these centripetal tendencies became more pronounced. At

5. Cf. M. Mollat, 1972, pp. 289–303.

certain times, three or more Hafsid rulers of various towns were claiming the throne in Tunis. Under these circumstances, the pendulum of power in the Maghrib swung westwards to the Marinids in Morocco; twice – in 1348 and 1357 – important parts of Hafsid territory, including the capital, Tunis, were occupied by Marinid forces. In neither case, however, did the occupation last for long, and the invaders were defeated by Arab nomads. At the end of the reign of Abū Isḥāḳ (1350–69), Bidjāya, Constantine and Tunis were governed by three independent Hafsid rulers, whereas the south, the south-east and a part of the coast (Sāhil) remained independent of Tunis.

The renaissance of Hafsid power commenced with Abu ʾl-ʿAbbās (1370–94) and continued under the long reigns of his successors, Abū Fāris (1394–1434) and ʿUthmān (1435–88). Abu ʾl-ʿAbbās succeeded in reuniting and reorganizing the country; he rescinded land grants, held local insubordination in check and restored the prestige of the dynasty. As a result of internal quarrels in Tlemcen and the open hostility between the Abd al-Wadids and Marinids, he had nothing to fear from the west. His son, Abū Fāris, completed the work of reunification and rooted out the local dynasties of Bidjāya, Constantine, Tripoli, Ḳafṣa, Tozeur and Biskra; he appointed governors there, chosen from among his freedmen. He subsequently gained control over the Abd al-Wadids of Tlemcen and intervened frequently in Morocco and even in Andalusia. This success was due mainly to Abū Fāris's policy of playing off the main sections of the population in the kingdom – the Almohads, Arabs and Andalusians – against each other. He showed tolerance towards the Jews, although he was himself a very devout Muslim. The popularity he enjoyed was due essentially to a number of factors: his concern for justice, the favours he bestowed on the pious – both the *ʿulamāʾ* and the *sharīf*s – his suppression of illegal taxes, his building achievements and his grandiose celebration of Muslim festivals.

Although the first years of the reign of Abū Fāris's grandson, ʿUthmān, were disturbed by a fight against rebellious relatives, his long rule was generally peaceful and this sultan managed to hold his realm together. The second part of ʿUthmān's reign, however, was clouded by famine and plagues, and by the revival of Arab unrest in the south. Nevertheless, he retained his hold on Tlemcen, although not without difficulty, and was recognized by the founder of the new Banū Waṭṭāṣ dynasty (the Wattasids) in Fez. The last years of ʿUthmān's reign are obscure, but he seems to have sown the seeds of future unrest by returning to the policy of appointing his own relatives to provincial governorships. Although his personality was strong enough to restrain the natural disposition of these relatives to seek independence, his successors were too weak to stem the tide of anarchy.

The second period of Hafsid power collapsed as suddenly as the first. By the end of the fifteenth and the beginning of the sixteenth century, the dynasty was again in a state of anarchy and was no longer capable of dealing successfully with the dangerous situation that arose from the rivalry between Spain and the Ottoman empire for supremacy in the Mediterranean. However, this forlorn struggle of the Hafsids to preserve their independence in the changing world belongs to the period covered by the next volume of this history.

The Marinids

'Originally from the desert, where they belonged to the noblest among the Zenāta, the Marinids came from the Zāb [a region of Algeria]. They knew neither silver metal nor money ... neither agriculture nor trade. All their wealth consisted of camels, horses and slaves.'[6] The Marinids, indeed, seem to offer the ideal model for Ibn Khaldūn's theory of the rise of nomadic dynasties and of their *ʿaṣabiyya*, the force which he saw as propelling the nomads out from the desert to conquer territories and found states. After the battle of Las Navas de Tolosa (1212) the Banū Marīn, who lived in the pre-Saharan steppes between Tāfīlālet and Figuig, started to invade north-eastern Morocco; finding the Almohad rule weak, they established their rule over the local agriculturalists and forced even towns like Tāzā, Fez and al-Ḳaṣr al-Kabīr to pay tribute. Although at first they were motivated merely by the natural desire of all nomads to enrich themselves at the cost of the sedentary population, their leaders gradually developed political ambitions.

Between 1240, when the Marinids were defeated at the siege of Meknes by the Almohad army, and 1269, when they conquered Marrakesh, the struggle was waged with intermittent success. The long-drawn-out progress of their conquest can be explained by their total lack of the religious motivation that had driven forward the Almoravids and Almohads to their rapid conquests. Nevertheless, their first drive was crowned with success in 1248, when their leader Abū Yaḥyā (1244–58) conquered Fez, Tāzā, Meknes, Sale and Rabat. Under Abū Yūsuf Yaʿḳūb (1258–86), the amir who can be regarded as the true founder of the Marinid sultanate, the last territories still under Almohad rule – the High Atlas, the Sūs and the region of Marrakesh – were gradually incorporated into the new realm and the conquest of Marrakesh in 1269 put an end to Almohad rule.

The new dynasty chose Fez instead of Marrakesh as its capital, and Abū Yūsuf founded a new town there, Fās al-Djadīd (New Fez), as distinct from the old city, thereafter called Fās al-Bālī (see Plates 4.1–4.3). Although they could not claim any religious legitimacy, the Marinids very soon looked upon themselves as heirs to the Almohads and attempted to re-establish that inheritance; their preference for its Iberian component did not prevent them from thrusting eastwards when the opportunity arose. It is a curious phenomenon, this attraction of the green hills and plains of Andalusia for these Berbers from the deserts, steppes and mountains, for Almoravids, Almohads and Marinids alike.

6. Ibn Abī Zarʿ, from the French transl. 1860, p. 401.

PLATE 4.1 *The Bou Inania Madrasa (the Koranic school) at Fez: detail of a courtyard window (14th century)*

PLATE 4.2 *The Bou Inania Madrasa (the Koranic school) at Fez: detail of a door panel (14th century)*

PLATE 4.3 *The Ḳarawiyyīn Mosque at Fez: restoration was carried out during the Almoravid era; in the courtyard, the main entrance of the prayer room*

Two high periods can be discerned in the history of the Marinids, as in that of the Hafsids, although they were of shorter duration. The first period occurred under the reigns of Abū Yūsuf Yaʿḳūb and his son Abū Yaʿḳūb Yūsuf (1286–1307), and the second was contemporaneous with the reigns of Abu ʾl-Ḥasan (1331–48) and his son Abū ʿInān Fāris (1349–58). However, it was only during the latter period that the Marinids could claim real supremacy in the Maghrib, and that only for a short space of time.

One of the most important developments under the Marinids was the growing importance of the Arabs in Morocco; already, under the Almohads, the Arab nomads had begun to penetrate into the country and to change its hitherto exclusively Berber character. The policy of the Banū Marīn towards the Arabs was dictated by the numerical weakness of their Zenāta followers, so they welcomed the support of the Arab nomads. The Zenāta themselves were to a high degree assimilated to the Arabs and the Marinid *ma<u>kh</u>zan* was composed of both groups. All this created the conditions for the expansion of the Arab domain in Morocco, where they settled mostly in the plains, and many Berber groups were Arabized. Contrary to the practice in the armies of the Almoravids and Almohads, where the Berber language was spoken, Arabic became both the common and the official language under the Marinids.

This process of expansion of the Arab nomads had also its negative side: the domain of the nomads increased and that of the cultivators diminished, with fields, gardens and forests being taken over as pasture by the nomads. The growth of nomadism contributed in large measure to the crystallization of the social structure that was to characterize Morocco for the coming centuries – the division of the population into nomads, townspeople and mountain dwellers.

Politically, this meant that only the towns and immediate countryside were under the firm administration of the sultans, whereas the *ma<u>kh</u>zan* tribes, both Arabs and Zenāta, enjoyed a large degree of autonomy and were allowed to levy taxes on the peasants in exchange for military service. However, since the loyalty and efficiency of these nomad contingents could not be taken for granted, the Marinid rulers, like their predecessors and neighbours, depended more and more on mercenary slave armies garrisoned in the larger towns. The Berbers of the Atlas, the Rīf and the <u>Dj</u>ibāl remained outside effective government, even though they sometimes recognized the sovereignty of the sultans; but in the period of the decline, they launched incursions into the *ma<u>kh</u>zan* lands (*bilād al-ma<u>kh</u>zan*) and took parts of them under their control or patronage, thereby enlarging the domain of the 'land of dissidence' (*bilād al-sibā*).

Urban life and civilization were given renewed vigour by the steady influx of the Andalusian immigrants, who brought with them a more refined style in architecture, arts and crafts and literature. The capital, Fez, became the leading cultural centre of Morocco, whereas the ancient capital, Marrakesh, went through a period of decline. The flourishing of urban culture, however, contributed further to the widening of the gap between the towns and rural areas, each of which led an independent life. This was very pronounced in the patterns of religious life. In Fez and other large towns, it was centred around universities such as al-Ḳarawiyyīn and the numerous *madrasas* where, under the official patronage of the Marinid sultans, the orthodox Mālikite rite was preponderant; the rural populations, on the other hand, were more and more attracted to the *zāwiyas*, the lodges of the mystic brotherhoods (*ṭarīḳas*), and to the shrines of local holy men or marabouts. This trend had already started under the Almohads, whose teaching incorporated the doctrine of al-Ghazālī (d. 1111), which merged mysticism (*taṣawwuf*) into the pattern of official Islam. Under the Marinids, mysticism was institutionalized by the establishment of the *Ṣūfī* orders, which were for the most part offshoots of the *ḳādiriyya*. This brand of popular Islam contributed significantly to the Islamization of the countryside, since it penetrated into the remotest parts of Morocco among the mountain Berbers, who had until then been only slightly affected by Islam.

Although the various aspects of the Christian challenge and the Muslim response it engendered in north-western Africa will be discussed later, the Marinid interventions in the Iberian peninsula have to be touched on briefly here. After consolidating his rule in Morocco proper, Abū Yūsuf Yaʿḳūb crossed the Straits of Gibraltar in 1275 and scored a decisive victory over the Castilians near Istidja' (Ecija). The sultan conducted three more campaigns in Spain; the Marinid navy defeated the Castilian fleet in 1279 and for a time the Christian threat to Granada and Morocco was frustrated. The fourth campaign resulted in the conclusion of an agreement, under which the king of Castile promised not to intervene in the affairs of the Muslim territories in Spain and also handed back Arabic manuscripts previously captured by the Christians. This compromise peace of 1285 was hailed by the Marinids as a victory.

Sultan Abū Yaʿḳūb had to deal with a succession of revolts in southern Morocco and was heavily involved in attempts to conquer Tlemcen and liquidate the Zayyānid dynasty. For these reasons, he was not inclined to disperse his armies and to intervene across the Straits. However, in 1291, when the king of Castile broke the agreement concluded in 1285, Abū Yaʿḳūb was compelled to embark on a short campaign, which failed to produce a positive result; the sultan then returned to his war against Tlemcen.

But Sultan Abū Yaʿḳūb was murdered and after his death the Marinid dynasty went through a period of eclipse, due mainly to the revolt of a dissident member who had seized large parts of southern Morocco and taken control of the trans-Saharan trade. The rebellion was suppressed only after the accession to the throne of Abu 'l-Ḥasan in 1331. During this period of internal dissension the Marinids were forced to abandon their offensive policy in both Spain and the Maghrib.

Abu 'l-Ḥasan was undoubtedly the greatest of the Marinid sultans;

shortly after his accession he reasserted the authority of Fez in southern Morocco, put an end to internal strife and revived the policy of conquest. In the first half of his reign, his efforts were centred on re-establishing Muslim sovereignty in Spain, all the more so as in 1337 the king of Castile had again embarked on a campaign against Granada. In 1333, the Marinid army crossed the Straits and conquered Algeciras. For the next six years Abu 'l-Ḥasan and the Nasrid amir of Granada prepared their forces for a final assault on Christian Spain. This threat led to the conclusion of an alliance between Castile and Aragon; but the Marinid fleet, aided by a number of Hafsid vessels, gained control of the Straits and won a decisive naval victory over the Castilian fleet in 1340. The Muslim army then laid siege to Tarifa, but the fortress held out until Christian forces came to its aid. In the fiercely fought battle at Rio Salada (1340) the Muslim force suffered a heavy defeat, its worst ever after that of Las Navas de Tolosa. In 1344, Algeciras was reconquered by the Christians. Although Gibraltar still remained in Marinid hands, the defeat at Rio Salada, followed shortly afterwards by other disasters in Ifrīḳiya, forced the sultan to abandon his Spanish venture. From this time onwards, neither the Marinids nor any other Moroccan dynasty were ever able to intervene actively in Spain. The sole remnant of the once glorious Muslim empire in Spain, the amirate of Granada, was thus left alone to continue its desperate struggle for survival.

The weakness of the Hafsids in the first half of the fourteenth century offered both the Zayyānids of Tlemcen and the Marinids of Fez an opportunity to expand their territories. Abu 'l-Ḥasan seized this opportunity in a clever way: on the pretext of coming to the aid of the Hafsids, who were being harassed by the Zayyānid ruler, he invaded the central Maghrib in 1335 and, after a two-year siege, conquered the Zayyānid capital, Tlemcen. This victory over his traditional rivals, which was duly announced to all his main fellow monarchs in the Muslim world, offered Abu 'l-Ḥasan a real prospect of realizing his dream of ruling over a reunified Maghrib. The Zayyānid territory was under Marinid occupation and the Hafsids became virtual vassals of the Marinid sultan. When the Hafsid dynasty subsequently went through another period of succession disputes, Abu 'l-Ḥasan entered Tunis in 1347 and annexed the Hafsid realm to his state. This was the high point of Abu 'l-Ḥasan's reign and, indeed, of Marinid history as a whole.[7]

The period that followed came as an anticlimax: Abu 'l-Ḥasan's policy of interfering with the Arab *ḳabīla* of Ifrīḳiya triggered off a widespread revolt; in 1348, his army was defeated near Ḳayrawān and he himself was besieged in the town. Although he managed to escape and restore his

7. The great historian, Ibn Khaldūn, for a long time nurtured hopes of seeing the Marinids reunify the Maghrib. Abu 'l-Ḥasan's failure came as a great disappointment to him. Cf. Ibn Khaldūn, French transl. 1852–6, Vol. 4, p. 253.

authority in Tunis to some degree, his defeat illustrated the fragility of Marinid power over the Maghrib. Tlemcen threw off his rule and the Hafsid princes of Bidjāya, Constantine and Annāba (the modern town of Bône) followed this example. Abu 'l-Ḥasan's son, Abū 'Inān, proclaimed himself sultan in Fez and deposed his own father. When Abu 'l-Ḥasan attempted to regain his throne with the remnants of his army, he was defeated in 1350 by Abū 'Inān and forced to seek refuge in the mountains, where he died a year later.

Abu 'l-Ḥasan's rise and fall can be seen as the epitome of the heroic and tragic history of the Maghrib under the Berber dynasties: a slow accumulation of forces, followed by a prolonged period of increasing successes and then suddenly, at the high point promising the final realization of the most audacious projects, a disaster and fall which dashed all the previous achievements and released all the forces of internal anarchy and dissent. The causes of Abu 'l-Ḥasan's final failure were similar to those that led to the decline of the Almohads, in that the human and material resources deployed in offensive campaigns came to be overstretched in two directions, compounded by the inability to come to terms with tribal and local particularisms and interests, by a precarious fiscal situation and by the lack of internal cohesion within the dynasty itself.

The first years of Abū 'Inān's reign were as successful as those of his father, twenty years earlier; with the same ambition as Abu 'l-Ḥasan, he assumed the caliphal title of *Amīr al-Mu'minīn* and was intent on reuniting the Maghrib. In 1352, he again conquered Tlemcen and a year later he annexed Bidjāya. The crowning point came in 1357, when he entered Tunis. However, his fall was as swift as his father's and for the same reasons, namely the opposition of the Arabs, who forced him to evacuate Ifrīḳiya and to return to Fez, where he was shortly to be murdered by one of his own viziers. With his death, the period of Marinid greatness came to an end; the remaining history of the dynasty until its demise in the fifteenth century is a tale of anarchy, revolts and widespread political, economic and cultural decadence.

No less than seventeen sultans reigned at Fez between 1358 and 1465, none of whom was able to check the forces of internal dissent or external threat. Viziers came to wield increasing power and from 1420 onwards that office was held by the members of the Banū Waṭṭāṣ clan, a collateral line of the Zenāta. The Wattasids, as they came to be called, steadily grew more powerful and became kingmakers for the next fifty years, until 1472, when Muḥammad al-Shaykh was proclaimed sultan at Fez after a six-year struggle against the *sharīf*s, who claimed descent from Idrīs II, the founder of Fez, and who aspired to take over political power. The rise of the *sharīf*s was associated with the cult of saints and with the belief in the *baraka* (the sacred blessing) inherent in the marabouts and to an even greater degree in the descendants of the Prophet Muḥammad. By contrast, the growing pressure exerted by the Portuguese against Morocco led to widespread popular discontent and opposition to the Marinid dynasty, which was incapable of effectively countering the incursions of the infidels.

Although the first Wattasid sultans, Muḥammad al-Shaykh (1472–1505) and his son Muḥammad al-Burtuḳālī (1505–24), succeeded in restoring the power of the sultanate of Fez to some degree and in suppressing the sharīfian movement, they were nevertheless unable to arrest Portuguese expansion along the Atlantic coast. Moreover, Wattasid authority was restricted to Fez and its environs; the southern part of Morocco remained virtually independent and beyond their control. It was in these regions that, at the beginning of the sixteenth century, the new popular forces led by a sharīfian family embarked on the holy war against the Portuguese forts on the coast and thereby simultaneously paved the way for the final overthrow of the Wattasid dynasty.[8]

The Zayyānids (Abd al-Wadids)

Another Almohad governor at Tlemcen, Yaghmurāsan b. Zayyān, who came from a minor Zenāta branch, broke away from the disintegrating empire in 1235; just as Abū Zakariyyā' had done in Tunis, he founded his own dynasty, which survived for over three centuries until 1554. From its very beginning, the existence of this kingdom was threatened by its stronger neighbours to the west and east, as well as by Arab nomads from the south. It was something of a miracle that the kingdom survived at all for so long a period; that it did so was due to the skilful policies of a number of very able rulers, the most successful of whom were the founder, Yaghmurāsan (1235–83), and Abū Ḥammū II (1359–89). Under their rule, the Tlemcen kingdom often went over to the offensive against the Marinids and Hafsids, in a bid to gain the Chelif valley and Bidjāya in the east and to penetrate as far as the approaches to Fez in the west. But, as often as not, the Zayyanids were driven to the defensive; Tlemcen frequently became the target of Marinid attacks and sieges and, in the fourteenth century, the Moroccans occupied much of the Zayyanid realm for several decades.

The periods of weakness were regularly exploited by the nomad Arabs, who systematically penetrated into the centre and were able to detach some of the outlying provinces. At the same time the Arabization of the Zenāta Berbers went on with increasing intensity, so much so that western Algeria lost its former predominantly Berber character.

The main weakness of the kingdom was its narrow and one-sided economic base: the state, whose territory comprised the less fertile parts of the Tell, was inhabited by numerically weak, sedentary populations and a host of nomad pastoralists, who in their turn were pressed by Arab incursions from the south and were steadily losing their pastureland. The instability that this created contributed greatly to the recurrent strife in

8. This pattern of events will be discussed in Volume V, Chapter 8.

society and within the ruling dynasty itself. It is little wonder that for long periods the Zayyanids were under the patronage of the Marinids, the Hafsids and, at an even later date, the kings of Aragon.

It seems scarcely feasible that, under such unfavourable political and economic conditions, the state should have survived until the Ottoman conquest in the mid-sixteenth century. Its main asset was the city of Tlemcen, which had replaced Tāhart as the main commercial entrepôt of the central Maghrib. It was located where the important north–south route, running from Oran (Wahrān) to the Saharan oases and further south to the Sudan, crossed the west–east axis between Fez and Ifrīḳiya; it soon eclipsed other centres as the focal point for trade between Europe and the Maghrib and the western Sudan. It also had direct links with Sijilmasa, the northern terminus of the trans-Saharan trade routes. The struggle between the rival dynasties – the Marinids and Zayyanids – might be partly accounted for as competition for the control of trans-Saharan trade. The person who was quickest to grasp the importance of that factor was Yag̲h̲murāsan b. Zayyan, who, after an unsuccessful attempt in 1257, conquered Sijilmasa in 1264 and held it for almost a decade, thereby bringing the two most important outlets of trans-Saharan trade, Tlemcen and Sijilmasa, under one authority for the first time. Although the Zayyanids soon lost Sijilmasa to the Marinids, Tlemcen still attracted the bulk of the trade.

This wealthy commercial city excited the envy of both the Marinids and the Hafsids, but it was the former who attempted to conquer it on many occasions. Between 1299 and 1307, Abū Yaʿḳūb besieged Tlemcen and built a new town opposite, which was called al-Manṣūra, but was generally known as New Tlemcen (Tilimsān al-D̲j̲adīd). This rapidly developed as a trade centre into which most of the trade was diverted. Even so, after Abū Yaʿḳūb's death the Marinid army retreated, Tlemcen was relieved and the first thing the Zayyanids did was to destroy the rival town of al-Manṣūra.

Over the next thirty years Tlemcen regained its commercial importance and again attracted merchants from Europe, the Maghrib and the eastern Muslim countries; at this time it had a population of about 40 000.[9] A proverb still current in Tlemcen in modern times recalls the memory of the wealth accruing to the town from the trans-Saharan trade: 'The best remedy against poverty is the Sudan.' The state was also able to recover greater political freedom and to launch an offensive policy against the weakened Hafsids, at a time when the Marinid dynasty was likewise involved in internal disputes.

The coming to the Marinid throne of Abu 'l-Ḥasan put an end to Zayyanid expansion; after a two-year siege, Tlemcen was conquered in 1337 and the terminal points of trans-Saharan trade fell under one controlling authority, that of the Marinids. However, as already mentioned,

9. At approximately the same period, Fez and Tunis had about 100 000 inhabitants each and Marrakesh some 60 000. Cf. Y. Lacoste, 1966, p. 50.

Abu 'l-Ḥasan's attempt to re-establish the unity of the Maghrib was short-lived, and during this sultan's struggles with his son Tlemcen recovered its independence.

Although the Tlemcen state flourished in the second half of the fourteenth century and enjoyed a period of prosperity under the able Abū Ḥammū Mūsā II (1359–89), it was twice occupied by the Marinid sultans and was harassed by Arab incursions and revolts. It was at this time that the great historian, Ibn Khaldūn, lived at Tlemcen and served as the intermediary of Abū Ḥammū with the chiefs of the Arab nomadic groups, thus gaining a deep insight into the mechanics of political life and changing alliances. He also left a testimony to Zayyanid culture: 'Here [in Tlemcen] science and arts developed with success; here were born scholars and outstanding men, whose glory penetrated into other countries.' The town was adorned by many monuments which have survived until the present day and have made Tlemcen the most important centre of Muslim architecture in the central Maghrib.

After Abū Ḥammū was dethroned by his own son Abū Tāshfīn II (1389–94), the Tlemcen kingdom entered a long period of decadence and was intermittently the vassal either of Fez or of Tunis, playing only a minor role in Maghrib politics. In the course of the fifteenth century it became virtually a protectorate of Aragon and by the end of the century it had disintegrated into a great many components, to the extent that the authority of the Zayyanid amirs of Tlemcen was confined to the town and its environs. Even then the amirs were plagued by conflicts over the succession and were increasingly compelled to seek the help of the Spanish and rely on their Christian mercenaries, who became the de facto rulers. In the following century, the Tlemcen kingdom was little more than a pawn in the great struggle between Spain and the Ottoman empire, and it finally disappeared under the onslaught of the latter in 1554.

The challenge of Christian Europe

From the thirteenth to the sixteenth century, the Muslim West came into much closer contact with Christian Europe than in the preceding period. However, it would be wrong to regard each side as a single homogeneous unit, engaging in a fixed policy of antagonism against the other. After the disappearance of the Almohads, the Muslim West was divided into the four political units discussed above: the Nasrid amirate of Granada, the Marinid sultanate of Morocco, the Zayyanid kingdom of Tlemcen and the Hafsid sultanate of Tunis. Their opponents from the northern shores of the Mediterranean were even more divided. In the Iberian peninsula there were the kingdoms of Castile, Aragon and subsequently Portugal; in Italy, moreover, Genoa, Pisa, Venice and Sicily (before it was annexed by Aragon) had independent and often mutually hostile policies. After the last unsuccessful crusade under St Louis, the French retreated into the background and played only a minor role in the Maghrib.

Since the multiplicity of states opened up many possibilities for the interplay of alliances, which often cut across religious boundaries, it would be over-simplifying matters somewhat if we were to see relations between the Muslims and the Christians in the western Mediterranean during the period under discussion merely in terms of a relentless warlike struggle between two uncompromising opponents, one inspired by the idea of the Islamic *djihād*, the other imbued with crusading fervour. This does not mean that these phenomena were not present; indeed, in some periods they were often the decisive motivating forces. But beneath them we can discern conflicting economic and commercial interests that account for the otherwise incomprehensible tangle of alliances and counter-alliances between Muslim and Christian states. Since Chapter 26 will deal with these underlying factors on a broad inter-continental scale, we shall confine ourselves here to the political aspects of Muslim–Christian relations.

A decisive point in the history of the western Mediterranean was reached in the mid-thirteenth century, when the Christian *reconquista* culminated in the conquest of the Andalusian heartland.[10] The following Muslim centres fell successively into the hands of various Iberian kingdoms: the Balearic Islands (Majorca) in 1229, Badajoz in 1230, Cordova in 1236, Valencia in 1238, Murcia in 1243, Djayyān (Jaén) in 1246, Seville in 1248, Gharb al-Andalus (Algarve) in 1249 and Ḳādis (Cádiz), Jeréz and Labla (Niebla) in 1260–2. From then onwards, some 90 per cent of the Iberian peninsula was under Christian control, and Muslim territory was reduced to the tiny Nasrid amirate of Granada, founded in 1232. Owing to the rivalry between Castile and Aragon, and at least partly to Marinid support in the first century of its existence, Granada managed to survive until 1492. Although the Nasrid amirs sometimes intervened actively in North African politics and accordingly helped to complicate the political situation, the role of Muslim Spain as an independent Mediterranean power was virtually ended.

At first, the changing balance of power was not apparent and the Marinids, as we have seen, attempted on several occasions to redress what, in their eyes, was only a temporary situation in Spain and to restore the Almohad empire to its full territorial extent. It was only in the middle of the

10. The term *reconquista* is used in Iberian (and European) historiography to denote the process of Christian resistance to Muslim domination and the wars to eliminate Islam from the peninsula. It covers the whole period between 722 (the battle of Covadonga) and 1492 (the fall of Granada). In recent years some Spanish scholars have begun to criticize the entire concept of the *reconquista* and have pointed out that, during the periods 722–1031 and 1252–1481, there were neither Christian conquests nor reconquests. They maintain that even the term 'conquest' ought properly to be applied only (a) to the period from 1035 to 1262, especially the years between the conquest of Toledo in 1085 and that of almost all Andalusia in 1249, and (b) to the later period from 1481 to 1492, prior to the fall of Granada. Cf. M. Cruz Hernández, 1970.

fourteenth century that the shift in the balance of power in favour of the Christian side became patently clear and the Maghrib was driven on to the defensive.

Some of the factors underlying the decline in the political and military strength of the Muslim states have already been mentioned. In all of them, the political power, which had been centralized at the beginning of the new dynasties, was constantly and increasingly eroded by a variety of centripetal forces, regardless of whether these represented dissident members of ruling families, heads of nomadic tribes, Christian mercenaries, Ṣūfī shaykhs or *ashrāf* (*sharīfs* or heads of noble families), all of whom wished either to have a share in power or to secure for themselves as much autonomy as possible, with no regard for a common purpose. The dichotomy between the coastal towns, geared to external trade, and the countryside, and between nomads and sedentary populations divided society to an even greater extent into factions that had very little in common.

There were also a number of intrinsic causes for the deepening crisis in the Maghrib. Compared with other Mediterranean countries the region was relatively underpopulated and the rate of population growth appears to have remained rather low in the crucial centuries.[11] The influx of Andalusian refugees was scarcely more than the population losses resulting from the Black Death in the middle of the fourteenth century. In many regions the feudal nature of the regime and the general instability led to the abandonment of cultivated lands. Written sources from the beginning of the sixteenth century onwards provide abundant evidence of the existence of deserted lands and the sparsity of population in formerly cultivated and inhabited parts. The gradual deterioration of the soil represented a further contributory factor; this was caused partly by the nomadic herds and partly by the decrease in fertility in arid zones that had been exhausted by over-intensive cultivation. Here again, the scarcity of labour had not made it possible to restore past productivity levels.

Trans-Saharan trade, which for centuries had been a reliable source of Maghrib economic prosperity, began from the 1350s onwards to be increasingly diverted towards Egypt. The repercussions of this change were felt not only by the commercial class, but to an even greater extent by the governments, because customs duty levied on trade formed one of the most accessible sources of revenue.

All this took place at a period when the Christian states were consolidating their political, military and economic power. Although at that time the eastern Maghrib under the Hafsids was not threatened by the Christians to such a dangerous degree as the more western parts, it nevertheless suffered as a result of occasional raids and campaigns. Charles of

11. The population of the whole of the Maghrib at the end of the sixteenth century was estimated at 3 million. At the same time, the population of the Iberian peninsula amounted to some 9 million, of France to some 15 million, and of Italy to some 12 million. Cf J. Monlaü, 1964, pp. 39–40.

Anjou had already occupied Collo in 1282, and the joint forces of Sicily and Aragon under Roger de Lauria seized Djarba, Kerkenna and Marsa al-Khāriz (La Calle). The island of Djarba remained in Christian hands until 1335 and became a thorn in the flanks of the Hafsid state. At the end of the fourteenth century, attacks by Christian fleets against coastal localities were renewed. The French, on this occasion allied with the Venetians, undertook an unsuccessful siege of al-Mahdiyya in 1390, and the fleets of Valencia and Majorca attacked Dellys in 1398 and Annāba in 1399. The Aragon army attacked Kerkenna and Djarba again in 1424 and 1432, and right up to the end of the century there were innumerable incursions, raids and attacks by the Genoese and Venetians on several of the ports between Tripoli and Algiers. Although these actions and the raids of the Maghrib pirates worsened political relations between the Hafsids and the Christian states, they never led to a total break and trade continued as briskly as before. Politically, the Italians did not represent any grave danger, as their interests were chiefly commercial and they did not aspire to territorial conquest. In general, the Muslim rulers maintained easier relations with the Italian traders than with the Iberians, whose ambitions were predominantly political.

The situation in the central and western Maghrib was both different and more complicated. In the course of the fourteenth century and the first half of the fifteenth, the kings of Aragon maintained friendly political relations with Morocco and exercised a strong influence in Tlemcen. Their policy was dictated by their rivalry with Castile as well as by their political ambitions elsewhere, in both Italy and the central Mediterranean. Castile and Portugal, on the other hand, were only waiting for an opportunity to intervene in Morocco. The victory at Rio Salado spelt the end of Moroccan involvement on Spanish soil: from then onwards, the struggle between Castile and Granada took on the character of a feudal dispute between suzerain and vassal rather than between the Christians and the Muslims. The Castilians looked upon the Muslims of the Maghrib as their real enemies and endeavoured to put an end to the twofold threat of a Moroccan invasion and the increasingly active privateers.

Piracy in the Mediterranean had existed from time immemorial and had been carried on by both Muslims and Christians in the Middle Ages. However, the Christian reconquest of Spain gave a religious colouring to an activity whose aim was primarily the amassing of booty. From the fifteenth century onwards, the Muslim corsairs, especially those exiled from Andalusia, regarded their own exploits as a kind of *djihād* and as a way of retaliating against their expulsion. In some of the principal ports of the Maghrib, the corsairs had founded independent 'republics', out of which they often operated in contravention of the wishes of the official state authorities. The Marinids, the Wattasids and the Hafsids had all adopted a policy towards the corsairs that fluctuated between giving them support and attempting to curtain their activities for fear of provoking punitive expeditions on the part of the Christian powers. Some of the raids on the North African coast were, in fact, acts of retaliation for the attacks launched by Muslim corsairs on Christian ships or on the Spanish seaboard.

When viewed in a historical perspective, Muslim privateering can be regarded as a kind of active response to the Christian challenge, at a time when the governments of the Maghrib states were suffering from internal weakness and were unable to offer any effective resistance to the European offensive. In some ways, the activities of the corsairs can be likened to the popular movements in the interior of Morocco in the fifteenth and sixteenth centuries, which were led by the *sharīf*s and marabouts against a central government that was incapable of expelling the Portuguese from the country.

However, the internal situation in Spain prior to the union of Castile and Aragon in 1479 did not at first enable any concentrated effort to be directed against the Maghrib. The temporary conquest of Tetuan in 1399 by the Castilians, when half its population was massacred and the remainder reduced to slavery, had long been the only serious Iberian incursion into Moroccan territory. A renewed offensive started only after the conquest of Muslim Granada in 1492.

The Portuguese proved to be far more dangerous and aggressive opponents both of the Maghrib and of Africa as a whole. After expelling the last Moors from their territories, the kings of the Avis dynasty, which came to power in 1385, decided to continue the struggle against non-believers on African soil. Their underlying motives were a complex combination of religious zeal, the expectation of territorial gains and rich booty, and the hope of suppressing Muslim privateering.

In 1415, the Portuguese fleet and army under the leadership of Prince Henrique (the future Henry the Navigator) and Prince Fernando, the sons of King João, conquered the Moroccan port of Ceuta after a short battle. This was the very first step in Portuguese overseas colonial expansion. The capture of Ceuta is widely regarded as an important landmark in European and even in world history, since it was purportedly the starting-point of the Europeans' expansion beyond the boundaries of their own continent in their bid for conquest and colonization. This judgement calls for qualification, however, since it should not be forgotten that the crusades had already represented a similar attempt at overseas expansion, control of eastern trade and exploitation of non-European countries and peoples. On the other hand, there can be no denying that the year 1415 marked the beginning of uninterrupted aggression by western European states, in the course of which they gradually gained control over other continents and discovered new lands which became the object of their efforts at colonization. As this general aspect will be dealt with more broadly in the introduction to Volume V of the *General History of Africa*, the discussion here will focus on the consequences of Portuguese aggression for north-western Africa and especially for Morocco.

The Portuguese had naturally planned not merely to capture a single port but to occupy the whole of Morocco, with the aim of taking over the lucrative gold trade. As already stated, the Marinid dynasty had proved incapable of withstanding that threat, and the vizier Abū Zakariyyā' al-Waṭṭāsī became the virtual ruler, who tried to mobilize the country. In 1437 the Portuguese, led by the two princes, again made an attempt to conquer Tangier (Tandja), but suffered a heavy defeat; they accordingly promised to return Ceuta to the victorious Moroccans, while Prince Fernando was retained in Morocco as a hostage. However, his brother, King Duarte, resolutely refused to abandon the Portuguese foothold on African soil and the unfortunate Fernando died in captivity at Fez.

The defeat at Tangier to some degree changed Portugal's expansion policy and projects, as it became clear that a frontal attack alone would not lead to the control of Morocco and the Sudanese trade routes. This compelled them to look for other approaches to the sources of gold; at the same time they nurtured hopes of finding an ally to the south of Morocco who could help them to encroach the Muslim enemy. This change of priorities did not, of course, mean that the Portuguese monarchs and bourgeoisie abandoned their projects in north-western Africa; but their attention was increasingly concentrated on the Atlantic coast. From the middle of the fifteenth century onwards, they successively occupied the following Moroccan coastal towns: al-Ḳaṣr al-Kabīr in 1458, Anfā in 1469, Arsīla in 1471, Massat in 1488, Agadir in 1505, Sāfī in 1508, Azammūr in 1513, Mazaghan in 1514 and Aghūz in 1519. In 1471, they had finally succeeded in conquering Tangier as well. From the Portuguese point of view, Morocco not only represented a stage in their expansion along the African coast, but was also intrinsically valuable, since the Portuguese treasury drew large profits from raids into the interior of the country, in the course of which many villages and towns (and even Marrakesh in 1515) were plundered and their inhabitants captured and sold into slavery. At the same time, they continued to engage in friendly trade with the Moroccans and purchased mainly cereals, horses and especially woollen textiles, which they subsequently bartered in West Africa for slaves and gold.

While the Portuguese were successfully expanding along the Atlantic coast of Morocco and further to the south in search of gold and an anti-Muslim ally (the legendary Prester John), thereby inaugurating the era of great discoveries and colonial empires, the Spaniards were finally consummating the union of Castile and Aragon under King Ferdinand and Queen Isabella. After a ten-year war, they conquered Granada and in the same year, 1492, Christopher Columbus embarked on his first voyage, in the course of which he discovered the shortest route to a New World which was later to be known as America.

Spain's expanding horizons overseas did not prompt her to neglect her more immediate enemies in North Africa. Under an agreement sanctioned by the Pope in 1494, the Maghrib was divided between the two Iberian kingdoms: the regions west of Ceuta were granted to Portugal and those further east to Spain. The Spanish were not slow to exploit both this agreement and the weakness of the Zayyanids and Hafsids. Between 1496 and 1510 they took possession of several major ports on the Mediterranean coasts, including Malīla (Melilla, still a Spanish possession), Mers al-Kabīr, Oran, Bidjāya (Bougie) and Tripoli. But they were unable to penetrate more deeply into the interior; their *presidios* were restricted to the ports and dependent on sea-borne supplies, thereby rendering them vulnerable to any strong sea power.

The end of the fifteenth century was thus a period when the fortunes of the Muslims in the Maghrib were at their lowest ebb: most of their ports, on both the Atlantic and Mediterranean coasts, were in the hands of the Christians; central governments were ineffective and weak; the countries themselves were divided into many rival factions; and their economies were precarious and subject to the strain of an evolving global balance of power. Although the Maghrib experienced a fresh lease of life in the following century, due to a strong popular movement in the West and to the intervention of the Turkish corsairs and subsequently of the Ottoman empire in the East, it never again attained the political, economic and cultural heights it had reached under the Almoravids, the Almohads and the early rulers of the Hafsid and Marinid dynasties.

5 Society in the Maghrib after the disappearance of the Almohads

R. IDRIS*

Although the historiography of the Maghrib is fairly advanced for the period that concerns us, its social history has yet to be studied. The scarcity of works of synthesis reflects this situation, and we need to get down to the task of research, analysis and interpretation of the documentary sources.[1] Generalizations about medieval Islam may still be of assistance in understanding the problems, but the differences between East and West and their different forms of development must be taken into account, even if these have emerged only dimly and slowly.[2]

The predominance of nomadism: life in the towns

The nomads

Since the eleventh century, the age-old but precarious balance between a sedentary and a nomadic mode of life had been upset in favour of the latter by the invasion of Arab nomads, the Banū Hilāl, who were followed, in the twelfth century, by the Banū Sulaym. At the beginning of the thirteenth century, their 'total devastation' ruined crops and brought anarchy to Ifrīḳiya and the central Maghrib.[3] The Almohads, for reasons of military and economic strategy, transferred them in large numbers to the Atlantic plains, which were given over to them, whereas other Beduin, the Banū Ma'ḳil, occupied the southern and eastern parts of the Moroccan Atlas range. The Maghrib was cut off from the east, its relations with the Sudan were disrupted, and its civiliza-

* This paper is published posthumously; Professor Roger Idris died on 29 April 1978.

1. There exist, however, two valuable works: G. Marçais, 1913, and R. Brunschvig, 2 vols, 1940 and 1947.

2. On urban history, which is of some importance in this article, reference may be made for comparative purposes to A. H. Hourani and S. M. Stern (eds), 1970 – a collection of studies of oriental towns.

3. Historians are far from unanimous concerning this thesis of 'total devastation'. A. Laroui, 1970, pp. 139–46, criticizes it to considerable effect.

tion, especially in the east and in the centre, was forced back towards the Mediterranean coast.

The rural population

Peasants – cattle breeders, cultivators, foresters, cash-crop growers and so on, depending on the territory concerned – made up the majority of the rural population, especially as there was some population drift between the small market towns and the countryside. The numerous workers required by an agriculture which had hardly progressed since ancient times were not serfs; small family farms predominated. Some powerful individuals possessed large properties, but the great majority of rural people held land collectively; joint ownership was frequent. Numerous plots were private or public *habous* which the recipients farmed themselves or leased to tenant-farmers.[4] Many farms, perhaps the majority, were cultivated under a contract entered into with the owner: plantations were leased out to numerous owners, and there were various forms of tenant-farming and share-cropping, most commonly for a fifth of the crops. The share-croppers (*khammās*) did not always proceed in attaining a subsistence level, and their condition was often quite wretched, particularly in years when the harvest was poor. Each family's meagre sustenance came from the land it owned or farmed for the owner. Farm produce, livestock, and rural and urban handicrafts were exchanged at rural markets – some seasonal, some weekly – which often grew into important market towns, centres for contact between residents, semi-nomads and nomads.

The lack of documentation makes it difficult to analyse the structure of village society. This varied rather widely according to the locality. It remained intact in those isolated areas which have retained the Berber language until recent times. Other places sustained the impact of nomads without being submerged by them, so that their new equilibrium was essentially a continuation of the past and remained unchanged for centuries.

The townspeople

Urban life has to be analysed separately in each of the three states of the Maghrib, beginning with the western region, whose influence was largely preponderant. First, however, a few general traits may be distinguished. There is no need to dwell on the characteristics of Muslim Arab society: the patriarchal family, the separation of the sexes, the veil

4. A *habous* or *wakf* is a religious endowment or bequest, private or public, in the form of property in mortmain, whose proceeds accrue only to its assigns (who may be the poor of a town, social groups, particular families or students).

PLATE 5.1 *Agadir (fortified granary) of Fri-Fri in the Tijnit region of southern Morocco*

worn by townswomen, polygamy, concubinage, endogamy, the distinctions between free men and slaves, between Muslims and tributaries and so on. There is also no need to dwell on the organization of traditional Muslim city life: the great mosque amid the *souk*s, the narrow, winding side streets, the *ḥammām*, the ramparts pierced by gates adjacent to the cemeteries, the markets and the suburbs.[5] Imported fabrics were stored in the cloth halls (*ḳaysariyya*) and other commodities in the caravanserai (*funduḳ*s), whose rooms gave on to an inner court. European merchants living in the ports were divided by nationality amongst the *funduḳ*s, each having their own consul. The corsairs brought back slaves

5. 'Ḥammām: lit. "heater" (Ar. *ḥamma*, "to heat", Hebr. *hāmam*, – "to be warm"), a hot steam bath. These are isolated buildings communicating with the street or market place by a more or less imposing door.' *Encyclopaedia of Islam*, 1st edn, Vol. 2, p. 253.

who were employed chiefly as domestics; Christian monks sometimes ransomed them.

As for the Jews, their numbers increased at the end of the fourteenth century following the arrival of numerous refugees from Christian persecutions. They played a leading role in the economy, thanks to their capital, their natural aptitudes and their connections with Jews remaining in Europe. Many settled in Tlemcen and Bidjāya (Bougie). They were well received in Ifrīḳiya but never occupied there the high office which they frequently managed to attain in Morocco. Pogroms broke out in Fez at the beginning and end of the Marinid dynasty. The Jewish community of the Tuat oasis was also subjected to persecution in the second half of the fifteenth century.

But the immigration of Muslim Spaniards following the *reconquista* was of special importance; the continual flow rose to its highest levels during the first half of the thirteenth century and at the end of the fifteenth. These Andalusians settled especially in the ports and constituted coherent groups whose members pursued diverse activities from top to bottom of the social scale: men of letters, musicians, lawyers, secretaries, soldiers, merchants, weavers, embroiderers, masons, gardeners and farmers; and the sultans frequently chose their favourites from among them.

Both in the cities and among certain rural or nomadic groups, some racial mixing resulted from the influx of black slaves of both sexes and Arab concubinage with black women.

The Arab–Berber 'symbiosis' began immediately after the conquest and was well advanced by the beginning of the ninth century.[6] But even in the cities, its most favourable environment, this did not extirpate a certain tribalism, which remained deep-rooted despite Islam. That religion, born in Arabia, in a city of commerce and caravans, is well known for its urban bias; therefore it is with reference to city life that one should depict the religious evolution of Maghrib society, which was fundamentally sacral, from the thirteenth to the sixteenth century.

The triumph of Mālikism: mystical tendencies

Almohadism failed to unsettle the Mālikism of the Maghrib; it appeared to be an unofficial religion legitimizing the power of the Maṣmūda and, as a consequence, was dealt a fatal blow by their downfall. Their successors, the Marinids and Abd al-Wadids, had no special religious doctrine and adopted Mālikite orthodoxy. They fostered this by founding numerous *madrasas* for lodging and instructing students, from among whom officials were chosen; the influence of the Andalusians quickly made itself felt in the *madrasas*. In the eastern Berber country, the situation was different. The Hafsids were Almohads who remained faithful to their

6. H. R. Idris, 1973b.

doctrine, which their first *madrasas* attempted to spread. In this they failed, because the Ifrīḳiyans remained profoundly Mālikite. Moreover in the second half of the twelfth century certain eminent doctors added fresh lustre to Mālikism, which took over all religious institutions, the magistracy and the instruction in the *madrasas*. Not only did the Hafsids allow this evolution to take place, but they also established a real collaboration with the Mālikite doctors and, thanks to the renowned Ibn ʿArafa, Mālikism triumphed in the second half of the fourteenth century.

Mālikism was not the only factor leading to religious unification: as early as the twelfth century, popular piety in the Maghrib became deeply imbued with mysticism. The Moroccan people had already suffered the constraints of the rigid, legalistic, narrow-minded and desiccated jurisdiction of the Almoravids, perpetrators of the *auto-da-fé* of the works of al-G̱hazālī. The Almohads were still vainly endeavouring to inculcate in them a more flexible but excessively rationalist doctrine, which proclaimed the sinless nature of the Mahdī and condemned jurisprudence, thus offending their ineradicable Mālikism; now the Moroccans slaked their frustrated thirst for piety with Ṣūfism. Upon the disappearance of the Almohads, this movement expanded considerably in Morocco under the influence of Andalusian Ṣūfism and a long tradition of local asceticism, which was rendered illustrious by a galaxy of leading mystics who had become popular holy men; thereafter it spread to the central Maghrib and Ifrīḳiya.

Abū Madyan al-Andalusī (Sīdī Bou Médine), who was born near Seville, studied mysticism with the Moroccans and then went to seek its source in the east. After a long sojourn at Bid̲jāya, he was summoned by the caliph of Marrakesh, who had become disquieted by his reputation; he died, however, en route to Tlemcen (1197–8). He had a rival in Nafṭī (Sīdī Abū ʿAlī al-Nafṭī) and his disciples included al-Daḥmāni (d. 1224), a Beduin originally from the Ḳayrawān (Kairouan) plains, and al-Mahdāwi (d. 1224) of Mahdiyya. Sayyidī Abū Saʿīd (Sidi Bou Said) (d. 1231) taught Ṣūfism in and around Tunis.

Another of Abū Madyan's disciples, Mulay ʿAbd al-Salām b. Mas̲hīs̲h, was a prominent holy man of the region. His pupil, Sīdī Abu ʾl-Ḥasan al-Sadīlī (Sīdī Belḥasen), born south of Tetuan (*c.* 1197), began preaching in the environs of Tunis, where he settled after a retreat at D̲jebel Zag̲houān, surrounded by large numbers of the faithful. However, suspected of being an ʿAlid agitator – he claimed to be a *s̲harīf* and a descendant of Ḥasan b. ʿAlī – he was forced to retire into the east, where he died in 1258, leaving a multitude of followers in Tunis. His fervent but unrefined Ṣūfism tended towards the cult of saints (maraboutism, *baraka*, thaumaturgy, poverty, eccentricity, life in a cell or a *zāwiya*) and religious brotherhood; it came to be known as Sadīlism.

Among the companions of al-Sadīlī, some fifty in number, mentioned by Hafṣid Ifrīḳiya, was a woman, Lalla Mannubiyya (d. 1267), whose behaviour was demented, although she was feared and venerated: the jurists demanded her arrest, which was opposed by the sovereign. Soon extravagances of this sort encountered no further opposition. Al-Murgānī (d. 1300), a *zāwiya* shaykh, maintained excellent relations with the court and the theologians.

This was the period when Sīdī Ben ʿArūs flourished (d. 1463). A native of Cape Bon, he first practised humble trades, while studying Ṣūfism in Tunisia and later in Morocco, where he spent a long period. Returning to Tunis, he lived as a marabout and a *gyrovague*;[7] he was also a thaumaturge, indulging in scandalous eccentricities and in *taha'ib* (the violation of moral and religious rules). Certain jurists were hostile to him, but he enjoyed great general popularity and several Hafsids took care of him. When he was buried in his *zāwiya*, the entire population, from the humblest to the greatest, mourned a saint whom they had from the first placed beside Sīdī Maḥrez, the patron saint of Tunis for five centuries. He left numerous followers, but the brotherhood of the ʿArūsiyya was not set up until the sixteenth century. Numerous ascetics spread throughout Ifrīḳiya, and *ḳabīla*s of marabouts were set up, such as that of the Saba'iyya, who eventually founded a marabout state, with Ḳayrawān as its capital; this later rose against the Spaniards and Turks. But it was in Morocco, the birthplace of its founder, that Sadīlism flourished most spectacularly, particularly in Aghmāt and Marrakesh. The Ragrāga founded a Sadīlite *zāwiya* in 1370, whose missionaries spread throughout the southern part of the country, both in the plains and in the mountains.

Finally, there was the advent of al-Ghazūlī (d. 1465), who was to give a fresh impetus to Ṣūfism, directing it towards the cult of marabouts and *sharīf*s. This Berber from the Sūs, who according to legend was descended from the Prophet, was a contemporary of the discovery in a Fez mosque in 1437 of a miraculously preserved body. This was immediately declared to be that of Idrīs II, whereupon Mulay Idrīs became the object of a fervent cult. In Meknes and Fez the Idrisid *sharīf*s formed powerful groups, whom the Marinids permitted to have a representative, a *naḳīb*. Al-Ghazūlī adopted and practised Sadīlism and soon had numerous followers, who were probably organized into a brotherhood. Southern Morocco produced a host of marabouts, who swarmed north and east as far as Tripolitania. The followers of *sharīf*s and marabouts became closely associated; scholars and jurists who had held aloof from Ṣūfism enrolled in the brotherhoods. On the death of al-Ghazūlī, one of his disciples organized a powerful revolt in the Sūs and for twenty years carried the body of his shaykh with him; he transported it in a bier.

7. *Gyrovague*, or vagrant: from the medieval Latin name given to monks who spent their lives moving from province to province and cell to cell, staying only three or four days in one place and living on alms; also known as Messalians.

Finally, in 1524, the Sa'dian *sharīf*, al-A'rag, had it transferred to Marrakesh with the body of his own father and placed it in the same mausoleum, thus sealing the alliance of the new dynasty with Ghazūlism and ensuring its triumph.

It was also in Morocco where the *mawlid* – the feast of the birth of the Prophet (12 Rabī' I), which had been celebrated in the east by the Ayyubids at the beginning of the thirteenth century – spread among the Berbers, in a frenzy of religious exaltation. This feast, first mentioned at Ceuta in the middle of the thirteenth century, was made official by the Marinid Abū Ya'ḳūb in 1292. In the middle of the following century the Abd al-Wadid Abū Ḥammū celebrated it with great pomp at Tlemcen. The Hafsid Abū Yaḥyā (1318–46) did likewise at Tunis, but met with such violent disapproval from the jurists that he had to renounce it. It was not until the reign of Abū Fāris (1394–1434) that Ifrīḳiya finally adopted the *mawlid* with much reciting of poems, songs, music and illuminations, as in Morocco and at Tlemcen. Here, again, it was chiefly the brotherhoods who initiated and then appropriated it, and with its celebration went increased prestige for the *sharīf*s.

Dynastic power and social structure

The Marinid, Abd al-Wadid and Hafsid dynasties were founded by conquering Berber tribes, and the victorious clan became identified with the state, the *makhzan*. This distinction between victors and vanquished was different from the traditional one between *khāṣṣa* (private individuals, courtiers, the politico-military aristocracy, the élite) and *'ammā* (commoners, the masses, plebs), a distinction created by the jurists, the historiographers and the ruling classes. Moreover, the fundamental egalitarianism of Islam is well known; *khāṣṣa* was often applied to the literate and *'ammā* to the illiterate. Meanwhile, in Fez, as in Tlemcen and Tunis, a middle class, a sort of petty bourgeoisie which had a great capacity for assimilation, was upsetting this theoretical bipartite structure and mitigating the spirit of caste. Anyone could raise his station in life through good fortune or education, or even through piety or the favour of a great man.

The Marinids

The Marinids recruited Zenāta from the central Maghrib and Arabs, but only in time of war; these were added to their small initial forces of cavalry. They had at their disposal some 8000 mounted mercenaries – Turkomans, Franks, Andalusians and renegades[8] – and a sultan's guard,

8. The renegades were mercenaries, usually apostates, and mostly from Spain, who had enlisted in the armies of the Maghrib.

probably Zenātian. The Zenāta formed the politico-military aristocracy, from which were drawn the high officials or viziers, members of increasingly influential rival families. The Banū Waṭṭāṣ family provided the regents for the last Marinid and founded a dynasty that controlled Fez and one part of the country. The chancellor's office and the accounts were entrusted to Moroccan or Andalusian secretaries (*kātib*). The chamberlains (*ḥādjib*), mostly freed slaves, had no political authority; but one, a Jew who was *ḥādjib* to Abū Ya'ḳūb Yūsuf (1286–1307), ended by becoming head of the government, and the last Marinid, in debt to Jews, placed two of them in charge of tax collecting. The *djandār* were stationed at the sovereign's door and carried out his orders;[9] their provost was the *mizwār*, who saw to the observance of official etiquette at the audiences given in the *dār al-'ammā* ('house of the people'). The heir apparent was closely associated with the exercise of power. The great provincial governors were princes of the blood, or chiefs of the Zenāta or Arabs.

The Atlas was virtually autonomous. Its docile *ḳabīla*s were commanded by powerful amirs selected from among the leading families devoted to the dynasty. The *ḳabīla*s had the right to levy taxes or *iḳṭā'*.[10] *Sharīf*s and holy men were entitled to a portion of the tax receipts and the brotherhoods were granted tax exemptions.

Fez reached its apogee in the middle of the fourteenth century. Once he was master of Morocco, Abū Yūsuf Ya'ḳūb left Marrakesh, capital of the conquered Almoravids, for Fez, where in 1276 he founded a new city, *Fās al-Djadīd* (New Fez), an administrative and military capital, comprising the prince's quarter, another area known as the Christian quarter and a third which was to become the *mallāḥ* (Jewish quarter). The Jews who became converts, rather than consenting to live in the *mallāḥ*, merged with the Muslim population and became wholesale traders. Numerous Andalusian refugees strengthened the intellectual, artistic and commercial élite.

To house, feed and instruct the students who flocked to Fez, Abū Yūsuf Ya'ḳūb founded in the old city the first of the famous Marinid *madrasa* endowed by *habous* foundations; four others were built between 1320 and 1323, a sixth in 1346–7 and Abū 'Inān (1349–58) added the one which bears his name (see Plates 4.1 and 4.2).

There was brisk trade with Spain, Portugal, Genoa and Venice. The Christian merchants were grouped together in one building under the authority of a sort of common consul (the *feitor* of Portuguese texts). The

9. *Djāndār* (or *djandār*): 'The *Nōbat al-Djāndāriyā* was in the Mamluk and Marinid kingdoms the bodyguard of the Sultan in his palace and on his journeys; it was their duty to conduct Amirs to the Sultan at audiences or paying of homage.' *Encyclopaedia of Islam*, 1st edn, Vol. 1, p. 1014.

10. The term *iḳṭā'*, like the legal and fiscal concept it represents, is difficult to express in European languages (see *Encyclopaedia of Islam*, new edn, Vol. 3, p. 1088). In this particular case it means the right to levy taxes.

Jewish community had its own leader and administration. The *muḥtasib* controlled commercial activity.[11] But the intellectual and economic prosperity of Fez declined with the dynasty. The accession of the Saʿdīs hardly helped, since they selected Marrakesh, long overshadowed and practically in ruins, as their capital and revitalized it.

The Abd al-Wādids

The Abd al-Wādids of Tlemcen, relatives and rivals of the Marinids, were likewise Zenāta, nomadic Berbers, who became leaders of a sedentary state. The founder of the dynasty, Yag͟hmurāsan (1235–83), lived under canvas until he was in his thirties, and could speak only Berber. The office of vizier was first entrusted to relatives of the sovereign, but from Abū Ḥammū I (1308–18) onwards, it passed into the hands of the money-changers whose family practised that profession at Cordova. They purchased and developed lands in the outskirts of Tlemcen; one of them, Mallāḥ, was Yag͟hmurāsan's minister of finance. The palace steward (*ḥadjib*), selected from among the jurists, was also in charge of the chancellor's office and accounts. Abū Tās͟hfīn (1318–73) appointed an Andalusian freedman, Hilāl the Catalan, as *ḥādjib* (master of ceremonies, palace chamberlain or prime minister) with supreme control over the administration.

Yag͟hmurāsan employed Turkish, Kurdial and Christian mercenaries who had served the Almohads (dispensing with the Christians after 1254), but the main part of the army was made up of Banū Hilāl; they were granted important fiscal concessions (*iḳṭāʿ*) and collected taxes, part of which they kept back for themselves. Yag͟hmurāsan was very pious and provided each of the great mosques of Tlemcen and Agadir with a minaret. The founding of the fortress of Maswār, where he lived, is attributed to him. His successor erected the mosque of Sīdī Bel Ḥasen (1296), and Abū Ḥammū I built a *madrasa* to enable two doctors to disseminate their knowledge; his son founded another *madrasa* and built three palaces. Tlemcen was then at the peak of its prosperity.

During the siege of Tlemcen (1298–1306), the Marinid Abū Yaʿḳūb Yūsuf built the camp town of al-Manṣūra, which Abū ʾl-Ḥasan again occupied and fortified during a later siege (1335). The Marinids ruled Tlemcen from 1337 to 1348 and fostered the cult of Abū Madyan, embellishing his mausoleum and adding to it the mosque of al-ʿUbbād and a *madrasa*. During the second Marinid occupation (1352–9), Abu ʿInān

11. '*Muḥtasib*, "Censor", an officer appointed by the caliph or his wazīr [vizier] to see that the religious precepts of Islam are obeyed, to detect offences and punish offenders ... In some respects his duties were parallel with those of the *ḳāḍī*, but the *muḥtasib*'s jurisdiction was limited to matters connected with commercial transactions, defective weights and measures, fraudulent sales and non-payment of debts.' *Encyclopaedia of Islam*, 1st edn, Vol. 3, pp. 702–3.

built a mosque with a *madrasa* and a *zāwiya* in honour of Sīdī ʾl-Halwī, a saint of Andalusian origin who had settled in Tlemcen at the beginning of the thirteenth century. The finest hours of the Maswār were under the reign of Abū Ḥammū II (1359–89): during the nights of the *mawlid* season, splendid receptions were given for dignitaries and for the people, at which the *mangana*, a monumental clock with moving figures, was much admired. He created a vast collection of religious foundations in the vicinity, including a family mausoleum, a *madrasa* and a *zāwiya*. Abū ʾl-Abbās (1430–61) built the mausoleum and mosque of Sīdī Lahsan, who died in 1453.

Through all its political vicissitudes, Tlemcen never ceased to shine, and its wealth seems not to have known any eclipse. The opulence of its merchants, both Muslim and Jewish, was based on its flourishing foreign trade. Near the Great Mosque, fabrics imported from Europe were stored in warehouses and sold in a *ḳaysariyya*. Genoese and Venetian merchants had their *funduḳ*s. Craftsmen were active, producing woollen fabrics, rugs, earthenware, harness and embroidered leather. The maritime traffic passed through Hunayn and Oran. Finally, Tlemcen seemed to supplant Marrakesh as the staging post for Saharan trade, which revived somewhat in the thirteenth and fourteenth centuries. Gold and slaves from Sijilmasa reached Tlemcen by a route controlled by the Banū Maʿḳil.

The Hafsids

Bidjāya, the mercantile port, corsair base, intellectual and religious centre and at times the capital, was, with Tlemcen, one of the poles of the central Maghrib. Its shipyards were supplied with wood and tar from the Kabylia forest. Apart from foreigners in transit, occasional sojourners and the Jewish and Christian communities, it was inhabited by Kabyle and Andalusian people. The city appears not to have had any *madrasa* or *zāwiya*, whereas Constantine, a city of equal size, had several. Furthermore, Constantine had a large Jewish community and a long-established and wealthy bourgeoisie.

In Eastern Barbary, the Hafsids perpetuated the Almohad order. Their kinsmen were grouped under the authority of one bearing the title of *mazwār al-garāba*. Those associated with the exercise of power, chiefly the provincial governors, bore the title of amir. Their children, brought up at court with those of the sultan and of the chief courtiers, acted as *ṣibyān* (waiters or pages) and were given a good education. Among the palace servants, the renegade Christians who had formerly been slaves played an increasing role in the military and civil high commands. The palace steward was a eunuch. The clan of the Almohad shaykhs, a military aristocracy, included the descendants of the original Almohad tribes; all obeyed the al-Muwaḥḥidūn shaykh, one of the most powerful pillars of the state, appointed for life, and each had at its head a *mazwār*.[12] The 'great shaykhs' were divided into groups: the Three, the Ten and the Fifty.[13] The 'lesser shaykhs' participated in ceremonies. In accordance with Almohad egalitarianism, each shaykh, including the sultan, was paid the same salary; they also received concessions of real property and an annual grant in cash and in kind. Their influence gradually decreased – to the advantage of the Andalusians and the freedmen – with some spectacular revivals. The council (*shūrā*) was composed of Almohads and other notables. The caliph held many meetings, both public and private, and every week held a council of the *ḳāḍī*s and *mufti*s, the jurists of the capital. He assumed personal responsibility for the repression of abuses (*raḍḍ al-maẓālim*).

As long as they were only Almohad governors, the Hafsids appointed as deputy a *kātib* (a sort of prime minister). Abū Zakariyyā' (1228–49) had three viziers: one for the army – the grand shaykh, or even the shaykh of the Almohads – who functioned as prime minister; one for finance; and one for the chancellor's office. At the end of the thirteenth century there emerged the essentially domestic office of chamberlain or *ḥādjib*, Spanish in origin and held by Andalusians, whose influence was constantly on the increase. In the fourteenth century, the *ḥādjib* became prime minister, and Ibn Tafrāgin (1350–64) was a dictator; following him, the title remained, but the office became honorary. The vizier of finance, formerly chosen from the Almohad shaykhs, was thereafter chosen from government officials or Andalusians. Starting with Abū Fāris at the end of the fourteenth and the beginning of the fifteenth century, *al-munaffid*, the controller of the expenditure of the royal household, finally gained supreme control over finance; after the disappearance of the shaykh of the Almohads and the *ḥādjib* in 1462, he took first place in the hierarchy of officials, whereas the vizier of finance was relegated to the function of treasurer. The *mazwār* – palace major-domo, usher and chief of the guards and servants – managed by the end of the fifteenth century to gain control of the administration of the army and to rank second after the *munaffid*. The Andalusians, who had constituted the majority of the scribes, were gradually supplanted by Ifrīḳiyans.

Initially, the Almohad shaykhs were in charge of the provinces; in the fourteenth and fifteenth centuries, they gave up this function to local officials, frequently of servile origin, the *ca'id*s (*ḳāḍī*s). The Hafsids selected the principal regional governors from among their kinsmen, especially their children (in particular, the eldest son was thus called on to serve his apprenticeship); to each they assigned an assistant, first known as the *kātib* and subsequently as the *ḥādjib*. The tribal shaykhs were chosen from

12. 'The term *mizwār* (or *mazwār*) is found early in the histories of the Maghrib in connection with Almohad institutions. There it means the head of a faction and the corresponding office seems at this time to be often confused with those of the *ḥafīẓ* or the *muḥtasib*.' ibid., p. 543.

13. For the origin of these various groups, see O. Saidi, Chapter 2 above.

the members of a family or clan that had gained supremacy and been invested by the sultan; they commanded the annual troop contingent from their *ḳabīla*, collected taxes for the treasury and were granted fiscal and property concessions.

The army was heterogeneous and included Almohads, nomadic Arabs, Berbers from the Maghrib or Ifrīḳiya, Orientals, Andalusians and Christian Franks; but the strength of all these was relatively slight compared with that of the Arabs of Ifrīḳiya, whose preponderance was strong. There are records of an urban militia, an Andalusian militia, a Turkoman force of mercenaries and a militia of Christian cavalry from Spain or Italy. (The latter, who made up the sultan's guard, continued to practise their religion and lived in a suburb of the capital.) In addition, Christian renegades, for the most part freed slaves, constituted a solid military element. The generals were often freedmen or renegades. Races for sailing ships, commissioned by the government or by businessmen, played an important role. Finding the sea to their taste, the Hafsids no longer thought of returning to the former capital of Ifrīḳiya, Ḳayrawān, which had been reduced to insignificance by the Banū Hilāl invasion. Its old urban population was diminished, drowned by the Beduin horde that submerged the plains. Its craftsmen remained active to some degree, due to the produce from pastoral nomads. Numerous *zāwiya* were founded in the city.

Tunis was a thriving metropolis. The Almohad *gasaba* or *ḳaṣaba* was modified by Abū Zakariyyā', who converted it into a small governmental city. Near the Great Mosque of the Zaytūna (see Plate 5.2) he built, around 1240, a *madrasa* (al-Samma'iyya) which is the oldest in North

PLATE 5.2 *The Ḳaṣaba Mosque at Tunis*

Africa. Beginning in the fifteenth century, some ten others were founded by princes and princesses. *Zāwiya* multiplied in the *madīna* and the suburbs. In the port area stood the *funduḳ*s of the Christian merchants, grouped by nationality. In the suburbs, numerous gardens and orchards were maintained by Andalusians. Parks and princely residences abounded; the Bardo is mentioned as early as 1420. It was at Tunis that the most representative character of his time, Ibn Khaldūn (1332–1406), was born. A few details from his life and reflections on his times may serve as a conclusion to the present sketch.[14]

The life and times of Ibn Khaldūn

The Khaldūn were Arabs of Yemeni origin, who had been settled since the conquest of Seville, in which they played a political role. They emigrated first to Ceuta and later to Ifrīḳiya, following the *reconquista*. Ibn Khaldūn's ancestor served Abū Zakariyyā' at Bône. His great-grandfather was minister of finance to Abū Isḥāḳ and his grandfather was successively *ḥadjib* to Abū Farīs at Bidjāya, prime minister to Abū Ḥafṣ, deputy *ḥādjib* to Abū 'Asīd and favourite of Abū Yaḥyā Abū Bakr. His father devoted himself to literature, *fiḳh* and piety; he died in the great plague of 1349. Ibn Khaldūn, then 17 years of age, had acquired a sound intellectual education in Tunis; he had had the advantage of instruction by the scholars who had flocked there at the time of the Marinid invasion (1347–9). The following year he was appointed writer (*'alāma*) to Abū Isḥāḳ II. Then, when the amir of Constantine invaded Ifrīḳiya, he fled to the west, at the start of a varied career, fertile in volte-faces and intrigues. After entering the service of the Marinid Abū 'Inān at Fez he completed his education, but joined in a conspiracy and was imprisoned for two years (1357–8). He then became secretary of the chancellor's office and eulogist to Abū Salīm and was thereafter appointed judge of the *mazālin*. Following certain intrigues, he left to spend a few years in Granada, where he was welcomed by his friend the vizier, Ibn al-Hatīb; he was placed in charge of an embassy to Peter the Cruel in Seville in 1364. The following year found him as *ḥadjib* to the Hafsid ruler of Bidjāya, who was shortly afterwards overthrown by his cousin of Constantine, to whom Ibn Khaldūn surrendered the city in 1366. He soon had to take refuge with the Dawāwida Arabs and then with the Banū Muznī of Biskra. He declined the offer of the sultan of Tlemcen, Abū Ḥammū II, to engage him as *ḥādjib*, stating that he wanted to devote himself to study; in fact he did so without relinquishing politics. He promoted the alliance between the Hafsid ruler of Tunis and the 'Abd al-Wadid ruler of Tlemcen against the Hafsid ruler of Bidjāya, and later recruited Arabs for the Marinid ruler of Fez.

14. See also Chapter 4.

After countless new tribulations in the central Maghrib, Fez and Granada, we find Ibn Khaldūn at Tlemcen in 1375, where the sultan, Abū Ḥammū II, entrusted him with a mission to the Dawāwida. He took the opportunity to go into retreat at Aḳl'a Ibn Salāma, near Tiaret, where for four years he worked on his famous *Muḳaddima*. To continue his work, he needed to gather documentation and obtained permission from the Hafsid to return to Tunis in December 1378, where he both taught and completed the draft of his *History*, a copy of which he offered to the sultan. A cabal directed by the jurist Ibn 'Arafa prompted him to undertake the pilgrimage to Mecca in 1382. He spent the remainder of his life in Cairo, where he taught and officiated on several occasions as the Mālikite Grand *ḳāḍī*. He was in Damascus a few years before his death, when it was besieged by Tamerlane, and thus had the opportunity to come into contact with the Mongol conqueror. The work of Ibn Khaldūn, however, was nurtured by his experience in the Maghrib from which he was inspired to draw conclusions of astonishing originality.

The *Muḳaddima* is the fruit of his prodigious reflections on fifty years of observation and experience. In drawing up this treatise on historical epistemology, he was conscious of founding 'a new science', the history of civilization. His intention was to understand and explain the way in which facts obey certain laws and to elaborate a philosophy of history. He considered two fundamental factors: ways of life and tribalism. He contrasted primitive nomadic life with civilized city life. The former, resting essentially on *ḳabīla* and group consciousness (*'asabiyya*), was a living force founding new empires and continually threatening established states; the latter first blossomed, then withered and finally disappeared beneath the impact of a new nomad force. For him, the consequences of the Banū Hilāl invasion and the great plague had so profoundly upset the life of the Muslim West that he spoke of a 'new world'. His cyclical view of evolution is neither pessimistic nor optimistic, but founded on the nature of things as he observed them. This also applies to his theory that sovereignty lasts for only four generations.

What strikes one about Ibn Khaldūn's thought is its realism, its lack of preconceived ideas and its scientific determination: in short, its modernity. One can understand why this inspired philosopher of history has been regarded as a precursor of 'total' history, of social economics, even of modern sociology and historical materialism, although, on the other hand, we find in him many traits peculiar to a man of his time and environment. It is sacrilege to insist on interpreting anachronistically such a monument, built with such a sense of proportion, maintaining a constant balance between a realism which was based on observation and a rationalism which explained and deduced ineluctable laws. His *Universal History* (*Kitāb al-'Ibar*) does not apply the method recommended in his 'Introduction to the profession of historian'; unlike traditional Muslim Arab chronicles, it studies first the history of the Arab *ḳabīla*s and their dynasties, and then that of the Berber tribes and their kingdoms. For the period closest to the author, it constitutes the fundamental documentary source.[15]

15. Ibn Khaldūn, French transl. in J. Cuoq, 1975.

6 Mali and the second Mandingo expansion

D. T. NIANE

The Mandingo are composed of a number of groups and subgroups scattered throughout the Sudan–Sahel zone, from the Atlantic to the Air, with deep projections into the forests of the Bight of Benin. At the beginning of the twelfth century, the Mandingo habitat was much less extensive. At the high point of the Ghana empire, at the end of the eleventh century, three major groups can be distinguished: the Soninke (Sarakolle), the founders of Ghana, who basically inhabited the provinces of Wagadu (Auker), Bakhanu and Kaniaga; the Soso to the south, at the foot of the Kulikoro mountains, with the city of Soso as capital; and still farther south, the Malinke of the country called Mande or Manding on the upper basin of the Niger, between Kangaba and Siguiri. The Soninke, who are also called Marka or Wakore (Wangara), were the founders of the Ghana empire, which was the first manifestation of Mandingo expansion.[1] According to Maḥmūd Ka'ti in the *Ta'rīkh al-fattāsh*, 'the Mali empire was set up only after the fall of the Kayamagha dynasty, whose power extended over the entire western region, including every province'.[2] When Ghana fell under the repeated attacks of the Almoravids, the Soninke had already spilled out of their native Wagadu and mixed with the populations along the banks of the Niger, where they created new settlements. The search for gold had led them far south towards the edge of the forests. It is believed that the town of Jenne – which reached its zenith in the fifteenth century – was founded by Soninke traders, probably well before the arrival of the Arabs.

Here we must digress for a few paragraphs about the development of Jenne. In recent years more and more has been learnt about the city and its surroundings; the ancient site of the town, called 'Jenne-Jeno', has been

1. The word Wangara (spelt Ouangara in French) is used by the Fulani and the Hausa to describe the Mandingo. Wangara and Wakore have the same origin, although Wakore is more generally used for the Soninke or Sarakolle. In the Ivory Coast forests, the Mandingo are called Dioula, which means 'trader' in Malinke. Wangara and Dioula are synonyms and refer particularly to those Mandingo engaged in trade.

2. From Maḥmūd Ka'ti, French transl. 1964.

besieged by archaeologists and the results have proved that the development of the city was not due to the trans-Saharan trade conducted by the Arabs from the ninth and tenth centuries onward. In point of fact, the oldest settlement of Jenne-Jeno goes back to the third century before the Christian era; it was created by farming peoples, along with herdsmen and iron-workers.[3] Outside Nigeria (the Bauchi plateau), the old town of Jenne-Jeno is the only place in West Africa with evidence of metal-working at that date. Rice was cultivated in the region from the first century of the Christian era, so the cultivation of the African variety (*Oryza glaberrima*) goes back at least that far; this definitely disproves the theory that it came from Asia. Jenne-Jeno was a major city with outlying farming hamlets around that period, in touch with the string of larger villages along the banks of the Niger and the Bani.[4] Trans-Saharan trade existed around the year 500, for copper objects of that date have been found at Jenne-Jeno: these could only have come from the Saharan mines at Takedda. At about that date, the city attained its largest area, some 34 hectares; archaeological excavations in 1977 showed that Jenne had heavily populated suburbs.

When and why did people leave Jenne-Jeno to settle in Jenne? It is probable that the Muslim nucleus of traders in the old town preferred to separate themselves from the mass of pagans. By about the year 800, the city was already a very important commercial centre, in touch with the countries of the savannah and the Sahel. Like Igbo-Ukwu on the Niger delta, Jenne was a major importer of copper, which it exchanged in the south for gold, kola nuts and ivory.[5] The discovery of copper at Jenne and Igbo-Ukwu dating from before the eighth century prove that the Arabs were responsible only for a wider extension of trans-Saharan trade. The commercial activities of the Wangara or Dioula preceded the coming of the Arabs; war and trade allowed them to expand their influence greatly in all directions.

After the fall of Koumbi Ṣāleḥ at the end of the eleventh century, we enter a period about which little is known. Between the capture of Koumbi by the Almoravids around 1076 and the victory of Sundiata in 1235, the birth date of Mali, we have few written sources on the western Sudan. The second Mandingo expansion corresponded with the emergence of Mali (see Fig. 6.1). From their base on the upper Niger, the Malinke clans made war as far as the Atlantic coast in the west. They settled in Senegambia; Mandingo traders in the fourteenth century introduced Islam into Hausa

3. See R. J. McIntosh and S. K. McIntosh, 1981.

4. Archaeology confirms the statement of the *Ta'ri<u>kh</u> al Sudan* that the region of Jenne was so populated and the villages so close to each other that the king's orders were called out from the top of the ramparts and transmitted by criers from one village to another. The silt deposited by the two rivers was extremely fertile and good for rice culture.

5. See Chapter 14, pp. 361–6 below on Igbo-Ukwu.

country and further south, striking deep into the forest areas, where they went to buy valuable kola nuts and gold from peoples untouched by Islam. This Mandingo expansion was both warlike and peaceful. Its agents among the Hausa and in the south were the merchants and marabouts; to the west, in Senegambia, warlike conquest came first, only to be followed by large numbers of traders and marabouts, so that the western provinces became an extension of old Mande. The Mandingo empire began to decline in the fifteenth century. Even so, the expansion towards the south continued and the Malinke founded a number of trading centres, among the most important being Begho in the Bron or Akan country, particularly rich in gold.

This study aims to identify the beginnings of the expansion and its development from the thirteenth to the fourteenth century, and will also attempt to distinguish the fundamental elements of Mandingo civilization. First, however, two questions must be answered. (a) What was the situation of the western Sudan at the beginning of the twelfth century? (b) How did the people and kingdoms of the region appear after the fall of Koumbi?

Kingdoms and provinces of the western Sudan in the twelfth century

Koumbi Ṣāleḥ, the capital of Ghana, fell to the Almoravids in 1076. We know little about the history of the Sudan in the twelfth century; after the valuable information supplied by al-Bakrī around 1068, there is a large gap until 1154, when the reports of the geographer al-Idrīsī were written.

None the less, since the West African states achieved independence, we have begun with the help of the oral traditions collected to learn something of the internal history of Ghana after the fall of Koumbi.[6] The Sudanese *Ta'rīkh*s in the twelfth century, based on oral traditions, include important sections on the western Sudan in general. Archaeology adds more and more significant contributions: the sites of Koumbi, Awdaghust and Niani have been centres of excavation for twenty years and have furnished a rich harvest of facts that confirm most of the oral traditions.[7]

Takrūr

The most important provinces, such as Mande (Manding) and Takrūr, had thrown off Ghana's domination as early as the middle of the eleventh century.[8] Wardjabi, king of Takrūr, had taken an active part as a Muslim convert in the holy war launched by the Almoravids; his son, Labi or Laba,

6. D. Sylla, 1975.
7. D. Robert, S. Robert and J. Devisse, 1970.
8. Al-Idrīsī, French transl., 1866; also Ibn Sa'īd in J. Cuoq, 1975.

PLATE 6.1 *Koumbi Ṣāleḥ: excavation showing parts of a mosque built between the 10th and 14th centuries*

continued this alliance with the Almoravids and fought beside them against the Godala in 1056.[9] Takrūr controlled the Senegal river, with a virtual monopoly on the gold of Galam, and for a time replaced Koumbi as a trading centre. Al-Idrīsī presents Takrūr as a powerful kingdom in the twelfth century, whose authority over the Senegal river was unquestioned. It annexed the city of Barissa, and also controlled the salt-mines of Aoulil. After Ghana, Takrūr was the kingdom best known to the Arabs in the twelfth century. Its traders had outstripped those of Ghana, who were hampered by the civil war which ravaged the Soninke provinces of Wagadu, Bakhunu, Kaniaga and Mema. The Senegal, which was navigable up to Gondiouru (region of Kayes), was a convenient means of communication used by merchants from Takrūr to exchange the salt of Aoulil for gold beyond Barissa.[10]

It becomes more and more apparent that the zenith of Takrūr was somewhere between the end of the eleventh century and the middle of the twelfth century. Before the emergence of Soso and Mali, Takrūr took the lead economically. Thus it is not surprising that the Arabs gave the

9. The Godala or Gdala formed part of the Sanhaja Ḳalīla Berbers, who lived in the Sahara.

10. Al-Idrīsī, loc. cit.; see also Ibn Saʿīd, loc. cit., pp. 201–5.

PLATE 6.2 *Toguéré Galia: general view of the butt intersected by the River Bani, taken from the west*

PLATE 6.3 *Toguéré Galia: excavation showing three funeral urns* in situ. *Post Period II (1600–?)*

PLATE 6.4 *Toguéré Doupwil: section C showing a funeral urn* in situ. *The cover is sealed with a clay roll. Period I (13th–14th century?)*

PLATE 6.5 *Toguéré Doupwil: section C showing the contents of a funeral urn* in situ. *An adult, thought to be male, in crouching position. Period I (13th–14th century?)*

name of Takrūr to the entire western Sudan. The towns of Sangana, Takrūr and Sylla were frequented by Berber Arab traders;[11] the fall of Koumbi did not interrupt the gold trade, but rather the reverse. Takrūr, which temporarily filled the vacuum left by Koumbi, was described by al-Bakrī as a metropolis including, like Koumbi, a Berber Arab quarter. The kingdom was, however, content to spread its influence through the Senegal river basin, without taking part in the struggle for supremacy that set the Soninke and Malinke against the Soso.

The Songhay

Ghana did not extend its domination over Songhay. This ancient kingdom had established relations with the Maghrib early on; its kings, converted to Islam around 1010, attracted Berber Arab writers and traders to Kūkya and Gao.[12] It was towards the end of the eleventh century that the Songhay went up the Niger river from Kūkya to the Dendi to occupy the Niger Bend. They moved their capital from Kūkya to Gao. Around 1100 (at the end of the fifth century of the Hegira) Timbuktu was founded by the Tuareg Magcharen. According to the *Ta'rīkh al-Sūdān*, 'They came into these countries to pasture their herds ... At first, travellers by land met seafarers there.'[13] The Songhay soon occupied the whole of the Niger Bend; their presence in Timbuktu made that new centre an important crossroads for trade. The kings of Gao were also determined to play a political role in the region; their progress toward the inner delta of the Niger illustrated that policy. But their time had not yet come.

The Soninke provinces

The capture of Koumbi provoked a series of wars and population movements among the Soninke. Before it fell to the Almoravids, Koumbi had sheltered many Muslim believers among its merchants; al-Bakrī tells us of one close to the king who was converted to Islam: 'The city of Aluken ... has a ruler called Canmer, son of Beci (the king). It is said

11. Al-Bakrī, al-Idrīsī and Ibn Sa'īd cite the towns of Takrūr, Sangana and Sylla, but no important research has been undertaken to locate the sites of these towns buried under the desert or destroyed by wars. The translation of al-Bakrī's book is an old one; looking at it again it is possible today to decipher the names of places and people. The towns of Sangana, Takrūr and Barissa, however, have not yet been located along the Senegal.

12. See Volume III, Chapter 3. King Za-Kosoi became a Muslim in 1010; see al-Sa'dī, French transl. 1964, p. 5. Al-Bakrī mentions Kūgha or Gao, 'whose inhabitants are Muslim. The goods brought there are mostly salt, cowries, copper and spurge.' From J. Cuoq (ed.), 1975, p. 365.

13. Translated from al-Sa'dī, loc. cit., pp. 36–7.

he is Muslim but hides his religion.'[14] We must not forget that as early as the eighth century Ghana had had trade relations with the Maghrib. Berber Arab Muslims had important positions in the court;[15] but the mass of the people generally remained true to their ancient religion. Complex struggles set one province against another and, within each of them, one clan against another.

The central province of Wagadu was torn by civil strife; certain groups of Soninke, who had remained faithful to the ancient rites, fled and settled in the province of Mema;[16] similar struggles divided the inhabitants of Kaniaga. Maḥmūd Ka'ti writes:

> There was in Kaniaga an old and important city which had been established earlier at Zara and which served as the capital; it was called Sain Demba; it was the main city of the people of Diafunu, who are called Diafununke. It had existed since the time of the Kayamagha and was ruined when they fell, in the course of the troubles which followed.
>
> It was after the destruction of the Kayamagha empire that Zara was built. Some of the inhabitants of the empire emigrated to Kussata and are called Kussa. The others went to Zara; they were conquered by the Kaniaga Faren, who seized their kingdom and subjugated the Arabs who belonged to it as far as Tututi, Tichit and Takanaka.[17]

The kingdom of Zara (Diara) took part in the struggles for domination and came into conflict with the Soso, then in full expansion.

Soso supremacy

This supremacy lasted a very short time, from 1180 to 1230. At the end of the twelfth century the Soso people, under the Kante dynasty, rose against the Muslims.

The Soso

The Soso were part of the Malinke group; according to tradition the site of their capital, Soso, was in the region of Kulikoro, in the mountains about 80 km north of Bamako.[18] But up to the present day there has been

14. Translated from al-Bakrī, loc. cit., p. 335.

15. See Volume III, Chapter 3.

16. N. Levtzion, 1973, pp. 46–9; C. Monteil, 1929, p. 353.

17. Translated from Mahmūd Ka'ti, loc. cit., pp. 70–1; see also C. Meillassoux, L. Doucouré and D. Simagha, 1967, p. 9, on the Kussa.

18. The city of Soso gave its name to the people. The Soso were a faction of the Malinke, the only difference being that the Malinke and their kings were favourable to Islam, whereas the Soso were distinguished by their hostility toward the new religion and their attachment to ancestral traditions.

no research to try to identify the ruins, as has been done for Ghana and Mali. In fact, the Soso were only a Malinke clan, who specialized in iron work. From the middle of the thirteenth century, this clan of smiths showed a clear desire to reject Islam and to take over the region of Soninke.[19] According to legend, the Soninke clan of the Diarisso gained its independence from Ghana even before the fall of Koumbi; the Kante took over in Soso and Kaniaga and founded a dynasty. The Soso king Kemoko unified Kaniaga and Soso into a single kingdom towards the end of the twelfth century; his son, Sumaguru (or Soumaoro) Kante succeeded him and continued his career of conquest.

Sumaguru Kante

Mandingo oral traditions recount the warlike feats of Sumaguru Kante (1200–35).[20] According to these traditions, after he had conquered the Soninke provinces, Sumaguru attacked Mande, whose kings put up a fierce resistance. Sumaguru is said to have 'broken' or sacked Mande nine times. Each time, the Malinke reformed their armies and led a counter-attack.[21] After the death of King Nare Fa Maghan, his eldest son, Mansa Dankaran Tuman, felt it would be wiser to make peace with the Soso. To mark his allegiance, he gave his sister, Princess Nana Triban, in marriage to Sumaguru. The rule of the Soso extended over all the provinces once controlled by Ghana, with the exception of Manding. Oral traditions emphasize Sumaguru's cruelty; he created a reign of terror in Manding so that 'men did not dare to meet in parley for fear that the wind might carry their words to the king'. Sumaguru impressed people as much by his military force as by his magical power; he was feared as a magician or sorcerer, and was called the Sorcerer King.[22] He is supposed

19. Levtzion, 1973, p. 51.

20. The chronology of Mali has been established by Delafosse on the basis of the length of reigns as stated by Ibn Khaldūn; it is only a relative chronology, whose cut-off point is the start of the reign of Magham III in 1390, mentioned by Ibn Khaldūn, who finished his *History* shortly after that date.

21. For the legend of Sumaguru, see M. Delafosse, 1913; C. Monteil, op. cit.; D. T. Niane, 1960; Premier colloque international de Bamako, 1975; G. Innes (ed.), 1974.

22. See Premier colloque international de Bamako, 1975. A tradition gathered by SCOA Foundation researchers from Wa Kamissoko, a *griot* of Kirina, says that at first Sumaguru only wanted to drive out the Soninke slave traders from his kingdom. But the Malinke rejected the Soso proposals. It is said to be possible still to gather reliable information on this period by studying the secret societies, the brotherhoods of hunters, who are the depositaries of unofficial traditions, like the descendants of *griots* who served the princes of Mali. *Note*: the French word *griot* has been retained here for the traditional minstrel (*dieli* in Bambara), although it is in some respects misleading. For a full account of the functions of the *dieli/griot*, and a translator's caveat, see A. Hampaté Bâ, in Volume I, Chapter 8, especially pp. 187–92.

to have invented the balafone (xylophone) and the dan, a four-string guitar used by the hunters' *griot*, or praise singer.

Another face of Sumaguru emerges from inquiries among the Kante smiths: it seems that Sumaguru wanted to suppress the Soninke slave trade, carried on with the connivance of the Malinke. In any case, he was clearly a ferocious opponent of Islam, who conquered and executed nine kings. The exactions of the Sorcerer King caused the 'Mandinka' to revolt yet once more. They appealed to Mansa Dankaran Tuman of Mande to take command, but fearing Sumaguru's reprisals he fled south to the forest, where he founded Kisidugu, the 'city of salvation', leaving a power vacuum. The insurgents then appealed to Sundiata, the second son of Nare Fa Maghan, who was living in exile in Mema.[23] Before discussing the wars and victories of the young prince, let us sketch a portrait of Mande, the heart of the Mali empire.[24]

Mande before Sundiata

Written sources

Al-Bakrī was the first to mention Mali, which he called Malel, and the kingdom of Do in the twelfth century.

> The Adjemm blacks, called Nungharmata [Wangara] are traders and transport gold dust from Irseni to other countries. Facing this city, on the other bank of the river [Senegal], is a great kingdom extending over eight days' journey, whose sovereign has the title of Dou [Do]. The people go into battle armed with arrows. Beyond this country is another called Malel, whose king has the title al-Muslimani.[25]

A century later, al-Idrīsī repeats al-Bakrī's information and adds interesting details. According to him, south of Barissa (the Irseni of al-Bakrī) there was the country of the Lem-Lem, which was raided by the people of Takrūr and Ghana in search of slaves. The Arab geographer mentions two cities, Malel and Do, which were four days' march apart.[26]

23. Niane, op. cit.

24. In the present study, in order to avoid confusion, the word 'Mande' is used to designate the original Malinke nucleus. The term 'Mandingo' denotes all the people who are linguistically related to the Soninke and Malinke. Under different names, there are Mande-speakers in Guinea, Mali, Senegal, Guinea-Bissau, Ivory Coast, Upper Volta, Liberia and Sierra Leone, etc. This expansion from a central nucleus took place between the twelfth and the nineteenth centuries.

25. Translated from al-Bakrī, loc. cit., p. 33. In the same passage he describes the circumstances under which the king of Mande was converted by a Muslim guest who lived in the king's court.

26. Al-Idrīsī, loc. cit., p. 132.

The two authors describe two political entities, Malel or Mand and Do; both speak of Wangara traders. It is interesting to note that al-Idrīsī speaks of the people of Ghana and Takrūr as participants in raids on the pagans to take prisoners and sell them as slaves; in the same passage, al-Idrīsī notes that the Lem-Lem marked their faces with stigmata or scarifications; many of the details he gives apply to the population of Upper Niger and Senegal.[27]

Oral sources

These sources tell us something of the internal history of the region; they have been collected in the whole savannah region over two decades. There are many centres or 'schools' of oral tradition in Mandingo country, including Keyla near Kangaba, which was run by the *griots* of the Diabate clan: Niagassola, Djelibakoro, Keita and Fadama (see Fig. 6.1).[28] The traditions taught in these schools, which are run by 'Masters of the Word' or *Belen-Tigui*, are variants on the corpus of Mali history, centred on the person of Sundiata. Give or take a few details, the essential points about the origins of Mali and the military exploits of the founder of the empire are found again and again, from school to school.

These sources confirm the initial existence of two separate kingdoms, that of Do and that of Kiri, or Mande, the name which was later used for the entire Malinke country. The kingdom of Do or Dodugu was inhabited by the Conde clan, and the Konate and Keita occupied the country of Kiri (Mande) to the south. The Camara clan had two principal cities, Sibi and Tabon, and gradually conquered the right bank of the Niger river; the Traore clan occupied a part of Kiri, but most of them lived in the province which was later called Gangaran.

The powerful Dodugu kingdom had twelve towns, whose names are not reported by oral tradition. The right bank of the Niger (or Bako or

27. Delafosse, op. cit.; C. Monteil, op. cit., pp. 320–35. Malel or Mali is the word used for the nucleus of the Malinke who went on to create the Mali empire.

28. Situated 10 km from the village of Kangaba in the Republic of Mali, Keyla is the village of the *griots* who preserve the oral traditions of the Keita royal family. The Diabate clan of Keyla organizes every seven years a ceremonial rebuilding of the roof of the museum-hut or Kamablon of Kagaba. During the ceremonies marking this rite, the Diabate clan recites the history of Sundiata and the origin of the Mali empire. Kita is another centre of oral tradition. Massa Makan Diabaté, of the great *griot* family of the region, has collected and transcribed the accounts of his uncle, the famous Kele Monzon; see M. Diabaté, 1970. A centre of oral tradition, run by the Conde *griots*, exists at Fadama on the Niandan, and another at Djelibakoro, both in Guinea. Oral traditions can also be collected at Niani, the little Keita village located on the site of the former capital (Guinea). In Senegambia the *griots* teach history; but in addition to the saga of Sundiata, great importance is given to Tiramaghan Traore, Sundiata's general, who conquered these regions and is considered to be the founder of the kingdom of Gabu, between Gambia and the Rio Grande.

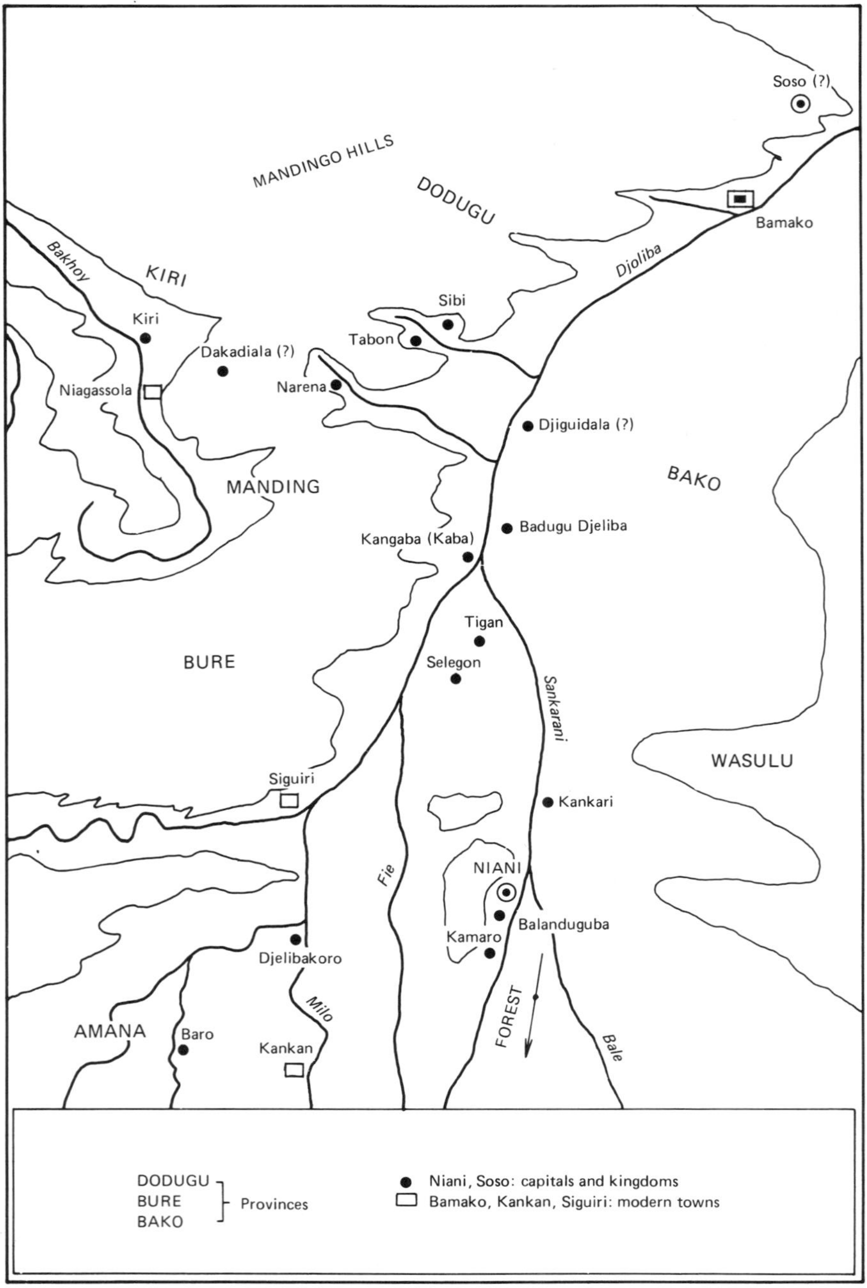

FIG. 6.1 *Old Manding (D. T. Niane)*

Mani) had four towns.[29] Thus, the historical traditions of the country confirm the evidence of the written accounts, that there were at least two kingdoms, Do and Malel (or Kiri in the oral tradition). Malel brought unity and the name Do disappeared. Al-Bakrī says that the king of Malel was converted to Islam before the fall of Koumbi, and Ibn Khaldūn provides the name of the king, Beremundana or Seremundana.[30] He may be identified with a Mansa Beremun in the list of Mandingo kings collected at Kita by Massa Makan Diabaté.[31] All the little kingdoms of the upper Niger were unified by the kings of the Keita clan during the eleventh and twelfth centuries. According to Ibn Khaldūn, King Beremundana was converted to Islam and made a pilgrimage to Mecca. We may suppose that by this time Do and Kiri had merged into a single kingdom, or else that 'Malel' was powerful enough for the king to undertake the journey to Mecca.

The Keita, who founded Mali, believed that they were descendants of Bilali Bunama (or Bilal Ibn Babah), the faithful servant of the Prophet Muḥammad and first muezzin of the Muslim community, whose son, Lawalo, settled in Manding and founded there the city of Kiri or Ki.[32] Lawalo had a son, Latal Kalabi, whose son was Lahilatul Kalabi. The latter was the first Mande king to make the pilgrimage to Mecca. His grandson, Mamadi Kani, was a 'master hunter' who expanded the Keita kingdom over Do, Kiri, Bako and Buri. Most of these kings were mighty hunters; in fact, it is likely that the first military force of the Mande consisted of hunters.[33] In Malinke country, until very recently, the hunters constituted a closed circle, and were believed to know many secrets of the bush and the forest. The title of *simbon*, or master hunter, was much sought after. The hunters, according to tradition, were the first defenders of the village communities. Mamadi Kani grouped them

29. There is a verbal refrain:

Do ni Kiri
Dodugu tan nifla
Bako dugu nani

which means 'Do and Kiri, country of twelve towns: Bako, kingdom of four towns'. C. Monteil, op. cit., pp. 320–1, believes the two kingdoms were northern Mali and southern Mali; the latter developed under Sundiata into the empire of Mali. The cradle of the Keita is in the mountains of Mande, around the towns of Dakadiala, Narena and Kiri. Even today a province of the region of Siguiri (Guinea) is called Kende (Mande). Mali is the Fulani version of the name Mande; Mellit is the Berber variant.

30. Ibn Khaldūn, in J. Cuoq, 1975.

31. Diabaté, op. cit.

32. See Levtzion, 1973, pp. 53–61; C. Monteil, op. cit., pp. 345–6. The adoption of Muslim ancestors from the Orient was common practice in the courts of the Sudan. It is worth noting that the Keita did not claim a white ancestor but rather an Abyssinian black, Bilal Ben Rabah. *Ki* means work; Kele Monson sings of the origin of Kiri and praises work: 'In the beginning, there was work.' See Diabaté, op. cit., p. 9.

33. Niane, op. cit., pp. 14–17.

together into an army, calling on all the clans – Camara, Keita, Konate and Traore. The reign of Mamadi Kani can be dated around the beginning of the twelfth century. He had four sons, one of whom was Simbon Bamari Tagnogokelin, whose son was Mbali Nene. The great-grandson of the latter, Maghan Kon Fatta or Farako Maghan Kegni or Nare Fa Maghan, was the father of Sundiata, the conquering founder of the Mali empire. Maghan Kon Fatta ruled at the beginning of the thirteenth century; the Soso were then at the height of their expansion under the Kante dynasty. After his death, his eldest son, Mansa Dankaran Tuman, ascended the throne, but Sumaguru, king of Soso, annexed Mande.

Tradition has it that sixteen kings preceded Sundiata on the throne.[34] The lists of his predecessors differ from school to school; the one supplied by Kele Monzon of Kita includes a Mansa Beremun, as we have seen, who can easily be identified with the Beremundana of Ibn Khaldūn. The oral traditions of Siguiri give the name of Lahilatul Kalabi as the first king of Mande to make the pilgrimage to Mecca. In any event, all the traditions agree that the first kings were master hunters or *simbon*, and they all emphasize the early introduction of Islam to Mande.

The hunters played a primary role in the origins of Mali; Sundiata's mother was given in marriage to Maghan Kon Fatta by the hunters of the Traore clan.[35] The members of these clans controlled a vast region, Gangaran, north-west of Bure, which was annexed to Mande shortly before the reign of Farako Maghan Kegni.

The gathering of the Malinke clans

During the reign of Mansa Dankaran Tuman, the Malinke rose once again against Sumaguru. When the king fled, as we have seen, they called upon his brother Sundiata. The war between Manding and Soso took place between 1220 and 1235.

Achievements of Sundiata

It is probable that, if Ibn Baṭṭūṭa in 1353 and Ibn Khaldūn in 1376 had not mentioned the great conqueror in their writings, European historians would have gone on regarding Sundiata as a mythical or legendary ancestor, so great is the part attributed to him by oral tradition in the history of Mali.

> The most powerful of these monarchs was the one who subjected the Soussou [Soso], occupied their city, and took over supreme authority from them. He was called Mari-Diata. With them the word

34. ibid.
35. Y. Cissé, 1964, pp. 175–6.

'Mari' means amir and 'Diata' means lion. This king, whose genealogy we have not discovered, reigned twenty years, I have been told.[36]

Ibn Khaldūn's information was sound. He was also the only writer of that period to mention the Soso, who were supreme in the Soninke–Malinke area.

But what else do we know of Sundiata? Literature tells us little, but oral tradition enlarges upon his notable activities.[37] He had a difficult childhood and was crippled for a long time, so that his mother, Sogolon Conde, was mocked by the other wives of the king. When he began to walk he became the leader of his age-group; persecuted by Dankaran Tuman, he had to flee with his mother and brother, Mande Bugari (Abubakar).[38] This exile, or *nieni na bori*, lasted many years. No Malinke chief dared offer them refuge, so he went to Ghana and was well received at Koumbi; but it was at Mema that he settled with his mother and brother. The king of Mema, Mansa Tunkara or Mema Farin Tunkara, appreciated the courage of the young Diata and gave him important responsibilities. It was at Mema that the Mandingo messengers found him; the king gave him a force of soldiers and he returned to Mande.

The battle of Kirina

The news of Sundiata's coming aroused great enthusiasm in the ranks of the Malinke. Every clan had formed its own army and the principal generals, such as Tabon-Wana (Tabon Ghana), were of the same age-group as Sundiata. Tabon Ghana or Wana was chief of one part of the Camara clan, and his cousin, Kamadian Camara of Sibi (between Siguiri and Kangaba), was chief of another. Faony Conde, Siara Kuman, Konate and Tiraman, all generals, agreed to work together for a common cause. The meeting with Sundiata took place on the plain of Sibi. The alliance was sealed and Sundiata took operational command.

The Camara, from the villages of Niani, Selegugu and Tigan, on the

36. Translated from Ibn Khaldūn, loc. cit., p. 344.

37. Since the appearance of *Soundjata, ou l'épopée mandingue*, the collection of oral tradition has been systematic. Cf. Innes, op. cit., who has gathered three versions of Sundiata's life in Senegambia. See also S. M. Cissoko, 1981a and 1981b, and M. Ly-Tall, 1977 and 1981; SCOA Seminars 1975, 1977, 1980; Senghor Foundation Seminar on 'The Oral Traditions of Kaabu', 1980.

38. Niane, op. cit., pp. 56–73. With few exceptions, the Sundiata saga of the different 'schools' is in agreement on essential matters: his difficult childhood, his exile in Mema, the sending of emissaries to find him, his return, the alliance and oath of the clan leaders, the defeat and disappearance of Sumaguru and the proclamation of Sundiata as mansa.

right bank of the Niger, had been the first to revolt and, under the leadership of Mansa Kara Noro, now put up a strong resistance against Sumaguru, whose victory over Mani was due to Fakoli, his nephew and general-in-chief. It was a fierce battle, for Mansa Kara Noro's army wore iron armour; but his queen betrayed him to Fakoli.

To celebrate this victory Sumaguru organized great festivities in Mani, in the course of which he quarrelled with Fakoli. Attracted by the culinary skill of Keleya Konkon, his nephew's wife, Sumaguru stole her from him. The outraged Fakoli, by way of revenge, crossed the Niger with his army and joined the allies gathered at Sibi. Sumaguru had thus lost his best lieutenant; but he attacked immediately, and after two indecisive battles the Malinke took courage. There was a decisive encounter at Kirina, a village difficult to locate, since oral tradition says it is a recent foundation. Sumaguru's army was numerous, though it is difficult to suggest any figure. Among his generals was Jolofing Mansa, king of Jolof and chief of the Tunkara of Kita, reputed to be a great magician. Sumaguru's cavalry was famous; its charge was irresistible.

But Sundiata's troops were full of enthusiasm, and the leader of the allies displayed great confidence. His sister, Nana Triban, who had been forced to marry Sumaguru, had managed to escape from Soso and joined Sundiata, with Balla Fasseke, *griot* to the Keita royal family, who now held the key to Sumaguru's strength. Magic entered into everything in ancient Africa. Sumaguru was invulnerable to iron, and his *tana* or totem was a white cockspur. He knew, since the flight of his wife and the *griot*, that his secret was now revealed. When he made his appearance on the battlefield he was downcast, and lacked the proud bearing that inspires an army. But he mastered his anxiety, and the battle began. The Soso were completely routed, and Sundiata pursued his enemy to Kulikoro, although he did not succeed in capturing him. He marched on the town of Soso and razed it to the ground.

The victory at Kirina was not just a military success for the allies; it also sealed the alliance between the clans. Although this war of magic and fetishes ensured the triumph of the Keita dynasty, paradoxically it was also a prelude to the expansion of Islam. For Sundiata, whose ancestors had been converted to Islam in the eleventh century, made himself the protector of Muslims; the delegation sent to find him in exile had included some marabouts. This unknown champion of Islam is not mentioned by any Arab author of the thirteenth century, and the battle of Kirina does not appear in the Arab chronicles. Nevertheless, Ibn Baṭṭūṭa tells us that Sundiata or Mari Diata was converted to Islam by a man called Mudrik, whose grandson lived at Mansa Mūsā's court.[39] Oral traditions speak only of the liberator of the Malinke.

39. Ibn Baṭṭūṭa, French transl. 1966, p. 63.

Sundiata's military conquests

Aided by brilliant generals, Sundiata conquered almost all the lands that had been controlled by Ghana; oral traditions record the names of Tiramaghan Traore and Fakoli Koroma. The former had been sent by Sundiata to Jolof to fight King Jolofing Mansa, who had arrested a caravan of traders sent by Diata to buy horses. After defeating the king, Tiramaghan waged war in Senegambia and conquered the Casamance and the highlands of Kaabu or Gabu, now Guinea-Bissau. Tiramaghan is considered by the western Mandingo to have been the founder of several kingdoms, the most important of which was the kingdom of Kaabu.[40] Fakoli Koroma conquered the southern regions stretching to the forest and the area of the upper Senegal river.[41] Sundiata personally defeated the kings of Diaghan or Diafunu and Kita, who were allies of Sumaguru. Thus he re-established the unity of the western Sudan. His conquests were continued by his son and his generals, who annexed Gao and Takrūr.

The constitution of Mali

Mandingo tradition attributes to the young victor of Kirina the codification of the customs and prohibitions which still govern relations between the Mandingo clans themselves, on the one hand, and between them and the other clans of West Africa on the other. Many things have been ascribed to this African Alexander which belong to a much later date. But the main outlines of the constitution and the administrative structures were essentially the work of Sundiata. He was a man of many names: in the Soninke language he was called Maghan or King Sundiata, and in Malinke, Mari (Lord) Diata (lion). He was also Nare Maghan

40. The episode of Jolofing Mansa is very important in the Sundiata saga. The king of Jolof had been an ally of Sumaguru and, like him, was hostile to Islam. He confiscated Diata's horses and sent him a skin, saying that he should make shoes out of it since he was neither a hunter nor a king worthy to mount a horse. Sundiata was furious and shut himself off from the world for several days. When he reappeared, he gathered his generals and ordered them to march on Jolof. Tiramaghan begged permission to go alone, arguing that there was no need to mobilize the whole army; when he insisted and threatened to kill himself, Diata granted his request and gave him a regiment. Tiramaghan conquered Jolofing Mansa and overran Senegambia and Kaabu. His deeds are sung by the *griots* of Kaabu in long poems accompanied by the *kora*. Several villages of Kaabu claim to be the burial place of Tiramaghan. But some Gangaran traditions maintain that the conqueror of Jolofing Mansa returned to Mali. (See Cissoko, 1981a and 1981b, and Ly-Tall, 1981.) The oral traditions of upper Gambia and East Senegal have yet to be collected; these regions contain sites and towns of considerable importance for a knowledge of Mandingo expansion westward.

41. His descendants are the Cissoko, Dumbuya and Koroma clans; the fetishes and war regalia of Fakoli can be found in the Koroma village of Norassoba, in the Republic of Guinea. In general, the Mandingo maintain small museums exclusively for a small group of initiates and privileged individuals. Some very ancient relics are thus preserved.

Konate, or king of the Konate, son of Nare Maghan; and Simbon Salaba, or master huntsman, whose head commands reverence.

According to tradition it was at Kurukan Fuga, a plain not far from Kangaba, that the Gbara or great assembly took place. It was in fact a constituent assembly of the allies after their victory, in front of whom the following took place.

(a) Sundiata was solemnly proclaimed mansa (in Malinke) or maghan (in Soninke), meaning emperor, king of kings. Each allied chief was confirmed in his province (farin); only the chiefs of Mema and Wagadu bore the title of king.

(b) The assembly decreed that the emperor must be chosen from the line of Sundiata and that the princes must always choose their first wife from among the Conde clan (in memory of the happy marriage between Nare Fa Maghan and Sogolon Conde, Sundiata's mother).

(c) In accordance with ancient tradition, the succession was to be fratrilineal.

(d) The mansa was to be the supreme judge, the patriarch, the father of all his subjects: hence the formula, 'M'Fa Mansa' (King, my father), for addressing the king.

(e) The Malinke and their allies were divided into 16 clans of 'quiver-bearing' freedmen or nobles (Tonta-Djon Tanni Moro).[42]

(f) The five marabout clans, the first of Sundiata's allies, including the Toure and the Berete, who had actively sought Sundiata in exile, were proclaimed the 'five guardians of the faith', or Mori Kanda Lolu. This group also included the Cisse of Wagadu, who had become Muslim converts and Sundiata's political allies.

(g) Men practising special trades were divided into four clans (Nara Nani), including the *griots*, the shoemakers and certain clans of smiths. The names of Mande clans were recognized as corresponding to the clan names of other ethnic groups of the Sudan. 'Joking relationships' were established, which continued after the time of Sundiata, and helped to reduce tension between ethnic groups.[43] The Niger boatmen, Somono and Bozo, were rewarded for their contribution to the war when Sundiata proclaimed them 'masters of the waters'. According to tradition, Sundiata 'divided

42. The bow and quiver were the symbols of freedmen. They alone had the right to bear arms. The Portuguese noted in the fifteenth century that the Malinke nobles had quivers laden with arrows when they walked in the town; they never laid down their arms, by which they were recognized.

43. For example, a man of the Conde clan among the Wolof is considered a brother by those of the Ndiaye clan, and a Traore is treated as a brother by the Diop. A Traore settling in Wolof country can take the clan name of Diop and vice versa. This fictional relationship, this clan fraternity, still plays an important role in the western Sudan. After Sundiata, new links were established between the Mandingo and the inhabitants of the lands where they settled, the forests of Guinea, Liberia and Ivory Coast.

up the world'; in other words, he established the rights and duties of each clan.

(h) A special measure dealt with the Soso: their territory was declared the property of the empire, and they were divided among the various craft clans or castes. Many of them emigrated to the west.

This constitution was very important in itself, and had far-reaching effects. It reproduced the social structure of the Ghana empire, in which the character of each region had been recognized. Furthermore, Sundiata codified the system of craft clans so that professions became hereditary. It seems that in the time of Ghana every man had practised the trade of his choice; but from now on the son had to practise the same trade as his father, especially within the four craft clans or castes.

Sundiata's government

Sundiata set up a government composed of his companions. Besides soldiers and war leaders, Sundiata surrounded himself with black scholars of the marabout clans, who were 'joking cousins' of the Keita clan. Probably some Arab traders frequented his court. Ibn Baṭṭūṭa says that Mari Diata was converted to Islam by a certain Mudrik whose descendants lived in Mansa Sulaymān's court; but tradition sees Sundiata as the liberator of the Mande and the protector of the oppressed, not as a propagator of Islam.

There were two kinds of province: those which had first rallied to his cause and whose kings preserved their titles, as in the case of Ghana (Koumbi) and Mema;[44] and the conquered provinces, where a governor or farin represented the mansa alongside the traditional chief. Sundiata respected the traditional institutions of the conquered provinces, so the administration was flexible and the empire resembled a federation of kingdoms or provinces rather than a centralizing empire. But the existence of Mandingo garrisons in the principal regions guaranteed security, while also acting as a deterrent force. Sundiata was probably responsible for the division of the empire into two military regions. 'The prince had under his orders two generals: one for the southern area and the other for the north; the first was called Sangar Zuma, the second Faran Sura. Each had a number of caids and soldiers under his command.'[45]

44. 'Throughout the kingdom of this sovereign [mansa], only the ruler of Ghana had the title of king and he was only the sovereign's lieutenant' al-'Umarī, French transl. 1927, p. 57. This passage refutes the statement of Delafosse that Mari Diata destroyed Ghana in 1240. Tradition is positive; the kings of Wagadu, Cisse and Mema were allies of Sundiata from the outset and for this reason enjoyed certain privileges.

45. Translated from al-Sa'dī, loc. cit., p. 20. 'Faran Sura' is certainly a corruption of the text. In Mandingo the name would be Sankaran Soma, or chief of Sankara, the southern province which included the basin of the upper Niger and its tributaries. Instead of Faran Sura, however, I suggest reading sura farin, or chief of the northern country.

Niani, capital of Mali

The town of Niani is in Camara territory, on the Sankarani. For many years, researchers have sought the location of the capital of Mali; many theories had been put forward before Maurice Delafosse read al-ʿUmarī's manuscript correctly. In fact, it is al-ʿUmarī's text which provides the correct interpretation of the name of the capital of Mali. It is Nyeni or Niani, which Delafosse places near the present village of Niani on the Sankarani, on the present border between Mali and Guinea.[46] We have seen above that the Keita had long been established at Dakadiala, Kiri and Kirina. In fact it was only after his victory over Sumaguru that Sundiata decided to set up his capital in the land of Mani, which was rich in gold and iron.[47]

The historian may wonder why Sundiata preferred Mani to the old village of Dakadiala, where several generations of kings had chosen to dwell. He had several reasons:

(1) The conqueror did not feel safe surrounded by his own clan at Dakadiala.
(2) The town was hemmed in by mountains and difficult of access.
(3) Niani was beautifully situated, with natural defences, on a huge plain alongside the Sankarani, surrounded by a semi-circle of hills traversed by passes and dominated by a rocky peak, the Mani Kuru. The Sankarani was deep and navigable all the year round.
(4) Last but not least, Mani or Niani was on the edge of the forest, a source of gold, kola nuts and palm oil, where Malinke traders came to sell cotton and copper goods. Hitherto it had been just a small town made famous by the resistance of its king against Sumaguru. Situated in the south, the new capital was far from the troubled areas of the Sahel nomads.

Niani developed rapidly in the vast plain. Two main trails started there: the Mande route northward (*Manding-sila*) and the caravan route to the north-east (*Sarakolle-sila*).[48] The latter went through the pass between

Sura refers to the Sahel regions occupied by the Mauretanians and the Tuareg, who were called people of Sura, or Suraka, in Malinke.

46. See M. Delafosse, 1912, Vol. 2, pp. 181–2 for the identification of Niani. Following the research of Vidal and Gaillard on the site and a painstaking analysis of Ibn Baṭṭūṭa's itinerary, Delafosse has rightly concluded that the capital of the mansas was indeed at Niani.

47. Niani is in that country. The first settlement of that name was established by the Camara of Sibi in the mountains on the left bank between Bamako and Kangaba. See Premier colloque international de Bamako, 1975 (paper by Y. Cissé).

48. The Malinke commonly called the Soninke *Marka* or *Sarakolle*. Soninke or Sununke in their traditional religion was a synonym of Malinke. In the traditional religion of Senegambia, Soninke was a synonym of Mandingo: there in fact the word Sarakolle was rarely used. *Mande sila* means the Mande road; *Sarakolle sila* means the Sarakolle road. The first went north and the second east.

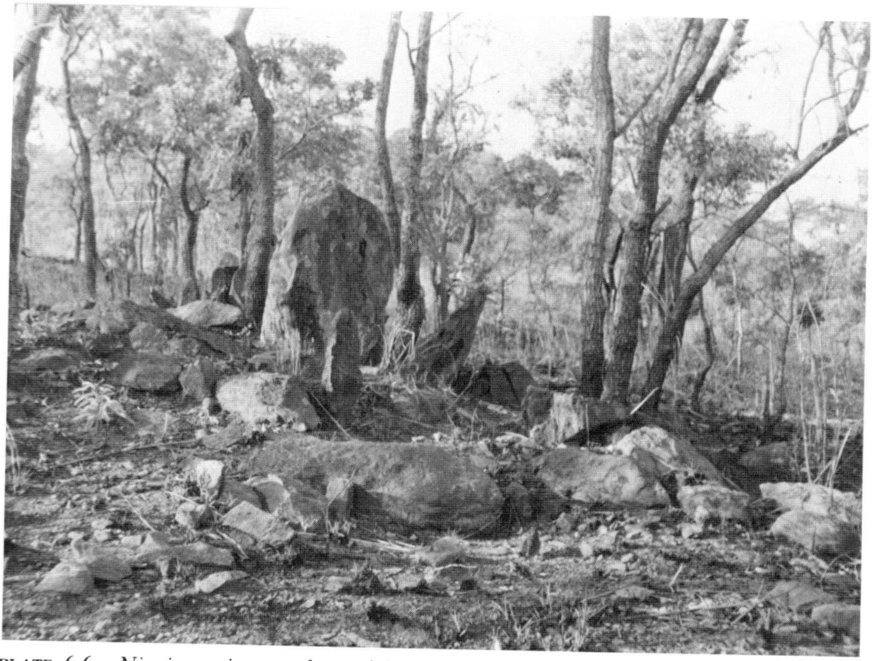

PLATE 6.6 *Niani: station 29, large dolerite rocks on the slope of Niani Kourou (where numerous potsherds have been discovered). Place of worship?*

PLATE 6.7 *Niani: station 1, a general view of the foundations of the huts in the inhabited area (level II)*

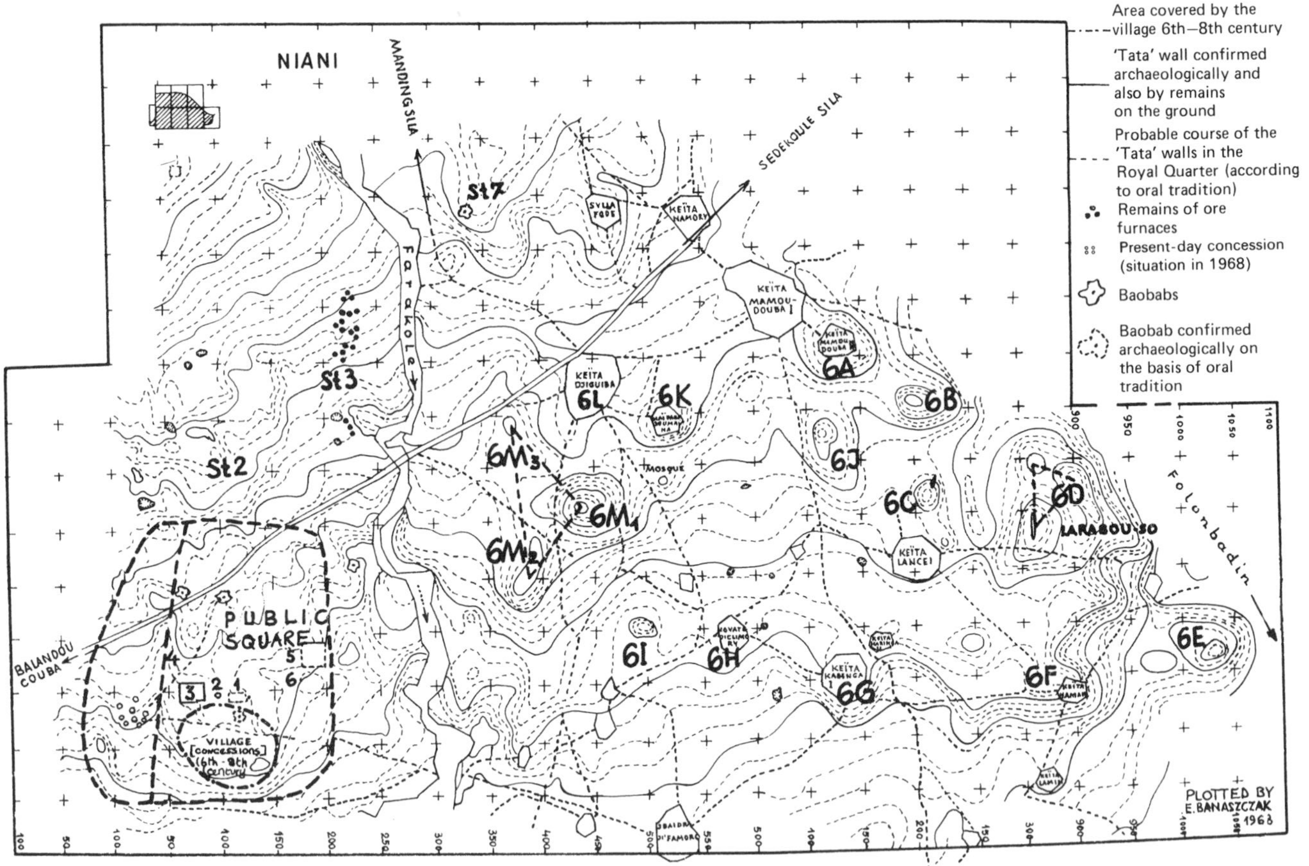

FIG. 6.2 *Map of site of Niani excavation (W. Filipowiak)*

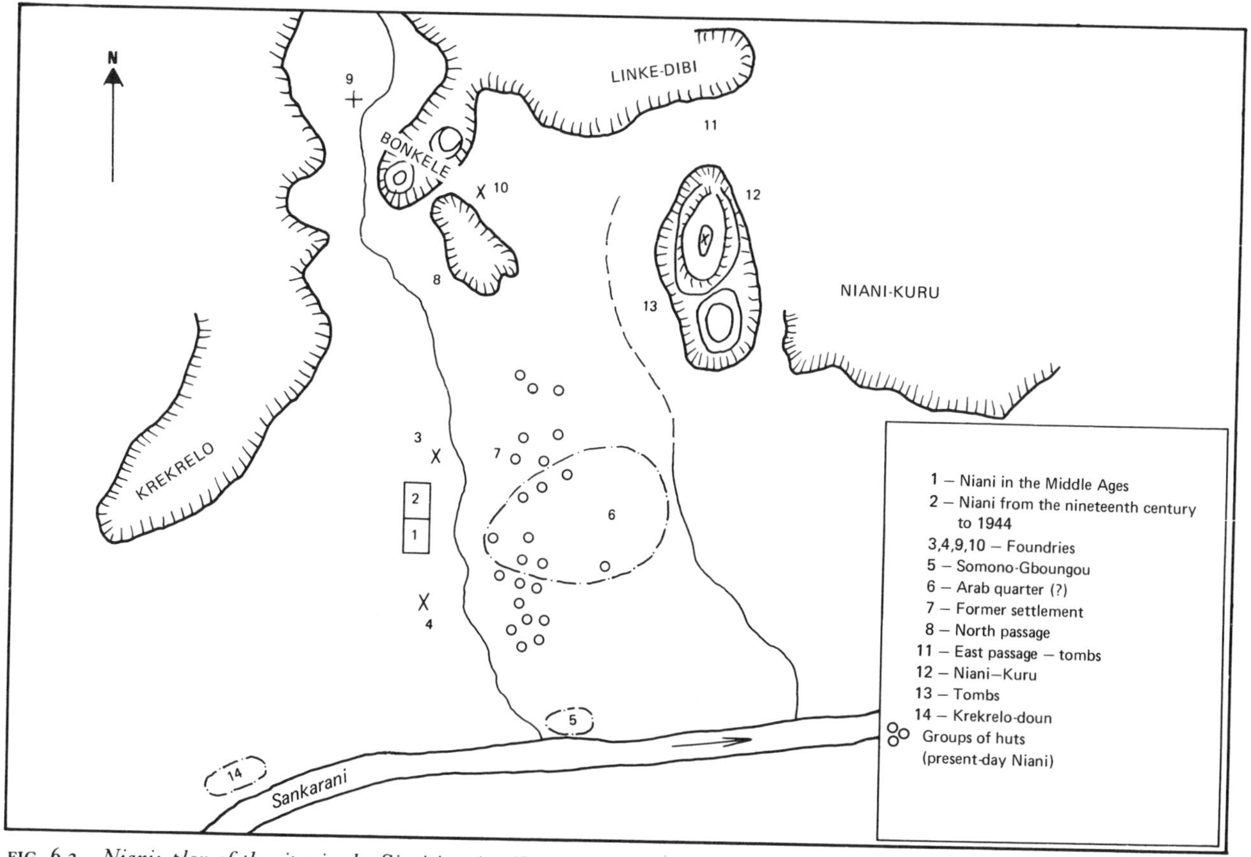

FIG. 6.3 *Niani: plan of the sites in the Siguiri region (D. T. Niane)*

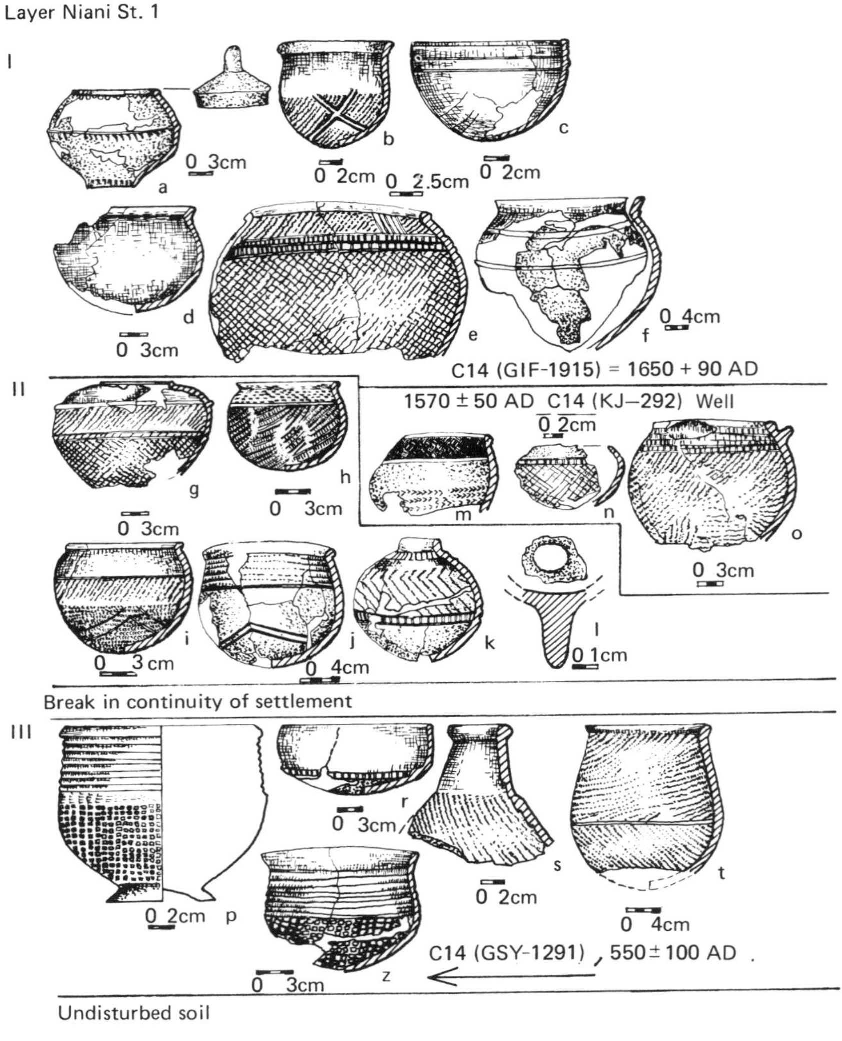

FIG. 6.4 *Niani: station 1, a selection of types of pottery found in radiocarbon-dated layers I–III (after W. Filipowiak, 1979)*

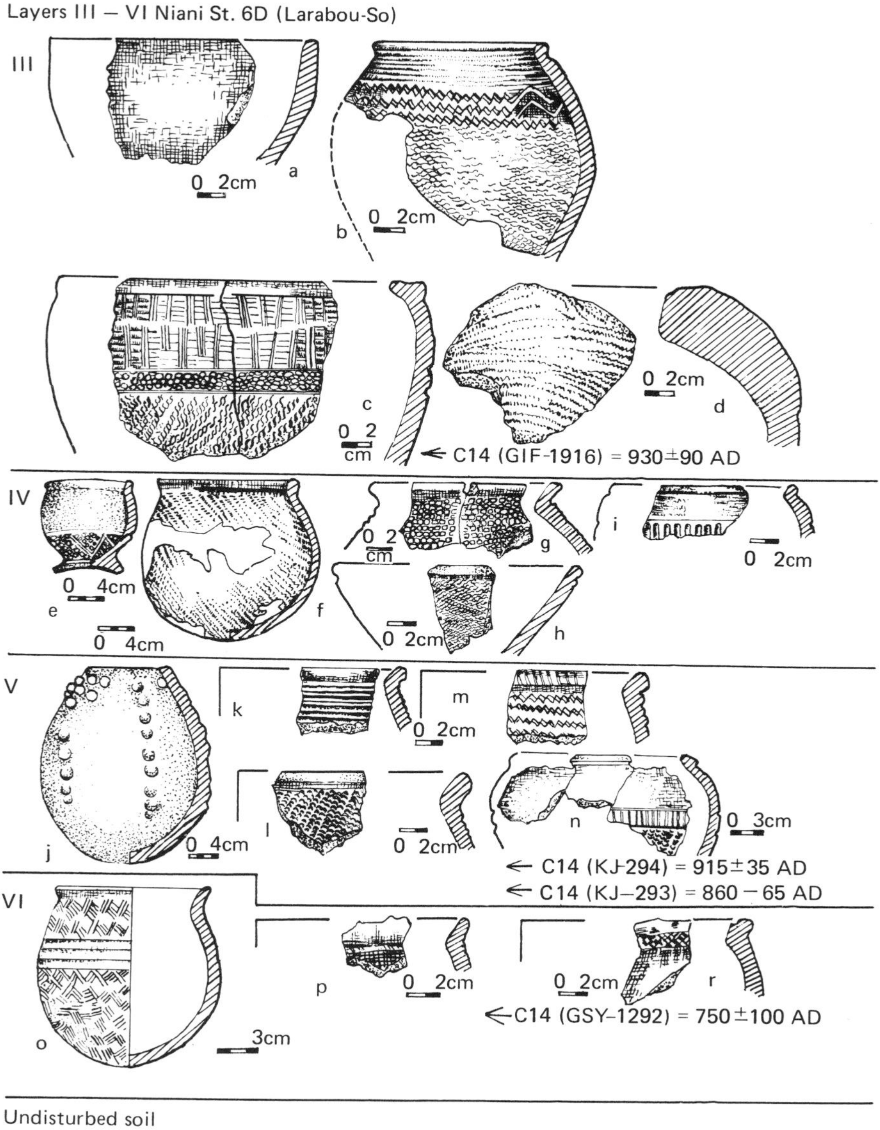

FIG. 6.5 *Niani: station 6D (Arab quarter), a selection of types of pottery found in radio-carbon-dated layers III–VI (after W. Filipowiak, 1979)*

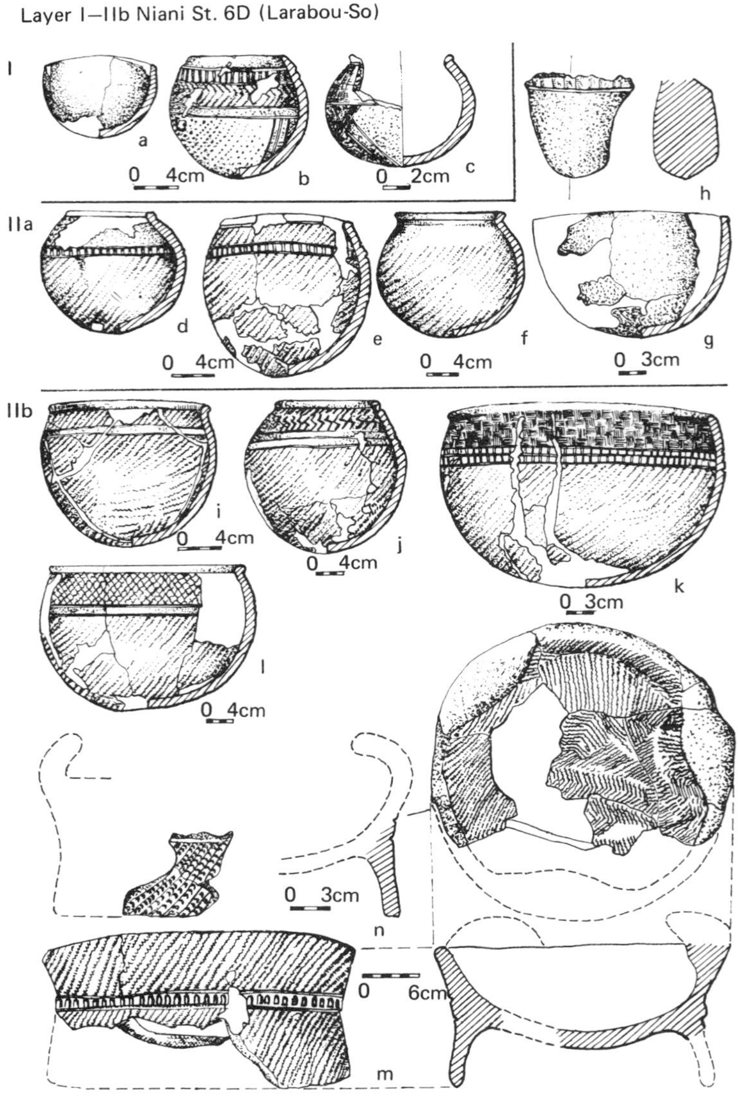

FIG. 6.6 *Niani: station 6D (Arab quarter), a selection of ceramics from layers I–IIb (after W. Filipowiak, 1979)*

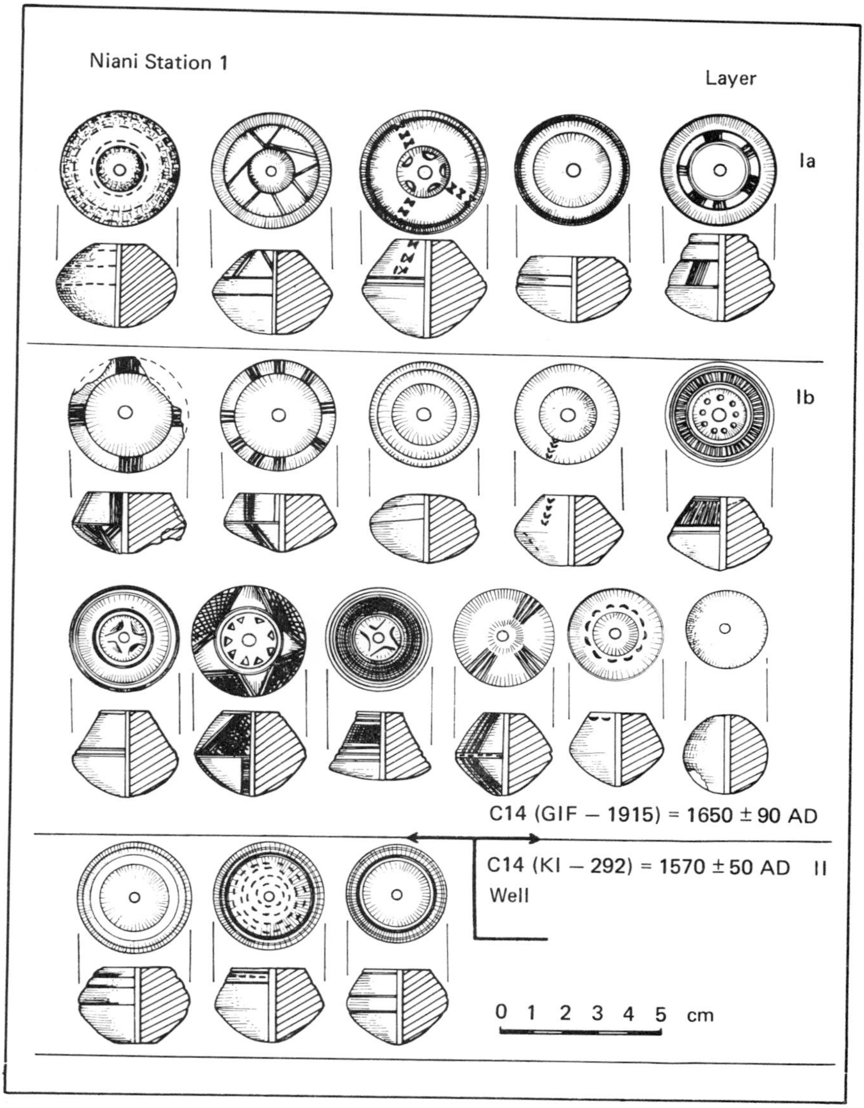

FIG. 6.7 *Niani: station 1, a collection of spindle-whorls found in layers in the residential sector of the Royal Quarter (after W. Filipowiak, 1979)*

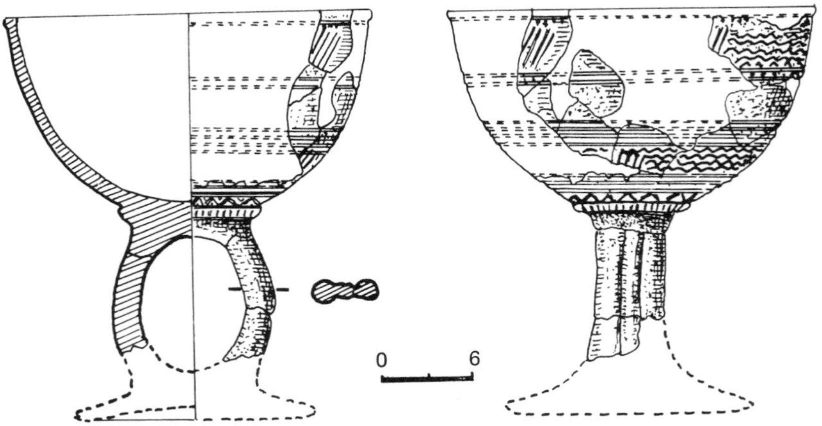

FIG. 6.8 *Niani: station 32 (cemetery), a clay cup from the bank of burial mound no. 1 (after W. Filipowiak, 1979)*

Mount Niani and Mount Dauleni Kuru (mountain of the red gate). The town became the political and economic capital of the empire.

Niani attracted both black merchants and Berber Arabs. Ibn Baṭṭūṭa, who visited the town in 1353, called it 'Malli'. But al-ʿUmarī gives us more details: 'The region of Mali is where the king's residence is located in the town of Nyeni, on which all the other regions depend; it is called Mali because it is the capital of the regions of this kingdom.'[49]

Since its identification in the 1920s the site of Niani has been visited by many researchers.[50] But it was not until 1968 that important excavations were undertaken: a Guinean–Polish mission has been working since then on the site. The Arab quarter and the royal villa have been identified and the archaeologists have exposed the foundations of stone houses as well as the foundations and *miḥrāb* of a mosque in the royal town (see Figs. 6.5, 6.6, 6.7). The wall around the villa has been traced. It is notable that all the buildings here were of bricks of beaten earth or banco, as al-ʿUmarī wrote:

> The houses of this town are built in layers of clay, like the walls of the gardens at Damascus. This is how they proceed: they build in

49. Translated from al-ʿUmarī, loc. cit., p. 57.

50. M. Gaillard, 1923, pp. 620–36; J. Vidal, 1924; R. Mauny, 1961; W. Filipowiak, 1970 and 1979.

> clay to a height of two-thirds of a cubit, then leave it to dry. Then they repeat the process until all is finished. The ceilings are made of beams and reeds. They are mostly in the shape of a cupola [i.e. conical] or a camel's hump, like vaulted arches. The floors of the houses are of earth mixed with sand.[51]

The style of construction described by al-ʿUmarī was used until the arrival of the colonizers, who introduced the brick mould; as is well known, conical roofs made of straw are still common throughout the Mandingo savannah, and the floors of the houses are still of beaten earth. Al-ʿUmarī's description is very precise and has guided researchers, who have compared it with traditional accounts. He adds:

> The town of Nyeni is the same in length and in breadth, being about one *berid* long and the same distance across. It is not surrounded by a wall, and the houses stand separately for the most part. The king has a group of palaces surrounded by a circular wall.[52]

Archaeologists have discovered that the dwellings were widely dispersed; around the royal town there was a host of hamlets or villages for various trade clans: smiths, fishermen and so on. The ruins stretch today from Niani up to Sidikila, 25 km away.

Sundiata declared Niani imperial territory, a common homeland for all his people.[53] The town's population was cosmopolitan; every province and every trade was represented. The conqueror revived the tradition by which the sons of farins and vassal kings were brought up at court, as in the days of the *Kaya Maghan*.

The death of Sundiata

There are several legends concerning the death of the hero. We can only theorize because those who guard the oral traditions are in disagreement. In any event, it is forbidden in Mandingo country to disclose the tomb of great kings, and there is no known cemetery or burial place for Mandingo rulers. According to a tradition heard by Delafosse, Sundiata was accidentally killed by an arrow during a ceremony. I believe that he was drowned in the waters of the Sankarani, in obscure circumstances, for it is known that some 10 km upstream from Niani there is a place called *Sundiata-dun* (Sundiata's deep water). This part of the river is very deep and has many eddies; the pirogues take care to avoid it. On each bank of the river the Keita have set up sacred places where, from time to time,

51. Translated from al-ʿUmarī, loc. cit., pp. 54–6.
52. Translated from the French; ibid., p. 57.
53. Tradition gathered by the author and reported to the Premier colloque international de Bamako, 1975.

chosen descendants of the conqueror meet to sacrifice fowls, sheep, goats and oxen.

A number of villages maintain places of worship in memory of Sundiata: at Kirina on the Niger, the 'traditionalists', the Mamissoko, offer sacrifices to him in a sacred forest. North-east of Niani, at Tigan, there is a pile of ashes in Camara country called 'Bundalin', under which there are believed to be shoes, a knife and a suit of armour which belonged to Sundiata. Then there is the ceremony held every seven years at Kangaba around the sanctuary called Kamablon, where there are also objects that belonged to Sundiata.[54] Finally, it is worth noting that classical Mandingo music began 'in Sundiata's time' (*Sundiata tele*). The saga of the hero is recited to the accompaniment of particular music. This saga, or *Sundiata fassa*, was composed by Balla Fasseke, the conqueror's *griot*. The song called *Boloba* (the great music) was composed by the *griots* of Sumaguru; Sundiata made it the music of every Mandingo warrior, which means that any Mandingo can ask a *griot* to play the music for him to listen or dance to it. The tune called *Janjon* ('glory to the warrior') was composed in honour of Fakoli after his feats on the battlefield; the *Tiramaghan fassa* celebrates the bravery and warlike deeds of the conqueror of the western provinces of the Mali empire.[55] *Duga*, an old warrior's chant, is much older than Sundiata and was reserved for the most distinguished warriors of the empire.

Sundiata's successors

We are indebted to Ibn Khaldūn for the complete list of the mansas of Mali from the middle of the thirteenth to the end of the fourteenth century (see Fig. 6.9). The list corresponds at many points with the list given in the historical traditions of Mande.[56] In his remarkable *History* and in his *Prolegomena*, Ibn Khaldūn acknowledges the political and economic importance of Mali in the Muslim world of the fourteenth century. His information on Mali was derived from good authorities – not only the Arab merchants but also Mali's embassies and consulates in Cairo. Conscious of the place of Mali in the Muslim world of the fourteenth century, he wrote at length on the history of the empire of the mansas.

The old principle of fratrilineal succession was not observed after Sundiata's death, when his eldest son, Mansa Yerelenku (or Oulin) seized power and reigned from 1250 to 1270. He preserved the unity of the army, and the generals continued their requests. It was probably under his reign that the Malinke took Takrūr and consolidated Tiramaghan's conquests in Senegambia; the Mandingo settled in these colonies. Mansa Oulin's pilgrimage to Mecca attracted the Arab countries' attention to Mali. After his

54. Tradition recorded by the author at Niani in 1968.
55. See above, p. 133, on Tiramaghan Traore.
56. On the chronology of the mansas, see N. Levtzion, 1963.

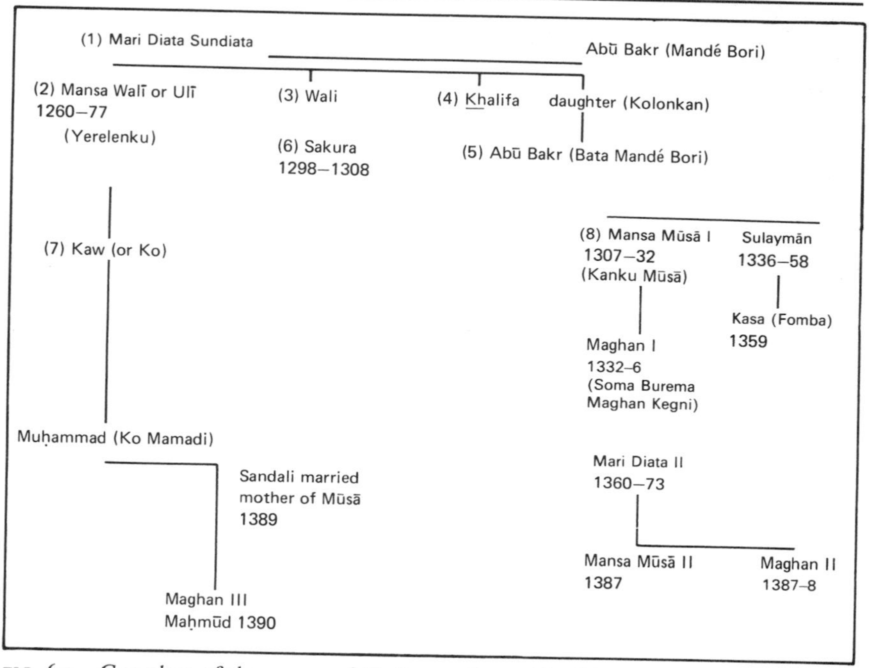

FIG. 6.9 *Genealogy of the mansas of Mali according to Ibn Khaldūn*
Note: the names given by oral tradition are in parentheses

death the empire was on the brink of destruction because of palace intrigues, but it was saved by Sakura, one of Sundiata's generals.[57] He resumed the conquests, subdued the Tuareg tribes, reaffirmed the authority of Mali over the valley of the Niger and took possession of Gao. Having thus restored order, he went to Mecca, but was murdered on the way home by Saharan robbers. His body is said to have been brought back to Mali and buried with royal honours.[58] His successors were weak, but in about 1307 Kanku Mūsā, a nephew of Sundiata, came to the throne. As Mansa Mūsā I he reigned until about 1337.

Mansa Mūsā's pilgrimage to Mecca in 1325 has been described by many authors. In his reign, Mali reached its apogee; he was succeeded by his son, Maghan I, or Soma Burema Maghan Kegni, who was overthrown in about 1336 by Mansa Sulaymān, brother of Mansa Mūsā I. He maintained the empire in all its splendour, but after him there was more intrigue at court.[59] Several political 'clans' formed around the descendants

57. Ibn Khaldūn, loc. cit., p. 345.
58. Delafosse, 1912, Vol. 2, pp. 185–6.
59. Ibn Baṭṭūṭa, loc. cit., pp. 62–3. The famous traveller recounts how Mansa Sulaymān's wife conspired to overthrow her husband. This internal strife weakened the empire.

of Mansa Mūsā I, Mansa Sulaymān and others, while the large Keita clan no longer hid its royal pretensions. Sulaymān's son, Fomba, remained on the throne only a year, and in 1359 he was dethroned by Mari Diata or Sundiata II, a despot, who 'ruined the Empire ... exhausted the royal treasury ... He sold the famous piece of gold regarded as one of the rarest treasures. This mass of metal weighed twenty *kinṭārs*. The spendthrift prince sold it for less than it was worth to Egyptian merchants.'[60] Mari Diata II was struck down by sleeping sickness and removed from power. He was succeeded by his son, Mansa Mūsā III (1374–87); however, the power really lay in the hands of his general, who restored order and put down a rising at Tiggida (Takedda), the famous copper-producing city. The end of the fifteenth century was disturbed by court intrigues fomented by the princesses. Provincial governors increasingly disregarded the central authority. But the empire's prestige survived for a long time.

The following is Maurice Delafosse's estimate of the dates of reigns from Sundiata to Mansa Mūsā I.[61]

(1)	Sundiata	1230–55
(2)	Mansa Oulin	1255–70
(3)	Wali	1270–4
(4)	Khalifa	1274–5
(5)	Abū Bakr	1273–85
(6)	Sakura	1285–1300
(7)	Kaw	1300–5
(8)	Muḥammad	1305–10

Triumph of Islam under Mansa Mūsā (1307–32)

Mansa Mūsā I is the best known of the emperors of Mali, largely because of his pilgrimage to Mecca in 1325 and the widespread fame of his visit to Cairo, where he gave away so much gold that the market for the precious metal was depressed for a long time.[62] The pilgrimage had important consequences for the subsequent history of the western Sudan, a region which haunted men's minds thereafter. Egypt, the Maghrib, Portugal and the merchant cities of Italy all took an increasing interest in Mali. Mansa Mūsā, who was very proud of his power, did much to make the rest of the world think of his empire as an El Dorado.

Once on the throne, Mansa Mūsā I set about consolidating the

60. Ibn Khaldūn, translated from the French of J. Cuoq, 1975, pp. 348–9.

61. Ibn Khaldūn says Mansa Mūsā's reign lasted 25 years, so a correction may be necessary to make the last reign 1307–32. See ibid., pp. 343–6.

62. Mansa Mūsā was attended by numerous followers; he took with him '80 packages of gold dust, each weighing 3 *kinṭārs* or 3.8 kg ... He was accompanied by 60 000 porters and 500 slaves, each carrying a golden staff weighing over 500 *mithkāl*, about 3 kg.' Translated from Delafosse, 1913. As early as 1375, cartographers depicted the Sudan with a portrait of Mansa Mūsā holding a gold nugget.

achievements of his predecessors and making the central authority be obeyed. He was ably assisted by an eminent general, Saran Mandian, who strengthened the emperor's authority not only in the valley of the Niger as far as Gao and beyond, but also throughout the Sahel, winning the submission of the Saharan nomads, who were often robbers and rebels; thus he facilitated Mūsā's journey to Mecca, for the Mali emperor had not forgotten the murder of Sakura by Saharan nomads.

Mansa Mūsā made elaborate preparations for his pilgrimage. In accordance with tradition he levied special contributions from every trading town and every province. He left Niani with a vast retinue. Although the figures given by the Arab writers are probably exaggerated, they give some idea of the power of the Mali emperor; there were said to be 60 000 porters and 500 servants decked in gold, each carrying a golden staff. At the beginning of the sixteenth century Maḥmūd Ka'ti related how, according to written tradition, the emperor was still in his palace when the head of his caravan arrived in Timbuktu. He was received in Cairo with the honours due to the great sultan he was, and created a great impression by his bearing and his generosity, worthy of the kings of the Arabian Nights.[63] He is one of the few kings of whom we have a physical description. According to al-Maḳrīzī: 'He was a young man with a brown skin, a pleasant face and good figure, instructed in the Mālikite rite. He appeared amidst his companions magnificently dressed and mounted, and surrounded by more than ten thousand of his subjects. He brought gifts and presents that amazed the eye with their beauty and splendour.'[64] Oral tradition says that Mansa Mūsā bought land and houses in Cairo and Mecca to accommodate pilgrims from the Sudan. But the important thing is that he established sound economic and cultural relations with the countries he travelled through.

Mansa Mūsā, builder and patron

Mansa Mūsā, impressed no doubt by the majestic palaces he saw in Cairo, returned home with a famous architect, Isḥāḳ al-Tuedjin, who built the great mosque at Gao, of which only a few remains of the foundations and a part of the *miḥrāb* survive. In Timbuktu the architect built another great mosque or *djinguereber*, and a royal palace or *madugu*. But his finest work was certainly the famous audience chamber at Niani, on which he lavished all the resources of his art. The emperor wanted a strong building covered with plaster, so al-Tuedjin 'built a square room surmounted by a cupola ... and, having covered it with plaster and decorated it with arabesques in dazzling colours, he produced a wonderful edifice. As

63. Maḥmūd Ka'ti, loc. cit.
64. Translated from al-Maḳrīzī, in J. Cuoq, 1975, pp. 91–2.

architecture was unknown in that country, the sultan was delighted and gave al-Tuedjin twelve thousand *mithkāl* of gold dust as testimony to his satisfaction.'[65] No doubt the emperor's architect had to use beaten earth, the most common material in that part of the Sudan. Buildings made of earth need constant repair and restoration in such latitudes as that of Niani. Further north, where rainfall is lighter, buildings last better, like the mosques at Jenne, Timbuktu and Gao. In the absence of stone, the banco or beaten earth is strengthened with wood; hence the characteristic Sudanese mosques bristling with bits of timber. With the successive destructions of Niani and the wearing away of the plaster under years of rain, the poet–architect's great achievement was finally reduced to a heap of clay and rubble.

In Cairo the mansa had been very ready to answer the questions of the courtiers and men of learning who flocked round him, and he described his empire in detail, not without some exaggeration. He said he had 'the exclusive right to gold, and that he gathered it in as tribute'. Ibn Amīr Adjib, governor of Cairo and Ḳarafa, whom the Mamluk sultan had appointed to look after the pilgrims, reported a great deal of what the emperor had said, and mentioned that his colours were yellow on a red ground. 'When he is on horseback they wave the royal standards, which are very large flags, over his head.' He had spoken of his empire: 'the inhabitants are very numerous ... a vast multitude ... Yet if you compare it with the black populations which surround it and stretch to the south, it is like a little white spot on the coat of a black cow.' Mūsā was well aware of the existence of large populations and powerful kingdoms to the south. He also mentioned that he had a town called Tiggida (Takedda, now Azelik), 'where there is a mine of red copper' which was brought in bars to Niani. ' "There is nothing in all my empire which is such a large source of taxes", the sultan told me, "as the import of this unworked copper. It comes from this mine and from no other. We send it to the lands of the black pagans where we sell one *mithkāl* of it for two-thirds of its weight in gold".'[66] Mūsā also said in Cairo that his predecessor on the throne had died at sea, 'for this king would not listen to those who told him it was impossible to get to the other side of the surrounding sea, and obstinately persisted in his purpose ... After the failure of 200 ships filled with men, and others filled with enough gold, water and provisions to last for years', the emperor himself took charge of operations, fitted out 2000 ships, and set off, never to return.[67] What the fate of this expedition was and how far Mūsā is to be believed are interesting questions, and writers such as Wiener and Jeffreys have raised the problem of whether the

65. Translated from Ibn Khaldūn, loc. cit., p. 348.

66. Translated from al-ʿUmarī, loc. cit., pp. 80–1. An interesting detail, which testifies to the intense commercial activity between Mali and the forest country, from which came palm oil, kola nuts and gold; see Chapter 25 below.

67. ibid.

Malinke discovered America.[68] In that case the blacks would have got there 200 years before Columbus![69]

But at least this anecdote shows that the Mandingo conquerors who settled on the coast, notably Gambia, were not indifferent to the problems of sea navigation. The great pilgrim attracted many men of letters to his court, and was himself skilled in Arabic, though he always spoke to Arabs through his interpreters. He had *ḳāḍīs*, secretaries and genuine *diwāns*, but this was mostly for show. After his famous pilgrimage, the Marinids of Fez and the merchant cities of the Maghrib began to take a lively interest in Mali, and the rulers exchanged gifts and ambassadors. Mūsā set up Koranic schools; he had bought many books in Cairo and the holy places. It was probably in his reign that Walata became important, and that Jenne and Timbuktu started to develop into cities that were to be world-famous a century later.

As a builder, Mansa Mūsā I left an enduring mark on all the cities of the Sudan, with their characteristic buildings of beaten earth strengthened with wood. The mosques at Jenne and Timbuktu were the prototypes of what is called the Sudanese style. As a patron and friend of literature, Mūsā helped lay the foundations of the Arabic literature of the blacks which was to bear its finest fruit in the cities of Jenne and Timbuktu in the fourteenth and sixteenth centuries.[70]

Mansa Sulaymān

After the short reign of Maghan I, the son of Mansa Mūsā, the throne passed to the legitimate heir according to tradition, Mansa Mūsā's brother, Mansa Sulaymān (1336–58). It was in his reign that the famous traveller Ibn Baṭṭūṭa visited Mali and stayed for nine months in the capital. His account complements that of al-ʿUmarī and gives us a lively picture of court life and the administration of the empire. Court ceremonies were governed by a very strict protocol, of which Ibn Baṭṭūṭa gives an extremely detailed account.

The mansa's role, like that of the *Kaya Maghan*, was first and foremost that of the dispenser of justice, the patriarch to whom all brought their

68. L. Wiener, 1920–2; M. D. W. Jeffreys, 1953b.

69. Ivan Sertima, an Afro-American researcher, has a theory that blacks were the first to sail to America. He has analysed minutely Mexican and Central American civilizations and finds Mandingo elements in these cultures. The theory is enticing, but unproved.

70. Oral traditions rarely mention Mansa Mūsā. Some even ignore him completely. After a long inquiry, it appears that Mansa Mūsā is considered 'unfaithful to ancestral Mandingo traditions'; his pilgrimage is well known to some bearers of tradition because he is blamed for wasting the imperial treasury. See SCOA Foundation, 1980 (no details available). It was during his reign that the secret Komo association was created by the Bambara (Banmana), who rejected the mansa's authority out of loyalty to traditional beliefs. See *Recueil de littérature mandingue*, 1980, pp. 215–27.

grievances. In the regions he was represented by the governors, but if they were guilty of injustice they were in principle deprived of office as soon as the mansa was informed. Subjects approached the mansa humbly, covering themselves with dust and saying 'M'fa Mansa' ('My lord, my father'). According to Ibn Baṭṭūṭa, the mansa held two audiences, one in the palace, in the famous audience chamber built for Mūsā I, and the other under a tree in the open air, on a throne mounted with gold and ivory. The lieutenant-general (Kankoro Sigui), the dignitaries, the governors, the priest and the legal experts took their places, and the *dj̲eli* or *griot* who acted as spokesman and master of ceremonies stood before the assembly in the audience chamber. Ibn Baṭṭūṭa described the mansa thus: 'The Emperor's turban is decorated with fringes, which these people arrange with great skill. Round his neck hangs a sabre with a gold sheath. He is booted and spurred; on this day, none but he wears boots. He holds two short iron-tipped spears, one of silver and the other of gold.'[71]

The open-air session, also described by Ibn Baṭṭūṭa, was no less solemn an occasion. It took place ritually every Friday after the midday prayers, when the *griot* 'spoke' the history and recalled the names and exploits of the kings. Oral tradition was then in its heyday. History was a continuing educational process, at the court as at home. The people swore their oaths in the name of the king, a practice which continued until the nineteenth century.

The Niani ceremonial was a revival in a more impressive form of the protocol of the *kaya maghan*, the novelty being that the emperor was now a Muslim and solemnly celebrated the great feasts of Islam. But the emperor also remained faithful to certain pagan customs, and Ibn Baṭṭūṭa was shocked by many unorthodox practices. Apart from the presence of Arabs and the slight Muslim veneer, what happened at the court of the mansa differed very little from what might have been seen at the courts of non-Muslim kings, for example those of Mossi.[72]

The dignitaries were splendidly attired, decked with gold, and they carried magnificent weapons, according to al-'Umarī. Soldiers were distinguished by their quivers – the nobles among them being descended from conquerors – judges and legal experts by their turbans. The black hermits were derived from the five guardians of the faith (Mori Kanda Lolu) and formed 'the nobility of the turban'.

Mandingo civilization

The peoples of the empire

At its height, under the reigns of Mansa Mūsā I and Mansa Sulaymān, the Mali empire covered the entire Sudan–Sahel region of West Africa.

71. Translated from Ibn Baṭṭūṭa, loc. cit.
72. See Chapters 9 and 10 below.

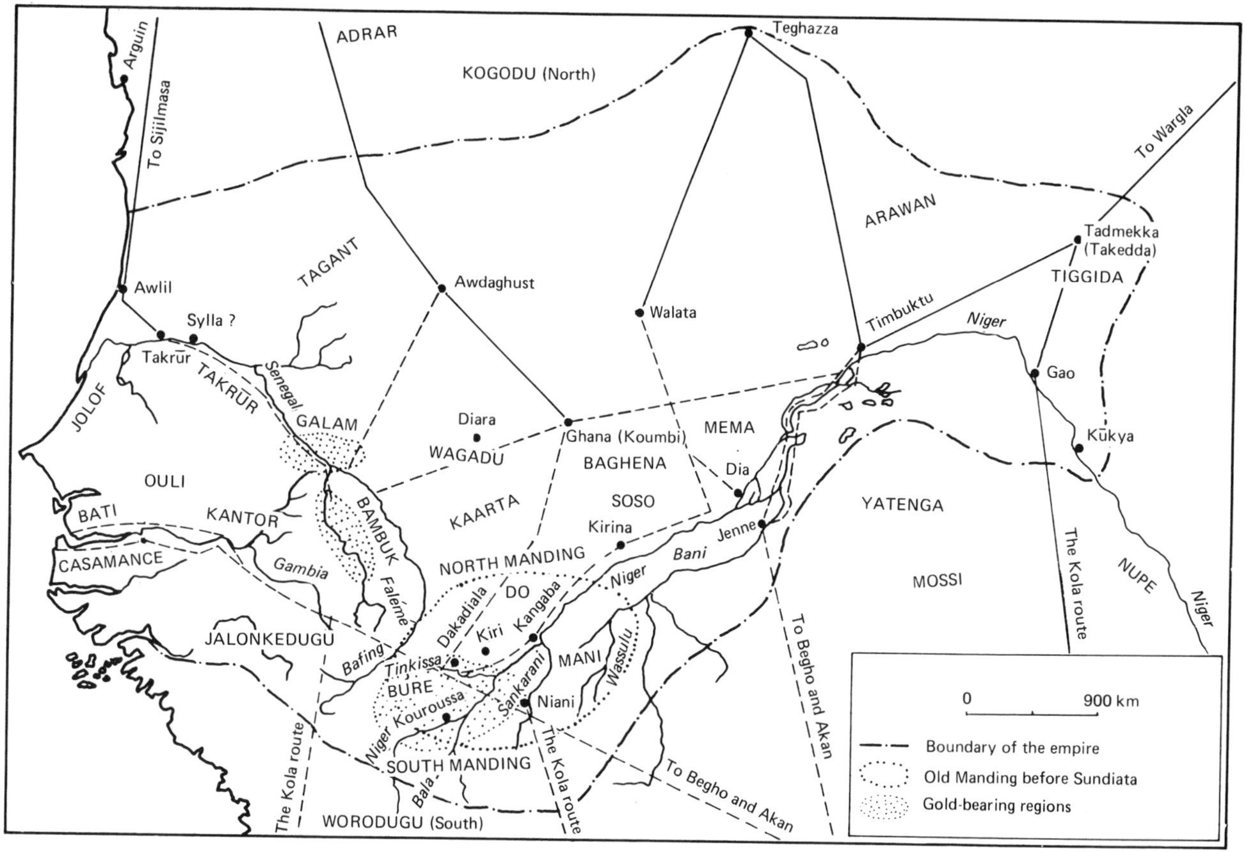

FIG. 6.10 *The Mali empire, 1325 (D. T. Niane)*

Many peoples and cultures were thus brought together under a single political head.

Nomads and herdsmen

The great Saharan nomads, particularly the Messufa, had a vast domain from the salt-pans of Teghazza to the city of Walata, a major intersection point for the trans-Saharan trade routes in Mali. The Messufa were the main commercial agents in the salt trade; caravan guides were recruited from among them because a perfect knowledge of the Sahara was needed to link the Maghrib with the Sudan. To the west, towards the Atlantic, were the Lemtima Sanhaja and the Godala, Berbers who occupied territory corresponding to the present Mauritania. Like the Messufa, they were involved in Saharan trade and exploited the salt-mines of Ijil. Between Walata and the Niger Bend was the territory of the Tuareg. All these great desert nomads were watched over by garrisons at Walata, Timbuktu, Gao and Koumbi. The vast Sahara domain was controlled by the military commander, *sura farin*.

The peoples of the Sahel

In those days, the climate of the Sahel was relatively mild and there was abundant pasture land. In this zone were located the northern cities of the Sudan such as Takrūr, Awdaghust, Koumbi, Walata and Timbuktu. The Fulani wandered from the Atlantic, on the Senegal estuary, to the Niger Bend. They were cattlemen and moved their pastures according to the seasons; nevertheless, by the fourteenth century, groups had filtered towards the south and were becoming sedentarized, particularly around Jenne and along the right bank of the Sankarani, around Niani, as well as in Takrūr.[73]

The Sahel farmer cultivators – the Toucouleur, or Takrūr people, the Soninke and Songhay[74] – had been converted to Islam much earlier (in the eleventh and twelfth centuries) and lived in large towns. Easy communication in the plains encouraged the establishment of new towns and a common culture, even if the people involved did not speak the same language.

The peoples of the savannah

The main groups, from west to east, were the Jolof, the Mandingo and the Soninke. The Malinke had also settled *en masse* in Casamance and

73. The Fulani occupation of the right bank of the Sankarani resulted two centuries later in the birth of the province of Wassulu. The Fulani of this area forgot their own language and spoke Malinke instead. Probably the Fulani infiltration at Futa-Jallon and Takrūr, in the Bundu and at Macina began around the eleventh and twelfth centuries and intensified after the fifteenth.

74. Toucouleur is a corruption of Takrūr. They themselves called each other *Hal pular-en* (those who speak Fulani); but their Jolof and Serer neighbours called them Toucouleur. They were farmers and traders rather than shepherds. Linguists classify Fulani, Jolof and Serer in the same west Atlantic linguistic family.

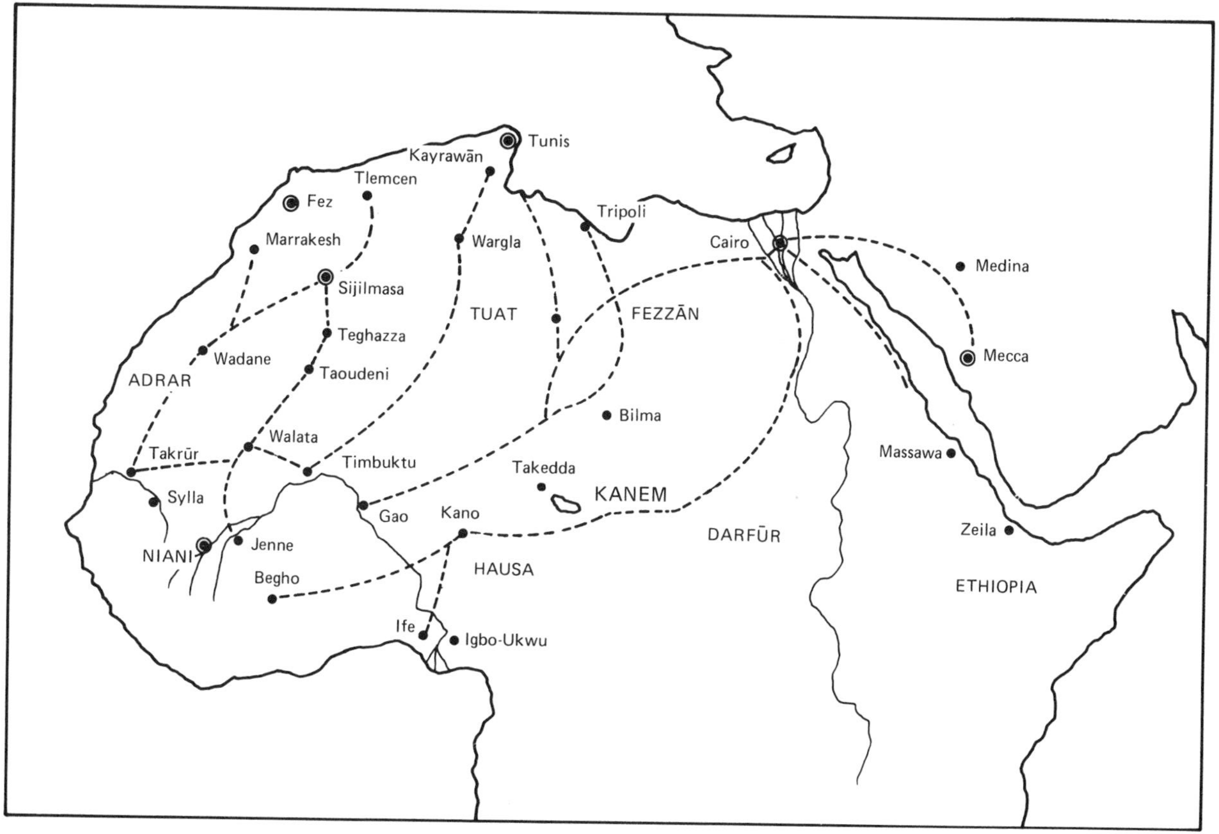

FIG. 6.11 *Main trans-Saharan routes in the 14th century (D. T. Niane)*

Senegambia, following Tiramaghan's conquests; these western regions had room for settlers. It would be interesting to know whether the Malinke were already in Senegambia before Sundiata; it is highly probable that traders and Soninke and Malinke hermits frequented the area well before the thirteenth century.[75] Along the coast from Gambia to the Rio Grande, the agricultural communities of Beafada, Balante, Felupe and Bainunke, noted for rice cultivation, were surrounded by the Malinke.

In the middle of the fifteenth century, Portuguese navigators made contact with the mansa when they arrived at the estuary of the River Gambia; from them, we know that these western regions had been strongly influenced by the Mandingo.[76] We also know from the historical writers of Timbuktu that Mali was densely populated. According to the author of the *Ta'rīkh al-Sūdān*,

> The territory of Jenne is fertile and populated; many markets are held every day of the week. It is said there are 7077 villages situated very close to each other.
>
> The following will give an idea how close they are. If the Sultan, for example, wishes to summon an inhabitant of a village near Lake Debo, the messenger sent goes to one of the gates of the ramparts and from there shouts the message he is to transmit. From village to village, people repeat the words and the message arrives almost immediately at its destination and the man in question goes to the meeting place.[77]

Although there may be some doubt about the number of 7077 villages in Jenne, one must note in passing the effectiveness of oral communication.

Maḥmūd Ka'ti declared that Mali 'has some 400 towns and its soil is most fertile. Among the kingdoms of the rulers of the world, only Syria is more beautiful. Its inhabitants are rich and live comfortably.'[78] These figures simply mean that the country was heavily populated; we can accept an estimate that the population of Mali was some 40–50 million. The river valleys of the Niger and the Senegal were virtually human anthills. The capital, Niani, had at least 100 000 inhabitants in the fourteenth century.[79] The Mali emperors do not seem to have been interested in the right bank of the Niger around Timbuktu, but this was not true of the rulers of Gao, who placed a governor at Hombori, at the foot of the mountains, near Dogon country.[80]

75. See Cissoko, 1981b, and M. Mané, 1981.

76. See Chapters 7 and 12; A. Donelha, 1977, pp. 107–21; I. B. Kaké, 1981.

77. Translated from al-Sa'dī, loc. cit., pp. 24–5. Archaeology confirms this description.

78. Translated from Maḥmūd Ka'ti, loc. cit., p. 67.

79. At the start of the sixteenth century, when Niani was no longer the great metropolis of the Sudan, Leo Africanus estimated that there were 6000 'hearths' there – or some 60 000 people, at an average of 10 persons per household, a minimum in Africa.

80. Maḥmūd Ka'ti, loc. cit., pp. 150, 254–5. Chi 'Alī died in 1492 on his return from a campaign near the country of the Tombo (Habe, or Dogon). A tradition collected at

The Dogon culture has been one of the most extensively studied in black Africa, but only from a limited ethnological perspective, so that we are unable to place the Dogon of earlier times in their historical context alongside other Sudanic populations. The work of R. M. A. Bedaux takes an original line in trying to establish relations between the Dogon and Tellen and the other peoples of the Niger Bend, placing them in a socio-historical perspective. Dogon art is world-famous; however, the finest works are not in Bamako, but in European museums and private collections in Europe and America.[81]

The Dogon[82]

The Bandiagara cliffs, part of the Hombori mountain range, are best known along the Niger Bend. The Dogon lived in this mountain area and the rulers of the savannah had little control over them. They lived in small villages clinging to the sides of the mountains. Every attempt to subject them ended in defeat. Who were the Dogon? According to their own oral tradition, they left Mande for the mountains and settled in the area of Sanga in the fourteenth and fifteenth centuries.[83] They are said to have found other mountain peoples there, whom they called Tellem (meaning 'we found them there'); these people are said to have left the region on the arrival of the Dogon, to settle in Yatenga. It is now agreed that the Dogon came from the southern regions (Mande), but many questions about both the Dogon and the Tellem remain unanswered. Comparative studies of Dogon pottery and that of the Malinke from Niani – the stemmed pottery – tend to confirm contacts between the two peoples.

A common culture linked the Sudan–Sahel populations. Within the framework of the empire, resemblances were accentuated and differences diluted by the system of corresponding names, by the bonds of kinship and by the joking relationships between Mandingo and Fulani, between Fulani and Jolof and between the Mandingo and the peoples of the coast in general.

Political and administrative organization

In the final analysis, this vast empire was a kind of confederation, with each province retaining a large degree of autonomy. As we have seen, the

Niani says that the Keita conquered land up to Kado Kuru, the mountains of Dogon. These victories are attributed to Sere Nandiugu, a seventeenth-century king, which is plausible, since by then the Niani chief no longer ruled the whole Malinke country; the empire had disintegrated.

81. See M. Griaule, 1938 and 1966; Cissoko, 1968; J. Rouch, 1953; R. M. A. Bedaux, 1972 and 1974; L. Desplagnes, 1907.

82. The Dogon are called Habe by the Fulani and Cado by the Malinke. Mandingo traditions say the Dogon came from Mande, but this remains to be proved.

83. R. M. A. Bedaux, 1977, pp. 87 and 92.

PLATE 6.8 *Pégué: a view of Tellem cave P; granaries of unfired brick (phase 3 Tellem, 12th–14th century)*

PLATE 6.9 *Pégué: a Tellem cup with four legs supported on base, from cave D (phase 2 Tellem, 11th–12th century)*

PLATE 6.10 *Pégué: a Tellem cotton tunic found in cave C (phase 2 Tellem, 11th–12th century)*

vassal kingdoms such as Ghana and Mema were linked to the central authority only by a rather symbolic allegiance.

The central power

The mansa was the head of government and the fount of all power; he was surrounded by high administrators and dignitaries, chosen from among the descendants of Sundiata's companions. In Mande itself the village or *dugu* was the basis of the political structure; in general, villages were inhabited by descendants of a common ancestor. A number of villages under the authority of a chief formed a province or *kafu* (*jamana*). Initially, the king of Mande was a chief among other chiefs; it was the unification of the provinces of Do, Kiri and Banko which made the Keita chief a powerful king. Through the conquests of Sundiata and his successors, the king of Mande became mansa or emperor, having a number of kings under him.

The descendants of Sundiata's generals, a military aristocracy surrounding the mansa, formed a council whose advice was important in the sovereign's decisions. The *griot* was a very important person; Ibn Baṭṭūṭa describes his functions in the court of Mansa Sulaymān. We know that the role was hereditary: the mansa's *griot* was always chosen from the Kouyate clan, descended from Balla Fasseke, Sundiata's *griot*. The *griot* was first and foremost the emperor's spokesman, 'for the latter speaks softly and the *griot* repeats his words loudly'. Couriers left Niani daily on horseback, and those who arrived from the provinces reported to the *griot*. He was the tutor of princes; it was he who conducted ceremonies and directed the court musicians.[84] In the fourteenth century, after the reign of Mansa Mūsā, the monarch had a staff of secretaries, but they were used only when the mansa sent messages to sultans or received communications. The rest of the time, messages were transmitted or received orally.

The emperor liked to play the role of 'father of his people', dispensing justice himself in solemn sessions; he listened personally to the grievances of his subjects against the governor or farin who represented him in each province. He decided lawsuits between individuals according to the country's laws.[85] Thus, despite all the outward forms of a Muslim court, the mansa remained the patriarch, the father, to whom anyone seeking justice could come. In the provinces, justice was rendered according to Koranic law by *ḳāḍī*s that he had chosen.

Officials

Apart from the *griot*, whose important role has been described by Ibn Baṭṭūṭa, we have little information on the other agents of the central power. The same author says that the mansa's second-in-command was a lieu-

84. Ibn Baṭṭūṭa, loc. cit., pp. 303–5.

85. Peasants walked many kilometres to complain about governors' exactions. The mansa decided that if the governor was at fault, he was to be recalled. ibid., pp. 303–9; al-'Umarī, loc. cit., pp. 57–8.

tenant-general, whose functions are not specified, although he seems to have been chief of the armed forces.[86]

The *santigui* (master of the treasury) was a kind of finance minister. Originally he was the guardian of the royal granaries. With the diversification of sources of revenue, he took charge of deposits of gold and other riches such as ivory, copper and precious stones. Earlier, these duties had been carried out by one of the mansa's slaves. We know from oral tradition that all trade clans were represented before the mansa by chiefs who received his orders and transmitted them to their members: thus the chief of the smiths, the boatmen or the fishermen was in reality the representative of a craft guild.

Provincial government

The empire consisted of provinces and vassal kingdoms. At the head of each province there was a governor (or farin). At its height, in the fourteenth century, the empire had twelve provinces.[87] The most important are listed below. Takrūr, situated along the middle and lower Senegal, was in fact a kingdom conquered by arms, and had many trading centres, such as Sylla and the eponymous town of Takrūr. Bambugu was famous for its gold-mines and almost entirely inhabited by Malinke. Zaga or Dia, the country of Diafunu, was situated in the valley of the middle Niger. Gao or Songhay was a kingdom which had been conquered by the successors to Mari Diata, but had shaken off the Mandingo yoke by the end of the fourteenth century, and whose capital, also called Gao, was in the fourteenth century a flourishing metropolis. Sanagana, mentioned by al-ʿUmarī, was the nomad territory of the Sanagana and Godala (now Mauretania). Finally, there were the kingdoms of Ghana and Mema, Sundiata's earliest allies. Mande, the seat of the capital, was directly under the mansa.

Each province had subdivisions, which were occasionally clan units. The provincial government was a small-scale model of the central government; the farin was surrounded by dignitaries and eminent persons, whose habits and customs he respected. The subdivision was made up of village communities grouped under the authority of a local traditional chief (*dugu-tigi*).

86. ibid., p. 304. See also Chapter 8 below. It does seem as if the Songhay were inspired by Mali's administrative structures. There were a number of ministries at Gao whose origins date from the time of Mali. Among them were the minister of finance, or *khalisse farma*, and the minister of whites (foreigners) or *korei farma*. The *kanfari* or *balama* was a kind of viceroy or inspector general of the empire. The *wanei farma* of the Songhay (head of sanitation) was the equivalent of the *santigui* of the Malinke. The *sao farma* was the Mandingo *tu tigui* or master of the forests. In Mali, the chief smith fulfilled the functions formerly held by a prince of the blood. The Songhay *hari farma* was the *dji tigui* of the Malinke or master of the waters (*somono* or *bozo*).

87. Al-ʿUmarī, loc. cit. Some of the provinces he mentions have not been identified, perhaps because the names were corrupt forms.

PLATE 6.11 *Mali empire: a group of horsemen, found in the Bamako region (probably 14th–15th century)*

PLATE 6.12 *Mali empire: statue of a horseman, found in the Bamako region (thermoluminescent dating: 680 ± 105 years before 1979; 1194–1404)*

This flexible provincial organization incorporating local leaders gave Mali considerable stability. The security of goods and of persons was guaranteed by effective policies and an army that long remained invincible.

The army

We do not know much about the number of soldiers in the army; Arab sources usually mention the figure of 100 000 men, but this indicates only an order of magnitude. The strength of the army lay in the warlike nature and sense of discipline of the Mandingo, who were the army's most important element. Garrisons were located in the principal cities of the empire, such as Walata, Gao, Timbuktu and Niani. The mansa's authority was effective as far as Teghazza; the respect that Mali inspired among the princes of the Maghrib can be measured by their pleas for help from Mansa Mūsā in recovering their thrones.[88]

The aristocracy or 'nobility of the quiver' were soldiers by choice. The cavalry was made up of *ton-tigui* or quiver-bearers; from Sundiata's time, it was an élite corps. For the most part, the horses came from Takrūr or Jolof, but horse-breeding prospered in the Niger valley. A Mandingo cavalryman would be armed with long spears and sabres in addition to his bow and arrows.[89] As an élite corps, the cavalry was directly under the orders of the mansa. The infantry was commanded by the minor nobility. They were armed with lances or quivers according to the area from which they came: Mande soldiers usually had bows and arrows; those from the Sahara carried skin shields and fought with lances. At its zenith, the empire does not seem to have had slave battalions; these appeared only later in the Mali army. Each province provided a contingent of freedmen; the existence of garrisons in the cities and numerous troops along the sensitive frontiers, such as the Sahel–Sahara, guaranteed the empire for many years against uprisings or the incursions of neighbours.

Economic life

Agriculture

The empire of the mansas was known abroad for its riches in gold; but the economy was essentially based on agriculture and cattle-rearing, which occupied the majority of the population. A number of Mandingo songs glorify agricultural life. Nobles did not disdain working in the fields. After war, farming was the ordinary occupation of freedmen. Hunting was closely linked to farming. These two activities were the only ones that a noble could undertake without loss of status. We do not know the details of rural activities; nevertheless Portuguese navigators' records of the four-

88. Ibn Khaldūn, loc. cit., p. 347; I. B. Kaké, 1980, pp. 46–51.
89. Kaké, 1980; al-ʿUmarī, loc. cit., pp. 57–9.

teenth century reveal that there was no shortage of foodstuffs. Rice was grown in the valleys of the Niger and Sankarani, in Senegambia and in Kaabu.[90] Millet, which grows best in dry terrain, was the main product of the Sahel, which received two or three months of rain. Beans and other vegetables were also grown. Ibn Baṭṭūṭa emphasizes the abundant supplies of food in Mali: the cost of living was low and travellers did not have to carry provisions, because they would find abundant food in each village.[91]

Thanks to this agricultural wealth, the mansa was able to maintain a large army and play the role of 'father of his people', offering them frequent feasts. At each harvest, a contribution, even if it was only symbolic, had to be given to the mansa or his representative: rejection of the authority of the mansa was demonstrated by a refusal to give the first fruits. In Mande, it was a tradition to give the chief the first yams of the season as a mark of respect; yam thieves were severely punished by the mansa. Cotton growing was widespread throughout the empire by the end of the fifteenth century; Portuguese sailors described the Casamance as rich in cotton, which was traded for iron.

Animal-rearing and fishing

Animal-rearing was the speciality of peoples of the Sahel such as the Fulani, but by the fourteenth century most of the Niger valley peasants were raising cattle, sheep and goats. By that period a number of Fulani groups had settled in Jolof, Takrūr and Mande, drawn by the rich pastures of the valley.

Fishing was the profession of very specialized groups, such as the Somono of the upper Niger, the Bozo on the middle Niger and the Sorko between Timbuktu and Gao in Songhay country. Smoked or dried fish were packed in large baskets for sale throughout the empire to the borders of the southern forest. It is not very long since fish from Mopti (the town which has replaced Jenne) were eaten in modern Ghana, in the Ivory Coast and Upper Volta.[92]

Craftsmen

Crafts were practised by certain clans. Iron-working was the business of the smiths. Iron was abundant in the Mandingo mountains as well as in the Niani region. The smiths manufactured farm implements (*daba*, sickles) and weapons.[93] The mansa had great forges at Niani. Skins and leather, handled by the shoemaker clans, were a rich resource which the countries to the north imported in large quantities. Goldsmiths were greatly

90. V. Fernandes, French transl. 1951.
91. Al-ʿUmarī, loc. cit. Yams store well and can be eaten through the winter.
92. See Chapter 8 below. The fees levied on fishermen and peasants were fixed by custom and paid by each family. They suggest serfdom rather than slavery.
93. Filipowiak, 1970. All around the Niani area, archaeologists have located iron-mines. The ore is of good quality.

PLATE 6.13 *Mali empire: statuette of a bearded figure, made from terracotta (thermoluminescent dating: 860 ± 180 years before 1979; 939–1299)*

PLATE 6.14 *Mali empire: terracotta statuette of mother and child (thermoluminescent dating: 690 ± before 1979; 1184–1394)*

PLATE 6.15 *Mali empire: coiled serpent in terracotta (thermoluminescent dating: 420 ± 65 years before 1979; 1494–1624)*

PLATE 6.16 *Mali empire: terracotta statuette of kneeling figure, from Bankoni region (thermo-luminescent dating: 1396–1586)*

honoured. Gold was worked in Mande by smiths called Siaki, who lived in the great urban centres. In Takrūr and Jolof the forging of precious metals was a tradition dating back the the *kaya maghan*. The craftsmen of these regions were among the most famous in West Africa.

Weaving also flourished; there was considerable trade among the provinces of the empire in rolls of cotton, which were exported to the peoples in the south. Cloth dyed with indigo quickly became a speciality of the Takrūr and Soninke peoples. A special clan, the Mabo, handled weaving and dyeing in Takrūr.

Craftsmen married within their clan. During the time of the mansas, the clans certainly had duties, but they also had carefully defined rights. Neither the emperor nor the nobles – and certainly not mere freedmen – could ask for more than was fixed by custom.

Trade

Gold, salt, copper and kola nuts were extremely important to Mali's economy. Mali had many gold-mines, which made it the largest producer of precious metals in the ancient world. Gold was mined in Bure, the province bordering Mande, whose people were occupied solely in mining the yellow metal. Bambuk, Galam on the upper Senegal river and the area around Niani also produced gold (see Fig. 6.10). As in the time of the *kaya maghan*, the mansa had an exclusive right to gold nuggets.[94] Mali also got gold from the forest regions to the south. Begho, in Bron land (present-day Ghana), was a major centre for trade in kola nuts, gold and copper.[95] Salt extracted at Teghazza and Ijil was retailed by the Dioula throughout the empire; the coastal regions of Senegambia produced sea-salt, but this did not reach the interior. Takedda was then a great centre for the production and sale of copper; cast in strips, the metal was exported to the south, whose people valued it more highly than gold. We now know that this copper was sold not only to the Akan, but also in the cultural region of Benin-Ife/Igbo-Ukwu.[96] Mali imported kola nuts from the countries to the south; the Soninke and Malinke specialized in this trade and thus came into contact with many of the forest people, including the Akan and the Guru (peoples who today inhabit Ghana and the Ivory Coast), who called them *dioula* or *wangara* (traders).[97]

As they searched for kola nuts and gold, the Mandingo built staging posts along the roads leading from the banks of the Niger to Kong (now in

94. Al-ʿUmarī, loc. cit.

95. M. Posnansky, 1974. It would be hazardous to venture an estimate of the quantities of gold sent annually to the countries of the north. Nevertheless, demand was very high in the fourteenth century all round the Mediterranean, with the adoption of the gold standard by the merchant cities such as Marseilles and Genoa.

96. See Chapters 11 and 25 below, for the trans-Saharan trade and commerce between the savannah and the forest.

97. For trade in kola nuts in the forest region, see J. Zunon Gnobo, 1976.

the Ivory Coast) and Begho (now in the Republic of Ghana). They propagated Islam and their Mandingo culture far to the south.[98] According to Hausa traditions, Islam was introduced into the central Sudan by the Wangara in the fourteenth century.[99] The Dioula or Wangara sent caravans of donkeys towards the forest, laden with salt, cotton goods and copper objects; they also used pedlars. Thus Valentim Fernandes reported that some Wangara from Jenne had up to 200 slaves transporting salt to southern countries in exchange for their gold.[100] This tradition and their keen business sense still characterizes the Mandingo today; they remain the moving spirits in West African trade.

98. The movement of the Mandingo towards the south accelerated at the end of the fifteenth century, when Mali lost its eastern provinces in the Niger Bend.

99. See Chapters 11 and 25 below.

100. V. Fernandes, French transl. 1938, pp. 85–6; see also Chapter 25 below.

7 The decline of the Mali empire

M. LY-TALL

Introduction

After the fourteenth century, dominated by the spectacular figure of Mansa Kanku Mūsā, Mali underwent a long period of decline. The fifteenth and sixteenth centuries were marked by a shift of the empire's centre of interest towards the west. Mali's trade, which had hitherto been with the Arab world, turned partially towards the coast, while the Muslim trading monopoly remained intact for other countries south of the Sahara, such as Songhay and Kanem. The markets of Sutuco and Jagrancura on the River Gambia replaced the markets of Jenne and Timbuktu, which had passed under Songhay control. It is therefore understandable that Arab sources do not tell us much about this period. Ibn Khaldūn, the principal source for the chronology of the Mali mansas, keeps us informed up to the end of the fourteenth century.[1] After him, more than a century passed before Leo Africanus' *Africae Descriptio* provided the last important Arab evidence on the Mali empire.[2]

The growing importance of the West can be explained by the Portuguese presence following the capture of Ceuta in 1415; the Arab Berbers were not the only ones to trade with West Africa. European sources, especially Portuguese travel accounts, took over from the Arabic sources and contain valuable information about the western provinces of Mali, especially Gambia and Casamance. The accounts of Ca da Mosto and Diogo Gomes, who went up the River Gambia in 1455 and 1456 respectively, are complementary.[3] For the early sixteenth century we have two pieces of evidence of nearly the same date, the *Esmeraldo de Situ Orbis* of Duarte Pacheco Pereira (1505–6) and the valuable account of Valentim Fernandes (1506–7).[4]

1. Ibn Khaldūn completed the bulk of the work on his *Kitāb al-Ibar* in 1393–4, although he was constantly revising it up to his death in 1406.

2. Leo Africanus, as he was known to Europe, or al-Hassan b. Muḥammad al-Wuzza'n (*c.* 1494–1552), does not seem to have actually visited all the countries he mentions; there are a number of clues that urge caution.

3. A. da Ca da Mosto, French transl. 1895; D. Gomes, French transl. 1959.

4. D. Pacheco Pereira, French transl. 1956; V. Fernandes, French transl. 1951.

But the most important source, which shows us the last flickers of power and the renown of Mali even in the last quarter of the sixteenth century, is the *Tratado Breve dos Rios de Guiné* by André Alvares d'Almada, a Portuguese born in Africa on the island of Santiago do Cabo-Verde, who often went to the coast of Guinea on business.

Alongside these written documents, Arabic and European, we have the oral traditions, which often give us valuable information despite the lapse of time. The Sudanese chronicles of the mid-seventeenth century, the *Ta'rīkh al-Sūdān* and the *Ta'rīkh al-fattāsh*, in spite of their authors' lack of impartiality, are extremely useful for knowledge of Mali after its break-up. As far as Mali's relations with Songhay are concerned, the chronicles are supplemented by all the Mandingo traditions from the Republic of Guinea, Mali and the Gambia. The traditions of the Siguiri region have a good deal to say about Niani Mansa Mamuru, who is identified with Mansa Muḥammad IV by Yves Person.[5] To the west, the traditions of the western Mandingo are particularly important because of the special economic role of the province of Gambia in the Mandingo empire in the fifteenth and sixteenth centuries. No less important are the traditions of the Mandingo kingdom of Kaabu or Gabu. The Fulani traditions of Futa Toro and Futa Jallon also shed a great deal of light on relations between the Mandingo empire and the Fulani state of Futa Toro. By using as yet unexploited Portuguese sources and by investigating the traditions more thoroughly, we can approach the history of the Mandingo empire in the fifteenth and sixteenth centuries from a new angle.

From the fourteenth century, Mali's relations with North Africa were strengthened as a consequence of Mansa Kanku Mūsā's celebrated pilgrimage to Mecca. There ensued an intense development both of the economy and of culture, a development which carried the influence of Mali well beyond its frontiers. But the customs of the country were somewhat disrupted by the massive introduction of Islamic culture. So long as energetic mansas like Kanku Mūsā or Sulaymañ were at the head of the empire, all went well. But with their successors, men of lesser parts, intrigues multiplied at the Mali court. The fourteenth century, when Mali attained the peak of its power, ended in a weakening of the central authority. Meanwhile a new power was developing along the lower Niger, which was to supplant the power of Mali in all its northern provinces: Songhay.

The Mali empire loses control of trans-Saharan trade

It was the Tuareg and the Berbers, before Sunni 'Alī and the Songhay troops, who struck the first blows at the Mandingo empire.

5. Y. Person, 1970. The first Muḥammad reigned from 1305 to 1310; the mansa who attacked Jenne in 1599 was the fourth of that name.

The Tuareg and the Berbers

At the pinnacle of its power in the fourteenth century, the Mandingo empire had various Berber groups under its rule. Some of these, such as the Kel Antessar, the Yantara, the Meddusa and the Lemtuna, had already begun to live a sedentary life as part of Mandingo society and to pay tribute to the mansa; others, however, living as nomads in the Aīr and the Adrar des Iforhas, were more rebellious. Their submission was effective only under certain mansas like Kanku Mūsā and Sulaymān. At the death of Mansa Mūsā II, about 1387, a period of crises over the succession began in Mande. The descendants of Sundiata – the senior branch of the royal family – tried to regain the power which since Kanku Mūsā had been held by the junior branch, the descendants of Sundiata's younger brother, Mande Bory.

These struggles for the succession, with two mansas assassinated in three years, greatly weakened the royal power and the central authority, especially in the Sahel regions. From the fifteenth century on, the Tuareg made many forays against the town of Timbuktu, which they captured around 1433, along with most of the Sahel cities, including Walata, Nema and possibly even Gao.

By thus depriving Mali of its former northern provinces, the southward drive of the Tuareg reinforced their role and position in trans-Saharan trade. But their military predominance did not last long. The emergence of the state of Songhay under Sunni ʿAlī was a decisive set-back for the Tuareg and explains the later ideological struggles between Sunni ʿAlī and the Timbuktu aristocracy of scholars and *ʿulamā*' who came for the most part from the Berber town of Walata.

The principal result of these Tuareg military activities and the supremacy of Songhay was a threat of economic suffocation. But the development of Atlantic trade following the arrival of the Portuguese provided a breathing space. The western provinces, which had hitherto seen the hinterland in the dominant role, found their commercial importance growing.

The western Mali provinces

There had been a fruitless attempt to sail the Atlantic under Mansa Abū Bakr, the predecessor of Mansa Kanku Mūsā;[6] but despite this the provinces of Senegambia and the ocean itself had played only a marginal role in the geopolitical and commercial orientation of Mali before the Portuguese discoveries. From the fifteenth century onwards, however, the sovereigns of Portugal and Mali established diplomatic relations, and commercial links were close.

Trade

The mansas of Mali remained in control of the Bure gold-mines; in addition, Wangara traders went in search of gold as far afield as Asante. Caravans

6. See Chapter 26 below.

PLATE 7.1 *The Kama-blon of Kangaba (septennial ceremonies hut), a general view*

PLATE 7.2 *The Kama-blon of Kangaba, façade*

PLATE 7.3 *View of Kamalia (south-west of Kangaba, Mali), from Mungo Park's* Travels in the Interior Districts of Africa (*1799*)

came periodically to the coast to exchange gold for copper, black and blue cotton cloth, linen, fabrics from India, red yarn, and even garments ornamented with gold and silver. It often happened that the Wangara had more gold than the value of the merchandise brought by the caravels, and returned with the remainder. They were in fact very shrewd dealers, who had weights and balances and were therefore no longer content with vague estimates. They thus succeeded in making the maximum profit from their gold.[7]

Very early on, the Europeans made use of the possibilities of exchange between various regions. They bought horses in Futa, which they sold in Gambia. The trade in horses, by strengthening the Mandingo armies, brought about the development of another trade, that in slaves. With the growing demand for horses by the kings of Jolof and the Mali governors of Gambia, the Portuguese, who were settling increasing numbers of

7. D. Pacheco Pereira, French transl. 1956, pp. 69 and 73; A. Alvares d'Almada, French transl. 1842, pp. 26, 27, 29, 30 and 43.

Negroes in Portugal, acquired the habit of exchanging horses for slaves (to begin with, one horse for eight slaves, but soon it was one for fifteen). Trade relations rapidly began to deteriorate, to the detriment of the Africans.

Trade thrived in the western provinces of the Mali empire until the end of the sixteenth century. Even in 1594, the Portuguese André Alvares d'Almada wrote that 'it is in Gambia that there is the largest volume of trade in all Guinea'; and Gambia was then still a province of Mali.[8] But trade provided an occupation for only one specialized group of the population, the Wangara. The great majority of people were peasants and animal rearers.

Agriculture and animal-rearing

The western provinces of Mali, well watered by rain and rivers, were an attractive sight in the rainy season, with their fine fields of cotton and rice, especially along the banks of the Gambia.[9] This majestic river becomes swollen with the abundant rainfall it receives throughout its length and deposits rich alluvial soil on its banks. Its floods at that time were so extensive that sometimes ships coming upriver were swept from the river bed and ended up among the trees.[10] The galleries of forests along its banks teemed with game, while further inland, where the trees were sparser, lived great herds of elephants, whose tusks supplied the ivory trade. Like the eastern Mandingo, those of the west were keen hunters, and hunting was inseparable from religion, since to win a reputation as a hunter one had to know the forest well, and this was associated with magic. In the western provinces, which were very damp, animal-rearing was linked with agriculture; the peasants were both herdsmen and cultivators. There were more and more Fulani shepherds in Gambia, who tended to settle down around the abundant pastures. Fulani communities became organized and began to play a political role towards the end of the fifteenth century, as we shall see. The role of animal-rearing was not negligible, but trade in skins developed much later.

Society and its customs

The family was based on matrilineal descent. As with the Soninke in Ghana, children belonged to their mother's lineage. In the political sphere, this meant matrilineal succession. For example, the chief of all Gambia, Farin Sangoli, was represented by one of his nephews at Niumi, near the mouth of the Gambia. Among the western Mandingo, according to Alvares d'Almada, several of the attributes of the mansas were linked to the royal blood, which explains why a nephew was chosen in order to preclude any

8. Alvares d'Almada, loc. cit., p. 35.
9. G. E. de Zurara, French transl. 1960, p. 346; A. da Ca da Mosto, French transl. 1895, p. 70.
10. Alvares d'Almada, loc. cit., p. 33.

mistake. The same explanation is given by al-Bakrī for matrilineal succession in Ghana.[11] Once he had been nominated by the Council of Ancients, the new farin was required, in regions such as Casamance, to purify himself by withdrawing for one year, during which the country was governed by regents. These were frequently generals of the preceding farin, but at least one was required to be a member of the royal family.[12] This obviously opened the door to political intrigue.

Another characteristic of the western Mandingo was to be found in their religious beliefs. They were deeply animistic[13] In lawsuits the charges always related to sorcery. Nearly all cases of illness were put down to this practice. The accused person was brought before the farin, who relied for proof solely on what was known as 'the red water judgement'. The two parties were given water to drink, coloured red with *cailcedra* roots; the one who vomited first won the lawsuit; the loser, thus recognized as a sorcerer, was either thrown to wild animals or taken into captivity, with all his family.[14] For the chiefs, this was obviously a very economical method of obtaining slaves.

It was among the chiefs that the greatest number of Muslims were to be found, but in most cases religion was only a veneer. For example, in Casamance, before embarking on a war, the Muslim mansa was in the habit of making the imam consult the soothsayers.[15] Also in Casamance, the Muslim chief made offerings to the dead; he never drank wine or *dolo* without pouring out some drops on the ground as a libation to the dead. In the fields, stakes daubed with rice and maize flour mixed with goat's or heifer's blood were supposed to ensure good harvests. Agrarian cults remained powerful. In the interior, on the Casamance and Rio Grande rivers, the Mandingo kingdom of Kaabu was fiercely attached to traditional religion in the fifteenth century. The king still depended on the central authority of Niani, but he had already subordinated almost all the Mandingo provinces. Kaabu traditions call the king 'Kaaba Mansaba' (the great king of Kaabu), but in Portuguese texts he was 'Farin Gabo'.[16]

Nevertheless, Islam made considerable progress in these regions, particularly in the sixteenth century.[17] Itinerant marabouts were to be found throughout the coastal regions, forbidding the eating of pork and distributing amulets. As in the fourteenth century, it was the chiefs in particular that the marabouts tried to convert, for once the chief had been converted his subjects followed, at least in name. However, this conversion was so

11. Al-Bakrī, French transl. 1965.
12. Alvares d'Almada, loc. cit., pp. 42 and 80.
13. Ca da Mosto, loc. cit., p. 40.
14. Alvares d'Almada, loc. cit., p. 40.
15. ibid., p. 39.
16. A. Donelha, Eng. transl. 1977.
17. This was probably related to changes in traditional religion; in Futa, the beliefs of the Hal Pulaar replaced those of the Denianke Fulani.

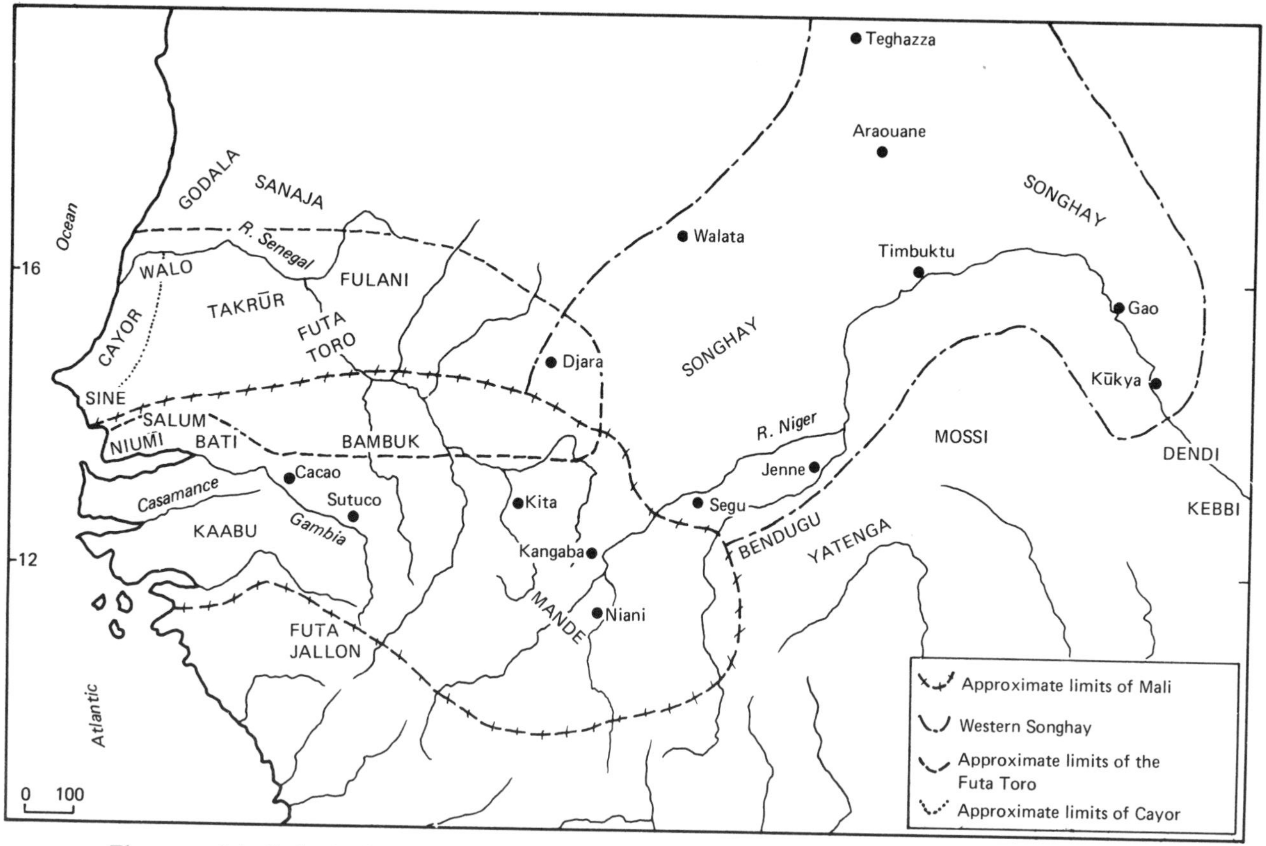

FIG. 7.1 *The states of the Sudan in the 16th century (after J. Bazin)*

superficial that the same chiefs had no hesitation in abandoning their new religion for Christianity at the first opportunity.[18]

Thus we see that western Mandingo society was faced with new realities, namely penetration by Muslim and even Christian culture. These outside influences necessarily disturbed the traditional equilibrium. But the most serious danger lay elsewhere, and was primarily military. While the peaceful Mandingo peoples thought of nothing but furthering the prosperity of their trade and agriculture, a formidable power was arising in the north, that of the 'Great Ful'.[19]

The emergence of the Fulani: the threat to Mali's western provinces

The Tengella family: 1490–1512

Ever since the thirteenth century the Fulani, who lived as nomads in Termes, had been infiltrating southwards, first in Futa Toro and thence towards the great *bourgo* reaches of Macina and the grassy plateaux of Futa Jallon. Starting as dependants of local chiefs, in the end they imposed themselves on the autochthonous populations and founded powerful states (see Fig. 7.1). This was how the Fulani state of Futa Toro was set up under the leadership of Tengella, whose son, Koly, is better known.

Koly Tengella is one of the African characters whose history has passed into the realm of legend. The Futa Toro traditions make him a son of Sundiata, and Tengella merely his adoptive father. This filiation can only be regarded as an attempt by legend to join these two great figures of West African medieval history. At the very most one may suppose, as some have done, that Koly had Mandingo blood.[20]

Under the leadership of Tengella and Koly, the Denianke (or Denian Kobe) Fulani invaded all of Senegambia. The route they followed is still debated. Some hold that they started from Futa Toro and went towards Futa Jallon.[21] Others claim that they went in the reverse direction.[22] In either case they must have come into confrontation with the Mandingo.[23]

The wars between the Denianke and the mansa of Mali are not precisely dated. They took place between 1481 and 1514. The Fulani armies were vividly remembered in the country's traditions. Nearly a century later,

18. See the spectacular conversion of the Mansa of Niumi in D. Gomes, French transl. 1959, pp. 42–4; see also Alvares d'Almada, loc. cit., p. 25.

19. The name given to the chief of the Denianke Fulani.

20. J. Boulègue, 1968, p. 186.

21. This is the theory of Delafosse, revised and corrected as far as dates are concerned by A. Teixeira da Mota.

22. Boulègue, op. cit., sets out the grounds for this view.

23. Perhaps the Ba-Keita connection between the two clans (Fulani and Mandingo) was established with reference to Koly Tengella's genealogy.

André Alvares d'Almada was told what great numbers of horsemen and camel-riders they had had, to say nothing of the herds of cattle that accompanied them. Koly not only conquered Futa but settled there, attracted by the fertility of the country.

Mali authority, hitherto exercised mainly in the foothills of Futa Jallon, now began to recede. Mali's lines of communication with the western provinces were falling back northwards, towards Gambia and Casamance.[24] In the late fifteenth and early sixteenth centuries, therefore, we have a narrowing of the corridor linking eastern and western Mali. Mandingo traders sent by the Mali mansa to sell gold at the Sutuco market in Gambia were no longer safe. They had to make many detours, so that their journey sometimes took six months.[25]

The armies of Koly and his father, swelled by reinforcements from all the Fulani settlements (especially in Macina), swept towards Bundu and from there towards Futa Toro.[26] They crossed the River Gambia at a place which was to be known, on that account, as 'Fulani Ford'. To give an idea of their number, the tradition says that to fill up the river, 5 km (or 1 league) wide, each soldier needed only to carry one single stone. After Bundu, father and son separated; Tengella headed towards the kingdom of Zara, while Koly began the conquest of Futa Toro.

The conquest of the kingdom of Zara (Diara)

We have seen that in the first two years of the sixteenth century the kingdom of Zara (Diara or Sankara) had fallen into the hands of the Songhay. Hastening to the aid of his brother 'Umar Komdiāgho, who was in difficulties in the Mandingo kingdom of Zara, Askiya Muḥammad conquered the mansa's local representative. He remained in the region for a long time to 'pacify' and organize it on a new basis.[27]

But peace was short-lived, for Fulani armies, already on the move, soon erupted into the Zara kingdom. The askiya's brother had to launch another campaign, which was more successful than that against the Mandingo. Tengella was vanquished and killed – in 1511–12 according to the *Ta'rīkh al-Sūdan*;[28] in 1512–13 according to the *Ta'rīkh al-fattāsh*.[29] The Songhay had shown once again how badly they wanted the kingdom of Zara, which would allow them to keep an eye on the Bambuku mines. Koly did not persist there, but went on towards the Futa Toro.[30]

24. Person, op. cit., p. 287.
25. Alvares d'Almada, loc. cit., pp. 30–1.
26. Boulègue, op. cit., pp. 186–9.
27. Al-Sa'dī, French transl. 1964, pp. 124–5.
28. ibid., p. 127.
29. Maḥmūd Ka'ti, French transl. 1964, p. 127.
30. Al-Sa'dī, loc. cit., p. 127.

The conquest of Futa Toro and Jolof

Futa was still marked by the Mandingo administration. The different farins who had had to submit to the king of Zara when he was under the authority of the Mali mansa became more or less emancipated when Zara was annexed by the Songhay. Koly had to fight against small local chiefs divided among themselves, which enormously simplified his task. He established his capital at Anyam-Godo. From there he led various attacks against the Jolof empire, several territories of which he conquered. According to traditions collected by Raffenel in 1846, he 'soon became the terror of all the neighbouring peoples and especially of the Jolof, whom he routed in several battles. The fine lands which he took under occupation were added to his conquests over the Moors; thenceforth the Jolof owned only the lands to the south, far removed from the river and its tributaries.'[31] The sovereignty of Futa over Jolof lasted until the first half of the eighteenth century.

Mali, then, was gradually stripped of its western possessions by the man whom the Portuguese vaguely designated as the 'Great Ful' – that is, the Silatigui of Futa. Nevertheless, the authority of the mansa of Mali held good from Gambia to Casamance until the end of the sixteenth century, as emerges from the testimony of André Alvares d'Almada. The mansa was known and obeyed more than 1500 km (300 leagues) from Sutuco, and passed into popular legend as the ruler of all the blacks. The inhabitants of El Mina called him 'the great elephant', but this was an elephant already stricken by old age.

The end of the Mali empire

The old empire, under attack from the east and from the west, had to face another threat which was no less dangerous for being veiled: Portuguese interference in the political life of West Africa.

Mali and the Portuguese: Mansa Maḥmūd II and Mansa Maḥmūd III

After their first, and particularly violent, contacts with black Africa, the Portuguese were forced to change their policy because of the coastal population's firm will to resist. They now settled down to winning the confidence of the local rulers.[32] Many diplomatic missions were sent by the kings of Portugal to their West African counterparts. For instance, between 1481 and 1495, John II sent embassies to the king of Futa, the *koi* of Timbuktu and the mansa of Mali.

31. Translated from A. Raffenel, 1846, pp. 317–18.
32. It was virtually a manhunt. See M. Ly-Tall, 1977, p. 17.

There were two embassies to Mali, which showed what importance the king of Portugal attached to that country. The first one went up the Gambia, the second left from Fort El Mina. The mansa who received them was called Maḥmūd. He was the son of Mansa Ule and the grandson of Mansa Mūsā.[33] Although already struggling with the Denianke Fulani, Mali was still very powerful. In a letter to the king of Portugal, Mansa Maḥmūd II estimated that his might was matched only by that of four sultans – those of Yemen, Baghdad, Cairo and Takrūr.[34] In 1534 Mansa Maḥmūd III received a mission sent by João de Barros, who represented the king of Portugal at Fort El Mina, to negotiate with the Mandingo ruler on various questions concerning trade on the River Gambia.

However, the Portuguese had already begun to meddle in the domestic conflicts of the coastal countries. For instance, around 1482, one Bemoy, a regent on the throne of Jolof, received aid from the king of Portugal against the legitimate heirs. These 'friendship' missions were also sources of information on the internal situation of the old empire. Another Portuguese policy was to give trading advantages to the small coastal chiefs and thus induce them to free themselves from the yoke of the Mande mansa. That was what happened in the kingdom of Salum.

Mali and the kingdom of Salum

Salum was most probably founded by M'Begane N'Dur, king of Sine, in the late fifteenth century, and it expanded greatly in the sixteenth. Towards 1566 it occupied the north of the River Gambia and a large part of Sine. The strength of its administrative and military structures made it one of the most powerful chiefdoms in the province of Gambia. The Portuguese trader, André Alvares d'Almada, was particularly struck by the efficiency of its military organization. Two captains-general, the *jagaraf*s (or *jaraf*), were set over all the village chiefs, or *jagodim*s: 'When the king wishes to raise an army he has only to tell the two *jagaraf*s, who transmit his orders to the *jagodim*s, and each of these assembles his men; so that in a short time he has raised a large army, including many horsemen on mounts purchased from the Fulani and the Moors.'[35]

The kingdom of Salum eventually freed itself from Gambian tutelage and even annexed several of the little riverside chiefdoms of which that kingdom was composed. In the early seventeenth century (1620–4), the Englishman Richard Jobson reported that the kingdom of Gambia was no longer spoken of in those parts.[36] In place of this important province

33. Note the frequency of the names Maḥmūd, Ule and Mūsā. Homonymy was common practice in the Mali royal family.

34. Mansa Maḥmūd II probably yielded to the temptation of slightly exaggerating his power.

35. Translated from Alvares d'Almada, loc. cit., pp. 26 and 28.

36. R. Jobson, 1932 edn.

of Mali there were now three kingdoms: Salum, Wuli and Cantor.[37]

What was left of the old Mali empire had just lost its only remaining window on the outside world. In one last effort in 1599, the mansa of Mali tried to regain his foothold in the central delta of the Niger. It was his swan song.

Mali's last bid: the defeat of Mansa Maḥmūd IV at Jenne, 1599

Mansa Maḥmūd IV tried to take advantage of the troubled situation created in the Niger delta by the Moroccan occupation. Strengthened by the support of most of the local Bambara and Fulani chiefs (the Kala Chaa of the Boka; the Kala or Hamadi Amina of Macina; and the canton chiefs of Farko and Oma), he marched on Jenne. But he was betrayed by the Kala Chaa, who, seeing that his two captains-general, the Zengar Zuma and the Faran Sura, were absent, chose to side with the Moroccans. But for this treason, the mansa of Mali might perhaps have succeeded in retaking Jenne. At all events, when the Moroccan reinforcements reached the city, they were impressed by the army of the Mali emperor, 'whose troops were so many that they stretched to the arm of the river where boats had to pass to reach the city'.[38]

Thanks to the judicious advice of the Kala Chaa, the Moroccans got the better of the Mandingo army after a violent bombardment. But even in defeat the mansa received the honours due to him. The Kala Chaa and the Sorya Muḥammad, 'having met him in a safe place, saluted him as sultan and bared their heads to do him honour, as was their custom'. Mansa Maḥmūd's final attempt at regaining control of the great commercial metropolis of West Africa thus ended in failure. The provinces that were still dependent on the mansa freed themselves one by one. This crumbling away was to give rise to five small kingdoms, according to al-Sa'dī.[39]

It was the Bambara (Bamanan) who profited from the collapse of Mali. Under the mansas, up to the early seventeenth century, they had set up fairly important centres in the kingdom of Zara and the inner Niger delta. Throughout the seventeenth century these were greatly strengthened by immigration, the most important waves of which were led by the two brothers Baramangolo and Niangolo to form the foundation of the Bambara kingdoms of Segu and Kaarta. Mali was reduced to a mere kingdom, Manding, and now included only the regions of Kaabu, Kita, Dioma and Kyumawanya.[40]

37. Boulègue, op. cit., p. 238; Donelha, loc. cit., revealed the existence of the kingdom of Kaabu or Gabu (Farin Gabo). It seems that after 1600 this Mandingo kingdom was the largest part of Senegambia.

38. Al-Sa'dī, loc. cit., p. 279.

39. ibid.; pp. 279 and 21.

40. Person, op. cit., p. 283.

Conclusion

The Mali empire underwent a long period of political decline. Shorn of its northern provinces in the first half of the fifteenth century, to the advantage first of the Tuaregs and then of the Songhay, it remained alongside this new state until the end of the sixteenth century, thanks to the economic strength of its western provinces. The vitality of the Wangara and the Dioula made the fifteenth and sixteenth centuries a period of cultural and commercial influence. The Europeans who visited western Mali have left us a picture of firm political, economic and social structures.

Administratively, the mansa of Mali was represented by a farin with many village chiefs under him – *niumi-mansa*, *bati-mansa*, *casamansa* and so on. In the mid-fifteenth century, the farin was called Sangoli and lived south-east of the village of Batimansa, ten days' journey to the south.[41] Some of these village chiefs were slaves attached to the royal family. Succession was usually matrilineal; thus Diogo Gomes tells us that Frangazik, chief of a village near the mouth of the Gambia, was the nephew of the Farin Sangoli.[42] But in the sixteenth century, with the conversion of certain local mansas to Islam, we find succession from father to son being introduced. Kaabu became a more powerful kingdom from the sixteenth century onward, asserting its independence and dominating the lands of Senegambia.[43]

The farin had a large retinue, including many slaves. To salute him, slaves had to take off their clothes; freed men discarded their weapons and knelt with their faces to the ground. Government officials, or *farba*, scoured the villages to raise taxes, the mansas' main source of revenue.

The area was irrigated by the Rivers Gambia and Casamance and abundantly provided with agricultural produce. All the Portuguese sources for the fifteenth and sixteenth centuries speak of the fine fields of cotton, the vast rice plantations, the lush forests of the kingdoms of Gambia and Casamance. But the most important economic activity was trade. Salt extracted at the mouth of the Gambia was sent to the interior to be traded for gold. Trade gave rise to towns with highly important markets along the Gambia – Sutuco and Jamnam Sura – which were regular stops for Portuguese traders selling horses, wine, Breton cloth, glass trinkets, beads, nails and bracelets. The Mandingo merchants whom they met there impressed them with their experience in trade.[44] Traffic in gold brought high profits, which led to the formation of a caste of rich traders, the Wangara. These precursors of the Dioula played a very important part

41. Ca da Mosto, French transl. 1937, p. 67.

42. Gomes, loc. cit., p. 34.

43. Alvares d'Almada, loc. cit., p. 8; Donelha, loc. cit., pp. 119–20.

44. Alvares d'Almada, loc. cit., p. 29; he says they used scales to weigh their gold and managed the weights 'perfectly'.

in disseminating Mandingo culture, particularly in the forest areas to the south (the present-day Ivory Coast, Ghana and Guinea).

In the fifteenth and sixteenth centuries the influence of Islam in the West remained weak.[45] Diogo Gomes did meet at Niumi Mansa's court a marabout from the western provinces of Mali, but his influence was so slight that the Portuguese traveller had no trouble in converting the mansa to Christianity.[46] It was only from the second half of the sixteenth century onwards that Islam began to penetrate deep into the kingdom of Gambia. Though the chiefs were often Muslim, they nevertheless preserved their animistic beliefs. Kaabu was the bastion of traditional religion in Senegambia. It barred the road to the Muslims, both Fulani and Sarakolle, until the nineteenth century.[47]

With the decline of the gold trade, many Mandingo withdrew towards the south, attracted by the kola trade.[48] The late sixteenth century saw many migrations of the Mandingo towards the south and the south-east, where they formed numerous settlements along the kola routes.[49] It was to these centres that Samory was to turn in the nineteenth century for support in founding his empire.

45. The great majority of the inhabitants of the Gambia were animists: J. Barros, Eng. transl. 1937, p. 70.

46. Gomes, loc. cit., pp. 42–4.

47. Alvares d'Almada, loc. cit., p. 28, S. M. Cissoko and M. Sidibé, papers presented at the Mandingo Conference, London, 1972.

48. There was a decline in the gold trade as the slave trade on the coast intensified.

49. Person, op. cit., p. 284.

8 The Songhay from the 12th to the 16th century

S. M. CISSOKO

After a long evolution lasting nearly 800 years, the Songhay, who had settled on both banks of the middle Niger, established a powerful state in the sixteenth century and unified a large portion of the western Sudan, thus making possible the flowering of a brilliant civilization which had been in the making for centuries. For the sake of greater clarity, we shall divide this evolution into two major periods, attempting to distinguish their main features as far as we are able to discern them in Songhay traditions, in Arab and European sources and especially in the two *Ta'rīkh*s of Timbuktu.[1]

Kingdom of Gao from the twelfth century to the advent of Sunni ʿAlī Ber in 1464

Little is known of the history of the Songhay before the reign of Sunni ʿAlī Ber (1464–92). The few Arab sources which exist concerning this period raise more questions than they answer. The oral traditions give only a very imperfect picture of what life was like in these ancient times. The study of this period will therefore be critical. It will raise more problems than it solves, and even the solutions put forward can be no more than hypotheses for research.

Kingdom of Gao in the twelfth century

By virtue of its geographical situation on the Niger, at the edges of the Sudan and the Sahel, Gao became in the twelfth century the capital of the newly established Songhay state and ended up by eclipsing the old city of Kūkya, or Kūgha as it is called by Arab writers. The salt trade with Tawtek (this place has not been identified), the merchandise brought from Libya,

1. Al-Saʿdī, French transl. 1964; Maḥmūd Kaʿti, French transl. 1964. These two works, written by Sudanese authors about the middle of the seventeenth century, are the fundamental source for the history of the Songhay and the western Sudan for the period under consideration.

Egypt and Ifrīḳiya via Tadmekka and the caravans from Tuat and beyond in the western Maghrib made Gao a great cosmopolitan market.

Arab sources are, nevertheless, not very accurate about the name of the town. Al-Bakrī, who transcribed the name 'Kaw-Kaw', wrote that the town was situated on the Niger.[2] Al-Idrīsī distinguishes the town from Kūgha, which he describes as 'populous and walled', on the north bank, 20 days' march from 'Kaw-Kaw' (Gao-Gao) to the north.[3] What should be noted is the existence, in the twelfth century, of both Gao and Kūkya.

The kingdom, which stretched along both banks of the Niger from Dendi to Gao, was governed by the Dia or Za, probably a Songhay minority who had intermarried with Berbers.[4] In any case, in the eleventh century the Dia bore the Songhay title of *kanta* or *kanda*. The major event was the conversion of the *Dia Kossoi* to Islam in 1019. His example does not appear to have been followed by the Songhay, who long remained faithful to their traditional religious beliefs and practices. The funerary stelae found at Gao-Sane bear Islamic names which differ from those in the *Ta'rīkh*s. For many reasons, they may be thought to have been brought into the region from outside. (See Plates 8.1 and 8.2.)

Mandingo domination and the Sunni dynasty: the thirteenth to the fifteenth century

Possibly about 1275, although more likely between 1285 and 1300,[5] the Mandingo armies conquered the kingdom of Gao. About 1324–5, Mansa Mūsā built a mosque in Gao on his return from a pilgrimage. The Mandingo organized the region of the Niger Bend under the direction of the farin or governors, and encouraged its economic development. Gao became a major commercial centre, one of the finest towns in the Sudan.[6]

Mandingo domination was not unbroken. The Dia of Gao was in point of fact a tributary, who took advantage of the difficulties in Mali to break away from it. It appears in any case that the end of the fourteenth century marked the cessation of Mandingo domination over Gao. A new dynasty, that of the Sunni, established by 'Alī Kolon in the thirteenth century, became independent and ousted the Mandingo.

The origin of this dynasty raises unsolved problems, but Boubou Hama

2. V. Monteil, 1968, p. 79.

3. Al-Idrīsī, French transl. 1866, section 3, pp. 12–14.

4. Al-Sa'dī, loc. cit., ch. 1, gives a legend concerning the origin of the Za or Dia, whose ancestor is said to have come from the Yemen. M. Delafosse, 1912, Vol. 2, thinks that the Dia were Lemṭa Berbers, converted to Christianity, who freed the kingdom of Gao from the marauding Sorko. B. Hama, 1968, considers the Dia to be a minority group of the northern Songhay, of mixed blood, converts to Islam.

5. Monteil, op. cit., clarifies the question through a careful criticism of Delafosse's thesis (op. cit.), which places the Mandingo conquest in 1324–5.

6. Ibn Baṭṭūṭa, French transl. 1966, p. 72.

PLATE 8.1 *Stela no 11 from Gao-Sane (SO 50–59 bis); rectangular quartz stela (height 0.38 m; width 0.28 m). 'This is the tomb of Muḥammad b. al-Gum 'a, God have mercy on him. He died on Friday 6 SHa'ban 496 [15 May 1103].'*

PLATE 8.2 *Stela no 14 from Gao-Sane (SO 50–54): yellow green shale stela (height 0.49 m; width 0.29 m). 'Every living being is perishable and must return unto God. This is the tomb of Hawa [?] daughter of Muḥammad, God have mercy on her. She died in the night of . . . Thursday 12 Ramadan 534 AH [1 May 1140].'*

thinks they came from Kūkya and drove the Mandingo out of Gao.[7] The Sunni, also known as Sii or Shi, were warriors. The last three of the line left Gao and carried the war westwards towards the rich Macina and the empire of Mali. Sunni Madawu, the father of Sunni ʿAlī, embarked on a great raiding expedition against Niani, the capital of the Mandingo empire, and sacked it, carrying off 24 slave tribes belonging to the mansa. His successor, Sunni Sulaymān Daama, in his turn invaded and destroyed Nema, the centre of the Soninke province of the Mali empire, and carried off considerable booty. The wars increased the monarch's scope for action. The king of Gao became the real master of the Niger Bend. The dynasty reached its peak with the accession of Sunni ʿAlī in 1464.

The Songhay empire in the fifteenth and sixteenth centuries

Sunni ʿAlī Ber or Sunni ʿAlī the Great (1464–92)

Sunni ʿAlī Ber changed the fortunes of the kingdom of Gao. He abandoned the raiding policies of his predecessors in favour of territorial conquest.[8] For this, he possessed a seasoned and well-organized army commanded by competent leaders. There was a flotilla on the Niger commanded by the *hi-koi* (the minister for the river and the fleet), a body of foot soldiers whose ranks were continually being swelled by the enlistment of conquered warriors, and above all a force of cavalry, whose great mobility spearheaded the conquests of the great Sunni. Throughout his reign, Sunni ʿAlī Ber patrolled every part of the Niger region at the head of his horsemen, taking his enemies by surprise, disconcerting them by his speed, and imposing his authority by violence and fear. In the minds of his contemporaries, he acquired a reputation of invincibility and was the living incarnation of the spirit of war. He was reputed to be a great magician and seen as an extraordinary and charismatic figure; the people conferred on him the title of *daali*.[9]

Like his predecessors, Sunni ʿAlī was attracted by the rich region of the west and the towns and central delta of the Niger. Step by step, he conquered Jenne – part of the Macina, where he slaughtered a large number of Fulani – and in 1468, most important of all, Timbuktu. He attacked the Tuareg and drove them back into the northern Sahel. In the south, he led several expeditions against the Dogon, the Mossi and the Bariba. In 1483 he encountered the Mossi king, Nasere I, who was returning from Walata laden with valuable booty, and conquered him near Jenne, thus putting a stop for ever to the Mossi threat in the valley of the Niger.

7. B. Hama, op. cit., ch. 3–5.
8. On the Songhay empire, see also A. W. Pardo, 1971, pp. 41–59.
9. Maḥmūd Kaʿti, loc. cit., p. 84, renders *daali* as 'le Très Haut' ('the Most High'), and thinks this title applicable to God.

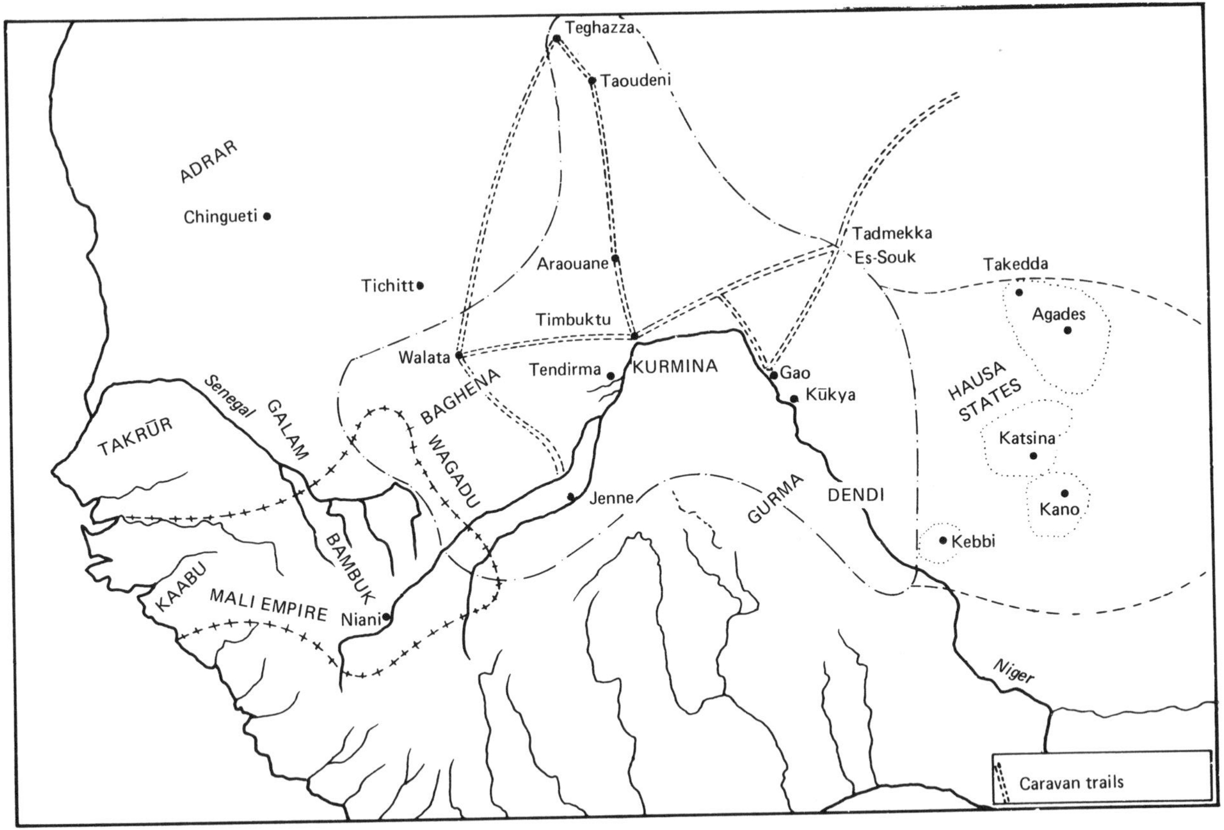

FIG. 8.1 *Songhay empire towards the end of the 16th century (D. T. Niane)*

At the time of his accidental death in 1492, Sunni ʿAlī was the master of a great empire based on the Niger, extending from Dendi to Macina. He organized it on the Mandingo pattern. He established new provinces which he entrusted to rulers called farin or *farma* in Mandingo and *koi* or *mondzo* in Songhay.[10] He appointed a *ḳāḍī* in Timbuktu and probably in other Islamic cities. All these agents in the east were directly responsible to Sunni. The patriarchal and customary state of Gao thus became a centralized state which controlled all the Niger regions. Sunni ʿAlī facilitated the economic development of the new empire. Although he failed in his attempt to dig a canal from the Niger to Walata, he is said to have built dykes in the river valley and encouraged agriculture.

Religious policy

Sunni ʿAlī encountered great difficulties with the Muslim aristocracy, especially in Timbuktu, whose *ʿulamā*ʾ, two centuries later, described him for posterity as a cruel, tyrannical and debauched sovereign. Sunni ʿAlī Ber has now been rehabilitated.[11] The reasons why he opposed the *ʿulamā*ʾ of the empire were political and ideological. He was not a good Muslim and never gave up the traditional religion of Songhay, having been educated in Faru (Sokoto), his mother country. The *ʿulamā*ʾ, for their part, continually criticized Sunni and many of them went over to the Tuareg of Akil Ak Melaul, against whom he was then fighting. Above all, Sunni ʿAlī was the symbol of traditional Songhay culture, confronting the new forces of Islam and the towns.

The dynasty of the askiyas (1492–1592)

Askiya Muḥammad I, the Syllanke[12]

Civil war broke out after the death of Sunni ʿAlī. Sunni Baare refused to become a convert to Islam. An Islamic faction led by the Hombori-Loi Muḥammad and his brother, ʿUmar Komdiāgho, rose in revolt against the new Sunni and overthrew him at Anfao, near Gao. Muḥammad Ture or Sylla seized sovereign power, assuming the title of askiya, and established an Islamic dynasty.

Askiya Muḥammad was of Soninke origin from the Ture or Sylla clan of Takrūr.[13] Although illiterate, he was a fervent Muslim, a balanced, moderate man and a far-sighted politician. His victory was the victory of

10. See pp. 196–202 below, on political and administrative instructions.

11. The defenders of Sunni ʿAlī – Rouch, 1953; Hama, op. cit.; C. A. Diop, 1960; R. Mauny, 1961; S. M. Cissoko, 1966; and other historians – have set right the injustice done to Sunni the Great and have placed his actions in their historical context.

12. Syllanke is a Soninke word meaning 'belonging to the Sylla family'.

13. Both names are given in the *Taʾrīkh*s. Askiya probably came from the Sylla clan. Ture was at that time a religious title, like Cisse, and was adopted by the Moroccan conquerors.

Islam and he drew support from the new forces in order to enlarge and consolidate the empire established by Sunni ʿAlī Ber. The outstanding event of the beginning of his reign was not so much his conquests as his pilgrimage to Mecca.

For reasons of both piety and policy, the new sovereign journeyed to Mecca in 1496–7. He was accompanied by an army of 800 horsemen and numerous *ʿulamāʾ*, and took with him the sum of nearly 300 000 dinars to cover his expenses. In Cairo, he visited one of the pillars of Islam, the grand master of al-Azhar, al-Suyūtī, who gave him advice on government. He purchased a concession in Mecca for pilgrims from the Sudan and obtained from the *sharīf* of Mecca the title and insignia of caliph of the Sudan, and the appointment of an ambassador, Sharīf al-Saklī, who was sent to his empire. He thus returned to the Sudan legitimized in Muslim eyes and with his power universally acknowledged.

Askiya Muḥammad continued the work of Sunni ʿAlī Ber. Assisted by his brother, ʿUmar Komdiāgho, he extended the empire on all frontiers. In 1512 he conquered Macina and Zara, where Tengella was killed, and was succeeded by his son Koly Tengella. Askiya Muḥammad became master of the Sahara as far as the mines of Teghazza and took Agades and the Hausa towns of Katsina and Kano. He unsuccessfully attacked the southern peoples, the Bariba, Mossi and Dogon. By his conquests, he consolidated the Songhay empire and extended it to its furthest limits, from Dendi to Sibiridugu to the south of Segu, and from Teghazza to the frontiers of Yatenga.

Askiya Muḥammad organized the empire in accordance with the tradition inherited from Sunni ʿAlī. He appointed as *Kurmina fari* his brother, ʿUmar Komdiāgho, who built an entirely new capital, Tendirma. He established new provinces, replaced Sunni ʿAlī's officials by men loyal to himself, and appointed *ḳāḍī*s to all the Muslim cities. He reorganized the court and the imperial council, established an order of precedence and protocol, and distributed the palace duties among his various servants. He set the standard for the *ʿulamāʾ* and *ḳāḍī*s at the court.

Askiya Muḥammad was an enlightened sovereign. He took an interest in everything that went on in his empire. He encouraged trade, which greatly enriched the empire. He made efforts to introduce accurate measuring instruments and provide for their inspection, to render prompt justice through the *ḳāḍī*s and to keep business in order by means of a large staff of market inspectors. He is said to have dug a canal in the Kabara–Timbuktu region.[14] He encouraged agriculture by setting up numerous farming settlements for slaves brought back from his wars, and particularly by easing the taxes on produce. He encouraged the advancement of learning by gifts or pensions to the *ʿulamāʾ* and especially by the respect with which

14. Oral tradition recorded in Timbuktu, where the course of a canal running from Kabara towards Timbuktu is still pointed out.

he surrounded them. In short, he established an alliance between church and state which was the foundation of the power of the askiyas. But he had the misfortune to have a large number of children and a long reign. When he was old and blind, he was overthrown by a conspiracy of his sons led by the eldest Mūsa, the *fari mondzo* (minister of lands), who was proclaimed askiya in 1528.

The successors of Askiya Muhammad

The sons of Askiya Muḥammad succeeded each other to the throne until 1583: Mūsā (1528–31), Muḥammad II Benkan Kiriai (1531–7), Ismāʿīl (1537–9), Isḥāḳ I (1539–49) and Dāwūd (1549–83). After this, the sons of Dāwūd took the succession: al-Ḥadj Muḥammad III (1583–6), Muḥammad IV (1586–8), Isḥāḳ II (1588–91) and Muḥammad Gao (1592). They had no more genuine conquests to carry out, but raided the neighbouring countries for booty. At home, the middle Niger was more than once the scene of bloodshed in the course of the struggles for the succession. Abroad, a new problem arose, that of the salt-mines at Teghazza, which was to embitter relations with the sultans of Morocco. We shall examine these problems during three major reigns.

Isḥāḳ I (1539–49) is described in the *Taʾrīkh*s as an authoritarian prince who commanded obedience. His brother Dāwūd led an expedition against the capital of the Mali empire and pillaged it. The problem of Teghazza began in the reign of Isḥāḳ I. The sultan of Morocco, the Saʿdī Muḥammad al-Shaykh, claimed ownership of the salt-mines, but failed in his attempt to occupy them. Isḥāḳ I reacted by organizing an invasion of the Moroccan Darʿa by Tuareg horsemen.[15]

Dāwūd (1549–83), another son of Askiya Muḥammad I, had a long and prosperous reign in which the Songhay empire flourished. The *Taʾrīkh*s describe Askiya Dāwūd as an intelligent prince, very wily, receptive to all and a friend of men of letters. He had held high political office and had been involved in all the problems of his brothers' reigns, which had given him great experience of affairs and men.

The empire reached its apogee in the reign of Askiya Dāwūd. It prospered economically and intellectual pursuits flourished. The river valley was intensively cultivated and the great trading towns were more active than ever. This was the time when the trans-Saharan caravan got the better of the Atlantic caravel, as Godinho puts it.[16] The askiya reaped considerable profit from the general prosperity and even established a treasury of coins obtained from taxes on business and the imperial estates. Into his storehouses poured thousands of tonnes of cereals collected throughout the empire. Dāwūd, like his father, was a great patron of the arts. He respected men of letters, and heaped honours and gifts upon them.

15. Al-Saʿdī, loc. cit., pp. 157–64. Cf. R. Mauny, 1949, pp. 129–40.
16. V. M. Godinho, 1969.

He contributed to the restoration of mosques and to the welfare of the poor.

On the military front the askiya conducted several pacification campaigns in Macina and the east, making fierce raids upon the Mossi. The most serious problem remained that of Teghazza. The sultan of Morocco, Mūlay Aḥmad al-Manṣūr, continued to claim the mines. It appears that a compromise was reached which safeguarded Songhay rights and ownership. Nevertheless, a Moroccan expedition occupied the mines in the reign of Askiya al-Ḥadj Muḥammad III (1583–6). The Tuareg went on to exploit Tenaudara (Taoud'eni), 150 km to the south of Teghazza, which fell into ruins.

On the death of Muḥammad III, his brother Muḥammad IV Bāno was proclaimed askiya in 1586. His accession sparked off a civil war. Several of the askiya's brothers revolted, among them al-Ṣaḍḍuḳ, the *balama* of the Timbuktu region. Al-Ṣaḍḍuḳ marched on Gao in 1588 at the head of all the forces of Kurmina and the western provinces. He was proclaimed askiya in Timbuktu, but met with defeat at the hands of the new askiya of Gao, Isḥāḳ II, who cruelly put down the rebellion and decimated the armies of the west. The empire was thus morally divided. The disillusioned west lost interest in Gao and many of the Songhay princes had no qualms about joining the Moroccan invaders in 1591, three years after the civil war. The Songhay empire thus collapsed, a victim of its own contradictions.

The civilization of the Songhay

Political and administrative organization

The Songhay empire was profoundly original in its political and administrative organization. The strong hierarchy of authority, the systematic centralization and the absolute monarchy gave the Gao dynasty a modern flavour and broke away from the traditional political system of a federation of kingdoms, as in the empires of Ghana and Mali.

The monarchy

The Gao monarchy, which had inherited a long tradition of government, was based on Islamic and customary values. On the one hand, according to the ancient customs of Songhay and the Sudan, the king was the father of his people, the wielder of semi-sacred power, and the source of fertility and prosperity. He was deeply venerated, and it was possible to approach him only in a prostrate position. On the other hand, by Islamic tradition, the kings of Gao, who had been Muslims since the eleventh century, had to govern according to the precepts of the Koran. These two traditions were combined and, as the character of the sovereigns varied, so one or other came to the fore: under Askiya Muḥammad and Askiya Dāwūd it was Islam, whereas Sunni 'Alī and most of the other askiyas were more Songhay than Muslim.

The emperor lived at Gao surrounded by a large court, the *sunna*, which included members of his family, high dignitaries, and Guesere and Mabo *griots*. He sat on a kind of raised platform surrounded by 700 eunuchs. The Wandu *griot* acted as a herald. A large number of servants, usually slaves, saw to the various domestic tasks under the direction of a mayor of the palace, the *hu hokoroi koi*. The master of the wardrobe was in charge of the king's clothes.[17] When the sovereign died, he was succeeded by his eldest brother. In practice, the succession was decided by the strength of the contestants, and this was the cause of periodic crises. The new askiya was proclaimed by the *sunna* and enthroned in the ancient capital of Kūkya.

The royal government was composed of nominated ministers and advisers, who could be dismissed by the askiya and were placed in order of rank according to their functions. A distinction can be drawn between the central government of the askiya and the government of the provinces.

Central government

The officials of the central government formed the imperial council, which discussed all the problems of the empire. A chancellor-secretary took the minutes of the council, dealt with the sovereign's correspondence, and saw to the drawing up and execution of his charters. Other officials, whose functions are known to a greater or lesser degree, were concerned with various administrative departments. There was no strict specialization of functions in the proper sense of the term. The *Ta'rīkh*s give us a list of the dignitaries of the central government, the main ones being the following.[18]

The *hi koi* was the 'master of the water' or commander of the fleet. His function was one of the oldest and most important, because of the role played by the Niger in the life of ancient Songhay. The *hi koi* became one of the highest dignitaries of court, a kind of minister of home affairs who controlled the governors of the provinces. At all events, under the reign of Askiya Isḥāḳ I, we find the *hi koi* reprimanding the powerful governor of Kurmina, Prince Dāwūd, and ordering him back to his province without delay.

The *fari mondzo* or *mondio* was the minister of agriculture. It is very likely that he was concerned with the management of the many imperial estates which were scattered throughout the empire and which brought in large revenues every year. This very important function was usually entrusted to princes of the blood or even to crown princes. Certainly the *fari mondzo* had to settle disputes over land. Similar functions were performed by the *hari farma* (commissioner of waters and lakes), the *sao farma* (commissioner of forests), and the *wanei farma*, who was responsible for property.

17. There were some 210 sets of silk, woollen and cotton garments. Maḥmūd Ka'ti, loc. cit., pp. 260–1.

18. A complete list of the officials of the imperial government is given by G. N. Kodjo, 1971, pp. 270–2, and J. Rouch, 1953, pp. 192–3.

The function of the *kalissa farma*, 'finance minister', is not clearly defined in the *Ta'rīkh*s. It must have been connected with the imperial treasury. We know that the askiyas were very rich and that their revenues in kind or in money were centralized in Gao. The *kalissa farma* was responsible for guarding the treasury and for the sovereign's expenses. There is no doubt that he was in charge of the treasury of coins set up by Askiya Dāwūd. The *kalissa farma* was assisted by the *wanei farma* or property master, the *bana farma*, responsible for wages, and the *doi farma*, the chief buyer.

The *balama* had a military function. The *Ta'rīkh*s do not say exactly what it was, although in former times the *balama* was the commander of the army. In the sixteenth century, the post must have diminished in importance; there is no mention of the *balama* at the head of the imperial armies. The *balama* became chief of an army corps stationed in the Kabara–Timbuktu region which was certainly dependent on the *kurmina fari*. The post seems to have been entrusted to princes of the royal blood.

Other departments co-ordinating the government of the empire must have existed in Gao, but they do not appear in the *Ta'rīkh*s. Among these we may mention the *korei farma*, the minister in charge of white foreigners, and the imperial commissioners sent periodically by the emperor into the provinces to settle urgent problems, to levy special duties on the traders of the big towns or to supervise local officials and provincial administrators.

Government of the provinces

The Songhay adopted two systems of government according to the territories concerned. The first group comprised those conquered provinces which were governed by chiefs appointed by the askiya and subject at any moment to dismissal by him. These governors, who formed a hierarchy, exercised all sovereign power except for justice, which was entrusted to the *ḳāḍī*. They were known by the titles of *fari*, *farma* or *farba*, derived from the Mandingo institution of farin or governor. The Mali empire had established these in the middle Niger, and Sunni 'Alī and the askiyas retained the post and the title. The *koi* was a Songhay term meaning a chief, and was thus of lesser importance. This was also true of *mondzo*, which could equally well apply to a locality (*Timbuktu Mondzo*) and to a ministerial department (the *fari mondzo*). We know nothing about the titles *cha*, *marenfa* and others.

The empire was divided into two major provinces, Kurmina in the west and Dendi in the south-east (see Fig. 8.1). The post of *kurmina fari* or *kanfari* was held, with very few exceptions, by princes of the royal blood and indeed often by the imperial crown prince.[19] The *kurmina fari*, who lived at Tendirma, ranked second in the state. We do not know exactly what the limits of his jurisdiction were. He seems to have been in charge of all

19. Including Askiya Muḥammad II Benkan and Askiya Dāwūd.

the provinces west of Timbuktu, but this is not certain because the governors of this region were appointed by Gao and were responsible to the askiya. Nevertheless, towards the end of the sixteenth century, the military power of the *kurmina fari* enabled him to extend his influence to all the western provinces, of which he became the *de facto* head. He had in fact a powerful army of almost 4000 men and was able to counterbalance the power of Gao, which he did on several occasions.

The *Dendi Fari*, the governor of Dendi, supervised all the provinces of Dendi, that is, the south-eastern part of the empire. He ranked third in the state. The holder of this post was usually an important dignitary of the court. His army must have been somewhat smaller than that of the *Kurmina Fari*. He was responsible for the defence of the empire's southern borderlands. Other secondary provinces were governed by chiefs appointed by the askiya. These included the *Bara Koi*, the *Dirma Koi*, the *Hombori Koi*, the *Arabinda Farma*, the *Benga Farma*, the *Kala Sha* and the *Baghena Farma*, who lost his title of askiya.

Trading towns like Timbuktu, Jenne, Teghazza and Walata enjoyed a certain autonomy under their *koi* or *mondzo* chiefs. Their commercial and craft activities and the size of their population required the presence of many administrative officials. In Timbuktu, besides the *ḳāḍī* responsible for justice and the *Timbuktu Koi*, or headman, there was a large staff which included the *asara mondzo* – a kind of superintendent responsible for policing markets and towns and for carrying out the sentences passed by the *ḳāḍī* – weights and measures inspectors, tax inspectors in the markets, customs officials from Kabara, masters of the various guilds, the chiefs of the various ethnic subdivisions (grouped together by neighbourhoods) and those in charge of the straw huts of the suburbs. All these constituted the kernel of an efficient administration in the large towns.

Indirect administration

The indirect administration involved the vassal or tributary countries. The chief of the country was installed in accordance with local custom and was recognized by the askiya. Disputes among claimants or rebellions against imperial authority nevertheless arose. In such cases, the askiya intervened and imposed his own candidate. Thus the *fondoko* of Macina, Bubu Mariama, was dethroned by Askiya al-Ḥadj Muḥammad III, who had him exiled to Gao.[20] Indirect rule was applied to the Hausa states of Kano and Katsina, the kingdom of Agades, the Tuareg Kel Antassar federation – referred to as Andassen by al-Sa'dī – and the federation of the 'Magsharen'. The latter were Tuareg of Sanhaja origin, from the Timbuktu–Walata region, but were not an ethnic group; they represented the nobility of Tuareg society.[21] The Mali empire was also a tributary, but Songhay

20. Al-Sa'dī, loc. cit., p. 189.
21. H. Lhote, 1955–6, pp. 334–70.

domination over Mali was never continuous. According to Leo Africanus, the mansa of Mali paid tribute to Askiya Muḥammad I. Although this domination was effective, it did not last; further expeditions against Mali were necessary in the reign of Askiya Isḥāḳ I. In fact, the mansa freed himself from the suzerainty of Gao. The border between the two empires, the Sibiridugu, must have been situated further to the south of Segu, on the border of Mande, at the level of present-day Kukikoro.[22] All these states were tributary to an extent that varied with Gao policy. Their sovereigns had periodically to pay tribute, provide contingents of warriors at the emperor's request and maintain good relations by visits, gifts and marriages.

By these various systems of administration – central, provincial and indirect – the empire of Gao managed to organize the peoples of the Niger region of the Sudan to provide security for themselves and their possessions, and to enable considerable economic development to take place. The monarchy of the askiyas, an organized and impersonal power rooted in Songhay and Islamic values, overcame many dynastic crises. If it had not been undermined by the Moroccan conquest, it could have evolved into a modern African state, guaranteeing the essential human freedoms in spite of its high degree of political centralization.

The state apparatus

The state had considerable resources which contributed to its strength and independence; the standing army was capable of protecting the empire, imposing the sovereign's will on his subjects, and crushing any rebellion. This powerful and stable state machinery was nevertheless not despotic. Justice, which was entrusted to virtually independent *ḳāḍī*s or to tribal chiefs, safeguarded the people's freedom and rights. A study of the machinery of the Songhay state brings out its modern character. The empire inherited a long warlike tradition; the Songhay were not farmers and tradesmen but warriors. 'The great men of the Songhay', writes Maḥmūd Ka'ti, 'were versed in the art of war. They were very brave, very bold and most expert in the deployment of military stratagems.'[23]

The vocations of the nobility were politics and war. They constituted the backbone of the cavalry, the spearhead of the Songhay army. Armed with long lances, sabres and arrows, the Songhay mounted warriors wore iron breastplates beneath their battle tunics. Horses were expensive (valued at about ten captives in the sixteenth century), so the cavalry were a privileged élite. The infantry, who were the most numerous branch of the army, were drawn from all ranks of society, including slaves, the lesser nobility and freed men. The infantry were armed with spears and arrows and carried leather or copper shields. The Niger fishermen, most of whom were Sorko,

22. This accords with the views of D. T. Niane, based on Mandingo traditions which he has recorded in the region of Niani.

23. Translated from Maḥmūd Ka'ti, loc. cit., p. 146.

made up a permanent flotilla of nearly 2000 dug-out canoes on the river. The army carried long trumpets (*kakaki*) and standards and had their own marching order and fan-shaped battle formation.

The true size of the army is not known. The reforms of Askiya Muḥammad I and Askiya Muḥammad Benkan increased the Gao standing army to some 4000 men, excluding the 300 warriors of the sovereign's bodyguard, the *sunna*.[24] Most soldiers were slaves of the askiya, who inherited them and was allowed to marry their daughters. The total army assembled in 1591 at the battle of Tondibi comprised nearly 30 000 infantry and 10 000 horsemen. It was the largest organized force in the western Sudan. It enabled the askiya to impose his will and, above all, it procured for him the spoils of war.

Financial resources

The sovereign of Gao was powerful and rich. The monarchy had reliable and permanent resources, levied in all parts of the empire and managed by a numerous administrative staff, at the head of whom was the *kalissa farma*. The imperial revenue came from a variety of sources. There were the revenues from the sovereign's personal property, the *zakāt* or tithe collected for the poor, taxes in kind levied on harvests, herds and fishing, taxes and customs duties on commercial activity, special levies on the merchants of the large towns and, above all, the spoils of almost annual war. The sovereign thus had inexhaustible resources, which he spent as he wished. A large proportion of his income went to the upkeep of the court and the standing army. The askiya also contributed to the construction or restoration of the mosques, supported the poor of his empire, and gave presents and alms to the great marabouts.

Justice

Justice was a royal prerogative. The askiya, as amir of the Muslims and father of his people, delegated its administration to representatives who were quite independent of the central power or its officials. In any case, a distinction should be drawn between the two kinds of jurisdiction, the Islamic and the customary.

The former covered the Muslim community. It was based on the Mālikite law taught at the Sudanese universities. The *ḳāḍī* was the supreme sovereign and judge, appointed by the emperor for life. The post was not greatly sought after and the askiya frequently coerced his nominees. In Timbuktu, the post was monopolized for the whole of the sixteenth century by the distinguished family of the *ḳāḍī* Maḥmūd ben ʿUmar al-Aḳit (1498–

24. Not to be confused with the *sunna* of the imperial council. The sovereign's bodyguard were soldiers of unswerving loyalty who had certainly sworn a special oath. The *sunna* could not flee from combat and thus were massacred at Tondibi in 1591.

1548), who also provided the imams of the Sankore mosque.[25] The post became hereditary in many towns. The *ḳāḍī* was aided by legal assistants such as clerks of the court, secretaries and notaries. Punishment was meted out by the *asara mondzo*, an official of the imperial power. The *ḳāḍī* sat in judgement on all matters, criminal and commercial, and there was no appeal against his sentences. In addition, he acted as a kind of registrar, recording such civil acts as the freeing of slaves, the division of inheritances and the validation of private documents. The *ḳāḍī* was the real head of the town of Timbuktu. His authority went beyond the strictly judicial domain and protected the freedom of the citizens.

Customary justice was the rule throughout most of the empire and even in the great Muslim towns people settled their disputes within the family or through the chief of their ethnic group in accordance with their own customs. At Gao, the imperial council sat as a political tribunal to pronounce judgement in the affairs of state, which generally involved conspirators, princes and their accomplices. To combat immorality, particularly adultery, which had become a scourge in the cultivated society of the middle Niger, Askiya Isḥāḳ II set up a special court to punish severely those taken *in flagrante delicto*. Particularly striking was the opportunity afforded to the people to administer justice for themselves through competent tribunals. This was the surest guarantee of order and freedom. In this way the Songhay state encouraged the flowering of a brilliant intellectual civilization and considerable economic and social development.

Economic development

The Songhay empire, in the midst of the Sahel region of the Sudan, was in a very favourable situation to benefit from trans-Saharan trade. The Niger, traversing the empire from west to east, facilitated communication and its fertile valley was intensively cultivated. A distinction can be drawn between two economic sectors, one rural and traditional and the other urban and commercial.

The rural sector

The *Ta'rīkh*s tell us little about rural activities. Agricultural techniques have not greatly changed since those times. The hoe (the Songhay *kaunu*), animal manure, the practice of horticulture in the valley and shifting cultivation in the savannah have stayed the same for centuries, but the valley of the Niger was then more densely inhabited by a population occupied in farming, fishing and stock-raising. Large estates belonging to the princes and *'ulamā'*s of the great towns were worked by slaves, settled in farming villages. The askiya was himself one of the great landowners. His fields,

25. On this family, see J. Cuoq, 1978, pp. 85–102.

scattered throughout the valley, were cultivated by communities of slaves working under overseers called *fanfa*. A sort of rent in kind was levied on the harvests and sent to Gao.[26] The same happened with private slaves.

Fishing was practised by the Sorko, Do and Bozo, and the fish caught were dried or smoked and sold throughout the empire. Similarly, the raising of cattle and goats in the Sahel border country in Macina and Bakhunu and beef cattle among the sedentary peoples of the Macina valley was an important source of milk and meat, particularly for town dwellers. In fact, a large proportion of the agricultural produce – grain, fish and meat – was marketed, enabling country dwellers to obtain vitally needed products such as salt.

The commercial sector

The towns of the Sudan and Sahel, such as Walata, Timbuktu, Jenne and Gao – centres of the great trans-Saharan trade – were in contact with the major markets of the Sahara, North Africa and beyond, as far as Mediterranean Europe. The trans-Saharan trade routes ran northwards from the Niger valley.[27] The principal ones were Timbuktu–Teghazza–Tuat to Tāfīlālet and western Algeria; Timbuktu–Walata–Tishit–Wadane to the Darʿa and Tāfīlālet; Gao–Tadmekka–Ghat to Libya and Egypt; Gao–Tadmekka–Ghadames to the Libyan and Tunisian coasts; and Gao–Hausa–Kanem-Bornu to the Nile valley. It appears that trade across the Sahara in the fifteenth and sixteenth centuries was directed principally towards Morocco, Algeria and Libya. In the centre, the Teghazza salt-mines and the Tuat and Ghat oases were the great commercial staging posts on the way to the Sudan.

Trade was in the hands of Berber Arab merchants (there were many merchants from Tuat and Ghadames in Timbuktu) and the Sudanese peoples – Wangara (Mandingo), Wakore (Soninke), Mossi, Hausa and Songhay. The meeting points were the towns, whose inhabitants made great profits from brokerage. Some merchants were well-organized, with branches in many towns, and made profits from the fluctuations in prices. They had a merchant fleet on the Niger and used pack camels and oxen to carry their merchandise. The port of Kabara was thus congested with all kinds of goods when Leo Africanus arrived at the beginning of the sixteenth century.[28]

Exchanges were effected by barter or more often through the intermediary of currency – cowries for small dealings and gold, salt or copper according to the market. The Sudan imported cloth, most of which came from Europe (Venice, Florence, Genoa, Majorca, England and France), salt

26. Maḥmūd Kaʿti, loc. cit., pp. 178–80.
27. Mauny, 1961, III C, 5.
28. Leo Africanus, French transl. 1956, Vol. 2, pp. 467.

from Teghazza and Idjil, arms, horses, copper, glassware, sugar and North African craft products, such as footwear and woollen goods. The mainspring of this trade was salt. It was carried in rectangular blocks weighing 25–30 kg, and distributed throughout the interior. The Sudan exported gold, slaves, ivory, spices, kola nuts and cotton goods. Gold dust (*tibar*) and nuggets came from mines in Bambuk, Bure, the Mossi country and particularly from Bitu in Asante. Gold was the pivot of trans-Saharan trade and was supplied to Europe as well.[29]

Trade within the Sudan involved local products. There were markets in all the large centres of population, where the peasants met to barter their produce and to buy salt, cloth and other wares from the pedlars who came from the north. Cereals from the central delta or from Dendi were carried to Timbuktu, Gao and the Sahel, and kola nuts and gold from the south were taken northwards to the starting-points of the trans-Saharan routes. Jenne played a considerable role as a collection and distribution centre for products from the whole of West Africa.

In conclusion, commerce helped to enrich the towns of the Niger and to bring a comfortable standard of living to the people living in the countryside; but unfortunately it involved only a small proportion of the local agricultural and craft products. The bulk of the trade involved the products of mining and gathering. Basically, trans-Saharan trade was more a matter of trading local produce for imported goods than a real market economy based on local production, and thus did not revolutionize the social structure or the techniques in use. It nevertheless enabled certain material improvements to take place in the living conditions of the people of the Niger and allowed a cultivated aristocracy to emerge. The long tunic (*bobu*) and slippers (*babush*), comfort in the home and a varied diet were the signs of progress in the society of the Niger.

Society

The underlying structures of Songhay society were similar to those of the other societies of the western Sudan. What was original about it was the development of a market economy which gave rise to an urban society with differentiated activities, although this was somewhat marginal, since society as a whole was predominantly rural.

Organization of Niger society

In town and country alike, the characteristic feature of Songhay society was the importance of the ties of kinship. The basic element which coloured

29. F. Braudel, 1946; J. Heers, 1958, pp. 247–55; and E. F. Gautier, 1935, pp. 113–23; these works adequately demonstrate the importance of Sudanese trade for the Mediterranean and European economy of the Middle ages. Cf. also Chapter 26 below.

all social institutions and daily life was the family. Clans were groupings of several families. The oldest were of Soninke origin (Ture, Sylla, Tunkara, Cisse, Jakhite, Drame and Jawara); only a few (Maiga) were Songhay. This raises the problem of the actual composition of the Songhay people, who had a considerable admixture of the blood of the Soninke, Berbers and other peoples like the Mandingo, the Gobir and the Hausa.

No mention is made of ethnic organization in the *Ta'rīkh*s, except to name the slave or rural populations tied to the soil or to trades organized by castes.[30] The most fundamental feature of Songhay society was its hierarchy, divided into nobility, free men, members of the guilds and slaves. This was a feature well known throughout the western Sudan, but here the nobility were more clearly distinguishable and were occupied almost exclusively with administration and warfare. The numerous slaves were assigned to domestic or agricultural tasks and had a subordinate political and military role.

Rural society

Outside the Niger valley, where there were large market towns, the Songhay and the peoples of the empire lived in the countryside and had rural occupations. The peasants of the fifteenth and sixteenth centuries, living in villages of round huts, differed only very little from those of today. The fundamental structures were not destroyed by a technical or any other kind of revolution. Living conditions have, of course, changed. The meagre information given by the *Ta'rīkh*s indicates a dense rural population in the Niger valley, particularly in the region of Jenne; the people lived primarily by agriculture. There were certainly guilds of artisans, such as smiths, carpenters and potters, but their work must have been seasonal and they lived for the most part by tilling the soil. The same must have been true of the fishermen of the Niger (the Sorko, Bozo and Somono), who cultivated the soil during the rainy season. Living conditions were probably not as wretched as Leo Africanus describes them.[31] Security was general and famine rare. The *Ta'rīkh*s give us a few glimpses of country life. There is virtually no mention of peasants' revolts. The rent demanded from the slaves by their masters was never crushing. The inventory of the wealth of an imperial steward in Dendi gives, on the contrary, the impression of a certain affluence in the countryside. The peasants even sold part of their produce in the local markets, obtaining products like salt or cloth and thus becoming involved in trade.

On the spiritual side, Islam did not take root in the countryside. The peasants remained attached to their own local values and most rural regions, Dendi and the south, were, despite a superficial conversion to

30. Maḥmūd Ka'ti, loc. cit., pp. 20–1.

31. Leo Africanus, loc. cit., Vol. 2, p. 472, describes wretched and ignorant peasants crushed by imperial taxation.

Islam, still attached to traditional cults. Thus although it was opened up to the market economy, the countryside remained somewhat closed to the spiritual values emanating from the town, which was the second major element in Niger society.

Towns and urban society

The great commercial expansion enabled an urban civilization to develop throughout the Sudan-Sahel region. In the fifteenth and sixteenth centuries, we find the towns of Walata, Jenne, Tenenku, Tendirma, Timbuktu, Bamba, Gao and Agades, and the Hausa towns of Katsina and Kano (see Fig. 8.1). These towns were generally open and unwalled. The market was inside the town and a suburb of tents and straw huts housed a shifting population. In the centre of the town were houses of one or two storeys, built of masonry in a Sudanese style; an entrance hall led to an inner courtyard with the rooms opening off it.

The three largest towns were Timbuktu, Jenne and Gao, concerning which more must be said. Conquered by Sunni ʿAlī Ber around 1468, Timbuktu reached the height of its expansion in the sixteenth century. It may have had some 80 000 inhabitants in the reign of Askiya Dāwūd.[32] It was at that time the economic capital of the empire and the holy city of the Sudan, famed for its holy men and its university. Jenne, an island in the central delta, economically and spiritually linked to Timbuktu and inhabited by some 30 000–40 000 people, was indeed the most important black settlement in the interior of the Sudan.[33] Dominated by its beautiful mosque, a pearl of Sudanese art, it was the great market of the south, in contact with the savannah and the forest country. Gao, which was the political capital and older than the others, was an immense town of nearly 100 000 inhabitants.[34] Because of its position, it looked towards the Hausa world, Dendi, Libya and Egypt.

All these towns of the Niger had a dominant Songhay nucleus, whose language was widely spoken. But they also had a cosmopolitan population of Berber Arabs, Mossi, Hausa, Mandingo (Wangara), Soninke, Fulani and others. Urban society was arranged in a hierarchy on the Sudanese pattern,

32. This is a very approximate figure. We nevertheless feel that it is closer to reality than the figure of 25 000 put forward by Mauny, 1961, p. 497. The town was very extensive in the sixteenth century. All oral tradition is unanimous in stating that the tomb of *Ḳāḍī* Maḥmūd, which today is far from the town, was his house at that time. The daily encroachment of sand on the town makes us sceptical as to the value of the aerial photographs of the old site. It should also be noted that Timbuktu was a town which spread upwards and that two-storey houses were very widespread. Living space was thus highly concentrated.

33. See S. Keech and R. J. McIntosh, 1980, which throws new light on the question of Jenne.

34. This figure is taken from the first census held in the town, towards the end of the sixteenth century, which gave a figure of 7626 houses, excluding the straw huts in the suburbs.

but differentiation was here along economic lines. Urban society contained three basic elements: the merchants, the craftsmen and the religious orders, all gaining a living directly or indirectly from commerce. The merchants were mostly foreigners. The craftsmen and small traders, an active and vigorous section of the population, were grouped together in guilds, each with its regulations and customs. Intellectuals, marabouts and students were men of breeding and enjoyed considerable respect socially.

Niger society was an ordered and cultivated society, at least at the level of the aristocracy. They liked ample garments and *babush*, the easy life of the home, highly spiced food and above all good company. This led to a certain moral laxity, as indicated by the numerous courtesans and the debauchery among the princely aristocracy.

Urban society thus represented a break with traditional rural society, and was never able to spread into the countryside. Its governing ranks were generally composed of foreigners and, as it was based on Islamic and commercial values, it seemed set apart from society as a whole. Nor did the merchant bourgeoisie ever manage to take firm root in the country, based as it was on an exchange economy. It was thus unable to have any profound and lasting effect on Songhay society.

Religious and intellectual development

Islam, which had entered the western Sudan in the eleventh century, made slow, uneven progress, finally establishing itself in the Niger Bend and the Sahel. Elsewhere, it was no more than a thin veneer over the older beliefs and never managed to take deep root. In urban areas, Islam gave rise to a literate élite which, by its great creative efforts, lent lustre to Islam and contributed to its reinterpretation. This development was made possible by the general prosperity of the Sudan, which attracted many foreign scholars from the fifteenth century onwards, and, above all, by the benevolent policy of the sovereigns of Gao, such as the founder of the dynasty of the askiyas, who heaped honours and gifts on the Muslim men of learning and bestowed on them a social prestige without parallel in the country. Askiya Muḥammad I practised a systematically Muslim policy and worked for the introduction and extension of Islam in the Sudan.

Religious life

Nevertheless, Islam was not the dominant religion in the fifteenth and sixteenth centuries. The great mass of the Songhay and the peoples of the empire living in the countryside remained attached to their ancestral beliefs. Askiya Muḥammad I, in a letter to al-Maghīlī, deplored and resisted this situation, although he was unable to change it.

The Songhay worshipped *hole* and spirits inhabiting nature, who had to be propitiated.[35] Their pantheon included several divinities, among whom were Harke Dikko, the god of the Niger ('Isā Ber), and Dongo, the thunder god. Their magical healers, the *sonianke*, who were considered to be descendants of the fallen dynasty of the Sunni, enjoyed popular veneration and protected society from evil spirits and sorcerers or *tierkei*. The cult of the dead was perpetuated by each clan chief. Traditional religion, so strongly alive in the countryside, thus served to ensure the protection, the psychic equilibrium and the continuity of society.

Islam, when added on to these beliefs, made little or no impact on the countryside. Although it was urban and aristocratic, it eventually became better adapted for widespread acceptance. This was a black and tolerant form of Islam; it gained ground through the activities of Askiya Muḥammad I and the Muslim doctors and through the peaceful expansion of trade, with which it was intimately linked from its very beginnings in black Africa. Askiya Muḥammad I followed the advice of the great doctors, al-Mag͟hīlī of Tuat and al-Suyūtī from Cairo;[36] with a glittering constellation of marabouts from his own empire he attacked the fetishes, hunted down the companions of Sunni, the 'bad Muslims', imposed a *ḳāḍī* and the Mālikite law on a number of communities and waged a *dj͟ihād* (holy war) against the Mossi infidels. The itinerant traders and merchants did the rest and took the religion with them right into the heart of the southern forest regions.

Thus, at the end of the sixteenth century, Islam was dominant throughout the middle Niger from Macina to Dendi, and elsewhere had made considerable advances. Religious life can be understood best by looking at the towns. Jenne and Dia in the central delta, Gao and Timbuktu had their mosques, imams, *ḳāḍī*s and cemeteries as well as many schools run by men of great piety and saints who are still venerated today in the Niger Bend. Timbuktu was a model city. It was known as the holy town of the Sudan by reason of its three great mosques – the Jingereber, the Sīdī Yaḥyā and the Sankore, the last two built in the first half of the fifteenth century – and the reputation of its holy men and doctors (S͟harīf Sīdī Yaḥyā, who died in 1464, *Ḳāḍī* Maḥmūd b. 'Umar Aḳiṭ, who died in 1548, and many members of his family, including *Ḳāḍī* al-Aḳīb, who restored the great mosques). Its university spread Islamic culture throughout the western Sudan.

Intellectual life

The Sudan of the Niger and the Sahel saw a great intellectual awakening in the fifteenth and sixteenth centuries. Sudanese humanism became a fundamental part of worldwide Islam. The Sudanese élite, trained in the fourteenth and fifteenth centuries in the universities of D͟jāmi' al-Ḳarawiyyīn in Fez and al-Azhar in Cairo, became emancipated and reached

35. J. Rouch, 1954 and 1960; J. Boulnois and B. Hama, 1954; these sources correct the Islam-centred interpretation of Songhay history.

36. E. H. R. Mbaye, 1972; J. O. Hunwick, 1970.

the heights of Islamic learning. The centres of this intellectual life remained the towns. The trade surplus made possible the development of a literate class devoted to worship and study. The general prosperity attracted scholars into the towns of the Niger region from all parts of the Sudan and the Sahel.[37]

The most famous university was undoubtedly that of Timbuktu, which gave us the two *Ta'rīkh*s; although written in the seventeenth century, these are the greatest historical works of the Sudan. The university, as a centre for the acquisition and dissemination of knowledge, was not an organized institution as were those of North Africa. It included a large number of independent schools, particularly the famous mosque of Sankore, which provided a higher education. In the sixteenth century, Timbuktu had some 180 Koranic schools and thousands of students from every corner of the Sudan and the Sahel, who lived with their teachers or as lodgers. The teachers were unpaid, but their material needs were provided for and they devoted themselves entirely to their studies by day and by night.

Study was at two levels: the elementary Koranic schools, based on the reading and recitation of the Koran; and the higher level, at which the student began to study Islamic subjects. The Sudanese university, like all those in the Muslim world at that time, taught the humanities, which included the traditional academic subjects – theology (*tawḥīd*), exegesis (*tafsīr*), traditions (*ḥadīth*) and Mālikite jurisprudence (*fiḳh*) – as well as grammar, rhetoric, logic, astrology, astronomy, history and geography. Scientific and mathematical knowledge must have been very rudimentary. Mālikite law was the speciality of the doctors of Timbuktu, who are referred to throughout the *Ta'rīkh*s as 'jurisconsults'. Teaching methods even now have changed little since the sixteenth century. The essential feature was exposition and commentary on the texts, following scholastic methods.

Instruction was provided by numerous teachers from the Sudan and the Sahara. In the fifteenth century, there were Shaykh Sīdī Yaḥyā and Moadib Muḥammad al-Ḳabārī, a native of Kabara, who trained the next generation of teachers. In the sixteenth century, there was a whole host of famous teachers in the Niger Bend. The greatest number came from the two great Berber families, the Aḳiṭs and the Anda Ag Muḥammads, who were connected by marriage. The most famous teachers were *Ḳāḍī* Maḥmūd b. 'Umar Aḳiṭ (1463–1548), a jurist and grammarian, his brother Aḥmad (who died in 1536), his cousin al-Mukhtār and his nephews, including the famous Abdul 'Abbās Aḥmad Baba ibn Aḥmad ben Aḥmad Aḳiṭ (1566–1627).[38]

Virtually nothing of the great intellectual activity of the fifteenth and sixteenth centuries has survived. The books whose titles we know were generally works of erudition, which should in no way be underestimated. The scholars of the Sudan, drawing on their own resources, attempted to

37. A. Cherbonneau, 1854–5.
38. ibid.; J. O. Hunwick, 1964 and 1966a.

understand and to interpret Islamic jurisprudence in theory and practice. This Islamic culture must nevertheless be seen in the general context of the Sudan. It was fundamentally the culture of an urban élite, which affected only a minority. It was based on the written language and did not absorb the native languages and cultures. It remained marginal to society and collapsed with the cities which gave rise to it.

9 The peoples and kingdoms of the Niger Bend and the Volta basin from the 12th to the 16th century

M. IZARD

The Mossi of the Niger Bend: chronology

In the present state of our knowledge, the history of the Niger Bend in the distant period considered here is necessarily centred around the emergence and territorial expansion of the Mamprusi, Dagomba and Mossi kingdoms; this happens for two reasons, which are in fact connected. The first is that the information available to us on this group of kingdoms is incomparably richer than anything we have for other historical formations in the same region, such as the Gurma, and *a fortiori* for societies without a centralized system of political power. The second is that any attempt to establish a formal history of the Mossi comes up against one fundamental problem, namely the identity of the 'Mossi' referred to in those classic chronicles, the *Ta'rīkh al-Sūdān* and the *Ta'rīkh al-fattāsh*. As we shall see, the definition of a satisfactory chronological framework for the whole of the area to be dealt with in this chapter depends upon the solution to this problem.

Our starting-point must be an analysis of the references to Mossi contained in the Sudanese chronicles. The *Ta'rīkh al-fattāsh* speaks of Mossi incursions into the territory of the Songhay kingdom of Gao around the middle of the thirteenth century, that is, during the first quarter of the period which it is proposed to cover in this volume. Za Baray, against whom the Mossi are said to have waged war, seems to be the Za Beirafoloko of the table of dynasties established by Jean Rouch;[1] his authority in the Niger valley extended from Gao to Tillaberi. It was during the reign of his successor, Za Asibay, that the kingdom of Gao passed under the suzerainty of Mansa Wali of Mali, who, according to Nehemia Levtzion, reigned from 1260 to 1277. The *Ta'rīkh al-fattāsh*, which gives no indication of where the territory of the Mossi was located, tells us that the latter sometimes invaded the western part of the Niger Bend, where Mali influence came up against that of the Tuareg from the north. The two brief fragments of the *Ta'rīkh al-fattāsh* to which I refer give us an important clue by speaking of a 'Mossi *koi*', in other words a chief or king of the

1. J. Rouch, 1953, p. 174, note 13.

Mossi.[2] Nothing in what has been handed down to us would point to bands of pillagers more or less out of control; on the contrary, everything indicates that we are dealing here with a people or a governing group with a strong political and military organization, perhaps on the lines of a state, and with a firmly established territorial base, which we can only locate somewhere within the Niger Bend without being sure exactly where. At all events, by the middle of the thirteenth century, this military society was able to challenge the principal hegemonies which shared the Niger Bend. Finally, these fragments speak of Mossi forays in the direction of Timbuktu; as we shall see, for the Mossi of the *Ta'rīkh*s the permanent objective throughout the succession of large-scale undertakings on which they embarked was to gain direct control of the trading centres in the north-west of the Bend.

Continuing in chronological order, we next meet the Mossi of the Niger Bend at the time of Mansa Mūsā (1312–37); the relevant events this time are reported by the *Ta'rīkh al-Sūdān*. The well-known passage relating to the taking of Timbuktu by the Mossi deserves to be quoted in full:

> It was, we are told, the Sultan Kankan-Moussa who caused the minaret of the great mosque of Timbuktu to be built, and it was during the reign of one of the princes of his dynasty that the sultan of the Mossi, at the head of a powerful army, launched an expedition against that city. Terror-stricken, the people of Melli took flight and abandoned Timbuktu to the assailants. The sultan of the Mossi entered the town, pillaged it, set fire to it, reduced it to ruins and, after putting to death everyone he could lay hands on and seizing all the wealth he could find, he returned to his country.[3]

The capture of Timbuktu by the Mossi is generally considered to have taken place around 1337;[4] thus, almost a century after the Mossi had threatened Gao, not only was this warlike people still in the limelight, but they even seem to have increased their power. From his mysterious country the 'sultan' of the Mossi launched far-flung expeditions and attacked large, probably well-defended cities, which suggests that he must have had a considerable potential in men, horses and weapons. Also in the *Ta'rīkh al-Sūdān* there is mention of a raid against Benka (west of the Niger Bend, upstream from Timbuktu), which probably took place shortly before 1433–4, the year Timbuktu was taken by the Tuareg.[5] Another hundred years had passed and the Mossi were still as menacing as ever. Rouch argues very convincingly that the raid against Benka was

2. Maḥmūd Ka'ti, French transl. 1913, pp. 333–4.
3. From al-Sa'dī, French transl. 1900, pp. 16–17.
4. C. Monteil, 1929, pp. 414–15.
5. See al-Sa'dī, loc. cit., pp. 45–6, on Benka; and Maḥmūd Ka'ti, loc. cit., pp. 118, 173 and 178, on the capture of Timbuktu by the Tuareg.

just one episode in a series of operations directed against the lake region.[6]

We now come to the best-known period in the history of the northern Mossi, corresponding to the reigns of Sunni ʿAlī and Askiya Muḥammad, which are dealt with in the two *Taʾrīkh*s whose references supplement each other. For the reign of ʿAlī (1464–92), we have the following points of reference.

(1) 1464/5: the accession of ʿAlī; war against the Mossi commanded by a 'king' named Komdao; the defeat of the Mossi, whom the Songhay pursued right into Bambara (Bamanan) country, while Komdao succeeded in regaining his capital, Argouma;
(2) 1470/1 to 1471/2: Songhay forays into Mossi country, led first by ʿAlī, then by Yikoy Yate; the destruction of Barkana, the place of residence of the king of the Mossi; and the death of a Mossi chief, to whom the *Taʾrīkh al-fattāsh* gives the title, *tenga niama*;
(3) 1477/8: Mossi penetration into Songhay territory, where they remained until 1483/4; the taking of Sama, a place situated between the river and Walata;
(4) 1480: the occupation of Walata by the Mossi after a month-long siege, then the withdrawal of the assailants, who had to abandon their prisoners to the inhabitants of the city;
(5) 1483/4: the battle of Kobi or of Djiniki-Toʾoi, which took place after the Songhay had captured members of the household of the chief of the Mossi and seized his war treasure; withdrawal of the Mossi to their country, pursued by the Songhay, who penetrated into it.[7]

What happened between the middle of the fourteenth century, marked in particular by the raid against Benka, and the middle of the following century, which seems to mark both the height of Mossi expansionism, with the taking of Walata, and the beginning of the reverses? On this whole century, the written sources are silent. However, the following at least can be gathered from the events which filled the latter half of the fifteenth century. When ʿAlī, a sovereign of exceptional stature, came to power, the Mossi represented such a danger to the Songhay empire that Songhay power could be consolidated only if the adversary were destroyed. During ʿAlī's reign it was no longer a question of occasional raids by the Mossi against the towns of the Niger Bend, nor of defensive ripostes on the part of the Songhay; we are confronted here with a long and implacable war between two great military hegemonies. At the end of his reign ʿAlī was victorious, but his successors were not content to let matters rest there; they undertook to annihilate completely the Mossi state in the north, which

6. Rouch, op. cit., p. 177.

7. On the Mossi of the Niger Bend and Sunni ʿAlī, cf. Maḥmūd Kaʿti, loc. cit., pp. 85–6 and 88–9; and M. Izard, 1970, pp. 38–44.

had lost the initiative on the accession of Askiya Muḥammad, but had not yet disappeared.

The fragments of the *Tar'ī<u>kh</u>*s relating to the history of the northern Mossi in the sixteenth century contain very few facts, but they do tell us something of capital importance: that with Muḥammad (1493–1529) and his successors, the Songhay wars against the Mossi were henceforth conducted in the name of Islam, the Mossi being 'pagans', like the inhabitants of Gurma.[8] In 1497/8 Muḥammad launched an expedition against the country of the Mossi, where the 'sultan' Naʿasira reigned; the Songhay army was victorious, but the Mossi lost many dead, their wives and children were taken away into captivity and their capital was destroyed. Dāwūd (1549–82) made war on the Mossi in the very year of his accession, then again in 1561/2, and finally around 1575. The 1561/2 campaign makes it possible to date with accuracy the almost complete disappearance of the northern Mossi power, which so far as we can judge had lasted for three centuries. The *Ta'rī<u>kh</u> al-Sūdān* tells us that, following Dāwūd's second expedition, 'the chief [of the Mossi] abandoned the country with all his troops'. Of the third and final campaign conducted during the reign of Dāwūd, that of 1575 (?), the same *Ta'rī<u>kh</u>* laconically informs us that the Songhay returned from it 'without having pillaged anything', which no doubt means that there was nothing left to plunder, and that the Songhay army had entered a country wasted by war and empty of inhabitants.[9]

Thus, in spite of the fragmentary nature of the information on which we are forced to rely, it is still possible to trace a fairly coherent picture of the history of the Mossi of the Niger Bend. For more than 300 years a conquering military society fought against the Songhay with a view to gaining control of the river, after establishing their ascendancy in the interior, and was finally defeated; the political antagonism was reinforced by religious antagonism after the reign of Muḥammad. Unfortunately we can formulate only very vague hypotheses concerning the identity of these Mossi and the exact location of their country, and, in the absence of any help from oral tradition, it is most unlikely that we shall know any more until the necessary archaeological investigations have been carried out.

Pending the exploration of new lines of research, there are a few items of information, not derived from the *Ta'rī<u>kh</u>*s, which can add to our knowledge, or at least strengthen our hypotheses. Boubou Hama alludes to a mysterious manuscript written in Arabic, entitled *Aguinass Afriquia*, which is said to date from the fifteenth century and whose presumed author was Abkal ould Aoudar. So far as I know, this chronicle, known as the *Ta'rī<u>kh</u> of Say*, has been neither published nor translated; although Boubou Hama summarizes its contents, he does not explicitly cite any passage from

8. Cf. Maḥmūd Kaʿti, loc. cit., pp. 114–15 and 134–5; al-Saʿdī, loc. cit., pp. 121–2 and 124.

9. Al-Saʿdī, loc. cit., pp. 168, 173 and 179.

it. According to Boubou Hama, basing himself on Aoudar, the Mossi, who had come from the east, founded on the left bank of the Niger a state by the name of Dyamare, the last capital of which was Rozi, in Dallol Boso. The state of Rozi is said to have remained in existence for 500 years, from the eighth to the twelfth century. By about the twelfth century the Mossi, without leaving the Hausa bank, created a second Dyamare with Minji as its political centre, since Rozi was abandoned under the pressure of the Berbers. The second Dyamare was but short-lived; soon afterwards, following a famine, the Mossi crossed the river and settled on the Gurma bank. After defeating the local populations – the Gurmankeyeba and perhaps the Kurumba – the Mossi founded the third and last Dyamare (see Fig. 9.1).[10]

Until we have the complete and authenticated text of the *Say Ta'rīkh*, we can neither make scientific use of the information supplied by Boubou Hama, nor, in particular, assess the validity of certain chronological pointers which he provides, such as the date 1132, which would correspond with the move from the second to the third Dyamare and which, for Tauxier, marks the beginning of the reign of Za Baray, the first Songhay sovereign to have fought the Mossi, according to the classical *Ta'rikhs*.[11] In another well-known Arabic document, the *Masālīk al-Abṣār fī Mamālīk al-Amṣār*, by Ibn Faḍl Allāh al-'Umarī, written in 1337 (the year Timbuktu is believed to have been taken by the Mossi), mention is made of a conversation between Mansa Mūsā and the future emir, Abu'l-Ḥasan 'Alī, one of the informants of the chronicler. When the Egyptian asks the sovereign of Mali to tell him with whom he is at war, the latter replies: 'We have a relentless enemy who, among the blacks, is for us what the Tartars are for you'. The king adds that these enemies 'are skilled in shooting arrows' and that they have 'gelded horses, with split noses'.[12] We may wonder whether these horsemen were Mossi from the north, although the practice of castrating horses was unknown within the Niger Bend.

We know that the Genoese merchant Antonio Malfante travelled in Tuat in 1447; a letter written in Latin to his compatriot Giovanni Mariono has been published by de la Roncière;[13] it contains a passage in which Yves Person saw an allusion to the Mossi of the north.[14] In connection with a town called Vallo (which Person identifies as Walata), mention is made of a 'fetishistic king with five hundred thousand men' who had come to besiege the town. Finally, to finish with the written sources, it will be recalled that João de Barros speaks of the 'Moses' people in his *Decadias*

10. B. Hama, 1966, pp. 205–15; cf. Izard, op. cit., Vol. 1, pp. 47–8.
11. L. Tauxier, 1924, p. 22.
12. Translated from a passage quoted in *l'Empire du Mali*, 1959, p. 61.
13. C. de la Roncière, 1924–7, Vol. 1, p. 156, gives the Latin text of the letter and a French translation.
14. Y. Person, 1962, pp. 45–6; it is to be noted that Person has 'Wallo' for de la Roncière's 'Vallo'; cf. Izard, op. cit., Vol. 1, pp. 50–3.

da Asia, dated 1552–3. The Portuguese author relates the visit made in 1488 by a Wolof prince named Bemoy to the court of Dom João II. Bemoy explained to the sovereign that the territory of the 'Moses' extended eastward from Timbuktu, which, for the Mossi of the north, does not contradict the information we may infer from the *Ta'rīkh*s. So great did the power of the king of the 'Moses' appear to Dom João II, he thought this must be the famous Prester John, dependant of the Queen of Sheba and legendary founder of the Ethiopian monarchy. Bemoy spoke of wars between the king of the 'Moses' and 'Mandi-Mansa, king of the Mandings', and described the customs of the 'Moses' in such a way that his listeners were convinced that they were Christians; at any rate they were not Muslims, which is where João de Barros is in agreement with the authors of the *Ta'rīkh*s.[15]

The account of João de Barros thus corroborates the Timbuktu chronicles in only one respect. As for the other written sources quoted, although they are not explicit, they at least confirm that, throughout the fifteenth century, a black and 'pagan' power confronted the Mali and the Songhay empires, and the other great hegemonies in that part of West Africa were in a permanent state of conflict with it. In addition, we are indebted to Claude Meillassoux for having collected some interesting Malian oral traditions;[16] these are interesting, though admittedly difficult to interpret, because they seem to relate to the Mossi of the north, of whom he finds traces in Hodh, Kaniaga and Wagadu, a region very remote from the Niger Bend. These oral traditions are so far the only ones which refer to the warlike people of the *Ta'rīkh*s. In Diankoloni, between Niamina and Niara, there is a line of wells said to have been dug by the Mossi, which hardly tallies with the purely warlike image we have of them. In this region the Mossi are said to have wiped out or assimilated the great majority of the Sumare clans, whereas the Dyariso clans held out victoriously against the invaders. The memory remains of a battle said to have been fought between the Mossi and the local population near the present site of Dangite-Kamara, some 100 km south of Mourdia. In Hodh, we are told, the Mossi occupied several places and set up a territorial command in Gara covering some forty villages; they are said to have invaded Daole-Guilbe, not far from the site of Koumbi Ṣāleḥ.[17]

15. From J. de Barros, French transl. 1909, pp. 6–18; cf. also L. Tauxier, 1917, pp. 84–5; and Izard, op. cit., Vol. 1, pp. 53–5.

16. Personal communication, cited in Izard, op. cit., Vol. 1, pp. 55–6.

17. Koumbi Ṣāleḥ, the presumed capital of the Ghana empire, 60 km south of Timbedra in Mauritania.

The Mossi of the Niger Bend and the Volta basin: the classical thesis

When the first authors began writing about the Mossi of the White Volta basin, they based their historical analyses on the oral tradition, which traces the descent of all the Mossi royal dynasties from a single ancestor, Naaba Wedraogo, and establishes an explicit relation between the origin of the Mossi kingdoms and that of the Mamprusi–Nanumba–Dagomba states. Delafosse, Frobenius and Tauxier were the first to attempt to trace the history of the Mossi: Delafosse through his study of colonial administrative monographs from 1909, and the other two on the basis of material collected directly.[18] In current Mossi traditions no trace can be found of former clashes with the Songhay or of a lasting Mossi presence within the Niger Bend. The authors mentioned above were familiar with the *Ta'rīkh al-Sūdān*; the *Ta'rīkh al-fattāsh*, however, was published and translated later than the other great Timbuktu chronicle and had not then been the subject of any comparable exegesis. Despite the silence of Mossi oral tradition regarding what we call the Mossi of the Niger Bend, there was no doubt in the minds of these true founders of Mossi historiography that the northern Mossi and those of the White Volta were one and the same people. It was of course possible, and even natural, that they should advance the hypothesis – for it was no more than a hypothesis, based almost exclusively on the similarity of ethnonym parallels – but, once it had been put forward, steps should have been taken to verify it and, if no decisive proof was forthcoming, it should have been abandoned. That hypothesis has never been verified, for it is not reasonable to consider as proof of its validity the possible relationship between, for instance, the name of a Mossi chief mentioned in one of the chronicles – Na'asira[19] – and that of one of the sovereigns of Yatenga, otherwise obscure.[20] Yet it is on such flimsy foundations that the history of the Mossi has been constructed, at the risk of obscuring the original features of the state or pre-state formations of the Mossi of the Niger Bend and, even worse, of emasculating historical research into them, by taking as resolved a problem which has not even been posed.

By equating the Mossi of the Niger Bend with those of the White Volta, Delafosse and Tauxier in particular provided an inexpensive chronological framework for the history of the present Mossi kingdoms; at the same time, they gave that chronology a far greater 'length' than can be inferred solely by considering the oral traditions of these kingdoms and the neigh-

18. M. Delafosse, 1912, Vol. 2, pp. 140–2; L. Frobenius, 1925, pp. 260–2; Tauxier, 1917, pp. 67–84.

19. Delafosse, op. cit., Vol. 2, pp. 141–2; Tauxier, 1917, p. 81.

20. The sovereign in question was Yatenga naaba Nasoda, whose no doubt short reign occurred in the first half of the seventeenth century.

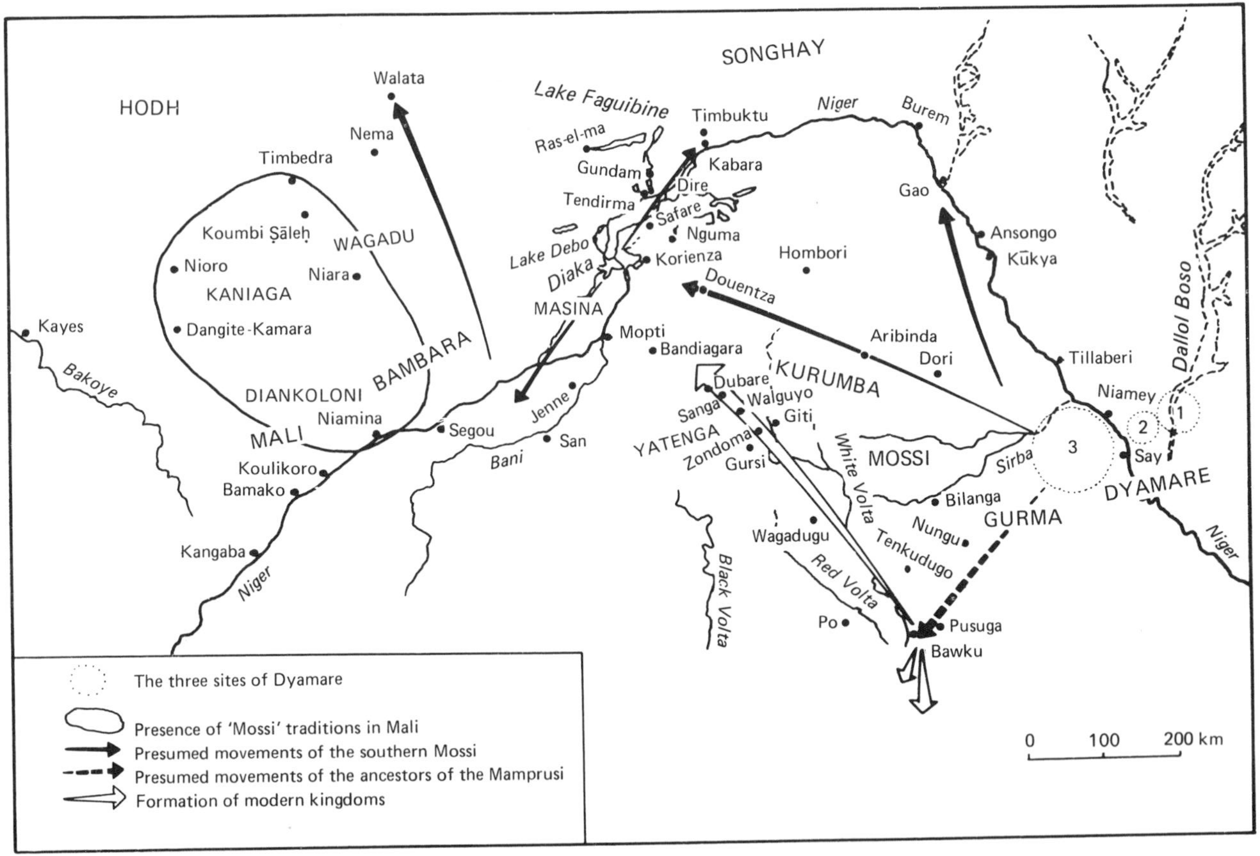

FIG. 9.1 *The Niger Bend and the Volta basin, 1100–1600*
Source: M. Izard in 'Introduction à l'Histoire des Royaumes Mossi' (doctoral dissertation, Paris University, 1970)

bouring historical formations. To maintain the validity of the dominant tradition concerning the southern origin of the present-day Mossi kingdoms and to make the Mossi of the White Volta the conquerors of Timbuktu, it was necessary to formulate the following complementary hypothesis: the Mossi were unable to embark upon their wide-ranging military campaigns until they had firmly established their power over the autochthonous populations of the Volta; the actions mentioned in the *Ta'rīkh*s could not have been conducted in the early stages of the history of the kingdoms. Delafosse, to give credibility to a hypothesis as hazardous as it was unverified, even placed the beginnings of the history of the present-day Mossi kingdoms around the end of the tenth century.[21] This involved either expanding considerably the average length of the reign of those Mossi sovereigns for whom this information is not directly given in the oral tradition, or taking the view that there are gaps in the dynastic lists found in Mossi territory, which is both unverifiable and unlikely if we consider only the wealth of genealogical material on the dynasties of kings and chiefs provided by current oral tradition.

A French military administrator, Captain Lambert, to his credit criticized as early as 1907 the tendency to equate the Mossi of the *Ta'rīkh*s with the present-day Mossi.[22] Unfortunately for Mossi historiography, Lambert's study – remarkable though it is – was never published, with the result that the theses of Delafosse and Tauxier were accepted as unquestioned dogma, no account even being taken of the divergences between the two authors, let alone the origin of those divergences.[23] It was not until 1964 that what may be called the 'classical' thesis – that of Delafosse and Tauxier – was the subject of radical criticism by the eminent British historian, John Fage. In a memorable article, Fage re-examined the classical thesis in detail and, after refuting it, proposed an overall reinterpretation of the history of the 'Mossi', in which he began by drawing a clear distinction between the Mossi of the Niger Bend and those of the Volta basin, although he did not rule out the hypothesis – presented with a great deal of qualification – of a possible relationship between those two groups.[24]

For Fage, the classical thesis comes up against one insurmountable difficulty in respect of chronology. Following an analysis of Dagomba oral traditions carried out with the late David Tait, Fage concludes that the traditional chronology of the history of the Mossi is too long and so too is the – generally accepted – chronology given by Tamakloe for the history of the Dagomba; he therefore proposes to date the beginning of

21. Delafosse, op. cit.

22. The original of Lambert's monograph is preserved in the archives of Senegal, in Dakar.

23. Delafosse, after the publication of his work in 1912, never re-examined it, differing in this from Tauxier, whose 1924 theories are more qualified regarding the interpretation of the *Ta'rīkh*s than those put forward in 1917.

24. J. D. Fage, 1964a.

the reign of Na Nyaghse, founder of the Dagomba state, at about 1480.[25] Thus, for Fage, the birth of the state formation from which the kingdoms which we are considering originated cannot have been earlier than the fifteenth century. Fage accepts the hypothesis of a common origin of the Mossi of the north and those of the Volta, but assigns the former to a pre-state phase, and the latter to a state phase, of the same history. Following the line traced by Fage, in 1965 Nehemia Levtzion presented a comparative chronological table for all the states of the Volta basin (except for Gurma, for which no information exists).[26] Levtzion's findings, compiled from a study of dynastic tables and based on acceptance of an average generation span of forty years, tally with those of Fage, since he places Na Nyaghse between 1460 and 1500, and the two previous generations in the periods 1380–1420 and 1420–60 respectively (first generation: foundation of the Mamprusi kingdom; second generation: foundation of the Nanumba kingdom).

I myself have sought to contribute to this debate and have proposed a chronological framework for the history of the state-like formations of the Volta based on an analysis of Mossi genealogical material, particularly that relating to the two principal present-day Mossi kingdoms; Wagadugu and Yatenga.[27] The method used consisted of first defining a pivotal date for the foundation of Yatenga by determining the average length of a generation, itself based on consideration of the lengths of the pre-colonial reigns, wherever this is possible. This gave me the year 1540 for the foundation of the Yatenga. I then went back from Naaba Yadega, founder of the Yatenga, to his ancestor Naaba Wubri, founder of the kingdom of Wagadugu, using the specific characteristics of the dynastic genealogy of Wagadugu for this extrapolation. This gave 1495 as the beginning of the reign of Naaba Wubri. To go back beyond the foundation of the kingdom of Wagadugu, I was forced, because of the poverty of the genealogical data and the uncertainties regarding the way in which power was transmitted, to propose an open chronology, the average length of a generation varying between fifteen and thirty years. Before Naaba Wubri the Mossi royal genealogies mention his 'father', Naaba Zungrana, the latter's 'father',

TABLE 9.1 *An open chronological table of five Mossi 'reigns'*

Years per generation	*15*	*20*	*25*	*30*
5 Naaba Wubri	1495	1495	1495	1495
4 Naaba Zungrana	1480	1475	1470	1465
3 Naaba Wedraogo	1465	1455	1445	1435
2 Yenenga	1450	1435	1420	1405
1 Na Bawa	1435	1415	1395	1375

25. The investigations carried out by Fage and Tait into the history of the Dagomba kingdom have not been published.

26. N. Levtzion, 1968, pp. 194–203.

27. Izard, op. cit., Vol. 1, pp. 56–70.

Naaba Wedraogo, and *his* mother, Yenenga, eldest daughter (?) of the founder of the Mamprusi kingdom, who was called Na Bawa or Gweba by the Mamprusi and Na Nedega by the Mossi and the Dagomba. This gives the results shown in Table 9.1, in which the dates indicated mark the beginnings of the 'reigns', whether real or fictitious (as with Yenenga at least).

It will be noted that in Table 9.1, each column corresponds to one standard average length for a generation, varying from fifteen to thirty years. It may be thought that in fact – and this is the most likely assumption – the length may have varied from one generation to another, so that a complete table would have to take into account every possible combination of length of generations. As presented, this open chronology is not at variance with that proposed by Levtzion since, on the basis of an average generation length of forty years, he places the reign of Na Bawa between 1380 and 1420, whereas, for the longest reigns, I place it either between 1400 and 1420 (for a generation length of twenty-five years) or between 1375 and 1405 (for a generation length of thirty years).

The origin of the states of the Volta basin: the present state of our knowledge

Let me recapitulate what can be learned from the various sources relating to the Mossi of the Niger Bend. During the first half of the thirteenth century, the proto-Mossi of Dyamare II (Minji) crossed the river in the region of Say and founded the third Dyamare. The early history of Dyamare III seems to have been dominated by wars against the Songhay of Gao, no doubt aimed at consolidating the new territorial formation. In the fourteenth century, once this had been achieved, the target of Mossi expansion was no longer to the east, but to the west of the Niger Bend, as shown by the 1337 expedition against Timbuktu. The fifteenth century opened with a new Mossi thrust towards the west and the north-west, with the raid against Benka. The second half of the fifteenth century was marked first by important Mossi successes, then by a vigorous and soon victorious Songhay counter-offensive, led by Sunni ʿAlī. Then, from the reign of Askiya Muḥammad to that of Askiya Dāwūd, for nearly a century, the Mossi, against whom the Songhay Muslim sovereigns preached holy war, were completely on the defensive. By about 1575, all organized resistance by the northern Mossi was at an end.

Until we have satisfactory information on Gurma, and until such time as archaeology comes to back up the study of texts and the collection of oral traditions, it will not be possible to propose valid hypotheses regarding the relationship between the Mossi of the north and those of the Volta basin, or, more broadly, between the Mossi of the Dyamare and the warriors present at the origin of the formation of the Mamprusi kingdom, from which came the Nanumba and Dagomba formations, on the one hand,

and the present-day Mossi formations on the other, and from which, finally, the present Nungu dynasty (Fada Ngurma) is perhaps derived. The question is an important one and in fact concerns the way in which a pattern of political organization was disseminated through a vast region of West Africa, perhaps from Bornu, with a possible staging post at Zamfara, in present-day Hausa territory. What does seem to be firmly established is that the ancestors of the Mamprusi sovereigns came from the east. According to northern Ghanaian traditions, the original direct ancestor of Na Bawa, the first Mamprusi sovereign (late fourteenth–early fifteenth century), was a 'red hunter', known by the name of Tohajiye. This is the predominant tradition, recorded by Tamakloe among the Dagomba in 1931.[28]

Tohajiye lived in a cave and hunted in a region bordering on the kingdom of Malle, itself close to Hausa territory. Being at war with his neighbours, the king of Malle called upon Tohajiye for help; when peace returned, the king, in return for services rendered, gave the hunter one of his daughters, Pagawolga, who had a limp. Pagawolga gave birth to a boy, Kpogonumbo, who according to some traditions had only one arm and one leg, but on whose gigantic stature all traditions agree. Kpogonumbo lived with his father until he reached manhood. In difficulty once again, the king of Malle requested from the son the help which he could no longer ask of the father. After waging war victoriously on behalf of his protector, Kpogonumbo decided to leave for the west rather than return to the paternal cave. After travelling for several days, he reached Biun, in Gurma. The 'master of the land' of Biun gave Kpogonumbo one of his daughters, Suhusabga or Sisabge. Five sons were born to that union: twins, who died in infancy, followed by Namzisielle, Nyalgeh and Ngmalgensam. Anxious to take command of Biun, Kpogonumbo put to death his father-in-law and had himself recognized as chief. This usurpation aroused the wrath of Daramani, king of Gurma, who went to war against the chief of Biun; unable to defeat Kpogonumbo, Daramani decided to make peace and gave his former adversary one of his daughters, Soyini or Solyini, as a surety; she gave birth to a boy, the future Na Bawa or Gbewa, known to the Dagomba and the Mossi by the name of Na Nedega. Of the immediate descendants of Kpogonumbo, this last son was the only one to leave Gurma to seek his fortune elsewhere. At the head of a large band of warriors, he entered what is now Kusasi territory and established his residence in Pusuga, from where he waged war against the Kusasi and the Bisa in order to establish his authority over the region.

Na Bawa had nine children: one girl, the eldest, called Kachiogo, and eight boys, named successively Zirili, Kufogo, Tohago, Ngmantambo, Sitobo, Sibie, Biemmone and Bogoyelgo. Although his successor should have been Zirili, the eldest son, Na Bawa arranged with his other children

28. E. F. Tamakloe, 1931.

to keep the heir from power, fearing his wickedness. Na Bawa chose as his successor his second son Kufogo, but, warned by his mother of what was being plotted against him, Zirili had the designated heir put to death; Na Bawa died when he learned of Kufogo's death. Na Bawa's eldest child, the girl Kachiogo, acceded to the throne, but Zirili succeeded in ousting her from the royal power, leaving her only, as consolation, the command of Gundogo. Zirili appears to have been the true organizer of the Mamprusi kingdom. On his death, a conflict over succession broke out between three of his younger brothers, Tohago (Tosugo), Ngmantambo and Sitobo. Tohago was driven from the kingdom of Na Bawa; he established Nalerigu and founded the present Mamprusi dynasty. Ngmantambo settled among the Nanumba, whose king he became. Sitobo settled successively in Gambaga, then in Nabare; during his lifetime his eldest son Nyaghse settled in Bagale and founded the Dagomba dynasty.

It goes without saying that what I have just summarized in a few lines merits development at much greater length, for strictly speaking all the many different variants of this general tradition should be taken into account. What is important here, however, is to seek in this material some general historical pointers.

If the chronology proposed by myself, or the very similar one proposed by Levtzion, is accepted, the proto-history of the Mamprusi was enacted in Hausa territory (that is to say, on the Hausa bank of the Niger), then in Gurma, during the fourteenth century, in other words during the period when the Mossi of the Niger Bend launched their first major expeditions towards the west. If there is any relationship between these Mossi and the ancestors of the Mamprusi, it can only be in a common but remote origin, which might date back to the time of Dyamare II (on the Hausa bank of the Niger) and Dyamare III (on the Gurma bank). It is perhaps possible to assign to the thirteenth century the period when, starting from the territorial base of the proto-Mossi, mercenary warriors entered Gurma, crossed it and reached the region of Pusuga. It will have been noticed that the Dagomba traditions related by Tamakloe speak of a king of Malle, a name suggestive of Mali. It will also be noted in this connection that the present-day Mossi of Yatenga distinguish between two 'Mandes', a western Mande corresponding to Mali, and an eastern Mande, from which the Kurumba of Lurum and the Mossi of the old minor command of Bursuma are said to have come.[29]

As I have said, Na Bawa is known among present-day Mossi by the name of Na Nedega, and Kachiogo, the eldest daughter of Na Bawa according to Dagomba tradition, can be equated with Yenenga, the eldest daughter of Na Nedega in Mossi tradition. What is important here is not so much

29. For an overall study of the Kurumba, see A.-M. Schweeger-Hefel and W. Staude, 1972, particularly pp. 19–127. Bursuma is a village in the centre of Yatenga whose inhabitants claim to be Mossi from eastern Mande; they are considered to be people of the land by the other Mossi.

the details of the traditions – which are highly complex, in any case – as our knowledge of two facts: (1) that a direct link exists between the formation of the Mamprusi, Nanumba and Dagomba states, on the one hand, and the Mossi states, on the other: (2) that this direct link is not through an agnatic relationship – the type of relationship prevalent among the north Ghanaian dynasties – but through a uterine relationship which, in a patrilineal society, is the undeniable mark of a solution of continuity, a dialectic of historical continuity and interruption.

I have found no less than fifteen versions of the legendary history of the origin of the Mossi kingdoms, and a careful collection of oral traditions would certainly bring many more to light. Let us examine what may be termed the dominant tradition, the one which largely prevails in Mossi country, particularly in the kingdom of Wagadugu. It relates that Na Nedega, king of the Dagomba (not of the Mamprusi), whose capital was Gambaga, had an eldest daughter, Yenenga, whom he refused to give in marriage, preferring to keep her with him because of her value as a warrior. The different versions of the dominant tradition seem unsure as to the reasons which led Yenenga, riding a stallion, into a forest near Bitu, where she lost her way. Did she flee her father's abode, little inclined to sacrifice her womanhood to his military designs, or did her horse bolt, separating her from the troop of horsemen she was leading? Whatever the reason, in the course of her desired or enforced ride through the forest she met a prince of Mande origin, Ryale or Ryare, an elephant hunter by trade. From that encounter a boy was born, known in Mossi country by the name of Naaba Wedraogo, from the More word *wedraogo*, which means 'stallion'. Naaba Wedraogo was to become the first of the Mossi, the common ancestor of an entire people.

The known traditions are silent about Ryale, who appears here merely as the sire of Naaba Wedraogo; socially speaking, Naaba Wedraogo has no 'father', he is only the son of Yenenga. The same traditions also have little to say about the end of Yenenga's life and her son's first steps upon the stage of history. Some relate, however, that, once old enough to bear arms, Naaba Wedraogo was introduced by his mother to his maternal grandfather, who placed his uterine grandson at the head of a troop of warriors. As will be recalled, this was probably in the middle of the fifteenth century.

There are many indications that the state of Gurma was already in existence, even if the sovereigns of that time did not necessarily belong to the present ruling dynasty. Rather than a single centralized state, Gurma must then have been – and, to a certain extent, has since remained – a confederation of territorial commands more or less independent of each other. We know that Gurma is mentioned in both the *Ta'rīkh*s. For instance, the last raid carried out by Sunni 'Alī was directed against that country at the end of the fifteenth century.[30] In the sixteenth century, all the

30. Al-Sa'dī, loc. cit., pp. 105 and 115–16.

Songhay sovereigns launched raids against the 'pagans' of Gurma. In the appendix to the *Ta'rīkh al-fattāsh* written by Ibn al-Moktar, grandson of the main author of the chronicle, Maḥmūd Ka'ti, there is mention of Askiya Isḥāḳ's entrance into Bilanga, the 'royal residence of the sovereign of Gurma'.[31] Apart from these very few facts, we are at present almost totally ignorant of the origins of the state of Gurma – or of the various states which succeeded each other in that same territory.

The dominant Mossi tradition, however, does have something to say about the origin of the dynasty of Nungu: it describes the first Nunbado (sovereign of Nungu), Dyaba, ancestor of the Lompo, as a son of Naaba Wedraogo, but this tradition seems to be a late one and almost certainly stems from Mossi ideological imperialism. In Durtenga, Junzo Kawada found a tradition according to which Dyaba was the son of Na Nedega, king of Gambaga.[32] It is significant that these traditions seem to be unknown in Gurma itself, where it is related that, like the first Kurumba king of Lurum, the first king of Nungu descended from heaven, a legend which at least has the interest of marking the independence of the history of the dynasty of Gurma from that of the northern Ghanaian and Mossi dynasties.[33]

The beginnings of the history of the Mossi kingdoms

During the sixteenth century the descendants of Naaba Wedraogo extended their sway over all the peoples of the valley of the White Volta; in the west they reached and crossed the Red Volta, and Boromo, in the valley of the Black Volta, marked the westernmost stage of the Mossi advance. This was followed by some regrouping and a stabilization of Mossi territory, the frontiers of which remained unchanged until the colonial period, when a new type of Mossi expansionism developed in the form of agricultural colonization.

The beginnings of the history of the Mossi kingdoms were for long obscure, largely owing to the delayed predominance exerted by the Tenkudugo (Tenkogodo) tradition over the older but now not very widespread traditions of the southern commands. Thanks to the work of Junzo Kawada, it is now possible to form a fairly precise idea of the complexity of the origin of the territorial commands in the south of Mossi territory.[34] Because of this complexity, it is not yet possible to obtain an overall view of that history; what is certain is that a long period of maturation preceded the actual conquest of the valley of the White Volta and the establishment of the great royal dynasties which we know today. According to Kawada,

31. Maḥmūd Ka'ti, loc. cit., 1898, pp. 275–6, note 1, p. 276, note 2.
32. J. Kawada, 1979.
33. W. Staude, 1961.
34. Kawada, op. cit.

the Mamprusi kingdom in its first form originated in Pusuga; Zambarga and Sanga were the first Mossi commands in the strict sense. The local dynasties of Durtenga and Komin-Yanga, whose chiefs were Gurmankyeba – or more accurately Yarse[35] – seem to have come directly from Pusuga and, as has been seen, the present Nungu dynasty might have originated in Durtenga. From the Zambarga command is said to have come the Kinzem command, which in turn led to those of Wargay, Lalgay and Tenoagen; it is supposed to have been from Kinzem that the first conquerors left for the north-west. The Gode dynasty, from which in turn the Tenkudugo dynasty was detached, is said to have come from that of Tenoagen.

After what appears to have been a period of preparation for ambitious politico-military undertakings, the setting for which was a southerly territory around Zambarga, Kinzem and a few other small places, the Mossi conquests developed rapidly. Two major figures in this early history, Naaba Rawa and Naaba Zungrana, whose actions can be situated in the second half of the fifteenth century, are placed by oral tradition in the generation of the 'sons' of Naaba Wedraogo. No doubt it is hardly necessary to stress that the filial – and hence fraternal – relationships which I have given for the first figures of Mossi history are highly problematical; this is particularly true where the association of Naaba Wedraogo with Naaba Rawa and with Naaba Zungrana is concerned. It is remarkable to note in this connection that the traditions relating to these two supposed sons of Naaba Wedraogo are mutually exclusive: where Naaba Rawa is known, Naaba Zungrana is unknown, and vice versa. Moreover, although there can be no doubt as to the historical existence of Naaba Rawa, in view of the great quantity of concordant information and evidence relating to him, that of Naaba Zungrana is much more open to question. Whereas traces of Naaba Zungrana can be found only in a few places in the south and centre of Mossi country, Naaba Rawa immediately assumes the stature of a great conqueror.

The musicians of Yatenga acclaim Naaba Rawa as the chief of Po (Kasena territory, known as Pugo in More), Zondoma, Sanga and Dubare, the last three places now being situated in the territory of the great Mossi kingdom of the north. Naaba Rawa was the founder of the sole Mossi political foundation in history to merit the name of 'empire', known by the name of Rawatenga.[36] For a very brief period this united under a single authority the greater part of present-day Mossi territory, with a large network of local commands in the central part of the country, the main ones being Nyu, Nanoro, Sao, Dapelego, Magé and Yubu. Rawatenga, too large and

35. In More the term *yanga* designates the east; the Yarse are people of the east in relation to the Mossi of the southern zone and are regarded as intermediaries between the Mossi and the Gurmankyeba.

36. In More the word *tenga* means the earth and also has the sense of 'territory'; such formations as Rawatenga, 'land of Rawa', Yatenga, 'land of Yadega' and Wubritenga, 'land of Wubri' are derived from it.

established at too remote a period, when the density of Mossi commands was still low and the submission of the autochthonous populations still partial, was unable to preserve its unity. Although a few sons or companions of Naaba Rawa long maintained commands in the centre of Mossi territory, the only coherent political formation which emerged from Rawatenga, even during Naaba Rawa's lifetime, was the kingdom of Zondoma, whose name was taken from one of Naaba Rawa's three residences in present-day Yatenga.

Naaba Rawa ended his conquests in the plain of Gondo, peopled by Dogon, whom he drove out of Yatenga in the direction of the Bandiagara cliff (Sanga and Dubare are now situated on the borders of Mossi territory and Dogon territory). In the north, Naaba Rawa set up numerous local commands, which he entrusted to sons, younger brothers and lieutenants. In Yatenga today there are many chiefs belonging directly or by assimilation to that lineage, including the chief of the village of Zondoma, where the tomb of the prestigious Naaba Rawa is located; they have there the status of 'masters of war' (*tasobanamba*) and throughout the kingdom's history have supplied many court dignitaries (*nayiridemba*). It was largely at the expense of the kingdom of Zondoma that the territorial development of Yatenga took place, from the second half of the sixteenth century. As has been said, Mossi historiography has but little to say at present about Naaba Zungrana, the younger 'brother' of Naaba Rawa; traces of him are to be found, however, at various points in the country, particularly in the southern region of Manga, and the two small kingdoms of Ratenga and Zitenga, bordering on Yatenga in the south-east, are reputed to have been founded by 'sons' of this little-known chief.

During this period, when the first Mossi political formations were being established, we can distinguish five major streams of penetration into the central area of the White Volta basin from the south. The first was in the western part of the area, with Naaba Pasgo and Naaba Silga, who crossed the White Volta and extended their influence over the regions of Kombisiri and Manga. The second had as its objective the region of Kugupela (Koupela). The third was on the shores of the lake of Bam, where Naaba Ratageba, founder of Ratenga, settled; not far from there his brother, Naaba Ziido, founded Zitenga. The fourth, with Naaba Gigma, was directed towards the region of Bulsa. The fifth ended in the heart of the central zone, where Wubritenga was to be founded, as its name indicates, by Naaba Wubri, 'son' of Naaba Zungrana. Among the conquerors and founders of dynasties of the late fifteenth and early sixteenth centuries, two figures stand out: Naaba Gigma and Naaba Wubri. According to the eastern traditions Naaba Gigma was an older brother of Naaba Wubri, who was ousted from power by his younger brother.[37] Naaba Gigma em-

37. The ousting of an elder by a younger brother is a frequently recurring theme in Mossi territory in the original traditions of the territorial commands.

barked upon the conquest of the eastern part of present-day Mossi territory and extended his influence northward as far as the present borders of Liptako.[38] It is interesting to note in this connection that the Mossi political formations of the east make up a single broad territorial strip running from north to south along the frontier of Gurma: it would seem that by then the Gurmankyeba were already organized on a sufficiently firm basis for their territory to have offered an insurmountable barrier to Mossi designs for expansion to the east.

Naaba Wubri was the founder of the present ruling dynasty of the kingdom of Wagadugu, whose sovereigns bear the title of *Moogo Naaba*, 'chief of the Moogo', that is to say of all Mossi country.[39] I have placed the political appearance of Naaba Wubri at the very end of the fifteenth century (1495, as a formal hypothesis); in practice, therefore, his reign covers the beginning of the sixteenth century. Naaba Wubri took possession of the region of Zinyare, which subsequently took the name of Wubritenga: it is related that his coming put an end to the incessant wars waged among themselves by the autochthonous peoples. From Wubritenga, Naaba Wubri extended his authority to the east and north-east; he made war on the people of Lay, and his conquests led him as far as Yako and Kudugo (Koudougou), into regions where the Mossi already had numerous local commands, some of which had belonged to Rawatenga. Naaba Wubri died in La, near Yako, which he had perhaps made his last residence; his remains were transferred to the village known since then as *wubriyaoge* ('place of Wubri's tomb'), and his relics were placed in Gilongu, Dabozuge-Yaoge and Lumbila, where sanctuaries of the kings of Wagadugu are to be found.

On the death of Naaba Wubri, the kingdom which he had founded included under one command nearly all the local divisions of the central region; his immediate successors were to continue his work, in particular by extending their influence westwards. In the reign of Naaba Nasbiire, the third son of Naaba Wubri to become king, the royal capital was La, where the founder of the dynasty had died. Two sons of Naaba Wubri set out in the direction of present-day Yatenga: Naaba Rimso, who established the Gambo command, and his younger brother, Naaba Wumtane, founder of the kingdom of Giti, who fought against the Dogon and enslaved the smiths. During the same period, a military chief, Naaba Swida, settled in Minima, near Gursi, where he was joined by another chief from the south, Naaba Warma.

The accession of Naaba Kumdumye, son of Naaba Nyingnemdo and grandson of Naaba Wubri, coincided with the departure of Naaba Yadega, son of Naaba Nasbiire, for the region of Gursi. Naaba Yadega, who had

38. It will be recalled that Liptako, a Fulani amirate whose capital is Dori, was constituted long after the period considered here; the population of this region of the north of the Upper Volta must have consisted of Songhay, Kurumba and Gurmankyeba.

39. The Mossi (*Moose*, sing. *Mooga*) call all the country which they control *Moogo*; the territory of the Mossi is, in practice, equated with the 'world'.

been brought up by Naaba Swida, chief of Minima, had been unable to get the better of Naaba Kumdumye in the struggle for power and went off to try his luck elsewhere, accompanied by his eldest sister, Pabre, who had stolen for him the regalia placed in her custody in her capacity as *napoko*.[40] My hypothesis is that these events took place in 1540: as already stated, this is our second pivotal date in the history of the Mossi. Naaba Kumdumye was to play a considerable role in the establishment of the present kingdoms. Under his leadership, the Mossi advance reached its highest point with a deep, though short-lived, penetration into Gurunsi territory. The direct descendants of Naaba Kumdumye were the founders of the present-day kingdoms of Konkistenga, Yako, Tema, Mane and Busuma. During the preceding generation, the present dynasty of Bulsa had been founded by a son of Naaba Wubri, Naaba Namende, who thus acquired part of the political heritage of Naaba Gigma. The kingdom of Kugupela was founded by a son of Naaba Namende, Naaba Kurita.[41] The foundation of the kingdom of Kayao can be attributed to another grandson of Naaba Wubri, Naaba Yelleku, son of Naaba Nasbiire and consequently brother of Naaba Yadega by the same father. With Naaba Kuda, the son of Naaba Kumdumye (second half of the sixteenth century), the central Mossi territory assumed its final shape; the main initiative of this sovereign, the last *Moogo Naaba* of the period under consideration here, was to send his son Naaba Tasango, founder of the present kingdom of Tatenga, into the mountains of Risyam.

By the time Naaba Yadega reached the region of Gursi, there were already a large number of Mossi commands in what is now Yatenga territory.[42] The principal political force in the region was the kingdom of Zondoma, the northern incarnation of Rawatenga, but it was rivalled by other formations, first among them the kingdom of Giti; in the south-west, on the borders of the newly-established Mossi territory and of Samo territory, the Minima and Gursi commands were merely the two principal Mossi strongholds of a series around which small regional commands were formed. From Gursi, Naaba Yadega set out to achieve three aims: to neutralize

40. On the death of a Mossi chief or king, between the official announcement of his death (not to be confused with the actual time of his death) and the appointment of his successor, his position is temporarily assumed by his eldest daughter, who is given the title of *napoko*, literally 'chief woman'; the *napoko* is a substitute for her father, whose clothes she wears.

41. The *kurita* is the representative among the living of a dead chief; the word *kurita*, which means 'reigning dead man' is constructed by analogy with *narita*, 'reigning chief'. The *kurita* is generally chosen from among the sons of the dead chief; he has no power by virtue of his title and he is debarred from the succession, but he can become a chief in an area outside his family's command; if a *kurita* becomes a chief, he retains the *nom de guerre* (*zab yure*) of *naaba kurita*.

42. Gursi today is an important place in south-west Yatenga; it seems to have been an important economic centre, a crafts and trading centre, and a staging post on the caravan route at a very early period.

his adoptive father, Naaba Swida; to form an alliance with the Gursi chief, Naaba Warma; and to extend his conquests in the direction of Samo territory. Firmly settled in Gursi, Naaba Yadega established a second residential area at Lago. Under Naaba Geda, the second son of Naaba Yadega, who was in power at the end of the sixteenth century, the young kingdom of Yatenga finally broke all its links with the kingdom of Wagadugu.[43] From that time on, the two great Mossi kingdoms, Wagadugu and Yatenga, were to have separate destinies and were to constitute the two territorial poles of the Mossi hegemony, each of them being surrounded by small vassal kingdoms constituting their zones of influence.

To sum up, the history of the Mossi kingdoms, which began in the first half or the middle of the fifteenth century, developed through three main phases during the period with which we are concerned: first, there was a phase of preparation (the second half of the fifteenth century); then came a phase of conquest (the first half of the sixteenth century); and finally, a phase of stabilization (the second half of the sixteenth century).

The Mossi political system

I shall here give only a very brief outline of the Mossi political system; indeed, we know very little about the history of Mossi institutions, which can be outlined only from the end of the eighteenth century for Yatenga and the beginning of the nineteenth for the kingdom of Wagadugu. In fact, the wealth of information available concerning the organization of the Mossi kingdoms, which began to be collected in 1907, makes it possible to describe how the public institutions functioned, but only at the very end of the pre-colonial period. The fundamental feature of the Mossi political system, as all observers agree, is the distinction made by society between those who held the mastery of the land (*tengsobondo*) and those who held the power (*naam*); the former, representing the autochthonous inhabitants, are also called 'people of the land' or 'sons of the land', the latter in principle are the Mossi. But here the distinction between the indigenous people and the conquerors is not always free of ambiguity; furthermore, at least where the 'people of power' are concerned, it is necessary to include with the Mossi proper (that is, the descendants of Naaba Wedraogo) the captives of the royal courts, who were for the most part of outside origin. Directly connected to this distinction between 'the people of the land' and 'the people of power' was the distinction made between 'the master of the land' (*tengsoba*) and the chief (*naaba*); it also had repercussions for religious ideology, since the people of the land, as their name indicates, were associated with earth worship, whereas the people

43. The founder of Yatenga, Naaba Yadega, held the royal insignia of Naaba Wubri, stolen by his eldest sister, the *napoko* Pabre, but we are told that Naaba Kurita and Naaba Geda, his two immediate successors, were enthroned at La, at that time the residence of the kings of Wagadugu.

of power recognized the divine supremacy of Wende, who was believed to be of celestial – perhaps solar – origin. The unity of society, in which religion was associated with the autochthonous people and power with the conquerors, was marked by the syncretic union of Naaba Wende and Napaga Tenga (*napaga*: chief's wife).

We know little about the identity of the pre-Mossi populations, except for Yatenga, the history of whose settlement has been established.[44] It appears possible to distinguish three main indigenous groups. First, there were the peoples known as Gurunsi, speaking the 'Voltaic' or Gur language; they may be linked, by reason of linguistic affinities, with the Kurumba, whom the Mossi called the Fulse and who constituted the principal pre-Mossi stock of Yatenga. There were also the Dogon (Kibse in More), whose former habitat seems to have been very extensive in Mossi territory but who, because of their armed resistance to the conquest, were the principal victims of the new power. Finally, there were the Mande peoples, the two main groups being the Samo (Ninise) and the Bisa (Busase), now separated territorially but having perhaps a common origin. Masters of the land, the autochthonous inhabitants were responsible for the annual fertility rites and in Yatenga, for instance, it was by means of sacrifices on certain land altars that a newly designated king, who like every holder of power bore the title of *naaba* (Yatenga *naaba*), could be enthroned and thus acquire the right to assume the title *rima*, which entitled him to be buried in the royal cemetery and allowed his sons or *rimbio* to aspire to the throne.

To continue with the example of Yatenga, the holders of power, apart from the king himself, may be divided into three categories: the 'people of the king's household' (*nayiridemba*); the 'masters of war' (*tasobanamba*); and the members of the royal lineage or *nakombse*, from which the sovereign was descended. The people of the king's household, or royal servants, and the masters of war might be either Mossi or royal captives; those who were of Mossi origin belonged to long-established families of chiefs, whose origin often went back to pre-Yatenga political formations (for instance, the kingdom of Zondoma). Thus it was from Mossi only remotely related to him, or from captives, that the king chose those on whom his power was directly based, whereas it was against those near to him, the *nakombse*, that the power was apt to be exercised. The Yatenga *naaba* lived in one of the country's four royal residences, surrounded by his wives and by Mossi or captive servants. The royal servants were organized in four groups for each of the royal residences; each of these groups was headed by a high-ranking dignitary called *nesomde* (plur. *nesomba*). For each of the four potential courts there was thus a college of four *nesomba*, three of Mossi origin (*togo naaba*, *balum naaba* and *waranga naaba*) and one of captive origin (*bin naaba* or *rasam naaba*).

One particular college of *nesomba* dignitaries appointed by the king, which

44. Cf. M. Izard, 1965.

was associated with the effective royal residence, constituted a veritable government of the kingdom and, on the king's death, played the part of an electoral college. It was responsible for choosing the new king from among the aspirants to the throne, within a system of devolution of power that had no automatic rule of succession. The transfer of power from elder brother to younger brother in fact made it possible for any king's son to aspire to the throne, or more accurately for any who was the eldest of a group of full brothers, sons of the same king, to do so. The history of Yatenga in the nineteenth century, now well known, shows that the laxity of Mossi custom regarding the transfer of power had the effect of triggering regular dynastic crises, which led to real civil wars between opposing factions belonging to the royal lineage. After the period of external conquest, the Mossi, we may conclude, became engaged in incessant struggles for power within their own frontiers, despite an ever-increasing centralization of authority and the ever-growing importance assumed by the state machinery, to the detriment of the nobility which supplied candidates to the throne.

From one end of Mossi territory to the other many variations in the details of institutions could certainly be found, but what is more striking is the remarkable linguistic and cultural unity of Mossi society, despite its historically composite nature; moreover, this unity can be seen in the coherence of the ideology of power, which may be regarded as a genuine and profound political philosophy. We have here one of the great civilizations of West Africa.

The peoples of the Volta basin without centralized political systems

Here again, it seems difficult to dwell at length on matters which certainly come within the province of history, but about which very little is known. It is true that we have a coherent picture of the non-state societies of the Volta basin, but it is a contemporary one. Their history remains to be established in most cases. The absence of a state structure often reduces the pre-colonial history of societies based on lineage or on village communities to a list of recent (nineteenth-century) migrations; or, if we look at societies organized as states, we are left with the effects on those societies of the policies of conquest and assimilation of the neighbouring kingdoms. In the great majority of cases – no doubt through lack of systematic research – what we know at present concerning non-state societies does not take us back beyond the end of the eighteenth or the beginning of the nineteenth century; between recent history and the founding myths there is generally an immense gap, which the historian still has to attempt to fill. In other words, we cannot possibly discuss with any certainty the history of the societies presented here for the period with which we are dealing.

Since this chapter is centred around the history of the Mossi kingdoms, it would seem legitimate to commence, in this paragraph, with the societies called 'Voltaic' or Gur, a name based strictly on linguistic classifications. The Gur languages have been widely studied – more, it is true, from the taxonomic than the genetic point of view – and we are indebted to Gabriel Manessy for having summed up our knowledge concerning this important family of languages.[45] The Gur group comprises a large number of languages spoken today in Upper Volta and in large areas in the north of the Ivory Coast, Ghana, Togo and Benin. De Lavergne de Tressan divides the Gur languages into three subgroups: More, Lobi-Bobo and Senufo, with the More subgroup comprising the More, Gurma, Tem and Gurunde languages.[46] Westermann and Bryan, like the former author, identify a separate Senufo subgroup, but considerably diversify the other subgroups, thus singling out Kulango, Lobi-Dogon (Lobi, Bobo and Dogon), Grusi, Gurma, Tem, Bargu and Mossi; Mossi in turn is associated with a group of languages comprising, in addition to Mossi proper, Dagomba, Nankanse, Talensi, Wala, Dagari, Birifo and Namnam.[47]

Greenberg proposes a classification similar to the preceding one by subdividing the Mossi-Grunshi or Gur subfamily into seven groups: Senufo, Mossi, Grunshi, Tem, Bargu, Gurma and Kilinga.[48] Köhler, whose classification has been reconstructed by Manessy, suggested a central nucleus of Gur languages, which he divided into three groups: Mossi-Dagomba (Mamprusi, Dagomba and Mossi, languages of the Atacora), Grusi (eastern Grusi: Kabre, Tem, Kala; western Grusi; northern Grusi: Kurumba) and Gurma.[49] Köhler also included Senufo and Bariba among the Gur languages, together with a number of residual languages of Togo and Dogon, a language which has lexical affinities with the Gur languages, but whose syntax is said to be of the Mande type.

Although there is far from being a consensus among the specialists, who in any case never provide a set of formal criteria for their classifications, it is generally considered that within the Gur languages it is possible to distinguish a large Mossi group comprising three subgroups: Mossi, Dagomba and Birifor-Dagari-Wile, with the Dagomba subgroup comprising Dagomba, Mamprusi, Nanumba, Nankana, Talensi and Kusasi. These problems of classification lead to even more complex problems of genetic affiliation between languages, to the study of which glottochronology has as yet made only a very slender contribution. Simply grouping languages together on the basis of the affinities between them shows at least that inter-related languages are spoken both in societies with and those without state structures: thus More (the language of the Mossi) is

45. G. Manessy, 1963.
46. M. de Lavergne de Tressan, 1953.
47. D. Westermann and M. A. Bryan, 1970.
48. J. H. Greenberg, 1955.
49. O. Köhler, 1958, and an unpublished work (untitled) quoted by Manessy, op. cit.

very close to Dagari. At most it can be noted that unification into a state generally results in few dialect forms, whereas non-centralized political systems have an extremely large number of dialects.

Linguistic classifications also raise the following problem: did the foreign conquerors, as was long believed in the case of the Mossi and as certain signs would suggest, impose their language on the conquered, who were forced to give up their own languages, or did the reverse phenomenon occur, the people in power being so to speak acculturated by the people of the land? Once we can give a precise answer to this question, we will undoubtedly have gone a considerable way towards understanding certain mechanisms fundamental to the establishment of centralized systems in Africa.

When considering the vast group of Gur languages, one is tempted to go on from a classification of languages to a classification of cultures. To do so is to assume that certain problems of method have been solved, which is not generally so; this explains why the endeavours of Delafosse, of Baumann and of Murdock are on the whole very disappointing.[50] It must also be remembered that the 'Voltaic' linguistic and cultural universes do not coincide exactly. To take but one example, the Bwa speak a Gur language but are of Mande culture, like their neighbours the Bobo, who speak a Mande language.

Oswald Köhler, already cited, has presented a very comprehensive picture of the societies of the Volta basin, but the groupings he makes are very close to his linguistic classification; thus he calls the Kurumba 'northern Grusi', although they are very far removed culturally from the group of peoples whom the anthropologists call 'Gurunsi' and who occupy a vast area to the west of Mossi territory. Less systematic in intention, but genuinely based on an anthropological approach to societies, the inventory made by Guy Le Moal has the merit of being free from *a priori* taxonomic assumptions.[51] Among the peoples of the Volta basin, Le Moal distinguishes the Mossi, Gurunsi, Bobo, Mande and Senufo groups on the basis of cultural and regional groupings and puts together under a common heading the peoples of the south-western part of present-day Upper Volta.

With the Mossi must be associated those pre-Mossi peoples whose identity has been to some extent preserved, for example the Kurumba, who undoubtedly established, in the kingdom of Lurum, a political formation comprising some elements of centralized power, initially based on the concept of 'divine kingship'. The Kurumba, under the name of Fulse, belonged to the groups of 'people of the land' of the Mossi kingdoms, Yatenga in particular, in the same way as the Maranse, who were Songhay, the Yarse, originally mainly Mande, or the Kambosi, who were of Bambare,

50. Delafosse, op. cit.; H. Baumann 1948; G. P. Murdock, 1959.

51. G. Le Moal, 1963.

Dafing or Dioula origin. With the Gurunsi, we leave the domain of states. Traditionally, anthropologists give the name 'Gurunsi' to the following six segmented societies: Lela, Nuna, Kasena, Sisola, Ko and Puguli. They are generally associated with societies settled on the present borders of Ghana and Upper Volta, like the Talensi, the Kusasi and the Nankansi; these may be considered culturally autonomous in relation to the neighbouring state formations, but from the point of view of those states they were dependent or tributary societies. Since the work of Meyer Fortes, these societies have, as we know, provided anthropological theory with the model of the political system 'segmented by lineage'.[52]

The peoples known as Bobo (with whom we may associate the Borom, of Mande origin) comprise essentially the Bwa (formerly called the Bobo-Wule) and the Bobo proper (formerly the Bobo-Fing). These societies, in which initiation linked to *do* worship played an important role, had a political organization based on autonomous village communities. The same was true of the Samo and the Bisa on the one hand, and the Dafing or Marka on the other. Dafing territory extended from the valley of Suru, in the north, to the region of Bobo-Dyulaso, in the south. The Dafing were Muslim traders and warriors, but large minorities had preserved their traditional religion. They were responsible for the establishment of numerous small centralized states; the way in which they came into the history of the valley of the Black Volta is comparable to the entry of the Dioula into the history of the region lying between Bobo-Dyulaso and Kong. The societies related to the Senufo – such as the Karaboro, the Tusya, the Turka, the Gwe and the Wara – borrowed numerous elements from that culture; thus the Tusya had a secret society, the *lo*, which had features similar to the *poro*.

Under the regional heading, 'peoples of the south-west', Le Moal brings together the Wile, the Dagari, the Birifo, the Lobi and the Dya, among others. These peoples originated in what is now Ghana and crossed the Black Volta in successive waves from the sixteenth century. The Wile, who were the first to arrive, drove back the Puguli; they were followed by the Dagari, who had linguistic and cultural affinities with the Wile but whose system of descent was bilateral, whereas that of the Wile was patrilateral. The Birifo arrived at the same time as the Dagari, that is to say after the Lobi; their system of descent was comparable to that of the Dagari. The Wile, the Dagari and the Birifo had a language belonging to the Mossi group; another characteristic was the importance assumed in their social life by the secret initiation into the *bagre*; the Birifo, immediate neighbours of the Lobi, took many of their cultural traits from them. Among the Lobi, matrilineal elements predominated largely over patrilineal ones; the importance of initiation into the *dyoro* played an essential role in social control. The Dya had close affinities with the Lobi and crossed the Black

52. M. Fortes, 1940.

Volta at about the same time. The peoples of the south-west had a segmented political organization but, unlike the Gurunsi, had no forms of centralized power based on 'divine kingship'.

Apart from these agricultural societies, it must not be forgotten that pastoral societies – the Fulani and the Tuareg – existed in the Niger Bend and the upper Volta basin. The Fulani, who were to be found in the valley of the Black Volta, the Suru valley, the Gondo plain, Jelgoji, Liptako and Yaga, set up numerous local commands (Dokwi, in the valley of the Black Volta; Barani, in the Suru valley; Jibo, Barabulle and Tongomayel in Jelgoji) and founded the state of Liptako. But here again, the history of the historical Fulani formations can be outlined only for a more recent period – starting in the seventeenth and eighteenth centuries – than that considered in this volume.

The economic approach

Looking at subsistence crops, we find that the dominant feature in the greater part of the area under consideration here was the cultivation of millet, which was replaced in the north by cultivated and wild varieties of *fonio*, and, in the south, by tubers. Cotton of the *Gossypium punctatum* type, still known today, had no doubt been cultivated for a very long time in the dry, shrubby, savannah zone. It seems clear that at the time of the foundation of the first Mossi kingdoms weaving was widespread, although long garments were reserved for the chiefs. In Mossi territory, the Yarse, of west Mande origin, are associated with weaving; according to the oral tradition of the Yarse of the kingdom of Wagadugu, a weaver made for Naaba Wubri a costume consisting of a loose shirt, trousers and a cap. The craft of dyeing, a Songhay speciality, was as old as weaving and complementary to it, the two principal dye plants being indigo and *Anogeissus leicarpus*, giving a dye khaki-yellow in colour.

The rearing of zebu cattle was the business of the Sahel herdsmen, the Fulani. The cultivators, for their part, raised only domestic farmyard animals: sheep, goats and poultry. The breeding of donkeys and horses, in which the northern part of present-day Mossi territory long played an important role, deserves special mention. Yatenga, for instance, exported donkeys to central and southern Mossi country, and the eastern zones of that kingdom were noted for the quality of their Dongolawi horses, introduced long before from Upper Egypt. The horse was the beast of war *par excellence* – the donkey being mainly a beast of burden for the caravans – and was represented by five races: those of Yatenga, Jelgoji, the Kurumba country, the Gondo plain and Barani.[53]

The two local industries, generally practised in association, were metalworking and pottery. Here again, Yatenga stands out from the rest of Mossi

53. Cf. de Franco, 1905.

territory in that it is rich in fairly high-grade iron ore, although the ore is also found throughout the western part of present-day Upper Volta.

We know virtually nothing of the early history of the long-distance trade. Conducted in the Volta basin by the Yarse, it seems to have been in existence when the Mossi arrived, although it developed considerably when the new states came into being. There is, however, a direct link between the development of long-distance trading and the technical mastery of weaving. The Yarse, who were both weavers and traders, used white or dyed cotton strips as local freight merchandise; in their inter-regional trade, which was conducted on a two-way basis between north and south, the north supplied mainly block salt from the Sahara – but also dried fish and mats – and the south mainly kola nuts. The currency of exchange was the cowrie (the heavy *Cyprea annulus* and the light *Cyprea moneta*), whose value may have been defined very early in relation to gold. In practice, many different standards of value were used for merchandise: a cubit of cotton fabric served as a unit of account for ordinary goods, whereas horses, for instance, were generally paid for in captives. The smiths of the metal-working centres themselves conducted the trade in finished products (tools and weapons) and balls of iron intended for refining.

The history of human settlement has provided evidence of the age of some of the trading centres. Unfortunately, in the absence of archaeological data, all that can be said of the economy of the Volta basin between the twelfth and sixteenth centuries is still only a hypothetical extrapolation, based on information gathered by European travellers in the nineteenth century: this is an area of research which it is essential to explore.

10 The kingdoms and peoples of Chad

D. LANGE

In the twelfth century, the major part of the region of Lake Chad lay under the sway of a powerful kingdom, Kanem. Other kingdoms probably existed in the area at the time, and a variety of peoples lived there in separate clans or ethnic groups. Kanem was known in very early times to Arab travellers and geographers and was the only political entity of international renown between the Nuba of the Nile valley and the Kaukau on the Niger Bend to the west. In view of the existing sources and the state of our knowledge, this survey will of necessity deal more with Kanem and the peoples living in that kingdom than with those outside, who did not attract the attention of the chroniclers and on whom, therefore, we have very little documentation.

Kanem, which is mentioned in various external sources from the ninth century onwards, is also distinguished by the existence of an internal source: the *Dīwān* of the sultans of Kanem-Bornu.[1] The origins of the *Dīwān* probably date back to the first half of the thirteenth century. At that time, the court chroniclers began to set down in writing certain facts relating to dynastic history that had formerly been handed down by word of mouth. But before moving on to the events of their own era, the chroniclers undertook to make a written record of the main elements of a tradition that dated back to the end of the tenth century. Subsequently, the work was brought continuously up to date until the end of the Sefuwa dynasty in the nineteenth century; on the death of each sovereign, a short paragraph was added relating to his reign. This method of composition might, after six centuries, have produced a voluminous work. In point of fact, the *Dīwān* in its present state consists of only 5½ pages. To be sure, the *Dīwān* informs us above all of the dynastic history of Kanem-Bornu, but it is possible to deduce from it certain elements of information relating to other aspects of the history of the central Sudan.[2]

There is, in addition, a certain amount of information provided by Arab geographers. Of particular value for the study of the history of the central

1. The text of the *Dīwān* has been translated with a commentary in D. Lange, 1977a.
2. ibid.

Sudan are the records of al-Idrīsī (writing in 1154), Ibn Saʿīd (d. 1286) and al-Maḳrīzī (d. 1442).[3] The two series of records largely complement one another: the African chroniclers provide the temporal framework and the Arab geographers the spatial dimension. (See the maps based on al-Idrīsī and Ibn Saʿīd, Figs. 10.1–10.3.)

The Sefuwa dynasty

It is shown in the previous volume of this series that Kanem was for several centuries under the rule of the Zag͟hawa.[4] This came to an end during the second half of the eleventh century with the advent of a new dynasty that bore the name of Sefuwa, claiming as it did to descend from the Yemenite hero, Sayf b. D͟hī Yazan (see Fig. 10.6). The founder of this dynasty was Hummay (*c*. 1075–1180). Everything suggests that he was a Berber; to judge by his name (derived from Muḥammad) and his genealogy, he came from a profoundly Islamized community. We know from al-Idrīsī that many of the inhabitants of Kawar were at that time *mulat͟ht͟hamūn* Berbers (wearing the *lit͟hām*).[5] Other sources indicate that the Islamization of this area dates back to before the middle of the ninth century.[6] It would be tempting to conclude that Hummay originated from Kawar, but it is also possible that he was descended from a Berber group that had already been integrated into Kanem at a time when that province was still ruled by the Zag͟hawa.

However, the claim to Yemeni ancestry clearly indicates that Hummay and his men were in contact with North African Berbers. The latter readily laid claim to Himyarite ancestors, to distinguish themselves from the Adnanite Arabs. Accordingly, it cannot be an accident that, among the presumed ancestors of Sayf b. D͟hī Yazan, only such names as relate to the northern Arab context are mentioned in the *Dīwān*. We find there the names of Ḳurays͟h (the eponymous ancestor of the tribe of the Prophet), Mecca (the place of pilgrimage) and Baghdad (the capital of the Abbasids), but no mention of Himyar, Ḳaḥṭān nor indeed of Yemen. At the start of the thirteenth century, Hummay's genealogy was clearly emptied of its Berber content and assigned a new function: instead of testifying to a Himyarite origin, the official genealogy of the Sefuwa kings was required above all to prove their long fidelity to Islam. The name of Sayf b. D͟hī Yazan had by that time become a fossil devoid of significance.[7]

3. Al-Idrīsī, French transl. 1866; Ibn Saʿīd, al-Maghrībī, French transl. 1958; al-Maḳrīzī, French transl. 1979; for the latter, see also J. Cuoq, 1975, pp. 382–9.
4. Cf. Volume III, Chapter 15.
5. Al-Idrīsī, loc. cit.
6. Al-Yaʿḳūbī, French transl. 1937, p. 205.
7. In a letter from Bornu dating from the end of the fourteenth century, Sayf b. D͟hī Yazan is also linked to the eponymous ancestor of the tribe of the Prophet. Al-Ḳalḳas͟handī comments: 'This is a mistake on their part, since Sayf b. D͟hī Yazan was a descendant of the Tubba of the Yemen, who are Himyarites.'

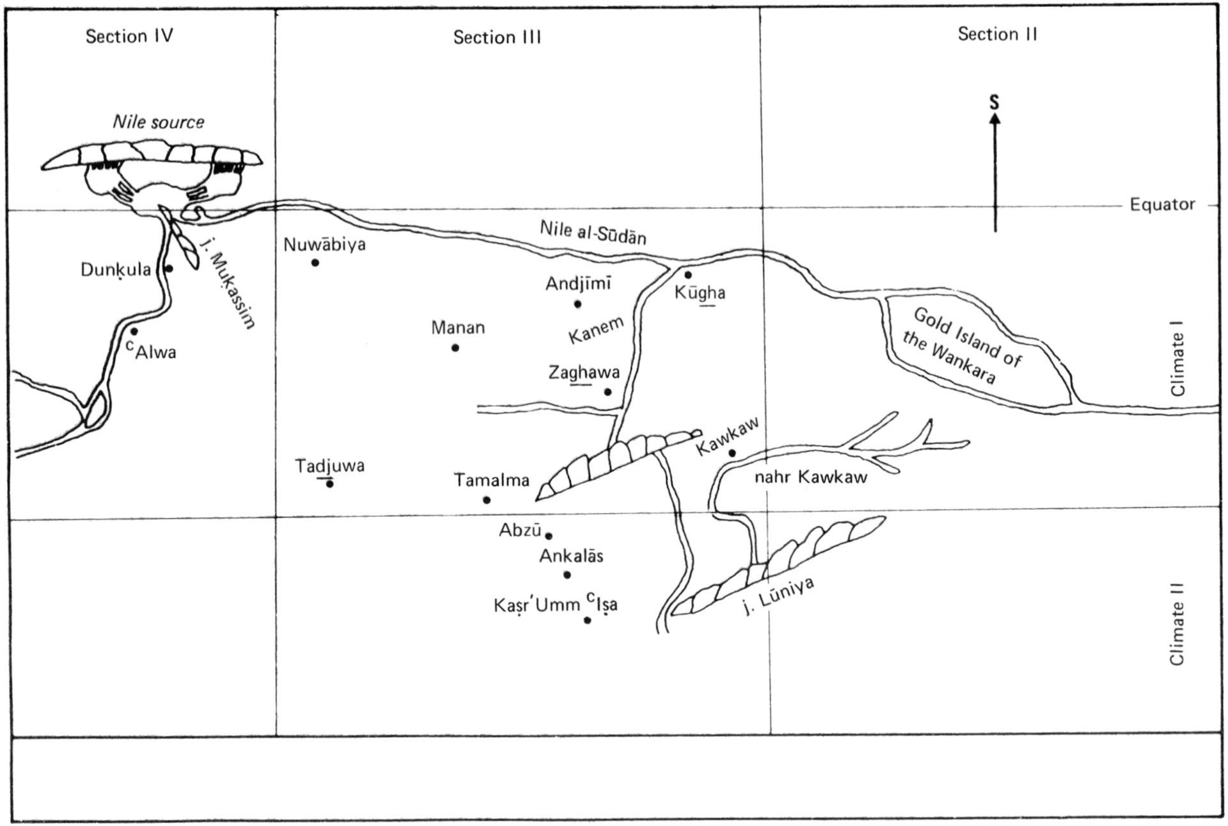

FIG. 10.1 *Simplified extract from the large map by al-Idrīsī (1154) (after the reconstruction of K. Miller in Y. Kamal,* Monumenta, 3 *(4), p. 867)*

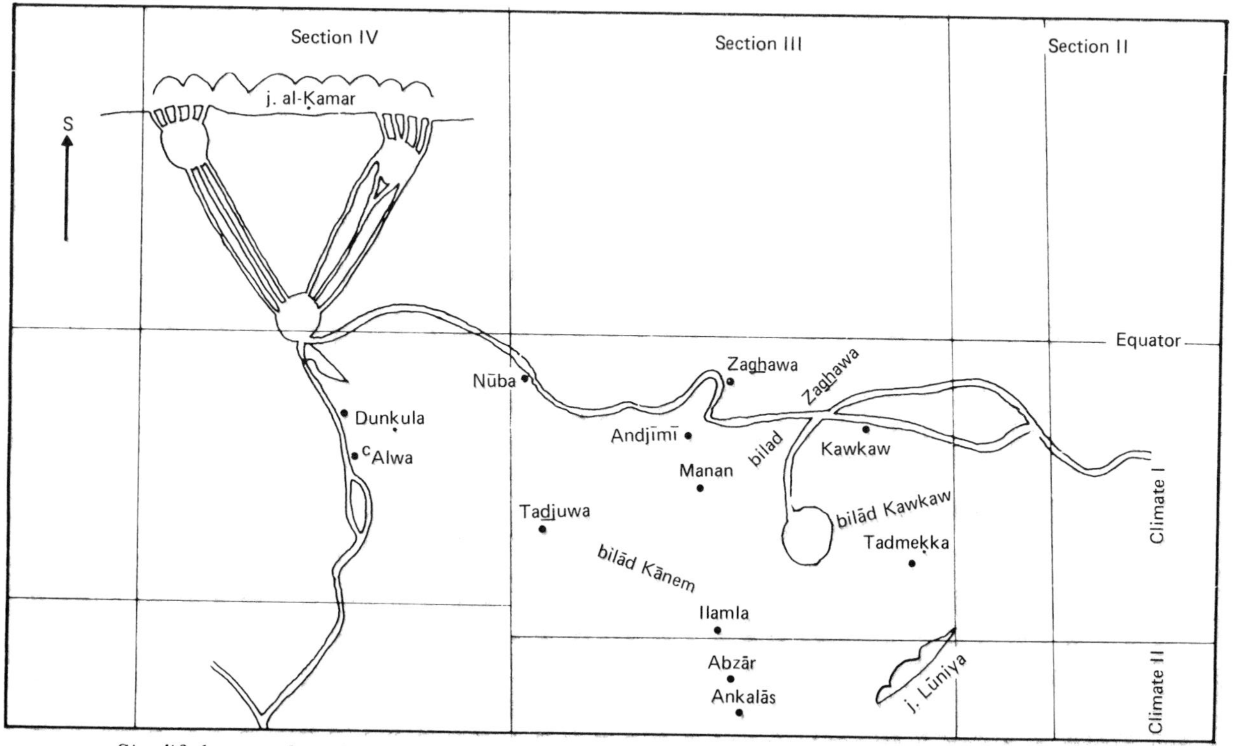

FIG. 10.2 *Simplified extract from the 'Shorter Idrīsī' (1192) (after the reconstruction by K. Miller,* Mappae Arabicae, I *(3), p. 99)*

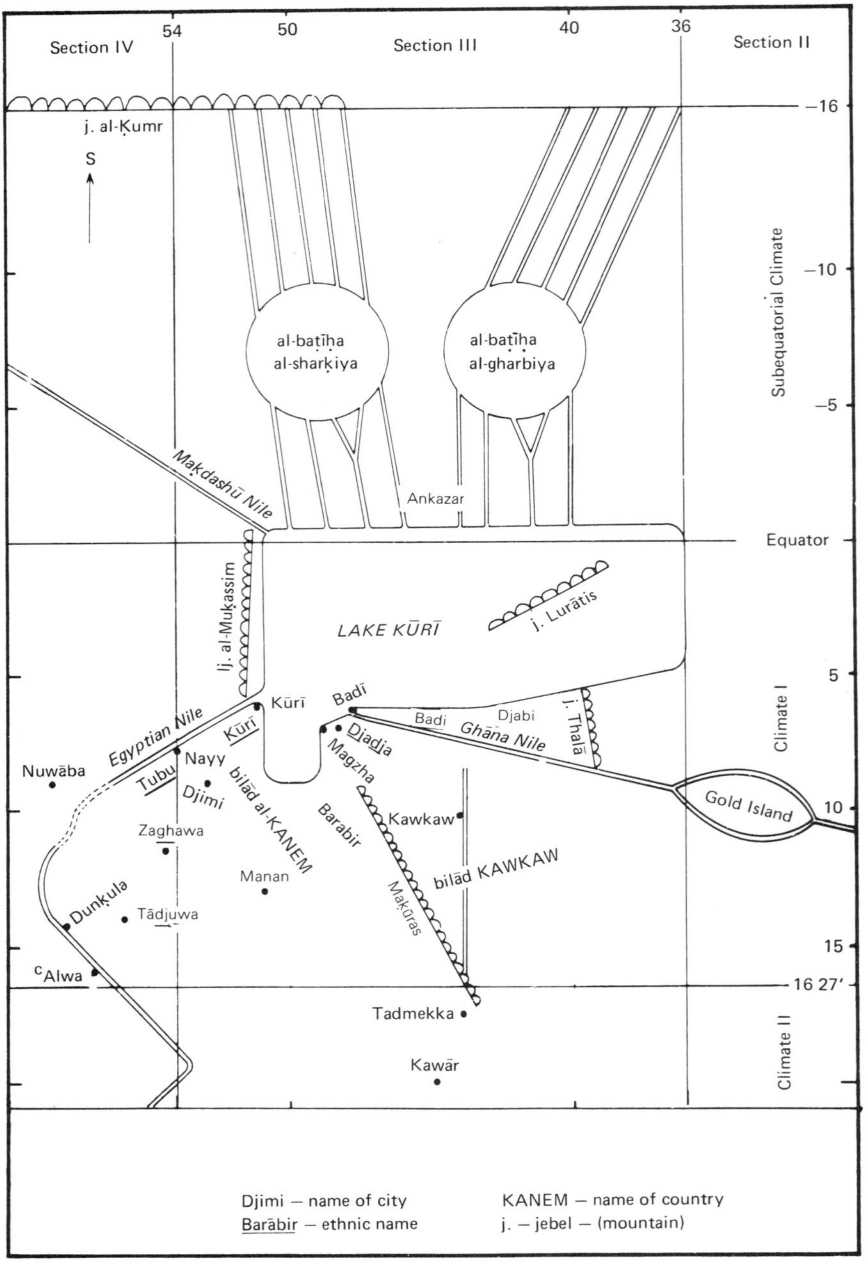

FIG. 10.3 *The Lake Chad area (Lake Kūrī) (after the reconstruction of an extract from the map by Ibn Saᶜīd (first half of the 13th century) carried out by the author of this chapter)*

Other evidence indicates that the Sefuwa kings wished their Berber origins to be forgotten; for example, the thirteenth-century chroniclers' record of Salmama b. 'Abd Allāh (*c.* 1182–1210), son of the great-grandson of Hummay, that he was 'very dark'. According to the chroniclers, 'no sultan has been born black since sultan Sayf until this one, but all were of the redness of Bedouin Arabs'.[8] To be sure, this information relates solely to the second dynasty. We might, however, have expected to find a reference to the Berber origins of the Sefuwa, but once again the chroniclers prefer to gloss over it, alluding to the Arabs rather than the Berbers. This example shows clearly that, in the chroniclers' eyes, a white skin was esteemed only in so far as it was associated with the Muslim religion. In other words, what mattered was not a man's colour but his religion.

A passage from Ibn Sa'īd shows that the foreign origins of the Sefuwa had rapidly faded in popular memory. Basing himself on the evidence of Ibn Fāṭima, who had himself visited Kanem, Ibn Sa'īd writes:

> The sultan of Kanem ... is Muḥammadi b. Djabl, of the lineage of Sayf b. Dhī Yazan. The capital of his infidel ancestors, prior to their conversion to Islam, was Manan; subsequently one of them, his fourth great-grandfather, became a Muslim under the influence of a jurisconsult, after which Islam spread throughout the country of Kanem.[9]

Now Muḥammad b. Djil was the name by which the great king Dunama Dibalami (*c.* 1210–48) was known to the outside world. (Ibn Fāṭima had stayed in Kanem during his reign, in the first half of the thirteenth century.) This means that at that time the Sefuwa were considered to be the direct descendants of the Duguwa (Zaghawa kings). Only the introduction of Islam – which had become a matter of peaceful 'conversion' – and the change of capital remained within the popular tradition to recall the political upheavals of the second half of the eleventh century.

It may be inferred from the continuity of the dynastic traditions, also borne out by the *Dīwān*, that Kanem was by that time a powerfully structured state with a firmly established territorial organization. The introduction of Islam and the dynastic change had apparently not impaired the foundations of this state, whose origins probably date back to the end of the sixth century.[10] Even the change of capital, which was either con-

8. *Dīwān*, para. 17.
9. Ibn Sa'īd, loc. cit, p. 95; Cuoq, op. cit., p. 209.
10. It has been noted that the tradition reported by Ibn Sa'īd is not very trustworthy. Al-Idrīsī, writing in the middle of the twelfth century, mentions both Manan and Djimi. According to him, Manan had been 'the seat of the prince and lord of the land' (of the Zaghawa?) whereas Djimi, which was smaller, is said merely to have belonged to Kanem. Quite clearly, al-Idrīsī has attempted to combine contemporary information with information stemming from the Zaghawa period. It is therefore not impossible that in his time Djimi was already the capital of Kanem.

temporary with or subsequent to the dynastic change,[11] appears to have had no major consequences for the political development of Kanem. The states of both the Zaghawa and the Sefuwa had permanent central capitals: Manan was the residence of the Duguwa kings for at least a century, and Djimi of the Sefuwa kings for three centuries. It was not until the end of the fourteenth century, when the Sefuwa were forced to leave Kanem, that Djimi lost its special status and became a city like any other.[12] As regards the change of capital that occurred in the second half of the eleventh century (or the beginning of the twelfth), it is important to note that Djimi was situated considerably further south than Manan. This shift might therefore be seen as evidence of the increasing influence of the sedentary peoples of Kanem, at the expense of the semi-nomads of the Sahel.

If we follow the matrimonial policy of the first Sefuwa kings, as this emerges from the information contained in the *Dīwān*, we discover that the 'de-Berberization' of the new dynasty – quite perceptible at the ideological level – went hand in hand with a progressive increase in the political weight of the sedentary peoples. Thanks to the care taken by the chroniclers to note the ethnic origins of the queen-mothers, the following list can be drawn up: the mother of Hummay (*c.* 1075–86) was descended from the Kay; the mother of Dunama b. Hummay (*c.* 1086–1140) was a Tubu; the mother of Bir b. Dunama (*c.* 1140–66) was a Kay (Koyam); the mother of ʿAbd Aḷḷāh b. Bir (*c.* 1166–82) was a Tubu; the mother of Salmama b. ʿAbd Aḷḷāh (1182–1210) was a Dabir; the mother of Dunama b. Salmama (*c.* 1210–48) was a Magomi (royal lineage). Subsequently, all the queen-mothers appear to have been Magomi, except the mother of Ibrāhīm b. Bir (*c.* 1296–1315) who was a Kunkuna.

A first point to be noted is that the Tomaghra, from whom two queen-mothers of the Duguwa period were descended, are no longer mentioned in connection with the Sefuwa kings. This may be evidence that they had lost their dominant position at the time of the dynastic change which occurred in the second half of the eleventh century. Subsequently, the Tomaghra undoubtedly continued to play a major role in the central Sudan, for they are today to be found in Tibesti and Kawar (the oasis of Bilma),

11. Cf. Lange, op. cit., ch. 7.

12. Apart from Djimi and Manan, the only cities in Kanem mentioned by external sources are Tarazaki (al-Muhallabī) and Nay (Ibn Saʿīd). Later, Ibn Furṭūwa, describing the martial expeditions of Idrīs Alawoma (1564–96), mentions a large number of localities situated in the Lake Chad area, including Djimi. Moreover, it should be noted that the *Dīwān* indicates the burial places of all the kings of Kanem-Bornu from the eleventh century. Some of these may have been fair-sized cities: in particular, Zamtam (*Dīwān* paras 17 and 38), Nanigham (paras 25 and 36) and Diskama (para. 20) were places situated to the west of Lake Chad but have otherwise not been identified. Djimi is mentioned as the burial place of four kings (paras 19, 21, 28 and 29).

where they predominate over other Tubu groups. They are also to be encountered in Kanem and in Bornu, where they are largely assimilated with the Kanembu and the Kanuri. According to the traditions collected in Bornu, it is from them that the dynasties of the Munio and Mandara originated.[13]

In contrast to the Tomaghra, the Kay are mentioned in connection with both dynasties. It would therefore seem that their political status was not affected by the fall of the Duguwa. It will be noted in particular that the mother of the founder of the new dynasty was a Kay. Today, the Kay – known by the name of Koyam – live to the north of Bornu, in the vicinity of the Komadugu Yoo. They are a sedentary people, but the fact that they continue to raise camels in an unfavourable environment is evidence of their northern, nomadic origins.

The Tubu are mentioned in the *Dīwān* solely in connection with the Sefuwa. This may be due to the nature of the information transmitted, as the chroniclers tell us only about the Duguwa reigns following that of Ayuma (*c*. 987–1007) with any degree of precision. None the less, the fact that the mother of Dunama b. Hummay – and hence Hummay's principal wife – was a Tubu appears significant; it is very possible that the Tubu contributed to the fall of the Duguwa. It must be acknowledged, however, that the relationship between the Tubu of the *Dīwān* and the Zag͟hawa mentioned in the external sources is far from clear. It is only the evidence of Ibn Fāṭima, dating from the first half of the thirteenth century and transmitted by Ibn Saʿīd, that enables a clear distinction to be made between the two ethnic entities. The Zag͟hawa, mentioned in conjunction with the Tadjuwa (D̲jad̲ja), are vaguely located between Kanem and Nubia, whereas the Tubu are situated very precisely in the vicinity of Baḥr al-G̲h̲azal.[14] There are a number of Tubu groups still living today in this region to the east of Kanem. They are collectively called Daza or Gorhan. The 'true' Tubu live in Tibesti and its vicinity. This mountain range is generally considered to be the country of origin of all the Tubu people (the name *tu-bu* is taken to mean 'inhabitants of the mountain'), but this is by no means certain.[15]

Two other ethnic groups mentioned in the *Dīwān*, the Dabir and the Kunkuna, no longer exist today. According to information collected by Nachtigal, the Dabir (more correctly, the Dibbiri) were a sedentary Kanembu people; after merging with Daza nomads, they are thought to have formed the Kadawa group, which is still living in Kanem. Barth and

13. G. Nachtigal, 1967 edn, Vol. 2, p. 338.

14. In the existing texts of the *K. al-d̲jug̲h̲rāfiyya*, the name Tubu appears in distorted forms. Cf. J. Marquart, 1913; see also Lange, op. cit., ch. 2, para. 13, no. 2.

15. Concerning the Tubu in general, see J. Chapelle, 1957. It should be noted, however, that the chapter on the history of the Tubu is not very trustworthy, in so far as the author has largely based himself on the hasty, superficial compilation by Y. Urvoy, 1949.

Nachtigal believe that the Kunkuna too were originally a sedentary Kanembu people, but neither authority has succeeded in establishing a clear line of descent to modern ethnic groups.[16]

Lastly, the Magomi – spelt M.gh.r.m by the chroniclers – constituted the patrilineage of the Sefuwa kings. If we are to believe the information contained in the *Dīwān*, the mother of Dunama Dibalami (*c.* 1210–48) was the daughter of a brother of ʿAbd Al̤l̤āh Bakaru (*c.* 1166–82). This may be seen as evidence of the gradual establishment of a lineage group that was later to constitute the nucleus of the Kanuri people. There is nothing to suggest that the Magomi existed before the reign of the Sefuwa, and it would certainly be mistaken to see in them the political force that enabled Hummay to accede to power. By contrast, it is highly likely that the Magomi in fact comprise all the descendants of the Sefuwa kings (in agnatic line), as their genealogies and the names of their different sub-sections suggest.[17] If these considerations are correct, the Magomi are the nucleus of a people (the Kanuri) that gradually established itself from a dynastic stock (that of the Sefuwa); however, the actual origin of the state of Kanem-Bornu would have antedated that of the people who today form its main substratum.

Before the emergence of the Kanuri people, the Kanem kings derived their power from different ethnic groups, comprising both nomadic and sedentary peoples, who spoke either Nilotic-Saharan languages – as do the Tubu, Zag͟hawa and Kanuri today[18] – or Chad languages.[19] In certain periods, the power of the Kanem kings must also have extended, as in the thirteenth century, to Berber-speaking groups; but these appear always to have been in the minority in relation to the Nilotic-Saharan groups.[20] If the meagre evidence contained in the *Dīwān* is to be believed, it would seem that there were three phases in the development and reinforcement of the ethnic base of the Sefuwa kings.

During the first phase, which extended from the advent of Hummay to the middle of the twelfth century, two nomadic tribes – the Tubu and the Kay – appear to have played a predominant role. In the second phase, the Dabir and Kunkuna – and probably other sedentary tribes – superseded

16. Concerning the Dabir, see Nachtigal, op. cit., Vol. 2, pp. 319–20.

17. Nachtigal, op. cit., Vol. 2, pp. 418–19, mentions the following sections: the Magomi Umewa (descended from Hummay), the Magomi Tsilimwa (from Salmama), the Magomi Biriwa (from Bir) and the Magomi Dalawa (from ʿAbd-Al̤l̤āh). See also *Dīwān*, paras 17–18.

18. The present-day Zag͟hawa no more resemble the Zag͟hawa mentioned by Arab authors before Ibn Saʿīd than the Kanuri resemble any Nilotic-Saharan group prior to the thirteenth century. Perhaps only the Tubu have preserved their ethnic identity from this period without major changes.

19. Among these are the Ngizim, Kotoko and Hadjeray languages of today.

20. Barth supposes the Tomaghra to be of Berber origin, just as he sees in the paramount role of the queen-mother (*g͟humsa*) a Berber survival. He also notes the absence of Berber borrowings in the Kanuri vocabulary.

the Tubu and the Kay as the main allies of the Sefuwa.[21] It was following this reversal of alliances that, during the third phase, the political power of the royal line of the Magomi became more firmly established; the mother of Dunama Dibalami (*c.* 1210–48) was a Magomi, as was one of his wives – the mother of Kaday (*c.* 1248–77). His other wife – the mother of Bir (*c.* 1277–96) – may also have been a Magomi, but the chroniclers do not specify her ethnic origin. In any case, the son and successor of Bir, Ibrāhīm Nikale (*c.* 1296–1315), had a Kunkuna mother. After this, the *Dīwān* ceases to indicate the ethnic origins of the queen-mothers, and it may be supposed that by the start of the fourteenth century the Magomi had finally eclipsed all the other sedentary groups of Kanem.

The closing of ranks around the royal line might go some way to explaining the power of the kingdom in the reigns of Dunama Dibalami (*c.* 1210–48) and his immediate successors. Moreover, it may also have been the cause – at least indirectly – of the long war against the Tubu that broke out during his reign. Barth believed that Dunama's second wife – the mother of Bir – came from an ethnic group bearing the name of Lakmama:[22] if this is true, the founding of rival lines by Dunama's two sons, Kaday (whose mother was a Magomi) and Bir, could be attributed to the power struggle between the sedentary groups of Kanem and the royal patrilineage of the Magomi. It is in any case highly significant that the peaceful period, marked by succession from father to son, came to an end when the Sefuwa kings ceased to take foreign women as their (principal) wives and married women descended from their own patrilineage instead.[23]

Kanem at its zenith

The development of the state of Kanem cannot be explained without reference to trans-Saharan trade. It is doubtless no accident that the greatest state of the central Sudan came into being at the southern terminus of the major caravan route passing through Fezzān and the oases of Kawar. This trail had probably been in use since Roman times: it was the most direct line of communication between the Lake Chad region and the

21. It would be tempting to attribute the transfer of the Kanem capital to this change of alliance. We should then have to accept that al-Idrīsī was right, and not Ibn Saʿīd (cf. n. 10 above).

22. H. Barth, 1857–9, Eng. transl. 1965, Vol. 2, p. 584. It has already been pointed out above that Bir's principal wife – the mother of Ibrāhīm Nikale – was not a Magomi.

23. The chroniclers say of the reign of Dunama Dibalami: 'in his time the sultan's sons split into different factions' (*Dīwān*, para. 17). These conflicts between the sons of Dunama may have been the expression, at the dynastic level, of the opposition between the Magomi and other ethnic groups. It is thus possible that this opposition was at the root of the first collateral succession in the history of the second Kanem dynasty. The first collateral succession may also be attributed to the weakening of the status of the principal wife, which may in turn have been a consequence of the slow 'de-Berberization' of the Sefuwa.

Mediterranean. To the east, only the extremely difficult trail that traversed the Kufra oases could be considered a potential rival and, to the west, the trail that passed through Takedda (later Agades).

Political structure

The *Dīwān* provides virtually no information on the political organization of Kanem. We may assume, however, that during an initial period, up to the reign of Dunama Dibalami (1210–48), the members of the royal family occupied the premier position in the machinery of the state.

That situation changed in the thirteenth century, according to the chroniclers, when the sultan came into conflict with his own sons, and later Ibrāhīm Nikale had his son executed.[24] We may infer from these indications that, from the thirteenth century onward, the Sefuwa excluded members of their family from key government posts, and depended rather upon officials who were unrelated, such as local chiefs. The *kagiama* (governor of the south) and the *yerima* (governor of the north) probably date from the period of Bornu. Both seem to have come from regions west of Lake Chad. Yeri was the name of a province north-west of Komadugu Yobe, and Kaga is the name of the area around the present town of Maiduguri.

In more recent times, the queen-mothers played a pre-eminent role in Bornu. It is not by chance that the *Dīwān* gives the ethnic origins of the queen-mothers of the first ten kings. It is worth noting that the support of the queen-mother's clan could be decisive at the time of a succession. Later, the *ghumsa* (the king's first wife) became the most important wife and the king designated his successor (the *shiroma*) from among her sons.

No precise information is available on the local administration, but we know that at the end of the fifteenth century the Sefuwa ruled over twelve vassal kingdoms.[25] Direct administration extended over a more limited area, and was probably exercised by slaves of the royal household. On military matters, the written texts indicate that the king maintained a standing army. They distinguish between a *djūnūd*, a soldier called up for a campaign and an *ʿaṣākīr*, or professional soldier.

Justice was dispensed by the king, as at the court of the mansa of Mali, despite the conversion of the rulers to Islam. Nevertheless, during certain reigns, attempts were made to base justice on the *sharīʿa*, as during the rule of Idrīs Alawoma.[26] Almost all the states in the area were influenced directly or indirectly by Kanem-Bornu, whose political organization was a model for the Hausa, the Kotoso and the Bagirmi.

24. *Dīwān*, para. 17.
25. See al-Maḳrīzī, loc. cit.
26. See Ibn Furṭūwa, Eng. transl. 1932.

Trade and commerce

Situated to the north-east of Lake Chad, Kanem inevitably sought to control the region to the west of Lake Chad, where Bornu was later to take shape, in order to secure a stranglehold on the trade routes from Kawar towards the south. However, Kawar was also accessible from Aīr (Takedda, subsequently Agades), and thus the control of this major staging post itself was bound to constitute a prime objective for the kings of Kanem no less than for those of Bornu. The control of Kawar assumed an even greater importance than its strategic location for trans-Saharan trade might suggest, for the extremely rich salt-mines at Bilma and Agram (Fachi) provided their owners with a large income from the massive export of salt to the countries of the Sahel. No other salt-mines of the central Sahara had a comparable economic value. We do not know, however, when these mines were first exploited. The authors of the *Dīwān* are perhaps referring to control of the salt-mines by Kanem, when they note that Arku (1023–67) established slave colonies at Dirku and Siggedim, but this is by no means certain.[27]

In the first half of the twelfth century, the inhabitants of Kawar enjoyed independence from their powerful neighbours to the north and south. Al-Idrīsī mentions the existence of several small towns inhabited by traders and salt-miners. The chiefs of these communities were Berbers (Ṭawāriḳ or Tuareg), wearing the *lit̲h̲ām*. According to al-Idrīsī, the inhabitants of Kawar were primarily occupied in the mining and marketing of alum (used for dyeing and tanning), which they transported as far as Egypt and westwards to Wargla.[28] This picture is undoubtedly falsified by the perspective of an outside observer. If the salt trade with the countries of the Sahel region was then in existence, it was certainly far greater in volume than the export of alum to the cities of North Africa. Moreover, it should be noted that al-Idrīsī makes no mention of the extensive trans-Saharan trade, for which Kawar was the sole staging post between Fezzān and the Lake Chad region. His silence on this point is perhaps indicative of the relative importance of these two types of commercial activity: the flourishing regional trade was perhaps not greatly inferior – at least by volume, if not by value – to the large-scale international trade.

The group of oases of the Fezzān were more important for long-distance trade than those of Kawar, being situated at the crossroads of two of the major trade routes of West Africa. Domination of the Fezzān made it possible to control both the north–south trade (Ifrīḳiya/Tripoli–Kanem-Bornu) and the east–west routes (Egypt–Ghana/Mali/Songhay). Kanem had no alternative for its long-distance trade with the Mediterranean countries

27. A recent study provides precise data concerning the enormous profits obtained by the Tuareg of Aīr, who today handle the transport of salt from Bilma and Fachi to the countries of the Sahel. P. Fuchs, 1974.

28. Al-Idrīsī, loc. cit.

(except for the far Maghrib); most imports and exports had to pass that way. Only merchants who traded with the countries of the Maghrib could bypass the Fezzān, taking the extremely arduous route passing through Djado and Tassili. Security on the north–south caravan route and control of the staging posts therefore had to be among the primary objectives of the kings of Kanem-Bornu.

What were the goods that Kanem traded with the north? On this subject, the sources yield scant information, but we may suppose that there was little change between the beginning of the Muslim period and the nineteenth century; slaves were probably always a major element. Our earliest information on this comes from al-Ya'ḳūbī, who records that in the ninth century Berber traders from Kawar brought black slaves, probably from Kanem, to Zawila, the capital of the Fezzān.[29] At the start of the sixteenth century, Leo Africanus gives us more precise information concerning the North African traders who travelled personally to Bornu to procure slaves in exchange for horses; they were frequently obliged to wait a whole year before the king had rounded up a sufficient number of slaves.[30] Apparently the king's slave raids against the pagan peoples south of Bornu did not suffice to meet the keen demand. When the kingdom became weak, the inhabitants of Kanem-Bornu themselves were in danger of being sold into bondage by external enemies, despite the fact that most of them had been Muslims since the thirteenth century. At the end of the fourteenth century, in a letter to Caliph Baybars of Egypt, Bir b. Idrīs (*c.* 1389–1421) complained of the Arabs who were reducing his Muslim subjects to slavery.[31] We know from D. Girard that in the seventeenth century certain inhabitants of Bornu suffered the same fate, as a result of Tuareg raids.[32]

Along with the slaves, the caravans travelling to the Fezzān and the Mediterranean centres also transported certain exotic products, such as elephant tusks, ostrich feathers and even live animals.[33] However, if the slave trade is to be assessed at its true value, it must be considered primarily in relation to productive activity as a whole. In this connection, there can be no doubt that Kanem-Bornu owed its prosperity more to its thriving agriculture, stock-raising and salt-mining than to the income derived from the slave trade. An important role was also played by craftsmen, some of whose products were exported to neighbouring countries. In the fourteenth century, Ibn Baṭṭūṭa recorded that, in addition to slaves, Bornu

29. Al-Ya'ḳūbī, loc. cit., p. 205.

30. Leo Africanus, French transl. 1956, Vol 2, p. 480.

31. Al-Ḳalḳashandī, French transl. in Cuoq, 1975, p. 40.

32. Cf. C. de la Roncière, 1919, pp. 78–88. With respect to slavery and the slave trade in central Sudan, see A. and H. Fisher, 1970.

33. We know that in 1268 'the sovereign of Kanem and lord of Bornu had dispatched to the Hafsid, Sultan al-Muṣtanṣir, a giraffe that created a considerable stir in Tunis.' From Ibn Khaldūn, French transl. 1852–6, Vol. 2, pp. 346–7.

exported embroidered garments.[34] Moreover, it should be borne in mind that, according to al-Idrīsī in the twelfth century, the alum of Kawar was much sought after in North Africa.[35]

Imports consisted mainly of horses, which were greatly valued for their military uses. The chroniclers state that the cavalry of Dunama Dibalami (*c.* 1210–48) comprised 41 000 horses.[36] Al-Maḳrīzī provides the interesting information that the horses of Kanem were particularly small: it seems permissible to infer from this the indigenous practice of horse-breeding in earlier times.[37]

Manufactured products such as garments and fabrics were also imported from the north, as well as iron weapons. Ibn Saʿīd notes in passing that in the age of Dunama Dibalami garments were imported into Kanem from the Tunisian capital.[38] Earlier, al-Muhallabī had mentioned that the king of the Zag̲h̲awa wore woollen and silk garments from Sousse. In the fourteenth century, local weaving was sufficiently well developed for the inhabitants of Kanem to use strips of cotton as a measure of value in their commercial activities.[39]

Furthermore, it may be supposed that copper was also one of the commodities transported to the central Sudan. We know that in the fourteenth century this metal was extracted – probably in small quantities – from mines situated close to Takedda.[40] By this time, the tin deposits of the Nigerian plateau had probably already begun to be mined. Petis de la Croix informs us that, at the end of the seventeenth century, tin was one of the exports from Bornu to Tripoli.[41] Copper and tin (as well as zinc) are of course essential for the manufacture of bronze; and it is known that in Benin and Nupe a remarkable art in bronze was flourishing well before the arrival of the Portuguese on the Atlantic seaboard.

The volume of north–south trade depended heavily upon the security of the central caravan route across the Sahara. In the first half of the twelfth century, this security was guaranteed by three different powers: in the north by the kingdom of the Fezzān, dominated since the beginning of the tenth century by the Berber dynasty of the Banū K̲h̲aṭṭāb; in the centre by the Berber chiefs of Kawar; and to the south by Kanem. When S̲h̲arīf al-Din Karāḳūs̲h̲, the Mamluk war leader, conquered the Fezzān in 1172–3, putting the country to fire and sword, the old equilibrium was gravely threatened.[42] The political vacuum created by the disappearance of the

34. Ibn Baṭṭūṭa, French transl. 1853–9, Vol. 4, pp. 441–2.
35. Al-Idrīsī, loc. cit., p. 39.
36. *Dīwān*, para. 17.
37. Al-Maḳrīzī, in H. A. Hamaker, 1820, p. 206.
38. Ibn Saʿīd, loc. cit., p. 95.
39. Al-ʿUmarī, French transl. 1927, p. 45.
40. Ibn Baṭṭūṭa, loc. cit., Vol. 4, p. 441.
41. Bibliothèque Nationale, Paris, *nouvelles acquisitions*, MS 7488 (hereafter referred to as B. N. Paris, *n.acq.*).
42. Al-Tīd̲j̲ānī, French transl. 1852, pp. 55–208, and 1853, pp. 101–68 and 354–424.

Banū Khaṭṭāḅ was sooner or later bound to lead the Kanem kings to intervene in the Fezzān.

In the thirteenth century, Ibn Saʿīd – whose information about Kanem refers to the reign of Dunama Dibalami (*c.* 1210–48) – recorded that the king of Kanem was in control of Kawar and the Fezzān.[43] The expansion of Kanem towards the north is confirmed by al-ʿUmarī, writing in the middle of the fourteenth century: 'The empire [of Kanem] commences on the Egyptian side at a town called Zella [north-east of the Fezzān] and ends on the other side at a town called Kaka; a three-month journey separates these two towns.'[44] The might of Kanem at that time is also attested by the traveller al-Tidjānī, who records that emissaries of the king of Kanem succeeded in 1258–9 in killing one of the sons of Ḳarāḳush who had invaded the Waddan, a region north of the Fezzān.[45]

However, for effective control of all trade between the central Sudan and North Africa, it was necessary to prevent the diversion of trade to secondary routes. In fact, Ibn Saʿīd states that the king of Kanem held the western town of Takedda (Tadmekka in the text) and ruled over the Tadjuwa (Dadjo) and the Zaghawa in the east.[46] The king of Kanem also ruled over the kingdom of Djadja, situated to the north-west of Lake Chad, and over the Berbers of the south (Tuwarik).[47]

It would be rash, however, to assert that in the thirteenth century Kanem was a vast empire with a strong territorial organization. In particular, we have no information enabling us to establish the precise nature of the power that Kanem wielded over the Fezzān. The *may* ʿAlī, whose tomb can still be seen today at Traghen, was in reality King Idrīs b. ʿAlī (*c.* 1677–96), who died in the Fezzān during the pilgrimage, and not, as was formerly thought, a governor or viceroy representing the king of Kanem.[48] Moreover, it is not certain whether Kanem extended to the east as far as the outskirts of Darfūr. Ibn Saʿīd himself says that the Tubu of Baḥr al-Ghazal – not far from Djimi – were an independent people.[49] Apparently Dunama Dibalami had not succeeded in subjugating them, despite the long war, lasting 'seven years, seven months and seven days', of which Ibn Furṭūwa speaks.[50]

43. Ibn Saʿīd, 1970 edn, pp. 114–15 and 127.

44. Al-ʿUmarī, loc. cit., p. 43. According to al-Ḳalḳashandī, Kaka was the name of the capital of Bornu; al-Ḳalḳashandī, French transl. 1913–19, p. 281. Kaka is probably the same as the 'Djadja' of Ibn Saʿīd (see p. 256, n. 69 below).

45. Al-Tidjānī, 1958 edn, p. 111.

46. On the problems of identification, cf. R. Bucaille, 1975, pp. 720–78.

47. Ibn Saʿīd, 1970 edn, pp. 94–5.

48. B. N. Paris, *n.acq.*

49. Ibn Saʿīd specifies that the Tubu were a black, infidel people. According to information collected by Nachtigal, the Tubu groups of Baḥr al-Ghazal were the first to adopt Islam (op. cit., Vol. 3, p. 213). Cf. p. 245 and nn. 14 and 15 above.

50. Ibn Furṭūwa, loc. cit., pp. 123–4.

The peoples living around Lake Chad and on the islands also continued to defend their independence successfully. Ibn Saʿīd asserts, from the information provided by Ibn Fāṭima, that 'Lake Kuri [Chad] is surrounded by unsubjugated infidels of the Sudan who eat human flesh'.[51] He places the Badi (Bedde ?) – who, according to al-Maḳrīzī, were organized in the form of a kingdom[52] – to the north of Lake Chad; the Ankazar (synonymous with the Kotoko?), to the south; the Djabi to the north-west; and the Kūrī to the north-east, at the mouth of the Baḥr al-Ghazal (today the latter are established on the islands). Moreover, there was on the shore of the lake a place called *dar al-sināʿa* (meaning 'the arsenal' or, by etymology, 'manufacture'), concerning which Ibn Saʿīd records: 'It is from here that, on most occasions, the sultan sets sail with his fleet on campaigns to the infidel lands on the borders of the lake, in order to attack their vessels, killing and taking prisoners.'[53] Al-Maḳrīzī, also basing himself on a thirteenth-century source, mentions the names of several pagan peoples living in the vicinity of Kanem. Among these, it is possible to identify the Bedde (?), the Afnu (a Kanuri name for the Hausa) and the Kotoko (written 'Kan.ku' in the text).[54] The same author records that about 1252–3 the king of Kanem came from Djimi to raid the Kalkin, a subgroup of the Mabna (the Mabba of the Wadday?), doubtless also for the purpose of taking prisoners.[55]

It seems permissible to infer from all this that the expansion of Kanem was limited to the northern region. In the south, relations with the non-Muslim peoples apparently had not changed. This need cause no surprise, since the prosperity of the kingdom – or at least the king's prosperity – depended directly upon the income derived from trans-Saharan trade rather than any increase in agricultural or pastoral production. Moreover, slaves constituted the main 'merchandise' exchanged for imports from the north, and they were obtained by organizing raids against the non-Muslim peoples of the south. It was therefore not in the interests of the kings of Kanem to facilitate the expansion of Islam beyond certain limits.

Even in Kanem, Islam did not take deep root before the thirteenth century. Al-Maḳrīzī, writing in the fifteenth century, considered Dunama Dibalami to have been the first Muslim king of Kanem, but he is certainly mistaken. The *Dīwān* contains information showing that all the Sefuwa were Muslims. If the chroniclers are to be believed, the second king of the Sefuwa, Dunama b. Hummay (*c.* 1086–1140), even made the pilgrimage twice and died during a third. Hummay himself, the founder of the Sefuwa

51. Ibn Saʿīd, 1970 edn, p. 94.

52. Al-Maḳrīzī, loc. cit., pp. 187–209.

53. Ibn Saʿīd, loc. cit., pp. 94–5.

54. The fortifications of the Kotoko towns are thought to date from the thirteenth century; at that time the towns would have been walled, to enable the inhabitants to resist raids from Kanem.

55. Al-Makrīzī, loc. cit., pp. 187–209.

dynasty, is reported to have died in Egypt. If this is true, it would suggest that he too had undertaken the pilgrimage.[56] It is also worth noting that, starting from the reign of Bir b. Dunama (*c.* 1140–66), the principal wives of various kings were Muslims, judging by their names – or the names of their fathers – as indicated in the *Dīwān*. However, it was probably not until the reign of Dunama Dibalami (*c.* 1210–48) that Islam, in its orthodox form, made any deep imprint on the people at large.

It may be inferred from the internal and external sources that Dunama Dibalami was a great Muslim reformer. The authors of the *Dīwān* pass over in silence the pilgrimages of two fourteenth-century kings and, with Ibn Furṭūwa, accuse Dunama Dibalami of having destroyed a sacred object called *mune*. This was probably the focal element of a royal cult handed down from pre-Islamic times. Ibn Furṭūwa – although himself an imam, writing in the sixteenth century – sees this 'sacrilegious act' as the cause of several disturbances, in particular, the lengthy war against the Tubu.[57] Moreover, Dunama Dibalami was probably also the founder of a *madrasa* in Cairo intended for the subjects of Kanem.[58] Ibn Saʿīd records that he was 'renowned for the holy war and for his praiseworthy actions', and states that his entourage was composed of Muslim jurists. He forced certain peoples of the central Sudan, notably Berbers, to accept Islam.[59] It is thus quite clear that, in the first half of the thirteenth century, the dissemination of Islam went hand in hand with territorial expansion.

Dunama Dibalami died around 1248 and was buried at Zamtam, a town north-west of Lake Chad. There is no source comparable with Ibn Saʿīd's *Kitāb al djughrāfiyya* to tell us of the extension of Kanem and the growth of Islam in the subsequent period. The *Dīwān* records the visit to Kanem of two 'Fellata' (Fulani) shaykhs from Mali during the reign of Bir b. Dunama (*c.* 1277–96), but does not even mention the pilgrimages of Ibrāhīm b. Bir (*c.* 1296–1315) or Idrīs b. Ibrāhīm (*c.* 1342–66).[60] Writing in the middle of the fourteenth century, al-ʿUmarī too gives little precise information. According to him, Kanem was an extremely weak empire whose resources were minimal and whose troops were very few. On the other hand, the religious zeal of the inhabitants of Kanem must have been remarkable, for he asserts: 'Justice reigns in their country; they follow the rite of Imām Mālik. They banish from their dress all that is superfluous, and have an ardent faith.'[61]

If al-ʿUmarī is to be credited, Kanem still dominated the Fezzān at

56. *Dīwān*, paras. 12–13.

57. Ibn Furṭūwa, loc. cit., pp. 123–7.

58. Al-ʿUmarī, loc. cit., p. 46. The *madrasa* was founded in the decade following AH 620 (1242–52 of the Christian era).

59. Ibn Saʿīd, 1970 edn, pp. 95–6.

60. In his letter to the caliph of Egypt, Bir b. Idrīs refers to them by the title of *hadjdj*. See al-Ḳalḳashandī, loc. cit., Vol. 8, p. 117.

61. Al-ʿUmarī, loc. cit., p. 43.

that time. Takedda, on the other hand, undoubtedly possessed an independent sultan.[62] It was doubtless as a result of the dynastic troubles that broke out in the second half of the fourteenth century that Kanem was forced to relinquish its exclusive control over the central Saharan caravan route. When, at the end of the fourteenth century, the Bulala succeeded in conquering Kanem and breaking its trading monopoly with North Africa, the Sefuwa entered the darkest period of their history.

From Kanem to Bornu

By the twelfth century at the latest, the different peoples of Kanem began to migrate westwards, settling in Bornu, west of Lake Chad. The Tomaghra, the Tura, the Kay (Koyam) and the Ngalma Dukko must have been among the earliest immigrants to Bornu. The oldest Magomi groups must also have originated in Kanem, while the groups formed after the end of the fourteenth century existed only in Bornu. In the second half of the sixteenth century, following the victorious expeditions of Idrīs Alawoma, a large number of Tubu and Arabs left Kanem in their turn for the more fertile and better protected lands west of Lake Chad. This migratory movement, which in the case of the semi-nomadic tribes was probably accompanied by political expansion, came to an end only at the beginning of the colonial era.[63]

West of Lake Chad, the groups that had come from Kanem encountered various sedentary peoples speaking Chad languages. We may follow Kanuri traditions in applying to them the collective name of Sao or Saw. Neither Ibn Saʿīd nor al-Maḳrīzī mentions any people of that name. However, the chroniclers record that in the middle of the fourteenth century four Sefuwa kings fell in battle against the Sao, two of them in Ghaliwa.[64] This town may tentatively be identified with the modern Ngala – south of Lake Chad – which is today inhabited by the Kotoko. According to oral traditions recorded in the nineteenth century, their early predecessors were the Sao.[65]

As far as written sources are concerned, the Sao reappear in the first half of the sixteenth century in the writings of Leo Africanus, who places them west of Lake Chad and south of Bornu.[66] Half a century later, Ibn Furṭūwa applies the name Sao to two ethnic groups: the Ghafata, living along the Komadugu Yoo, and the Tatala, who were settled on the western shore of Lake Chad. Idrīs Alawoma (1564–96) launched a series of

62. Ibn Baṭṭūṭa, loc. cit., Vol. 4, pp. 441–2.

63. Nachtigal, op. cit., Vol. 2, pp. 415–47, provides much information concerning the settlement of Bornu.

64. *Dīwān*, paras. 22–5 and 66. The last chroniclers write the name of the town as *Ghala*.

65. Nachtigal recorded the existence at Ngala of a large mausoleum containing the tombs of 45 Kotoko kings. He took this to be the number of kings who had reigned at Ngala since the Kotoko replaced the Sao. Nachtigal, op. cit., Vol. 2, pp. 426–7.

66. Leo Africanus, loc. cit., Vol. 1, pp. 5 and 53; Vol. 2, p. 480.

murderous attacks against these two peoples and forced the survivors to abandon their ancestral homes.[67] Some took refuge on the islands of Lake Chad. In 1582, the Italian geographer G. L. Anania applied to Lake Chad the name 'Sauo'.[68] Today, the name Sao (So or Saw) designates, in the culture of the Kanuri, the peoples who preceded them – whether in Kanem, Bornu or Kawar – concerning whom there is no longer any certain knowledge.

It is difficult to determine the nature of the relations that existed between Kanem and Bornu before the end of the fourteenth century. One thing is certain: between the beginning of the thirteenth century and the end of the fourteenth, Bornu gained in relative importance. Ibn Saʿīd mentions a kingdom west of Lake Chad; although he gives only the name of its capital, Djadja, the geographical situation suggests that it was Bornu.[69] He notes: 'The town of Djadja is the residence [*kursi*] of a separate kingdom, possessing towns and lands. At present, it belongs to the sultan of Kanem.'[70]

There is therefore a strong possibility that before the thirteenth century Bornu was an independent kingdom. Al-Maḳrīzī, who knew a text by Ibn Saʿīd that has since disappeared, uses the same ambiguous term *kursi*, but applies it to both Kanem and Bornu. According to him, Ibrāhīm b. Bir (*c.* 1296–1315) held the thrones (*kursi*) of Kanem and of Bornu.[71] Ibn Khaldūn, writing of the year 1268, mentions 'the sovereign of Kanem and lord of Bornu'.[72] Ibn Baṭṭūṭa, who visited Takedda – to the south of Aïr – in 1353, knew of a Sefuwa king of Bornu, but the distance he gives to its capital brings us to the east of Lake Chad, to Kanem.[73] These different statements can be reconciled, if it is accepted that Kanem and Bornu were initially two separate kingdoms, but from the thirteenth century on were brought under the rule of a single dynasty, that of the Sefuwa.

However, writing in the middle of the fourteenth century, al-ʿUmarī asserts that the Mamluk sultans of Egypt exchanged letters with both the king of Kanem and the king of Bornu.[74] From this it may reasonably be inferred that Bornu had preserved a measure of autonomy, despite the suzerainty of the kings of Kanem, and that the old dynasty probably continued to play an important role there. When the power of the Sefuwa declined, the authority of the local kings was strengthened; but when the

67. Ibn Furṭūwa, Eng. transl. 1926, pp. 63–9.
68. D. Lange and S. Berthoud, 1972, pp. 350–1.
69. Djadja was probably the town called Kaka by al-ʿUmarī; loc. cit., p. 43.
70. Ibn Saʿīd, 1970 edn, p. 94. On the subject of Kawar, Ibn Saʿīd expresses himself in almost identical terms, but in this case the existence of earlier chieftaincies is confirmed by al-Idrīsī, loc. cit., p. 114.
71. Al-Maḳrīzī, 1820 edn, p. 207.
72. *Kitāb al-Ibār*, translation 2, pp. 346–7; Ibn Khaldūn, 1925, 1956, pp. 346–7.
73. Ibn Baṭṭūṭa, loc. cit., Vol. 4, pp. 441–2.
74. Al-ʿUmarī, 1894 edn, pp. 27 ff.

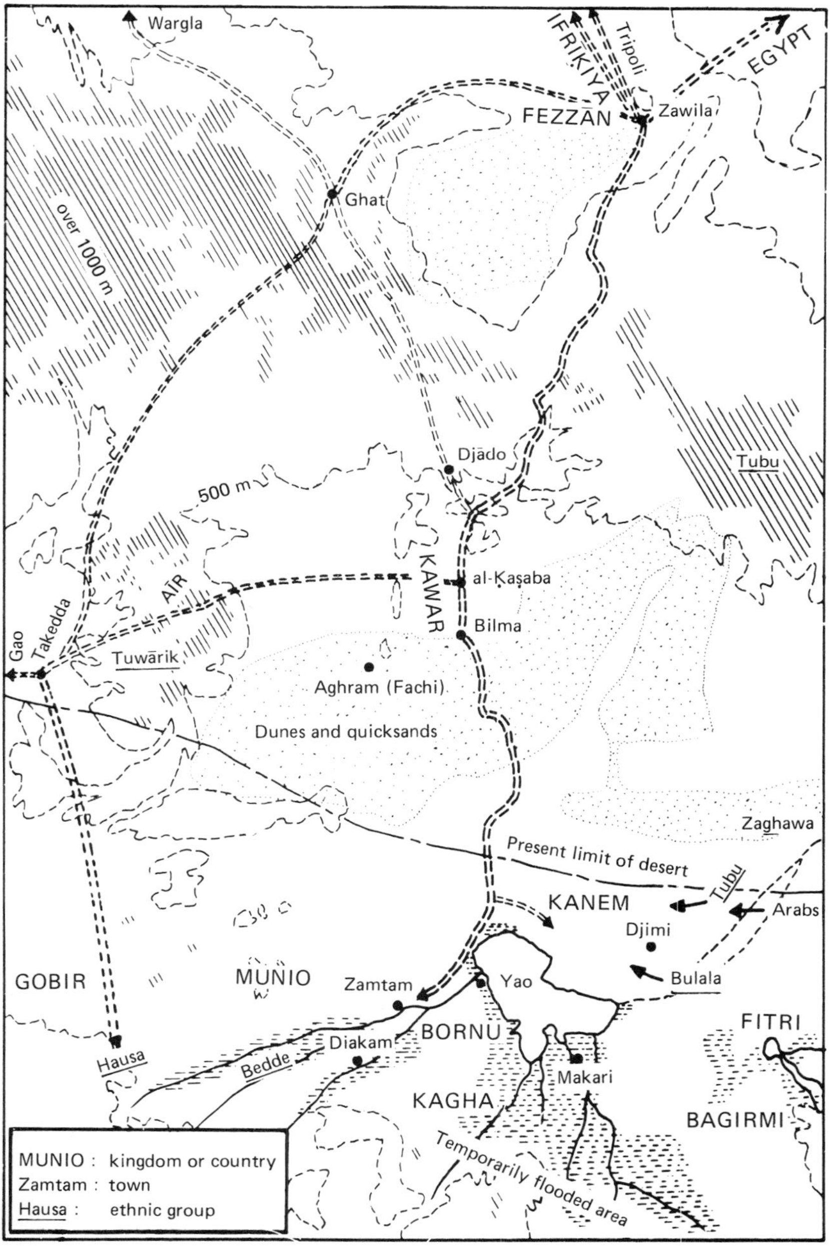

FIG. 10.4 *Peoples and kingdoms of Chad in the 14th century (D. Lange)*

Sefuwa were strong the latter had less room for manoeuvre. Nevertheless, the ethnic substratum must have been the same, otherwise how could Ibn Baṭṭūṭa have used the name Bornu to designate the Sefuwa empire?

This situation must have changed towards the end of the fourteenth century, when the attacks launched by the Bulala forced the Sefuwa to abandon Kanem and settle finally in Bornu (see Fig. 10.4). The Bulala were a pastoral people who were probably already settled in the region of Lake Fitri, where they live today, before their incursions into Kanem.[75] There they ruled over the Kuka, a people speaking a language allied to Sara. Was their drive towards Kanem perhaps connected with the westward migration of certain Arab tribes that followed the dislocation of the Christian kingdom of Nubia at the beginning of the fourteenth century? At the end of the sixteenth century, Arabs were to be found among the allies of the Bulala, according to Ibn Furṭūwa. At the end of the fourteenth century, one of the Sefuwa kings had fallen in battle against the Arabs.

It appears that the immediate reason for the intervention of the Bulala in Kanem was the weakening of the Sefuwa kingdom by the dynastic conflict between Dāwūd b. Ibrāhīm Nikale (*c.* 1366–76) and the sons of his brother and predecessor, Idrīs. Dāwūd himself was killed by the Bulala king, ʿAbd al-Djalīl. His three successors were all killed fighting against the Bulala. The fourth, ʿUmar b. Idrīs (*c.* 1382–7), finally had to leave Djimi and seems to have abandoned Kanem entirely.[76] According to a letter written by his brother, Bir b. Idrīs, he was killed by Djudhām (Djuhayna?) Arabs.[77] Two further Sefuwa kings were to die fighting the Bulala before the threat of these redoubtable foes of the Sefuwa empire was finally averted during the long reign of Bir b. Idrīs (*c.* 1389–1421).

These events did not pass unnoticed in the other Muslim countries. Al-Maḳrīzī summarized them in the following terms:

> About the year 700 [= + 1300], their king was al-Hadjdj Ibrāhīm, a descendant of Sayf b. Dhī Yazan. He held the thrones of Kanem and Bornu. After him, his son, al-Hadjdj Idrīs, reigned, then his brother, Dāwūd b. Ibrāhīm, then ʿUmar, son of his brother, al-Hadjdj Idrīs; lastly, his brother, ʿUthmān b. Idrīs, who reigned shortly before the year 800 [= + 1397–8]. But the people of Kanem revolted against them [i.e. the kings] and renounced the faith. Bornu remained in

75. Ibn Furṭūwa, loc. cit., pp. 4–5. According to Barth, the Bulala were descended from a certain Djil Shikomeni, said to be a son of Dunama Dibalami: R. Barth, 1857–9, Eng. trans. 1965, Vol. 2, pp. 545 and 586; it is more likely, however, that there were no kinship ties between the Bulala and the Sefuwa; Nachtigal, loc. cit., Vol. 3, pp. 38–9.

76. *Dīwān*, paras. 27–31.

77. The name of Djudhām had fallen into disuse in the fourteenth century (*Encyclopédie de l'Islam*, 1st edn, Vol. 1, pp. 1090–1). The Djuhayna, by contrast, played a major role in the dismantling of the Christian kingdom of Nubia. They subsequently moved towards the south and west. H. A. MacMichael, 1922, pp. 187 ff.

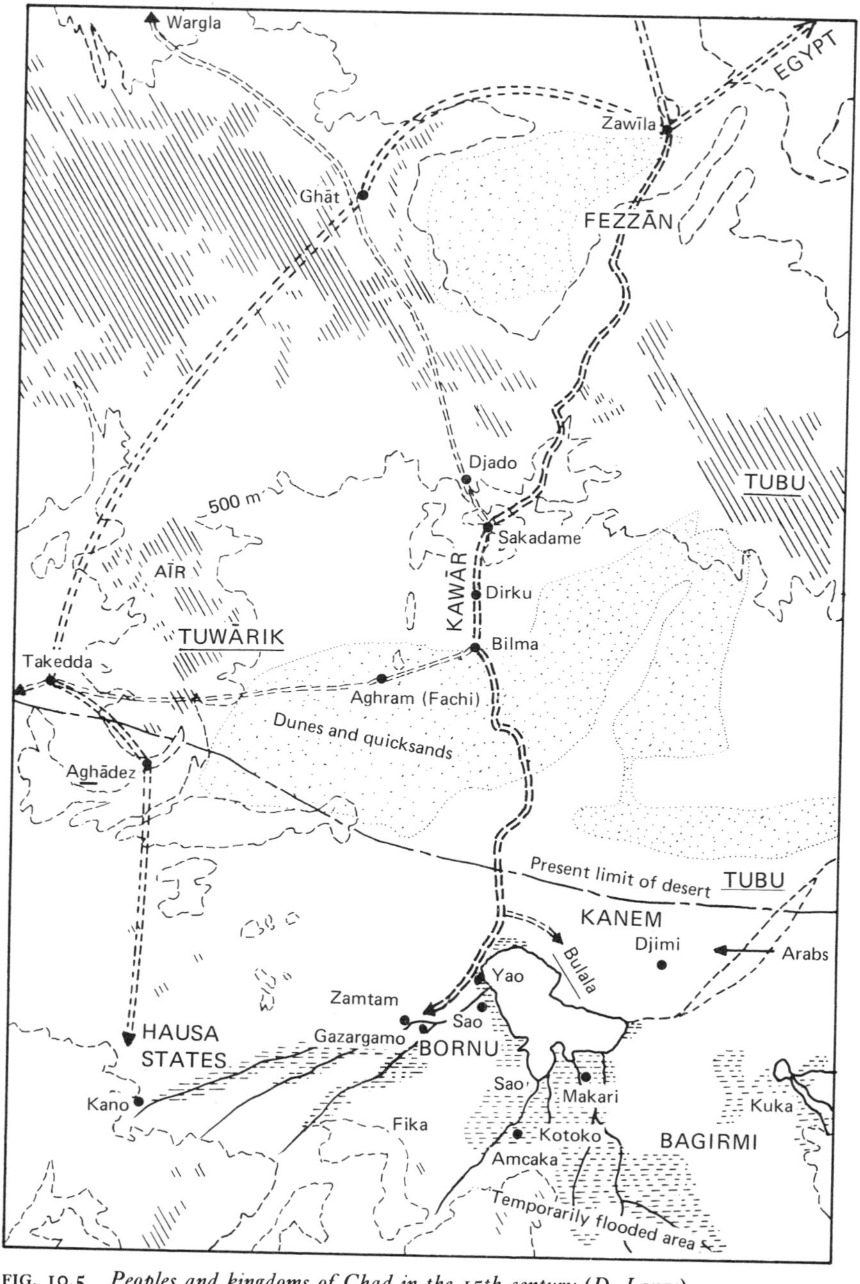

FIG. 10.5 *Peoples and kingdoms of Chad in the 15th century (D. Lange)*

their empire. Its inhabitants are Muslims and wage holy war against the people of Kanem. They have twelve kingdoms.[78]

Al-Maḳrīzī's statement might lead us to suppose that the Bulala were pagans, but neither the *Dīwān* nor Ibn Furṭūwa corroborates this. More credible is the information relating to the new Sefuwa empire, with Bornu as its centre; many local chiefs appear to have sworn allegiance to it. Kaka became the new capital.[79] Seemingly, Bir ('Uthmān) b. Idrīs was sufficiently strong to carry the war into enemy country.

Turning to the Bulala, we know that they founded a powerful kingdom in Kanem and that, as Ibn Furṭūwa tells us, Tubu and Arab tribes were their allies. Leo Africanus knew their kingdom by the name of 'Gaoga', doubtless derived from Kuka.[80] According to his report, Kanem was more extensive and powerful than Bornu; its king enjoyed excellent relations with the caliph of Egypt.[81] This description cannot refer to the beginning of the sixteenth century – when Leo Africanus claims to have visited the kingdoms of the Sahel[82] – but might correspond to the situation prevailing at the end of the fifteenth century, as described to him by traders from North Africa. It is known that the Bornu forces recaptured Djimi around the beginning of the reign of Idrīs Katakarmabi (*c.* 1497–1519), 122 years after having been expelled from it.[83] The Bulala were not, however, decisively defeated until Idrīs Alawoma achieved this in the second half of the sixteenth century.

Dynastic and political crises

Most of the information contained in the *Dīwān* concerns dynastic history, which is therefore the best-known aspect of the history of Kanem-Bornu. (See Fig. 10.6.) As a rule, the *Dīwān* provides only information relating to the succession (successive paragraphs are devoted to successive reigns); but this is enough to enable us to determine the lines of descent linking

78. Translated from al-Maḳrīzī, in B. N. Paris, *n. acq.*, MS 3744. Previous translations of this passage were made on the basis of a defective text (Hamaker, 1820, p. 207). Note that in the *Dīwān* (para. 34) 'Uthmān b. Idrīs is called Bir b. Idrīs.

79. Al-Ḳalḳashandī, loc. cit., Vol. 5, p. 281. Kaka is also mentioned by al-'Umarī and may be identical to the Djadja referred to by Ibn Sa'īd and to the Kagha mentioned in the *Dīwān* (para. 31). See p. 252, nn. 43 and 49 above.

80. This is an ethnic group and not the city of Gao or Gao-Gao, often spelt Kawkaw.

81. Leo Africanus, loc. cit., Vol. 1, p. 10; Vol. 2, pp. 479–83.

82. The numerous errors contained in his 'description' of the kingdoms of central Sudan rule out any possibility of Leo Africanus having himself visited this region. He calls the king of Bornu 'Habraam' (Ibrāhīm) and mentions two kings of the 'Gaoga', Mose (Mūsā) and Homara ('Umar). The only sovereign by the name of Ibrāhīm to have reigned in Bornu during the fifteenth and sixteenth centuries was Ibrāhīm b. 'Uthmān (*c.* 1431–9). Neither name – Mūsā or 'Umar – is confirmed for any Bulala kings of this period.

83. Ibn Furṭūwa, Eng. transl. 1932, fol. 5.

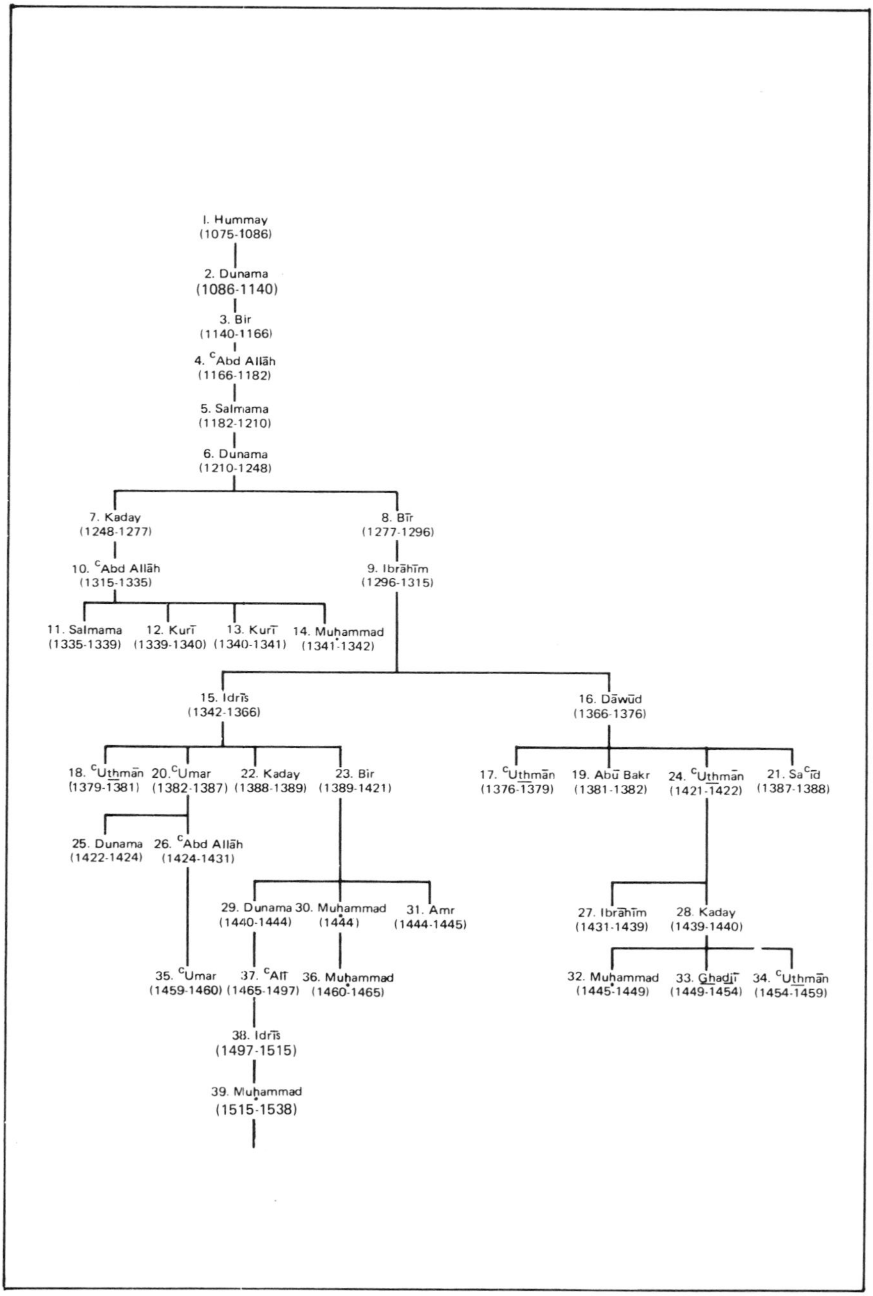

FIG. 10.6 *Genealogy of the Sefuwa (D. Lange)*

the different kings (their genealogy) and the evolution of the rules of succession. It was on the basis of such rules – or rather, of the precedents – that a successor to a deceased king was chosen. Although the balance of power between the different dynastic groups was also taken into account, it was conformity with existing rules that conferred legitimacy upon a successor. These unwritten rules proved more durable than our modern constitutions. They varied only over long periods and as a result of major changes. The dynastic groups were formed with reference to these rules, and were unable to manipulate them as they pleased. A reconstruction of the rules of succession, and of their variations, will facilitate an understanding not only of dynastic history – in the narrow sense of the term – but also of certain aspects of the historical process.

According to the *Dīwān*, the first six Sefuwa kings succeeded one another in direct line, from father to son. The chroniclers indicate a similar method of succession in the case of the Duguwa kings, but the duration of successive reigns shows that the kings could not have belonged to different generations. This patrilineal succession is therefore thought to have originated among the chiefs of Kawar, the probable ancestors of Hummay, who founded the new Sefuwa dynasty.

It was in the generation of Dunama Dibalami's sons that we find the first case of collateral succession (one brother succeeding another); however, it should be noted that Kaday b. Dunama (*c.* 1248–77) and Bir b. Dunama (*c.* 1277–96) were born of different mothers. Kaday's mother was probably a Magomi, whereas Bir's mother may have been descended from one of the ancient tribes of Kanem. This interpretation should be seen in the light of an important observation of the chroniclers regarding the reign of Dunama Dibalami: 'In his time, the sultan's sons split into different factions; formerly, there had been no factions.'[84] It is perhaps permissible to infer that the rivalry between the Kaday line and the Bir line reflects dynastic conflicts that were already breaking out in the first half of the thirteenth century. Probably, as we have seen, the growing antagonism between the royal line of the Magomi and the sedentary tribes of Kanem was at the root of these conflicts.

It should also be borne in mind that the first collateral succession in the history of the Sefuwa occurred, according to the chroniclers, after the first violent death of a Kanem king in Kanem (Dunama b. Hummay was killed during the pilgrimage). Kaday in fact died fighting against the *'andakama dunama* – doubtless one of the kingdom's great vassals. His brother Bir, on the other hand, died a natural death in Djimi. Ibrāhīm Nikale (*c.* 1296–1315) succeeded his father, following the patrilineal pattern, but was himself defeated by another great vassal, the *yerima* Muḥammad b. Ghadī, and power passed into the hands of his cousin, 'Abd Aḷḷāḥ b. Kaday (*c.* 1315–35). Then the former principle of succession was re-

84. *Dīwān*, para. 17.

established when, on ʿAbd Al̤l̤āḥ b. Kaday's natural death in Djimi, he was succeeded by his son, Salmama (*c.* 1335–9). From this it may be inferred that, during the second half of the thirteenth century and the beginning of the fourteenth, patrilineal succession was still the dominant pattern – one, moreover, that could be broken only by resorting to violence.

Increasingly, from that time, collateral succession prevailed. Four sons of ʿAbd Al̤l̤āḥ wielded power in turn, but they were all killed in battles against the Sao after very short reigns. Seemingly incapable of defeating the Sao, the descendants of Kaday b. Dunama relinquished power to a grandson of Bir, Idrīs b. Ibrāhīm Nikale (*c.* 1342–66). This king may well have been more conciliatory towards the indigenous people of Bornu, as he himself was a descendant of the line of Bir b. Dunama, which enjoyed close relations with the non-Magomi people of Kanem. In any case, he appears to have succeeded in establishing a *modus vivendi* with the Sao tribes and in bringing order to Bornu.

On the death of Idrīs, the problem of succession became more acute than ever: who was to succeed him, a son or a brother? A brother, Dāwūd, born of a different mother, was in fact chosen, in preference to sons;[85] but the latter were not reconciled and during the reign of Dāwūd 'war broke out between the son [or sons] of the sultan and the sultan himself'.[86] It may be supposed that it was this war of succession and the consequent weakening of the Sefuwa that provoked the intervention of the Bulala: between 1376 and 1389, seven successive kings fell fighting the invaders.[87] It also resulted in the polarization of two lines of descent, the Dawudids and the Idrisids, who, in their frequently violent struggles for power, dangerously weakened the kingdom of the Sefuwa. It was another century before the problem of the succession was finally solved, by the total elimination of one of the two lines.

The immediate consequence of the external invasion was to trigger a defensive reflex: ʿU<u>th</u>mān (*c.* 1376–9) succeeded his father Dāwūd without difficulty, and Dawudids and Idrisids subsequently reigned turn and turn about until the end of the fighting in Kanem. During this period, collateral succession tended increasingly to become the rule: ʿU<u>th</u>mān b. Idrīs succeeded ʿU<u>th</u>mān b. Dāwūd, and ʿUmar b. Idrīs succeeded Abū Bakr b. Dāwūd. Clearly, the principle of legitimate succession was subordinated to the political imperatives of the moment.

In these circumstances, not surprisingly, it even became possible for

85. In contrast to the sons of Dunama Dibalami, the sons of Ibrāhīm Nikale do not appear to have represented two different groups; according to the *Dīwān*, the mothers of Idrīs and Dāwūd were in fact sisters. They were very probably Magomi.

86. *Dīwān*, para. 17. It might have been supposed that the sons in question were the sons of Dāwūd; in that case, however, the chroniclers would probably have written: 'war broke out between the sultan and his son(s)', as they did concerning the reign of Dunama Dibalami.

87. ibid., paras 27–33.

a non-Sefuwa to accede to the throne. A 'king' (*malik*, not sultan), Saʿīd (*c.* 1387–8) in fact succeeded ʿUmar, who had been forced by the Bulala to abandon Kanem. Saʿīd was therefore the first king to reign over Bornu alone. He was probably chosen because he represented the interests of the inhabitants of that part of the ancient kingdom better. It is indeed tempting to see in him a representative of the ancient Bornu dynasty. Both he and his successor, Kaday Afnu b. Idrīs (*c.* 1388–9), were also killed fighting the Bulala, before Bir (ʿUthmān) b. Idrīs finally succeeded in repelling the invaders.

It might have been supposed that this victory would give the Idrisids sufficient trump cards to enable them to exclude the descendants of Dāwūd once and for all from power. By that time, the Dawudids had already been ousted from the succession three times, and the long reign of Bir (ʿUthmān) b. Idrīs (*c.* 1389–1421) rendered their return to power still more doubtful. Nevertheless, ʿUthmān Kalnama b. Dāwūd (*c.* 1421–2) was able to succeed Bir (ʿUthmān); but this was because the real holders of power at that time were clearly no longer the Sefuwa, but some of the kingdom's top-ranking officials.

The *Dīwān* informs us that Bir (ʿUthmān) had himself already had to fight the *kayghamma* (chief of the army), Muḥammad Dalatu. ʿUthmān Kalnama, his successor, was removed from power after only nine months by the *kayghamma*, Nikale b. Ibrāhīm and by the *yerima* (northern governor), Kaday Kaʿaku. Power then passed into the hands of two of ʿUmar b. Idrīs's sons, Dunama (*c.* 1422–4) and ʿAbd Aḷḷāḥ (*c.* 1424–31), before returning to two Dawudids, Ibrāhīm b. ʿUthmān (*c.* 1431–9) and Kaday b. ʿUthmān (*c.* 1439–40). This oscillation of power between the two lines was undoubtedly due to the manipulation of the succession by the officers of the kingdom and, in particular, by the *kayghamma*. The chroniclers leave us in no doubt regarding the great power wielded by the *kayghamma* in that era. ʿAbd Allāh b. ʿUmar was dethroned by the *kayghamma*, ʿAbd Aḷḷāh Daghalma, who set up in his place the Dawudid Ibrāhīm b. ʿUthmān; but after the death of the latter, the *kayghamma* reinstated ʿAbd Aḷḷāh b. ʿUmar. For at least twenty years, the real masters of Bornu were thus the military chiefs and not the princes of royal blood.

It is perhaps no accident that the growing influence of the officers, and in particular of the *kayghamma*, began to make itself felt precisely during the reign of Bir (ʿUthmān), at a time when the external threat represented by the Bulala had been averted. Once hostilities had ended, it was tempting for the chief architects of the consolidated kingdom to turn to account their influence with the reigning dynasty. They were too weak – and probably too disunited – to attempt to substitute their own rule for that of the Sefuwa.[88] However, by exploiting the existing cleavages

88. The names of the different *kayghamma* do not permit the inference that their office was at that time hereditary. However, Abdullahi Smith has put forward the hypothesis that the *kayghamma* were the chiefs of Kagha (in the southern part of Bornu) and that they

between the dynastic groups for their own purposes, they helped to revive the dynastic crisis, which might have been successfully settled after the long reign of Bir (ʿUthmān).

For the next twenty years direct confrontation continued between Dawudids and Idrisids. Dunama b. Bir (*c.* 1440–4) attacked Kaday b. ʿUthmān and reconquered the kingdom for the descendants of Idrīs. Two brothers – Muḥammad b. Matala and ʿAmr b. ʿA'isha bint ʿUthmān[89] – succeeded him, but their two reigns combined lasted for less than two years before the Dawudids returned to power. It is not known in what circumstances Muḥammad b. Kaday (*c.* 1445–9) succeeded ʿAmr, but it is probable that he imposed himself by force. He was also succeeded by his two brothers, Ghadjī b. Imāta (*c.* 1449–54) and ʿUthmān b. Kaday (*c.* 1454–9). The latter was defeated by ʿAlī Ghadjideni, with whom the Dawudids as a political power ceased to exist. The great dynastic conflict that had rent the country for almost a century thus ended with the complete victory of the Idrisids.

However, ʿAlī Ghadjideni, the son of Dunama b. Bir, was not necessarily assured of the succession. Apparently, two older members of his line had stronger claims. ʿAlī Ghadjideni did not in fact accede to the throne until after ʿUmar b. ʿAbd Allāh (*c.* 1459–60) and Muḥammad b. Muḥammad (*c.* 1460–5). It must be supposed that during the long-drawn-out struggle between Dawudids and Idrisids the two dynastic groups became strongly structured and that collateral succession, by seniority, down to the last surviving member of each generation, had become so binding a rule that even the conqueror of the Dawudids could not be exempted from it.

Very little reliable information has reached us concerning the reign of ʿAlī Ghadjideni (*c.* 1465–97). All that is known with certainty is that he built the city of Gazargamo (situated between Kano and Lake Chad), which was to remain the capital of the Sefuwa for over three centuries. Nevertheless, the importance of his reign may be measured by the fact that it saw a transformation of the rules of succession in favour of his direct descendants, his son Idrīs Katakarmabe (*c.* 1497–1515) and his grandson Muḥammad b. Idrīs (*c.* 1515–38). After the long period of troubles, the return to patrilineal succession must have seemed to the inhabitants of Bornu like a return to the golden age.

resented the encroachment of the Sefuwa on their own territory. H. F. C. (Abdullahi) Smith, 1971, p. 180. Since there is no evidence of the military function of the *kayghamma* until the second half of the sixteenth century (Ibn Furṭūwa), this hypothesis remains perfectly plausible.

89. If the chroniclers do not indicate the agnatic line of descent, this is doubtless because it was presumed to be known. It cannot be inferred from this that Muḥammad and ʿAmr were usurpers.

11

The Hausa and their neighbours in the central Sudan

M. ADAMU*

The area traditionally inhabited by the Hausa is contained within a region extending from the Air mountains in the north to the northern edge of the Jos plateau in the south and from the border of the ancient Bornu kingdom in the east to the Niger valley in the west. In this area, from very early on, Hausa was the only known indigenous language. As if to emphasize the importance of that language, the territory had no particular name and was simply called *kasar hausa* – the country of the Hausa language. However, through migrations and assimilation, the area in which Hausa was used as the main vehicle of communication expanded towards the south and west, and, in the north, a number of non-Hausa peoples, especially the Tuareg, the Zabarma/Djerma and the Fulbe/Fulani entered the territory and settled there.

Hausa is now the dominant language of the savannah belt of the central Sudan. It is spoken by diverse groups who have intermingled over the course of history, so that they eventually took on a single, unique cultural identity and gave rise to a brilliant civilization. Indeed we may agree with Guy Nicolas that 'the Hausa, who speak the same language, follow the same customs and obey the same political institutions, comprise one of the most important ethnic groups of Africa. Many were the neighbouring peoples who, drawn by their culture, abandoned their own language and customs to become part of them.'[1] But where did they come from? What was their origin? These are the questions which will be discussed in the first part of this chapter, before we examine the establishment and evolution of the Hausa states up to the sixteenth century. Subsequent sections will attempt, in particular, to highlight the political and administrative organization of the Hausa states, as well as their social and economic structure. The nature and quality of the relations which existed both between the individual component states and with neighbouring states, especially Songhay and Bornu, will also be examined in the course of the chapter.

* The Bureau decided to revise this chapter using a contribution from A. Salifou. The chapter was finalized by a subcommittee composed of Professors J. Devisse, I. Hrbek and Y. Talib, appointed by the International Scientific Committee.

1. Translated from G. Nicolas, 1969, p. 202.

Hausa origins

Several theories, often mutually contradictory, have been put forward about the origins of the Hausa people. These may be summarized as follows.

The first theory, based on an erroneous interpretation of the Bayajida (or Daura) legend, claims that the ancestors of the Hausa people were originally Arabs from Baghdad in Iraq.[2] Recently Salifou has given us another version of the legend, and Hallam has interpreted it as being an account of the emergence of new dynasties in Hausaland at the beginning of the present millennium.[3] According to Abdullahi Smith, 'if the Bayajida legend means anything, it is rather the Bornu influence on the political institutions of the Hausa which is perhaps to a certain extent proved by the Kanuri words in the Hausa vocabulary'.[4] Historians no longer subscribe to this theory of Arabic origin.

The second theory maintains that the Hausa people originally resided in the southern Sahara before it became a desert and that later they moved southwards.[5] After entering present-day northern Nigeria, either they pushed back the autochthonous people to the Bauchi plateau, or they found the territory so sparsely populated that there was room for all to live there without displacing the original inhabitants. This explains why there are now numerous small ethnic groups on the plateau, whose languages belong to language family groups quite different from Hausa. The theory of the Saharan origin of the Hausa is plausible but not conclusive, since it is not based on any factual data and therefore remains only a hypothesis.

The third theory is diametrically opposed to this view, and states that the ancestors of the Hausa were the hunting, fishing and farming inhabitants on the western shore of the great Lake Chad.[6] When the lake began to shrink eastwards to its present location, these people chose to remain where they were as sedentary cultivators. According to the theory put forward recently by Sutton, the territory which constituted the Daura, Kano, Rano and Garun Gobas kingdoms was the place where 'Hausa-ness' first developed, from which it later spread westwards and northwards to include the Katsina, Zazzau, Gobir, Zamfara and Kebbi areas. Sutton summarizes his theory as follows: 'Put simply, the history of Hausaland in the present millennium has been a westward push from the Hadejia–Daura–Kano region to that of Sokoto and beyond.'[7] He thus rejects completely the

2. H. R. Palmer, 1928, Vol. 3, pp. 133 ff.

3. A. Salifou, 1971, pp. 321–45; W. K. R. Hallam, 1966.

4. H. F. C. (Abdullahi) Smith, 1970a; on the influence of Kanuri on the Hausa language, see J. H. Greenberg, 1960.

5. Smith, op. cit.

6. The present-day Lake Chad is a relic of an old inland sea which occupied an area of 400 000 km² in prehistoric times. The lake reached its maximum height about the year 10 000 BP (*c.*–8000), a level which lasted until about 4000 BP (*c.*–2000). *Cf.* Vol. I, Chap. 16.

7. J. E. G. Sutton, 1979, pp. 184–5.

northern (Saharan) origin of the Hausa people advocated by Smith. However, Sutton's theory has not yet been conclusively proved.

A fourth theory on the origin of the Hausa people was recently proposed by Adamu.[8] The main argument in favour of this theory is that, although no section of the Hausa people has ever had a tradition of migration from any place outside Hausaland, locally recorded traditions speak of the ancestors of the Hausa as 'coming out of holes in the ground'. This type of tradition, which is also encountered in many other parts of Africa, is interpreted as meaning that the ancestors of the people were autochthonous to the area. So it appears that the origin of the Hausa people must be located precisely in the territory now known as Hausaland. The Hausa ethnic group benefited greatly, of course, from the large-scale immigration of people from the north and east; at a later date, various Wangarawa (Dioula) and Fulani peoples also came from the west to settle in Hausaland. There is nothing to disprove this theory, which indicates that both the Hausa language and the Hausa ethnic group first developed in Hausa territory, although the process of ethnogenesis is now obscure, owing to the distance in time.[9]

However, it is very likely that the territory inhabited by the Hausa peoples in earlier times included some parts of the southern Sahara, especially Azbin (or Air).[10] Various sources indicate that this area was conquered as late as the fourteenth or fifteenth century by the Tuareg, who forced the majority of its original Hausa inhabitants to move southwards to Gobir. The pressure from the north led to the general shift of the Hausa southwards to regions inhabited by other ethnic groups, who gradually adopted the Hausa language and customs in the course of the following centuries.

The term Hausa as the ethnonym for the peoples of Hausaland has appeared in the written sources only since the sixteenth and seventeenth centuries. Until that time, these peoples were known by the names of their particular cities or kingdoms – Kanawa, Katsinawa, Gobirawa and so on. At the beginning of the sixteenth century, Leo Africanus wrote that the common language in the area which today forms northern Nigeria was Gobir.[11] However, the Egyptian historian al-Suyūtī (1445–1505) used the term 'Hausa' for the territory in his *Epistles to the Kings of the Sudan, Hausa and al-Takrūr*.[12] Likewise the Timbuktu authors of the *Ta'rīkh*

8. M. Adamu, n.d. Even H. F. C. (Abdullah) Smith, op. cit., argues that the Hausa-speaking people have lived in their present area of settlement from a very early period.

9. We have left on one side the far-fetched theories of the Coptic, Nubian or Berber origins of the Hausa, proposed by C. K. Meek, 1931b, Vol. 1, pp. 61–87; C. R. Niven, 1957, pp. 265–6; or H. R. Palmer in his many writings. All of them are offshoots of the now defunct 'Hamitic myth'. On this, see Volume I, Chapter 1, pp. 35 ff.

10. R. Mauny, 1961, p. 144, suggests that the present Harratin of the Saharan oases are the remains of these ancient blacks, who formed part of the Hausa-speaking population.

11. Leo Africanus, French transl. 1956, Vol. 1, p. 9.

12. See H. R. Palmer, 1914, pp. 407 ff.

al-fattāsh and the *Ta'rīkh al-Sūdān* regularly employed the term Hausa to refer to the areas on the left bank of the Niger inhabited by the Hausa people, contrasting it with Gurma, which they used to describe those on the right bank.[13]

Originally, the term Hausa referred only to the mother tongue of the inhabitants of Hausaland, whereas the people actually called themselves 'Hausawa' (that is, speakers of the Hausa language).[14] Sometimes, however, Hausa referred merely to the territory made up of the former Zamfara, Kebbi and Gobir kingdoms, thereby indirectly confirming the Sudanic chronicles, since these kingdoms were the nearest Hausa lands to Songhay.

There are non-Muslim groups in both Nigeria and Niger who speak only Hausa and who share the Hausa culture, but who refuse to be called Hausa people. In Nigeria these people call themselves, and are called by the other Hausa, Maguzawa (or Bamaguje), whereas in Niger they are known by the name Azna (or Arna) – the Hausa word for 'pagan'. These Azna also regard the geographical coverage of the name Hausa as being confined to the Zamfara, Kebbi and Gobir areas. Since the name Maguzawa is probably derived from the Arabic *madjūs* (originally 'fire-worshippers', then 'pagan' generally) it is possible that the polarization between Hausa and Maguzawa/Azna began only with the spread of Islam among the common people in Hausaland, after the seventeenth and eighteenth centuries.

In this chapter, the term Hausa is used to denote all those whose mother tongue is Hausa, regardless of their place of residence or their religion.

The birth and evolution of the Hausa states

The common Hausa legend of origin recounts the westward journey of Prince Bayajida from Baghdad to Kanem-Bornu.[15] It was there that the *mai* (king) gave Bayajida his daughter, the *magira*, in marriage, but deprived him of his followers. Bayajida fled to the west in fear of the *mai* and after some time, came to a town whose inhabitants were prevented from drawing water by a great snake known as *sarki* (chief). He slew the snake with his sword;[16] as a reward, the local queen, Daura, married him and also

13. Maḥmūd Ka'ti, French transl. 1913–14, pp. 53, 178 and 330; al-Sa'dī, French transl. 1900, pp. 41, 152 and 232; cf. also N. Skinner, 1968, pp. 253–7.

14. D. A. Olderogge, 1960, p. 68, connects the ethnonym Hausa with the Hausa word, *hausa*, for language or tongue; cf. *na gane hausarka*, 'I understand your language'.

15. Both H. R. Palmer, 1936, pp. 273–4, and W. K. R. Hallam, op. cit., pp. 47–60, regard this Bayajida as having some historical connection with Abū Yazīd, who led a kharijite Berber revolt against the Fatimids in North Africa in the first half of the tenth century. Abū Yazīd was probably born in the western Sudan to a slave-girl from Tadmekka and was killed by the Fatimids in 947.

16. The legend of the heroic snake-killer is also found among the Mandingo tales of the origins of the Wagadu kings.

gave him a Gwari concubine. The son of the marriage with Daura was called Bawogari, while the concubine bore him a second son called Karbogari or Karafgari (town-seizer). The town became known as Daura. Bawo, who succeeded his father, had six sons, three sets of twins, who became the rulers of Kano and Daura, Gobir and Zazzau (Zegzeg or Zaria) and Katsina and Rano respectively. Together with Biram, which was ruled by Bayajidda's son by the Bornu princess, these seven states formed the *hausa bakwai* (the seven Hausa states). Karbogari's sons established another seven states, namely Kebbi, Zamfara, Gwari, Jukun (Kwararafa), Yoruba, Nupe and Yawuri, which were together called *banza bakwai* (the seven bastards or worthless ones).[17]

Even though this legend contains some ancient details, it reflects a situation which prevailed in northern Nigeria in the sixteenth century. The states which came to form the *hausa bakwai* were those that survived centuries of successful struggle against neighbouring rival groups. As Abdullahi Smith has emphasized, the dynasties and centralized governments in Hausaland did not emerge as a result of the handiwork of a civilizing hero who came from the east with a superior culture, for the legend of Bayajidda itself recognizes that when he arrived at Daura he found a queen there.[18] The same story is told, moreover, of Kano, where there was already a royal dynasty in power before the coming of Bagauda, the son of Bayajidda, who is regarded as the founder of Kano. All this implies that the real meaning of the legend of Daura has not yet been revealed.

The relatively late origin of the legend is shown by the interesting description of the division of functions among the Hausa cities. According to this, Kano and Rano became *sarakunan babba* (kings of indigo), since their main occupation was the production and dyeing of textiles, whereas Katsina and Daura were called *sarakunan kasuwa* (kings of the market), since trade was concentrated in those towns. Gobir was *sarkin yaki* (the king of war), because its duty was to defend the others against external enemies. Finally Zazzau (Zaria) became *sarkin bayi* (the king of slaves), since it supplied slave labour to the other Hausa cities.[19] This reflects the general situation after the establishment of the main Hausa city-states, once they had attained a high level of economic growth.

The appearance of centralized states seems to have been closely linked with the establishment of great cities called *birane* (sing. *birni*) as the centres of political power. The Hausa cities varied in importance at different times, and for this reason we shall only discuss the evolution of those which

17. Cf. Palmer, 1928, Vol. 3, pp. 132–4. Various versions of this 'Daura' legend differ as to the composition of these two groups of seven: among the *hausa bakwai* we sometimes find Zamfara, Kebbi and Bauchi (Biram and Rano are excluded), whereas Gwambe, Bauchi, Gurma, Zaberma and Borgu may be included in the list of *banza bakwai*. Cf. Olderogge, op. cit., pp. 72–3, where all these differences are tabulated.

18. Smith, op. cit., pp. 329 ff.

19. A. J. N. Tremearne, 1913, p. 141.

played a significant role, especially after the fourteenth century, including Kano, Katsina, Zazzau (Zaria), Gobir and Kebbi.

Kano

The history of Kano is undoubtedly the best known, thanks to its chronicles and the wealth of oral tradition.[20] The territory which later formed the Kano kingdom was initially ruled by small chiefdoms, each headed by individuals whose authority over the rest of the people was based on ritual jurisdiction. The most important of these chiefdoms were Sheme, Dala and Santolo. At Dala, there were six generations of rulers before the coming of Bagauda.

The entry of Bagauda into the Kano area took place, according to Palmer, in the year +999; that dating has not yet been revised, although Palmer's chronology is plainly arbitrary and very approximate.[21] Bagauda lived and died at Sheme after compelling the local people to recognize his political rule. It was his grandson, Gijimasu (1095–1134), who first established the present city of Kano, when he built his settlement at the foot of Dala hill. He also started to build the city walls, but it was not until the reign of his son Tsaraki (1136–94) that they were completed. By 1200, the Kano rulers had subdued nearly all the independent chiefdoms in the area, with the exception of Santolo, which remained independent for another 150 years.

Under Yaji (1349–85) the process of subjugating the country and people around the city was brought to a successful conclusion, although many groups in Kano and outside occasionally rose in revolt. Outward expansion was marked by the conquest of the still independent chiefdoms of Zamnagaba and the occupation of Rano for two years. From that time onwards, although Rano continued to exist, it never regained its sovereignty.

In his war against Santolo, Yaji was aided by a large group of Muslim Wangarawa/Dioula people who arrived in Kano during that period, according to the *Kano Chronicle*. They not only joined his army in the attack, but also offered prayers for the success of the campaign. Santolo was finally captured and the religious centre of the city, where traditional sacrifices had been performed, was completely destroyed. This conquest completed the territorial definition of the kingdom of Kano.

It is interesting to note that the *Kano Chronicle* depicts the struggle

20. The *Kano Chronicle*, written in Arabic, was apparently composed about 1890, but it is based upon earlier, pre-*d̲j̲ihād* records. It gives an account of 48 Hausa (after 1807, Fùlani) *sarakuna* or kings, from Bagauda to Muḥammad Bello. An English translation was published by H. R. Palmer, 1909, pp. 58–98, and was reprinted in Palmer, 1928, Vol. 3, pp. 92–132 (used for citation hereafter). A Hausa translation, 'Tarihin Kano', was published in R. M. East, 1933. A variant list of the kings of Kano is to be found in the anonymous *Song of Bagauda*; see M. Hiskett, 1964–5.

21. Palmer, 1928, Vol. 3, pp. 92 ff.

between the ruling class and the commoners – who repeatedly rebelled against an increasingly despotic rule – as a conflict between Muslims and followers of the traditional religion.[22] This, however, is clearly a late interpretation of the process of centralization. The expansion of Kano was directed southwards; Santolo was followed by other campaigns in regions to the south, where Kano's armies clashed for the first time with the Kwararafa/Jukun. The outcome appears to have been indecisive, since the Kwararafa refused to pay allegiance to Yaji, but agreed to hand over 100 slaves.

Kananeji (1390–1410) continued the policy of expansion and in two campaigns subdued Zazzau, whose king was killed in the battle. Relations with Kwararafa were seemingly peaceful and Kano exchanged its horses for slaves. External contacts were stepped up, as shown by the introduction of *lifidi* (the quilted protection for war-horses), iron helmets and coats of mail.[23] Under Dauda (1421–38), the foreign influence became more marked with the arrival of a refugee Bornu prince with his men and a large number of *mallam*s. Apart from such regalia as horses, drums, trumpets and flags, it seems that the Bornu people also brought with them more sophisticated concepts of administration, and it was from that time onwards that Bornu titles such as *galadima*, *chiroma* and *kaigama* came into use in Kano.

Although wars and raids continued throughout the whole of the fifteenth century, the growing commercial activities of the Kanawa represented a more important development. A road from Bornu to Gwanja (Gonja in modern Ghana) is said to have been opened in the 1450s; camels and salt from the Sahara became common in Hausaland; and a profitable trade was started in kola nuts and eunuchs. The growing prosperity of the kingdom, as well as the more pronounced Islamic character of the ruling class, attracted many Muslim clerics to Kano. In the 1450s, the Fulani came to Hausaland from Mali, bringing 'books on divinity and etymology' (formerly only books on law and the traditions had been known); the end of the century witnessed the arrival of a number of *rif* (descendants of the Prophet Muḥammad) and the vigorous Muslim cleric, al-Maghīlī.[24] On the other hand, the kings of Kano were forced to pay tribute to Bornu and became involved in a century-long war with Katsina.

The *Kano Chronicle* ascribes to Muḥammad Rumfa (1463–99) a number of innovations of varying importance, among them the extension of the city walls and the building of new gates; the appointment of eunuchs to state offices; the establishment of Kurmi market, the main market in Kano; and the setting up of a council of nine leading office-holders (*tara-ta-Kano* –

22. ibid., pp. 102 ff. The *Kano Chronicle* also mentions the introduction, at this time, of long trumpets in Kano and of a national anthem, *Zauna daidai Kano garinkine* ('Stand firm, Kano is your city'). ibid., p. 104.

23. Palmer, 1928, Vol. 3, p. 107.

24. ibid, p. 111. On al-Maghīlī and his role, see pp. 290–1 below.

'the Nine of Kano') as a kind of ministry. Some of these innovations mark Rumfa's ambition to emulate the manners of the Bornu or even of the courts of the Maghrib, such as the construction of a new palace (*gidan rumfa*), long trumpets and ostrich-feather fans as symbols of royalty, the establishment of a secluded harem with 1000 wives and, last but not least, the official festivities at the end of the Ramadan fast (*'Īd al-fiṭr*).

It was in Rumfa's reign that the first war took place with Katsina; this lasted eleven years, with neither side gaining the upper hand. His successors, Abdūḷḷāhī (1499–1509) and Muḥammad Kisoki (1509–65) continued his policy and, although they fought without much success against Katsina, they defeated Zaria. The growing might of Bornu still loomed menacingly over Hausaland, and Kano was not spared the humiliation of its *sarki* before the *mai*, but it managed on other occasions to defend its territory.

Katsina

In general, there is much less information on the early history of Katsina;[25] but it seems to have closely paralleled that of Kano, albeit with a considerable time-lag. In the thirteenth and fourteenth centuries the territory which later came to be known as Katsina consisted of independent chiefdoms, all of them Hausa-speaking; that at Durbi-ta-Kusheyi was the most important. It was from Durbi that the centralized city-state of Katsina eventually developed. With Sarki Muḥammad Korau (1445–95), who was probably the founder of a new dynasty, we are on firmer historical ground. While still at Durbi, Korau identified an important meeting point of several trade routes, the site of an iron-mine and an important shrine, known as Bawada; and as *sarki*, he established there a new walled city (*birni*) called Katsina.[26]

The new settlement soon became attractive to both settlers and passing traders, and thus brought more power and wealth to its ruler. Little by little, the surrounding chiefs came to pay him tributes in the form of iron bars, and this was the beginning of *haraji* or poll-tax in Katsina. With such a strong economic and political base, Muḥammad Korau began to raid far and wide, until he had carved for himself a large domain, the kingdom of Katsina; he is traditionally regarded as its first Muslim ruler.[27] It was during his reign that al-Maghīlī visited the city; the Gobarau mosque, part of which still stands, was built during the same period, modelled on the mosques of Gao and Jenne. Katsina's military campaigns outside Hausaland were concentrated, like those of Kano, in the territory to the

25. H. R. Palmer, 1927, published a list of Katsina kings; see also Palmer, 1928, Vol. 3, pp. 78–82. The most recent work on the history of Katsina is a doctoral dissertation (University of Zaria) by Y. B. Usman.

26. Y. B. Usman's research has disproved the assertion of some earlier writers that the city of Katsina was founded by Wangarawa immigrants; ibid.

27. H. F. C. (Abdullahi) Smith, 1971, pp. 196–8.

south of the kingdom. The *Katsina Chronicle* records that Muḥammad Korau waged war against Nupe, which then had a common frontier with Katsina;[28] this war perhaps arose from the same nascent Nupe expansionism which had precipitated conflict between the Nupe and the Yoruba.

Among Korau's successors, Ibrāhīm Sura (1493–9) is remembered as a severe taskmaster who forced his subjects to pray and imprisoned those who refused; he also corresponded with the celebrated Egyptian historian, al-Suyūtī (d. 1505). 'Alī, who succeeded Ibrāhīm and whose long reign covered the first quarter of the sixteenth century, was called *murābiṭ* ('man of the *ribāṭ*'), perhaps to commemorate his fortification of the city.[29]

Zazzau

The picture we have of the early history of Zazzau is even more clouded than that of Katsina. The historical materials are too limited to allow for any reasonable reconstruction of the political history of the area, and the interpretations given to the few sources available are contradictory. According to Abdullahi Smith, the Hausa people 'had lived in Zazzau for more than a millennium before a central government emerged in the area, based initially at Turunku'.[30] From there, the chiefs expanded the territory, annexing the smaller neighbouring chiefdoms and then establishing their new headquarters at the site of the present city of Zaria, probably at the end of the fifteenth century.

Recently M. Last has put forward a completely different picture of Hausa rule in Zazzau. He suggests that as early as the year 1200 there existed a kingdom in that territory, but that it went by the name of Kankuma (Kangoma or Kwangoma as now pronounced) and that the rulers were not Hausa but Kamuku. This Kangoma federation was 'heir to the Nok culture and its economy was based on trade in metals'. When this federation broke up, 'the kingdom of Kangoma (which had emerged from the split) at Turunku became known in the sixteenth century as Zegzeg'. It was only in 1641 that the Hausa people began to rule Zegzeg or Zazzau, with Zaria as the capital.[31] This is a rather bold theory, not without its weak points (mostly linguistic), and it must remain in the realm of conjecture until more convincing arguments have been advanced in its support.

Abdullahi Smith gives us a more satisfactory picture of the history of Zazzau in this period, which can be summarized as follows. Not long before the fifteenth century, on the plain of Zazzau in the extreme south of Hausaland, several urban centres arose, which evolved a city-state type of administration. In the course of political development, two towns,

28. Palmer, 1928, Vol. 3, pp. 79–80. Cf. also Y. B. Usman, 1972, pp. 175–97.

29. Early Katsina chronology is rather confused. H. F. C. (Abdullahi) Smith, 1961, uses the reference to an eclipse during the reign of Aliyu Karyagiwa (dated by Palmer between 1419 and 1431) to prove that Palmer's dates are over 100 years too early.

30. H. F. C. (Abdullahi) Smith, 1970b.

31. M. Last, in M. Adamu (ed.) (forthcoming, b).

Turunku and Kufena, came to exercise authority over the others. These two towns were initially independent of each other and remained so until the end of the fifteenth century, when a Turunku ruler, Bakwa, seized power also at Kufena. Later, the kings of Zazzau, who ruled the former territories of Kufena and Turunku, settled permanently in the new capital built at the eastern end of the Kufena *birni*, which was called Zaria after a daughter of Bakwa. (Princess Zaria and the celebrated Amīna were sisters.)

With the merger of Turunku and Kufena, the Zazzau kingdom had really come into being. From the beginning of the sixteenth century, Zazzau embarked on territorial expansion in the west and south. According to historical tradition, the Zazzau army was led in some campaigns by the *gimbiya* (Princess) Amīna, daughter of Bakwa, who also fortified Zaria and Kufena with wide city walls. There is nothing in the literature or the non-palace oral traditions to show that Amīna was ever a monarch in Zazzau. Her name is not found on any of the lists of Zazzau kings; she lived and died a princess – admittedly a very influential one – but never a queen. The legend depicts her as a great warrior who campaigned beyond the frontiers of Zazzau as far as Nupeland in the south-west and Kwararafa in the south-east. The *Kano Chronicle* states that 'the *Sarkin Nupe* sent her [the princess] forty eunuchs and 10 000 kola nuts. She was the first in Hausaland to own eunuchs and kola nuts. In her time all the products of the west were introduced into Hausaland.'[32]

Gobir

Whereas Zazzau was the southernmost Hausa state, Gobir was furthest north. The original homeland of the Gobirawa was situated even further north and stretched from the region of Agades up to and including the Air massif. The Hausa name for the area is Azbin (correctly pronounced Abzin), whereas Gobir was used to refer to the political entity formed by the Gobirawa.[33] The various groups into which they were divided had been under pressure from the Tuareg since the twelfth century and had been driven southwards. Some of them settled on the plains, in an area now called Adar, and became known as the Adarawa. Other groups of Hausa-speakers, who later became the Gobirawa, also migrated southwards and established the Gobir kingdom, in different places and at different times. Thus, in the period up to about 1405, this kingdom was located in what is now the Republic of Niger (with its centre at Marandet?); later it moved

32. Palmer, 1928, Vol. 3, p. 109. According to the *Kano Chronicle*, Amīna was a contemporary of Dauda of Kano (1421–38). Some modern scholars are inclined to accept this date, for example, R. A. Adeleye, 1971, and H. J. Fisher, 1977; others claim that she lived in the sixteenth century: S. J. Hogben and A. H. Kirk-Greene, 1966, pp. 216–18, place her after 1576; Abdullahi Smith, 1970b, gives the beginning of the sixteenth century. This is also the opinion of the editors of this chapter.

33. According to some oral traditions, all the Hausa come from the Air massif, see D. Hamani, 1975.

again to the south and established its capital at Birnin Lalle for some time. The *Kano Chronicle* mentions the arrival of the Abzinawa in Gobir in the mid-fifteenth century and adds that it was from that time onwards that salt became common in Hausaland.[34]

The paucity of the written and oral sources does not enable us to reconstruct a more coherent history of Gobir or of the process by which a centralized state first developed there. The same is true of the chronology, since none of the currently available versions of the list of kings is of any value. However, Marandet was already, by about the ninth century, an important commercial and industrial centre based on the trans-Saharan trade with Gao, so it is possible that Gobir had become a centralized state by that time. In spite of continuous pressure from the Tuaregs, the Gobirawa were successful in their role as defenders of Hausaland's northern borders, both during the period under discussion and also at a later stage.

Rano

In most works on the early history of the Hausa states, Rano is presented as one of the kingdoms established early in the present millennium, which subsequently lost its sovereignty to Kano. Recently, however, Murray Last has drawn attention to the fact that, if the *Kano Chronicle* is examined carefully, no evidence can be found for the existence of a kingdom of Rano before the fifteenth century.[35] There was, in fact, a Hausa chiefdom called Zamnagaba (or Zamnakogi) which was independent of Kano. According to the *Kano Chronicle*, it was Sarkin Kano Yaji (1349–85) who drove its chief from his capital and then went on to Rano and Babu, where he lived for two years.[36] Last suggests that before this conquest Zamnagaba was part of the political system of Santolo, which was still independent of Kano at that time and was conquered by Yaji only towards the end of his reign. There would seem therefore to be a need to reconsider the inclusion of Rano among the early Hausa states and to engage in further research on Rano's relationship with Santolo and Kano respectively. Zamnagaba should perhaps take the place of Rano among the list of the early *hausa bakwai*.[37]

Zamfara

It was only at the beginning of the sixteenth century that the Zamfara kingdom can be said to have clearly emerged as a state. Before that time, the main chiefdoms in its territory were Dutsi, Togai, Kiyawa (or Kiawa) and Jata. Unfortunately, none of the available sources illustrates the process

34. *Kano Chronicle*, in Palmer, 1928, Vol. 3, p. iii.
35. M. Last, in *Kano Studies*, 1979, pp. 13–15.
36. Palmer, 1928, Vol. 3, p. 104.
37. The meaning of the name Zamnakogi also needs investigating. This is given in the *Daura Chronicle* as the name of the founder of Kano; ibid., p. 134.

by which a system of centralized government first developed here, but it seems that the areas that were administered from an early date were also places where iron ore was smelted and where hills of some religious significance were situated.[38] The centralization process started with the rulers of Dutsi, who had brought the other chiefdoms under their control. The establishment of Birnin Zamfara as the permanent capital of the kingdom may have occurred early in the sixteenth century, for in the middle of that century Zamfara began to campaign in a southerly direction; these campaigns took them to Yawuri in the Niger basin, although they did not occupy it permanently. Until 1600, the main concern of the Zamfara rulers was to consolidate their domestic power.[39]

Kebbi

Although Kebbi, the westernmost part of Hausaland, was inhabited by Hausa-speaking peoples from early times, local traditions of origin do not include its people among the *hausa bakwai*, but lists them among the *banza bakwai*. According to M. Muḥammad Bello, 'the people of Kebbi are descended from a Katsina mother and a Songhay father'.[40]

Kebbi appears in history at the time when the area first came under Songhay rule, during the reign of Sunni ʿAlī (1464–92). At this time the lower Rima valley was administered by clan chiefs with the title of *magaji* (successor), but shortly afterwards immigration started from other Hausa areas. One of the immigrants was a certain Muḥammadu Kanta from Kuyambana in southern Katsina. Through his military prowess, he soon eclipsed the local *magaji*s and became the *de facto* governor of the Songhay sub-province of Kebbi.[41] He joined the Songhay army as a *barde* (captain) and participated in the successful campaign against the Sultan of Agades, where much booty was captured. Because Kanta did not receive his expected share of the spoils, he and his followers broke away from the Songhay empire and were declared rebels. This happened in 1516; a series of military engagements with Songhay followed, lasting for several years, but Kanta managed to preserve his independence.[42]

Kanta then established his capital at Surame and encouraged the small villages to merge together into towns, which were then fortified with city walls for defensive purposes. He himself grouped together nine separate settlements to found Birnin Leka, and later founded another town, which

38. N. Garba, 1977.

39. K. Krieger, 1959.

40. M. Muḥammad Bello, Eng. transl. 1922, p. 13. The exclusion of Kebbi from the 'Seven Hausa' may arise from the fact that, in the sixteenth century, the Kebbi kingdom was an ally of Songhay and led many campaigns against the other Hausa states, which consequently regarded it as an enemy.

41. An account of the early history of Kebbi, including the rise and fall of Kanta, is given in an unpublished thesis by M. B. Alkali, 1969.

42. Al-Saʿdī, loc. cit., pp. 129–30.

came to be known as Birnin Kebbi, to serve as a base for defence against Songhay.[43]

After thus consolidating his system of defence, Kanta turned his attention outwards. He occupied Air/Agades and seized control of that area from Songhay. Muḥammad Bello credited him with conquering the whole of Hausaland and parts of Bornu;[44] other sources recount his invasions of Yawuri and Nupe in the south.[45] Kanta does not appear to have evolved any administrative machinery for integrating the conquered territories with the metropolitan province. It was enough for him that the vassal states paid their tribute to him and acknowledged Kebbi's overlordship.[46]

In the sixteenth century Kebbi became a major power, functioning as a sort of buffer between Hausaland and the Niger basin. The Bornu kingdom, alarmed by the rise of a new and powerful state, attempted to subdue it and invaded the Hausa states under Kanta's rule; but the Bornu army was crushed. It was on his return from another victorious campaign in western Bornu, in 1556, that Kanta died. After his death, the Hausa states stopped sending tribute to Kebbi and became independent again, and Aḥmadu, the eldest son and successor of Kanta, did not take up arms to compel them to resume payment. At the end of the sixteenth century, even the overlordship of Agades was no longer firmly in the hands of the Kebbi rulers, since Kano and Katsina had intervened there in support of a claimant who was Kebbi's enemy. Kebbi thus had shrunk from an 'empire' to a local kingdom, whose paramountcy over Hausaland was completely ended.

It can be seen from the foregoing that the period between 1200 and 1600 must be considered crucial in the history of the Hausa people. During that time they established centralized governments in half a dozen states, based on walled capital cities, which also became important as commercial centres. Some of these states had already begun to expand and to attack other peoples, both in Hausaland and beyond.

Relations of the Hausa with neighbouring peoples

The Hausa were not, of course, the only people inhabiting the central Sudan, that is the territory stretching from Lake Chad in the east to the Niger basin in the west, and from the Sahel in the north to the Benue basin in the south. It was within these perimeters that the Hausa people developed contacts with other ethnic groups. The Daura legend – the Hausa myth of origin – enumerates some of the neighbouring non-Hausa peoples with whom the Hausa had established relations by the year 1500. Although various lists of the *banza bakwai* ('the worthless seven') sometimes include

43. Alkali, op. cit., pp. 55 ff.
44. Muḥammad Bello, loc. cit., pp. 13–14.
45. R. M. East, 1933, Vol. 1.
46. Adeleye, op. cit., p. 564.

Hausa-speaking societies (Kebbi and Zamfara), the main representatives of these were the Jukun, the Kwararafa, the Gwari, the Yoruba, the Nupe and the Yawuri. It is interesting to note that none of these lists contains the names of the greater and more important neighbours – Kanem-Bornu and Songhay – whose influence in Hausaland must have been considerable from a very early date.

As a rule the Hausa used the name Barebari (or Beriberi) to refer to all the peoples of the Kanem-Bornu empire. Thus the names of Kanembu, Kanuri, the Shuwa Arabs, Bolewa, Ngizim and so on were not widely known in Hausaland before the modern period. Among the Barebari, the social classes dominating Bornu's relations with Hausaland – the rulers, merchants and Muslim clerics – were predominantly of Kanuri ethnic origin, and certain features of Kanuri culture accordingly came to be seen as representative of the Beriberi people.[47]

In the history of Hausaland, the relationship with Kanem-Bornu is of great significance because it was from that state that many important cultural elements and new ideas were borrowed, which later became an integral part of Hausa culture and civilization. Contacts between the Hausa and the Kanuri peoples began when the latter were still in Kanem; but when they became firmly established in Bornu, to the south-west of Lake Chad, these contacts took on a new dimension.[48]

In the second half of the fifteenth century, after a long period of uninterrupted conflict, the Bornu kingdom settled down to a new-found stability. This stabilization was associated with the establishment of a permanent walled capital at Ngazargumu, to the west of Chad, which formed a suitable base for the later extension of Bornu power westwards into Hausaland.[49] In about 1425 ʿUth̲mān Kalnama, a deposed ruler of Bornu, sought refuge in Kano, with his retinue; he played an important role there under the reign of Dauda (1421–38) and Abdūḷḷāhī Burja (1438–52). The *mai* of Bornu could scarcely ignore this threat coming from Hausaland, and he reduced Kano and other parts of Hausaland to vassal status, so that many towns had to pay tribute to Bornu. About the same time, Katsina was to some extent subject to Bornu and was also forced to send an annual tribute of 100 slaves to Ngazargumu.[50] It is not clear to what degree the whole of Hausaland became dependent on Bornu, nor for how long. M. G. Smith inclines to the view that, initially, only Biram and Kano were the vassals of Bornu, since Kano was the leading Hausa state on Bornu's borders and would thus have been the first to engage the attention of the Kanuri.[51] On the other hand, according to the *Sokoto Provincial Gazetteer*, 'Yawuri sent annual tribute to Zaria, its immediate

47. Usman, op. cit., pp. 185–97
48. Cf. M. Adamu, 1979; the history of Kanem-Bornu is discussed in Chapter 10 above.
49. Smith, 1971, p. 182.
50. *Kano Chronicle*, in Palmer, 1928, Vol. 3, pp. 109–10 and 83.
51. M. G. Smith, 1964a.

superior, and therefore to Bornu. All other Hausa states sent their tribute to Daura for Bornu.'[52]

The true nature of the suzerainty of Bornu over Hausaland and its various parts in the period under discussion still requires further research. Nevertheless, it has already been established that from this time onwards the influence of Bornu became stronger and was channelled mainly through Kano, thereby enriching the cultural development of Hausaland.

During the sixteenth century, the rise of Kebbi as the most warlike state of the central Sudan led it into a prolonged struggle with the rulers of Bornu. Muḥammad Kanta emerged victorious from this struggle, which had as its main objective the domination of Air (Agades), the important crossroads of trans-Saharan routes leading to Hausaland. It is difficult to discern to what extent the Hausa states were involved in this power game, but Kanta seems to have imposed his suzerainty on at least some of the city-states and thus eliminated Bornu's political tutelage.

The other powerful state on the borders of Hausaland was the Songhay empire. Mali, its predecessor in the hegemony of the central Sudan, never played any political role in Hausa history, although its cultural influence – mainly through the activities of the Wangarawa traders and clerics – must have been felt strongly from an early date.[53]

Until recently, most historians believed that Askiya Muḥammad (1492–1528), the powerful ruler of the Songhay empire, had conquered all of Hausaland in the first years of the sixteenth century and imposed his rule over Kano, Katsina, Gobir, Zamfara and Zazzau. According to this theory, the Hausa region became in subsequent decades the setting for a prolonged struggle between two imperial states, Songhay and Bornu, although the emergence of an independent kingdom, Kebbi, weakened the direct hold Songhay had over Hausaland from 1515. But, as H. J. Fisher has persuasively shown, the only source for the alleged Songhay invasion and occupation is the account of Leo Africanus, the Moroccan Arab traveller who claimed to have visited some parts of the western Sudan in 1510 and 1513.[54]

It cannot be denied that Leo's description of the Songhay invasion is very vivid and provides a great many details about the fate of the Hausa rulers, their crippling tributes and their marriage alliances.[55] On the other hand, the Hausa chronicles are silent about this event, which was so important for the political history of Hausaland, and it cannot be explained away simply by the chroniclers' deliberate suppression of any reference to a humiliating débâcle, since the *Kano Chronicle* frequently recounts defeats of the *sarkin kano* on various occasions by less powerful states

52. Quoted in ibid.

53. Songhay is often referred to in Hausa chronicles as 'Melle', in the sense of 'the western empire'.

54. H. J. Fisher, 1978.

55. Leo Africanus, loc. cit., Vol. 2, pp. 473 ff.

such as Katsina, Zaria or Kwararafa. Even more important is the fact that the Timbuktu chronicles, which tell the tale from the Songhay point of view, do not mention this allegedly victorious campaign of their favourite hero, Askiya Muḥammad. They refer only very briefly to a minor expedition against Katsina in 1514, shortly after Leo's visit.[56] It now appears more than likely that the Songhay conquest of Hausaland never took place and that the states of this area never came under Songhay domination.

The Jukun now live to the south-east of Hausaland, along the middle reaches of the River Benue. Although today they are not very numerous, in the past they played a considerable role in the history of central and northern Nigeria, and exercised a lasting influence on many of their neighbours.

According to the generally accepted view, the Jukun moved into their present area of settlement from the north-east. The traditions diverge concerning the country from which they came; some mention the Nile valley and Kordofan, others look as far as Arabia or the Yemen. One tradition claims that the Jukun arrived at the same time as the Kanuri.[57] Although these traditions of remote origin must be considered highly suspect, it seems more plausible that the Jukun came from the north-east through the country between the Mandara highlands and Lake Chad. However, the linguistic evidence shows that the Jukun language belongs to the Benue-Congo subfamily, together with the Tiv, Ibibio, Efik and the majority of Cross River languages; this points rather to a southern origin, although the possibility cannot be ruled out that the Jukun may have been the last wave of a general migratory movement from the north and north-east to the south.

Two theories have been put forward to identify the region of Nigeria which formed the first power base of the Jukun people. The first suggests that it was on the middle Benue basin, south of the river channel, that the Jukun established the Kwararafa empire often mentioned in traditional Hausa texts.[58] Ruins of the city, which went under the name of Kwararafa, can still be seen in the area. Kwararafa is the Hausa name for the Jukun people and their capital, as well as for their kingdom.[59] When the city was abandoned at the end of the eighteenth century,[60] its still-extant successor town, Wukari, grew up in the same region. It was from the southern Benue basin that the Jukun expanded northwards into the Gongola valley

56. Maḥmūd Ka'ti, loc. cit., pp. 77 and 147; al-Sa'dī, loc. cit., pp. 78 and 129.

57. C. K. Meek, 1931a, p. xv.

58. ibid.

59. Kwararafa is derived from *kororo-afa*, meaning 'the salt people', since Jukun territory was well known for its salt-mines. Cf. W. B. Baikie, 1856, p. 455. The terms Kororofa or Kororofawa, which appear in the literature, may refer to the peoples of the Benue valley in general and not necessarily to the same people (the Jukun) on each occasion. See T. L. Hodgkin, 1975, p. 31.

60. For the decline and break-up of the city of Kwararafa, see Meek, 1931a, pp. 32 ff; M. Adamu, 1978, pp. 38–43.

and later into Kasar Chiki.[61] This northward expansion has not yet been dated, but it occurred before the evacuation of the city of Kwararafa. Early Hausa–Jukun relations first developed in this area of the southern Benue basin. The Jukun language has been shown to have originated south of the Benue basin and to have spread northwards.[62] The southern origin of Jukun political power is further supported by oral traditions from different towns in Kasar Chiki, which claim descent from Jukun immigrants from the south (Kwararafa and Wukari).

According to the second theory, it was in the Gongola valley to the north of the Benue and in parts of the upper Benue basin that the Jukun first organized their political power and initially established military and commercial relations with the Hausa people. Jukun rule south of the River Benue developed only later. However, there is as yet no documentary evidence as to when and how this developed.[63]

These two theories are not entirely incompatible; the Jukun seem to have had two centres of political power, the southern Benue basin and the Gongola valley. For reasons that are still unclear, the southern Benue basin politically overshadowed all the other areas containing Jukun settlements. Some of the attacks on the Hausa states that were mounted from the Gongola valley may have been initiated on the orders of the *aku*, the supreme ruler of the Jukun people based on the southern area in the now abandoned city of Kwararafa.[64] On the grounds that the Hausa and Kanuri called their common enemy by different names (Kwana in Kanuri, Kwararafa in Hausa), Riad has suggested the existence of two Jukun states, one in the north, bordering Bornu (Kwana), and the second further to the south, more closely involved with Hausaland. These states were not contemporary with each other; the southern one was mentioned in the *Kano Chronicle* as having existed in the fourteenth century.[65]

Unfortunately, the Jukun people recorded their history neither in writing nor in 'drum history'.[66] The majority of the present-day Jukun, with the important exception of the Pindiga group, no longer remember the details of their warlike past. Nevertheless, various sources clearly show

61. Kasar Chiki is the lowland part of the present Plateau State of Nigeria, covering Wase (Langtang), Shendam and Awe local government areas. In Hausa the literal meaning of *kasar chiki* is 'the territory between'; the origin of the term has not yet been investigated.

62. K. Shimuzu, 1971, unpublished dissertation on the Jukun language.

63. The Gongola theory is supported by H. F. C. Smith, 1971, and more recently by S. Abubakar, 1980, pp. 168 ff.

64. The *aku* owed his position to his religious role, in that he was believed to be divinely appointed and to function as the intermediary between the gods and the people. See M. W. Young, 1966.

65. M. Riad, 1960, pp. 483 ff.

66. Drummers and singers are the bearers of the oral traditions of many communities in West Africa. Historical accounts are usually preserved in the form of songs and citations, and are passed down from father to son in the families of the traditional bards of *griots*. Most of such accounts relate to political histories, because it was the kings and chiefs

that the Jukun people were already established in the middle Benue basin and also in the Gongola valley during the period 1200–1600. It is even possible that their expansion into Kasar Chiki had already started in the sixteenth century. During the period under discussion they had established a powerful state, which by 1600 was approaching the peak of its military might. The early importance of the Jukun is also suggested by the fact that there are some ethnic groups which either claim descent from the Jukun or have copied many aspects of their culture, directly or through the Igala. In addition to the Igala themselves, these include the Idoma, Ankwe, Montol, Igbirra and a number of others.[67]

With the Nupe, we reach the southernmost part of the central Sudan. Both linguistic evidence and oral tradition, however, suggest that the earliest significant links were with the south rather than the north. By virtue of its geographical location, the Nupe country was, nevertheless, predestined to form a link between the savannah of the north and the forest regions of the south and to become a meeting point of influences from both directions. By all indications, the Nupe people were autochthonous in their present-day area of settlement, near the Niger–Benue confluence.

Even the story of Tsoede – 'the culture hero and mythical founder of the Nupe kingdom'[68] – merely refers to the emergence of one central government for the Nupe people and not to the genesis of the Nupe as a people.[69] Before the era of Tsoede (Edegi was his other name, particularly among the Hausa), the Nupe were divided into five subgroups or clans: the Ebe, Beni (or Bini), Ebagi, Bataci (or Batache) and Dibo (or Zitako, who were also known as Gana-Gana among the Hausa). These formed a loose association, called the Beni confederacy. The sources make it clear that there were kings before Tsoede's time and some of these are specifically named. M. D. Mason argues that Tsoede is 'simply the personification of a chain of events that led to the founding of a supratribal state'.[70] This period was revolutionary, in the sense that 'Tsoede' brought about the unification not only of the sedentary Nupe represented by the Beni confederacy, but also of the riverine Kyedye (or Kede) who 'ruled the water' and other subgroups, many of whom were assimilated Yoruba, Gwari, Kanuri or Igala immigrants.

Tsoede himself is believed to have flourished in the early part of the sixteenth century, but this date is quite uncertain. Even if the pattern

---

who could afford to offer continuous patronage to such bards. The songs are usually recited at ceremonies. In the Hausa states there are also drum histories, but these have not yet been systematically collected. Most historians draw their information from palace courtiers and Muslim clerics (*mallams*), as well as from written documents.

67. Details of these claims can be found in O. S. M. Temple, 1922, and Meek, 1931a.

68. S. F. Nadel, 1942, p. 72.

69. M. D. Mason, 1970–1, pp. 32–3.

70. ibid.

of state formation cannot at present be fitted into any firm chronological framework, references to the Nupe in Hausa sources date back to the fifteenth century and some of these may perhaps refer to the Beni confederacy. From that century onwards the Nupe people were therefore members of a very rapidly expanding ethnic group, which grew numerically by encouraging the settlement and subsequent assimilation of immigrants from Yoruba territory, from Igala (people who came allegedly with Tsoede) and from Bornu, along with Gwari and some Kambari people. Culturally, the fifteenth and sixteenth centuries represented a period when a dynamic culture for the Nupe as a whole was forged at the expense of the local cultural loyalties formerly entertained by small ethnic groups. The Tsoede tradition was central to this development. During this period the Nupe kings established diplomatic and commercial contacts with many neighbouring states, and especially with the Hausa cities.

Another group of people who had relations with the Hausa during this period were the inhabitants of Bauchi; this is the Hausa term used to refer to the territory due south of Hausaland – *kasashen bauchi*. It comprised the area covered by the present-day states of Bauchi, Plateau, Southern Kaduna, Northern Niger and Southern Sokoto (Zuru and Yawuri).[71] There are many peoples who regard this vast territory as their traditional homeland and, with the exception of the Kambari, all are composed of small ethnic groups.[72] Their traditions – again, with the exception of the Kambari – claim origin from either Hausaland or the Bornu territory.

It is difficult to reconstruct the relationships which developed between the Hausa and the Bauchi peoples during the period up to the sixteenth century, because historical sources are so meagre. The main trend seems to have been the Hausa migrations into Bauchi territory; many peoples ventured southwards for trading or military purposes, and some also went there as refugees.[73] Apart from the soldiers, the majority of migrants into the *kasashen bauchi* settled there and did not return. Some of the settlers retained their Hausa language; the descendants of other groups lost it and became linguistically assimilated by the indigenous host people, whether Kambari, Gungawa, Dakarawa, Gwari, Kamuku or Warjawa. On the other hand, Bauchi was a favoured territory for slave raiding from both Kano and Zazzau, and thus a large number of local people entered Hausaland.

Only the Kambari and Kamuku among the Bauchi peoples seem to have established some kind of centralized government before the sixteenth century. The political history of Yawuri shows that when the Hausa people began to settle in that area, towards the end of the fourteenth century, they found the Kambari chiefdom of Maginga, which they took over and

71. For a brief discussion on the traditional usage of the term Bauchi, see Adamu, 1978, p. 23.
72. Cf. C. K. Meek, 1925, and Temple, op. cit.
73. Adamu, 1978, pp. 39–40.

have ruled ever since. It is possible, therefore, that Maginga already existed as a kingdom of the Kambari by the year 1200. Owing to the lack of material it is difficult to ascertain what relations it might have had with the emerging Hausa states at so early a date. It is nevertheless noteworthy that the first Hausa to establish their rule in Yawuri in the fourteenth century were traders from southern Katsina, resident in the area.[74]

As for the Kamuku, it may be possible to identify them with a people called Karuku, mentioned by al-Maḳrīzī (d. 1442) in *al-Khbar an adjnas al-Sūdān* ('The Races of the Sudan'), together with the kingdom of Kankuma (Kwangoma or Kangoma).[75] It is still uncertain whether this kingdom – where the Kamuku are alleged to have been the dominant people – existed by 1200 and formed the predecessor state of Zaria, as suggested by M. Last.[76] Nevertheless, the evidence of al-Maḳrīzī points to the existence of some form of political organization among the Kamuku people as early as the fourteenth or fifteenth century.

Major developments in Hausaland

Immigration

One of the major developments of this period was the large-scale immigration into Hausaland of peoples and groups coming from different directions at different times and for different purposes. The areas from which Hausaland received most of its immigrants were the Sahel in the north, Bornu in the east and the Mali and Songhay empires in the west. The categories of immigrants included herdsmen, fishermen, agriculturalists, merchants and traders, Muslim clerics and scholars (known as *mallam*s in Hausa) and some aristocrats.

The first immigrant herdsmen were the Fulani/Fulbe, followed by the Tuareg. Although a great deal has been written on the early history of the Fulani in the central Sudan, no generally accepted reconstruction of their migration has emerged, except that most scholars agree that they reached this area from the west. However, the chronology and the routes they took still remain obscure. According to Yusūfū Usman, the Fulani first came to Katsina during the reign of Sarkin Katsina Jabdayaki (*c.* 1405–45).[77] Shortly afterwards, their arrival is mentioned in the *Kano Chronicle* in these words:

> In Yak'ubu's time (1452–63) the Fulani came to Hausaland from Melle, bringing with them books on divinity and etymology. Formerly our doctors had, in addition to the Koran, only the books of the law and the traditions. The Fulani passed by and went to Bornu, leaving

74. Cf. Adamu (forthcoming, a), ch. 2.
75. See the English translation in Palmer, 1928, Vol. 2, p. 6.
76. Last, in Adamu (ed.) (forthcoming, b).
77. Y. B. Usman, 1979b.

a few men in Hausaland, together with some slaves and people who were tired of journeying.[78]

Although some of these Fulani were Muslim clerics, as appears from the quotation, the vast majority of the immigrants were nomadic pastoralists, holding traditional religious beliefs, who came to Hausaland in search of new and better grazing for their cattle, sheep and goats. It is impossible to state with any certainty how many Fulani came to present-day Northern Nigeria during this period, but they do not appear to have been very numerous; the places in Hausaland where the Fulani were found at this time included central Kano, northern Katsina and the Rima valley (parts of Zamfara and Kebbi). The Muslim clerics lived mostly in Hausa urban centres, where their presence contributed significantly to the strengthening of Islam, particularly in Kano and Katsina states.

The Tuareg entered Hausaland through Azbin in the late fourteenth century, when they began to clash with the Hausa people of Gobir. It has already been noted that they had later dislodged the Hausa ruler of Gobir from the Azbin area and had established their sultanate in Agades in 1495.[79] As pastoralists, the Tuareg were not greatly interested in territorial occupation and settlement; their main concern lay in exchanging their products for agricultural commodities and also in engaging in raids on settled communities to the south of Azbin. However, some groups of Tuareg immigrants continued to penetrate into Hausaland in search of grazing, but it was only at a later period that this immigration became more intensive.

Movements of people from the Bornu area to Hausaland probably represented a very long-standing process, but it is only from the fifteenth century that documentary evidence exists for these.[80] Apart from the refugee aristocrats from Bornu, referred to in the *Kano Chronicle*, many more people, especially merchants and scholars, continued to come to Hausaland.[81] They settled in all parts of the country, but chiefly in Kano, Katsina and Zaria;[82] however, the immigration before 1600 was admittedly far less dense than in later periods. There is no evidence of craftsmen among the early immigrants of Bornu, but that possibility cannot be ruled out.

Another wave of immigrants into Hausaland was that of the Wangarawa/Dioula. As their arrival is closely linked with the problem of the introduction of Islam into the area and its dating is still open to question, it will be discussed in a later section. The first wave – whether it came in the fourteenth or the fifteenth century – was followed by subsequent groups of Wangarawa, particularly of merchants. Some of these settled at Yandoto

78. Palmer, 1928, Vol. 3, p. 111.
79. J. O. Hunwick, 1971b, pp. 218–22.
80. Adamu, 1979.
81. Palmer, 1928, Vol. 3, p. 109.
82. Usman, 1972, and Last, in Adamu (forthcoming, b).

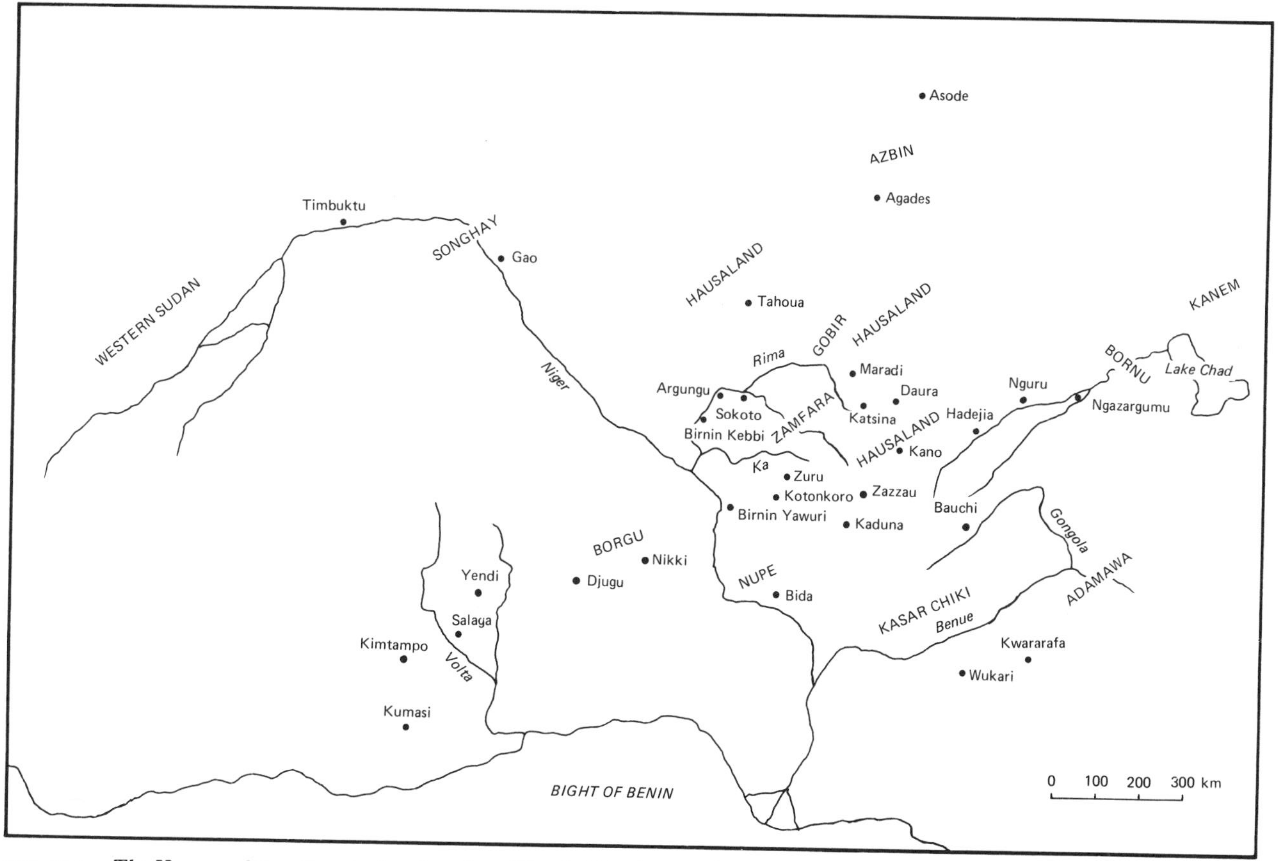

FIG. 11.1 *The Hausa and the other peoples of northern Nigeria (M. Adamu, 1981)*

and Kuyambana in Katsina Leka, others in the urban centres of Zazzau, and many, of course, in Kano.[83] The Wangarawa who came to the central Sudan soon became absorbed into the Hausa social system, even though they did not lose control of their economic activities and for some time formed a special social group.[84]

Another group of immigrants from the west were the Songhay fishermen, who entered the lower Rima valley and settled there to engage in their traditional occupation. At the time they arrived they possessed a higher degree of technology as regards fishing gear and methods;[85] they also practised some agriculture. Like other foreign groups, they eventually shed all traces of their Songhay culture and became Hausa, thereby creating what might be termed the western marches of Hausaland (see Fig. 11.1).

The last category of immigrants to be considered are the Arab and Berber merchants and scholars who came from North Africa and the Timbuktu area. They began to enter Hausaland in the second half of the fifteenth century, at about the same time as the Fulani; Kano and Katsina were again the main areas of intake. Kano in particular became a pole of attraction for Muslim scholars from distant regions. This influx was connected both with the growing prosperity of the Hausa states and with the adoption of the Islamic religion by further groups and strata of the urban population.

Emigration

While Hausaland was receiving immigrants from different directions, the territory was also losing people, on no mean scale. The majority of the emigrants moved southwards and westwards.[86] The movement of people from Hausaland into the territories lying immediately to the south seems to have been a very prolonged process, but no records of it have survived. The first recorded instances of the Hausa moving southwards in large numbers relate to military campaigns mounted by the rulers of Kano, Katsina and Zaria. In the course of the fourteenth century, the non-Hausa peoples in present-day Bauchi and Gongola, such as the Kudawa, Warjawa and Kwararafa/Jukun, were attacked by the armies of those Hausa states. During the fifteenth and sixteenth centuries, the campaigns were not only stepped up in intensity but became more diversified.[87] The territories raided included the plateau highlands, the area now known as southern

83. Usman, 1979b; Last, in Adamu (forthcoming, b).

84. The most noticeable aspect of this social adaptation was the dropping of the use of *nisba*s or clan names while in Hausaland. That is why names such as Kamara, Cisse, Traore or Watara were never current in Hausa territory. Hausa became the only language of communication used by the Wangarawa, at least in public.

85. See Alkali, op. cit., p. 49. But A. Augie, in his doctoral dissertation on the history of the Rima basin before the Sokoto *dj̱ihād* of 1804, disagrees (no further details available).

86. A detailed discussion of these movements is to be found in Adamu, 1978, chs. 3 and 5–7.

87. ibid., pp. 24–5.

Zaria, and the Yawuri area. Some of these campaigns involved sieges and other prolonged stays for mopping-up operations. The *Kano Chronicle* records that many non-military Hausa people left their homes and followed the armies; they bought and sold goods and also provided paid services for the soldiers.[88] Since many of these people never returned to Hausaland, the military campaigns contributed to the emigration and spread of the Hausa outside their original homeland.

Other categories of emigrants included traders and Muslim clerics. This was how the people from the Kuyambana area of southern Katsina established Hausa rule in Yawuri in the second half of the fourteenth century.[89] Bornu, too, received some Hausa migrants from Kano in the early fifteenth century according to the *Kano Chronicle*.[90] Although such Hausa movements started during this period, it was only after the sixteenth century that they became a more spectacular Hausa diaspora in various parts of West Africa.

The spread of Islam

The initial introduction of the Islamic religion into Hausaland is still the subject of scholarly controversy. Many authors have uncritically accepted the statement of the *Kano Chronicle* that Islam was first introduced into the area in the middle of the fourteenth century by the Wangarawa, who came from Mali during the reign of Sarkin Kano Yaji (1349–85). Although this is the first recorded mention of Islam in Hausa written sources, it is more than likely that Islam entered Hausaland at a much earlier date. In the first place, Islam had already existed in Kanem-Bornu since the eleventh century;[91] it is also an established fact that the Hausa were in continuous contact with that state long before the fourteenth century.[92] It would be more than surprising, therefore, if that religion had failed to reach Hausaland during the long period preceding the fourteenth century. Islamic influences from Kanem-Bornu were present in Kano from an early period, judging by the linguistic evidence. Many Arab words connected with religion were introduced into Hausa through the intermediary of Kanuri, which indicates that Islam penetrated Hausaland from the east earlier than it did from the west.[93]

Second, oral traditions recently collected at Kano indicate that Islam existed in the city of Kano long before the first arrival of the Wangarawa.[94] Third, the trade route from Fezzān to Gao, which existed from the ninth century onwards, went through Gobir territory, where Marandet had grown

88. Palmer, 1928, Vol. 3, p. 110.
89. Cf. Adamu, 1979.
90. Palmer, 1928, Vol. 3, p. 108.
91. H. F. C. (Abdullahi) Smith, 1976, pp. 165–6 (no further details available).
92. Adamu, 1979.
93. Greenberg, 1960.
94. J. Paden, 1973, pp. 48 ff.

up as a major commercial centre, and the influence of North African Muslim merchants can accordingly be expected to have led to the introduction of Islam into Gobir well before the fourteenth century. Fourth (although this is admittedly not a strong argument), allowance has to be made for the fact that, even before Yaji's time, there were many people in Kano who bore Islamic names such as Daud (a Bagauda variant), Maidawaki, Abdūḻḻāhī, Zakar, Salmata or Usman.[95]

A recently discovered and published Arabic document, the *Wangarawa Chronicle* (*Aṣl al-Wangariyīn*), dated 1650–1, does not shed any new light on the question of the first introduction of Islam into Hausaland, in spite of the expectations it aroused initially. This document describes in detail the arrival of the Wangarawa Muslims in Kano during the reign of Sarkin Kano Rumfa (*c.* 1463–99) and makes it contemporary with the arrival of the famous al-Maghīlī. This has led A. al-Hajj Mbaye to the conclusion that it was at the end of the fifteenth century that this Wangarawa Islamizing mission reached Kano and that the fourteenth-century dating given in the *Kano Chronicle* is to be rejected.[96] But it is quite clear that the *Wangarawa Chronicle*, by situating them both in Rumfa's time, combined two events which were, in reality, more than a century apart.[97] As the *Aṣl al-Wangariyīn* went through several revisions and contains a number of internal inconsistencies, its contents cannot be accepted uncritically.[98] Preference therefore has to be given to the indications of the *Kano Chronicle*'s dating of the arrival of the Wangarawa in the fourteenth century. Regardless of which date is correct, however, it is obvious that Islam was introduced into Hausaland much earlier, either by way of Air and Gobir or, more probably, via Kanem-Bornu. And it cannot be ruled out that Muslim traders from the west (Mali and Songhay) were actively spreading Islam among the Hausa traders and some of the ruling élite in Hausaland before the arrival of the Wangarawa, who were immigrant Muslim scholars and missionaries and who later helped to establish a stronger and more widespread Islamic tradition.

On the other hand, although Islam was widely known in Hausaland before the fourteenth century, it evidently remained largely a religion of expatriate traders, small groups of local merchants and the ruling élite; for the most part, the masses continued to practise their traditional religion. Nevertheless, in the fifteenth century a strong Islamic tradition appears to have been established, especially in Kano and Katsina. This trend was strengthened not only by the Wangara scholars, but also by Muslim Fulani clerics, who brought with them new books on theology and law.

It is precisely from this time that we have accounts by many Muslim scholars from outside the region who were active in Hausaland. The best-

95. See *Kano Chronicle*, in Palmer, 1928, Vol. 3, p. 99–100 and 103–4.
96. A. al-Hajj Mbaye, 1968, pp. 7–16.
97. Cf. Fisher, 1977, p. 296.
98. Cf. E. Sa'ad, 1979, pp. 52–6.

known and most significant of these is undoubtedly al-Maghīlī, who came from Tuat in the Sahara.[99] Celebrated for his earlier career in the Maghrib as a scholar, controversialist and persecutor of Jews, he travelled in the 1490s to visit Agades, Takedda, Kano, Katsina and Gao. His role in Hausaland was of considerable importance, although in Katsina his work is remembered only in vague outline and accounts of it are rather contradictory. According to some reports, al-Maghīlī himself converted the *sarki* there;[100] other sources indicate that the commoners responded to al-Maghīlī's preaching of Islam more readily than the ruling class. One of al-Maghīlī's pupils, Muḥammad al-Tazakhtī (d. 1529/30), a Timbuktu scholar, later became *ḳāḍī* at Katsina after going on the pilgrimage to Mecca.

In Kano, al-Maghīlī wrote an essay on 'The Obligations of Princes', apparently to guide Sarkin Kano Muḥammad Rumfa in his administration as a Muslim ruler.[101] Shortly before his visit to Kano in 1491–2, al-Maghīlī had engaged in a correspondence with the *sarki*, in which he set out his own concepts of an ideal government.[102] It is difficult to determine to what degree Muḥammad Rumfa followed al-Maghīlī's advice and exhortations, since the evidence is conflicting. Some of the 'innovations' mentioned in the *Kano Chronicle* seem to correspond to Islamic principles as preached by al-Maghīlī, whereas others run counter to them.[103] The *Hausa Chronicle* accuses Rumfa of 'dishonest ways', including his turning away from Islam and his introduction of customs that were explicitly forbidden by Islamic law.[104]

Among other leading figures who played a role in strengthening the Islamic tradition and way of life in Kano, mention should be made of Aḥmad ibn 'Umar Aḳīt of Timbuktu – ancestor of the famous Aḥmad Bābā – who visited Kano and taught there *c.* 1487. At some time between 1504 and 1518–19, 'Abd al-Raḥmān Suḳḳayn from Morocco, a pupil of the historian Ibn Ghāzī, arrived from Egypt to teach in Kano, and his colleague, Makhlūf al-Balbalī (died after 1534), was also active in education in Kano and Katsina. As Hunwick has put it: 'The teaching activities of these scholars seem to mark the emergence of Kano as a Muslim city; its "conversion" is symbolised by the cutting down of the sacred tree, an event which both the *Kano Chronicle* and Wangara sources attribute to the reign of Muḥammad Rumfa (1466–99).'[105]

99. Muḥammad ibn 'Abd al-Karīm al-Maghīlī, on whom see A. A. Batran, 1973, pp. 381–94.

100. Muḥammad Korau, probably a contemporary of Rumfa of Kano, is reported to have been the first Muslim ruler of the state. Owing to the uncertainties of Katsina chronology, it is not known who was its ruler at the time of al-Maghīlī's visit. See H. F. C. Smith, 1961, p. 7.

101. English translation by T. H. Baldwin, 1932.

102. See the English translation by H. R. Palmer, 1913–14.

103. Cf. pp. 272–3 above.

104. *Hausa Chronicle*, English transl. R. S. Rattray, 1913, Vol. I, pp. 10–16.

105. Hunwick, 1971b, pp. 216 ff.

At the same time, Islam also found its way to other Hausa states. In Zaria, the late fifteenth-century *sarki* Muḥammad Rabo is traditionally regarded as having been the first Muslim ruler;[106] in Kebbi the first *sarkin kebbi*, Muḥammad Kanta (*c.* 1516–54), and some of his chiefs are believed to have accepted Islam. This is quite probable for, as a former military leader under the pious Askiya Muḥammad, Kanta must have been exposed to Islamic influence. Many of his successors bore Muslim names, so that at least a very thin Islamic veneer remained, although the majority of Kebbawa continued to practise their traditional religion for a long time to come. As for the other parts of Hausaland, our information about Islamization at this period is rather meagre. In Yawuri, we can only surmise the existence of small groups of Muslims before 1600, since kola-nut traders stopped there on their journey between Bornu and Gonja, and Muslim traders are known to have spread Islam along their trade routes and founded small colonies at the more important places.[107]

In general, Islamization during this period was chiefly confined to the ruling élite and to trader groups, and it was only in cities and larger centres that Islam had much impact. Even so, most of the so-called Muslims were only half-hearted in their allegiance to Islam and still believed in other gods, whom they invoked in their shrines at sacred rocks and trees.

Islam can be said to have been incorporated into the African religious scheme of things and was not regarded as a strange religion or one incompatible with the Hausa religious outlook. More important, Muslim society at this time did not claim exclusivity for its religious ideology and was prepared to accommodate without objection many features of traditional beliefs or customs. This was probably the general attitude of the majority of local converts and their descendants. At one extreme an élite group of expatriate scholars and their pupils attempted to observe Islamic law and customs more strictly; at the other, the rural population adhered to the traditional religion, magic and witchcraft for a very long time. No opposition to the new religion seems to have existed, at least so long as the Muslim clerics did not demand changes in some of the old patterns of social and cultural life.

In the political sphere, Islam contributed to the process of centralization in various Hausa states by weakening the traditional political structure based on the control of important places of worship. Before the rise of centralized states, political control in the small chieftaincies was closely bound up with the religious performance of the chiefs. The *Kano Chronicle* – written from the Muslim point of view – is full of accounts of the opposition of local chiefs, who are depicted as 'unbelievers', to the centralizing attempts of the Kano rulers, who are regarded as true Muslims. The conquest of these chieftaincies was followed by the deliberate large-scale

106. H. F. C. Smith, 1971, pp. 196–8.
107. S. A. Balogun, 1980, p. 216.

destruction of the important ancient places of worship, so that the chiefs were deprived of their main source of power. In Kano, Santolo was the last of such ancient sites to be destroyed, during the reign of Yaji (1349–85).

Another effect of the spread of Islam was the influx of scholars and clerics from various parts of Africa. This occasioned the spread in Hausaland of new political, social and cultural ideas and the growth of literacy, defined as the ability to read and write in the Arabic language, and later also in Hausa, using the Arabic script (the *ajami* system).[108] In turn, this helped improve the state administration, as well as various commercial practices and operations. Last, but not least, the introduction and spread of Islam linked Hausaland more closely to a large and developed cultural area.

Political and administrative organization

In spite of some regional differences, Hausa political organization, both in its formative stages and in its subsequent development, followed a similar pattern everywhere, based on a common socio-economic and cultural identity, as expressed in the common language. At the same time, the administrative system which had emerged in the Hausa states since the fourteenth century bore witness to the marked influence of Kanem-Bornu, from where many institutions and functions were borrowed, sometimes even with their Kanuri/Kanembu names. In point of fact, Bornu long served as a model of superior civilization and culture, and its influence was steadily strengthened by immigration from the Lake Chad area.

It is interesting to note that, in spite of many campaigns and incursions by the rulers of Bornu and the tribute paid by the Hausa states, the Hausa never looked upon Bornu as an enemy – in contrast to Songhay, Kebbi or Kwararafa – and they appear to have tacitly acknowledged its predominance as being in the natural order of things. On the other hand, the political and administrative structure, at all but the highest level, was original and grew out of local circumstances.

Throughout the country, small rural communities (*kauyuka*, sing. *kauye*) were composed of groups of families (*gidaje*, sing. *gida*) under the authority of a chief (*maigari*). These communities consisted, in fact, of farming hamlets that were generally quite small and in some cases of a shifting nature. At the next level came the villages (*garuruwa*, sing. *gari*), which were larger and permanent. At their head they had a *sarkin gari* or *magajin gari* (village chief), who may on occasion have had district leaders (*masu-unguwa*, sing. *mai-unguwa*) under him. At the apex of the structure stood the *birni* (plural *birane*), the district capital, which was ruled not by a *sarkin birni* (the expression does not exist in Hausa), but a *sarkin kasa* or chief

108. However, it should be noted that no Hausa *ajami* manuscript written before 1600 has yet been discovered.

of the 'country', whose authority naturally extended over all the lower-level chiefs.

Several factors seem to have played a decisive role in the development of *birane* as seats of a new form of political power. These were, first, the very wide variety of farming and craft resources in Hausaland; second, the expansion of long-distance trade, especially after the fifteenth century; and finally, the existence of city walls, which afforded protection for the people and fields in the city-states and into whose shelter the neighbouring rural population fled in time of war. The *birane* were also noteworthy for the cosmopolitan character of their population as a result of trade, and for the slow pace at which they appear to have been established.[109]

At the head of the country, the *sarki* or king was absolute. In theory, at least, his physical person was sacred, since the fortunes of the kingdom were linked to his own. As a rule, he was chosen from among the members of the ruling lineage; although father–son succession was common, it is noteworthy that the *Kano Chronicle* indicates the name of each ruler's mother, which may point to surviving vestiges of a matrilineal system. The *sarki* shared power with high officials, who belonged partly to his own lineage and partly to leading lineages of the old regime now transferred into a hereditary aristocracy. Among this élite, some were members of the council of state appointed by the monarch. In Gobir, this council was called *tara ta Gobir* (or *tarar Gobir*) 'the nine of Gobir' and when the king died any candidate for the succession had to accept their decisions.[110] Similarly, as mentioned above, the Kano council bore the name of *tara ta Kano*, 'the Kano nine'. These councils are reminiscent of the council of twelve in the old Sefuwa empire of Kanem-Bornu.[111]

As already observed, Sarkin Kano Rumfa was the first to appoint slaves, and even eunuchs, to important offices of state, placing them in control of the treasury, the town and palace guards, and communications with free office-holders; they also performed various household functions, such as control of the harem.[112] Foremost in importance among the state officials was the *galadima*, a kind of prime minister or grand vizier in whom the conduct of all affairs of state was vested.[113] This office was sometimes occupied by the heir apparent and, in very many instances, the *sarki* became only a puppet in the hands of a powerful *galadima*. Under the latter were a host of officials and dignitaries, each of whom took charge of a specific locality or territorial unit, ranging from an entire province to a group of villages.

109. Cf. H. F. C. Smith, 1971, pp. 187–91; according to tradition, it took no less than 200 years for the city-state of Kano to become really established.

110. Nicolas, op. cit., p. 207.

111. Cf. Temple, op. cit., p. 467; Y. Urvoy, 1949, pp. 37–42.

112. See *Kano Chronicle*, in Palmer, 1928, Vol. 3, p. 112.

113. The title was borrowed from Bornu, but there it designated the governor of the western provinces, that is, those nearest to Hausaland.

It is impossible to reconstruct the precise process by which the Hausa administrative system developed, owing to lack of evidence. From about 1350 onwards, as pointed out by M. G. Smith, many factors, including Islam, and especially slaves – their capture, their role as tribute paid and as exports, their settlements and their appointment as officials, eunuchs and concubines – played a decisive role in the development of centralized and sometimes dictatorial governments.[114] The appointment of slaves to high office could be interpreted as a further step taken to weaken the position of leading lineages and to give the ruler more absolute power. Some of Rumfa's 'innovations' – the seizure of women and property or the right to mobilize subjects for forced labour – illustrate the increase in royal prerogatives, and at the same time point to far-reaching changes in the social structure.

Economic development

The potentialities for economic development in Hausaland can be summarized thus. First, the region had rich and fairly well distributed deposits of iron ore. This is indicated not only by the *Kano Chronicle* as far as Kano itself was concerned, but also by archaeological research in other areas.[115] Almost all these deposits were located very close to wooded areas, where firewood and charcoal were produced in large quantities for smelting the ore, and they were all being worked during the period in question. The iron of Dalla Hill was certainly an important element in attracting the settlement of the area which was to become Kano.

Secondly, almost the entire territory of Hausaland was endowed with rich and fertile soils. Early sources such as Ibn Baṭṭūṭa and Leo Africanus, who skirted the fringes of Hausaland, and all subsequent studies emphasize that agriculture was the most important economic activity throughout the Hausa states.

Thirdly, although there are no statistical data available for the population density of Hausaland, to judge from the numerous villages and towns in the various Hausa states, there are grounds for thinking that the country was not sparsely populated. Population distribution was evenly balanced, in the sense that the states were not all crowded together in one part of Hausaland.

A fourth factor was the geographical location of Hausaland, which lay between the Sahel and the Sahara to the north and the savannah and tropical forest to the south, and thus had the advantage of being an intermediary in the exchange of products between these areas. As a result of these factors, Hausaland was able to embark on the development of crafts and long-

114. M. G. Smith, 1964a and 1964b.

115. For iron-working in Zazzau, see J. E. G. Sutton 1976 and 1979. For Gobir, see D. Grebenart, forthcoming.

distance trade quite early. However, more research is needed to reconstruct the economic history of Hausaland since the beginning of the present millennium.

Despite the general impression that the Hausa people were overwhelmingly engaged in trade, every Hausa was primarily a farmer, and agriculture was essential to the economic life of the region. Land belonged to the community – hamlet, village or town – whose chief supervised its use. Land was never sold and those who cultivated it enjoyed the usufruct. On the authority of the communal chief, people from outside the community could acquire and work land. Later, with growing feudalization, the *sarki* had the possibility and right to assign land to anyone, whether autochthonous or foreign. The farmers (*talakawa*, sing. *talaka*) were directed in their agricultural activities by a leader – *sarkin poma* (chief of crops) – who was responsible for closely watching for the onset of the rainy season and for making appropriate sacrifices to local gods in order to ensure a good harvest.

In the course of time, three kinds of farms developed in Hausaland: *gandum sarkin*, the king's field, characterized by its large size; *gandum gide*, the family field, generally known as *gona*, the generic name for any field; and lastly *gayauna* or *gayamma*, the individual field.[116] Slave labour played a major role on the *gandum sarkin* as well as on the large estates of the state dignitaries. Under the reign of Sarkin Kano ʿAbdūḷḷāh Burja (1438–52), thousands of slaves lived in Kano and its environs and certainly a very high proportion of them were employed in agriculture. His *galadima* is said to have founded twenty-one towns, in each of which he settled 1000 slaves. Although no hint is given as to their occupation in the *Kano Chronicle*, we can surmise that they were assigned to farming the newly conquered land.

Many crops were grown in Hausaland, including various strains of millet (*Pennisetum typhoideum*), sorghum, fonio, rice (particularly in Kebbi and the western districts) and other food crops. Of special importance was the cultivation of commercial crops, chiefly cotton and indigo, especially in the state of Kano.[117]

After agriculture, handicrafts occupied an important place in the Hausa economy well before the fourteenth century. A comparatively high level of output had been attained through the division of labour and specialization. The leading place was occupied by textile production, and cotton cloth was manufactured from a very early date. All stages in the manufacturing process – ginning, carding, spinning, dyeing and weaving – were performed locally. The leather workers and shoemakers of Hausaland made a wide range of articles, including a variety of bags, footwear, saddles and

116. In time, the word *gayamma* came to be applied only to a field given to a woman, who cultivated it and disposed of the fruit of her labours as she wished.

117. 'In that province [Kano], many kinds of corn and rice and also cotton are grown.' Translated from the French version of Leo Africanus, loc. cit., p. 476.

cushions, which they supplied both to the countries of the Sudan and to markets in North Africa.[118]

Metal-working was a long-established craft and blacksmiths were especially important figures. Cast iron was obtained by melting large amounts of ferruginous gravel in furnaces which the Hausa called *marmara*. From this raw material the smiths – those in Kano being particularly renowned – manufactured all the implements needed by the community, such as cooking utensils, farm tools, knives, axes, arrowheads, spears and so on. Pottery was also a widely practised craft and provided most of the receptacles needed for preserving liquids and grain.

Most of the craft occupations were governed by guilds, each of which had a leader appointed by the king, occasionally on the nomination of the guild members, whose basic task was to collect the various taxes levied on the craftsmen. They also exercised control over admission into the guild, production methods, standards of workmanship and prices.

The preferred venue for commerce among the Hausa was the market fair (*kasuwa*) and, as trade became one of the most important activities of the urban population, it also fulfilled other roles, as 'a high-point of social life, a meeting place and rendezvous where one finds relatives and friends, where one makes contact with foreigners'.[119] The person in charge of the market was known as the *sarkin kasuwa*, who with his assistants kept order in all the markets, settled disputes between merchants and buyers, and also collected taxes, either in money or in kind on behalf of the king.

From a very early date, the merchant class was divided into various categories. The Hausa drew a distinction between the market or local trade, called *ciniki*, which involved the products of agriculture and small-scale crafts and was conducted chiefly by the producers themselves, and *fatauci* or wholesale trade. This was in the hands of professional merchants called *fatake* (sing. *farke* or *falke*), who were engaged in long-distance commerce. Midway between the two were the *yan koli* (sing. *dan koli*), who went from one market to another buying and selling cheap goods or retailing those imported by the *fatake*. The *ciniki* was in the hands of the so-called *yan kasuwa* (sing. *dan kasuwa*) who were basically confined to their home towns. Within these general categories, there were other specialists such as meat dealers and grain dealers.

A special function in all Hausa markets was that of the broker (*dillali*, plur. *dillalai*) who knew the prices prevailing in each market in the region, could predict the fluctuations of supply, demand and prices, and engaged in speculation on the basis of that knowledge. He was paid a percentage on the sale price for his services.

118. Leo Africanus said of Gobir: 'There are among them those who make shoes like those formerly worn by the Romans. These shoes are exported to Timbuktu and Gao.' Translated from the French version, ibid., pp. 477 ff.

119. Adamu, 1979, p. 1.

Although the market-place played an important role, business was often conducted outside it; for example, the craftsmen's workshops were in their homes, to which customers came to buy. On the other hand, merchandise, largely imported, was brought to the homes of the upper classes or to the royal court, since such persons were precluded by their rank from appearing in the market-place. Another feature of the Hausa commercial system was the role of women, whether married or single, who ran food shops near the markets or sold cotton cloth.

Little information is available about the currency used in these commercial activities and it can be surmised that, in the period in question, barter predominated in regional exchanges. The principal currencies were bands of cotton cloth (known as *sawaye* in Hausa), salt and slaves. As for cowrie shells (in Hausa *farin kudi*, or white money), the date of their introduction into Hausaland is unknown; to the west, in Mali and Songhay, cowries were in circulation from an early date, but they were introduced into Kanem-Bornu only much later, in the nineteenth century. Until recently, it was thought that cowries began to circulate in Hausaland in the eighteenth century,[120] but a recently published sixteenth-century source mentions that in Katsina 'they use sea shells, which are very white, as money to buy small objects, as is the case among all the blacks, and gold is exchanged for its weight in goods brought by the merchants'.[121]

Owing to the slower evolution of centralized government in Hausaland, the network of long-distance trade reached this area later than its neighbours to the west (Mali and Songhay) and the east (Kanem-Bornu). But, once they had the prerequisites, the Hausa people fully exploited the opportunities offered by the geographical location of their country. The Wangarawa were undoubtedly the pioneers of the long-distance trade in Hausaland, but their role seems to have been somewhat exaggerated by some authors.[122] In point of fact, the North Africans, the Tuareg, the Kanuri and others also participated in this trade. From the fifteenth century, which appears to have seen the beginning of the transformation of the Hausa economy, the Hausa people launched out into commerce and took over certain routes, especially those leading to the south.[123] The emergence of Kano and Katsina as important but rival cities is closely connected with the rise of long-distance trade and the increasing participation of Hausa merchants in it. Hausa trade radiated outwards in several directions, taking advantage of geographical location and of the variety of products needed in the different countries. As a rule, the mainstream trade followed the north–south axis of earlier times, whereas its lateral spread was the work of later centuries.

120. M. Johnson, 1970, p. 33.

121. D. Lange and S. Berthoud, 1972, p. 335.

122. For example, see P. E. Lovejoy, 1978.

123. The possibility cannot be ruled out that further research will reveal the existence of Hausa trade routes to the east.

The main commodities in Hausa trade can be classified according to their places of origin, as follows.

(1) Local products of Hausaland included cotton cloth, hides and leather, agricultural products (mainly millet) for the oases of the Sahara, musk from the civet cat, ostrich feathers and probably gum.

(2) Products of North Africa, and partly of Europe, included metalware, arms, horses, beads, glassware and some luxury cloth.

(3) Mineral products of the Sahara included tin bars from the Takedda (Azelik) mines, but principally salt and natron from Bilma and other salt-mines in the Sahara. The main centres of the salt trade were Agades and Gobir.[124]

(4) (a) Slaves were primarily imported from the regions to the south of Hausaland and were either victims of raids or paid as tribute from neighbouring countries. They fulfilled various roles, being used as currency and goods, as domestic servants, soldiers and guards, and in agriculture and craft work. Some of them were retained in Hausaland; others were sold for export to other parts of Africa, mainly the Maghrib.[125]

(b) The second main commodity exported from the south was kola nuts. The main centre of kola production was Gonja/Gwanja, in present-day northern Ghana. The main trade route to Gonja from Hausaland passed through Zaria and Borgu.

No information as to how long-distance trade was actually organized has come down to us from this period. In the present state of our knowledge all that can be said is that North African merchants occupied a preponderant place in trans-Saharan trade, whereas the southern – and part of the east–west – trade was in the hands of the Hausa merchants. A more important consideration appears to be the fact that some Hausa cities, especially Kano and Katsina, served as entrepôt centres for trade flows between north and south, in that they were termini of the trans-Saharan route. The ruling class of the Hausa states plainly took advantage of this burgeoning trade to enrich itself, and its prosperity is reflected in the opulence of the courts from the fifteenth century onwards. It was also as a result of this prosperity that Muḥammad Rumfa was able to undertake an extensive building programme and introduce a host of administrative, political and religious reforms, as already described.

124. The Hausa vocabulary contains more than fifty words for various kinds of salt, which indicates the importance of this commodity in trade and daily life.

125. The Hausa made a distinction between two kinds of slaves: the *bayi*, who had been captured or bought and who had few rights, and the *cucenawa*, a second generation, who occupied a position that was more akin to serfdom than to chattel slavery. On slavery, see A. G. B. Fisher and H. J. Fisher, 1970, passim.

By the end of the sixteenth century, after the fall of the Songhay empire, the commercial route to the west became unreliable and relations between Songhay and Air petered out. On the other hand, commercial dealings between the north and Hausaland were stepped up, particularly since Katsina, the terminus of the trans-Saharan caravans, had become, more than ever before, the backbone of the economy of Hausaland and indeed of the whole of the central Sudan.

12 The coastal peoples: from Casamance to the Ivory Coast lagoons

Y. PERSON*

General features of the region

The term Guinea refers to the western coast of Africa from the mouth of the Gambia to the Niger delta. This was the term – synonymous with 'Ethiopia' or 'the country of the blacks' – commonly used by the first Portuguese navigators to write about the area. Upper Guinea comprises the countries between the mouth of the River Gambia and the Bandama. This coast and its hinterland was outside the area which interested the Arab travellers and writers; nevertheless, it is probable that, from the time of the empire of Ghana, there were trade relations between the savannah and these forest-covered areas. This is not the dense or equatorial forest, but the environment is very different from the savannah. One characteristic of the region is a population fragmented into a large number of ethnic groups.

With the growing influence of the Mandingo, the vanguard of the advancing migrations from the Sudan pushed southwards into the land of kola nuts, gold, slaves and salt. Then suddenly, in the fifteenth century, the Atlantic seaboard was no longer a backwater, unused except for coastal fishing and local trade. Instead, it became a 'second front' of contact with Europe, along which the slave trade to the Americas was soon to be the dominant activity. From then onwards, the history of upper Guinea forms a pattern in which these two historical currents were intertwined, although they did not really merge. Between the threads in this pattern, the autochthonous peoples endeavoured to lead their lives in their own way, increasing their efforts to preserve their identity and to keep control of their own destiny.

The civilization of the Sudan and the Sahel, one of whose main sources was Mandingo, was shaped from the eighth and ninth centuries onwards by the autochthonous peasant societies which had to contend with the problems of the newly reorganized trans-Saharan trade, following the conversion of North Africa to Islam. A network of long-distance trade soon covered the entire Sudan region, its best-known agents being the

*This paper is published posthumously; Professor Person died in December 1982.

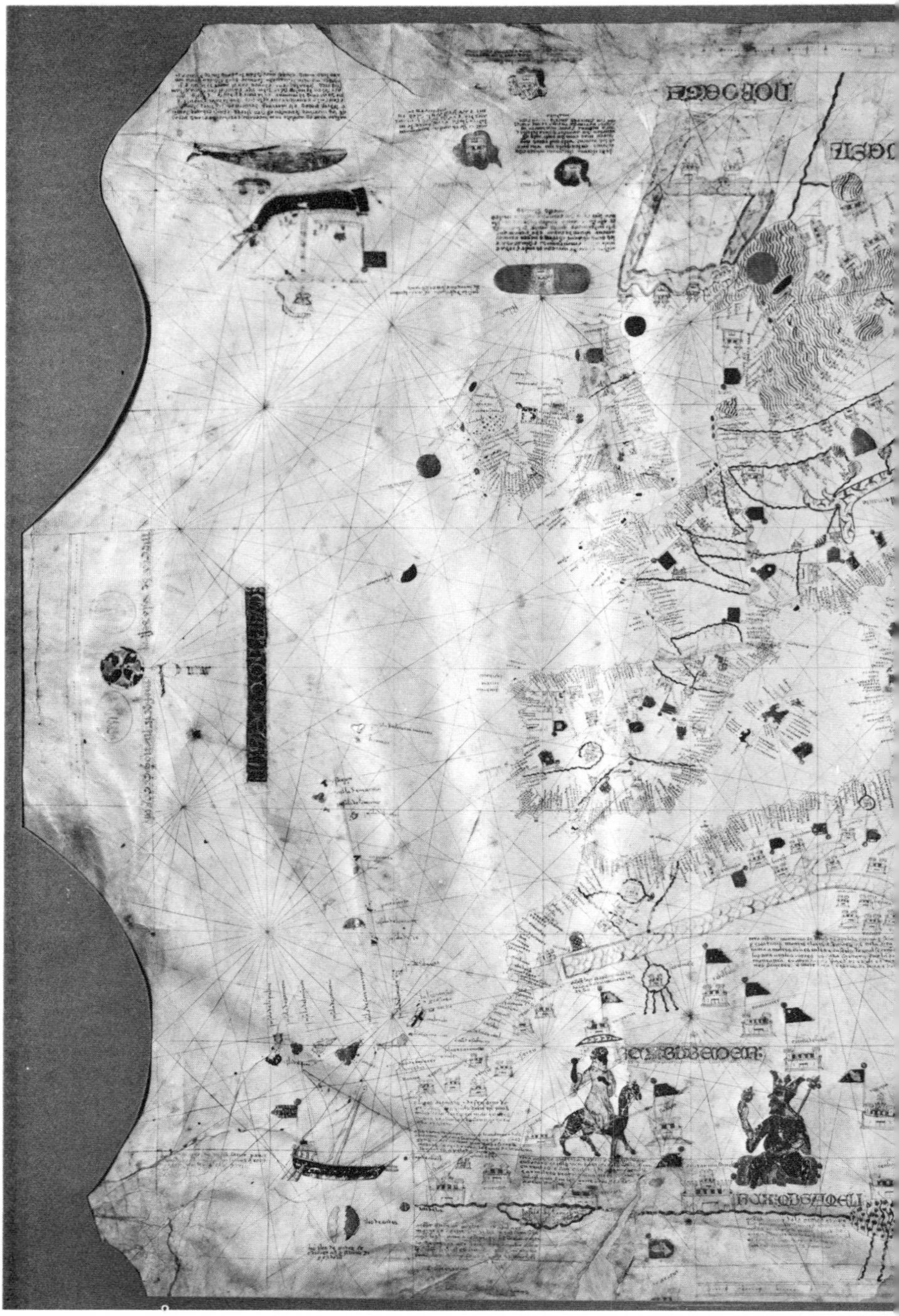

PLATE 12.1 *Portolano of Mecia de Viladestes, 1413 (a coloured, hand-drawn map on parchment)*

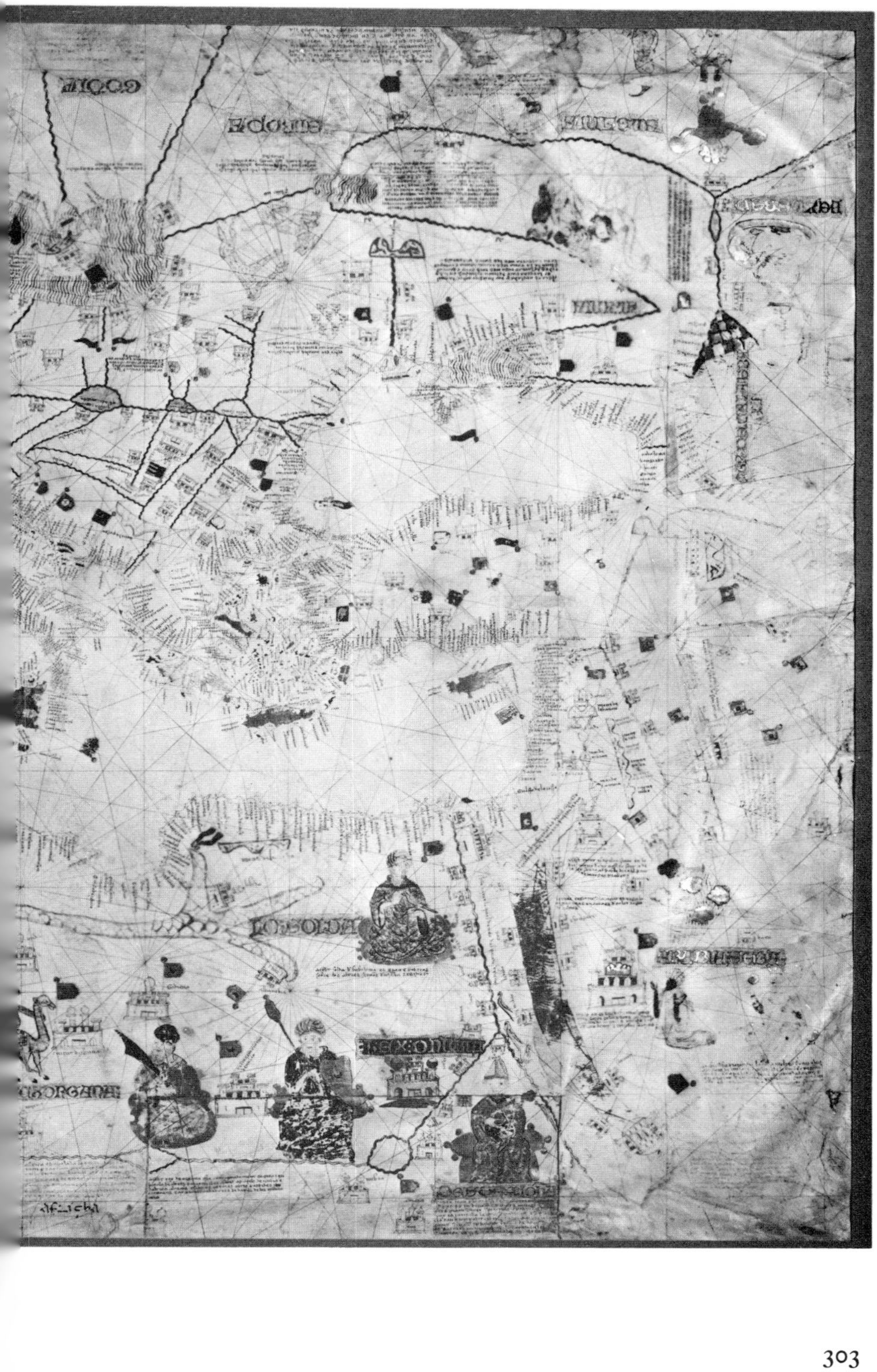

famous Malinke traders. As early as the twelfth century, this network was already sufficiently organized to enable that eminently perishable product, the kola nut, to be exported to North Africa.

Judging from what we know of later periods, the network extended to the forest fringes, where business was transacted through brokers. Further into the forest, producers organized in kinship guilds traded in relays, passing goods on from one group to the next without using specialized traders. This is certainly how the kola-nut trade grew up. It was also how Malaguetta pepper was marketed in the fourteenth and fifteenth centuries; although it grew only in southern Liberia, it reached Europe (in particular the Iberian peninsula) by way of the Sudan region and the Maghrib. The Portuguese later diverted this trade to the coast.

These navigators, who sailed along the coast in short stages between 1450 and 1500, left detailed accounts of the local population which are very helpful to this study. In general, the coast was low-lying and swampy, with muddy areas highly suitable for the growing of rice; it was watered by numerous streams, which flowed out of Futa to the sea after several hundred kilometres. The sea did not play a major role in the lives of these coastal people, who were basically farmers; nevertheless some of them engaged in short-distance sea trade and were involved in the extraction of salt for sale to the population inland.

However, all these commodities supplied long-distance, though mainly regional trade, and adjustments had to be made, as soon as the Muslim influence opened up the Saharan routes, to cater for large-scale trade with the outside world. As we know, the latter was primarily based on the search for gold in the Sudan, as the Mediterranean world had suffered from a shortage of that metal since ancient times. Slaves and ivory were the second most important commodities.

Gold was not of direct relevance to upper Guinea, since the main mining areas lay outside the region, either in the Senegal or Niger basins in such areas as Bambugu or Bure, or else in the Lobi and Akan areas of the Volta basin to the east. Only the relatively unimportant mines of the Guerze at Kpele in today's Republic of Guinea come within the region, but there is no evidence to suggest that these were worked at an early date.

The Portuguese were drawn to upper Guinea, once it had been 'discovered' and the 'second front' opened up, by the commodities for which there was an international demand. Naturally the chief of these was gold, which, although not mined in the region, had to be sent through it once exports were routed to the seaboard instead of northwards. However, it will be seen that the leading place was soon to be taken over by the slave trade.

Development of the countries of upper Guinea

Having outlined the framework, we shall first ascertain what we know about the peoples and cultures involved in the five centuries concerning us here.

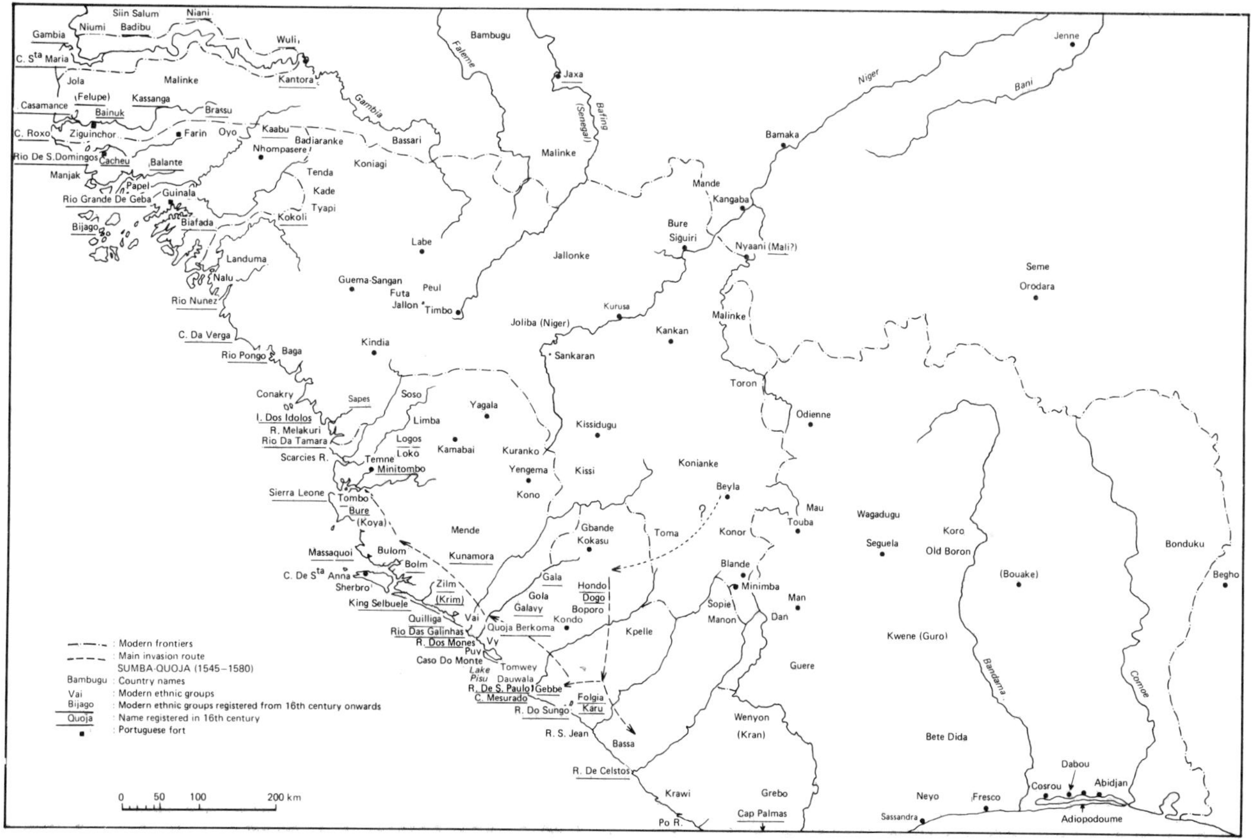

FIG. 12.1 *Upper Guinea in the 15th century (Y. Person)*

The survey is bound to be tentative, since the period goes too far back for most of the oral traditions, and written documents shed light only on the concluding century. Archaeological research, which should one day provide us with the information we are seeking, is still in its infancy. Therefore we have to make considerable use of the retrospective method, based on anthropological and linguistic data.

From Casamance to Mount Kakulima

In the north of upper Guinea, bordering on Senegambia, in the network of inlets and estuaries of Casamance and the Rio Cacheu, are found the Balante, the Dioula and the Felupe – all rice-growing, autonomous rural communities.

In this area, the Bainuk (the Banhum of the Portuguese writers) are also considered autonomous. Until the middle of the sixteenth century the authority of the Mande mansa (emperor of Mali) reached all along this coast.[1] The Biafada (who called themselves Dioula) and the Kokoli (or Landuma) farther south were independent chiefdoms. They spread rapidly as far as the sea in the mid-fifteenth century. They clashed with the Bijago, who lived on fortified islands and used their naval superiority to raid and dominate the mainland, right up to colonial times. The Bijago were able to build large boats capable of carrying 90–120 people.

Further in the interior, from upper Gambia to the foothills of the Futa Jallon, the ancestors of the Tenda peoples – the Bassari, Koniagi and Badiaranke – controlled a vast area and remained organized in autonomous rural communities. Some of them had taken part in the military ventures of Tengella, founder of the Denianke empire, at the end of the fifteenth century; they still offered stubborn resistance to attempts by the Fulani and Mandingo to dominate them.[2] The Tenda practised shifting agriculture; their villages were farming camps.

The lands of the Baga, Landuma, Nalu, Tyapi and Temne extended from the Rio Grande to the Rio Pongo. They were rice-growers and fishermen, whose villages were built in the middle of the mudflats or occasionally on dikes, and they spoke the Mel language. From the fifteenth century onward the first three groups were virtually in their present location, with the Baga along the coast of the modern Republic of Guinea from Rio Nunez to Mount Kakulima. It was probably under pressure from them that the Temne moved south of Tumbo island to found a new settlement.[3]

The Portuguese navigators who landed on these coasts in the middle of the fifteenth century confirmed that they were densely populated. But

1. V. Fernandes, French transl. 1951, pp. 83–9.
2. Cf. Chapter 7 above.
3. Fernandes, loc. cit., pp. 69–105; V. Monteil, 1966; D. Pacheco Pereira, French transl. 1956.

there were no extensive kingdoms among the Felupe, the Balante, the Landuma, the Nalu or the Baga. Those whom the navigators called kings were rather patriarchs or clan chiefs with very limited powers.

In his description of the west coast of Africa, Valentim Fernandes wrote: 'The kings of all the villages get no revenue from their subjects nor tribute money, but if they want to plant, sow or harvest their subjects help them free of charge; when they build houses, fence their land or go to war, all answer their call.' But the power of the king was limited by his council: 'If the king wishes to declare war, he calls together the elders and forms a council. If they decide that the war is not justified or that the enemy is too strong, they tell the king that they cannot help him and they insist on peace, despite the king.'[4]

These people practised the traditional religion; there was no Islamic influence south of the Rio Grande. The Portuguese correctly noted the common basis of all the religions encountered along the coast. The people paid honour to idols carved out of wood; the chief divinity was called Kru; they also practised worship of the dead, who were embalmed before burial. 'It is usual to make a memento for all those who die: if he was a notable person, an idol is made resembling him; if he was merely a commoner or a slave, the figure is made of wood and is put in a thatched house. Every year, sacrifices of chickens or goats are made to them.'[5] This is the oldest description we have of the religious and funerary rites of the coastal peoples; the statuettes in question are the *nomoli* or *pomta* (sing. *pomdo*) carved out of soft soapstone, which are to be found in the ancient burial places of the Republic of Guinea and in Sierra Leone (see Plates 12.2–12.5).

From Mount Kakulima to Kru country

The Temne, descendants of the Sapes, ruled the area south of Mount Kakulima. There is only a vague memory of them in the Republic of Guinea today, since the Temne are now concentrated in Sierra Leone. Beside them were the Limba, the Bulom and, in the interior, the Kissi; these last two groups spoke the Sherbro language.

Like the others, these peoples were organized in kinship groups and autonomous villages. Their political structure was dominated by esoteric 'mask' societies, which were responsible for initiation, like the Simo society in the north among the Baga and the Landuma. The Portuguese did not note any significant differences between these coastal populations. Villages were numerous among both the Bulom and the Temne; each had approximately 150–300 inhabitants, although some accounts speak of

4. Fernandes, loc. cit., p. 83.

5. Monteil, op. cit; cf. Pacheco Pereira, loc. cit., p. 47; Fernandes, loc. cit., pp. 69, 105.

PLATE 12.2 (*above*) *Nomoli statue of Sierra Leone (steatite)*

PLATE 12.3 (*above*) *Nomoli statue of Sierra Leone (steatite)*

PLATE 12.4 (*below*) *Nomoli statue of Sierra Leone (steatite)*

PLATE 12.5 (*above*) *Nomoli statue of Sierra Leone (steatite)*

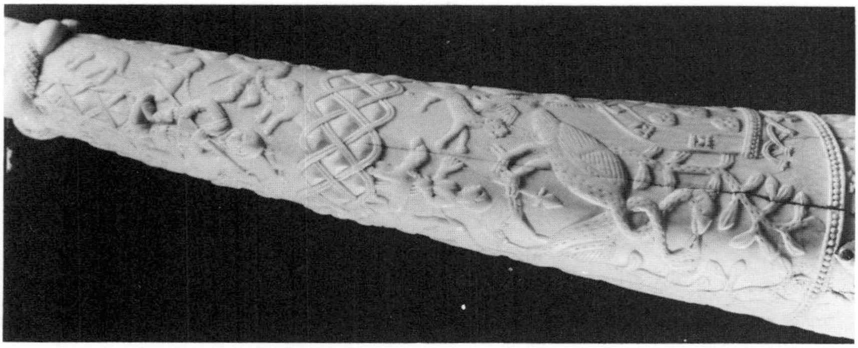

PLATE 12.6 *Ivory tusk with hunting scenes*

PLATE 12.7 *African ivory of Portuguese ship and warriors, general view*

Bulom villages of 1000–3000 people. Each village had its patriarch (*bai*). Rice-growing was well developed along the coast; by the end of the fifteenth century the Portuguese were shipping the Sierra Leone surplus to the north. The Bulom, like the Bijago, built large boats and had a successful fishing industry; they developed wood sculpture and were adept at carving ivory (see Plate 12.6). The Portuguese frequently ordered works of art from them, such as salt cellars and spoons.

At some point, a time not yet precisely determined but probably in the thirteenth or fourteenth century, the Temne language and culture spread inland from the coast from north-west of Futa Jallon to Rokel in Sierra Leone. When the Portuguese arrived, they still held the region from the latitude of Conakry southward, but the Mande vanguard, the Soso (the Susu of Futa Jallon) were already tending to push them southwards. Although the Portuguese spoke of the 'empire of Sapes', there was never a structured state, but a series of chiefdoms united by a common culture. Archaeological findings will doubtless enlighten us one day on their early movement towards the south, although this should not be regarded as a sudden and massive population shift – the old view of migration – but rather as a slow cultural diffusion, certainly lasting several centuries.

Along the coast, beyond the domain of the Temne and the Bulom, we find the Kru peoples, whose power stretched as far as the arm of the Bandama; they lived in an essentially forest environment that was virtually impenetrable until the sixteenth century. Little is known about this group for the period in question; it is remarkably original from both the linguistic and the anthropological standpoints. Like the Nalu, the Landuma, the Baga and the Bulom, they were active in fishing along the coast and practised an agriculture that was less developed than that of their northern neighbours. Rice may have come from their Mandingo neighbours inland, but it was not widely grown. Their territory was much more extensive than it is today, especially in that it encroached on the savannah near Seguela, where from the sixteenth century they gave way to the Malinke. At all events, the Portuguese found both the Bassa and the Kru well established on the coast in the fifteenth century.

The influence of the savannah

If we look at contacts with the Sudan, the main peoples involved were the Mandingo, since the Fulani came on the scene only marginally at the end of the period. The southern Mandingo had been in contact with the people of the region from very ancient times and had been culturally influenced by them to a considerable degree. In the thirteenth and fourteenth centuries the Mandingo continued to advance towards the sea between the Rio Grande and the Liberian coast.

The Mandingo – the peoples speaking the Malinke, Bambara, Juula

PLATE 12.8 *African ivory of Portuguese ship and warriors, in detail*

and other languages – formed the core of the Mande world, and they made their collective mark on history in the thirteenth century, when they built the celebrated empire of Mali. They were interested very early in upper Guinea. The Malinke and the Bambara were organized in large patrilineal village groups, which were in turn grouped together to form *kafu* or *jamana*, small state-like territorial units. Although these units probably did not antedate the Mali empire, they were remarkable for their continuity. At the village level, political life was sustained by large initiation societies or *jow*. Islam was omnipresent, a minority faith but indispensable because of its connection with long-distance trade. Social stratification was relatively highly developed and the tradition of state organization, in the form of a superstructure exacting tribute from the *kafu*, was more or less universal.

The Mali empire, which survived until the first half of the seventeenth century, was centred on the Niger and oriented towards the great open spaces of the savannah and the control of trans-Saharan trade. Long-distance trade, particularly in kola nuts and slaves, must have stimulated an interest in the southern routes to the edge of the forest, but the empire does not seem to have established unbroken political sway beyond a line running from Kurusa through Kankan to Odienne. Nevertheless, the rulers seem always to have encouraged good relations with the forest chiefs.

To the east of Futa Jallon, which seems always to have escaped the domination of Mali – its barren sandstone plateaux were difficult for access, and the sea itself remained an unnavigable obstacle – the Malinke expansion seems to have taken place outside the imperial framework. In the areas closest to the empire, it seems that the gradual advance of the peasantry under the discipline of soldiers led to the absorption of the indigenous peoples. Great and noble lineages shared out power amongst themselves, and there was no political centralization except for periods of military supremacy, among the Konde of Sankaran on the upper Niger, at least as early as the fourteenth century, or the Malinke clans, Kuruma and Konate of Toron, from Kankan to Odienne, not later than the fifteenth.

Further south, the firstcomers seem to have been Juula traders, who went to the edges of the forest in search of slaves, kola nuts, gold and, in the west, Malaguetta pepper. Outside the region, towards the east, they reached the Gulf of Guinea – the 'Gold Coast', now Ghana – before the Portuguese. With them came the first seeds of Islam. Their disputes with the indigenous population subsequently led them to call on Malinke warriors, who organized the country politically and brought in peasants to assimilate the existing population (the Kuranko, in what is now the Republic of Guinea and Sierra Leone, not later than the fifteenth century; the Konianke and Mau towards the end of the same century; and the Wagadugu in the sixteenth and seventeenth centuries). Some of them – the Kono and the Vai – penetrated as far as the sea as early as the fifteenth century. It was almost certainly the Camara of Konianke who were responsible for the great Somba invasion which reached the coast of Liberia and Sierra Leone in 1540–50.

On the Bandama, this great Malinke expansion was to meet the advance guard of the Juula who, from as early as the fourteenth century, had reconnoitred the routes from Jenne to the Akan gold-mines at Begho, and as far as the Gulf of Guinea at ancient Boron, Wagadugu and Koro. From the end of the sixteenth century, there was an outlet to the sea on that side, near the lower Bandama.

However, the new world of the southern Malinke, from the source of the Niger to the Bandama, was oriented not towards the sea, but towards the Sudan, the Sahel and the north; and it did not suffer until much later the impact of the slave trade. It was only at the end of the seventeenth century that the influence of the sea became significant, and the Muslim and commercial elements grew in importance. At that point, the people of the upper Niger, by gaining access to the Atlantic, disrupted the culture of the indigenous Soso and Temne inhabitants and destroyed the equilibrium of their own land.[6]

The Mandingo states or provinces of the coast

A series of major events appears to have taken place in the north-west from the first half of the thirteenth century onwards. These culminated in the formation of a centre of Malinke culture in Kaabu (Gabu) stretching from the Gambia to the Rio Grande. The Mali empire, which controlled the gold-bearing areas of the upper Senegal and upper Niger, seems to have imposed its hegemony over the whole of Senegambia, but did not survive the crisis which it underwent a century later.

However, further south, from the Gambia to the foothills of Futa Jallon, the influence of Mali was more enduring, since it was based on a new influx of population and a far-reaching transformation of the indigenous societies. According to tradition, this upheaval was the work of Tiramaghan Traore, Sundiata's general, who is said to have conquered and organized Kaabu. This large state, which was to survive into the nineteenth century – until 1867 to be precise – was originally the western government of Mali. It ranged as far as the Bambugu gold-mines in the west and provided an outlet to the sea which, although only of value for supplying salt and fish, seems already to have been a source of fascination to the Malinke of the Sudan.

Kaabu was surrounded by a host of vassal states, some of which were peopled by acculturated non-Mandingo groups, such as the Tyapi, Biafada and Kassanga (the eastern Bainuk) or the kingdom of Brass (Oyo on the Rio Cacheu). The Portuguese encountered a series of Gambian kingdoms in the fifteenth century; these were, from the river-mouth upstream, Niumi,

6. See W. Rodney, 1970, and K. C. Wylie, 1977.

Badibu, Niani and Wuli. The Balante, who were hostile to any form of centralized power, kept to themselves and were only partly subdued. Although the Mandingo language and culture were dominant and have continued to flourish until the present day, the political system established was largely independent of the centre, on the upper Niger. One noteworthy feature is that the aristocracy of Kaabu, under the influence of the indigenous inhabitants, adopted the matrilineal system of succession. This accounts for the origins of the Gelowar lineage, who founded the Serer kingdoms at a date unknown, but certainly prior to the arrival of the Portuguese in 1446.

Towards the lower Casamance, the vassal kingdom of the Bainuk-Kassanga preserved its identity until it was destroyed by the Balante in 1830. It was from the title of the king – Kasa-Mansa – that the Portuguese derived the name of Casamance, which they gave to the river.

The event which had the most marked impact on western Malinke was clearly the arrival of the Portuguese in the period between 1446, when they discovered the Gambia, and 1456, when they reached the Rio Grande. Thenceforth, the seaboard became the main frontier of acculturation and its significance to the empire of Mali changed completely. The Gambia was a waterway on which navigation was remarkably easy, and it was to remain one of the main access routes into the heart of the continent until the nineteenth century.

This was the route through which gold from Bambugu and even from Bure was exported; it was soon followed by large numbers of slaves. At the end of the fifteenth century, the same route was taken by the Portuguese missions that visited the emperor of Mali in 1484–5, 1487 and 1534. At the end of the fifteenth century, an alliance was formed against the Denianke Fulani of Tengella, who threatened the route by conquering upper Senegal from the Futa Jallon. But the threat receded and the Denianke eventually settled in Futa Toro. However, as the Serer kingdom of Salum gained in strength in the early sixteenth century, the Malinke states in the north of the Gambia, from Niumi to Niani, came under its sway. From that time until the eighteenth century they lived by the rhythm of the slave trade.

Kaabu preserved its authority only south of the River Gambia, and made a bid to communicate directly with the Portuguese further south, along the Rio Cacheu and the Rio Grande. However, all the evidence suggests that, despite the ordeals of the sixteenth century, Kaabu still remained loyal to the Mali empire. This empire, though reduced in size and deprived of its Sahel dependencies, was still in existence, contrary to what has long been believed. The date when this historic connection was broken can almost certainly be identified. It appears, after careful checks, that Bambugu with its gold-mines remained under the control of Mali until 1599, when Mansa Mamudu was finally defeated in front of Jenne. It was then conquered on behalf of the Denianke of Futa Toro, who had formed the 'empire of the great Ful', by a band of Portuguese renegades recruited by the celebrated Ganagoga, a Jew from Crato who had been converted to Islam and was the son-in-law of the *silatigi* (king) of the Denianke.[7] From that time, about 1600, communication between Kaabu and the upper Niger became impossible, and Mali was eventually dismembered in the next twenty-five years.[8]

Further south, the hinterland of the Sapes was occupied by the vast sandstone massif of the Futa Jallon, the watershed of West Africa, where the broad plateaux cut through by deep valleys are infertile, but the climate is suited to stock-raising. From very early times, no precise date is yet known, this region had been the home of two closely related peoples, the Jallonke and the Soso (or Susu), speaking two dialects of the same Mandingo language, close to Malinke but nevertheless quite distinct.

The Fulani and the peoples of the Futa Jallon

The Jallonke, who lived on the northern and eastern sides of the Futa Jallon range and spread eastwards into Bure, the gold country, had a Mandingo type of civilization and were traditionally organized in patrilineal kinship groups, villages and small chiefdoms analogous to the *kafu*. They were probably at least partly tributary to Mali during the heyday of the empire, until the disturbances at the end of the fifteenth century and those of the upper Niger, which took place probably near the end of the sixteenth century.

By contrast the Soso, who lived in the western and southern parts of the massif, seem to have led an isolated existence in small groups and to have changed their culture under the influence of those who spoke the Mel language. Thus their political organization, much less highly structured, assigned an important role to the Simo initiation society, which was Temne or Baga in origin. Their language, however, gradually became dominant among the peoples of the coast. At that time, the Baga and the Nalu were very numerous in the valleys of the Futa Jallon; they left the region only in the eighteenth century, during the Fulani *djihād*.

As peasants and hunters living on the fringes of the Sudan world, the Soso were for a long time unacquainted with Islam and were compelled to lead a rather inward-looking existence, until two new factors came to disrupt their isolation and to bring major trade routes through their territory. These were the incursion of the Fulani and the arrival of the Portuguese on the coast.

The Fulani, who were semi-nomadic herdsmen speaking a western Atlantic language closely related to Serer, made their first appearance in the region in the middle of the fifteenth century. When Mali was loosening

7. A. Teixeira da Mota, 1969. Cf. also A. Donelha, Eng. transl. 1977, pp. 268–9.
8. See Chapter 7 above.

its grip over the Sahel, groups of Fulani left the Futa, in the east of present-day Mauritania, to cross the upper Senegal, and then the River Gambia by the Niani ford, which is still remembered in the traditions. About 1450, Dulo Demba attacked the Biafada, who were still vassals of Mali, on the western confines of the Futa Jallon. Some time afterwards, the Temmala (Tengella) group settled on Jallonke land in the region of Guema-Sangan. From there they set out at the end of the century to do battle with the Malinke of Kaabu and Gambia, and later, in the early sixteenth century, to conquer upper Senegal and the Futa Toro, where Koly Tengella was to found the Denianke dynasty.

The Futa Jallon was only symbolically linked to the empire of the 'great Ful' at the end of the sixteenth century, but the Denianke did not take all the Fulani with them when they left. These herdsmen, who at that time practised their traditional religion, settled on the high plateaux among the Soso and the Jallonke. About 1560 they joined with the Soso of Benna, on the borders of Sierra Leone, to halt the Mane invasion, which had just overrun the regions to the south. However, they were content with their marginal role in society until they received an influx of Muslims at the end of the seventeenth century. (They then went on to subjugate the Jallonke, whose name the region still bears, during the *d̲j̲ihād* of Karamoxo Alfa, which began in 1727.)

However, it was the arrival of the Portuguese, with the sudden impetus this gave to coastal trade, that completely changed the destinies of the Soso. From the end of the fifteenth century, the region was crossed by the heavy traffic of the Djakana caravans linking the Bambugu gold-fields on the upper Senegal and the Bure mines on the upper Niger with the riparian coast. The Soso, following this movement, pushed back the Baga and Temne towards the Rio Pongo and Benna, which they had reached by the mid-sixteenth century. The first small Islamic groups were among them, but it was not until the end of the seventeenth century and the beginning of the eighteenth that the influence from the Sudan brought about a far-reaching cultural and social mutation, as it had among their southern neighbours.

Mandingo pressure on the coast – the advance of the Malinke

The forest front from the upper Niger to Sassandra was occupied by a variety of true Mandingo groups, such as the Kuranko and the southern Malinke (the Konianke and the Mau). On this side, the network of trade in kola nuts was probably set up by the Juula at a very early date; it included a brokerage zone where contact was made with the producers, who were all regarded as forest 'barbarians', whether they spoke Mande – like the Guro, Dan, Kpelle and Toma (Loma) – or a Mel language like the Kissi.

This region was far removed from the political centres of the Mali empire, and it is not known to what extent and at what periods the central authority really held sway. But although the dates are not known with precision, it can be stated that settlements of warriors, peasants and traders were slowly established and came to form the bulk of the population, while the indigenous inhabitants mentioned above were either assimilated or driven out. There are indications that the main movements occurred in the fourteenth and fifteenth centuries;[9] this was the time when the retreat of Mali to the north turned men's energies towards the south instead. The main thrust seems to have taken place before the Portuguese discovery, or at least without reference to it. However, the way in which the Mane refer to the Mali empire suggests that the Konianke still theoretically recognized its authority in the mid-sixteenth century.

East of the upper Niger, the settlement of Sankaran and Toron, in contact with the Kissi and Toma, probably dates back to the fourteenth century. The settlements of the Konianke, and of the Mau at Touba in the Ivory Coast, although more recent, must go back at least to the end of the fifteenth century, if the Mane invasion is to be intelligible. Emphasis must be placed on the importance of this high plateau, where conditions are healthy and favourable for stock-raising, surrounded as it is by mountains dominating the southern equatorial forest and within easy distance of Monrovia and Freetown. The situation would suggest a thrust to the coast as soon as this acquired some commercial importance. The region was inhabited by Malinke clans under the domination of the Camara-Diamande, whose legendary ancestor, Feren-Kaman, had driven back or assimilated the original Kpelle inhabitants. These highlands subsequently attracted many Fulani clans, especially in the seventeenth century, but the new immigrants adopted the Malinke language. Once settled on the forest front, the Mandingo were to drive through it on at least two occasions to reach the seaboard, although the circumstances were very different on each occasion.[10]

The Kono and the Vai

These people were Mandingo and settled in the forest zone in present-day Sierra Leone and Liberia before the Portuguese discovery, that is to say in the 1460s. Their settlement may even have taken place in the previous century, but the fact that the Kono and Vai languages remain close to Mandingo suggests that the date was relatively recent.

9. If the genealogies are taken at their face value, the mid-sixteenth century would seem to be a more likely date; but if a comparison is made with the Keita of the upper Niger, it can be proved that it is structurally impossible for the Malinke to trace their history back more than four centuries by that method. Calculations based on the number of generations only give the minimum length of the period.

10. This twofold drive led me, in an earlier work, (Y. Person, 1961) to divide the Mane invasion, incorrectly, into two. The first drive was the origin of the Massaquoi clan and the second of the Fahnbule clan, both of which remain dominant to this day among the Vai (the Mandingo people of Liberia).

In any event, it was from the upper Niger, probably from Sankaran, that some Malinke clans set out and made for the sea, which they reached in the border area between present-day Liberia and Sierra Leone. They were led by the Camara and hence, according to tradition, related to those who were subsequently to settle in Konianke. Some who dropped out on the way became the Kono people; they lived in a highland region similar to the Konianke.[11] The others, who according to tradition were led by Kamala the younger, Fangoloma and Kiatamba, reached the sea at Lake Pisu, near the present-day Robertsport, where they became the Vai. The Portuguese, who were impressed by the number of their poultry, called them 'Gallinas'.

These former inhabitants of the Sudan adjusted their civilization to forest life, but they appear to have kept a fairly centralized political structure. By the same token, they adapted quite quickly to the new commercial world created by the arrival of the Portuguese, although their reasons for migrating in the first place were probably connected with the search for salt and fish. They were soon to submit to the incursion of another Sudanic people, the Mane, although the latter, who were probably of the same origin, did not upset the social balance.

The Mane or Mande invasion

The second great Mandingo thrust towards the sea corresponds to the celebrated invasions of the Mane-Sumba and Kwoja-Karu. There is a vast amount of documentation on this subject, but it is complex, variable in quality and often only superficially studied. It has not yet been correlated with the ethnography or the history of the peoples concerned, and the many studies prompted by events still do not provide a complete picture.

The Mane invasion was one of those great movements that have periodically shaken the history of certain regions of Africa, like that of the Jaga in Angola some fifty years later or the Zulu in the nineteenth century. All these movements had a more disruptive effect on institutions and relations between peoples than on the ethno-linguistic map. This is true of the Mane invasion, which played a less significant role than that of the Vai, although it was doubtless responsible for the spread of the Mandingo language in the south and for the origin of the Loko group. But, above all, it contributed to the dissemination of centralized political institutions and to the extension of the long-distance trading network of the Sudan.

Some scholars, like Professor Hair, may still appear to be doubtful;[12] but it seems clear that the Mane invasion was originally launched by

11. *Kono* in Mandingo means 'wait'. According to the tradition of Fadama (the centre of Mandingo tradition), these immigrants got their name because they were waiting; but having heard nothing from the vanguard they remained in the high plateaux of Sierra Leone.

12. P. E. H. Hair, 1967.

Mandingo groups who were already familiar with long-distance trade and the eastern gold routes (allusion is made to a war with El Mina). Since their movement emerged more than eighty years after the Portuguese discovery, we may accept that the desire to open up a direct trade route to the coast was not unrelated to it. Although their political and military organization was superior, the invaders were few in number and ill adapted to the forest environment. They were successful only because they progressively mobilized the people they conquered and thus produced such a snowball effect that within a short space of time they were only a small minority carried forward by the momentum of the movement they had unleashed. This accounts for the duality which struck Portuguese observers from the very outset.

The Cape Verde Islands

The arid, desert lands of Cape Verde were first settled in 1462 on the model of Madeira; the islands, however, were returned to the Portuguese crown after 1484. From the very beginning, the capital was established at Santiago, the island closest to the mainland, which became the residence of the governors and, from 1535, of the bishop, whose jurisdiction extended down the coast from Senegal as far as Cape Mesurado in Liberia.

In view of its climate, the archipelago was quickly populated by a majority of slaves, purchased in Senegambia and upper Guinea. Later, in 1582, the two main islands, Fogo and Santiago, had 1600 white inhabitants, 400 free blacks and 13 700 slaves. The economy of the islands in the sixteenth century was based on stock-raising, cotton-growing and weaving, using African techniques. Very soon the islands, not content with importing slaves for their own use, began to ship them to America too. While São Tome and Kongo supplied Brazil, the Cape Verde Islands turned towards trade with Spanish America from 1530–40. In the second half of the century, the number of slaves exported may be estimated at 3000 a year, partly in exchange for cotton cloth from Cape Verde.

As soon as we look at this trade with the mainland and with America, we must take into account the specific features of Portuguese colonization. It was based on the idea of a royal monopoly of trade, granted to concessionaires for clearly defined periods and regions. Thus the Charter of 1466 granted the inhabitants of the islands the right to trade with 'Guinea de Capo Verde', that is with the coast as far as Cape Mesurado. In 1514, however, the code promulgated by King Manuel prohibited travel to Guinea without a licence, and even stronger prohibitions applied to settlement.

At the beginning of the sixteenth century, the main concern of the Portuguese authorities was the struggle against their emigrants, who had settled on the continent with the agreement of the African sovereigns, intermarried and set themselves up as commercial middlemen. These people

PLATE 12.9 *European traders making contact with the inhabitants of Cayor at Cape Verde (etching)*

PLATE 12.10 *An African village*

were known as *lancados* (from *lancar*: to launch out on an adventure) or *tangomãos* (people who had adopted local customs).[13] In 1508, a special decree was aimed at those living in Sierra Leone. They were considered criminals, and certainly many of them came from the fringes of society, especially the 'new Christians', the Jews who had been converted by force.

13. J. Boulègue, 1968.

PLATE 12.11 *Negro township of Rufisco*

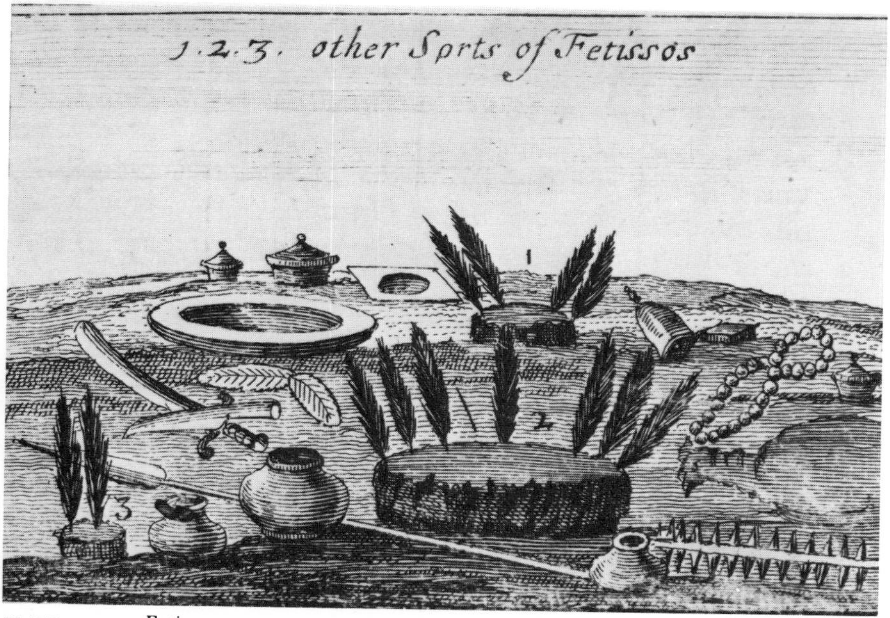

PLATE 12.12 *Fetisso*

PLATE 12.13 *Fetisso*

PLATE 12.14 *The king of Sestro (in the 17th century)*

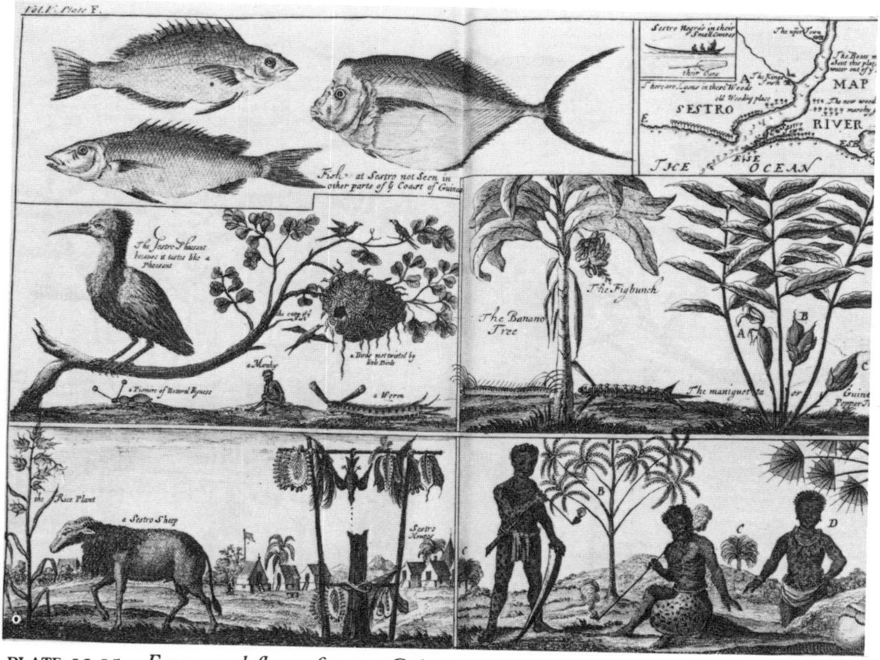

PLATE 12.15 *Fauna and flora of upper Guinea*

Conclusion

The coastal regions are still virgin territory for research. The Portuguese navigators provide written records from the fifteenth century onwards and the Lisbon archives have recently been opened to researchers. Archaeological studies have barely begun. The study of some traditions has already proved that this region was not closed in on itself; trade in kola nuts and other forest products attracted the Mandingo very early to set up powerful trading communities or kingdoms, such as those of Kaabu and the Konianke on the edge of the forest. Many of the coastal peoples were noted for their sculpture, such as the Nalu, the Baga and the Bulom. Their knowledge of rice cultivation made the region into a true granary for the men and women of the savannah, whose kings usually maintained good relations with the local chiefs.[14]

14. There is a Malinke saying: 'If you want palm oil and kola, do not make war on the king of Kissi.' Savannah warriors rarely penetrated into this region; the forests and swamps prevented the widespread use of cavalry.

13 From the Ivory Coast lagoons to the Volta

P. KIPRE

The country

From Cape Palmas the coast curves from west to east in an arc that forms the Gulf of Guinea; as we approach the Equator the vegetation becomes more and more dense and the forest takes over. A notable feature is the appearance of lagoons along the coast. In fact, the region can be divided into three areas:

(1) east of the estuary at Cape Palmas to the Tano river – a continuous chain of twelve lagoons runs parallel to the coast;[1]
(2) from the Tano to the Accra plain – a few hills give the illusion of an uneven landscape (Cape Three Points);
(3) towards the mouth of the Volta – the countryside appears more arid and the forest has practically given way to clearings dotted with occasional trees.

The region has an equatorial climate with heavy rainfall, averaging 2000 mm annually. There is a rainy season from March to July, followed by two months of dry weather, with a shorter rainy season in October and November, and finally a dry season from December to March. The atmosphere is always heavy with humidity, even during the dry season. The influence of the forest hangs heavily over the whole country.

The problem of sources

The region has begun to interest historians only recently; for a long time, attention was focused on the countries of the savannah and the Sahel further north, the former seat of empires whose history was full of pomp and ceremony. Muslim travellers and historians who visited the Sudan between the tenth and the sixteenth centuries did not know the forest regions; thus written records are lacking. Archaeology is only now begin-

1. The twelve lagoons – Noni, Tadio, Make, Ebrié, Aghien, Kodio-Boué, Ono, Potou, Ehi, Hebo, Tagba and Aby – constitute a vast body of water covering 2400 km^2.

ning to explore the area. Traditions are abundant, but they present certain problems.

Written sources

These are for the most part accounts of voyages by Portuguese navigators from the fifteenth to the seventeenth century; their interest is therefore limited to the end of the period with which we are now concerned. From 1471 to 1480, the land between Cape Palmas and the mouth of the Volta was explored by the Portuguese, who came into contact with the local population; in 1481, they began to build the fort of El Mina, which assured them effective control of the coastal trade. For all this there are two essential sources: the works of the Portuguese navigator Duarte Pacheco Pereira, who took part in the exploration of the coast and in 1505–6 wrote his *Esmeraldo de situ orbis*, which describes the West African coast from Morocco to Gabon; the second is the description of Africa by the Dutchman O. Dapper, who collated a whole series of accounts and presented a synthesis of Africa in the seventeenth century. What can we learn from these sources?

They describe the coastal peoples and provide details of their activities. At Cape Palmas, Pacheco Pereira met people whom he called Eguorebo, none other than the Grebo. The rivers flowing into the ocean are carefully noted; the Santo Andre or Sassandra has 'harrari or rice fields'. Towards the east, his Rio Pedro can be identified as the River Tabu; Rio Laguoa is our great Lahu. Beyond Rio Laguoa, Pacheco Pereira noted seven villages with many hostile people: these were the Kru – 'bad men', says the navigator. All the way to the River Mayo (La Comoe) the foreigners got an unfriendly welcome: 'We know nothing about trade in this area, but we know that it is densely populated.'[2] They built a small fort, named after St Antony, at Axim, and soon afterwards the one at El Mina. The discovery of gold in the region was the motivating force. To build the fort, the king of Portugal sent nine ships laden with stone and lime; the fort was built despite the continuing threats of the local people, who quite naturally resented this Portuguese enterprise. The king of Portugal had found a source of gold that he intended to exploit on his own.

El Mina rapidly became a trading centre which attracted many merchants; 'these merchants belong to many nations, such as the Bremus, Attis, Hacanys, Boroes, Mandinguas, Cacres, Anderses or Suzos and others whom I omit to name, to avoid too long a recital'.[3] We can identify in that list the Attie, Akan, Bron or Abron and the Mandingo. The influx of merchants to El Mina is proof of the importance of trade; before the Portuguese arrived, the Mandingo were the best customers of the 'forest

2. From D. Pacheco Pereira, French transl. 1956.
3. ibid., p. 123.

people'. It is worth noting that the Akan, Attie and Bron were interested in this trade because there certainly were gold-bearing deposits in their countries. The majority of these sixteenth-century peoples have been identified. The country from the River Bandama to Cape Three Points was called the Tooth (Ivory) Coast or Quaqua Coast. The Gold Coast (present-day Ghana) stretched from Cape Three Points to the Volta and many villages are named in the Portuguese accounts. The village of Sama with its 500 inhabitants is described as a large village, whereas the ports of 'Little Fante' and 'Great Fante' are obviously in Fanti country. This region, with El Mina, became an important gold market at the end of the fifteenth century.

Here and there, the Portuguese give valuable information on customs, but many gaps must be filled before we can reconstruct people's lives within the framework of their own institutions.

Archaeological sources

Archaeological research has begun only recently; some sites have been opened up in Ghana and the Ivory Coast and the first results indicate that they will provide fruitful information, even for the seemingly impenetrable forest areas. At the northern edge of the forest, where it meets the savannah, excavations in Bron country at Begho indicate that many cultural objects came from Jenne, and prove that there was intense trading activity with the valley of the middle Niger; Posnansky thinks that these relations were long standing.[4] Begho was a trading centre between the forest and the savannah, and an area where an important colony of Malinke or Dioula settled beside the Bron. Excavations since 1970, particularly in the Nyarko area of Begho, would seem to indicate that this site was inhabited around 1100.[5] What is certain is that in the fourteenth century Begho was one of the most important kola-nut markets. Posnansky thinks it probable that in the same period Akan society was structured in such a way that it could serve as an intermediary between the Mandingo and the southernmost kola-producing areas. There is evidence that in the fourteenth century Begho and Mali traded in gold, which must have come from further south. Relations with the forest areas became more important in the fourteenth century (the high point), when the demand for gold was very strong.

On the western side, in Guro country, Mandingo infiltration started much earlier. The kola trade now appears to have been much older than previously thought; the 8° latitude line was the contact area between savannah and forest, and most of the trading centres were located along this line. Finds discovered around Oda in Ghana and at Séguié in the

4. M. Posnansky, 1974, p. 48.
5. M. Posnansky, 1975b.

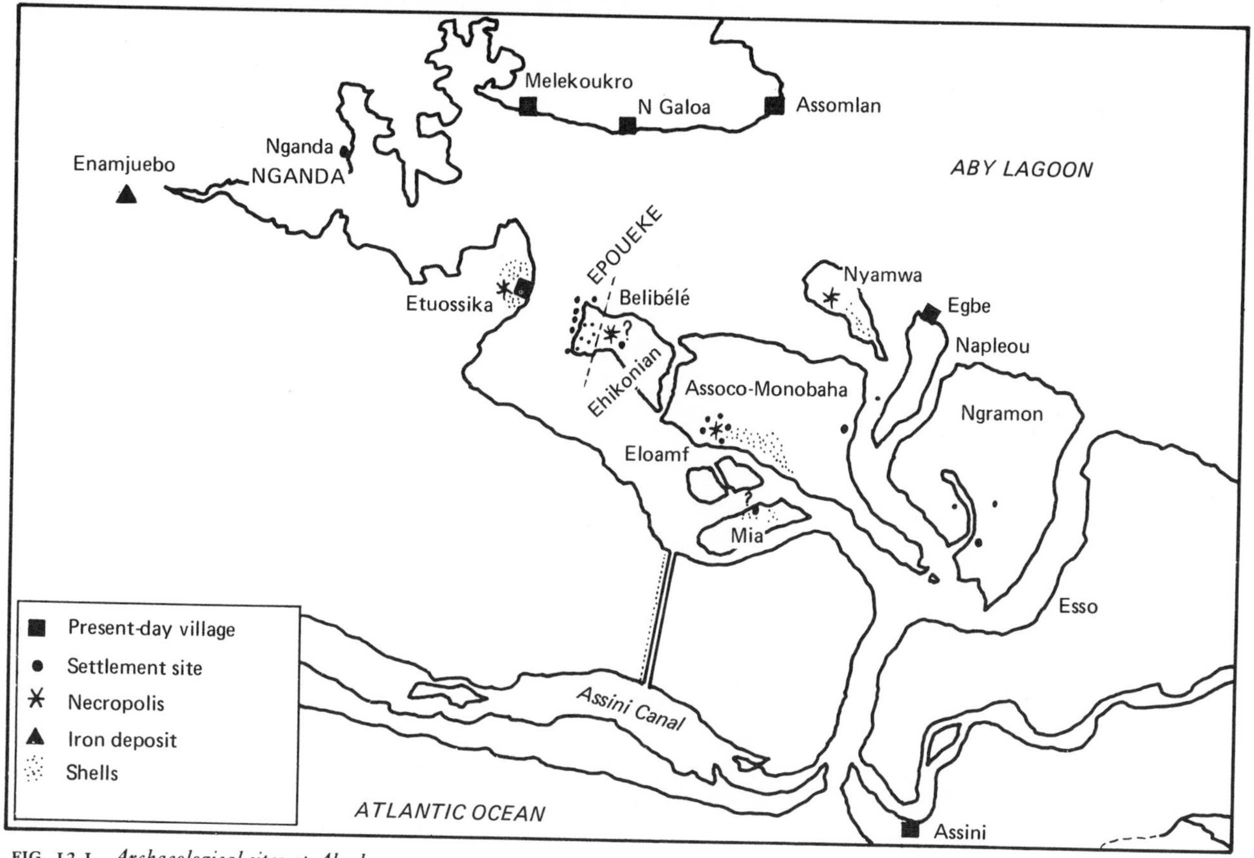

FIG. 13.1 *Archaeological sites at Aby lagoon*
Source: Revue Godo-Godo, 2 (*Abidjan, 1976*), *p. 123*

PLATE 13.1 (*above*) *Pipes found at the site of Séguié (sub-prefecture of Agboville)*

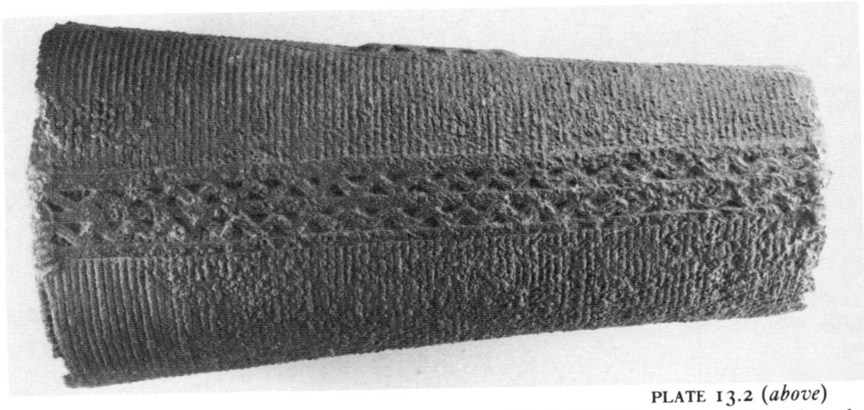

PLATE 13.2 (*above*) *Forearm sleeve bracelet found at the site of Séguié*

PLATE 13.3 (*left*) *Vase found in the necropolis of Nyamwa*

PLATE 13.4 *Vase found in the necropolis of Nyamwa*

PLATE 13.5 *Pipes found in the necropolis of Nyamwa*

Ivory Coast have not yet been dated. At Séguié there are great oval-shaped ditches which resemble defensive areas; they vary in depth from 4 m to 6 m. Excavations have uncovered a vast quantity of pottery;[6] but the dating is uncertain (see Plates 13.1 and 13.2). A comparative study is needed of pottery from these sites and from neighbouring areas. The present inhabitants, the Abe, say their ancestors found the ditches when they arrived and they do not know who made them. Traditions tell us that the Abe arrived shortly before the great Akan migration of the eighteenth century.[7] At all events, the existence of these remains, deep in the forest, is an indication that interesting finds are possible. All we can say is that a gap in our knowledge remains to be filled. We have found from the Portuguese sources that the coast was inhabited by fishing and farming communities; research should be concentrated directly on the coast and towards the forest, precisely in the areas noted by the navigators.

The Institute of Archaeology and Art of the University of Abidjan has been probing the lagoon area, but research is difficult in the mangrove swamps, where there are heavy accumulations of dead leaves. Nevertheless Aby lagoon has been investigated, with soundings at three islands; Belibélé, Assoco and Nyamwa (see Fig. 13.1). Piles of neolithic shells were left by the first inhabitants of the coast;[8] beside them, large kitchen middens have been found. Three burial places have been partially explored, and bones, bracelets, beads and pottery collected, although these have not yet been dated (see Plates 13.3–13.5). Whatever the outcome, it has been demonstrated that there are interesting sites along the lagoon banks.[9]

Oral sources

These are abundant because each ethnic group has a myth of origin or an epic or account of migration. The ethnic fragmentation has been extreme and one finds groups of less than 20 000 scattered among small hamlets in the forest. Oral sources therefore present serious problems for researchers, and there are certain particularities worth noting. First, the recollections of some groups do not go back beyond the eighteenth century. Secondly, frequent borrowings are found between ethnic groups, which confuse the record. Many groups claim that their ancestor came down from heaven, one by means of a gold chain, another by an iron chain, and so on. Others again have their ancestors coming out of a hole in the ground or an anthill. Cross-cultural contamination also occurs where clans treat others as their 'brothers'; the Avikam, for example, consider the

6. J. Polet, 1974, pp. 28–44.
7. Posnansky, 1974, p. 46.
8. See Volume III, Chapter 16.
9. J. Polet, 1976, pp. 121–39.

Alladian to be their brothers. But most peoples say they originated outside the countries where they now live, and recount tales of migration; the Adiukru, for example, believe they came from the west in eight large waves of migration. But where was their country of origin? When was the first migration? When did the movement cease? These questions cannot be answered in a short survey.

Other, numerous peoples of the Akan group place their origin within the Republic of Ghana. The traditions of the Akwamu say their origins lie in the northern savannah, at Kong. Similarly, the Fanti of the coast say their ancestors came from Tekyima in north-west Ghana. The problem is not simple. First, a systematic collection of legends is needed, which would identify and locate each ethnic group. Various disciplines would have to co-operate to disentangle and to classify common cultural traits, for none of these peoples is a separate entity, each being linked to a larger group. After this stage of collection and classification, historians could reconstruct the past, using the normal methods of their discipline.

Here, above all, we see the need for co-operation between linguists, archaeologists, anthropologists and historians. Encouraging examples of such collaboration in research have been set by the University of Abidjan and the University of Ghana at Legon. This was well brought out during the Bonduku Seminar in January 1974 on 'The Peoples common to the Ivory Coast and Ghana'. Researchers from both countries, looking at the different data provided by oral tradition, archaeology and anthropology, came to the conclusion that it was possible not only to write the history of the peoples concerned, but also to discern the process by which their interaction in the same area had created a new culture.

Before ending this section on oral tradition, it should be noted that the fragmentation referred to took place between the seventeenth and nineteenth centuries. The traditions appear at first sight to be of little help here, since very few go back before the seventeenth century. Yet the Akan, Kru and Bron were settled in the fifteenth century, when the village of Accra also existed. A typical example is that of the Ndenye. Their traditions say that they were led to their present settlement by an ancestor called Ano Asena. They came from a country called Anyanya, situated in east Ghana. 'Ano Asena brought law to the people; before him ... there were no trees, there was nothing. In front of him, a copper basin descended from heaven at the end of a chain.' The tradition also says that Ano Asena taught men farming by giving them the banana and the yam. After inquiry and cross-checking with several different traditions, Claude Perrot has found that Ano Asena belongs to the seventeenth century. He has traced documents in Europe which date this ancestor of the Ndenye with some precision around 1690.[10]

It is tempting to go back to the distant past for the date of this man

10. C. Perrot, 1974.

who taught mankind agriculture. But what really happened? At the end of the seventeenth century a war broke out in the kingdom of Aowin in Ghana. Ano Asena, a clan chief, left the country with his men and settled around Assini, the present habitation of the Ndenye, who belong to the great Akan clan. There the people reconstructed an ancient myth of origin around the figure of Ano Asena and gave him the attributes of a mythical ancestor. This rearranging of tradition created a new history which the people adopted, banishing to the distant past the events which preceded their migration.

This example is given to urge caution in the use of tradition; it is interesting to see how a research worker has collated the different oral, written and even archaeological sources concerning Ano Asena in order to arrive at a reconstruction of the past.

It is by collating the different data in this way that we shall attempt to sketch the history of the region between the twelfth and sixteenth centuries. There remain many lacunae in our knowledge, given the state of the evidence, but guidelines can be indicated for future research.

The peoples of the coast and the interior

Traditionally, the peoples of the area fall into two groups: those of the lagoons and forests, and those of the interior (low forest and savannah). The first were called palaeonegritic because they were supposed to be the prehistoric black people who settled in the forest and on the coast. But this picture does not stand up to the new facts provided by anthropology and linguistics. Indeed, it now appears that the inhabitants of the lagoons and the people of the interior both belong to the Kwa language group. It may be recalled that the Portuguese navigators called part of the coast 'the coast of the Quaqua' (see map of Akan migrations, Fig. 13.2).[11]

In a remarkable study entitled 'Who are the Akan?' Professor Adu Boahen, while bringing out the varied elements of Akan culture, draws upon the most recent linguistic studies to assert the linguistic unity of the peoples called Akan and to trace the stages of migration which have brought them to their present settlements.[12] It is worth recalling that, in our time, the Akan constitute 45 per cent of the population in Ghana and 33 per cent in the Ivory Coast. Among the Akan in Ghana, Boahen lists the following groups: the Bono, Asante, Kwahu, Akyem, Akuapim, Wasa, Twifo, Assini, Akwamu, Buem, Sefwi, Aowin, Nzima, Ahanta, Fanti, Gomwa and the Azona; in the Ivory Coast, the Abron (Bron), Anyi, Sanwi, Baule, Attie (Akye), Abe, Abidji, Adiukru, Ebrie, Ega

11. O. Dapper, 1668.

12. A. A. Boahen, 1974. The Ghanaian historian refutes the old theories that the Akan came from Mesopotamia, Libya or ancient Ghana. He takes Greenberg's linguistic theories into consideration in situating the Akan country of origin in the Chad–Benue region.

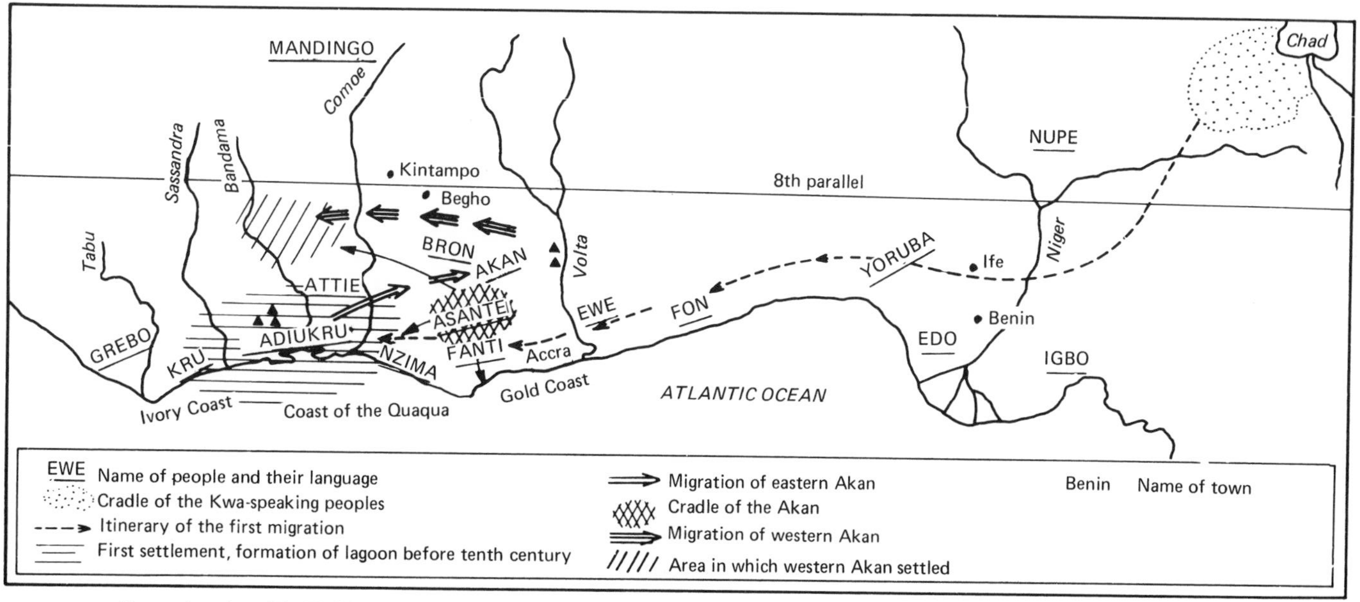

FIG. 13.2 *Akan migrations (D. T. Niane)*

(Dra), Eotile, Abure, Agwa, Avikam and the Alladian.[13] The Akan thus form a vast linguistic group. For the period we are studying, the fragmentation of groups had probably not yet occurred, even though certain dialects had become distinct.

The people of the lagoons and the Akan belonged to the Kwa group. Both were part of the Volta-Comoe linguistic family. The ancestors of the Kwa-speakers presumably came from Chad–Benue by stages, passing by way of the lower Niger and crossing present-day Benin and Togo before arriving at the lagoons.[14] There they created the institutions which govern them today. Many migrants left Adansi for the west and mingled with the people of the lagoons, giving rise to the Baule, Nzima, Sefwi and Anyi.[15]

As a result, three centres of population (or dispersal) must be noted: the Chad–Benue region of origin; the lagoon country, the point of departure for the Akan of Ghana; and Adansi, the origin of the last wave which peopled the west (Ivory Coast). Archaeology throws little light on these population movements, but we have seen that as early as 1300 the Akan (Bron section) around Begho were organized into well-structured communities for trade in gold and kola with the Mandingo.[16]

The people of the lagoons

When were these people settled? Probably well before the twelfth century.[17] We have seen that the Portuguese made contact with the Kru, the Fanti and other coastal peoples. In the fifteenth century, the Kru formed independent lineage-based communities. 'The blacks of the coast are great fishermen and have pirogues with deckhouses in the front and they use cloaks for sails.'[18] The Kru, as is well known, have remained excellent sailors until our time. The Portuguese noted that the coast was densely populated and had large villages. We learn that the people of 'Little Fante', 'Sabu' and 'Great Fante' spoke the same language as the people of El Mina. But the communities were independent of one another. The accounts of the navigators show that the chiefs were, above all, religious leaders.[19] The Kru clan, which dominated the western regions, managed to preserve its kinship society, owing to the efficient protection offered by the lagoons and the forest.

13. ibid., p. 66.
14. J. M. Stewart, 1966.
15. Boahen, op. cit., pp. 76–81
16. Following Posnansky, Boahen thinks that it was between 1000 and 1500 that the Akan developed the fundamental structures of their society.
17. Cf. Volume III, Chapter 9.
18. Translated from Dapper, loc. cit., pp. 302–4.
19. Dapper mentions a king who was feared all along the coast for his magic powers; ibid.

Through the Portuguese, we know that the people of the lagoons traded with the people of the interior: the people of Rio Lahou sold salt to the people of the interior, with whom they had 'a great trade in clothing'. By all the evidence, the people of the lagoons were not cut off from the nearby forests and savannahs; exchanges involved salt, fish, fabrics, gold and copper.

At the end of the fifteenth century the people of the lagoons lived in kinship communities under the authority of a patriarch whose power was more religious than temporal. The Kru were the original stock which, according to Professor Harris, gave rise to the Ahizi (of Abra, Nigui and Tiagha), the Adiukru (Bubury and Dibrimon), and the Ebrié-Abia.[20] It seems difficult, however, given the present state of knowledge, to say when these ramifications occurred and in what conditions. Thus, at the beginning of the sixteenth century, the western Akan group, essentially people of the lagoons, formed distinct kinship communities. We know little about their institutions; the chiefs, however, had a clear tendency to assert their political power.

The origins of Akan society

We have seen that in reality the Akan formed the basic population of this region, since the people of the lagoons were the oldest stock. Anthropologically speaking, the people of the forest region were relatively homogeneous. According to Professor Harris, this was due to the fact that initially three stocks produced the populations which intermingled. From the Akan stock, the most fertile, whose principal centre was in Ghana, came – in addition to the Anyi – the Baule, Akye, Abure, Mabto, Abe, Alladian, Nzima, Ebrie, Adiukru, Akradio and the Akan. Professor Harris also mentions the Kru stock, to which we have already referred, and finally the peoples who were settled there much earlier, such as the Ewotire, Agwa, Kimpa, etc.[21]

The date when these different subgroups broke off from the mother clan remains a problem. Nor do we know whether the development of the institutions and principal elements of eastern Akan culture (Ghana) occurred before the fifteenth century. Posnansky's study of Akan society postulates that the seventeenth century was a turning-point. He believes that along the coast, as well as in the forest, new pottery finds confirm a notable evolution. Some of the baked ware has anthropomorphic decorative elements or animal subjects.[22] The working of copper and gold began very early, even though archaeology has not found any fourteenth or fifteenth-century objects from the Bron states, which date from the

20. M. F. Harris, 1974, p. 135.
21. ibid.
22. Posnansky, 1974, pp. 46–8.

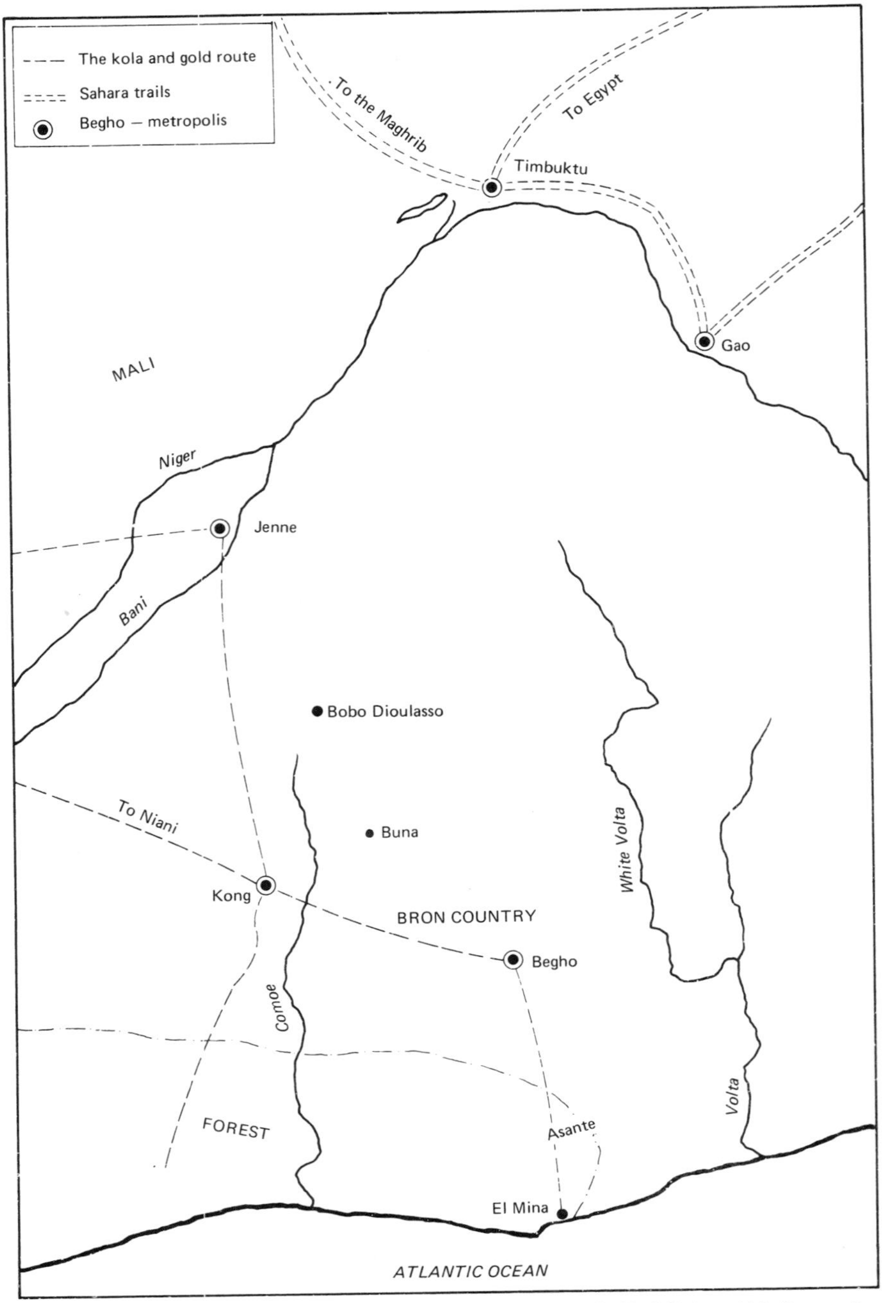

FIG. 13.3 *Map of the area between the Niger valley and the Gulf of Guinea (M. Posnansky, Bonduku Symposium, 1974)*

beginning of the fifteenth century. Cultural objects found in excavations have to be analysed in the light of the evidence of tradition, and of anthropology and other disciplines. To fill in the lacunae between the fifteenth century, when the Portuguese arrived, and the seventeenth century, which saw the expansion of the Akan kingdoms, more information must be collected from the guardians of oral tradition; subsequent excavations may also produce additional evidence on the material culture of the people.

Nevertheless, one may reasonably assume that the Akan kingdoms at the beginning of the fifteenth century had begun to develop both on the coast and inland: on the coast, the kingdoms of Asebu, Fetu, Aguafo and Fanti, although still modest in size at the end of the fifteenth century, were organized for the working and trading of gold; inland, Begho was the capital of a Bron kingdom much inclined toward trade with the Mandingo (see Fig. 13.3).

Foundations of Akan society

The eastern Akan groups are universally considered to have developed most of the aspects of culture that concern us here. The wars of the seventeenth and eighteenth centuries provoked migrations towards the west, and many groups carried with them the essential cultural elements.

(1) A common language with numerous local dialects. (At the end of the Bonduku Seminar, Professor Wondji emphasized that henceforth researchers should use the word 'Akan' in a political sense and the word 'Twi' should denote the linguistic group which belongs to the Kwa family.)[23]

(2) The system of matrilineal inheritance of power (from uncle to nephew on the mother's side).

(3) The system of giving children two names, one for the day of the week on which it is born, the second selected by the father's clan.

(4) The Akan calendar, which has a 42-day month. It appears that this may have arisen from the combination of the original Akan six-day week and the Muslim seven-day week; but the origin of this calendar remains controversial.[24] According to Niangoran-Boah, it concerns a 'ritual month which has a well-defined number of days. This month serves for the organization by provincial peoples of their religious activities.'[25]

Akan music and dance are the same for all; they have festivals and other feasts at the yam harvest. Every Akan has two clans, matrilineal and patrilineal; there are eight of the former and twelve of the latter. In the

23. C. Wondji, 1974, p. 680.
24. J. Goody, 1966.
25. Niangoran-Boah, 1967, pp. 9–26 (no further details available), as cited by Boahen, op. cit., p. 69.

Akan cosmogony, according to Professor Boahen, the two clans complement each other; the matrilineal clan is supposed to give the blood, whereas the patrilineage determines the character, spirit and soul of a person.[26] The Akan world is easily distinguishable by these cultural traits that have shaped the people.

The Akan state appears to have been highly centralized. Each state comprised a certain number of towns and villages, placed under the authority of a king and a queen. Each Akan state had its own pantheon of gods and the king paid careful attention to the words of the priest. The presence of the queen beside the king at the solemn sessions of the court is noteworthy. Originally, according to Mme Diabaté, power was held by the queen and it appears that it was after the birth of kingdoms that men took power, while continuing to associate the queen with its exercise.[27] Probably the clans accepted the queen at their head in the fourteenth and fifteenth centuries, when they 'lived independently, in isolated units, having no need of a common chief';[28] but when it became necessary to fight more often in order to survive or to expand, they preferred a leader who was always ready for war.[29]

We may conclude that the kingdoms were fully structured by the end of the sixteenth century. The requirements of defence meant that the role of the queen had to be reinforced by a war leader who shared power with her; the appearance of the king thus marks the passage from a kinship society to a kingdom. Henceforth, the king's role was more political than ritual.

Conclusion

The lagoon zone from the twelfth to the fifteenth century saw the development of autonomous kinship societies that were independent of each other. The social division of labour had begun; for example, the Kru probably caught enough fish to sell the surplus to their neighbours. Then the commercial current flowed northward from the coast. The coastal people sold salt, others offered special fabrics. Gold exerted a great attraction for the Mandingo, who had long traded in kola nuts; after 1500 they moved beyond Begho across Bron country as far as El Mina, to enter once again into contact with the Portuguese, whom they had already met in Senegambia. The Akan people formed the majority of the population and they had set up kingdoms and city-states before the arrival of the Portuguese, towards the end of the fifteenth century.

26. ibid., pp. 70–1.
27. H. Diabaté, 1974, pp. 178–80.
28. R. S. Rattray, 1929, p. 81.
29. Diabaté, op. cit., p. 185.

14 From the Volta to Cameroon

A. F. C. RYDER

Ecology and language

Eight hundred years ago the coastal fringe of the region between the Volta and Cameroon presented an appearance little different from that which one sees today. Further inland, however, the freshwater swamp, which covers most of the Niger delta, and also the rain-forest belts were far less affected by intensive settlement. Tree felling and dry-season burning have since converted almost half of the original forest area into derived savannah. In Togo and Benin, where the original forest was less extensive than in Nigeria, annual burning of the vegetation cover has virtually destroyed the primary forest. East of the Niger, cultivation has obliterated hundreds of square kilometres of the original rain forest and replaced it by oil-palm bush (see Fig. 14.1).

The labour of clearing the primary forest began when peoples of Negro stock first settled in the region thousands of years ago. It was much accelerated by the diffusion of iron-working techniques, which aided the transition from a hunting and gathering economy to one based on agriculture. By the fifth century of the Christian era the use of iron had penetrated to almost all parts of the forest and the density of settlement was thereby much increased. Such traditions are particularly strong among the Yoruba – historically perhaps the most significant group of the whole area – and yet dialect analysis of their language suggests that the direction of their expansion has been from the forest into the savannah. There is obviously a contradiction between linguistic analysis and historical tradition. It has been proposed that this contradiction could be explained by the movement of secondary populations from the forest to the savannah and vice versa.

Three main groups of Yoruba dialects have been identified.[1] The two believed to exhibit the characteristics of greatest antiquity, and hence of older settlement, are the central group (comprising the Ife, Ilesha and

1. A. Adetugbo, 1973.

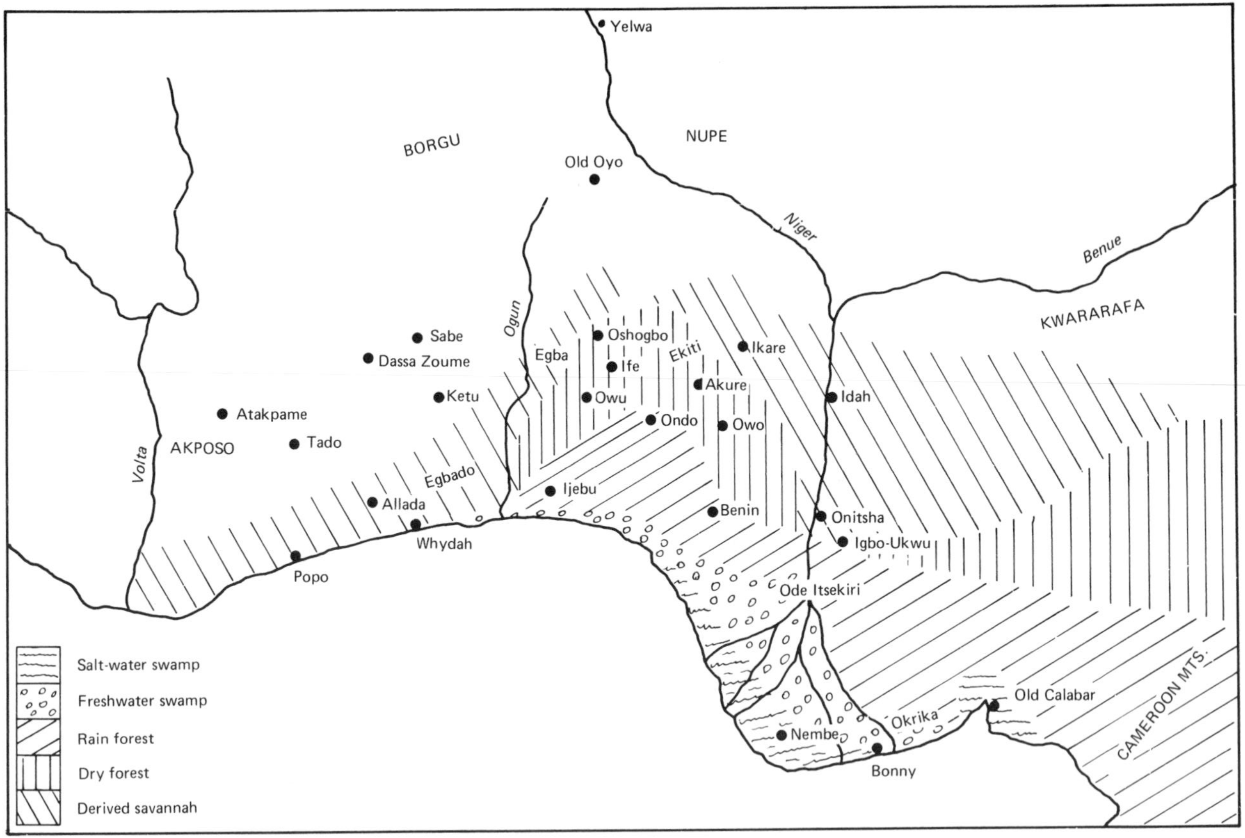

FIG. 14.1 *Map of the area between the Volta and the Cameroon, 1100–1500 (A. F. C. Ryder)*

Ekiti areas) and the south-eastern group (the Ondo, Owo, Ikale, Ilaje and Ijebu areas). In the twelfth century all these areas fell entirely within the forest zone. The third group of dialects embraces Oyo, Osun, Ibadan and the northern Egba area; this north-western group, historically associated with the Oyo empire, shows fewer traces of antiquity than the other two. This analysis harmonizes with the Ife myth, which places the creation of the earth at Ile-Ife, whereas the Oyo-based myth recorded by Samuel Johnson towards the end of the nineteenth century postulates Yoruba origins in a migration from the east.[2]

A similar analysis of the Edo language shows that its dialects can be grouped into a northern and a southern cluster; the dialect of the Benin kingdom, the focus of political and cultural development, falls into the latter group. However, it has not yet been determined whether this division corresponds to a historical sequence of settlement and dispersion.[3] A systematic dialect analysis of Igbo has still to be carried out, but the hypothesis has been advanced that the Ibo people expanded to the north, north-east, west and south from a homeland in the neighbourhood of Owerri-Umuahia.[4] Ijo migrations have been traced to points in the central Niger delta and adjoining areas. In short, the evidence at present available strongly suggests that many of the peoples who have played a major part in the historical developments of the past thousand years have their origin within the forest.

At the beginning of the period covered here, the languages of the region had certainly not assumed their present forms, nor did their distribution correspond to the existing pattern. In form they were probably closer together than today; the technique of glotto-chronology, which postulated a separation of several thousand years between the major Kwa languages, has been largely discredited. Also they were probably more numerous, for many must have been obliterated by the expansion of the more vigorous and successful language groups. Some evidence of this survives in a cluster of languages – each spoken in no more than one or two villages – which appears to have survived between the advance of Yoruba and Edo as a result of the remote and difficult terrain.[5] The years between 1100 and 1500 witnessed crucial developments in the process whereby some groups expanded to establish the hegemony of their language, and sometimes their political control, over wide areas previously occupied by weaker peoples or else uninhabited. The most striking manifestation of this expansion was the formation of major territorial states such as Oyo, Benin and Ife, but it did not always lead to such a con-

2. S. Johnson, 1921.
3. B. O. Elugbe, 1974.
4. S. Ottenberg, 1961.
5. Personal communication from Professor Carl Hoffman of the Department of Linguistics and Nigerian Languages, University of Ibadan. The nature and interrelationships of this language cluster are still uncertain.

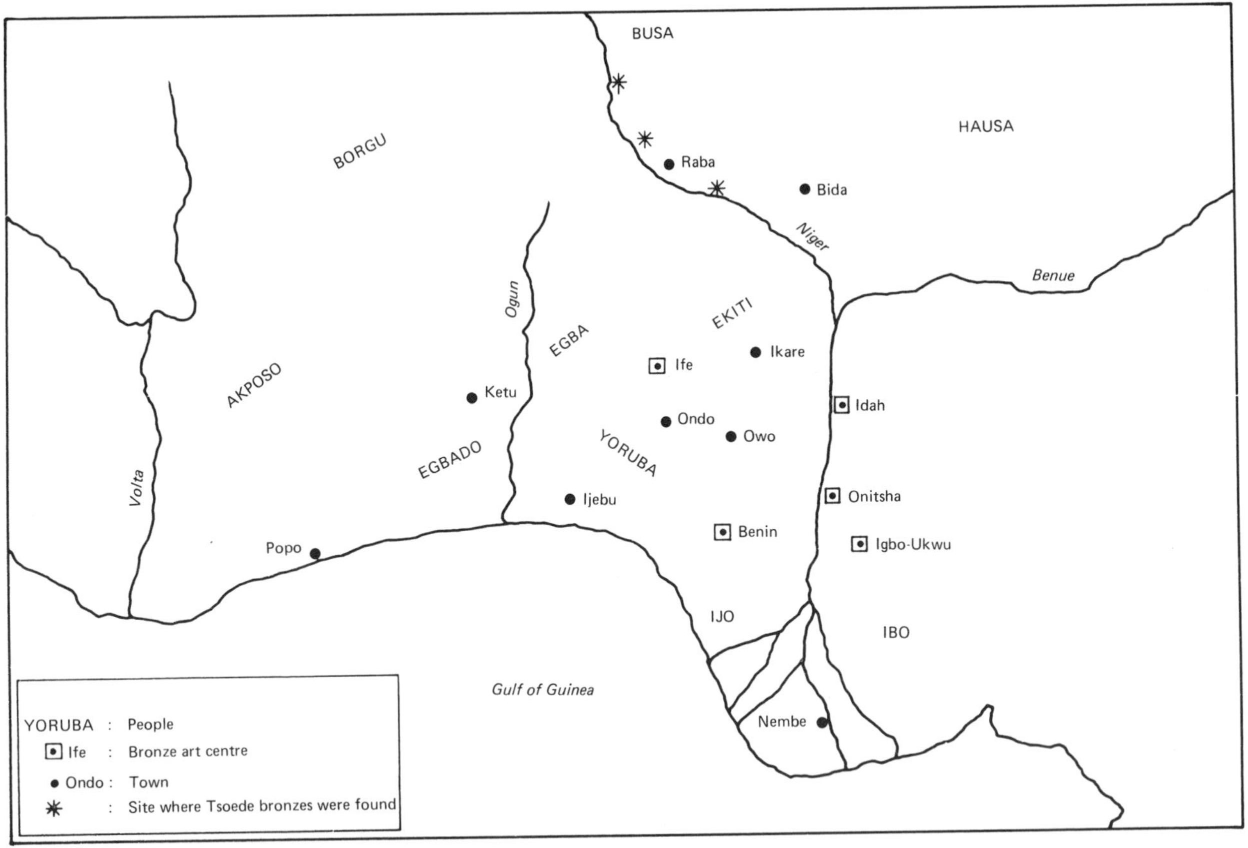

FIG. 14.2 *Populations of the Niger delta (D. T. Niane)*

clusion; the dispersion of the Ibo, for example, resulted not in the establishment of a large Ibo state, but in a host of independent settlements based on the homesteads of small lineage segments (see Fig. 14.2).

Kinship societies

This is the name given to societies without central organization, in which clans or lineages live side by side in complete independence. The authority of the patriarch or clan chief was not absolute and each group exploited a more or less large territory. Some agricultural techniques were rudimentary and the search for good soil caused migrations. It was intensive cultivation of the yam and oil palm which enabled the Ibo to colonize and transform most of the forest zone east of the Niger. The forest zone was driven back by clearing operations in some Ibo areas.[6] This expansion also resulted in more intensive cultivation of the soil and the birth of large village agglomerations. Without explanation states and well-structured cities developed, with individual political authority.

Among the Ibo, many kinships remained independent; in contrast to them were societies where the lineage group had at its head a central power – a king with attendant dignitaries and a court. One can therefore distinguish lineage societies, on the one hand, and city-states or kingdoms with better-developed political powers, on the other. A more common form is the dispersed, territorially defined community, the outcome of a situation in which the peripheral land supply available to an expanding people is very unequal, and in order to obtain land for settlement some groups have to separate from their closer kin and beg land from others with whom they acknowledge little or no genealogical relationship.

In the forest, alongside the kingdoms and cities, lineage groups are to be found who have preserved their independence and live under the authority – more ritual than political – of patriarchs. The protection afforded by hilly country may have helped the Akposo of Togo to preserve their 'stateless society'. Most peoples, however, found themselves constrained to abandon that form of organization and to consolidate adjacent lineages in larger village-type communities in order to offer an effective defence against enemies. In some places the enemy was the autochthonous inhabitants, struggling to maintain their territory against intruders. Ife traditions of an early, prolonged conflict with the indigenous Igbo may refer to such a situation.[7] Owo has a similar legend of struggle against a people known as the Efene. Defence may not, however, always have been the motive for adopting a village as distinct from a dispersed form of settlement.

6. E. J. Alagoa, 1972, pp. 189–90.

7. The Igbo of Ife legend must not be confused with the Ibo who now live in eastern Nigeria.

For example, those Ijo who migrated from the freshwater delta to the salt-water swamp were consequently forced to abandon a fishing and farming economy for one based on fishing and salt-boiling. In the earlier environment they had lived in autonomous settlements governed by an assembly of all adult males presided over by the oldest man. In the new fishing village, composed of several unrelated lineages and competing with other villages for scarce settlement land, the criterion for headship changed from age to ability and membership of the dominant lineage – usually that of the founding ancestor.

Besides evolving new forms of authority, the village encouraged the emergence of institutions that cut across the lines of lineage affiliation. The most characteristic were age grades and secret societies. Age grades brought together the men and – much more rarely – the women of the village in groups that served the whole community. Basically they divided the males into younger men and elders; sometimes a threefold system made a further distinction between youths and mature adults. Mature adults constituted the fighting force of the village and the elders its governing council. Initiation ceremonies in each grade helped to emphasize village as against lineage solidarity; they also played a very important role in the process whereby secret societies weaned their members from ties of family to prime allegiance to the community.[8]

Just as the welfare of the family group was believed to be safeguarded by ancestral spirits, to whom the senior man of the lineage ministered on behalf of his kin, so the village head came to stand in a special relationship with the spiritual forces which could bring good or ill to the whole community.

The emergence of religious concepts specifically related to the community is well illustrated by the cults of Ama-teme-suo and Amakiri among the Ijo. That of Ama-teme-suo is especially significant, for it represents 'the very character and living spirit of the community itself, and the destiny (and history) of the community may be said to depend on it'.[9]

How widespread was the village form of organization by the twelfth century? The fact that the oldest territorial states of which we have certain knowledge had their beginnings about that time argues that in some areas at least, and especially in the dry forest, the village must have been already well established. Archaeological evidence does not give much help at present in answering the question because there is seldom any means of determining whether an early deposit belongs to a village or a dispersed settlement. Thus we cannot tell which type of settlement produced the charcoal, carbon-dated to a period between +560 and +980, which has been excavated from pits at Ile-Ife. Similar uncertainty surrounds the

8. The age grades and secret societies are to be found in most African societies from Senegal to Zambia, including Nigeria and Cameroon. Age grades are the ideal framework for collective labour such as hunting and ploughing.

9. Alagoa, op. cit., p. 200.

site at Yelwa on the banks of the Niger, where archaeological deposits indicate a prolonged occupation from +100 to +700. Only very extensive investigation of large sites is likely to demonstrate the indubitable existence of villages and fix the time of their emergence.[10]

Another possible approach to the problem is a careful study of traditions of origin and migration and of religious, social and political institutions. Investigations of this kind among the Ijo have made it possible to plot the dispersion of this people through the Niger delta and to establish with some certainty that it began no later than the end of the twelfth century. To that period we may also ascribe the introduction of village-type settlements among the Ijo for, as explained above, it was the dispersion into a new environment which produced the new political structure.

If it is difficult to distinguish on archaeological evidence between a dispersed farming settlement and a village of the first millennium, it is still harder to affirm the existence of political units larger than the village in that period. Nevertheless, it is reasonable to assume that they did exist and it is unnecessary to seek for outside influences, even from the Sudan, to account for the evolution of the 'stateless' village into the city-state within the forest zone of West Africa. Horton's model for the transformation of the segmentary lineage settlement into the compact village shows how, in the process, the rudimentary organs of a 'state' may begin to appear by internal adaptation.[11] Leadership loses its transient character, founding lineages acquire greater authority, institutions emerge with a community not a lineage orientation, and principles of political integration founded on common residence and common laws lay the foundation of the principle of sovereignty.

Kingdoms and cities

Once the village has stabilized, it grows rapidly if the soil is rich and becomes an important community; this, in turn, necessitates the establishment of an effective military organization. It is most probable that commercial routes and exchanges played a major role in the development of cities, even in the forest region. Once formed, the city becomes an active economic centre attracting traders. Everything tends to confirm that the cities were formed in a competitive, if not hostile, climate. The most aggressive enlarged their lands by absorbing other cities and lands. None the less the forest remained a brake on such expansion. It also contributed to restricting the domains of the city; rare are those which exercise power beyond 60 km from the capital. Beyond that, the city is dependent upon 'vassals' or kinship chiefs.

10. The materials first used in building homes were wood and reeds; probably around +900 beaten earth or banco was used. In the clearings and savannah, villages multiplied rapidly in a network of paths and communication routes.

11. R. Horton, 1971.

The foregoing insistence on an indigenous origin of the forest state should not be interpreted as a denial of all external influence. An embryo state might even have borrowed a ruler. Examples of this happening among the forest states themselves are well authenticated – the diffusion of Benin swords of state and chieftaincy titles is one among many – so there is no reason to suppose that a similar exchange did not take place between states of the forest and those of the savannah. The period when Ghana dominated the western Sudan may have witnessed such a transmission of rites and institutions between centres of power in the savannah and the forest, just as high-priced commodities like copper and salt passed between them at that time.

During the twelfth and thirteenth centuries the expansion of the peoples of the savannah towards the forest is indicated by the importance of trade in kola, gold and copper. The Mandingo or Wangara, as well as the Hausa, had early contacts with the forest people – contacts which were military as well as commercial.[12]

An example of state evolution, apparently uninfluenced to any important extent by outside forces, can be found in the conversion of the Ijo autonomous, stateless village into a community with the characteristics of a state. In the fishing villages of the eastern Niger delta, headmen acquired the significant title of *amanyanabo* ('owner of the town'); the need to sell their fish and salt in exchange for foodstuffs which they could not grow themselves stimulated the trade of these villages with the Ijo and Ibo of the interior, and this trade, in turn, strengthened the authority of state institutions. The village grew into a city, whose chief became king or 'owner of the town'.

The Yoruba

The most important complex of states was that associated with the Yoruba-speaking peoples, for it extended from Atakpame in the west to Owo in the east, from Ijebu and Ode Itsekiri in the south to Oyo in the north. Its origins are less easily discerned than those of the Ijo states because the prestige attaching to two of the Yoruba states – Ife and Oyo – has effectively coloured tradition in the others. For example, it has been suggested that the claim of the Popo to Ife ancestry may date only from their conquest by Oyo in the eighteenth century, when it became important for the conquerors to establish the link with Ife in order to justify their rule over a 'Yoruba' people.[13] Obviously all claims to an Ife origin, whether made by peoples or dynasties, cannot be taken at their face value.

Again, it is instructive to turn to the Ijo states, where we find numerous claims to a Benin origin. Of these it has been said:

12. It is almost certain that as early as the ninth or tenth century copper from Takedda reached Ife and Benin as well as Igbo-Ukwu.

13. R. C. C. Law, 1973.

> The claims to Benin and other distant places of origin, in fact, reflect a peculiar attitude to origins among the Ijo, that is, the deep prejudices against individuals and groups ignorant of their antecedents. Accordingly, where a group no longer remembers a prior place of origin, it is likely to choose one that was reputed powerful, old and distant enough to pose no danger to its autonomy.[14]

Such a cherishing of antecedents is not in any way peculiar to the Ijo; similar considerations almost certainly influenced the Yoruba and many other peoples who have been moved to claim an Ife origin. In some places the installation of a ruler from Ife, or indeed from another Yoruba state, seems to have led the whole population to claim Ife descent.[15]

If we accept that the original homelands of the Yoruba were the areas covered by the central and south-eastern groups of dialects, we have to look there for the origins of Yoruba state institutions. The claims of Ife to have been the first Yoruba state are clearly impressive. Numerous extant versions of the legend of Oduduwa, the founder of that state, including even those derived from Oyo, all acknowledge the primacy of Ife, and there are no rival legends which seek to claim that distinction for any other state. Radiocarbon dates for charcoal from the Ita Yemoo site in the town lend support for this idea, since they range from +960 to +1160 and are earlier than those for any other urban Yoruba site.[16] A further consideration favouring the Ife claim is the relative proximity of the town to the northern limit of the forest, which could have exposed its inhabitants earlier than others to pressure from savannah-dwelling peoples.

Origins

According to Ife legend, a first generation of Yoruba states arose under the grandchildren of Oduduwa, who had migrated from Ife; these states were Owu, Ketu, Benin, Ila, Sabe, Popo and Oyo. It is, however, highly unlikely that they all came into being at the same time and in the manner described in the legend. The case of Popo has already been commented upon. The list of Sabe kings contains only twenty-one names, compared with the forty-nine remembered in Ketu and the forty-seven of Ife. On the other hand, Ijebu, which is not numbered among the company of primary Yoruba states of legend, appears to be one of the oldest, having a list of fifty-two rulers. Clearly there is still much to be learned about the order and manner in which these states came into being.

The typical Yoruba state was small, often comprising no more than one town and its surrounding villages. In recent centuries there were no

14. Alagoa, op. cit., p. 187.

15. A study of place-names would help to throw light on the origin of states. At present it is a field of inquiry almost entirely dominated by folk etymology.

16. It must be admitted that there are few archaeological excavations of Yoruba sites.

fewer than sixteen or seventeen kingdoms in the Ekiti area alone, and there is no reason to believe that the units had ever been substantially fewer and larger. The Egbado towns seem never to have constituted themselves into a larger state or federation, whereas the Egba, like the Ijebu, formed a federation of small states rather than a centralized kingdom. The 128-km course of the *eredo* earthquake may well delimit the territory of Jebu proper. Ife itself appears not to have extended its sway over a large area.[17] The Akoko, on the north-eastern fringe of Yoruba influence, evolved no political organization larger than the village.

The striking exception among this congeries of small states was the kingdom of Oyo, and even that developed its 'imperial' character quite late, perhaps in the early seventeenth century. This unique development may be explained by the typical savannah environment in which the Oyo empire flourished, for it permitted greater ease of movement than the forest and hence the effective deployment of cavalry and large troops of foot soldiers over comparatively great distances. Oyo in fact may have been more influenced in its development by the neighbouring savannah states of Borgu and Nupe than by the Yoruba states of the forest. It had to establish itself first against these northern rivals before it was free to turn to conquest among the Yoruba. On the basis of the Oyo king-list, a founding date early in the fifteenth century has been suggested for the kingdom. An abandonment of the capital under Nupe pressure in the second quarter of the sixteenth century is fairly well established. The earliest archaeological evidence so far discovered seems to relate to a period after the capital had been reoccupied around the end of that century. In short, it is unlikely that Oyo had attained any great consequence by the end of the fifteenth century.

Ife

Considering the central place it occupies in the general history of the Yoruba, we know surprisingly little about the history of Ife. After the comparative wealth of detail attached to the legendary founder of the state, Oduduwa, and his immediate successors, we encounter a very spare and broken narrative in the oral traditions for subsequent ages. The archaeological record has done something to fill the gaps, but this research is in its infancy. A first phase in the history of the state, opening around the eleventh century, is characterized by a scattered settlement pattern, the widespread use of floors made of potsherds set on edge, a glass-bead industry and a very fine terracotta art which specialized in the production of naturalistic figures, especially human heads. Because of this latter feature, a link has sometimes been posited between the cultures of Ife and Nok, despite the thousand years which stand between them. More significant

17. Adetugbo, op. cit., p. 193.

PLATE 14.1 *Terracotta head (Owo, Nigeria)*

is the very close resemblance which the terracotta art of Ife bears to that discovered in other centres of Yoruba culture. Heads in a style related to that of Ife have been found at Ikinrun and Ire near Oshogbo, at Idanre near Ikare, and most recently and interestingly at Owo, where a large number of terracotta sculptures have been excavated in a fifteenth-century context (see Plate 14.1). This wide distribution of the style may indicate the extent of Ife influence, but it may also be that it marks the spread of a cultural trait among the Yoruba associated with religious rites rather than with Ife kingship. In other words, Ife is only one among a number of centres which produced such works and the exclusive identification of this art style with Ife is becoming steadily less tenable.

The potsherd floors, which in Ife have often been discovered in association with terracotta figures, are likewise not a unique feature of that city; similar floors have been found at Owo, Ifaki, Ikerin, Ede, Itaji Ekiti, Ikare and much further afield at Ketu and Dassa Zoume in the Republic of Benin and in the Kabrais district of Togo. At Yelwa they occur in a site that was occupied until *c.* +700, at Daima near Lake Chad among eighth-century deposits and in Benin in a fourteenth-century context. The earliest potsherd floors so far discovered in Ife date to about +1100 and the latest bear maize-cob impressions, which means that they cannot be earlier than the sixteenth century.[18] The subsequent disappearance of the floors, and apparently also of the terracotta art, probably reflects some catastrophe which overwhelmed Ife in the sixteenth century. The twenty-five Ife 'bronze' heads (they are in fact made of brass and copper), which bear so striking a stylistic resemblance to the terracottas, may have been made in the years immediately before the disaster, when imports of brass and copper by the Portuguese had made casting metal relatively plentiful. We can at present only surmise the nature of the events which destroyed this culture; conquest by an alien dynasty seems the most likely explanation.

If the above interpretation of Ife history is correct, the dynasty which now reigns there is that which established itself in the sixteenth century, built the palace on its present site and threw up the earliest of the walls around the central area of the town. Perhaps the new dynasty has preserved some of the political and social institutions of its predecessor, but we cannot assume that the earlier regime resembled the later in its political arrangements any more than it did in its art, so that it is impossible to describe with any certainty the form of government which existed in Ife before the sixteenth century. The question also arises whether the relationship with Ife claimed for many Yoruba states refers to the earlier or later period of Ife history. Because the modern pattern of installation ceremonies and royal insignia are so similar throughout most of Yoruba-

18. Maize originated in the New World and was introduced into Africa by the Portuguese in the sixteenth century.

land, including Ife, and because these insignia bear little resemblance to those worn by supposedly royal figures in the earlier phase of Ife history, we can conclude that modern Yoruba kingship derives from the later phase, even though states may originally have been formed on the pattern of early Ife.

It is possible that the rise and fall of states in the western Sudan in the fifteenth and sixteenth centuries directly influenced state formation in the Guinea forest zone. The fifteenth and sixteenth centuries saw the formation or, more probably, the reconstitution of several major states to the north of those with which we are concerned in this chapter; the most important were the kingdoms of Borgu, Idah and Kwararafa.[19] Their appearance and expansion may well help to account for the upheavals which happened about that time in the adjacent southern states. We know that the Nupe drove the Yoruba from Old Oyo early in the sixteenth century, and that, before they returned to their capital three-quarters of a century later, the Oyo had reorganized their military forces so as to give greater prominence to the cavalry, the striking force of armies in the savannah states. From the Nupe the Oyo borrowed the *Egungun* cult of ancestors, and certain features of their revivified state may have come from the same source.

The kingdom of Benin

Benin was the first state that the Portuguese visited on the coast; they soon established diplomatic as well as trade relations. Situated south-east of Ife, Benin probably became a kingdom early on, perhaps in the twelfth century. A transformation, in some ways resembling that which befell Ife in the sixteenth century, appears to have occurred in Benin in the fifteenth. Although some form of state may have existed among the Edo before the thirteenth century, the definitive establishment of a kingdom is attributed by both Benin and Yoruba tradition to Oranyan, a scion of the prestigious ruling family of Ife, who is said to have been sent to Benin by the king, his father, probably around 1300, at the invitation of a number of the Benin chiefs.

Tradition depicts the first rulers of the Ife line as strictly limited in their authority by the power of the hereditary order of indigenous chiefs known as the *ozama*. However, it is possible that this order received its titles and organization from the dynasty itself, for the titles bear a resemblance to some of the commonest Yoruba titles – a feature which can only be explained by imitation on one side or the other.[20] The six

19. We know little about the relations between savannah and forest. In view of the importance of trade, which is becoming more and more evident, it is possible that relations then were closer than today. Cf. T. Shaw, 1970, p. 254.

20. Unless both Yoruba and Benin titles derived from a common outside source. The Edo titles are *oliha, edonen, ezomo, ero, eholo nire* and *oltoton*. Their Yoruba counterparts are *olisa, odofin, ojomo, aro, osolo* and *oloton*.

ozama chiefs appear to have played a political role very similar to that later attributed to the seven holders of the title of *oyomesi* of Oyo. On Horton's hypothesis of state formation we might expect such variations on the same basic pattern, of a balance of power between a king and chiefs representing descent groups, to have been very widespread. Tradition has it that the fourth ruler of the Benin dynasty contrived to alter the balance in his favour after an armed struggle with the *ozama* chiefs. He thereupon moved to a more spacious palace, where he organized a sizeable court and created a number of non-hereditary titles for its leading men; but still he and his successors were hardly more than *primus inter pares* in face of the powerful *ozama*.

In the fifteenth century a major upheaval transformed this limited monarchy into an autocracy and the small state into a large kingdom. Tradition attributes the changes to a ruler known as Ewuare, who acquired the throne by ousting and killing a younger brother; in the course of the struggle much of the capital is said to have been destroyed. This explanation of events in terms of an elder/legitimate versus younger/usurping brother relationship looks suspiciously like an attempt to preserve the necessary line of legitimacy in a dynastic genealogy, which in all other respects loses credibility at this point. One is rather inclined to see in the violence of Ewuare's accession, and in the fundamental changes which followed, a conquest of Benin by an alien power.

The city

Ewuare rebuilt his capital to a new plan and gave it the name of Edo, which it has borne to this day.[21] In the centre of the city a huge ditch and rampart were thrown up, cutting across older structures as did the city wall of Ife. Within the rampart a broad avenue separated the palace from the 'town' – the quarters which housed numerous guilds of craftsmen and ritual specialists who served the ruler. The palace itself was organized into three departments – the wardrobe, the ruler's personal attendants and the harem – each with a staff graded into three ranks analogous to the age grades of the Edo villages. Each of the 'town' guilds had a similar grade structure and was affiliated to the appropriate palace department. Members of the senior palace grades bore individual titles conferred for life. There are grounds for believing that Ewuare associated all his free-born subjects with the palace organization by making a period of retainer service in its lower ranks obligatory. Having completed their service, the majority of the men returned to their villages. The personal attachment of all free-born subjects to the ruler was further emphasized by the facial

21. The name 'Benin', by which the city and kingdom are known to all non-Edo, is something of a mystery. Folk etymology does not explain it satisfactorily. Possibly the first Portuguese to arrive on the coast picked up the name *beni*, meaning 'water dwellers', from the Ijo and applied it in error to the Edo.

scarification which Ewuare introduced and by dubbing them 'slaves of the *oba*'.

Ewuare's government

The government of Benin, as refashioned by Ewuare, rested upon the ruler and three bodies of titled chiefs: the hereditary *ozama*, the palace chiefs, and an order of 'town' chiefs created by Ewuare himself. These senior members of the hierarchy formed the council, which deliberated with the ruler on any matter he cared to lay before it. Each of them was also entrusted with the supervision of a number of the tributary units into which the kingdom was divided. Junior grades furnished messengers, soldiers and other executants of the royal will. Another important constitutional development at this time was the application of the principle of primogeniture to succession to the throne; Ewuare gave his heir apparent the title of *edaiken*, which he added to the *ozama* order. In the realm of religion, too, Ewuare, who is remembered in Benin as a great magician, gave greater potency to the mystical powers attributed to the ruler by introducing the annual *Igwe* festival, during which his vital forces were renewed.

Ewuare's other achievement – the creation of a large kingdom – involved him in constant war with his neighbours. Leading his armies in person, he conquered other Edo peoples, many of the Ibo living west of the Niger, and some eastern Yoruba, including, it is said, the towns of Akure and Owo. The more distant conquests managed to maintain a degree of independence by paying tribute to Benin; others were subjected to governments modelled on that of Benin, with princes of the Ewuare dynasty at their head; only those within a radius of some 64 km of the capital were brought under the direct rule of Benin. In this central region – the kingdom proper – the king alone could impose the death penalty.

Tradition does not record any fundamental military reform associated with Ewuare which would explain his successful career of expansion. The secret of his victories may therefore lie in the manner in which he mustered the service of his subjects. Not only could he thus have assembled forces superior to those of his opponents, but his very success in incorporating a large proportion of his able-bodied subjects in a war machine would have necessitated repeated forays to sustain it with booty and tribute.

For more than a century a series of warrior rulers who succeeded Ewuare led regular military expeditions into the frontier provinces and beyond. Most of the northern Edo peoples were brought under the sway of Benin. The eastward expansion of Yoruba influence recoiled before a powerful Edo incursion into Yoruba territory. Pushing beyond Owo and Akure, the Benin armies brought large areas of Ekiti into a tributary relationship. Ijebu, one of the most ancient of Yoruba states, is reputed in Benin to have fallen temporarily under Edo suzerainty. Although this claim is not confirmed in Ijebu, certain features of Ijebu government – the *ifore* palace association, for example – bear a strong resemblance to those of Benin. Other parallels of this kind may be found in the adjacent Yoruba state of Ondo. Conquest by Benin could explain these common features, but it is also possible that some Yoruba states voluntarily accepted, or even asked for, a ruler from Benin after Ewuare had established the prestige of his dynasty. This happened with the Itsekiri, an eastern branch of the Yoruba, who received Ewuare's grandson Iginua as their ruler. Iginua settled among them with a number of Edo followers and established a kingdom on the Benin pattern, which acknowledged the seniority of the parent dynasty over many centuries.

The character of the Benin state as reformed by Ewuare has here been examined in what may seem undue detail, partly because of its crucial importance for Edo history, partly because it had so much influence upon all neighbouring peoples and partly because it is the only state in this region for which we have any reasonably certain knowledge of institutions prior to the sixteenth century. That our knowledge of the early history of Benin is so much more detailed than that of any other state is due to the richness of the oral tradition preserved by the court, to the information gathered by European visitors in the sixteenth and seventeenth centuries, and to the archaeological investigations carried out in the city during the past two decades.

Archaeology has confirmed the traditions which assign the construction of the great wall of Ewuare and a major rebuilding of the palace to the fifteenth century (see Plate 14.2). It has also shed light on the development of the renowned Benin art of *cire perdue* (lost-wax) casting in brass and bronze. All brass objects found in a pre-sixteenth-century context prove to have been made by a smithing not a casting process. Although the *cire-perdue* technique may have been known at an earlier date, it would seem, both from the archaeological evidence and from a stylistic study of the very large body of Benin brasswork still in existence, that only in the sixteenth century, with the import of large quantities of European brass, did this art become important.[22]

Ife art and the Gulf bronzes

Until now, African art has been considered almost solely from an aesthetic point of view; little attention has been paid to the sociological context of its creation. With the Ife–Benin civilization, we have the opportunity to study an African art in its historico-sociological context.

22. One of the best-known pieces attributed to the early period of Benin brass casting is the head of an *iyoba* or 'queen-mother'. If the identification is correct, the head cannot be earlier than the first decades of the sixteenth century, when the ruler Esigie created the title of *iyoba* for his mother.

PLATE 14.2 *An excavation into the deepest part of the Benin city walls*

In general, wood sculpture dominates black African art, so that most of the works that stir the enthusiasm of aesthetes are of comparatively recent origin; the Ife–Benin civilization is the brilliant exception, in that one finds works of art in terracotta and in bronze which accounts for the particular importance of this region in the general evolution of black African art.

We noted earlier that objects in brass were either forged or made by the *cire-perdue* technique, which was known at Fié probably earlier than the thirteenth century. In the light of the most recent research, a natural link unites the terracotta art illustrated by naturalistic figurines, particularly human heads, with the culture of Nok, which goes back to the Iron Age (the fifth century before the Christian era). This is most important and underlines the widespread diffusion of the Nok culture, which cannot be restricted merely to the Bauchi plateaux; moreover, we have evidence of

PLATE 14.3 *Benin plaque, depicting the ceremonial slaughter of a cow by Oba's attendants*

PLATE 14.4 *Benin: bronze flute-player*

exchanges and continuing contacts between the countries of the savannah and those of the forest to the south. Thus the well-known bronzes and naturalistic brass of Ife and Benin are the culmination of an artistic evolution begun at least as early as the Iron Age in a vast cultural region.

We shall spare the reader all the theories elaborated by the colonialists, who sought an extra-African source for these masterpieces of a naturalism so pure that a European specialist in Yoruba art writes: 'If one examines the head reproduced [it is of an Oni of Ife of the thirteenth century], one is tempted at first sight to exclaim "this is surely a Renaissance Masterpiece".'[23]

It was the German Leo Frobenius who discovered the sculptures of Ife in the course of a journey in Africa in 1910. But at the end of the last century an event occurred which cannot be passed over in silence: Ife was sacked by an English column and the city was pillaged by the conquerors, who took to England many sculptures from the Ife palace.

Leo Frobenius brought the masterpieces of Ife to the attention of the cultured world; soon artists and ethnographers launched into the most extraordinary theories to explain the so-called miracle of Ife.[24] In 1939, an important group of bronzes was discovered not far from the palace of the Oni at Ife; since then, a number of other discoveries have been made in Ife as well as in Benin.

Characteristics and development of Benin art

Bernard Fagg conducted excavations at Abiri in 1949, not far from Ife.[25] He discovered three terracotta heads in a tomb at Abiri: one was completely naturalistic whereas the other two were stylized in the extreme. As William Fagg has noted, there is 'in Ife's culture a strange phenomenon, extremely rare in the history of world culture. It is the coexistence in the same culture of a completely naturalistic art with one that is almost completely abstract, a phenomenon which is inconceivable in the classic periods of the Renaissance in Europe.' He considers one of the heads to be the best example of realistic or naturalistic Ife style. All the measurements are exact and 'one can even see the occipital bump'. The face is calm with an interior equilibrium that confers upon it a striking density of expression. Next to it, in the same tomb, were the two other heads, of an extreme stylism:

> two holes represent the eyes and a horizontal slash the mouth. The stylism is emphasized ... and yet these three objects, four in the same tomb, are of the same origin ... Matter and firing tech-

23. W. B. Fagg, 1963, p. 105.

24. W. B. Fagg writes: 'It has often been said that these bronzes were the work of the Egyptians, or a wandering Roman or Greek artist, even of a Renaissance Italian or of Portuguese Jesuits.' ibid., p. 105.

25. See, for example, B. E. B. Fagg, 1956, 1959, 1969 and 1977.

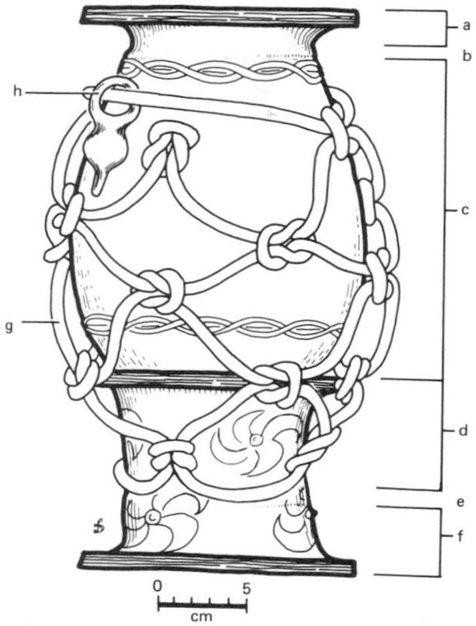

(a) rim section
(b) run-in between rim section and body of pot
(c) body of pot
(d) upper part of the stand
(e) run-in between upper and lower parts of the stand
(f) lower part of the stand
(g) rope-work cage
(h) travelling handle

FIG. 14.3 *Schematic drawing of the bronze roped pot (after T. Shaw, 1970)*

PLATE 14.5 *Bronze roped pot*

PLATE 14.6 *Bronze altar stand*

PLATE 14.7 *Ritual calabash*

> nique and the state of preservation are all identical. It is evident that one must attribute the two very different expressions of the human spirit not to a race foreign to Africa but rather to a mystical belief of the ancient Yoruba religion.[26]

It is certain that Ife and Benin art, from the beginning, had a basically religious character.

What do these heads represent? For the most part, they represent the Oni, the religious chief of Ife. The works were executed after the Oni's death, to be placed in his tomb. At the palace museum of the Oni are exposed:

> hundreds of fragments of heads in terra cotta of the same style as the bronzes, some of them artistically the equal or even superior to the beautiful bronze busts and almost all these heads and all these fragments were discovered, not in the course of organized excavations but by pure luck in two or three of the hundred temples of Ife. Many of them are obviously for ritual purposes for this art was closely linked to the life of the community.[27]

Tradition holds that the Oba of Benin requested and received from the Oni a skilled sculptor who taught the craftsmen of Benin the technique of modelling bronzes; thus Ife is truly the mother city whence came the religion and art by which one honours the ancestors. The worship of ancestors was the basis of traditional religion and Ife created an art to perpetuate the remembrance of 'those who watch over the living'. The great number of figurines found in the temples suggests also that certain figurines were the objects of worship in the temples and were not intended to be buried. But this art was not restricted to the Ife–Benin areas. Discoveries have been made not only in the delta but even to the north, at the borders of Nupe.

Igbo-Ukwu

Discovered in 1939 in the east of Nigeria, the site of Igbo-Ukwu was explored in 1959 by Professor Thurstan Shaw; some 800 bronze pieces have been brought to light which are completely different from the Ife–Benin bronzes. Igbo-Ukwu is an urban complex in the middle of which were the palace and temples. Different buildings have been uncovered: a great room where plates and objects of worship and treasures were stored; a burial chamber of a great priest, richly decorated; and an enormous hole in which were deposited pottery, bones and other objects.

26. W. B. Fagg, op. cit., p. 106.
27. ibid, p. 104.

Certainly there are some differences between the bronzes discovered at Igbo-Ukwu and the works of art of Ife. Nevertheless, a number of shared traits show that the two centres were part of the same culture. Indeed, we are in the presence, as at Ife, of a ritual monarchy.[28] The virtuosity of the Igbo-Ukwu artists is remarkable, with regard to both terracotta and bronze. They manipulated the materials with a skill that resulted in the form desired and a richness of detail which is just short of affectation. Bronze bowls in the form of gourds and ceramic vases ornamented with serpentine motifs are handled with mastery (see Plates 14.5, 14.8–14.9, 14.11–14.13).

It is believed that Igbo-Ukwu was the religious capital of a very vast kingdom, and that the treasures were stored there under the keeping of a priest-king, Ezi Nzi.[29] Information is lacking on the culture of Igbo-Ukwu; inquiries among those who guard oral tradition are continuing, and archaeologists see an extension of the area of bronze manufacture. Nevertheless, Igbo-Ukwu, with its ritual kingship and abundance of *cire-perdue* castings, appears to contradict the foregoing hypothesis about the development of brass casting, and indeed much of what has so far been postulated about state formation; on the evidence of radiocarbon dates, this highly sophisticated culture had evolved by the ninth century among Ibo peoples who otherwise maintained a 'stateless' form of society. In other words, the Igbo-Ukwu culture antedates those of Ife and Benin, and all others of comparable complexity so far discovered in the forest region, by at least two centuries.

If it were not for the radiocarbon dates, one would confidently have ascribed a sixteenth or seventeenth-century date to Igbo-Ukwu on the evidence of the material found there. The nearby Onitsha kingship was founded about that time under Benin influence; the Igala state, which is said to have influenced the development of chiefship among the Umueri – the group to which Igbo-Ukwu belongs – did not itself come into existence before the fifteenth century. How much reliance can be placed upon the radiocarbon dates? When they are obtained from charcoal they need to be treated with great caution, because a surface deposit of charcoal may already be ancient when it becomes buried in a pit or any other form of excavation. Moreover, a fundamental query has been raised about the reliability of radiocarbon dates in the vicinity of the Equator.[30] One of the five Igbo-Ukwu dates, it should be noted, comes out at 1445 ± 70; this agrees very well with a date of 1495 ± 95 for an excavation 24 km to the east, which yielded some bronze bells cast in a style similar to that of Igbo-Ukwu. Thus Igbo-Ukwu poses a conundrum of great significance which has still to be solved, either by a refinement of the

28. T. Shaw, op. cit.
29. See F. Willett, 1967, pp. 172–3.
30. P. Ozanne, 1969.

PLATE 14.8 *Large bronze bowl, viewed from above*

PLATE 14.9 *Large upturned bronze bowl, viewed from side*

PLATE 14.10 *Heavy knotted bronze wristlet*

PLATE 14.11 *Pottery: general view*

PLATE 14.12 *Pottery: general view*

PLATE 14.13 *Pottery: detail*

technique of radiocarbon dating or by a general revision of current hypotheses on the evolution of states in this region.[31]

The Nupe bronzes

Further north along the Niger, between Busa and the confluence of the Benue, bronzes have been discovered at several sites (see Fig. 14.4 and Plate 14.15). They are called the 'Tsoede bronzes', after the founder of the Nupe kingdom in the sixteenth century. According to tradition, these bronzes were brought from Idah, capital of Igala, by Tsoede. It is further said that Tsoede was accompanied by smiths, who taught the people of Nupe the *cire-perdue* technique.[32]

Figurines have been found at Tada, Jebba and Gurap. Each of these centres has its own style, but there is a certain resemblance which testifies to the influence of Ife or Benin, as F. Willett writes: 'In the history of the forging of bronze throughout the valley of the Niger, there is not merely one or two threads to unravel. It is rather a piece of fabric which will demand a long time to separate the threads of the warp and the woof.'[33]

Thurstan Shaw has indicated some directions for research to find the source of the copper used throughout the region of the lower Niger.[34] According to Shaw, great attention should be devoted to the study of north–south relations between the region and the Arab-Muslim world; trade could have started before the tenth century and it was precisely to control this trade route from south to north that the centre of power moved from Ife to Old Oyo. Thus the bronzes found at Jebba/Tada are in the zone of contact, on the Niger.

To sum up, considerable research is necessary to establish a chronological table and to understand better the different schools of bronze. The region produced no copper; the nearest source was the mine of Takedda. The dossier on relations between Niger, Benue and the Sudan is far from closed.

31. Several dates obtained with carbon dating have been furnished: 1075 ± 130 (tenth–thirteenth century); 1100 ± 110 (tenth–thirteenth century); 1110 ± 145 (tenth–thirteenth century). The chronology of the whole region must be re-examined. From all the studies, it is evident that the Niger delta had close links with the Nupe to the north and beyond there with the savannah of central Sudan, through which came the copper from Takedda to Ife–Benin and Igbo-Ukwu. The great currents of trade between the savannah and the forest probably existed far back in antiquity.

32. King Tsoede is a legendary personage. One tradition says he arrived at Nupe in a bronze pirogue. He represents a synthesis: he is said to have been born in 1463; in 1493 he was taken as a slave to Idah; in 1523, he fled that city to become king of Nupe in 1531 and died in 1591. That means he would have lived 128 years.

33. The period in question is obviously mythic, according to Willett. 'It is possible that Tsoede belonged only to the end of the period, or perhaps to the very beginning and that his existence was "stretched" to fill the "gap" which separates him from the historic king', op. cit., p. 212.

34. T. Shaw, 1973.

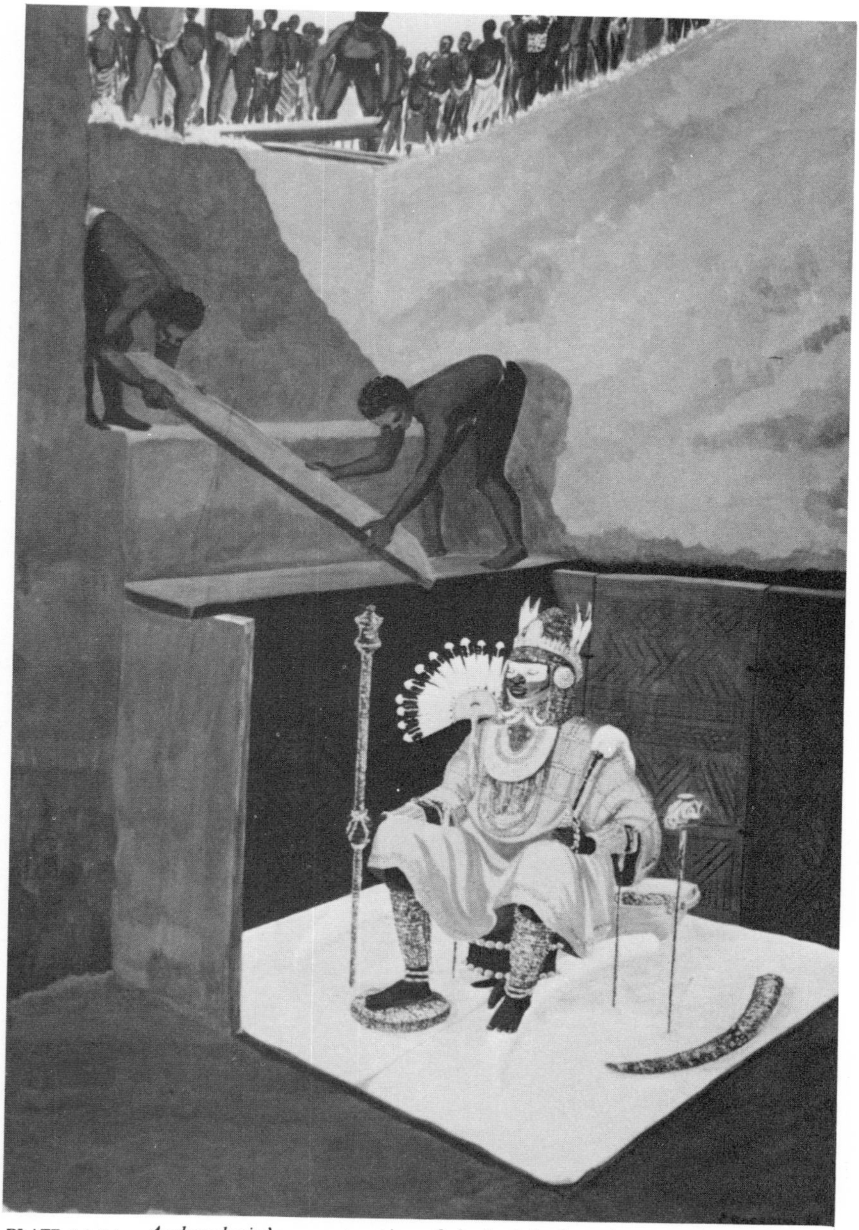

PLATE 14.14 *Archaeologist's reconstruction of the burial of a ruler at Igbo-Ukwu*

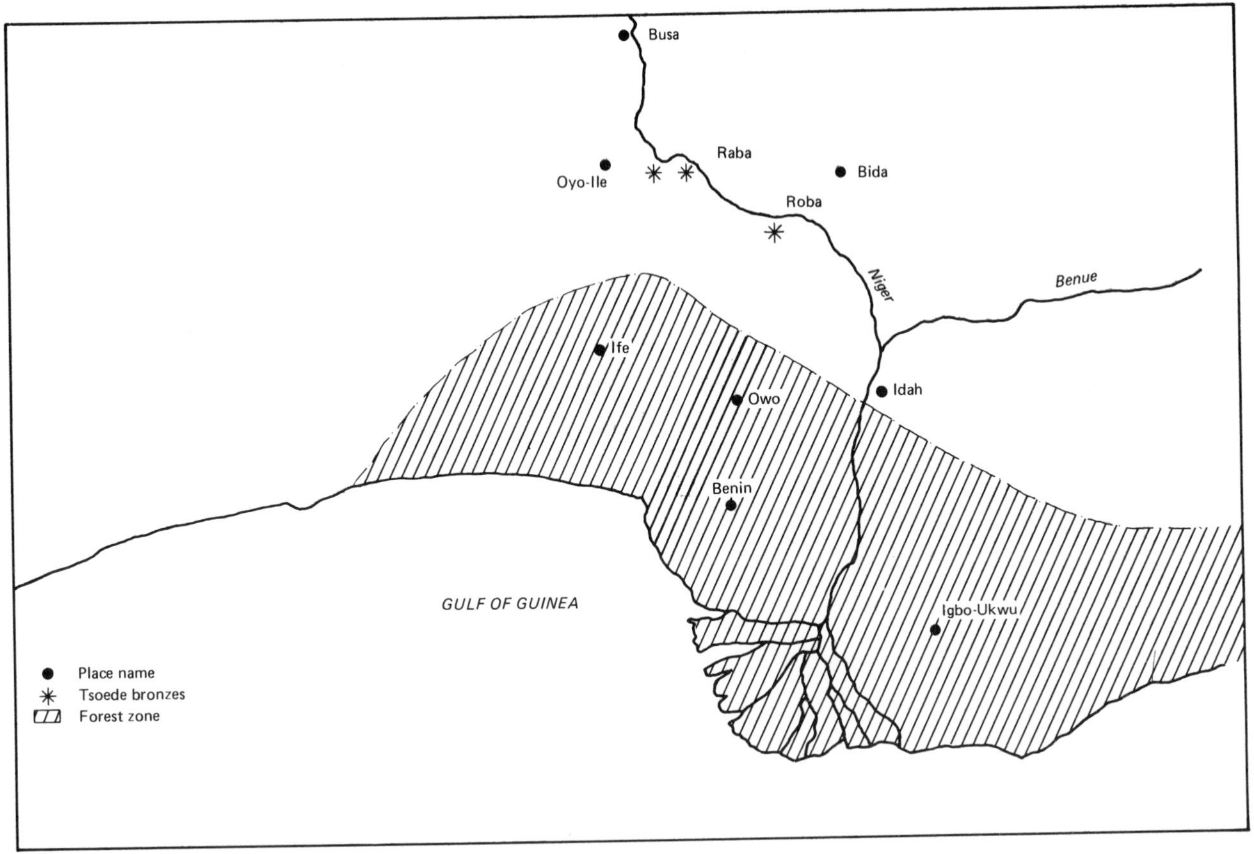

FIG. 14.4 *Sites of the Tsoede bronzes*
Source: T. Shaw in 'A note on trade of Tsoede bronzes', West African Journal of Archaeology (*Vol. 3, 1973*), *p. 234*

PLATE 14.15 *Bronze of a Tsoede seated figure*

Conclusion

At the end of the fifteenth century, when the Portuguese reached the coast, Oyo and Benin were the most important states; there were also independent cities which were quite well structured and which incorporated kinships in less complex governments. Benin and Oyo were on the way to becoming powerful, expansionist kingdoms. The process of state formation had quickened the tempo of cultural interaction between peoples, encouraging the diffusion of institutions, ceremonial practices and objects, religious cults and probably technology. The technique of *cire-perdue* casting, for example, was a jealously guarded secret associated with divine kingship, and yet it became widely diffused.

Economic relationships, too, acquired a new intensity and complexity. States required and permitted a greater degree of economic specialization than the stateless community: the palace of the ruler, with its demands for provisions and specialized services, played a key role in stimulating this development. Also, states were better equipped to organize external trade, to provide markets, to arrange the collection and transport of produce, and to ensure the safety of traders travelling over long distances. Ijo trading states were sending large canoes far into the interior to exchange the salt they manufactured for the foodstuffs they could not produce for themselves. The king of Benin was able to organize a large-scale trade in slaves, ivory and pepper. Ijebu cloth found its way into markets over a wide area. Oyo, owing to its frontier position between the forest and savannah states, controlled much of the trade that passed between the two zones.

So it happened that when the Portuguese first appeared on the coast at the end of the fifteenth century they found at Ijebu, Benin and among the Ijo well-established states with economies already adapted to the needs of international trade. How the challenge of commercial, cultural and political contact with European states was met becomes one of the major themes in the history of all the peoples of this region over the next four centuries.

15

Egypt and the Muslim world

J. C. GARCIN

To the superficial observer, the time span falling between the end of the twelfth and the beginning of the sixteenth century may appear to be the least 'African' in Egyptian history. The regime established in Cairo in +1171 took over the reins from the Fatimid caliphate, which had originated in the Maghrib and found its definitive axis of power in the Nile valley. The country then became the main source of strength of an empire – first Ayyubid, then Mamluk – spreading as far as the Euphrates and the passes of the Anatolian Taurus and conducting its chief enterprises outside Africa; at other times even the status of a province merged in an Ammayad, Abbasid or Ottoman complex seemed to cut Egypt off from the African continent less completely. All this may be true, but this period in which the predominance of Egyptian power was asserting itself in the Middle East was also a time during which the routes across the Sahara were bringing the princes of Kanem, Mali and Songhay to Cairo on their way to the Muslim holy places of the Ḥidjāz, while Egyptian merchants were taking the same routes to the centre of Africa.

There is no doubt that these particular centuries of Egypt's history were those which counted in the evolution of a great part of Africa, that part which was to fall under the sway of Islam. Within Ayyubid and Mamluk Egypt, Sunni Islam took its final form, and from it most African Muslims drew in various degrees their principles of conduct and their framework of thought. Nor is the ancient Islamic heart of the Maghrib less indebted to this Egyptian period, for the disappearance of the Shī'ite caliphate from the Nile valley in some ways brought closer together the Maghrib and the Muslim East – the traditional fount of culture and religion – thus contributing to the uniform aspect of Islam in Africa. Of that Islam, Cairo was the major school. All the political and cultural developments arising thereafter on the banks of the Nile were of concern to much of Africa: Ethiopia and the central and western Sudan.

The resurgence of Egypt after the fall of the Fatimids (Ṣalāḥ al-Dīn and the rise of a new political territory)

The lands which constituted the territorial base of the Ayyubid (and later, give or take a few regions, the Mamluk) sultanate were brought together under the authority of Ṣalāḥ al-Dīn Yūsuf ibn Ayyūb (known in the western world as Saladin), in his struggle against the crusaders. It is on record that neither the Abbasid caliph of Baghdad, then dominated by the Turkish Seldjuḳ amirs of Iraq, who had recently arrived from the Asian steppes to serve the caliphate and were already divided, nor the Fatimid caliph of Cairo, also under the sway of his military chiefs and threatened by the Abbasid campaign of reconquest conducted by the Seldjuḳs in Syria, could or would resist the implantation of westerners in Palestine and on the upper Euphrates in the final years of the eleventh century, or their settlement there throughout the twelfth century between the two caliphates. The reactions of the Muslims, who at first did not apprehend the nature of the implantation, had been slow, and the spirit of the *djihād* (holy war) hardly survived in Islam; the counter-offensive undertaken by the amirs who governed Mosul had led to the reunification of the reconquered areas of the upper Euphrates with the territories of inland Syria (from Aleppo to Damascus) under the authority of the Turk Nūr al-Dīn, one of their number; but the Egyptian caliphs sustained these efforts of their rivals only from time to time.

War against the Latin kingdom of Jerusalem would doubtless have lasted longer had not the rivalry for real power – that is, the vizierate – in Egypt itself led the competing chiefs of the Fatimid armies to seek armed help from outside, from Damascus and Jerusalem. It was to ward off a definitive installation of the troops brought from Jerusalem into Egypt that the caliph himself agreed to the elevation to the Fatimid vizierate of Shirkuh, the man who led the army corps sent from Damascus, an amir of Kurd origin, who after his sudden demise was replaced by his nephew, Salāḥ al-Dīn (1169). Two years later, this last vizier of the Egyptian Fatimids proclaimed the fall of the Shīʾite caliphate; the unity of allegiance to the Abbasids, under the authority of Nūr al-Dīn, was restored in the East in opposition to the crusader states. The political dimensions of the new Muslim empire had begun to appear.

In point of fact the theoretical submission of the Egyptian amir to the prince of Damascus would not have prevented the rivalry of the two powers within the Abbasid sphere. In anticipation of a conflict, Ṣalāḥ al-Dīn even sought to ensure a possible line of retreat to the south: first in Nubia, the attempted conquest of which he soon abandoned, then in Yemen, which he rapidly mastered in 1174 as the future advance post of Egyptian prosperity on the shores of the Indian Ocean. In that same year (1174), however, Nūr al-Dīn died, leaving as his heirs individuals unqualified to carry on his task. Within months Ṣalāḥ al-Dīn was in Damascus; by 1182 his sway extended as far as Aleppo; in 1186 the last territories of the Euphrates basin, which had hitherto held out, were added to the realm; and in the following year the victory of Hattīn and the reconquest of Jerusalem brought the existence of the crusader kingdom to an end. Real unity had been established, but this time Egypt lay at the centre of the new empire; until then barely involved in the struggle against the crusaders, now it was to become the main focus of resistance to the West and the target of the onslaughts to come.

The ideology of the new power

These events and the personality of Ṣalāḥ al-Dīn, for whom the rebirth of Islam represented a total political ideal, played a great part in the 'reconstruction' of Egypt – for it was indeed a reconstruction of Muslim Egypt that was undertaken after the fall of the Fatimids. Shī'ism had not spread greatly among Egyptian Muslims except perhaps in Upper Egypt, where it took some time to disappear; but, as it was considered to be both a political schism and a betrayal of true Islam, it was held largely responsible for the weak state in which the Muslim world found itself in the face of western attack. What was needed was the firm establishment within the political structure, within society and within men's minds, of the Islam of tradition and of the community, the Sunni form. The distant Abbasid caliphs, now regaining genuine political independence in the admittedly narrow frame of the Iraqi regions, by reason of the weakening of their Seldjuḳ overlords, became thenceforth the object of a certain respect. The Mecca pilgrimage, which the existence of the crusader kingdom of Jerusalem had impeded, was made easier for pilgrims by protecting them better against the abuses to which they were exposed at the hands of local authorities in Egypt or the Ḥidjāz, the latter falling increasingly under Egyptian influence; the reputation of Ṣalāḥ al-Dīn thus spread to the westernmost confines of Muslim Africa.

Within Egypt itself, the new power went to great lengths to create a class of men versed in religious, legal and literary disciplines who could provide a solid backing for the Sunni state. The system of teaching in *madrasas*, imported from the Seldjuḳ east, was now installed permanently in Egypt; these were designed essentially for training the reliable men, devoted to Sunni Islam, who were required.[1] To give this undertaking a favourable start, recourse was frequently had to lawyers and teachers originating from militant Muslim circles in Syria and further east; but, little by little, the role of the purely Egyptian leadership became dominant and a social category arose which was qualified to act as a link between governors and people.

1. A small number of *madrasas* did in fact exist before Ṣalāḥ al-Dīn, in Alexandria and old Cairo (al-'Fustāt).

Mystics also made their appearance, not only from the East but also from the Maghrib, especially in Upper Egypt with its Mālikite majority. Living either in groups in convents (*khānkā*) or in solitude in the *ribāts* of Upper Egypt, they undertook to bring about the rebirth of a more orthodox spiritual life among the Muslim population, or more simply to provide them with that elementary religious instruction which was often lacking, especially in the countryside. When the Maghrib mystic Abu 'l-Ḥasan al-Shādhilī settled in Alexandria towards 1244, he was only adding his own efforts to those already expended in building up a Sunni Egypt. Such was the inspiration which provided the underlying motive force for the political endeavour of the Ayyubids, conceived as a form of resistance to the external and internal foes of Islam. It culminated in the creation of sturdy socio-cultural structures which were to survive the regime which had helped to build them.

The Ayyubid peace

The construction of Sunni Egypt, begun under the momentum of the counter-crusade, proceeded in an atmosphere of political détente and more broadly in a time of peace and economic prosperity favoured by the ending of hostilities. The destruction of the kingdom of Jerusalem, with the reduction of the crusader presence in a few strongholds along the coast (1187), was a flash of violence which provoked a vigorous reaction on the part of the European princes in the shape of the Third Crusade, the effects of which Ṣalāḥ al-Dīn had some difficulty in containing. The crusaders, though unable to reconquer Jerusalem, settled once again firmly on the Syrian and Palestinian coasts, and, before his death in 1193, Ṣalāḥ al-Dīn acknowledged this as a *fait accompli*. In reality, the narrow proportions and strategic vulnerability of the coastal belt now held by the westerners reduced from then on the threat implicit in their presence. It was not only military men who were now established but also merchants, who might even contribute to the economic prosperity of the Ayyubid states.

The successors of Ṣalāḥ al-Dīn also sought to ensure peace, though not without murmurings in Muslim circles; among the westerners, however, especially those now settled in the East, awareness of the many benefits of all kinds that would attend the maintenance of the status quo carried more weight than their sharply declining crusading spirit. Aggressive action was still undertaken, such as the establishment of a striking-point at Damietta from 1218 to 1221 (the Fifth Crusade), aimed this time at the heart of the power that inhibited western undertakings. But the Muslims were ready for concessions, going so far as to cede Jerusalem back to the West in 1225, on condition that it remained an open city. As a result of this policy, the Syrian provinces of the Ayyubid empire enjoyed notable prosperity in their relations with the Christian traders on the coast.[2]

Egypt itself also benefited from the peace and was able to increase its profits from a less disturbed trade with the westerners, in addition to the wealth it was deriving both from its traditional agricultural production and from sugar-cane, the cultivation of which was at that time expanding. Like its Fatimid predecessor, the Ayyubid state needed that trade, for it lacked goods as important as iron, structural timber and pitch, all essential for building a war fleet. These goods were sought from the merchants of Venice, Pisa or Genoa, who supplied them despite the religious embargo on the sale of strategic materials likely to be used against the crusaders.[3] Egypt, however, could offer in return the alum needed by textile producers in the West, and above all the valuable products of the Far East.

In this context the Ayyubid state benefited especially from the efforts made by the Fatimid caliphs to bring back to the Red Sea and Nile valley routes the historic Indian Ocean trade which had created the wealth of Graeco-Roman Egypt. In the second half of the eleventh century the spice road had found its way across Egypt, along paths that were to persist for three centuries (see Fig. 15.1). The precious Oriental merchandise, after crossing the Red Sea, was unloaded at the port of ʿAydhāb, carried by caravan as far as the Nile, to Kūs – then the capital of Upper Egypt, a little to the north of Luxor – and was sent downriver from there to Alexandria, where the western merchants had to wait for it. Cairo itself had been closed to them by Ṣalāḥ al-Dīn; *a fortiori* they could not reach the Red Sea. So Egypt had complete control of this trade and had nothing to fear on the Red Sea; an Ayyubid prince governed the Yemen until 1231. The Karim or Karīmī merchants who specialized in this major Oriental commerce – their generic name and origin have not yet been fully explained – had built up links with Yemen that must have been very close. They are referred to in the correspondence of Jewish traders in Egypt as early as the close of the Fatimid era, and make a sudden appearance in Muslim documents from the beginning of the Ayyubid period. This trade, which gave rise to the movement of goods and people up and down the Nile, benefited not only those who derived financial profit from it, including the customs revenues, but also contributed to the prosperity and unity of the Nile valley as a whole.

The state and its organization: the military class in power (the successors of Ṣalāḥ al-Dīn)

Although the history of the political evolution of Ayyubid Egypt has yet to be written, it can be assumed that government and administration forced

2. From the beginning of the thirteenth century, the crusading spirit lost its momentum. Although the followers of the two religions continued to fight each other, their leaders were increasingly guided by commercial considerations.

3. See Chapter 26 below, on the western mastery of the Mediterranean.

no break with Fatimid traditions. Despite the clear Muslim orientation of the political structure, the Egyptian Christians or Copts were still very numerous and continued, as under the Shī'ite caliphs, to bear a great part of the administrative burden, inheriting a bureaucratic technique which had survived the change of rulers. The Ayyubid government with its ministerial functions (*dīwān*) was a continuation of the Fatimid system; the founder of the dynasty had also been the last vizier of the Cairo caliphs, and the Ayyubid and Mamluk sultans bore – and were frequently addressed by – an ancient title of the viziers, *malik*, which was symbolic of sovereignty.[4]

Ṣalāḥ al-Dīn was also, however, a Kurd amir, born of a family in the service of the Seldjuḳs. His political mission, and later the stability of his power, like that of his successors, rested upon the army. This naturally took the place of the Fatimid military caste, already in existence during the second century of the caliphate, which was financed by the *iḳṭā'* system; that is to say, to each amir was allocated, under strict public control, the tax revenue of one or more areas, depending upon the importance of the particular amir and the number of men he was obliged to maintain under arms. This system, with a few variations, was then in force throughout the Orient. Yet the army, composed as it was of Kurds and Turks, was often regarded by the Egyptians as a foreign body. In fact it was mainly the structure of political power which spread beyond the Egyptian geographical scene and which obeyed concepts hitherto unknown on the banks of the Nile. Ṣalāḥ al-Dīn held a familial view of the political structure, like other Iranian or Turkish amirs before him, who had placed the strength of their armed following at the service of the Abbasid caliphate and ended by holding power in their own hands; he gave each of the various members of the agnatic group sovereign power over a province or township, under the authority of the chief. The empire thus resolved itself into a federation of autonomous principalities, and the governance of each was entrusted to a family which had deserved well of Islam; it was not unknown for a prince to be shifted from one capital to another, if higher interests so dictated. Egypt, by reason of its importance, had the privilege of being generally the chosen domain of those who exercised – or claimed – power as head of the group.

Yet this system of choosing different family groups to defend and govern the Muslims (except at Aleppo, where the princely succession passed from father to son) involved the risk of deepening within each principality the gulf between governors and governed which was already marked at the ethnic level. An uncertain division of responsibility was the chief cause of rivalries and armed conflicts between the princes, in which third parties were invited to intervene – notably Christians from the Syrian and Palestinian coast – and thus to become involved in the Middle Eastern

4. See G. Wiet, 1937.

political game. In 1193 Ṣalāḥ al-Dīn bequeathed Egypt to his son al-Mālik al-ʿAzīz, but before long his own brother, al-Mālik al-ʿĀdil, then governing the provinces of the Euphrates, gave proof of greater authority in arbitrating disputes between relatives, and also of greater ambition. After the death of al-Mālik al-ʿAzīz in 1198, he finally settled in Cairo in 1200 and ruled the Ayyubid princes with a firm hand until his death in 1218 at Damascus, just when soldiers of the Fifth Crusade were landing at Damietta. In the circumstances, his son al-Mālik al-Kāmil had no difficulty in securing the succession in Cairo. He sought to pursue his father's policy towards relatives, but met with far less success, especially because of his conciliatory attitude towards westerners. When he died in 1237, he had failed to rebuild the family unity which had marked the days of Ṣalāḥ al-Dīn and al-Mālik al-ʿĀdil, and had even at one moment seen all the Ayyubid princes in league against him, except for one of his sons, al-Mālik al-Ṣāliḥ, whom over-precocious ambitions had led into exile in the Euphrates provinces. Yet it was this son who, after incredible adventures, finally succeeded to the leadership in Cairo in 1240.

From his experiences al-Mālik al-Ṣāliḥ drew the lesson that, in order to gain the upper hand in such bitter political contests, it was necessary to have a faithful army at one's disposal – an asset which other Ayyubid notables had also tried to secure – and that for this purpose such an army was best composed of men dependent upon their leader in every respect, that is, of men bought and trained by him, whose survival was linked with his own success: 'Mamluks' or slaves of white race, in this particular case Turks. Quartered on the island of Roda in Cairo, the regiment of Mamluks or Bahri (from the word *Baḥr*, which is used in Egyptian Arabic to designate the Nile)[5] soon became the vital support of the last great prince of the Kurd dynasty, whose principles of devolution of authority had given rise in Egypt to a dominant power group, the like of which had been seen before only in the Muslim Orient.

The Turkish Mamluks

The Mamluk regime represents the establishment, at the head of Muslim society in Egypt, of that powerful military caste which henceforward chose the sultans from among its own ranks. Although it is customary in this context to speak of 'dynasties', this was a regime no longer much concerned with such continuity, except where an immediate political advantage was to be gained. The armed group which the Ayyubid prince held at his own disposal was now self-sufficient: it had its natural chiefs and constituted, together with rival groups, the only political class in which a sultan could emerge from the power struggle. This finalized the breach between the

5. This appears to be the genuine etymology of Bahri (in Arabic, *Baḥriyya*). The theory by which *baḥr* means the sea, as in classical Arabic, which would imply that they came from beyond the sea, does not appear valid.

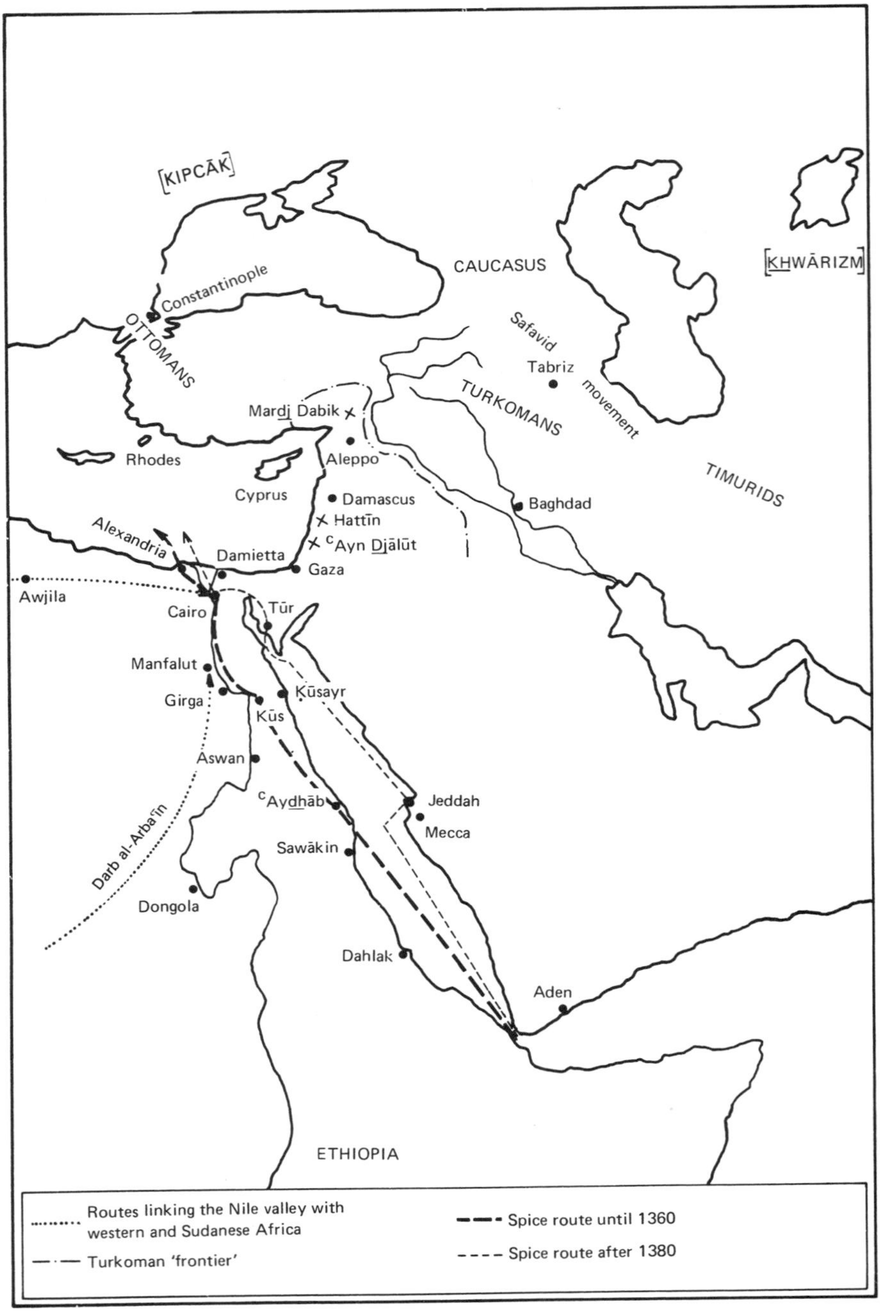

FIG. 15.1 *The Near East during the Mamluk period (J. C. Garcin)*
Note: The situation of the Asian powers is that of the second half of the 15th century

governors and the governed, who came to know their rulers first as 'the Turkish Mamluks' – that is, the group known to western historians as Bahris, even though the term strictly applies only to the regiment created by al-Mālik al-Ṣāliḥ – and later, from 1382 onwards, as 'the Circassian Mamluks'.

The origins of their power: the struggle against the Mongols and the Crusading West

The seizure of power by the military caste resulted from the appearance of a new and terrible danger, the westward advance of the Mongols. This was at first only discernible in some of its unexpected repercussions. When the first great invading wave reached Hungary in the 1240s, installing on its way in the plains of the lower Volga basin the Mongol khanate of Kipcāk, only the Iranian provinces such as the sultanate of Khwārizm and those beyond had been touched. Armed bands had fled for their lives from those provinces and al-Mālik al-Ṣāliḥ had even thought of finding among those bands the military strength he was trying to gather in order to assert his dominance over the other Ayyubids. He soon rejected these uncontrollable Khwārizmians, however, in favour of the white slaves of Turkish origin whom the Mongol settlements in Kipcāk were throwing on to the market in great numbers: it was these men who constituted the Bahri regiment.[6] The ravages committed by the Khwārizmians in the Syrian and Palestinian provinces, including the massacre of Christians in Jerusalem in 1244, led to a strong western reaction. In 1249 the army of the Sixth Crusade, led by King Louis IX of France, landed at Damietta, once again holding Egypt responsible for events in the East.

The situation became very serious when al-Mālik al-Ṣāliḥ died while the prince who was to succeed him, Turan Shah, was campaigning on the Euphrates. It was the Bahri regiment which saved Egypt from invasion by defeating Louis IX and taking him prisoner. When the new sultan arrived the victory was secure, and the Bahris emerged as the principal force in the state. Turan Shah was assassinated in May 1250. He was the last Ayyubid ruler of Egypt, and power was restored to the Mamluks; but in order to forestall the reactions of other Ayyubids, they appointed the widow of al-Mālik al-Ṣāliḥ to the sultanate for a period, in association with one of themselves. This move, however, did not save them either from war with the princes of the Ayyubid family or from the intrigues which the latter managed to foment among them, and the Mamluks might well have failed to maintain their hold, had not a second wave of Mongol aggression enabled them to demonstrate that they alone could defend Islam. Baghdad fell to the Mongols in 1258, and the Abbasid caliph was executed

6. The take-over of power by a military class in Egypt was not an isolated phenomenon; cf. the Selpukids in Iraq. From the thirteenth to the fifteenth century, until the age of Tamerlane, Asia exerted pressure on the Middle East.

by order of Hulagu, the grandson of Ghenghis Khan; the Ayyubid principalities were rapidly overrun and the invaders penetrated as far as Gaza. Their further progress into Egypt was halted only by reason of internal Mongolian politics.[7] But Kuttuz, the Mamluk sultan, took advantage of the situation to defeat the remaining Mongol forces at ʿAyn D̲j̲ālūt, near Nablus (September 1290). The Mongols had to retreat across the Euphrates and the future of the Mamluk regime was assured.

The power of the Turkish Mamluks thus arose from services rendered to Islam, while their masters, the Ayyubid princes, had failed to ward off the dangers of both Christians and Mongols. The Mongol threat, and the shock administered to the Muslim world when it was already stricken by the tragic end of the caliphate, left a lasting mark on the structure of the Mamluk sultanate, and on its policy: the Mamluk state was only the perpetuation of a *de facto* socio-military organization arising out of resistance to external aggression and rendered viable by the military and political genius of Baybars, one of the amirs of the Bahri regiment, who took command by force in 1260.

The appearance of the Mongols on the scene profoundly altered the situation in the East. The western princes, hoping to benefit from the variety of religions followed by the newcomers, thought to build up a coalition against Islam with these unexpected allies who had disposed of the caliphate. Consequently the Christian fiefs of the Syrian–Palestinian coastlands again constituted a danger; even though they had mostly remained neutral during the Mongol invasion, they might still serve as bases of operations for later attacks, and must therefore be destroyed. The Mongol threat was a fearful one, having regard to the military strength which the Mamluks could set against it. Fortunately for the Mamluks, however, the Mongols were divided among themselves: Hulagu and his descendants, the Persian Il̲k̲h̲āns, with their capital at Tabriz, were in conflict with the Khans of Kipcāk, who allowed the Mamluk state to recruit Turkish slaves in their midst and who had adopted the Islamic faith.

Anatolia was the cause of the conflict; as elsewhere in the East, Turkoman tribes had penetrated this area in the course of the eleventh century, and, as a result of the more or less passive attitude of Byzantium, had settled there under the leadership of princes who had broken away from their Sel̲d̲j̲uḳ allegiance (these were the so-called 'Rum' Sel̲d̲j̲uḳs, those installed in the former Byzantine lands, as distinct from the 'great' Sel̲d̲j̲uḳs of Iraq). After a brilliant beginning, this sultanate had been overwhelmed in 1243 by the first Mongol wave, that of the Kipcāk Mongols. But in the distribution of roles within the great Asian empire it was the Iranian Mongols who were allotted supervision over Turkoman Anatolia. Numerous conflicts resulted, in which the Mamluk state was saved several times.

7. Principally the death of the great Khan Mongke, brother of Hulagu, which occurred after the capture of Aleppo and Damascus by the Mongols. Hulagu returned to Persia for opportunist reasons, leaving only a part of his army in Syria.

It is when we take account of this whole situation, dominated as it was by the Mongolian factor, that we can best understand the policy of the new sultan, al-Mālik al-Zāhir Baybars (1260–77). Profiting from the periods of respite afforded to the Muslims by struggles between rival khanates and by the internal stirrings caused whenever one Mongol prince succeeded another, Baybars reduced the most dangerous bases of operations of the Christians in Syria and Palestine between 1265 and 1268, and again in 1270, on the occasion of a new western attack which, however, was diverted to Tunis at the last moment. By 1277 he was already leading an expedition into Anatolia, where Turkoman tribes were restive under Mongol domination, thereby affirming the role which the new power intended to play in the protection of all Muslims. The great sultans who were to follow him – al-Mālik al-Manṣūr Kalāʿūn (1279–90) and al-Mālik al-Nāṣir Muhammad ibn Kalāʿūn (1310–41) – continued his endeavour.

But the Mongols persisted in their purposes: they reached Homs in 1282 and Damascus in 1300; in 1310 they again crossed the Euphrates, which had by then become the state border. On the Mamluk side, the capture of St John of Acre in 1291 – the last Christian stronghold on the coast of Palestine – was by way of answer to fresh projects of alliance between Mongols and western kings. The removal of this danger and the conversion to Islam of the Persian Ilkhāns in 1295 appeared to show that the existence of the Muslims was no longer threatened. On the other hand, the goodwill shown by the Ilkhāns towards Shīʾism (1310), though not continuous, was beginning to lead to a confrontation between a mostly Sunni Middle East and an Iranian/Mongol block with Shīʾite leanings, which could only inspire apprehension; although the threat was less total, it remained alive.

Peace only became a reality in 1323 with the decline of the Ilkhān state. The Mamluk empire had now overcome the dangers which had given rise to its existence; its writ extended to the borders of Anatolia, itself liberated from the Mongols, and Turkoman turbulence was dissipated in encounters with numerous principalities, including the Ottomans in the north – not yet of great account – who had resumed their ancient tradition of hostility and ambiguous relations with what remained of Byzantium. The Mamluk state, in fact, appears at this time to have been the great power of Islam.

Mamluk power and Africa

It is not surprising to find this power, won so strenuously against the threats of both Europe and Asia, asserting itself in Africa. The paths of Mamluk prosperity lay chiefly on African soil. The great trade with the Far East once again followed the route along the Red Sea and the Nile valley; Yemen had to acknowledge Egyptian hegemony, which also sought to control the minor trading posts, through an alliance with the amirs of Dahlak or through reclaiming sovereignty over Sawākin and Musawwar.[8]

8. On Dahlak, see G. Wiet, 1951–2, pp. 89–95.

The Mongol enemy had attempted to switch this profitable traffic back to the Persian Gulf route, and for a while the spice trade also used the Mongol roads. But the merchants of Venice, Genoa and Barcelona had to acknowledge the facts: from the 1340s onwards, the Red Sea route as feeder to the Egyptian ports and the re-emerging Levantine harbours had no rival worth mention. It was down the great African river that the spices came. The Karīmī merchants made fortunes from it and extended their activities into West Africa, where, according to the chronicles, one of these magnates of international trade met his death in Timbuktu in 1334.[9]

These African relationships formed an integral part of the overall pattern of political and cultural connections. African princes and their subjects had been making pilgrimages to the Ḥidjāz and passing through Cairo since at least 1261, when Baybars came to power. Noting their visits, the educated public thereafter became aware of the existence of the African Muslim kingdoms. It was during the fourteenth century that Ibn Faḍl Allāh al-ʿUmarī wrote his geographical encyclopaedia, which today provides in its section on Africa a historical source of prime importance.[10] As for the ordinary people of Cairo, what they noticed most were the signs of wealth: the founding of a Mālikite *madrasa* at Fustāt by the ruler of Kanem or the gold distributed by Mansa Mūsā during his pilgrimage of 1324. Mali gold continued to supply the Egyptian mint. The sultans therefore extended a warm welcome to the African princes – a welcome not unrelated to their desire to extend Egypt's political influence which, they reckoned, would spread into Africa in the wake of the valuable textiles, the official manners of the court and the books that visitors found in the great metropolis.

Egyptian influence thus spread naturally in Africa through the greatness and prosperity of the Mamluk empire. But it also asserted itself more deliberately and brutally in the areas closest to Egypt; the northern part of the Christian kingdom of Nubia was annexed in 1275, and vassal princes were installed at Dongola and gradually established there. Moreover, the Egyptian state found effective auxiliaries in its march forward, namely the Beduins: the Banū 'l Kanz, ancestors of today's Kenouz, were soon established between Aswan and the Sudanese frontier; they contributed actively to the downfall of the Christian kingdom of Dongola and became its rulers after formally adopting Islam in 1317.[11] By that time the Djubayna tribes and other southern Arab groups, such as the Bali, Djudhām and Tayy,

9. Scholars are not agreed on the meaning of the word *Karīmī*. Either it is a defective reading or else the term denotes the merchants of Kanem (Kanimi). If the latter hypothesis is correct, Kanem played a hitherto unsuspected role in the development of trade in the East. But see also Chapter 26, p. 653, n. 55 below.

10. See al-ʿUmarī, 1894 edn, or French transl. 1927.

11. The Dongola church (*Dunḳula al-'adjūz*), which was transformed into a mosque, has an inscription giving the exact date: 29 May 1317 (16 Rabīʿ I, 717). See Chapter 16, pp. 403–4, for details of the succession.

had moved further south in great numbers into Darfūr and Central Africa, starting with the provinces of Asyut and Manfalut. The Nubian obstacle was removed, and it appeared that Egyptian power, which until the days of al-Mālik al-Nāṣir Muḥammad had as far as possible discouraged mass movements of nomads, now considered such shifts advantageous; the departure of turbulent groups gave Egypt provisional relief, while the peoples concerned became vassals in the far south with whom the Cairo chancellery remained in contact. From 1320 onwards Manfalut contributed out of its tax revenue (*iḳṭāʿ*) to the sultan's private treasury, while at the same time it had become a slave market. That was only a beginning, however, and Mamluk Egypt exerted a stronger influence on African Muslims through the pattern of civilization which it presented.

Islam in Egypt

The underlying motive force of the Mamluk state could only perpetuate the Ayyubid era. The important point was still to defend Islam from attack, although the internal foe hardly existed any more. Sunni teaching had spread in Egypt. In Cairo, Alexandria, Kūs and even in small settlements in the Egyptian countryside, *madrasa*s had been set up, in some cases as prestige structures designed to glorify their founders – amirs or wealthy merchants – in others as modest premises with resources barely sufficient to pay the teachers' salaries and the subsistence of the students, but always contributing to the creation of the class of learned and devout men at which Ṣalāḥ al-Dīn had aimed. A Sunni environment that was specifically Egyptian had thus come into being and the provinces could participate in the life of the capital through their élite. Spiritual life was inspired by an orthodox mystique faithful to the teachings of al-Ghazālī; fraternal groups or *shadili*s were formed and history came to life again in the teaching of Muslim traditions through the biographical collections or encyclopaedic summaries of such authors as al-Udfuwī, al-Nuwayrī, Ibn ʿAbd al-Zāhir or Ibn al-Furāt, to name only Egyptians. In the higher posts of the state chancellery recourse was still had to the services of Syrians, such as the Banū Faḍl Allāh al-ʿUmarī, but the work of such men as al-Ḳalḳashandī towards the end of the fourteenth century proved that Egyptian society was ready to resume the great tradition of the Abbasid secretaries to the caliphate. Sunni Islam had thus built its Egyptian bastion.

It is true that the Mamluk military caste, heir to the Ayyubid regime, did not always find among these Egyptian lawyers, teachers and divines the unqualified approval to which it felt entitled on the grounds of its glorious defence of Islam. It seemed to the Egyptians, on the other hand – for, unlike the Syrians, they had never suffered directly from Mongol attacks – that the protection of the Muslims hardly justified the luxurious living of the amirs sustained by the resources which the military caste exacted from the country. These lawyers considered themselves in some degree the representatives of the Egyptian people *vis-à-vis* the foreign

PLATE 15.1 *Cairo: tomb of Kayt Bay (1472–4) (Mamluk architecture)*

PLATE 15.2 *Great porch of Kansuh-al-Ghūri Mosque (built 1504)*

PLATE 15.3 *Cairo: interior of Mosque of Djawhar-al-Lāla (of Ethiopian origin) (1430)*

Mamluks and a financial administration which remained to a large extent in Christian hands. Amirs risen from the ranks were uncouth, often insolent; they had had no more than the rudiments of religious training and were more fluent in Turkish than in Arabic; their calling was war. Yet the common people were conscious of the prestige of Muslim victories and of the beauty of the edifices built by Baybars, Kalā'ūn or al-Mālik al-Nāṣir Muḥammad. The pomp of the sultans, inherited from the Fatimid splendours, won all hearts; the spectacular displays of strange fraternities – though of doubtful orthodoxy – from the Far East, protected by the amirs, delighted simple souls. The Islam of the common people merged with the Islam of the military caste, with few points of difference, and the unity of the Mamluk political edifice was thereby strengthened. Was not the all-important task now to preserve the social cohesion which had been achieved, and thereby to affirm the glory of Islam?

That glory was nowhere more evident than in Cairo, for the city had become the seat of the restored Abbasid caliphate. Baybars had welcomed a member of the former caliph's family who had escaped from the massacre and who was seeking help in recovering his capital; but he obtained no more than token assistance and died in combat. But, as at Baghdad in the eleventh century, in the days when a sultan held power at the head of the military caste on behalf of the caliph, Baybars received from the Abbasid the official investiture which legalized his sultanate. Another escapee then obtained recognition of his Abbasid lineage and his claim to the caliphate; having renounced the former as a fruitless enterprise, he became caliph of Islam in 1262 and thereafter had his seat in Cairo, where prayers were said in his name. Conflicts soon broke out between sultan and caliph, for the lawyers were inclined to see the latter as the only legitimate prince; but having no other support, the Abbasid lived on under surveillance. Such was often the lot of his successors, but the sultans never dared to rid themselves of these symbolic caliphs, however unwelcome was the reminder that the sultanate was only a *de facto* power in Islam: for outside Egypt, and particularly among African Muslims, the caliph's presence in Cairo added lustre to the sultan's glory.

Cairo, where the 'Tales of a Thousand and One Nights' were nearing completion, was the new Baghdad. Clearly, it was not just the capital of Egypt nor of the Mamluk empire alone; from Syria and from all the countries of Islam there flowed into the *madrasa*s a culture to which Egyptian intellects were only beginning to contribute. This culture was doubtless less rich than in classical times and its inspiration was more uniformly Sunni in character, but it was eager to preserve the heritage of the past, to record it, to assimilate such parts of it as the new, militant spirit of Islam was willing to retain, compiling for the purpose enormous collections, of which the 'Universal History' of Ibn Khaldūn, who reached Egypt in 1382, is one of the outstanding examples. The inspired teaching of that conservative aristocrat, several times appointed the great Mālikite *ḳāḍī* of Egypt, was only one example of the learning handed down in the *madrasas* of Cairo.

The Mamluk political system

This flowering of Muslim society took place under the protection of the Turkish Mamluks, and it was within that group, constantly renewed, of some tens of thousands of men devoted to the defence of the empire, that the real political game was played. The Turkish Mamluks came mostly from Kipcāk; Genoese traders brought them from the shores of the Black Sea to Alexandria by ship, and the great merchants of the Muslim East imported them overland. But there were also deserters from a great variety of origins, including Mongols. The cohesion of the group depended upon the constant nature of the education its members received: not only physical and military training, but also the rudimentary learning which would transform these young slaves into Muslims, perhaps one day to be freed and to aspire to the highest positions. The support of the military continued to depend upon the changing distribution of *iḳṭā*ʿ from the different areas: the sultan was entitled to a portion of the proceeds, and that portion was increased by al-Mālik al-Nāṣir Muḥammad to strengthen his own power base. Other amirs shared the remainder in accordance with their rank.

But these receipts also contributed indirectly to the development of the towns, for the Mamluks lived in provincial centres and in the capital itself. In Cairo, the amirs accumulated within their residences stocks of money, provisions and the rich artefacts of urban craftsmen, along with the men who stood ready to answer the call of the sultan from the Ṣalāḥ al-Dīn citadel which dominated the city. The political apparatus ensured ruthless selection.[12] Baybars and Kalāʿūn had both risen from the ranks of the Bahri regiment. Following the Ayyubid example, they had acquired their own Mamluks; it became the first concern of every subsequent amir who attained the sultanate to build up a force which would enable him to exercise power effectively. They did not all succeed, for any of them could be overthrown before he had acquired enough followers. But when they did, political stability was assured: a new group of Mamluks was formed, bearing the name of the sultan who had recruited them and attached closely to his person until his death, when links of comradeship and personal merit might lead to the emergence of a new sultan from among them. Each new ruler therefore provided the occasion for the emergence of a new group which was determined to maintain its grasp on the major levers of state and which threatened the power of the next ruler, while that generation lasted.

In these circumstances it will be obvious that dynastic continuity was only apparent, despite the wishes of many successive sultans and although the Turkish Mamluks were often described as the 'dynasty of the Kalāʿūn

12. A. Darraj, 1961.

family'. In fact Kalāʿūn (1279–90) was more fortunate than Baybars (1260–77), from whom he seized power, for he succeeded in handing the sultanate over to his son al-Mālik al- ʿAs͟hrāf K͟halīl (1290–3), the vanquisher of St John of Acre, although not for long. His brother Muḥammad twice became sultan, because twice the amirs seeking power did not yet feel strong enough to succeed against their rivals; it was due to his own energy that he won his third and longest sultanate (1310–41). After Muḥammad's death his twelve children and grandchildren (1341–82) never exercised the full powers of that office for more than a few months, since each was very young at the time of accession; in fact government was conducted during this period by the great amirs, Kūsūn, Tāz and S͟hayk͟hū, whose prestige has remained alive in the urban architecture of Cairo in the form of buildings which bore witness to their power. In contrast, the beautiful mosque of al-Mālik al-Nāṣir Hasan (1356–62) is the only major building by a sultan. The history of this period has yet to be told, but one may ask whether respect for the dynasty alone prevented these three amirs from aspiring to the sultanate. Was it not rather some failure of the system which deprived them of sufficient power to succeed? When, in 1382, the amir Barḳūḳ became sultan, he began a reign which, with one brief interruption, lasted until the end of the century (1399) and re-established the great Mamluk tradition; but he was a Circassian, and a new kind of bond, ethnic in origin, sustained his power.

Egypt up to the end of the fifteenth century – African contacts (the Circassian Mamluks)

Little is known about the evolution of the Mamluk sultanate in its second stage, corresponding roughly to the fifteenth century, and much of the story must be based on conjecture. The dividing-point between the two stages is generally taken as the year 1382, when power shifted to the Circassian Mamluks, and there is no doubt that contemporary witnesses had the feeling that political life was from that date onwards obeying different rules. But the change ran deeper and began before that date. On the other hand, it was only later, following the serious crisis which affected Egypt and the sultanate at the beginning of the fifteenth century, that the Mamluk regime took on a new aspect and that a new Egypt began to emerge, which was no longer the Egypt of the Middle Ages.

Far-reaching changes

There was a change in the recruitment of the Mamluks. The khanate of Kipcāk was in decline throughout the second half of the fourteenth century and was no longer an abundant source of supply. The main source from that time onwards was the Caucasus region, and the Circassians, already present in the Mamluk army, began to dominate the other groups by dint of their sense of ethnic and familial solidarity.[13] Their exclusiveness in relation to other races reduced still further the genuine political nucleus or group from which it was possible to select a sultan; race now conferred as important a right of access as did the strict military training. Even though urgent needs still dictated repeated purchases of Mamluks from various sources, these recruits did not take part in the political game, which was reserved to the Circassians; they were solely intended to bear arms and adjusted the degree of their loyalty to the amount of their pay.

While the composition and structure of the military caste were changing, the traditional resources derived from the *iḳṭāʿ* were also changing and shrinking. Egypt, like Europe, was beginning to be affected by epidemics: the Black Death in 1349, another in 1375, and again frequently during the fifteenth century. These took a heavy toll among the Mamluks, who had to be replaced more quickly, but the city-dwellers and peasants of Egypt also suffered. The yield of the soil, and hence the *iḳṭāʿ*, could not but decline.

To these enduring changes, resulting from situations to which Mamluk power had to adapt itself, were added the consequences of the policy adopted by the Turkish sultans in Upper Egypt, which proved no less decisive. Beduin tribes had been allowed to settle there and to send forays to the south and into Central Africa; for example, the D̲jud̲h̲ām were then raiding the Bornu.[14] They became powerful in Upper Egypt and after ten years of disturbances and unsuccessful reprisals following the death of al-Mālik al-Nāṣir Muḥammad, their presence had to be reckoned with. They went so far as to force the withdrawal towards Aswan of the Banū ʾl Kanz who had settled in Nubia. As a consequence, the route from ʿAyd̲h̲āb to Kūs became impassable and fell out of use in the 1360s. For a while Ḳūsayr replaced ʿAyd̲h̲āb as a port of entry for the spice trace; but before long, in a land in which amirs, who saw their revenue falling off, frequently resorted to arbitrary extortions, merchants thought it best to land their precious wares as late as possible, that is, as far north as possible, at El Tūr on the coast of the Sinai peninsula, which came into use after 1380. Hence the spice trade no longer moved down the Nile, and the use of Egyptian territory was thereby affected (see Fig. 15.1).

At the time of Barḳūḳ's accession to power these numerous changes were not yet discernible, except in some disorder in the conduct of the state, in a loss of authority and in some turbulence on the part of impoverished amirs. The sultanate of al-Mālik al-Zāhir Barḳūḳ (1382–99)

13. The Circassian Mamluks got their name of *burd̲j̲iyya* or *burd̲j̲i*s from a political and military practice of Sultan al-Manṣūr Kalāʿūn, who quartered a regiment of his own Mamluks in the towers (*abrād̲j̲*; singular *burd̲j̲*).

14. In 1391, the king of Bornu wrote a letter to Sultan Barḳūḳ in which he complained of the bad behaviour of the D̲jud̲h̲ām and other Arab clans, who were attacking his subjects and selling them to merchants in Egypt, Syria and other countries. See al-Ḳalḳas̲h̲andī, 1913–19 edn, Vol. 1, p. 306 and Vol. 8, pp. 116–18.

was, however, distinguished by a stiffening of control in the provinces, by the transfer of the Hawwāra Berbers from the western delta to Upper Egypt to balance the Arab tribes, and by a gradual strengthening of the central authority. This government appears to have followed the traditions of the great Turkish sultans; their style of public building was revived in Cairo.

The crisis at the beginning of the fifteenth century

The real crisis broke on the death of Sultan Barḳūḳ. It was both external and internal, and it nearly brought the Mamluk sultanate to an end. Externally, the regime's authority was threatened in Anatolia. One Turkoman principality, that of the Ottomans, had taken on a new dimension as a result of the war it was waging against the Christians, thrusting as far as the Balkans. (Since 1366 Europe had been considering an expedition to rescue Constantinople.) The Ottomans claimed the succession to the Seldjuḳ sultanate of Rum and were seeking gradually to reduce the other principalities; their troops had just intervened in areas under Mamluk protection when a further danger, even more formidable, arose. In Central Asia Tamerlane, an officer of the Mongol princes, had undertaken the task of restoring the great empire, this time under the banner of Islam purified by the sword. The terrible westward march of the Mongols was resumed. In 1400 Tamerlane attacked the Mamluks; he soon reached Damascus and could have invaded Egypt without difficulty, had he not elected first to devote himself to the re-establishment of Mongol domination over Anatolia. He crushed the Ottomans in 1402; but other problems then called him back into Asia.

Once more, Egypt had escaped invasion and the Mamluk sultanate had again found in the East circumstances favourable to its own cause: the Ottoman expansion was broken for a long time, and the Turkoman principalities in Anatolia resumed their traditional rivalries, as did others more recently installed in Iraq. But to what domination could the Mamluk sultanate now aspire? The Mongols had spontaneously withdrawn from its ravaged territories, and this time the Turkoman princes owed their restored autonomy to the invaders. Spared by a miracle, the Mamluk empire had proved unable to play any role and this impotence remained, by reason of the evils which were destroying it from within.

After the death of Sultan Barḳūḳ, his Mamluks obviously contested the transfer of power to his son Faradj; but, either because political solidarity, previously forged in the long communal apprenticeship of the barracks, was now no longer strong enough to allow one amir to take the lead, or because, as before Barḳūḳ's days, not one of them was sufficiently powerful, the military caste broke down into lengthy, bloody and fruitless rivalries. Their spirits were so troubled that, when Faradj lost both the contest and his life in 1411, the sultanate was for a short while entrusted to the Abbasid caliph. It looked as though the regime was tottering. To make matters worse – and this accounts for the time taken in resolving the political crisis – Egypt was struck by disaster. In 1403 the Nile floods failed, leading to famine, and in 1405 plague reduced the population, ruined the towns and paralysed the administration. In Upper Egypt, the Beduin – Berbers or Arabs – asserted themselves, imposing their will virtually without any restraint from Cairo during the whole decade. Egypt faced a crisis of a magnitude seldom paralleled in its history. The Mamluk state was bound to be either overthrown or transformed.

Egypt facing the Christian danger: the struggle against the Portuguese

In these perilous circumstances one of Barḳūḳ's Mamluks became Sultan al-Mālik al-Mu'ayyad (1412–21) and initiated counter-action in every sector with the utmost energy. He was succeeded by another of Barḳūḳ's Mamluks, al-Mālik al-'Ashraf Bārsbāy (1422–38), who completed the task of restoring order. The administration began to function more regularly. Upper Egypt, with the probable loss of the devastated province of Aswan, returned to the control of the Mamluk government, thanks to the co-operation of the Hawwāra Berbers, who had installed their authority at Girga while Cairo's control had lapsed. It was essential for the government to find some way to offset the loss of income caused by the crisis to the sultanate, for epidemics had continued until the close of Bārsbāy's administration and broke out again later in the century.

There was one area where Egypt had no competition to fear, particularly while the Mongol wars continued: the spice trade. Coming from Aden, these wares were now taken across Egypt by the shortest routes, from El Tūr to Alexandria, Rosetta or Damietta, or else to the Syrian ports. In 1425 Bārsbāy made it his business to capture the profits of this trade for the sultanate exclusively; to eliminate any loss, the goods were to come solely through Jeddah, the Ḥidjāz port which was now an integral part of the empire (some contemporaries even said, of Egypt), where they would be taxed before being sold to western merchants through official channels only. These steps were clearly detrimental to the interests not only of the Yemenite princes who controlled Aden, but also of the great private merchants (including the Karīmī, although they were then in decline) and of the western traders, especially the Venetians, who in the fifteenth century claimed to control two-thirds of Egyptian imports. All these found themselves compelled to buy at prices fixed by the sultan. Reactions were heated, but the sultan stood firm. He had, in addition, an official duty to protect this trade, chiefly in the Mediterranean where Catalan and Genoese corsairs harried the coasts; Cyprus, a Christian kingdom suspected of conniving with the pirates, was raided and its king taken prisoner in 1425; similar though less successful expeditions were undertaken against Rhodes in 1440. This monopoly hold provided Bārsbāy and his successors with the resources they needed, and the Egyptian community with a different economic basis, detectable by many indicators.

Once the amirs had been reduced to living off the smaller revenues yielded by the *iḳṭā*ʿ, the sultan had acquired a new dominance which no opposition was ever dangerous enough to threaten again, except in a few isolated instances. The only remaining problems posed by the military caste were the new recruits, who were being reduced, through the exclusiveness of the Circassian group, to the status of mere mercenaries – too quickly trained, greedy and demanding. The character of the sultanate was changing: gone were the amirs, young or in the prime of life, who with the active help of their men could seize power and exercise their aptitudes and ambitions; in their stead were mature or older men, who took on responsibilities sometimes too heavy for them and behaved more as politicians than as soldiers. They also claimed to be good Muslims, for the antagonism between the military caste and the men of learning and religion was dwindling. The legitimacy of the sultans was no longer contested, and this removed much of the significance of the increasingly unobtrusive presence of the Abbasid caliphs.

The ratio of Muslims to Christians appears to have greatly increased at this time in Egypt; during the hard years of the first quarter of the century, when the common people were inclined to blame all their ills upon minorities, conversions had been numerous. Egypt was becoming more uniformly Muslim in the face of pressures from the West. These pressures included not only the corsair raids upon the coasts (there was even talk of a secret alliance between western Christians and the Negus of Ethiopia, aiming to attack Islam once again from the rear), but also the presence of the merchants, who now came freely to Cairo, with their gold coins and their costly fabrics. Altogether it seems that this renewal of the sultanate, through the fullest possible exploitation of the great international commerce, gave the Mamluk society of Egypt a new strength, a stability and a peace which it had never known before, while at the same time imparting a fragility, as yet dimly perceived, and a dependence upon the West which lay at the heart of the trade relations that bound them together.

Yet the western travellers who ventured beyond the *funduḳ*s of the coastal towns, whose memoirs remain invaluable to the historian, were not the most numerous strangers in Cairo. Travellers from West Africa constituted a shifting colony on the periphery, vulnerable to epidemics, staying there for shorter or longer periods or stopping altogether, on their way to the Ḥidjāz. It appears that African pilgrims were particularly numerous towards the middle of the fifteenth century and, like other countries' official delegations to the holy places, they now had their 'pilgrimage amir'. The Sunni allegiance of the masters of Cairo or the Ḥidjāz masters, referred to in the *Ta'rīkh al-fattāsh* and the *Ta'rīkh al-Sūdān*, [15] had borne fruit and had attracted social support in Africa, as previously in Egypt. This was henceforth to influence the political life of the African kingdoms; the pilgrimages undertaken by princes invested by the Abbasid caliph, such as Askiya Muḥammad in 1496, bear witness to this. The Mamluk sultans, for their part, were now levying heavy taxes on the pilgrims and viewed them mainly as a source of gold.

Contacts with Africa were also made through Upper Egypt. The Beduin amirs had become landed proprietors, wholesale merchants and good Muslims in their turn. They acquired an increasing hold on the country and became wealthy through trade: the horses they bred and the slaves they sold to Cairo were important items of commerce.[16] Spices, on the other hand, no longer passed through Upper Egypt, which became a different world from the delta. The Christian population remained numerous and life moved at a slower pace. It was now chiefly in the delta that the contrasts of wealth, which distinguished the Egypt of the Circassians, the commercial bustle in the towns against the poverty of the countryside, were most marked. Buildings of a new style arose in great numbers. In this respect, the long sultanate of al-Mālik al-'Ashraf Kayt Bay (1468–96), who completed the task of giving Cairo the appearance it has preserved to this day, represents a summit: the brilliant conclusion of Circassian achievement (see Plates 15.1–15.3).

There can be no doubt that the 1480s were a turning-point in the history of the sultanate and of Egypt. External problems began to put this lengthy process of rehabilitation at risk, but the fifteenth century in Egypt already ranks, despite difficult conditions, as a period lacking neither in style nor in originality. The influence of Egypt had been maintained through the majestic regulation of the state and the blossoming of her culture; the Egyptian school of historians had reached the height of their fame from al-Maḳrīzī, still a witness to the dark years of the early century, through al-Aynī, Ibn Ḥadjar al-Askalānī, Ibn al-Taghrītoiroī and al-Sakhāwī – all Egyptians and sons of Mamluks of mixed blood – down to the chroniclers of the difficult times to come, Ibn Iyās and the prolific al-Suyūtī, who was proud to see his fame spread as far as Takrūr.

A new international context

The balance of power in the East favoured the Circassians for a long time. The successors of Tamerlane, the Timurids – peaceful princes and friends of the arts who ruled Iran and central Asia – abandoned any real warlike attitude. The return to the former political fragmentation of the Turkoman groups enabled the reorganized Mamluk state, without great risk, to resume

15. Maḥmūd Ka'ti (before 1593), French transl. 1913–14; al-Sa'dī, 1656, French transl. 1964.

16. Maḥmūd, Ka'ti, loc. cit.; al-'Umarī, loc. cit.

its traditional policy of intervention in Anatolia. Once again, the sultans had their protégés. Besides, the ebullient Turkoman people required supervision and the Timurids' territorial borders were being pushed back by the Turkomans of Iraq. The sultans always kept a watchful eye on the numerous conflicts, while clearly conscious of the limitations of their power as demonstrated in a succession of minor incidents. By seeking to control the political evolution of these newcomers to Islam – with whom the Mamluks must have felt some affinity – the Cairo sultanate was playing its part as a great power; but in seeking results which were bound to be uncertain, in the Turkoman context of shifting forces seeking unity, it was bringing upon Egypt, and thereby upon the whole of North Africa, the dominance of an ethnic group which had not at first sought such a broad area in which to settle. The Ottomans, defeated and divided, began to rebuild their strength only with the utmost caution. Not before Meḥmed II (1451–81) was the Ottoman drive resumed: the fall of Constantinople in 1453 was celebrated in Cairo, but it gave the newly expanding state a glamour embarrassing to a champion of Islam. On the other hand, the Turkoman protégés of the Mamluks in Anatolia were rendering their cause indefensible by coming to terms with the West in order to avoid their own absorption by the Ottomans. A clash between Mamluks and Ottomans was inevitable. It came in 1468, under Kayt Bay: the first confrontation, up to 1472, was indirect and fortunately it was concluded through the intervention of the Iraqi Turkomans, against whom the Ottomans had to gather all their forces. This was followed by open war between the two sultanates from 1483 to 1491. The Mamluk victory was very hard won; at the cost of the internal stability of the state, it once again halted the progress of the Ottomans. The latter now concentrated all their efforts upon the Mediterranean, in a *d̲jihād* against the westerners, from whom they learnt how to handle firearms. Yet the Turkoman people remained restless, and were set in turmoil by the S̲hīʾite movement among the Safavids, who in 1501 united Iranians and Turkomans; Iran, now officially S̲hīʾite for the first time, threatened its Ottoman rivals, who were Sunnis. To exploit such a situation, which might prove both perilous and advantageous, the Mamluk sultans needed to prove their clear-sightedness and, above all, to exercise their power – which, already shaken by reason of the recent wars, abruptly failed them.

It was at this very time that Portuguese expansion in the Indian Ocean, striking simultaneously at Venetian trade and at the resources of the Mamluk economy which depended upon it, began to undermine the material foundations upon which the political structure of the Circassians was built. The presence of the Portuguese made itself felt following Vasco da Gama's voyage of 1498. They bought spices and organized a blockade of the Red Sea. By circumventing both Africa and Islam, the damage they inflicted upon Mamluk power in Egypt brought into relief its identity of interest with Africa as a whole. The last great Circassian sultan, al-Mālik

PLATE 15.4 *Egyptian lamp in enamelled glass (Mamluk era)*

al-ʿAs̲h̲raf Kansūh al-G̲h̲ūrī (1501–16), attempted to strike back. His Ottoman rival, anxious to play his part as defender of Islam and with an eye to the danger which threatened the Ḥidj̲āz, even helped him to build a fleet; but after the defeat of the Egyptian squadron at Diu on the west coast of India in 1509, the Mamluk empire was reduced to the defence of the Red Sea. This lack of power should have ruled out any provocative attitude towards the East, where the situation was rapidly changing.

The Safavids, encouraged by the West, were in fact placing the Ottomans in a difficult position. When Selim, the new Ottoman sultan, attempted to retaliate, he did not find the Mamluks at his side, even though he was helping them on the Red Sea; the old reflexes of Turkoman policy had prevailed over clear-sightedness in Cairo. Selim fought alone and, as a result of using firearms, with which the Ottomans were now familiar, he was able to contain the expansion of S̲h̲īʾism in 1514 and limit it to Iran. He then decided to put an end to the harmful influence which his Mamluk rival, now incapable of protecting Islam and the Sunni faith, refused to surrender in the Turkoman areas. The fate of the Mamluk empire was decided by a single battle, at Mardj̲ Dabik to the north of Aleppo, on 24 August 1516, when modern weapons prevailed over the Circassian horsemen who despised them. The death in battle of the ageing Mamluk sultan, intrigues within the military caste, the prestige of the new defender of Sunni Islam and the indifference of the Egyptian people turned what had at first been no more than a limited settlement of account into total conquest, easily achieved.

Conclusion

When, in 1517, the domination of the Ottomans extended to Egypt, it was a whole political power that collapsed; having become the preserve of a small political group that had difficulty in renewing itself, it had lost the power of survival and the legitimacy derived from its efficient defence of Islam. An Ottoman governor was installed in Cairo, and the authority of a Beduin amir was confirmed at Girga, thus formalizing the distinction, destined to endure, between coastal Egypt and the upper lands. Yet social structures were not affected in any way, and were to survive for a long time. Mamluk society itself also survived – the vestige of a political and cultural enterprise which had been its justification and which holds a high place in the history of both Islam and Africa.

16 Nubia from the late 12th century to the Funj conquest in the early 15th century

L. KROPÁČEK

Decline and disappearance of the Christian Nubian states

In world history we can find few instances of a bilateral international arrangement maintained for as long as the *baḳt*, which for six centuries was taken as a legal basis for peaceful relations between Muslim Egypt and Christian Nubia.[1] Despite occasional small-scale raids and counter-raids the truce was observed, and reciprocal obligations including conventional supplies were fulfilled in a way that, in principle, did not leave doubts about the validity of the agreement. With all modifications and temporary withholdings, the *baḳt* was a convenient formula for economic interdependence.

Under the Fatimids, Egyptian–Nubian relations seem to have best realized the much-sought pattern of neighbourliness and some co-operation. It served the needs of the Fatimid – slaves for the army and a peaceful southern border – as well as those of Nubia, which attained the height of its political power and cultural achievements. The period of the Ayyubids (1171–1250) and the Mamluks (1250–1517) in Egypt, which corresponds to the span of our interest in this chapter, was characterized – in comparison with that of their predecessors – by a progressive deterioration of relations with Nubia. Eventually the northern factor, in a comprehensive sense, proved decisive in Nubia's eclipse. Two interconnected processes may be discerned: on the one hand, the direct pressure of the Egyptian rulers on the weakening Nubian power and, on the other hand, the increasing penetration of Arab nomadic groups and their destructive effect on the Nubian social fabric.

Our knowledge of the political history of Christian Nubia is almost entirely derived from the written Arabic sources of Egyptian provenance.[2] Local records of late Christian times are scarce and not very relevant. The significance of the archaeological evidence has, however, been enhanced in the 1960s by the salvage programmes necessitated by the con-

1. For legal aspects of the *baḳt*, see *Encyclopaedia of Islam*, new edn, Vol. 1, p. 966.

2. Virtually all available Arabic sources have been reliably explored and analysed in Y. F. Hasan, 1967.

struction of the High Dam at Aswan. The campaign in Lower Nubia led to a careful preoccupation even with such otherwise unattractive sites as humble domestic remains, resulting in a number of stimuli for the interpretation of Nubian history with the emphasis on internal developments.[3]

According to the Arabic sources, the political geography of Nubia in the twelfth and thirteenth centuries was still the same as described in the earlier records. Two riverain kingdoms were distinguished: al-Muḳurra (in Graeco-Coptic, Makuria) with its capital in Dunḳula (Old Dongola); and 'Alwa (Alodia). The frontiers dividing the two lie between the Fifth and Sixth Cataracts (see Fig. 16.1). The northernmost outpost of 'Alwa is often mentioned as al-'Abwāb ('the Gates', or modern Kabushiya). In both kingdoms succession to the throne was predominantly regulated by the principle of matrilineal descent, which provided for the hereditary right of a son of the previous ruler's sister. To a great extent the Nubian social and political institutions were essentially ethnic in character, which seems to have been largely misunderstood both in the sources and in interpretative accounts.

Muḳurra

As has been suggested earlier, we have good reason to believe that the relations between the Fatimid rulers in Egypt and Nubia were fairly friendly. There is enough evidence, both documentary and material, of Egyptian–Nubian trade flourishing at that period. Study of the excavated pottery, to take just one example, reveals movements of people in both directions as well as the influence of Fatimid designs on Nubian manufacture. The reciprocal exchanges under the *baḳt* arrangement, which in this period probably took its classical shape, symbolized the mutual advantage of security and trade. The difference of religion was not considered a major obstacle. Arabic sources report the undisturbed communication between the patriarchate of Alexandria and the Nubian king acting as his protector, the just punishment of the anti-Nubian slander concerning alleged anti-Muslim measures and the warm reception and hospitality offered to the retired Nubian King Solomon in Cairo in 1079.

A possible explanation of the goodwill of the Fatimids towards their southern neighbours may be their feeling that the Shī'ite regime was isolated in the world of Islam. From the Nubian side, this goodwill seems to have been occasionally answered by direct help. Thus Egypt in the tenth century suffered from Nubian incursion at the same time as the Fatimid campaign of conquest, and these raids were resumed only after the Ayyubids overthrew the friendly regime. The Nubians also showed co-operation in handing over runaway slaves and political fugitives from Egypt. Again, the provisions of the *baḳt* in this respect reflect the conventions of Fatimid times.

3. See, in particular: P. L. Shinnie, 1965, pp. 263–73; W. Y. Adams, 1966 and 1967.

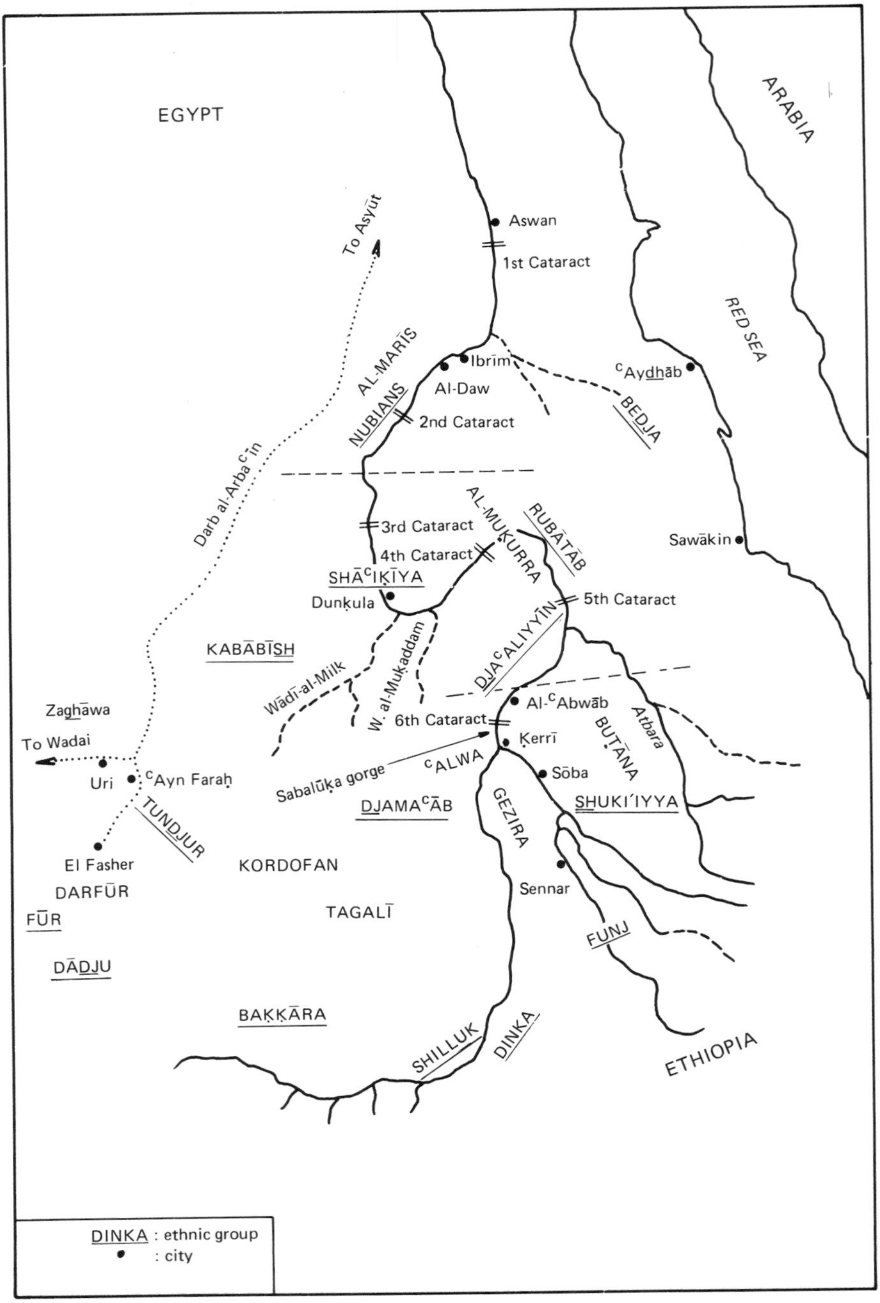

FIG. 16.1 *Nubia from the late 12th century until the Funj conquest at the beginning of the 16th century (L. Kropáček)*

An important element in the military power of the Fatimids was the role of black troops of Sudani origin, largely obtained from Muḳurra and 'Alwa. After a period of great prominence, due especially to favour shown them by the Khalifa al-Mustanṣir's black mother, in the latter half of the eleventh century, their Turkish and Berber rivals drove many of them to Upper Egypt, where later they often came into conflict with their political enemies. The black troops, however, remained staunch supporters of the Fatimid regime and in its last years showed stubborn resistance to the rising power of the Ayyubids.

Arab troops, who were to become a serious source of trouble in later periods, proved obdurate and rebelled on several occasions. Some of them probably managed to escape to the south from the repression that followed, but their numbers and conduct remained manageable. In their handling of the Arab problem of Banū Hilāl the Fatimids are best known for their ingenious solution of sending them westward to North Africa. On the southern border they had to quell Banū 'l-Kanz aspirations to independence by a punitive campaign in 1102–3; the rebellious Kanz al-Dawla, seeking refuge in Muḳurra, was extradited by the Nubian king to the Egyptians. Then troops were stationed at Aswan to guard the frontier, whose peace was not disturbed by any major event until the overthrow of the Fatimids. Indeed the Arab chroniclers did not find anything worth recording about Egyptian–Nubian relations throughout the last seventy years of Fatimid rule, which serves to confirm the regular course of peaceful coexistence and interchange.

Trade went on undisturbed. The provisions of the *baḳt* indicate that it was customary to permit free travel and offer protection to Muslim merchants, whereas settlements were usually tolerated only in the northern borderland. In the long run, as in the western Sudan, trade paved the way for Islamization. The continuing movements of the merchants increased their knowledge of the country, which was passed on to those interested. The private zeal of the merchants did more for the spread of Islam than the official propaganda agents (*du'āt*) charged by the Fatimids with the diffusion of the Shī'ite creed. In the Nile region, official action was limited to 'Aydhāb, and most missionary work was spontaneously and inconspicuously carried on by traders.

The history of Egyptian–Nubian relations under the Ayyubids begins in 1172 with a Nubian attack; the Ayyubid army under Ṣalāḥ al-Dīn's brother Tūrān Shah counter-attacked and succeeded in capturing Ḳaṣr Ibrīm, which they occupied for a time. It has been suggested that the Nubian initiative might have been a consequence of a possible alliance between the Fatimids and the Nubians.[4] A little later the Ayyubid army defeated the rebellious Arabs, Banū 'l-Kanz, and compelled them to retreat from Aswan to al-Marīs, the northern portion of Muḳurra. There is ample

4. P. L. Shinnie, 1971b, p. 46.

evidence of the progressive Arabization and Islamization of this area between the ninth and twelfth centuries. The presence and intermarriage of the Banū ʾl-Kanz (who were themselves of mixed Arab–Nubian origin) in Nubia was just one aspect – though a major one – of this twofold process.

The southward movement of *ḳabīla*s from Egypt was proceeding on an unprecedented scale. Heavy pressure was exerted on the Arab nomadic and semi-nomadic *ḳabīla*s under the Ayyubids, and even more under the Mamluks, which brought about serious clashes. The major punitive campaigns of the Mamluk troops against the refractory *ʿurbān* – or Beduin, as it became customary to label them – are recorded as taking place in 1302, 1351, 1353, 1378 and 1395. They were relentlessly hunted down and only one escape route remained open to them: into the Sudan. Other dangers, from outbreaks of famine and plague, pushed them in the same direction. Thus marauding nomads in ever-increasing numbers approached riverain Nubia through the deserts, a disruptive force marching through inhabited zones, plundering and starting fights against both individual settlements and the established power, as well as among themselves. In Egypt and Nubia they were feared as a serious danger.

The history of Nubian relations with Mamluk-dominated Egypt has to be viewed against this background. Exposed to depredations and gradually losing internal cohesion, Muḳurra proved increasingly unable to sustain the expected role of a co-operative neighbour assuring the peace of the southern borders. The Mamluks, in their turn, intensified a policy aimed at reducing Muḳurra to a vassal kingdom. Their interventions were facilitated by the discord within the ruling family, which at a later stage assumed a new significance when some of them were converted to Islam.

It seems reasonable to assume that the inauguration of an active policy of intervention in Nubian affairs by Sultan Baybars (1260–77) was to a great extent motivated by consideration of the safety of Egypt. Also, it has been suggested that the large amount of plunder collected from the Nubian campaigns and from the *ʿurbān* in Upper Egypt may be indicative of an economic motive behind the repeated interventions.[5] Contemporary chroniclers record a diplomatic overture resulting in the sultan's demand for resumption of deliveries of the *baḳt*, which had been suspended from a date unknown. King Dāwūd of Nubia instead undertook a number of incursions into Egyptian domains, culminating in 1272 with the capture of ʿAyd̲h̲āb, a Red Sea port of primary importance for Egyptian commerce. A suggestion has been made that this act was meant to support the crusaders, but there is no evidence for this. More likely incentives were the immediate prospect of booty and revenge for the Mamluks, having gained control over Sawākin a few years earlier. The concurrence of Mamluk campaigns in Syria and Nubia is, however, worthy of note.

5. Hasan, op. cit., p. 114.

In 1276 Baybars sent a large punitive expedition, which defeated Dāwūd, and conferred the throne of Muḳurra upon Dāwūd's cousin and rival, whose name is given as S͟hakanda or Mas͟hkad in the sources. In return for Mamluk help, S͟hakanda took a solemn Christian oath binding him to a number of obligations that would practically have replaced the traditional *baḳt* relationship by complete vassalage.[6] Calling himself the sultan's *nā'ib* or representative, S͟hakanda promised to pay an annual tribute consisting of half the country's revenue and a specific number of Sudanese animals. Marīs, or more probably its revenue, was assigned to the direct control of the sultan. Nubians who did not agree to embrace Islam were bound to pay a yearly poll tax, *djīzya*. Arab nomads seeking refuge in Nubia were to be extradited. Moreover, S͟hakanda's policy was to be subject always to the sultan's approval.

In addition to the humiliating political and economic terms of the agreement, Nubia had to suffer a considerable drain on human resources, although the sources certainly exaggerate the number of captives brought to Egypt as slaves, which they put at 10 000. It is politically significant that the prisoners included hostages from the royal family and the former King Dāwūd, given up by the ruler of al-ʿAbwāb, where he had sought refuge. Some interest in his fate is shown in the correspondence between Baybars and Yekuno Amlak of Ethiopia.

Reduced to a state of vassalage under a mighty suzerain, Muḳurra still experienced internal disorder. Punitive expeditions followed in due course. This ruthless policy of repeated intervention was bound eventually to prove short-sighted, in terms of Nubia's role as a buffer state against the predatory nomads. Mamluk troops devastated and depopulated the country. The resistance capacity of the riverain state organization *vis-à-vis* the nomads was thus weakened to the point of inefficiency. Numerous Arabs took the opportunity to join the Mamluk troops in search of booty and a better living outside Egypt. Ibn al-Furāt estimated the number of such participants in 1289 at 40 000 tribesmen, the figure doubtless including both men and camp followers.[7] Banū 'l-Kanz had been engaged to support the Mamluk campaigns right from the outset.

King Shamāmūn was a stubborn adversary of the Mamluks. Twice defeated, he attacked the Mamluk garrison left at Dunḳula and killed both their nominee and the traitors. In 1290 he wrote to Sultan Ḳalā'ūn asking pardon and offering to pay an augmented *baḳt*. It seems that the sultan's commitments in fighting the last remnants of the crusaders led him to consent to this state of affairs.

For over a decade after that Nubia was spared military operations. In 1305 another expedition was sent from Cairo on the request of King Ammy, looking for help with internal troubles. Later Ammy's successor, Karanbas,

6. Hasan, op. cit., p. 109, gives the full text of the agreement, as transcribed by al-Nuwayrī and preserved in al-Maḳrīzī's *Kitāb al-sulūk*; see also J. S. Trimingham, 1949, p. 69.
7. Ibn al-Furāt, 1936–42 edn, Vol. 8, p. 83, quoted by Hasan, op. cit., p. 114.

either refused or was unable to pay the expected tribute and in due course a punitive expedition was sent with a new pretender to replace the disobedient king. For the first time the candidate was a Muslim, King Dāwūd's nephew, whose name is given by the sources as Sayf al-Dīn ʿAbdallāh Bar<u>sh</u>ambū (or Sanbū). Karanbas reacted by proposing another Muslim candidate, the then Kanz al-Dawla (or chief of the Banū ʾl-Kanz) Shujāʿ al-Dīn, who had a better right to the succession as Karanbas's own sister's son.

Sanbū's accession to the throne at Dunḳula marks the beginning of the official conversion of Muḳurra to Islam. The event is commemorated by a tablet in Arabic recording the conversion of the old royal cathedral of Dunḳula into a mosque, opened by Sayf al-Dīn ʿAbdallāh al-Nāṣir on 16 Rabīʿ I, 717 (29 May 1317). The new king's reign, however, was short. Kanz al-Dawla managed to gain popular support among Nubians as well as among the Arab *ḳabīla*s and thus to defeat and kill his rival, the distant relative sent from Cairo.

The sultan was afraid of a possible wider alliance that could be shaped around a ruler of mixed Nubian and Arab descent, and resorted to the promotion of a new candidate. After the latter's premature death another expedition, in 1323–4, restored to the throne King Karanbas, who had embraced Islam during his temporary captivity in Cairo.[8] Kanz al-Dawla, however, drove out his uncle and took back the power into his own hands. It is not clear why the Mamluks did not intervene again.

Further dynastic history is not clear either. From the sources we have for the events of 1365–6, it appears that the internal struggle for power continued with strong Arab involvement. A great role was played by the Banū ʾl-Kanz, their allies the Banū ʾl-ʿIkrima, and the Banū Jaʿd, who took control of Dunḳula. The king sought refuge in the castle of al-Daw in Marīs, while Dunḳula was left in ruins. Mamluk troops, sent for by Nubian envoys in Cairo, accomplished their mission by slaughtering Arabs, taking prisoners in the northern areas and enforcing the submission of the Banū ʾl-Kanz and the Banū ʾl-ʿIkrima. The Nubian kings retained their residence at al-Daw, and the larger part of Muḳurra was left in disorder, without central authority. The last written reference to the Nubian king, dating from 1397, concerns another request for help with internal troubles.

Thus the last days of the Nubian kingdom are veiled in obscurity and Egyptian sources are silent on the matter. The other available evidence from the Sudan – from both oral tradition and genealogies – is concerned with the making of new ethnic patterns in the riverain and adjacent areas and does not show any interest in the disappearance of the former rulers.

8. Hasan, op. cit., p. 120, following the authority of Ibn <u>Kh</u>aldūn and al-ʿAynī. It is interesting, however, to note that a pious Greek graffito in Old Nubian script from 'St Simeon' monastery at Aswan, dated 1322, praises King Kudanbes, great Christian monarch, 'president of caesars'. Cf. F. L. Griffith, 1928.

The recorded facts indicate that Nubia was never annexed. The Egyptian invasions cannot be viewed as a systematic attempt at either destruction or colonization. Nevertheless their effect was that Mukurra lost a great deal of vitality and efficiency as an organized state. Referring to the Islamization and Arabization of the royal family, a modern Sudanese historian writes that the 'Nubian kingdom was not so much overthrown as turned inside out'.[9] Others speak of 'the submergence of Christian Nubia';[10] or the absorption of its power by immigrants.

An important vehicle of Arabization was intermarriage. By virtue of the Nubian matrilineal system, sons of Arab fathers and Nubian mothers acquired the rights of succession to leadership as well as a share in land and other property. We have seen this system in operation in the political ascendancy of the Banū 'l-Kanz. The gradual conversion of the people to Islam was another facet of the same complex process at work within the seemingly chaotic state of affairs left behind after the disappearance of central governmental authority.

Cumulative evidence obtained from recent archaeological work has made it possible to envisage the hostile phases of the process in terms of some concrete ascertained facts.[11] The growth of insecurity from about the middle of the twelfth century is paralleled by the development of defensive architecture and settlements intended to provide protection for larger concentrations of the Christian population. Inspection of habitation sites reveals the general adoption of features that can be best explained as devices for the protection of property and food from marauders, while the population probably preferred escape. Defensive surrounding walls and watchtowers (see Plate 16.1) are commonly found only in upper Nubia and in the very late Christian sites upstream of the Second Cataract. Numerous vestiges of late Christian communities are found on islands. The landward defensive orientation of such island settlements, as well as the southward view provided for the watchtowers in the cataract region, seems to indicate that the enemy was expected from the desert, mainly from the south, and probably unaccustomed to water barriers.[12]

Hence it seems reasonable to conclude that the main danger came from the predatory groups from the desert, mainly Arabs but possibly also Berbers, Zagbāca and others. Thus, on the one hand, contemporary sources written from the Egyptian viewpoint tell us of villages destroyed, waterwheels broken and people carried off into slavery by invading armies from the north; a scorched earth policy on the part of the retreating Nubians

9. Hasan, op. cit., p. 90.

10. P. M. Holt, 1970, p. 328.

11. Adams, 1966.

12. Adams, 1966, p. 150: 'The further south one goes, the more fortification is encountered and the earlier in the Christian period it makes its appearance.' Adams, however, admits that this assertion is based on his own unsystematic observation of Christian sites in the Batn al-Hadjar and upper Nubia.

themselves is also mentioned. On the other hand, in the light of archaeology we see the greater importance of another danger, stretching over a much longer span of time and more acutely felt. It was this factor – the penetration of the Arabs – which did most to destroy the old social and political organization and to set in motion a far-reaching process of culture change.

ʿAlwa

The history of ʿAlwa is even more obscure than that of the last days of organized Christianity in Muḳurra. The usual image of a flourishing kingdom draws mainly on the accounts of Ibn Sulaym (from 975) and Abū Ṣāliḥ in the early thirteenth century, supplemented by information obtained from Muslim merchants, for ʿAlwa was a good market for the purchase of slaves. Abū Ṣāliḥ's description shows the kingdom in full prosperity, with some 400 churches including a spacious cathedral in Sōba.

In the Mamluk period references to ʿAlwa become extremely rare. The only person frequently referred to is Adur, the ruler of al-ʿAbwāb, who several times extradited fugitive Nubian kings in an endeavour to ensure the goodwill of the Mamluk sultans. In 1287 an ambassador of the sultan was sent at Adur's invitation on a mission to investigate complaints against the king of Dunḳula. In 1290, as recorded by the same medieval author, the sultan's help was requested against an external enemy, most probably from the south.[13]

The decline of ʿAlwa probably resembled that of Muḳurra. Arab immigrants penetrated to marginal areas and deeper into the heartland, intermarried with the local population and assumed control over the pastures, eroding in this way the social fabric and undermining central authority. Attacks by black peoples from the south constituted another threat and a strain on the country's potential and human resources, probably already weakened by the slave trade. The Church, moreover, stagnated in isolation. In the second half of the fifteenth century the overall deterioration permitted the Arabs to settle in the very heart of the country near Sōba. The most southerly point of Arab expansion in the Gezira was the town of ʿArbad̲j̲ī, founded about 1475.

Until recently it has been customary to date the fall of ʿAlwa to 1504, which is the year of the establishment of the Funj sultanate with its centre at Sennar. The two events, however, need not have occurred at the same time, and there is insufficient reason to discard the old tradition that Sōba was captured by the Arabs acting alone, probably at an earlier date.[14] The tradition describes the action as being organized and led by Chief ʿAbdallāh, nicknamed Jammāʿ, 'the gatherer' of the Ḳawāsima section of

13. Ibn ʿAbd al-Zāhir, 12th cent., quoted in Hasan, op. cit., p. 13.

14. See P. M. Holt, 1960; H. N. Chittick, 1963b. Chittick thinks that after the fall of ʿAlwa a Christian general escaped to Ḳerrī, which would seem to be the stronghold referred to in the ʿAbdūllābi chronicle.

the Rufā'a Arabs. The attack was directed against the alleged tyranny (*zula*) of the kings of 'Alwa, called 'Anadj. Sōba was conquered and probably destroyed and the inhabitants dispersed. 'Abdallāh's descendants – the 'Abdallābi – gained supremacy over the nomadic *ḳabīlas* and Arabized Nubians in a fairly large area around the confluence of the two Niles and further north. The capital of the new rulers was established at Ḳerrī (near the Sablūḳa gorge), which assured a position of command over the main Nile.

The supremacy of the Arabs did not remain unchallenged for long. At the beginning of the sixteenth century another wave of newcomers suddenly appeared in the Gezira on a migratory move down the Blue Nile. They were cattle-herding nomads named Funj, who at that time were practising their traditional religion. Their remote origin has given rise to a number of speculative hypotheses, from their identification with the Shilluk to a search for their home somewhere in Bornu or in northern Ethiopia.[15] The Arab–Funj relationship is referred to in two contradictory traditions concerning the events of 1504. Whereas the first, preserved in a nineteenth-century revision of a *Funj Chronicle*, speaks of an alliance between the Funj chief 'Amāra Dūnḳās and 'Abdallāh Jammā' against Sōba, the second, known through James Bruce, informs us of a battle between the two parties near 'Arbadjī. Both sides obviously contended for grazing rights in the southern Gezira as well as for political supremacy.

Victory and power fell to the Funj, whereas the 'Abdallābī chiefs obtained a subordinate position. The Funj rule, in partnership with the 'Abdallābi Arabs, extended over a large proportion of the Nilotic Sudan and opened a new period in the country's history. The degree of political stability achieved facilitated the further growth of Arab prestige and an effective Islamization.

The triumph of Islam

The passing away of Christianity

The conversion of Nubia from Christianity to Islam was not a straightforward sweeping process, proceeding continuously from north to south. The spread of Islam started well before the period of our review, continued at unequal speed in different areas and was roughly completed only under the Funj. The means of Islamization were numerous: they included the activity of Muslim traders admitted to the country for centuries, the infiltration of the Arabs, as well as direct pressure and the opportunist search for advantage in later periods, for example in Shakanda's treaty and the conversion of the royal house of Dunḳula.

15. The earliest authority for the Shilluk theory was James Bruce (1790), who visited Sennar in 1772. The Bornu theory was propounded mainly by A. J. Arkell. For a detailed analysis of the problem see P. M. Holt, 1963.

Similarly, the Christian faith did not disappear in one breath together with Nubia's governmental system, but persisted much longer. The tomb of a bishop buried with his Coptic and Arabic scrolls, discovered in Ḳaṣr Ibrīm in the early 1960s, has shown that church dignitaries were still in office in 1372. The Christian community may have survived for several further generations. In the 1520s a Portuguese chaplain, Francesco Alvares, travelling in Ethiopia, heard from his companion, called John of Syria, an account of the land of the 'Nubiis':

> that he had been to this country and that there are in it 150 churches, which still contain crucifixes and effigies of Our Lady, and other effigies painted on the walls, and all old: and that the people of this country are neither Christians, Moors nor Jews, and that they live in the desire to become Christians. These churches are all in old ancient castles which are throughout the country, and as many castles there are, so many churches.[16]

Alvares also writes of a Christian embassy sent from the same country to the Ethiopian court to ask for priests and friars to teach them; however, the Ethiopian 'Prester John' could not do this in view of his own dependence on the patriarch of Alexandria. The usual view that the country referred to is ʿAlwa has recently been questioned, and the Dunḳula area suggested instead. The question remains open. Archaeological work seems very likely to produce further discoveries attesting to the long persistence of local Christian communities in Nubia.

As regards the chronology of the advance of Islamization, most of the evidence, although it is controversial, comes from the northern areas. The Muslim minorities probably lived long in peace with their Christian neighbours, both sharing the same material culture. The absence of Arabic tombstones after the middle of the eleventh century has given rise to a suggestion that Muslims may have been persecuted by Christians, which would seem to be corroborated by an inscription about the individual conversion of a Muslim to Christianity, though insufficiently so for a more definite statement.[17]

Later indications of anti-Christian violence accompanying invasions suggest that such action was incidental rather than preconceived or prompted by widespread religious hatred: for example, the chroniclers' account of the conversion of the church into a mosque, the capture and torture of the bishop and the slaughtering of pigs, following the Ayyubid conquest of Ḳaṣr Ibrīm. In general, the Christian monuments of Nubia do not bear many traces of destructive violence, although some were probably plundered by the *ʿurbān*. Nor do the written sources reveal that Christianity *per se* would have been an object of attack. To quote

16. F. Alvares, Eng. transl. 1881, pp. 351–2.

17. The inscription found at Meinarti is mentioned in W. Y. Adams, 1965, p. 172.

PLATE 16.1 *The church and monastery at Faras (Nubia) surrounded by Arab fortifications, seen from the east*

PLATE 16.2 *The city wall of the Arab citadel of Faras, reconstructed with ancient bricks*

W. Y. Adams: 'the Christian population of Nubia was caught between Muslim forces, Egyptian and nomadic, whose hostility was directed as much at each other as it was at Nubians. If Nubian Christianity was nevertheless destroyed in the process, it was more by accident than by design.'[18]

Yet there were also significant internal causes for the weakness of Nubian Christianity. According to widespread opinion it was essentially the religion of an élite and did not strike deep roots among the mass of the people. To a great extent worship was associated with Coptic clergy and a foreign culture, and lacked indigenous saints and martyrs. The tombstones are nearly all in Greek or Coptic. In Trimingham's view, the Nubian Church 'never became indigenous in the sense that Islam is today'.[19] All the same, the frescoes in excavated churches occasionally reveal the dark faces of indigenous Nubian bishops. Pious inscriptions in Nubian cannot be disregarded, although the devotion of the clergy is hardly indicative of the feelings of the peasantry. The persistence of older, pre-Christian beliefs is attested in Ibn Sulaym's account (written in the tenth century) as well as in their further continuation in popular Sudanese Islam today.

The Nubian Church was an elaborate urban culture closely associated with the state, but largely isolated by Muslim neighbours from Christianity abroad. We should not, however, be too dogmatic on this point. Nubian art seems to indicate contacts with Byzantium and even perhaps with the crusaders.[20] Besides the predominant Monophysitism and ties with the Coptic patriarchate, there is also evidence of Melkite rites, even for later periods.[21] The isolation, however, tended to increase. By the middle of the thirteenth century the links with the patriarchate of Alexandria had been cut and Coptic priests were probably not sent any more. Yet as late as the fourteenth and fifteenth centuries Nubian pilgrims were noticed in their chapel in the Church of the Holy Sepulchre in Jerusalem and later at services in Galilee.

Thus, in a situation not easy to survey, the external factors, especially the mass immigration inimical to the maintenance of independent Christian states, must have been decisive in inducing change. With the eclipse of the Church as a social force, conversion to Islam, which the powerful newcomers elevated into a new sign of prestige, became a gradual but generalized process for all sections of the population, as a part of social reintegration.

18. Adams, 1966, p. 151.

19. Trimingham, op. cit., p. 76.

20. The Byzantine influence was brought to light particularly by Polish excavations at Faras. There are also traces of Persian influence. For details see K. Michalowski, 1965 and 1967.

21. This has also been confirmed by the excavations at Faras. The nature of Nubian Christianity has been reviewed in D. W. Kilhefner, 1967.

The Arabization of the Sudanese

A great part of the migrations of the Arab *ḳabīla*s into and within the Sudan, as well as the vigorous recombinations of the Sudanese peoples into new groups, came about during the span of time of our review. The resulting situation, as it emerges from the dark period following the disappearance of the Nubian states, attests a large-scale racial mixing, with Arabic language and culture ultimately prevailing. The Arabization of the indigenous population, however, ran parallel with an equally intensive Africanization of the immigrants, obvious today in their racial characteristics, as the newly acquired cultural traits of the Sudanese Arabs were better suited to the environment of their new homes.

The sources available for the historical study of the individual moves leading to the making of the modern peoples of the northern Sudan can be used only with great circumspection. Most of them are legends and genealogical traditions, whose present form is of recent origin. These genealogies, known as *ansāb* or *nisba*s, were preserved by oral transmission, or in some cases in written form as valued pieces of private property.[22] The origin of some of the pedigrees can be traced far back into the past. The best-known originator of a great number of *nisba*s is al-Samarḳandī, a somewhat legendary figure of the sixteenth century, who is said to have compiled a book of genealogies for the Funj. It was designed to convince the Ottoman sultan of the well-founded Arab and Muslim background of the Sudanese and so to dissuade him from hostile plans. The same purpose – to show a descent from a noble Arab forefather – makes a great many genealogies, especially their older sections, suspect and unreliable.

In general, the *nisba*s pay little regard to the factual aspects of blood inheritance, whereas family groups take pride in identifying themselves with ancient *ḳabīla*s and confederations. For example, the historical D̲juhayna claim south Arabian (Ḳaḥṭānī) origin, and the D̲ja'aliyyīn look to north Arabia ('Adnānī) in claiming descent from the Prophet's uncle al-'Abbās and hence kinship with the Abbasid dynasty, whereas the black Funj conceal their obscure origin behind a tendentious claim to 'Umayyad ancestry. Another highly pretentious claim appears in some Sudanese clans and families of religious teachers, who represent themselves as 'As̲h̲rāf, that is, descendants of the Prophet and his close kin. Supplementary and corrective information obtainable from medieval Arab writers is, unfortunately, fragmentary and less impressive than the elaborate *nisba*s.

It goes beyond the scope of the present survey to follow the movements of the numerous ethnic groups. Their infiltration, going on for centuries in a mostly peaceful way, grew into a massive influx from the twelfth century onwards. A number of ethnic names, frequently mentioned in medieval sources, entirely disappeared later, and new units came into ex-

22. The richest collection of *nisba*s has been made and published by H. A. MacMichael, 1922.

istence. The fluid nature of the ethnic groupings over longer periods should always be kept in mind. The routes which the Arabs followed on their long march, whether with large flocks or in poverty, are partly identifiable through traces left to this day.

Thus the suffix *-āb*, which frequently occurs in the ethnic names east of the Nile, is a loan-word from Tu-Bedawie (Bedjāwī) meaning family or clan, and hence indicates the passage of *ḳabīla*s through the Bedja country. This area was probably the first to experience Arab immigration both across the Red Sea and from Egypt. The country was unattractive for the settlement of a large pastoral population, and the Bedja-Arab contacts, including intermarriage, did not end in complete fusion. The *ḳabīla*s headed further, to the rolling plains of the Butāna and the middle Nile, where they met others pouring through Nubia. Many finally settled in the Gezira.

Numerous groups moved south through the Nile valley. It has been mentioned that some of them willingly participated in Mamluk expeditions. Their further infiltration into the steppe region south of Dunḳula followed more than one direction. Some groups headed westward. Convenient routes must have been Wādī al-Milk and Wādī al-Muḳaddam. For penetration into Darfūr another possibility was the Darb al-Arbaʿīn ('forty-day route'), starting from the Egyptian oases in the Western Desert.

According to their respective *nisba* claims most Arabic-speaking Sudanese groups class themselves with one of two comprehensive groups, Djaʿaliyyīn or Djuhayna. The Djaʿaliyyīn group includes predominantly sedentary peoples in the middle Nile valley and in Kordofan, in particular Djawābra, Bedayriyya, Shāʿiḳīya, Batāhīn, Djamaʿāb, Djamāʿīya and Djawāmiʿa, besides the Djaʿaliyyīn proper, who live between Atbara and the Sabalūḳa Gorge. Their common eponymous ancestor was Ibrāhīm Djaʿal, an ʿAbbāsī who may have lived some time in the twelfth or thirteenth century. His nickname Djaʿal is explained by a popular tradition of his generous hospitality, which made him say to the hungry: *Djaʿalnākum minnā*, 'we have made you ours'.[23] The preserved *nisba*s can be considered fairly reliable only from the sixteenth century onward.

On the whole, the Djaʿaliyyīn are Arabized Nubians, with only a small proportion of Arab blood. Their homeland is the middle Nile region south of the Fourth Cataract, where their reintegrative settlement may have started somewhere between the lands under the control of the two Christian states. The names Djamaʿāb, Djamāʿīya, Djawāmiʿa and the like suggest the etymological association with the Arabic verbal root *djamaʿa*, 'to gather';[24] they indicate the mixed composition of the Arab immigrants, who continued to mingle with the indigenous population; this point is entirely ignored by the *nisba*s.

At some time in the early sixteenth century some of the Djaʿalī groups

23. MacMichael, op. cit., pp. 28 and 128.
24. Cf. Swahili, *ujamaa*.

migrated further west to Kordofan, where they became absorbed into local black races, although they retained their name and their consciousness of Ḏjaʿalī identity. Marriages of their chiefs with daughters of local notables are a common theme of popular legends about the rise of governments in the area. A claim to Ḏjaʿalī ancestry is made by the rulers of Taḳlī in the Nuba Mountains, in Darfūr, Wadai and Bornu, as well as by the Nusabbaʿāt of Kordofan.

The Ḏjuhayna have a better right to consider themselves Arabs. Unlike the Ḏjaʿaliyyīn, they preferred the nomadic life, for which they found favourable conditions in the grazing plains of the decaying ʿAlwa. Systematizing zeal has misled the genealogists into classifying all the nomadic and non-Ḏjaʿalī groups with the Ḏjuhayna. Thus in the present-day, broad meaning they include the Arabs of Satāna (Shukriyya and Rufāʿa), those of the Gezira (Kināna and Mesallamiyya) and even the camel-owning nomads of Kordofan (Kabābīsh, Dār Hāmid and Hamar) and the cattle-owning Baḳḳāra. They all claim descent from a common ancestor, ʿAbdallāh al-Ḏjuhanī.

The penetration of the Arabs into Kordofan probably took longer. In the fourteenth century there is evidence of westward penetration beyond Darfūr into the savannah of Chad. The pioneers of this push were the Ḏjudhām Arabs, whose name later fell into disuse. The Kabābīsh seem to have originated from various components, who came to express their unity by creating a fictitious eponymous ancestor, Kabsh ibn Hamad al-Afzār. *Kabsh* means 'ram', which is symbolic among pastoralists. Kabsh's brother is said to be the ancestor of the Fazāra, whose name, frequently encountered in older sources, fell into disuse after the Mahdist period.

The generic name Baḳḳāra (from *baḳara*, 'cow') includes the cattle-breeding groups whose present habitat stretches to the south of the main Sudanese east–west route. This zone is not climatically suitable for either camels or sheep, which led the Baḳḳāra to abandon them in favour of bulls. They rode upon these, however, and generally treated them as they had been accustomed to treat camels. As late arrivers, they probably found the northern pastures occupied and had to acquire a new way of living. Like the Kabābīsh, they absorbed some of the former clans of the Ḏjudhām. Their very dark colour is evidence of their intensive mixing with local Negroid peoples.

The incoming route of the Baḳḳāra is not clear. Some of them claim that their ancestors came from Tunis and Fezzān. Migratory, commercial and cultural movements along that route and further to Darfūr are indicated in a number of local traditions. It seems possible that the Baḳḳāra may have originated from an amalgamation of the Ḏjudhām, coming from the Nile, and other groups coming through Fezzān and Chad. A vigorous tradition relates that the Baḳḳāra forefathers, perhaps some ten generations ago, travelled west and then returned east to the present habitat. Alleged links with Banū Hilāl may reflect equally well the lasting cultural contacts with North Africa as well as the presence of smaller Hilālī groups among the peoples pushing southward from Egypt to Nubia.[25]

In addition to the Arabs, the waves of newcomers into the Nilotic Sudan included also Berbers and Arabized Berbers, although they were less numerous here than further to the west. The sources report movements of partly Arabized Howara in Egypt in the fourteenth and fifteenth centuries. Small Howari settlements are found both in Kordofan and Darfūr. The supposed migratory movements from the Maghrib must also have included Arabized Berbers besides Hilālī or other Arabs.

Social and cultural change

Nubia was always an important zone between the advanced civilizations of the Mediterranean and those of tropical Africa. The disappearance of central government and the change of religion, along with large-scale intermingling and recombination of racial and ethnolinguistic groups, made the country – the northern Sudan of modern times – once again a crossroads of multiple influences, all to be absorbed and reworked into a new, comprehensive and unique whole. The emerging society already bore a recognizable resemblance to the present-day ethnic and cultural characteristics which make Sudan a unique Arab–African entity or, in other words, a microcosm of the northern part of Africa.[26]

The first consequences of the eclipse of state power must have been impoverishment and a decline in security. In addition to the historical reasons already discussed for the depression of living standards, modern research has indicated a probable climatic deterioration, which was manifested about this time by the sinking of the level of the Nile.[27]

Earlier records of the material well-being of the Nubians reflect wide divergences in the opinions of eyewitnesses, depending on their different backgrounds and bias. Thus a report of an Ayyubid envoy from the twelfth century speaks of a poor country with only sorghum and date-palm cultivation and with a ridiculous princeling, whereas at about the same time the Armenian ʿAbū Ṣāliḥ speaks with admiration of the elaborate urban culture. Modern archaeological work has confirmed the latter view, while considerably enlarging our appreciation of Nubian art, especially church frescoes and pottery. Although the painting points to Byzantine inspiration, the pottery followed the local Neroitic tradition. A substantial change came only with Islam.

Pending further archaeological research, the developments in Nubia proper (Muḳurra and Marīs) in the dark period between the destruction of Dunḳula and the stationing of Ottoman garrisons in the early sixteenth century remain an open question. W. Y. Adams has recently formulated

25. Cf. Hasan, op. cit., pp. 169–71.
26. On this theme see in particular ʿAbd al-Raḥīm, 1970.
27. Cf. J. de Heizelin, 1957.

a hypothesis that Middle Nubia (between Maharraḳa and the Third Cataract), being a poor area, was probably abandoned by its Christian population by the end of the thirteenth century. After some 300 years of nomadism in the rainfall belt further south, they returned to their earlier homes as Muslims. This may explain the anomalous difference between the Nubian dialects spoken by the Maha in Middle Nubia and those spoken further north by the Kenūz and further south by the Danāḳla. Both the latter dialects are closely related and both are different from the Mahasī dialect, although the Mahasī homeland lies between the areas inhabited by these two peoples. In Adams's view, Islamized speakers of Kenzī had been infiltrating the largely depopulated area south of the Third Cataract since the last days of the vanishing kingdom and had thus imposed their speech, whereas the Maha in their supposed temporary nomadism preserved a dialect closer to Old Nubian. The hypothesis, however, is not unanimously accepted.[28]

In general, it seems probable that a considerable part of the earlier sedentary population turned nomad or semi-nomad in the dark period, as the margin of cultivation shrank. For Ibn Khaldūn, who was contemporary to the decay of Christian Nubia, the developments in the country neatly fit into his sociological scheme of sedentary life as the last stage of civilization and the starting-point of decay, contrasted with the courage and vitality of the Beduin. The developments also seemed to confirm his opinion of the quick death of a defeated nation. After describing how the Arab *ḳabīla*s, in particular those of the Djuhayna, brought about the disintegration of the kingdom and a generalized state of anarchy, Ibn Khaldūn writes: 'And there remains no trace of central authority [*mulk*] in their lands because of the change wrought in them by the influence of Arab beduinization through intermarriage and alliance.'[29] In spite of the realism of this account, it would, however, be an over-simplification of a complex situation to deduce that Nubia witnessed a general nomadization.

The cultural influence of Arabs and Islam brought about a number of interconnected innovations. Some of them have been mentioned already, in particular the change from matrilineal to patrilineal organization and the general self-identification as Arabs. The linguistic movement to Arabic affected all but Nubia proper, from Aswan southwards to just beyond Dunḳula, and even here bilingualism became widespread. On the other hand, spoken dialects of Arabic throughout the area from Bornu to the Nile show marked African influences. Islamic *sharīʿa* rules came to be implemented only gradually, under the Funj and later. The position of women changed as they were ousted from public life. New customs developed in weddings and other ceremonies of family life or social and religious occasions.

28. Adams, 1966, pp 153–5. For Shinnie's opinion, see his contribution to Y. F. Hasan (ed.), 1971, p. 44.

29. Ibn Khaldūn, quoted from Hasan, 1967, p. 128.

The visual arts and architecture of Christian times came to an end. The Beduin immigrants, in conformity with Ibn Khaldūn's view, had little regard for fine arts and did not bring with them anything of the delicacy of taste and refined skills of their sedentary co-religionists from the central lands of Islam. In this respect, the Sudan remained a neglected periphery. On the other hand, indigenous African aesthetic traditions did not fade out and continued to be felt in minor arts and handicrafts.

Ibn Khaldūn also mentions that conversion to Islam relieved the Nubians of the duty to pay *djīzya*. We do not know to what extent this part of Shakanda's agreement was ever put into practice. Certainly, the people who embraced Islam were protected against enslavement. In the past the invasions, the deliveries under *baḳt* and the occasional gifts and sales of slaves to Muslim merchants had often affected the Nubian population, especially when captives who practised the traditional religions were in short supply. Under the altered circumstances, following the expansion of the *dār al-ʿIslām*, the hunting and purchasing grounds had to be sought further to the south and west. On the other hand, there was probably little change in the employment of domestic slave labour, which continued to be of only subsidiary importance in economic life. Nor is there any evidence of change within the simple technology of agricultural work.

The disappearance of central government, the impoverishment of the population and the preponderance of nomadism were sure symptoms of a temporary social regression. Ethnic structures were strengthened, to the detriment of the potential growth of feudal-type state institutions. In return, the new social and cultural patterns which the emerging Sudanese peoples acquired and developed, through the dark period and after, conditioned them for further historical advancement within the bridge area between Arab and African cultural orbits.

Nubia in Africa

A strong and justified feeling has arisen amongst contemporary historians of the Nilotic Sudan that in the past the northern, or Arab, factor was asymmetrically overemphasized at the expense of both indigenous developments and contacts with Negro African cultures.[30] This particular example of cross-cultural influence to and from the Sudan belt has for some time been a fruitful field for abundant speculation.

An obvious reason for the uneven distribution of attention has been the nature of available evidence. Arabic literary sources constitute the most considerable body, whereas archaeological work has only made its first steps. None the less, coupled with the exploitation of oral tradition and

30. Cf. P. E. H. Hair, 1969. The need for reconsideration in Sudanese studies was one of the main stimuli of the first international conference sponsored by the Sudan Research Unit in Khartoum in February 1968. See Hasan (ed.), 1971.

the comparative study of institutions, archaeology has already yielded some interesting results, in particular along the east–west axis of the Sudan. On the other hand, there still remains a danger of misrepresentation, based on the false identification of seemingly similar ethnic and local names or on other kinds of incorrect interpretation of cumulative evidence.

In relation to Egypt, it is only fair to stress once more the high degree of Nubia's creative cultural independence *vis-à-vis* the comparable Coptic communities. Both were, of course, in close contact over a long period. In time of persecution Coptic monks sought refuge in Nubia.[31] There is also sufficient evidence of reciprocal Nubian influence in Upper Egypt. The most interesting fragments of Nubian documents have been found in Coptic monasteries, and other discoveries from Egypt include a number of sherds of characteristic Nubian pottery, known as Dongola ware. Suffice it to say that evidence of commercial contacts between the neighbouring countries is abundant, both in literary sources and in excavations. To the east, Nubia's activities also resulted in contacts with Egypt and the Arabs. Little is known about Nubian policy towards the Bedja, who probably did not refrain from occasional raids against the settled riverain areas. According to Ibn Khaldūn, some of them adopted Christianity. The whole problem of the Nubian presence in the eastern desert still awaits elucidation.

As a result of the diligence of Arab writers, more is known about the trade via the Red Sea, which in the period of this review flourished considerably; the Fatimids had made the Red Sea the principal route for commerce with India and it remained so until the Portuguese breakthrough in the early sixteenth century. The main ports on the Sudanese coast were ʿAydhāb and Sawākin, both developed by Muslim merchants. The trade between the ports and the Nile valley was entirely in the hands of the Arabs, and the Bedja, through whose country the traffic flowed, seem to have been mainly, though not entirely, passive. Their goodwill and the safety of the caravan routes were guaranteed by treaties and, in some cases, by a share of revenues apportioned to the local chiefs. In the ʿAydhāb area this share tended to increase, from the Fatimid times to the fourteenth century, when Ibn Baṭṭūṭa visited the flourishing port.[32]

ʿAydhāb provided trade links mainly with Egypt. It was also used by pilgrims to Mecca, especially during the time of the crusaders' presence in Palestine, which constituted a danger for the Sinai route. The second half of the fourteenth century witnessed a considerable decline in eastern trade passing through ʿAydhāb, due to the rise of Jeddah on the opposite (Asian) shore. Permanent unrest in the hinterland probably also played its part. Finally, in the 1420s, Sultan Bārsbāy in an act of retaliation against

31. The presence of Coptic monks is shown, for example, by grave *stelae* found at Ghazālī. See P. L. Shinnie and H. N. Chittick, 1961, pp. 69 ff.

32. Hasan, 1967, p. 73.

the local Arabs and Arabized Bedja dealt the port a fatal blow.[33]

In view of its geographical position Sawākin was probably a more important commercial outlet for Nubia than its northern rival. From the nature of the available written sources it follows, however, that our information concerns only its relations with Egypt. In 1264–5 Sultan Baybars punished the Arab ruler of Sawākin by military action, but later consented to appoint him as a Mamluk representative. For some time the token of the Sawākin ruler's submission was an annual payment of 80 slaves, 300 camels and 30 *ḳintārs* of ivory – typical Sudanese commodities, always in high demand.[34] In the middle of the fifteenth century Sawākin was captured again by a Mamluk army and made subject to their more direct authority.

However strange it may appear, knowledge about Nubia's relations with Christian Ethiopia is very scanty. Mention has been made of some isolated instances of contact, such as the unsuccessful Nubian mission to the Ethiopian court reported by Alvares. In spite of the lack of evidence, it may still be presumed that the political relations between Nubian and Ethiopian Christians were closer than has so far been proved. Perhaps more evidence is yet to be found from the Ethiopian side.

To the south the picture is also obscure. It cannot even be said with certainty how far the limits of ʿAlwa extended. At present the southernmost sites of the same culture have been discerned near Wad Hedani, although a further extension is fairly probable. It may also be supposed that slaves were frequently obtained from areas in this region. Arab authors writing about ʿAlwa distinguish the Nūba from other blacks. An ethnic name that occurs more than once is Kursī, Kersa or Karsā.[35] We are told that they were naked – or, from another source, that they dressed in skins – and made the local spirits reap the harvest for them. Other black and probably naked people beyond ʿAlwa are mentioned as Takunna or Bakunna.[36] From Ibn ʿAbd al-Zāhir we learn that at about 1290 the country of the ʿAnadj (that is, ʿAlwa), was attacked by an enemy. Y. Fadl Hasan supposes that this attack must have come from the south, perhaps from the ancestors of Funj, whereas A. J. Arkell suggests that the invaders were from Kanem or Darfūr.[37] The attacks from the south were surely not of rare occurrence. Finally, the Funj are said to have advanced into the Gezira from the south down the Blue Nile. On the whole, it is tempting to imagine that there may be some connection between the collapse of Christian Nubia and what

33. A tradition about the destruction of ʿAydhāb was recorded by Leo Africanus about 1526; see French transl. 1956, pp. 484–5. ʿAydhāb is by mistake called Zibid or Zabid.

34. Hasan, 1967, p. 85, citing the authority of al-Nuwayrī.

35. Mentioned by Ibn Sulaym, Ibn Hawḳal and Ibn ʿAbd al-Zāhir. A. J. Arkell, 1961, p. 195, suggests they might be people of Darfūr or identical with the Maba of Wadai.

36. Mentioned by Ibn al-Faḳih and al-Masʿūdī. See Hasan, 1967, p. 7. Arkell, 1961, pp. 189–90, suggests that their name may survive in those of Jebel Kon in Kordofan, of the Junkun in Nigeria or even of Ghana.

37. Hasan, 1967, p. 130; Arkell, 1961, p. 199.

seems to have been a chain reaction of population movements everywhere in the neighbourhood, including perhaps even the southward push of Nilotes from the upper Nile to the equatorial lakes.[38]

To the west, Nubia's contacts and reciprocal influences are more easily traceable. Just as uncritically as ancient Meroe used to be credited with the spread of iron-smelting, medieval Nubia was viewed as a centre for the diffusion of Christianity as far as West Africa. Some reservations, though not total scepticism, are called for here. Very many Christian traditions from the west have been collected by U. Monneret de Villard;[39] and the idea of a large-scale diffusion of Christianity from Nubia is also maintained by contemporary scholars.[40] Sceptical voices, however, have been numerous, pointing either to other possible routes for Christianity across the Sahara, for example through the Goraan, or to a probable misunderstanding of Islamic influence.[41]

In fact, the evidence for the westward influence of Christian Nubia is a little clearer than that for the spread of culture from Meroe, once expounded so vigorously by A. J. Arkell. Nubia definitely brought to maturity a superior civilization, equal to those of the empires of the western Sudan, and could be viewed as a desirable model. The numerous traditions of the West African peoples about their eastern origin cannot simply be disregarded. Shinnie says of them: 'With such a mass of material all suggesting eastern contacts it is unlikely that all is fiction or myth and it is possible that they contain elements of truth and suggest that at least some cultural influence came from the East.' Since oral tradition rarely goes back more than 500 years, Shinnie suggests that these influences should be ascribed to medieval Nubia rather than Meroe.[42]

Arab writers provide little information on this point. Ibn Hawḳal in the tenth century wrote of two western peoples: *al-D̲jebāliyyūn*, subject to Dunḳula, and *al-Aḥādiyyūn*, obeying ʿAlwa. They lived in a land called Amḳal, rode camels, bore arms and wore sandals like others of the West (*mag̲h̲āriba*), whom they resembled.[43] This information is certainly rather confused and not easy to interpret.

The material evidence for Nubian influence on countries to the west is scattered. It includes a graffito in Old Nubian and, notably, red-brick structures at Zenkor and Abū Ṣufyān, along the east–west route through northern Kordofan. The pottery from Zenkor resembles that of Sōba. Both sites are still waiting for more than mere survey and surface collections.[44]

38. See the stimulating article by M. Posnansky, 1971, pp. 51–61.
39. U. Monneret de Villard, 1938.
40. For details, see I. Hofmann, 1968. The theme of the joint Byzantine, Persian Kisra and Nubian role in Christianizing Africa has been, in Frobenius' footsteps, rehabilitated in T. Papadopoulos, 1966. See also the relevant review article of D. F. McCall, 1968.
41. See C. H. Becker, 1913.
42. Shinnie, 1971b, p. 48.
43. Ibn Hawḳal, 1938–9 edn, p. 58.
44. For details see A. E. D. Penn, 1931; W. B. K. Shaw, 1936.

Red-brick structures of the same type continue further through Darfūr and Chad ('Ayn Galakka) to Bornu, the westernmost site being Nguru in northern Nigeria. In Darfūr there is the royal palace at Uri, some 900 km from Dunḳula, which Arkell suggests may have been one of the places visited by Sultan Ḳalā'ūn's envoy in 1287 on Adur's request, since only the consonants of the names have been preserved in the Arabic account.[45] At 'Ayn Faraḥ in northern Darfūr, ruins of red-brick buildings, identified after some hesitation as a monastery and churches, were found to contain potsherds of Nubian origin from between the eighth and eleventh centuries, decorated with Christian symbols. The buildings are tentatively dated from the same period up to the thirteenth century.[46] Of this chain of similar sites, the only one that may be dated with some precision is Birnin Gazargazo in Bornu, from the fifteenth or sixteenth century.

Pottery showing medieval Nubian influence and dated after the year + 1000 has been found on sites at Koro Toro and Bochianga in Chad, over 1450 km from the Nile.[47] It has not yet been decided whether they indicate trade with Nubia or with a local settlement. It is also worthy of note that both sites provide evidence of iron-working, which raises anew the question of the spread of this technique from the Nile valley.

The extent of Nubia's relations with Kanem-Bornu, and perhaps with the western Sudan, remains uncertain pending further systematic archaeological work. The key area for investigation is Darfūr, whose early history prior to the establishment of the Fūr Kayra power, from about 1640 onward, is largely a matter of controversial legend and speculation. There is general agreement only on the fairly peaceful succession of power from the Dādju in the south to the Tundjur in the north and finally to the Fūr.[48] The origin of the former two and the dating of their respective periods of rule have aroused a great deal of speculation.[49] In view of their different locations, their power may have flourished for some time simultaneously. Their available genealogies and traditions are clearly fictitious within the well-known schemes of Arab noble ancestry.

Most of the work on reconstructing the medieval history of Darfūr has

45. Arkell, 1961, p. 198.

46. For details of 'Ayn Farah, see A. J. Arkell, 1960; also R. de Neufville and A. A. Houghton, 1965, which emphasizes the Muslim character of the buildings superimposed upon older remains.

47. R. Mauny, 1963.

48. For a brief summary of the reliable knowledge available, see H. G. Balfour-Paul, 1955. Longer accounts are G. D. Lampen, 1950, and notably Arkell's numerous studies (see n. 50 below).

49. As regards the Tundjur, there is evidence for traces of Christianity amongst them; see H. A. MacMichael, 1920, pp. 24–32 and 1922, pp. 66 ff. The tradition of their Hilālī descent has been recorded by G. Nachtigal, 1879–81, and H. Carbou, 1912. H. Barth, on the contrary, records traditions of their coming from the Nile, whereas Becker, op. cit., attempts to reconcile both traditions. A great deal of speculation may be found also in numerous writings of H. R. Palmer.

been undertaken by A. J. Arkell. Whereas his earlier hypothesis dated the Tund̲jur hegemony during 1350–1535, the verification of Christian influence at ʿAyn Faraḥ led him to restate it, saying that Tund̲jur rule was under Nubian protection, and dating its heyday between the eighth and tenth centuries.[50] Should Ibn Hawḳal's information be understood to support this view? Moreover, Arkell traces the derivation of the same Tund̲jur back to 'Muḳurra' and also sees possible links with the name of the 'wise stranger' of Darfūr legends, Aḥmad al-Maʿḳūr. About 1240, he believes, Darfūr was conquered by the great king Dunama of Kanem, whose power extended as far as the Nile in Marīs, at the point of closest approach to the desert route Darb al-Arbaʿīn. This hypothesis presumes a strong Bornu influence over Darfūr for the next 400 years, especially under the rule of Mai Idrīs.[51]

There is clear internal evidence of similarities among the institutions found in all the emerging Muslim states between the Nile and the savannah of Chad, which may be interpreted in terms of Bornu cultural influence, but not necessarily of political supremacy. The influence seems noticeable, *inter alia*, in the fourfold divisions of administration, in some aspects of architecture, and the imposition of the queen-mother in government. The latter feature, however, may be also found in Nubia.

Uri in northern Darfūr, in Arkell's view, was a centre of Tund̲jur rule and later for that of Kanem. It was probably an important emporium of long-distance trade at the crossroads of Darb al-Arbaʿīn and the east–west savannah route, known in Arabic as *tarīḳ al-Sūdān*. Within the span of time under review we may presume that there were higher and lower levels of trade along this road at different times, but it does not seem probable that it would have been used for the traffic of pilgrims to Mecca prior to the sixteenth century. Written sources do not contain any allusion to this. All known pilgrimage traffic of the period from the western and central Sudan, including the famous travels of the rulers of Mali, Songhay and Bornu, went towards the North African coast and on through Egypt, often by way of ʿAyd̲h̲āb. The internal overland route along the populated Sudanese belt, employed for trade and migration, seems to have been adopted for pilgrimage only later, after the important changes of the sixteenth century. Although, on the one hand, the Moroccan invasion of Songhay and the decline in security had a negative influence on the western Saharan routes, favourable conditions, on the other hand, were created in eastern Sudan by the disappearance of the Christian establishment in the Nile valley and the rise and consolidation of Islamic power in Sennar, Darfūr and Wadai. Yet the pilgrims' movement along the Sudan road was in-

50. See A. J. Arkell, 1936, 1937 and 1946 (earlier view); 1959 (restatement). More recently, Arkell (1963) has expressed the view that, besides Darfūr with its headquarters at Uri, the legendary Tund̲jur 'pagan kingdom' of Wadai with its capital at Wara may actually have been another province of Muḳurra.

51. See Chapter 10 above.

creasing only slowly and took a long time to acquire major proportions.[52] As to Darfūr, the general assumption is that Islam may have appeared as a court religion under the Tundjur, but certainly it gained currency only under the Kayra Fūr.

Meanwhile, the whole area between the Nile and Chad had been greatly affected by the penetration of Arab populations. Further cultural, commercial and political development cannot be properly understood without an awareness that their presence was increasingly being felt among the peoples of the Sudan. In 1391 Sultan Barḳūḳ in Cairo received a letter from the king of Bornu complaining of the misbehaviour of the Djudhām and other Arabs, who were attacking his people and indiscriminately selling them to slave dealers from Egypt, Syria and elsewhere. The document, preserved by al-Ḳalḳashandī, is among others a unique testimony of far-reaching political as well as commercial contacts in this part of the world.[53]

As in the Nile valley, though to a lesser extent, the presence of Arabs modified the ethnic map of the area from the Nile to Chad. Conditions became more favourable for the progress of Islamization and the rise of new Sudanic states in an easterly extension of the chain. In the complete absence of older written records, these new beginnings are reflected in the intricate aggregations of colourful legendary material, in which the area abounds. A systematic archaeological investigation is badly needed to disentangle them.

52. Cf. U. A. al-Naqar, 1971.
53. Al-Ḳalḳashandī, 1913–19 edn, Vol. 1, p. 306 and Vol. 8, pp. 116–18.

17 The Horn of Africa: the Solomonids in Ethiopia and the states of the Horn of Africa

T. TAMRAT

The political geography of the Horn

The political geography of the Horn of Africa had become extremely complex by the last quarter of the thirteenth century. The most widely known state in the area was the Christian kingdom in the northern highlands of Ethiopia, which had just passed from the hands of the Zagwe to those of the Solomonid dynasty in 1270. The borders of this kingdom at that time extended roughly to the northern districts of Shoa in the south, the region east of Lake Tana and the upper Blue Nile in the west, and the edge of the Ethiopian plateau in the east. Besides this Christian state, however, there were several other political units of various sizes in the area. Immediately to the north-west of the former Zagwe kingdom, beyond the River Tekeze, the Falasha (the so-called 'Jews of Ethiopia') seem to have constituted an independent state of their own, which was in continuous struggle against attempted Christian conquest. The kingdom of Gojjam, which is mentioned in the traditions, seems to have existed in the mountainous area to the immediate south of Lake Tana. More important still, there are strong indications in the historical traditions of the area that a powerful state called 'the kingdom of Damot' controlled an extensive territory south of the Blue Nile gorge. Almost nothing is known about this very ancient African kingdom, but the traditions referring to it clearly show that long before the advent of either Christian or Muslim principalities in the area the kings of Damot had effective hegemony over the whole region of the Shoa plateau.

There were also Muslim principalities in the area, along the coast from the Dahlak archipelago in the Red Sea to the Somali town of Brava on the Indian Ocean. Their geographical location would seem to have depended upon the strategic importance of the coast for trade between the rich plateau of central and southern Ethiopia, the East African coast, the Gulf of Aden and the Red Sea. By the end of the thirteenth century, as a result of this trade, powerful Muslim communities had emerged which were to constitute various well-organized principalities and states: the most important in the interior were Shoa, Ifat, Fetegar, Dawaro, Hadya, Bali

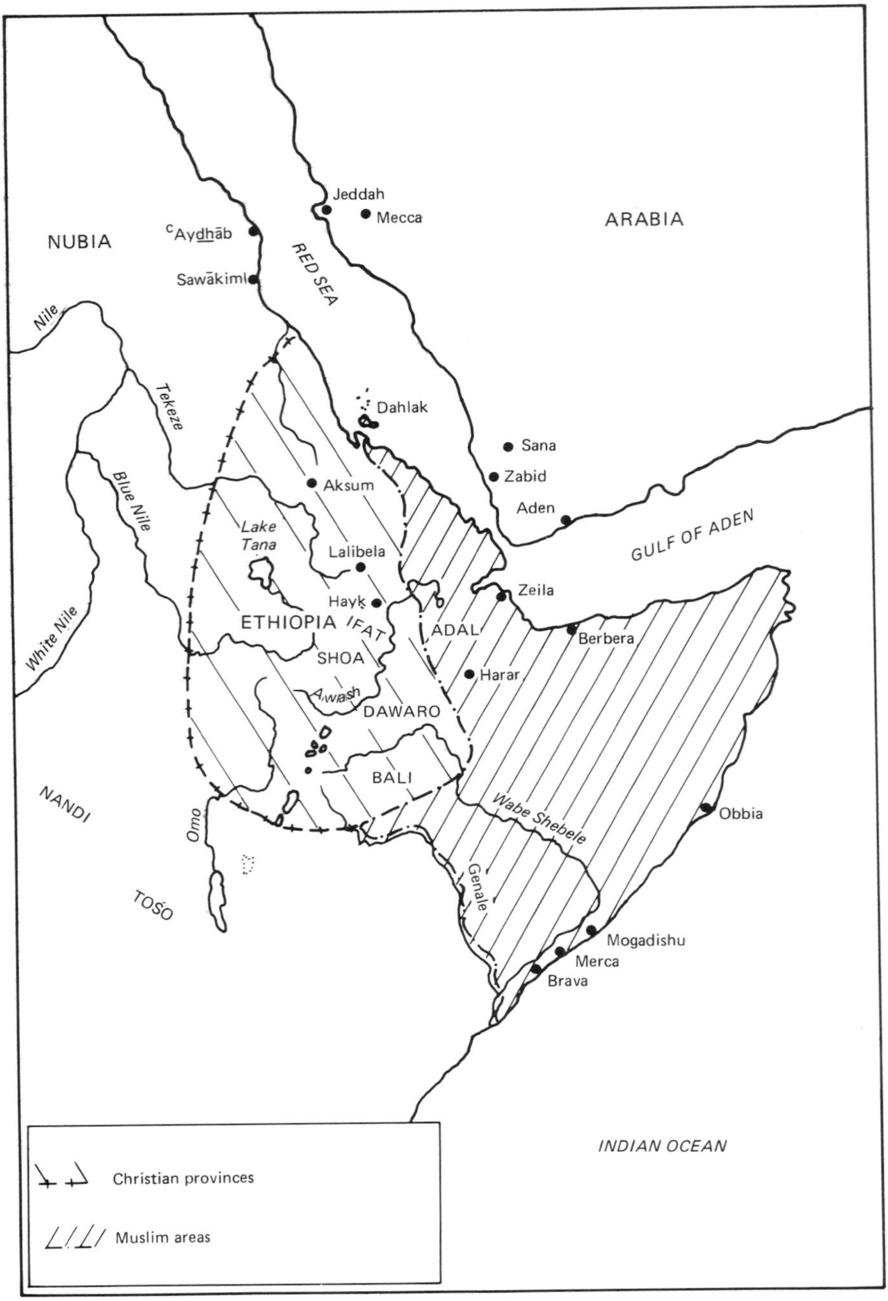

FIG. 17.1 *Ethiopia and the Horn of Africa* (*T. Tamrat*)

and Adal.[1] Although the main settlements – Dahlak, Zeila, Berbera, Mogadishu, Merca and Brava – seem to have been more deeply imbued with Islamic culture than their counterparts in the interior, it was these communities of the hinterland that most persistently – and successfully – set out to create a real Muslim empire in the Horn.

Peoples and languages

The well-known Italian historian, Conti Rossini, has very aptly described Ethiopia as a 'museum of peoples'. This truly reflects the great antiquity and complexity of the linguistic and ethnic picture of Ethiopia and the Horn as a whole. Apart from the Congo–Kordofan and Khoisan groups, the two other 'super-families' of African languages, Afro-Asiatic and Nilo-Saharan, are profusely represented in the area. The Afro-Asiatic group is the more important of the two in terms of distribution and relevance, and three out of its six branches – namely Semitic, Cushitic and Omotic – are spoken there, each with a large number of highly diversified dialects.[2]

It seems clear that throughout the period with which we are concerned in this chapter the large majority of the peoples of the Horn of Africa were speakers of Cushitic, which is generally subdivided into North Cushitic (Beja), Central Cushitic (Agew) and Eastern Cushitic.[3] The Beja, in what is today the northern part of Eritrea, constituted the northernmost inhabitants of the area. To the south of the Beja lived speakers of different dialects of Agew, in the central and southern highlands of Eritrea (Bilen/Bogos), in parts of Tigrai, in the homelands of the Zagwe in Wag and Lasta, in the Falasha country west of the River Tekeze, and in the mountainous areas of Gojjam south and south-east of Lake Tana. It is quite possible that there were still some enclaves of Agew-speaking communities in Amhara in the thirteenth and fourteenth centuries. By far the largest area in the interior of the Horn, however, was occupied by speakers of the various languages and dialects which constitute Eastern Cushitic, of which the two major subdivisions are Burgi-Sidamo and Lowland Cushitic. Burgi-Sidamo seems to have been distributed in what are today portions of southern Shoa, Arussi, Bali and parts of the Harar plateau; Lowland Cushitic was spoken in the dry, hot lowlands between the edge of the Ethiopian plateau and the Red Sea in the north, throughout the predominantly Somali-inhabited interior of the Horn and

1. Though al-ʿUmarī (in French transl. 1927, p. 2) omits Adal, he nevertheless lists seven 'Muslim kingdoms in Abyssinia': Ifat, Dawaro, Arababni (or Arabayni), Hadya, Sharkha, Bali and Dara. This list was repeated quite unchanged and in this order by al-Maḳrīzī, who calls them 'kingdoms of the Zeila country'; 1895 edn, p. 5.

2. Specialists in the subject are by no means agreed on the classification of African languages.

3. M. L. Bender, 1976.

in the portions of present-day Ethiopia to the immediate south and south-east of Lake Chamo, from around which the expansion of the Galla-speaking peoples apparently started in the sixteenth century.

Omotic, which was known as Western Cushitic until very recently,[4] was probably spoken by the inhabitants of south-western Ethiopia between the southern part of the Blue Nile gorge and the basin of the River Omo. Although most of the highly diversified Omotic languages and dialects are now concentrated within a rather small area in the Omo basin, the existence of the related Shinasha and Mao languages, in the south-western parts of Gojjam and in Welega respectively, seems to indicate that Omotic was more widely distributed throughout south-western Ethiopia before the sixteenth-century expansion of the Galla.

The third branch of the Afro-Asiatic group of African languages represented in Ethiopia and the Horn is Semitic, and in the period between the thirteenth and sixteenth centuries the politically and culturally dominant peoples in the area were mostly Semitic-speaking. The Semitic languages of Ethiopia, known collectively as Ethio-Semitic, are many and diversified. The old notion that they were introduced by South Arabian immigrants in northern Ethiopia after −700 no longer seems plausible. More recent studies indicate that their history is much older than has hitherto been assumed; the two branches of Ethio-Semitic, North and South, are now believed to have separated at least three centuries before the rise of Aksum. It is apparent that, by the end of the thirteenth century, the present-day distribution of these languages had already begun to take shape. One of the three North Ethio-Semitic languages, Ge'ez, had been the literary language of the Ethiopian Church ever since the fourth century, and as such it has continued to survive to the present day with all its ancient forms still intact. The other two, Tigre and Tigrigna, were and still are spoken in what were once the most important provinces of the Aksumite empire: Eritrea and Tigrai. Except for some Tigre-speaking communities in the coastal and northern parts of Eritrea, the remaining areas originally inhabited by speakers of both Tigre and Tigrigna during the Aksumite empire were inherited almost intact by the Christian kingdom of Ethiopia in the thirteenth century.

In clear contrast with this, the many languages and dialect groups which constitute South Ethio-Semitic had a more complicated historical development, of which the details are still obscure. The latest attempts to classify South Ethio-Semitic distinguish two major branches, known as 'outer' and 'transversal' South Ethio-Semitic.[5] Speakers of 'outer' South Ethio-Semitic (the Gafat and the northern, western and central Gurage) seem to have been the earliest spearhead of Semitic expansion in central

4. Harold Fleming has made a most important contribution by showing that Omotic, previously classified as Western Cushitic, is a separate Afro-Asiatic family: H. C. Fleming, 1964.

5. See Bender, op. cit.

Ethiopia and in the period under discussion they had come to occupy a more or less continuous geographical area between the upper Awash basin and the Blue Nile gorge, in what is today western Shoa. Their earlier history is unknown, but it seems clear that they had moved into this area before the establishment of the Christian Church in Aksum and before the expansion of the new religion in the south. As late as the fourteenth, fifteenth and sixteenth centuries some groups of these people are described as being still at war with the Christian state of Ethiopia.

The earliest references to speakers of 'transversal' South Ethio-Semitic (Amharic, Argobba, East Gurage and Harari) also indicate that even the Amhara were not yet completely converted to Christianity at the beginning of the ninth century. From that period onwards, however, the Amhara began to be part of the Christian kingdom, which they finally came to dominate at the end of the thirteenth century, with the advent of the so-called Solomonid dynasty. The early history of other branches of 'transversal' South Ethio-Semitic (Argobba, East Gurage and Harari) is much more difficult to reconstruct; but they appear to have been distributed south and south-east of the Amhara, and they may very well have constituted the first bases for the early expansion and development of Muslim communities in Shoa and Ifat,[6] and probably also in Fetegar and Dawaro. It is important to note in this connection that the ancient walled city of Harar and its environs, where Harari and Argobba are now spoken, were precisely the new political centres established by the Muslim Walasma princes exiled from Ifat when, as we shall see later in this chapter, their former realms were finally annexed by the Christians at the end of the fourteenth century.

Besides these branches of Ethio-Semitic, which were thus distributed in the Ethiopian interior throughout the long corridor from the highlands of Eritrea to the upper Awash basin, Arabic was also spoken; it was the religious and commercial language used in all the settlements on the Red Sea, the Gulf and the Indian Ocean, as well as along the major trade routes and in the market centres of the interior, in some parts of which tombstones with Arabic inscriptions have been found.

The Muslim principalities of the coast

Apart from the Christian kingdom of Ethiopia and some of the more powerful Muslim principalities, almost nothing is known about the many states that certainly existed in the area at the end of the thirteenth century. The old African states (Falasha, Gojjam and Damot), like the many Islamized peoples on the coast and in the interior of the Horn, only figure in the history of the area if they were militarily subjugated by more powerful Christian or Muslim neighbours. Hence – since the purpose of this chapter

6. E. Cerulli, 1941, pp. 32–4.

is to bring out as far as possible the interactions between these different political entities – let us make it clear at once that the data available for reconstructing the political and cultural history of the peoples of the Horn relate only to Ethiopia and the most powerful of the Muslim states, such as the sultanates of Ifat, Dawaro, Adal and Dahlak. Generally speaking, the local history of these ancient states has been sorely neglected. A great deal of linguistic and archaeological research will need to be done before we can speak with greater certainty about the cultural and political dynamics of these peoples.

Although in the present state of our knowledge it may be difficult to determine the broad lines or structural features of the development of many of the peoples of the Horn during the period, the use of some Arabic sources affords us a summary list of the various Muslim coastal principalities that came into being as a result of trade and were more or less well known and frequented by Arab merchants and traders.

The Dahlak Islands off the northernmost part of the Horn, which command the Massawa Channel, together with the Farasan Islands off the coast of the Arabian peninsula, are a virtual bridge between the Yemen and the coast of Eritrea, and also an important port of call for north–south movement along the Red Sea. This had been their role even in antiquity; very early on, in the seventh century, the Muslims occupied the largest of them, Dahlak al-Kabīr, which was used as a prison and place of exile under the ʿUmayyad and Abbasid caliphs, before falling into the hands of the Zabid dynasty of the Yemen in the ninth century.[7]

Taking advantage of the internal dissensions of the Muslim world in the thirteenth century, the archipelago was able to regain its independence and set itself up as an amirate. It engaged in trade and piracy, and succeeded in neutralizing the threats of the Mamluks of Egypt by active diplomacy and an efficacious policy of opportunist alliance with the Mamluks themselves, against attempts at hegemony by the Yemeni and Ethiopian rulers. This policy on the part of the kings of Dahlak bore fruit, for the archipelago still seems to have been independent when the Portuguese arrived, at the beginning of the sixteenth century.[8]

Ibn Baṭṭūṭa skirted the whole of the east coast of Africa from the Egyptian Red Sea coast to Kilwa, and from his account we have some information for the fourteenth century concerning the area between Zeila and Mogadishu (Makdis͟hu).[9] Zeila was a town inhabited by a black community, the Berbera, undoubtedly the Berābir (that is, Somali) referred to by Yāḳūt.[10] The town was actively engaged in trade, in camel and sheep-breeding and in fishing. The general prevailing atmosphere was

7. For the Dahlak Islands, see *Encyclopaedia of Islam*, new edn, Vol. 2, pp. 90–1.

8. G. Wiet, 1951–2.

9. Ibn Baṭṭūṭa, 14th cent.; see, in particular, French transl. 1922, Vol. 2, pp. 179–91; and partial French transl. 1966, pp. 22–6.

10. Yāḳūt, German edn 1866–73, Vol. 1, p. 100; Vol. 2, p. 966; and Vol. 4, p. 602.

really that of a large conurbation faced with town-planning and sanitation problems.

The town of Makdishu was a large commercial centre. Sheep-breeding enabled its inhabitants to make 'the cloth that takes its name from this town and has no peer. From Makdishu it is exported to Egypt and elsewhere.'[11] They also grew bananas, mangoes and vegetables as well as rice, the staple food. The town's harbour was a port of call for many boats, which were surrounded on arrival by a swarm of *sunbuk* – small craft no doubt used both for fishing and for retail transport of goods to the outskirts of the town. The town is depicted as a very civilized community in which the conviviality and hospitality characteristic of the world of trade were highly developed. It was dominated by a large aristocracy of powerful merchants, lawyers and officials of the sultan. The sultan himself, who according to Ibn Baṭṭūṭa was a shaykh, was at the apex of a firmly established organization undoubtedly designed to ensure the best possible trading conditions. We have little information about the political development of the dynasty or about politicians at that time, but all the evidence is that the sultan's court included various viziers with well-defined administrative functions.

In this cosmopolitan world, Arabic coexisted with the language of the country, about which the author tells us nothing; but it displayed all the strength of African cultural structure, even though with the progress of Islamization the teaching of the Koran was very highly developed. Ibn Baṭṭūṭa lays great stress on the large number and assiduity of the *ṭabala* and the fact that the Shāfiʿī rite was preponderant among the people.

Arab geographers also tell us something about three other trading cities on the Somali coast of the Horn: Berbera, Merca and Brava. Berbera was in fact well known in antiquity as an important port. The town and its hinterland are well described in the *Periplus of the Erythraean Sea* and also by Ptolemy and Cosmas Indicopleustes. Its importance as a port can certainly not have declined by the period with which we are concerned, for its name was long used to denote the Gulf of Aden; Arab geographers themselves referred to it indifferently as the Sea or Gulf of Barbara. According to these geographers the Berābir who inhabited the country (and who, as most of them pointed out, were not the same as the Berbers) were quite distinct from the Waswahili and the Abyssinians. We have every reason to think that they were indeed Somali.[12] Politically also, between the ninth or tenth and the fourteenth centuries Berbera seems to have developed hand in hand with the other Muslim communities in the area, particularly Zeila, which was relatively close, and the sultanate of Adal.

11. From Ibn Baṭṭūṭa, partial French transl. 1966, p. 23.

12. The word Somali appears for the first time only at the beginning of the fifteenth century, in an Ethiopic hymn dating from the reign of Negus Yeshak. *Encyclopaedia of Islam*, new edn, Vol. 1, pp. 1172–3.

At the other end of the Horn, the towns of Merca and Brava seem to have belonged to the trading empire of Mogadishu and its fleet, which is partly explained by redistribution and a fairly large regional trading area. Hence it would appear that there was a relatively dense network of trading exchanges between Mogadishu and the other two ports (that is, Brava and Merca), which were much less important for inter-regional trade.

These various Muslim communities were key pieces on what André Miquel has described as a 'commercial chessboard'. Their importance was also closely linked to the existence of an enormous, active, rich hinterland.

The Christian and Muslim states in relation to the communities practising traditional African religions

The development of the trade routes from the Gulf of Aden to the interior of the Horn of Africa from the tenth century is one of the most significant factors in the history of all the peoples of the area. Even when they were a bone of contention among the main powers in the region, which vied for their control, these routes undoubtedly helped to bring about all kinds of interaction between local peoples of different cultural, religious and linguistic affiliations. Groups of people from almost all corners of the region played a part in the economic and political developments generated by the opening of these routes, particularly during the protracted movements of conquest and expansion of the leading Christian and Muslim states in the period under consideration. By the middle of the thirteenth century even the Christian Zagwe kingdom in northern Ethiopia no longer regarded the sultanate of Dahlak as its only outlet to the Red Sea, and had started to use the Zeila route through its southern provinces. This vital change in the economic significance of Zeila may be seen as a key factor not only in the emergence of Ifat as the leading Muslim state between the Gulf and the Shoa plateau, but also in the gradual southward shift of the political centre of Christian Ethiopia, which resulted in the rise of the Solomonid dynasty.

The founder of the new Solomonid dynasty, Yikunno-Amlak, was a local leader in Amhara about whose origin and early career very little is definitely known. But the traditions unanimously identify him as the man who put an end to the Zagwe dynasty in 1270. The traditional polemics between the Zagwe and the Solomonid rulers dominate the annals of the period; much of the story about Yikunno-Amlak is designed to establish the legitimacy of his rule as a restoration of the ancient Solomonid dynasty of Aksum. This approach has somewhat obscured the practical reasons, which seem to provide a better explanation for the success of Yikunno-Amlak and his supporters. The Christian settlements in the southernmost provinces of the Zagwe kingdom had long been part of a great network of commercial relations with the Muslim principalities strung out between the Gulf of Aden and the Shoa plateau. The whole of the upper and middle Awash basin was a frontier area in which Christian, Muslim and traditional religious communities had been interacting for at least three centuries.

The area seems to have formed part of the domains of the famous 'king of Damot' – referred to by Ibn Khaldūn[13] – whom Christian traditions recall as a dominant power in the thirteenth century. The 'king of Damot' (known as Motelami in Christian traditions) practised the traditional religion; the existence of the Christian and Muslim settlements in the Shoa plateau north of the upper Awash still depended on his goodwill. This pattern of relationships between the traditional religious communities, on the one hand, and their Christian and Muslim neighbours, on the other, had begun to take shape between the tenth and eleventh centuries at the latest. Christians from northern Ethiopia and Muslim merchants from the Gulf of Aden had by then established their respective communities in the area. With the revival of Christian Ethiopia under Zagwe rule in the twelfth century the Christians appear to have become increasingly confident and even to have asked the Zagwe to intervene on their behalf. The Zagwe tradition about an armed expedition against Damot most probably refers to such a situation.[14] The expedition was a failure: Damot did not fall under the sway of the Zagwe king, and he and many of the Christians he had led against Damot lost their lives in the battle. Yet Zagwe ascendancy over the Christian communities seems to have been strengthened, and the Christians in the area thenceforth considered themselves the subjects of the Zagwe kings. Their contacts with the Christian provinces in Amhara, and further north in Angot and Tigrai, increased.

Many of the Christian settlers in Shoa were involved in long-distance trade with Tigrai in the north. According to an early source that refers to the thirteenth century, these traders travelled to Tigrai to get salt, which they exchanged for horses and mules in Shoa.[15] This appears to indicate that the relatively few Christians settled at that time, in what is today northern Shoa, had acquired a major share in the internal trade of the Ethiopian plateau north of the upper Awash. They also engaged in mixed farming, and very early traditional references portray some of them as prosperous farmers with large families, including a certain number of slaves. Dispersed over a wide area, they were organized into small chieftaincies, which all seem originally to have been tributaries of the kings of Damot. There was a very strong sense of common identity and interdependence among these scattered settlements, and in the heyday of Zagwe power in Lasta they seem, with their neighbours in Amhara, to have constituted a larger Christian province in what is today Wello.

13. Ibn Khaldūn, partial French transl. 1852–6, Vol. 2, p. 108.
14. C. Conti Rossini (ed.), 1904, pp. 22–6.
15. T. Tamrat, 1972a, p. 82.

Side by side with these Christians lived the Muslim families settled in the eastern foothills of the Shoa plateau. Since both these religious communities had originally been subjected to the rulers of the area who practised the traditional religions, there was probably no well-defined territorial demarcation at first between their respective settlements. Like the Christians, the Muslims had a strong sense of identity and shared the tradition that the founders of their communities were Arabs from Mecca.[16] In the thirteenth century, however, they formed a number of independent, competing political entities, which tended gradually to break away from the authority of the ruler of Damot. One of these was the 'sultanate of Shoa', which actually comprised many rival principalities dominated by small family groups descended from a common Arab ancestry. The area later known as Fetegar may also have formed part of these closely associated settlements. The other important Muslim community was Ifat, which came into prominence mainly in the thirteenth century. Since their establishment, each of these settlements had been strengthened by an increasing number of local conversions to Islam. According to linguistic analysis of the names of the rulers and later reports by al-'Umarī, the dominant section both of the Muslim population and of the nearby Christian communities, at least in Shoa, spoke Ethio-Semitic.[17]

Like their Christian neighbours, these Muslims led relatively comfortable lives, based both on mixed farming and also, to a much greater extent than the Christians, on long-distance trade. In the latter respect the Muslims had an advantage, in that the caravan routes from the Gulf of Aden to Shoa passed through areas which had been predominantly Muslim since the thirteenth century. Thus they were in firm control of international trade. Nevertheless, to take their trade further inland to the centre of the Zagwe kingdom they no doubt had to co-operate with the Christians of Shoa and Amhara, who seem to have acted as middlemen for the stage across the Christian high plateaux in both directions. This interdependence obviously gave rise to a strong bond of interest between the Christian and Muslim communities in the area. As a result of the growing importance of the port of Zeila on the Gulf as the main trading outlet from central Ethiopia, this link became increasingly close and profitable. Although aware of their respective identities, a spirit of mutual toleration existed between the two groups, so that there were probably no major conflicts on religious grounds in these frontier areas during that early period.

On the eve of Yikunno-Amlak's coming to power, therefore, all the evidence suggests that the Christian communities in Amhara and Shoa played an important part as middlemen between the Muslim areas and the rest of the Zagwe kingdom in the north. Their economic co-opera-

16. E. Cerulli, 1931, p. 43; and 1941, pp. 15–16.
17. Al-'Umarī, loc. cit., pp. 1–2.

tion with the merchants enhanced their influence both at the Zagwe court and in the rest of the Christian lands. It certainly seems that before he actually became the new ruler of Christian Ethiopia, Yikunno-Amlak had made firm alliances with both the Muslim and Christian communities in Shoa. It is significant that the more plausible traditions about him emphasize the role of his 'warriors', who came from several districts in northern Shoa.[18] Moreover, in a letter to the Egyptian Sultan Baybars (1260–77), Yikunno-Amlak declared that he had many Muslim horsemen in his army.[19] One of the very few paintings of the new king depicts him seated on a raised throne and surrounded, according to the caption on the canvas, by 'Muslims and slaves'.[20] All this seems to show that what enabled Yikunno-Amlak to depose the Zagwe was not so much the legitimacy of his claims to restore the Solomonid dynasty of ancient Aksum as his much stronger economic, political and military position.[21] The main result of his success was to shift the centre of Christian Ethiopia southwards, to Amhara and Shoa; from then on, the kingdom could play a more direct part in the rapid development of trade between the Gulf and the Ethiopian interior.

The kingdom of Ethiopia under the Solomonids

The early days of Solomonid rule were a very difficult period, during which the new dynasty had to consolidate its authority both within the Christian kingdom and in its relations with the neighbouring peoples. Two of the thorniest problems facing it were, first, the making of consistent rules for the succession to the throne and, secondly, the drawing up of an effective policy for Muslim–Christian relations both in the interior of Ethiopia and in the rest of the Horn. The succession problem was resolved by setting up a new institution on Mount Geshen, henceforth known as the 'mountain of the kings'. All Yikunno-Amlak's male descendants except the reigning monarch and his direct offspring were detained in the inaccessible heights of the mountain, with several hundred incorruptible warriors guarding its foothills and passes. There the princes were treated with all the honours due to members of the ruling family and, within the limits of Mount Geshen, enjoyed all kinds of amenities. Isolated from the outside world, and effectively deprived of any genuine social or political relationships with

18. J. Perruchon, 1893, p. 368; C. Conti Rossini, 1922, pp. 296–7.
19. Mufaḍḍal, French transl. 1973–4.
20. W. Wright (ed.), 1877, fol. 75b–6.
21. This strength was certainly noticed by various contemporary geographers and cartographers of Mediterranean Europe. Marco Polo, describing the war between Yikunno-Amlak and the Muslim principalities, notes that the Abyssinians 'are reported to be the best fighters in the whole province'; from French transl. 1955, pp. 292–3. Similar reports were to be repeated and amplified throughout contemporary Mediterranean cartography; Y. K. Fall, 1978, pp. 300–10.

the rest of the kingdom, most of these princes took up the study of religion, in which they excelled, and were noted as writers of Ge'ez poetry and composers of sacred music. When a reigning monarch died without leaving a viable heir among his immediate relatives, one of the princes on Mount Geshen was selected and ascended the throne. Thus, the 'mountain of the kings' was an ingenious constitutional device which, throughout the period covered by this chapter, helped to safeguard both the stability and the continuity of the Christian kingdom.

But a much more arduous task was to establish good relations with the increasingly powerful Muslim settlements and groups in the area between the Gulf of Aden and the Awash valley. During the first fifty years of Solomonid hegemony, relations between Christians and Muslims reached a position of forced equilibrium; it was only in the crucial reign of Yikunno-Amlak's energetic grandson, Amde-Siyon (1314–44), that the Christian kingdom gained the military dominance over the area that was to continue throughout the period under discussion. At the time of Amde-Siyon's accession to the throne Christian Ethiopia was seriously divided within itself: its territories were limited to the old Zagwe possessions, with some unimportant recent acquisitions in the Shoa area, and there was continual insecurity on all sides, both among the Muslim sultanates in the east and south-east and in the Jewish (Falasha) communities and those where the traditional religions were practised, that stretched from the north-west to the south-west and south.

Amde-Siyon was a warrior king *par excellence*, and he quickly set out to tackle each of these problems personally and systematically. The exact chronology of his early campaigns is not known, but he himself tells us in a land-grant deed that he led expeditions against the rulers of Damot and Hadya in 1316–17, and against Gojjam soon afterwards. The area north of Lake Tana, whose best-known inhabitants were the Falasha, also seems to have been first annexed at about this time. Each of these campaigns was successful, and the areas in question were integrated into the Christian kingdom. The conquest of these inland provinces gave Amde-Siyon enormous manpower reserves for his army, and firm control over the termini of the trade routes from the Gulf of Aden. The king was thus in a strong position to impose his rule over the chain of Muslim communities from the Gulf to the Awash valley. Besides Ifat, which since the reign of 'Umar Walasma had become the most important Muslim principality, the Muslim townships of Dawaro, S̱harḵẖa and Bali lived mainly on the trade with distant lands that went on in the area Amde-Siyon had just taken over.

This new economic subjugation to the Christian king, which began to make its effects felt, seems to have created an atmosphere of uneasiness and hostility towards the conqueror in most Muslim circles. Among these communities, Ifat had come into political and military prominence during the reign of 'Umar Walasma, who was Yikunno-Amlak's contemporary.

Some years before 1332, Amde-Siyon had complained that 'Umar's grandson, Haḳedin, was restricting the freedom of movement of his Christian subjects, one of whom was said to have been seized by the Muslims and sold as a slave. The incident gave the Christian army an excuse to invade Ifat and its dependencies. The town was sacked and the sultan killed in the battle; although his son, Deradir, courageously went on fighting, with the help of the Muslim herdsmen in the plains east of Ifat, all resistance was soon broken. Amde-Siyon reduced Ifat, for the first time in its history, to the rank of a tributary state, and military garrisons occupied the key points in the territory. The other big Muslim principalities then hastened to make their peace with Amde-Siyon, and at least two of them, Dawaro and Sharkha, are said to have made a treaty of friendship with him. The military victory over Haḳedin thus took on its full meaning; and, as the result of his earlier conquests of the principalities of Hadya, Damot and Gojjam, after less than ten years of his reign King Amde-Siyon found himself at the head of a Christian kingdom enlarged by an enormous area.

We shall briefly examine below the administrative structure by which the king kept such a vast empire under his firm control and governed it efficiently. But it should be noted here that revolts against Amde-Siyon's authority remained rife not only in the newly annexed provinces, but also in other areas relatively more integrated into the kingdom. In about 1320, for instance, Amde-Siyon had to go and put down a local rebellion by the Christians in northern Tigrai, and soon afterwards he seems to have gone campaigning as far as the Eritrean coast.[22] But the most serious uprisings he had to face broke out in 1332, when simultaneous revolts took place in widely separated areas, which led to his famous conquests of that year. The campaigns and conquests of 1332 are well documented.[23] Briefly, however, their main achievements were to reduce the great Muslim principalities of Ifat, Dawaro, Sharkha and Bali to stricter tributary status, and to strengthen the Christian military position on all fronts. From that time onwards the fame of Amde-Siyon's exploits spread far and wide in the Middle East, and the Arab historian al-'Umarī, who was his contemporary, wrote of him: 'It is said that he has ninety-nine kings under him, and that he makes up the hundred.' Although these are almost certainly fanciful figures, al-'Umarī explicitly included among Amde-Siyon's tributaries what he called 'the seven Muslim kingdoms of Ethiopia', including Ifat, Dawaro, Sharkha and Bali.[24]

The Muslim states and Ethiopia

The vast empire built up by Amde-Siyon and ruled, with few territorial additions, by his descendants down to the sixteenth century was neverthe-

22. B. Turaiev, 1906, p. 53; Tamrat, op. cit., pp. 95–6.
23. J. Perruchon, 1889.
24. Translated from al-'Umarī, loc. cit., pp. 25–6.

less not a unitary state. At best, it was a loose confederation of a large number of principalities of differing religious, ethnic, and linguistic affiliations; its coherence depended mainly on the supremacy of the central power.

Every time the authority of the court slackened, however little, each of the vassals was only too ready to go its separate way. During much of the period under review, most of these principalities continued to be administered by their hereditary princes under the supreme authority of the Christian emperors. The best contemporary description of the relationship between the Christian rulers and their newly conquered tributaries is again given by al-'Umarī:

> Although all the sovereigns of these kingdoms transmit their power on the basis of heredity, none among them has effective authority without being invested by the king of the Amhara. When one of these kings dies, if he has any male issue they all go to the king and employ all possible means to gain his favours; because it is he ... who has supreme authority over them, and before him they are only lieutenants.[25]

Al-'Umarī had only the Muslim tributary states in mind when he wrote this, but this description reflects the basic organization of the whole Christian empire at the time. The large army which the Christian emperors always kept as a symbol of their power was indispensable in ensuring the continued allegiance of the vassal territories. Contingents of the army were often stationed at such places, particularly in the early days of the conquest; they were commanded by a hierarchy of titled officials who acted without reference to the local hereditary princes and remained closely linked to the emperor's court. As a general rule, the troops for such garrisons occupying newly conquered territories were recruited in other ethnic and linguistic areas, so that any chance of a conflict of loyalties was minimized. These garrisons ensured that the smallest local rebellion was immediately suppressed, that the annual tribute to the emperor was duly paid, that the main trade routes stayed open and were safe and, finally, that the emperor's wishes were carried out in all respects. If local disturbances became too much for the garrison to suppress, their commander reported this to the emperor, who sent reinforcements of troops from stations in neighbouring territories. If the matter was very serious, as in 1332, he would personally lead an expedition against the rebels.

This system essentially characterized the Solomonid period until the early sixteenth century; the empire had then become so heterogeneous and difficult to govern that the kings could prevent its dismemberment only by keeping the court continually on a war footing, ready to move in any direction required by the latest emergency. More than anything else, this

25. ibid. (translated from the French), p. 19.

was the reason for the continuous mobility of the court and the absence of any large urban areas during the period.

The political structure of the Ethiopian empire

The Solomonid kings administered their vast territories from these mobile camps. Despite its mobility, however, the emperor's court always remained the focal point of the political and economic life of all his subjects, and tended to serve as a melting pot for their cultural and linguistic variety. Its internal structure and organization have been set out more fully elsewhere.[26] Suffice it to say here that the functions of the mobile court were exactly the same as those of a fixed capital. Large numbers of people from all corners of the empire always drifted along with it. Permanently attached to it were numerous troops and royal guards, recruited from all the dependent territories and commanded by officers who always had to accompany the monarch wherever he went. Besides these, there were thousands of retainers of the monarch and his household, as well as those of his many high officials. A special contingent of priests always followed the court, to staff its many royal chapels and serve the religious needs of the king and his followers. Wherever it was located, the royal camp also tended to be a major centre for the exchange of goods and supplies; thus merchants, artisans and craftsmen – both Christians and Muslims – all converged there with their merchandise and services. During the dry season, when travelling was much easier, the court was regularly visited in addition by many people from the provinces: vassal chiefs and local governors bringing their tribute, and many others seeking decisions from the monarch and his officials on awkward cases. Thus the actual number of individuals in the royal camp at any one time could easily approximate to the size of an average town.

Just like an ordinary urban centre, the royal camp had an important integrative function in bringing together thousands of people of different linguistic, ethnic and religious affiliations. In a sense it actually played this role much better than even a permanent settlement. In the case of a fixed town, the immigration of new residents from rural areas is one-way traffic. In the case of a mobile camp, however, not only did it receive residents from the countryside, but it was also continually moving from one part of the empire to another, so that it had a much more dynamic relationship with the areas through which it passed. It thus exercised its integrative functions within a much wider area.

This regular traffic between court and country no doubt contributed to the cultural assimilation and political integration of thousands of Ethiopians of sundry origins who happened to come into contact with it. This was particularly so with the large number of prisoners of war taken from

26. Tamrat, op. cit., pp. 103–6 and 269–75.

the newly conquered territories. Many of these were recruited into the Christian army; the rest entered the service of the monarch's own large household or of those of his countless officials. It is also apparent that members of the hereditary ruling families of the dependent principalities resided with the emperor either as outright hostages or just on prolonged visits to their overlord. In time many of these people developed deep personal loyalties to the emperor and his family, and became available for appointment to key positions of responsibility either at the royal court or in the provinces. However, the court remained in one area for only a relatively short period of time and its contacts with the local people were therefore transitory, superficial and even oppressive. Considerable demands seem to have been made on the area to supply sundry provisions and services, and the whole experience of being visited by the emperor and his huge entourage could not have been a very pleasant one for the majority of the local inhabitants. Thus the integrative role of the mobile court was seriously limited.

In fact, the basic nature of the control which the emperors could exercise over their dependent territories was always one of indirect rule. Even though they appointed a galaxy of titled officials both at the royal court and at the various local levels, no centralized system of imperial administration ever emerged, and the everyday life of the peoples of the different principalities and chieftaincies was highly localized. It was also partly to temper this localization that the emperors, followed by their unwieldy court, had to make occasional visits to every major part of their realm.

Amde-Siyon's conquests not only increased the size of his court and his army, but also made him and his successors very wealthy monarchs. Much of this wealth was derived from the regular tribute imposed upon all dependent territories. Failure to send tribute was considered a serious act of treason and often led to the disgrace, arrest and even execution of many a vassal. The historical records of the period are not very helpful in elucidating the economic basis of the empire, but the many land grants which are attributed to the Solomonid kings of the time seem to indicate that a major source of their power lay in their distribution of fiefs among their numerous followers in return for specific services. After their conquest of the Muslim areas along the eastern frontiers, however, there is some evidence to show that their control of trade had given them yet another lucrative source of wealth. They had gained absolute military control over the interior, which traditionally supplied the Muslim Near East with the highly priced *ḥabasha* slaves. Ivory and gold were also obtained from some of the newly conquered lands, and they are often cited as the two important items of trade in the region. In addition, the rich agricultural areas of the Ethiopian plateau also supplied the coastal towns on both sides of the Red Sea with much-needed cereals and fresh fruit.

From these commercial activities in the whole region, the emperors raised revenue in two ways. First, they imposed what amounted to import and export taxes on each of the items of trade. Secondly, they soon began to participate and invest directly in long-distance trade by sending out well-supplied caravans, led by their own commercial agents. In the long run, however, this Christian success in the inland provinces only generated the reorganization and revival of Muslim power in the area between Zeila and the frontiers of Ifat, Dawaro and Bali. The leadership of this Muslim revival was once again provided by a break-away branch of ʻUmar Walasma's family, who moved the headquarters to the Harar plateau and from there built up a remarkable network of Muslim alliances in the vast hinterland between the Dahlak Islands in the Red Sea and the Somali coast on the Indian Ocean, as well as throughout the neighbouring Arab countries. This development has been described elsewhere in greater detail; it need only be pointed out here that the fire of Muslim opposition to Christian rule was kept alive in the area until it finally erupted in the sixteenth-century *dji̱hād* (holy war) of Imam Ibn Ibrāhīm (*c.* 1527–43), also known as Gragn.

The revival of the Ethiopian Church

Besides the conquests and territorial expansion which we have reviewed briefly in earlier sections, another important result of the growing power of the Christian state under the Solomonid emperors was the revival of the Ethiopian Church and the renewed attempts it began to make to evangelize the Ethiopian interior. When the Solomonid dynasty took over in 1270 the Church was firmly established only in the ancient provinces of central and southern Eritrea, Tigrai, Wag, Lasta, Angot, Amhara and parts of the highlands of Shoa between the basins of the Rivers Abbay and Awash. As a general rule, the further south the location, the weaker and more precarious was the position of the Church in those days. All the major Christian educational centres were still located in Tigrai and the Zagwe homeland of Lasta, where the Egyptian bishops also held their episcopal court. Thus advanced religious training and ordination into the priesthood could only be achieved by spending many years in those parts of the Zagwe kingdom. Evidently very few individuals in the remote southern parts of the kingdom could undertake this, and the existence of the Church in northern Shoa was due not so much to a strong religious leadership by the local clergy as to the persistent loyalties of the few Christian families unevenly spread all over the area. Even in Amhara, further north, it was only on the eve of the rise of the Solomonid dynasty that, according to the traditions, the influential monastic school on the small island in Lake Hayḳ was established by a remarkable monk from Lasta, Iyesus-Moʻa, who had his own religious training in the ancient monastery of Debre-Damo in Tigrai.

With the advent of the new dynasty and the southward shift of the centre of the kingdom, however, many more religious and educational institutions began to flourish in Amhara and northern Shoa, and these soon emerged as centres for the propagation of the Christian faith in all directions. The two important propelling forces behind this expansionist movement were, first, the internal reawakening within the Church itself, which seems to have already started during the Zagwe period, and secondly, the special commitment of the Solomonid emperors to the establishment of the Church throughout their realms. Although most of the Zagwe kings were also equally committed to the Church, their Solomonid successors certainly had more extensive authority and much vaster resources with which to back the efforts of the Ethiopian clergy.

Almost all the new monasteries which began to develop in Amhara and Shoa from the last quarter of the thirteenth century onwards had some relationship with Iyesus-Mo'a's island school on Lake Hayḳ. Their founders were either themselves his pupils or had received their early instruction from someone who had connections with him. During the first fifty years of Solomonid rule, before the extensive conquests of Amde-Siyon, only Amhara and northern Shoa were safe for these monastic developments.

From the very beginning, the Ethiopian Church had been deeply imbued with the monastic traditions of the Egyptian deserts and the Nile valley, and Iyesus-Mo'a's pupils strictly followed the ancient coenobitic models of Sts Anthony and Pachomius in establishing their communities. A study of the historical traditions of these communities clearly shows that at the beginning the overriding motive of their founders was not so much the propagation of Christianity as their own search for personal salvation. Almost invariably the founder simply 'abandoned the world' by withdrawing from his own village and establishing an isolated hermitage, which often consisted of a natural cave on an uninhabited hillside; the usually inaccessible locations of most of Ethiopia's ancient monasteries seem to have been a result of this historical genesis. At first the founder was either alone or accompanied by only a few younger followers. For the first few years these anchorites led a severely ascetic life, entirely devoted to prayer or meditation, inflicting upon themselves considerable sufferings of hunger, thirst and even physical pain. They lived on wild fruits, but later started clearing the land around the hermitage and grew some vegetables and other plants. Gradually, they came into contact with the local people, who soon began to admire the religious zeal of the community and carried to neighbouring areas accounts of the reputation for sanctity of the founder and his companions. The curious as well as the genuinely religious began to visit the hermitage. Some ended up by joining it directly; others merely established spiritual connections with the founder, asking for his blessing and prayers and giving offerings to his community. In time, the spiritual influence of these monks grew and, given favourable geographical locations, even spread to include the households of the provincial governors and the court of the Solomonid emperors.

The community received endowments of land, cattle and other goods from individual families and local officials, and probably also from the emperors. As it grew more prosperous, the community would erect a more respectable church building and many huts to serve as living quarters for the inmates and for schools and other communal needs. Besides the increasing number of religious devotees who joined the community for purely spiritual reasons, the poor, the aged and orphans came to the monastery in search of food and shelter. Hagiographical traditions about the sanctity of the place and its residents spread far and wide, and many individuals with physical and mental ailments were brought there to be miraculously cured by the holy men. The monastery became the centre of a regular pilgrimage. In addition, most of the leading monasteries had convents under their spiritual guidance, often located some miles away. The community had to cater for all these elements and soon grew into quite a sizeable village with hundreds of permanent residents. In contrast to its simple beginnings, a complex set of rules was developed to guide the life of the community, and a hierarchy of monks was democratically elected to administer these rules and manage the property of the monastery, which grew continually richer.

Another important dimension of the spiritual fame of these monasteries was their role as educational centres. Each monastery supported a number of resident scholars, who gave traditional courses in reading, writing, the highly developed sacred music of the Ethiopian Church, Ge'ez poetry and grammar, church history and the exegesis of the holy scriptures.[27] Masters of calligraphy and religious painting were especially well patronized. The great monasteries vied among themselves to attract the best specialists in each of these fields, and maintained them with great honour and generous remuneration. In an attempt to render the cultural milieu more conducive and continuously challenging to the assembled scholars, assistance was given to needy and promising students, who could eventually join the ecclesiastical leadership either as members of the monastic clergy or as married priests and other church functionaries.

It was not only potential clergymen who underwent the very rigorous training provided in such schools. As the only educational institutions in the country until modern times, the monastic schools were an essential preparatory ground for national leadership. Apart from being born into a rich and powerful family, gaining meritorious distinction as a religious scholar was the most reliable way of joining the Christian élite. As we have seen above, the members of the Solomonid family detained on Mount Geshen were provided with similar educational facilities, and most of the officials in the provinces and at court were also products of church schooling. More than anything else, it was this key position of the Church in the educational

27. The best recent review of the history of Ethiopian Church education is Sergew Hable Selassie, 1972, pp. 162–75.

PLATE 17.1 *Lalibela: St George's Church, a general aerial view of the excavated church*

PLATE 17.2 *Lalibela: St George's Church, the upper section of the church during excavation*

PLATE 17.3 *Lalibela: St George's Church, vertical elevation*

PLATE 17.4 *Lalibela: the window of the 'Saviour of the World' Church*

system which enabled its influence to permeate the whole power structure of Christian Ethiopia throughout the centuries.

Such religious, cultural, and educational facilities had been provided in the ancient monasteries of northern Ethiopia since the days of Christian Aksum. But it was only in the last quarter of the thirteenth and the first half of the fourteenth centuries that they began to be available to many parts of Amhara and northern Shoa. During this early period, the communities established by Iyesus-Mo'a's pupils made steady progress. The most important of these were Debre Asbo (later renamed Debre Libanos), founded by Abba Tekle-Haymanot (*c.*1215–1313) in Shoa; Debre Col, started by Abba Anorewos and Beselote-Mika'el in Amhara; and the island monastery of Daga in Lake Tana, traditionally attributed to another pupil of Iyesus-Mo'a, Hirute-Amlak. The hagiographical traditions of these monastic schools indicate that their graduates went further into the interior and started their own communities. Monasteries grew up all over the area, particularly in Shoa, and an increasing number of well-trained clergymen began to be available. In the northernmost parts of Ethiopia a similar process of monastic reawakening was being led by the resourceful saint, Abba Ewostatewos, whose evangelical activities eventually affected the Christian areas of Bogos, Marya, Hamasen, Serae and some parts of Kunama in what is today Eritrea.[28]

At a time when Amde-Siyon was annexing many non-Christian territories, this expansion within the Church was a real blessing. With the emperor's approval, the Egyptian bishop who was the head of the Ethiopian episcopate at the time, Abune Yaikob, apparently began systematically to organize the major monastic orders and to demarcate specific dioceses for each of them, so that they could be responsible for the evangelization and general religious welfare of their respective spheres of influence. We have seen above that Amde-Siyon established garrisons in newly conquered areas. The emperor and his Egyptian bishop strengthened this expansion movement by recruiting priests from the monasteries and settling them in the new territories together with the Christian troops. Thus churches and monasteries gradually developed in Falashaland, Gojjam, Damot and even in the Muslim fiefs of Ifat, Dawaro and Bali. Generous land grants were made to them and the local people were under an obligation to the Christian emperor to protect the churches and facilitate their religious activities. Violations of this obligation were often cited as a major reason for punitive expeditions undertaken by the emperor's army.

Although this political and military protection initially speeded up the formation of Christian communities throughout the length and breadth of the Solomonid empire, the very close ties which the Church always

28. Further details of these movements of Church expansion are given in Tamrat, op. cit., pp. 156–205.

had with the power structure were in the long run a serious liability to it in a number of ways. Regarded by the dependent territories as a limb of the expanding and oppressive empire, it never gained the heart and soul of the conquered peoples. Even with the massive support it had from the state, the Church always continued to face persistent opposition from the traditional religious leaders of these peoples;[29] its fortunes were inextricably linked with those of the empire. Entirely dependent economically on the Ethiopian feudal system, it could never assert its spiritual and moral independence; and, outside the limits of the ancient provinces of the north and the major centres of Christian power in the annexed territories, its influence was minimal indeed. The hard truth of this situation was particularly evident when the empire collapsed under the pressure of the *dj̲ihād* in the first and second decades of the sixteenth century.

The considerable expansion of the Church during this period did not bring about any changes in its basic organizational structure. Spiritual dependence on the patriarchate of Alexandria continued and Egyptian bishops were brought in to head the ecclesiastical hierarchy. A very important development was the emergence of two leading monastic orders, the so-called 'houses' of Tekle-Haymanot and Ewostatewos. Tekle-Haymanot's 'house' tended to be more established in the sense of its closer ties with the royal court, and with Debre Libanos of Shoa as its base it had the allegiance of most of the churches of the empire. The 'house' of Ewostatewos started as a militant minority group in the early fourteenth century and, although it also established additional communities in Tigrai, Falashaland, Gojjam and Shoa during the fifteenth century, its main bases of power remained the monasteries founded by Ewostatewos's pupils in Eritrea, among which Debre Bizen later emerged as the leading centre.

It is important to note here that, just like the Christian empire itself, the Ethiopian Church was highly decentralized. Although they tended to have a hierarchy of spiritual and historical importance attached to them, each of the major monasteries was essentially self-sufficient and almost completely independent of the rest. This was largely true even of the relationships of monasteries within the same order. The Egyptian bishops and emperor always attempted to reduce this decentralization and increase their direct control over the monasteries through economic preferment and the use of the bishop's unique power of granting holy orders. This attempt had the desired effect in the case of the numerous secular churches, which were staffed by married priests and were susceptible to lay control even at the local level. The major monasteries, however, jealously protected their autonomy and successfully thwarted the evolution of a strong national hierarchy. Both at the royal and the episcopal courts there were, of course, a number of ecclesiastical officials who wielded considerable power as religious advisers to the emperors and their Egyptian bishops. Throughout

29. T. Tamrat, 1972b.

much of the period under discussion the emperors recruited their most prestigious ecclesiastical official, the *aḳabe-seat*, from the island monastery of Hayḳ, and the abbots of Debre Libanos (later given the title of *echege*) began to step into this role towards the beginning of the sixteenth century. But it was mainly by virtue of their position as officials of the imperial court and not as members of a national hierarchy with widely recognized spiritual powers that these ecclesiastics exercised their influence throughout the empire.

This period was the most productive in the history of the Ethiopian Church. Although it could not gain a permanent foothold in all the territories recently annexed by the empire, it had clearly established itself very firmly in many areas where it had been either weak or altogether non-existent at the end of the thirteenth century. Despite their frequent rivalries, the orders of Tekle-Haymanot and Ewostatewos contributed much to this expansion movement. But much more important was the internal spiritual and cultural reawakening of the Ethiopian Church. Excellent studies have already been made by Guidi and Cerulli of the Ethiopic literature of the period.[30] The extent of artistic achievement during those centuries can also be seen in the relatively few illuminated manuscripts, diptychs and church murals as well as the many crosses and ceremonial croziers with very elaborate designs which have survived for many centuries under the jealous protection of the medieval monastic centres of Ethiopia.[31] (See Plates 17.5–17.7.)

This cultural revival was closely supervised and encouraged by the emperors, some of whom were themselves men of great learning. The most notable among them was Emperor Zera-Yakob (1434–68), who personally participated in literary developments and is believed to have been the author of a number of theological treatises. The numerous hagiographical traditions of the period further testify to the intensity of religious activity in the monastic communities, in some of which a whole process of re-thinking the ecclesiastical, liturgical and doctrinal legacies of the Church seems to have been undertaken. Doctrinal controversies as well as disputes over liturgical practices were rife throughout the period, and the leadership of Alexandria in all these matters was seriously challenged. So greatly had the spirit of Ethiopian self-sufficiency been enhanced, and so far had confidence in the Egyptian bishops declined, that in the last quarter of the fifteenth century there was a strong but unsuccessful movement to break away entirely from the Alexandrian patriarchate.[32]

Struggles between Christians and Muslims

The traditional links with the patriarchate of Alexandria were invaluable

30. I. Guidi, 1932; E. Cerulli, 1956.

31. For a detailed review of Ethiopian art during the period see: J. Leroy, 1964; S. Chojnacki, 1971.

32. Tamrat, 1972a, pp. 243 n. 4, 230 n. 4, and 245–7.

PLATE 17.5 *A 15th-century Ethiopian manuscript, portraying the tree of life (Monastery of Kebran)*

PLATE 17.6 *A 15th-century Ethiopian manuscript, portraying the Crucifixion (Monastery of Kebran)*

PLATE 17.7 *A 15th-century Ethiopian manuscript, portraying the Annunciation* (*Monastery of Yahya Giyorgis*)

to the Christian empire. Although this allegiance kept the Ethiopian Church under continual supervision by the Coptic hierarchy in Egypt, these connections were nevertheless the only lines of communication with the old Christian centres of the Holy Land and the rest of the Christian world. This fact had always been appreciated by the emperors and their leading advisers, and hence the occasional periods of friction between the Egyptian bishops and the Ethiopian clergy throughout the centuries were never allowed to lead to a permanent schism. The religious alienation of their country from the neighbouring peoples on either side of the Red Sea and the Gulf of Aden always presented Ethiopian emperors with a major dilemma in formulating their foreign policy. There was, on the one hand, the natural desire to exploit their Christian identity, establish contacts and military alliance with Christian Europe and even participate directly in the later crusades; on the other hand, they could try to work out a more realistic policy of peaceful coexistence with their Muslim neighbours.

As the most prestigious and powerful state in East Africa, in firm control of the international routes to the Mediterranean, Mamluk Egypt held the key to these contradictory political options. Thus the Solomonid emperors began their rule by pursuing very cautious diplomatic policies towards the court in Cairo and the neighbouring Arab countries, particularly the Yemen, with which regular commercial contacts were maintained. They sent 'slaves of both sexes, gold, and other presents' to the Mamluk sultans whenever they needed to request a new Egyptian bishop.[33] Letters were written to the sultans entreating them to facilitate the passage of Ethiopian pilgrims to the Holy Land and their safe return home.

But this cautious policy was not always consistent with the new sense of power which Christian Ethiopia began to acquire after Amde-Siyon's annexation of extensive Muslim areas. Indeed, throughout the period following Amde-Siyon's reign we can clearly discern an increasingly aggressive stance being adopted by the Ethiopian emperors in their relationships with the Mamluks. Since the sultans of Egypt always claimed to protect the interests of Islam in Ethiopia, Amde-Siyon and his successors began to reciprocate by demanding that the freedom of worship and other civil rights of Coptic Christians be respected and that the Mamluks take firm action to stop the persecution of the Copts in Egypt. Ethiopian and Coptic traditions indicate that this conflict began to intensify in the reign of Amde-Siyon's son and immediate successor, Seyfe-Ar'ad (1344–70), whom a fifteenth-century Italian traveller in Ethiopia describes as having led an army as far as the Nile valley in an attempt to reinforce the siege of Alexandria by the king of Cyprus, Pierre de Lusignan, in 1365.[34] Al-Maḳrīzī reports that Seyfe-Ar'ad's son, Dawit (1380–1412), 'had invaded the territory of Aswan, defeated the Arabs and ravaged the lands of

33. Translated from E. M. Quatremère, 1811, Vol. 2, pp. 268–71.

34. C. Schefer, 1892, p. 148. For Seyfe-Ar'ad's other conflicts with Egypt, see Perruchon, 1893, pp. 177–82, and E. A. W. Budge, 1928, Vol. 1, pp. 177–9.

Islam'.[35] It was, however, the Emperor Yishak (1413–30) whom al-Maḳrīzī particularly described as the sworn enemy of Islam, who sought to establish a strong alliance with Christian Europe in order to end Muslim supremacy in the Near East.[36]

Another fifteenth-century Arab writer, Ibn Taghrībirdī (1409–70), describes more fully the story of Yishak's secret delegation to Europe, which was apprehended by the Egyptian authorities in Alexandria on its way back to Ethiopia. The leader of the mission, a Persian resident in Ethiopia, was publicly hanged in Cairo, and the goods confiscated by the Egyptians included 'a large number of uniforms on which were embroidered (the symbol of) the Cross and the name of the *Hati* written in golden letters. These were uniforms for the soldiers.'[37] Normal relations were restored some time after this. But when Zera-Yakob (1434–68) was told that fresh persecutions of the Copts had resulted in the demolition of the famous Coptic church of Mitmak (al-Magtas), he sent a letter of strong protest to Sultan Jaḳmaḳ (1438–53). When Jaḳmaḳ sent an envoy with a sarcastic letter in reply, Zera-Yakob arrested the Egyptian diplomat and detained him for four years.[38] These displays of arrogance by the Ethiopian emperors of the fifteenth century stand in stark contrast to the rather obsequious style of the founder of the Solomonid dynasty, Yikunno-Amlak (1270–85), who wrote to Baybars describing himself as 'the most humble of the servants of the sultan'.[39] But it was a true reflection of the tremendous developments since the end of the thirteenth century.

These developments had a number of international implications for Christian Ethiopia. Despite the great personal difficulties they had to face, an increasing number of Ethiopian monks were undertaking the pilgrimage to the Holy Land. An isolated piece of evidence for the period between the fourteenth and the beginning of the sixteenth centuries indicates the existence of a chain of small Ethiopian communities: in some Egyptian monasteries in the Nile valley, on Mount Sinai, at various places in the Holy Land, in Armenia, on the islands of Cyprus and Rhodes and in a number of Italian cities such as Venice, Florence and Rome. Wherever they went, these Ethiopians boasted to their fellow Christians of the conquests and expanding empire of Amde-Siyon and his successors. They may also have exaggerated the great wealth, inexhaustible resources and tremendous power at the disposal of the Ethiopian emperors. But it was precisely in the early part of this period that the legendary Prester John of the Indies began to be identified with the Christian monarchs of Ethiopia.

Moreover, serious consideration seems to have been given by some

35. Al-Maḳrīzī, translated from the French of Quatremère, op. cit., pp. 276–7.

36. Al-Maḳrīzī, French transl. 1790, p. 8.

37. Quatremère, pp. 277–8; Ibn Taghrībirdī, French transl. in Quatremère, op. cit., pp. 277–8; Eng. transl. 1957–60, pt. 4, pp. 59–61.

38. Al-Sak͟hāwī, 1897 edn, pp. 71–2 and 124–5.

39. From Mufaḍḍal, loc. cit., pp. 384–7.

strategists to the possibility of drawing Christian Ethiopia into the later crusades. This appears feasible, not only because of reports that the Ethiopian rulers were adopting an aggressive policy towards Egypt, but also because the Mamluks were clearly anxious to cut all communication between Ethiopia and Europe. According to a fourteenth-century traveller to the area, the Christians of Ethiopia 'would willingly have communicated with us Latins, but the sultan of Babylonia [i.e. Egypt] never lets a single Latin pass into their country, lest they should enter into a treaty to make war against him'.[40] Nevertheless, the stronger and more prosperous the Ethiopians felt, the greater was their determination to establish closer contacts with the rest of the Christian world; hence, despite the failure of Yishak's ill-starred delegation of 1427–9, his brother and successor Zera-Yakob sent another mission to Europe in 1450. This was more successful than the first; it visited Rome and Naples at least, and probably also returned safely to Ethiopia with a number of European artisans and craftsmen.[41]

In the final analysis, however, the Ethiopians were fighting a losing battle, for they had no possible way of ending their isolation. Besides its ultimate control over the international routes to the Mediterranean, Mamluk Egypt could exercise considerable pressure on the patriarchate of Alexandria. Firm action against the patriarch could easily shake the whole religious and political foundations of Christian Ethiopia. This was attempted on many occasions throughout the history of Ethiopian–Egyptian relations; but when it came to the point, the Ethiopians always had to retreat from their extreme position. In the fifteenth century the arrogant policies of the Ethiopian rulers towards the Mamluks caused the patriarchs in Cairo much embarrassment and humiliation. We have just referred above, for instance, to the arrest and imprisonment by Zera-Yakob of an Egyptian envoy sent to his court by Sultan Jaḳmaḳ. In retaliation, the sultan summoned the patriarch, had him beaten, and probably forced him to ask Zera-Yakob for the release of his prisoner. Moreover, after the return of the envoy, the sultan apparently instructed the patriarch in 1448 to have no more dealings with Ethiopia without express permission.[42]

The impact of this religious sanction was felt in Ethiopia for more than three decades, and no replacement was sent for the last of Zera-Yakob's Egyptian bishops, who died before 1458. It was not until 1480–1, in the reign of his grandson, Iskindir (1478–94), that a new bishop was enthroned, and then only after the Ethiopians had made supplication by sending the customary presents to the Egyptian sultan. The basic vulnerability of Ethiopia in this connection, and the great public satisfaction when the deadlock was finally broken, are both reflected in the king's chronicle,

40. From E. Cerulli, Italian transl. 1943, 1947, Vol. 1, p. 133.
41. F. Cerone, 1902–3; C. M. de Witte, 1956.
42. Al-Sak͟hāwī, loc. cit., p. 210.

which describes the effect of the bishops' arrival as follows: 'The priests became many, the Churches were restored, and happiness filled all the land.'[43] Ethiopia was too remote from Christian Europe, and too much a part of the Near East, to hope to succeed in establishing meaningful and sustained relations with western Christendom.

The decline of Ethiopia

The traditional superiority of the Christian empire in the balance of power within Ethiopia and the Horn was also beginning to show some signs of decline in the last three decades of the fifteenth century. Zera-Yakob's reign had marked the high point of Christian domination throughout the territories conquered by his ancestors over the preceding century and a half.[44] Within the Christian kingdom itself he had worked out a reconciliation with the militant monastic order of Ewostatewos, whose estrangement from the rest of the Ethiopian Church for about a century had had important political and regional implications. He had sought thoroughly to reorganize the Ethiopian Church in the best way to meet its evangelical responsibilities throughout his realms, where he proclaimed the elimination and active suppression of all traditional religious beliefs and practices. A genuine theological scholar himself, he had imposed an end to the serious doctrinal controversies within the Church and persecuted all the recalcitrant monks without mercy. He had even tried to stop the continual moves of the royal court by founding a new capital at Debre-Birhan in Shoa, where he set up a highly centralized administration.

In defence of the empire Zera-Yakob had repelled the continued attacks on his eastern frontier provinces by the kingdom of Adal, crushed the rebellion led by his Muslim vassal, the sultan of Hadya, and strengthened his military control over the remote dependent territories by reorganizing the frontier garrisons and posting very loyal troops to them. On what is today the Eritrean plateau, he founded a colony of Maya soldiers recruited from a famous warlike people in Shoa; and he had a harbour dredged out at Girar on the Red Sea, not very far from the site of present-day Massawa.[45] Zera-Yakob tackled most of these large problems successfully. His reign marked the true culmination of the cultural, political and military development of late medieval Ethiopia.

But the implementation of Zera-Yakob's many projects was very difficult, and the emperor had to face organized resistance from all quarters. His own books, the chronicles and some of the hagiographical traditions dealing with the period show that his tireless activity had aroused much political unrest, and that there were even some attempts to depose him.

43. Translated from J. Perruchon, 1894, p. 340.
44. Zera-Yakob's career is discussed more fully in Tamrat, 1972a, pp. 220–47.
45. Conti Rossini (ed.), 1903, pp. 181–3; J. Kolmodin, 1912–14.

They also show that he used strong repressive measures to crush all such opposition, and there are many stories of high ecclesiastical and other court officials being exiled to remote places of detention. One of the first public acts of his son and successor, Beide-Maryam (1468–78), was in fact to pardon many of these political prisoners and relax Zera-Yakob's centralization of power in the new capital city of Debre-Birhan. Soon afterwards, however, the loosening of Zera-Yakob's iron grip led to fresh rebellions on many fronts and, although the young king made remarkable efforts to stem the tide, his stature was not equal to his father's great authority.

Serious internal divisions followed the short reign of Beide-Maryam; he died leaving two sons who were minors, not yet able to assume imperial responsibilities. The resulting conflicts over the succession between the supporters of these two princes lasted for several years, and undermined the power of the Christian empire.[46] The first serious defeat of the Christian army on the Adali front occurred in Beide-Maryam's reign, and in a sense the decline in Christian power in Ethiopia and the Horn worsened from then on, until the final collapse brought about by Imam Aḥmad's *d̲j̲ihād*.

46. T. Tamrat, 1974, pp. 526–33.

18

The development of Swahili civilization

V. V. MATVEIEV

In the history of the islands and coast of East Africa the period from the twelfth to the fifteenth century stands out as that of the formation of what may best be termed the Swahili ethnic community. There were undoubtedly states in the region at that time and the first known records of them date back to the tenth century. Another important fact is that the historical and cultural development of East Africa between the twelfth and fifteenth centuries was not subject to disruptive outside influences. The appearance in East Africa in the early sixteenth century of Portuguese conquerors upset this process and altered the conditions and character of later development. These circumstances, together with the constant growth and development of culture, make it reasonable to regard the period under consideration as the heyday of Swahili civilization, particularly when set against subsequent regression and decline.

During the twelfth century the Swahili people did not form a homogeneous community either ethnically or socially. Ethnically, it was a community built on the Bantu-speaking population of the region. This basis was added to by people from neighbouring parts of the hinterland and emigrants from the countries of the northern shore of the Arabian Sea and the Indian Ocean, comprising Arabs, Persians and Indians. There were social disparities, since in addition to the main body of ordinary, free members of the community, there existed a distinct and isolated élite. Institutions based on clan and ethnic group accounted for the formal structure of the community, which nevertheless contained the elements of a class society. Thus the élite was supposed to be, but was not in fact, equal to the other members of the community. It was rich and enjoyed the influence stemming from traditional functions.

Alongside this élite the community included other individuals who were rich, but did not wield traditional power and influence. Their wealth was derived from trading. The commoners formed the majority and the main body of the Swahili people. Furthermore, Swahili society in the early twelfth century probably also included slaves. We can surmise their existence from the accounts of Arab writers describing the export of slaves. Their role in Swahili society is unclear. They were perhaps merely the commodity of the slave trade. But by the end of the fifteenth century they must have been taking some part in economic activity, judging from an anonymous Portuguese report that at Kilwa they cultivated various plants.[1]

The civilization established by the Swahili population was as heterogeneous as Swahili society itself. We can distinguish the traditional and popular culture of the ordinary people, and the culture of the élite; our knowledge of this civilization, however, is incomplete for want of sources.

Economy and commerce

Three main occupations underlay Swahili civilization: namely, farming, fishing and gathering seafood, and trading.

Agriculture and fishing

Farming was carried on by ordinary people. Together with fishing and the gathering of seafood, it was the basis of the very existence of Swahili society. The tenth-century author al-Mas'ūdī lists the following local crops: bananas, durra, yams (al-kalari), coleus and coconuts.[2] Others tell of sugar-cane and tamarinds. For the fifteenth century, the anonymous Portuguese writer cited above mentions that Kilwa Kisiwani had coconuts, sweet oranges, lemons, various vegetables, small onions and aromatic herbs, betel nuts, various species of peas and maize (probably durra or sorghum). He also says that domestic animals were kept, including cattle, sheep and goats, and that cotton was grown. The latter information, coupled with the finding of clay spindles, indicates that spinning and weaving were practised. The coconut palm was also an important agricultural item for the inhabitants of the East African islands and coast.

The existence and importance of fishing and the gathering of seafood is indicated by Arab authors, who frequently refer to the local consumption of fish, marine animals and molluscs. The resources of the ocean did not merely provide food. We know from Arabic records that pearls, shells, turtle shells and amber were gathered and sold. The fish caught was not only consumed, but also offered for sale, which suggests that catches were fairly substantial. It is known that shells were used to make vessels, spoons and beads. As a rule, when Arabic sources mention fishing, they refer to the entire coast without any geographical details. But al-Idrīsī writes of the basic occupations of the inhabitants of several towns and speaks of fishing in a section on Malindi.[3]

The development of navigation is closely bound up with fishing and the gathering of seafood. This development was to take two directions:

1. G. S. P. Freeman-Grenville, 1962b, p. 217.
2. Al-Mas'ūdī, French transl. 1861–77, Vol. 1, p. 334, and Vol. 3, pp. 7, 11 and 29. See also V. V. Matveiev, 1971, pp. 26–7.
3. V. V. Matveiev and L. E. Kubbel, 1965, p. 304. This is a compilation of tenth to twelfth-century Arabic sources on Africa south of the Sahara, with Russian translation.

advances in boat-building and the improvement of seafaring techniques, particularly navigational astronomy. The latter could only have been developed by sailing the Indian Ocean, and there is every reason to suppose that African seafarers made their contribution to it.[4]

As to boat-building, it may be supposed that there were other boats besides the *mtumbwi* dug-outs and the stitched *mitepe* craft. The same anonymous Portuguese source speaks of many large boats in the harbour at Kilwa, close in size to the 50-tonne caravel, but unfortunately he does not say to whom they belonged. An indirect indication of the existence of various types of boats is the fact that there are several names for them in Kiswahili, probably reflecting their particular purposes, and that in the early twentieth century there were still a great many sorts of boats. If the supposition is correct, it should cast doubt on the conjecture that the inhabitants of East Africa did not sail the Indian Ocean trade routes.

Trade and urban development

The common Waswahili lived in huts which they made from sticks and clay and thatched with palm leaves or grass. These huts were grouped to form villages and towns. In all probability Arabic sources had just such people in mind when they spoke of people hunting for leopards and wolves, of the working of iron ore for the sale of iron, of their ability to cast a spell on fierce animals so that they did no harm and to charm lions and leopards into not attacking, of the red dogs they used for hunting wolves and lions, and of the huge barrel-like and fearful-sounding drums to which they bowed down.[5]

However, this was not the sum of the culture of the East African coast. Another aspect is reported in Arabic sources. This was the more advanced culture of the towns of the East African islands and coast, related to the development of maritime trade. This difference in cultural level was remarked upon by Arab authors, and Abu ʾl-Ḳāsim al-Andalusī says that amongst such peoples as those of East Africa, only the town-dwellers 'take spiritual delight in the study of philosophy'.[6] These towns probably consisted for the most part of huts, but they also had stone buildings, and the wealthy and noble members of Swahili society lived there. The important point was that the towns were trading centres where local wares were assembled and ships from overseas put in. These towns were at the same time centres of Islam on the coast. The trade carried on there was extremely profitable, the main reason being the varying estimates of the value of the goods. Imported goods not produced locally, chiefly luxury items, took on a greater value in the eyes of the buyers than they really had. On the other hand, the abundance of such highly prized goods as

4. V. M. Misiugin, 1972, pp. 165–77.
5. Matveiev and Kubbel, op. cit., p. 305.
6. Translated from the Russian version, ibid., p. 194.

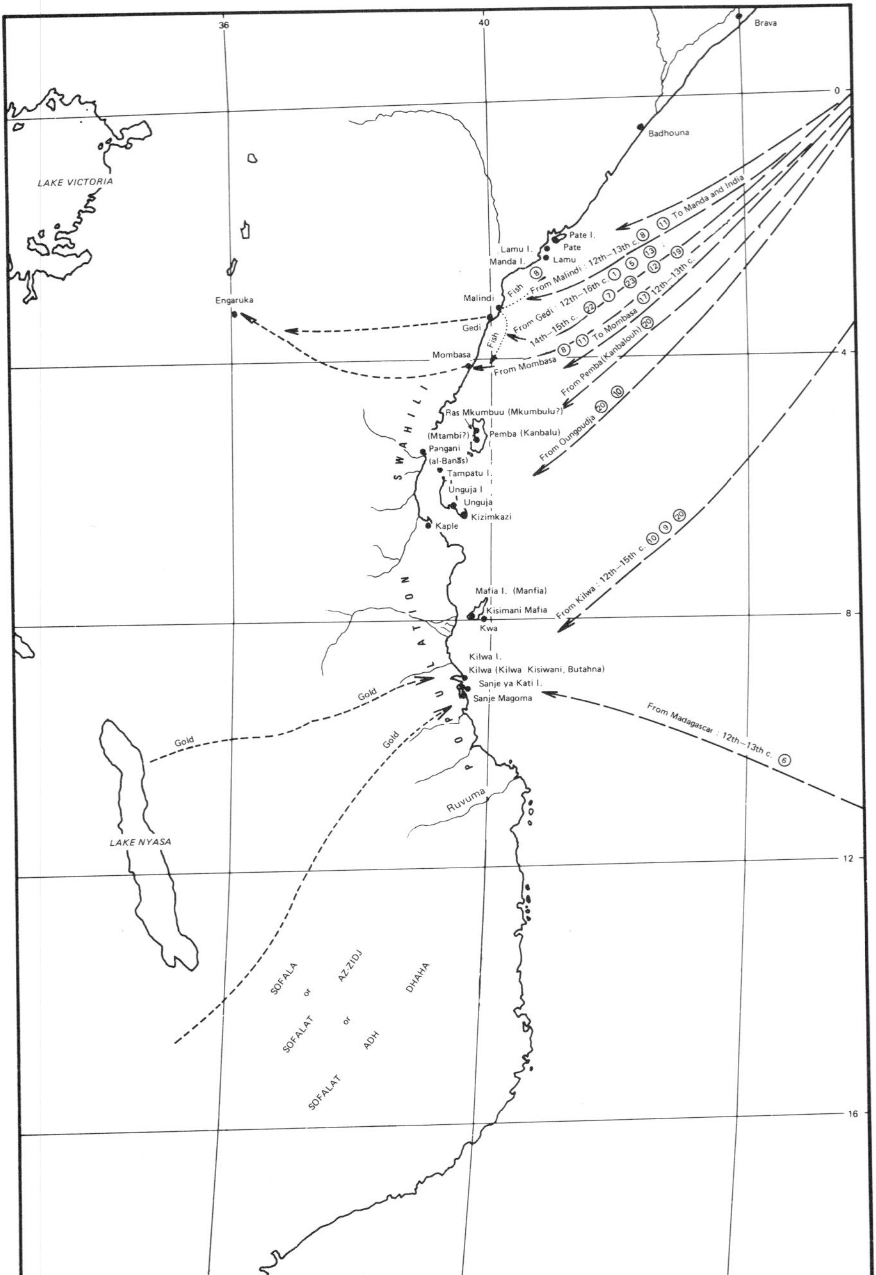

FIG. 18.1 *Internal and transoceanic trade in the coastal towns of East Africa between the 12th and 15th centuries (V. V. Matveiev)*

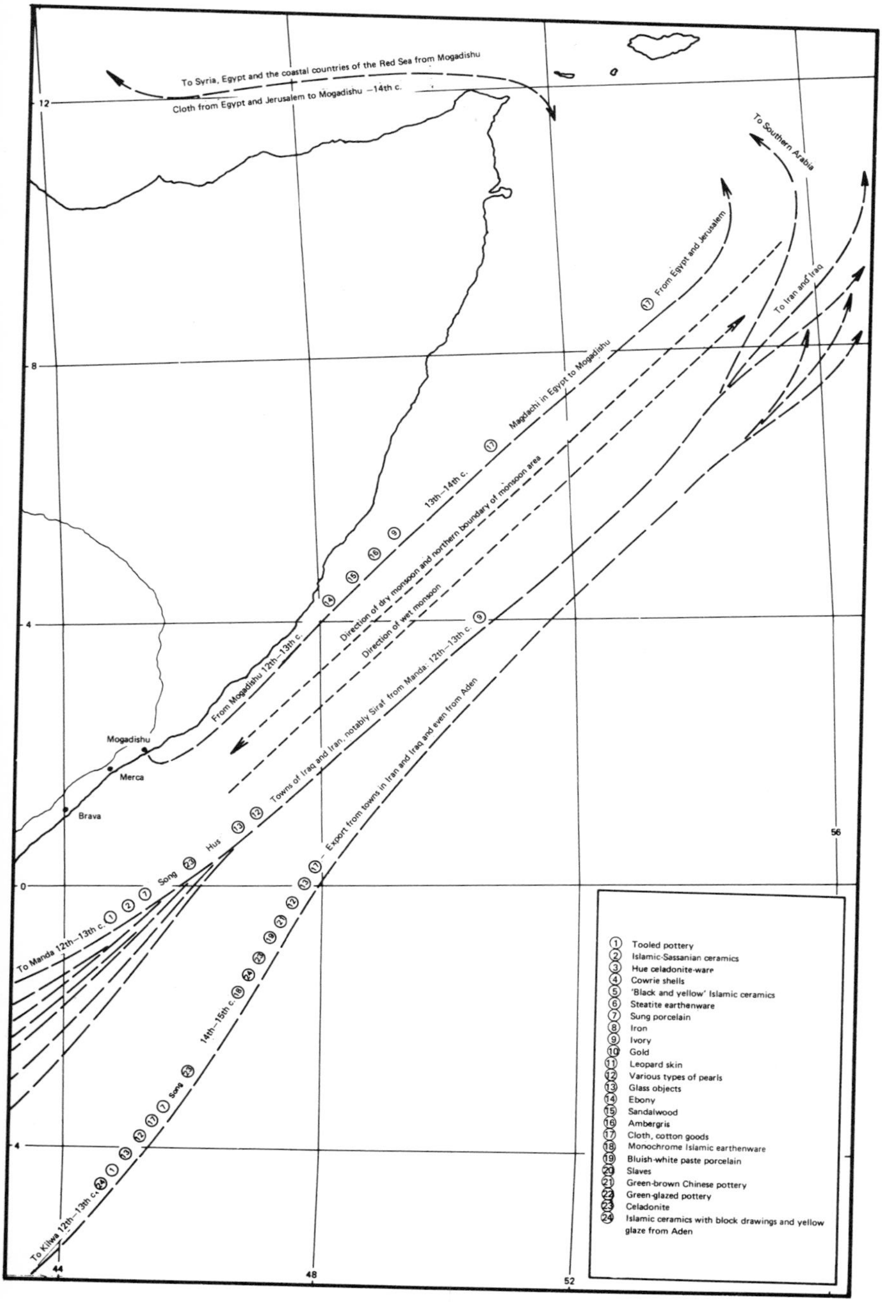
To Syria, Egypt and the coastal countries of the Red Sea from Mogadishu
Cloth from Egypt and Jerusalem to Mogadishu –14th c.
12
8
4
0
4
44
48
52
56
To Southern Arabia
From Egypt and Jerusalem
To Iran and Iraq
Magdachi in Egypt to Mogadishu
13th–14th c.
Direction of dry monsoon and northern boundary of monsoon area
Direction of wet monsoon
From Mogadishu 12th–13th c.
Towns of Iraq and Iran, notably Siraf from Manda: 12th–13th c.
Export from towns in Iran and Iraq and even from Aden
Mogadishu
Merca
Brava
Hus
Song
To Manda 12th–13th c.
14th–15th c.
Song
To Kilwa 12th–13th c.
1 Tooled pottery
2 Islamic-Sassanian ceramics
3 Hue celadonite-ware
4 Cowrie shells
5 'Black and yellow' Islamic ceramics
6 Steatite earthenware
7 Sung porcelain
8 Iron
9 Ivory
10 Gold
11 Leopard skin
12 Various types of pearls
13 Glass objects
14 Ebony
15 Sandalwood
16 Ambergris
17 Cloth, cotton goods
18 Monochrome Islamic earthenware
19 Bluish-white paste porcelain
20 Slaves
21 Green-brown Chinese pottery
22 Green-glazed pottery
23 Celadonite
24 Islamic ceramics with block drawings and yellow glaze from Aden

FIG. 18.1 (*cont.*)

gold and ivory, together with the assumption that it would always be possible to replenish stocks, brought down their price. The convenient geographical position – the whole coastal zone of East Africa practically coincides with the area affected by the monsoon winds – made it possible to sail the Indian Ocean and accounted for the very existence of trading in that part of the world.

It seems that in the twelfth century the main trade flow to and from Africa was via the Lamu archipelago and Zanzibar; archaeological excavations and surveys have shown that the chief centre for this area was the town of Manda on Manda Island, which prospered in the ninth and tenth centuries and continued its trading activity in the twelfth and thirteenth centuries.[7] After that, most of the trade evidently went through Kilwa. The wealth and prosperity of the town of Manda are indicated by the large quantity of imported goods, including Sassanid-Islamic pottery, Yueh celadon, and sgraffito. Many of the unglazed and glazed items are similar to those excavated at Siraf.

Finds of slag indicate that iron was smelted. It seems difficult, however, to form an idea of the scale of smelting on archaeological data alone. It is possible that the reference in al-Idrīsī's work to the town of Malindi – 'Iron is their main source of revenue and main item of trade'[8] – concerned this region and that iron was taken from Malindi to Manda. The chief article of export accounting for the wealth of Manda was ivory.

Al-Idrīsī tells us of other towns of the coast and the islands, naming Merca, Brava, Malindi, Mombasa, Pangani (al-Banās) and Unguja (ancient Zanzibar). According to a recent and seemingly accurate identification, al-Idrīsī mentions Kilwa as Butahna, beyond Pangani.[9] This mention probably means that Kilwa had already been in existence for a certain time, but had not yet become one of the main trading centres. Arabic sources of an earlier period also refer to Sofala, whence gold was exported. By comparing them, it is possible to locate these territories in the Kilwa region.

Archaeological work carried out at Kilwa Kisiwani provides a picture of fairly developed trading.[10] Finds have included a large quantity of cowrie shells, which were used as money, imported pottery of the yellow sgraffito type with a cream shading and also with dark green glazing, and glassware. A small quantity of glass, cornelian and quartz beads and steatite vases from Madagascar have also been found. The main export item here was gold. In the mid-twelfth century Kilwa started to import Chinese Sung porcelain, together with a small amount of celadon.

7. H. N. Chittick, 1967b.

8. Translated from Matveiev and Kubbel, op. cit., p. 304.

9. M. A. Tolmacheva, 1969, p. 276.

10. For the brief account of archaeological finds in East Africa and for the subsequent outline of East African Swahili architecture, the following are the main works drawn upon: J. S. Kirkman, 1954a; H. N. Chittick, 1961, 1966 and 1967b.

The most typical imports of that period at Gedi were Muslim black and yellow pottery, yellow and green sgraffito wares, and various types of celadon. Arabic sources do not mention Gedi. The town of Mogadishu was probably already in existence too, although al-Idrīsī does not refer to it. Two trading centres of lesser importance were Malindi and Mombasa, which exported iron and leopard skins. Fish was also exported from Malindi.

In the early thirteenth century Yāḳūt calls Mogadishu one of the most renowned cities of East Africa and writes that its inhabitants were Muslim Arabs living in communities. At that time Mogadishu exported sandalwood and ebony, ambergris and ivory. Yāḳūt notes the mixed character of the population of Mogadishu: he also mentions the towns of Mtambi and Mkumbulu on Pemba Island. 'Each has its own sultan independent of the other. On the island there are many villages and hamlets. Their sultan maintains that he is an Arab and descended from people who emigrated to the island from Kufa.'[11] Yāḳūt is also the first to mention the towns of Kilwa (by that name) and Mafia, which he situates not on the island but on the coast, and Tampatu Island, in his account of Zanzibar Island (Lanjuya-Unguja). According to him, there was an independent state on Zanzibar and the town of Unguja was the trading centre where ships put in. He speaks of the inhabitants of Tampatu as Muslims.

At that time the Shirazi dynasty ruled at Kilwa and it seems that Mafia Island came under its sway. In the mid-thirteenth century Kilwa fought the Shanga people, who were most probably the inhabitants of the island of Sanje ya Kati. The likely cause of the struggle was rivalry to control local trade. As related in the *Kilwa Chronicle*, Kilwa ultimately prevailed.[12] This victory probably underlay the subsequent rapid development of Swahili trade and the Swahili civilization, which can be reckoned to have begun in the early fourteenth century and to have coincided with the rise at Kilwa of a new dynasty associated with the name of Abu 'l-Mawāhib.

At that time Gedi continued to deal in the same principal articles of trade. As in the previous period, the chief trading partners of both Manda and Gedi were the Persian cities, particularly Siraf. At Kilwa there was a sharp rise in the volume of imports, which comprised large quantities of sgraffito pottery, usually dark green with various kinds of decoration, and sometimes greenish-yellow. There was also an increase in the quantity of Chinese porcelain of the Sung dynasty, among which a little celadon is to be found. A great deal of glassware was imported, mainly bottles, which were sometimes decorated in relief, most probably for perfume and kohl. The forms and decoration of the glassware found in excavations at Kilwa resemble other items of the same period from Gedi, also mostly

11. Yāḳūt, 13th cent., German transl. 1866–73, Vol. 4, pp. 75–6; Vol. 5, pp. 302 and 699.

12. *Kilwa Chronicle*, Eng. transl. in G. S. P. Freeman-Grenville, 1962a, pp. 34–49 and 1962b.

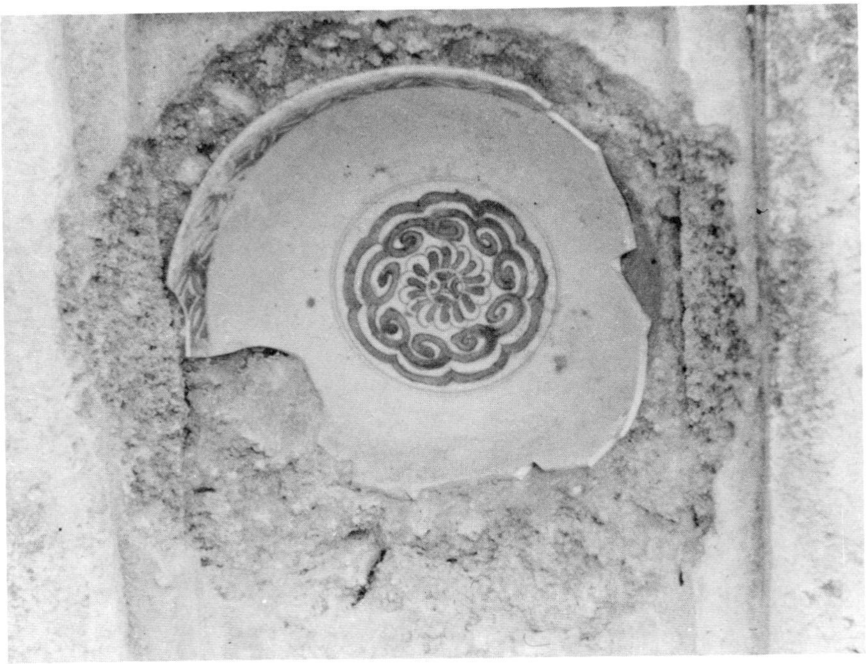

PLATE 18.1 *Chinese porcelain plate set into tomb at Siyu, Pate Island*

PLATE 18.2 *Chinese porcelain plates inset into kibla of Juma Mosque on Mafia Island*

bottles of various sorts. Like most of the ware from Gedi, they probably originated in Iraq or Iran. More steatite vases from Madagascar were imported. There was also a considerable increase in the import of glass beads, chiefly 'wound' beads of three types and occasionally 'cane' beads.

In the fourteenth century the volume of trade was, it seems, at its height. Our main source in Arabic for that period is Ibn Baṭṭūṭa, who visited East Africa.[13] He describes Mogadishu as a major trading centre and relates that it was customary for each merchant who arrived to choose from among the citizens a confidential agent to manage his affairs. This practice is also referred to by Yāḳūt, but he does not go into it in detail. In addition to the goods mentioned by Yāḳūt, Mogadishu exported *maḳdāshī* (cloth, of Mogadishu). Mogadishu's trade links were distinct from those of the other towns further south. Thus *maḳdāshī* was exported to Egypt, whereas other textiles were imported from Egypt and from Jerusalem. The other towns of East Africa did not have relations with Egypt and Syria.

Manda had already declined in importance at that time. Nor were Malindi, Mombasa or other towns of great significance. The excavations carried out by H. N. Chittick indicate that it was only then that the town of Pate came into being on Pate Island.[14]

Exchanges: centres, products, quantity

In the fourteenth century Gedi began to import new goods. Blue and green glazed ware with a fine lustrous surface supplanted the sgraffiti and the yellow and black pottery, which continued to be imported until the middle of the fourteenth century. These new goods probably came from Iran. Other imported items were various types of celadon and white porcelain ware, together with many kinds of beads, made of red clay (round or cylindrical), glass ('cane' and 'wound'), faience and other types.

Kilwa was the main trading centre. The overall quantity of imported ceramics had grown still further. Muslim pottery was imported in small quantities, the most typical ware being poor-quality vessels with a yellow matt glaze and black design. It is supposed that this sort of pottery was made in and exported from Aden. The second half of the fourteenth century saw the first of the Muslim monochrome ceramics; these were almost spherical, thick vessels with a thick body, a simple rounded edge and light green glazing on the body.

Chinese porcelain was imported in much larger quantities and consisted mainly of celadon, often of a bluish shade. 'Lotus-shaped' celadon vessels were widely used and there was some distribution of Chinese earthenware; the latter had a cinnamon yellow glaze and beneath that a colour close to black with a scratched design on it. A great many glass beads were

13. Ibn Baṭṭūṭa, French transl. 1853–9, Vol. 2, pp. 176 ff.
14. Chittick, 1967b, pp. 19–27.

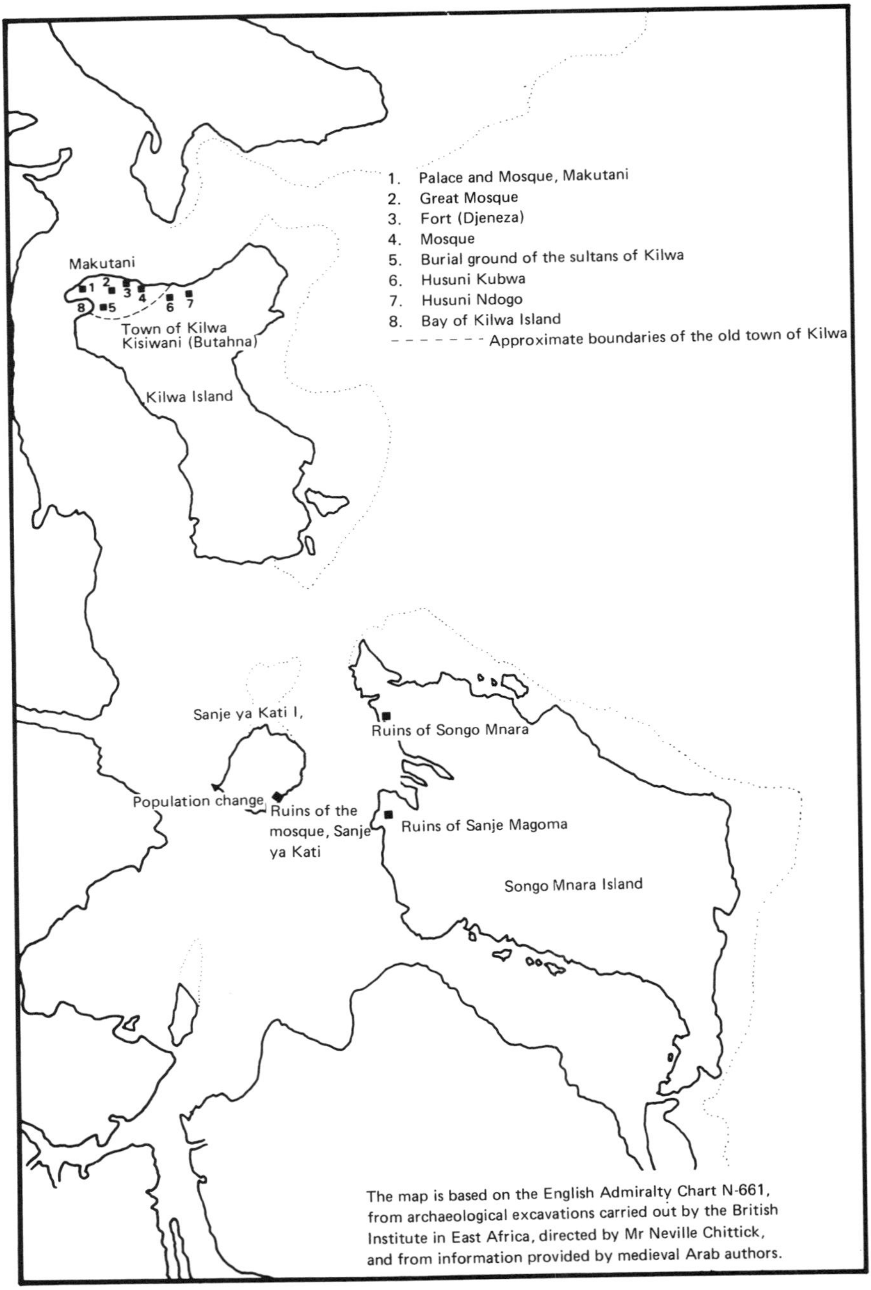
1. Palace and Mosque, Makutani
2. Great Mosque
3. Fort (Djeneza)
4. Mosque
5. Burial ground of the sultans of Kilwa
6. Husuni Kubwa
7. Husuni Ndogo
8. Bay of Kilwa Island
Approximate boundaries of the old town of Kilwa
Makutani
Town of Kilwa Kisiwani (Butahna)
Kilwa Island
Sanje ya Kati I,
Ruins of Songo Mnara
Population change
Ruins of the mosque, Sanje ya Kati
Ruins of Sanje Magoma
Songo Mnara Island
The map is based on the English Admiralty Chart N-661, from archaeological excavations carried out by the British Institute in East Africa, directed by Mr Neville Chittick, and from information provided by medieval Arab authors.

FIG. 18.2 *Island and town of Kilwa (V. V. Matveiev)*

also imported and the proportion of 'cane' to 'wound' beads increased; at the same time, a new cobalt-blue variety of the former appeared. The import of steatite vessels ceased, although the same kind of glassware as before was apparently in use.

In the fifteenth century Gedi continued to import the white and green Muslim pottery with a fine lustrous glaze. A new item was white and blue porcelain, which appeared in the region for the first time and was decorated in a style characteristic of the Ming period in the fifteenth century. The beads imported were very much the same as in the previous century. The amount of glassware imported in that period was small. The fifteenth century is usually regarded as a time of moderate decline for Kilwa, brought about by the internal political power struggle of the various groups of the upper level of society. Nevertheless, imports continued to increase. Muslim monochrome pottery was of somewhat better quality and became the most usual type, its colour ranging from blue-green to green. There was twice as much Chinese porcelain as Muslim earthenware. Here, too, the most widespread types became celadon and blue and white porcelain, occurring in almost equal quantities. Glass vessels, mainly bottles, were also fairly common. Nearly all glass beads were of the red 'cane' type.

The main export items were, as before, ivory and gold, in addition to slaves (slave raids were referred to by Ibn Baṭṭūṭa), rhinoceros horn, ambergris, pearls, shells and, in the northern part of the coast, leopard skins. There was yet another important article which was partly imported from overseas and partly produced locally; this was cotton cloth, and the volume of trade in it was probably very great. We know of a huge quantity of cloth arriving at Mombasa and Kilwa for onward dispatch to Sofala in the fifteenth century.[15] The part played by cloth in the early period is clear, for instance, from the account in the *Kilwa Chronicle* of the purchase of Kilwa Island for a length of cloth equal to the island's total circumference.

The maritime trade between the East African coast and islands and the countries on the northern shores of the Indian Ocean provided mutual links and contacts between the peoples concerned, and enriched them. It was part of a world-wide process, since it represented one of the branches of the major trade routes linking west and east. The East African ports were not the terminals of this route, which led on to Madagascar. There were undoubtedly links between the coast and the inland gold-bearing regions near Lake Nyasa, whence the gold was brought to Kilwa. In the fourteenth century certain gold-bearing areas of Sofala came under the control of the sultans of Kilwa, who sent their governors there. The existence and antiquity of such links is indicated by the excavation of objects originating on the coast or even in countries outside Africa.

15. J. Strandes, 1899, pp. 97–100. (See also Eng. transl. 1961.)

G. Caton-Thompson noted that lemon-yellow beads excavated at Zimbabwe were identical with beads found in a number of places in India, which she reckoned to date back to about the eighth century.[16] It is also possible that the blue and green glass found at Zimbabwe came from India, since it is very similar to Indian and Malay items.

J. S. Kirkman concluded from his study of the local pottery found at Gedi (classes 1 and 2) and on the basis of its resemblance to one of the types of pottery from Zimbabwe that there were also relations between the coast and the owners of the gold-mines in the interior of the continent.[17] The gold-bearing regions near the Zambezi, in the heart of the continent and on the territory of what is now Zambia, were probably the first with which trade links were established. This is indicated by finds of cowrie shells, which were exchanged for gold and ivory, at Gokomere and Kolomo. In the Engaruka area of present-day Tanzania, excavation of a trading settlement has yielded the same type of cowrie shells and beads of the fifteenth and sixteenth centuries as in excavations at Kilwa and other coastal towns.

There is a direct indication of the existence of caravan trading with the inland regions in the work of al-Idrīsī, relating to the twelfth century: 'Since they have no pack animals, they themselves transport their loads. They carry their goods on their heads or their backs to two towns – Mombasa and Malindi. There they sell and buy.'[18]

In this trade it was cowrie shells more than anything else which provided a medium of exchange. They are found in all excavations and, as indicated, not only on the coast but also in the interior of the continent. The same purpose seems to have been served by beads and, at a later date, by china. Where commercial activity was most intense, a new medium of exchange was introduced in the form of coins. The minting centres seem to have been Kilwa and Mogadishu. In Kilwa coins came into use, according to research by Chittick, with the accession of the Shirazi dynasty, which he puts at the end of the twelfth century.[19] The coins were made of copper and silver. The only coin from Mogadishu is dated, unlike the Kilwa coins, and was minted in 1322.[20] Coin finds along the coast are not evenly spread. Freeman-Grenville notes that none have been found on the stretch of coast between Mnarani and Kilwa Masoko, and suggests that this may be due to a lack of archaeological research in the area.[21] Of course, it may be that coins were not minted and were not in circulation in these places.

16. G. Caton-Thompson, 1931, p. 81.
17. Kirkman, 1954a, pp. 72–3 and 78–9.
18. Al-Idrīsī, translated from the Russian version in Matveiev and Kubbel op. cit., p. 305.
19. H. N. Chittick, 1965.
20. H. N. Chittick, 1971, p. 131.
21. G. S. P. Freeman-Grenville, 1957 and 1960a.

The fact remains that coins are found in the major trading centres such as Kilwa Kisiwani, Kisimani Mafia, Kwa on Juani Island, and the islands of Zanzibar and Pemba; individual specimens have been found in Kenya. The presence of coins suggests that there was an intensive and well-developed local trade on the coast and islands of East Africa which required them. It may also be supposed that coins had a greater exchange value than cowries and that their introduction is a likely indication of the large scale of business done. This is borne out by the fact that the main article of trade in Kilwa was gold, with its very high intrinsic value. At that time the abundance of gold and its role in commerce as an article of trade obviously precluded its use as a medium of exchange. The areas over which coins are found should serve as an indication of the geographical extent of local trade. The fact that Kilwa coins carry no indication of place and date of minting or of value may possibly be explained by the fact that when a piece of business was transacted using cowrie shells, all that was necessary was to count the number of shells.

The trade of the East African towns was enormously profitable and was the basis of their wealth. It underlay the social and cultural development of Swahili society. Trading contacts familiarized the Swahili people with the cultural achievements of others, including Arabs, Persians and Indians. Despite the vast quantity of goods of Chinese origin found in the course of excavation, the Chinese did not take a direct part in trade with Africa until the early fifteenth century. Recent research by a leading authority on Chinese written sources, V. A. Velgus, indicates not only that between the fifth and the eleventh centuries Chinese trading vessels did not sail in the region of the Persian Gulf, but also that they did not venture southward or westward of Sumatra and Java, let alone to the East African coast.[22] The first known voyages of Chinese fleets to the East African coast took place in 1417–19 and 1421–2, under the command of Cheng-Ho.

Swahili civilization from the thirteenth to the fifteenth century

This wealth and these contacts influenced the economic, social and cultural development of East Africa. A consequence of the development of trade was the transformation of originally small settlements into large towns. Another important result of such development was the appearance of an influential group in Swahili society competing for power with the old aristocracy, whose sway and influence was based on the discharge of various kinds of traditional public functions. The rise of this new, influential group and its endeavour to consolidate its position called for a new ideology. This was provided by Islam, which had become known through contacts

22. V. A. Velgus, 1969.

with the Arabs and Persians. On the principle that, if necessary, what has been achieved elsewhere may be taken over and adapted to one's own needs rather than reinvented, the Islamic religion, which had been offered by historical circumstances, gained ground in East Africa. We know nothing of the actual conditions of its spread, but can confidently state that, in general, Islam was not imposed by force in East Africa, as it was in the course of Arab conquests elsewhere. It seems also that there was no special propaganda in favour of conversion to Islam. This suggests that Islam was embraced voluntarily and met the internal demand of society for a new ideology.

The penetration of Islam seems to have begun at the end of the seventh or eighth century. In the tenth century al-Masʿūdī reports the presence of Muslims on Kanbalu Island speaking an African language. That is the period to which the spread of Islam on the East African islands is usually attributed. In the thirteenth century Islam spread to the coast itself. East African Islam should evidently not be put on a par with that of the Arab countries, for instance. In all probability, as shown by J. S. Trimingham for a much later period, this form of Islam basically meant that people were numbered among the Muslims, while it coexisted with traditional cults.[23] This fact in itself is very important, since it illustrates the disruption and destruction of a number of traditional social ties and the emergence of new ones. People probably also embraced Islam out of a desire to distinguish themselves from other, non-Muslim Africans. To a great extent, Islam was merely a matter of appearances; but in the course of time its influence grew and deepened and the number of adherents increased. An outward indication of this kind of change was the rise in the number of mosques.

The progress and distribution of Islam

The start of the extension of Islam should probably be dated no later than the last decades of the twelfth century, and its full development must have coincided with the fourteenth and fifteenth centuries. Thus in 1331 Ibn Baṭṭūṭa describes Mogadishu as a profoundly Islamized town. Of the inhabitants of Kilwa, he says that 'faith and righteousness are their foremost qualities' and that their sultan exalted the faithful and noble.[24] We know of the existence of mosques at Mogadishu, Gedi, Kaole, Kilwa, Sanje Magoma and elsewhere at that time. Those adopting Islam evidently looked on their conversion as a transition to a new quality and way of life, necessarily bound up with initiation in outward patterns of conduct. A practical manifestation of this was the wearing of Muslim clothes and the assumption of Muslim names and titles. This was of particular significance in demon-

23. J. S. Trimingham, 1964, pp. 24–8 and 46–7.
24. Ibn Baṭṭūṭa, translated from the French, loc. cit., Vol. 2, p. 194.

strating new social links. How gradual the process was is evident from the fact that new and old titles existed side by side, both Muslim and African, such as sultan and *mfalme*; later the African titles died out. It may also be supposed that in practice the prescriptions and prohibitions of Islam were by no means all respected, since the customs and rites peculiar to traditional forms of worship continued to exist.

The first to adopt Islam were probably the rich merchants. Their example was followed first by the old aristocracy and only later by some sections of the common people, who in so doing wished to put themselves on an equal footing with their rich co-religionists.

The adoption of Islam was bound up with the assimilation of those cultural attainments which were applicable to the local context. Judging by the reference in Ibn Baṭṭūṭa's work to the *ḳāḍīs* of Mogadishu and Kilwa, Swahili society assimilated some elements of Muslim law, but probably not the entire legal system.[25] The spread of Islam under conditions of intense commercial activity was accompanied by much borrowing from Arabic, particularly with regard to trade, religion and law. The demands of trade and religion, with the need to keep accounts, to observe a number of Muslim religious ceremonies and to fix the rights and privileges of the various sections of Swahili society, led to Kiswahili being put into a written form based on Arabic script. As shown by the research of V. M. Misiugin, to be able to read this writing it was essential to know Kiswahili, so that it can have been devised only by the Waswahili themselves. In his view, this was done in the period from the tenth to the thirteenth century.[26]

Swahili architecture

A consequence of the development and spread of Islam among the Waswahili was not only the construction of mosques, but also the development of building in stone. The archaeological work of Kirkman and Chittick provides a general picture of the development of building and architecture on the islands and coast of East Africa. Their beginnings date back to the twelfth century in Gedi, Zanzibar and Kilwa. This initial period had its own building methods, which consisted simply of laying coral blocks on red clay. The only edifice from that period to have survived to this day is the Great Mosque of Kilwa, but it was rebuilt a number of times and is now a completely different building. This mosque is the only building referred to in written sources. Another vestige of the twelfth century is the inscription of 1107 from the mosque of Kizimkazi on Zanzibar, which now adorns an eighteenth-century mosque.

For the thirteenth century, we know of three mosques in Kisimani Mafia,

25. ibid, pp. 183–4.
26. V. M. Misiugin, 1971, pp. 100–15.

PLATE 18.3 *The two adjoining buildings of the Great Mosque at Kilwa*

the northern part of the Great Mosque of Kilwa, a small mosque on the island of Sanje ya Kati, two minarets near Mogadishu, one of which is dated 1238, and a mosque of Fakhr al-Dīn with an inscription in the *miḥrab* dating from 1269. The building methods of that time had changed somewhat: large and rather crudely shaped cubic blocks of coral, measuring 25–30 cm across, were laid in mortar, the lime for which was obtained by calcination of the coral.[27]

In the fourteenth century the main trading centre of Kilwa underwent a period of growth and prosperity in architecture as well as in commerce, and building methods developed further, simply using undressed stone of more or less uniform size, which was placed in mortar. This method evidently simplified and facilitated the process of construction, although the masonry was naturally of lower quality than in the thirteenth century. More carefully worked stone was used only for finishing *miḥrab*s and door and window casings. New construction elements included spherical and pointed cupolas, semi-cylindrical vaults, stone columns and various ornaments. But it seems that those elements were then only to be found at Kilwa. Elsewhere flat roofs continued to be the rule.

A remarkable monument of that time is the palace fortress or palace

27. These details are based on H. N. Chittick, 1963a, pp. 179–90. For information on architecture, building techniques and the results of the archaeological excavations at Kilwa, see particularly the remarkable work by Chittick, 1974, on which the following paragraphs draw.

trading centre of Husuni Kubwa. Chittick dates it in the fourteenth century from a mention of the name of Sultan al-Ḥasan Ibn Sulaymān II (1310–33), and suggests that these edifices of Husuni Kubwa served as models for the rich dwelling houses which were built in that century. As a rule, these houses faced north or east and had adjacent courtyards in front. The house itself consisted of a few long narrow rooms. The long wall of the first of them – probably an antechamber – abutted on the courtyard and had a door in it. The other rooms were parallel to the first. Their number varied, but generally there was a main room beyond the antechamber, and a bedroom beyond that. In the rear right-hand part of the house was the lavatory, together with washing facilities. There were no windows except in the front overlooking the courtyard, and so the inner rooms were dark. Houses like this have been found at Gedi, Kisimani Mafia and Kaole, and on Kilwa Island. Similar dwellings occupied much of Husuni Kubwa. Another part of that complex was apparently taken up by a pool. Husuni Kubwa has no parallel and is a true masterpiece of East African architecture, although its purpose is not entirely clear.

In the course of the fourteenth century Kilwa became a large town; many stone houses were built there, which undoubtedly reflected the growing wealth of the town. In the first half of the fifteenth century this activity continued at Kilwa and was accompanied by further improvement in building methods. The mortar was poured into casing and rubble was added. Even cupolas were built in this way. Monolithic columns were replaced by columns of stone and mortar. The basic type of house remained the same, but houses of two or three floors made their appearance. A characteristic detail of building at that time was the custom of adorning vaults and cupolas with glazed vessels of Chinese and Persian porcelain set into the body of the construction. A monument of that period at Kilwa is the house with a mosque within the bounds of Makutani. In the reign of Sultan Sulaymān Ibn Muḥammad al-Mālik al-ʿĀdil (1412–42) the Great Mosque of Kilwa was reconstructed in its present form, and it is a very fine example of East African Swahili architecture (see Plate 18.3).

Views on this architecture differ. Freeman-Grenville points out the similarity of the ground plan of certain buildings in Kilwa (particularly the eighteenth-century palace) to that of the ordinary mud-walled house, which suggests that the stone buildings were of local African origin.[28] Kirkman and Chittick suppose that the spur to development was provided by the Arabs and the Persians. At the same time they note that a number of details in the buildings are incompatible with the stipulations of Islam for buildings in Arab countries. Thus Kirkman notes the presence in the Gedi mosque of a decoration in the form of a spearhead, which would have been impossible in Arabia or Iran. Chittick writes: 'Materially, and especially in the architecture, the people of the coast evolved a civilization

28. Freeman-Grenville, 1962b, p. 92

that was in many respects peculiar to themselves, a civilization which it is best to refer to as early Swahili.'[29]

Sutton and Garlake express a similar view, and Sutton writes: 'In its plans and styles for both religious and domestic buildings, in its masonry techniques ... in its dressed stone mouldings and decorative motifs, the architecture of the Swahili coast maintained over the centuries its own traditions distinguishing it from that of Arabia, Persia and any other Muslim land.' They seem to wish to emphasize the non-African origin of this architecture and speak of its 'non-creative' character, maintaining that it was the work of master masons rather than of real architects.[30] Although I have not had direct access to Garlake's book, I should like to point out that what he apparently calls the non-creative character of this architecture may to a certain extent be due to a conscious endeavour to follow certain models; for example, the development of building methods indicates a rational adaptation to local materials and an ability to make better use of them.

According to Portuguese sources, the narrow streets of mud-walled houses in Kilwa were covered over with protruding palm leaves, which formed the roofs of the houses. The streets with stone houses were also narrow; by the walls of the houses there were stone benches. The palace was an important edifice, which probably had two and, in part, three floors. The buildings had wooden doors and probably other details in wood which was richly adorned with carving. Work of this kind has come to light in various parts of the coast, particularly Bagamoyo and Zanzibar. The fact that the high standard of this art is mentioned in the work of Duarte Barbosa suggests that it had also been practised in previous centuries.[31] As we know, the Portuguese were impressed by the towns, the appearance and architecture of which did not fall short of anything they had at home, and by the wealth of the inhabitants who came to meet them and were elegantly dressed in rich, gold-adorned clothes and in silk and cotton cloth. The women wore chains and bangles of gold and silver on their arms and legs, and earrings set with precious stones.

The high level of development of Swahili civilization also seems to be indicated by the ceramic lamps found in excavations, which must have been used for lighting the dark rooms, and suggest that the inhabitants probably engaged in reading, writing, keeping accounts and so forth. Candles were also used. The furniture consisted of carpets and mats, and sometimes stools and luxurious beds inlaid with ivory, mother-of-pearl, silver and gold. The rich made everyday use of imported pottery from Iran, Iraq and China, as well as from Egypt and Syria. Cooking was done with local earthenware, which was also used for all purposes by the poorer sections of the community. Throughout the period from the twelfth to

29. Chittick, 1971, p. 137.
30 J. E. G. Sutton, 1967 (review of P. S. Garlake, 1966).
31. D. Barbosa, Eng. transl. 1918 and 1921, Vol. 1, pp. 17–31.

PLATE 18.4 *Gateway of fort at Kilwa Kisiwani: general view*

PLATE 18.5 *Detail of gateway of fort at Kilwa Kisiwani*

PLATE 18.6 *Ruins of Nabkhani Mosque on Songo Mnara Island*

PLATE 18.7 *Mihrab of Great Mosque at Gedi*

the fifteenth century this earthenware showed fairly numerous variations in details of form and decoration. There were two basic types of vessel: those with a round or pointed base, designed to be placed on the fire; and broad shallow vessels, resembling bowls or saucers, which were probably for eating.

Power structures

The East African Swahili towns were not only centres of trade and Islamization, but often administrative centres too; the capitals of the small states ruled over by the local Muslim dynasties. The clearest example of such a centre is provided by Kilwa, which is better known from the two versions of its *Chronicle*.[32] According to this, the dynasty – whose members were not Africans but Persians – originally came from the town of Shiraz. We know of similar legends in nearly all the towns of East Africa. The question that arises is: who were, in fact, the rich Islamized ruling classes of the Swahili towns? The answer is of considerable significance in determining whether the Swahili civilization was African or brought to African soil by strangers from outside.

From myth to historic fact

At present there are two distinct theories on the subject. According to one, the civilization established on the East African coast was the work of Persians and Arabs, who either built towns there, introduced Islam and spread their own culture, which was superior to that of the Africans, or paved the way for and fostered such development. The local population is considered to have played a passive part, according to this view; the settlers surrounded themselves with large African households of wives, servants, and so on, and thus became more or less rapidly assimilated in the local setting. Their cultural heritage did not develop but gradually regressed and, had it not been for newcomers from abroad, the whole historical movement of Africa would generally have been reduced to a closed circuit.

This theory was put forward by J. Strandes at the end of the nineteenth century.[33] It was based on Hegel's philosophy of history, according to which the peoples of the world are divided into those who have a historical influence and those who are passive, have no creative powers and are condemned to be led by the activists. With a number of variants, the theory has survived to the present day and still has some currency. Nearly all specialists concerned in one way or another with the East African

32. See G. S. P. Freeman-Grenville, 1962a and 1962b.
33. Strandes, op. cit.; Eng. transl. 1961.

past have shared this erroneous concept to some extent, so that its ingredients are to be found in the works of historians such as J. M. Gray, Gervase Mathew, Roland Oliver and especially G. S. P. Freeman-Grenville;[34] and those of the archaeologist J. S. Kirkman.[35]

The other concept, advanced in the West by the archaeologist H. N. Chittick and in the Soviet Union by V. M. Misiugin, continues to receive elaboration.[36] The opinion of the African scholars J. Ki-Zerbo and Cheikh Anta Diop also come close to it.[37] This theory hinges on the assumption of an active African participation. It affirms the basis of research that the ruling dynasties in the towns were dynasties of local African origin.

The system for the transfer of power

The subject of V. M. Misiugin's research was the *Chronicle* of the town of Pate. Misiugin shows that before the Nabkhani dynasty in Pate there was a state governed by an old African aristocratic clan called 'Wapate', which had the privilege of royal power and bore the title of *mfalme*.

> In order to preserve ancient, time-honoured legal standards relating to the title and office of *mfalme*, the ruling clan of Pate maintained as a necessary survival the division of kinsmen into groups according to a system of reckoning kinship. Within the groups belonging to the Wapate clan, the men of the clan who bore and transferred to one another in turn the title of *mfalme* considered that the most important relations of kinship were those which linked in a united group – *ndugu* – the representatives of one age category [one generation] . . . In these circumstances, within the noble clan Wapate the title of *mfalme* was transmitted not to an individual person but to the whole generation, that is, the whole group comprised by the term *ndugu*. Where there was a closed aristocratic clan, the *ndugu* group could not be very large. It might, however, include a number of men. The title of *mfalme* was accordingly not bestowed for life, but was transferred within the limits of one generation from one *ndugu* man to another on his majority.
>
> A person formally reached majority upon marriage. Because of the closed nature of the aristocratic clan, the men married women from the same clan, who in turn represented the *ndugu* group of the same generation. The wedding also served as the ceremony of transfer of the title of *mfalme*. In accordance with these ancient customs, the

34. J. M. Gray, 1962, p. 622; G. Mathew, 1953, pp. 212–18, and 1956, pp. 50–5; R. Oliver and G. Mathew (eds), 1963; R. Oliver, 1962, pp. 305–21; G. S. P. Freeman-Grenville, 1958 and 1962a.
35. J. S. Kirkman, 1954b.
36. H. N. Chittick, 1974; V. M. Misiugin, 1966.
37. J. Ki-Zerbo, 1972, pp. 10–12 and 190–2; C. A. Diop, 1955, p. 19.

> title of *mfalme*, giving the right to supreme power, was the property of the entire Wapate clan. All its men fulfilled for a certain time the functions attaching to the title, while all the women of the clan were the depositories of this right. Thus Sulaymān, the founder of the Nabkhani dynasty, received the title of king of Pate when he married a woman from the al-Bataviyuna [Wapate] clan, in accordance with ancient custom. He received the title not because he married the king's daughter, which was a coincidence, but because she was one of the women belonging to the next *ndugu* generation.[38]

From the fact that *ndugu* rule was maintained, it does not follow that Swahili society was a clan society.

> The social nature of the *ndugu* rule originally meant that in former times the waPate clan, on the strength of its superiority over other clans in terms of property, limited or closed off within itself a part of the scheme of clan social relations, thereby depriving the other clans of the right to occupy the supreme office.[39]

Thus the accession of Sulaymān, the first representative of the Nabkhani dynasty, and the fact that he received his power through marriage indicate the already long-standing development of class relations on the coast. However, Sulaymān did not belong to the royal clan of Pate. Therefore, after the title had passed to him through his wife, he was linked to the traditional clan only through a woman. Such a situation could involve the risk of loss by the royal clan of its right to the title, for according to the *ndugu* rule it went to the husband's brothers, who might not be married to representatives of the royal clan. In these circumstances the king's wife, as representative of the royal clan, became the depositary of the abstract right to the title of king, the office of which was discharged by her husband. It mattered little who in fact the husband might be; the important thing was that he simply became a part of the existing system, which had arisen on the African coast and was African in origin.

We have attempted to apply these research methods to the *Kilwa Chronicle*, and it seems that the *ndugu* rule governed succession in that town as well. This is particularly clear from the first chapter. We have a reference to this where the texts says that Muḥammad Ibn ʿAlī reigned first, then his third brother Bas<u>kh</u>āt Ibn ʿAlī, succeeded by his son ʿAlī, who had usurped the power over the heads of his paternal uncles Sulaymān, al-Ḥasan and Dāwūd. Here we have a clear indication of infringement of the legal norms, according to which the rightful ruler should have been not ʿAlī Ibn Bas<u>kh</u>āt but his uncle.

A similar allusion is to be found in the third chapter of the *Chronicle*, dealing with the mutual rights to the sultanate of the two

38. Misiugin, op. cit., p. 8. This quotation is translated from the Russian.
39. ibid., p. 63.

brothers al-Ḥasan Ibn Sulaymān al-Matūn and Dāwūd. In fulfilling the functions of sultan, Dāwūd regarded himself as the deputy of his absent brother and recognized his duty to obey him, should he return. This seems to us of special interest, since al-Ḥasan Ibn Sulaymān and Dāwūd Ibn Sulaymān belonged to the Abu 'l-Mawāhib dynasty, which was said to have originated in Yemen. Its consolidation at Kilwa is held to underlie the high level of development of the various branches of culture in the town. It is also interesting to note that the Swahili version of the *Kilwa Chronicle* and the *Pate Chronicle* record that the new Persian sultan married the daughter of a local chief.

The fact that succession to power was subject to the *ndugu* rule bears out the thesis of the local origin of the machinery of government in the African towns, for the rule stemmed from local African social institutions. Accession to power in towns other than Pate and Kilwa through marriage to the ruler's daughter is known to have occurred, and Freeman-Grenville gives several examples of this. All this justifies the belief that much the same situation as at Pate obtained all along the coast under the apparent dominion of Islam and its customs and standards.

Islam and the ideology of power

The supremacy of Islam was bound up with the growing role of those sections of Swahili society that had grown rich on trade. Their position probably improved to the extent that the old aristocracy tried to strengthen its position through marriages to rich Muslims, who in turn, in order to keep even with the old aristocracy, tended to claim that they were descended from Arabs, and sometimes from illustrious Arab and Persian families prominent in the history of Muslim countries.

> In this way the old Swahili legends of the migration of more or less considerable groups of Muslims to the East African towns in the seventh, eighth, ninth and tenth centuries are transformed into tales of the migration from Arabia and Persia of ancestors of the ruling dynasties of many Swahili towns and their foundation by Arabs or Persians.[40]

Such legends are by no means unique, and a number of them are given in the collection of traditions, *Kitāb al-Zanūdj*.[41] The same sort of legends occur at other times and in other places in Africa and elsewhere. One example is the version that has come down to the present day, attributing the origin of the ruling dynasty in Ethiopia to King Solomon and the Queen of Sheba. African tribes of eastern Sudan claim descent from Arab

40. Translated from the Russian; ibid., p. 67.
41. For an Italian version, see E. Cerulli, 1957–9.

tribes that penetrated into Africa. The emergence of the state of Kanem is linked to the name of the first king, Sefe, who according to tradition was the king of Yemen, Sayf Dhu Yazan. The pedigree of the ruling Keita clan in Mali is traced back to the entourage of the Prophet Muḥammad. Even in Nigeria there is a legend that the ancestors of the Yoruba people were Canaanites from Syria and Palestine. As we can see, all these legends attribute to white strangers who came to Africa long ago the origin of entire peoples, the foundation of states and the establishment of ruling dynasties, without explaining them by purely African factors and events. Here we are clearly concerned with a general phenomenon peculiar, in certain cases, to the historical process at the stage of transition from the pre-class to the class society. Further indirect evidence of such a practice is provided by certain researchers, particularly A. H. J. Prins, who gives examples of ethnic groups claiming Arab or Shirazi ancestry despite their indubitably African origin.[42]

It seems clear, however, that the East African Swahili civilization was the fruit of commercial development. It was trade that prompted the growth and progress of civilization, but also underlay its weakness, for it was not tied in with the development of the productive forces of the region. From the occupation of the population, it can be seen that the Waswahili people as a whole did not endeavour to develop their productive forces beyond the level which probably obtained in traditional Swahili society before the advent of trade on a substantial scale. This is also evident from the fact that few iron tools or other metal instruments have come to light in excavations. Almost all the goods produced by the Waswahili were intended not for local consumption but for sale and export. This was also true of hunting and the mining of gold and iron. At the same time, trade alone was an insufficient basis and stimulant for a civilization. The loss of former trade routes and the disruption of commercial relations threatened to bring trade to a standstill, with the inevitable consequence of a rapid depletion of wealth and of the civilization's vital force. This, as we now know, was what the future held in store for the East African towns.

Various circumstances are considered to have contributed to the decline of Swahili civilization. There was the Zimba invasion, and it also seems that a decrease in rainfall and the consequent upsetting of the water balance hindered the further development of the coastal towns. It is possible that all these factors did actually sap Swahili civilization. However, the chief cause, in the writer's view, was the disruption of maritime trade by the Portuguese. Being well fitted out, equipped with artillery and built for the purpose of naval warfare, the Portuguese ships were an invincible force. Their constant presence in the region under the command of Ruy Lorenso Ravasco, the seizure of twenty vessels laden with goods, the defeat

42. A. H. J. Prins, 1961, pp. 11–21.

of Zanzibar's large fleet of light craft, and the plundering and destruction of the coastal towns, particularly Kilwa, were all blows from which East African maritime trade never recovered, and the medieval Swahili civilization perished with it.

19 Between the coast and the great lakes

C. EHRET

At the beginning of the twelfth century of the Christian era in the East African interior, the signpost of the previous pathways of historical change was the striking correlation of ecology and ethnicity. Bantu-speaking societies were still relatively few in number, despite the major migrations of Bantu settlers into eastern Africa over the course of the first millennium of the Christian era, and they were almost wholly restricted to the better-watered regions with, at the lowest, 900–1000 mm of rainfall a year.[1] It must be concluded that, even though grain cultivation and often general livestock keeping had been taken over by most of the East African Bantu during the first millennium, Bantu communities still maintained the primacy of the agricultural tradition, based upon root and tuber crops, which had been brought by the earliest Bantu immigrants.[2] In contrast, on the plains and highlands of the Kenya interior and of Tanzania, East African mixed farming, with its combined grain cultivation and extensive cattle-raising, predominated. Through the northern parts of this belt of generally drier environments, the majority of societies spoke Nilotic languages, whereas Southern Cushites were the more numerous through the southern portions.[3]

The immediate interior

Along the immediate interior of the East African coast, three major clusters of Bantu can be identified: the Sabaki-speakers, the Seuta-speakers and the Ruvu. The Sabaki language had three dialects, spoken along a very narrow strip of land behind the Kenyan coast. The ancestral Miji-Kenda dialect was spoken south of the River Tana, probably immediately inland from Mombasa and south from there to the far north-east point of Tanzania. Near the mouth of the Tana, and possibly also in the Lamu hinterland,

1. Unless otherwise noted, Bantu groupings, locations and culture histories in the following pages are based on data and conclusions contained in D. Nurse, 1974; D. Nurse and D. W. Phillipson, 1974; T. Hinnebusch, 1973; and C. Ehret, n.d.
2. C. Ehret, 1974a.
3. C. Ehret, 1974b.

can be located the community which spoke the proto-Kipokomo dialect of Sabaki.[4] The third dialect, proto-Kiswahili, had earlier emerged in the commercial centres along the coast itself.[5]

As the coastal strip gave way to the drier eastern Kenyan interior, Sabaki communities gave way to different peoples with quite different subsistence adaptations. To the north of the Tana were pastoralists, speaking an early form of Somali. Along and south of the Tana can be placed the Southern Nilotes, similarly pastoral in economy.[6] An important Sabaki cultural feature, which may derive from Bantu interactions with such interior populations, were the age-grade systems of the Miji-Kenda and Pokomo peoples. The general suggestion has been that those systems arose under Galla influence in the seventeenth century; nevertheless, among the Pokomo, certainly, Southern Nilotic ideas were the primary stimulus to age-grading, and that influence must therefore be placed before 1600.

Both the pastoralists of the interior and the Bantu along the coast co-existed with hunter-gatherers, and that pattern has been maintained in varying degrees until the present. To the north of the River Tana the modern Boni, who speak their own quite distinct Somali dialect, can be understood as hunter-gatherers who took up Somali speech from dominant pastoralists as long as a thousand years ago, but retained their food-gathering subsistence pattern.[7] Along the Lamu interior, the vocabulary of the Southern Cushitic-speaking Dahalo hunter-gatherers shows loan-word evidence of their continuous interaction with, yet separate existence alongside, dominant Pokomo and Swahili peoples over a period of many centuries, extending back as early as the first millennium.

The second Bantu cluster, the Waseuta, lived to the south of the early Sabaki communities, behind the modern north-eastern Tanzanian coast, in the area roughly between the lower Pangani and Wami rivers. The proto-Seuta people of 1100 had already added crops of Indonesian origin to their more ancient African planting tradition. Such crops included Asian yams, taro and bananas. Similar agricultural developments can probably also be assumed for contemporary Sabaki groups. It is not clear, however, that the intensive cultivation of bananas, such as appears among the later highland Kishambaa descendants of the proto-Seuta, had yet come into being. Over the next 500 years the original Seuta grouping gradually diverged into three sets of communities. The Kishambaa dialect emerged along the north-west of the Seuta area, among migrants pushing into the highland environment of the Usambaras. Proto-Zigula-Ngula had emerged by the mid-millennium as the dialect of those Seuta communities which had spread up the River Wami toward the Ngulu mountains; in the original

4. ibid., Table 2–1; loan-words attributed there to Nyika (Miji-Kenda) come instead from early Kipokomo.

5. See Chapter 18 above.

6. Ehret, 1974b, chs. 2, pt 2 and 4, pt 2.

7. H. C. Fleming, 1964.

heartland of the Seuta settlement, an early form of the dialect known today as Bondei was spoken.

As in Kenya, the well-watered coastal strip of north-east Tanzania gave way to increasingly drier interior areas. From the proto-Seuta era, and probably throughout the period 1100–1600, Seuta communities lived as near neighbours to Southern Cushites, who spoke a Mbuguan language. From the assumed Mbuguan adherence primarily to cattle-raising and secondarily to grain cultivation, it seems best to place them in the eastern portions of modern Seuta country, hence between the Maasai steppe and the coastal strip.

Along the River Wami watershed to the south of the Seuta lived the Ruvu Bantu; by the twelfth century they consisted of two sets of communities with two kinds of agricultural adaptations. The East Ruvu communities, from which derive the modern Wakutu, Wakwele, Wados, Wazaramo, Wakami and Walugulu, can be seen as originally keeping to the wetter lowland areas behind the coast. In consequence, they would have emphasized the sort of combined African and Indonesian agriculture that has been postulated for their Bantu neighbours to the north. The West Ruvu peoples, from whose dialects come the modern Kikagulu and Kigogo languages, departed from this background in the course of their expansion westward towards the upper sources of the Wami. They diverged in subsistence practices by shifting towards a greater emphasis on grain cultivation and livestock-raising. They may have diverged in culture through their interactions with pre-existing Southern Cushitic groups in that region, although this proposition cannot yet be demonstrated. The particular Cushites who interacted with the early West Ruvu communities seem to have been the southerly extension of the Mouguan people, who were the neighbours of the proto-Seuta.

From Lake Nyasa to Lake Victoria

A second region of considerable Bantu population at the beginning of the twelfth century was along the southern fringe of East Africa, about and near the north end of Lake Nyasa. In the highlands of the north-east tip of the lake can be placed the proto-Njombe society. The Njombe language was ancestral to the modern Kikinga, Kikehe, Kibena and Kisangu tongues. A second Bantu society, speaking an ancient form of Kinyakyusa, resided to the west of the Njombe in probably much the same area as the modern Wanyakyusa. To the north-west of them, along the highland corridor between Lake Tanganyika and Lake Nyasa, two other Bantu peoples spoke divergent dialects of a single corridor language: nearby the Wanjombe and early Wanyakyusa were the proto-Wanyiha, and to the west of the proto-Wanyiha were the proto-Walapwa. At the other, south-eastern end of this belt of Bantu peoples, the proto-Wasongea and the early Wapogoro lived as the southern and eastern neighbours respectively of the Njombe; peoples speaking the dialects ancestral to the Kiyao, Kimakonde and Kimwera languages were spread out along the River Ruvuma eastward, probably even then as far as the Indian Ocean seaboard.[8]

The whole region around the north end of Lake Nyasa was both a source of major outward expansion of Bantu and an area of considerable internal migration over the centuries between 1100 and 1600. In the western half of the corridor the Lapwa communities entered an era of expansion about midway through the period, which spread the Kilapwa language over much of its present territory and led to the differentiation of Kilapwa into its three modern dialects: Kinyamwanga, Kimambwe and Kifipa. There is considerable evidence to suggest that Kilapwa-speakers spread partly by absorbing an interlacustrine, central Sudanic people.[9] But by far the most extensive movements were those of eastern Songea Bantu groups; these people settled across the vast dry lowlands that stretch between the River Rufiji and the wetter Ruvuma river belt, a region where the annual rainfall is less than 1000 mm. Their latter-day descendants include the Wamatumbi, Wandengereko, Wangindo and Wabunga among others. Their ability to establish themselves in country marginal at best for the earlier Bantu crops, and unsuitable for cattle-rearing, shows that even in the eleventh and twelfth centuries the eastern proto-Wasongea were turning their primary agricultural emphasis towards grain and other seed crops. Their fast advance and extremely low, present-day population densities suggest that only hunter-gatherers preceded them through most or all of the lowlands south of the Rufiji.

The major internal population movements, in contrast, came from the Njombe area. The early Wakinga intruded southward into former Songea Bantu lands, and a major Njombe component was absorbed into the proto-Wanyiha society. Later, in the sixteenth century, the two major princely lines of the Wanyakyusa and the ruling house of the Kinyakyusa-speaking Wangonde were each established by Wakinga immigrants.[10]

Also late in the period, the corridor region itself began to receive Bantu immigrants from elsewhere, in particular from the west and south-west. All the Bantu of the region had long maintained some sort of chiefly principle of leadership, but the local political unit had been extremely small and relatively unstable. The princes of the Wanyakyusa described by Charsley may have been the prototype of earlier corridor leaders.[11] The western and south-western immigrants frequently seem to have disrupted the previous accommodation between communities and so precipi-

8. Percentages of core vocabulary cognition among Songea languages, calculated by the writer from the standard list used in Nurse and Phillipson, 1974, range no lower than 70 per cent. Comparison with Nurse and Phillipson's dating suggests that the beginning of the divergence in Songea was no more than a thousand years ago. Wayao, Wamakonde and Wapogoro share lower percentages of cognates with each other and with Songea, and therefore were already distinct by that time.

9. C. Ehret, 1973. 10. M. Wilson, 1959a, Chart I. 11. S. R. Charsley, 1969.

tated the formation of new, larger chiefdoms with the leaders of the immigrants taking over the chiefly positions. The Kyanwanga chiefdom was thus created in the sixteenth century, but the western and south-western factor was mostly to gain great importance only in the seventeenth century and after.[12]

A third area of continuous Bantu settlement at the beginning of the present millennium was along the eastern shores of Lake Victoria. In the twelfth century, south-east Victoria Bantu communities could be found probably from Mara in the south to the Kavirondo Gulf in the north. Along the northern margins of that gulf and in an area north-west along the east side of Busoga was the north-east Victoria proto-network of Bantu-speaking communities. The south-east Elgon Bantu, a detached outlier of the north-east Victoria group, inhabited an area on the south or south-east side of Mount Elgon. Along the north side of the lake, north-east Victoria Bantu territory merged into the Lacustrine Bantu-speaking regions.

Despite contiguity on the north with Lacustrine Bantu, east Victoria societies were distinctly different from Lacustrine societies, and this difference reflected several previous centuries of interaction and acculturation between Bantu and non-Bantu peoples along the eastern side of Lake Victoria. At about the beginning of the twelfth century all the east Victoria Bantu practised male circumcision, and south-east Victoria peoples, or so comparative ethnographic evidence suggests, had female circumcision as well. Both these practices were entirely unknown among the Lacustrine Bantu, but universal among the Southern Cushitic and Southern Nilotic peoples, who were eastern neighbours of the east Victoria Bantu. Moreover, east Victoria societies all seem to have been organized into small local units on a clan or lineage basis. Chiefship, as also among their non-Bantu neighbours, was entirely lacking, whereas chiefly or kingly leadership was the rule among contemporary Lacustrine societies and can be shown to be a much more ancient Bantu organizational principle.[13]

For south-east Victoria communities, with the lake on one side, the Nilotes and Cushites on their remaining flank were perforce a continuing factor in their cultural history, from the twelfth to the seventeenth century. Growth by absorbing former Southern Nilotes was an especially prominent trend among the peoples speaking the Mara dialect of the south-east Victoria language; the process led eventually – among the ancestors of the modern Wakuria, Wazanaki, Waikoma and others – to the grafting of a Southern Nilotic cyclical age-set system on to the earlier, south-east Victoria, clan-based, social and political organization. With the merging of Bantu and Southern Nilotes into one society came the merging of ideas of social structure drawn from both backgrounds, although Mara speech predominated as the language of the amalgam.[14] Among the Musoma subgroup

12. B. Brock, 1968.
13. Cf. J. Vansina, 1971.
14. C. Ehret, 1971, ch. 5.

of the south-east Victoria communities, Southern Nilotic contacts are also clearly attested;[15] but it is not yet apparent that these contacts had the same degree of impact on cultural change. For the Gusii branch of the Mara subgroup, in contrast, it was not Southern Nilotes but rather Plateau Southern Cushites who had the greatest impact. The very early Gusii-speaking community apparently grew by absorbing Plateau people and hence never took up the Southern Nilotic type of age-organization as did the other Mara communities.[16] Even after 1600, during the era of close relations between the Gusii and the Kipsigis – a Southern Nilotic people – the adoption of Gusii identity meant maintenance of the type of local community organization which became stabilized in the period before 1600.

During the same period (twelfth–seventeenth century), north-east Victoria societies were involved in a more diverse set of cultural contacts. Along the west of their territory, Lacustrine Bantu immigrants would seem to have affected social practices and ethnic distribution in varying degrees. The decline, for instance, of circumcision and non-cyclical age-set systems among the western Baluhia can be attributed to the periodic movement out of the Lacustrine-speaking regions of people lacking those ideas. On the west slopes of Mount Elgon, an Itung'a people earlier inhabiting the area was gradually replaced between 1100 and 1600 partly by speakers of the Gisu dialect of north-east Victoria, but also partly by a second Bantu society, the Syan, that coalesced around immigrants coming from modern Busoga or Buganda. Conversely, linguistic evidence demonstrates that north-east Victoria immigrants pressed eastward in considerable numbers into Busoga during the same period. The Kintu period in Busoga and Buganda oral history, it can be convincingly argued, represents a major settlement of north-east Victoria people, dating perhaps to the fourteenth century, such as would account for the linguistic evidence.[17] There seems no reason to doubt the claim of tradition that the Kintu movements introduced the banana to Buganda and Busoga, if we understand that it was not the first introduction of the banana that is meant, but rather the introduction of the sort of intensive cultivation and utilization of bananas that had already developed by this time in the Mount Elgon region.

Among northern and eastern communities in the north-east Victoria network, however, Nilotic contacts predominated. The confluence of ideas drawn from the West Elgon Itung'a and the Kitoki Southern Nilotes, who lived along the south of Mount Elgon throughout most of the period, contributed to the growth in importance of cattle in the proto-Gisu subsistence repertoire. In the sixteenth century and continuing even later, the encounter of Luyia and Kalenjin-speaking Southern Nilotes below the Nandi escarpment led to the formation of Bantu-speaking communities which maintained the older territorial clan basis of social and political

15. ibid., app. D4.
16. Ehret, 1974b, ch. 2, pt 6.
17. D. W. Cohen, 1972.

structure, but with appended cyclical age-set systems of Kalenjin origin. An additional, very late development was the sixteenth-century intrusion of Luo immigrants into the far southern part of the region near the Kavirondo Gulf. At first relatively unimportant, the Luo were to rise rapidly to great importance in later centuries.

Inland zones of Kenya and Tanzania

Although most Bantu communities of the interior of Kenya and Tanzania were established in areas with more than 1000 mm of annual rainfall, a few were already adapting in the eleventh century to drier climates. One such were the West Ruvu people, previously discussed. Another possible set of communities were those speaking the proto-Takama language of western Tanzania. The linguistic geography of the modern Kitakama languages – Kinyaturu, Kinyiramba, Kinyamwezi-Kisukuma and Kikimbu – fits best with the postulate of a proto-Takama homeland somewhere along the west of the River Wembere, a region with annual rainfall ranging from approximately 600 mm to 1000 mm. If in some parts of that territory a few of the older African crops were cultivable, they could hardly have been dependable staples, and thus already among the proto-Takama the shift towards a greater reliance on grains must have been made.

Throughout the rest of interior Kenya and Tanzania a variety of Nilotic and Southern Cushitic societies predominated in the twelfth century, interspersed with a few scattered concentrations of Bantu. All the Nilotes and Cushites had a special bias in favour of livestock-raising, but it would be a mistake to think of them as pastoralists to the exclusion of cultivation. Indeed, to judge from the usual pattern among more recent societies like these, grain cultivation in most cases probably provided the major part of their actual sustenance. Nevertheless, in certain limited regions of extremely low and/or poorly distributed rainfall, such as the Maasai steppe and large parts of north-eastern Kenya, cultivation may, in fact, have been completely or almost completely superseded by stock-raising.

A particular contrast with present-day conditions was the vast spread and importance of Southern Cushitic populations; of these, the East Rift peoples were by far the most numerous. At the height of their importance in the first millennium, the East Rift societies were dominant in a broad belt of country running from Kilimanjaro and the Pare Mountains southwards to the Dodoma region of modern Tanzania. They herded cattle, sheep and goats and raised bulrush millet as their staple grain, together with sorghum and, where rainfall permitted, eleusine. By 1100 the once continuous East Rift territory had been broken by the expansion of the Dadog (Dadio, Dago) and the Ongamo, both Nilotic peoples.

In central Maasailand, one small East Rift community, whom I have called the Asax, persisted in spite of Dadog dominance there; however, it persisted only because it was a hunter-gatherer group.[18] The hunter-gatherers with their radically different economy had been able to coexist socially with the once dominant East Rift population even as they adopted the East Rift language. When Dadog absorbed or drove out the East Rift pastoralists, the Asax continued to survive as a separate social unit and to maintain their own Cushitic language.

Southward from central Maasailand, two major East Rift societies continued the herding and grain-cultivating life of their ancestors of the first millennium. One of these groups, the Kw'adza, were direct descendants of the former dominant East Rift society of Maasailand and spoke a dialect closely related to Asax.[19] Their territory probably included parts of the South Maasai, Mpwapwa and Dodoma areas of Tanzania.[20] The second East Rift people, who can tentatively be called the Iringa Southern Cushites, had territory of uncertain extent. It would appear, however, that they were southern neighbours of the Kw'adza and that they were spread far enough and in sufficient numbers to have had significant influence on the proto-Njombe of the period around 1100, and also to have been an element in the formation of the Hehe (Wahehe), Bena (Wabena) and Sangu peoples in the centuries since then.

For several centuries after 1100 the aridity of Kw'adza and Iringa country continued to deter Bantu expansion. But at the same time increasing numbers of Bantu communities, whether by absorbing earlier Southern Cushitic peoples or through trade and general cultural interchange, supplanted their earlier agriculture with mixed farming like that of the Iringa and Kw'adza. One such Bantu group formed the Njombe communities of the southern highlands of Tanzania, another the West Ruvu of the Kilosa area, and still another the various Takama communities to the west of the Kw'adza. By the sixteenth century major expansions of Bantu settlers from all three regions were under way. In the southern highlands the remaining East Rift communities gave way not only before the primary push of Wanjombe immigrants, who spoke the ancestral Kibena-Kihebe dialect, but also before the pressure of West Ruvu migrants, although this latter movement may have begun no earlier than 1600. In the Dodoma region the Kw'adza began to come under pressure from all three directions. The Kigogo language brought in by West Ruvu immigrants eventually predominated, but Kigogo vocabulary evidence as well as Gogo historical traditions, point to equally significant increments of population from Uhehe to the south and from Takama country to the west – so many in total as to swamp their Kw'adza predecessors.[21] In 1600, however, these processes were just beginning and the Kw'adza remained a factor in central Tanzanian history.

18. In previous works the Asax have been referred to as the 'Aramanik'.
19. Kw'adza is a correction of the previous spelling, 'Qwadza'.
20. Ehret, 1974b, ch. 2, pt 4.
21. P. Rigby, 1969, esp. chs. 2 and 3.

The spread of Takama immigrants into the Dodoma area was only one aspect of much wider Takama expansion through western Tanzania, which began as early as 1000. By the first centuries of this millennium, the initial stages of spread had led to the division of the proto-Takama into three sets of communities. The Wembere society, speaking a dialect of Takama ancestral to modern Iramba and Nyaturu, had emerged among Takama settlers on the dry plateaux to the east of the River Wembere. The ancestral Kikimbu-speaking communities took shape perhaps to the immediate south of the upper Wembere, whereas the proto-Wanyamwezi-Wasukuma resided somewhere to the north-west of the Wembere area.[22] The fact of greater dialect diversity within modern Usukuma than in Unyamwezi implies that the proto-Wanyamwezi-Wasukuma homeland lay within the general area of Usukuma.[23] The number of Southern Cushitic loan-words in Kinyamwezi-Kisukuma vocabulary shows that the proto-Wanyamwezi-Wasukuma society arose in part through the amalgamation of Takama-speakers and an as yet unidentified Southern Cushitic people formerly residing south of Lake Victoria.[24] There is little evidence, on the other hand, of Southern Cushitic influence on the proto-Kiwembere and early Kikimbu-speakers, and it seems probable therefore that Wawembere and Wakimbu settlers moved into territories which had previously been only sparsely populated by hunter-gatherers. The Hatsa of Lake Eyasi appear thus as the last unassimilated remnant of such earlier communities. The nearby Sandawe would be another such people, but they escaped assimilation by turning to an agricultural life.

The pattern of the period 1100–1600 was one of continuing spread and differentiation of the Takama group of peoples. Early on, the Wawembere began to develop a north–south division, which was to give rise respectively to the later Iramba and Nyaturu societies. But by far the most important expansion was that of the Wanyamwezi-Wasukuma communities until, by 1600, people speaking dialects of that language had spread from the shores of Lake Victoria almost as far south as modern Ukimbu. Perhaps as early as 1600 Wakimbu immigrants were also beginning to filter south and south-westward into their present-day territory. It was as part of these late stages of Takama expansion that some Takama settlers were to move eastward and merge with other Bantu settlers in the Dodoma region.

Mountain regions: Kilimanjaro and Kenya

To the north of central Maasailand, on the slopes of Kilimanjaro, one or more additional East Rift Southern Cushitic communities carried on life as usual in the twelfth century, and yet another, or possibly two, East

22. See Nurse and Phillipson, op. cit., for this tripartite division of Takama (their 'South Lake').

23. D. Nurse, personal communication, July 1974.

24. Probably Nyanza Southern Cushites; cf. Ehret, 1974b, ch. 2, pt 6.

Rift groups can be located in the Taita Hills.[25] The shared feature of these East Rift societies, it seems probable, was their reliance on irrigation and manure to carry on a basically grain agriculture. These two practices provided the essential underpinnings of a major event in East African agricultural history, the development of an intensive highland agriculture with bananas as the staple crop. It was Bantu-speaking communities that, in the course of absorbing Southern Cushites, successfully merged the Bantu planting tradition, with the addition of the Indonesian banana, into the Cushitic procedures of cultivation. When and where the resulting new highland tradition first emerged is unclear, but early in the second millennium it had taken hold among the then small Bantu communities of Kilimanjaro, Mount Kenya and the Pare Mountains. The further diffusion of the highland tradition allowed the beginning of the Shambaa settlement in the Usambara range by 1500. The highland East Rift communities may have become familiar with some crops of the highland tradition, but their full adoption of that agriculture probably came only with their assimilation into the expanding highland Bantu communities.

In the twelfth century the highland East Rift groups were restricted to the highland zone by the spread of the Ongamo through the Kaputie plains north of Kilimanjaro, southward around the mountain itself, and apparently among the fringes of the Pare ranges as well.[26] The Ongamo spoke a language closely related to, and at that period still mutually intelligible with, the proto-Maasai of the Mount Kenya region. Ongamo vocabulary-retention from their common ancestry with the Maasai demonstrates not only their raising of livestock, but their cultivation of sorghum and eleusine. Yet although Ongamo control of the plains may have restricted the East Rift people to the mountains, the direct pressure against East Rift lands came from small Bantu communities, equally hemmed into the mountains by the Ongamo.

Around 1100, the proto-Chagga were most probably settled on the south-east slopes of Kilimanjaro, although a primary settlement area in nearby North Pare is also possible. They already possessed a fully developed highland agriculture that gave extraordinary importance to the banana within that system. The immense productivity of the highland tradition, it is argued here, was the crucial advantage that allowed the rapid spread of the Chagga over the next five centuries, absorbing both East Rift and Ongamo communities in the process. Out of the initial stages of Chagga dispersion, there emerged four sets of Chagga communities.

Three of these were settled on Kilimanjaro – the West Wachagga along the south side of the mountain, the Central Wachagga near modern Moshi, and the Rombo on the east side. The early Wagweno, on the other hand, emerged in North Pare, where there is some evidence of a prior East Rift

25. Ehret (in 1974b, ch. 2, pt 4 and Tables 4.6 and 4.7) described these as simply 'Rift'. But Ehret, n.d., has shown conclusively their East Rift affiliations.

26. Ehret, n.d., and 1974b, Table 8.2.

population. Continuing expansion of Wachagga settlement until 1500 encouraged the division of the Rombo Wachagga into several separate communities along the east of the mountain, and, at the same time, some West Wachagga immigrants crossed from Kilimanjaro to the highland forests of nearby Mount Meru. By the sixteenth century, East Rift communities remained prominent only at the far south-west of Kilimanjaro, as can be seen from the Southern Cushitic loan-words in the Siha dialect of West Wachagga.[27] Ongamo were still numerous on the lower eastern slopes of Kilimanjaro, but apparently no longer a factor outside that zone.

The Taita Hills, even more than Kilimanjaro, would seem to have had a history between 1100 and 1600 which was dominated by the problems of accommodation between East Rift and Bantu. East Rift communities preceded the proto-Taita people in that region and continued to be an important population element, even as the proto-Taita diverged into separate Dawida and Sagala societies during the early centuries of the second millennium. Not until more recent centuries can one be sure of the final absorption of the East Rift people into the growing Bantu communities of the Taita Hills. An additional divisive factor, especially among the Sagala, was the intrusion of other Bantu immigrants from the Sabaki-speaking areas at the coast and from the Pare Mountains. So strong was the coastal element among the Sagala that their language took up many Sabaki loan-words and, most startlingly of all, went through sound-changes found in the more distantly related Sabaki languages but not in closely related Dawida. But this coastal factor began to affect the Taita Hills only as the East Rift factor declined, probably no earlier than the sixteenth century. Its social and political dimensions belong more properly to later periods which are not covered in this volume.

The movement of Sabaki groups into the Taita Hills was presumably an offshoot of the same set of immigrations around which the Akamba ethnic identity crystallized in sixteenth-century Ukambani to the north of the Taita Hills.[28] But in Ukambani the southern immigrants merged into a Bantu population with Mount Kenya antecedents and a Thagicu language. By about 1100 the ancestral Thagicu had formed a small set of Bantu communities on the south slopes of Mount Kenya. Like the contemporary proto-Chagga society, they were wedged between Southern Cushites – here Kirinyaga in language[29] – and more pastoral peoples, in this case the Southern Nilotes, on the plains lower down. The proto-Maasai lived probably to the north-west beyond the forests of Mount Kenya, but Maasai-speaking peoples do not seem to have had any discovered impact on Thagicu communities until after 1600.

Between 1100 and 1500 Thagicu communities expanded their territory

27. Nurse and Phillipson, op. cit.
28. K. A. Jackson, 1972.
29. Ehret, 1974a, ch. 2, pt 7.

by cutting back the forest and spreading out along the south of the mountain. At the same time the original proto-Thagicu language was dividing into several dialects; these developed among the Thagicu migrants, who moved south away from Mount Kenya and into north-central Ukambani.

By the sixteenth century the modern ethnic divisions among the Thagicu were beginning to become apparent. The major expansions of later centuries were to come from two of these already emergent societies – the Kikuyu at the gap between Mount Kenya and the Nyandarua range, and the Neru at the other extreme of Thagicu settlement, on the east of Mount Kenya. At the same time the Sabaki immigrants were interacting with the established Thagicu of Ukambani, fashioning a society which was Thagicu in language, but one which in many aspects of culture resembled not those of the Bantu of Mount Kenya but that of the Taita or the coastal Bantu. Examples are the Akamba replacement of the spear with the bow and arrow as the standard weapon and their lack of the age-set principle of political and social organizations, which was so important on Mount Kenya. Southern Cushitic communities still remained along the east of the mountain, a few of them possibly as neighbours to the early Kikuyu; the hunter-gatherer bands controlled the forested slopes of the Nyandarua range to the south of the Kikuyu. The pre-Bantu populations of Ukambani are as yet not satisfactorily accounted for, but the presence of at least a few Southern Nilotes – probably close kindred to the Southern Nilotes of the adjoining dry plains of north-eastern Kenya – seems required in eastern Ukambani by the presence of a small Southern Nilotic loan-word set in the modern Kitui dialect of Kikamba.

To the west of a line running through Mount Kenya and Kilimanjaro lay the one large region of interior Kenya and Tanzania, in which the general trend towards Bantuization in the 1100–1600 period did not operate. Dominant through most of the region until after 1500 were Southern Nilotic societies, in particular the Kalenjin and Dadog. Around 1000 the proto-Kalenjin, and the closely related Kitoki Southern Nilotes, controlled the territory stretching from the immediate south of Mount Elgon eastward through the Uasingishu plains. During the next two or three centuries the Kalenjin spread across the breadth of the Uasingishu plateau and east and south-eastward into the Rift Valley areas of central and southern Kenya. Continuing Kalenjin expansion over the next several centuries only reinforced the dialectal and ethnic differences beginning to emerge in different parts of Kalenjin country.

Along the south-east of Mount Elgon the early Elgon Kalenjin society diverged from the common Kalenjin pattern through its incorporation of the south-east Elgon Bantu people. For instance, territorial clans, as among the north-east Victoria Bantu, superseded cyclical age-sets as the basic organizational principles of Elgon Kalenjin society. For the same reasons the Elgon Kalenjin began to shift to an agriculture based on the cultivation of bananas and, with that advantage, began to spread around the forested slopes of Mount Elgon.

To the east of the mountain, by 1500, the ancestral Pokot people were coming under the cultural dominance of their Itung'a neighbours to the north; and the proto-Nandian society had taken shape along the western edge of the Uasingishu plateau, just south of the Pokot. The early stages of Nandian growth were accompanied by the incorporation of Plateau Southern Cushites; one of the probable Southern Cushitic contributions to their Kalenjin descendants and successors is the practice of irrigation agriculture among the Keyu and Marakwet, Nandian-speaking peoples who reside today along the Elgeyo escarpment. Then, around 1500, the direction of Nandian expansion swung around southward into the forest and plains of the River Nyando country. From these Nandian settlers the later Nandi and Kipsigi communities would, in part, derive.

But the most explosive and far-reaching ethnic spread of the era was that of the South Kalenjin. The ancestral South Kalenjin communities evolved on the far south fringe of the earliest Kalenjin expansions. From central southern Kenya they expanded rapidly southward, first along the plains to the east of the Rift wall, and then through the Maasai steppe to the east of the Kondoa highlands. By no later than 1500, South Kalenjin immigrants had settled as far south as the borders of the West Ruvu Bantu country. In northern and central Maasailand it was the once-dominant Dadog who gave way before the Kalenjin advance. In South Maasai it was the Kw'adza who were assimilated or driven out by the South Kalenjin. The Rift escarpment in northern Tanzania remained a barrier to South Kalenjin expansion, for the Dadog continued to control the Loita and Ngorongoro highlands and, one suspects, the Serengeti and Mara plains to the west. Not until the seventeenth century was Dadog power to be broken in those regions and then not by Kelenjin, but by Maasai invaders.

In the Kondoa and Mbulu highlands, West Rift Southern Cushites, together with one Bantu society, the proto-Irangi, remained unaffected by the South Kalenjin expansion to their east. Little is yet known about the history of the peoples of the region between 1100 and 1600, with the exception of the West Rift Cushitic people, the Iraqw. The penetration of Iraqw settlers northward along the Rift escarpment into the shatter-zone between the Dadog and South Kalenjin is clearly attested in Iraqw loan-words in Kisonjo.[30] The Wasonjo, a Bantu-speaking people, held the unique position of being predominantly cultivators, isolated in small enclaves where irrigation was possible, among predominantly pastoral Dadog and South Kalenjin. The Iraqw settlers can be envisaged as moving into the same sort of niches along the edge of the Rift and pursuing the same sort of livelihood. By their own traditions, the Sonjo are to be placed

30. ibid., ch. 2, pt 4.

before 1600 on the edges of the Rift Valley below the Loita highlands.[31] The isolated Iraqw groups were presumably southern neighbours of the Wasonjo, living possibly in such locations as those of the modern Sonjo settlements above Lake Natron and probably at the famous archaeological site of Engaruka.

At the other extreme of Kalenjin territory, in Baringo and the Laikipia plateau, the proto-Maasai were evolving during the period into three separate societies: the Samburu, Tiamus and Maasai. The southernmost of the three, the Maasai, began to make inroads into former Kalenjin lands along the Rift Valley in central Kenya as early as the sixteenth century. By 1600 they may have spread as far south along the line of the Rift as the northern edges of Tanzania and, from there, were beginning to threaten the Dadog and South Kalenjin dominance further south.

Population movements and cultural interchange

From this complexity of events, population movement stands forth as a repeated motive force for historical change in the Kenya and Tanzania interior. Yet immigrants between 1100 and 1600 were probably never moving into entirely empty land. Hence the history in which they participated was one of societies in conflict and of the resulting give and take of ideas between peoples in the course of forming new social and political groupings. An integral part of the explanation for the special expansion of Bantu-speaking territories was the growing agricultural adaptability of several of the earlier Bantu populations. In large parts of central and western Tanzania, it was the willingness of Bantu immigrants to shift their emphasis in eating habits from root crops to the bulrush millet and sorghum favoured by their Cushitic and Nilotic neighbours which enabled them to settle among, and by stages absorb, the prior populations. In several highland portions of northern East Africa it was a very different adaptation – highland agriculture – which encouraged Bantu expansion.

Not the least of the side-effects of Bantu agricultural adaptability was the opening up of new areas heretofore occupied only by food-gathering communities. In other parts of western Tanzania as well, for instance in the areas immediately east of the River Wembere, the agricultural way of life may have been finally established only by the settlement of grain-cultivating Takama communities during the period between 1100 and 1600. In the north, the highland farming tradition allowed the utilization of forest zones previously left to hunter-gatherers, and on Kilimanjaro the early Chagga may have expanded not so much by moving in directly on the lands of their agricultural predecessors as by cutting back the forest and moving in alongside and above their competitors, and then progressively assimilating them.

31. A. Jacobs, personal communication, September 1976.

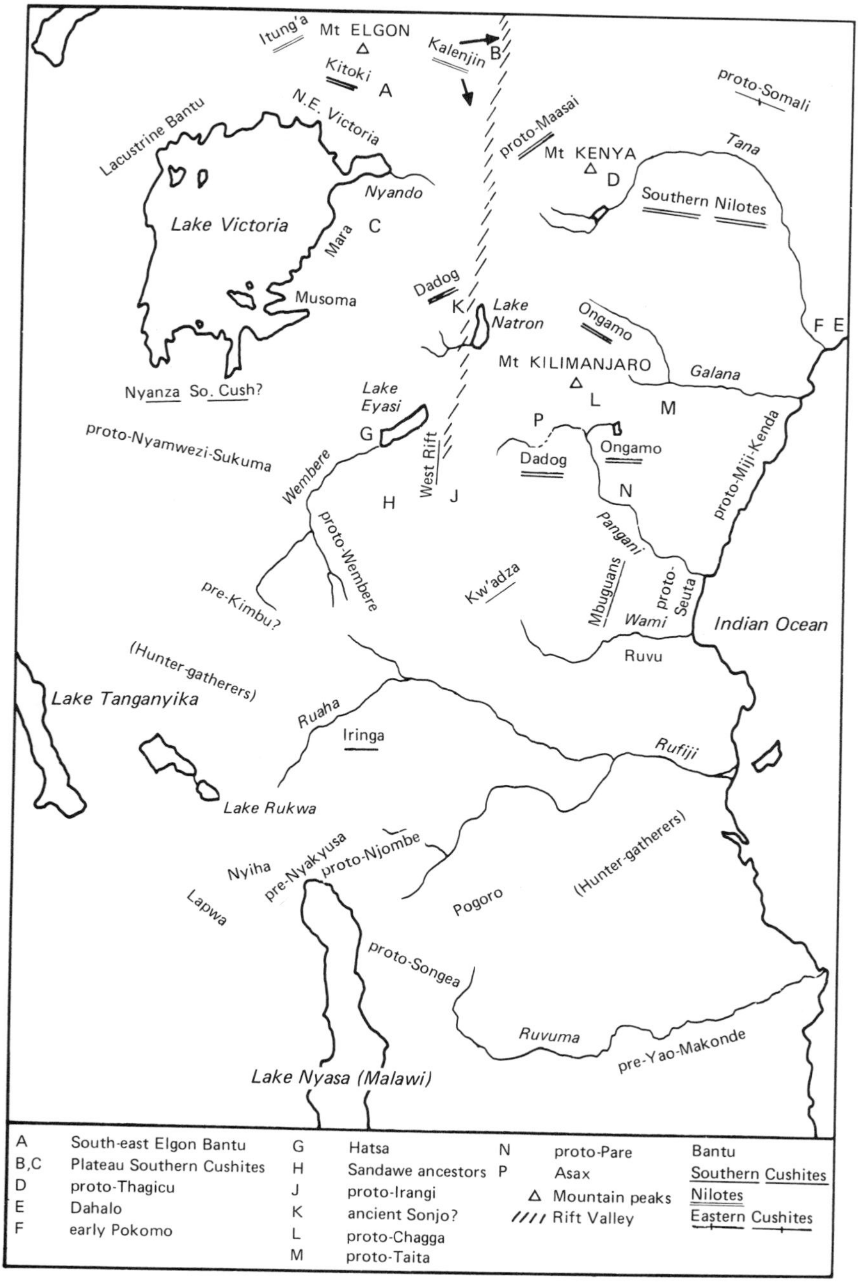

FIG. 19.1 *Probable approximate locations of peoples in the East African interior in the 12th century* (C. Ehret)

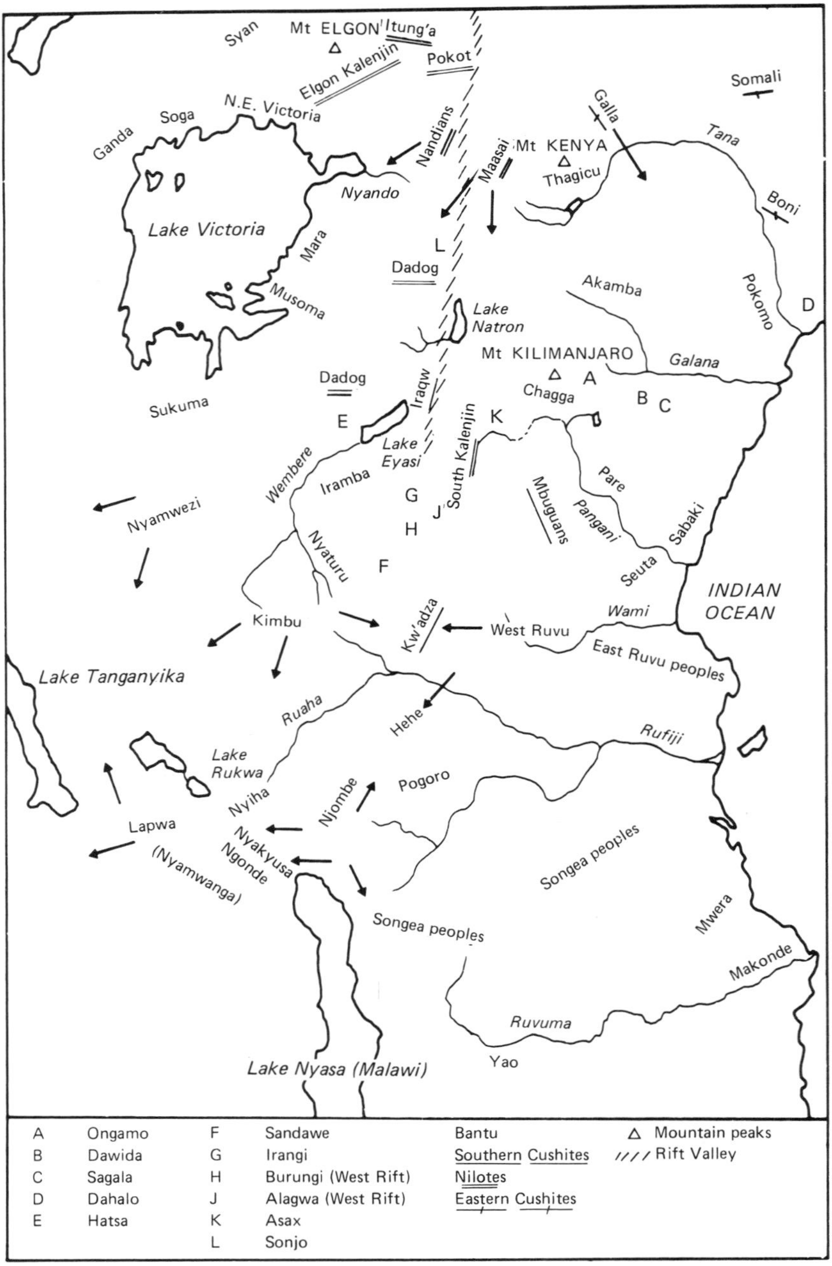

FIG. 19.2 *Probable approximate locations of peoples in the East African interior in the 16th century* (*C. Ehret*)

Alongside these major cultural and ethnic shifts some sort of limited exchange of goods between people must have taken place from time to time all through interior East Africa. In only one region, however, did so great a difference in kinds of surplus production exist side by side as to precipitate the creation of formal markets. The region was that of Mount Kenya and Kilimanjaro, where intensive highland agriculturalists lived next to intensive cattle-keepers, and both cultivators and pastoralists frequently coexisted also with hunter-gatherer bands.[32] The pastoralists produced a surplus of hides and could also manufacture leather clothing desired by the highland farmers. The highlanders, in turn, had the timber from which to make large wooden vessels, such as beehives and watering troughs, and cultivated the gourds from which calabash containers, so important to the plains communities, were made. At times of the year when food was in short supply, the highlanders could offer their surplus crop production in exchange for livestock from the people of the drier plains nearby. The hunter-gatherers might occasionally have been able to offer surplus hides or honey from their subsistence activities.

Another factor was the uneven distribution of metal deposits. Even in the sixteenth century the Wagweno of North Pare were integrally tied to the highland–plains trading system through their role as the major supplier of iron and iron tools;[33] the Thagicu may have had a similar position for areas around Mount Kenya. For most of the rest of the interior of Kenya and Tanzania, however, markets were not to appear as a regular feature of economic life until well after 1600, and even then because of external rather than local influences.

32. The reconstruction of the institution of markets is based on the antiquity of the terms for market in the region; proto-Thagicu and early (if not proto-) Chagga terms exist.

33. I. N. Kimambo, 1969.

20 The Great Lakes region

B. A. OGOT

A historian attempting to reconstruct the history of the interlacustrine region of East Africa between 1200 and 1500 of the Christian era is faced with several major problems. First, the 300 years represent an era for which we have scant oral tradition or linguistic data. Nor do we have any adequate archaeological data. The oral traditions, for example, are replete with legendary father-figures who are variously identified as gods, fathers of all the people, founders of clans, or as introducers of food crops (such as banana or millet) or of cattle. The stories of their exploits have been forged into popular traditions whose historical validity is difficult to establish. It is not surprising, therefore, that historians such as C. Wrigley have concluded that the Chwezi myths, for example, contain no valid information about the early history of the interlacustrine region. To accept that the Chwezi spirits referred to in myth and cult were actual kings of a fifteenth-century kingdom in the interlacustrine region is, he says, like believing that Odin and Freya were kings of ancient Sweden, even though the *Ynglinga Saga* assures us that they were.[1]

Secondly, the historians working in this region face a major problem of bias with regard to the relationships between the agriculturalists and pastoralists. In many history books and articles the pastoralists are portrayed as civilizing conquerors who introduced law and order where anarchy formerly reigned supreme. The agriculturalists, on the other hand, are painted as docile and silent majorities who neither initiated any developments nor founded any state. Rwanda provides an excellent example of this bias, and Kagame, for instance, finds it difficult to believe that the state of Rwanda could have borrowed any institution from the agriculturalists. Nor is he prepared to accept the idea that any 'Hutu' ruled over noble, 'Hamitic' pastoralists.[2] We hope to show in this chapter that state formation among the agriculturalists in this region antedates the advent of most pastoralists. We also hope to show that for a long time there was peaceful coexistence between the agriculturalists and the pastoralists

1. C. Wrigley, 1958 and 1973.
2. A. Kagame, 1955, p. 112.

prior to the major state formation processes of the fifteenth century, which to a large extent were responsible for the creation of social classes or castes in this region. In this connection, it is important to emphasize that the terms 'pastoralists' and 'agriculturalists' are occupational and not ethnic terms. The interlacustrine traditions reveal that when pastoralists lost their cattle and were unable to recoup those losses, they became cultivators; and when cultivators acquired cattle, they became pastoralists.[3] This change of occupation was continually occurring in the region, both at the individual and at the group levels.

Another problem facing a historian working in this region during this period is chronology. For the last twenty years several scholars, working with a combination of the generational principle, tie-in references and eclipses mentioned in traditions, have done a great deal of work on Bantu and Nilotic chronologies. But a closer reading of this voluminous literature shows that there is no general agreement either on the chronology of individual states or on a general chronological framework for the whole interlacustrine region. For example, the reliability of the Bito genealogy in Bunyoro has recently been called into question by Henige.[4] In Rwanda also, the problem of chronology is of fundamental importance. Kagame has argued for a founding date in the tenth century of the Christian era, offering a royal genealogy from 959.[5] Vansina, however, maintains that the first seven names of Kagamé's list, with the possible exception of Gihanga, are not historical persons. According to Vansina, the state of Rwanda was founded during the latter part of the fifteenth century.[6]

But even if we were to be able to solve the question of the chronologies of individual states, we should still have to integrate the chronologies of Rwanda, Gisaka, Bunyoro, Kiziba, Mpororo, Buganda, Busoga, Nkore, Karagwe, Ihangiro, Kyamutwara, Buzinza and Sukuma into a basic chronological structure covering our period. And that is a very difficult task.

The final problem facing a historian working in this region is that most of the published histories until recent times were court-centred. They discussed the origins and development of centralized states in the interlacustrine region on the basis of court traditions. For instance, in Rwanda, the works of Pagès, de Lacger and Kagame are largely based on court traditions. Such histories are bound to be limited, especially with regard to sections of society living away from royal enclosures.

Having noted the major problems, we should now turn to the history of this region, which for historical convenience is discussed under four

3. See S. R. Karugire, 1971.

4. D. P. Henige, 1974.

5. A. Kagame, 1959. The genealogy begins as follows: Gihanga I (959–92), Gahima I (992–1025), Musindi (1025–58), Rumesa (1058–91), Nyanume (1091–1124), Rukuye (1124–57), Rubanda (1157–80).

6. J. Vansina, 1960.

headings: the Kitara complex, the Kintu complex, the Ruhinda complex and the Rwanda complex. The term 'complex' has been used to emphasize both the multi-ethnic nature of the region and the confluence of cultural traditions that constitutes its history. But, at the same time, the four complexes are interconnected and merge into a general history of the region.

The Kitara complex

The history of the Kitara complex, which covers geographically most of the present Bunyoro, Toro and neighbouring portions of Nkore, Mubende and Buganda, has recently been studied by Dr Carole Buchanan.[7] It is probably the oldest state system of the interlacustrine region, and its history is usually conceptualized in terms of three groups of invaders: the Batembuzi, the Bachwezi and the Bibito. We should note that this historical conceptualization, which to a large extent reflects the historical division of the Kitara complex into three main periods, is significantly silent about the Bantu-speaking peoples, whose languages dominate the area. Are we to deduce from this that the Bantu-speaking majority rarely observed history and never participated in it?

In order to answer this question, it is essential to remember that the arrival of most Bantu-speakers predated that of the three groups. Dr Buchanan has postulated that the period between 722 and 1200 of the Christian era witnessed some of the earliest remembered migrations into the Kitara complex. The first cluster of clans to settle in this area was probably of central Sudanic origin, and thus originally from the north or north-west.[8] There is no unanimity among scholars about the early history of the central Sudanic peoples, but the linguistic evidence suggests that they were probably in this area before the earliest Bantu-speakers. If this is the case, it would mean that, on the basis of archaeological evidence, they were in the area before the fourth century of the Christian era.[9] The first Bantu-speaking clans seem to have come from the region to the west of Lake Mobutu (Albert) and to have settled throughout the region south of the Nile. According to their traditions, they were predominantly agriculturalists, cultivating eleusine and sorghum, although some of them kept livestock. Buchanan has suggested that these early Bantu migrations into the interlacustrine area occurred in the tenth and eleventh centuries, on the grounds that the oldest strata at Kibiro (*c.* tenth century) showed no evidence of the dimple-based pottery which has been linked to the presence of Bantu-speaking peoples.[10]

7. C. A. Buchanan, 1974.
8. C. Ehret, 1974c, p. 8.
9. C. Ehret, 1967, p. 3; J. E. G. Sutton, 1972, pp. 11 and 23.
10. S. Pearce and M. Posnansky, 1963; S. Chapman, 1967; J. Hiernaux and E. Maquet, 1968, p. 43.

Some of these Bantu clans were later involved in the formation of a number of small agricultural states, which Buchanan associates with the Batembuzi period of Kitara history and tentatively dates from *c.* 900 to 1300.[11] If she is right, then it would provide an answer to the question posed above regarding the role of the Bantu-speakers in the history of this region. The answer would be that, at least in the case of the Batembuzi, we are not dealing with invaders in the sense of some immigrant pastoralists; rather, we are dealing with the earliest Bantu groups in the area.

Buchanan's work represents the first serious examination of the pre-Bachwezi period. Hitherto historians and other scholars have referred to the Batembuzi period as 'the reign of the gods' and have considered the Batembuzi to belong more to mythology than to history. According to Kinyoro tradition, there were nineteen *Abakama Abatembuzi* or 'pioneer kings';[12] whereas Nkore tradition records only four, to whom no collective name is applied. Some of these kings, such as Hangi, Kazoba and Nyamuhanga, were ancestor spirits worshipped by the Bachwezi.

Buchanan was able to penetrate the thick mist of the Batembuzi only by placing less reliance on court traditions than on clan histories. One of the earliest political units she identifies was the chiefdom of Bugangaizi, established by the Bagabu clan, who are remembered in tradition as Batembuzi and whose founder was Hangi. The Bayaga – whose original name was Basehe – are another pre-Bachwezi clan who probably migrated from the Semliki valley at about the same time. Their traditions associate them with the coming of cattle (probably not long-horned) into the area and the salt-work site at Kiboro on Lake Mobutu. Another group whose pre-eminence seems to have had an economic basis is the Basita clan. This clan is among the largest in the interlacustrine region. The people are identified with Sitta, a founder of one of the clans of Bugisu, with the Abendega (sheep) clan of Buganda and Busoga, with the Baswaga of Bakonjo, and with the Byabasita of Kibale; they figure significantly in the traditions of Nkore, Kiziba and Buhaya states, where they are associated with an earlier form of chiefship, predating the Bahinda. Their rise to power and their extensive dispersal would appear, from their traditions, to have been due to the fact that they were iron-workers. The place-name 'Mbale' or 'Kabale', which is found in Mwenga, in Bugisu (in Uganda), in north-western Tanzania and in western Kenya, is linked in the traditions with settlements of the Basita.

By about 1250 there was already a number of small Bantu chiefdoms east of the Ruwenzori Mountains, either offshoots of the Batembuzi of Bugangaizi or created in imitation. For instance, according to Lwangira, the first king of Kiziba lived between 1236 and 1263.[13] But at the same

11. See also J. Nyakatura, 1947. His genealogy would suggest 869–96 for the first Batembuzi and 1301–28 for Isaza, the last.
12. ibid., pp. 6–65.
13. F. X. Lwamgira, 1949, p. 65.

time there were several other Bantu-speaking societies organized into smaller political units such as lineages and clans.

The history of the Baranzi clan provides a link between the Batembuzi and the next dynasty in the Kitara complex – the Bachwezi. According to Kinyoro tradition, the founder of the clan, Bukuku, was a commoner and an official in the court of Isaza (*c.* 1301–28), the last of the 'pioneer kings'. He is supposed to have taken over from Isaza and at the same time he is regarded as the grandfather of Ndahura (*c.* 1344–71), the great ruler of the Bachwezi period. The clan itself had the grasshopper and the civet cat as its totems and it probably came from the Busongora area into the west. As is explained below, both totems are important in Buganda and Busoga history as names of pre-Kintu, and therefore pre-Bachwezi, groups that moved from west to east across the grasslands to the shores of Lake Victoria.

As we have said, Bukuku, an agriculturalist, provides a genetic relationship between the pioneers and the Bachwezi. Ndahura's foster-father was, according to Bunyoro and Nkore traditions, a potter by trade, who came from a Bakopi clan.[14] Hence Ndahura's other name, Karubumbi (from *mubumbi* or potter). Perhaps these traditions were intended to legitimize the position of Bukuku, a commoner who rose to great fame. Nevertheless, such traditions are widespread in the region, and they should be interpreted to mean that the origins and developments of the centralized states in the interlacustrine region cannot be accounted for entirely in terms of alien pastoral aristocracies. Internal factors, including local initiatives, might provide a more convincing theory.

The succession of Bukuku to Isaza's throne was resisted by several chiefs, who objected to being ruled by a commoner. Bukuku crushed the rebellion, although dissatisfaction became widespread and provided an opportunity for Ndahura to seize the throne and found the Bachwezi dynasty. The traditions of Bunyoro and Nkore are agreed that this dynasty consisted of two rulers – Ndahura and Wamara – and a regent, Murindwa, who acted as such when his brother Ndahura was away on war expeditions. In spite of this unanimity on the names of the rulers, and despite the existence of voluminous literature on the Bachwezi dynasty, there is still no agreement among historians about the validity of this literature. Huntingford suggests that the Bachwezi might have been of 'Hamitic' stock, related to the Sidama of south-western Ethiopia.[15] Oliver asserts that the Bachwezi were historical figures and that 'on the whole it seems likely that the Ganda Kingdom of Chwa was identical with that of the Chwezi, and that what the Bito conquered was already ... a single political unit dominated by the Hima pastoralists under the kings of the Chwezi clan'.[16] Earlier, Crazzolara had thundered that the Bachwezi and the Bahima were

14. Nyakatura, op. cit.; A. G. Katate and L. Kamugungunu, 1967 edn.
15. G. W. B. Huntingford, 1963, p. 86.
16. R. Oliver, in R. Oliver and G. Mathew (eds), 1963–76, Vol. 1, pp. 181–2.

the same people, and that both groups were Luo.[17] Posnansky, on the basis of archaeological evidence, accepts the historical existence of the pastoralist Bachwezi, and the correlation of the Bachwezi with the Bigo culture, which he dates at 1350–1500. Indeed he goes further, to identify Bigo as the capital of a pastoral kingdom ruling over western Buganda, between 1350 and 1500.[18]

Although all the above authors accept the historicity of the Bachwezi, Wrigley, almost alone, still maintains that they constituted nothing but 'a pantheon of a familiar kind, a collection of named and individualized divinities, imagined as a human kin-group writ large, and mostly associated with the more prominent features and forces of the natural world'.[19] In this chapter, we accept the historicity of the Bachwezi. We therefore proceed to discuss the major developments which took place in the Kitara complex from 1350 to 1500 as part of East African history, and not as an aspect of East African mythology.

There are two major theories about these developments. There are those historians who argue, like Oliver, that the Bachwezi empire was founded following the incursion of the pastoralist Bahima. They disagree, however, as to where the Bahima came from. The older view was that they came from the north-east, probably from southern Ethiopia. Recently, some members of this historical school have suggested that the Bahima might have come from the south. Thus Chris Ehret, discussing the cultural influence of the Southern Cushites in the interlacustrine region, has opined:

> This late continuation of Southern Cushites as important pastoralists in the southern half of the lacustrine region raises the intriguing possibility that the latter-day Tutsi and Hima pastoralism, most significant in the southern half of the region, is rooted in the Southern Cushitic culture and so derived from the east rather than the north.[20]

This infiltration of the region by the Bahima is supposed to have occurred in the thirteenth and early fourteenth centuries. Then, during a period of instability, they and their allies amongst the earliest settlers gradually acquired an aristocratic status over the agricultural population and in the fourteenth century established their loosely structured state.

The other theory, which is rapidly gaining ground, is that the Bachwezi were local rulers who emerged as a result of the economic and demographic changes that were taking place in the interlacustrine region. It is clear that the empire of Kitara was created by Ndahura (*c.* 1344–71), a great warrior king, who extended the small chiefdom of Bugangazi over a vast area which included Bunyoro, western Buganda, Toro, northern

17. J. P. Crazzolara, 1950–4, Vol. 2, pp. 94–7 and 102–3. In this chapter, I shall use the correct spelling, Luo, and not the old, Europeanized version, Lwoo.
18. M. Posnansky, 1966, pp. 4–5.
19. Wrigley, 1973, p. 226.
20. Ehret, 1974c, p. 11.

Kigezi, the Sese Islands, Nkore, Kiziba, Karagwe, part of north-eastern Rwanda and part of western Kenya. He lacked the military power, the bureaucracy and the means of quick communication to be able to establish a centralized state over this vast area. He therefore relied more on agents who were appointed to represent the king in the various areas. This loosely organized empire seems to have had salt, cattle and iron as its economic mainstay.

King Ndahura, who often led his own army, was captured during an invasion of Ihangiro in Bukoba, when an eclipse of the sun caused panic among his troops. On his release, he preferred to migrate westwards rather than return as a disgraced king to his capital at Mwenge. Tradition is silent on his subsequent fate.

He was succeeded by his son Wamara (*c.* 1371–98), who on security grounds moved his capital from Mwenge to Bwera. Wamara's reign was even more turbulent than that of his father, largely because it witnessed the advent of several immigrant groups. Among those were the Jo-Oma (or Bahima), most of whom came from the Agoro mountain region; the Bantu-speaking clans from the east associated with the Kintu complex (see pp. 518–24 below); an invasion from the south which probably represented an advance group of the Bashambo clan; and the Luo, who began to infiltrate into Kitara from north of the Nile. There is as yet no agreement as to whether the Jo-Oma were Luo or Bahima, although recent research by Webster and his team at Makerere would favour the latter.[21] Be that as it may, the important point to emphasize is that, according to the historical reconstruction we are outlining here, the Bachwezi were not Bahima or Luo: they were a Bantu aristocracy who emerged in western Uganda in the fourteenth and fifteenth centuries. As a result of the arrival of the Bahima pastoralists (whether from the north only or from the north and south) and of the Luo during the reign of the last Bachwezi king, the loosely structured empire became multi-ethnic and multilingual. Internal tensions arising from the problems of political integration developed which could not be resolved, and the empire collapsed.

King Wamara had attempted to enlist the support of the immigrants by appointing them to important political posts. For instance, Miramira of the Bashambo clan and Rugo and Kinyonyi of the Balisa clan were appointed Wamara's representatives around Lake Masyoro in the areas which became Kitagwenda, Buzimba and Buhweju. Ruhinda, a Muhima, was placed in charge of the royal herds; Nono, a member of the Basita clan, became a deputy chief in Karagwe; Kagoro, a Luo, became the chief military commander; and Wamara formed a blood brotherhood with Kantu, who had emerged as the leader of the Bantu clans of eastern origin. All these overtures, however, were construed as appeasement by the immigrant communities, who soon developed into over-mighty subjects.

21. See J. B. Webster, 1978.

Then there occurred a great famine, followed by a cattle disease which spread all over the empire. Dissatisfaction became widespread. Kagoro, Wamara's military commander, seized the opportunity to stage a coup against the Bachwezi, who were mercilessly massacred and their bodies thrown into water. The Bachwezi aristocracy, which in any case could not have been a large one, was thus annihilated or, as tradition put it, 'disappeared'. The coup marked the end of the Bachwezi empire. It was replaced by two conglomerations of states: the Luo–Babito states of Bunyoro-Kitara, Kitagwenda and Kiziba; and the Bahinda (Bahima) states further south in Karagwe, Nkore, Kyamutwara, Ihangiro and possibly Gisaka (see Fig. 20.2).

The collapse of the Bachwezi empire led to a fierce struggle between the Luo and the Bahima (the Babito and the Bahinda) for the political control of the region; the history of the successor states for the next three centuries should be viewed in the context of this struggle for political hegemony.

Beginning with the Luo successor states, it is important to emphasize the theory advanced in this chapter, that historical developments in western Uganda cannot simply be explained in terms of a conquest theory which regards successive waves of pastoralist conquerors as the carriers of civilization.[22] As already mentioned, the Luo started to arrive in Kitara during the reign of Wamara. But before this, the Luo-speaking peoples had already dispersed from their land of birth, probably in the southern Sudan. The northern Luo apparently remained in this region, but the central and southern Luo moved south into the area of the Agoro mountains. A glotto-chronological study of the Luo dialects has suggested that this separation occurred in 870 (± 200), that is, between 670 and 1070.[23]

Oral tradition indicates that the Luo-speakers continued their gradual expansion and dispersal during the thirteenth and fourteenth centuries (see Fig. 20.1). These dates receive corroboration from linguistic evidence, which suggests that the proto-central and southern Luo separated between *c.* 1170 and 1470.[24] By the end of the fourteenth century, four Luo communities had emerged: one group lived near the Agoro mountains; another lived along the Nile near the north end of Lake Mobutu – the Pakwac triangle; a third occupied the area between Nimule and Shambe (Baar); and the ancestors of the Joka-Jok lived somewhere south of Mount Agoro.[25]

According to Luo traditions, they encountered several non-Luo groups in the Agoro mountain area. On arrival, they found the Muru, amongst

22. See Oliver and Mathew, op. cit., p. 180; B. A. Ogot, 1967, Vol. 1, pp. 46–7; Posnansky, op. cit., p. 5.

23. B. Blount, and R. T. Curley, 1970. I am of course aware that many linguists no longer believe in glotto-chronology.

24. ibid.

25. Ogot, op. cit. – the Joka-Jok were already in western Kenya in the late fifteenth century.

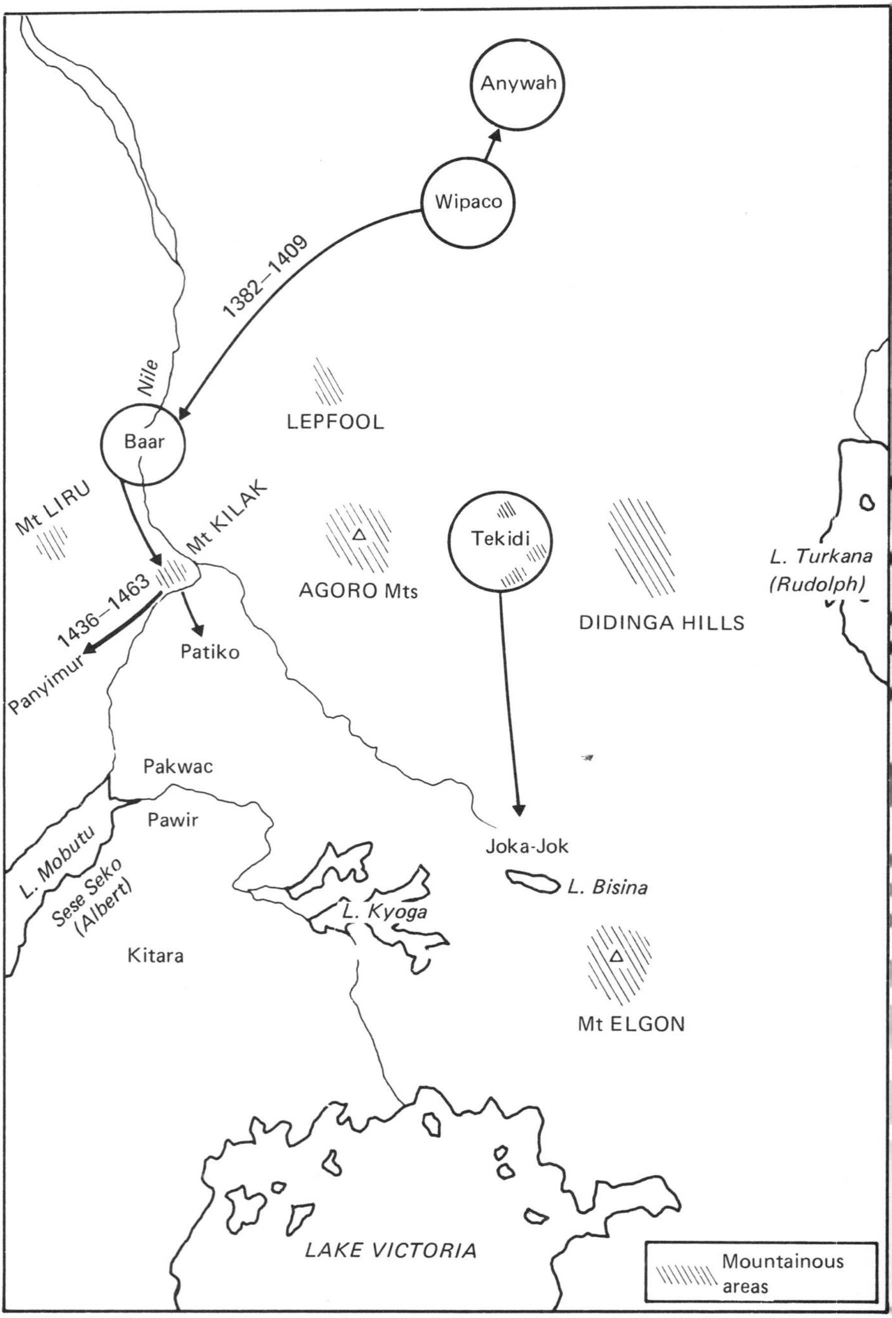

FIG. 20.1 *Early migrations of the Luo (B. A. Ogot)*

whom they settled and with whom they extensively intermarried. It was from this mixed population that the Joka-Jok and the Pawir-Pakwac groups, who moved away, derived. The Luo-speakers who stayed behind in the Agoro mountain area were later joined by the Jo-Oma (Bahima) about 1320–60. At this time the former were primarily hunters and agriculturalists, and they seem to have learnt about cattle-keeping from the Bahima pastoralists. Following the outbreak of a cattle disease in the area, a large number of these pastoralists were later forced to migrate. They crossed the Nile into the Bachwezi empire during the reign of King Wamara, as we saw above. Those who remained behind were absorbed by the Luo-speakers who, under their king, Owiny I (1409–36), had established Tekidi, one of the earliest Luo states.[26] According to Luo traditions, Owiny married Nyatworo, a Muhima girl, by whom he had a son, Rukidi. Later, Prince Rukidi broke away from his father and, with his followers, migrated towards Pakwac. After Kagoro's coup, he was invited by earlier Luo migrants into Kitara to assume political leadership there. He and his followers became known as the Babito, and he founded the new Babito dynasty of Kitara (*c.* 1436–63) as related below. From these accounts of life in Tekidi we can infer that at this time it was extremely difficult to know who was a Luo and who was a Muhima, given the mixed descent of the population. It is probably because of this that Crazzolara and other writers refer to these Luo-speaking Bahima as Luo.

Further north, in Baar, a similar ethnic fusion was taking place between the Luo and the Madi. Several royal clans such as Patiko, Nyimur, Padibe, Atyak (Kwong), Koc and Pagaya, which were to play significant roles in the history of the northern part of this region, emerged from this historical crucible. For example, we know that the Patiko, led by Labongo from Pari-Baar, migrated to the Nile in the Pakwac triangle. Some of them, including another clan called Anywagi (Anywah), accompanied Rukidi on his march into Kitara. We are also told that the Bakwonga (predominantly of central Sudanic origin), Bacwa and Bagaya (both clans of northern Luo origin) migrated southwards and crossed into the Kitara empire. Buchanan contends that this must have occurred at least one generation before Rukidi.[27] Thus the idea of a Luo army marching into the Kitara empire must be discarded as without foundation. Small groups continued to expand northwards into the Sudan, westwards into Zaïre, eastwards into Ethiopia, and southwards into Kitara, Busoga, Bukedi and western Kenya.

From the traditions of Bunyoro, Kiziba, Nkore and Karagwe, it is evident that the Babito and the Bahinda found it easier to topple Wamara's government than to control the empire. The new rulers created and propagated the myth of Bachwezi disappearance. They also tried to legitimize their positions by claiming genetic links with the Bachwezi. Unfortunately, such

26. Buchanan, op. cit., p. 181.
27. ibid.

propaganda failed to impress their subjects. The Bachwezi-appointed chiefs sought to control their areas. The Barisa royal clan, for example, succeeded in creating independent chiefdoms in Buzimba and Buhweju.[28] Also in Pawir, the Luo royal clan succeeded in retaining its political independence, although very much under the shadow of Bunyoro-Kitara. In all the other places, a mixture of force and guile had to be used in the establishment of Luo and Bahima rule.

In Kiziba, for example, the struggle went on for over a generation before Kibi (*c.* 1417–44), a Luo hunter, succeeded in establishing a Luo hegemony. Through political intrigues and generous distribution of game meat, he managed to win the support of several important clans such as the Bagaba – the old royal clan of the Batembuzi – the Basiita and the Baranzi.[29]

The struggle in Bunyoro-Kitara lasted even longer. Although Kagoro had organized a successful coup, he was unable to unite the Luo, let alone the whole state. He ensured, however, that the royal regalia such as drums were left behind for the Babito. In the end, the Luo sent for Rukidi, who agreed to come, accompanied by his followers, the Babito. He found that in several parts of the country the people were hostile. In Bwera, for instance, the hostility towards the new regime was such that Rukidi was forced to remove his capital from there to Bugangaizi, the heart of the old Batembuzi state. He was also faced with the problems of legitimacy and of creating an integrated state from a multi-ethnic society. This situation did not stabilize until after 1500, when Bunyoro began to expand towards the Bahinda states and Rwanda.[30]

As we saw earlier, the Bachwezi had appointed Miramira of the Bashambo clan and members of the Balisa clan as chiefs in the area around Lake Masyoro. Following Wamara's death, there ensued a struggle for supremacy. Two Babito brothers – Wakole and Nyarwa – managed to kill Miramira and to establish the state of Kitagwenda, with the collaboration of the Bashekatwa.[31]

The Ruhinda complex

The geographical focus of this complex is the present Kigezi district, Ankole, the Bukoba district in Tanzania and parts of Burundi and Rwanda. During the period under consideration, the main states that were involved were Nkore, the Buhaya states of Karagwe, Ihangiro, Kiyanja, Buzinza and Kyamutwara, as well as some parts of the future kingdom of Rwanda

28. K. K. Nganwa, 1948, pp. 6–7; P. K. Kanyamunyu, 1951.
29. Lwamgira, op. cit.
30. On the expansionist policy of Bunyoro-Kitara, see B. A. Ogot, Volume V, Chapter 26.
31. See A. Wheeler, 1971.

such as Ndorwa (see Fig. 20.2). Despite the existence of international boundaries and language barriers, the region possessed a historical coherence which dates back to the period under consideration. For instance, the impact of the Bahima/Batutsi pastoralists seems to have been greatest in this area. Several old clans, such as the Basiita, Bagahe, Basigi, Bazigaaba, Bakimbiri, Bashambo, Baitira, Batsyaba, Bagyesera, Baishekatwa, Bungura and Babanda, are widely scattered throughout the area. This is particularly important in this region where clans, especially the larger ones, tended to represent chiefdoms with mixed populations, rather than exogamous descent groups.[32] Many Bahima have been incorporated into Bantu clans, and Bantu families incorporated into Batwa clans and vice versa. This homogeneity is confirmed by the fact that today most inhabitants of the area speak Rukiga, Ruhororo, Runyankore or Runyambo – all closely related dialects – or Runyarwanda. Another factor which has fostered historical coherence is that most groups in the area had some experience of the expanding Rwanda state. But that story is outside the scope of this section.

By about 1200, traditions suggest that the forest belts were much more widely spread than they are today and that the Batwa, a group of forest hunters and gatherers, occupied the belts. They hunted large game, including elephant and buffalo.[33] Gradually Bantu agriculturalists began to move into the region, largely from the south and west. They cleared the forest and established permanent settlements, where they grew millet and sorghum. They also hunted and worked iron. For instance, the Barongo were pre-eminently iron-workers and hunters long before the advent of the Bahima in Buzinza.[34] We also learn from the traditions of the Basinga clan that their ancestor Kasinga was a blacksmith and a sorcerer in Karagwe. He was chased away by his brother, Muhaya, and he took refuge in Ndorwa before the coming of the Batutsi.[35]

Initially, the Bantu-speakers organized themselves on an extended family basis, with the heads of families constituting the highest authority. Sitting together, they looked after the welfare of, and administered justice for, the group. But as more immigrants moved in, clan organization developed. We should, however, emphasize that when we speak of clans in this region, we are not necessarily talking about people descended from the same ancestors. The custom of blood brotherhood, for instance, encouraged newcomers to join old families and some incoming groups sought the protection of powerful clans by joining them and adopting their languages and customs. Indeed, changing from one clan to another seems to have been an accepted practice in this region.

In this way, the clans became political organizations with territorial

32. F. Géraud, 1977, p. 24.
33. See Z. Rwandusya, 1972.
34. I. K. Katoke, 1975, p. 14.
35. Géraud, op. cit., p. 28.

boundaries. The chief of a clan was also the chief of the land, and the area was named after the dominant family. Thus Busigi, for instance, was occupied largely by the Basigi, Bugahe largely by the Bagahe, and so on. Large clans such as the Bazigaaba, the Bagyesera, the Basigi and the Babanda had a king or chief (*mwami*), who was both a political and a religious leader. He was responsible for the well-being of people, livestock and plants. Most of them were also rain-makers.[36] For instance, we learn from tradition that the Bagahe in Ndorwa around Lake Bunyoni, the Basigi in Busigi (an area now in Rwanda) and the Babanda in Kinkizi were rain-makers.

By the beginning of the fifteenth century, it would appear, some of these Bantu clans had established dynasties. For instance, we know that members of the Basiita clan ruled in Nkore, Karagwe and in other Buhaya states before the Bahinda took over. Rwanda historical traditions refer to a group of people called the Barengye, who were agriculturalists. They are regarded as being among the earliest inhabitants of the Rwanda region, concentrated particularly around Nduga in what is now western Rwanda. They employed huge and rather crude iron hoes.[37] The Barengye are supposed to have been wiped out by the Babanda long before the arrival of the Batutsi.[38] Fortunately, we know that today the Barengye are found in north-west Tanzania and in western Uganda, from Bufumbira to Toro. It would therefore appear that this ancient, Bantu-speaking, iron-working community was widely distributed in Rwanda and in south-western Uganda prior to the arrival of the pastoralists. In most of these areas they provided ruling families.

Another ancient clan of cultivators, who were probably amongst the earliest inhabitants of Rwanda and south-western Uganda, are the Bungura, who according to d'Hertefelt were numerically strong in Ruhengeri (north-western Rwanda) in 1960.[39] Unfortunately, no traditions relating either to migration or to state formation have been recorded among the Bungura – a fact which suggests antiquity.

The Bazigaaba also seem to have formed part of the earliest agricultural stratum in the region. We know that in Rwanda they established the Mubari state in the far east of Rwanda, which had a king (Kabeija) and a royal drum (sera) when the Banyiginya first appear in history.[40] But they are also found in large numbers in Nkore and in the Rujumbura county of Kigezi. In each of these three areas they have a different totem: the leopard in Rwanda, the antelope in Rujumbura and a striped cow in Nkore. As Professor Denoon has pointed out:

36. 'In Rwanda the rain-makers are mostly descendants of the local kings of the Bantu clans', A. Pagès, quoted by Géraud, ibid., p. 30.
37. J. K. Rennie, 1972, pp. 18–19.
38. Géraud, op. cit., p. 27.
39. M. d'Hertefelt, 1971, table 8.
40. M. Pauwels, 1967, p. 208.

> This distribution and diversity points firmly towards the existence of a multi-clan state (presumably Mubari) whence a diaspora migrated over a long period of time, retaining the name Bazigaaba initially as a political term and ultimately as a social category, and retaining the totemic signs of the original clan composition of the Bazigaaba state.[41]

There were other Bantu-speaking groups, such as the Banyangwe, Basiita, Banuma and Baitira, who played significant roles towards the end of the fifteenth century, when the Bahinda began to rule Nkore.

The only other clan that should be mentioned in order to illustrate the kind of politics which had evolved in the western lacustrine area by the beginning of the fifteenth century is the Baishekatwa, whose totem was *ensenene*. They are found in Rwanda (where the Bahondogo, who once ruled Bugyesera, are supposed to be an offshoot), Kigezi (where they are the oldest inhabitants of Rujumbura), Toro and Nkore. We also learn from Buganda traditions that the *ensenene* clan of the Buganda entered Buganda from the west, accompanying Kimera, as outlined below. It would appear therefore that the Baishekatwa are a very old, western Uganda clan, extending from the Busongora to southern Rwanda.

So far the discussion has been confined to the Bantu-speaking cultivators. Attention should now be turned to the pastoralists. First it is important to reiterate what has already been said, that the origin of the pastoralists in this region is uncertain. A northern origin has been postulated, but, as Rennie has pointed out, 'one should not rule out the local development, perhaps in or around Karagwe, of pastoralism as a way of life'.[42] Secondly, the widely held belief that the pastoralists in this area came in as conquerors who, from the very beginning, established pastoral aristocracies over the agricultural populations needs modification in this area, as in Kitara. Several instances of peaceful coexistence between the pastoralists and agriculturalists can be cited.[43] Indeed, until the fifteenth century, when several pastoralist states emerged (as related below), it was mostly the agricultural clans, as has already been shown, that provided ruling dynasties.

A group like the Bariisa, for example, is regarded as one of the oldest pastoral clans in the region. According to their traditions, they migrated from the north, possibly from Bunyoro, to Karagwe in the south. From Karagwe they moved back northwards through the present Kigezi and western Nkore. When they reached Mpororo, the clansmen dispersed in all directions. Amongst them was a family consisting of three brothers – Kateizi, Kinyonyi and Rugo – and a sister, Iremera, who were led by an eagle to the court of King Wamara, the last of the Bachwezi rulers. One of the brothers, Kateizi, dropped out and settled in Buhweju, where he married local women, adopted agriculture and founded the sub-clan

41. D. Denoon, 1972, p. 6.
42. Rennie, op. cit., p. 23.
43. Karugire, op. cit., pp. 122–3.

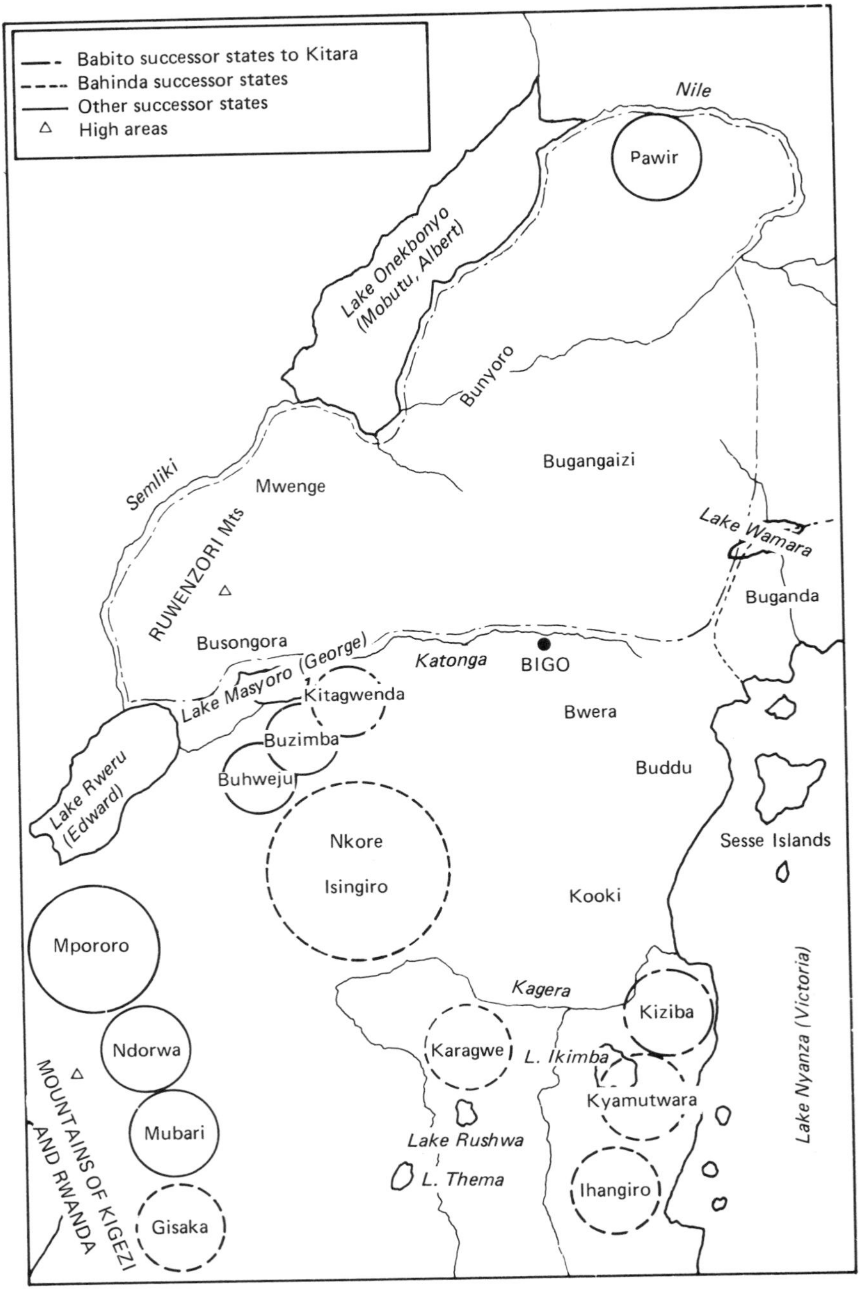
Babito successor states to Kitara
Bahinda successor states
Other successor states
High areas
Nile
Pawir
Lake Onekbonyo (Mobutu, Albert)
Bunyoro
Bugangaizi
Semliki
Mwenge
RUWENZORI Mts
Lake Wamara
Buganda
Busongora
Lake Masyoro (George)
Katonga
BIGO
Kitagwenda
Bwera
Buzimba
Buhweju
Buddu
Lake Rweru (Edward)
Nkore
Isingiro
Sesse Islands
Kooki
Mpororo
Kagera
Kiziba
Karagwe
L. Ikimba
Ndorwa
Kyamutwara
Lake Nyanza (Victoria)
MOUNTAINS OF KIGEZI AND RWANDA
Mubari
Lake Rushwa
L. Thema
Ihangiro
Gisaka

FIG. 20.2 *The Bachwezi and the immigrants* (*B. A. Ogot*)

of the Bateizi. The other two brothers and their sister finally reached the Bachwezi court. Iremera married the king, Rugo was appointed to rule over Buzimba, and Kinyonyi became Wamara's agent in Buhweju. Each was given a royal drum and a hundred head of cattle by the king.[44] From this tradition, it is clear that not all pastoralists started as rulers. Nor did they all end up as rulers, as the fate of the Bateizi illustrates.

Among the later pastoralist immigrants are three clans – the Bashambo, the Basiita and the Bahinda – that played leading roles in the founding of new clans in Nkore, Karagwe, Ihangiro and Kiziba. Tradition has it that the Bashambo came from the north and settled in and around Ndorwa in north-eastern Rwanda, from where they dispersed northwards and eastwards into Nkore and eastern Kigezi.[45] They were probably Bahima who entered the Bachwezi state before or during the Bachwezi reign. The Basiita were apparently moving in the opposite direction to the Bashambo. They seem to have spread northwards from a centre in or around Karagwe. During Bachwezi times, they provided rulers in Karagwe and Nkore, where Nono and Karara acted as agents of the Bachwezi.

There is much controversy surrounding the origin of the final group, the Bahinda. Nkore traditions claim that the Bahinda were descendants of the Bachwezi and that Ruhinda, the founder of a series of dynasties in Karagwe, Kyamutwara, Nkore and Ihangiro, was the son of Wamara, the last king of the Bachwezi.[46] De Heusch, on the other hand, has suggested that the Bahinda were Nilotes. He argues that, when the Luo invaded Bunyoro, they defeated the Bachwezi, who then retreated southward into Bwera and Nkore, which were protected from the incursions of the Luo by the fortifications of Bigo. A branch of the Luo, the Bahinda, outflanked the retreating Bachwezi and descended upon them from behind, via Karagwe. They finally defeated King Wamara in Nkore and then provided new dynasties for Nkore, Karagwe, Ihangiro and Kyamutwara. This theory has been convincingly refuted by Karugire.[47]

Denoon has advanced the theory that 'Ruhinda was a Mugyesera, from Gisaka, either extending the power of that state, or breaking away from it'.[48] He supports this by pointing out that the Bagyesera and the Bahinda share the same monkey totem; that the Bafumbira and Batoro refer to Nkore as 'Bugyesera' – the kingdom of the Bagyesera; that the total absence of the Bagyesera clan in Nkore, which is nevertheless surrounded by the Bagyesera diaspora, can only be explained by accepting Bahinda as the local name for the Bagyesera; and finally that the known magnitude of the Bagyesera power is compatible with the theory. They were the dominant

44. Kanyamunyu, op. cit.

45. The Bashambo women are supposed to have married the Bachwezi. See Géraud, op. cit.; L. de Heusch, 1966.

46. Karugire, op. cit., pp. 126–7.

47. ibid.

48. Denoon, op. cit., p. 10.

power in western Nkore and eastern Kigezi until the late seventeenth century, and they raided as far north as Busongoro and Mwenge. All that Denoon has shown, however, is that there was a dominant pastoral group in this region who could perhaps be identified as the Bagyesera. Whether it is possible to go a step further and identify the Bagyesera with the Bahinda is not clear from his account, especially as he has not demonstrated the connection between Ruhinda and the Bagyesera.

It would appear that Bunyoro traditions, as recorded by Nyakatura, provide an acceptable account of Ruhinda's origin. According to him, Ruhinda was a rich pastoralist (Muhima) who lived during the reign of King Wamara.[49] He gained eminence at the Bachwezi court and was appointed chief herdsman. When Kagoro staged his successful coup, Ruhinda drove away some of the royal herds into Karagwe. It was Ruhinda and his followers, according to Karagwe tradition, who introduced long-horned cattle into Karagwe. At this time the Basiita and Banyangwe clans, who had been given drums as symbols of authority by the Bachwezi, ruled this southern area. Nono, a member of the Basiita clan, ruled in Karagwe; Nkombya and Karara, both of the Banyangwe clan, ruled in Ihangiro and Nkore respectively.

Few kings of the early years can be dated as firmly as Ruhinda. Dynasties of four states – Buzinza, Kyamutwara, Karagwe and Nkore – claim descent from his sons. Calculations based on the four genealogies give Ruhinda a composite date of *c.* 1405–47. Kiziba tradition refers to Ruhinda in the generation *c.* 1417–44. When Ruhinda reached Karagwe, he used his great wealth in cattle to oust Nono from power. He then proceeded to establish a firm base of operations in Karagwe, whence he later moved north to Nkore. There he secured political control by concluding a political deal with the large and influential Banyangwe clan. In return for their acceptance of his leadership, the Banyangwe were guaranteed freedom from persecution or confiscation of their goods. Like Rukidi, Ruhinda also tried to persuade his subjects through carefully worked-out propaganda that he was a descendant of the Bachwezi.

He left his son, Nkuba, in charge of Nkore and turned his attention to Kyamutwara and Ihangiro. In the former, he killed Mashare, Wamara's agent, and installed Nyarubamba, another of his sons. In Ihangiro, he probably worked through collaborators, who poisoned Ihangiro of the Abayango clan, another agent of Wamara. He sent his youngest son, also called Ruhinda, to rule over Ihangiro. Finally, he moved to Buzinza, deposed Nshashame and installed another son.[50] Thus, having gained a foothold in Karagwe, Ruhinda quickly overran the surrounding area, deposing Bachwezi agents and replacing them with his sons. He was well on the way to creating a Bahinda state in the south similar to the Babito state

49. Nyakatura, op. cit., pp. 65–6 and 290; see also F. X. Lwamgira, 'History of Karagwe, Ihangiro, Nyamitwara, etc', unpublished MS, pp. 1–3.

50. Karugire, op. cit., pp. 130–1 and 137–42.

in the north or the Rwanda state created by the Banyiginya of Buganza, when he died in Buzinza. With his death, the large area of his influence became fragmented. His sons, who had acted as his agents, now became independent rulers of their respective areas and founded the dynasties of Karagwe, Ihangiro, Kyamutwara and Buzinza. These Bahinda successor states of Kitara were small and were to remain so for a long time.

From this survey, it is evident that the period following the 'disappearance' of the Bachwezi saw the emergence of several states in the interlacustrine regions: Gisaka, the Bahinda states, Rwanda, Ndorwa of the Bashambo, the Babito states and Buganda (which we have not yet considered). With the possible exception of Buganda, most of the new states had a marked pastoralist element. Ruhinda was a herdsman, whereas the Bagyesera, Banyiginya and Bashambo were pastoralists. The Babito, though initially hunters and agriculturalists, rapidly acquired the characteristics of pastoralist rulers.

The Rwanda complex

In discussing the early history of Rwanda, we shall adopt Vansina's outline, as modified in a major interpretative essay by J. K. Rennie.[51] In doing so, we are fully aware of the immense influence of the works of Kagamé and of the White Fathers generally.[52] But these works suffer from two major defects: first, they are court-centred, and therefore tell us little about the reactions of the societies that were being incorporated into the Rwanda state; and secondly their objectivity is severely limited by the authors' belief in the outmoded Hamitic theory.

Briefly stated, Kagamé and the White Fathers maintain that the present Rwanda was formerly occupied by a motley of Bantu families and clans that exhibited little political organization. Into the region came a cohesive group of pastoral 'Hamitic Tutsi' from the north, who introduced pastoralism, iron-working, concepts of kingship, a caste society and a number of new crops. Under their leader, Gihanga, they established a number of Tutsi dynasties from the tenth century of the Christian era, which were eventually incorporated into the Rwanda state. Through diplomacy, conquest and economic power, based on the Tutsi control of cattle, their state gradually expanded to include all of modern Rwanda. Through a system of vassalage in which the Bantu ('Hutu') received the use of cattle in return for services and loyalty, the conquered were assimilated into this state. It also marked the origin of the class system in Rwanda or what the sociologist Maquet has termed *The Premise of Inequality in Rwanda*.[53]

In order to have a balanced picture of the early history of Rwanda, it is imperative that we should examine the histories of the pre-

51. Vansina, op. cit.; Rennie, op. cit.
52. A. Kagame, 1954, 1959, 1961 and 1963.
53. J. J. P. Maquet, 1961.

Nyiginya states and societies. According to tradition, the first inhabitants were almost certainly forest hunters and gatherers, represented by the Batwa. Besides hunting, they practised pottery and basketwork. Later, when the agriculturalists began to arrive and to clear the forests for permanent settlements, the hunters brought skins and meat to them in exchange for salt and iron goods. The Bantu-speaking agriculturalists grew sorghum, kept livestock and bees, hunted and developed village industries. They wore goat skins and barkcloth and they organized themselves into lineages and clans under the leadership of lineage heads or chiefs respectively.[54]

By the fifteenth century, many of the Bantu-speakers were organized into small states. Each state comprised several different lineages under a ruling lineage headed by a *mwami* (chief or king), who was both a land chief as well as a ritual leader in charge of rain-making.[55] The position was thus similar to that already described in the Ruhinda complex. There is evidence that some of these lineages – for example, the Rubunga lineage of the Singa clan and the Heka lineage of the Zigaba clan – had acquired cattle before the establishment of the Nyiginya clan in Rwanda, and that several major states had emerged before the advent of the Nyiginya clan. Each of them was controlled by a dominant clan, although we should reiterate that clan names at this time were more in the nature of political labels than names of exogamous groups descended from some eponymous ancestor.

It is generally agreed that seven major clans had pre-Nyiginya states. These were the Singa, Zigaba, Gesera, Banda, Cyaba, Ongera and Enengwe.[56] Of these seven, three – the Singa, Zigaba and Gesera – are recognized as *abasangwabutaka*, that is those who were there before anybody else, or the original owners of the land in Rwanda.[57] What was the nature of these states and how were they incorporated into Rwanda? The first part of this question will be discussed below, but the second part in most cases falls outside the scope of the present discussion.

According to Tutsi traditions, the oldest state in Rwanda was probably established by the Renge lineages of the Singa clan. Although loosely organized, it covered most of modern Rwanda except the eastern section. History has not, however, preserved any name for this area. What is clear from the traditions is that the Renge had developed a complex concept of ritual kingship. We learn that at the end of the sixteenth century a body of ritual experts known as Tege, and claiming descent from Nyabutege, were incorporated into the state institutions of Rwanda. Nyabutege is supposed to be a descendant of Rubunga, a Renge ritual specialist from whom Gihanga, the founder of the Tutsi clans of Rwanda, adopted the

54. M. d'Hertefelt, 1962, pp. 41–4; Vansina, op. cit., p. 78.
55. Vansina, op. cit., pp. 77–8.
56. Kagame, 1955.
57. Kagame, 1954, p. 56.

drum and the Renge ritual code of royalty.[58] By the middle of the seventeenth century, all the Renge states had been absorbed into the expanding Rwanda state.

In the far east of Rwanda was the Mubari state of the Zigaba clan, which apparently covered an extensive area. The Nyiginya clan is first mentioned in the history of Rwanda, receiving the hill of Gasabo from the Zigaba rulers.[59] The former were allowed to have their own chief, but he was to be under the jurisdiction of the latter. At this time, the two groups intermarried freely. However, the Mubari state of the Zigaba lost its independence by the end of the sixteenth century, when the Rwandan ruler Yuki II Gahima took their drum Sera from them. In spite of the loss of political independence, the dynasty managed to survive until the latter part of the eighteenth century, when Kigeri III Ndabarasa (1765–92) killed the king and ended the dynasty. Small groups of the Zigaba migrated to different parts of south-west Uganda, where they played leading roles, as shown above.

Closely related to the Zigaba were the Gesera, who ruled over the powerful state of Gisaka in south-east Rwanda, and probably over Bugyesera as well. Gisaka managed to maintain its independence until the nineteenth century, when it finally disintegrated and was annexed by Mwami Rwogera (*c.* 1830–60). But Gesera rule continued until the twentieth century in two small states which had broken away from Gisaka: Busozo in the south-west of Rwanda, which was apparently founded in the early seventeenth century, and Bushiru in the north-west.[60] In north-central Rwanda was another state, Busigi, under a rain-making chief. Busigi was not finally incorporated into Rwanda as a state until the early part of the twentieth century.[61]

Several other smaller states could also be mentioned, but enough evidence has been given to show that the new state of Rwanda was not being established over stateless peoples. For a long time Gisaka, for instance, was as well organized as the young state of Rwanda. These states, varying in size and strength, had evolved institutions of kingship as well as ritual power over the land and rain. Some of these political and religious institutions were incorporated into the new state of Rwanda as it expanded during the next three centuries. Indeed, court rituals in Rwanda were politically effective largely because they incorporated agriculturalist and pastoralist rituals, and a number of agriculturalists were given important ritualist positions in society. They therefore developed a vested interest in the system.

From about the fifteenth century, the number of pastoralists increased sharply in these states. Initially, they were not a dominant caste, and in

58. Kagame, 1955, p. 13.
59. Kagame, 1954, pp. 53–4.
60. A. d'Arianoff, 1952.
61. Pauwels, op. cit., p. 223.

some areas they may even have been clients of the cultivators. Vansina has produced enough evidence to show that, in the north-east, north-west and west of Rwanda, there was a peaceful coexistence between the pastoralists and the agriculturalists. The system of vassalage that was to characterize the relationship between the two groups developed after 1500, during a period when both groups had to be incorporated into a new Rwanda state.

Although it is always risky to argue from the present to the past, it is generally accepted that at least nine of the major Rwandan clans are Tutsi, and hence probably originally pastoralist. The nine clans are the Sindi, Nyakarama, Ega, Shambo, Sita, Ha, Shingo, Kono and Hondogo; they have evolved a nationalist charter which traces the origin of all Tutsi clans back to Gihanga, a mythical founder.

These pastoralists did not move in large cohesive groups. They came in small groups until by the end of the fifteenth century they were numerically strong enough to form powerful lineage organizations in the south, where they soon clashed with the agriculturalists. But, with the exception of two groups, none of these lineages was strong enough in the fifteenth century to form an independent state. The exceptions were the Hondogo and the Nyiginya. The former had settled around Lake Mugesera in the south and had established a political organization which enabled them to drive the Gesera eastwards into Gisaka. The second group, the Nyiginya, were to form the ruling dynasty of Rwanda. They had come from Mubari in the east and settled, as we have seen, at Gasabo in central Rwanda around Lake Muhazi. By the end of the fifteenth century they had succeeded in establishing a centralized state with institutions that incorporated both pastoralists and agriculturalists. The creation of an independent territorial state of Rwanda, its consolidation and expansion are themes which fall outside the period under consideration.[62]

The Buganda, Busoga, Mount Elgon region

According to Cohen, the period between 1100 and 1400 witnessed the movement of a number of Bantu-speaking clans from the Mount Elgon/Lake Victoria region. It is not clear what caused this major dispersal. Kiwanuka has suggested that the 'south-eastern advance of the Luo had some influence on these migrations'. It is evident from Luo tradition, however, that this movement predates the earliest Luo migration in this area by at least a century. These Bantu-speaking groups were to have a significant role in the political developments in their new homelands after 1100. One section of this migration included the Kintu complex of clans, which Cohen suggests migrated south of Lake Kyoga and were re-

62. According to Rennie's chronology, which is a modification of Vansina's, only three kings fall within our period: Ndahiro Ruyange (1424–51), Ndoba s/o Ndahiro (1451–78) and Samembe s/o Ndoba (1478–1505).

sponsible for the founding of a number of tiny states, including Buganda, along the northern shores of Lake Victoria.[63]

It is not clear whether a person called Kintu ever lived. What seems to be evident is that the Kintu figure is associated with a complex of Bantu-speaking clans whose totems are the leopard and the lion. According to Buganda traditions, the major stopping places of Kintu – such as Nnono, Buvvi, Bukesa, Mangira, Magonga and Butwala – are identical with the leopard clan lands in Buganda. Similarly, Kanyanya and Lwadda, which today are among the most important lands of the lion clan in Buganda, are traditionally regarded as Kintu's stopping places.

The lion–leopard complex of clans had been preceded on the northern coast of Lake Victoria by a number of Bantu-speaking clans, among them the *manis*, civet cat, colobus monkey, bird, lungfish and reedbuck. In Buganda, the clans are called the *banansagwa* or those 'found in the place'. Politically, these groups had clan heads who operated independently of one another. Only the reedbuck clan had created a multi-clan chiefdom of Bugulu, headed by the *igulu* in what is today southern Busoga. The chiefdom was centred on a large pottery industry and an important religious shrine, both controlled by the ruling lineage of the AbaiseIgulu. The clan had been migrating in an east–west direction along the northern coast of Lake Victoria. Its first encounter with the lion–leopard complex was in Bugulu.

Another group of the *banansagwa* who met the Kintu complex of clans in the Bugulu area was the lungfish clan. According to their traditions, collected by Cohen in Busoga, Buganda and on the islands on Lake Victoria, they left a place called Bumogera between Kisumu and Mount Elgon, where they were important fishermen and iron-workers. (For the clans and places mentioned in this account, see Fig. 20.3.) It is not clear when they left their original home or why. From Bumogera they crossed Lake Victoria: some went to south Busoga; others to the Buvuma Islands; others to Busagazi on the Kyaggwe coast, from where Mubiru, a lungfish leader, passed inland to Mangira, where he found Kintu.

The section of the clan that went to south Busoga was led by Walumbe; they met the Kintu group at Bugulu. It would appear at this time that the Kintu figure or symbol emerged as the leader of the lion–leopard complex. He married Nambubi, the daughter of Walumbe, and thus began the important relationship between the lion–leopard and the lungfish clans. The *igulu* was obviously uneasy about these immigrant groups. According to tradition, he was the person who, perhaps using an oracle, advised Kintu or the lion–leopard families to leave.

Kintu and his followers decided to travel westwards until they came to Buswikira, which is still regarded in Busoga traditions as the 'landing place' of Kintu and Nambubi in their travel from Ggulu or 'heaven'. It

63. D. W. Cohen, 1972, esp. pp. 70 ff.; M. S. M. S. Kiwanuka, 1971, p. 33.

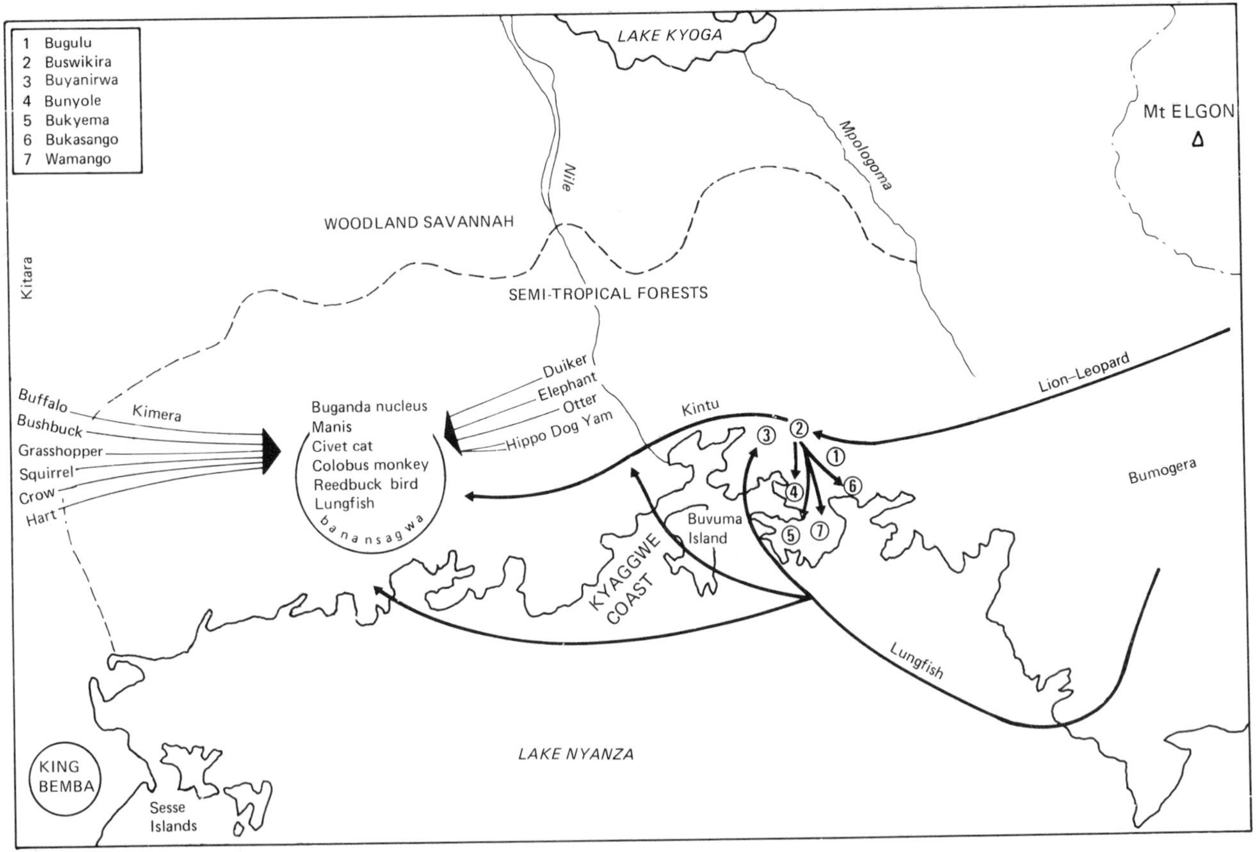

FIG. 20.3 *Kintu to Kimera (B. A. Ogot)*

would appear that what is referred to in the Buganda genesis story as Ggulu or 'heaven', which Kintu left behind, is a symbolic representation of Bugulu and her shrine. Soon they were followed to Buswikira by their in-laws, the lungfish clan led by Walumbe. But there soon developed a struggle between lion–leopard and lungfish groups over the distribution of lands, which eventually drove the Walumbe contingent a few miles west to Buyanirwa, where they established a permanent settlement. The traditions of the AbaiseMaganda of Busoga record that Walumbe is their most important deity, whose shrine is still closely guarded by the lungfish clan. According to Busoga traditions, Buswikira was the centre of Kintu's activities in Busoga. The traditions further claim that the AbaiseIsumbwa and AbaiseKyema ruling groups, who founded the chiefdoms of Bunyole, Bukasango and Bukyema on the lakeshore, are descended from Kintu's sons.

From Busoga, Kintu moved westwards into what was to become the nucleus of Buganda. Besides the leopard–lion clans, other groups that tradition records as having accompanied Kintu or followed in his wake from the east were: elephant, otter, duiker, hippo, dog and yam. They also encountered the section of the lungfish clan led by Mubiru, who had already arrived in the area, and who were hostile to Kintu and his followers. But a more serious threat facing Kintu came from King Bemba of Buddu. Besides the chiefdom of Bugulu, which has already been considered, the chiefdom of Bemba located in Buddu was the only other pre-Kintu, Bantu, multi-clan, political organization in modern Busoga and Buganda. A clash between Kintu, who had allied himself with one of the indigenous clans – the colobus monkey clan – and King Bemba soon ensued. The latter was killed, and Kintu or his successor proceeded to establish the nucleus of what was to develop into the state of Buganda.

This reconstruction of the histories of Buganda, Busoga, eastern Uganda and western Kenya during this period has also helped to bring out the point which has been made repeatedly in this chapter, that several small states were established in the interlacustrine region by Bantu-speaking agriculturalists before the pastoralists became politically important. In the area under discussion, and during the period 1200–1500, it would appear that the activities of the pastoralists were peripheral. Buganda, in particular, and the small states of Busoga to a certain degree, emerged as forest states whose economies depended more on agriculture than on a combination of pastoralism and agriculture with the resulting caste systems and class structures. Even demographically, we know that the *banansagwa* or the original inhabitants of Buganda were agriculturalists; the Kintu complex of clans were also agriculturalists, and Kimera and his followers from the west, whose story is related below, became primarily agriculturalists.

Both Cohen and Buchanan have noted that some of the clans of the

Kintu complex seem to have moved west into the Kitara complex.[64] Since the entry of the Kintu groups into the centre of what is today Buganda appears, according to Cohen, to have occurred immediately before the emergence of the Bachwezi rule in western Uganda, it is therefore quite plausible that the section migrating west could have arrived in Kitara during King Wamara's time, as discussed above.[65] By this time a person by the name of Kantu had already emerged as the leader of the eastern immigrants. As already noted, King Wamara made blood brotherhood with him, as part of his strategy of incorporating immigrants into the established system. But this eastern group seems to have posed a special threat to Wamara. Their leader, Kantu, was killed, an event which, according to Bunyoro traditions, greatly affected the stability of the empire.[66] Feeling insecure, groups of clans began to move away towards the equatorial forests along the northern shores of Lake Victoria. This west–east migration to Buganda brings us to one of the unresolved historical problems of the interlacustrine region – the Kimera complex.

Kimera (*c*. 1344–74) is often identified with the Kitara area. Even more important, he is identified as the founder of a new dynasty in the small chiefdom of Buganda.[67] Much of the controversy surrounding Kimera has been concerned with the identity of his clan. One tradition has linked him with the bushbuck clan of Luo origin. Another tradition links him to the grasshopper clan of the Bahima. Kiwanuka, for instance, relying on a history of the grasshopper clan written by Kaggwa, argues that Kimera was probably a member of the Basonga dynasty, who had established themselves at Kisozi. In any case, he adds, quoting Gorju approvingly, 'Kimera's coming to Buganda seems to have antedated the arrival of the first Babito rulers in Bunyoro.'[68] What would appear to be important is not the personal identity of Kimera. We should try to understand the meaning of the Kimera traditions, or what we have called the Kimera complex.

It would appear that the Kimera traditions deal with the migrations of several refugee groups that were fleeing from the Bachwezi empire into the equatorial forests from the time of Ndahura to the collapse of that empire. Initially, they were apparently escaping from the general insecurity which had been generated by Ndahura's military activities. Kimera himself seems to have left Kitara at this time. With the death of Kantu, followed later by the collapse of the Bachwezi rule, more refugees left Kitara to seek refuge in Buganda, just as they sought refuge in Nkore and other areas which offered political stability.

Tradition is silent on the routes followed by these refugees. It is quite possible that the earlier groups, such as the one which included

64. Buchanan, op. cit.
65. D. W. Cohen, in Webster, op. cit.
66. Nyakatura, op. cit.
67. Kiwanuka, op. cit., pp. 36–41.
68. ibid., pp. 40–1; A. Kaggwa, 1905; J. L. Gorju, 1920.

Kimera, may have established settlements or even states en route, in the same way as the lion–leopard families were doing in Busoga. Moreover, the refugee groups were multiclan and multilingual. Some of them were probably indigenous Bantu-speaking groups of Kitara; some were pastoralist Bahima; some were Luo hunters and agriculturalists; and some were Bantu clans originally of the Kintu complex. According to Buganda traditions, the Kimera complex included the following clans: buffalo, bushbuck, grasshopper, squirrel, crow and hart. So if a researcher collected the tradition of the bushbuck clan in Buganda, as Crazzolara did, he would conclude that Kimera and his followers were Luo. If he restricted himself to the grasshopper clan, as Kaggwa and his translator, Kiwanuka, have done, he would conclude that they were Bahima.[69] Moreover, in using the date of the establishment of Bito rule in Bunyoro–Kitara as an argument against regarding Kimera as a Luo, one should remember that, as already indicated, many Luo groups preceded the Babito in Bunyoro.

As people fleeing from various regimes, their ideology was understandably anti-Bachwezi, anti-Babito and anti-Bahima. It is not surprising that traditions linking Buganda to any of the three groups have been suppressed, even where the evidence is overwhelming. For instance, when we compare the Bachwezi traditions of Bunyoro and Nkore with the traditions of Buganda, which rarely refer to the Bachwezi, we find several similarities which historians cannot afford to ignore. In Bunyoro and Nkore the gatekeeper of King Isaza of Kitara was Bukulu of the Balanzi clan. On the Sesse Islands the traditions of the otter clan – which is the same as the Balanzi clan – name one Bukulu. In Bunyoro and Nkore, the daughter of Bukulu, and hence the mother of King Ndahura, was Nyinamwiru. The Kiganda equivalent is Namuddu, who is widely found in Sesse legends. From the west we learn that Bukulu's grandson was called Mugasha, and in Buganda tradition gives the name of Bukulu's grandson as Mukasa. We learn from the traditions of Nkore that Mugasha disappeared in Lake Victoria; according to Bunyoro tradition, King Wamara disappeared into the lake and he was also responsible for the construction of Lake Wamala. In Buganda, Wamala, who is a descendant of Bukulu, is associated with the making of the same lake. Moreover, just as the Bachwezi spirits are deified in the Kitara complex area, the Buganda deify the spirits of the descendants of Bukulu, such as Nende and Mukasa. Is it not possible, therefore, that the descendants of Bukulu in Buganda were Bachwezi?

To go back to the fleeing clans that constituted the Kimera complex, it would appear that, just as they left Bunyoro at different times, they also arrived in Buganda at different times. Unfortunately, all these refugee clans, irrespective of when they reached Buganda, now regard themselves as part of the Kimera migration, largely because people like to associate

69. Crazzolara, op. cit.; A. Kaggwa, 1971.

themselves with success. Kimera, the leader of refugee groups, founded a new dynasty and a state that brought together the thirty-five clans that had settled in the area from different directions. Each clan wanted to participate in the monarchy, and therefore there arose in Buganda the custom of each clan presenting wives to the Kabaka, giving each the opportunity to provide his successor.[70] By 1500 the migration and settlement period of Buganda history had ended. The consolidation and expansion of the new kingdom belonged to the future.

70. Kiwanuka, op. cit., pp. 91–110.

21 The Zambezi and Limpopo basins: 1100–1500

B. M. FAGAN

Cultures and societies of the Iron Age around the year 1000

By the end of the first millennium of the Christian era, Iron Age peoples were settled over most of the savannah woodland between the Zambezi and Limpopo rivers, eastwards as far as the Indian Ocean, and north of the Zambezi into what is now Zambia and Malawi.[1] Surviving remnants of later Stone Age hunting populations still lived in remoter pockets of the savannah woodland, interacting sporadically with their farming neighbours and dwelling in rock shelters or small open camps, where their implements have been found in association with Iron Age pottery. Hunting and gathering populations, ancestors of modern San groups, also occupied much of the Kalahari region to the south and west of the savannah woodlands, an area where they were to roam freely until modern times. Most of the Iron Age peoples of this large area of South Central Africa were subsistence farmers, basing their food production on both domesticated cattle and small stock, combined with the cultivation of cereal crops such as sorghum and millet. Hunting and gathering played an important role in their economies, and only simple forms of shifting cultivation were in use, probably involving the careful selection of particular soil types.

Although the first Iron Age settlement of South Central Africa took place as early as +200, and the initial occupation took place over a relatively short period of time, early agricultural populations were widely scattered in areas free from tsetse fly, and general population densities were extremely low. The distribution of tsetse belts was affected by the pattern of shifting agriculture, which in turn soon affected population distribution. Throughout the first millennium the agricultural population increased slowly and more land was taken into cultivation as forest clearance and cultivation methods slowly improved. The settlement of new areas was, in part, caused by wasteful methods of shifting cultivation, which, by analogy with modern figures, used well under 50 per cent of every acre of woodland cleared.

1. B. M. Fagan, 1967–9.

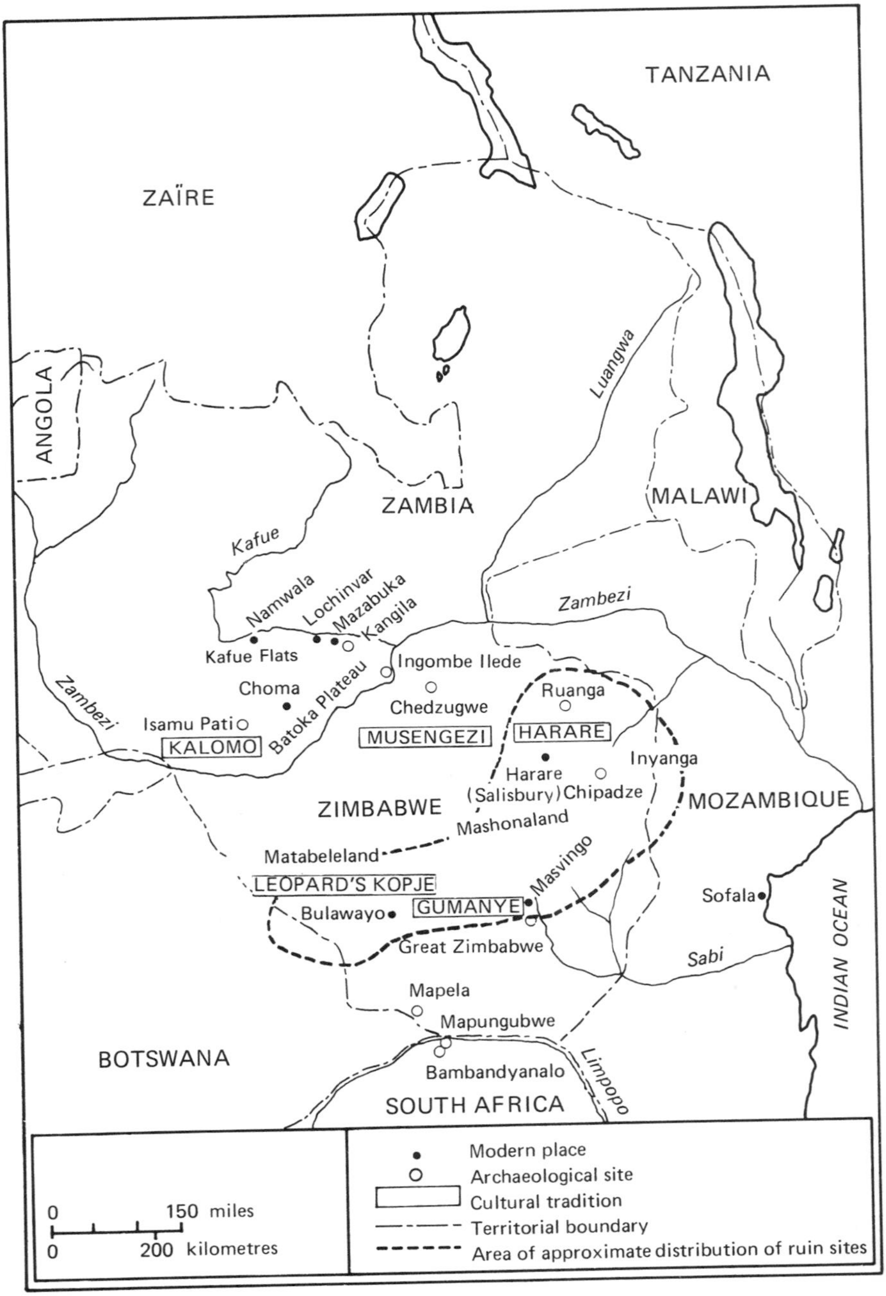

FIG. 21.1 *Sites and archaeological traditions mentioned in the text (B. M. Fagan)*

Technologically, the Iron Age farmer enjoyed a simple level of iron metallurgy; copper was smelted for ornaments, and later for wire. Simple but well-made pottery was used everywhere. Like all subsistence-farming cultures, those of South Central Africa were well adapted to the almost ubiquitous savannah woodland environment, based on an intimate knowledge of soil, climate and vegetation and on the use of local raw materials for building and for the domestic economy. Each community was largely self-sufficient, drawing on neighbouring villages and local trade for more specialized needs.

The Early Iron Age cultures of South Central Africa have been studied in some detail by a number of archaeologists, whose work has concentrated mainly on pottery styles and radiocarbon dating.[2] The simple grooved and incised pots of the earliest agriculturalists show considerable variation from one end of South Central Africa to the other, and a number of regional variations, 'traditions' and 'cultures' have been proposed to classify them. The details of these various societies need not concern us here; suffice it to say that Early Iron Age cultural traditions and settlements persisted in many parts of South Central Africa until well into the second millennium of the Christian era, with their simple iron technology, hoe agriculture

PLATE 21.1 *Isamu Pati mound (Zambia) during excavations*

2. See particularly D. W. Phillipson, 1968 and 1974.

and their political and social organization entirely based on small villages of mud and thatch huts. Early Iron Age peoples were the direct ancestors of the more elaborate cultures of later centuries.

A thousand years after Early Iron Age farmers had settled by the Zambezi, some new cultural traditions had emerged on both sides of the river. One distinctive tradition was centred on the Batoka plateau of southern Zambia. There the savannah woodlands gave way to open grassland areas, providing good grazing for cattle. These highland tracts, free of tsetse fly and well-watered for much of the year, had been settled by Early Iron Age peoples by the fourth century of the Christian era. Towards the end of the first millennium, their settlements were occupied by 'Kalomo culture' farmers with a somewhat similar way of life, although they placed considerable emphasis on cattle-herding. In contrast to the grooved and incised ware of earlier centuries, the new pottery was simple and decorated with only a few horizontal incised or finely stamped bands. Many of the vessels were bag-shaped.

One settlement, Isamu Pati, near the modern town of Kalomo, has been excavated on a large scale (see Plate 21.1). Like most Iron Age sites on the Batoka plateau, Isamu Pati is a large mound, consisting of subsoil and occupation debris accumulated over several centuries. Although the mound was the site of small settlements for at least two hundred years from the seventh century, the later villages on the mound were much larger. By the year 1000 the Kalomo culture was in full swing at the site. The last village at Isamu Pati, abandoned in the thirteenth century, consisted of a series of mud-and-pole huts, built around a central cattle enclosure on the summit of the mound. The inhabitants placed a major emphasis on cattle and cereal agriculture, but this was based on only a simple iron technology used to make implements of tillage, arrowheads and other such utilitarian objects. At each Kalomo culture village – and they have been recorded in the middle and upper Zambezi valley as well as on the Batoka plateau – there are a few signs of local or long-distance bartering. Copper strips and beads have been found in several villages, obviously traded from areas some hundreds of miles away, where copper was smelted and found in surface outcrops. More significantly, a handful of imported, east-coast glass beads and very rare cowrie shells have come from Kalomo culture settlements and burials; these provide evidence of long-distance bartering and trade in this remote corner of Central Africa. These were probably too few in number to affect the social structure of Early Iron Age society.

The origins of Kalomo culture in all probability lie in the Early Iron Age cultures of the upper Zambezi valley. The technology and economic strategies of the Kalomo people closely resemble those of Early Iron Age farmers, arguing for a long continuity of Iron Age culture on the Batoka plateau. Conceivably the Iron Age population spread rapidly over a wide area as a result of village fission and pressures on agricultural and grazing land.[3] The new adaptation was a success, for the Kalomo culture appears to have survived as late as 1450 in some areas near Choma and in the Zambezi valley. In the northern and north-western parts of the Batoka plateau the Kalomo culture does not occur at all, for reasons that remain obscure.

Another series of settlements, none of them as substantial as the Kalomo mounds, occurs in the region of Mazabuka and Lochinvar. This Kangila tradition, named after a settlement near Mazabuka, is best represented at the Sebanzi site on the edge of the Kafue Flats, where it merges over a period into the modern Ila-Tonga culture that has flourished on the entire Batoka plateau for some centuries. There are some parallels in pottery styles between Kalomo and Kangila vessels that have caused some authorities to feel that both pottery traditions are to be attributed to Ila-Tonga-speaking peoples, already known to be one of the oldest linguistic groups north of the Zambezi. This would mean that Ila-Tonga peoples arrived in their present homeland at least a thousand years ago. In the Namwala district, at the extreme north-western corner of the Kafue Flats, another series of large mounds contains an as yet ill-defined later Iron Age pottery type, linked to both Kalomo and Kangila ware. That all these three represent early Ila-Tonga occupation of southern Zambia seems at least a viable hypothesis pending further research.

Later Zambian history is overlaid by the intensive population movements and political manoeuvrings of the past five centuries that have brought new cultural traditions from Zaïre to obscure and absorb earlier Iron Age cultures. But in northern, western and eastern Zambia, Early Iron Age peoples survived well into the second millennium. David Phillipson has identified two major ceramic traditions that are thought to have emerged in Zambia early in the second millennium. The Luangwa tradition covers the central, northern and eastern parts of the territory and extends into Malawi, whereas the Lungwebungu tradition is found in western Zambia. Both have survived until recent times; little is known of their origins, but they are quite distinct in their modern forms from Early Iron Age traditions.

Economic and social transformations in the eleventh and twelfth centuries

South of the Zambezi, the Early Iron Age cultures of the first millennium were replaced in several areas by new societies during the eleventh and twelfth centuries. The best-known is the so-called Leopard's Kopje tradition, which extends from the Limpopo valley northwards into the Bulawayo region and the central parts of the Limpopo–Zambezi watershed (see Fig.

3. See Phillipson, 1968, pp. 191 and 212.

21.1).[4] Leopard's Kopje villages are smaller than earlier farming settlements, conceivably as a result of ecological changes induced by man. Unlike Early Iron Age sites, many of them were occupied several times. Cattle herds seem to have been larger. Ox figurines and the inclusion of cattle bones in some human burials would seem to suggest that cattle were more important than in earlier centuries. Leopard's Kopje shows such a marked break with earlier Iron Age traditions that it seems almost certain that its makers were immigrants, with few direct cultural relationships with the earlier inhabitants.

No traces of the Leopard's Kopje people have been found north of the Zambezi. It has been suggested that they entered their homeland from grasslands in the archaeologically unknown regions of Botswana and Angola, but this is pure speculation. Like their predecessors, the early Leopard's Kopje people relied heavily on subsistence farming – millet and sorghum – as well as hunting and gathering. Like their Kalomo neighbours, they practised a simple iron technology. A few imported glass beads and sea shells reached their scattered villages. During the late twelfth and early thirteenth centuries the population expanded and began to till the more fertile but heavier soils of the Matabeleland gold belt. Much longer-lived villages were founded, a development that may have coincided with the first mining and working of gold, for the earliest gold workings south of the Zambezi are thought to date around the twelfth century. Some of these Leopard's Kopje settlements, like that at Bambandyanalo in the Limpopo valley, were of very considerable size, with a central cattle enclosure. At another settlement at Mapela Hill, 111 km away, a hill (92 m) was terraced with roughly piled-up stones – stonework so extensive that substantial community effort must have been needed to construct it. Furthermore, a group of huts on the highest terrace was much more substantially constructed than the rest of the village, so solid that they were probably the houses of important personages who enjoyed a privileged position in society, a contrast to earlier cultures where there is no evidence of any social ordering or status. Glass beads and other imports are more common, too, as if the tempo of long-distance trade had increased significantly.

Later Leopard's Kopje culture shows every sign of a much more diversified and controlled economy, based on mining, metallurgy and trading as well as subsistence farming; political power and wealth was concentrated in the hands of relatively few people, who lived in major population centres of important settlements. This is clearly demonstrated at the famous Mapungubwe site, where in the fifteenth century a small group of wealthy rulers occupied the summit of a long, low hill overlooking the Limpopo valley. There are extensive village deposits in the shadow of the hill, where a much larger population dwelt.[5] Gold beads and sheets have been found

4. T. N. Huffman, 1974b.
5. B. M. Fagan, 1964.

at burial sites on the hill, together with numerous glass beads and other imports. The rich copper deposits of the Limpopo valley were obviously an important source of wealth for the rulers of Mapungubwe, whose steep dwelling place has been held sacred until the present day. Whether Mapungubwe was ruled by a minority group who exercised political and religious sway over the local farmers is still a matter for debate, as is the nature of the relationships between the Limpopo site and Great Zimbabwe to the north-east. These general trends towards cultivation of heavier soils and larger, longer-lived settlements are still little understood; indeed, even provisional hypotheses to explain the phenomenon are still lacking.

There are also signs of new farming cultures in other regions south of the Zambezi. To the north-east, the Musengezi tradition flourished near the southern fringes of the Zambezi valley and on the northern plateau, and the Harare tradition is found in the Harare (formerly Salisbury) area. Both are peasant-farming cultures with more of the social and cultural elaboration characteristic of Leopard's Kopje after the twelfth century. The ceramics of both groups are closer to later Iron Age styles than those of the Early Iron Age, and the subsistence farmers of the Inyanga region to the east are perhaps also within the same later traditions, maintaining a simple hillside-farming culture into modern times.

Each of these cultural traditions, apparently a fresh development at the end of the first millennium, conceivably sparked by external population movements or technological innovations, survived with considerable changes into recent times. The Leopard's Kopje tradition separated into northern and southern branches, and the latter continued into the nineteenth century. Highly tentative but plausible attempts have been made to correlate these archaeological traditions with the linguistic groups still living between the Zambezi and Limpopo today. Shona is the largest linguistic family represented there, with at least six dialect clusters within the family (Kalanga, Karanga, Ndau, Manyika, Zezuru and Korekore). The remaining languages include Ndebele (a nineteenth-century introduction), Tonga, Hlengwe and Venda, all of which have origins outside the area. Shona itself has no direct relationship with south-east Bantu. Several of the cultural traditions just described are thought to have close links with one or other of the Shona dialect clusters. The Leopard's Kopje people are linked with the Kalanga, the Harare culture with the Zezuru. Although links between Karanga, Korekore, Ndau and Manyika and archaeological sites or pottery traditions are still lacking, there is some reason on the basis of oral tradition to believe that most of the later Iron Age cultures between the Zambezi and the Limpopo just described can be associated with Shona-speakers. It was among the Shona-speakers that significant political and economic developments occurred after the twelfth century.

Origins of Zimbabwe culture

The famous Great Zimbabwe ruins near the modern town of Masvingo (formerly Fort Victoria) are the symbol of the most vigorous of these developments and are celebrated both for the excellence of their architecture and also for the extravagant theories that have surrounded their origin.[6] All serious scholars now perceive Great Zimbabwe as an essentially African development, built of local raw materials and according to architectural principles that have endured from the use of these media over many centuries. But the ultimate causes of the emergence of the economic, political and religious organization that lay behind this and other sites of this type between the Zambezi and the Limpopo remain cloaked in mystery.[7]

Archaeological discoveries and the oldest settlement

Traces of Early Iron Age occupation at Great Zimbabwe are confined to the lowermost levels of the long cultural sequence on the so-called Acropolis Hill that overlooks the Great Enclosure, most spectacular of all the Great Zimbabwe structures, and to a few scatters of pottery in the valley below. The Acropolis Early Iron Age level has been dated to before the fourth century of the Christian era, but no one could describe the Early Iron Age settlement at Great Zimbabwe as really significant. In all probability, the valleys between the well-watered hills provided, to quote Peter Garlake, 'good hunting grounds and open country with light, easily tilled soils'. It was not until about the tenth or eleventh century – the date is still uncertain – that later Iron Age peoples settled at Great Zimbabwe. Little is known about these folk, for few of their sites have been discovered, except for the Gumanye settlement at Great Zimbabwe itself. The pottery is quite unlike Early Iron Age ware and has been compared to Leopard's Kopje vessels, although there are significant differences.

The Gumanye tradition still possesses only a shadowy identity, which will remain so until more settlements of this type have been found and excavated. Its owners occupied Great Zimbabwe before the great stone walls were built and are thought to represent another, later Iron Age culture tradition along the lines of Leopard's Kopje, with which Gumanye shares some common features. But whatever the precise definition of Gumanye itself, by the twelfth century the culture of the people had undergone significant change. The pottery became better finished, clay human figurines were made, and many more glass beads and other imports appear. Much more solid mud-and-pole buildings were constructed, copper, bronze and gold ornaments began to proliferate, and stone walling came into extensive use at Great Zimbabwe. These developments are paralleled, at

6. See R. Summers, 1963, for a criticism and overview of these theories.

7. On this question, see P. Garlake, 1973.

least in part, in Leopard's Kopje sites such as that at Mapela, already mentioned. By 1300, the foundations of a powerful and influential state had been laid, a state centred on Great Zimbabwe that extended over a wide area of central and southern Mashonaland. That this state in its early stages shared many common cultural traditions with the Leopard's Kopje tradition seem unquestionable, a fundamental identity that probably also extended to a common language, Shona. To quote Peter Garlake again: 'From about the late twelfth century, diversification, expansion, affluence, and, a concomitant of these, increased social, economic and functional specialization took place in both cultures so that in the end, entire settlements could, like areas within sites, be built and used for limited functions by certain groups or clusters of people.'[8] Great Zimbabwe may well have been such a settlement.

Before describing Great Zimbabwe itself, it is as well to look more closely at some of the hypotheses put forward to explain the formation of the Great Zimbabwe state. Two major theories have been adduced to explain the new state. The first, proposed by the historian Donald Abraham, sees the Shona as immigrants at the end of the first millennium of the Christian era who not only introduced mining techniques and other technological innovations, but also brought their own ancestor cults with them. This led them to establish shrines, the principal of which was built on a hill called Mhanwa, and named *Dzimba dzemabwe* (houses of stone). By astute political manoeuvring, Abraham believes, the Shona leaders established ascendancy over a loose confederacy of vassal chieftains, who paid them tribute in ivory and gold dust. Arab traders from the East African coast were in contact with this powerful alliance and used it as a vehicle for expanding the gold and ivory trade. But the central power of the state lay in the hands of the chiefs and priests who controlled the *Mwari* cult and the complex ancestor-worship rituals associated with it, by acting as intermediaries between *Mwari* and the people. This so-called religious hypothesis is based on research into Shona oral tradition, details of which remain unpublished.[9]

An alternative hypothesis sees the primary origin of the Karanga state in intensified trading activity. Many more glass beads and other imports were used at Great Zimbabwe during the fourteenth century, together with Syrian glass, Persian faience and Chinese celadon – all evidence of much-expanded trade. Gold and copper objects also proliferate at Great Zimbabwe, for gold and copper mining was now widespread south of the Zambezi. It was at about this period also that the Arab coastal town of Kilwa experienced a marked jump in prosperity, a quantum leap perhaps connected with increased gold and ivory trading with the Sofala region on the coast of Mozambique, for centuries the coastal entrepôt for gold

8. Garlake, op. cit.
9. D. P. Abraham, 1961.

trade with South Central Africa. Perhaps it is not without significance that, when the Arab traveller Ibn Baṭṭūṭa visited Kilwa in 1331, he referred to the gold trade of Sofala, trade which originated at 'Yufi in the land of the Limis', one month's journey into the interior from Sofala.[10]

The trade hypothesis takes the evidence of intensified exports and imports, and assumes that in a lineage society with some social stratification the chief is the most wealthy person. But part of his wealth is recycled through society by means of ceremonial functions, weddings, funerals and so on. As trading contacts are intensified, the amount of wealth not recycled through society increases, leading to more and more concentration of both wealth and political authority in the hands of a few individuals, a situation that is potentially destructive in the long term. Eventually it is possible for a wealthy ruler to pay people to carry out public works, or, by political fiat, to engage the population in state works as a form of taxation by labour, a system once used, for example, among the Lozi of Zambia. Thus, in the case of Great Zimbabwe, the increasing wealth of the rulers led to greater redistribution of wealth, the concentration of the population at a major commercial centre and the organization of labour forces to build the great, free-standing walls of the Great Enclosure and the Acropolis. The trade hypothesis relies heavily both on the expansion of the east-coast trade as a primary cause of state formation and on the assumption that economic power equals political authority, an assumption that may be only partially true. It also assumes that enormous labour forces were needed to build stone walls, which to judge from analysis elsewhere may not have been the case.

Political and economic power in the formation of the Great Zimbabwe state

Both the religious and the trade hypotheses take little account of the realities of subsistence agriculture and of the complex decision-making mechanisms that control, at least within the broadest limits, the general directions of social development. The beginnings of the Great Zimbabwe state lie long before surviving oral tradition; all the evidence comes from archaeological sites or from the most generalized of linguistic information. Archaeologists have established that Shona-speakers may have been responsible for the later Iron Age traditions between the Zambezi and Limpopo. By the thirteenth century, both the Leopard's Kopje and Gumanye traditions were showing signs of considerable elaboration, derived both from extensive trading contacts and more centralized political authority. Population densities rose in some areas to higher levels than ever before, levels that could have resulted in some improvements in the methods of shifting agri-

10. Ibn Baṭṭūṭa, Eng. transl. 1958–62. This site has not been identified beyond question. The file on relations between Kilwa and Zimbabwe contains a coin discovered in Great Zimbabwe dating from al-Ḥasan b. Sulaymān (around 1320–33).

culture, conceivably by the adoption of more advanced forest clearance and burning techniques that would permit longer intervals between the fallowing of vegetable plots. But, even if there was some concentration of population at Great Zimbabwe and other centres, most of the people must have been scattered in smaller villages, settlements that were both situated and moved according to the needs of subsistence agriculture and cattle-herding. When a major centre like Great Zimbabwe attracted a denser rural population, the long-term consequences of higher population densities per square kilometre must have been serious in terms of land fertility, over-grazing and environmental degradation.

The subsistence-farming society in Iron Age Africa was basically self-sufficient, although it may have obtained some raw materials such as iron ore or hut poles from a fairly wide local radius. There was little or no incentive for longer-distance trading, except within the context of religious or economic motives, the latter being difficult to discern in a basically self-sufficient village community. To possess these motives on a limited scale is quite a different proposition from unifying a scattered rural population under a single religious, political or commercial umbrella. Although the demand for raw materials stimulated by the East African coastal trade obviously led to new economic initiatives, this trade by itself could not unify the people under a single political or religious authority. This process involved not only the religious or political acumen of a few families, but also a move – conscious or unconscious – by society as a whole to adopt a more hierarchical social and political organization, even if the process of doing so seemed quite unselfconscious at the time. It is a mistake to conceive of the origin of the Great Zimbabwe state or any other African kingdom in terms of a single religious or commercial motivation. Rather, both these factors, and many others difficult to identify in the archaeological record, carried weight in Iron Age societies as their political and economic perspectives widened from a village level to a larger canvas.

Whatever the fundamental causes behind the rise of Great Zimbabwe, there is no doubt that it is a most impressive monument.[11] The site is dominated by the Acropolis, a long, granite hill covered with enormous boulders (see Figs. 21.2 and 21.3). Successive generations of occupants linked the boulders together with stone walls, making small enclosures and narrow passages. The westernmost enclosure is the largest, enclosed by a thick, free-standing stone wall. It contains a long sequence of later Iron Age occupation that provides the basis for subdividing Great Zimbabwe's history into at least three stages. The most intensive occupation began in about the eleventh century; but no stone walls were built until the thirteenth century, when the small pole-and-mud huts of earlier times were replaced by more substantial mud houses. The stone retaining wall for the western enclosure was also built at that time, as more imports appear

11. Cf. T. N. Huffman, 1972.

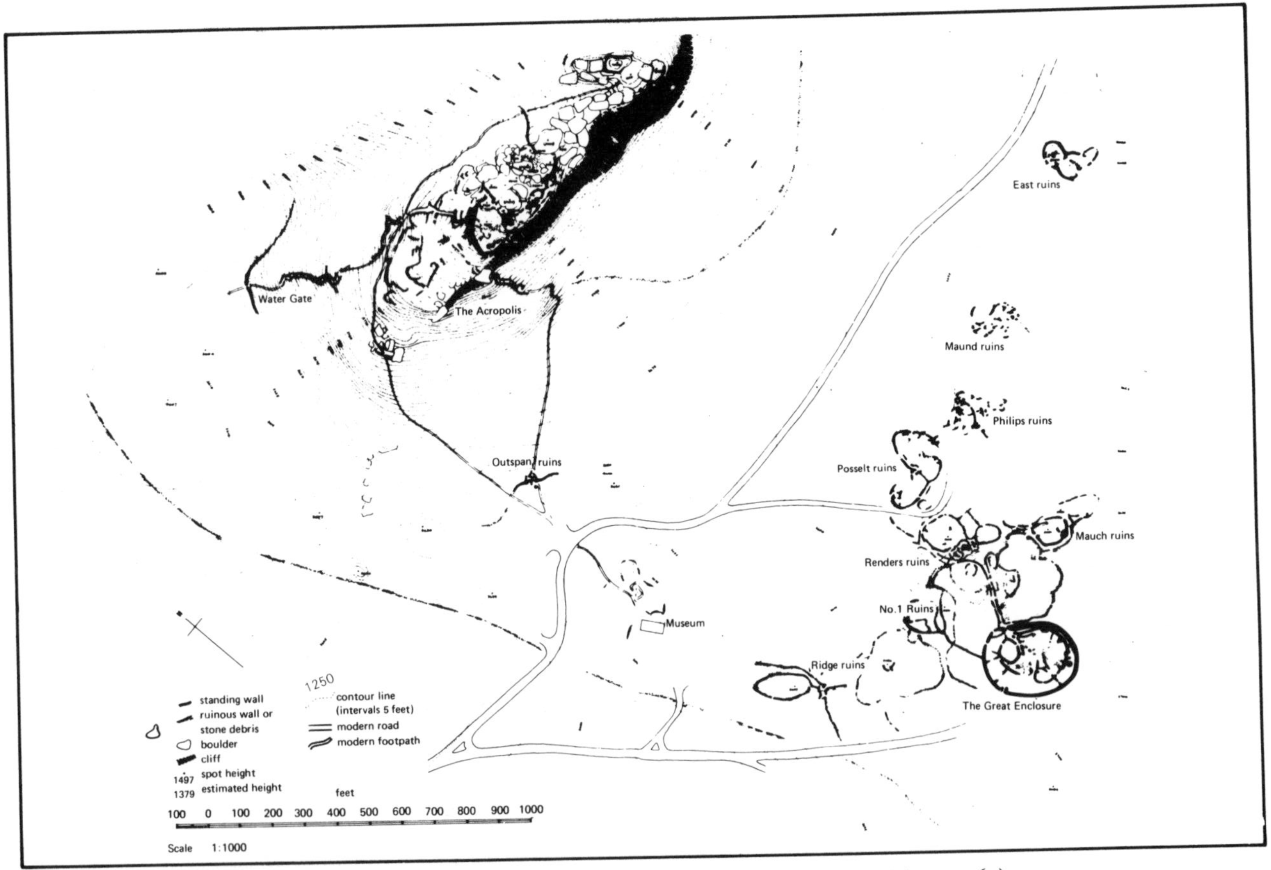

FIG. 21.2 *Great Zimbabwe ruins* *Source: R. Summers*, Zimbabwe, a Rhodesian Mystery (Nelson, 1963)

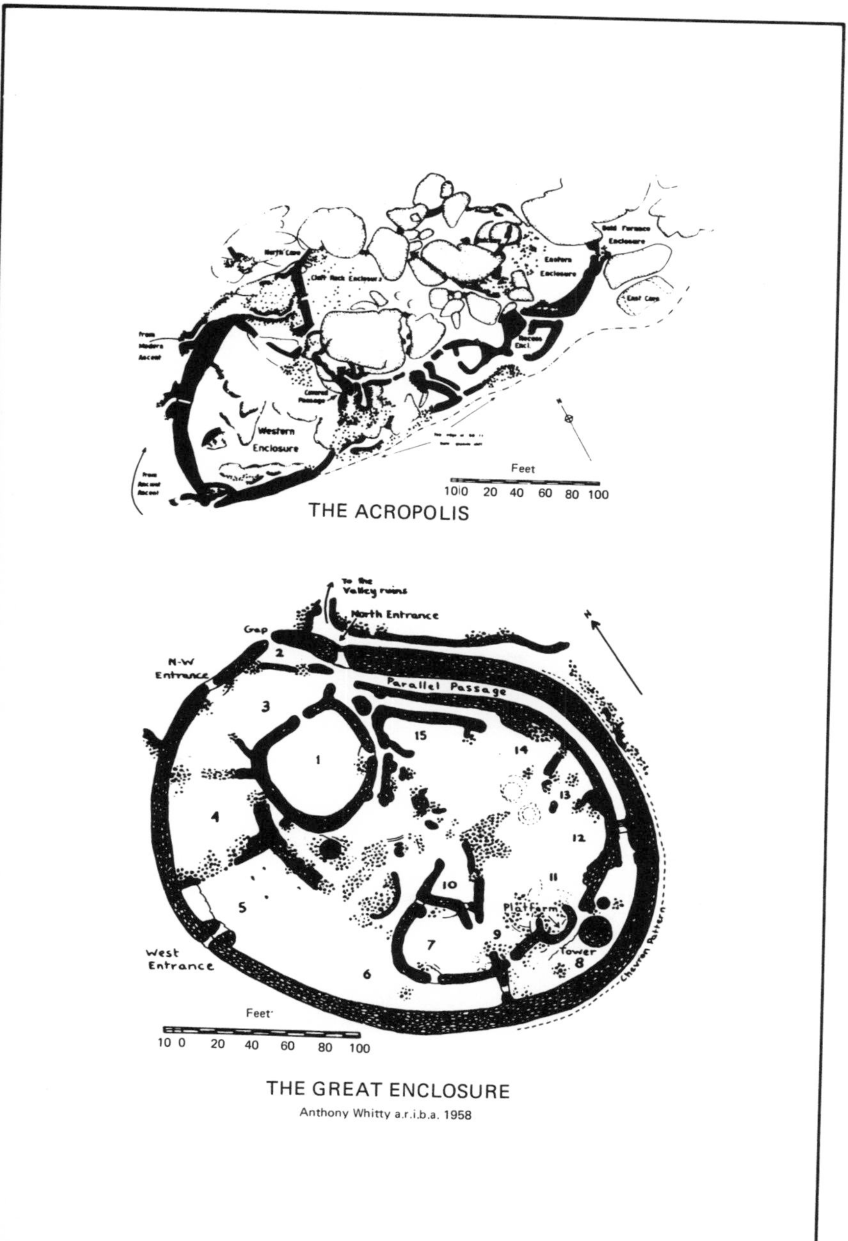

G. 21.3 *Great Zimbabwe: the Acropolis and the Great Enclosure*
ource: R. Summers, Zimbabwe, a Rhodesian Mystery *(Nelson, 1963)*

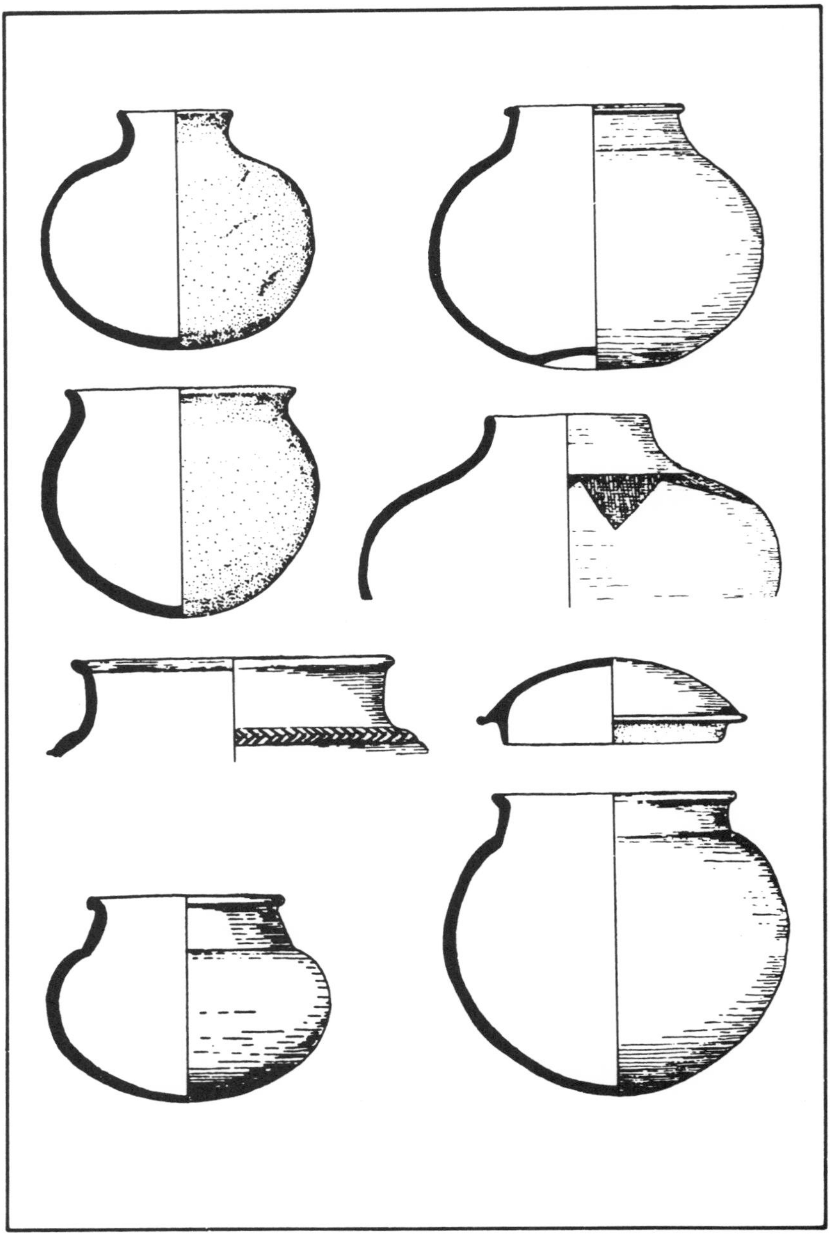

FIG. 21.4 *Pottery excavated from the later levels on the Acropolis, Great Zimbabwe*
Source: Peter Garlake

PLATE 21.2 *Interior view of the elliptical rampart leaving the top of the external wall of Great Zimbabwe*

in the deposits. It was during the thirteenth or fourteenth century, also, that the first buildings were constructed in the valley below the Acropolis.

The Great Enclosure with its massive free-standing walls was built progressively during the following century (see Fig. 21.3). The enclosing wall of the Great Enclosure has an average height of 7.3 m, is 5.5 m thick at the base and between 1.3 m and 3.6 m at the top. The wall itself has a rubble core, bounded on each side with horizontal, free-standing masonry. A length of 52 m is decorated with a chevron pattern (see Plate 21.3). Inside is an unfinished enclosure wall which was evidently replaced by the present one and which helps to form a narrow defile between the two walls, leading to a skilfully constructed conical tower that dominated the Great Enclosure (see Plate 21.5); its significance is unknown. The Great Enclosure itself was divided into a series of smaller enclosures, in which the foundations of substantial pole-and-mud houses are to be seen. It was presumably the dwelling place of the rulers of Great Zimbabwe, an impressive and politically highly significant structure.

The deposits of the Great Enclosure, as well as the upper levels of the Acropolis, contained many gold and copper ornaments, and fine soapstone bowls and carvings, removed by early treasure hunters. Large quantities of imported glass beads, as well as Chinese, Persian and Syrian china, glass and porcelain, dating back to the fourteenth century, have also been recovered. Clearly, by that time the East African coastal trade had penetrated far into the interior. Great Zimbabwe was an important centre for the trade, and its rulers presumably enjoyed a substantial monopoly of commerce. After all, it paid the foreign trader or his agent to work through the political rulers of the interior, both for his own security and also for maximum profit. Indeed, in a situation where the miners and their products were under the political control of Great Zimbabwe, bound to its ruler by religious and tribute ties, they had no option. It is difficult, however, to assess the extent to which the Arab masters of the trade played a significant political role in Zimbabwe's affairs, or influenced either the architecture or technology of the African state.[12]

One school of thought claims that the Arabs played a leading role in the design of the Great Enclosure, compares the conical tower to East African mosques and argues that the level courses of stone used at Great Zimbabwe are quite different from the normal, simple mud-and-pole architecture of Shona villages. The architecture of Great Zimbabwe, however, is a logical extension of the large enclosures and chiefs' quarters which were built of grass, mud and poles in other African states, but merely constructed here in stone. Stone was used because it was more durable and also because abundant granite was exfoliated in natural layers about 50–100 cm thick near Great Zimbabwe. The builders were able to obtain unlimited numbers of suitable blocks with minimal dressing of the stone

12. On trade relations between East Africa and the Orient, see the works of H. N. Chittick, 1968, 1970 and 1974; and also H. N. Chittick and R. I. Rotberg, 1975.

PLATE 21.3 *The wall of the Great Enclosure at Great Zimbabwe*

PLATE 21.4 *Soapstone sculpture of a bird on a monolith found in the Philip's ruins in the valley of Great Zimbabwe*

PLATE 21.5 (*left*) *The conical tower of Great Zimbabwe*

either from natural exfoliation or by accelerating the process with fire and water.

With the exception of the conical tower, which is a unique structure of unknown significance, there is nothing in Great Zimbabwe architecture which is alien to African practice. Indeed, free-standing walls, terraces and decorated stonework were used at many other sites not only contemporary with, but later than, Great Zimbabwe. It is the scale of the ruins that impresses the visitor and gives rise to many of the myths about their ancestry. Unmistakable Arab influence in either Great Zimbabwe's construction or in the Great Zimbabwe culture as a whole is almost impossible to detect. The leaders of the state should certainly not be regarded as puppets who played to an Arab tune, manipulated by foreigners for their advantage. Nor is it likely, despite claims to the contrary, that more than a very few Arabs or their agents actually resided within the frontiers of Great Zimbabwe's sphere of influence. The long-distance trade must have been, at best, sporadic, conducted through regular, perhaps seasonal, visits rather than by constant commercial activity.

Great Zimbabwe's expansion and its regional supremacy

Great Zimbabwe is a unique site only on account of its scale, for it is the largest of an estimated 150 ruins in the granite country that forms the Zambezi–Limpopo watershed. There are other ruins with between one and five enclosures, at least partially surrounded with free-standing walls and with mud-and-pole huts inside them, built near Zimbabwe and in Mashonaland. The regularly coursed masonry is in the Great Zimbabwe style. Those that have been excavated contain occasional gold objects, copper-wire bracelets, glass beads, and the fire pots and spindle whorls characteristic of the Great Zimbabwe culture. At the Ruanga and Chipadze ruins, cattle were important. Five of the excavated ruins have produced dates that suggest they were all built and occupied between the beginning of the fourteenth and the end of the fifteenth centuries. Some have been dated as late as the sixteenth century. All these ruins are small, having had but a minimal population. They were normally built near hills that were a plentiful source of stone, too small to be viable economic units, probably built by external labour from surrounding villages that were able to support themselves by shifting agriculture on the savannah. Peter Garlake has pointed out that no unwalled site has yielded artefacts of the type found in the ruins. 'The settlements that provided such labour,' he writes, 'must have had a material culture that looks unrelated to that of the ruins although there is no evidence in the ruins of other cultural groups.' He goes on to argue that the assistance that was given took the form of intermittent tribute, a hypothesis that is as yet far from proven.

At Nhunguza ruins there was a single, very large hut, divided into three rooms. One of the rooms was big enough to hold a large number of people, a second contained a single seat, a third was a 'completely secluded room that must have contained objects of special value including . . . what must have been a monolith set in a grooved stone platform'. This unusual structure may well have been the location where a prominent religious authority held sway, an authority that was not only the reason for the building of the isolated enclosure, but also the human cement that held together the Great Zimbabwe state. One has a sense of an extremely strong and unquestioned political and religious authority whose hold over the scattered rural population was based on some form of unifying faith in the powers of the divine *Mwari* or some other religious catalyst that reached out to every family. Long-distance trade, however regularly maintained, cannot have been such a powerful device, affecting as it did only a minority of the population.

The borders of the Great Zimbabwe state are still ill-defined, although its heartland was in central Mashonaland. Some Great Zimbabwe-style ruins occur in what is now Matabeleland, where Great Zimbabwe people infiltrated Leopard's Kopje territory. But it was not until after the decline of Great Zimbabwe in the fifteenth century that Mashonaland became a major centre for political and commercial initiatives, developments that lie outside the scope of this chapter.

Commercial ties with the East African coast

The influence of Great Zimbabwe and its tributary settlements were felt far outside the immediate, relatively limited boundaries of the state itself. The prosperity of Kilwa on the East African coast was closely tied to the fluctuations in the gold trade with Sofala. Already in the tenth century the Arab geographer al-Mas'ūdī was writing of Kilwa and the gold trade. Four centuries later Ibn Baṭṭūṭa described Kilwa as one of the most beautiful cities in the world, a town whose prosperity depended on the southern gold trade.[13] Without question the wealth of the rulers of Great Zimbabwe waxed and waned with the fortunes of the coastal trade. Kilwa itself went through commercial vicissitudes, reaching the height of its prosperity in the fifteenth century with the reconstruction of the famous Great Mosque and its elaborate domed and vaulted roof. But a century later Kilwa, the East African coast and Great Zimbabwe itself had all declined. When the Portuguese arrived at Sofala the coastal trade was but a shadow of its former self. For all its isolation, Great Zimbabwe's trading connections and the gold within its borders contributed not only to prosperity and economic growth on the East African coast, but also in much remoter lands as well.

The mechanics of the coastal trade itself are little understood, for few trading sites in the interior have been excavated or have escaped the insidious attention of early treasure hunters. In the fourteenth and fifteenth

13. Al-Mas'ūdī, French transl. 1962; Ibn Baṭṭūṭa, loc. cit., Vol. 2, pp. 379 ff. Cf. also *Encyclopaedia of Islam*, new edn, Vol. 5, pp. 106–7.

centuries, however, there was considerable trading activity in northern Mashonaland and the Zambezi valley, which is reflected in some remarkable archaeological discoveries. This region was settled during the Early Iron Age, which survived until the end of the first millennium. Between the twelfth and fourteenth centuries northern Mashonaland was occupied by the makers of Musengezi ware, subsistence farmers with minimal trading contacts, thought to be Shona-speakers. Their culture is a far cry from the wealth of their southern neighbours at Great Zimbabwe, although more trade goods occur in later Musengezi settlements. But the same is certainly not true of the extreme north-western corner of Mashonaland and the lower part of the middle Zambezi valley, where large settlements and the working and trading of copper assumed great importance. The Chedzugwe site in the fertile Urungwe district covered over 24 hectares of fine grassland; abundant cattle and game bones testify to the importance of pastoralism and hunting. But copper and iron-working was of considerable significance, both ores being abundant nearby. Copper was made into standardized ingots of two fixed weights; wire bracelets made from copper and tin alloy were commonplace. Textiles were also in use, and extremely fine pottery was made, with a finish and delicacy of decoration on shallow bowls and beakers that is almost unparalleled elsewhere (see Fig. 21.5).[14]

Archaeology and the limits of Zimbabwe's influence

The people of Chedzugwe were not only in touch with Great Zimbabwe, but also with the Zambezi valley. Their fine copper ingots and delicate pottery are found at the isolated Ingombe Ilede settlement, where the complex mechanisms of long-distance and local trade were partially revealed by some spectacular discoveries in 1960. Ingombe Ilede is situated on the summit of a low hill on the Zambezi floodplain, some distance from the north bank of the river. Now the site of a pumping station, the Iron Age settlement was discovered during the construction of large water-storage tanks. Eleven richly decorated burials were found on the summit of Ingombe Ilede, fortunately recovered before the construction of the tanks. The skeletons lay in close juxtaposition, deposited with an astonishing array of domestic and trade goods. One richly decorated body wore a necklace of *conus* shells, an East African sea-shell traditionally associated with chiefship, as well as strings of gold, iron, copper and imported glass beads, worn at neck and waist. Another *conus* shell and two wooden amulets, thought to have Islamic associations, lay at the waist of the same burial. Iron gongs, ceremonial hoes and sets of wire-drawing tools lay at the head or foot of several skeletons, together with copper cruciform ingots (see Plate 21.6). The limbs were swathed in copper-wire bangles, presumably made with the wire-drawing tools found with the same bodies. The copper

14. P. S. Garlake, 1970.

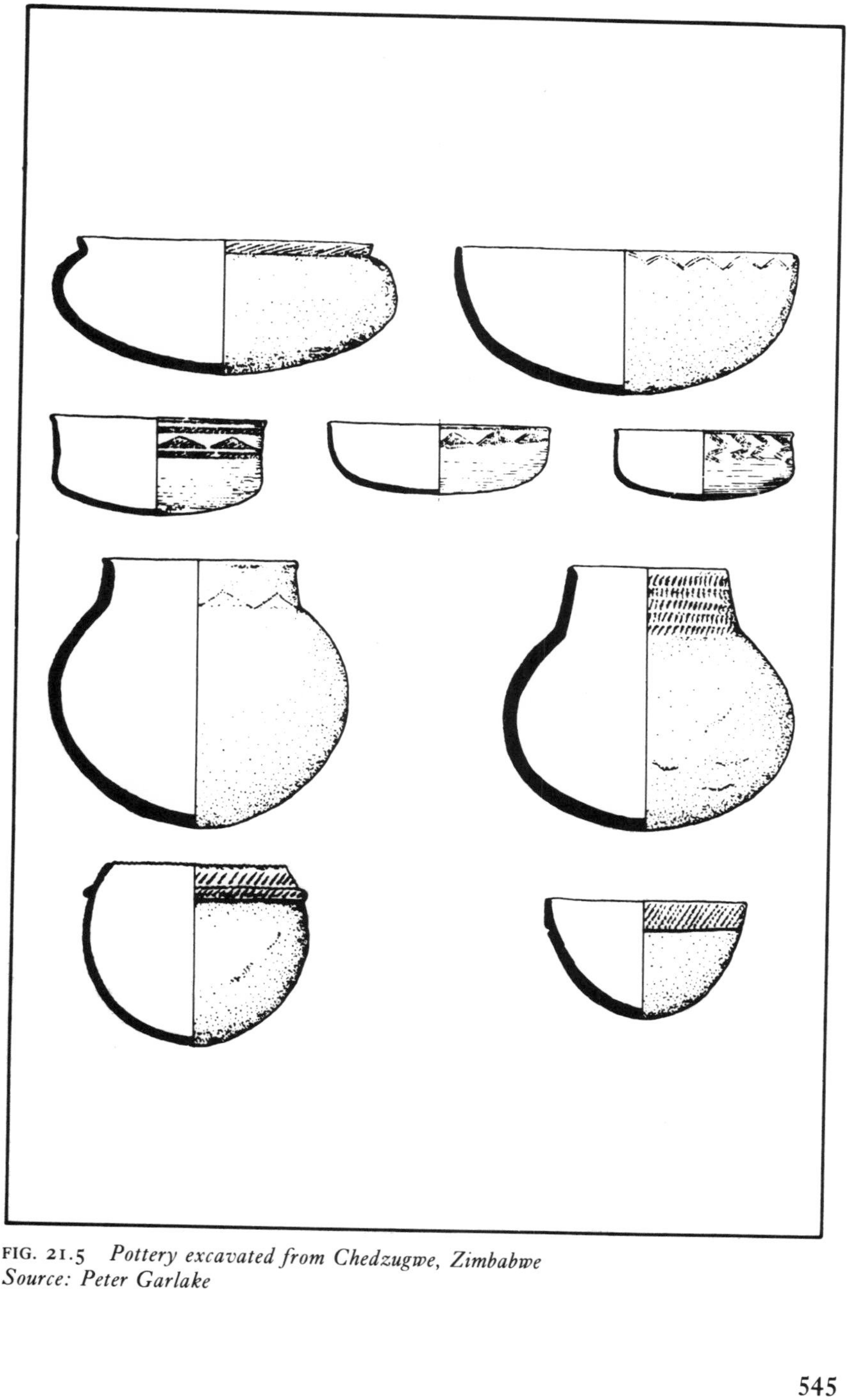

FIG. 21.5 *Pottery excavated from Chedzugwe, Zimbabwe*
Source: Peter Garlake

PLATE 21.6 *Two copper cruciform ingots from Ingombe Ilede, Zambia (post-11th century)*

acids of the bangles had preserved several layers of cotton and bark cloth that presumably formed part of the owners' garments. Spindle whorls were abundant in the upper levels of Ingombe Ilede, so at least some of the cloth was woven locally.

The remarkable thing about these burials is that, with the exception of the pottery, almost all the grave furniture consists of artefacts or materials obtained by long-distance trade. There are no significant copper, gold or iron-ore deposits in this area of the Zambezi valley, although both salt and elephant ivory were easily obtained, both being essential trading commodities, the former for domestic consumption. The copper ingots are identical to those from Chedzugwe and the fine pottery discovered with the burials is virtually the same as that from the Urungwe district site. Glass beads are, however, more abundant at Ingombe Ilede. On the face of it, there seems no good reason for a site like Ingombe Ilede to be involved in long-distance trade, for there are no local sources of metal ore. The explanation may lie in the abundant salt deposits of the River Lusitu, for cake salt was a highly prized commodity in the Iron Age, one that was bartered extensively at the local level. Control of the salt deposits may have brought the Ingombe Ilede people into contact with other communities on the plateau to the north and south of the Zambezi, who would accept salt in exchange for their precious metals, which Ingombe Ilede could in turn barter for imported luxuries obtained from the east-coast trade. This middleman role for Ingombe Ilede is a purely hypothetical construction, for it is, of course, equally possible that both the imported luxuries and the copper, gold and iron were obtained by barter from Urungwe and Great Zimbabwe, Lusitu salt being the medium of exchange.

Considerable uncertainty has surrounded the date of the Ingombe Ilede burials, for it has proved difficult to obtain radiocarbon dates for the skeletons. It is known that a large pole-and-mud structure was built on the summit of the village, the foundations of which were largely removed by the tank construction work before excavations began. The gold burials were deposited under the foundations of this hut, which may have been destroyed as part of the burial rites. The skeletons date back to the closing years of Ingombe Ilede, a village that had been occupied, perhaps intermittently, from as early as the seventh century of the Christian era. Towards the end of the first millennium the site was abandoned by the subsistence farmers who had occupied it, people with some connections with agriculturalists on the Batoka plateau to the north. Ingombe Ilede was certainly not a trading village during the first stages of its existence. But in about 1400 the settlement was reoccupied for a fairly short time, at the end of which the gold burials were made in the fine ash midden on the summit of the hill. It is to this final period of occupation that the imported goods – gold, copper and delicate pottery – found at Ingombe Ilede may be assigned. This was the period when Great Zimbabwe was at the height of its importance and prosperity and when Arab control of the east-coast trade was well established. But even if Ingombe Ilede was a trading village, the wealth and profits of the barter were definitely concentrated in the hands of a few individuals, those buried on the summit of the hill. The southern boundaries of the site have yielded thirty-one more burials contemporary with the gold-laden individuals of the summit. Only a few of these hastily buried bodies bore any adornment at all – a few glass or freshwater-shell beads or a copper bracelet. That some degree of social stratification was in existence at Ingombe Ilede seems unquestionable.

Ingombe Ilede probably represents a northern frontier of trading activity between the Limpopo and Zambezi valleys, a frontier dictated by the vagaries of the coastal trade and the complicated political networks of the state of Great Zimbabwe and its neighbours. It has so far proved impossible to link the Ingombe Ilede gold burials with any known historical group, except for some tantalizing references in sixteenth-century Portuguese documents. In 1514 Valentim Fernandes made a pioneer journey into the far interior beyond Sofala, where he visited chiefs and described the gold trade in operation. He reported hearing tales of a great river to the north of the kingdom of Monomotapa, where the people of 'Mobara' traded copper for cloth, crossing the river in canoes to trade with the Arabs. A connection between Ingombe Ilede and these sixteenth-century Mbara is widely accepted.

The beginning of the fifteenth century; mutations and transformations

With the state of Great Zimbabwe at its apogee of power and prosperity, South Central Africa lies at the threshold of historical documentation and oral tradition. Towards the end of the fifteenth century Great Zimbabwe fell into disuse and was largely abandoned. The forces of economic and political power shifted southwards and westwards under the leadership of the powerful Rozwi clan. Oral traditions refer to the emergence of hereditary rulers, the first *Mwene Mutapa* (master pillager) being Mutota.[15] His son Mutope expanded the territory of the Mwene Mutapa northwards, moving his headquarters northwards away from Great Zimbabwe. Subsequently, about 1490, the southern portions of the kingdom broke away, under Changamire, to become a powerful state in their own right. The Mwene Mutapa himself was left with a strip of territory nearer the Zambezi extending to the Indian Ocean. His domains eventually came under Portuguese influence in the sixteenth and seventeenth centuries.

But these political events do not, in themselves, explain the reason for a sudden abandonment of such an important site as Great Zimbabwe. The same religious practices and economic activities were pursued at other locations. The population was still supported by subsistence farming, based on shifting cultivation. Herein may lie the key to the abandonment of Great Zimbabwe, for the surrounding countryside may no longer have been able to support even a scattered network of small villages, let alone the elaborate superstructure of the non-agricultural population that dwelt at Great Zimbabwe itself. The intensification of agriculture is only possible through irrigation or by artificial fertilization of the soil. Neither method was practised nor was practicable in the savannah woodland near Great Zimbabwe. Once the available agricultural land was exhausted, there was only one recourse – to move away to new tracts of woodland where fresh food plots could be cleared to support the existing population. Once fallow periods were shortened and cattle and small stock were permitted to graze on regenerating vegetation, vital agricultural cycles were interrupted, with

15. For certain authors, Mwene Mutapa means 'master pillager', whereas for others it means 'lord of metals'.

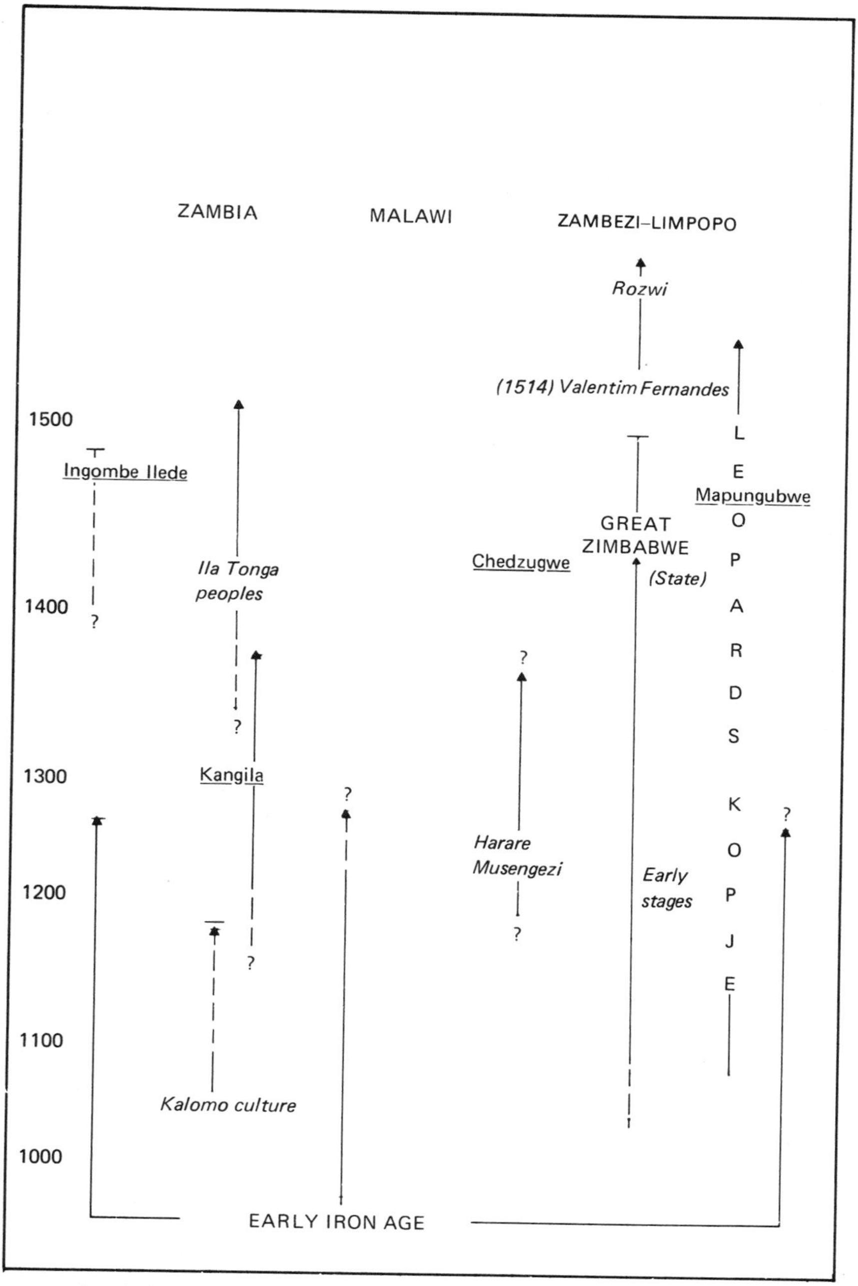

FIG. 21.6 *Archaeological traditions and phases (B. M. Fagan)*

the inevitable results of environmental degradation, over-grazing, and large-scale population shifts into new areas. Once this had happened around Great Zimbabwe, the Mwene Mutapa had to move, however sacred his dwelling place or imposing his stone enclosure walls. It seems very likely that the unsettling political changes of the late fifteenth century were closely tied to the environmental limitations that always beset complex political or religious organizations based on subsistence agriculture and a scattered rural population.

By 1500 South Central Africa had experienced major political and economic change. A degree of political unity and of social stratification had come into being between the Zambezi and Limpopo, fostered in part by intensified long-distance trading and the demands of remote market-places, but also by the internal development of African societies themselves – the greater concentration of wealth in a few hands, the increased centralization of political power at a level that transcended the village, and the creation of an elaborate panoply of state, whose secular and religious authority was concentrated in the person of the chief, himself considered to be of divine descent. These developments were peculiarly African, and found in many vigorous states in Central Africa and other parts of the continent. But their viability depended upon the maintenance of vigorous trading networks and upon an adequate system of subsistence agriculture to feed the population. In the first analysis, these were among the most important variables that affected the growth and prosperity of Great Zimbabwe and of its successor state, Rozwi. And, despite the rise and decline of small and large chiefdoms, the basic thread of Iron Age life continued to be the subsistence farmer with his patchwork of cultivated land and herds of cattle and small stock, a thread well documented by archaeological research.

22 Equatorial Africa and Angola: migrations and the emergence of the first states

J. VANSINA

The present state of knowledge

To try to reconstruct the past of so vast a region of the continent over the period from 1100 to 1500 presents historians with a challenge which they could well do without, in view of the few contemporary sources available. The first extant manuscript goes back only to 1492, and the excavations in the Shaba and Bas-Zaïre provinces and elsewhere are still in their early stages and do not yet give a complete enough chronological picture. The later written sources only deal with the kingdom of Kongo. These become more frequent in the period after 1550, and accounts dating from 1587, 1624 and later have been used here when they relate to the period before 1500 or, better still for the present purposes, before 1483.

Among non-contemporary sources relating to Kongo are oral traditions that were first recorded in 1624, and others dealing with the coastal kingdoms were noted by Dapper and Cavazzi between 1641 and 1667 – that is, two or three centuries after the events. Oral traditions from other regions were not recorded until the end of the nineteenth century at the earliest, but such recording has tended to become systematic since independence (1960). They have proved to be an essential source for understanding both history and culture.

For the period in question and for the preceding one, the use of linguistic data could be crucial, even if, as I believe – although not everyone agrees – this period comes after the era of the Bantu migrations. At all events, everyone does agree that the period under examination begins well after the end of the proto-Bantu society, whose main features can be reconstructed from its vocabulary. The study of the differentiation of languages and the processes of state formation is in its infancy, but it promises to be very fruitful. As for the languages spoken in the northern savannahs, belonging to Greenberg's Adamawa-Eastern branch and the central Sudan, historical linguistics have not yet been applied in depth.

There remains the evidence of ethnography. The data here are difficult to establish. First, the field has to be rigorously cleared so as to get back at least to the situation on the eve of colonization; then, an extremely careful methodology needs to be applied, as has been proved by the efforts of historical anthropology since the end of the last century. Nevertheless, a thorough ethnological study, together with a study of linguistic borrowing and diffusion, throws light on many aspects of history. As with languages, so in ethnography it is necessary not only to establish detailed descriptions where these do not already exist, but also to try to obtain data which are as objective as possible.

Chronology is the great stumbling block with all such later material not dated either by radiocarbon or by written documents. Not even a relative chronology is supplied by linguistic or ethnographical evidence, and dating can only be achieved by comparing the results obtained with those of archaeology. Oral traditions do give a relative sequence, but this is valid only for periods after the genesis stories. So the chronology for this period in this area, with the exception of the coast, remains uncertain, and it can be improved only by means of intensive excavations and radiocarbon dating in large blocks.

Under the conditions described, the only possible approach is to try to reconstruct history on the basis of the archaeological and linguistic data we possess for the preceding period and the period under study, together with the evidence dating from after 1500. We then obtain a picture in which the earliest and the most recent threads are joined, although the resulting fabric merely consists of hypotheses.

Population

If the expansion of the Bantu languages reflects the great migrations, these ended well before 1100. It is true – according to Professor Oliver, following the linguist, Professor Guthrie – that the great mass of the Bantu-speaking peoples originated in Shaba and the adjoining region in north-east Zambia. In the west, the area they came from may even have stretched as far as the Atlantic. According to Oliver, it was there that a 'Bantu' way of life developed, based chiefly on a cereal-based agriculture and the extensive use of iron. As a result of these developments the population multiplied, according to this theory, and moved up the rivers and coast into the forest, where as late as the year 1000 scattered populations of hunters and fishermen still lived at a pre-agricultural level.[1] This irruption from the south probably ended around 1500, although even nowadays there are vast expanses where planters speaking non-Bantu languages exist along-side pygmy hunters.[2] In Angola, hunter groups are also found; perhaps they are some of the San people who have not been driven south.

This theory is rejected by many linguists, who follow Professor Greenberg in maintaining that the Bantu tongues originated in the region between

1. R. Oliver, 1966; M. Guthrie, 1962.
2. For this Bantu expansion, see B. Fagan, Volume III, Chapter 6.

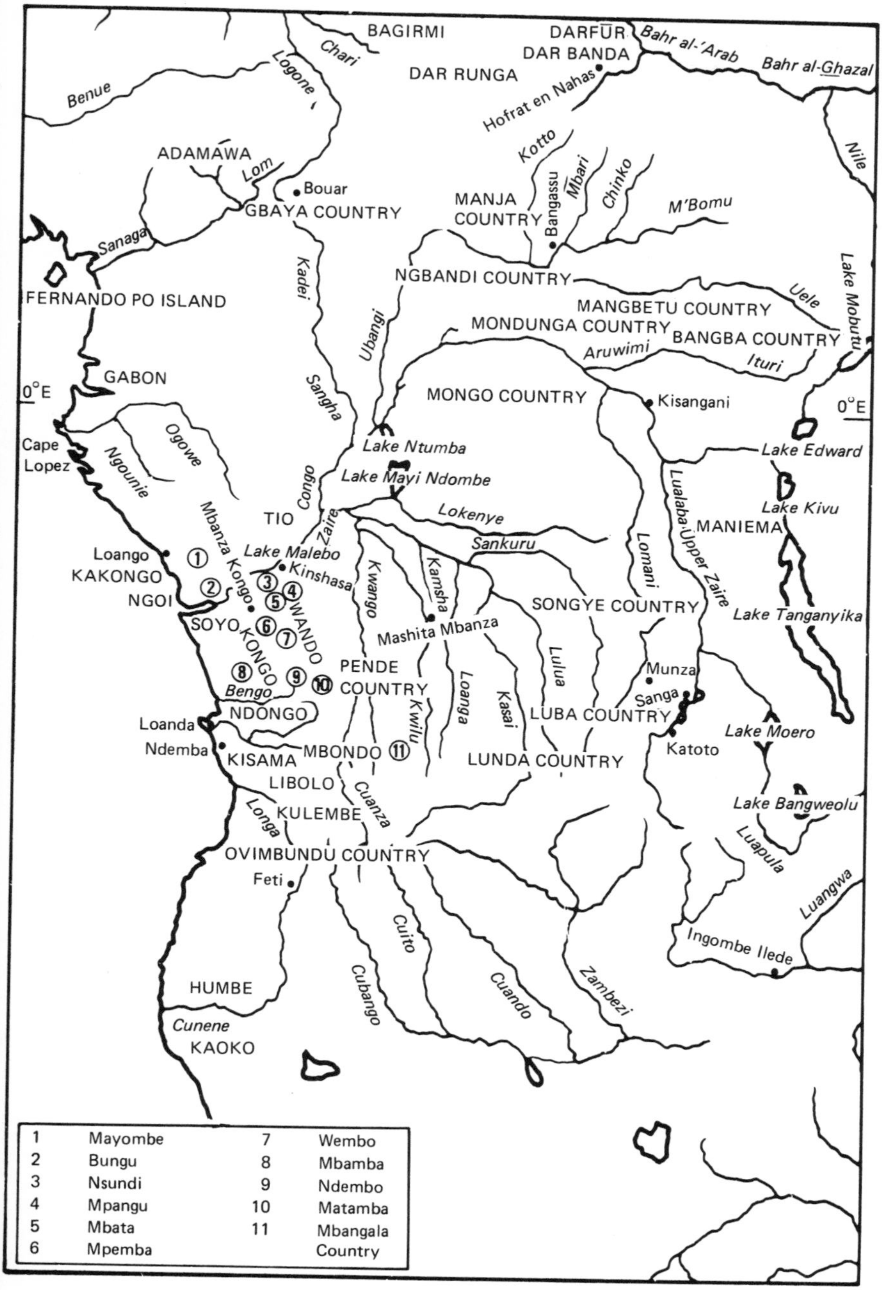

FIG. 22.1 *Central Africa, c. 1500 (J. Vansina)*

the Rivers Benue and Cross. According to them the Bantu-speakers moved gradually south, colonizing the region between the Sanaga and the Ogowe long before 1000, and perhaps even before the beginning of the Christian era. There was a parallel movement along the Ubangi–M'Bomu during the same period. After this, there was a sort of language explosion, fanning out from a secondary nucleus in the region of the Kongo languages, either in Shaba or in the Great Lakes area, since one branch of the first Bantu-speakers is thought to have travelled east along the borders of the great forest and then gone up the Ubangi and the M'Bomu. But even this movement outward from a secondary nucleus was over long before the year 1000, because Kiswahili too is among the derived languages, and al-Djakhis noted the first Bantu vocable in Kiswahili before 868. In my view, the most recent linguistic studies offer the best explanation, and I accept the thesis that in the regions under consideration the migrations came to an end before 1000.[3]

It is also probable that the impact of peoples speaking the eastern languages of the East Adamawa group broke up the mass of the central Sudan well before the year 1100. But in the north-east corner of the forest, to the north of the Niger Bend and in the Ubangi basin, mutual confrontation continued between languages, including Bantu; sometimes one drove out another, probably without any great movements of population. The central Sudanese languages never assimilated Bantu-speaking peoples, or vice versa, and the oldest languages of the region, which belonged to the eastern group of East Adamawa, were eroded by the others. The pygmies chiefly adopted central Sudanese. All this suggests that the parties concerned were about equally matched on the cultural front, and that if we knew the whole story it would be one of centuries of minor and fluctuating gains and losses on either side. Elsewhere, Bantu had succeeded in displacing the autochthonous tongues or was in the process of doing so, but it is probable that in this process the Bantu-speaking immigrants incorporated into their civilizations many cultural complexes derived from the original inhabitants. All this could have taken place without any great migrations; such migrations seem to be the exception rather than the rule in the history of the region.

Probably well before 1500 the first regional ethnic groups had been formed. The best-known example is that of the Imbangala, comprising the Lunda, the Luba, the Ovimbundu and the Ambundu.[4] The influence of communications is observable in particular in the central basin, where a triple division of labour linked together farmers, hunters (chiefly pygmies) and fishermen. The latter had frequent contact with the 'landsmen', to whom they sold fish and pottery in exchange for vegetable produce and meat; but they were also in constant communication with other fishermen

3. J. H. Greenberg, 1963, pp. 30–8; B. Heine, H. Hoff and R. Vossen, 1977; A. Coupez, J. B. Evrard and J. Vansina, 1975, p. 152; D. W. Phillipson, 1977.

4. J. C. Miller, 1972a.

in neighbouring river reaches through the network of waterways. The configuration of this network explains why the Mongo languages remained so uniform throughout the basin. In the Maniema forest, although communications were difficult because of the mountainous terrain and the particularly dense vegetation, we find two large groups, the Lega and the Komo, whose cultural unity has been preserved.[5]

The lasting influence of the autochthonous peoples is of course most clearly seen in the north-eastern forest area and the area between the Zaïre, the Ubangi and the M'Bomu. One is even tempted to think that the various groups deliberately cultivated linguistic differences as a visible sign of their wish to distinguish themselves from one another. Ehret goes even further and maintains that the central Sudanese occupied not only the north-east but all the country east of the Lualaba. They were already divided into separate peoples before the coming of the Bantu-speakers, and not only did they leave a mark on the languages of the region but, according to Ehret, they transmitted their spirit of individualism to those whose language they adopted. It is still too soon to judge the validity of this theory or to evaluate its results.[6] The impact of the central Sudanese and others appears clearly on the map of the northern savannahs and explains the presence of 'ethnic' islands, although we must never lose sight of the fact that today's map represents the situation arising from the great migration which overwhelmed the region from the seventeenth to the nineteenth century.

Thus the Banda immigration, originating in the Dar Banda just south of the Baḥr al-ʿArab in the Sudan, swept away the Sabanga and Kreish groups throughout the east and in the centre of the empire. By about 1900 the Sabanga were only little islands lost among the great mass of the Banda, and largely assimilated by them. Out of the whole group only the Nzakara kingdom was strong enough to survive. The Banda then emigrated because of the intensified raids of the slave traders, who came first from Darfūr and then directly from the Nile. At the same time the west of what is now the Central African Republic was convulsed by a massive Gbaya migration caused by Hausa slave raids from Adamawa.

The history and civilization of the region

Agriculture

The known ecological and archaeological data make it possible to say that even before 1100 agriculture was practised everywhere, except in the interior of southern Angola, which was too close to the Kalahari Desert,

5. M. Guthrie, 1953, with a map that clearly shows this distribution; J. Vansina, 1966a, pp. 93–103 and 105–14.
6. C. Ehret, 1974a.

and in some forest areas. The cereals cultivated were chiefly red sorghum and other millets (*saa-sanga*). Among root crops, many kinds of African yam predominated, the Asian coco-yam was probably very rare, whereas bananas and sugar-cane, also from Asia, were grown mostly in the forest, though also in the savannah. Among other vegetables grown were beans and groundnuts (*voandzia*). Necessary proteins were provided by hunting, fishing and the gathering of caterpillars and grubs. Domestic animals – chickens, goats and dogs – were found everywhere. South of the forest, sheep were kept and, round the lower part of the river at least, horned cattle and pigs. Farming methods certainly differed between the forest and the savannah, cereals being the staple food in the latter and bananas and yams in the former. There were even special areas for the growing of raffia and borassus palms.

But it is essential to remember that the forest was interspersed with natural intercalary savannahs, along the coast, between the Gabon and upper Zaïre rivers, and within the bend of the latter; cereals were probably grown there too. The only reason why cereals might not have been grown in these areas is because the humidity near the Equator would have been very high. This question will have to be resolved by archaeologists and botanists. Around these intercalary savannahs, as on the edges of the forest, man enjoyed the advantages of *two* environments that were often complementary. It was here, above all, that harvests could be relied upon, that one might expect to find a population increase beginning with the introduction of agriculture and the use of iron tools. Before the year 1000 this increase must have led to movements of population towards less-crowded regions.

It was not only in the forest that people were able to exploit a double environment. In the wooded part of the savannah, strips of forest or intercalary woods played exactly the same role as the intercalary savannahs in the forest, especially in the valleys of the Ubangi, the Kasai and the Lualaba. Moreover, along these rivers and the Chari, the abundance of fish favoured a growth and even concentration of population. The higher-protein diet here may also have increased the fertility rate and so made a further contribution to population growth.

Crafts and trade

By 1100, craft techniques everywhere had acquired the characteristics they were to preserve until about the end of the nineteenth century: iron metallurgy was well developed, and other activities included pottery, wickerwork, raffia weaving, cooperage, the production of rock and sea-salt, and the extraction of salt from plants and salt marshes. The excavations at Bouar in the Central African Republic and those at Sanga provide proof of metal-working. It is possible that the iron-mines at Munza (Shaba) were exploited very early and that this is linked to the expansion of the classical Luba kingdom.[7]

With these techniques was born a regional trade. The first evidence of the use of cross-shaped copper ingots as money appears in the copper belt around the year 1000, and the practice spread from the Zambezi to the Lualaba before the mid-fifteenth century. The Portuguese found a currency unit of account, called the *nzimbu*, in the Kongo in 1483; about 1500, raffia squares were circulating as units of value on the trade routes throughout the southern savannah facing the Atlantic. Rock-salt from Kisama was used as money in the next century.[8] The first carriers were probably fishermen, who produced not only fish but also the pottery that can be found along the navigable reaches of the region's many rivers. There may have been specialized copper miners/traders in Shaba and upper Zambia. Doubtless there was a limited trade in iron; finally, no doubt the native hunters in the forest were themselves becoming accustomed to bartering game for iron arrowheads, bananas and salt.

Society and the organization of power

With the growth in population from the time of the expansion and the spread of craft techniques and trade, society was organized in patrilineal lineages. At first the Bantu-speakers were grouped in fairly compact villages. It is quite possible that matrilineal tendencies were marked within the group and developed in the southern savannah before the period under consideration. In fact, not only do we see once more the matrilineal belt of Central Africa, stretching from Namibia to the Zambezi and from the Ogowe to Lake Tanganyika, but Murdock and others have argued that the peoples of the forest west of the Lualaba were all matrilineal, like the Luba of Shaba. Perhaps this was still the case around the year 1000. At all events, the forest population was patrilineal in the fifteenth century, but the Luba of Kasai and probably also those of Shaba were still matrilineal. The pattern of succession changed only after 1500.[9]

The Bantu matrilineal system was in fact accompanied by the principle that men possessed authority over women, and this often resulted in what amounted to virilocal residence, the result of which was a fragmentation of the clans. The lineages remained weak, but this strengthened the structure of the village, since order and community life had to be maintained. This village authority was based on territorial, and therefore

7. P. Vidal, 1969; P. Vidal and N. David, 1977, have identified another Iron Age site at the confluence of the Nana and the Mode in the Central African Republic; P. de Maret, F. van Noten and D. Cahen, 1977; T. Q. Reefe, 1975.

8. R. Gray and D. Birmingham, 1970; M. S. Bisson, 1975.

9. G. P. Murdock, 1959, p. 287; J. Vansina, 1978, pp. 105–10. These data imply that the Luba (of whom the Kete form part) were matrilineal.

political, principles. From the beginning, the Bantu-speakers had political leaders at this level.

In contrast, the patrilineal non-Bantu-speakers scattered through the Central African Republic lived in hamlets ruled by the men of a lineage, although there were no real chiefs among them. Villages were replaced by a scatter of hamlets, and society was in fact very egalitarian. But in other regions, among the patrilineal forest-dwellers along the Ubangi and Chari rivers, there were large residential groupings, the lineages were much stronger and some chiefs were recognized.[10]

Lords of the land were recognized throughout the southern savannah and on the borders of the forest, both north and south. Because they stood in a privileged relationship with the land through the spirits whose priests they were, these rulers enjoyed an authority which was in reality political. Whether the spirits they dealt with were natural or ancestral is of little importance. These lords of the land seem to have governed groups of villages, each forming a canton or territorial unit, an embryonic kingdom.

The process which led to these land chiefs gaining recognition as political chiefs derived from the growth of the lineage groups. At the same time the increase in revenues from the lineage reinforced its chief's authority. Thus the patriarch became lord of the land, and later founder of a state, by absorbing other lineages or imposing his authority by force of arms. At the village level, the production of a surplus freed the village chief from manual work. Demographic growth provided additional hands to work and also liberated the family heads, who formed a council around the patriarch; from that point, the state was in gestation.

The state was therefore born from the reinforcement of the authority of a lineage chief who dominated other lineages; it was a territory that included a certain number of villages recognizing the political authority of a chief, whose entourage of agents and dignitaries formed his council. In the early days the king, as a political leader, still retained the religious attributes of chiefship, which explains his 'sacred' character. Once past this stage, as the chief in the process of becoming a king acquired an increasing number of counsellors, judges, dignitaries and bodyguards, a system had to be set up for redistributing the producers' surplus to provide for the needs of the state. These kings, chiefs and counsellors acquired followers through their generosity, especially in distributing wine or beer. That is why, in many states, the ritual of 'the king's drink' later became the very token of the king's supremacy. Since more than the normal surplus was required, and since technology did not change but land was abundant, more hands were needed. Labour was the only factor that could be varied; hence, probably, the emergence of the domestic slave. A slave was a servant who produced under the orders of a master and also added a unity to an agricultural labour force composed chiefly of women. The first slaves

10. P. Kalck, 1959, pp. 45–54; Vansina, 1966a.

were no doubt prisoners of war. Fighting must have become more frequent as feudal domains developed into states, since in order to grow they had to absorb other domains or patrilineages. Another possible source of slaves was the pardoning of criminals.[11]

There were cases where a state did not come into being, despite favourable social and ecological conditions. Then we see different political systems developing. Some prized equality above everything else and refused to depart from it. Others partly safeguarded this spirit by forming lineage confederations based on ritualized associations without chiefs. It is difficult to say whether a group that created such a state, or one that did not, was the more inventive. The most spectacular example of this 'choice' is probably that of the Ngbandi, who provided lineages of rulers elsewhere, but did not transform themselves into a state. A more usual case is that of the Gbaya, who lived in contact with ethnic groups like the Mbum, who were organized into states, but did not follow their example. Similarly, the Sara helped to form the Bagirmi kingdom, but their society developed within the framework of lineages alone.

Throughout the zone, certain religious characteristics were probably common to cultivators: the existence of sorcery, fertility rites conducted by the master of the land, the importance of local and ancestral spirits and the respect accorded to diviners and healers. All this has already been demonstrated for the proto-Bantu world.

All forms of authority, from the paterfamilias to the sovereign or association, have a sacred aspect. It is not surprising that all royalty has a sacred character, nor that all conceptions of the sacred are similar, since the religious bases underlying them all are alike. This uniform principle has been rather hastily christened 'sacred kingship' (or divine right), and people have tried to find a single origin for it. But that is to overlook crucial features which differ from one kingdom to another in so far as they have developed independently. This is exactly the case with the Luba kingdoms or the states of the Atlantic coast, to name only the most familiar examples.

The formation of the larger political groups has been discussed at length because it was between 1000 and 1500 that states were finally established, especially in the southern savannah.

The northern savannahs: the population

The oral tradition of the Ngbandi, who now live in the bend of the Ubangi and are organized in patrilineal lineages – in fact the equivalent of seigniories or feudal lordships – goes back to the period before 1500. On interpretation, these myths of origin state that the people came from a neighbouring region of the Dar Banda, in the present-day Republic of

11. E. De Jonghe and J. Vanhove, 1949; S. Miers and I. Kopytoff (eds), 1977. Cf. also C. Meillassoux (ed.), 1975.

Sudan, and settled by the Banda in the nineteenth century. This country is bounded on the north by the Baḥr al-ʿArab, a tributary of the Baḥr al-Ghazal, and is close to the copper deposits of Hofrat in Nahas. No one knows how long these have been worked, but they are not mentioned.

By about 1300, groups of Baḳḳara Arabs had arrived to the north of this river, and perhaps it was they who drove out the Ngbandi. The myths speak of whites armed with bows and arrows, spears, knives, darts and even guns; they are called Azundia and Abara. The conflict is supposed to have taken place in the fifteenth century, and then a migration that continued for two centuries brought the Ngbandi into an area close to Bangassu. Towards the end of this migration they met the Bantu-speaking peoples to the north of M'Bomu, between Chinko and Mbari.[12]

It would appear that the Zande became localized about 1500, between Kotto and Dar Runga, and that the western part of the present Central African Republic was then occupied by the Manja/Ngbaka and the eastern part by the Bantu. The people of the central Sudan were already divided into at least two blocs: one including the Sara and the future Bagirmi, and the other located around the upper Nile and in the north-eastern forest. Some groups of people in the central Sudan, such as the Kreish and the Yulu, would already have been settled in Dar Banda and close to the native land of the Ngbandi.

In the sixteenth century a Ngbandi lineage founded the Nzakara kingdom, whose subjects spoke Zande; the other Ngbandi built up great lineages under feudal lords.[13] The analysis of linguistic evidence for the forest region of Uele shows that the Ngbandi are the best-known example of a slow movement that took the western peoples towards the east, and those of the north towards the south. The complexity of the way this region was populated has been demonstrated by Larochette;[14] however, he still underestimates the cultural and historical movements that took place in the region.

It would be erroneous to attribute all these linguistic expansions and contractions to spectacular migrations. Costermans has proved for the Bangba that their migratory history consisted of a wandering movement of families, shifting very slowly; this process is perhaps more common than vast migrations, for which the direct evidence is in fact nowhere to be found.[15] Instances of linguistic acculturation certainly also played a part. The pygmies, for example, all adopted the languages of the central Sudanese. At least part of the confusion could be unravelled by pursuing linguistic, cultural and purely historical studies, and the cultural sequences

12. B. Tanghe, 1929, pp. 2–37; H. Burssens, 1958, pp. 43–4. But in fact the oral traditions of the Ngbandi group only relate to the country of the Chinko and the Mbari.

13. E. de Dampierre, 1967, pp. 156–81.

14. J. A. Larochette, 1958.

15. J. Costermans, 1953.

could be dated by archaeological research. Pending such investigations, we have to be content with the limited data mentioned here.

A. de Calonne-Beaufaict, who worked in this region before 1914, maintained that the Iron Age had not penetrated there prior to 1500 and that, even in his own day, polished haematite axes were still found stuck in the trunks of very old trees. These polished stones, polishers and half-moons form the Uelian Neolithic, which is perhaps related to similar industries in the Central African Republic and even as far down as central Cameroon. The archaeologist van Noten was able to prove that this was a survival of the use of stone alongside iron. The tools were made of haematite containing a high proportion of iron. Presumably the melting down of the ore and its conversion into raw iron did not, in many cases, produce a superior tool, at least compared with the amount of work entailed in the process. Stone tools with a very high iron content accordingly held their own for a very long time.[16] In any event it is not certain that the appearance of iron-working techniques immediately ended the use of stone.

The great equatorial forest

The forest was not a barrier between the northern and southern savannahs, as too many authors have assumed, but rather a filter. At least two main routes crossed it: one along the coast and the other by river, from the Kadei Sangha by way of the Ubangi and the Congo/Zaïre down to Lake Malebo (Stanley Pool). Sea voyages were undertaken even before the year 1000, as demonstrated by the presence of the Bubi people on Fernando Po. It can be argued that the production of polychrome wooden statuary by peoples all along the Gulf of Guinea, from Yoruba country to Loango, indicates the gradual spread of these influences by sea.[17] When the Portuguese arrived, the whole coast was inhabited by fishermen. Within the river system, the confluence of the Ubangi, Sangha and Zaïre formed a vast marshy area of flooded forest where only fishermen could live. Here, too, there are traces of influences that have crossed the forest, probably items carried by the fishermen.

Movements through the forest

To mention only the best-known examples, simple bells without clappers are known to have crossed the forest, probably from north to south, well before the year 1000. They were followed by double bells of similar type, before 1450 (see Plate 22.1). These products involve a knowledge of sheet-metal working and of soldering. The double bells were used to reproduce

16. A. de Calonne-Beaufaict, 1921, p. 135; F. van Noten, 1968; de Maret, van Noten and Cahen, op. cit., pp. 486 and 498.

17. F. M. Olbrechts, 1941. He noted the facts but attributed them, wrongly, to the period after the Portuguese arrival.

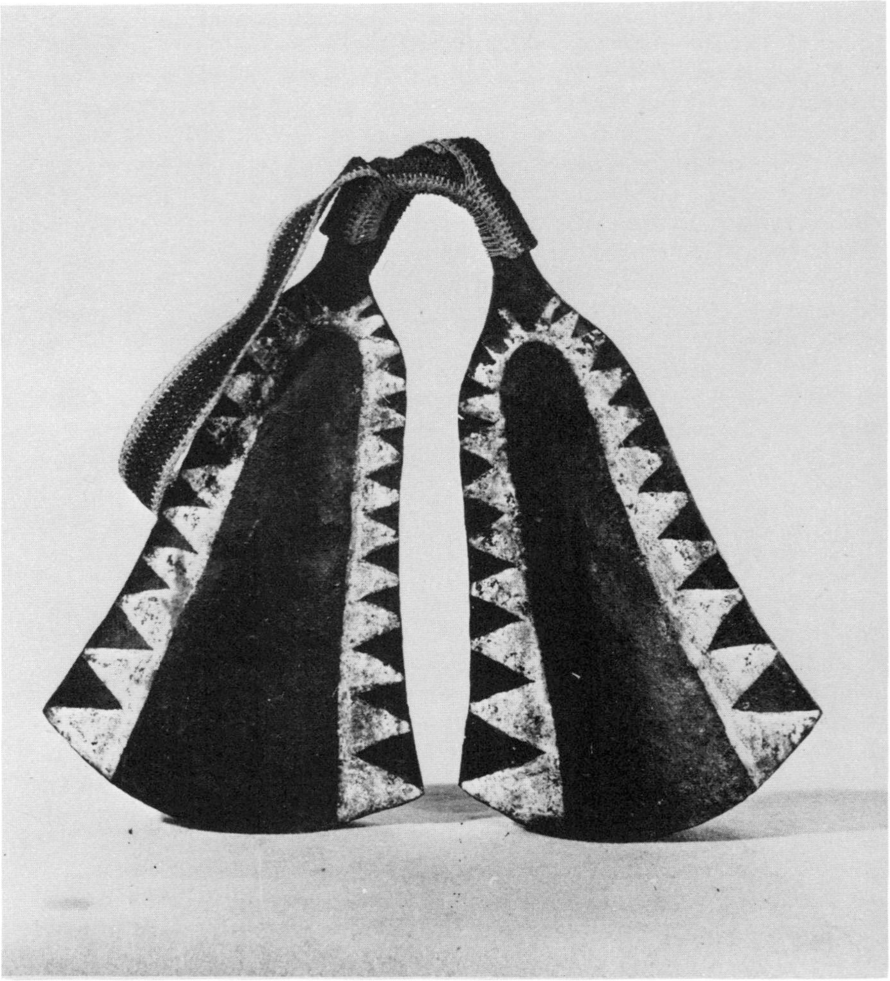

PLATE 22.1 *Double iron bell from Mangbetu (Zaïre)*

the tones of the spoken language, and indicate the existence of tonal (Bantu) languages in the forest and further south. Furthermore, the functions of these objects were similar in the region from Nigeria to Zambia; the double bell was always one of the symbols of the political chief. Knives for throwing were also sent from the north to the south, where they were reported by observers around 1587. Other objects, including bobbin-holders, certain types of knives and a kind of slit drum for sending messages, have been found in Benin and at least as far as Malebo, although it is impossible to say which came from the north and which from the south. The important aspect of this distribution is that it shows that the forest and the southern savannah were not completely isolated from the rest of the continent. With these objects, ideas could travel, and they crossed the forest in both directions.[18]

The most important development in the forest itself during this period was the penetration and diffusion of the idea of the political chief, as distinct from the 'kinship chief'. In the Mongo languages, the word for the right of blood relationship is *mpifo*, whereas the right of the first occupier, the lord of the land, is *okofo*. Among the Mongo, feudal lords, or rather lineage chiefs with well-defined authority, developed very early. The *mpifo* or lord who was able to increase his revenues, attract a growing clientele of people whom he fed, and impose his authority over other lords, could thus become king.

Social organization in the forest and the clearings

Before 1500 there was also a slow but considerable expansion of people speaking Mongo-type languages in the south of Sankuru and Kasai. Some groups penetrated very far along both sides of the Loanga, between the Loanga and the Kasai, and on both banks of the Kamsha. For the drift from north to south, from Lokenye to Sankuru, then southwards to the Lulua, evidence already exists in the form of oral traditions cross-checked by linguistic analysis. It has been possible to reconstruct the way of life here in these small chiefdoms or *nkumu*. Often the village was ruled by councils of elders who also assisted the chief. At the village level, there may have been two spokesmen, one for either side of the main street. Relations with the pygmies were ambivalent. Some groups seem to have lived in symbiosis, and in other cases farmers and pygmies fought each other. As regards social structure, the concepts of age and authority were practically identical and there was a clear division between generations. In comparison with the Mongo in general, these southern groups had begun to develop regulations, linked with matrimonial alliance, which implied less stress on the primary lineage as an organized group, and strengthened territorial unity. On the economic plane the most notable facts were the growing of sorghum (millet) in intercalary savannahs in the forest, and the forest people's well-known ability to work in iron. The Songye admit that the Luba, who came from the forest, taught them how to smelt iron. Whether this is true or not, ethnographic evidence shows that iron-working was a well-established technique in the forest environment. By burning trees of very hard wood they were able to produce high temperatures, and they had even discovered how to make steel.[19]

Very little is known about the history of the forest from Gabon/

18. J. Vansina, 1969; D. Cordell, 1973.
19. Vansina, 1978, pp. 90–103 and *passim*.

Cameroon to the Republic of the Congo. A gradual population drift started, from north of the Sanaga towards south Cameroon. The so-called Pahwin migration was in reality a very slow movement which started before 1500.[20] Political structures of the *nkumu* type also evolved in this region from about that date. Lastly, it is known that a large part of the forest in north-eastern Gabon was probably uninhabited, or at least was not inhabited by cultivators, since it remained primary forest until a short time ago.

To the east of the upper Zaïre, in the Maniema, there were some gradual population movements, but there is no means of dating them. Here again, the movements were due to the very high mobility of small groups who were familiar with agriculture, but chiefly engaged in fishing and who absorbed whole communities of pygmy hunters.

Before 1500, the southern part of the Maniema was probably already the home of the ancestors of the Lega population. It is possible that these people had already evolved the socio-political associations known as *bwami*. These consisted of a complex hierarchy of grades, in which the members of the highest grade constituted a collective political and moral authority for the entire region participating in their *bwami*. It is on the basis of these *bwami* that western interlacustrine groups living between Lakes Kivu and Tanganyika, on the western border of the Graben, are believed to have developed the concepts of chiefship and of kingship. Once again, therefore, a primary impulse in the elaboration of political structures came from the forest. Similar forest associations may also have been the origin of the elective feudal 'lordships' that developed among the Songye in the south. If the connection was indeed from north to south, this process too would certainly date from before 1500.[21]

The savannahs of Shaba

In the savannahs to the south of the basin, one can clearly distinguish between an eastern and a western tradition on the Atlantic coast. The first can even be subdivided into a Luba tradition and a tradition of upper Kasai and upper Shaba. Traditions tell of the birth of the Luba and Lunda empires. But how far are they to be believed? Some people maintain that they are pure fantasy, or merely reflect and justify structures of the nineteenth century. Professor de Heusch accepts that they are myths, but myths that came into being when the empires they tell of were born.[22] In fact, these opinions are not based upon the analysis of tradition – that still has to be undertaken.

Sanga is the main site bearing witness to the early development of metal-working techniques. We must await the results of current investigations

20. P. Laburthe-Tolra, 1977, pp. 79–414.
21. D. Biebuyck, 1973, pp. 11–12 and *passim* on the *bwami*.
22. L. de Heusch, 1972.

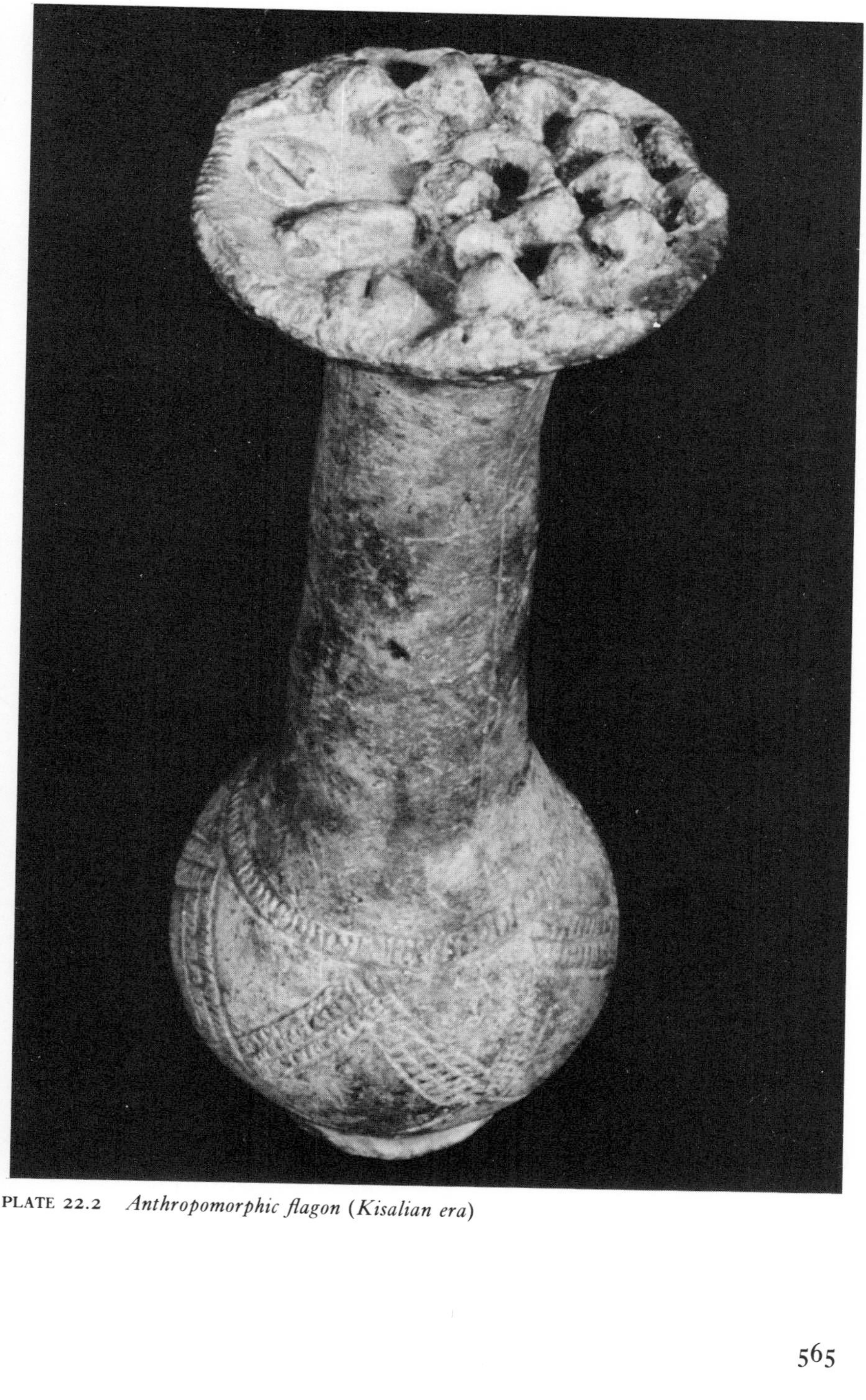

PLATE 22.2 *Anthropomorphic flagon (Kisalian era)*

PLATE 22.3 *Tomb of Kikulu (KUL-T2) with a small cross clearly visible on the body's thorax (Kabambian A tomb of 14th–16th century)*

before proposing a precise chronology. Nevertheless, it can be stated that from the fifteenth century onwards there are traces of considerable social differentiation which indirectly confirm the growth of chiefdoms. A trade network was established very early extending from the Lualaba lakes to the middle stretch of the Zambezi, in which cross-shaped copper ingots were used as money. These crosses first appeared on the present-day border between Zambia and Zaïre, in the copper belt, between the ninth and

PLATE 22.4 (*above*) *Contents of classical Kisalian tomb at Kanga site (12th century)*

PLATE 22.5 (*left*) *Stone 'Ntadi Kongo' statue, from Mboma, Lower Zaïre*

twelfth centuries. They made their appearance, therefore, shortly after the beginning of the Late Iron Age in this region. In view of the connection of the Ingombe Ilede site with the east-coast trade, there can be little doubt that this regional network was linked to that of the Indian Ocean from before 1500.[23]

The oral traditions speak of 'Luba' chiefs in Malawi and northern, central and eastern Zambia at various dates, those for Malawi being the earliest. It is through these same traditions that we learn of the foundation of the Luba and Lunda states and, as a result of Miller's research, one Lunda state is known to have existed from before 1450.[24] It is possible that small groups of craftsmen migrated into these regions; regional trade favoured such an expansion.

The Luba and Lunda kingdoms

Oral sources and knowledge of the country

In the southern savannahs, the kingdoms of Luba and Lunda took shape very early. These state formations developed near the Lualaba lakes. In Shaba, a mining area with rich agricultural resources, chiefdoms emerged very early and, as they perfected their structure, gave birth to kingdoms. The ease with which commerce took place in the savannah region may have been a stimulus to the formation of states.

It was the Luba and the Lunda who first organized states. For the most part our information here comes from oral sources and it is particularly abundant on these groups. Nevertheless, we do not yet possess a corpus of tradition; this is being collected all the time.

According to tradition, the kingdom of Luba was founded by a certain Kongolo, who established his capital near Kalongo; the myth of origin provides certain useful information in the light of other traditions on the culture, if not the history, of the Luba. It has been vaguely estimated that the state of Luba emerged before 1500. It was the result of the fusion of several clans under the authority of a single chief. The political organization of the kingdom is little known, but it is certain that the people were organized in patrilineages. Each lineage had its villages and the chiefs owned slaves. The *kiloto* or chief of the lineage recognized the king's authority. The latter was surrounded by dignitaries, of whom at least two are known: the guardian of emblems, called *inabanza*, and the military chief or *twite*. Luba royalty was founded on the principle of *bulopwe* or 'sacredness', inherent in the royal blood, which is called *mpifo* by the Luba.[25]

23. Phillipson, op. cit., summarizes all the data prior to 1977. Cf. P. de Maret, 1967; also de Maret, van Noten and Cahen, op. cit., pp. 487–9. See also B. Fagan, Chapter 21 above.

24. J. C. Miller, 1976.

25. J. Vansina, 1966b, pp. 71–87; A. Roberts, 1976, pp. 36–41; T. Q. Reefe, 1977,

The Shaba region's resources of salt and metals were favourable to trade, the mixing of populations and the emergence of large towns. Here there is a continuity with the developments of the first millennium. The penetration of the systems of patrilineal kinship, insisting more strongly on purity of blood, favoured the establishment of feudal overlords in the reigning patrilineages, and facilitated territorial cohesion. *Bulopwe*, the Luba sacral principle, still depends upon the royal blood.

Political institutions

Here the ideological principle of the Luba empire differs markedly from the political principles of the Songe, who maintained an elective kingship, founded on the richness of lineages, often limited in time, and dependent upon the council of an esoteric association, the *bukishi*. Among the matrilineal eastern Luba, esoteric associations constituted the mechanism of government. Geographically, all this is very close to the world of the Lega forest, and one is tempted to suggest a link between *bwami* and these forms of government, a link very different from the cultural ties that existed between the Songye and the central Luba. *Bulopwe* seems to have been invented solely by the latter, perhaps in the region of the Lualaba lakes. Besides, there were several Luba kingdoms; in addition to Kikonja in the lake region, we know of the Kalundwe feudal lordship.[26]

As for the Lunda, we may accept, until the contrary is proved, that the whole region of upper Kwango to upper Kwasao, southern Shaba and the regions adjoining Zambia were already practising perpetual kingship, a complex system whereby the successor actually 'became' his predecessor, adopted his name, his relations of kinship, his duties and prerogatives.[27] This system denied the passage of time in order to ensure the unfailing cohesion and continuity of the whole social order. It permitted the perpetuation of power relations derived from matrimonial alliances, conquests, integration, and mutual or 'fraternal' agreements between chiefs. After 1500 it was to become a powerful tool in the forging of a true empire, the grouping of several kingdoms under Lunda authority.

It may be noted that this region between Kasai and Kwango is poor in natural resources and was probably sparsely populated, whereas salt-

---

denies that the Luba influenced the Lunda, but J. Hoover (personal communication) and Ndua Solol do not accept his arguments. H. W. Langworthy, 1972, pp. 28–30 and pp. 21–7.

26. A. Wilson, 1972, does not believe that there was a very extensive Luba state prior to about 1800, but this is partly contradicted by J. Yoder, 1977, pp. 67–97 and 120–53. For Kuaba, see Yoder, op. cit. pp. 56–7, and compare with J. Weydert, 1938, and G. Wauters, 1949; see also the doctoral thesis of N. J. Fairley, 1978, on the Ben 'Eki. Reefe, 1981, is the most recent work.

27. J. C. Miller, 1972b, pp. 45–68, 81–2 and 166–8.

mines and copper deposits were being developed between the Lualaba and the Luapula in the east. Towards the south, the upper Zambezi valley boasted more resources than Lunda country but, all things considered, rather less than southern Shaba. Nevertheless, the complex Lozi state was to grow up in this region. Its foundation can be acknowledged as having been partly prompted by the Lunda, but the period of its development is not known.[28]

Angola

In the basin of the Lui, a tributary of the upper Kwango, chiefdoms developed early (well before 1500), and the inhabitants were ruled by the Pende. Here, too, Miller sees a regular growth in the size of the chiefdoms.[29] The country surrounding the Lui basin consisted predominantly of salt-pans.

Finally, shortly after 1500 at the latest, on the plateau south of Libolo, a Kulembe state was seen, perhaps one of the first Ovimbundu states. It was differently organized, and a characteristic feature was the *kilombo*, a military initiation association. It was either at Libolo or at Kulembe that the first of the complex stone tombs was built, the ruins of which remain but have yet to be excavated. Perhaps the other Ovimbundu states were also familiar with the *kilombo*, which is also encountered in the founding tradition of Humbe, a state in the south of Angola that came into existence at an unknown date. Perhaps, on the other hand, the *kilombo* was introduced to Humbe by the Imbangala, who did not form a separate ethnic group until the sixteenth century. The Ovimbundu speak a south-west Bantu language, and groups such as the Huambu point to the southern edge of the plateau as their place of origin, in particular a site called Feti, where excavations have supplied radiocarbon dates of 710 ± 100 and 1250 ± 65. The second dating no doubt refers to the Ovimbundu group, but is only a possibility; excavations must be resumed. It is possible that the formation of some of the fourteen Ovimbundu states may well have begun before the sixteenth century; the language, the presence of cattle and the system of kinship link this civilization with those of the Bantu-speakers of southern Angola and Namibia.

These have three main branches: the Nyanyeka-Humbe, the Ambo and the Herero. The first, who are closely related culturally to the Ovimbundu, were not organized in large states, with the exception of the Humbe. Petty chiefdoms were frequent. The other two groups are also found in Namibia. There was some agriculture among the Ambo, but life really turned on the possession of long-horned cattle. In the nineteenth century, Ambo political organization consisted of twelve states, three of which possessed

28. M. Mainga, 1973, pp. 16–21; G. Prins, 1980.

29. Miller, 1972b, pp. 55–88; B. Heintze, 1970 and 1977; the latter article criticizes some of Miller's views.

considerable military strength. The chiefs reigned in fortified capitals. All offices were hereditary in the maternal line. Power was denoted by possession of the sacred fire and by an economic structure based on possession of cattle. The Herero were nomads like their neighbours the Khoi of Namibia, living off their herds of cattle and sheep, their hunting and their crops. Like the Khoi, they did not use iron until the nineteenth century. They spoke Bantu, however, and their double descent also distinguished them from the Khoi. Southern Angola and central and northern Namibia also had groups of San hunters, and some black hunters, the Twa – including the *bergdagai* ('black men of the mountains'), the smiths of Namibia – who spoke Khoi–San languages.[30]

This was the situation in about 1850. What was the history of these peoples? The Nyanyeka-Humbe say they are autochthonous; the Ambo and the Herero say they came from the east. It may be accepted that they came from the Zambezi and, with cattle they had acquired there, moved westward by way of the Cubango. The Herero got their sheep from the Khoi, unless we date their migration in the first half of the first millennium, which seems too early. In any case, the cave paintings associated with sheep definitely depict Khoi. The Ambo assimilated many Twa hunters and are not ashamed of it, whereas the Nyanyeka-Humbe, who assimilated both Twa and other unspecified hunters, do not care to admit it. The Herero also seem to have assimilated many Twa, for Kaokovela, which the southern Herero occupied for about two hundred years, is really called Otwa, 'the land of the Twa'.

At one time, therefore, the black hunters with a San culture who occupied the coast as far as latitude 13°S travelled round the central plateau from the south to join other San groups in the east. In the south they occupied all the northern coastal region of Namibia. In the interior they were neighbours of the San and the Khoi. Some of these groups acquired the art of smelting iron. It may be supposed that it was about this time that the Bantu-speakers of the south-west occupied the central plateau of Angola at a few points to the south and to the west, and in the east they lived in the valleys of eastern Angola, leaving the land between the rivers to the San. Towards the north and the sources of the Cuito and Cuando, where the country is better watered, there were Iron Age agricultural peoples belonging linguistically to the Lunda–Guangella–Cokwe group. The Ambo and the Herero still lived in the valleys.

The savannahs of the south-west

The Portuguese found two great kingdoms on the coast, Kongo and Loango, and another in the interior, the Tio kingdom of the 'great Makoko'.

30. Cf. C. Estermann, 1960; H. Vedder, 1938; and C. H. L. Hahn, H. Vedder and L. Fourié, 1966.

The traditions record that the first two were formed by the slow amalgamation of lesser states, and that the Kongo dynasty originated north of the river, not far from the Loango dynasty. It seems probable that these kingdoms were founded between the thirteenth and fourteenth centuries. According to Dapper, all these kingdoms originated in the regions to the north of Lake Malebo, that is, the area of the Tio. This is not unlikely, especially because one common tradition concerning a person or a place, Nngunnu, linked the Tio, Loango and Kongo peoples – a tradition which was probably purely aetiological. According to this, any descendant of a former king could (in theory) make the same claim to the throne as any other. It may also be noted that the birthplace of the Kongo is just west of Maniango, under the Bateke (Tio) regime.

If this common origin is true, the first states north and north-west of Malebo must have been in existence before the fourteenth century, perhaps even around 1000. Only excavation of the earliest known burial grounds of the Kongo, Vili and Tio dynasties, and of Mbanza Kongo (San Salvador) can supply a date and a fuller background. It is not unreasonable to suggest that the civilizations of this region first acquired a character of their own in the north, on the border of the forest or in the forest of Mayombe. They adapted to the savannah and even, in the case of the Bateke high plateau, to the steppe. Their expansion, including that of their language, showed another 'swelling' around two initial centres, one for the Kongo and one for the Tio (Bateke). The Kongo spread south of the river, the Vili of Loango along the coast towards the north and north-east as far as the Ngounie, a tributary of the Ogowe, whereas the Tio, who came from the edge of the forest near the Equator itself, occupied all the high plateaux towards the south, the wooded areas in Gabon and the region of the river cataracts.

When it was recorded for the first time in 1624, Kongo tradition indicated a period of gradual occupation of the country south of the river, a territory occupied by Ambundu (or Ndembo) chiefdoms. Kongo conquered them to the extent of including both the Matamba and the Ndongo, at least as irregular tributaries, for the kingdom proper probably stopped at the Loje, while including the coast around Loanda, the island and the land opposite between the rivers Cuanza and Bengo. We have fewer details about conquests or the formation of states in other regions, although there is a list of the independent feudal lordships that were incorporated to form the central provinces of Loango. A fairly regular political evolution is discernible, but there is no record of its stages before the coming into existence of greater lordships like Ngoi, Kakongo, the nucleus of Loango, Bungu, Nsundi and Mbata. We may assume that the pattern was the same as in the equatorial forest: big matrilineal villages with chiefs and counsellors (one for each lineage), the formation of chiefdoms through inter-village marriages and perhaps through conquests or spiritual supremacy (using spells, spirits and so on), and then varieties of circumstances whereby some chiefdoms grew and others disappeared in the course of the creation of small kingdoms such as those that have been mentioned. Everywhere there was worship of spirits – spirits of the earth – and of ancestors, both being treated as gods. Trade seems to have developed early in this sector too, for coins were circulating in 1483 when the Portuguese arrived. There was an aristocracy, and slaves did the farm work. Excavations under way in Kinshasa and on the island of Mbamu may well enable us to settle the precise dates.

The kingdom of Kongo before 1500 – its institutions[31]

Kongo deserves a longer description, not because it was the largest or most powerful state, but because it is the best-known by tradition. Lukeni Nimi founded it when he crossed the river on leaving Bungu in Mayembe, and went on to conquer the Ambundu chiefdom of Mbanza Kongo. He 'shared' power there, and eventually conquerors and natives mixed, 'nobles with nobles, commoners with commoners'. We also have an interesting 'Description of the kingdom of the Congo and surrounding countries' by two Portuguese writers at the end of the sixteenth century:

> The Kingdom is divided into six provinces: Bamba, Sogno, Sundi, Pango, Batla and Pemba. Bamba, the largest and richest, is governed by Dom Sebastião Mani Mamba, a cousin of King Dom Alvaro, who died recently; it is situated along the coast from the river Ambrize in the south to the Coanza river; there are many dependent lords, of whom the most important are Dom Antonio Mani Mamba, brother of Dom Sebastião and lieutenant governor, Mani Lemba, Mani Dandi, Mani Bango, Mani Luanda, who is chief of the Island of Luanda, Mani Corimba, Mani Coanza and Mani Cazzani. All these lords have authority in the coastal part of the country. In the interior, on the Angola side, we hear of the Ambundo, who are also the responsibility of Mani Bambre: these are the Angasi (Ngasi), Chinhengo (Kungengo), Motolo, Cabonda and many others of less noble blood. Note that the word *mani* means 'Lord' and that the second part of the name denotes the country, the lordship. Thus, for example, Mani Bamba means 'Lord of the region of Bamba' and Mani Corimba, 'Lord of Corimba', Corimba being part of Bamba, and so it is for the other lords ...
>
> Bamba, as we said, is the main province of the Congo; it is the key to the kingdom, its shield and its sword, its defence, its bastion against the enemy ... its inhabitants are courageous and always ready to take up arms, to drive back the enemies from Angola ... in case of need an army of four hundred thousand warriors can be mustered.[32]

31. The fullest bibliography and the most precise description to date are to be found in W. G. L. Randles, 1968.

32. Translated from the French version (1965) of F. Pigafetta and D. Lopes (eds), 1591. (There is also an English translation, 1881.)

This passage describes sufficiently the administrative divisions; the figures for the army that the king could recruit in Bamba are surely an exaggeration, but they indicate that the country was densely populated with a strong administrative structure. The *mani* or governor lived at Banza, the name given to the chief's residence.[33]

Provincial government and organization

The Kongo king exercised great authority, but did not have absolute power. He nominated the governors, except for that of Mbata, 'elected by the people and the dignitaries of the Nsaku family, with royal confirmation'. In the province of Soyo, the governor was hereditary. It seems that the sovereign of the Kongo had a much more extensive kingdom before 1500; he continued to claim sovereignty over Kisama, Ngoi, Kakongo, Loango and the chiefdoms and kingdoms of Teke and Suku.

The governors collected taxes and tributes which they handed over to the king. The tribute comprised *nzimbu* (shells used as money), raffia squares (also used as money), sorghum, palm wine, fruit, cattle, ivory and animal skins (leopard and lion). Taxes and tribute were thus partly in currency, partly in provisions, partly in trade goods and one part was symbolic (the leopard and lion skins).

Around 1530 the king of Kongo still claimed sovereignty over Kisama, Ngoi, Kakongo, Loango, the Teke chiefdoms and kingdoms, Kongo ria Mulaza (around the Kwango) and Suku. But that was probably an exaggeration. Around 1483, the heart of the kingdom was made up of six provinces: Soyo, between the river and the sea; Mbamba, to the south of Soyo; Nsundi, in the north-east; Mpangu, south of Nsundi; Mbata, in the east; and Mpemba, which included the capital, in the centre. In addition, several chiefdoms extending towards the Wembo and perhaps the Wando depended directly upon the king (see Fig. 22.1, with numbered inset).

The king was assisted by a central administrative body, also subject to dismissal. It included, in the capital, the chief of the palace who acted as viceroy, a supreme judge, a receiver of taxes together with his treasurers, a chief of police, a messenger service, and another officer with the title *punzo*, whose function is unknown. This serves as a reminder that the manuscripts only give those offices which were easily understood by Europeans who noted them down. Outside this administrative corps there was the lord *kabunga*, who acted as high priest, and whose ancestor had been lord of the land in the capital before Nimi Lukeni.

Provincial governors were often immediate relatives of the king. The king made his favourite sons governors of Nsundi and Mpangu. They thus had a strong base from which to contest the succession when the

33. O. Dapper, 1668, p. 219; J. Vansina, 1973, pp. 339 and 345; Randles, op. cit., pp. 17–25; P. Martin, 1972, pp. 3–11.

king died. The governors nominated the lesser lords, who in turn ruled over the *nkuluntu*, the hereditary village chiefs.

The tombs of the ancestors were very close to the capital and were the object of great veneration. Power was sacred, but not the person of the king, even though he was called *nzambi mpungu* or 'superior spirit'. He was not like ordinary mortals. By committing incest with his sister he put himself outside his own family and thus became the only person capable of ruling equitably over all families. By this act and by his initiation, he acquired great power over magic spells, a power comparable to that of the sorcerers. Among other things his insignia included first of all a head-dress, with a drum, a bracelet made of copper or ivory, the tax purse and a throne in the form of a square stool; all these symbolized his position as first lord of the kingdom and holder of the supreme power which set him apart. The pre-eminence and uniqueness of the king was emphasized by a complex code of etiquette.

We know the capital of Kongo rather well as a result of the accounts of Portuguese writers, who described it often, as well as court life in the fifteenth century. However, the site of the capital has not yet been excavated thoroughly.

> Although the capital of the kingdom of the Kongo is within the country of Pemba in a certain way, the city and its environs within a circumference of some twenty miles are governed personally by the king and may be considered a special district ... in the language of the country, [the city] is called Banza, which means, in general, 'court, residence of the king or governor'.[34]

Located in the centre of the country, the city was also a fortress from which 'aid could rapidly be sent to all the region'. Banza, a well-built city with stone walls, which the Portuguese later named San Salvador, was also a major commercial metropolis, the meeting place for the principal trade routes from the interior and from the coast.

In theory, the king's successor was supposed to be chosen and advised by a college of electors, made up of either nine or twelve members. The lord *kabunga* had a right of veto, and the governor of Mbata, who was ineligible as successor, was an ex-officio member, as was later the chief of Soyo. The other electors were probably not members of the royal family. They usually confined themselves to approving whichever of the deceased king's sons seemed to have the greatest power when his father died. During a reign the council, which might include members of the administrative corps, reserved the right to oversee the king, especially in such matters as war, the nomination or deposition of governors and trade (they could declare routes open or closed).

The payment of 'salaries' to officials is evidence of the commercialization of production and its control by the state, which supervised the output

34. Translated from Pigafetta and Lopes, loc. cit., pp. 78–9.

of *nzimbu* shells. There must have been a long and fairly intensive period of commercial development, and the articles exchanged seem to have been necessities such as iron tools, pottery, sea-salt, mats and basketwork, together with prestige goods including copper and ivory trinkets, raffia squares and fibre fabrics from the coast. If there were slaves, the trade in them must have been limited before 1483. There was no full-time specialization in any one craft, and the two most prestigious activities, iron smelting and the weaving of raffia, were reserved for the nobility.

The main trade routes went to the capital: one brought the *nzimbu* from Loanda to the capital; another brought sea-salt and the products of lower Zaïre (fish, pottery, wickerwork); another those of the Malebo area (raffia and various goods including pottery); another copper from Mbamba, and perhaps copper and lead from north of the river cataracts; and finally, one brought goods from Matamba. Excavations at San Salvador, in Kinshasa, in the provincial capitals, on the island of Loanda and in other locations where a market-place might be expected are essential to give us a better picture of economic life in the kingdom before 1483.

Society

We know little about the social structure of the time. Even the matrilineal principle is not clearly demonstrated, although it may be supposed to have existed by then. We are certain only about the royal succession, because the name of the first king was composed of one name connecting him to his father and another to his mother's father. But these are clan names which are still known, as is that of Mbata. This leads one to suppose that there were groups of single-line descent which were more than likely to have been matrilineal clans. All that is really known is that the villages, ruled by *nkuluntu*, were small, and were distinct from centres governed by feudal lords. The provincial centres might have had the character of towns, and in fact the texts use that word to refer to Mbanza Kongo, to the residence of the governor of Soyo, and later to Kinshasa. The stratification of society is clear: there were three orders, the aristocracy, free men and slaves, and the aristocracy formed a caste which did not intermarry with plebeians. Within the two free orders, marriages served as instruments of alliance between families, and preferential marriages seem to have occurred. Among the aristocracy were the *kitomi*, former lords of the land, who played the same role in the provinces as the *kabunga* played in the capital, and who probably formed an aristocracy connected with other lords by preferential marriages of the kind which united the dynasty to the Mbata and the *kabunga*.

General conclusions

The period from 1100 to 1500 will become better known only when extensive excavation has taken place and considerable progress has been made in linguistic and ethnographical research. From the general impression produced by what is already known, two major features emerge; the importance of the omnipresent forest, a powerful ecological force; and the early development of state systems. The second was suspected already; after the end of the migrations and the upheavals they caused, and after the introduction of the use of iron, it seemed probable that kingdoms would arise.

The importance of the forest has hitherto been completely misjudged. It was not realized that both the forest with its intercalary savannahs and the forest fringes offered a doubly rich environment, comparable to that of the galleried forests to the north and south. In particular, all the earliest state formations may be attributed to this kind of environment, with the exception of the earliest Luba centre, although this too was very favourably situated with its lakes, its lowlands which must have been partly covered by forests, and its savannah plains.

Let us note in conclusion that not all the possible sources have yet been drawn upon; the systematic study of the traditions and of the myths of origin, together with linguistic research, is only just beginning, as is archaeological work. Great perspectives are opening up for historical research in this region, which was long believed to be undocumented.

23 Southern Africa: its peoples and social structures

L. D. NGCONGCO *in collaboration with* J. VANSINA

The writing of history and the problem of sources

The history of southern Africa presents a number of problems. It was for this reason that Unesco, as sponsor of the *General History of Africa*, called together a group of experts on 'Historiography of Southern Africa' in 1977 at Gaborone.[1] The existing political situation in the region is hardly conducive to historical research. Because of apartheid, the history of the black peoples south of the Limpopo has been studied less than that of other African populations. In the *General History of Africa*, Volume VIII, the problem of apartheid will be treated in the context of contemporary Africa, but it is also essential to examine here its unfortunate effects on the writing of the history of the region.

As was stated at the Gaborone meeting, 'The tendency to concentrate on the past of the dominant white minority has been accentuated by the rigid positions adopted by South African universities and South African publishers in general who refuse to accept the validity of non-written sources for historical reconstruction.' Furthermore, white historians in South Africa have refused the aid of such sciences as archaeology, anthropology and linguistics. Even more serious is the fact that the official historians of the country of apartheid draw from the archives material which relates only to the whites, deliberately putting aside documents referring to African peoples. To sum up the way in which history is written in the region dominated by apartheid, the Unesco experts noted: 'The rich Portuguese archives that have contributed so much to the understanding of African histories of many East African societies, especially those along the coast, documents which have also illuminated the study of the pre-colonial history of the societies of Zimbabwe, as well as those of Angola and Mozambique, have been studiously neglected by Southern African scholars.'[2] Not

1. Unesco, 1980b.
2. ibid., contributions by L. D. Ngcongco, pp. 18–19, and D. Chanaiwa.

only do these historians reject oral traditions as a non-valid source, but they also demonstrate 'a troubling selectivity' among written records, which is unscientific.

All the historical material accumulated by four generations of South African historians is written against the history of African peoples. It has not always been easy to gather the documentation to write this contribution to the *General History of Africa*, but in the present instance we are confronted with a considered policy of ignoring or destroying existing documents! The active negation of African culture and history is a dangerous weapon in the hands of the controllers of apartheid.

Nevertheless, changes are occurring in the environment of southern Africa: the independence of Zimbabwe in 1980 has opened a wide field for research. Since independence, Angola and Mozambique also offer new perspectives for research, and studies are already beginning in neighbouring states such as Malawi, Zambia, Botswana, Swaziland and Lesotho. Conferences and seminars abound and a real effort is being made to integrate oral traditions.

The state of knowledge

Two problems dominate the history of southern Africa: first, the dates when the various peoples settled there or, in other words, the movements or migrations of peoples; and second, the nature of power, which implies the need to define its structures. It thus becomes necessary to go back to the origin of kingdoms or states.

In the first place, it must be said that the most recent research has demonstrated how long ago the Khoikhoi peoples settled in the region;[3] some even maintain that the peoples settled in the region of the Cape were important sheep-raisers. At Lydenburg, in eastern Transvaal, splendid pottery heads have been uncovered (fifth century of the Christian era) along with irrefutable proof of the existence of farming. It was this period which saw the start of the first Iron Age, which ended towards 1100. Inskeep, using radiocarbon-dating methods, places the earliest date for the appearance of iron between the Zambezi and the Limpopo around the years 20 ± 80 before the Christian era. The culture of this Early Iron Age spread throughout southern Africa: pottery has been discovered in many places.

Towards 1100, the second Iron Age began, otherwise known as the Middle Iron Age. This one was intimately linked with the migrations of Bantu-speaking peoples. The experts at Gaborone looked into this question and rejected the old theory about Bantu migration. A group of researchers with Professor Ehret (using a modified corpus of 90 words

3. Khoikhoi is the name given to themselves by those often called Hottentot. The term 'Hottentot' has derogatory connotations.

specially adopted from Morris Swadesh's 100 universal words) studied the correlations between two groups of languages in the central areas of South Africa. One of these groups comprised very different Shona dialects, spoken between the Limpopo and the Zambezi, and the other, the Sotho, Nguni, Tsonga, Chopi and Venda dialects, the latter being called the south-east Bantu language. According to Ehret, 'the first populations of Shona speakers settled in what is now Zimbabwe while the proto-Bantu of the south-east occupied an area farther south, probably in the north of the Transvaal'.[4]

The period between 1000 and 1500 formed a crucial era in the past of southern Africa. New ways of life were spreading after 1100. The Khoikhoi became pastoralists and expanded over a huge area. The importance of cattle also dramatically increased among the other peoples, who probably spoke Bantu. It is to this period, or earlier, that we must look for the origin of the major cultural traditions that are so characteristic of the Bantu-speakers living in the region, the Sotho/Tswana and the Nguni.[5] By about 1500 some of these traditions were taking shape, which were inherited by the main ethnic groups known in the nineteenth century. These changes deeply influenced the lives of the coastal fishing communities, the shepherds near the Cape and the hunters.[6]

But we still lack adequate information on this crucial period. Written evidence is extremely scarce and touches only on the last years of the period. Rock art remains mainly undated and poses problems of interpretation that are difficult to overcome. Oral tradition lacks chronological benchmarks when it goes back as far as this period. Linguistic data have not yet been sufficiently exploited; in particular, we need to reconstruct early Nguni and early Sotho vocabulary, and it would be very rewarding to study Khoisan loan-words in Bantu languages and vice versa.[7] Comparative anthropological work on regional problems, within a time perspective, has only just begun.[8]

There are real problems in collating evidence derived from many sources,

4. Unesco, op. cit., p. 20.

5. Sotho/Tswana and Nguni are ethnic labels coined in the nineteenth century. They are universally adopted for the two cultural blocs in South Africa that are Bantu-speaking and live south and west of the Venda and Tsonga. Cf. M. Wilson, 1969a, pp. 75–6 and 1969b, pp. 131–3; M. Legassick, 1969, pp. 94–7; S. Marks, 1969, pp. 126–7.

6. By hunters we mean those people of southern Africa formerly called Bushmen or San. *San* is a Khoikhoi word meaning 'client', 'robber', 'vagrant', and is not used by any of the hunting groups to refer to themselves. Cf. R. Elphick, 1977, pp. 19–20 and 23–8.

7. Khoisan is used to denote the non-Bantu languages of southern Africa. Cf. O. Köhler, 1975, pp. 309–13. We shall also use the word in a biological sense, as biologists unfortunately use it for a group of related populations in southern Africa. Cf. J. Hiernaux, 1974, pp. 98–112.

8. A. Kuper, 1975.

including archaeological finds. It has been customary to establish a parallel between a common tradition of pottery and related linguistic or ethnographic material, but often on the most slender of evidence. This chapter will rely essentially on the results of archaeological excavations, but such finds will be associated with cultural and linguistic groups only when the available data justify this. Such a rigorous approach will preclude the criticisms that can be applied to much earlier work, namely, that in the many treatises and monographs that have appeared on various peoples, speculation is often raised to the level of scholarly hypothesis and even presented as evidence. We shall examine, in turn, the evolution of the southern Bantu languages, their development both north and south of the Drakensberg and the expansion of the Khoikhoi.

The evolution of the southern Bantu languages

The Bantu languages of southern Africa belong to the following groups: Venda, Sotho, Tsonga, Nguni and Inhambane.[9] Although formerly some authors grouped all of these together with Shona as a subdivision of Bantu, later research clearly shows that this was an inaccurate classification. The lexico-statistical method shows Shona, Venda, Tsonga, Inhambane and Sotho-Nguni to be some of the co-ordinated branches within eastern Bantu. It means that the overwhelming majority of the Bantu-speakers of southern Africa belong to a single group, distinct not only from Shona but also from Venda in the northern Transvaal, Tsonga and Inhambane in southern Mozambique and the Transvaal plains.

Ehret and his collaborators have found the strongest correlation between Venda and Shona (55 per cent), then between Tsonga and Shona (41 per cent), followed by Chopi (38 per cent), Sotho (37 per cent) and Nguni (35 per cent). According to them, since the Shona and the south-east Bantu form two distinct sub-groups linguistically, it is evident that there were two centres from which the Bantu language spread through the vast regions of the south-east. Ehret's group see in the correlation between Shona and the other south-eastern Bantu languages the proof that proto-Nguni and proto-Sotho-Tswana spread rapidly from the original region where the Sotho-Chopi-Tsonga languages were spoken, which still remain confined to the lower valley of the Limpopo. By contrast, Nguni and Sotho-Tswana are widely diffused on both slopes of the Drakensberg.[10] The linguistic differentiation between the Sotho and the Nguni language groups is much more recent than the others and occurred within the general area where the speakers now live, that is, within South Africa itself, long after Bantu-speakers had settled there. As we shall see, typical patterns of settlement for the Tswana and other Sotho

9. C. M. Doke, 1954.
10. C. Ehret, 1973.

and for the Nguni had developed by about 1500, and it is not unreasonable to suggest that the separation of the languages had already taken place, which would give us a limiting date of 1600. This would be consonant with the very rare oral traditions, which are mainly concerned with genealogies going back to the seventeenth century and earlier.

It is impossible to establish a direct link between archaeological data and the appearance of Bantu-speaking peoples. Until recently archaeologists as a whole equated Bantu-speakers with agricultural and metal-working communities, so that they placed their arrival in the first centuries of the Christian era. More recently, however, Inskeep and Phillipson have placed in parallel the spread of the later Iron Age, which began about the year 1000, with the spread of Bantu languages in southern Africa. They limit themselves to the observation that the spread of these languages, and that of the later Iron Age pottery, represent major cultural upheavals and the *last* such upheaval in the record. Hence the arrival of Bantu-speakers cannot be linked with any later archaeological period.[11]

It is not certain that the Bantu brought superior agricultural techniques or better tools everywhere. What should be emphasized, though, is that perhaps these new techniques contributed to increased production and favoured new forms of settlement. The arrival of the Bantu was not quite the 'event' that early researchers reported.

It must be admitted that for a long period there was interaction between the Shona, Venda and Tsonga languages in the region between the Zambezi and the Limpopo. This could explain the large number of related words in Nguni and Sotho, as well as the considerable resemblance in social habits (patrilineal inheritance, circumcision and polygamy).[12] The same customs and the same forms of socio-political organization are the result of a long cohabitation. It should be noted that all the other groups have totems corresponding to lineages or clans, but the Nguni have not.

Historians are in agreement on the Bantu migrations in southern Africa, but we must look to the evidence that there was no invasion, rather an infiltration of small groups. Oral traditions have not been sufficiently examined or judiciously criticized; they could provide information going back to the sixteenth century and even earlier. These data should not be ignored by archaeologists.

North of Ukhahlamba

The second or Middle Iron Age occurred between 1100 and 1600. This period is represented by villages uncovered in the region of Olefantspoort, at Melville Koppies and at Platberg. Each consists of ten or twenty houses

11. R. R. Inskeep, 1979, pp. 124–8 and 153; D. W. Phillipson, 1977, pp. 197–209, esp. 206. Apart from this unfortunate hypothesis, these two works are the most recent and up-to-date on the archaeology of our region.

12. Inskeep, op. cit.; Ehret, op. cit.; Phillipson, op. cit.

laid out in a circular fashion; they were surrounded by a fence and had beaten-earth floors. In the ruins were found teeth of cattle, sheep and goats, iron tools and 'well-preserved burnt millet seeds'.[13]

The cultures dating back to the Middle Iron Age were certainly Bantu-language communities (1100–1600) and almost certainly those of Sotho–Tswana peoples, according to Mason. In these villages are to be found some huts with stone walls. Except in the case of the Leopard's Kopje style, it has not been possible to find a site where the passage from the beginning to the last period of the Early Iron Age is clearly apparent.

It may be that the archaeologists will have to abandon this important distinction, at least in its present form. The only site where the transition may be verified is at Eiland in central Transvaal, where salt was worked throughout the period. Early Iron Age pottery was replaced in the eleventh or twelfth century by Mapungubwe ware (in the Leopard's Kopje tradition) and later by Phalaborwa pottery.[14] The nearby site of Silver Leaves (Tzaneen) shows the same development (see Fig. 23.1).

A very different pottery and way of life appeared at Phalaborwa, one of the two main centres of copper production in Transvaal at that time. It lies near a tributary of the Limpopo, the Olifants river – which Vasco da Gama called 'the river of copper' in 1498 – some 80 km east of the Drakensberg in the Transvaal. Mining had gone on at least since the eighth century, but the earliest site so far discovered goes back to between 960 and 1130. The style of the pottery has no equivalent from the Early Iron Age, but is virtually similar to pottery made by the people of Phalaborwa today. Several centuries before the beginning of the period under consideration, this pottery had established its present character, which is also found among the Lobedu, some 90 km to the north.[15] This proves that pottery is not a barometer of cultural change. Over several centuries Lobedu society has become noticeably differentiated from that of Phalaborwa, especially in the political field (it is famous for its rain queens). Phalaborwa itself is now in the cultural orbit of the northern Sotho, but in 1700 it was, like Lobedu, part of the Venda kingdom. There is reason to believe that in the seventeenth century at least, if not later, the speech of these people was close to Venda, rather than Sotho. Major changes have occurred since then, but these are not reflected in the pottery tradition.[16]

Continuity in the region was provided by the miners and traders, who were also the potters, the indigenous inhabitants of the oral traditions, in which they are called the 'Salang of Shokane', and are claimed – perhaps because they were of Tsonga culture – to be different from and far inferior to their conquerors, people linked to the Venda political tradition. More-

13. R. J. Mason, 1973.
14. Inskeep, op. cit., p. 132; Phillipson, op. cit., p. 204; M. Klapwijk, 1974.
15. N. J. Van Der Merwe and R. T. K. Scully, 1971–2.
16. See R. T. K. Scully, 1978a, for details of development from about 1700.

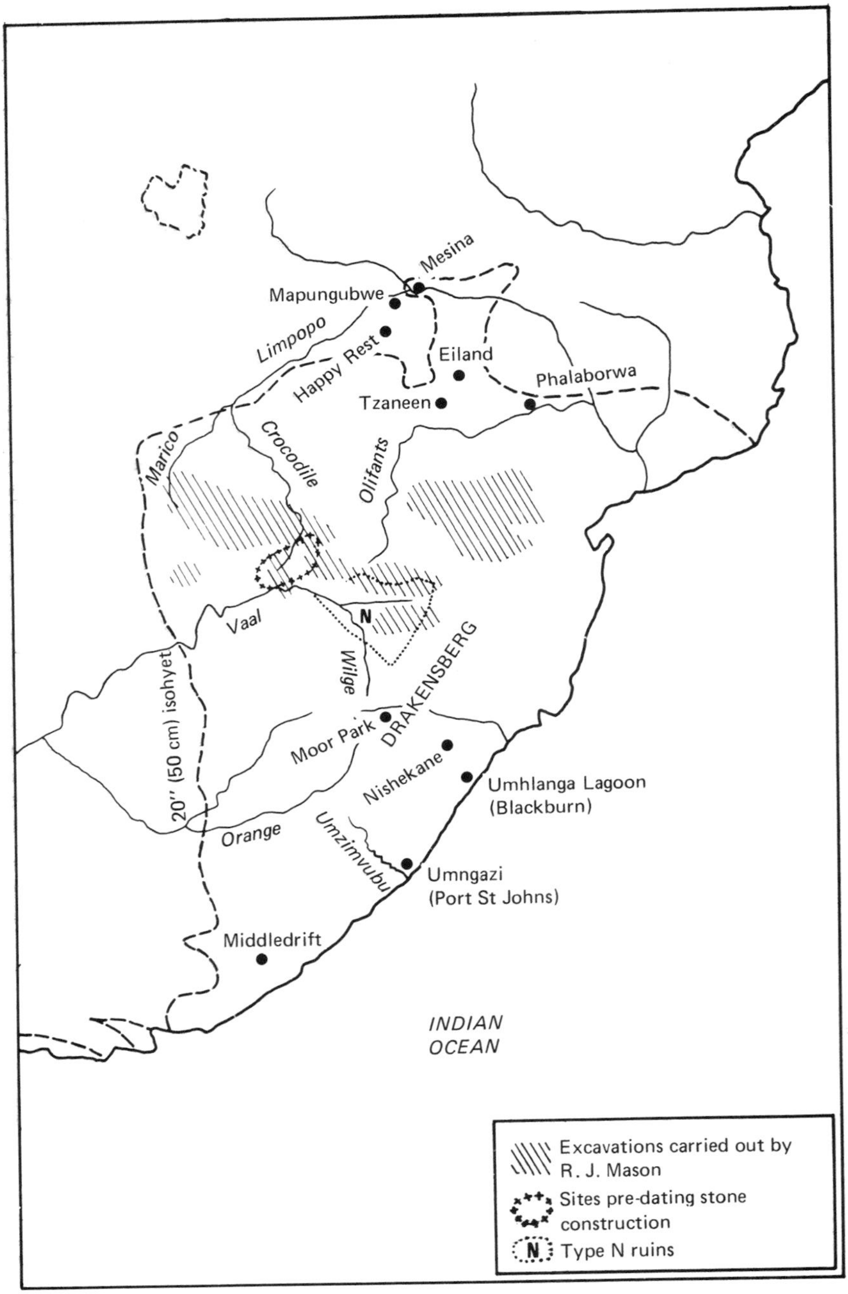

FIG. 23.1 *Archaeological sites of southern Africa, 1100–1500 (J. Vansina)*

over, some accounts of contacts with non-Bantu-speaking hunters, which have recently begun to proliferate in the region, may well be based on an authentic tradition. It seems therefore that between 1100 and 1500 there were agricultural settlements on the Transvaal low veld that traded among themselves and exchanged their craft products. The Phalaborwa mines were a source of iron objects, within a radius of at least 32 km, and a source of copper over much greater distances. Probably some of it found its way as far as the lower Limpopo and perhaps overland to the coast. Tzaneen provided salt for the area and, further north, the Mesina copper-mines were certainly trading their products over a wide area. Scully has put forward the hypothesis that the society became a state as a result of the development of metal-working at Phalaborwa and the trade that followed. The chiefdoms that grew up all over the Transvaal plain were on a small scale at first, but still had to cope with roaming bands of hunters and competing neighbouring chiefdoms. But after the end of this period, or perhaps in the seventeenth century, the Venda polity subdued them all and united them in a single kingdom.[17]

In the triangle bounded by Rustenburg, Klerksdorp and Johannesburg, north of the Vaal, traces have been found of a group of villages of the same tradition, ranging in date from 1060 to 1610; some excavations have been carried out there by Mason.[18] On the plastered floors of the round houses were platforms, also plastered, whereas the walls were of perishable materials, probably palisades of wood or, given the scarcity of wood on the high veld, reeds coated with mud. Millet was cultivated and livestock, including sheep and goats, were kept. The houses were located around an oval or circular space, about 1 hectare in area, which presumably was the cattle kraal. The villages were small, consisting of only ten to twenty huts, at least in the three sites excavated. This type of settlement is very significant because it preceded building in stone, which on present evidence became quite widespread on the high veld of the Transvaal in the seventeenth century.[19] As only four of the hundreds of settlements that have been identified in central and southern Transvaal have been excavated, it is quite possible that future research will find some stone-walled sites dating to the period before 1500. It is all the more likely because in the Orange Free State one type of settlement built in stone, the 'N' type, is at least as early as 1400–50.

Type N sites occur north and south along the upper Vaal river, as far west as the Wilge river and as far south and east as the Drakensberg. The area enjoys good rainfall and rich grasslands. The patterning of granaries, byres and houses within a wall surrounding the whole settlement is strong evidence of a mixed economy of agriculture and stock-raising.

17. R. T. K. Scully, 1978b, p. 25. Cf. also Inskeep, op. cit., p. 135.
18. R. J. Mason, 1962 and 1973.
19 Phillipson, op. cit., pp. 198–200. The pottery found on these sites is known as Uitkomst ware and seems closely related to Buispoort ware from the Rustenburg area.

After 1600, type N was to develop into other types of settlement that spread across that part of the Orange Free State that lay north of modern Lesotho. One variant of these later types is clearly Tswana and appears at the latest around 1600.[20]

Only future research will determine whether the Rustenburg/Klerksdorp/Johannesburg pre-stone sites, and perhaps the undated village site at Lydenburg, further east, are in fact prior to the stone settlements of type N or those of the Transvaal proper. The distribution of both the pre-stone sites, and those of type N and related stone settlement sites north of the Vaal, reaches right into the region between the Marico and Crocodile rivers, a territory associated with the dispersal of some Sotho groups, at least since the sixteenth century.[21] The data at our disposal now are tantalising, but perhaps Inskeep's view, which identifies these pre-stone and stone settlements with the Sotho way of life and indirectly with the Sotho-language group, may still be premature. Earlier attempts by Mason to link distinct pottery styles of the period 1100–1500 in these villages with distinct Tswana groups have not stood the test of time.[22] Only future research will solve this question.

Still, the present evidence looks impressive. The stone settlements of type N predate the later groups, which include one very typical bilobed house which is equally clearly Tswana. One can draw valid parallels between the diffusion of new patterns of architecture and oral traditions which relate the movements of ruling families, at least after the sixteenth century. In the region that corresponds to modern Zimbabwe, the rulers built in stone during the period under consideration, and the stone ruins there or in Mozambique are linked with the expansion of ruling groups. The idea of using stone for walls may come from there. It may also have been a local invention in the Johannesburg area, where grazing is good, but wood is scarce. Even so, the example of political leaders, adopting this architecture, doubtless set standards of prestige and fashion that would ensure the spread of the new type of settlements.

The settlement sites north of the Drakensberg show obvious and dramatic changes after 1100. In comparison with earlier known sites, the role of cattle in the economy had dramatically increased. The scale of local organization also increased, because during this period the size of settlements also grew markedly. The general impression derived from oral tradition – that by the sixteenth century states were beginning to be formed – corresponds with the available data. When we compare the situation here with the low veld (Phalaborwa) or with Botswana, the extent of change near the Vaal is even more spectacular. Changes here in

20. T. M. O.'C. Maggs, 1976a and 1976b.

21. Inskeep, op. cit., p. 138, makes some excessive generalizations; cf. Legassick, op. cit., pp. 100 and 103.

22. See the comments of B. M. Fagan, 1969, pp. 60–2; Mason, 1962.

settlement patterns and pottery seem to have been quite well marked. How are we to explain this?

The key to the riddle may well lie in Botswana, where Denbow's research has uncovered well over 150 sites, dating from +800 to +1300. Excavations at two sites show a continuous local development of the Zhizo phase of Gokomere pottery (Early Iron Age) into Tautswe ware. Most of the sites in central Botswana (north of Mahalapye) contain strong evidence of intensive herding of cattle. Some manure deposits there are up to 1 m thick.[23] These people were semi-pastoralists and the environment was very favourable to this activity because of the sweet veld and the nutritious *mopane* leaves. It is here, and not in Natal as Huffman believed, that the multiplication of livestock seems to have occurred. After the year 100, the sites in Botswana show less evidence of trade with the East African coast, which is not surprising since Zimbabwe, and later also Mapungubwe to the east, began to centralize trade. After *c.* 1300, the number of sites diminishes rapidly, perhaps because the climate became drier (the Kalahari is not far away) or because of a shift in the tsetse-fly belt, which would have forced an emigration of the cattle and their masters.

It is more than tempting to associate this decline of population with the apparent demographic growth which occurred in the western Transvaal and the evidence of large-scale cattle-keeping there. Some of the semi-pastoralists could have moved with their animals into the better environment near the Vaal and would then have used their cattle to absorb Early Iron Age groups into their communities. The introduction of *lobola* (bride-wealth paid in cattle) and of clientship contracts for cattle would have made this possible, and favoured the owners of the largest herds. *Lobola*, along with cattle clientship and the payment of tribute in the form of cattle, are characteristic of the later Sotho and Tswana cultures. The crossing of the Vaal was accompanied by the adoption of a pastoral and agricultural economy and the introduction of milking. The indigenous inhabitants may have kept some cattle, but probably only for meat, not for milk production.

It can be argued against this hypothesis that so far there is no link between Tautswe pottery and that made on the banks of the Vaal during the Later Iron Age. No comparative study, however, has yet been made of the two, and the new styles along the Vaal do not necessarily have to be the old styles of the immigrants.[24] A new style could have developed out of the contact between the indigenous and the imported styles.

This, we believe, is what occurred. Later, a change in the environment of central Botswana, natural or human (the rise of the Zimbabwe political organization), led to immigration near the Vaal and the appearance of

23. J. R. Denbow, 1979.

24. On innovation in pottery, see Inskeep, op. cit., pp. 132–3 and table 9, which I find interesting, but too dogmatic.

the typical Sotho-Tswana ways of life and languages. As we shall see, it is likely that other pastoralists and semi-pastoralists moved further south and east, influencing the whole population of south-east and south-west Africa.

South of the Ukhahlamba

Only three sites so far testify to the existence of a Later Iron Age south of the Drakensberg. This territory is now occupied by Nguni-speakers, whose way of life is more centred on cattle than among the Sotho-Tswana; their settlements are much smaller and less nuclear and their culture differs also in other ways from that of the Sotho-Tswana.

Blackburn, near Umhlanga lagoon, some 15 km north of Durban, has been excavated. It consisted of a village with a dozen or so houses, two of which were dug up.[25] Built on a circular plan, with a diameter of *c.* 5.5 m, the structures appear to have been beehive-shaped and supported internally by one or more central posts. The frame was probably made of twigs and the whole covered with thatch. In this they closely resemble both Nguni architecture and Khoikhoi buildings. The size of the village also corresponds with known Nguni and Khoikhoi practice. The site contained a few scraps of iron. Food remains included game bones, shellfish and a few fish bones. The site could then be just as well ascribed to the ancestors of the Khoikhoi or even coastal fishermen as it could be a Nguni site. Since the Nguni, like the Sotho-Tswana, are well known for their taboo on the eating of fish, the evidence means either that the taboo developed after the eleventh century or that the site belonged to coastal, Khoisan-speaking hunters. The pottery, known as NC 2 ware, bears a vague resemblance to Thembu (Nguni) pottery. More to the point, the same ware has also been found in a large area of the ruins near the Vaal; thus a connection may have existed between the populations of these two regions. All of this certainly provides food for thought, but cannot easily be accounted for at this time, especially in view of the dearth of other sites. Inskeep therefore wisely refuses to speculate further in this connection.[26]

The site at Moor Park near Estcourt dates back to the thirteenth or fourteenth century. It is located on a promontory and surrounded by a wall which encloses not only the houses, but also clearings and terraces. The settlement was obviously located in a strong defensive position. The remains of the houses seem to indicate a rectangular floor plan. If that is correct, it is unique in the whole of southern Africa. The inhabitants used iron, cultivated sorghum, hunted game and herded cattle. The pottery has not yet been securely linked with other ware. Were it not for the

25. O. Davies, 1971.
26. Inskeep, op. cit., p. 145.

apparently rectangular floor plans, the site would conform more closely with the supposed economic activities of the ancestors of the Nguni than does the Umhlanga lagoon find.[27]

A last set of sites was found in 1978 near the Umngazi river mouth in the Transkei. These represent Early, Middle and Late Iron Age occupations. Evidence of iron smelting and a hut floor of baked clay resembling the floors of the high veld have also been found. No radiocarbon dating is reported and age is inferred from the types of sherds discovered. Confirmation of an early date for the hut floor and the smelting could well have revolutionary implications for our understanding both of the links between the societies north and south of the Drakensberg and of the time when the presumed ancestors of the Nguni settled this far south.[28]

At present our earliest information about the Nguni comes from survivors of shipwrecks along the Natal and Cape coasts in the sixteenth century.[29] Information gathered from oral traditions indicates that the Transkei was inhabited by Xhosa organized in small and unstable chiefdoms by the sixteenth century at the latest. Before that, the ruling families had lived for generations on the upper reaches of the Mzimvabu river, specifically near the now unknown Dedesi stream. Wilson has argued from comparative evidence that they had lived there since at least *c.* 1300.[30] But that does not represent a definite date, only an order of magnitude. Certainly by 1500 the Nguni had occupied almost the whole territory in which they were living in 1800, although in the western parts they were mixed with the Khoikhoi, whom they were gradually to assimilate.

The Khoikhoi have left a deep imprint on both the eastern and the western Nguni languages. Lanham maintains that this influence started only after the Xhosa and Zulu language clusters began to separate.[31] This would be late, because just before 1600 a sailor, shipwrecked on the coast, claimed that the languages were merely dialects on a single continuum, and he had followed practically the whole coast.[32] Khoikhoi influences were very strong on both Zulu and Xhosa, amounting to about 14 per cent and 20 per cent of the vocabulary respectively. Khoikhoi influence transformed the Xhosa phonemic system, which means that these influences existed when the Xhosa began to differentiate themselves from

27. O. Davies, 1974.
28. Matiyela, 1979.
29. M. Wilson, 1969b, gives a summary, pp. 78–95.
30. M. Wilson suggests that the date was 'within the period covered by the genealogies, i.e. since 1300, and it may well have been centuries before that' (1959b, p. 178). The substance of the argument is repeated in Wilson, 1969b, but without mentioning the date. However, a date of 1686 for the rule of Togu, a Xhosa chief, has served as a basis for most calculations (as in Wilson, 1969b, p. 95), but it remains an uncertain estimate. See also J. B. Peires, 1973; and G. Harinck, 1969, pp. 154 and 155 n. 30.
31. L. W. Lanham, 1964.
32. Wilson, 1969a, on the Santo Alberto wreck of March 1593.

the eastern Nguni. The Khoikhoi must have occupied tracts of land deep into Natal, so that even the eastern Nguni tongues were affected.[33]

The Nguni became semi-pastoralists, preferring the breeding of cattle to agriculture, certainly as a result of Khoikhoi influence. But their cattle were not directly acquired from the Khoikhoi, since the latter tended to keep Afrikander cattle, and the Nguni the Sanga breed, which is also common north of the Drakensberg. Khoikhoi behaviour was strongly influential in matters of breeding, and milking was learned from them, as the vocabulary loans indicate. From them the Xhosa leaders also learned to ride and to use pack oxen.[34] The Khoikhoi also influenced the Xhosa in religious matters, which Lanham takes as a proof that they used to live in Nguni lands, a presence further attested in the western border regions by the survival of Khoikhoi place-names. Other indications of Khoikhoi influence can perhaps be found in the pattern of residence, and certainly in the practice of lopping off a portion of the little finger.

Physically the Nguni today represent a cross between 'Negro' and 'Khoisan'.[35] The cross is very pronounced among the Xhosa, who seem to derive 60 per cent of their genes from Khoisan stock. But that is also true of the Tswana. The eastern Nguni reach less high percentages, but the relationship still remains very strong. This is not unexpected as far as the western Nguni are concerned, or even the Tswana, as their interaction with hunters and Khoikhoi is well documented; but it is amazing to find such strong evidence for intermixture with the eastern Nguni.

Taking the linguistic evidence (which points to Khoikhoi) and the biological evidence (which could be due to hunters or Khoikhoi) together, one must reach the conclusion either that at one time many Khoikhoi lived in Natal, or that Nguni and Khoikhoi strongly interacted even before the Nguni settled in Natal; the latter seems less likely, since in that case the common share of Khoikhoi words in both eastern and western Nguni would have been higher. The moral of this story is that the Khoikhoi played a more important role than historians have allowed for up to now. As we shall now see, their influence was not restricted to the Nguni, but extended over huge portions of South Africa and Namibia.

The Khoikhoi

In 1488 Bartolemew Dias discovered the Cape of Good Hope; he visited and saw Africans, with whom he made contact. At the end of 1497, during an expedition by Vasco da Gama, contact was made with Africans north of the Cape of St Helena Bay and also at Mossel Bay. In 1510, the Viceroy of India, Dom Francis de Almeida, was killed together with sixty Portuguese soldiers at Table Bay; the skirmish pitted the Khoikhoi against

33. Lanham, op. cit.; Harinck, op. cit., pp. 150–3.
34. Wilson, 1969b, pp. 96, 103–5 and 107–9.
35. Hiernaux, op. cit., pp. 107–10.

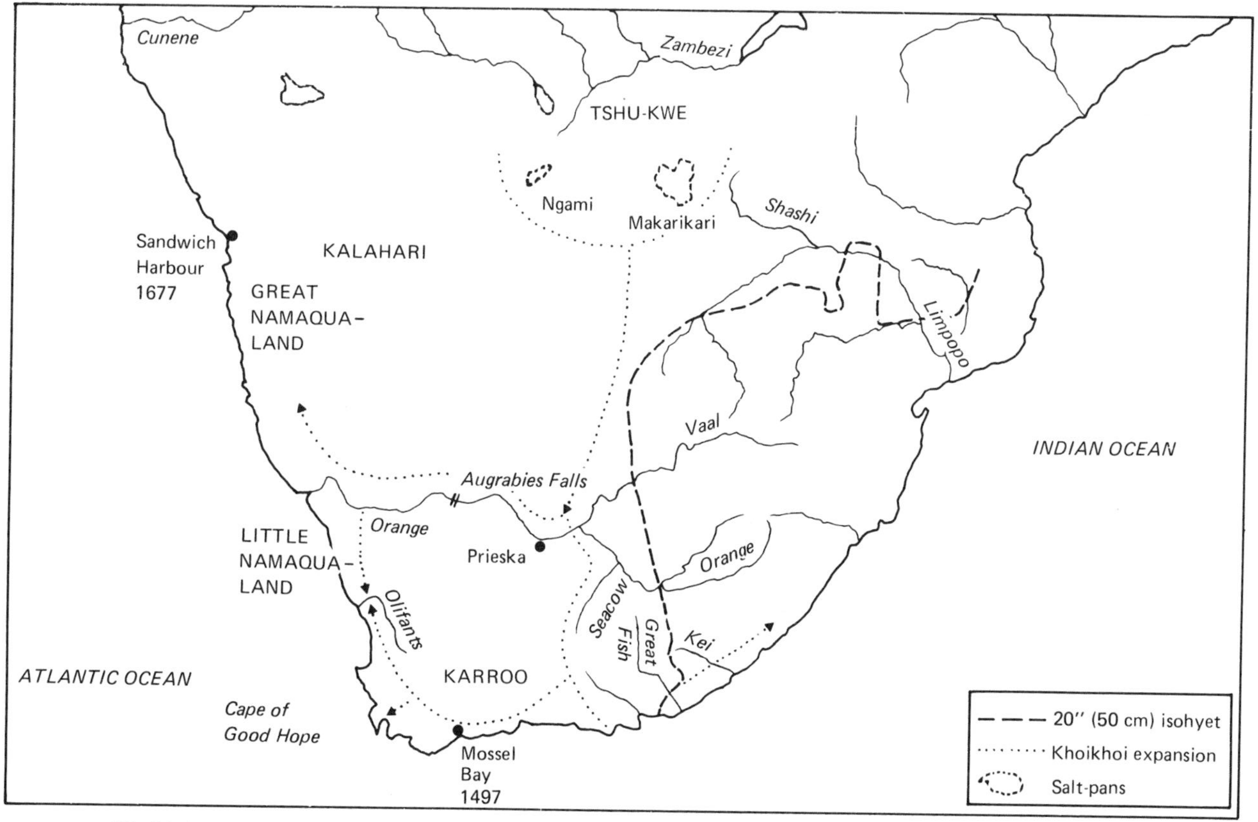

FIG. 23.2 *Khoikhoi expansion (J. Vansina)*

the Portuguese.[36] This proves that they were well enough organized to wipe out a Portuguese column which had guns. A century and a half later, the Khoikhoi confronted would-be Dutch settlers at the Cape. This began a long war of extermination.

More recently it has become quite evident that linguistically they belong to the Tshu-Kwe group of the Khoisan family of languages. This also includes a number of languages spoken on the southern coast of Angola.[37] In effect a single Khoikhoi language, divided into two or three dialects, was spoken over a territory which, in later times, spanned the area from northern Namibia to the Cape and then east to the River Fish. Moreover, as the influence of their speech on the Nguni shows, it must once have been widely spoken in Natal as well. Elphick notes that this makes Khoikhoi one of the most widely diffused tongues in Africa; and the linguistic homogeneity of this group points to a relatively recent and swift dispersal from the Tshu-Kwe homeland. The Khoikhoi pastoralists kept cattle and fat-tailed sheep, rode cattle and used oxen to pack their belongings and poles for their houses. This gave them a high degree of mobility, a characteristic that fits nicely with the dispersion of their language. Despite notable differences from the hunters, their physical characteristics also fit in the 'Khoisan' group.[38] Most of the differences are to be attributed to the effects of a different diet (milk), although others, such as the serological peculiarities, are not so easily explained. Despite divergence on these points of detail, all physical anthropologists now accept that the Khoikhoi and the hunters form one somatic whole. This reinforces the conclusions drawn from linguistics. The Khoikhoi belong to the South African hunting populations and are not derived from any other part of the continent.

Khoikhoi were present in the southern Cape by 1488. But they had not been there for very long, as is evident from the low population density of the Cape Khoikhoi in the seventeenth century and their apparent absence from good pastures near the mountain range of the Central Cape Province at about the same time. This, plus the homogeneity of language over such vast distances, leads Elphick to reckon that they had not arrived at the Cape long before 1488, although at least a century must have elapsed before then to bring them from Botswana to the Cape.[39]

36. See E. Axelson, 1973a and 1973b.

37. E. O. Westphal, 1963; Köhler, op. cit., esp. pp. 305–7 (on the Hamitic theory) and 322–30 (on the Tshu-Kwe, called by him Khoe).

38. Elphick, op. cit., pp. 8–10; Hiernaux, op. cit., pp. 100, 103–7 and esp. 106–7.

39. Elphick, op. cit., pp. 12–13. No rock paintings of cattle exist in the western Cape or in Namibia. But then only five such paintings of sheep, which have been kept there since the beginning of the Christian era, have ever been discovered. More extensive research should make it possible to ascertain the date at which the Khoikhoi arrived in the extreme south of the region. In the seventeenth century, however, the Boers did not find it completely unpopulated.

The ancestors of the Khoikhoi acquired cattle in large numbers in northern Botswana, probably developed the Afrikander breed there, learnt to forge metals, but not to smelt them, and partially abandoned their hunting and gathering way of life. It is very tempting to propose that some of the sites found by Denbow in Botswana are remnants of early Khoikhoi settlements and not just camps left by Bantu-speakers. The controversial evidence from the physical remains of Bambadyanalo on the Limpopo also seems to point to people who were both at least semi-pastoralists and physically like the Khoikhoi in the eleventh century.[40] The decrease of population in Botswana after 1300 gives us a date for the dispersal not only of probable Bantu-speakers who went to the Vaal, but also for the beginning of Khoikhoi expansion (see Fig. 23.2).

The Khoikhoi expanded south and south-eastwards from the high veld, travelling along rivers wherever possible.[41] Once they reached the Vaal/Orange confluence, one section followed the Orange downstream and expanded into Namaqualand and Namibia, where they reached Sandwich Harbour before 1677. Another branch headed south along the rivers from the confluence, crossed the Sneeuwberge and split into two branches: one travelled eastwards and inland from the coast to Natal, the other went westwards to reach the superb pastures of the Cape area. An offshoot of this last group then trekked along the coast north to River Olifants and finally met some of their brethren from Namaqualand.[42]

Only one discordant point remains to be mentioned before this picture can be accepted: the evidence from Middledrift. This open-air occupation site on River Keiskamma dates from the eleventh century.[43] Domestic cattle were kept there, but the tools do not belong to the Iron Age. Only pottery fragments and stone tools have been found. If Middledrift is seen as a Khoikhoi site, the hypothesis outlined so far must be abandoned, because the date is so early, and also perhaps because of the technology involved. But there is no reason for accepting it as Khoikhoi, either, just because it does not fit our present ideas about the culture of Bantu-speakers. We may provisionally accept Middledrift as a site where hunters had acquired cattle, just as their brethren, a millennium before along the Cape coast, had perfected sheep-herding. The people of Middledrift were assimilated or swept away by the Khoikhoi.

The Khoikhoi expansion deeply affected the life of all the inhabitants of southernmost Africa. We have mentioned their impact on the Bantu-speakers of the eastern Cape and Natal. Usually we are told that the Nguni

40. Denbow, op. cit.; Elphick, op. cit., p. 11. For Bambadyanalo, cf. Fagan, op. cit., pp. 145–6.

41. Elphick, op. cit., pp. 18–19; in part based on the behaviour of the Korana along the River Riet and the archaeological material there, although its date is later than 1500. Cf. Inskeep, op. cit., pp. 145–6.

42. Elphick, op. cit., pp. 14–21.

43. R. M. Derricourt, 1973.

found no Khoikhoi in Natal and gradually pushed back or absorbed those they found in the eastern Cape. But the overall evidence tells a different story. The Khoikhoi met scattered farming settlements east of the Kei, but overran them to become the dominant power in the Transkei and perhaps even in parts of Natal. It took a century or perhaps two for the farming communities to reach a density, in the lowlands between the Drakensberg and the sea, high enough to shift the relative weight of the populations involved and the direction of absorption and dominance. This explains why the Xhosa adopted so many traits from the Khoikhoi and it does not contradict the emergence of Xhosa dominance during the sixteenth century.

To the west, the Khoikhoi were to affect the Herero in a different, but equally significant way. The Herero did not take to the Khoikhoi language, but borrowed their whole way of life as pastoralists from the Khoikhoi and probably part of their clan organization as well. On the whole, it seems that these speakers of western Bantu languages met the Khoikhoi in western Botswana, from which they too emigrated to Namibia, but to the north of the Khoikhoi. When this happened we cannot say, but a date before 1500 is not to be excluded.[44]

Politically, the Khoikhoi were divided into sets of clans and, when the cattle stock waxed, they formed larger political units, under the leadership of hereditary chiefs. Thus links of tribute between different chiefdoms were to be found on a large scale, at least by the seventeenth century, since all the Khoikhoi from the Cape to the Kei were involved in a single tribute system. But the political organization was founded on individual wealth, and the system of inheritance and marriage practices only partially kept the wealth of a family for the descendants. Moreover, despite the pronounced gap between rich and poor, reversals of fortune could occur, so that the rich could become poor in a generation and vice versa. The very poor could and did drop out of this way of life. They reverted to a hunting and gathering life, as happened among the *strandlopers* at the Cape. A coalition of poor people in one political unit could also attack a neighbouring unit to raid cattle and better their fortunes.

As long as stock was waxing, the political system grew stronger, but as soon as it was waning, either for lack of rain or because of an epidemic or a revival of thieving by poor cattle rustlers, tensions overrode the common ties, strife increased and the wealthier chiefs became the prime targets for thieves, reducing their wealth and their ability to lead their set of clans. So, although it is easy to see how the Khoikhoi could at first overawe the less mobile and less well-organized farmers, longer-run fluctuations of climate and cattle diseases – as well as the strong social

44. D. Birmingham and S. Marks, 1977, p. 607. The known Herero traditions have been summarized by H. Vedder, Eng. transl. 1938, pp. 131–53. He holds that the traditions indicate migration from northern Botswana and gives a tentative date, *c.* 1550 (pp. 151–3).

inequality among the Khoikhoi proper – worked in favour of the farmers, at least to the east of the Kei.[45]

The Khoikhoi affected the aboriginal hunters and sheep-herders and the hunters of the seashore even more strongly, because they all competed for the same resources to a greater degree than happened between farmers and herders. Between 1100 and 1500 the aborigines – all nomads and, in principle, all hunters – followed several avocations. Along the coast they had become almost sedentary and lived off the produce of the sea.[46] Along the shores of the western Cape and along the lower Orange river, between Augrabies Falls and Prieska, they herded flocks of fat-tailed sheep; in the interior, others mainly lived from hunting and the gathering of *veldkos*. In those centuries the driest areas of the Karroo, the sand of the Kalahari and the coldest uplands in the mountain ranges were probably uninhabited. In a few places to the east, as at Middledrift perhaps, a few hunters had even taken to keeping cattle.

With the arrival of the Khoikhoi, the sheep-herders and the possible cattle-herders lost their stock and reverted to hunting or became clients of the Khoikhoi. The coastal groups living on sour veld and on the beaches survived long enough to teach the most impoverished Khoikhoi how to become *strandlopers*, but eventually they too came under Khoikhoi dominance. Pastoralists and hunters competed in the interior with varying degrees of success and admixture. To the Khoisan the hunters were but 'robbers' (*san*) and the hunters no doubt viewed the herdsmen as illegal 'poachers', who were driving them from their best water supplies and from the choicest hunting grounds. In general, the larger scale of the Khoikhoi social organization gave them an edge over the small bands of their competitors. But when environmental conditions became ever so slightly more adverse, the hunters regained a measure of equality, as many herders were forced to turn more to hunting and some merged with existing hunting bands. Nevertheless, the Khoikhoi way of life was gradually gaining the upper hand. Khoikhoi had, by the seventeenth century, become the *lingua franca* for the whole western Cape, and that constitutes evidence of a form of cultural domination. Whatever the details, there can be little doubt but that the Khoikhoi expansion had transformed the lives of all the aboriginal hunting bands. No group in the nineteenth century or today can be considered as 'pristine' hunters, either north or south of the Kalahari Desert.

Conclusion

Perhaps the dominant fact in the period under consideration here was the Khoikhoi expansion into southernmost Africa. This was probably

45. For the socio-political structure, cf. Elphick, op. cit., pp. 23–68, and Harinck, op. cit., pp. 147–8.

46. Inskeep, op. cit., pp. 114–17.

caused by a climatic deterioration along the edge of the Kalahari in Botswana or by a major shift in the tsetse belts, if not both. Whatever the cause, by 1300 the regions of central and northern Botswana, where an original pastoral economy had been fashioned, were being abandoned. Some of the peoples there were not Khoikhoi, but Bantu-speakers. They and their cattle left as well.

In the region of Zimbabwe and in the high veld south of the Limpopo, cattle were absorbed into the farming economy and the immigrants, at least among the later Sotho-Tswana, came to power and began to set up chiefdoms north of the Drakensberg. Whether any of these migrants ever reached further south, we do not yet know. It is possible that the ancestors of the Nguni acquired more cattle than they had before, but that the number of immigrants remained limited. Whatever the cause, the Nguni were to develop an economy more strongly based on cattle-herding than that of the Sotho-Tswana. This was an adaptive innovation, induced by observing the way of life of those Khoikhoi who had successfully invaded their lands.

The historical record still remains very patchy. Even if all the hypotheses we put forward here are confirmed by future research, we still have not accounted for the development of a pastoral economy in northern Botswana itself, perhaps between 800 and 1300. Nor do we know to whom to attribute this evolution. Bantu-speakers were probably not responsible, because so many cattle-keeping terms in southern Africa are not of eastern Bantu origin. They could be of Khoisan origin, and one scholar traces them back to central Sudanese languages.[47] The evidence adduced to date for such a conclusion, however, remains far too slender. For this evidence must prove a huge, far-flung expansion of central Sudanese-speakers from an area in the north-east corner of Zaïre all the way to Botswana and Zimbabwe, an expansion that preceded that of the Bantu-speakers. We are rather inclined to think that the vocabulary is Tshu-Kwe in origin and that it was the ancestors of the Khoikhoi who, over five centuries, perfected a pastoral way of life. They had accepted cattle, but did not want to abandon their nomadic and hunting traditions.

47. C. Ehret, 1972 and 1973.

24 Madagascar and the neighbouring islands from the 12th to the 16th century

F. ESOAVELOMANDROSO

The essential constituents of the population of Madagascar were present by the end of the twelfth century, even though further waves of migration occurred until the sixteenth century. The settlement of Madagascar formed part of the vast framework of relations between South-East Asia and Africa, across the Indian Ocean. Recognizing the importance of this question, the International Scientific Committee for the drafting of a *General History of Africa* organized a meeting of experts in July 1974 at Port Louis (Mauritius) on 'Historical relations across the Indian Ocean'.[1] The problem concerning the peopling of Madagascar was the subject of a chapter in Volume III of the *General History of Africa*. Nevertheless, a number of questions still remain to be answered; among them, for example, the comparative contributions of Africans, Arabs, Indians and Indonesians to the population and culture of Madagascar are still being actively discussed by research workers.[2]

Rather than attempting in this chapter to present a definitive synthesis of the civilization and history of Madagascar between the twelfth and sixteenth centuries, an effort will be made to elucidate the slow and complex interaction, both ethnic and cultural, which finally produced, at the beginning of the sixteenth century, an original identity for the Great Island. It seems to be well established that after the twelfth century Madagascar welcomed more Arabs, Indonesians and Africans. In this connection, oral traditions of the Merina and Betsileo regions tell of wars which the kings, at the head of the newcomers, had to wage before they could oust the 'Vazimba' population and push them inland.[3] These traditions include

1. Unesco, 1980a.
2. See Volume III, Chapter 25; see also R. K. Kent, 1970 – an attempt, on the basis of linguistic analysis, to evaluate the African contribution politically as well as culturally.
3. On Imerina, see R. P. Callet (ed.), 1908. The Tantara, which form one of the most important collections of oral traditions in Merina country, were collected by Father Callet between 1868 and 1883 and give valuable information on the Merina people. A critical study of the Tantara has been carried out by A. Délivré, 1974. On the Betsileo region, see J. Rainihifina, 1975, and P. Ratsimbazafimahefa, 1971.

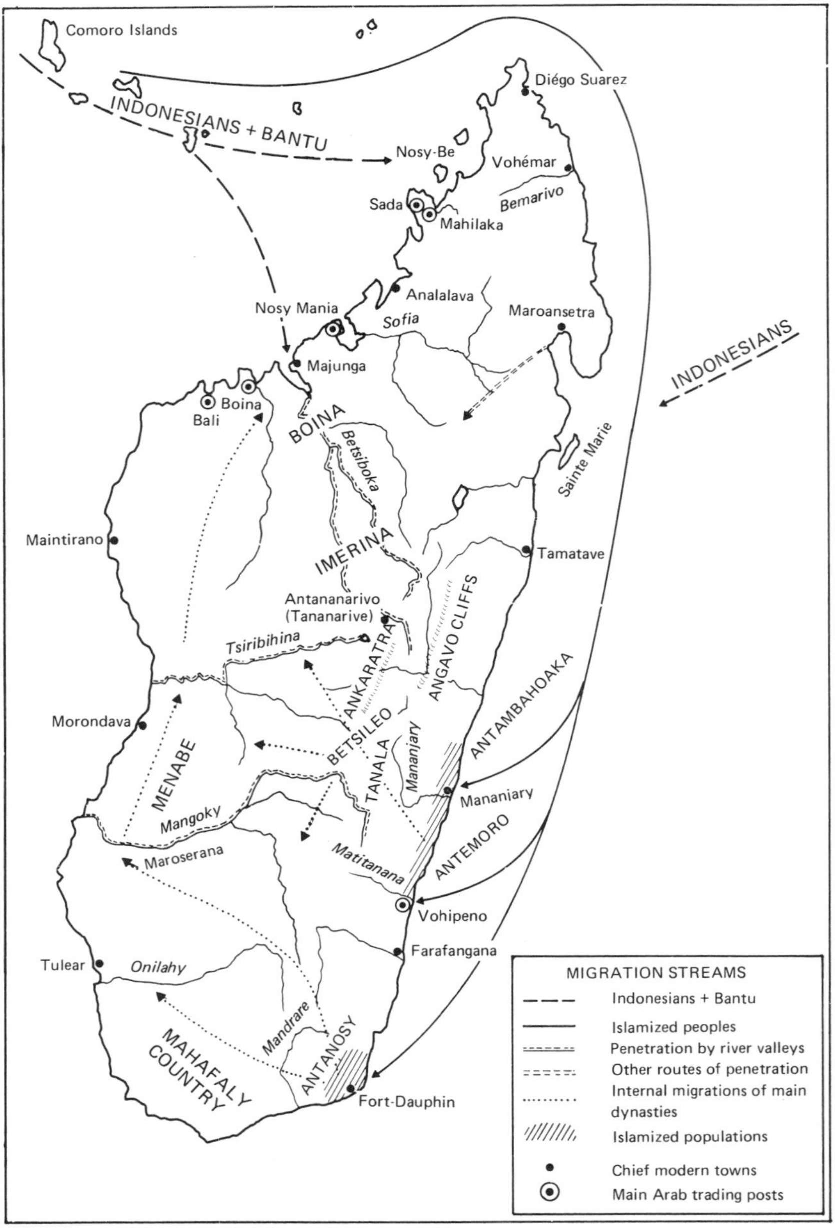

FIG. 24.1 *Madagascar: migration streams and peopling*

Source: F. Esoavelomandroso with the collaboration of T. Rajaona, using elements from the Atlas de Madagascar *by S. Ayache (pl. 20 and 20 bis) and the* Atlas du peuplement de Madagascar *by F. Ramiandrasoa*

Notes: The last migratory waves of Indonesians came between the 12th and 13th centuries. The Islamized peoples (Swahili and Arabs) had their main base in the Comoros from where they circumnavigated the island by the north

genealogical lists that may go back as early as the fourteenth century or even the thirteenth.

Nevertheless, a number of experts think that the neo-Indonesian migrations of the thirteenth and fourteenth centuries involved only the Merina; doubts have been expressed about the existence of the Vazimba, their enemies according to oral tradition. Some believe, in fact, that the word *vazimba* means 'ancestors' and does not therefore designate a people; the term would rather be a vague reference to the earlier, doubtless black, inhabitants of the central highlands who preceded the Indonesians.[4]

On the island's population, the *sorabe* carefully preserved by the Antemoro (a people of the south-eastern region) speak of the arrival and settlement of Arabs from Mecca.[5] These more recent migrations appear to have played a decisive role, both directly and indirectly, in the establishment of well-defined political structures, even though they found people already grouped in kingdoms. When did these latecomers arrive? A critical study is needed of the various written and oral traditions, particularly when they come from dynasties that have a natural tendency to insist on their antiquity.

From the fifteenth and the early sixteenth centuries, Portuguese sources describe the people and kingdoms of the island. They were well established when the Portuguese arrived, but there is still the problem of when they were created. Were they there before the twelfth century? How did they take shape? A number of theories exist and it must be admitted that the present state of knowledge and the lack of research in this area do not provide definitive answers.

Was it the blacks, probably the first occupants, who laid the foundations for the kingdoms or was it the immigrants from Indonesia who founded them? Muslim elements played an important role very early; in view of the extent and depth of Arab influence, the theory of an Arab or Muslim origin of the kingdoms has not been ruled out by some scholars, as will be seen.

The origins of the kingdoms of Madagascar

There was no Vazimba people; probably the traditions mentioning them are evidence of the prior existence of certain populations, which are difficult

4. Discussions about the 'Vazimba' take their point of departure from linguistic arguments; see G. Ferrand, 1891–1902. The ancient populations designated by this term do not appear to have had certain techniques (metal-working and cattle-raising, for example); see P. Boiteau, 1958. For the most recent study of the population of Madagascar, see C. Ravoajanahary in Unesco, 1980a.

5. The *sorabe*, which are manuscripts written in Arabic characters but in the Antemoro language, are a compilation of the traditions of the *katibo* (the scribes, guardians of tradition). These manuscripts are preserved in libraries in Britain, France and Norway. Cf. L. Munthe, 1977.

to identify. The traditions about the Vazimba simply serve as a starting-point, to indicate that the institution of royalty did not exist before the last waves of migrants. Betsileo regional traditions also tend in the same direction: the autochthonous populations had no king and nominated chiefs only in time of war.

Traditions and theories

Ottino believes that the people who came from Indonesia can be identified by cultural characteristics and not by a chronological time-scale according to the order of their arrival. According to this writer, some immigrants had a popular culture 'derived from Malay–Polynesian tradition', whereas others came from an aristocratic culture 'typical of Indonesian Hinduism regarding the separate roles of royalty and the state'. Dynastic festivals among the Merina are reminiscent in fact of those found in the Hindu regions of the Indonesian archipelago. Many traditions emphasize the recent character of this wave of immigrants, distinguishing them from earlier ones. Ottino places the arrival of this aristocracy in the twelfth century.[6]

According to this thesis, the aristocracy of Imerina is notable for its Hindu culture. Lombard, however, insists that 'the constitution of large scale political units in the south and west is a result of the arrival of Arabized groups'.[7] This theory of the 'Arab' origin of royal or monarchical institutions is supported by a number of authors, who all insist on the innovations brought by Muslims to the societies in the south-east, the only area where clan groups were known.

It should be noted that a number of different sources of influence may have existed simultaneously and that in any event we are confronting a biological as well as a cultural and political symbiosis. For example, Muslim influence can be found in the political institutions of the Merina, although it is difficult to ascertain when contacts took place between Andriana and the immigrants who settled in the south-east. Domenichini notes, rightly, that the African contribution must not be forgotten; he also points out that it is very wrong to link the origins of the kingdoms with the arrival of the Muslims; each region's institutions should be analysed. Only three of the fourteen royal *sampy* come from the south-east. Working from the oral traditions regarding the discovery of other *sampy* and from the very nature of these magic charms, the author concludes that 'the institution of the *sampy* preceded the diffusion of Muslim religion and culture in Madagascar, even though later this institution was subject to such influence'.[8]

In the west, Ottino says that the first kingdoms, 'of small geographical

6. P. Ottino, 1975.
7. J. Lombard, 1973.
8. J. P. Domenichini, 1971b.

extent and doubtless without any clearly defined notion of political succession', appeared before the arrival of the Maroserana. He links these 'pre-Sakalava' kingdoms with the first matrilineal Bantu immigrants, people who lived by agriculture, whereas the Sakalava kingdoms were founded by pastoral groups (patrilineal Bantu).[9] Caution should be exercised regarding these studies; they call, in particular, for research into the various components of a culture, which will throw light on the different contributions and the ways in which they combined. Everything indicates that the kingdoms appeared after the twelfth century; before that date there may have been strongly organized clans here and there that contained the nucleus of royalty. The kingdom may well be nothing more than the regrouping of these clans into larger and more strongly hierarchical units.

It is true none the less that Raminia, the founder of the Islamic kingdom of the south-east, and his descendants had great influence. According to Ottino, the founder of the kingdom must have come from south-west India. Studying the inter-related western dynasties (Maroserana, Andrevola), Fagereng attributes to them a common Indo-Arabic origin, adopting in part Grandidier's hypothesis, which Kent criticizes.[10] The traditions of these dynasties link them with foreigners who arrived at a late period in the southern part of the island and who later emigrated towards the west.

The tangle of internal migration is even more difficult to unravel. It appears that, once they had arrived, the newcomers moved around. Even if they maintained their ethnic identities, the melting-pot effect is obvious, as demonstrated by the cultural unity of the island.

The arrival of the Merina and the occupation of Imerina; birth of the Merina kingdom

The highlands are occupied today by the Merina, the Sihanaka, the Betsileo and the Bezanozano; some traditions say they all have the same origin, although the Merina form an inner aristocracy, whose ancestor Andriantomaza led the expedition which landed at the Bay of Antongil. From that point, the newcomers gradually won the central highlands.[11] Whether they came directly from South-East Asia to Madagascar or voyaged in stages via the African continent and the Comoro Islands, they seem to have come ashore at the Bay of Antongil.

The arrival of the last immigrants from Asia may be dated between the thirteenth and fifteenth centuries. It was probably at the end of this period that the newcomers, who may have come in a succession of small waves, spread through the island along a route punctuated by a number

9. Ottino, op. cit.
10. See E. Fagereng, 1971; Ottino, op. cit.; Kent, op. cit.
11. E. Ramilison, 1951–2.

of sites which have now been identified and studied. From Maroansetra, they went inland and came to a halt at the sources of the Varahina on the western edge of the Angavo escarpment. Vohidrazana to the north of Tamatave and Ambatomasina Vohidrazana of Noramanga were some of the staging points on this march.[12]

The accounts of Arab travellers of the thirteenth century, and even of Europeans in the sixteenth, confirm the hypothesis that Indonesian immigrants arrived on the east coast at a relatively late date.[13] The traditions of the Betsileo region also speak of immigrants led by the Iarivo, the founders of the local dynasties, who took the same route from the coast to the sources of the Mahatasiatra. This was a slow penetration, with no traces of a brutal or massive invasion, as the analysis of tradition shows clearly.

The newcomers did not start fighting the existing inhabitants as soon as they settled in the region. The *Tantara ny Andriana* start by referring to the long period during which the two communities lived side by side in Imerina. It was only after two reigns – from Andrianaponga to Andriamanelo – that the newcomers, according to tradition, unleashed a war upon their hosts. In so vast a region, which was probably largely covered by forest and sparsely populated, it was possible for scattered human groups to live for quite a long time in isolation without competing with each other, so long as none of them made any specific territorial or political demands. However, contact was gradually established and intermarriage occurred. Although the traditions clearly distinguish the Merina, the Betsileo and the Sihanaka from the Vazimba, other accounts continue without a break from a genealogy of so-called Vazimba kings to that of the Merina kings. Did the latter present themselves as the heirs and legitimate successors of the early kings? It is not impossible that the latest arrivals found a state framework with which they collaborated and which they then took over and re-formed. The later conflicts which broke out between the *tompon-tany* (masters of the land) and the newcomers were very bitter. According to a tradition quoted by Callet, Merina political ambitions were at stake, as they found it difficult to share the most favourable land with the original occupants and masters of the land.[14] The victor, King Andriamanelo, is said to have won because of the superiority of his soldiers' iron weapons, since the masters of the land did not know the use of this metal. An important question arises: how and when was iron introduced to Madagascar?[15] According to accepted theories, it was introduced before the end of the first millennium of the Christian era. The problem is that the latecomers credit themselves with this major invention.

12. A. Mille, 1970.
13. G. Ralaimihoatra, 1969 and 1971.
14. Callet, op. cit.
15. See Volume III, Chapter 25.

For my part, with regard to the Vazimba, I accept willingly the ingenious theory offered by Hébert.[16] According to this explanation, the Vazimba were merely the people of the interior with whom the latecomers (Merina) and also the Sakalava established joking relations, 'which assumes privileges of which not the least curious was the gratuitous insult (even today, *manazimba* means to insult)'.[17] Thus, Vazimba could mean a mixed group of black and Indonesian population who occupied the highlands before the Merina.

Most of the Merina and Betsileo traditions speak of the vanquished fleeing westwards as far as the Menabe region. After being driven out by the kings of the highlands, they settled in Sakalava country. The memory of this movement is still clearly recalled by their descendants. When questioned on their origins, the Mikea, a people living in the forest of southern Befandriana in the Tulear region, said that they were descended from the Vazimba, who had been driven out by the Merina kings.[18] However, the hypothesis that the autochthonous people fled, leaving behind only tombs that were both feared and venerated, cannot be accepted without question.[19] The fact that the Antehiroka clan, self-styled descendants of the Vazimba, still live in the Merina heartland to the west-north-west of Antananarivo disproves the theory that the original inhabitants were completely evicted. Although some of them left Imerina, Betsileo and Menabe – the Zafisoro, a people formerly living in the west, are said to have emigrated eastwards after the Sakalava conquest – the majority remained. It was indeed in the interests of the latest immigrants to come to an understanding with those groups which, on account of their earlier presence, were regarded as being *tompon-tany*. Marriage alliances increased in number and a *modus vivendi* was established between victors and vanquished. The former were thus assured of the support of the earlier inhabitants and the favours of the earth gods; the latter hoped to gain less rigorous treatment through their submission. In the west, 'the alliance between the immigrants and the *tompon-tany* group of the Andrambe gave

16. J. C. Hébert, 1958. Hébert links the words *Vazimba* and *ziva*, a term denoting a joking relative, and puts forward the hypothesis that there was a *fizivana*-type alliance between the 'masters of the soil' and the newcomers.

17. The theory is appealing. In West Africa, the joking relationship has an important role; it relaxes social tensions in many cases. In Senegal, Mali, Guinea and the Ivory Coast, the Mandingo and the Fulani have special feasts at which joking relations exchange gifts and insults in an atmosphere where barriers no longer exist between rich and poor, great and small. (Note by Volume Editor)

18. Survey conducted by the University Centre of Tulear in September 1974. Further information on the origins of these people is provided by earlier or later surveys. The Mikea regard themselves as refugees who fled the authority of the Maroserana, the royal dynasty of the colonizers. Cf. J. Dina and J. M. Hoerner, 1975.

19. According to a Betsileo tradition reported by Dubois, there is no trace of the Vazimba in the royal families or in those of their subjects. The Vazimba are all supposed to have withdrawn to the west. H. M. Dubois, 1938.

rise to the first historical figure in the Andriambolamena dynasty'. Thus the Menabe kingdom was set up by the Andrambe and a ritual was established whereby prayers were addressed to the king's ancestors by an official called *mpitoka*.[20]

Thus the newcomers – Merina, Betsileo and others – gradually became masters of the country and created kingdoms. These also reinforced the economic and cultural contribution of the Muslims, who are known to have frequented the Comoro Islands and Madagascar as early as the ninth century. It was particularly in the twelfth, thirteenth and fourteenth centuries that Arab or Muslim influence became very powerful in Madagascar and the surrounding islands, an influence that was at once political, economic and cultural.

The Islamic penetration of Madagascar and the Comoro Islands

Groups of Muslims from the east coast made regular visits to the Comoro Islands and Madagascar, following the rise of the trading settlements along the East African coast and the spread of Swahili seafaring culture.[21] A flow of trade between both sides of the Mozambique Channel was further consolidated by the fact that 'colonies' of Muslim converts settled in the Comoro archipelago and in some regions of Madagascar. In occupying islands that served as staging points between the Swahili settlements on the east coast of Africa and Madagascar, the Comorans were better able to preserve the cultural traditions of their region of origin. In Madagascar itself, however, the situation was less clear-cut. The south-eastern region of the island, furthest from the centres of Swahili civilization, was progressively integrated into the Malagasy tradition, while retaining some of its original characteristics. By contrast, the descendants of the Islamized groups who settled in the north-west of the island remained in close contact with their fellow Muslims who were trading with the Comoro Islands and the African settlements, and have maintained up to now their true original character, derived from their power, their ancestry and their traditions of seafaring.

Comoran and Malagasy traditions, moreover, speak of ancestors of Arab origin, compelled to leave their country of origin because of their religious convictions. The Antemoro *sorabe* recount the arrival of Ralitavaratra, the ancestor of the Antemoro-Anakara, in about the fifteenth century:[22] he is said to have been the custodian of sacred relics, bequeathed by Moses to

20. Lombard, op. cit., pp. 10–11.

21. According to Chittick, the coastal strip stretching from Mogadishu to Sofala began to come under Islamic influence only with the establishment of Muslim settlements in Pemba and Zanzibar in about the tenth century; in a good many towns people were still practising the traditional religions in the twelfth century. H. N. Chittick, 1967a.

22. The Antemoro-Anakara were a noble Antemoro caste whose powers were religious.

his family, and coveted by the Sultan of Mecca, 'Alī Tawarath, who had to seek refuge elsewhere with some thirty loyal retainers. After many adventures, they eventually found the 'promised land' on the banks of the River Matitanana. Other traditions preserved among the Antambahoaka and Antanosy in south-eastern Madagascar also speak of the arrival from Mecca of a common ancestor, Raminia.[23] A Comoran tradition recounts the arrival in Anjouan in about the fourteenth century of a group of Sunni Muslims who had been forced to leave Persia because of Zeidit domination.[24] These accounts clearly reflect the determination of the individuals concerned to attach themselves to the most celebrated sources of Islam in a bid to impose themselves and better establish their ascendancy both with Muslim and Arab credentials.[25]

Although the traditions insist on religious reasons for the migrations to the south, the attraction of the Comoro Islands and Madagascar was strong. More and more of the migrants were interested in trade with the Swahili world. Numerous factors – the study of Arab voyages in the western Indian Ocean, a knowledge of the East African trading settlements, the existence in the Comoro Islands and north-western Madagascar of cultural traditions very close to those of the Swahili world, and the discovery at sites in the north-east and south-east of the island of objects clearly demonstrating the existence of trade relations between this country and the African ports – all these make it necessary to approach in a different way the problem of the migrations of these Islamized peoples.

The staging post of the Swahili world

The cities and islands of the African seaboard stretching from Mogadishu to Sofala were the setting for intense commercial activity even before the Muslim settlements were established.[26] These ports, which became increasingly prosperous from the twelfth and thirteenth centuries onwards, looked seawards rather than towards the interior, and extended their influence well beyond the coast. The trading settlements acted as staging posts between Arabia – and perhaps even India – on the one hand, and Madagascar and the Comoro Islands on the other. Moreover, many of the Islamized immigrants arriving in the region were so imbued with Swahili culture that there can be no doubt that the African cities played a key role in the spread of Islam in the island.

However, although the written material does not provide much information, there are grounds for believing that the African influence was considerable. Archaeological research has shown that the cities of the coast were indeed founded by Africans, and not by Arabs. References to Muslim

23. E. de Flacourt, 1661.
24. C. Robineau, 1962.
25. This tendency to claim an Arab origin is found among almost all the Islamized dynasties of East Africa and the Sudan.
26. H. N. Chittick, 1974.

PLATE 24.1 (*above*) *View of Antongona (15th–18th century) taken from a late 19th-century engraving. The villa on top of the hill, surrounded by aviavy and amontana* (ficus) *trees, was the residence of the princes; the entrance is cut into the dry-stone fortifications*

PLATE 24.2 (*left*) *Antsoheribory, on the Bay of Boina: the architecture of this dressed coral entrance to an Antalaotse tomb shows the cultural similarities of the east coast of Africa*

influence have likewise to be qualified, since the Arabs were not necessarily involved. There is no reason not to acknowledge that long-standing relations existed between the black peoples of the island and those of the continent.

Trading posts

The trading posts of north-western Madagascar and the Comoro Islands had many features in common with the towns of the East African coast, as regards both their configuration and the life-style of their inhabitants. The ruins of ancient fortifications, the remains of mosques and the old houses with richly carved doorways which still exist in Anjouan all bear witness to a life deeply marked by Islam and by Arab civilization in the settlements of Mutsamudu, Wani, Domoni and Sima.[27] Despite their prejudices, the Portuguese have left interesting descriptions of life in the ports of north-western Madagascar in the early sixteenth century.

One of the most important settlements, Nosy Langany, was described thus: 'The population consisted of Muslims who were more civilized and wealthier than those living at other points along the coast, since their mosques and most of their houses were built of limestone, with balconies after the style of Kilwa and Mombasa.'[28] Remains of fortifications comparable to those on the east coast of Africa have been discovered at the Mahilaka site.[29] (Fig. 24.2 shows the plan of a fortified hill location in Imerina.) The deep bays which indent the north-west coastline of the island, such as Ampasindava, Mahajamba and Boina, were the sites of a number of trading settlements – Mahilaka, Sada, Nosy Langany, Nosy Boina, and so on – which maintained close relations with the Comoro Islands and Africa and formed part of the Swahili seafaring culture.

The dhows were loaded on the coast of Madagascar with rice and soapstone objects (funeral vessels, such as long-stemmed drinking cups, and three-legged cooking pots), which were made mainly in Iharana, on the north-west coast of the island.[30] The Malagasy trading stations imported Indian pearls, fabrics and Chinese ceramics – plates and bowls often found among burial possessions. These stations on the north-west coast were active in redistributing the goods imported, and the excavations at Rezoky and Asambalahy have brought to light artefacts that are characteristic of Swahili sites.[31] Despite European competition from the sixteenth century onwards, these Islamized settlements continued to go about their highly lucrative business.

27. P. Vérin, 1967a and 1967b.
28. Quoted by C. Poirier, 1954.
29. L. Millot, 1912; P. Vérin, 1972.
30. E. Vernier and J. Millot, 1971.
31. P. Vérin, 1980.

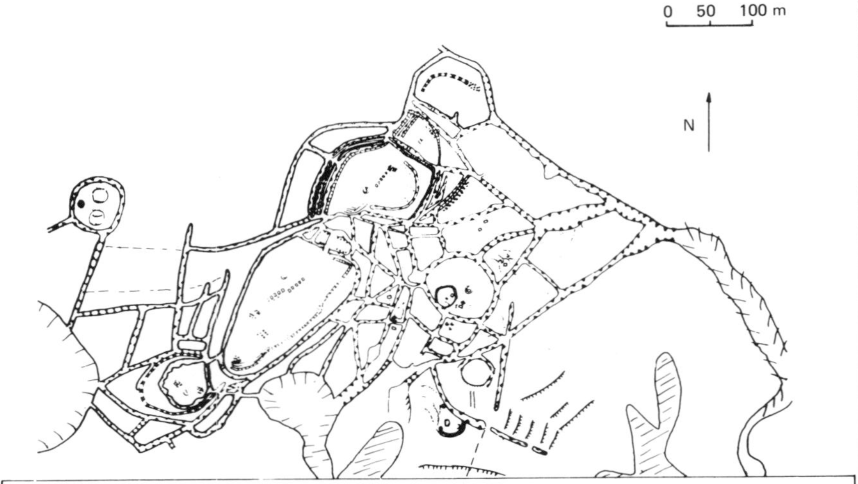

Complex network of fortifications (moats sometimes reinforced with dry-stone walls) of a hill site dating from *c.* fifteenth century.

FIG. 24.2 *Ambohitrikanjaka, Imerina (J. P. Domenichini and D. Rasamuel)*

The peopling of the Comoro Islands and the Antalaotse group

Although the Comoros, and the island of Anjouan in particular, probably received Indonesian and Bantu immigrants, these were swamped by successive waves of Islamized settlers from the east coast of Africa. Following the classic pattern, the newcomers imposed their rule by force and claimed that they were the defenders of the true faith in a land where 'believers remote from the sources of Islam had tended to become lax in their religious observances'.[32] While striving to establish political domination over the original settlers, the newcomers gave a fresh impetus to religious life.[33]

The Islamized settlements in north-western Madagascar formed the Antalaotse group. This group was economically dominant and represented a powerful commercial bourgeoisie that was organized in true city-states, headed by chiefs whose functions were both political and religious.[34]

Malagasy civilization from the twelfth to the sixteenth century

We must begin by saying that we know very little about the Vazimba epoch except for the oral accounts of those who drove back the first settlers

32. Robineau, op. cit.

33. By building mosques, for example. This was true of the 'Shirazian', Hassani Ben Muḥammad, who built the Sima mosque in the fifteenth century.

34. The city-states were modelled on those on the East African coast, which were symbols of Swahili maritime culture. Cf. M. Mollat, 1980.

and laid the foundations of the kingdoms. Much may be expected from the archaeologists, whose work is only just beginning; systematic excavation projects under the aegis of the Museum and Centre of Art and Archaeology of the University of Antananarivo are getting under way. Important work is in progress in Androy.[35] The reader should refer to Volume III of the *General History of Africa*, in which the first settlement of Madagascar and the culture found there by later immigrants in the twelfth century is discussed.

Between the twelfth and the fifteenth centuries, as newcomers arrived on the island, they were integrated into existing groupings or organized themselves following autochthonous models. The interaction between African and Asian ethnic groups followed a procedure which eludes us; on the other hand, written documents show Swahili Muslims settling in the Comoro Islands and Madagascar and still keeping their contacts with the Swahili coast.

Material culture

Field research by archaeologists shows that agriculture existed before the period under discussion. After the twelfth century, the cultivation of rice, yams, bananas and cocoa spread through the island. Domestic animals – cattle and poultry – were of African origin. It would be hazardous to try to discern extensive social distinctions at this time.[36] As Madagascar became more populated, villages multiplied and clans took shape. Fishing was very important and the outrigger canoe gave the islanders mastery of the sea. Rice growing was important and furnished the staple food.

The material culture of the southern and western regions and a part of the north seems to have been predominantly African. According to Ravoajanahary, paddy-rice growing is an Indonesian technique, whereas the raising of zebu cattle and the growing of yams is typically African.[37] This author shows that it was the last arrivals of the fourteenth century who introduced political and ritual models which, from the fifteenth century onwards, favoured the formation of the first Malagasy kingdoms, initially in the south-east, but then on parallel lines in the south, the west and the highlands. We may suppose that the basic structures were in existence by the fifteenth century: families were grouped in clans, and clans in more or less independent villages.

Archaeological research has brought to light numerous examples of pottery (see Plate 24.3), but no worthwhile conclusions can be deduced from them; at best, one can define the types of ceramics which are related

35. G. Heurtebize and P. Vérin, 1974; see also J. P. Domenichini, 1979a, and T. Wright, 1977.
36. P. Boiteau, 1974.
37. C. Ravoajanahary, 1980, pp. 91–2.

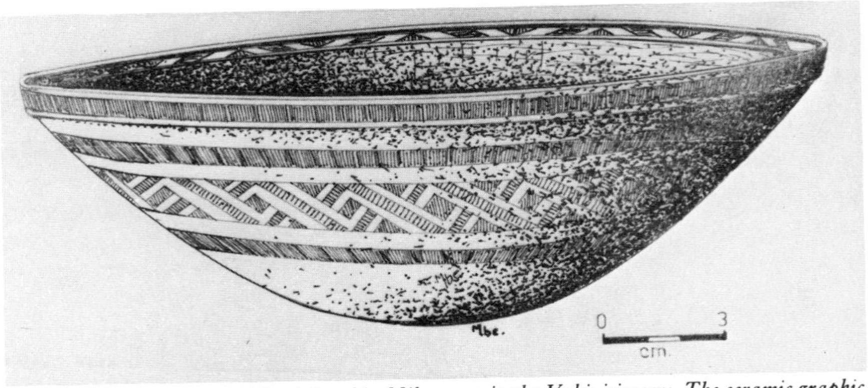

PLATE 24.3 *Reconstructed bowl found in Milangana in the Vakinisisaony. The ceramic graphic is typical of the products of Imerina in the 15th century*

to Indonesia and others in the African style. Numerous radiocarbon datings will have to be made in order to fill the gaps in our knowledge.[38]

Royalty and its institutions

From the clan to the kingdom

Clans organized around chiefs or patriarchs seem to have taken shape very early. Terms such as *foko*, *troki* or *firazana* designate the clan's principal characteristics: a shared community (*foko* = community) and a common ancestry for the members (*firazana*=ancestry and *troki*=maternal breast). The clan is the basic unit of the kingdom just as it, in turn, depends on the villages or the farmland. Most traditions emphasize the struggles between clans during the formation of the kingdoms. Within the clan, authority is vested in the elders, whose spokesman is the patriarch, the oldest man. Culture and religious rites are the mortar that binds the clan, in addition to linguistic unity.

The first kingdoms and their evolution

Although the Arab origin of the princes who, in the Comoro Islands, superseded the *fani* – the first Islamic chiefs who had originally succeeded the *beja* of pre-Islamic times – does not appear to present any problem, the conquering Malagasy dynasties pose several. Many traditions speak of the kinship links existing between the dynasties of the west and south (the Maroserana, Sakalava and Mahafaly, and the Zafimanara of the Androy region) and those of the south-east (the Zafiraminia of the Anosy region). The area in which the Arabized groups were settled appears to have

38. Vérin, 1980, p. 116.

been the cradle of a large number of Malagasy dynasties. Tradition recalls the memory of east–west migration, on the one hand from Antemoro country (the Tanala Zafiramba) and from the Anosy region (the Maroserana) on the other. The route taken by the future sovereigns of the Menabe followed the River Itomampy, passed to the north of the Onilahy, and crossed the Fiherenana and the Mangoky before reaching Bengy.[39]

Let us then try to see what would constitute, in the monarchical context, an exclusively African or Indonesian heritage – in so far as the institutions of royalty can be said to have partly resulted from the dynamic character of the first societies – and what would enable us to define more clearly the part played by Arabs and Muslims in the formation of the Malagasy kingdoms. The study of the African aspects of Malagasy culture has thus prompted historians to look to the mainland for the origins of certain basic institutions, such as the cult surrounding the relics of dead kings (the cult of the *dady* in Sakalava country). Kent sees a similarity between the famous empire of Monomotapa and the kingdom of the Maroserana Volamena, although he does not conclude that the latter were African in origin. After severely criticizing the 'myth of the white kings' of Asian origin propounded by Grandidier, Kent puts forward the hypothesis that the Andriana Merina were of very mixed origin. In his view, they descended from the *tompon-tany*, from new immigrants of unknown origin, and perhaps even from Arabized Zafiraminia.[40] The political institutions are accordingly derived from a synthesis of African, Asian and Muslim influences, enriched by the Islamic contribution of unknown latecomers.

Political institutions reflect various influences. Most authors are agreed today in bringing to light the important role played by the Arabs in the political and social history of Madagascar. Written texts make it clear that in the fourteenth century new conceptions were introduced with regard to political power, particularly in the division of the kingdom into 'homogeneous territorial units'. We have ourselves seen the importance assigned by tradition to the dynasties of Zafiraminia, which are of Arab–Indian origin, and the importance of other Temoro groups, including certain elements that came directly from Mecca – the Antanpansemac ('people of the sands of Mecca').[41] On this question, much more work has to be done in order to understand better the establishment of power in Madagascar; what is certain is that these royal dynasties became strong in the fifteenth century, with a marked Islamic influence.

Religion

This represents a marriage of African and Indonesian elements, together with the Islamic influences which remained dominant, especially in the

39. Lombard, op. cit.
40. Kent, op. cit.
41. de Flacourt, op. cit.

Comoro Islands. It is often difficult to separate the different groups of migrants, but what is important is the symbiosis that makes Madagascar unique.

Gods

In the Malagasy pantheon, first place is reserved to the principal god from Indonesia: Zanahary or Andriananahary in the coastal regions, Andriananitra (perfumed lord) in the interior. He is the most powerful divinity; he created the world, formed society and bestowed customs. He is the first god invoked in prayers, but he is too distant. To reach him, men seek the intercession of secondary gods or *djinn*s – of the waters or of the forest. The spirit of the ancestors is also invoked: prayers are addressed to the Vazimba, masters of the land. Forests, rocks, great trees, all can be places of worship.

Offerings

Sacrifices were offered to the gods; the sacrifice of a buffalo was very common, but less so than that of a cow, which was practised everywhere and in various events of life.[42]

Sorcerers

In talking of beliefs, the sorcerer must be mentioned; he was greatly feared in society. It is difficult to decide whether the sorcerer is of Asian or African origin; the name given him, *inpamosary*, is Asian, but sorcerers with the same characteristics as in Madagascar can be found in Africa.

Funerals

In Madagascar, there are double funerals, as in Indonesia. Among the Betsileo, the pallbearers dance as if possessed, moving in zigzag fashion towards the tomb.

All these elements probably date back to this period of synthesis between the twelfth and sixteenth centuries.

Conclusion

Much remains to be done if we are to understand better this period in the history of the Great Island, a period that was essential for the formation of a Malagasy people who enjoy an undeniable linguistic unity, yet who still pose problems. We are grateful to Unesco for having organized the meeting in Mauritius, which stimulated interest in the general question of historic relations across the Indian Ocean. Madagascar is so

42. What is the origin of the sacrifice of a cow? It is thought that the blacks introduced cattle into the island. It is a practice which goes far back into the past.

closely involved that its culture and its history will be elucidated only as we deepen our understanding of these relations. Archaeological research and the collection of oral traditions, on a more diversified but also a systematic regional basis, will help us to comprehend the many different elements which make up Malagasy culture.

The present study inevitably has a number of gaps. Obscure areas still remain and certain *fady* (taboos) will have to be lifted, in particular those relating to the famous tombs of the Vazimba. Madagascar provides an example of symbiosis, the study of which is even more interesting than the history of Africa. Arabia, India, Africa and Indonesia have all come together on this island, which offers to the world a striking example of biological and cultural intermixture, and whose offspring are so handsome.

25 Relationships and exchanges among the different regions

D. T. NIANE

Between 1100 and 1500 Africa was a privileged partner in inter-continental relations with the Old World. Across both the Mediterranean Sea and the Indian Ocean, Europe and Asia were linked with Africa by an active trade, usually conducted by Muslims. It must be emphasized that various types of organized trade within the continent are known to have been carried on since prehistoric times. As will be seen in this chapter, research is gradually providing more and more precise detail, especially on the scale of these inter-regional exchanges. However, with the present state of knowledge, it is still impossible to give an exhaustive account of relations between the different regions of Africa from the twelfth to the sixteenth century.

It would appear that the economic and commercial expansion of Africa was in full spate in the fourteenth and fifteenth centuries; but the contacts with the West which were opened up by the slave trade meant the breaking off of a lively start which, if trade had developed in other merchandise, might have changed the course of African history. Great currents of cultural exchange crossed the continent in every direction, sometimes mingling with the cross-currents of trade. There were no isolated regions, for neither deserts nor forest presented impassable barriers any longer. Today, archaeological excavations and the study of African languages and oral traditions are opening new vistas for historical research, and this is already shedding light on the problem of migrations, transfers of technology, and trade relations between widely separated regions.

The role of Islam, both in the spread of ideas and in trade, was of paramount importance at this time, as illustrated by Ibn Baṭṭūṭa's travels in China and in East and West Africa. In the period under consideration, the works of Arab geographers, travellers and historians make an appreciable contribution to our knowledge of the peoples concerned.

The Sahara and the Sahel: a privileged space in external relations

Until the middle of this century, European historians have sought to explain the present technological backwardness of Africa by the existence of the

Sahara which, they claim, cut off black Africa from the Mediterranean world. In actual fact, the Sahara, even when it became a desert, has never acted as a barrier. In the first place, the Sahara was not uninhabited. It was the home of nomads, who maintained very close relations with the sedentary peoples to the north and south. There is no doubt that between 1100 and 1500 the Sahara served as a privileged thoroughfare and this can be said to have been the golden age of trans-Saharan trade. From the tenth century, West Africa's gold trade with North Africa developed rapidly. The Sahara has been rightly compared to a sea, with the Sudanese Sahel and the southern fringes of North Africa as its shores. In the south, Tichit, Walata, Timbuktu, Tirekka and Gao were the major termini for caravans from Tamdult, Sijilmasa, Tlemcen, Wargla and Ghadames. Only the dromedary could be used to cross the desert, a journey which took at least two months. This explains the importance of the great pastures to the north and south of the Sahara, reserved for feeding and rearing dromedaries, as well as the sometimes violent disputes between the nomads for control of these fields.

Both north and south of the desert, trans-Saharan commerce extended much further than the 'ports' mentioned; the Tuat and the Ghura, the Tunisian Djerid and the Libyan oases were just as important as the 'ports' themselves in the trans-Saharan trade. From the Sahel to the forest savannah, tracks and waterways completed the trans-Saharan system. That is certainly true of present-day Senegal, where we are already well acquainted with the system within the upper Niger basin.[1] Recent research in Upper Volta, Ghana and Nigeria suggests that trade had developed between Africa south of the Sahara and the Maghrib. The area in question lies in the savannah and there is much archaeological evidence that it was well frequented.[2] In the north of modern Nigeria these trade routes certainly crossed those from Chad, which will be discussed later.

The nomads, masters of the desert, profited greatly from the trans-Saharan trade, for the caravans brought them grain and cloth in exchange for meat, salt and water. The nomads and the sedentary peoples thus complemented each other. In the immensity of the Sahara, caravans needed guides and these were provided by the nomads, who knew the crossing routes and were paid a golden price. The crossing of the Sahara had to be prepared in minute detail; the camels were fattened up during long

1. Polish and Dutch archaeologists think they have found an important indication of movements of people and of trade in the upper Niger (where Niani was situated) as far as Dogon country, in the occurrence of pottery so similar that the connection is indisputable. The question remains, in which direction did the pottery travel?

2. See M. Posnansky, 1974, and A. A. Boahen, 1974. The Akan come from the region between the Benue and Lake Chad, demonstrating clearly that the movements between the north and the forest regions of the south were no myth; by linguistic and toponymic analysis, migration patterns and trade routes can be deciphered. Cf. T. Shaw, 1970, Vol. 2, pp. 280–7.

weeks. In order to reach the Sudan, Ibn Baṭṭūṭa went to Sijilmasa, an assembly-point for those leaving Morocco, and noted: 'In this city I purchased camels that I fed on forage for four months.'[3] The caravan was placed under the authority of a chief who was in command of everyone, like a ship's captain. Once the caravan moved off, no one was to lag behind or to advance too quickly, still less to stray from the group, lest he should lose his way in the immense desert.

Nomads such as the Messufa specialized in trans-Saharan trade and provided guides and messengers for the caravans. Let us follow the caravan that took Ibn Baṭṭūṭa to Niani (Malli), the capital of the empire of the mansas. After 25 days of travelling, the caravan arrived at Teghazza, an important Saharan salt-mine. There, men and animals rested and built up their strength again. After ten days the caravan set off again towards Walata. Ten days out of Walata, the caravan dispatched a messenger to that city. The messenger carried letters addressed to correspondents 'that they may rent houses to them and come to meet them with a provision of water at a distance of four days' travel'.[4] The messenger was very highly paid – 100 *mithḳāl*, according to Ibn Baṭṭūṭa. The caravan was doomed, if the messenger did not make it to Walata, but that seldom happened as the Messufa knew the desert well. In 1964, Theodore Monod discovered a large quantity of cowries, copper bars and scraps of cloth, buried in the sand in Mauritania; this may well have been the merchandise of a caravan that came to grief in the desert.[5]

Ibn Baṭṭūṭa arrived in Walata, the first city of Mali, after two months of travelling. A governor, representing the emperor of Mali, lived there and the caravan had to observe customs formalities at this stage. Walata was also a trading centre where black African and Berber Arab merchants met. This would account for Ibn Baṭṭūṭa's long stay in that city, some 51 days. From Walata, after 24 days, the traveller reached 'Malli' (Niani), capital of the mansas. The routes were safe and within the limits of the empire it was possible to travel alone without fear of thieves or brigands.

The traveller on the roads of the ancient world greatly appreciated this security. So long as a strong authority reigned in the Sudan, the nomads were content to turn to account the services they could render the caravans. When that authority weakened, bringing about the ruin of the towns, the nomads left the desert and came to prowl around the cities.

The gold trade

In the tenth century the king of Ghana was, in the eyes of Ibn Hawḳal, 'the richest sovereign on earth ... he possesses great wealth and reserves of gold that have been extracted since early times to the advantage of

3. Ibn Baṭṭūṭa, from the French transl., in J. Cuoq, 1975, pp. 292–3.
4. ibid.
5. Radiocarbon dating gives the year 1165 ± 110 (that is between + 1055 and + 1275).

former kings and his own'. In the Sudan it was a long-standing tradition to hoard gold, whereas in Ghana the king held a monopoly over the nuggets of gold found in the mines: 'If gold nuggets are discovered in the country's mines, the king reserves them for himself and leaves the gold dust for his subjects. If he did not do this, gold would become very plentiful and would fall in value ... The king is said to possess a nugget as big as a large stone.'[6]

However, the Sudanese always kept the Arabs in the most complete ignorance regarding the location of the gold-mines and how they were worked. Mansa Mūsā himself did not offer much enlightenment to the inhabitants of Cairo, who questioned him on his fabulous empire; he did not lie, but he hid the truth among many different explanations. This would explain how the king maintained his reputation of extraordinary wealth. A generation after his pilgrimage, the mansa appears holding his gold nugget in the famous Majorcan atlas made for Charles V of France. The Majorcans could only have known of this from the Muslims. It is virtually established now that, in addition to the known locations of Galam, Bowe and Bambuk, gold from the pre-forest and forest regions – present-day Ivory Coast, Ghana and Nigeria – fed the northern trade at that time. Mali's gold trade is known to have been very important in the Middle Ages, but it would be hazardous to put forward estimates of the quantity of gold exported. The bounty of the mansas gives grounds for thinking that the amount of gold accumulated was considerable. In the Sudan, gold was considered 'sacred', or at least endowed with mysterious power. In traditional thought, only the king could master the 'spirit' of gold. The same view prevailed in the southern forest regions, where the chiefdoms were also extremely rich in gold.

Salt and other merchandise

Salt held a dominant position in the trans-Saharan trade, as in other regions of Africa. Successive rulers in West Africa constantly tried to lower its price.[7] Customs officials rigorously controlled salt imports and exports. The mines of Teghazza supplied salt for the western Sudan; the Senegal river region obtained rock-salt from Aouli, but its distribution scarcely went further than the Niger Bend in the interior.

Salt taxes accounted for a large part of crown revenues. Things were still much the same in the fourteenth century. Ibn Baṭṭūṭa, who visited Teghazza, tells us with great exactness: 'The Sudanese come all the way here [to Teghazza] to replenish their salt supplies. The load comes from Iwalatan [Walata] at a price of 8–10 *mithḳāl* and is sold in the city of

6. Ibn Hawḳal, from the French transl., in Cuoq, op. cit., p. 74. As for this nugget, which the mansa had inherited, Ibn Khaldūn says a ruler of Niani sold it cheaply to Egyptian traders. Ibn Khaldūn, French transl., in Cuoq, op. cit., pp. 340–7.

7. J. Devisse, 1972, pp. 50 ff. and 61 ff

Malli for between 20 and 30 and sometimes 40 *mithkāl*.' Salt served as a trading currency for the Sudanese, just like gold and silver. They cut it into pieces to market it. Despite the small size of the market town of Teghazza, a large quantity of gold dust was traded there.[8]

Salt was very expensive in the Sudan; the price was four times as high in Walata as in Niani, and the forest peoples probably paid even more for it. Rock-salt cut into small pieces served as tokens or small change for itinerant traders. Likewise, kola nuts from the forest served as currency in village markets. It begins to appear likely that the people of the forest obtained salt by other means, for example, by burning saliferous plants. Salt also came from the coast, though in small quantities.[9] 'Salt is lacking in the interior of the Sudan; some individuals bring it in secretly and people exchange it for an equivalent pile of gold.'[10] There is certainly some truth in this Arab account, even if it is partly exaggerated; it is easy to imagine the Wangara or the Hausa dealing with customers in the forest, where they went to buy kola nuts, gold and slaves.

Copper, too, was a major item of trade in West Africa and in other regions of the continent. Research in recent years has been making known the early patterns of the copper trade in West Africa.[11] Ownership of a copper-mine in the fourteenth century still had great economic significance. The mansa of Mali demonstrated this in his 'interview' with the people of Cairo, when he said:

> In the city of Tigida, there was a mine of red copper, which was exported in bars to the town of Niani, providing a special and unequalled source of revenue. In fact we send this copper to the pagan Sudan, where we sell it at a rate based on the weight of a *mithkāl* of gold, i.e. 100 *mithkāl* consisting of two-thirds gold.[12]

This is extremely precise. The Sudanese *mithkāl* weighs approximately 4.25 g. If copper was thus sold for almost its weight in gold, Mali must have enjoyed a particularly fruitful trade with 'the people of the forest', whom the emperor refers to as 'pagan'.

The account of Ibn Baṭṭūṭa, who spent many months in Niani, gives the impression that the towns of the Sahel and the Sahara were organized to serve as both staging posts and trading centres. This was true of Teghazza and also of Takedda ('Tigida'), which served as the main trading centre for copper.[13] The great traveller informs us that copper was shaped into

8. Ibn Baṭṭūṭa, loc. cit., pp. 288–90.
9. O. Dapper, French transl. 1686, p. 280.
10. Al-'Umarī, French transl., in Cuoq, op. cit., p. 282.
11. See Volume III, Chapter 14. The antiquity of copper production and trade is now generally conceded, especially in the Sahel area. It is worth recalling the importance of recent discoveries in Aïr concerning the antiquity of copper smelting and probably trade. Cf. also S. Bernus, P. Gouletquer and D. Kleinman, 1976.
12. Al-'Umarī, loc. cit., p. 282.
13. Ibn Baṭṭūṭa, loc. cit., p. 295.

both thick and thin bars. The former were sold at the rate of 1 gold *mithkāl* for 400 bars and the latter at the rate of 1 *mithkāl* for 600 or 700 bars. In the region, copper bars served as currency for the purchase of wood, meat, sorghum, butter and wheat. Ibn Baṭṭūṭa also says that the people of Takedda had 'no other occupations beyond trade'. Every year they travelled to Egypt, whence they imported all kinds of fine fabrics and other things. The inhabitants were prosperous and lived a life of ease, having large numbers of slaves of both sexes. Educated women slaves were sold only rarely, and then at a high price. Ibn Baṭṭūṭa found it difficult to acquire one, since those who possessed such slaves refused to sell them.[14] He recounts that one inhabitant who agreed to sell him one was subsequently so full of regret that he almost 'died of a broken heart'. Unfortunately he does not tell us what constituted the education of these women slaves who were so much in demand. It is highly probable that they were sought after on account of their talents as cooks or for their great beauty.

From Takedda Ibn Baṭṭūṭa set off for Tuat with a large caravan comprising approximately 600 women slaves. This is highly revealing, for it tells us how many slaves a caravan could transfer from the Sudan to the Maghrib, and also that the object of the slave trade was to provide domestic servants for the Berber Arab aristocracy, these being sometimes highly specialized in certain activities. Similarly, the Sudanese sovereigns imported slaves from Cairo, especially to serve as their personal guards. When the mansa sat on his throne in the public square, 'behind him stand some thirty Turkish [Mamluk] or other mercenaries, purchased for him in Cairo. One of them holds a silk parasol in his hand, surmounted by a cupola and a gold bird representing a sparrow-hawk.'[15] For both sovereigns and aristocracy, what counted was to have a gifted and loyal retinue.

Certain authors have sought to attribute a probably unwarranted importance to the export of slaves to Arab countries. In the period under consideration, this trade could not be regarded as a haemorrhage, because what interested the Arabs above all in the Sudan was gold, which was very urgently needed for coinage around the Mediterranean. Raymond Mauny has tentatively estimated the number of black slaves exported to the north at 20 000 a year or 2 million for the century.[16] The need for manpower was not so strongly felt by the Berber Arabs, as their demand was not so high. It is worth recalling here the famous treaty, called the *baḳt*, signed by Egyptian rulers with the kings of Nubia. This stipulated that the king of Nubia should send 442 slaves to Cairo annually, distributed as follows: 365 for the public treasury, 40 for the governor of Cairo, 20 for his deputy at Aswan, 5 for the Aswan judge and 12 for the twelve

14. ibid., p. 318. On copper in Takedda, see S. Bernus and P. Gouletquer, 1976.
15. Al-'Umarī, loc. cit., p. 269.
16. R. Mauny, 1961.

notaries of the town. This tribute exacted by the sultan of Cairo proves that court needs were not enormous.

The Berber Arab traders sought not only gold, but ivory. Elephant tusks from Africa were especially prized in Arabia and India, being much softer and more easily carved than those of Indian elephants.[17] The Sudan also sold skins, onyx, leather and grain to the Sahara oases. In the fourteenth century, when Mali was at the height of its power, the most travelled route was the one Ibn Baṭṭūṭa had used, but another trail led from Timbuktu to Ḳayrawān, via Wargla; this was the one often used by pilgrims from Mali.

In the towns of the Maghrib, as in Ghadames and Egypt, there were dynasties of rich traders, true 'privateers', who loaded up the trans-Saharan caravans. A notable example was that of the al-Maḳḳarī brothers of Tlemcen, who achieved a judicious division of labour. Two of them were based in that city, one in Sijilmasa and two others in the Sudan; between them they succeeded in creating a vast commercial network under the protection of the mansas of Mali.

> The one in Tlemcen dispatched to his Saharan brother such merchandise he requested, and the Saharan sent him skins, ivory, [kola] nuts and gold dust. As for the one in Sijilmasa, like the needle of a balance, he informed them of downward and upward trends in prices and wrote to them about the situation of the various traders and local events. And thus their wealth increased and their situation improved considerably.[18]

The al-Maḳḳarī brothers thus constituted a veritable Tlemcen corporation, which had branches in Sijilmasa and Walata, with its own information network and its own liaison officers. Mandingo and Hausa merchants probably organized their businesses and firms similarly in their relations with the trading centres of the savannah and the forest.[19]

A major role was probably played in this trade by Jewish communities. Lewicki's research has revealed the role played by Jews in Tuat as early as the eighth and ninth centuries.[20] Is the *Taʾrī<u>kh</u> al-fattā<u>sh</u>* to be believed when it speaks of Jewish farmers in the region of Tendirma on the Niger? At all events, references to Jews abound: early in the sixteenth century, the Portuguese navigator, Valentim Fernandes, also speaks of very rich but oppressed 'Jews' in Walata.[21]

17. Shaw, op. cit., Vol. 2, pp. 272–85.

18. Ibn al-<u>Kh</u>aṭīb, translated from the French version, in Cuoq, op. cit., pp. 324–6.

19. Today sociologists can observe family groups and associations among the Hausa and the Soninke. Brothers and cousins based at Dakar, Bamako, Abidjan, Accra, Kumasi, Kano and Lagos share control of the trade in kola, cloth and many other goods.

20. C. de La Roncière, 1924–7, Vol. 1, pp. 143–59.

21. V. Fernandes, French transl. 1951, p. 85; T. Lewicki, 1967; C. Monteil, 1951, pp. 265–98.

In the fifteenth century, with the offensive of the *reconquista*, the Christians settled in the Maghrib. Several Italian traders were drawn to the Sudan, as the riches in gold there had passed into legend. A certain Benedetto Dei, a Florentine traveller and writer, claimed to have ranged as far as Timbuktu in 1469–70.[22] A Genoese, Antonio Malfante, was renowned for his famous letter sent from Tuat to his Genoese business house. Malfante visited Tuat and gathered valuable information about the Nigerian Sudan and about Tuat, which was a crossroads for trade.[23] But it was by way of the Atlantic that direct contact between Europe and the Sudan was established in the fifteenth century, as a result of the Portuguese navigators.

Ibn Khaldūn informs us that there were caravans of 12 000 camels going from the Sudan to Egypt.[24] It was difficult to cut directly across the Sahara, because sandstorms swept along the Niger–Nile diagonal, so such caravans were rare. On the normal routes from the Niger to the Maghrib, the caravans averaged 1000 camels.

The spread of ideas and techniques

As a result of the trans-Saharan trade, many Berber Arabs settled in the cities of the Sudan and established their homes in Walata, Niani, Timbuktu, and Gao amongst others;[25] most of these towns had an Arab quarter. Marriages took place, creating the kinship ties which Sudanese genealogists take pleasure in unravelling. Historians still debate whether it was contact with Islam that introduced patrilineal inheritance into the Sudan. In the time of the empire of Ghana, the succession to the throne was not in the direct but in the collateral line, passing from uncle to nephew (the sister's son). Mali in the fourteenth century had difficulty in accepting direct inheritance from father to son.[26] Arab influence was not the deciding factor here. If one looks at the forest regions of the south, one finds both types of descent, and it would be hard to speak of Islamic influence in the Congo at that time.

The Islamization of black Africa was not accomplished by violence, but took place peacefully, through the influence of the Berber Arab traders, the Wangara and the Hausa. Apart from the warlike episode of the Almoravids, there were few wars for the purpose of propagating Islam. The new religion took account of the ancient practices of the traditional societies; but Ibn Baṭṭūṭa was struck with admiration by the piety of the black Muslims, their assiduous regularity of prayer and their faithfulness to group worship, obliging even their children to follow their example. The

22. C. de La Roncière, op. cit., Vol. 1, pp. 143–59.
23. Mauny, op. cit., pp. 50–2; C. A. Diop, 1960.
24. Ibn Khaldūn, loc. cit., p. 349.
25. Ibn Baṭṭūṭa, loc. cit., pp. 312–23.
26. See Chapter 6 above.

Wangara, always on the move from village to village, built mosques in various centres, like landmarks, along the kola routes. Because of the natural tolerance of Africans, they could say their prayers even in villages where the traditional religions were practised. Arabic became the language of the literate and the courtiers; Mansa Mūsā spoke it correctly, according to al-ʿUmarī, and can be regarded as responsible for the introduction of Muslim culture into Mali.[27]

An African literature in Arabic came into being, but it bore its finest fruits in the sixteenth century, under the askiyas of the Niger Bend. Scholarly exchanges between the universities of the Sudan and the Maghrib took place constantly from the fourteenth to the sixteenth century. But during the fourteenth century Cairo strongly attracted the Sudanese; situated on the pilgrim route, the city had many black inhabitants.[28]

The rulers of the Sudan were surrounded by Arab jurists and counsellors who were for the most part followers of the Mālikite rite. However, in the fourteenth century Ibn Baṭṭūṭa mentions the existence of whites (Khāridjites) among the Diafuno of Mali.[29]

The cultural and economic role of the Muslims was most remarkable south of the Sahara. On returning from his pilgrimage, Mansa Mūsā I had writers and an architect in his retinue, whom he employed to build the famous audience chamber where Ibn Baṭṭūṭa was received in 1353 by Mansa Sulaymān, his brother and successor.[30]

Relations between Chad and the Mediterranean

Historians have concentrated to a large extent on the western Sudan in dealing with the relations between Africa south of the Sahara and the Mediterranean. This is because of the numerous sources on that part of the continent. Many Arab travellers, including Ibn Hawḳal and Ibn Baṭṭūṭa, went to the Sudan along the western routes. Nevertheless, central Sudan and the countries of the Lake Chad basin also had very active relations with the Maghrib, Libya and Egypt. During the period in question, this region also included large political groupings such as the kingdom of Kanem-Bornu, whereas the rich Hausa cities conducted a flourishing trade between Lake Chad and the Niger.[31]

In the fourteenth century, the kingdom of Kanem stretched from Fezzān

27. Apparently it was during the reign of Mansa Mūsā that the cleavage began between Malinke and Bambara. The latter refused to accept Islam and created a secret society, 'Koma', in reaction to imperial policy. The Bambara (*ban-ma-na*) are 'those who reject the mansa'.

28. Ibn Khaldūn, loc. cit. This famous Arab historian got his information generally from a literate Malian who lived in Cairo.

29. Ibn Baṭṭūṭa, loc. cit., p. 311.

30. Ibn Khaldūn, loc. cit., pp. 347–8.

31. See Chapters 10 and 11 above.

in the north to Wadai in the east. The policy of Kanem's rulers was to make overtures towards the north, sending embassies to the kings there, with rich presents.[32] There were several main routes from Chad to the north. The first was the route from Kanem to Egypt: it went from Lake Chad towards Fezzān after crossing Kawar and its salt-pans; after Zawila in the Fezzān, the route crossed the Libyan oases (*sokna*) to reach Cairo by skirting the coast. The second route from the lake passed through Bilma, then headed eastward across the Tibesti, where gems were mined in the fifteenth century, to reach Aswan and finally Cairo. The third route left Kanem for Ghat and Ghadames; from there one branch went towards Tunis and the other to Tripoli. These routes were as much used as the western routes. They were most active in the fifteenth and sixteenth centuries, however, with the rise of the Hausa cities and Bornu, but when Arab groups settled at Darfūr to engage in the slave trade, commercial relations deteriorated.

In the areas between the Niger and Lake Chad and its environs, the major exports were leather, slaves and elephant tusks. The Hausa were the active initiators of trade in the central Sudan, where they acted as middlemen between the savannah and the forest, like the Mandingo in the west. It is quite possible that the Hausa were involved very early in trade with the kingdoms and cities of the Niger delta: Oyo, Ife, Benin and even Igbo-Ukwu; more and more researchers believe that a large part of the copper used in Ife, as in Igbo-Ukwu, came from the Sahel (Takedda). Thurstan Shaw, who conducted the first Igbo-Ukwu excavations, supports the hypothesis of extensive trade between the delta and the savannah.[33] In any event, the Hausa were involved in long-distance trade in these regions. Zaria, the southernmost city, was the bridgehead towards the forest regions.

The savannah and the forest

Not so very long ago the forest was considered an environment hostile to all forms of human settlement, and the particularly dense equatorial forest was described as a barrier just like the Sahara, if not even more hostile. It is now known that the forest did not stand in the way of either migrating peoples or ideas and techniques.

32. In 1391, Mai Abū ʿAmr ʿUthmān b. Idrīs, sultan of Bornu, corresponded with Sultan Barḳūḳ. See Chapter 10 above.

33. T. Shaw, op. cit., pp. 279–83; and 1973, pp. 233–8. The large quantity of copper objects at Igbo-Ukwu poses a problem, because there are no deposits of copper in the area; the nearest mine is at Takedda.

West Africa

Arab geographers, including Ibn Saʿīd and Ibn Khaldūn, thought that the desert began south of the savannah.[34] The peoples of the savannah, who could have enlightened the Arabs, preferred to keep silent about that region, which supplied a large proportion of the gold marketed in the Sudanese towns; however, Mansa Mūsā let it be clearly understood in Cairo that he drew great profits from the copper he mined. Copper from Mali was traded in the forest regions for gold, ivory, kola nuts and also slaves. This trade between the empires of the Sudan and the southern forest is beginning to be the subject of very serious research. Trade routes crossed the forest in every direction, and it is becoming increasingly clear from archaeological, linguistic and anthropological research that, in the past, the savannah and the forest complemented each other. The forest peoples refer to the Mandingo as Dioula (Ivory Coast) or Wangara (Ghana), both words meaning 'trader'. The kola trade routes are dotted with villages, populated partly or wholly by Dioula or Hausa. It is very likely that before the fourteenth century the Mandingo had established contact with the forest peoples. The kingdoms of Kong and Begho, situated in the wooded savannah, were outposts of the kola and gold markets of the forest regions.[35] There is a break in the forest around the Gulf of Guinea, and in Ghana and Nigeria there are wide clearings all the way down from the north to the Atlantic Ocean. In these areas, therefore, contacts with the Sudan were easier and more constant. The Wangara and Hausa traders had reached Asante territory at this time, and also Yoruba land via Bono Manso.

Again, we cannot say how much merchandise came from the savannah nor how much was sent from the forest regions to the Sudan. However, until very recently, the Mandingo and Hausa used to sell beads, salt, amber, copper pans and smoked or dried fish from Jenne and Mopti at village fairs in the forest. The West African forest is not dense, and can easily be penetrated; the Wangara crossed it with their donkey caravans. But more often the Wangara and Hausa settled in large villages on the fringes of the forest; there were other peoples, intermediaries between them and the deep south, who had a monopoly of the kola trade.

Kola nuts played an important role in West African social life at that time and do so even now. They were found as far as the Kongo, as Pigafetta

34. Ibn Khaldūn: 'The equatorial and more southerly regions were empty of inhabitants', *al-Muḳaddima*, from French transl., 1967–8, p. 100.

35. Oral traditions say the city of Kong dates from the Sundiata period. However, the archaeological excavations currently being carried out at the site have not confirmed this. Joint research by the Universities of Abidjan and Accra on the peoples common to their two countries show the antiquity of savannah–forest relations; so does Thurstan Shaw's work. This specialist in Igbo-Ukwu bronzes believes that the copper trade between the savannah and the forest may date back to the ninth and tenth centuries. Shaw, 1970, pp. 268–70.

noted.[36] This trade involved the activity of many different ethnic groups. Although the detailed operation of this trade is unknown for our period, the description of Zunon Gnobo is suggestive; he reports that the kola lands were divided by sectors according to the quality of the fruit.

> In the north, the wooded savannah, poor in kola, in the south, the sectors of Gbalo, Bogube, Yokolo, Nekedi, Ndri, which were noted for the quality of their kola. It was the focal point of the north–south circuits and those of the Bete interior. The Guro screen prevented direct trade relations between the Dioula and the Zebuo. These Malinke traders could only reach the Guro markets, where they stocked up in kola from the south. The Guro suppliers went down to meet the Zebuo women, who gathered the kola in the Bete and Guro ethnic areas of the south.[37]

In any case, we are here in the presence of a very ancient trade between the savannah and the forest; the Mandingo were more interested in gold than in kola and it was the search for that commodity that led them to create staging points in the wooded savannah that later became major trade centres.[38] Gold was abundant in the southern regions; research is gradually allowing us to uncover the gold circuits in these regions. At present we only have data for later periods; the Akan and Baule kingdoms hardly go back earlier than the seventeenth century.

Thus the forest was not a barrier, but it played the part of a filter for economic currents, ideas and techniques. (See Fig. 25.1.) It also is evident, from the study of oral traditions, that many of the forest peoples came originally from the savannah; the currents of trade go back very far into antiquity. It may be noted that many peoples of the savannah recognize the superiority and even the profundity of the knowledge of the forest people in their herbal pharmacopoeia and in the esoteric art of drum language.

The northern part of the tropical forest was encroached upon by agriculture, and receded on several fronts in Guinea, Ivory Coast, Liberia and Ghana. In Nigeria, major communication routes ran from Nupe to the delta and, in several places where the population cleared the land, Yoruba cities flourished and grew in the spaces thus opened up.

East and Central Africa

A number of questions still require further research before they can be answered in a satisfactory manner. It may be asked, for example, how

36. F. Pigafetta and D. Lopes, Eng. transl. 1881.
37. Translated from J. Zunon Gnobo, 1976, p. 79.
38. Located in the north-west of the Republic of Ghana, Begho was a hub of trade at the edge of the forest. It was linked to Jenne and the upper river as early as the twelfth century and had an important Malinke colony as well as Hausa traders.

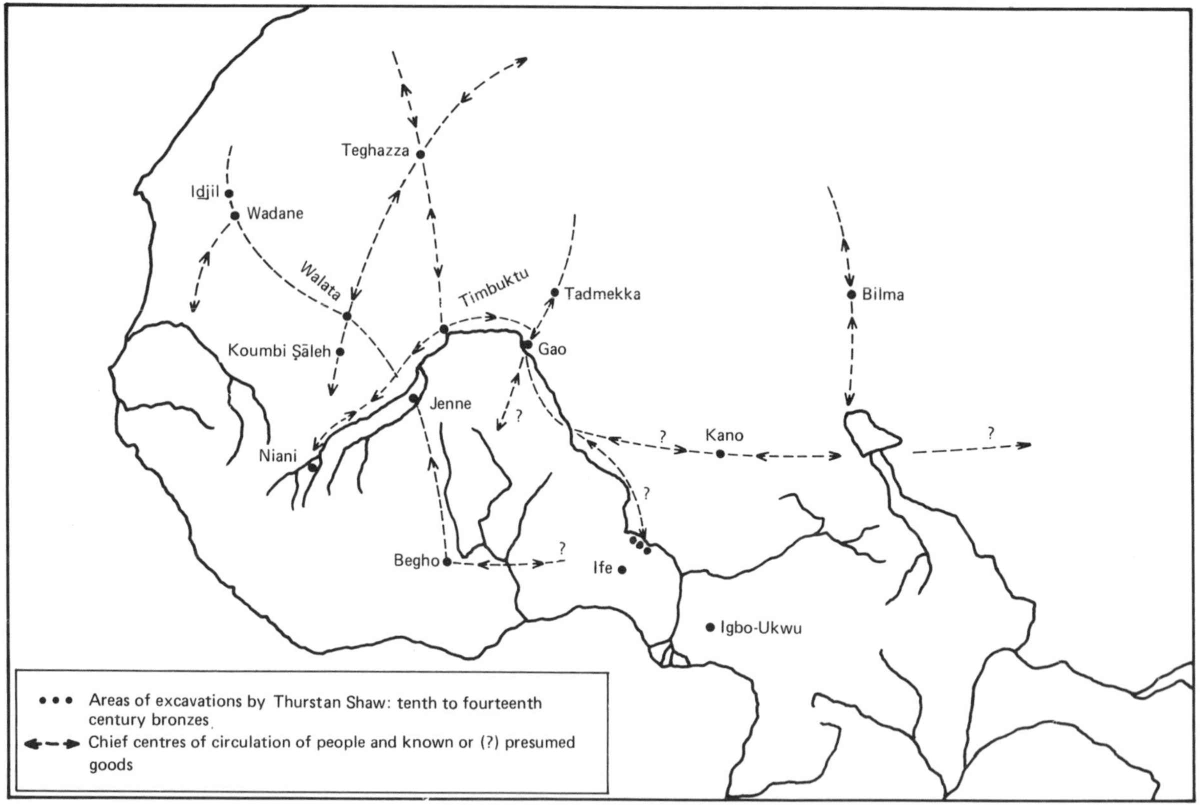

FIG. 25.1 *Circulation of men and techniques in West Africa (J. Devisse)*

the products exported from the coastal regions to the Muslim world and Asia were collected, and what kind of organization existed over the centuries for the trade in ivory or wild-animal skins. We know the importance of this for earlier and later centuries, but little is yet known concerning the period under study here. Were there regular transport networks for these products? Through whose hands did they pass? What commodities came in return to the interior of the continent from the eastern coast? In comparison with West Africa, where there is evidence of such imports, what proportion of the materials imported by the coastal trading centres were redistributed in the interior?[39]

It would also be useful to know the quantity of cowrie shells landed annually on the coast and where they went.[40] Up to now, very few traces have been found outside Zimbabwe of the luxury articles which arrived at the Indian Ocean ports; does this mean that none were sold or given to the people of the interior or that research has not yet permitted us to find the evidence?

At least certain trade flows can now be distinguished clearly throughout the interior, from Ethiopia to the Zambezi. One example of this is the salt trade. We have seen above the importance of different kinds of salt in the trans-Saharan trade. From Idjil to Bilma, from Taoudeni to Aïr, all types of production were in competition to supply Africa with salt.[41] Beyond the examples that have been studied and are well known, how many other sources of salt, from surface deposits or small inland lakes, played a more obscure but even more lasting role? Bankalie salt was one of the Aksumite exports as early as the third or fourth century of the Christian era;[42] and it is unlikely that this did not continue in subsequent centuries. Such salt production probably never reached major proportions;[43] but it is more than likely that it was distributed, at least in neighbouring regions, during the centuries with which we are concerned here.

It would also be useful to study the most probable ancient forms of salt-mining along the southern coast of Somalia and in the north of Kenya, up to the island of Pate. According to Grottanelli, many deposits of sea-salt were found there, which were gathered by women and children.[44] There were also large concentrations of rock-salt, which seem to have been traded.

Written sources rarely mention such facts, which are nevertheless essential. When by chance they do, little is made of it. Vasco da Gama, for

39. See P. Vérin, 1975, p. 77

40. Archaeological evidence of their penetration has been found in Zambia and southern Zaïre.

41. On Aïr salt, see Bernus and Gouletquer, op cit., pp. 53–65; Bernus, Gouletquer and Kleinman, op. cit.; H. J. Hugot and M. Bruggman, 1976, pp. 129 ff.

42. G. Gerster (ed.), 1974, pp. 197–210.

43. The production has been estimated at 10 tons per annum for the years 1964–6.

44. V. L. Grottanelli, 1965, p. 92.

example, explains in the account of his first voyage that the Africans with whom his men came into contact in the south of the continent carried gourds of sea water to obtain salt by evaporation. There is much evidence that similar methods of salt production existed a very long time ago on the Atlantic coast, at least around the Gulf of Guinea, but there has been no systematic study in support of this precisely dated evidence provided by Vasco da Gama. Similarly, in the same passage, he explains that the men carried iron spears and daggers with ivory hilts; but this information, of great significance for the history of iron and ivory transport, has never been exploited. Here is at least one very typical example where recourse to oral traditions concerning commercial exchanges seems indispensable. In fact, oral traditions often allow us to make a single leap backwards over many centuries.

We have more information on the mining of salt in the south of present-day Tanzania.[45] The salt-pans of Uvinza in the south-east of the country are still in use today and stretch over more than 15 km. The first archaeological research has shown that there was intense activity in the preparation and sale of salt before 1500 at Uvinza. Receptacles have been found in which boiling produced salt by evaporation. Radiocarbon dating indicates that mining started towards the fifth or sixth century of the Christian era and that it has been continued. At Ivuna, in the same area, it is certain that production was carried on from the thirteenth to the fifteenth century (see Fig. 25.2).

Researchers are unanimous in thinking that the salt was exported to distant regions and that it probably provided material for regular trade and barter. Comparable research should be undertaken further north on lesser salt-pans – at Saja, 230 km north of Ivuna; in Uganda, at Kabiro; and also in Zambia, with regard to the salt springs of Bazang, which seem to have been exploited from very early times. An extremely interesting experiment was undertaken recently in Burundi, in the region of Kumozo;[46] vegetable salt was extracted from salt plants well known to the guardians of oral tradition, using methods they had committed to memory. It seems quite reasonable to suppose that, for many regions of East Africa, the production of vegetable salt, banned by European colonizers, was for a long time an important source of sodium. In the kingdom of Kongo, salt was a royal monopoly. Work is needed on the salt deposits of Mpinda, near the Zaïre estuary, and of Ambriz, in the north of Angola (see Fig. 25.2).

With the progress of research we will be able to discover how medium and long-distance trade, in addition to gifts and local barter, ensured the movement through eastern Africa of valuable cattle. It would be interesting, too, to undertake inquiries in these regions about the circulation of gems,

45. B. M. Fagan and J. E. Yellen, 1968; J. E. G. Sutton and A. D. Roberts, 1968.
46. L. Ndoricimpa *et al.*, 1981.

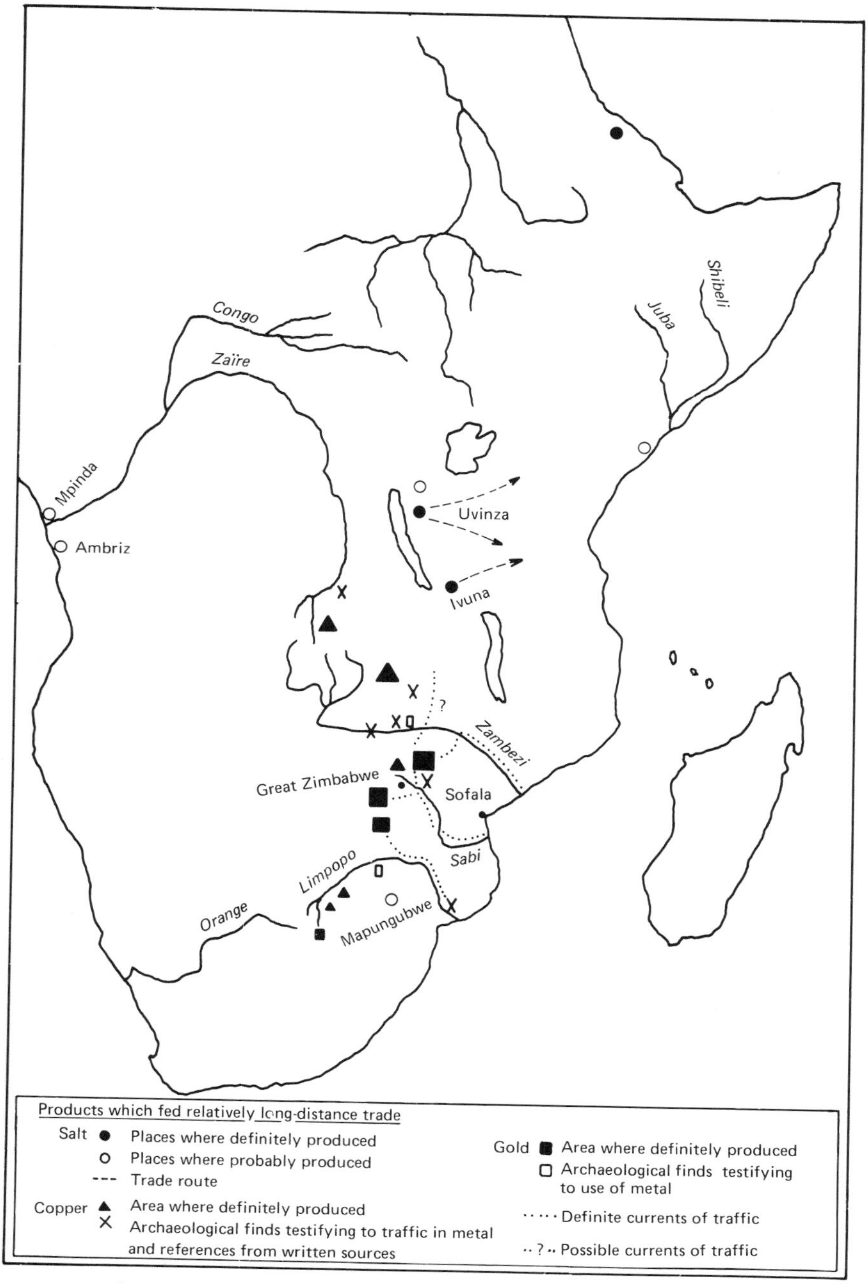

FIG. 25.2 *Central, East and Southern Africa, 11th–15th centuries (J. Devisse)*

Products which fed relatively long-distance trade

Salt   ● Places where definitely produced
       ○ Places where probably produced
      --- Trade route

Copper ▲ Area where definitely produced
       X Archaeological finds testifying to traffic in metal
          and references from written sources

Gold ■ Area where definitely produced
      □ Archaeological finds testifying
         to use of metal

····· Definite currents of traffic

··?·· Possible currents of traffic

which were the objects of a flourishing trade.[47] It would also be appropriate to inquire into the different types of money which facilitated the exchange activities, presumed to have been active and widespread. The Kongo shells, whose production was a royal monopoly when the Portuguese arrived, are probably not unique.

The thick, equatorial forest, long thought to be an impenetrable, impassable barrier, did not hinder relations between the northern and southern savannahs, especially where climatic changes and the work of man opened up large gaps. Jan Vansina, in his study of bells – one of the prerogatives of the kings of the savannah – has shown that they crossed the equatorial forest from north to south. Thus, bells have been found at Ife and much later, after 1400, in Zimbabwe.[48] Those who specialized in the sending of messages used these bells to reproduce the tones of speech. Further research has revealed that knives made for throwing were transmitted to the southern peoples from the north through the great equatorial forest. Thus techniques, objects and ideas were able to cross the forest both from north to south and from south to north. Peoples migrated in all directions without the forest hindering their movement.

In these high forest regions, the rivers provided permanent axes of communication; although each section was controlled by dominant, coherent ethnic groups, these waterways, largely due to the fishermen, contributed to the transfer of techniques and ideas.

On the Atlantic coast from the mouth of the River Congo (in Zaïre) all the way to Angola, the local populations were involved in the coastal trade, and experts think that certain influences spread by way of the sea. Thus, according to Vansina, the polychrome statuettes to be found in an area extending from Nigeria to Angola bear witness to the seaborne dissemination of a particular technique. It is quite possible, in fact, that this maritime trade was more active in the past than people today imagine.

One can only regret that, despite all the theoretical discussion of the ancient economy and society of Africa, so little concerted effort has so far been put into research, even though we already have evidence of the important results of research into the forms, techniques and values of early production and trade. How many prejudices regarding the 'immobility' of African societies in relation to development and innovation would fall away if, instead of using as a reference point the centuries of contact with Europeans, during which Africa was overwhelmed by the socio-economic effects of the slave trade, a very serious attempt was made to explore the period with which we are concerned and to increase our knowledge of the political, social and economic structures about which, paradoxically, we know so little. The area open to research in this field is immense, but it is virtually unexplored, apart from the work of a small group of archaeologists.

47. An example of West African research is given by Lewicki, op. cit. Another important example of jewellery as a stimulus for trade is in Vérin, op. cit., p. 7.

48. J. Vansina, 1969. See Chapter 22, pp. 561–3 above.

Yet it is this Africa which should be known, through its socio-political structures, in order to establish a new society which would be deeply rooted in the values of its civilization.

Copper and gold, the bases of exchange in southern Africa

We know with certainty today that the mining of copper started in a number of regions of southern Africa during the first centuries of the Christian era.[49] The metal was extracted principally from sites in Shaba, in the north-west of present-day Zambia, on the central plateau of Zimbabwe and, to a lesser extent, on the upper Limpopo. Archaeological discoveries and datings of recent years leave no doubt about the long-distance trade in copper bars and crosses as well as copper alloys.

The first name given by the Portuguese to the Limpopo, when they began their explorations, was the 'copper river'; their urgent need to find copper mines at all costs, in order to free themselves from dependence on the European producers of this metal, and the importance of their exports of copper to Africa, where the metal was much in demand from the end of the fifteenth century, all explain why the prospect of finding the mineral in southern Africa was so attractive.

For a long time, copper was also highly appreciated by the Africans; there is much evidence of this.[50] It was used first as jewellery: very early, the *Compendium of Marvels* noted that the wives of the blacks wore 'copper rings on their wrists and ears' and that they dressed their hair 'with copper and shell rings'. Probably we should think in terms of copper jewellery when Ibn Baṭṭūṭa describes the people who came occasionally to the mansa's court as 'wearing great ear-rings half a span wide'. The widespread use of copper and its alloys as marks of political prestige in various regions of the continent is probably also ancient. These facts alone convince us that there was a long-distance trade in this 'semi-precious metal'. Nor should anyone dismiss the idea that copper crosses may have acted as money in southern Africa in the same way as the copper bars produced at Takedda, of which Ibn Baṭṭūṭa speaks, probably did.[51]

South of the equatorial forest, in the wooded savannah, the mineral riches of Shaba probably attracted numerous peoples. It was no doubt there that the technique developed of working ferrous and non-ferrous metals. Consequently, long-distance trade rapidly expanded there. The Luba kingdoms and the Lunda empire developed in this area of Shaba before 1500. Research on languages and population migrations and the

49. See Volume II, Chapter 25, p. 632 and Chapter 27, pp. 678 and 688; Volume III, Chapter 23; and Chapter 22 above.

50. From the ninth century, worked copper was an important element in Muslim trade with black Africa.

51. Ibn Baṭṭūṭa, loc. cit., pp. 313, and 718. For an example of copper jewellery found in graves, see J. O. Vogel, 1971, p. 99.

analysis of myths of origin and the kinship system already make it possible to form an idea of the socio-cultural problems of the region.[52] It is becoming increasingly clear that men travelled in all directions, both in the forest and in the savannah. It emerges in the light of this research that Shaba was a cultural pole with a vast sphere of attraction; the Luba influence was felt as far as the provinces of the Zambezi.[53]

As early as the tenth century, al-Mas'ūdī speaks of the position of gold in southern Africa in these terms: 'at the limits of the sea of Zanguebar lies the country of Sofola and of al-Waḳwaḳ, lands which produce gold in quantity'.[54] This text suffices to show that in the tenth century the Muslims were aware of the gold in southern Africa which was already being mined and probably exported.

Archaeology, once again, confirms and illuminates the written sources. Although his conclusions may be disputed, it is difficult to contest the basic chronological and quantitative information reported by Summers on the exploitation of gold on the Shona plateau.[55] A systematic examination of the traces of mining, test borings and datings have enabled the author to draw accurate maps. Mining seems to have started around the seventh century immediately south of the Zambezi, in the Mazoe valley, and to have spread between the ninth and eleventh centuries to the whole of the plateau, from which it reached the Limpopo area only in the fifteenth century. According to Summers, most exports went to the coast through the Sabi valley, towards Sofala; but two other trade routes went along the Zambezi and the Limpopo (see Fig. 25.2). Randles, who generally follows Summers's conclusions, believes – together with several other historians – that the prosperity of Zimbabwe in the fourteenth and fifteenth centuries may be explained by the concentration of trade upon the Sabi, in the hands of a rich minority, and that the profound transformations in navigation on the Sabi after the fifteenth century can account for the decline in trade via Zimbabwe and the weakening of Sofala.[56]

One should therefore not link the exploitation of and trade in gold exclusively with the fate of Zimbabwe alone, as is too often done. As in West Africa, where the rivalries for the control of gold production and trade explain much of the history of the tenth–fifteenth centuries, it is probable that gold from the south reached its Muslim buyers by many different routes, despite all the efforts of the rulers of Zimbabwe, particularly

52. See Chapter 22 above.

53. A. Wilson, 1972. A number of authors consider the oral traditions of these regions (Luba–Lunda) as literary developments or amplifications of legends to legitimize the status quo in the fourteenth century. It would be more scientific to proceed to an analysis in greater depth.

54. Al-Mas'ūdī, French transl. 1962, Vol. 2, pp. 322–3.

55. R. Summers, 1969.

56. W. G. L. Randles, 1975, pp. 14 ff.

during the fourteenth and fifteenth centuries, to establish a monopoly.

However that may be, and even if Summers's estimate of gold production in the eleventh century (approximately 9–10 tons per annum) is to be treated with caution, it is certain that the southern gold reached the north earlier than most historians, interested primarily in the fate of Kilwa and in the coinage of the precious metal, have believed up to now. This gold probably played an important role in African commerce as early as the eleventh century.

Muslim navigators were conducting coastal trade up to Sofala from that time; it was not interrupted until after the arrival of the Portuguese, even when the rivalry between coastal cities made it perhaps more difficult. This cabotage, which reached Aden, was both a generator of the export trade in products from the interior of Africa to the Muslim, Indian and Chinese worlds and a creator of shipyards of which we know practically nothing today.

Although the size of the gold trade in the eleventh century is debatable, nobody questions its importance from the thirteenth to the fourteenth century. From estimates of its volume, made when the Portuguese arrived at Sofala, it is permissible to believe that during those centuries several thousand tons of gold went each year from south to north. Excavations of the fortified quarter of Great Zimbabwe, known so unfortunately as the Acropolis, have uncovered the places where the precious metal was smelted; it is probable that it was also refined before export.

Gold therefore occupied a dominant place in the fourteenth and fifteenth centuries in the merchandise exported from the Shona plateau and among the products sold to the aristocracy which ruled Zimbabwe. Nevertheless, most historians today agree that gold was not the origin of the wealth of Zimbabwe and one should probably think of the considerable development of cattle-raising on the grassy plateau which was free of tsetse fly. A major drought in the thirteenth century contributed to the drift of the graziers up to the more hospitable plateau. As the sacrificial kings of cattlemen, the masters of Zimbabwe may have originally built their power and wealth on cattle, a century or two before they expanded it considerably by the greatest possible control of the gold trade. That is, unless we should follow an ancient but still occasionally accepted distinction between 'miners', 'cattle-raisers' and 'builders': the first group would have been exploiting gold, copper and other metals before 1100; the third may have been responsible for the famous stone buildings of Great Zimbabwe. Neither their ethnic origin nor their language is known: nothing, however, prevents us from believing that these 'builders' and 'miners' were the direct ancestors of the people who live on the Zimbabwe plateau, that is the Sotho and the Shona.[57]

Unfortunately, we do not know enough about any of these questions.

57. R. Summers, 1960 and 1963.

The existence of the racist states of Rhodesia and South Africa[58] has blocked research. The prehistory of these regions is well known, thanks to the work of Anglo-Saxon researchers, but everything is confused when one reaches historical times. Everything has been done to deny that the blacks originated the flourishing cultures which developed before 1500.

Items gathered here and there, however, prove that these civilizations were interlinked and present an undeniable unity. Towards the east, the valley of the Zambezi was a route for the penetration of northern influences, including those of the Bantu. In the kingdoms that spread across the savannahs of the south, metal-working and trade played a primordial role. South of the Zambezi, two areas of intense cultural activity may be distinguished: the Zimbabwe plateau and, in the far south, the Lughveld plateau.[59]

Another aspect of inter-African trade has assumed great importance in recent years. Vérin was the first to insist on the frequent contacts between Madagascar, the Comoro Islands and the east coast of Africa; he has suggested that, if numerous influences reached the islands from the coast, certain products, like the objects carved from Madagascar's chloritoschist, could well have spread along the coast as far as Kilwa.[60] If Vérin's intuitions and hypotheses are confirmed by future research, it will be necessary to reassess seriously what has often been said about the southern limits of African and Arab navigation zones in the Indian Ocean. The vigorous resumption of archaeological research in Madagascar since 1977, judging from the first published results, will undoubtedly contribute important elements to our knowledge of these regions.

58. When the Republic of Zimbabwe gained independence, this opened new prospects.
59. See Chapter 21 above.
60. Vérin, op. cit., pp. 72–3; Cf. J. P. Domenichini, 1979b.

26 Africa in inter-continental relations

J. DEVISSE *in collaboration with* S. LABIB

Africa as seen by the rest of the world

It is difficult to tell how Africans living in the interior of the continent during the four centuries from 1100 to 1500 thought of themselves in the light of both their changing cultural context and their centuries-old traditions. One must not give up trying, however; although difficult, this inquiry is of fundamental importance. We are beginning to discern what changes have been made by successive acculturations from the point of view of the perception of space in Africa; it would be fascinating to know, for instance, how an African merchant of the fifteenth century visualized his own environment. However, we can now state that the merchants of Takrūr in Mali – who were in fact Wangara[1] – had a fair idea of the geography of the Muslim world and perhaps even of the entire known world of the time. In the fifteenth century, the Wangara merchants were literate, or at least there were a large number of literate people among them who had a very clear knowledge of their environment. The Wangar used the term Saheli or Kogodugu (land of salt) to refer to the north, whence Arab or Berber merchants came with camels loaded with slabs of salt. The terms Worodugu (land of the kola nut) or Tu-Koro (forest) denoted the south, whose forests, difficult of access, supplied the precious kola nut. The thinly-wooded Gbe Kan ('clear country'), stretching from east to west, was the land through which the Wangara merchants plied their trade on foot, horse or donkey-back.

Owing to the royal pilgrimages, many people of the Sudan region had

1. Wangara: this word is written in various ways by Arab writers – Wankāra, Wanghāra, Wangāra, Wangarāta and perhaps even Amdjara (Mas'ūdī in the tenth century). The Wangara are sometimes confused with the Gangara, to whom are attributed, rather vaguely, some ancient ruins in the Sahel. The Wangara do not appear in Arab sources before the eleventh or twelfth century. They are said to have mined and traded in gold in upper Niger. In the fourteenth century their name was often associated with Jenne and their zone of influence extended far to the east, according to Ibn Khaldūn. Later the word Dioula tends to replace the earlier name, and is still used to designate the Mandingo-speaking traders of the savannah zone extending up to Ghana.

an accurate knowledge of the Maghrib, Egypt and even Arabia, from the thirteenth century onwards. There are no figures on which to base an estimate but, to judge from the documents available, the fact that black ambassadors were resident in Cairo at the end of the fifteenth century suggests a strong Sudanese presence in that town. On the seaboard of the Indian Ocean, the Zandj and Swahili were thoroughly familiar with the eastern Arab world, with India and perhaps even with distant China. Black merchants from the Sudan and East Africa very probably went on trading missions to Arab towns and provinces. Geography was taught in the schools of Timbuktu, and the basic textbooks were no doubt the same as in Cairo. Al-ʿUmarī says a sovereign such as Mansa Kanku Mūsā had a clear idea of the extent of the lands of the black peoples and Mali's place within them.

For the time being, we have more knowledge of the way in which peripheral cultures knew and, above all, 'saw' the African continent. To speak of peripheral cultures is to group together under the same heading the Muslim world, both African and non-African – we shall see the considerable implications of this – and the Asian, Byzantine and western worlds.

The Muslims knew Africa. But in the fourteenth century their cultural tradition, passed on from generation to generation, still reflected outdated ideas and incomplete knowledge. This scholastic picture, as we shall see, contrasted with the process of discovery of the continent, which, already actively under way in the eleventh century, developed remarkably in the fourteenth. Even the great Ibn Khaldūn admitted that his sources for whole regions were still Ptolemy and al-Idrīsī. Ibn Khaldūn tells us the philosophers had concluded that 'the equatorial regions and those further south were uninhabited', on account of the heat and the dry climate of the first two parts of the world.[2] However, the great historian admits his perplexity, since 'observation and continuing tradition support the opposite view. How can one decide?' Having assessed the arguments on both sides, he concludes that 'there may be a civilization in the equatorial regions and further south, as people say, but it cannot amount to much'.[3]

To understand the mental attitude of cultures based on monotheistic religions towards Africa and its surrounding seas, we must bear in mind two sets of ideas to be found among all the writers – Jews, Christians and Muslims alike – during the centuries with which we are concerned. The first follows from the belief that the earth is encompassed with the waters of an ocean. 'The waters receded', says Ibn Khaldūn again, 'from certain parts of the world in which God wished to create living beings and which he wished to populate with the human race.' Africa, the south-

2. Ibn Khaldūn, from the French transl. 1967–8, p. 100. According to the learned Ptolemaic and Muslim tradition, the world was divided into seven parts or 'climates', from the south (equatorial) region to the north (boreal) region. The 'first two parts' mentioned here correspond, roughly speaking, to the equatorial and northern tropical regions of Africa (see Fig. 26.1, which shows these divisions).

3. Ibn Khaldūn, from the French transl., loc. cit., pp. 103–4.

ernmost of the known continents, was washed by very extensive and as yet unexplored seas.[4] The inheritors of Greek culture, whether Arabs or westerners, regarded the equatorial regions, both land and sea, with their overwhelming heat, as the limits of the world in which man could bear to live. In addition, all these heirs of the Mediterranean cultures, as Ibn Khaldūn again puts it, thought that 'the cradle of civilization lies between the third and the sixth parts of the world' – neither in the north nor in the south.[5] No better information on the Atlantic Ocean and its islands is to be found in the traditional teaching of cloistered scholars, either Muslim or Christian. The Islands of the Blest – the Canary Islands – in the Atlantic were the western boundary of the known world. Many pre-fourteenth-century Arab writers thought them uninhabited. Dhu 'l-Ḳarnayn (Alexander the Great) once visited them, but did not manage to sail further west, 'either on account of the thick fog or for fear of getting lost and perishing'.[6]

The Muslim travellers had a totally different approach, at least after the tenth century, as they gradually penetrated south of the Tropic of Cancer, by sea along the eastern coasts, and overland in West Africa.[7] Many observations give the lie to the stereotyped channels of book learning; this direct information from the fourteenth century is derived mainly from Ibn Baṭṭūṭa and al-ʿUmarī.[8] From the Indian Ocean, moreover, the Muslim world learnt all the Asian sciences of navigation and astronomy.

For writers mainly concerned with West Africa, many problems remain unsolved which we would like to see tackled and resolved; this is the result of both the mystery with which African cultures, jealous of their autonomy, could be seen to surround themselves, and the limitations imposed by the authorities on uncontrolled entry by Muslim traders and missionaries into the Sahel area and the savannah.

4. ibid., pp. 90 ff. and 111–12. 'The first part of the world lies immediately north of the Equator. To the south, there is only the civilization mentioned by Ptolemy and, after that, wastelands and sandy deserts until the circle of water called the Ocean is reached.'

5. ibid., pp. 101 and 117. Ibn Khaldūn speaks of the part of West Africa which is frequented by Moroccan traders. The southern parts, he says, are a reserve of 'Lamlam' slaves, 'with scarred faces. Beyond, in the south, there are only men who are nearer to animals than to reasonable beings. They cannot possibly be counted as human beings' (p. 166). The way of life of these men is due to 'their living so far away from the temperate zone ... which means that their nature becomes closer to that of the brute beasts and that much further away from the human race'.

6. On the Canary Islands, for example, see al-Idrīsī, French transl. in J. Cuoq, 1975, p. 127; Ibn Saʿīd, ibid., pp. 202 and 212.

7. The exception for West Africa was the hypothetical voyage of Ibn Fāṭima along the African coast, as recounted by Ibn Saʿīd (ibid.) and others, which will be discussed below.

8. We must take care not to ignore the major inquiries undertaken in the tenth century by al-Masʿūdī, in the eleventh by al-Bakrī and in the twelfth by al-Idrīsī. Lewicki's remarkable study of the last-named shows clearly how carefully the information had been put together by the director of a large team; T. Lewicki, 1966.

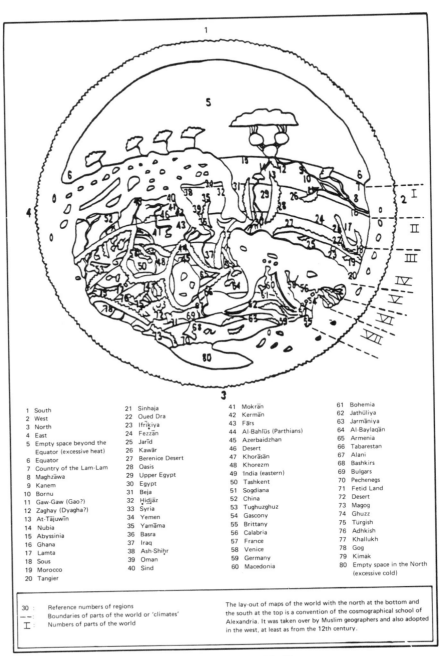

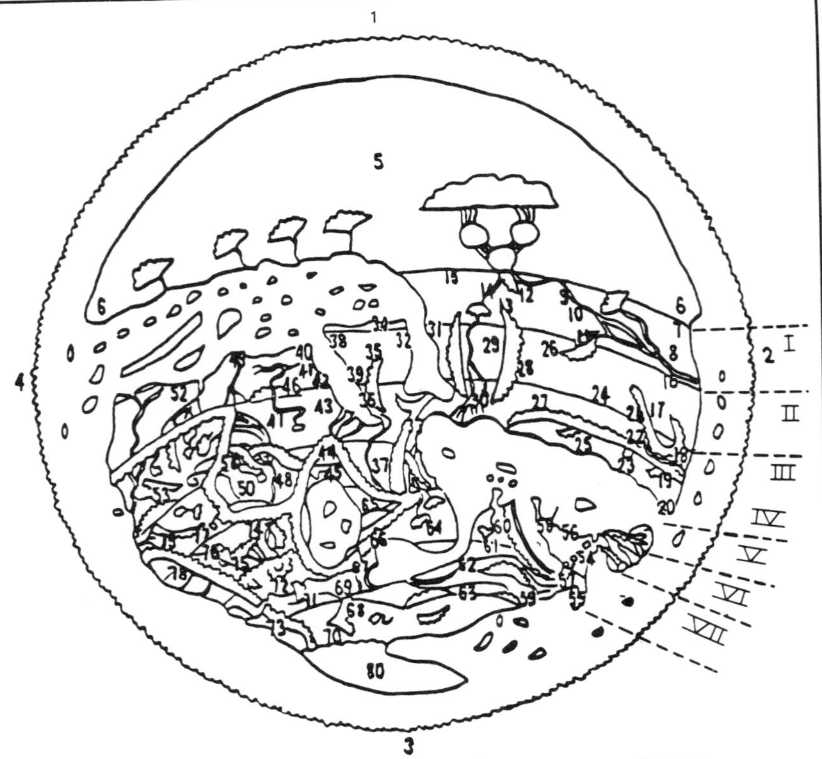

1 South
2 West
3 North
4 East
5 Empty space beyond the Equator (excessive heat)
6 Equator
7 Country of the Lam-Lam
8 Maghzāwa
9 Kanem
10 Bornu
11 Gaw-Gaw (Gao?)
12 Zaghay (Dyagha?)
13 At-Tājuwīn
14 Nubia
15 Abyssinia
16 Ghana
17 Lamta
18 Sous
19 Morocco
20 Tangier
21 Sinhaja
22 Oued Dra
23 Ifriḳiya
24 Fezzān
25 Jarīd
26 Kawār
27 Berenice Desert
28 Oasis
29 Upper Egypt
30 Egypt
31 Beja
32 Ḥidjāz
33 Syria
34 Yemen
35 Yamāma
36 Basra
37 Iraq
38 Ash-Shiḥr
39 Oman
40 Sind
41 Mokrān
42 Kermān
43 Fārs
44 Al-Bahlūs (Parthians)
45 Azerbaidzhan
46 Desert
47 Khorāsān
48 Khorezm
49 India (eastern)
50 Tashkent
51 Sogdiana
52 China
53 Tughuzghuz
54 Gascony
55 Brittany
56 Calabria
57 France
58 Venice
59 Germany
60 Macedonia
61 Bohemia
62 Jathūliya
63 Jarmāniya
64 Al-Baylaqān
65 Armenia
66 Tabarestan
67 Alani
68 Bashkirs
69 Bulgars
70 Pechenegs
71 Fetid Land
72 Desert
73 Magog
74 Ghuzz
75 Türgish
76 Adhkish
77 Khallukh
78 Gog
79 Kimäk
80 Empty space in the North (excessive cold)

30 : Reference numbers of regions
— — : Boundaries of parts of the world or 'climates'
I : Numbers of parts of the world

The lay-out of maps of the world with the north at the bottom and the south at the top is a convention of the cosmographical school of Alexandria. It was taken over by Muslim geographers and also adopted in the west, at least as from the 12th century.

FIG. 26.1 *The world according to al-Idrīsī and Ibn Khaldūn*

At least Arab writers could visit, reflect upon and describe an unbroken stretch of land, from the shores of the Mediterranean to the Niger Bend, to the sources of the Senegal and the Niger, to Chad and to the north of what is now Nigeria. The area remaining unknown to them – mainly the forest zone – contained far more unusual characteristics, compared with the 'Mediterranean norm', than the desert or the steppe. The forest region, with its own peculiar climatic mechanisms, was precisely the area which the Europeans, who were almost entirely ignorant of the interior of the continent, were to discover. Africa still suffers from the consequences of the heterogeneous nature of the areas discovered, almost haphazard, by various parties.

In the Christian West, little interest was shown in Africa as such.[9] Traders wishing to penetrate the secrets behind the 'Muslim curtain' cast a utilitarian eye on it. Some carefully examined the efforts made by cartographers to assemble the information received from the Arabs and transmitted through Spain in the form of coherent maps, in which the shape of Africa, north of the Tropic of Cancer, is fairly accurate. The Majorcans, who inherited Arab science through Jewish emigrants from Spain, gave concrete form to the knowledge they acquired in the most famous of the first great marine charts.[10] In 1339 Angelino Dulcert's famous map revealed to Christians the existence of a 'Rex Melli', rich in gold. At the end of the same century, the accurate maps of the Cresques, father and son, clearly showed that, for their authors, the key to the south was to be found at Tlemcen, and also that the routes leading to the 'land of the blacks' were beginning to be known.[11]

Parallel with this effort to summarize existing knowledge, attempts were made to open up the way to the land of the blacks through the Saharan trade routes; such attempts were undoubtedly numerous and were probably doomed to eternal oblivion. The expedition made by Malfante of Genoa to Tuat in 1447 belongs to this series of 'probes', which produced few results.[12] For their part, the Egyptians had very effectively prohibited

9. See F. de Médeiros, 1973. Among the picturesque curiosities known as *mirabilia* in Latin must be included Dante's mention of the Southern Cross and Petrarch's allusions to the Canary Islands, R. Hennig, 1953–6, Vol. 1, pp. 369 ff. Similarly Ramon Llull's reference, in a famous novel of the late thirteenth century, to 'Gana' and to the blacks who surrounded this town – numerous, idolatrous, cheerful and stern lovers of justice – must be considered, like many other comparable details given by other authors, a literary flight of fancy.

10. See J. Vernet, 1958.

11. It is naturally only possible here to give a very cursory outline of this question. It has already been the subject of many publications, and deserves the further attention of research workers, since many more useful observations could still be drawn from these documents.

12. C. de la Roncière, 1924–7, Vol. 1, pp. 144 ff. The version of the text published by de la Roncière would repay careful revision from the manuscript. Regarding this author's interpretation of this voyage, see J. Heers, 1971, pp. 66 ff.

all Christian penetration south of Cairo and in the Red Sea since the end of the twelfth century. But the Christians were far more interested for many years in the Muslims living in Africa than in the continent itself.

This state of affairs continued until Portuguese expansion brought Europeans into contact with many non-Muslim blacks for the first time. The founding of the College of Miramar in the Balearic Islands in 1276 and of a centre for the study of Arabic and Islam in Ifrīḳiya at the end of the thirteenth century correspond to the Dominicans' and Franciscans' desires and hopes to convert the Muslims. As a side-effect, some new features were added to the existing knowledge of Africa.

It was quite unusual for the Popes to intervene in the continent itself. In certain cases, at the end of the eleventh century, papal interventions were aimed at preserving the last vestiges of Christianity, which was disappearing from Ifrīḳiya. In others, they were aimed at ensuring, through diplomatic representations to Muslim sovereigns, the continuing life of the churches or even – in Morocco – the bishoprics created for the European communities of merchants and mercenaries resident in the Maghrib. On occasion, such representations took a more indiscreet turn and constituted direct interventions in the life of the Maghrib.[13] The Christians of the Iberian peninsula were to leave a decisive mark on European knowledge of Africa. As seekers of precious metals and enemies of the Muslims, they believed they had found in 'Prester John' – a figure familiar to the crusaders, whom the rest of Europe was beginning to forget – an African 'ally' against Islam.

Although Asians knew the east coast of Africa long before the great, decisive expansion of the fifteenth century, they paid little attention, according to the documents so far available, to the African continent.[14]

An expanding area: from Mediterranean diplomacy to Afro-European exchanges

Until quite recently, historians paid attention only to diplomatic relations and warfare between African and western Islam. There is no point here in repeating well-known facts. It may simply be mentioned that although Muslim resistance to the onslaughts of the Christians are not well coordinated, the Christians were no better placed to act in a coherent and united manner themselves. From west to east, with various dynasties reigning over territories of different sizes, the Muslim states of Spain, Morocco, Tlemcen, Ifrīḳiya and Egypt, after the disappearance of the Almohads, were usually fighting among themselves. Although a powerful spiritual

13. This was the case in 1251, when Innocent IV called for the creation of Christian sanctuaries on the Moroccan coast; in 1290, when Nicholas IV addressed an encyclical to all Christians in North Africa; and in 1419, when Martin V addressed the Christian hierarchy in Morocco.

14. J. J. L. Duyvendak, 1949; T. Filesi, 1962a and 1962b; Chou Yi Liang, 1972.

and cultural unifying force, Islam was not, in political and military terms, cohesive enough to counteract the divergent interests of the princes. Similarly, economic interests brought the Christian states, from Castile to Italy, into open conflict, in spite of their common ideology.

On the face of it, the diplomatic, military and political history of the Mediterranean region during these centuries does not seem to have been very logical. Genoa constantly supported the kingdom of Granada against Castile. Granada, in spite of its appeals, received little assistance from Morocco or Egypt. The rivalry between the inhabitants of the two sides of the Straits of Gibraltar for control of this essential gateway to the Atlantic explains the diplomatic conflicts between the Marinids and Granada.[15] The interests of Egypt, a client state of Castile and Aragon, show why its support for Granada was so half-hearted. The Marinids entered into conflict with their neighbours of Tlemcen, while the Hafsids tried to push the latter back westwards and prevent any strong Marinid expansion. The difficult and contradictory relations existing between the Venetians and the Genoese, on the one hand, and Mamluks and Ottomans, on the other, remain incomprehensible unless one looks beneath the surface of diplomatic relations. The realities lie at other levels and are on a different scale.

The Muslims, already the masters of trade between Asia and Europe simply by virtue of their politico-economic sphere of influence, also brought the Sahel economy into close connection with world changes. Both directly and indirectly, North Africa drew very considerable resources, particularly gold, from further south, possibly from as far south as the verge of the forest zone. This happened slowly at first, from the seventh to the tenth century, and more rapidly during the eleventh and twelfth centuries. The southerly or 'oblique' routes were now linked with the main arteries of Muslim trade.[16] West Africa was involved, under the Mali and the Ghana empires; but so also were Air, Chad, Darfūr and the middle Nile.[17] In the Sahel area the consequences were far reaching.[18] In the north, from the eleventh century onwards, states grew up at each point of convergence of the southern routes, and each was in competition with its neighbours. Economic competition developed between the princes, usually without

15. The treaty signed in 1285 by Castile and the Marinids marked a profound change of balance. The Marinids renounced their claims both to Spanish land and to a naval presence. In exchange – and the fact remains of considerable cultural importance to us – Fez took delivery of thirteen shipments of books from Cordova; C.-E. Dufourcq, 1966, p. 206.

16. The Fatimids, followed by the 'Umayyads of Spain, the Almoravids and then the Almohads, successively benefited from the advantages of hegemony over the most important terminal points of the southern routes. See D. Robert, S. Robert and J. Devisse, 1970; and J. Devisse, 1972.

17. An enormous amount remains to be done to clarify the history of the movements of people and goods in the regions in question.

18. I have developed this point elsewhere; see Devisse, op. cit.

benefit to the population except where, as at Tlemcen, a commercial bourgeoisie appeared.

From the twelfth century onwards, the Christian states took advantage of this competition and of the decline in political and military strength which it entailed. The Muslim lands and their southern annexes found themselves linked up to a much vaster area, in full economic expansion: the western Mediterranean countries, and then the whole of Europe. The most remarkable effects of this 'revolution' were felt from the thirteenth to the fifteenth century.[19] Mali and Songhay organized a careful system for controlling exports and taxing imports. Furthermore, the diversification of export routes and customers, systematically sought by the mansas of Mali and the sovereigns of Gao, certainly contributed in no small measure to developing relations of all sorts between the Sahel and its rivals/partners in the north of the continent. The frequent sending of embassies, the journeys and exchanges of letters begin to give us an idea of the active and able diplomacy of the black sovereigns, who were trying to avoid the disastrous consequences of a monopoly over the purchase of their products.[20] This new situation had far-reaching and increasing repercussions on relations between northern and tropical Africa, and also on the internal position of the Muslim kingdoms of the north. The successes and failures of the Marinid, Wattasid and Sa'dian dynasties in Morocco, for example, were largely connected with the interruption or improvement of relations with the south.

Christian military and commercial pressure was increasing. The number of treaties and the number of times they were renewed show the stubbornness of the merchants and kings of the north and the supple resistance of the Maghrib (see Fig. 26.2). The increasing numbers of trading settlements, more or less isolated from their context in the Maghrib and in constant rivalry with each other, show the importance Europe attached to trade in Africa (see Fig. 26.3). From this time onwards the north treated Africa as part of the economically exploitable south, right down to the forest belt.[21] Egypt alone managed to control European trade in its ports in such a way that its successive dynasties managed to secure a balance of advantage.[22]

While competing fiercely with each other, the Europeans did not apply the same methods in their trade with Africa. All sought to obtain the most advantageous balance of trade, but their economic and strategic possibilities differed widely. Venice remained faithful until the end of the fifteenth century to a type of trade which was beginning to give way to more modern forms. Venetian merchants bought Asian spices in Egypt and Syria and resold them at high prices. Safe in the knowledge that they

19. R. S. Lopez, 1974, p. 252.
20. See Devisse, op. cit.; and more recently M. Abitbol, 1979, p. 370.
21. Devisse, op. cit., p. 369.
22. See C. Cahen, 1965.

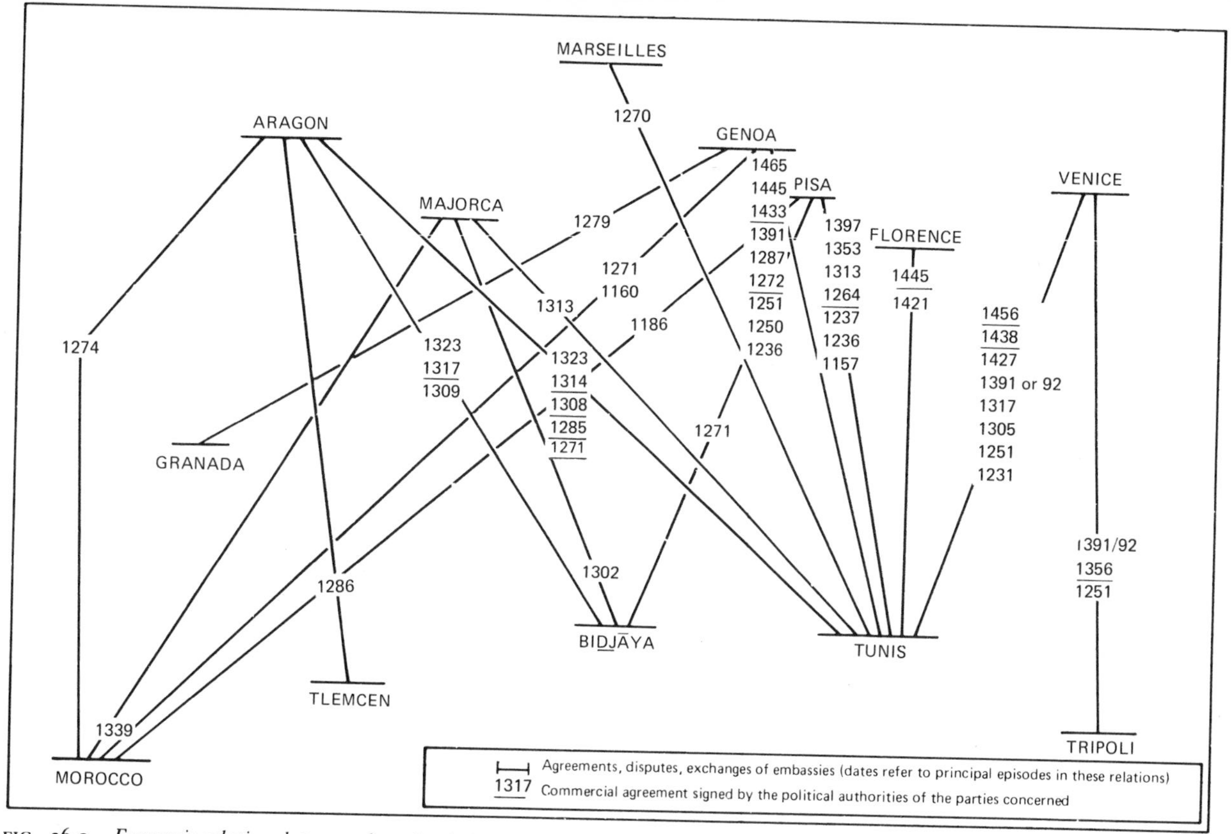

FIG. 26.2 *Economic relations between places bordering the western Mediterranean (J. Devisse)*

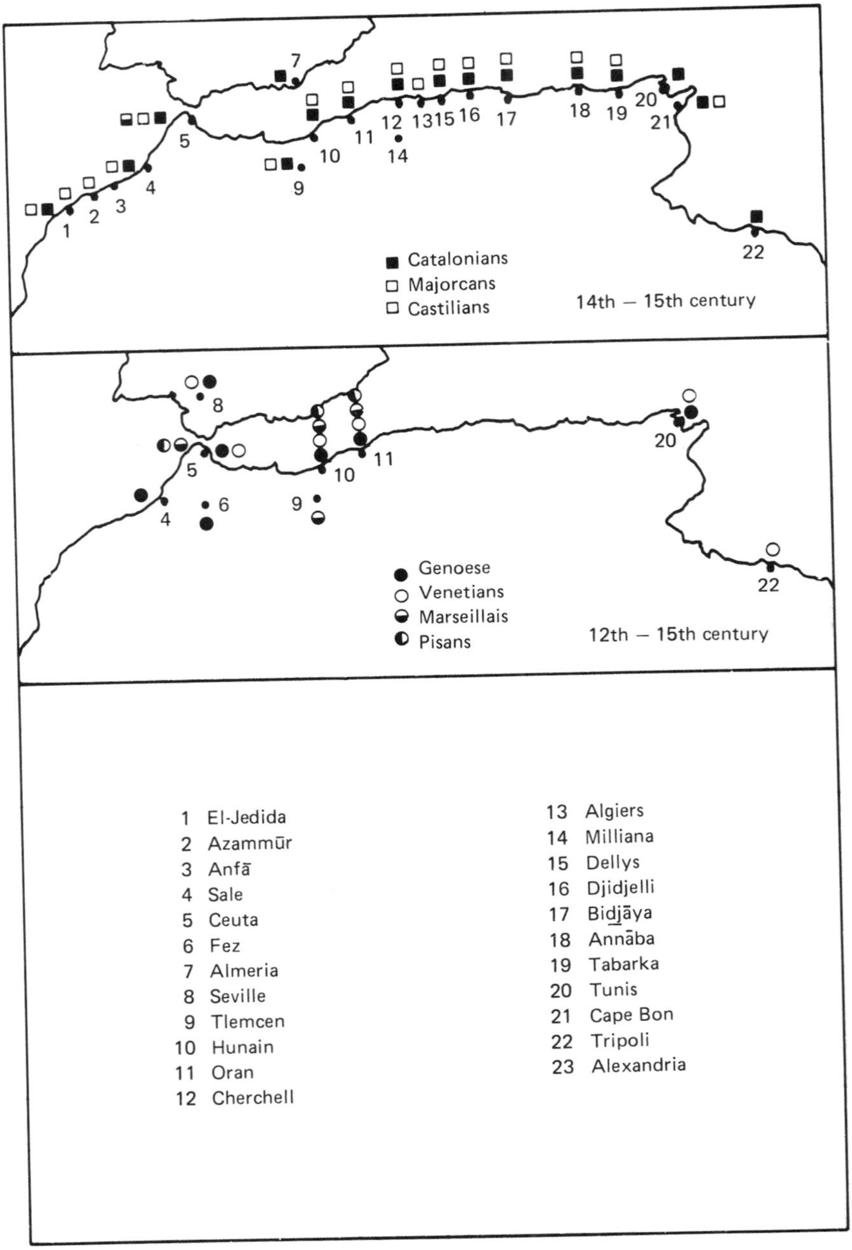

FIG. 26.3 *Search for African gold by European merchants in the 12th–15th centuries (J. Devisse)*

held a sales monopoly in a market which could not be saturated, they did not care to import large quantities and could thus ask the most exorbitant prices. From this point of view, Egypt and the eastern Mediterranean countries were most important to Venice.[23] When difficulties arose in the fifteenth century, however, the Venetians had no objection to supplying Tripoli and Tunis with glassware and textiles, copper and coral, in exchange for gold. As a result of their monopoly of sugar from the East, from Cyprus and from Crete, the Venetians also had considerable opportunities for adding to their wealth. For many years they were more interested in Egypt and the eastern basin of the Mediterranean, the termini of the Asian and Middle Eastern trade routes, than in Africa itself.[24]

In the fourteenth century the Genoese were selling wheat and slaves to these same eastern regions.[25] From England they obtained woollens of fairly low quality, which could be sold cheaply.[26] Without making a large profit on each transaction, they multiplied their volume of sales and thus built up quite a considerable trade in terms of value.[27] Like the Catalonians, but for a longer time and on a larger scale, the Genoese chartered their ships to Muslims for the transport of people and goods between Egypt and Spain. North-west Africa and the eastern Mediterranean had already assumed considerable importance for them. The Ottoman conquest drove them away from the latter area, and from this time onwards they relied entirely on trade with northern Africa. To compete with the Venetian sales of sugar, they asked far lower prices and, for the first time in history, developed a bulk trade in this commodity. But from that time they needed to control, directly or otherwise, the sugar-producing areas. It was the Spaniards – Muslims or Christians – who were the first to supply substantial quantities.[28] This naturally brought a *rapprochement* with

23. On the consequences of this choice for the Venetians, see R. Romano, A. Tenenti and V. Tucci, 1970, pp. 109 ff.

24. From the fifteenth century, when the Venetians were also constrained by the Ottoman expansion, they attached great importance to trade with Tripoli – especially the import of gold – as we are only just beginning to discover.

25. The Genoese controlled the export of wheat from the Black Sea, as the Byzantines had done before them, using it as a means of pressure on the Fatimids of Egypt. Now it became a trump card for the Genoese in dealing with the Mamluks. It would be interesting to discover if other forms of 'wheat diplomacy' existed, in the Maghrib for example, which would again constitute a means of pressure on countries with irregular harvests. The whole question of the grain trade in the interior of Africa in this period has yet to be studied. There are a few rare references to it in documents of the fourteenth century. In 1477, a ship carried 640 tonnes of cereals from Oran to Genoa; also in the fifteenth century, wheat was transported from the Atlantic coast of Morocco to Portugal.

26. European textiles penetrated far into the south. We know that Ibn Baṭṭūṭa referred to them in describing clothing of the mansas of Mali; Ibn Baṭṭūṭa, 1357, p. 305.

27. In 1445, 90 kg of cowries were recorded among the merchandise confiscated by the Granada from the Genoese. On these matters, see J. Heers, 1957, p. 120

28. From this point of view, the downfall of the kingdom of Granada in 1492 certainly constituted a considerable, although temporary, set-back to the Genoese sugar sales policy,

the Genoese, who were subsequently associated closely with the Portuguese policy of discovery, with the introduction of sugar-cane growing in the Atlantic islands occupied by the Portuguese and with the marketing of sugar from Madeira and the Canary Islands. As a natural consequence, this Genoese policy brought the Italians out into the Straits of Gibraltar and the Atlantic, interested them in the intense research into shipbuilding then being developed, especially in Portugal, and led to their more or less direct participation in exploration.[29]

These facts deserve to be emphasized since they explain all the mechanisms of future Portuguese expansion in the Atlantic and foreshadow the consequences of this expansion for Africa. The Catalonians, the last to arrive on the scene, did not attain the same level of power as their great Italian rivals; they engaged in a large number of small, low-yield operations.[30] The other western ports and countries exhausted themselves trying to keep up with these examples.

But this is not the most interesting point. It was not just the small quantities of kola nuts, malaguetta pepper and other more or less decorative products, including ivory;[31] it was through the gold and the slaves torn from its bosom that the African presence became most clearly visible in the Mediterranean economy. No thorough inquiry has yet been made on either of these subjects, and the most that can be done is to outline a number of results already obtained.

From the tenth to the twelfth century, African gold contributed above all to the excellence of the Fatimid, 'Umayyad, Almoravid, Almohad and Hafsid coinages.[32] Gold continued to flow towards North Africa, with a few fluctuations about which too little is known, until the end of the fifteenth century (see Fig. 26.4). It still provided the rulers, who controlled its circulation with varying degrees of success, not only with the raw material for minting coins, but also with political prestige and a degree of luxury at their courts which the Arab writers describe. But new developments gradually modified the position to the advantage of the Europeans.

It is now known that by the end of the tenth century, Spanish Christians had begun to obtain gold from the south, by methods which were then very primitive. But from the thirteenth century onwards, things

and it probably contributed to the intensification of production in the Atlantic islands. See Heers, 1971, pp. 89 ff. and 170.

29. C. Verlinden, 1966b.

30. On Catalonian trade, see Dufourcq, op. cit.

31. V. L. Grottanelli, 1975, has shown that European imports of African ivory preceded the Portuguese expansion. This fact has been too little studied and merits attention from researchers; it suggests that the influence of African art in Europe predates the fifteenth century.

32. A great deal has been published on this. See especially *Journal of Economic and Social History of the Orient*, the publications of the British Royal Numismatic Society and those of the American Numismatic Society of New York.

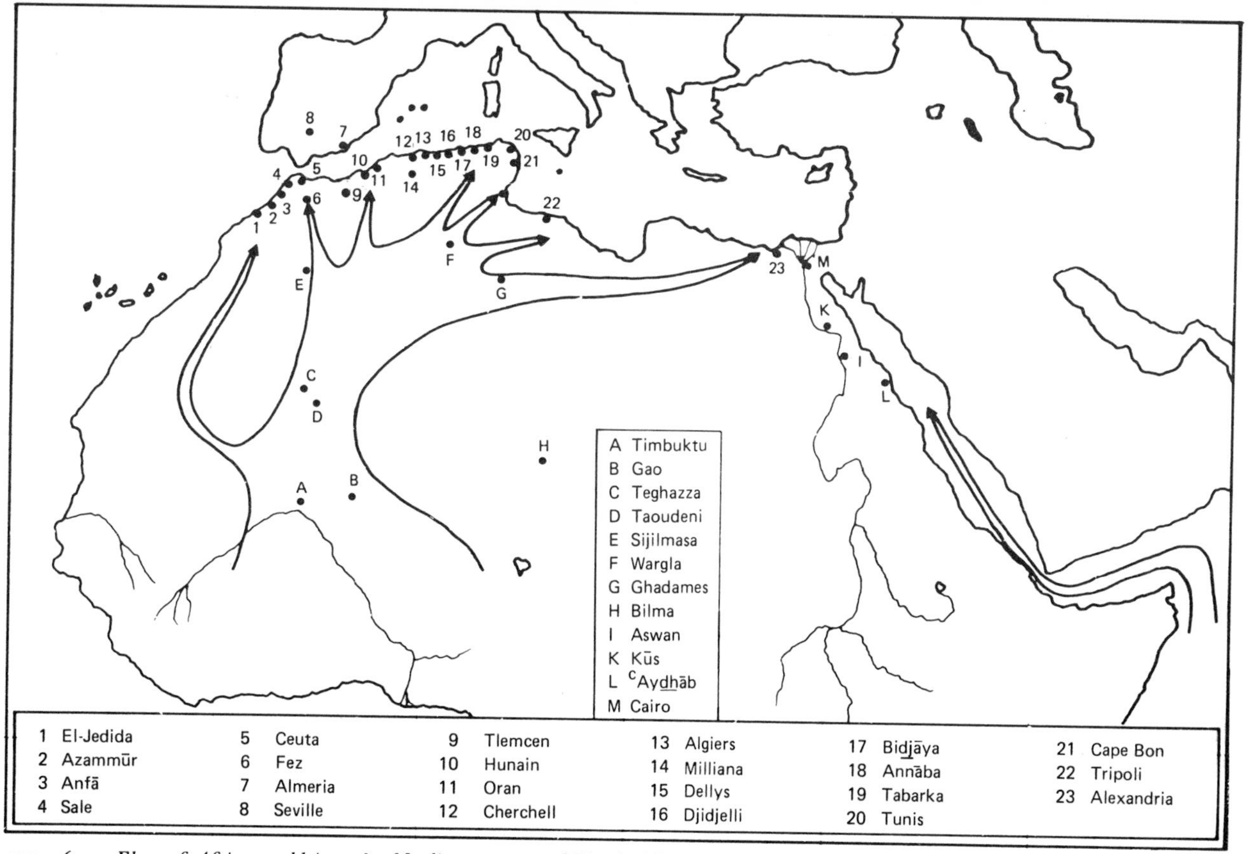

FIG. 26.4 *Flow of African gold into the Muslim economy of North Africa (J. Devisse)*

changed and the profits accumulated. Trade with Tunisia was then reputed to be bringing the Christians roughly 20 000–60 000 dinars a year and trade with Bidjāya (Bougie) from 12 000 to 24 000 dinars. In 1302 and subsequent years, Majorca received some 2000 dinars in gold from its trade with Bidjāya. In 1377, Genoa imported 68 000 poundsworth of gold, most of which had passed through Granada or Christian Spain; 75 years later, Genoa was making some 45 000 ducats a year through the same channels.[33] The overall value of Catalonian exports to the Maghrib as a whole – and not simply its profits – is reckoned to have been, in the fifteenth century, 400 000 or 500 000 dinars a year; Barcelona had an annual revenue of the order of 120 000 dinars.[34] Unfortunately, no estimates are available for the eastern trade of Venice and Genoa, which must certainly have brought in considerable amounts of cash. It is not surprising in the circumstances that an active merchant class should have come into being in the great Christian ports of the Mediterranean and in certain large cities such as Milan and Florence. Since profit breeds profit, the power of these 'capitalists' – increasing with the establishment of business firms – enabled them to undertake shipbuilding on a large scale and to arm fleets of ships of increasing tonnage.[35]

At the same time, of course, the minting of gold coins, which had been interrupted for centuries in the West, started again after the middle of the thirteenth century.[36] This was undoubtedly due partly (to an extent yet to be estimated) to the African gold obtained from Muslim ports. The study of the scientific and economic aspects of these currencies is now being carried out and will certainly advance our knowledge of these questions. Be that as it may, even taking into account the inflow of eastern gold from North Africa through Egypt, the amount of gold coming into Europe remained inadequate to meet the needs of the West in a period of full economic expansion.[37]

The 'thirst for gold' was to be a powerful contributory factor, motivating the Europeans to set out on the conquest and economic

33. P. Bonnassié, 1975–6, Vol. 1, pp. 372 ff.; P. Vilar, 1974, p. 42; Dufourcq, op. cit., p. 429; Heers, 1957, p. 101, and 1971, p. 177; R. Arié, 1973, p. 363.

34. Dufourcq, op. cit., pp. 555–6. He gives the value for Ifrīḳiya as about 125 000 dinars, for the central Maghrib as 30 000–70 000 dinars, and for Morocco as about 200 000 dinars.

35. Shipbuilding became difficult for the Muslims, owing to the shortage of timber, when they no longer had access to the rich timber resources of the Mediterranean islands and Spain.

36. Genoa had a stable coinage from 1330 to the end of the century. In 1443, after a period of crisis, it reformed its monetary system in relation to gold. The other Italian towns, particularly Venice and Florence, did the same. Majorca minted a gold *real* of 3.85 g from 1310 onwards. Under Alphonse X, Castile adopted the weight of an Almohad dinar (4.60 g) for its gold doubloon.

37. Dufourcq, op. cit., reckons that some 70 kg of African gold came into Aragon every year. Heers considers that 200 kg of gold was brought into Genoa annually. On the amount of gold circulating in the economy in relation to real needs, see Vilar, op. cit., pp. 32–3.

domination of the world. The interest shown by the Mediterranean Christians in African gold, which sent Malfante and many others out in search of the gold routes in the interior of the continent, is easier to explain in this context. The profits from trade, which were not negligible for the kings themselves, were not the westerners' only means of obtaining African gold. The tributes imposed by the Christian conquerors in exchange for a largely illusory protection also brought in comfortable profits, in this case to the rulers.[38]

In the twelfth century, the kings of Tunis paid 33 000 gold bezants a year to Sicily. After 1282 Aragon tried in vain to impose the renewed payment of this tribute. (In the fourteenth century, Ifrīḳiya began to pay again, but only small amounts – of the order of 20 000 dinars – and only irregularly.) The naval alliance with the Catalonians, which the Marinids requested for a short time in 1274, cost the Moroccans some 40 000 dinars. In 1309, the support provided by Aragon cost them a further 7000 dinars. To appreciate the value of these 'presents', it should be recalled that an embassy from Granada returned from Cairo in the fourteenth century with a gift of 2000 Egyptian dinars for the Nasrid sovereign. It has recently been shown that Granada, which received some of the African gold, transmitted between 10 000 and 40 000 dinars annually to Castile – including the levies exacted when Castile won a military victory. During the fifteenth century, these sums were reduced, perhaps because gold had become scarcer in Granada. Bidjāya promised – but failed – to pay 1000 dinars a year to Aragon in 1314 and 1323, and paid 8000 dinars in 1329. Tlemcen paid the same king of Aragon between 2000 and 6000 dinars a year from 1275 to 1295.[39]

These payments were, of course, largely a reflection of the real balance of power between Muslims and Christians. Other methods, such as hiring out fleets or troops, proved to be even more profitable. There were many examples of the hire of ships. In 1304 Morocco chartered a fleet from Aragon for 30 000 dinars. In 1302 and again in 1309, James of Aragon offered fully equipped ships for hire to the Marinids at 500 dinars per month per ship. He did the same for the Hafsids in 1309, and the actual monthly profit amounted to some 250 dinars. Dufourcq calculates that the cost of building a ship could have been amortized in four or five months at this rate. In 1313, Tlemcen hired six galleys for a year for 35 000 dinars. In 1377, Peter IV of Aragon provided ships with crossbowmen to Granada

38. On signing agreements with their Muslim counterparts, the Christian kings sometimes obtained the refund of part of the customs duties paid by their merchants in Africa: in 1229–30, the king of Aragon thus received some 500 dinars from Tlemcen; in 1302 Bidjāya promised to refund him one-quarter of its duties, some 1500 dinars a year; Ifrīḳiya returned 50 per cent of these duties to Aragon at the beginning of the fourteenth century. On the monetary effects of these negotiations, see Vilar, op. cit., pp. 42–3.

39. G. Yver, 1903, p. 135; Dufourcq, op. cit., p. 179; Arié, op. cit., pp. 119 and 214.

for 900 dinars a month. Turning to soldiers, from the middle of the thirteenth century onwards, the Catalonians supplied the Hafsids with Christian troops. Part of the amount paid for the mercenaries was made over to the king of Aragon, who thus made a profit of some 4000 dinars a year; a similar system was organized at Tlemcen, and also in Morocco, where the price paid was 10 000 gold dinars in 1304.[40] Dufourcq has estimated that from the end of the thirteenth century onwards the income earned in these various ways by the king of Aragon amounted to 15 000 dinars, or over 10 per cent of crown revenues.[41]

On the basis of this information, and pending a fuller account, there are adequate grounds for supposing that the proportion of African gold which passed into the European commercial circuit was by no means negligible. Even though the amounts involved only represented a very small proportion of the amount of gold – perhaps between 4 and 8 tonnes – exported annually from the west and south of Africa to the north of the continent, and even though these amounts were ridiculously small in relation to the real needs of the European economy, they still constitute a considerable input. Moreover, European pressure in the trading enclaves gave ample evidence that everyone concerned was conscious of the profits to be made there. Economic pressure was accompanied by a new effort to establish religious communities, particularly in Morocco, at a time when the old structure of the African church was finally disappearing in Ifrīḳiya;[42] the half-hearted efforts made by Rome in the fifteenth century to establish relations with Ethiopia had had practically no results.

It is not surprising that the Muslim kingdoms of North Africa accepted such a situation, when we recall that they did quite well out of it. The customs duties levied on European imports usually amounted to 10 per cent, apart from the privileges granted by treaty. Trade with Catalonia alone would have brought in 6000 dinars a year to the Marinid coffers and considerable amounts to Tlemcen as well. During the fifteenth century, the Hafsid custom-house at Tunis produced an annual revenue of 150 000 dinars.[43] It was still profitable for these dynasties, even if Europe grew richer at their countries' expense, to pay for the troops needed to keep the roads safe, particularly south of Tlemcen, and to collect taxes. The more clear-sighted of the rulers of the Maghrib accused European commercial colonization of throwing their economies increasingly off balance; but most of them drifted with the tide.

Since the seventh century, the raiding of enemy territory and the capture of slaves – some of whom were sold again and the rest employed

40. Dufourcq, op. cit., pp. 103, 149 ff., 541; Arié, op. cit., p. 269.

41. Dufourcq, op. cit., pp. 560 ff.

42. L. Jadin, 1966, pp. 33–69. The mendicant orders appeared in Morocco and bishops were appointed to Fez and Marrakesh for the Christian mercenaries. See also A. Mahjoubi, 1966, Vol. 1, pp. 85–103.

43. Dufourcq, op. cit., pp. 563 ff.

on a great variety of tasks – had been one of the customary features of the warfare between Muslims and Christians. In the tenth and eleventh centuries, this 'market' was particularly favourable to the Muslims of Spain. The trend was reversed, from the twelfth century onwards, as the military and naval pressure of the Christians on the Muslims increased. The growing imbalance left the Christians with growing numbers of slaves to be used or sold; they included not only people of the Maghrib, but also blacks from North Africa or from further south.[44]

It is certain that 'Sudanese' or Nubian slaves were imported into all the countries of northern Africa. This is well known for Egypt, but less so, at present, for West Africa.[45] There is no doubt that the first contacts between Christians and blacks occurred through the intermediary of the Muslim world. Iconography, for example, reveals the place occupied by 'blackamoors' in the armies of Muslim Spain which fought the Christians;[46] Ibn 'Abdūn tells us in his manual, *Ḥisba*, in the twelfth century that these blacks were present in Almoravid Seville and were reputed to be dangerous.[47]

During the fourteenth and fifteenth centuries, this shameful trade was mainly in the hands of Christian merchants. The Catalonians were past masters at it; the merchants of northern Spain were sending black slaves to Roussillon from the fourteenth century. In 1213 a black Christian woman slave was sold by a Genoese merchant to one of his colleagues. In the fifteenth century, according to the sources, the western basin of the Mediterranean – and Venice to a lesser degree – increased their imports of black labour, and Cyrenaica played an essential role in this trade, at least from 1440 to 1470. In the second half of the century, 83 per cent of slaves in Naples were black. There were also many blacks in Sicily.[48]

An important fact was the appearance on the Mediterranean market of blacks from 'Guinea'.[49] The competition among Europeans was already

44. During the twelfth and thirteenth centuries, sources reveal the presence of blacks in Sicily: for example, 23 slaves at Catania in 1145, and one black Christian slave at Palermo in 1243. In the twelfth century, the Muslims given by the Norman king to the abbey of Monreale include about thirty names which could be those of blacks. (Information, partly unpublished, from young research workers at the University of Paris VIII.)

45. See, for example: al-Ya'ḳūbī (891), French transl. in Cuoq, op. cit., p. 49; al-Istakhrī (951), ibid., p. 65; al-Muḳaddāsī (946–88), ibid., p. 68; al-Birūnī (973–1050), ibid., p. 80; al-Bakrī (1068), ibid., p. 82; al-Zuhrī (1154–61), ibid., pp. 115 ff.; al-Idrīsī (1154), ibid., pp. 127 ff.; Ibn 'Idharī al-Marrākūshī (fourteenth century), ibid., p. 220; al-'Umarī (1301–49), ibid., pp. 255 ff.; Ibn Baṭṭūṭa (1356), ibid., pp. 380 ff.; al-Maghīlī (1493–6), ibid., pp. 399 ff. See also R. Mauny, 1961, pp. 336–43, 377–9 and 422–4.

46. See especially A. Steiger, 1941.

47. Ibn 'Abdūn, French transl. 1947, para. 204.

48. C. Verlinden, 1966a, pp. 335–43, gives these and many other examples. See also C. Verlinden, 1977, pp. 200 ff.

49. First mentioned in Barcelona in 1489; Verlinden, 1966a, p. 338.

keen. As early as 1472, the Portuguese Cortès was demanding that the re-export of slaves – a trade that had begun towards the middle of the century, initially through raids on the Mauritanian coasts – should be strictly supervised and that such manpower should be used primarily for the agricultural development of Portugal and the islands it controlled. But this was to overlook the spirit of enterprise among the Italians and Catalonians. From 1486 to 1488, Bartolomeo Marchionni, a Florentine living in Portugal, noted the trade increasing on the Slave Coast;[50] and slave imports grew. The Genoese, whose control of finance and shipping gave them an important share of Portuguese business, and the Catalonians re-exported and resold this labour. The slave market at Valencia was well supplied from 1494 onwards. In 1495–6, some 800 slaves were sold there, including a considerable number of blacks who had come through Portugal.[51] Some of these slaves were of Senegalese origin.[52]

The consequences of this influx were very serious. First of all, prices collapsed: black slaves were sold at the lowest prices and their fate was described as the most miserable of all. It became customary to consider black labour, which was tough and reliable, as particularly suited to hard agricultural work; the consequences quickly appeared. Certain social classes in Mediterranean societies adopted a contemptuous and aloof attitude towards these unfortunate blacks, an attitude which was not shared at that time by northern Europe.[53]

During the fifteenth century, the economic growth which Africa had seen in the previous hundred years was jeopardized by the serious events occurring on the periphery. The struggle for the control of the Indian Ocean and the Ottoman expansion were among the factors which upset the former balance. European expansion towards the Atlantic was to be another factor and to have even graver consequences for Africa; it was to be responsible for the brutal interruption, over several centuries, of the growth which had begun in the fourteenth century.

50. From 15 June 1486 to 31 December 1493, 3589 slaves arrived in Lisbon, at least 1648 of whom were intended for the Florentine merchants. See also V. Rau, 1975.

51. See V. Cortés-Alonso, 1964. 62 Canary Islanders were sold in 1489 at Valencia and 90 at Ibiza in the Balearic Islands; 21 in 1493 at Valencia, 130 in 1494, 99 in 1496 and the last 26 in 1497. Regarding the Guanche trade, see C. Verlinden, 1955a, pp. 357, 550, 561, 562–7 and 1028. The numbers of African blacks were: in 1484, over 200; in 1490, about 50; in 1491, nearly 350; in 1492, about 180; in 1493, about 180; in 1494, about 150; in 1495, about 650; in 1496, about 150; in 1497, about 110. Supplies were then interrupted until 1502.

52. Cortés-Alonso, op. cit., pp. 56 ff. They were often young, aged 9, 12 or 15 years old.

53. We hope to enlarge on this material by the publication in the near future of a long study on the iconography of blacks in the West.

Africa, Asia and the Indian Ocean

The preceding volumes have shown that relations with the rich Asian production centres led to the opening of major trade routes, by land and sea, all of which led to western Asia. The Muslims had controlled these routes since the seventh century, but competition remained acute between the route terminating at the bottom of the Arab/Persian Gulf, which fed Mesopotamian and Syrian trade, and the route ending at the Red Sea, which led, through the Nile, to the development of the delta ports. There was incessant rivalry between the two terminal points. During the era with which we are concerned, upheavals of all sorts occurring in Asia and the collapse of Muslim domination in Mesopotamia left the field open for Egypt, which was then in control of the eastern trade and enjoying its most sumptuous period under the Fatimids and the Mamluks.[54]

The Mediterranean was, in effect, abandoned to the Christians after 1100. However, their military and commercial efforts to reach the main international trade route to the Red Sea, via Egypt, remained fruitless. In any case, the Egyptians and their successive sovereigns seldom had the opportunity of direct access to the great trade of the Indian Ocean. They were nearly always obliged to go through the intermediary of the various dynasties which succeeded each other at Aden, the hub of this trade.

At all events, from the twelfth century onwards, the specialists in this great trade were the Karīmī, who established the traffic in spices, precious stones, gold and copper between Asia and Africa, on the one hand, and Aden and Egypt, on the other.[55] Their prosperity grew steadily for three centuries. Until the time of the Ottoman conquest, they and the Muslim merchants who imitated them enjoyed great prosperity, the benefits of which were felt in the Mediterranean ports of Egypt, where westerners came to buy these rare and precious objects.

Under the Ayyubids (1171–1250), ʿAydhāb became one of the busiest ports in the world.[56] Ibn Djubayr passed through it on the pilgrimage in 1183. He gave up counting the caravans present, they were so numerous. The political and naval unification of the Red Sea was never very durable, however, and neither the Ayyubids nor their successors really succeeded in realizing it. The true unifying factor was the merchants, particularly the Karīmī, who were based at Aden, whence they transported,

54. S. Y. Labib, 1965.

55. The name of the Karīmī has occasionally been linked with the Kanim (Kanem) of Chad. Recent research supports this connection. On this question see *Encyclopaedia of Islam*, new edn, under 'Karīmī', Vol. 4, pp. 640–3. In Tamūl, *karya* means 'business'; it is not impossible to see an interesting connection there. See also S. D. F. Goitein, 1966, esp. ch. 17 and 18; and cf. J. C. Garcin, Chapter 15, p. 382 n. 9 above.

56. On the growth of this port, see J. C. Garcin, 1972, pp. 189–209, and A. Paul, 1955.

bought and sold products from Asia, Africa and the Mediterranean. The Karīmī acted as diplomatic intermediaries when conflicts arose between the masters of Egypt and the dynasts of Aden. They also negotiated agreements between Asian and Egyptian princes. The Egyptian authorities granted these essential auxiliaries safe conduct for themselves and their goods, and the right to import western products freely into Egypt. The flow of spices and of slaves towards the entrepôts of the Nile was thus ensured. Egyptian economic hegemony was extended under the Mamluks to the ports on the west coast of the Red Sea, Sawākin, Massawa and Assab.

Aden was also the main point through which another trade had to pass – the trade with the east coast of Africa, which was developing less spectacularly and was less generally known than the Asian trade; the profits also appear to have been smaller.[57] It is likely, however, that the many proofs of interest shown in this African trade by members of the Fatimid family and Egyptian merchants were not unconnected with Egypt's need for gold in the twelfth century, when the mines of Wadi al-Allaḳ were becoming exhausted and it was difficult or impossible to obtain West African gold.[58]

According to al-Idrīsī, intense commercial activity already existed in the twelfth century on the East African coast. Iron was exported at a great profit, particularly to India, whose high-quality steel required considerable imports of raw materials. In about 1240, Ibn al-Wardī wrote of the country around Sofala: 'it is an immense country with mountains containing iron deposits exploited by the inhabitants. The Indians come and buy this metal from them at a very high price.' Ivory, collected in the interior and much sought after for the Muslim, Chinese and Indian markets, hides, iron and gold constituted the most important export products. Timber will probably have to be added to this list when studies comparable to those already undertaken in respect of the Mediterranean

57. See *Unesco General History of Africa*, Volumes II and III. While waiting for other studies to be published on this question, it is worth noting that, according to Goitein, some commerce did not go through Aden: op. cit., p. 355, and 1967. Arabic and Chinese sources will also provide important additional information; see P. Wheatley, 1959.

58. The problem of the import of gold from the south has not yet been tackled with all the attention it deserves, owing to lack of collaboration among the specialists, but it is apparent from the most important publications that mining and export had certainly begun by the year 1000. See, in particular, R. Summers, 1969, who appears convinced that production started in ancient times, and also T. N. Huffman 1974a, with an important bibliography. This author stresses that large-scale gold mining began in the eleventh century. At the other end of the line, the very scholarly articles by A. S. Ehrenkreutz, 1959 and 1963, should be read to appreciate the true scale and quality of the Fatimid coinage, presupposing an abundant supply of gold which the Fatimids could not have obtained from Egypt, Nubia or West Africa at the time. It is only fair to point out that there are still very few specialists who accept the antiquity of this gold trade with Egypt.

have identified the important place occupied by Africa in this international trade, second only to Asia.[59]

Gold from the south, exported through Sofala but marketed at Kilwa, assumed a dominant place in this trade. R. Summers estimates South African output at 10 tonnes a year during these centuries, with a decline starting in the fifteenth century.[60] But even if one accepts more modest figures, it must be admitted that this gold certainly played a part – very little studied as yet – comparable with that of West African gold in the world economy.

Ships brought various products to this coast; the following are of particular interest because of their provenance: cowrie shells, new plants which quickly became acclimatized in Africa, clothing and glass beads which sold at a high price to the Africans.[61] This was mainly a coastal trade, carried in ships of varying types and tonnage, which probably used Kilwa as their home port.[62] The more southerly areas, as far as the Mozambique Channel, where meteorological conditions were very different from the familiar conditions of the northern Indian Ocean, had not been systematically explored and exploited by Muslim sailors before the fifteenth century. 'The south', indeed, remained shrouded in mystery, first of all because, according to Ptolemy, it was more oriental in character than truly southern, and also because it was there that a mysterious country – Waḳwaḳ – rich in promises and threats, awaited the intrepid traveller. There was also a 'land's end' about which very little was known (see Fig. 26.1).

Using the summer monsoon winds, Muslim ships sailed from Mombasa or Malindi to Asia every year. These ships played an important part in developing navigation techniques, which improved considerably from the thirteenth to the fifteenth century. Navigation by the stars, which was derived largely from the inventions and observations of the Chinese; the use of the compass, which was probably borrowed from the Chinese at about the same time by Arab and Mediterranean sailors; the knowledge of winds, currents and variations in marine fauna and flora; and the drawing up of navigation charts, in which the Muslim pilots noted their observations: all these constituted a valuable store of science and tech-

59. M. Lombard, 1972, pp. 153–76.

60. Summers, op. cit., p. 195.

61. Ibn Baṭṭūṭa makes a lengthy study of trade in cowrie shells from the Maldive Islands on the east coast. He also writes on plants. For a more recent account, see H. N. Chittick and R. I. Rotberg (eds), 1975, and Unesco, 1980a.

62. At Kilwa and Sofala, Swahili traders bought cotton, silk and woollen fabrics in exchange for their gold. In the thirteenth century, 67 per cent of customs duties levied at Kilwa came from imported cotton. It seems that in this region of Africa, as in the western region, copper ornaments were valued at least as highly as gold ones. Recent studies (Randles; Summers), however, stress the caution shown by the Muslims in collecting gold in the south. These authors note the contrast between their slow pace – even if, in the long run, they found considerable amounts of gold – and the feverish search for the same gold when the Portuguese settled in the south of the continent.

nology, from which the Portuguese were to benefit when they arrived at Mombasa.[63]

All in all, this trade, which was obviously very much against the interests of the Africans of the interior, enriched all the African and non-African middlemen established in the coastal enclaves. (Kilwa was striking coins from the thirteenth century.) African sailors were employed on coasters and other ships plying between Asia and Africa, at least if certain paintings on manuscripts are to be believed (see Plate 26.1). Others left Africa, more or less voluntarily, perhaps, and set up colonies in southern Arabia and even as far as the west coast of India, where their historical importance is only just beginning to be studied.[64]

Over fifty towns, from Cape Gardafui to Sofala, demonstrated the vitality of the urban phenomenon in the Swahili zone even before the arrival of the Arabs. From the twelfth century onwards, as clearly indicated by archaeology and the critical study of sources, small groups of emigrants came from the Muslim world into these towns and the islands along the coast, although there was no uniform or systematic effort at colonization. The linking of these towns with the large-scale trade that was growing in the Indian Ocean via Aden or on the direct line between Africa and Asia, aided by the monsoons, led to the development in the coastal towns of a rich merchant aristocracy, Muslims for the most part, who occasionally challenged the power of the traditional authorities. As in West Africa, these towns were an ethnic and cultural crucible, whose nature was progressively transformed by Islam and in which Arabic and Swahili mingled together. The coastal towns themselves, burgeoning at other points further south, helped to spin the tangled web of the origins of this very mixed population, now almost impossible to unravel.[65]

Their ruling classes enjoyed a degree of prosperity which is confirmed by archaeology. Beautiful stone mosques and palaces, magnificent glassware imported from the Persian Gulf, ceramics from across the seas and from China, all clearly indicate their affluence. The sovereigns and the wealthy classes amassed in their palaces precious faience from Sultanabad and Nishapur, pale green Chinese Sung porcelain and splendid, decorated Ming plates, pearls and precious stones from India, gold and ivory figurines, jade and copper jewellery as well as carpets from the Middle East.

63. There are an increasing number of studies on this aspect. See, for example, L. A. Barradas, 1967; G. R. Tibbetts, 1969.

64. See Unesco, op. cit.

65. It was only at a much later date, beginning in the fifteenth century at the earliest, that the traditions associated with the founding of these towns were deformed to link them up to Asian origins. The 'Shirazi myth', which continues to be widespread today, is, in its rigid formulation, of even more recent date. See Chapter 18 above. Among many other relevant works, some awaiting publication, see: W. Hirschberg, 1931, and V. L. Grottanelli, 1955.

PLATE 26.1 *A 13th-century Arabic manuscript, showing that there were Africans on the boats sailing in the Indian Ocean*

It should not, of course, be concluded from these atypical examples that the whole population in these towns was rich. The towns themselves were undoubtedly poles of attraction: they made possible the import of new techniques and the emergence of a life-style which contrasted with that of the Africans of the interior as described by al-Masʿūdī in the tenth century. They also undoubtedly played their part in uprooting and impoverishing those who rashly crowded into them. A study by Chittick and Rotberg gives a clear picture of one of the most prosperous of these towns, Kilwa, which Ibn Baṭṭūṭa described as 'one of the most beautiful towns in the world' and whose four and five-storey houses are described by fifteenth-century Chinese sources.[66]

The Chinese indeed visited this coast of Africa in force during the fifteenth century. There is evidence, too, of the arrival of Africans in China, possibly as early as the sixth or seventh century;[67] paintings of the T'ang era show black Africans in Buddhist grottoes; and a thirteenth-century compilation probably refers to Swahili country. But it is only archaeological finds that indicate traces of a 'Chinese presence' in East Africa from the eighth century onwards.[68] Even then, there is no proof that they originate from a direct link in ancient times between the Chinese and the Africans. Everything changed in the fifteenth century: as early as 1402 a Korean map gave an approximately correct, non-Ptolemaic outline of southern Africa; in 1470 the Ming chronicles gave a precise description of a zebra; and a Chinese painting of 1444 depicts a giraffe – no doubt the one that had arrived at the imperial court some years earlier (see below). In addition to the slave trade, Chinese sources mention four major articles exported from East Africa: gold, amber, yellow sandalwood and ivory.

A Chinese fleet of ships, which were enormous for their time, under the command of Cheng Ho, a Muslim from Yunnan, made seven great voyages across the Indian Ocean from 1405 to 1433; these ships called at the African coast twice, once between 1417 and 1419 and once between 1431 and 1433.[69] During the first voyage, the fleet sailed as far as Malindi, bringing home a delegation which had been sent to present a giraffe to the imperial court at Peking in 1415.[70] The towns of Brava and Mogadishu are mentioned in the reports on the second voyage. These voyages were considered the crown of China's maritime enterprise, but they were suddenly interrupted by domestic events in China. Nevertheless,

66. H. N. Chittick, and R. I. Rotberg, (eds), op. cit. On another of these cities, Shungwaya, see Grottanelli, 1955.

67. Chou Yi Liang, op cit., see also F. Hirth, 1910; W. W. Rockhill, 1915; C. E. Frip, 1940, 1941; Lo Jung Pang, 1955; T. Filesi, 1962a, 1962b.

68. Chou Yi Liang, op. cit.

69. The ships were of 1500 tonnes, whereas the first Portuguese ships to sail the Indian Ocean were only 300 tonnes.

70. See Duyvendak, op. cit.

as a result of Arab, Persian and Gujarati marine traffic between China, South-East Asia and West Africa, Chinese products such as porcelain and silk continued to be sold on the markets of East Africa after these expeditions, as they had been earlier.[71] On the coral island of Songo Mnara, near Kilwa, Mathew discovered glazed earthenware from Thailand as well as large quantities of Chinese porcelain dating from the end of the Sung period to the beginning of the Ming period (approximately 1127–1450).[72] Between 1440 and 1449 in China, Wang Ta Yuan wrote a book in which he spoke of the Comoro Islands and Madagascar.

Around 1450, a stable system of commercial exchange between the east coast of Africa, north-west Madagascar – which at the time was linked to Kilwa by regular traffic – Egypt, Arabia and Asia contributed to the prosperity of the trading settlements and the whole of the Indian Ocean region. In 1487, Pedro de Covilham, on a secret mission for the king of Portugal in the eastern Mediterranean, learned of the scale of the east-coast traffic as far as Sofala. On 24 July 1488, Bartholomew Diaz rounded the southernmost tip of Africa and became convinced that the shape of the continent beyond that point was not that attributed to it since the time of Ptolemy. In 1497–8, Vasco da Gama's fleet was laid up for repairs for thirty-two days on the south-east coast. The navigators noted that iron was used for arrows and assegais, that salt was produced by evaporating sea water, that daggers had ivory handles and that some of the women, who were more numerous than the men, wore lip ornaments. On 2 March 1498, Vasco da Gama met his first Arabic-speaking Africans in Mozambique and was surprised by their fine clothes. On 7 April, the sultan of Mombasa extended a warm welcome to the Portuguese. Seventeen days later, they left for India, guided by Ibn Mas<u>dj</u>id, the compiler of a sea chart.[73] In September 1499, a few survivors of this first expedition returned to Portugal. A completely new era in the history of the Indian Ocean and of the east coast of Africa was about to open, an era that had been preceded by considerable upheavals on the Atlantic coast.

The mastery of the Atlantic and its consequences for Africa

The 'Atlantic Mediterranean'

This was the name often given in the sixteenth century to the part of the eastern Atlantic bounded by the western coasts of the Iberian peninsula and Africa, Madeira, the Azores and the Canary Islands.[74] Arabic

71. See G. S. P. Freeman-Grenville, 1955; J. S. Kirkman, 1967; Chittick and Rotberg (eds), op. cit.

72. G. Mathew, 1956.

73. The Arabic text has been published: G. Ferrand, 1921–8. Cf. n. 63.

74. On the Atlantic, see *Encyclopaedia of Islam*, new edn, Vol. I, p. 934. The texts by

sources show that, as with continental Africa, the authors confined themselves to transmitting previous knowledge and were often ignorant of this region of the world; even the Canary Islands remained little known, although merchants and navigators were active there.[75] We have every reason to believe that Muslim ships were in many cases the first to link the coasts and islands, although there is no written record of their passage.[76] The importance of the sea for the inhabitants of the coast cannot be doubted. Thus Ibn Saʿīd remarks that 'tunny fish is the staple food of the people of Morocco and al-Andalus: it is cut in two, crosswise, and then hung up to dry'. In the eleventh century, al-Bakrī notes the production of amber on the coast of black Africa and, in the twelfth century, al-Idrīsī mentions the salt trade between Aulil and Senegal.[77] The area explored was probably not very extensive, for the travellers did not venture far from the shore.[78] It is beyond question that the sea was habitually regarded as a highway and a source of food; the first Portuguese sailors noted the presence of fish-eating people on the West African coast, who were thoroughly despised by the hunters of the interior.

The conquest of the 'Atlantic Mediterranean' by the Europeans was not due to technical superiority. The real reasons for it must be sought elsewhere. In the twelfth century, the Almohad fleet had such a reputation that Ṣalāḥ al-Dīn (Saladin) sought its support against the Christian navies in the eastern Mediterranean. At the end of the thirteenth century, the naval power of the Marinids was exhausted, following the great battles for the Straits of Gibraltar. An even more decisive factor was that the Christians now held nearly all the major areas producing timber for shipbuilding in the western Mediterranean.[79]

---

al-Idrīsī (French transl. in Cuoq, op. cit., p. 143) and Ibn Khaldūn (French transl. in Monteil, 1967–8, p. 115) suffice to show the poor quality of the information handed down to them. It should be stressed here that the Arabs' poor knowledge of the seas to the west of Africa is in sharp contrast to their mastery of the Indian Ocean and its shores.

75. In the twelfth century, the 'Lisbon adventurers' may perhaps have reached the Canary Islands: R. Mauny, 1960, p. 91; 1965, p. 61. In the thirteenth century Ibn Fāṭima's voyage, as recounted by Ibn Saʿīd (French transl. in Cuoq, op. cit., p. 212) shows that the Muslims were trying to explore the African coast. Ibn Fāṭima's account reveals that their expansion was by no means disinterested and they were not bent on scientific research. South of Morocco the navigator discovered a region which is difficult to place, a sandy desert but 'excellent for the cultivation of sugar-cane'. In the next century, al-ʿUmarī tells us that a vizier of Almeria tried to explore the African coast; in Cuoq, op. cit., p. 281.

76. We feel that there is some exaggeration in the approach of a Chinese author, drawing on Chinese sources. His suggested identification of these regions would need to be supported by more consistent scientific evidence. Hui Lin Li, 1960–1.

77. In Cuoq, op. cit., pp. 83, 128 and 212.

78. Regarding the North Atlantic, Heers recognizes the importance of the discoveries made by fishermen on whole segments of future transatlantic routes and quotes the example of the Lisbon fishermen who, in the sixteenth century, reached Hudson Bay; J. Heers, 1966, p. 230.

In addition, in the Christian ports, the accumulation of capital required for shipbuilding was in the hands of the merchants and their associates more often than in the hands of those holding political power. Shipbuilding policy was directly linked here with accelerated economic expansion from 1200 to 1600. This spread to the North Atlantic after 1277. The Genoese and then the Venetian fleets linked mercantile Italy, via ports of call in the Balearic Islands, Seville, Lisbon, Madeira and Bayonne, with industrial Flanders and England. Here economic power played the determining role.[80] The Muslims did not respond to the growing European challenge, as much because of the weakness of the kingdoms of the Maghrib – apart from the short-lived Hafsid or Sa'dian interludes – as because, in general, the sea was not essential to the success of Muslim economic ventures. Caravans brought back far more gold than the caravels ever would; and the traders and authorities of the countries of the Maghrib had no obvious economic reason in the fourteenth and fifteenth centuries to compete with the Christians at sea, at the cost of heavy investment. This explains the unequal efforts made to conquer the 'Atlantic Mediterranean': it took a century of investment, of persistent efforts and failures, to achieve that conquest at the end of the fourteenth century, although the technical difficulties bore no comparison with those awaiting explorers south of Cape Bojador. This explains the preponderant role played by the Italians in this phase of expansion. During this early stage, Portugal did not have the merchants and bankers capable of putting up the necessary capital.[81]

Most of the voyages of European discovery made in this area will remain unknown to us for ever; occasionally, by chance, historians bring one of them to light. Out of prudence, historians are increasingly using the word 'rediscovery' when referring to the first well-documented European expedition leading to the occupation of a given territory.[82] The reasons why the Christians established themselves in the 'Atlantic Mediterranean' so rapidly are obvious today. The search for gold may have played a part in it,[83] but clearly a much more important motive was the hope of large-

79. Lombard, op. cit., pp. 153–76.

80. During the fifteenth century, the volume of traffic on this sea route represented approximately forty times the volume of the former overland traffic between Italy and Flanders through Champagne.

81. See V. de Magalhães Godinho, 1962 and 1969; Heers, 1966, pp. 273–93; Rau, op. cit., pp. 447–56; Verlinden, 1955b, pp. 467–97, and 1961.

82. A. Cortesão, 1971, 1972 and 1973; Y. K. Fall, 1978. The latter cites many telling arguments in support of the strong probability that many other navigators, Muslim and Christian, had sailed beyond Cape Bojador before the Portuguese did so.

83. Contradictory views are expressed by Godinho, 1962 and 1969; and Heers, 1957 and 1971, concerning the expedition of the Vivaldi brothers. It is certain that the Portuguese needed gold; between 1387 and 1416, the gold price there rose by 12 per cent. The minting of gold coins did not start again in Portugal until 1436, and Muslim models were used until 1456.

scale production of useful crops – wheat, vines and sugar-cane – in the Atlantic islands. Madeira, the Canary Islands and for a time the Azores, before the expansion south of Cape Bojador, became sugar-growing countries.[84] The role of the sugar trade as an engine of expansion has not yet been fully studied. As early as the thirteenth century, Morocco exported sugar to Flanders and also to Venice. The development of the Moroccan plantations, which had seen an explosion in the Sa'dian era, had continued since the ninth century; but until the time of the Sa'dians, output, investment and sales organization were not sufficient to give Morocco a large share in the competitive sugar trade. The Moroccan effort came rather late, at a time when, under pressure of the Genoese, heavy investment had led to a marked increase in sugar production in the islands. This expansion came a few decades earlier than that of American sugar production in the sixteenth century.

The export of African labour was directly linked with this effort. Beginning in the fourteenth century, the Guanches of the Canary Islands had preceded black Africans into slavery, tied to sugar and profit-making agriculture.[85]

South of Cape Bojador

The exploitation of a maritime region

The Atlantic of the trade winds and anticyclones, as Mauny has clearly shown, raised technical problems of a quite different order from previous ones.[86] From 1291 to 1434, at least on the Christian side, many of the naval exploration efforts south of Cape Bojador ended in failure. Mauny's argument, that it was impossible for ships which sailed too far south of Bojador to return, has recently been challenged again;[87] but the fact remains that, to be successful, these voyages called for considerable effort and investment and heavy sacrifices in men and material in the fifteenth century. Experience gained in the 'Atlantic Mediterranean' helped to suggest solutions; but these were inadequate and it was found necessary to carry out scientific and technical research in the western Mediterranean, often on the basis of Arab achievements, to master the new conditions.[88] Financial needs were even greater than previously.[89] In addition, navigation by the

84. By 1455, Ca da Mosto reported that the Madeira sugar-cane plantations were in full production. In 1508, the island produced 70 000 arrobas of sugar.

85. See Godinho, 1962 and 1969. At the end of the fifteenth century, Guanche slaves were sold at Seville; F. Perez-Embid, 1969, p. 89. After 1496, the numbers were vast. On their sale by Christians of Salé, see the evidence of Ibn Khaldūn, loc. cit., p. 115.

86. R. Mauny, 1960.

87. For example, by R. Lonis, 1978.

88. See G. Beaujouan, 1969; A. Teixeira da Mota, 1958; and E. Poulle, 1969.

89. Heers, 1966.

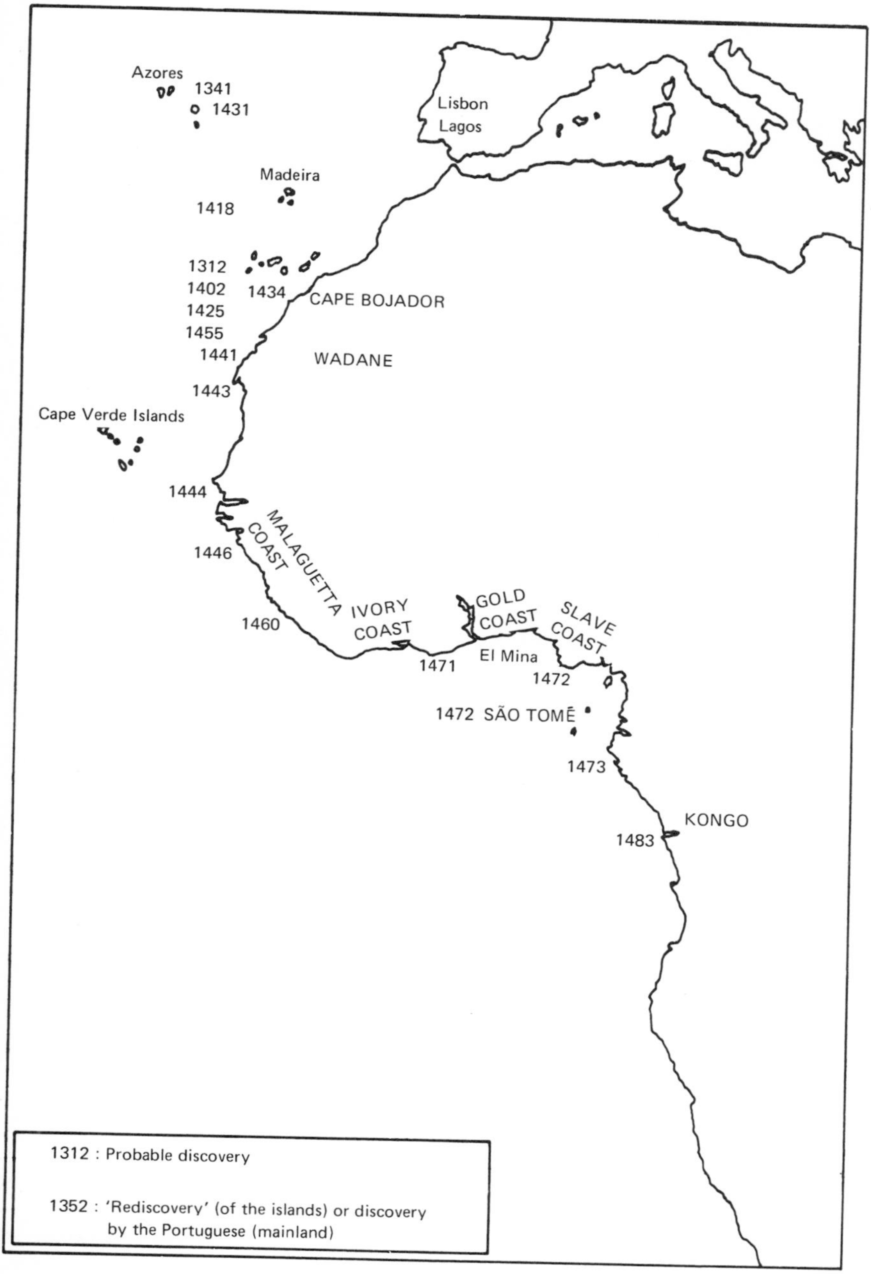

FIG. 26.5 *The Portuguese encirclement of Africa in the 15th century (J. Devisse)*

stars or at least with the use of the compass and marine charts had to be mastered;[90] and it also proved necessary to build small and manoeuvrable ships.[91] The tonnage of the caravels was two or three times less than that of Venetian cargo ships. Caravels were well adapted to Atlantic winds and could sail up rivers, but they were useful only during the brief period when the question of the tonnage to be transported hardly arose. In the sixteenth century, heavy galleons were to replace caravels for trade with Asia.

As soon as all the conditions for success were met, systematic exploration developed very rapidly. Such exploration mainly concerned Europe, but in certain respects it had a very serious effect on the life of Africa in the fifteenth century. Although the complete outline of Africa had now been discovered for the first time, its discoverers paid little attention to the continent itself. The Portuguese, disappointed at getting little gold, most of which remained in the hands of the Muslims in the north and east, rapidly reduced Africa to a single role – that of supplying manpower. Thus, just when the isolation of centuries had been broken for the western seaboard, the export of a considerable part of the population of Africa to America began. The New World's economic prospects seemed infinite; Asia, which had at last been reached by bypassing Islam, now supplied spices, precious stones, fabrics and porcelain. Both eclipsed the 'dark continent' in the minds of the whites.

Before pursuing this point, special attention should be paid to a text by al-ʿUmarī which, like many others, has aroused a great deal of sometimes unscientific controversy. Al-ʿUmarī reported Mansa Kanku Mūsā's account of his predecessor on the throne of Mali as follows:

> He did not believe that the ocean was impossible to cross. He wished to reach the other side and was passionately interested in doing so. He fitted out 200 vessels and filled them with men and as many again with gold, water and food supplies for several years. He then said to those in charge of embarkation, 'do not return until you have reached the other side of the ocean or if you have exhausted your food or water'. They sailed away. Time passed. After a long time, none of them had returned. Finally one vessel, only one, returned. We asked its master what he had seen and heard: 'We sailed on and on for a long time until a river with a violent current appeared in the middle of the sea. I was in the last vessel. The others sailed on and when they reached that spot they were unable to return and dis-

90. In use in the Mediterranean from 1317, marine charts only started to include the Atlantic in the fifteenth century. The first to give a satisfactory picture of West Africa and its ocean dates from approximately 1470; the first to mention the islands of Cape Verde and São Tomé dates from 1483. See C. de la Roncière, 1967; M. de la Roncière, 1967.

91. P. Gille, 1970.

appeared. We did not know what had happened to them. For my part, I came back from that place without entering the stream.'

The sultan rejected his explanation. He then ordered 2000 vessels to be fitted out, 1000 for himself and his men and 1000 for food and water. He then appointed me his deputy, embarked with his companions and sailed away. That was the last we saw of them, him and his companions.[92]

Attempts have been made to find in this very interesting document evidence of an eventual discovery of America by Mali sailors before Columbus.[93] Sometimes it is even taken as proof of a seamanship which might have allowed the blacks to reach the Indian Ocean from the Atlantic.[94] In this 'competitive' vein, there are few chances of reaching sound and reliable conclusions. Countering these interpretations, Mauny has repeatedly stressed that the technical conditions prevailing at the time in West Africa made such a voyage impossible, and that in any case it seems to have had no known consequences or lasting effects.[95]

Leaving these matters aside, we would like to suggest some complementary lines of thought. First of all, the 'technical debate' needs to be defused. Navigation had certainly existed for a considerable length of time on all the coasts of Africa, and there is no reason to suppose that Africans had given less thought than others to the techniques required to overcome the real and considerable difficulties it presented. Fishing, coastal trade and the activities carried on along the coasts which were described by the first European navigators leave no room for doubt here: a certain area of the sea, both to the west and to the east, had been mastered by Africans. It remains true, however, that the sea did not occupy a leading place in the economy and the political organization of the African powers. Africa lived within itself: all the economic, political, cultural and religious decision-making centres were a long way from the coasts.[96]

92. Al-'Umarī, from the French transl., in Cuoq, op. cit., pp. 274–5. On this text, there is an old bibliography in Hennig, op. cit., Vol. 3, pp. 161–5.

93. L. Wiener, 1920–2; see also M. Hamidullah, 1958, which borrows from M. D. W. Jeffreys, 1953a, an argument that cannot be considered conclusive in the present state of knowledge; namely, that the 'river' mentioned was the Amazon. This overlooks two facts: first, that before reaching this 'river in the sea', the vessels would have run into several currents, the most powerful of which flowed towards the Caribbean and not towards Brazil; secondly, that the outflow of the Amazon would have pushed the vessels back and not drawn them towards the coast of what is now Brazil. It is true, however, that these currents, if they could be used, could carry ships across the Atlantic westwards on the latitude of Dakar, but would make the return journey impossible. Is this what al-'Umarī's account means? See also C. L. Riley, 1971.

94. J. H. Hutton, 1946.

95. R. Mauny, 1971.

96. Mali's interest in its 'maritime provinces' of Casamance, Gambia and even more probably Sierra Leone should, however, be strongly stressed. This interest appears more and more clearly, particularly in recent studies carried out by young African historians.

It is all the more interesting to see a mansa taking an interest in the Atlantic. It must first be pointed out that Muslim acculturation had probably not yet affected the Mali ruling classes. The Ptolemaic inheritance, with its attendant inhibitions, would probably not have influenced the mansa's outlook: the ocean was an area to be explored, like the desert or the forest.[97] Moreover, we must take account of the role played by Mali's maritime provinces, of the efforts made by Mali to diversify the economic relations of the Sahel with its partners and, finally, of the number of Muslim or European 'probes' carried out in the thirteenth and early fourteenth centuries. It does not seem at all surprising that a mansa should have tried to explore and to gain a mastery of this ocean, which others were beginning to discover. The very tone of the narrative shows that Mansa Mūsā himself considered this operation unrealistic – perhaps simply because it had failed. The economic consequences of his pilgrimage with its massive export of gold reveal a failure no less significant than his predecessor's. Restored to such a context, this venture deserves to be taken seriously, with a study of its causes and possible human consequences – for example, a small landing in South America.[98] Its economic consequences, on all the evidence, were non-existent.[99]

Expansion, disappointment, exploitation

Once they had obtained a firm hold over the coastal trading enclaves in Morocco, whence they imported cloth, horses and gold, the Portuguese rounded Cape Bojador in 1434. It took them nine years to master the techniques of returning by way of the Azores; in 1443, expansion along the African coasts became possible (see Fig. 26.5). Fifty-four years later they reached the south of the continent, and within sixty years they were sailing the Indian Ocean regularly. During the second half of the fifteenth century, three phases – expansion, disappointment and exploitation – were superimposed on Africa.

Brutality and pillage marked the early stages of expansion, which became

97. To help forward the discussion of this subject, it would be useful to make a systematic collection of the traditions concerning the ocean to be found among the Mandingo. To our knowledge, no such effort has ever been made. It is rather entertaining to quote here the reply attributed to those whom Prince Henry had ordered to explore the regions south of Cape Bojador: 'How could we go beyond the boundaries set by our fathers? And what benefit can the Prince derive from the loss of our souls as well as our bodies, for it is obvious that we would be committing suicide? It is plain to see that there are neither men nor inhabited places beyond this cape. . . . The currents are so strong there that no ship which rounded the cape would ever be able to return.' G. E. de Zurara, 1960 edn, pp. 69–70.

98. For some unfortunate, unfounded attempts in this field, see Jeffreys, op. cit.

99. See *Unesco General History of Africa* Volume V, for a study of the controversial question of the existence of a pre-Colombian, African maize, and of the possible introduction of American maize by Muslim or black mariners who are supposed to have discovered America before Columbus.

more organized after 1450; trade took the place of raids. To varying degrees, Arguin and El Mina were the ports of call for Portuguese trade on the African coast. Small quantities of products which sold well, such as leather, amber and gum, were sent from there to Europe. But the most sought-after articles turned out, one after the other, to be disappointing in volume compared with the initial trials. Expansion was first carried out under the control of the crown and partly for its benefit. When it became too much of a burden, individual concessions were granted.[100] But the Portuguese crown never entirely abandoned its policy of direct control, although it did not have the means to exercise this, nor, above all, the means to defend its theoretical monopoly against the other European countries.[101]

Disappointments of all sorts soon piled up. The first was linked with the very nature of the trade: annual expeditions by a small number of small ships were hardly likely to bring in high profits. The attempts to penetrate the interior of the continent all ended in failure. In 1481, John II of Portugal, trying to find a waterway leading to gold, vainly ordered the Felou rapids on the River Senegal to be cleared with gunpowder. Another disappointment occurred in 1483, when it was found that the River Zaïre, which was so wide that it looked as if it would offer easy access to the interior, was barred by the impassable Yelada rapids. In 1487, they attempted to establish a trading post at Wadane to secure some of the gold which was known to pass through it on the way from Timbuktu to Morocco; but this met with general hostility. At Cantor, on the Gambia, trade was too firmly controlled by the Mali to be very profitable; and further south, as far as the Grain Coast, foreigners were not made welcome at all and moorings were unsatisfactory.

The attention of the Europeans was held for a considerable time by the search for African gold.[102] We now know that the Portuguese did not succeed in channelling the bulk of gold production towards the coasts. The amounts they obtained never exceeded, and perhaps never even attained, 1 tonne a year from all the Atlantic coasts.[103] After the first years, and in relation to the needs of the rapidly growing European economy, the disappointment was great. The Mediterranean ports, as we

100. Arguin was to remain under constant close royal control. South of the Gambia, contracts were signed on several occasions with private shipowners. In exchange for a fee payment and the annual exploration of a certain length of the coast, local profits were left to them.

101. The most famous example in the fifteenth century was the voyage to the Gold Coast of Eustache de la Fosse and his companions (1479–80), which ended in tragedy; they were captured and threatened with hanging for having ventured to El Mina without royal permission. See E. de la Fosse, ed. R. Fouché-Delbosc, 1897 (no further details available).

102. In 1447, Malfante's expedition to Tuat may have been financed by the Genoese bank of the Centurioni, which was anxious at the same time to open up a land route to Asian spices through Russia and Asia.

103. See Godinho, 1969; Devisse, op. cit. It should be recalled here that Mauny, 1960, estimates the gold trade between West and North Africa at less than 4 tons a year.

are slowly learning, continued to obtain African gold, brought in by caravans. Malaguetta and black pepper from Benin replaced gold for a time;[104] but as far as the international traders at the end of the fifteenth century were concerned, although malaguetta pepper still sold well, African pepper could not compete once Asian pepper had appeared on the market.

All in all, from the economic point of view, trade was very modest, although the accounts of preceding centuries had led people to expect marvellous things of Africa. Fairly small quantities of silver – which was rare south of the Sahara – of textiles manufactured in the Moroccan trading settlements, of horses and of copper kept the balance of trade even.[105]

Disappointments were no less severe outside the economic sphere. The kingdom of the famous Prester John, whom the Portuguese and the Spaniards had dreamed of as an ally against the Muslims since the fourteenth century, was nowhere to be found in West or North Africa. In the middle of the fifteenth century, an anonymous Franciscan had confidently declared the kingdom of salvation to be in Africa. Diego Cao thought he had found the way to it through the mouth of the Congo in 1483. But no part of black Africa appeared to be Christian or ready to fight against Islam.

The immediate disappointment caused by the exceptional climate was to have more positive results for the future, as it sharpened the sense of observation of the mariners and traders.[106] The continuous summer rains in the Benin region, first observed by Ca da Mosto, were in contrast with the arid conditions in more northerly regions.[107] This appeared to bring all agricultural activity to a standstill at a season which, in Europe, was harvest time. And yet, as Ca da Mosto observed, they sowed before the rains and harvested after them. This was a strange kind of agriculture for someone from the Mediterranean. Observation of the pattern of winds, which had been necessary for navigational purposes, revealed a disconcerting mechanism – the appearance and disappearance of both the north-east and the south-east trade winds.[108] The fact that temperatures

104. See Mauny, 1961, pp. 249–50.

105. Silver was worth more than gold in Africa and was imported from Christian countries. Even the Maghrib, for international economic reasons, was an excellent market for silver at this time. V. Fernandes, French transl. 1938, p. 97. Textiles were manufactured in spite of the fact that the earliest travellers noted with understandable interest that the inhabitants of Africa went about naked or only lightly clad.

106. See S. Daveau, 1969.

107. In Arguin, 'it only rains for three months in the year, August, September and October': Ca da Mosto, from the French transl. 1895.

108. Times of sailing would soon have to be calculated with reference to these winds. At the beginning of the sixteenth century, Duarte Pacheco Pereira noted: 'There are three months in the year, January, February and March, in which ships which are to sail to the Indies must be absolutely ready to leave; and of these three, February is the best.' Duarte Pacheco Pereira, from the French transl. 1956. It should perhaps be recalled here that in winter there was little sailing in the Mediterranean.

hardly varied was no less disconcerting. The customs of the inhabitants, the uneasy and sometimes amused observation of traditional religious ceremonies, gave rise to the first ethnological comments, for example, by Valentim Fernandes.[109] The word 'fetish', which was later to have an unjustified popularity, had not yet appeared.[110]

These observations were of a sort which could lead to useful discoveries, as happened with navigation, but in this respect the sea was more productive than the land.[111] Initially the Portuguese had hoped to acclimatize European plants, wheat and vines, as well as men, to the soil of Africa; but the geographical environment rejected the agricultural transplants and the climate dismayed the men.[112] The revolution against the Ptolemaic cultural heritage had started;[113] but Africans found that the prejudices inherent in that outlook had not evaporated.

The transfer of European agriculture to Africa soon proved to be impossible, but the possibility remained of establishing new sugar-cane plantations on virgin soil such as that of São Tomé, which had been occupied in 1472; the sugar market was still growing. The idea of 'bringing in the manpower required' emerged as a matter of course from the scheme, and captured blacks were also transported to other sugar-growing islands of the 'Atlantic Mediterranean'.[114]

The slave trade had, in fact, developed an annual rhythm on the African coasts about thirty years before this deportation to the islands began.[115] From 1440 onwards, slaves captured at various points on the present Mauritanian coast were the objects of a barter which was justified by Zurara in terms which might well appear cynical, if he had not, first

109. V. Fernandes, French transl. 1951, Vol. 2, pp. 71, 73, 77, 83 and 101. He described the idols worshipped by Africans, among other less interesting notes.

110. On 'fetish', see R. Arveiller, 1963, pp. 229–30. The Portuguese adjective *feitico*, which originally meant 'artificial', was not used in the same sense as the French *factice* ('fake') in the thirteenth century. *Feitico* gave birth to a whole series of words in other languages. 'Fetishist' comes from a French translation (1605) of a Dutch travel book of 1602 (P. de Marees); 'fetish' appears only in 1669. The word should be studied in Portuguese and Castilian.

111. It was initially for utilitarian reasons that the West emerged from its ethnocentrism – the discovery of geographical differences led to research into the reasons for them; but the scientific approach followed only very slowly after the first rich crop of observations.

112. Duarte Pacheco Pereira observed that the climate on the coast of Benin was very unhealthy throughout the year, and was particularly unbearable in August and September, when it rained without stopping; 'all these rivers are rank with fevers, which are very harmful to us white men'. Pacheco Pereira, from the French transl., loc. cit.

113. 'The whole African coast from Benin to the Congo is heavily wooded and populated. This land is near the equatorial circle which our ancestors said was uninhabitable, but we have found by experience the contrary to be true': ibid.

114. Verlinden, 1955a, pp. 630–1.

115. ibid., p. 617; and Verlinden, 1967, pp. 365–77.

and foremost, revealed the profound contradictions of the European outlook:

> It should be noted here that these blacks, although they are Moors like the others, are none the less their slaves by virtue of an ancient custom which I believe comes down from the curse laid on his son Ham by Noah after the Flood. . . . [However] although their skin is black they have a soul like the others and, besides, these blacks are not of Moorish but of pagan blood, so that it should be easier to guide them on to the path to salvation.[116]

The profit motive backed up their conscience;[117] so there were few people who seem to have had qualms either about the exchange of one white Moor for several blacks, or about the direct enslavement of the blacks.[118] In 1444, a company was set up at Lagos, Portugal, to exploit the slave trade. In the same year, 240 slaves were shared out at Lagos between Henry the Navigator, the church of Lagos, the Franciscans of Cape St Vincent and the merchants.

In 1448, 'regular trade' – consisting of the exchange of goods for human beings – was established at Arguin, which probably supplied several hundred slaves a year until the fifteenth century. Further south, the organization was no less 'profitable': after 1460, some 1000 slaves were taken from the land lying between Cape Verde and Sine Salum. Still further south, estimates are difficult to establish for the fifteenth century.[119]

Arrivals in Portugal, at Lagos and at the royal Casa dos Escravos in Lisbon, are estimated by Verlinden as amounting to some 880 a year.[120] Castile had recognized the Portuguese monopoly over this trade since 1474, but bought slaves in Lisbon. At the end of the century it is certain that there was a regular flow of slaves into Portugal, although reliable figures cannot be given regarding their numbers.[121] The organization of the barter system was stabilized at the end of the fifteenth century. The

116. Zurara, loc. cit., p. 90.

117. A bull dated 8 January 1454 addressed by Pope Nicholas V to Alphonso V of Portugal authorized the latter to deprive of their freedom 'all the Moors and other enemies of Christ', no exception being made for 'Guineans'. See Verlinden, 1955a, p. 618.

118. An additional advantage was that the blacks who had been converted would return to their countries and spread Christianity. Prior to this, they would have supplied all the information they had about the little-known continent of Africa, where gold was to be found in abundance.

119. The Florentine Bartolomeo Marchionni, who had been given the concession for slave-trading on the Slave Coast from 1486 to 1488, paid a lease of 45 000 ducats a year.

120. Verlinden, 1955a, pp. 617 ff.; see also ibid., pp. 358–62.

121. The best informed work on this subject (P. D. Curtin, 1969, pp. 17–21) estimates that 175 000 slaves were taken from Africa in the fifteenth century. Add to that the number given by Verlinden, 1977. Numerous published studies by Portuguese and Spanish authors should also be consulted, for example, V. Cortés-Alonso, 1963, 1964 and 1972, pp. 123–51; A. Franco Silva, 1979. See also A. Teixeira da Mota, 1981.

barter value of slaves had fluctuated widely during the early years; but it was now set at the same level practically everywhere, roughly six slaves for a horse.[122] As in the interior of the continent, the horse was a highly prized object of barter; but in some places, particularly in the equatorial regions, copper gradually replaced the horse.[123] For centuries, unfortunately, the African slave trade was to remain by far the most profitable commercial transaction for Europeans on the coasts of Africa.

During the fifteenth century as a whole, the Europeans made a great impact on the various archipelagos of the Atlantic coast of Africa, but barely penetrated into the interior. They did not upset the old-established trading systems nor the main political balance in any lasting way. Their attempt to make contact with the mansa of Mali by sending an embassy there between 1481 and 1495 does not seem to have met with any success. It is difficult to ascribe to these moves any influence on the drift of the Fulfulbe towards the south, which started around 1480–90. Their relations with the king of the Kongo, Nkuwu, although closer, remained ambiguous and did not have any decisive consequences at the time. In 1483, in response to a Portuguese embassy, the king requested a mission. He received one in 1491, including some Franciscans, who baptized him on 3 May of that year; there were also carpenters, stock-breeders and stone masons to supervise and teach their trades. Serious difficulties arose in 1493 or 1494, when the king preferred apostasy to giving up polygamy. The introduction of Christianity had no more success, for the time being, on the coast of Benin or in Senegambia.[124] A Christian institutional framework was set up in the islands only – for example, the Canary Islands had a bishop – with the exception of Morocco, which was a special case.[125]

By contrast, the indirect influence of the European presence on the African coasts very soon made itself felt, even if only over a comparatively small geographical area. In Senegambia, the Portuguese found a dual balance already established, apparently since long before their arrival. On the one hand, by imposing a sort of blockade on iron, as noted by Portuguese travellers, the mansas of Mali had for some time asserted their hegemony

122. Ca da Mosto shows that in the north 14 slaves were exchanged for a horse at first. In Senegambia the number varied between 10 and 12. At the end of the fifteenth century, at Sine Salum, the number still fluctuated between 6 and 15 per horse.

123. This problem is so important that it concerns more than the African coasts. (Professor D. McCall is preparing a monograph on it.)

124. There were Franciscan efforts in Guinea-Bissau from 1469. In 1489, an attempt was made to convert a Serer chief, who was assassinated on his return from Europe by his own Portuguese escort. In 1484, the Dominicans settled in Benin.

125. In accordance with a treaty entered into by Morocco and its various European partners in 1225, Christians had been allowed to settle in various parts of Morocco. The mendicant orders endeavoured – in vain – to make converts, bishops were installed at Fez and Marrakesh, and churches were opened in the coastal trading enclaves to serve the groups of Christian mercenaries. On these questions, see Jadin, op. cit., pp. 36–68.

over the Casamance region as far as the north of Gambia; and, on the other, they abandoned the region lying between Senegal and Gambia to the powerful Jolof state. The arrival of European iron, even in small quantities, altered this balance. Portuguese trade acted even more strongly in dissolving existing political and social relations, first in Senegambia, followed by a repeat performance, after 1500, on the coast of Benin and especially in the Kongo. The Burba of Jolof had managed, probably for several centuries, to obtain recognition of his power by the Cajor and the Baol. From 1455 onwards, the Burba demanded horses from new arrivals, and by 1484 this practice had become regularized.[126] But then the Jolof ruler turned his attention away from internal trade to participate in coastal trade. As the future was to show, the geographical advantage in this respect clearly lay with the Cajor and the Baol.

The social consequences of this new situation, however, were very soon seen to be at least as important as the political repercussions. The Senegambian society described by writers at the time of its discovery included a number of very typical occupations, such as *griots*, weavers, blacksmiths and cobblers, but no merchants. In the absence of the latter, it was the king who organized trade with the newcomers, and this trade provided him with the means of strengthening his power at a time when, for many reasons, it was starting to be challenged. Horses and iron – even though the hypocritical ban on the export of the latter to non-Christian lands was officially repeated – called for their *quid pro quo*, slaves.

The sources certainly show that 'slavery' existed in the various societies at the latter half of the fifteenth century, probably for a variety of reasons which historians are gradually bringing to light – wars, debts and famine – but the structure of this society was not based on slavery and the status of these dependants in Senegambia probably remained of a private nature. Things obviously changed very rapidly, however, once it became necessary to 'deal in slaves' to pay for imports. The royal and aristocratic ruling circles derived personal profit but social and moral disrepute from this practice. In all likelihood, social relations and relations with neighbouring peoples were profoundly altered in a short space of time.

Strongholds of resistance against Islam still existed in Senegambia; except in the ancient land of Takrūr, few chiefdoms had yet been converted. Among the Jolof, Islam was to spread among the common people as a potential challenge to traditional authority, and the kings, like the rulers of the Wattasid dynasty in Morocco, were already giving way to the temptation to let Europeans become involved in internal problems, between kingdom and kingdom and between one social stratum and another.

126. See J. Boulègue, 1968.

27 Conclusion

D. T. NIANE

This volume of the *Unesco General History of Africa* ends with the beginnings of European predominance and expansion. The fifteenth and sixteenth centuries were a turning-point not only in the history of black Africa but also in the general history of our planet. A new era was indeed dawning for mankind; gunpowder, the compass and the easily handled caravel, with its flexible sail system, gave Europe control of the seas and of world trade.

The ports of the Mediterranean – that lake of the ancient world – sank one by one into lethargy, despite the immense efforts made by the Italian merchants and particularly the Genoese, who throughout the fifteenth century had tried to gain access to Sudanese gold through the traders of the Maghrib. In 1447, the famous trader Antonio Malfante succeeded in reaching the Tuat; from his stay in that area he brought back to Genoa valuable information on distant Sudan and on the gold traffic. But, as we know, it was the Spaniards and the Portuguese who discovered the sea routes to Sudan and the Indies; it is noteworthy that the Portuguese and Spanish kings were able to realize their dream only through the Italian navigators in their service. With the circumnavigation of the world, the Muslims, who until that time had played a predominant role, gave way to the Spanish and Portuguese Christians. It was not by chance that the maritime discoveries were made by the Portuguese and the Spaniards, for they inherited Arab science after long contact both in war and in peace, as shown by Professor Talbi.[1]

From the twelfth to the sixteenth century Africa played a leading part in the world economy: the discovery of America in 1492 by Christopher Columbus opened up to Europeans new sources of gold and silver; the mines of Peru and Mexico soon surpassed those of Bure, Bambuk, Ngalam and the Mwene Mutapa in the supply of precious metals.

Three major realities marked the history of Africa during the period under review; these were, first, religious and political; secondly, economic and cultural; and thirdly, a historical dynamism.

1. See Chapter 3 above.

Religious and political aspects

First came the development of kingdoms, empires and cities. Islam had asserted itself through the gradual Arabization of northern Africa. South of the Sahara it had become the official religion for a number of kingdoms and empires, but the Arabs did not gain control of black Africa, where Islam was a political rather than a religious factor. However, Islam stimulated trade relations everywhere. In the Sudan the large volume of trade led to a rapid social development and a new social class of black merchants and scholars emerged. South of the Sahara, Islam adapted itself; more precisely, it was a thin veneer covering only the court and the merchants in contact with the Berber Arabs. The traditional religion, based on ancestor worship, remained as strong among the peoples whose rulers were converted to Islam as among those whose kings were not Muslims. The similarity of the court ceremonial at Koumbi, at Niani and in the Yatenga is significant. In all these cases, the subjects covered themselves with dust and prostrated themselves before addressing their sovereign.

Everywhere the ruler was held responsible for the happiness and prosperity of the empire. That was the basis of the respect which the subjects imposed upon themselves, and from there it was only a short step to using the terms 'sacred kingship' or 'divine royalty', as some specialists came to do. Lastly, stress must be laid on the spirit of tolerance shown by the early black kings, who encouraged the settlement of the Berber Arabs in the towns, even before they themselves had been converted to Islam. But their conversion in no way involved a rejection of ancestral religious practices. In some regions, it gave rise to an original symbiosis: for instance, the Sudanese traditional background contains many traces of the influence of Islam, whose myths, heroes and history have been presented in forms differing considerably from those of the ancient model. The same applies to Christianity and the traditional African background in Ethiopia. But the two revealed religions, Islam and Christianity, were to remain on a war footing for centuries. Despite this tension between Muslims and Christians in the Horn of Africa, however, traders never lost their rights.[2]

> The development of the trade routes from the Gulf of Aden to the interior of the Horn of Africa from the tenth century is one of the most significant factors in the history of all the peoples of the area. Even when they were a bone of contention among the main powers in the region, which vied for their control, these routes undoubtedly helped to bring about all kinds of interaction between local peoples of different cultural, religious and linguistic affiliations ... By the middle of the thirteenth century even the Christian Zagwe kingdom

2. See Chapter 17 above.

in northern Ethiopia no longer regarded the sultanate of Dahlak as its only outlet to the Red Sea, and had started to use the Zeila route through its southern provinces.[3]

Thus the religious conflicts, and the episodic wars to which they gave rise, in no way prevented the mingling of populations, and cultural and economic exchanges were not broken off.

In the political sphere, clans and ethnic groups were in the main sufficiently well structured to resist the temptations of assimilation: even when one of the groups emerged and imposed its law, the result was not so much a fusion of groups around the victorious clan as the creation of a federation of clans, each retaining its own identity according to the extent to which it was structured. This is a remarkable fact; for example, in the Maghrib the Marinid, Hafsid and Sa'adite kingdoms were in fact formed by groups of *ḳabīla*s (clans) around that of the sovereign. The same happened in Mali, where the Mandingo clans joined together with the other clans, and also in Mossi, in Rwanda and among the Mwene Mutapa.

In the north and north-east of the continent, the Maghrib and Egypt became distinct, individual parts of the Muslim world; after the brief period of unity in the Maghrib under the Almohads, three states began to take shape: Morocco in the far west, Tunisia and Algeria. The personality of each took shape after the break-up of ephemeral political unity. It is notable here that Arabization spread slowly; the *ḳabīla*s were a political and social reality and the sovereign had to take into account the s̲h̲ayk̲h̲s and clan chiefs. Between the Gulf of Gabès, which delimits Ifrīḳiya or Tunisia, and the valley of the Nile, the Libyan area was a zone of shifting allegiance between the sovereigns of Tunis and those of Cairo. The latter, particularly the Mamluk dynasty, gave Egypt supremacy in the Muslim world. Cairo was a political capital whose voice was heard in the west as well as the east.

Islam was the mortar between the Maghrib, Egypt and the Muslim east: but no region attempted to impose itself or to re-create the Muslim unity of the preceding era. At the end of the period under study, Islam suffered a net retreat on the political level: the Christians took the offensive in Italy and in the Iberian peninsula. Granada, the last Arab kingdom in Spain, fell. Christians crossed the Mediterranean and landed in the Maghrib; St Louis's Crusade was an example. The Portuguese, in the van of this Christian offensive, settled in Ceuta at the end of the fifteenth century, obviously intending to make Morocco a bridgehead for their penetration of Africa. At the end of the fifteenth century, the rulers of the Iberian peninsula took the initiative from the Muslims by land and sea, and sought the access routes to the Sudan, rich in gold.

3. Chapter 17, p. 430 above.

The case of Nubia, where Christianity was uprooted after a long struggle, deserves particular mention.[4] Professor Kropáček writes:

> According to widespread opinion it [Christianity] was essentially the religion of an élite and did not strike deep roots among the mass of the people. To a great extent worship was associated with Coptic clergy and a foreign culture, and lacked indigenous saints and martyrs ... All the same, the frescos in excavated churches occasionally reveal the dark faces of indigenous Nubian bishops. ... The persistence of older, pre-Christian beliefs is attested in Ibn Sulaym's account (written in the tenth century) as well as in their further continuation in popular Sudanese Islam today.[5]

But here, as elsewhere, Arabization was not completely peaceful; the invaders had to quell several revolts, for in fact the blacks were submerged by waves of Arab immigrants.

> A strong and justified feeling has arisen amongst contemporary historians of the Nilotic Sudan that in the past the northern, or Arab, factor was asymmetrically overemphasized at the expense of both indigenous developments and contacts with Negro African cultures. This particular example of cross-cultural influence to and from the Sudan belt has for some time been a fruitful field for abundant speculation.[6]

Recent research proves that Nilotic Sudan has always been a transit zone and an area of contact between many clans or Negro ethnic groups. From one year to another, archaeology brings to light the Negro element in the black culture of Sudanese civilization.

Clans existed in the deserts: in the Sahara each clan had its own territory in which it moved about; the extreme mobility of the population, imposed by natural factors, prevented the establishment of centralized states. The same happened in the equatorial forests, where the pygmies survived in extremely difficult conditions, camping here and there, always in pursuit of game. The same applies to the Khoikhoi, the San and all the peoples that were pushed back either into the desert or into the forests by the Sudanese or Bantu populations, who were better armed since they had discovered the use of iron and wielded lances.

To conclude these few general remarks on political development, let us say that everywhere in Africa before 1600 the clan stage had been reached or passed and that, wherever conditions permitted, towns, kingdoms and viable empires were founded. Original political formations, enriched from outside, took shape; many forms of government were known. The African past contains a wealth of political experience, the study of

4. On this, see Chapter 16 above, which also sheds new light on cultural and social transformations in Nubia during the same period.

5. Chapter 16, p. 410 above.

6. ibid., p. 416 above.

which has hardly been touched upon. The different stages of political development show an evolution from clans, to clan groupings, to kingdoms, which in turn became grouped into empires. From now on, it is possible to undertake a study of political institutions in many regions of Africa.

In the southern tip of the continent, south of a line from Namibia to the mouth of the Limpopo, it is certain that even before the twelfth century kingdoms and empires came into being. Archaeological research continues, but the existence of the Republic of South Africa has put a brake on historical research. There is indeed little information on the forest regions and the southern savannahs, although archaeological studies have already thrown considerable light on material culture in this region. The analysis of Professor Vansina, the specialist in Bantu traditions, demonstrates that during the period under study the state (that is to say, a structured political entity) was a long-established reality in the regions in question:

> The states must be very old. It is not by chance that the great necropolises of Sanga and Katoto are on the Lualaba lakes just south of the very heart of the Luba empire, which might well have been their later manifestations. But the necropolises date from before 1000 of the Christian era. It is certain that towns as densely populated as those whose traces remain in Sanga were not regulated by mere inter-clan relationships. Moreover, the antiquity of the Luba-type states would account for the vast extension of related languages covering all eastern Kasai, the greater part of Shaba, north-east Zambia, the Zambian Copper Belt, and part of north-west Zambia.

It should be mentioned that at the beginning of the present century a 'Rhodesian Ancient Ruins Ltd' or 'Ancient Ruins Co.' was established by the British. In the course of a few decades, this notorious company pillaged the royal tombs of the Zimbabwe–Mapungubwe civilization, and the treasures from several tombs were systematically removed. This southern African civilization seems to have had much in common with that of Zimbabwe. It, too, was a mining civilization with stone buildings, like that of Manykeni in Mozambique. In the former Transvaal, the Sotho and Shona built mighty stone monuments and, according to the latest research, the Mapungubwe civilization achieved a symbiosis between the cultures of the Bantu people and more ancient peoples such as the Khoi-khoi. The use of iron was widespread well before the tenth century, and we have every reason to believe that the tombs of the Mapungubwe hill and its surroundings belonged to a civilization which flourished at least between the eleventh and fifteenth centuries, if not even earlier, before going into a long, slow and painful decline under the effects of the political and social instability caused by the slave trade.

There is something faulty in the reasoning of certain researchers, who tend to date the introduction of iron into southern Africa only around the ninth and tenth centuries, in spite of the facts that (a) relations between the Nile valley (Meroe Napata), the lake region and the savannahs of the Limpopo were continuous; (b) there was no major obstacle to population movement; nor (c) consequently to inter-regional exchanges, either on the cultural or on the strictly commercial level. Most recent research indicates that iron may have been worked in southern Africa even before the Christian era, which has upset a number of theories.

Several points concerning the origin and development of these regions during the period under consideration still remain obscure. But if we still ask questions about Zimbabwe, it is no longer to find out whether blacks or whites were the creators of these cyclopean monuments. These stone buildings are entirely the work of the Shona; that has been established. But what were the political institutions of this kingdom? What was its social structure? How was the trade organized between Zimbabwe and the coast? So many questions are still unanswered.

Economic and cultural aspects

The most striking feature here is the intensity of inter-regional and intercontinental relations, constantly stimulated by Arab, Persian, Berber, Chinese, Mandingo and Hausa merchants. In the south, the Shona and other populations of the sub-equatorial savannahs carried on a flourishing trade, both in the direction of the Atlantic and towards the Indian Ocean through the Congo, the lake region and the area of the Mwene Mutapa.

The black rulers were well aware of the economic and political role of metals such as gold, copper and iron, and their exploitation was controlled. This point is most important, for many studies and articles on Africa give the impression that Africa was a reservoir of gold for Berbers, Arabs and Persians, as if the African kings were only there to serve the foreigners; this is an implicit negation of the existence of any organized states. It was no accident that African monarchs banned Arab travellers from gold-bearing areas.

Each partner benefited from trade conducted on a basis of equality. It was certainly not by chance that the greatest ruler in the Sudan was known as *Kaya Maghan*, the 'king of gold'; to the south, his counterpart for the countries rich in gold, copper and iron, was called Mwene Mutapa, 'lord of metals'. These rulers and their people were well aware that the prosperity and fame of their kingdoms were based on the precious metals. They knew the role of minerals in their external relations; the *Kaya Maghan* had exclusive rights to gold nuggets and strictly controlled exports of the precious metal. It must have been the same in Zimbabwe with the Mwene Mutapa. This must be emphasized, since some Africanists would have us believe that Africans and their rulers yielded their treasures to the first traders who arrived and had no conception of the public interest.

These rulers knew how to play on the attraction of gold to secure the service of foreigners; thus Mansa Mūsā attracted architects to his capital as well as writers and priests, to whom he gave pensions paid in gold. The monarchs of Zimbabwe had to pay in gold for the Chinese porcelain and other luxury products much used by the court. As a result of the presence of gold, copper and ivory, the African kings secured for their countries foodstuffs and basic essentials, such as salt – which was, if necessary, bought for its weight in gold – Chinese porcelain, brocades, silks and fine weapons, all things which could bestow more brilliance on the court.

Northern Africa and the east coast of the continent played a particularly important intermediary role; through northern Africa passed products and merchandise from Europe, and the precious metals which gave life to trade relations in the Mediterranean world. Surely the privileges of such a position explain the bitter rivalry between the merchant cities of the Maghrib for control of the routes along which Sudan's riches flowed! Ibn Khaldūn understood this phenomenon perfectly in that part of his *Universal History* in which he dealt with the Berbers. This is probably why he made such a long and detailed inquiry into the history of the countries of the blacks, upon whom the trade and activities of the towns of the Maghrib and Egypt largely depended.

The eastern side of the continent, from the Horn to Sofala, looks on to the Indian Ocean, which put Africa into direct contact with the East and the Far East. Seaborne trade led to the building of trading towns on the coast. The kings of the interior, in particular the Mwene Mutapa, also built cities – monuments now described as cyclopean, so imposing are their size and architecture, which show no signs of outside influence.

Trade during the period with which we are concerned depended on the exchange of cloth, weapons and various products from the depths of the savannah and the forests, which were sold to countries as far away as China and Indonesia. This was the importance of the ocean that washes the shores of Madagascar; the Great Island, like the coastal towns, achieved a symbiosis of eastern and African cultures at all levels, linguistic and economic. Trade brought new plants to Africa, especially from Asia; for example, cotton, which was introduced into the Sudan by the Arabs before the tenth century.

Never before had cultural activities and inter-regional exchanges been so important; the book trade flourished in Gao and Timbuktu. A Negro-Muslim literature emerged throughout the Sudan, from the Atlantic coast to the Red Sea. The kingdoms of Abyssinia, Bornu, Songhay, Takrūr and Mali developed an original literature in which theology and history occupied an important place. The south Saharan towns maintained cultural relations with those of the north by means of pilgrimage or trade.

It was between the twelfth and sixteenth centuries that the Bantu-speaking peoples spread throughout Central Africa, with their improved agricultural techniques as a result of iron tools. To the south, the influence of Bantu culture was continually increasing. When Vasco da Gama rounded the Cape in 1498, the southern tip of the continent was the site of outstanding civilizations; agriculture and stock-raising were thriving there. But, to justify the early settlement of Europeans in the southern tip of the continent, scholars had no hesitation in declaring that this part of Africa was almost empty. This was a highly convenient justification *pro domo*, but it did not stand up to the evidence provided by historical research. The fact is that, from the seventeenth century onwards, the Dutch and then the British pushed the Africans back towards the infertile regions, and in the nineteenth century there was a surge towards the mining areas of Zimbabwe and Transvaal, which five centuries earlier had been under the dominion of the powerful sovereigns of Mwene Mutapa, Mapungubwe and Manykeni in Mozambique.

Despite the importance of minerals during the whole of this period, agriculture provided one of the principal economic bases of the kingdoms south of the Sahara; production rested on the family farm. Here and there, however, there were enslaved population groups who worked on behalf of the rulers. In black Africa there was a system of serfdom, tributes and dues being fixed by custom; in the southern Maghrib slaves and peasants worked the land for the benefit of the lords or rulers. Plantations were developed in the islands off the east coast of Africa. But nowhere throughout this period were there hordes of slaves being systematically exploited.

While stock-raising was a speciality of certain societies, in the humid, grassy regions, it was closely linked with agriculture. Herdsmen roamed the Sudan and the Sahel; some groups went far to the south, where they tended to become sedentary, like the Fulani at Macina and Futa Jallon. Various crafts were practised by members of castes in black Africa, at least in the Sudanese belt; elsewhere, as in the Maghrib or Egypt, craft guilds, true corporations, were organized. The lack of written documents makes it impossible to speak of the organization of crafts in southern Africa, where metal-working had, however, reached a high level. A careful study of tradition could provide valuable information on the organization of labour in these regions.

In general, the patriarchal mode of production prevailed almost everywhere. The clan chief, the head of the *ḳabīla*, the king or the emperor were not tyrants at all, but products of a custom which protected each individual from exactions or arbitrary acts of the rulers. In the Maghrib, revolts of the *ḳabīla* against the sultan's tax collectors were frequent in the fourteenth and fifteenth centuries.

One particularly important fact is the existence of a merchant class – a bourgeoisie in embryo. These merchants, whether converted to Islam or not, furthered relations between different regions and peoples. This fact has been emphasized in many chapters of the present volume. It was in this period that the trading propensities of people like the Mandingo and Hausa developed.

If comparison is permissible, we might say that everywhere in the ancient world, from Africa to China, by way of Arabia, Europe, the Atlantic and the Bosphorus, kingdoms and empires had reached a high level of development; the European adventure which began in the fifteenth century could have been undertaken either by Africa or China, especially the latter, where the compass and gunpowder had been discovered long before. Did not a Mali emperor try to discover where the Atlantic Ocean, the 'surrounding sea', ended?[7] But the wheel of history had spun, and pointed to Europe. For nearly five centuries western Europe, that leading edge of the Asian land mass, was to be preponderant.

The historical dynamism of Africa

In the light of these observations, we cannot fail to observe that, for the period under review, the main characteristic of the continent was its own historical dynamism. The development of the civilizations which then flourished on the continent cannot be explained solely by the influence of Islam, as has been maintained up to now. We have seen that the brilliant civilizations of Benin, of the Congo (Zaïre), of Mapungubwe and Great Zimbabwe give the lie to such a theory. Even the states converted to Islam drew their moral strength less from Islam than from the basic African traditions, which were more alive than ever. In northern Africa the indigenous populations, while accepting Islamic and Arab influences, nevertheless retained their own cultural identity. Thus the Berbers were able to preserve their language and much of their culture, even when they accepted Islam.

The political instability which may be noted here and there was due to internal causes, and the way the problems were solved reflected the underlying tendencies of the population. One typical case was the introduction of Islam into West Africa. The Almoravid movement was essentially Negro-Berber; in the Sudan, for example, its development led to the dislocation of the old empire of Ghana. There followed a series of wars between the provinces, which led to the restoration of the empire under the rule of Mandingo, whose kings were converted in the eleventh century. The new empire of Mali acquired new provinces and spread its influence well beyond Ghana's sphere of interest. Set in a frame with Islamic gilding, this new evolution was a prelude to the founding of new towns and a new society, soon to be dominated by an aristocracy of black merchants and scholars. Many examples could show the internal dynamism of African societies. Ethiopian Christianity is a striking example; cut off from the rest of the Christian world, Ethiopia shaped a Church according to its ancient values.

In the theoretical sphere, there is still much controversy over the defini-

7. See Chapter 26, pp. 664–5 above.

tion of the mode of production that prevailed in pre-colonial Africa. But how can anyone characterize a type of production, when the very outlines of its history are unknown? The past must first be re-created, by showing the interplay of institutions and presenting the components of society, which implies much more research.[8]

As we have said above, although gold, copper and ivory were the most important materials for trade between tropical Africa and the rest of the world, for the *Kaya Maghan*, the mansa and the Mwene Mutapa, the foundation of the economy was agriculture, because peasants and craftsmen were in the majority.

The merchants and the nobles at court and in the towns formed an aristocracy which was numerically small in comparison with the mass of the peasants and stock farmers. The main fact to bear in mind in respect of black Africa is that private ownership of land did not form the basis of social and economic development as it did in Europe. Up to the present time in black Africa, before the monetary economy developed, land was considered to be the indivisible property of the community. The kings and emperors had 'human estates', that is, lands worked by subjugated communities; but closer examination shows that this was a system of serfdom rather than slavery. For instance, in the empire of Mali and later in that of Gao, the subjugated peoples or ethnic groups were obliged to pay a fixed rent per family. Professor Mody Cissoko shows this clearly:

> Agricultural techniques have not greatly changed since those times. The hoe (the Songhay *kaunu*), animal manure, the practice of horticulture in the valley and shifting cultivation in the savannah have stayed the same for centuries, but the valley of the Niger was then more densely inhabited by a population occupied in farming, fishing and stock-raising. Large estates belonging to the princes and '*ulamā*'s of the great towns were worked by slaves, settled in farming villages. The askiya was himself one of the great landowners. His fields, scattered throughout the valley, were cultivated by communities of slaves working under overseers called *fanfa*. A sort of rent in kind was levied on the harvests and sent to Gao. The same happened with private slaves.[9]

In some regions, however, the slaves played a key part both in the economy and in the exercise of power. That was the case in central Sudan between Niger and Chad. The Hausa cities were largely populated by slaves collected in the south. André Salifou also distinguishes between slaves of the crown and slaves of the house. Slaves of the crown were chosen from among the servants and most devoted associates of the king. Young slaves whose parents had been captured, sold, or even killed in a fight were usually brought up at the court with the princes of the country;

8. Hasty generalizations should be particularly avoided, since only the broad outlines of the overall history of certain regions are visible.

9. Chapter 8, pp. 202–3 above.

growing up in the sultan's shadow, they came to recognize only him as 'father'. They were neither sold nor maltreated, and they filled important posts in the country's military and civil services.

These facts are not new. Frequently, to counterbalance the influence of the aristocracy, the king assigned important positions to slaves who were naturally devoted to the person of the monarch and lacked political ambition. There are well-known cases of powerful slaves in the Maghrib, Egypt and Mali. Generally speaking, slaves never exceeded peasants as a proportion of the population. Free men worked the soil on their own account, but free men and tributaries both owed services to the ruler or to the local lord.

In the present state of research, the three following propositions can be asserted, each of which is discussed in turn.

(1) Although the economy was based on agriculture and stock-raising, nowhere did private ownership of property become general; the principal right of ownership belonged to the community.

(2) A certain accumulation of capital began with the merchant class, but this did not result in a true bourgeoisie.

(3) Africa was not an under-populated continent.

This is an extremely important point, and a distinguished historian has written: 'civilization is born of numbers'. Without these 'numbers', the emperors of Ghana would never have been able to build the great palaces of Koumbi, nor would the rulers of the Maghrib have built the beautiful mosques of Fez and Ḳayrawān and the great storehouse of Sijilmasa. Without these 'numbers', the emperors and kings of the south could never have built Great Zimbabwe. The continent was therefore densely populated, especially south of the Sahara: in the Senegal valley, in the interior of the Niger delta and around Lake Chad there were hundreds of farming villages, trading centres and towns.

The first archaeological excavations in these regions permit a categorical statement on this question. The gigantic monuments were not the work of 'hordes of slaves'; it was the piety of the subjects and their concept of royalty – which made each think of himself as the son of the king – that made possible these major endeavours. The coercion of 'hordes of slaves' appears more and more a superficial explanation, just as if we tried to explain a Gothic cathedral or a Roman basilica as the product of slaves working under the whip. Faith has strong echoes in the hearts and spirits of men.

We have some indications of the population of certain regions. According to Maḥmūd Ka'ti, Mali had 400 towns or large population centres; the farming villages stretched in a continuous line along the waterways. Agricultural production was very extensive. Professor Cissoko, whom we have already quoted, has drawn attention to the extent of rice production; for example, among the Songhay in the fifteenth and sixteenth centuries, a single *fanfa* or overseer, directing the work of a community of tributaries, could supply the king with more than 1000 *sounu* (large leather sacks which held about 70 kg). The royal stocks of food were immense; we may gain some idea of them from the fact that the king of Gao had a regular army of 100 000 men, garrisons near the main commercial towns and a very large court, and that all these people were fed and maintained by the king almost entirely from his agricultural revenues. It is difficult to estimate the size of the population, but the large number of well-populated trading towns and constructions on the scale of the Great Zimbabwe monuments would suggest that the population was dense. Over the whole continent, at this period of commercial expansion, the towns perhaps accounted for 10 per cent of the population.

Africa was far from being under-populated; but, from north to south and from east to west, the population was unevenly distributed, owing to the existence of deserts and thick forests. At this time Africa must have suffered epidemics, periods of drought and major floods, but the documents available make little mention of famine. Arab travellers – for example, Ibn Baṭṭūṭa, the fourteenth-century globe-trotter – noticed the abundance of food on the east coast and in the Sudan. For the whole of the continent, the population in Ibn Baṭṭūṭa's lifetime may be estimated at 200 million at a minimum.[10]

(3) The slave trade was carried on in Africa before 1600, but the numbers involved were limited.

There is no comparison with the slave trade the Europeans imposed on the black world from 1500 onwards. The latter had good commercial relations with Sudanese rulers as well as those of Guinea and the Congo. Around 1550, the Portuguese were driven out by the Dutch, English and French, who each built factories and forts on the African coast in order to turn the slave trade to better account.

If we are to gain a better understanding of the history of the period from the twelfth to the sixteenth century, research must be based on archaeology, linguistics, anthropology and also on oral traditions, which provide information from the interior. The latter can, on the one hand, be compared with written records and, on the other, can guide archaeologists in the field, as in the case of Koumbi and Niani. The search for manuscripts should continue; it appears that there is much more written material on this period than used to be thought. The need for a systematic collection of the oral traditions of black Africa cannot be overemphasized.

The example of Somalia is noteworthy, where children's songs, folk songs, magical incantations and other traditions have been systematically collected and virtually nothing has been ignored. We may also mention

10. The countries which supplied the most slaves were among those with the largest population – the coast of the Gulf of Guinea (from the Ivory Coast to Nigeria); the mouth of the Congo/Zaïre; Angola; and so on.

an unpublished work by the late Musa H. I. Galaal, a member of the Scientific Committee for the History of Africa, entitled 'Stars, seasons and weather'.[11] In Somalia, the study of the stars and constellations – referred to in the Somali language as *xiddigo* – is based on a series of short poems, and the same is true of the formal study of the sky and the stars visible at certain seasons of the year, from which a calendar is drawn up. It is most interesting to see the study of astronomy thus intimately related to the life of the people. I read with very great pleasure the text which Musa Galaal was kind enough to lend me. It confirmed my belief that we still have much of interest to learn from the study of oral traditions. This work contains the elements of Somali astronomy, and shows that peasants and herdsmen alike possessed an advanced knowledge of the cosmos. All the constellations and planets are described in brief songs; the calendar of agricultural activities and the migrations of nomads were based on sound knowledge which was the outcome of many centuries of experience. I have no doubt that when Musa Galaal's study is published it will inspire many Africans to investigate 'traditional' science.

Our own long experience of oral tradition entitles us to state that much remains to be done in this field, only recently opened up, which is all too often considered merely from the historical and literary points of view. The Dogon of Mali and many other peoples have made careful studies of the sky and the constellations; other peoples have devoted particular attention to the study of soils and plants. Oral traditions can be investigated from several angles. They should be studied not only by historians and men of letters, but also by scientists, jurists and even political scientists, all of whom are interested for various reasons in ancient black African institutions. It must be admitted, however, that it is difficult to enter the world of the oral traditions, since the initiates live in a world to which it is difficult, if not impossible, to gain access. It is for African states to create the best possible conditions for the full participation of those who hold our patrimony in the development of our changing society.

There are still many 'wise men' living in villages hidden in the most isolated regions. Little has yet been lost; but everything remains to be done. In the last analysis, this is a matter not so much for individual research workers as for the governments of Africa, which must draw up a research policy and place resources at the disposal of African experts, and at the same time prepare the people to take part in a massive project, in which everyone can feel involved. Knowledge of the land and of local culture is indispensable for those who wish to help the people of the countryside.

Before leaving the question of tradition, let us note that Africa's artistic traditions have their roots precisely in this period which saw the birth and development of the peoples and states from which modern Africa

11. Musa H. I. Galaal, n.d.

has grown. Muslim art in the Maghrib and Egypt produced in this period such masterpieces as the mosques of Fez, Tunis, Tlemcen and Egypt in the fourteenth and fifteenth centuries. If works of art from Africa south of the Sahara are rare for this period, that is due partly to the fact that sculptors, for example, worked mainly in wood. The scarcity is also partly a result of our ignorance. There are masterpieces in the museums of Paris, London, Brussels, Berlin, Lisbon and the Vatican of which Africans are not even aware.

On the other hand, the civilization of Ife-Benin has left us famous bronzes and brass heads which are known all over the world. The art of Ife-Benin is of such a pure naturalism that 'Africanists' began by denying that they could have been made by Africans. But today we know that Ife is not an isolated case; the bronzes of Igbo-Ukwu and of Nupe prove that the technique of brass casting was widespread, as shown by the recent discovery of figurines made of bronze in Guinea-Bissau. The problem of how this technique was diffused is thus posed in a larger context.

What will the Zimbabwe excavations, and those of southern Africa, reveal in artistic terms? At all events, the most sanguine hopes are permissible.

Members of the International Scientific Committee for the Drafting of a General History of Africa

The dates cited below refer to dates of membership.

Professor J. F. A. Ajayi
(Nigeria), from 1971
Editor Volume VI

Professor F. A. Albuquerque Mourao
(Brazil), from 1975

Professor A. A. Boahen
(Ghana), from 1971
Editor Volume VII

H. E. Boubou Hama
(Niger), 1971–8 (resigned)

H. E. M. Bull
(Zambia), from 1971

Professor D. Chanaiwa
(Zimbabwe), from 1975

Professor P. D. Curtin
(USA), from 1975

Professor J. Devisse
(France), from 1971

Professor M. Difuila
(Angola), from 1978

Professor H. Djait
(Tunisia), from 1975

Professor Cheikh Anta Diop
(Senegal), from 1971

Professor J. D. Fage
(UK), 1971–81 (resigned)

H. E. M. El Fasi
(Morocco), from 1971
Editor Volume III

Professor J. L. Franco
(Cuba), from 1971

The late Mr M. H. I. Galaal
(Somalia), 1971–81; deceased 1981

Professor Dr V. L. Grottanelli
(Italy), from 1971

Professor E. Haberland
(Federal Republic of Germany), from 1971

Dr Aklilu Habte
(Ethiopia), from 1971

H. E. A. Hampate Ba
(Mali), 1971–8 (resigned)

Dr I. S. El-Hareir
(Libya), from 1978

Dr I. Hrbek
(Czechoslovakia), from 1971

Dr A. Jones
(Liberia), from 1971

The late Abbé Alexis Kagame
(Rwanda), 1971–81; deceased 1981

Professor I. M. Kimanbo
(Tanzania), from 1971

Professor J. Ki-Zerbo
(Upper Volta), from 1971
Editor Volume I

M. D. Laya
(Niger), from 1979

Dr A. Letnev
(USSR), from 1971

Dr G. Mokhtar
(Egypt), from 1971
Editor Volume II

Professor P. Mutibwa
(Uganda), from 1975

Professor D. T. Niane
(Senegal), from 1971
Editor Volume IV

Professor L. D. Ngcongco
(Botswana), from 1971

Biographies of Authors

INTRODUCTION D. T. Niane (Senegal); specialist in the Mandingo world; has published a number of works on West Africa at the time of the great empires, from the eleventh to the sixteenth century; former Director of the Fondation L. S. Senghor, Dakar; researcher.

CHAPTER 2 O. Saidi (Tunisia); specialist in the history of the Almohads; has published various works on the classical history of the Maghrib, of Tunisia in particular; teaches history at the Faculty of Arts and the Ecole Normale Supérieure of the University of Tunis.

CHAPTER 3 M. Talbi (Tunisia); Islamologist; has published many works and articles on the various aspects of Islamic religion and culture; teaches at the Faculty of Arts, Tunis.

CHAPTER 4 I. Hrbek (Czechoslovakia); specialist in the Arab sources of the history of Africa, particularly West Africa, as well as specialist in Islam; has published many works and articles in these fields; researcher at the Oriental Institute, Prague.

CHAPTER 5 R. Idris (France); specialist in Arabic language and literature; taught the history of the Muslim West; deceased.

CHAPTER 6 D. T. Niane.

CHAPTER 7 M. Ly-Tall (Mali); specialist in the history of Mali; has published works on the Mali empire; teaches at the Ecole Normale Supérieure, Bamako; researcher.

CHAPTER 8 S. M. Cissoko (Senegal); specialist in the history of medieval Timbuktu; has published various works on the history of West Africa; Assistant Lecturer at the Faculty of Arts, Dakar.

CHAPTER 9 M. Izard (France); specialist in the history of the Volta Basin and particularly that of the Mossi kingdoms; has published many works on the pre-colonial, colonial and modern history of this region; Senior Researcher at the Centre National de la Recherche Scientifique, Paris.

CHAPTER 10 D. Lange (Federal Republic of Germany); specialist in the pre-colonial history of the central Sudan; has published various works on this period; teaches at the University of Niamey.

CHAPTER 11 M. Adamu (Nigeria); specialist in the history of the Hausa; has published works on this subject; Director of the Centre for Nigerian Cultural Studies of Ahmadu Bello University, Zaria.

A. Salifou (Niger); specialist in the history of the Hausa; has published various works on Niger and Nigeria; teaches in Niger.

CHAPTER 12 Y. Person (France): specialist in the history of Africa, particularly the Mandingo world; has published many works on the history of Africa; Professor at the University of Paris I, Panthéon-Sorbonne; deceased.

CHAPTER 13 P. Kipre (Ivory Coast); specialist in modern and contemporary history of the Ivory Coast; has published various articles based on oral tradition; teaches at the Ecole Normale Supérieure, Abidjan.

CHAPTER 14 A. F. C. Ryder (UK); specialist in the history of West Africa; has published many works on the pre-colonial and colonial periods of this region; Professor at the University of Bristol.

CHAPTER 15 J. C. Garcin (France); specialist in the history of Muslim Egypt; has published various studies on the history of Egypt under the Mamluks and on Muslim Upper Egypt; teaches at the University of Provence, Aix-en-Provence.

CHAPTER 16 L. Kropáček (Czechoslovakia); specialist in the social, political and religious history of the Sudan; has published various works on Darfūr; teaches at the Department of Oriental and African Studies of Charles University, Prague.

CHAPTER 17 T. Tamrat (Ethiopia); specialist in the medieval history of Ethiopia; has published various studies on this period; teaches at the University of Addis Ababa.

CHAPTER 18 V. Matveiev (USSR); historian and ethnologist; has published many works on the Arab sources of the history of Africa; Senior Researcher at the Institute of Ethnography of the Academy of Sciences of the USSR, Leningrad.

CHAPTER 19 C. Ehret (USA); linguist and historian of East Africa; has published many works and articles on the pre-colonial and colonial history of East Africa; teaches at the University of California, Los Angeles.

CHAPTER 20 B. A. Ogot (Kenya); specialist in African and particularly East African history; has published many works and articles on the history and archaeology of East Africa; teacher, researcher, former Director of the International Louis Leakey Memorial Institute for African Prehistory.

CHAPTER 21 B. M. Fagan (UK); anthropologist, archaeologist; has published many works on the Iron Age and Stone Age cultures in East and Southern Africa; Professor of Anthropology at the University of California, Santa Barbara.

CHAPTER 22 J. Vansina (Belgium); specialist in oral tradition; has published many works on the history of Equatorial and Central Africa; teaches at the University of Wisconsin, USA.

CHAPTER 23 L. Ngcongco (Botswana); specialist in the pre-colonial history of Southern Africa; has published various studies on Botswana in pre-colonial times; taught at the University of Botswana; Director of National Institute of Research, Gaborone.

J. Vansina.

CHAPTER 24 F. Esoavelomandroso (Madagascar); specialist in the history of Madagascar; has published various studies on the history of Madagascar from the sixteenth to the eighteenth century; teaches at the Faculty of Arts, Antananarivo.

CHAPTER 25 D. T. Niane.

CHAPTER 26 J. Devisse (France); specialist in the history of North-West Africa from the fourth to the sixteenth century; archaeologist; has published many articles and works on the history of Africa; Professor of African History at the University of Paris I, Panthéon-Sorbonne.

S. Labib (Egypt); specialist in the medieval history of Africa; has published various works on the social and economic history of this period; teaches at the University of Utah (USA) and the University of Kiel (Federal Republic of Germany).

CHAPTER 27 D. T. Niane.

Bibliography

Foreword

This bibliography has been edited to meet the needs of scholars from many countries; it includes only works cited in Volume IV. Entries are listed alphabetically by author where known, otherwise by title. To reconcile the diverse systems of cataloguing works which are part of a general series, all entries appear under the author's name and the series title is appended to publication details. Contrary to the pactice of some bibliographers, the first date given for each work is, wherever possible, the date of first publication (or completion, for Arabic MSS). This is done in order to distinguish more clearly between early works and modern editions or translations. First names are given only for Arabic authors, who are listed under the Arabic names by which they are most commonly known and/or cited in the text; some cross-references, however, are given to alternative Arabic names and familiar names.

Names and titles originally written in Arabic script have been transliterated according to the system followed in the *Encyclopaedia of Islam*, English edition, whch has been a valuable source of reference. (But the transliterations used by editors and translators have not been altered in their titles.) Other bibliographical information has been taken from the following catalogues: Library of Congress, Bodleian Library, British Library, Bibliothèque Nationale, University of London School of Oriental and African Studies, Northwestern University Melville J. Herskovits Library, Oxford University Oriental Institute Library, Chicago University Oriental Institute Library, University of Utah Middle East Catalog and the Library of Rhodes House, Oxford. The following bibliographies have also been consulted: Bibliographie ethnographique de l'Afrique subsaharienne, Current Bibliography of African Affairs, International African Bibliography, International African Institute and Cumulative Bibliography of African Studies.

Abbreviations and list of periodicals

AA *African Affairs*, London: OUP
AB *Africana Bulletin*, Warsaw: Warsaw University
AEA *Anuario de Estudios Atlanticos*, Madrid
AEDA *Archivo Espanol de Arqueolologia*, Madrid
AEO *Archives d'études orientales.*
AESC *Annales-Economie, Sociétés, Civilisations*, Paris
AFRCD *Afrique française: renseignements coloniaux et documents*, Paris: Comité de l'Afrique française et Comité du Maroc
Africa–(L) *Africa*, London
Africa–(R) *Africa*, Rome
Africana Linguistica *Africana Linguistica*, Tervuren: Musée royal de l'Afrique centrale
Africanist *The Africanist*, Washington DC: Howard University, Association of African Studies
Afrika Museum Groesbeck, Netherlands
AHES *Annales d'histoire économique et sociale*, Paris
AHS *African Historical Studies* (later: *International Journal of African Historical Studies*), Boston University: African Studies Center
AI *Annales islamologiques*, Cairo
AIEOA *Annales de l'Institut d'études orientales d'Alger*, Algiers
AJ *Antiquaries Journal, Journal of the London Society of Antiquaries*, London: OUP
AL *Annales Lateraniensis*, Vatican City
ALS *African Language Studies*, London: School of Oriental and African Studies
al-Andalus *al-Andalus, Revista de las Escuelas de Estudios Arabes de Madrid y Granada*, Madrid
AM *Afrikana Marburgensia*, Marburg
Ambario *Ambario*, Tananarive
ANM *Annals of the Natal Museum*, Natal

Annales islamologiques
Annales du Midi *Annales du Midi: revue de la France méridionale*, Toulouse
Anthropos *Anthropos: Revue internationale d'éthnologie et de linguistique*, Fribourg
Antiquity *Antiquity*, Gloucester
Arabica *Arabica: Revue d'études arabes*, Leiden: Brill
Archiv Orientalni *Archiv Orientalni, Oriental Archives: Journal of African and Asian Studies*, Prague
Arnoldia *Arnoldia*, Salisbury: National Museums of Rhodesia
ARSP *Archiv für Rechts-und-Sozialphilosophie*, Berlin, Leipzig
AS *African Studies*, Johannesburg: Witwatersrand University Press
ASAM *Annals of the South African Museum*, Cape Town
ASp *Afrika Spektrum, deutsche Zeitschrift für moderne Afrikforschung*, Pfaffenhofen: Afrika Verlag
ASPN *Archivio Storico per la Province Napoletane*, Naples
A–T *Africa – Tervuren*, Tervuren
AU *Afrika und Übersee*, Hamburg: Universität
AUA *Annales de l'université d'Abidjan*, Abidjan
AUM *Annales de l'université de Madagascar*, (*Série lettres et sciences humaines*), Tananarive
Awraḳ *Awraḳ* (Arabic & Spanish texts), Madrid: 1978– Instituto Hispano–Arabe de Cultura
Azania *Azania*, Nairobi: British Institute of History and Archaeology in East Africa
BA *Baessler Archiv*, Berlin: Museum für Völkerkunde
BAM *Bulletin de l'Académie Malgache*, Madagascar
BARSOM *Bulletin de l'Académie royale des sciences d'outre-mer*, Bruxelles
Ba-Shiru *Ba-Shiru*, Madison: Wisconsin University, Department of African Languages and Literature
BCEHSAOF *Bulletin du Comité d'études historiques et scientifiques de l'Afrique occidentale française*, Dakar
BCGP *Bolletino Culturale da Guiné Portuguesa*, Bissau
BEO *Bulletin d'études orientales*, Damas: Institut français
BHSN *Bulletin of the Historical Society of Nigeria*, Ibadan
BIBLB *Boletim Internacional de Bibliografia Luso-Brasileira*, Lisbon: Fondaçâo Calouste Gulbenkian
BIE *Bulletin de l'Institut d'Egypte*, Cairo
(B)IFAN *(Bulletin de l')Institut fondamental d'Afrique noire* (previously: (Bulletin de l')Institut français d'Afrique noire), Dakar
BLPHGAM *Bulletin de liaison des professeurs d'histoire et de géographie d'Afrique et de Madagascar*, Mejec-Yaoundé
BM *Bulletin de Madagascar*, Tananarive
BNR *Botswana Notes and Records*, Gaborone
Boston University Papers in African History Boston University: African Studies Center
BPH *Bulletin Philosophique et Historique*, Paris: Comité des travaux historiques et scientifiques, section d'histoire et de philologie
BRAH *Boletin de la Real Academia de la Historia*, Madrid
BSACH *Bulletin of the Society for African Church History*, University of Aberdeen, Department of Religious Studies
BSOAS *Bulletin of the School of Oriental and African Studies*, London
CA *Current Anthropology*, Chicago
CEA *Cahiers d'études africaines*, The Hague: Mouton
China Review *China Review*, Hong Kong
CHM *Cahiers d'histoire mondiale*, Paris: Librairie des Méridiens
CJAS *Canadian Journal of African Studies* (*Revue canadienne des études africaines*), Ottawa: Carleton University, Department of Geography, Canadian Association of African Studies
CNRS Centre National de la recherche scientifique, Paris
COM *Cahiers d'outre-mer*, Bordeaux: Institut de la France d'outre-mer
CRTSASOM *Compte-rendus trimestriels des séances de l'Académie des sciences d'outre-mer*, Paris
CSIC Consejo superior de investigaciones cientificas: Madrid
CSSH *Comparative Studies in Society and History*, Cambridge: CUP
CUP Cambridge University Press, London to 1978, Cambridge thereafter
Der Islam *Der Islam: Zeitschrift für Geschichte und Kultur des Islamischen Orients*, Berlin
EAPH East African Publishing House
EAZ *Ethnographisch-Archäologische Zeitung*, Berlin
EcHR *Economic History Review*, London, New York: CUP
EHR *English Historical Review*, London: Longman
EM *Etudes maliennes*, Bamako

EP *Etnografia Polska*, Wroclaw: Polska Akademia Nauk, Instytut Historii Kultury Materialny
Ethiopiques *Ethiopiques, Revue socialiste de culture négro-africaine*, Dakar: Fondation Léopold Senghor
Ethnos *Ethnos*, Stockholm: Ethnographical Museum of Sweden
EV *Etudes Voltaïques, Mémoires*, Ouagadougou
FEQ *Far Eastern Quarterly* (later: *Journal of Asian Studies*), Ann Arbor, Michigan
FHP *Fort Hare Papers*, Fort Hare University
Garcia da Orta *Garcia da Orta*, Lisbon: Junta de Investigações do Ultramar
GJ *Geographical Journal*, London
GNQ *Ghana Notes and Queries*, Legon
Godo-Godo *Godo-Godo: Bulletin de l'Institut d'histoire d'art et d'archéologie africaines*, Université d'Abidjan
HAJM *History in Africa: a Journal of Method*, Waltham, Mass.
Hespéris *Hespéris*, Rabat: Institut des hautes études marocaines
HJAS *Harvard Journal of Asiatic Studies*, Harvard
H-T *Hespéris–Tamuda*, Rabat, Université Mohammed V, Faculté des lettres et des sciences humaines
IAI International African Institute
IFAN see *BIFAN*
IJAHS *International Journal of African Historical Studies* (previously: *African Historical Studies*) Boston University: African Studies Center
IIALC International Institute of African Languages and Cultures
IRCB Institut royal colonial belge
JA *Journal asiatique*, Paris
JAH *Journal of African History*, London, New York: OUP
JAI *Journal of the Anthropological Institute*, London
JAL *Journal of African Languages*, London
JAOS *Journal of the American Oriental Society*, New Haven
JAS *Journal of the African Society*, London
JATBA *Journal d'agriculture traditionnelle et de botanique appliquée*, Paris: Museum National d'Histoire Naturelle
JEA *Journal of Egyptian Archaeology*, London
JES *Journal of Ethiopian Studies*, Addis Ababa
JESHO *Journal of Economic and Social History of the Orient*, London
JHSN *Journal of the Historical Society of Nigeria*, Ibadan
JMAS *Journal of Modern African Studies*, London: CUP
JMBRAS *Journal of the Malayan Branch of the Royal Asiatic Society*, Singapore
JNH *Journal of Negro History*, Washington DC: Association for the Study of Afro-American Life and History
JRAI *Journal of the Royal Anthropological Institute of Great Britain and Ireland*, London
JRAS *Journal of the Royal Asiatic Society of Great Britain and Ireland*, London
JRASB *Journal of the Royal Asiatic Society of Bengal*, Calcutta
JSA *Journal de la Société des africanistes*, Paris
JSAIMM *Journal of the South African Institute of Mining and Metallurgy*, Johannesburg
JSS *Journal of Semitic Studies*, Manchester: Manchester University, Department of Near Eastern Studies
KO *Kongo Overzee*, Antwerp
KS *Kano Studies*, Kano, Nigeria
Kush *Kush, a Journal of the Sudan Antiquities Services*, Khartoum
L'Homme *L'Homme: Cahier d'éthnologie, de géographie et de linguistique*, Paris
MA *Moyen âge*, Paris
Man *Man*, London
MIO *Mitteilungen des Instituts für Orientforschung*, Berlin: Akademie der Wissenschafte
MNMMR *Memoirs of the National Museums and Monuments of Rhodesia*, Salisbury
MSOS *Mitteilungen des Seminars für Orientalische Sprachen an die Friedrich Wilhelm Universität zu Berlin*
Muslim Digest *Muslim Digest*, Durban
MZ *Materialy Zachodnio-Pomorskie*, Warsaw
NA *Notes africaines*, Dakar: IFAN
NAk *Nyame Akuma*, Calgary: University of Calgary, Department of Archaeology
Nature *Nature*, London, New York
NC *Numismatic Chronicle*, London: Numismatic Society
NED *Notes et études documentaires*, Paris: Direction de la Documentation

OA *Oriental Art*, London
OCP *Orientalia Christiana Periodica*, Rome
Odu *Odu: Journal of West African Studies* (previously: *Journal of African Studies*, Ife; preceded by *Journal of Yoruba and Related Studies*, Ibadan), Ife: University of Ife
OL *Oceanic Linguistics*, Carbondale: Southern Illinois University, Department of Anthropology
OSA *Omaly sy anio*, Tananarive: University of Madagascar
OUP Oxford University Press
PA *Présence africaine*, Dakar
Paideuma *Paideuma, Mitteilungen zur Kulturkunde*, Frankfurt-am-Main
PAPS *Proceedings of the American Philosophical Society*, New York
RASGBI Royal Asiatic Society of Great Britain and Ireland
RBCAD *Research Bulletin of the Centre of Arabic Documentation*, Ibadan
RDM *Revue des deux mondes*, Paris
REAA *Revista Espanola de Anthropologia Americana*, Madrid: Universidad
RES *Revue d'ethnographie et de sociologie*, Paris
RGM *Revue de géographie du Maroc*, Rabat: University Faculty of Geography
RH *Revue historique*, Paris: PUF
RHC *Revista de Historia Canarias*, Las Palmas
RHCF *Revue de l'histoire des colonies françaises* (later: *Revue française d'histoire d'outre-mer*), Paris
RHCM *Revue d'histoire et de civilisation du Maghreb*, Algiers: Société Historique Algérienne
RHES *Revue d'histoire économique et sociale*, Paris
RHSP *Revista de Historia*, São Paulo
RIBLA *Revue de l'Institut des belles lettres arabes*, Tunis
RNADA *Rhodesian Native Affairs, Departmental Annual*, Salisbury
ROMM *Revue de l'occident musulman et de la Méditerranée*, Aix-en-Provence
RRAL *Rendiconti della Reale dell'Accademia dei Lincei*, Classe de Scienze Morale, Storiche e Filologiche
RS *Revue sémitique*, Paris
RSACNM *Recueil de la Société archéologique de Constantine, notes et mémoires*, Constantine
RSE *Rassegna di Studi Etiopici*, Rome
RSO *Revista degli Studi Orientali*, Rome: Scuola Orientale dell'Universita
SAAB *South African Archaeological Bulletin*, Cape Town
Saeculum *Saeculum*, Freiburg
SAJS *South African Journal of Science*, Johannesburg
Sankofa *Sankofa*, Legon (Ghana)
Savanna *Savanna: a Journal of the Environmental and Social Sciences*, Zaria: Ahmadu Bello University
Scientia *Scientia, Rivista di Scienza*, Milan
SHG *Studia Historica Gandensia*, Ghent
SI *Studia Islamica*, Paris
SM *Studi Magrebini*, Naples
SNED Société nationale d'édition et de diffusion, Algiers
SNR *Sudan Notes and Records*, Khartoum
SOAS London University, School of Oriental and African Studies
South Africa *South Africa*, Pretoria
SS *Sudan Society*, Khartoum: Khartoum University
Swahili *Swahili*, Nairobi: East African Swahili Committee
SWJA *South Western Journal of Anthropology* (later: *Journal of Anthropological Research*) Albuquerque, University of New Mexico
Taloha *Taloha, Revue du Musée d'art et d'archéologie*, Tananarive
Tamuda *Tamuda*, Rabat
Tantara *Tantara*, Tananarive: Société d'histoire de Madagascar
THSG *Transactions of the Historical Society of Ghana* (previously *Transactions of the Gold Coast and Togoland Historical Society*), Legon
Times *The Times*, London
TJH *Transafrican Journal of History*, Nairobi: East African Literature Bureau
TNR *Tanzania Notes and Records* (formerly *Tanganyika Notes & Records*), Dar es Salaam
TNYAS *Transactions of the New York Academy of Sciences*, New York
T'oung Pao *T'oung Pao, Revue internationale de sinologie*, Leiden: Brill
UCLA University of California Los Angeles
Ufahamu *Ufahamu, Journal of the African Activist Association*, Los Angeles
UJ *Uganda Journal*, Kampala

Universitas *Universitas*, Legon: University of Ghana
WA *World Archaeology*, Henley-on-Thames
WAAN *West African Archaeological Newsletter*, Ibadan
WAJA *West African Journal of Archaeology*, Ibadan
Zaïre *Zaïre*, Kinshasa
ZDMG *Zeitung der Deutschen Morgenländischen Gesellschaft*, Leipzig

Bibliography

ʿAbd al-ʿAzīz b. Muḥammad b. Ibrahīm al-Ṣinhādjī al-Fishtālī (16th cent.) *Manāhil al-Safā' fi akhbār al-Mulūk al-Shurafā*; 1964 ed. ʿAbd Allāh Gannun (Tetuan).
ʿAbd al-Bāsiṭ b. Khalīl, al-Malati (15th cent.) *al-Rauḍ, al-Bāsim*; 1936 ed. and French transl. R. Brunschvig, *Deux récits de voyage inédits en Afrique du nord au 15e siècle* (Paris: Larose).
ʿAbd al-Raḥīm, M. (1970) 'Arabism, Africanism and self-identification in the Sudan', *JMAS*, **8**, 2, pp. 233–49.
ʿAbd al-Rahmān b. ʿAbd Allāh, al-Saʿdī: see al-Saʿdī
ʿAbd al-Wāḥid al-Marrākushī (1224) *al-Muʿdjib fī talkhīs Akhbār al-Maghrib*, 1963 ed. M. S. al-Iryan (Cairo); 1847, 1881, Eng. transl. R. Dozy, *The history of the Almohads* (Leiden: Brill); 1893 French transl. E. Fagnan (Algiers); 1955 Spanish transl. A. Huici Miranda (Tetuan: Editora Marroquí).
Abitbol, M. (1979) *Tombouctou et les Arma: de la conquête marocaine du Soudan nigérien en 1591 à l'hégémonie de l'empire peul du Macina en 1833* (Paris: Maisonneuve et Larose).
Abraham D. P. (1961) 'Maramuca: an exercise in the combined use of Portuguese records and oral tradition', *JAH*, **2**, 2, pp. 211–25.
Abū ʿAbd Allāh Muḥammad al-Wazīr al-Andalusī (16th cent.) *al-Ḥulal al-sundusīya fī 'l akhbār al-tunisīya*; 1870 edn and transl., *A history of Africa, especially of Tunis*, 4 vols (Tunis).
Abubakar, S. (1980) 'Peoples of the upper Benue basin and the Bauchi plateau before 1800', in O. Ikime (ed.) *Groundwork of Nigerian History* (Ibadan/London: Heinemann), pp. 165–86.
Abu 'l-Fidā (14th cent.) *al-Mukhtaṣar ta'rīkh al-bashar*; 1869–70 edn, 2 vols (Istanbul); 1907 edn (Cairo).
Abu'l-Maḥāsin b. Taghrībirdī (15th cent.) *al-Nudjūm al-Zāhira fī Mulūk Miṣr wa 'l Ḳāhira*; Eng. transl. W. Popper, *History of Egypt (1382–1469 AD)* (Berkeley: University of California Press; Publications in Semitic Philology, 13–14, 17–19, 22–3).
Abun-Nasr, J. M. (1971, 1975) *A history of the Maghrib* (London: CUP).
Abū ʿUbayd al-Bakrī: see al-Bakrī
Adams, J. (1904) *Légendes historiques du pays de Nioro* (Paris: Challamel) (no further details available).
Adams, W. Y. (1965) 'Sudan Antiquities Service excavations at Meinarti, 1963–1964', *Kush*, **3**, pp. 148–76.
Adams, W. Y. (1966) 'Post-Pharaonic Nubia in the light of archaeology, 3', *JEA*, **52**, pp. 147–62.
Adams, W. Y. (1967) 'Continuity and change in Nubian cultural history', *SNR*, **48**, pp. 1–32.
Adamu, M. (1976) 'The spread of Hausa culture in West Africa', *Savanna*, **5**, 1, pp. 3–13.
Adamu, M. (1978) *The Hausa factor in West African history* (Zaria: Ahmadu Bello University Press and OUP).
Adamu, M. (1979) 'Distribution of trading centres in the central Sudan in the eighteenth and nineteenth centuries', in Y. B. Usman (ed.), *Studies in the history of the Sokoto caliphate: the Sokoto Seminar Papers* (Zaria: Ahmadu Bello University Department of History for the Sokoto Caliphate Bureau), pp. 59–104.
Adamu, M. (forthcoming a) *The Hausa kingdom of Yawuri* (Zaria: Ahmadu Bello University Press).
Adamu, M. (forthcoming b) *History: essays in honour of Professor Abdullahi Smith* (Zaria: Ahmadu Bello University Press).
Adeleye, R. A. (1971) 'Hausaland and Bornu, 1600–1800', in J. F. A. Ajayi and M. Crowder (eds), *History of West Africa* (London: Longman), Vol. 1, pp. 485–530.
Adetugbo, A. (1973) 'The Yoruba language in Yoruba history', in S. O. Biobaku (ed.), *Sources of Yoruba history* (Oxford: Clarendon Press), pp. 175–204.
Aḥmad b. Mādjid al-Nadjdī: see Ibn Mādjid al-Dīn Aḥmad
Ahmad, A. A. R. (1973) *La femme au temps des mamlouks en Egypte* (Cairo: Institut français d'archéologie orientale; Textes arabes et études islamiques, 5).
Ahmed Ibn Fartua: see Ibn Furṭūwa, Aḥmad

Ajayi, J. F. A. and Crowder, M. (eds) (1971, 1974) *History of West Africa*, 2 vols (London: Longman).
Alagoa, E. J. (1972) *A history of the Niger delta: an historical interpretation of Ijo oral tradition* (Ibadan: University Press).
Albatenius: see al-Battānī
Alberuni: see al-Bīrūnī
Alfonso X, el Sabio, King of Castile and Leon (n.d.) *Libros de acedrex dados e tablas*; 1941 ed. Arnald Steiger, *Das Schachzabelbuch König Alfons des Weisen* (Geneva: Droz).
Alkali, M. B. (1969) 'A Hausa community in crisis: Kebbi in the nineteenth century' (unpublished M.A. dissertation, Ahmadu Bello University, Zaria).
Allan, W. (1965) *The African husbandman* (Edinburgh: Oliver and Boyd; New York: Barnes and Noble).
Alvares d'Almada, A. (1594) *Tratado Breve dos Rios de Guiné*; 1946 Portuguese ed. L. Silveira (Lisbon); 1842 French transl. V. de Santaren (no further details available).
Alvares d'Almada, A. (16th cent.) *Asia*; 1934 edn (London: Hakluyt Society).
Alvares, F. (16th cent.) 1881 ed. and Eng. transl. Lord Stanley of Alderley, *Narrative of the Portuguese embassy to Abyssinia during the years 1520–1527* (London: Hakluyt Society).
Arianoff, A. d' (1952) *Histoire des Bagesera, souverains du Gisaka* (Brussels: Institut royal colonial belge; Mémoires de l'Académie royale des sciences d'outre-mer, classe des sciences morales et politiques, **24**, 3).
Arié, R. (1973) *L'Espagne musulmane au temps des Nasrides (1232–1492)* (Paris: de Boccard).
Arkell, A. J. (1936–46) 'Darfur antiquities', *SNR*, **19**, 1, pp. 301–11; **20**, 1, pp. 91–105; **27**, 3, pp. 185–202.
Arkell, A. J. (1950) 'Gold Coast copies of fifth to seventh century bronze lamps', *Antiquity*, **24**, 93, pp. 38–40.
Arkell, A. J. (1951–2) 'The history of Darfur: 1200–1700 A.D.', *SNR*, **32**, pp. 37–70 and 207–38; **33**, pp. 129–55, 244–75.
Arkell, A. J. (1959) 'The medieval history of Darfur in its relation to other cultures and to the Nilotic Sudan', *SNR*, **40**, pp. 44–7.
Arkell, A. J. (1960) 'A Christian church and monastery at Ain Farah Darfur', *Kush*, **7**, pp. 115–19.
Arkell, A. J. (1961) *A history of the Sudan from the earliest times to 1821* (London: Athlone Press).
Arkell, A. J. (1963) 'The influence of Christian Nubia in the Chad area between AD 800–1200', *Kush*, **11**, pp. 315–19.
Arnett, E. J. (1910) 'A Hausa chronicle: (*Daura Makas Sariki*)', *JAS*, **9**, 34, pp. 161–7.
Arveiller, R. (1963) *Contribution à l'étude des termes de voyage en français 1505–1722* (Paris: d'Artrey).
Ashtor, E. (1971) *Les métaux précieux et la balance des paiements du Proche-Orient à la basse époque* (Paris: SEVPEN).
'Ashūr, Sa'īd 'Abd al-Fattāh (1965) *al-'Asr al mamālīkī fī misr war al-sham: The Mameluke period in Egypt and Syria* (Cairo).
Asín Palacios, M. (1941) *Huellas del Islam: Sto Tomás de Aquino* (Madrid: Espasa-Calpe).
al-Athīr: see Ibn al-Athīr, 'Izz al-Dīn
Avempace: see Ibn Badjdja
Averroës: see Ibn Rushd
Axelson, E. (1973a) *Congo to Cape: early Portuguese explorers* (London: Faber).
Axelson, E. (1973b) *Portuguese in south-east Africa, 1488–1600* (Johannesburg: Struik).
Ayalon, D. (1953–4) 'Studies on the structure of the Mamluk army', *BSOAS*, **15**, 2, pp. 203–28, 3, pp. 448–76; **16**, 1, pp. 57–90.

Badawi, A. R. (1972) *Histoire de la philosophie en Islam*, 2 vols (Paris: Vrin).
Baikie, W. B. (1856) *Narrative of an exploring voyage up the rivers Kwora and Binue* (London: Murray).
al-Bakrī (Abū 'Ubayd al-Bakrī, 'Abd Allāh b. 'Abd al-'Azīz b. Muḥ b. Ayyub) (11th cent.) *Kitāb al-Masālik wa 'l Mamālik*; 1911, 1913 ed. and French transl. MacG. de Slane, *Description de l'Afrique septentrionale* (Algiers: Jourdan; Paris: Geuthner); 1965 reprint (Paris: Maisonneuve et Larose); 1968 ed. 'Abd al-Raḥmān (Beirut).
Balfour-Paul, H. G. (1955) *History and antiquities of Darfur* (Khartoum: Sudan Antiquities Service; Museum pamphlet 3).
Balogun, S. A. (1980) 'History of Islam up to 1800', in O. Ikime (ed.) (1980), q.v.
Barbosa, D. (1812); 1918, 1921, edn and Eng. transl. *The book of Duarte Barbosa: an account of the countries bordering on the Indian Ocean and their inhabitants*, 2 vols (London: Hakluyt Society).
Barbour, N. (1974) 'The Emperor Frederick II, king of Jerusalem and Sicily, and his relations with the Muslims', in J. M. Barral (ed.), *Orientalia hispanica* (Leiden: Brill), Vol. 1, pp. 77–95.
Barges, J. J. L. (1859) *Tlemcen, ancienne capitale du royaume de ce nom* (Paris: Duprat).

Barges, J. J. L. (1877) *Complément à l'histoire des Beni-Zeiyan, rois de Tlemcen* (Paris: Leroux).
Barradas, L. A. (1967) *O sul de Moçambique no roteito de Sofala do piloto Ahmad ibn-Madjid* (Coimbra: Junta de investigações do Ultramar; Agrupamento de estudos de cartografia antiga, 20).
Barros, J. de (1552) *Decadas da Asia*, Vol. 1; 1937 partial Eng. transl. in G. R. Crone, q.v.
Barth, H. (1857, 1858) German edn, *Sammlung und Bearbeitung*, (including Centralafrikanischer Vokabularien), 3 parts in 2 (Gotha: Perthes); Eng. edn, *Travels and discoveries in North and Central Africa; being a journal of an exploration undertaken under the auspices of HBM's government in the years 1849–1855*, 5 vols (London: Longman); 1965 Eng. reprint, 3 vols (London: Cass).
Barth, H. (1965a) 'Authenticity and general character of the discovery of Bornu', in *Travels and discoveries*, 1965 edn (see above), Vol. 2, pp. 15–35.
Barth, H. (1965b) 'Chronological table, containing a list of the Sefuwa, or kings of Bornu', in *Travels and discoveries*, 1965 edn (see above), Vol. 2, pp. 581–605.
Bathily, I. D. (1961) 'Notices socio-historiques sur l'ancien royaume Soninké de Gadiage', *BIFAN*, B, **31**, 1, pp. 31–105.
Batran, A. A. (1973) 'A contribution to the biography of Shaikh ... Al-Maghili, Al-Tilimsani', *JAH*, **14**, 3, pp. 381–94.
al-Battānī, Abū 'Abd Allāh Muḥammad b. Djābir, also known as Albatenius (*c.* 900) *Kitāb al-Zīdj*; 1896 edn of astronomical tables, *Le tabelle geografiche d'al-Battānī* (Turin: Bona); 1899, 1903, 1907, ed. and Latin transl. C. A. Nallino, *al-Battānī sive Albatenii opus astronomicum*, 3 vols (Milan: U. Hoeplium).
Baumann, H. (?1948) 1957, 1967 French transl. L. Hamburger, *Les Peuples et les civilisations de l'Afrique*, with French transl. of D. Westermann, 'Les langues et l'éducation' (Paris: Payot).
Baumann, H. (1956) 'Die Frage der Steinbauten und Steingräber in Angola', *Paideuma*, **6**, 3, pp. 118–51.
Bautier, H. R. (1955) 'Les relations commerciales entre l'Europe et l'Afrique du nord et l'équilibre économique méditerranéen du 12e au 14e siècle', *BPH*, pp. 399–416.
Bayle des Hermens, R. de (1972) 'Aspects de la recherche préhistorique en République centrafricaine' *A–T*, **18**, 3–4, pp. 90–103.
Beattie, J. (1960) *Bunyoro: an African kingdom* (New York: Holt).
Beaujouan, G. (1969) *L'astronomie dans la péninsule ibérique à la fin du Moyen Age* (Coimbra: Junta de investigações do Ultramar; Agrupamento de estudos de cartografia antiga, 24).
Beaumont, P. and Schoonraad, M. (1971) 'The Welgelegen shelter, eastern Transvaal', in *Rock paintings of Southern Africa*, *SAJS*, special issue no. 2, pp. 62–9.
Becker, C. H. (1910) 'Zur Geschichte des östlichen Sudan', *Der Islam*, **1**, pp. 153–77.
Becker, C. H. (1913) 'Leo Frobenius und die Brille des Islam', *Der Islam*, **4**, pp. 303–12.
Bedaux, R. M. A. (1972) 'Tellem: reconnaissance archéologique d'une culture de l'Ouest africain au Moyen Age: recherches architectoniques', *JSA*, **42**, 2, pp. 103–85.
Bedaux, R. M. A. (1974) 'Tellem: reconnaissance archéologique d'une culture, de l'Ouest africain au Moyen Age: les appuie-nuques, *JSA*, **44**, 1, pp. 7–42.
Bedaux, R. M. A. (1977) 'Tellem', *Afrika Museum* (Groesbeck, Netherlands).
Bel, A. (1903) *Les Bénou Ghânya; derniers représentants de l'empire almoravide et leur lutte contre l'empire almohade* (Paris: Leroux; Bulletin de correspondance africaine de l'école des lettres d'Alger, 27).
Bel, A. (1937) 'Les premiers émirs mérinides et l'Islam', in *Mélanges de géographie et d'orientalisme offerts à E. F. Gautier* (Tours: Arrault) pp. 34–44.
Bel, A. (1938) *La religion musulmane en Berbérie: esquisse d'histoire et de sociologie religieuses* (Paris: P. Geuthner).
Bello, M.: see Muḥammad Bello, M.
Bender, M. L. (ed.) (1976) *Language in Ethiopia* (London: OUP).
Béraud-Villars, J. M. E. (1942) *L'empire de Gâo: un état soudanais aux 15e et 16e siècles* (Paris: Plon).
Bernus, S. and Gouletquer, P. (1976) 'Du cuivre au sel: recherches ethno-archéologiques sur la région d'Azelik (campagne 1973–1975)', *JSA*, **46**, 1–2, pp. 7–68.
Bernus, S., Gouletquer, P. and Kleinman, D. (1976) 'Die Salinen von Tegidda-n-tesemt (Niger)', *EAZ*, **17**, 2, pp. 209–36.
Bertrandon de la Broquière (1892) tr. C. Schefer, *Le voyage d'outre-mer de Bertrandon de la Broquière*, (Paris: Leroux).
Betbedder, P. (1971) 'The kingdom of Buzinza', *CHM*, **13**, 4, pp. 736–62.
Bezzola, R. (1944–63) *Les origines et la formation de la littérature courtoise en Occident: 500–1200*, 5 vols (Paris: Champion).
'Bibliographie de l'histoire des grandes routes maritimes', (1968–73) in: *Boletim internacional de bibliografia luso-brasileira* (Lisbon: Fondação Calouste Gulbenkian)
Allemagne: **9**, 2, pp. 189–252

Danemark: **9**, 2, pp. 254–72
France: **9**, 2, pp. 274–352; **9**, 3, pp. 433–57
Pologne: **9**, 3, pp. 457–71
Etats-Unis: **10**, 4, pp. 509–62; **11**, 1, pp. 5–153
Espagne: **13**, 1, pp. 7–149; **13**, 3, pp. 373–446
Grèce: **13**, 3, pp. 447–98
Royaume-Uni: **14**, 1, pp. 5–162, **14**, 3, pp. 359–544, **14**, 4, pp. 673–711

Biebuyck, D. P. (1973) *Lega culture; art, initiation, and moral philosophy among a Central African people* (Berkeley: University of California Press).

Bikunya, P. (1927) *Ky'Abakama ba Bunyoro: History of Bunyoro* (London: Sheldon Press).

Birkeli, E. (1936) *Les Vazimba de la côte ouest de Madagascar: notes d'ethnographie* (Tananarive: Imprimerie Moderne de l'Emyrne; Mémoires de l'Académie malgache, fasc. 22).

Birmingham, D. (1965) 'The date and significance of the Imbangala invasion of Angola', *JAH*, **6**, 2, pp. 143–52

Birmingham, D. (1966) *Trade and conflict in Angola: the Mbundu and their neighbours under the influence of the Portuguese, 1483–1790* (Oxford: Clarendon Press).

Birmingham, D. and Marks, S. (1977) 'Southern Africa', in R. Oliver (ed.), *Cambridge History of Africa* (London: CUP), Vol. 3, pp. 521–620.

al-Bīrūnī, Abu 'l-Rayhān Muḥammad b. Aḥmad (1030) *Kitāb Ta'rīkh al-Hind*; 1887 ed. E. Sachau; 1888 Eng. transl. E. Sachau, *Alberuni's India; an account of the religion, philosophy, literature, geography ... of India about AD 1030* (London); 1964 reprint (Delhi: S. Chand).

Bisson, M. S. (1975) 'Copper currency in Central Africa: the archaeological evidence', *WA*, **6**, 3, pp. 276–92.

Blount, B. and Curley, R. T. (1970) 'The southern Luo languages: a glotto-chronological reconstruction', *JAL*, **9**, 1, pp. 1–18.

Boahen, A. A. (1974) 'Who are the Akan?' in Bonduku Seminar Papers, q.v.

Boelaert, E. (1957–8) *Lianja-verhalen*, 2 vols (Tervuren: Annales du musée royal du Congo belge: Sciences de l'homme: Linguistique, 17–19).

Boiteau, P. (1958) *Contribution à l'histoire de la nation malgache* (Paris: Ed. sociales).

Boiteau, P. (1974) 'Les droits sur la terre dans la société malgache pré-coloniale', in *Sur le mode de production asiatique* (Paris: Ed. sociales), pp. 135–69.

Bonduku Seminar Papers (1974) 'Colloque inter-universitaire Ghana – Côte-d'Ivoire: Les Populations communes de la Côte-d'Ivoire et du Ghana' (Bonduku: University of Abidjan).

Bonnassié, P. (1975–6) *La Catalogne du milieu de 10e à la fin du 11e siècle: croissance et mutations d'une société*, 2 vols (Toulouse: University of Toulouse-le-Mirail, Série A, 23, 29).

Boulègue, J. (1968) 'La Sénégambie du milieu du 15e siècle au début du 17e siècle' (doctoral dissertation, University of Dakar).

Boulègue, J. (1972) *Les luso-africains de Sénégambie, 16e–19e siècle* (Dakar: University of Dakar, Department of History, Travaux et documents, 1).

Boulnois, J. and Hama, B. (1954) *Empire de Gâo: histoire, coutumes et magie des Sonrai* (Paris: Maisonneuve).

Bourouiba, R. (1972) *L'Art musulman en Algérie* (Algiers: Sned).

Bourouiba, R. (1973) 'La Doctrine almohade', *ROMM*, **13–14**, pp. 141–58.

Bourouiba, R. (1976) 'Le problème de la succession de 'Abd al-Mumin', *RHCM*, **13**, pp. 23–9.

Bousquet, G. H. (1954) *L'Islam maghrébin; introduction à l'étude générale de l'Islam* (Algiers: Maison des livres).

Bovill, E. W. (1927) 'The Moorish invasion of the Sudan', *JAS*, **26**, pp. 245–62, 380–7; **27**, pp. 47–56.

Bovill, E. W. (1933) *Caravans of the old Sahara; an introduction to the history of the western Sudan* (London: OUP for IIALC); revised edn 1968, *The golden trade of the Moors* (London: OUP).

Boxer, C. R. (1963) *Race relations in the Portuguese colonial empire, 1415–1825* (Oxford: Clarendon Press).

Brasio, A. D. (1952–71) *Monumenta missionaria africana: Africa ocidental*, 12 vols (Lisbon: Agência geral do Ultramar).

Brasseur, G. (1968) *Les Etablissements humains au Mali* (Dakar: IFAN; Mémoires, 83).

Braudel, F. (1946) 'Monnaies et civilisations: de l'or du Soudan à l'argent d'Amérique: un drame méditerranéen', *AESC*, **I**, pp. 9–22.

Bréhier, E. (1971) *La Philosophie du Moyen Age* (Paris: Albin Michel).

Brett, M. (1972) 'Problems in the interpretation of the history of the Maghrib in the light of some recent publications', *JAH*, **13**, 3, pp. 489–506.

Brignon, J., Amine, A., Boutaleb, B., Martinet, G. and Rosenberger, B. (1967) *Histoire du Maroc* (Paris: Hatier).

British Museum (1877) *Catalogue of the Ethiopic manuscripts*: see Wright, W. (ed.)

Brock, B. (1968) 'The Nyiha', in A. Roberts (ed.), *Tanzania before 1900* (Nairobi: EAPH), pp. 59–82.

Broecke, P. van den (1605–14); 1842 French transl., 'Voyages au Cap Vert', in C. A. Walcknaer (ed.), *Collection des relations de voyages par mer et par terre ... depuis 1400 jusqu'à nos jours*, 21 vols (Paris: Walcknaer), Vol. 2, pp. 300–5; 1880 Eng. transl. Charles, *Stirring adventures in African travel* (no further details available).

Bruce, James (1790), *Travels to discover the source of the Nile in the years 1768, 1769, 1770, 1771, 1772, 1773*; 1964 reprint (Edinburgh: Edinburgh University Press).

Brunschvig, R. (1940, 1947) *La Berbérie orientale sous les Hafsides: des origines à la fin du 15e siècle*, 2 vols (Paris: Maisonneuve).

Brunschvig, R. (1948) *La Tunisie dans le haut Moyen Age: sa place dans l'histoire* (Cairo: Institut français d'archéologie orientale).

Bucaille, R. (1975) 'Takadda, pays du cuivre', *BIFAN*, B, **37**, 4, pp. 720–78.

Buchanan, C. A. (1974) *The Kitara complex: the historical tradition of western Uganda to the sixteenth century* (doctoral dissertation, University of Indiana, Bloomington).

Budge, E. A. W. (ed.) (1928) *The books of the saints of the Ethiopian Church, Mashafa Sĕnkĕsâr*, 4 vols (London: CUP).

Burssens, H. (1958) *Les Peuplades de l'entre Congo-Ubangi: Ngbandi, Ngbaka, Mbandja, Ngombe et Gens d'Eau* (Tervuren: Annales du Musée royal du Congo belge, sciences de l'homme. Monographies ethnographiques, 4).

Buzurg b. Shariyār (10th cent.) *Kitāb 'Adjā'ib al Hind*; 1883 ed. P. A. van der Lith (Vol. 1) and 1886 French transl. M. Devic (Vol. 2), *Livre des merveilles d'Inde* (Leiden: Brill).

Ca da Mosto, A. da (15th cent.) 1895 French transl., *Relations des voyages à la côte occidentale de l'Afrique d'Alvise da Ca' da Mosto, 1455–1457* (Paris, Leroux); 1937 ed. and Eng. transl. G. R. Crone (q.v.); 1948 Italian text with Portuguese transl., *Viagens de Luís de Cadamosto e de Pedro de Sintra* (Lisbon: Academia portuguesa da história).

Cahen, C. (1960) 'Ayyūbids', in *Encyclopaedia of Islam* (q.v.), new edn, Vol. 1, pp. 796–807.

Cahen, C. (1965) 'Douanes et commerces dans les ports méditerranéens de l'Egypte médiévale d'aprés le Minhadj d'al-Makhzumi', *JESHO*, **7**, 3, pp. 217–314.

Callet, R. P. (ed.) (1908) *Tantara my andriana eto Madagascar: documents historiques d'après les manuscrits malgaches*, 2 vols (Tananarive: Imp. officielle).

Calonne-Beaufaict, A. de (1921) *Azande; introduction à une ethnographie générale des bassins de l'Ubangi-Uele et de l'Aruwimi* (Brussels: Lamertin).

Campbell, D. E. H. (1926) *Arabian medicine and its influence on the Middle Ages*, 2 vols (London: Kegan Paul, Trench, Trubner).

Canard, M. (1939–41) 'Relations entre les Mérinides et las Mamelouks au 14e siècle', *AIEOA*, **5**, pp. 41–81.

Carbou, H. (1912) *La région du Tchad et du Oudai*, 2 vols (Paris: Leroux; University of Algiers, Faculté des lettres et des sciences humaines, 47–8).

Cardinall, A. W. and Tamakloe, E. F. (1931, 1970) *Tales told in Togoland, by A. W. Cardinall. To which is added: The mythical and traditional history of Dagomba, by E. F. Tamakloe* (London: OUP).

Carreira, A. (1972) *Cabo Verde: formação e extinção de uma sociedade excravocrata (1460–1878)* (Lisbon: Memorias do centro de estudos da Guine portuguesa, 24).

Carreira, A. (1978) *Notas sobre o tráfico português de excravos: circunscritos a costa ocidental africana.* (Lisbon: Universidade Nova, ciencias humanas e sociais).

Carrère, C. (1967) *Barcelone, centre économique à l'époque des difficultés, 1380–1462*, 2 vols (Paris: Mouton).

Casciaro, J. M. (1969) *El diálogo teológico de Santo Tomás con musulmanes y judíos* (Madrid: CSIC).

Castries, H. de (1923) 'La conquête du Soudan par El-Mansour', *Hespéris*, **3**, pp. 433–88.

Caton-Thompson, G. (1931) *The Zimbabwe culture: ruins and reactions* (Oxford: Clarendon Press); 1971 edn (London: Cass).

Cavazzi, G. A. (1965) *Descrição histórica dos três reinos do Congo, Matamba e Angola, de João António Cavazzi de Montecúccolo, G. M. de Leguzzano* (Lisbon: Junta de investigações do Ultramar; Agrupamento de estudos de cartografia antiga, Secção de Lisboa, Publicações, 2).

Cerone, F. (1902–3) 'La politica orientale di Alphonso di Aragona', *ASPN*, **27**, pp. 31–93; **28**, pp. 154–212.

Cerulli, E. (1931) *Documenti arabi per la storia dell'Etiopia* (Rome: Memorie dell'Accademia nazionale dei Lincei, classe di scienze morali, storiche e filologiche, serie 6, **4**, 2).

Cerulli, E. (1941) 'Il sultanato della Scioa, nel secolo XIII secondo un nuovo documento storico', *RSE*, **1**, pp. 5–42.

Cerulli, E. (1943, 1947) *Etiopi in Palestina: storia della communita etiopica di Gerusalemme*, 2 vols (Rome: Lib. dello stato).

Cerulli, E. (1949) *Il 'Libro della scala' e la question delle fonti arabo-spagnole della Divina Commedia* (Vatican City: Biblioteca apostolica vaticana).

Cerulli, E. (1956) *Storia della letteratura etiopica* (Rome, Nuova academia editrice).

Cerulli, E. (1957, 1959, 1964) *Somalia: scritti vari editi ed inediti*, 3 vols (Rome: Amministrazione Fiduciaria Italiana della Somalia).

Césard, E. (1927) 'Comment les Bahaya interprètent leurs origines', *Anthropos*, **22**, pp. 440–65.

Césard, E. (1937) 'Le Muhaya (l'Afrique orientale)', *Anthropos*, **32**, pp. 15–60.

Chanaiwa, D. (1980) 'Historical traditions of southern Africa', in Unesco (1980b), (q.v.), pp. 25–44.

Chapelle, J. (1957) *Nomades noirs du Sahara* (Paris: Plon).

Chapman, S. (1967) 'Kantsyore Island', *Azania*, **2**, pp. 165–91.

Charsley, S. R. (1969) *The princes of Nyakyusa* (Nairobi: EAPH for Makerere Institute of Social Research).

Chaunu, P. (1969) *L'expansion européene du 13e au 15e siècle* (Paris: PUF).

Cherbonneau, A. (1854–5) 'Essai sur la littérature arabe au Soudan d'après le *Tekmilet ed dibadji* d'Ahmed Baba le Tombouctien', *RSACNM*, pp. 1–42.

Chéron, G. (1924) 'Contributions à l'histoire du Mossi: traditions relatives au cercle de Kaya', *BCEHSAOF*, 7, 4, pp. 634–91.

Childs, G. (1964) 'The kingdom of Wambu (Huambo): a tentative chronology', *JAH*, **5**, 3, pp. 365–379.

Chittick, H. N. (1959) 'Notes on Kilwa', *TNR*, 53, pp. 179–203.

Chittick, H. N. (1961) *Kisimani Mafia: excavations at an Islamic settlement on the East African coast*, (Dar es Salaam: Government Printer).

Chittick, H. N. (1963a) 'Kilwa and the Arab settlement of the East African coast', *JAH*, **4**, 2, pp. 179–90.

Chittick, H. N. (1963b) 'The last Christian stronghold in the Sudan', *Kush*, **11**, pp. 264–72.

Chittick, H. N. (1965) 'The Shirazi colonisation of East Africa', *JAH*, **6**, 3, pp. 275–94.

Chittick, H. N. (1966) 'Kilwa: a preliminary report', *Azania*, **1**, pp. 1–36.

Chittick, H. N. (1967a) 'L'archéologie de la côte occidentale africaine', in P. Vérin (ed.), *Arabes et islamisés à Madagascar et dans l'Océan indien* (Tananarive: Revue de Madagascar), pp. 21–38.

Chittick, H. N. (1967b) 'Discoveries in the Lamu archipelago', *Azania*, **2**, pp. 37–68.

Chittick, H. N. (1968) 'The coast before the arrival of the Portuguese', in B. A. Ogot, (ed.), *Zamani: a survey of East African history* (Nairobi: EAPH), pp. 98–114.

Chittick, H. N. (1969) 'A new look at the history of Pate', *JAH*, **10**, 3, pp. 375–91.

Chittick, H. N. (1970) 'East African trade with the Orient', in D. S. Richard (ed.), *Islam and the trade of Asia* (Oxford: Cassirer; Philadelphia: University of Pennsylvania Press), pp. 97–104.

Chittick, H. N. (1971) 'The coast of East Africa', in P. L. Shinnie (ed.), *The African Iron Age* (Oxford: Clarendon Press), pp. 108–41.

Chittick, H. N. (1974) *Kilwa: an Islamic trading city on the East African coast*, 2 vols (Nairobi: British Institute in Eastern Africa, Memoirs, 5; London: distrib. by Thames and Hudson).

Chittick, H. N. and Rotberg, R. I. (eds) (1975) *East Africa and the Orient: cultural syntheses in precolonial times* (New York: Harvard University Press; London: Africana Publishing Co.).

Chittick, H. N. with Shinnie, P. L.: see Shinnie, P. L. and Chittick, H. N. (1961)

Chojnacki, S. (1971) 'Notes on art in Ethiopia in the sixteenth century: an inquiry into the unknown', *JES*, **9**, 2, pp. 21–77.

Chou Yi Liang (1972) 'Early contacts between China and Africa', *GNQ*, **12**, 6, pp. 1–3.

Chrétien, J. P. and Coifard, J. L. (1967) 'Le Burundi', *NED*, 3364.

Cissé, Y. (1964) 'Notes sur les sociétés de chasseurs malinkés', *JSA*, **34**, 2, pp. 175–226.

Cissoko, S. M. (1966) *Histoire de l'Afrique occidentale, Moyen Age et temps modernes, 7e siècle–1850* (Paris: Présence africaine).

Cissoko, S. M. (1968) 'Famines et épidémies à Tombouctou, et dans la boucle du Niger du 16e au 18e siècle', *BIFAN*, B, **30**, 3, pp. 806–21.

Cissoko, S. M. (1969) 'La royauté (mansaya) chez les Mandingues occidentaux d'après leurs traditions orales', *BIFAN*, B, **31**, 2, pp. 325–38.

Cissoko S. M. (1972) paper presented at Mandingo conference, London.

Cissoko, S. M. (1975) *Tombouctou et l'empire Songhay: épanouissement du Soudan nigérien aux 15e–16e siècles.* (Dakar: Nouvelles éditions africaines).
Cissoko, S. M. (1981a) 'De l'organisation politique du Kabu'; and (1981b) 'Introduction à l'histoire des Mandingues de l'ouest'; both in *Colloque international sur les traditions orales du Gabu* (Dakar: Ethiopiques, Numéro special, October 1981), pp. 195–206, 73–92.
Clark, J. D. (1970) *The prehistory of Africa* (London/New York: Thames and Hudson).
Cohen, D. W. (1970) 'A survey of interlacustrine chronology', *JAH*, **11**, 2, pp. 179–202.
Cohen, D. W. (1972) *The historical tradition of Busoga, Mukama and Kintu* (Oxford: Clarendon Press).
Cohen, R. (1967) *The Kanuri of Bornu* (New York: Holt).
'Colloque inter-universitaire Ghana-Côte-d'Ivoire' (1974): see Bonduku Seminar Papers
Connah, G. (1969) 'Archaeological work in Bornu, 1964–1966, with particular reference to the excavations at Daima Mound', in *Actes du premier colloque international d'archéologie africaine, 11–16* Dec., 1966 (Fort Lamy: Institut national pour les sciences humaines; Etudes et documents tchadiens, mémoires, 1), pp. 112–24.
Connah, G. (1971) 'Recent contributions to Bornu chronology', *WAJA*, **1**, pp. 55–60.
Conti Rossini, C. (ed.) (1903) 'Gli atti di Abba Yonās', *RRAL*, serie 5, **12**, pp. 177–201, 239–255.
Conti Rossini, C. (ed.) (1904) *Vitae Sanctorum Antiquiorium: I: Acta Yared et Pantaleon* (Paris: Corpus scriptorum christianorum orientalum, 36–7; Scriptores aethiopici, 9–10).
Conti Rossini, C. (ed.) (1922) 'La caduta della dinastia Zagué et la versione amarica del Be'ela nagast', *RRAL*, serie 5, **31**, pp. 279–314.
Cordell, D. (1973) 'Throwing knives in equatorial Africa: a distribution study', *Ba-Shiru*, **5**, 1, pp. 94–104.
Cornevin, R. (1967) *Histoire de l'Afrique des origines à nos jours*, 3 vols; Vol. 1, *Des origines au 16è siècle* (Paris: Payot).
Cortés-Alonso, V. (1963) 'La trata de esclavos durante los primeros descubrimientos (1489–1516)', *AEA*, **9**, pp. 23–50.
Cortés-Alonso, V. (1964) *La esclavitud en Valencia durante el reinado de los reyes católicos, 1479–1516* (Valencia: Ayuntamiento).
Cortés-Alonso, V. (1972) 'Procedencia de los esclavos negros en Valencia (1482–1516)', *REAA*, **7**, 1, pp. 123–51.
Cortesão, A. (1971) *Descobrimento e cartografía das ilhas de Sao Tomé e Principe* (Coimbra: Junta de investigações do Ultramar; Agrupamento de estudos de cartografía antiga, Secção de Coimbra, publicações, 62).
Cortesão, A. (1972) *Descobrimento e descobrimentos* (Coimbra: Junta de investigações do Ultramar; Agrupamento de estudos de cartografía antiga, publicações 72).
Cortesão, A. (1973) *A história do descobrimentos das ilhas da Madeira por Roberto Machim em fins do século 14* (Coimbra: Junta de investigações do Ultramar; Agrupamento de estudos de cartografía antiga: secção de Coimbra, serie separata, 85).
Cortesão, J. (1958, 1961) *Os descobrimentos portuguêses*, 2 vols (Lisbon: Arcadia).
Costermans, J. (1953) *Mosaïque bangba: notes pour servir à l'étude des peuplades de l'Uele* (Brussels: IRCB; Mémoires de l'Académie royale des sciences d'outre-mer, **28**, 3).
Coupez, A., Evrard, J. B. and Vansina, J. (1975) 'Classification d'un échantillon de langues bantoues d'après la lexicostatistique', *Africana Linguistica*, **6**, pp. 131–58.
Cour, A. (1920) *La dynastie marocaine des Beni-Wattâs, 1420–1544* (Constantine: Braham).
Crazzolara, J. P. (1950–4) *The Lwoo*, 3 vols (Verona: Ed. Missionaria Italiana).
Crone, G. R. (ed. and Eng. transl.) (1937) *The voyages of Cadamosto, and other documents on Western Africa in the second half of the fifteenth century* (London: Hakluyt Society).
Cruz Hernández, M. (1970) 'La estructura social del período de occupacion islámica de al-Andalus (711–755), y la fundación de la monarquía omeya', *Awrak*, **2**, pp. 25–43.
Cuoq, J. M. (ed.) and French transl. (1975) *Recueil des sources arabes concernant l'Afrique occidentale du 8e au 16e siècle (Bilād al-Sūdān)* (Paris: CNRS, Sources d'histoire médiévale, 3).
Cuoq, J. M. (1978) 'La famille Aquit de Tombouctou', *RIBLA*, **41**, 1, pp. 85–102.
Curtin, P. D. (1969) *The Atlantic slave trade: a census* (Madison: University of Wisconsin Press).

Dampierre, E. de (1967) *Un ancien royaume bandia du Haut-Oubangui* (Paris: Plon).
Dandouau, A. and Chapus, G. S. (1952) *Histoire des populations de Madagascar* (Paris: Larose).
Daniel, F. de F. (1940) *History of Katsina* (London: Colonial Office Library).
Daniel, N. (1962) *Islam and the West; the making of an image* (Edinburgh: Edinburgh University Press).
Dapper, O. (1668) *Naukeurige Beschrijvinge der Africaensche gewesten van Egypten, Barbaryen, Libyen, Biledulgerid* ... (Amsterdam: Van Meurs); 1970 Eng. transl. and adaptation, J. Ogilby, *Africa: being*

an accurate description of the regions of Aegypt, Barbary, Lybia, etc. (London); 1670 German transl., *Beschreibung von Afrika* . . . (Amsterdam: Van Meurs); 1686 French transl., *Description de l'Afrique* . . . (Amsterdam: Wolfgang, Waesberge *et al.*).

Darraj, A. (1961) *L'Egypte sous le règne de Barsbay, 825–841/1422–1438* (Damascus: Institut français de Damas).

Datoo, B. A. (1970) 'Rhapta: the location and importance of East Africa's first port', *Azania*, **5**, pp. 65–76.

Daux, P. (1952) *Histoire du pays gourmanché* (Paris: Challamel).

Daveau, S. (1963) 'Géographie de l'expansion portugaise', *COM*, **16**, pp. 313–18.

Daveau, S. (1969) 'La découverte du climat d'Afrique tropicale au cours des navigations portugaises (15e siècle et début du 16e siècle)', *BIFAN*, B, **31**, 4, pp. 953–87.

Davidson, B. (1959) *Old Africa rediscovered* (London: Gollancz).

Davidson, B. (1964) *The African past: chronicles from antiquity to modern times* (London: Longman; Boston: Little, Brown).

Davidson, B. and Bush, F. K. (1965, 1967), *The growth of African civilisation: a history of West Africa 1000–1800* (London: Gollancz).

Davies, O. (1961) 'Native culture in the Gold Coast at the time of the Portuguese discoveries', in *Actas do congresso internacional de historia dos descobrimentos* (Lisbon), Vol. 3, pp. 97–9.

Davies, O. (1971) 'Excavations at Blackburn', *SAAB*, **26**, 103–4, pp. 165–78.

Davies, O. (1974) 'Excavations at the walled Early Iron Age site in Moor Park near Estcourt, Natal,' *ANM*, **22**, 1, pp. 289–324.

Davis, R. W. (1970) 'The problem of possible pre-Colombian contacts between Africa and the Americas: a summary of the evidence', *GNQ*, **6**, 2, pp. 1–7.

De Craemer, W., Vansina, J. and Fox, R. C. (1976) 'Religious movements in Central Africa: a theory', *CSSH*, **18**, pp. 458–74.

De Jonghe, E. and Vanhove, J. (1949) 'Les formes d'asservissement dans les sociétés indigènes du Congo belge', *BARSOM*, Section des sciences morales et politiques, **19**, pp. 483–95.

De la Fosse, E., ed. R. Fouché-Delbosc (1897) 'Voyage à la côte occidentale d'Afrique, au Portugal et en Espagne, 1479–1480', *RH*, **4**, pp. 174–201.

Delafosse, M. (1912) *Le Haut Sénégal–Niger*, 3 vols; 1972 ed. M. F. J. Clozel (Paris: Maisonneuve et Larose).

Delafosse, M. (1913) 'Traditions historiques et légendaires du Soudan occidental, traduites d'un manuscrit arabe inédit', *AFRCD*, August, pp. 293–306; September, pp. 325–9, 355–69.

Delafosse, M. (1922, 1941) *Les noirs de l'Afrique* (Paris: Payot); Eng. trans. F. Fligelman, *The negroes of Africa* (Port Washington: Kennikat Press).

Delafosse, M. (1924) 'Les relations du Maroc avec le Soudan à travers les âges', Hespéris, 4, pp. 153–74.

Delgado, J. A. (1950) 'La navegacion entre los Canarios prehispanicos', *AEDA*, 79, pp. 164–74.

Délivré, A. (1974) *L'histoire des rois d'Imérina: interprétation d'une tradition orale* (Paris: Klincksieck).

Denbow, J. R. (1979) 'Iron Age research in eastern Botswana', *NAk*, **14**, pp. 7–9.

Denoon, D. (1972) 'Migrations and settlement in south-west Uganda', Makerere Seminar Papers.

Derricourt, R. M. (1973) 'Archaeological survey of the Transkei and the Ciskei: interim report for 1972', *FHP*, **5**, 4, pp. 449–55.

Deschamps, H. J. (ed.) (1970–1) *Histoire générale de l'Afrique noire*, 2 vols (Paris: PUF).

Deschamps, H. J. (1972) *Histoire de Madagascar*; 1972 4th edn (Paris: Berger-Levrault).

Deschamps, H. J. and Vianes, S. (1959) *Les Malgaches du sud-est: Antemoro, Antesaka, Antambahoaka, peuples de Farafangana* (Paris: PUF).

Desplagnes, A. M. L. (1907) *Une mission archéologique et ethnographique au Soudan français: le plateau central nigérien* (Paris: Larose).

Deverdun, G. (1959, 1966) *Marrakech des origines à 1912*, 2 vols (Rabat: Editions techniques nord-africaines).

Devic, L. M. (1883) *Les pays des Zendjs, ou la côte orientale d'Afrique au Moyen Age.* (Paris: Hachette).

Devisse, J. (1972) 'Routes de commerce et échanges en Afrique occidentale en relation avec la Méditerranée: un essai sur le commerce africain médiéval du 11e au 16e siècle', *RHES*, **50**, pp. 42–73, 357–97.

Dez, J. (1967) 'De l'influence arabe à Madagascar à l'aide de faits linguistiques', in P. Vérin (ed.), *Arabes et islamisés à Madagascar et dans l'Océan indien* (Tananarive: Revue de Madagascar), pp. 1–20.

Dez, J. (1971) 'Essai sur le concept de Vazimba', *BAM*, **49**, 2, pp. 11–20.

Diabaté, H. (1974) 'A propos de la reine-mère dans les sociétés akan', in Bonduku Seminar Papers, q.v.

Diabaté, M. (1970) *Kala Jata* (Bamako: Editions populaires).

Diaby, K. (1972) 'Inventaire partiel des manuscrits de la bibliothèque de Kadi Muhammed Mahmud à Tombouctou', in 'Tombouctou, la ville la plus riche en documents historiques et sociologiques sur l'Afrique de l'ouest', *EM*, 3, pp. 1–20.

Diagné, P. (1965) 'Royaumes sérères: les institutions traditionnelles du Sine Saloum', *PA*, 54, pp. 142–72.

Dias de Carvalho, H. A. (1890ff) *Expedição portuguêsa ao Muatiânvua*, 6 vols (Lisbon: Imp. nacional).

Dieterlen, G. (1955) 'Mythe et organisation sociale au Soudan français', *JSA*, **25**, 1, pp. 39–76.

Dina, J. and Hoerner, J. M. (1975) 'Etude sur les populations miké du sud-ouest de Madagascar', *OSA*, 3–8, pp. 269–86.

Diop, C. A. (1955, 1965) *Nations nègres et cultures* (Paris: Présence africaine).

Diop, C. A. (1960) *L'Afrique noire précoloniale: étude comparée des systèmes politiques et sociaux ...* (Paris: Présence africaine).

al-Djilali, 'Abd al-Raḥman b. Muḥammad (n.d.) *Ta'rikh al-Djazā' ir al-amm*; 1934–60 edn (Algiers).

al-Djinhānī, al-Ḥabīb (n.d.) *al-Ḳayrawān 'abra 'usūr izdihār al-hadārah al Islāmiyāh*; 1968 edn (Tunis).

Documents on the Portuguese in Mozambique and Central Africa, 1497–1840; also *Documentos sobre os Portugueses em Moçambique e na Africa central, 1497–1840*; 1962, Vol. 1, *1497–1506* (Salisbury: National Archives of Rhodesia and Nyasaland; Lisbon: Centro de estudos historicos ultramarinos).

Doke, C. M. (1954) *The southern Bantu languages*, (London: OUP for IAI).

Domenichini, J. P. (1971a) 'Artichiroka et Vazimba: contribution à l'histoire de la société du 16e au 19e siècle', communication, séance plénière de l'Académie malgache.

Domenichini, J. P. (1971b) *Histoire des palladium d'Imérina d'après des manuscrits anciens* (Tananarive: Travaux et documents du musée d'art et d'archéologie de l'Université, 8).

Domenichini, J. P. (1979a) 'L'écuelle de Milangana, 15e siècle' *Ambario*, 1, pp. 127–31.

Domenichini, J. P. (1979b) 'La plus belle énigme du monde', seminar paper, Colloque de Tuléar, 9–15 Avril 1979.

Donelha, A. (1625) *Descrição da Serra Leõa e dos rios de Guiné do Cabo Verda, 1625*; 1977 eds and Eng. transl. A Teixeira da Mota and P. E. H. Hair, *An account of Sierra Leone and the rivers of Guinea of Cape Verde, 1625* (Lisbon: Junta de investigações do Ultramar, Centro de estudos de cartografia antiga, secção de Lisboa, 19).

Dramani-Issifou, Z. (1975) 'Les relations entre le Maroc et l'empire songhai dans la seconde moitié du 16e siècle' (Doctoral dissertation, University of Paris).

Dubois, H. M. (1938) *Monographie des Betsileo (Madagascar)* (Paris: Institut ethnologique).

Dufourcq, C.-E. (1966) *L'Espagne catalane et le Maghrib aux 13e et 14e siècles, de la bataille de Las Navas Tolosa (1212) à l'avènement du sultan mérin ide Abou-l-Hassan (1331)* (Paris: PUF; Bibliothèque de l'Ecole des hautes études hispaniques, fasc. 37).

Dufourcq, C.-E. (1968) 'Les relations du Maroc et de la Castille pendant la première moitié du XIIIe siècle', *RHCM*, **5**, pp. 37–62.

Dufourcq, C.-E. (1979) 'Commerce du Maghreb médiéval avec l'Europe chrétienne et maxime musulmane: données connues et problèmes en suspens', in *Actes du Congrès d'histoire et de civilisation du Maghreb* (Tunis), pp. 161–92.

Dunbar, A. R. (1966) *History of Bunyoro-Kitara* (Nairobi/London: OUP for East African Institute of Social Research).

Duncan-Johnstone, A. C. and Blair, H. A. (1932) *Inquiry into the constitution and organisation of the Dagbon kingdom* (Accra: Government Printer). Reviewed in *Africa*-(L), **5**, pp. 497–8.

Dupuis, J. (1974) 'La Diffusion du maïs dans l'ancien monde et hypothèse de voyages arabes en Amérique précolombienne', *CRTSASOM*, **34**, 2, pp. 381–406.

Duyvendak, J. J. L. (1938) 'The true dates of the Chinese maritime expeditions in the early fifteenth century', *T'oung Pao*, **34**, pp. 341–412.

Duyvendak, J. J. L. (1949) *China's discovery of Africa* (London: Probsthain).

East, R. M. (1933) *Labarun Hausawa da Makwabtansu*, 2 vols (Lagos: CMS Bookshop); 1970 reprint (Zaria: Northern Nigerian Publishing Co.).

Ehrenkreutz, A. S. (1959) 'Studies in the monetary history of the Near East in the Middle Ages', *JESHO*, **2**, pp. 128–61.

Ehrenkreutz, A. S. (1963) 'Studies in the monetary history of the Near East in the Middle Ages: 2. The standard of fineness of western and eastern dinars before the crusades', *JESHO*, **6**, pp. 243–77.

Ehret, C. (n.d.) 'Comparative culture vocabularies of Eastern, Southern and Central African languages' (unpublished typescript).

Ehret, C. (1967) 'Cattle keeping and milking in Eastern and Southern African history: the linguistic evidence', *JAH*, 8, 1, pp. 1–17.

Ehret, C. (1971) *Southern Nilotic history: linguistic approaches to the study of the past* (Evanston: Northwestern University Press).

Ehret, C. (1972) 'Outlining Southern African history: a re-evaluation AD 100–1500', *Ufahamu*, 3, 1, pp. 9–38.

Ehret, C. (1973) 'Patterns of Bantu and central Sudanic settlement in Central and Southern Africa (*ca* 100 BC to 500 AD)', *TJH*, 3, 1, pp. 1–71.

Ehret, C. (1974a) 'Agricultural history in Central and Southern Africa (*ca* 1000 BC to 500 AD)', *TJH*, 4, 1, pp. 1–26.

Ehret, C. (1974b) *Ethiopians and East Africans: the problem of contacts* (Nairobi: EAPH).

Ehret, C. (1974c) 'Lacustrine history and linguistic evidence: preliminary considerations' (Los Angeles: UCLA seminar paper).

Ehret, C. (1976) 'Aspects of social and economic change in western Kenya, 1500–1800', in B. A. Ogot (ed.), *Kenya before 1900* (Nairobi: EAPH), pp. 1–20.

Ehret, C. (1980) *The historical reconstruction of southern Cushitic phonology and vocabulary* (Berlin: Reimer).

Elphick, R. (1977) *Kraal and castle: Khoikhoi and the founding of white South Africa* (New Haven: Yale University Press; Yale historical publications, miscellany, 116).

Elugbe, B. O. (1974) 'A comparative Edo phonology' (Ibadan: unpublished PhD thesis).

L'Empire du Mali (1959) *NA*, 82, pp. 1–63; 83, pp. 64–70.

Encyclopaedia of Islam (1913–38) 4 vols and supplement (London: Luzac; Leiden: Brill).

Encyclopaedia of Islam (1960–78) new edn, 4 vols; 1979–82, Vol. 5 in progress (Khe–La) (Leiden: Brill).

Encyclopédie de l'Islam (1913–38) 4 vols and supplement; 1960–78, new edn, 4 vols; 1979–82, Vol. 5 in progress (Paris: Klincksieck; Leiden: Brill).

Estermann, C. (1960) *Etnografia do sudoeste de Angola* (Lisbon: Junta de investigações do Ultramar; Junta das missões geograficas e de investigações do Ultramar, memórias, serie antropologica, 4–5), 2nd edn.

Everbroeck, N. van (1961) *M'bom 'ipoku le seigneur à l'abîme: histoire, croyances, organisation clanique, politique, judiciaire, vie familiale des Bolia, Sengélé et Ntomb'e njalé* (Tervuren: Musée royal de l'Afrique centrale; Archives d'ethnographie du musée, 3).

Evers, T. M. (1975) 'Recent Iron Age research in the eastern Transvaal', *SAAB*, 30, pp. 171–82.

Evers, T. M. and Van den Berg, R. P. (1974) 'Recent mining in southern Africa with reference to a copper mine in the Harmony block, northeastern Transvaal', *JSAIMM*, 74, pp. 217–26.

Eyre-Smith, St J. (1933) *A brief review of the history and social organization of the peoples of the Northern Territories of the Gold Coast* (Accra: Government Printer).

Fagan, B. M. (1964) 'The Greefswald sequence: Bambandyanalo and Mapungubwe', *JAH*, 5, 3, pp. 337–61.

Fagan, B. M. (1965) *Southern Africa during the Iron Age* (London: Thames and Hudson).

Fagan, B. M. (1967) *A short history of Zambia: from the earliest times until AD 1900* (Nairobi: OUP).

Fagan, B. M. (1967, 1969) *Iron Age cultures in Zambia*, 2 vols (London: Chatto and Windus; Robins series, no. 5).

Fagan, B. M. (1969) 'The Later Iron Age in South Africa', in L. Thompson (ed.), *African societies in Southern Africa* (New York: Praeger), pp. 50–70.

Fagan, B. M. and Yellen, J. E. (1968) 'Ivuna: ancient salt-working in southern Tanzania', *Azania*, 3, pp. 1–44.

Fage, J. D. (1952) 'Some general considerations relevant to historical research in the Gold Coast', *THSG*, 1, 1, pp. 24–9.

Fage, J. D. (1955) 'Some problems of Gold Coast history', *Universitas*, 1, 6, pp. 5–9.

Fage, J. D. (1956) 'Some notes on a scheme for the investigation of oral tradition in the Northern Territories of the Gold Coast', *JHSN*, 1, pp. 15–19.

Fage, J. D. (1964a) 'Reflexions on the early history of the Mosi-Dagomba group of states', in *The historian in tropical Africa* (London: IAI; proceedings, fourth international African seminar, Dakar, 1961), pp. 177–91.

Fage, J. D. (1964b) 'Some thoughts on state formation in the western Sudan before the seventeenth century' (Boston: University papers in African history, 1), pp. 17–34.

Fagereng, E. (1971) *Une famille de dynasties malgaches: Zafindravola, Maroserana, Zafimbolamena, Andrevola, Zafimanely* (Oslo: Universitetsforlaget).

Fagg, B. E. B. (1956) 'A life-size terracotta head from Nok', *Man*, 56, 95, p. 89.

Fagg, B. E. B. (1959) 'The Nok culture in prehistory', *JHSN*, **1**, 4, pp. 288–93.
Fagg, B. E. B. (1969) 'Recent work in West Africa: new light on the Nok culture', *WA*, **1**, 1, pp. 41–50.
Fagg, B. E. B. (1977) *Nok Terracottas* (Lagos: Nigerian Museum; London: Ethnographica).
Fagg, W. B. (1963) *Nigerian Images* (London: Lund Humphries; New York: Praeger); French transl., *Les Merveilles de l'art nigérien* (Paris: Editions du Chêne).
Fairley, N. J. (1978) 'Mianda ya Ben'ekie: a history of the Ben'ekie' (Doctoral dissertation, University of New York at Stonybrook).
Fall, Y. K. (1978) 'Technologie et Idéologie au Moyen Age. L'ecole cartographique majorquine et la représentation de l'Afrique' (thesis, Paris University, roneo.)
al-Fashtālī: see 'Abd al-'Azīz . . . al-Fishtālī
Fernandes, V. (1506–7) 1938 French transl. P. de Cenival and T. Monod, *Description de la côte d'Afrique de Ceuta au Sénégal (1506–7)* (Paris: Larose; Publications du Comité d'études historiques et scientifiques de l'Afrique occidentale française, 6).
Fernandes, V. (n.d.) 1951 eds T. Monod, A. Teixeira da Mota, R. Mauny, French transl. P. de Cenival and T. Monod, *Description de la côte occidentale d'Afrique (Sénégal du Cap de Monte, Archipels)* (Bissau: Publicações do centro da Guiné portuguesa, 11).
Ferrand, G. (1891–1902) *Les Musulmans à Madagascar et aux îles comores*, 3 vols (Paris: Leroux; Bulletin de correspondance de l'Ecole des lettres d'Alger, 9).
Ferrand, G. (1921–8) *Instructions nautiques et routiers arabes et portugais des 15e et 16e siècles*, 3 vols (Paris: Geuthner).
Fiedler, R. (1978) 'Arab rock inscriptions and drawings in the Czechoslovak archaeological concession in Nubia', *Archiv Orientalni*, **46**, pp. 38–45.
Filesi, T. (1962a) *Le relazioni della Cina con l'Africa nel Medio Evo* (Milan: Giuffrè).
Filesi, T. (1962b) 'Testimonianze della presenza cenesi in Africa', *Africa–*(R), **17**, pp. 115–23.
Filipowiak, W. (1970) 'Niani poraz drugi in z otchlani', *Wikow*, 1.
Filipowiak, W. (1979) *Etudes archéologiques sur la capitale du Mali* (Stettin: Museum Narodin).
Filipowiak, W., Jasnosz, S. and Wolaeiewicz, R. (1970) 'Les recherches archéologiques polono-guinéennes à Niani en 1968', *MZ*, **14**, pp. 575–648.
Fisch, R. (1913) 'Die Dagbamba', *BA*, **3**, pp. 132–64.
Fisher, A. G. B. and Fisher, H. J. (1970) *Slavery and Muslim society in Africa: the institution in Saharan and Sudanic Africa and the Trans-Saharan trade* (London: Hurst).
Fisher, G. A. (1957) *Barbary legend: war, trade and piracy in North Africa, 1415–1830* (Oxford: Clarendon Press).
Fisher, H. J. (1977) 'The eastern Maghrib and the central Sudan', in R. Oliver (ed.), *Cambridge History of Africa*, Vol. 3 (London: CUP), pp. 232–330.
Fisher, H. J. (1978) 'Leo Africanus and the Songhay conquest of Hausaland', *IJAHS*, **11**, 1, pp. 86–112.
Fisher, R. B. (1911) *Twilight tales of the Black Baganda* (London: Marshall); 1970 repub. (London: Cass).
al-Fishtālī: see 'Abd al-'Azīz . . . al-Fishtālī
Flacourt, E. de (1661) *Histoire de la grande île de Madagascar* (Paris); 1905 edn (Troyes: Oudot)
Fleming, H. C. (1964) 'Baiso and Rendille: Somali outliers', *RSE*, **20**, pp. 35–96.
Ford, J and Hall, R. de Z. (1947) 'The history of Karagwe, (Bukoba District)', *TNR*, **24**, pp. 3–27.
Forstner, M. (1979) *Das Wegenetz des zentralen Maghreb in islamischer Zeit: Vergleich mit dem antiken Wegenetz* (Wiesbaden: Harrassowitz).
Fortes, M. (1940) 'The political system of the Tallensi of the Northern Territories of the Gold Coast', in M. Fortes, E. E. Evans-Pritchard (eds), *African political systems* (London: IAI), pp. 239–71.
Franco, de (Capitaine) (1905) *Etude sur l'élevage du cheval en Afrique occidentale* (Paris) (no further details available).
Franco Silva, A. (1979) *La esclavitud en Sevilla y su tierra a fines de la Edad Media* (Seville: Diputación Provincial de Seville).
Freeman-Grenville, G. S. P. (1955) 'Chinese porcelain in Tanganyika', *TNR*, **41**, pp. 62–5.
Freeman-Grenville, G. S. P. (1957) 'Coinage in East Africa before the Portuguese times', *NC*, **17**, pp. 151–79.
Freeman-Grenville, G. S. P. (1958) 'Swahili literature and the history and the archaeology of the East African Coast', *Swahili*, **28**, 2, pp. 7–25.
Freeman-Grenville, G. S. P. (1959) 'Medieval evidences for Swahili', *Swahili*, **29**, 1, pp. 10–23.
Freeman-Grenville, G. S. P. (1960a) 'East African coin finds and their historical significance', *JAH*, **1**, 1, pp. 31–43.
Freeman-Grenville, G. S. P. (1960b) 'Historiography of the East African coast', *TNR*, **55**, pp. 279–89.

Freeman-Grenville, G. S. P. (1962a) *The East African coast: select documents from the first to the early nineteenth century* (Oxford: Clarendon Press); 1975 2nd edn (London: Rex Collings).

Freeman-Grenville, G. S. P. (1962b) *The medieval history of the coast of Tanganyika* (London/New York: OUP).

Freeman-Grenville, G. S. P. (1981) 'Kilwa', in *Encyclopaedia of Islam* (q.v.), new edn, Vol. 5, pp. 106–107.

Frip, C. E. (1940, 1941) 'A note on medieval Chinese–African trade', *RNADA*, **17**, pp. 86–96; **18**, pp. 12–22.

Frobenius, L. (1912–19) *Und Afrika sprach ...*, 4 vols (Berlin: Vita).

Frobenius, L. (1925) *Dichten und Denken im Sudan* (Jena: Diederichs).

Fuchs, P. P. (1974) 'Sozio-ökonomische Aspekte der Dürre-Katastrophe für die Sahara-Bevölkerung von Niger', *ASp*, **9**, 3, pp. 308–16.

Fuglestad, F. (1978) 'A reconsideration of Hausa history before the Jihad', *JAH*, **19**, 3, pp. 319–39.

Gaden, H. (1912) 'Légendes et coutumes sénégalaises d'après Yoro Dyao', *RES*, **3**, 3–4, pp. 119–37; 5–6, pp. 191–201.

Gaillard, J. (1923) 'Niani, ancienne capitale de l'empire mandingue', *BCEHSAOF*, **6**, pp. 620–36.

Galaal, Musa H. I. (n.d.) 'Stars, seasons and weather' (unpublished).

Garba, N. (1977) 'Rise and fall of Zamiara' (dissertation, University of Zaria).

Garcin, J. C. (1972) 'Jean Léon l'Africain et Aydhab', *AI*, **11**, pp. 189–209.

Garcin, J. C. (1974) 'La méditerranéisation de l'empire mamelouk sous les sultans bahrides', *RSO*, **48**, 1, pp. 75–82.

Garcin, J. C. (1976) *Un centre musulman de la Haute-Egypte médiévale: Qûs* (Cairo: Institut français d'études d'archéologie orientale; Textes arabes et études islamiques, 6).

Garlake, P. S. (1966) *The early Islamic architecture of the East African coast* (Nairobi/London: OUP; Memoirs of the British Institute of History and Archaeology in East Africa, 10); 1966 reviewed in *TNR*, **67**, pp. 60–2.

Garlake, P. S. (1970) 'Iron site in the Urungwe district of Rhodesia', *SAAB*, **25**, 97, pp. 25–44.

Garlake, P. S. (1973) *Great Zimbabwe* (London: Thames and Hudson; New York: Stein and Day).

Gautier, E. F. (1935) 'L'Or du Soudan dans l'histoire', *AHES*, **7**, pp. 113–23.

Géraud, F. (1977) 'The settlement of the Bakiga', in D. Denoon (ed.), *A history of Kigezi in south-west Uganda* (Kampala: National Trust, Adult Education Centre), pp. 23–55.

Germain, R. (1965) *Les biotopes alluvionnaires herbeux et les savanes intercalaires du Congo équatorial* (Brussels: Mémoires de l'Académie royale des sciences d'outre-mer), n.s., **15**, 4.

Gerster, G. (1974) *L'Ethiopie, toit de l'Afrique* (Zurich: Editions Atlantis).

Gevrey, A. (1972) *Essai sur les Comores* (Tananarive: Travaux et documents du musée d'art et d'archéologie de l'université, 10).

al-Ghazālī (1095) *Tahāfut al-falāsifa*; 1947 edn (Cairo); 1962 edn (Beirut: Imprimerie catholique); 1927 French transl. M. Bouyes (Beirut: Imp. catholique); 1958 Eng. transl. S. A. Kamali, *The incoherence of the philosophers* (Lahore: Pakistan Philosophical Congress).

al-Ghazālī (11th cent.) *Iḥyā' 'ulūm al-dīn*; 1888 edn (Cairo); 1967–8 edn, 5 vols (Cairo); 1978–9 Eng. transl. M. Fazul ul-Karim, 3 vols (Lahore: Sind Sagar Academy).

Gille, P. (1970), 'Les Navires des deux Indes: Venise et Portugal, évolution des types, résultats économiques', in *Méditerranée et Océan indien: travaux du sixième colloque international d'histoire maritime*, 1962 (Paris: SEVPEN), pp. 193–202.

Godinho, V. de Magalhães (1943–56) *Documentos sôbre a expansão portuguêsa*, 3 vols (Lisbon: Gleba).

Godinho, V. de Magalhães (1952) 'A economia das Canarias nos seculos 14–15', *RHSP*, **10**, pp. 311–348.

Godinho, V. de Magalhães (1962) *A economia dos descobrimentos henriquinos* (Lisbon: Sá da Costa).

Godinho, V. de Magalhães (1969) *L'économie de l'empire portugais aux 15e et 16e siècles* (Paris: SEVPEN).

Goes, D. de, *et al.* (15th cent.) 1749 ed. R. Boache (Lisbon); 1926 ed. J. M. Teixeira de Carvalho and D. Lopes (Coimbra: Scriptorum Rerum Lusitanorum); (n.d.) ed. and French transl. in V. de Castro e Almeida, *Les Grands Navigateurs et colons portugais du 15e et du 16e siècles* (Brussels: Desmet-Verteneuil), Vol. 4, pp. 191ff.

Goitein, S. D. F. (1966) *Studies in Islamic history and institutions* (Leiden: Brill).

Goitein, S. D. F. (1967–78) *A Mediterranean society; the Jewish communities of the Arab world as portrayed in the documents of the Cairo Geniza*, 3 vols (Berkeley: University of California Press).

Goldenberg, S. and Belu, S. (1971) *Epoca marilor descoperiri geografice* (Bucharest: Ed. Stiintifica).

Goldziher, I. (1887) 'Materialen zur Kenntnis der Almohadenbewegung in Nord-Afrika', *ZDMG*, **41**, pp. 30–140.
Goldziher, I. (1903) 'Moḥammed ibn Toumert et la théologie d'Islam dans le nord de l'Afrique au 11e siècle', preface to R. Luciani, *Le Livre d'Ibn Toumert* (Algiers).
Gomes, D. (15th cent.) 1937 Eng. transl. in G. R. Crone (q.v.); 1959 French transl. T. Monod, R. Mauny and G. Duval, *De la première découverte de la Guinée, récit* (Bissau).
González Palencia, A. (1926–8) *Los Mozárabes de Toledo en los siglos 12 y 13*, 3 vols (Madrid).
González Palencia, A. (1945) *Historia de la literatura arábico-española* (Barcelona: Ed. Labor); 1955 Arabic transl. H. Mones, *Tar'īkh al-fikr al-Andalusi* (Cairo).
Goody, J. (1966) 'The Akan and the north', *GNQ*, **9**, p. 20.
Gorju, J. L. (1920) *Entre la Victoria, l'Albert et l'Edouard* (Rennes: Oberthür).
Goytom, W. M. (1970) *An atlas of Africa* (Addis Ababa) (no further details available).
Les Grandes Voies maritimes dans le monde, 15e–16e siècle: Rapports présentés au 12e Congrès international des sciences historiques par la Commission internationale d'histoire maritime, à l'occasion de son 7e colloque (Vienne, 1965) (1966) (Paris: SEVPEN).
Grandidier, A. (1903) 'Ouvrages ou extraits d'ouvrages portugais, hollandais, anglais, français, allemands, italiens, espagnols et latins relatifs à Madagascar: 1500–1613', in *Collection des ouvrages anciens concernant Madagascar* (Paris: Comité de Madagascar), Vol. 1.
Gray, J. (1935) 'Early history of Buganda', *UJ*, **2**, 4, pp. 259–70.
Gray, J. (1963) 'The solar eclipse in Ankole in 1492', *UJ*, **27**, 2, pp. 217–21.
Gray, J. M. (1950) 'Portuguese records relating to the Wasegeju', *TNR*, **29**, pp. 85–97.
Gray, J. M. (1962) *History of Zanzibar from the Middle Ages to 1856* (London: OUP).
Gray, R. and Birmingham, D. (1970) *Precolonial African trade: essays on trade in Central and Eastern Africa before 1800* (London/New York: OUP).
Gray, W. (1826) *Voyage dans l'Afrique occidentale pendant les années 1818, 1819, 1820, 1821, depuis la rivière Gambie jusqu'au Niger* (Paris: Gastel).
Grebenart, D. (forthcoming) Paper presented to 1979 Seminar on the History of the Central Sudan before 1804.
Greenberg, J. H. (1947) 'Islam and clan organization among the Hausa', *SWJA*, **3**, pp. 193–211.
Greenberg, J. H. (1955) *Studies in African linguistic classification* (Bradford: Compass Pub.).
Greenberg, J. H. (1960) 'Linguistic evidence for the influence of the Kanuri on the Hausa', *JAH*, **1**, 2, pp. 205–12.
Greenberg, J. H. (1963) 'The languages of Africa', *JAL*, **29**, 1, (Part 2); repub. as Publication of the Bloomington Research Center in Anthropology, Folklore and Linguistics, 25.
Griaule, M. (1938) *Masques dogons* (Paris: Institut d'ethnographie).
Griaule, M. (1966) *Dieu d'eau: entretien avec M. Ogotemmêli* (Paris: Fayard).
Griffith, F. L. (1928) *Christian documents from Nubia* (London: Proceedings of the British Academy, **14**, pp. 117–46).
Grottanelli, V. L. (1955) 'A lost African metropolis: (Shungwaya)', in J. Lukas, (ed.), *Afrikanistische Studien* (Berlin: Akademie Verlag), pp. 231–42.
Grottanelli, V. L. (1965) *Pescatori dell'Oceano Indiano; saggio etnologico preliminare sui Bagiuni, Bantu costieri dell'Oltregiuba* (Rome: Cremonese).
Grottanelli, V. L. (1975) 'Su un'antica scultura in avorio della Sierra Leone', *Africa*–(R), **30**, 4, pp. 475–505.
Guerrero-Lovillo, J. (1949) *Las cantigas estudio-arqueologico de sus miniaturas* (Madrid: CSIC).
Guidi, I. (1932) *Storia della letteratura etiopica* (Rome: Istituto per l'Oriente).
Guillain, C. (1845) *Documents sur l'histoire, la géographie et le commerce de la partie occidentale de Madagascar* (Paris: Imprimerie royale).
Guthrie, M. (1948) *The classification of the Bantu languages* (London: IAI).
Guthrie, M. (1953) *The Bantu languages of western Equatorial Africa* (London: IAI).
Guthrie, M. (1962) 'Bantu origin: a tentative new hypothesis', *JAL*, **1**, pp. 9–21.
Guthrie, M. (1967–71) *Comparative Bantu* . . . 4 vols (Farnborough: Gregg International).

Hahn, C. H. L., Vedder, H. and Fourié, L. (1966) *The native tribes of South-West Africa* (London: Cass).
Hair, P. E. H. (1964) 'Christianity in mediaeval Nubia and the Sudan: a bibliographical note', *BSACH*, **1**, 3–4, pp. 67–73.
Hair, P. E. H. (1967) 'Ethnolinguistic continuity on the Guinea coast', *JAH*, **8**, 2, pp. 247–68.
Hair, P. E. H. (1969) 'How African is the history of the Sudan?', *SS*, **4**, pp. 39–58.
Hair, P. E. H. (1974) 'Barbot, Dolpper Davity: a critique of sources on Sierra Leone and Cap Mount', *HAJM*, **1**, pp. 25–54.

al-Hajj Mbaye, A. (1968) 'A seventeenth-century chronicle on the origins and missionary activities of the Wangarawa', *KS*, **1**, 4, pp. 7–42.

Hājjīyāt, 'Abd al-Hamid (1974) *Abū Hammū Mūsa al-Zayyani, hayātuhu wa-ātharuh* (Algiers).

Hallam, W. K. R. (1966) 'The Bayajida legend in Hausa folklore', *JAH*, **7**, 1, pp. 47–60.

Hama, B. (1966) *Enquête sur les fondements et la génèse de l'unité africaine* (Paris: Presence africaine), including 'Un manuscrit inédit de Abkal Aould Aoudar', pp. 205–15.

Hama, B. (1967) *Histoire du Gobir et de Sokoto* (Paris: Présence africaine).

Hama, B. (1968) *Histoire des Songhay* (Paris: Présence africaine).

Hamaker, H. A. (ed.) (1820) *Specimen catalogi codicum Mss. orientalium bibliothecae Academiae lugduno-batavae* (Leiden: Luchtmans).

Hamani, D. (1975) *Contribution à l'étude de l'histoire des états hausa: l'Adar précolonial (République du Niger)* (Niamey: Institut de recherches en sciences humaines).

Hamann, G. (1968) *Der Eintritt der südlichen Hemisphäre in die europaïsche Geschichte. Die Erschliessung des Afrikaweges nach Asien vom Zeitalter Heinrichs des Seefahrers bis zu Vasco da Gama* (Vienna: Böhlau; Veröffentlichungen der Kommission für Geschichte der Mathematik und der Naturwissenschaften, 6).

Hamidullah, M. (1958) 'L'Afrique découvre l'Amérique avant Christophe Colomb', *PA*, 18–19, pp. 173–83.

Harinck, G. (1969) 'Interaction between Khasa and Khoi: emphasis on the period 1620–1750', in L. Thompson (ed.), *African societies in Southern Africa* (London: Heinemann; New York: Praeger), pp. 140–70.

Harris, M. F. (1974) paper presented at Bonduku Seminar (q.v.) (no further details available).

Hartwig, G. W. (n.d.) 'The Bakerebe', *CHM*, **14**, 2, pp. 353–76.

Hasan, Ali Ibrahim (1944) *Dirāsāt fi ta'rīkh al-Mamālīk al-Bahrīya* (Cairo).

Hasan, Y. F. (1967) *The Arabs and the Sudan: from the seventh to the early sixteenth century* (Edinburgh: Edinburgh University Press).

Hasan, Y. F. (ed.) (1971) *Sudan in Africa: studies presented to the first international conference sponsored by the Sudan Research Unit, February 1968* (Khartoum: Khartoum University Press).

Hazard, H. W. (1952) *The numismatic history of late mediaeval North Africa* (New York: American Numismatic Society).

Hébert, J. C. (1958) 'La parenté à plaisanterie à Madagascar', *BM*, **142**, pp. 175–216; **143**, pp. 268–336.

Heers, J. (1957) 'Le Royaume de Grenade et la politique marchande de Gênes en Occident: 15e siècle', *MA*, 1–2, pp. 87–121.

Heers, J. (1958) 'Le Sahara et le commerce méditerranéen à la fin du Moyen Age', *AIEOA*, **16**, pp. 247–55.

Heers, J. (1966) 'Le Rôle des capitaux internationaux dans les voyages de découverte aux 15e et 16e siècles', in *Les Aspects internationaux de la découverte océanique aux 15e et 16e siècles: Actes du cinquième colloque international d'histoire maritime, 1960* (Paris: SEVPEN), pp. 273–94.

Heers, J. (1971) *Gênes au 15e siècle: civilisation méditerranéenne, grand capitalisme et capitalisme populaire* (Paris: Flammarion).

Heine, B. (1973) 'Zur genetischen Gliederung der Bantu-Sprachen', *AU*, **56**, 3, pp. 164–85.

Heine, B., Hoff, H. and Vossen, R. (1977) 'Neuere Ergebnisse zur Territorial-Geschichte der Bantu', in W. J. G. Möhlig (ed.), *Zur Sprachgeschichte und Ethnohistorie in Afrika* (Berlin: Reimer), pp. 57–72.

Heintze, B. (1970) 'Beitrage zur Geschichte und Kultur der Kisama, Angola', *Paideuma*, **16**, pp. 159–86.

Heintze, B. (1977) 'Unbekanntes Angola: der Staat Ndongo im 16 Jahrhundert', *Anthropos*, **72**, pp. 749–805.

Heizelin, J. de (1957) 'Pleistocene sediments and events in Sudanese Nubia', in W. W. Bishop and J. D. Clark (eds), *Background to African evolution* (Chicago: Chicago University Press), pp. 313–28.

Henige, D. P. (1974) 'Reflections on early interlacustrine chronology: an essay in source criticism', *JAH*, **15**, 1, pp. 27–46.

Hennig, R. (1953–6) *Terrae incognitae; eine Zusammenstellung und kritische Bewertung der wichtigsten vorkolumbischen Entdeckungreisen an Hand der darüber originalberichte Vorliegenden*, 4 vols. (Leiden: Brill).

Hertefelt, M. d' (1962) *Les Anciens Royaumes de la zône interlacustre méridionale: Rwanda, Burundi, Buha* (London: IAI; Tervuren: Musée royal de l'Afrique centrale; Monographies ethnographiques, 6).

Hertefelt, M. d' (1971) *Les Clans du Rwanda ancien* (Tervuren: Annales du Musée royal de l'Afrique centrale, série in octavo, sciences humaines, 70).

Heurtebize, G. and Vérin, P. (1974) 'Première découverte sur l'ancienne culture de l'intérieur de l'Androy (Madagascar): archéologie de la vallée du Lambòmaty sur la haute Manambovo', *JSA*, 44, 2, pp. 113–21.
Heusch, L. de (1966) *Le Rwanda et la civilisation interlacustre* (Brussels: Université libre)
Heusch, L. de (1972) *Le Roi ivre, ou l'origine de l'état: mythes et rites bantous* (Paris: Gallimard).
Heyd, W. von (1959) *Histoire du commerce du Levant au Moyen Age, 1885–1886* (Leipzig: Harrassowitz) 2 vols (Amsterdam: Hakker).
Hiernaux, J. (1968) 'Bantu expansion: the evidence from physical anthropology confronted with linguistic archaeological evidence', *JAH*, 4, 4, pp. 505–16.
Hiernaux, J. (1974) *The people of Africa* (London: Weidenfeld and Nicolson).
Hiernaux, J. and Maquet, E. (1968) *L'Age du fer à Kibiro* (*Uganda*) (Tervuren: Musée royal de l'Afrique centrale; Annales: série in octavo: sciences humaines, 63).
Hinkel, F. W. (1977) *The archaeological map of the Sudan: a guide to its use and explanation of its principles* (Berlin: Akademie Verlag).
Hinnebusch, T. J. (1973) *Prefixes, sound change and subgrouping in the coastal Kenyan Bantu languages* (Los Angeles: University of California Press).
Hirschberg, W. (1931) *Die arabisch-persisch-indische Kultur an der Ostküste Afrikas; ihre Beziehungen nach dem Inneren des Kontinents* (Vienna: Mitteilungen der anthropologischen Gesellschaft, 6).
Hirth, F. (1910), 'Early Chinese notices of East African territories', *JAOS*, 30, pp. 46–57.
Hiskett, M. (1962) 'An Islamic tradition of reform in western Sudan from the sixteenth to the eighteenth century', *BSOAS*, 25, pp. 577–96.
Hiskett, M. (1964, 1965) 'The song of Bagauda: a Hausa kinglist and homily in verse', *BSOAS*, 27, 3, pp. 540–67; 28, 1, pp. 112–35; 28, 2, pp. 363–85.
Historia do Reino do Congo (*c.* 1624) MS 8080 da Biblioteca nacional de Lisboa; 1969 ed. A. Brasio (Lisbon: Centro de estudos historicos ultramarinos); 1972 ed. and French transl. F. Bontinck and J. Castro Legovia, *Histoire du royaume du Congo* (Louvain, Nauwelaerts; Etudes d'histoire africaine, 4).
Historical relations across the Indian Ocean: see Unesco (1980a)
Historiography of southern Africa: see Unesco (1980b)
Hodgkin, T. L. (1970, 1975) *Nigerian perspectives; an historical anthology* (London: OUP).
Hofmann, I. (1968) 'Die historische Bedeutung der Niltalkulturen zwischen Aswan und Sennar', *Saeculum*, 19, 27, pp. 109–42.
Hogben, S. J. and Kirk-Greene, A. H. M. (1966) *The emirates of Northern Nigeria: a preliminary survey of their historical traditions* (London: OUP).
Holt, P. M. (1960) 'A Sudanese historical legend: the Funj conquest of Suba', *BSOAS*, 23, pp. 1–17.
Holt, P. M. (1963) 'Funj origins: a critique and new evidence', *JAH*, 4, 1, pp. 39–55.
Holt, P. M. (1970) 'The Nilotic Sudan', in *The Cambridge History of Islam* (Cambridge: CUP), Vol. 2, pp. 327–44.
Hopkins, J. F. P. (1958) *Medieval Muslim government in Barbary, until the sixth century of the Hijra* (London: Luzac)
Horton, R. (1971) 'Stateless societies in the history of West Africa' in J. F. A. Ajayi and M. Crowder (eds), *History of West Africa* (London: Longman), Vol. 1, pp. 78–119.
Hourani, G. F. (1951) *Arab seafaring in the Indian Ocean in ancient and early medieval times* (Princeton: Princeton University Press; Oriental Studies, 13).
Hourani, A. H. and Stern, S. M. (eds) (1970) *The Islamic city: a colloquium* (Oxford: Cassirer; Philadelphia: University of Pennsylvania Press).
Huffman, T. N. (1972) 'The rise and fall of Zimbabwe', *JAH*, 13, 3, pp. 353–66.
Huffman, T. N. (1974a) 'Ancient mining and Zimbabwe', *JSAIMM*, 74, 6, pp. 238–42.
Huffman, T. N. (1974b) *The Leopard's Kopje tradition* (Salisbury: Memoir of the National Museums and Monuments of Rhodesia, 6).
Huffman, T. N. (1978) 'The origins of Leopard's Kopje: an 11th century *difawuane*', *Arnoldia*, 8, 23.
Hugot, H. J., and Bruggman, M. (1976) *Sahara: dix mille ans d'art et d'histoire* (Paris: Bibliothèque des arts).
Huici Miranda, A. (1949) 'La leyenda y la historia en los orígenes del imperio almohade', *al-Andalus*, 14, pp. 339–76.
Huici Miranda, A. (1954) 'El reinado del califa almohade al-Rashid, hijo de el-Ma 'mun', in *Hespéris*, 41, pp. 9–45.
Huici Miranda, A. (1956a) *Las grandes batallas de la reconquista, durante las invasiones africanas* (*Almoravids, Almohades y Benimerines*) (Madrid: CSIC).
Huici Miranda, A. (1956b; 1956–9) *Historia política del imperio almohade*, 2 vols (Tetuan: Editora Marroquí).

Hui Lin, Li (1960–1) 'Mu Lan p'i: a case for precolombian transatlantic travel by Arab ships', *HJAS*, 23, pp. 104–26.
al-Ḥulal al-Mawshiyya fī dhikr al-akhbār al-Marrākushiyya (1381) (?) attrib. to Abū 'Abd Allāh Muḥammad b. Abi 'l-Ma'ālī Ibn Sammāk; 1936 ed. I. S. Allouche (Rabat: Institut des hautes études marocaines; Collection des textes arabes, 6).
Humblot, P. (1918, 1919) 'Du nom propre et des appellations chez les Malinké des vallées du Niandan et du Milo (Guinée française)', *BCEHSAOF*, 3–4, pp. 519–40; 17–23, pp. 393–426.
Huntingford, G. W. B. (1963) 'The peopling of the interior of East Africa by its modern inhabitants', in R. Oliver and G. Mathew (eds), *History of East Africa* (Nairobi: OUP), Vol. 1, pp. 58–93.
Hunwick, J. O. (1962) 'Ahmad Baba and the Moroccan invasion of the Sudan, (1591)', *JHSN*, **10**, pp. 311–22.
Hunwick, J. O. (1964) 'A new source for the biography of Ahmad Baba al-Tinbukti (1556–1627)', *BSOAS*, **27**, 3, pp. 568–93.
Hunwick, J. O. (1966a) 'Further light on Ahmad Baba al-Tinbukti', *RBCAD*, **1**, 2, pp. 19–31.
Hunwick, J. O. (1966b) 'Religion and state in the Songhay empire, 1464–1591', in *Islam in tropical Africa: studies presented at the fifth international African seminar, 1964* (London: IAI), pp. 296–317.
Hunwick, J. O. (1969) 'Studies in the Ta'rīkh al-Fettach: its author and textual history', *RBCAD*, **5**, 1–2, pp. 57–65.
Hunwick, J. O. (1970) 'Notes on a late fifteenth century document concerning al-Takrur', in C. Allen and R. W. Johnson (eds), *African perspectives: papers in the history, politics and economics of Africa presented to Thomas Hodgkin* (London: CUP), pp. 7–34.
Hunwick, J. O. (1971a) 'A little known diplomatic episode in the history of Kebbi (*c.* 1594)', *JHSN*, **5**, 4, pp. 575–81.
Hunwick, J. O. (1971b) 'Songhay, Bornu and Hausaland in the sixteenth century', in J. F. A. Ajayi and M. Crowder (eds), *History of West Africa* (London: Heinemann), Vol. 1, pp. 202–39.
Hunwick, J. (1973) 'The dynastic chronologies of the central Sudan states in the sixteenth century: some reinterpretations', *KS*, **1**, 1, pp. 35–55.
Hutton, J. H. (1946) 'West Africa and Indonesia, a problem in distribution', *Man*, **10**, p. 134.

Ibiraa (n.d.) 1970 French transl. Issaka Dakoussoul, *Histoire du Dawra* (Niamey: Centre de recherche et de documentation pour la tradition orale, 2).
Ibn 'Abd al-Ẓāhir, Muḥyī 'l-Dīn (12th cent.) *Tashrīf al-ayyām wa 'l-uṣūr fī sīrat al-Malik al-Manṣūr*; 1934, 1955, ed. and French transl. E. Lévi-Provençal, in *Documents arabes inédits sur la vie sociale et économique en Occident musulmane au Moyen Age* (Cairo); 1961 ed. M. Kamil (Cairo).
Ibn 'Abdūn Muḥammad b. Aḥmad, al-Tudjībī (12th cent.); 1947 French transl. E. Lévi-Provençal, *Séville musulmane au début du 12e siècle: la traité d'Ibn Abdun sur la vie urbaine et les corps de métiers* (Paris: Maisonneuve et Larose).
Ibn Abī Dīnār, al-Ḳayrawānī (1681 or 1698) *Kitāb al-Mu'nis fī akhbār Ifrīḳiya wa Tūnis*; 1861–2 edn (Tunis: Imprimerie du gouvernement); 1845 French transl. Pellissier and Remusat, 'Histoire de l'Afrique', in *Exploration scientifique de l'Algérie pendant les années 1840, 1841, 1842* (Paris: Imprimerie royale), Vol. 7.
Ibn Abī Zar', Abu 'l-'Abbās Aḥmad al-Fāsī (before 1320) *Rawḍ al-Ḳirṭās* (*al-Anīs al-muṭrib bi-Rawḍ al-Ḳirṭās fī akhbār mulūk al-Maghrib wata'rīkh madīnat Fās*); 1843, 1846 ed. and Latin transl. C. J. Tornberg, *Annales regum Mauritaniae* (Uppsala: Litteris academicis); 1936 edn, 2 vols (Rabat); 1860 French transl. A. Beaumier, *Histoire des souverains du Maghreb* (*Espagne et Maroc*) *et annales de la ville de Fès* (Paris: Imprimerie royale); 1975 partial French transl. in J. Cuoq (q.v.), pp. 228–39.
Ibn al-Aḥmar, Ismā'īl b. Yūsuf (n.d.) *Rawḍat al-nisrīn*; 1917 transl. G. Bouali and G. Marçais, *Histoire des Benī Merīn, rois de Fās* (*Le Jardin des Eglantines*) (Paris: Leroux; Bulletin de correspondance africaine de l'Ecole des lettres d'Alger, 55).
Ibn al-Athīr, 'Izz al-Dīn (*c.* 1231) *Kitāb al-Kāmil fī 'l-ta'rīkh* ('Universal history'); 1851–76 ed. and Latin transl. C. J. Tornberg, *Chronicon, quod perfectissimus inscribitur*, 14 vols (Leiden: Brill); 1876–91 reprint; 1898, 1901, partial French transl. E. Fagnan, *Annales du Maghreb et de l'Espagne* (Algiers: Jourdan); 1975 partial French transl. in J. Cuoq (q.v.), pp. 189–94.
Ibn Badjdja, Abū Bakr Muḥammad b. Yaḥya b. al-Ṣa'ighal Tudjībī al-Andalusī al-Saraḳusṭī, also known as Avempace, or Ibn al-Ṣā'igh (12th cent.) *Tadbīr al-Mutawaḥḥid*; 1859 French transl. S. Munk (Paris); 1946 Spanish transl. M. Acín Palacios, *El régimen del solitario* (Madrid: CSIC).
Ibn Bashkuwāl, Abu 'l-Ḳāsim Khalaf b. 'Abd al-Malik (1139) *Kitāb al-Ṣila fī ta'rīkh a'immat al-Andalūs*; 1955, 1966, edns, 2 vols (Cairo).
Ibn Bassām al-Shantarīnī, Abu 'l-Ḥasan 'Alī (12th cent.) *al-Dhakhīra fī maḥāsin ahl al-Djazīra*; 1975 edn, 4 vols (Beirut).
Ibn Baṭṭūṭa (1357) *Tuḥfat al-nuẓẓār fī gharā' ib al-amṣār wa'adjā' ib al-asfar*; 1853–9, 1922–49, ed. and

French transl. C. Defremy and B. R. Sanguinetti, *Voyages d'Ibn Batoutah*, 4 vols (Paris: Imprimerie impériale; Collection d'ouvrages orientaux publiée par la Société asiatique); 1960 edn (Beirut); 1958, 1962, 1971, Eng. transl. H. A. R. Gibb, *The Travels of Ibn Baṭṭūṭa*, 3 vols, in progress (Cambridge: Hakluyt Society); 1966 partial French transl. R. Mauny *et al.*, *Textes et documents relatifs à l'histoire de l'Afrique: extraits tirés d'Ibn Batuta* (Dakar University: Publications de la section d'histoire de la faculté des lettres et sciences humaines, 9); 1975 partial French transl. in J. M. Cuoq (ed.), 1975 (q.v.), pp. 289–323.

Ibn Faḏl Allāh al-'Umarī: see al-'Umarī

Ibn al-Faraḏī Abu 'l-Walīd 'Abd Allāh b. Muḥammad (before 1013) *Ta'rīkh 'ulamā' al-Andalūs*; 1954 edn, 2 vols (Cairo).

Ibn Fartua: see Ibn Furṭūwa, Aḥmad

Ibn al-Furāt, Nāṣir al-Dīn Muḥammad b. 'Abd al-Raḥīm (before 1405) *Ta'rīkh al-duwal wa 'l-mulūk*; 1936–42 ed. Q. Zuqayq (Beirut: Faculty of Arts and Sciences of the American University of Beirut, Oriental series, 9).

Ibn Furṭūwa, Aḥmad (16th cent.) *Ta'rikh mai Idrīs wa ghazawātihi lil Imām Aḥmad Burnuwī*, 1932 ed. H. R. Palmer (Kano: Amir's Press); 1926 Eng. transl. H. R. Palmer, *History of the first twelve years of the reign of Mai Idris Alooma of Bornu (1571–1583), by his Imam* (together with the 'Diwān of the sultans of Bornu') (Lagos: Government Printer).

Ibn Furṭūwa, Aḥmad (16th cent.) 'Kanem wars of Mai Idris Alooma', 1928 Eng. transl. H. R. Palmer in *Sudanese Memoirs* (q.v.), Vol. 1, pp. 15–72.

Ibn Furtūwa, Aḥmad (16th cent.) 'Ghazawāt sultan Idrīs fī balad Bornu', ed. H. R. Palmer in *Hadhā al-kitāb huwa min sha'n sultān Idrīs Alawma* (Kano, 1932); Eng. transl. J. W. Redhouse, *JRAS*, **19**, pp. 43–124, 199–259.

Ibn Ghalbūn: see Muḥammad b. Khalīl

Ibn Ḥawḳal, Abu 'l-Ḳāsim b. 'Alī al-Naṣībī (10th cent.) *Kitāb Ṣūrat al-arḍ* (or, *Kitāb al-Masālik wa'l Mamālik*); 1938 ed. J. H. Kramers, 2 vols in 1 (Leiden: Brill; Bibliotheca geographorum arabicorum, 2); 1964 French transl. J. H. Kramers and G. Wiet, *Configuration de la terre* (Beirut; Paris: Maisonneuve et Larose; Collection Unesco d'oeuvres représentatives, série arabe). 1975 partial French transl. in J. Cuoq (q.v.), pp. 70–6.

Ibn 'Idhārī al-Marrākushī, Aḥmad b. Muḥammad (14th cent.) *Kitāb al-Bayān al-mughrib fī akhbar al-Andalūs wa 'l-Maghrib*; 1848, 1851, 1st 2 parts ed. R. P. A. Dozy, *Histoire de l'Afrique et de l'Espagne, intitulée al-Bayano 'l-Moghrib*, 2 vols (Leiden: Brill); n.d. (1929?) 3rd part ed. E. Lévi-Provençal (Beirut: Dar Assakafa), 1930 reprint (Paris: Geuthner; Textes arabes relatifs à l'histoire de l'Occident musulman); 1948, 1951, new edn of Dozy's text with new MSS, G. S. Colin and E. Lévi-Provençal, 2 vols (Leiden: Brill); 1961 further parts ed. A. Huici Miranda, *Hespéris*, pp. 46–59; 1972 selections ed. Iḥsān Abbās (Rabat); 1949 ed. M. S. Iryan (Cairo); 1901, 1904, French transl. of Dozy's text, E. Fagnan, *Histoire de l'Afrique et de l'Espagne*, 2 vols (Algiers: Imprimerie orientale Fontana); 1975 partial French transl. in J. Cuoq (q.v.), pp. 219–24.

Ibn al-Ḳāsim (8th cent.) *al-Mudawwana*; A. H. 1323 edn, 15 vols (Cairo); A. H. 1325 edn, 4 vols (Cairo).

Ibn al-Ḳaṭṭān, 'Alī b. Muḥammad (n.d.) *Djuz' min Kitāb Naẓm al-Djuman*; 1925 partial edn E. Lévi-Provençal, in 'Six fragments inédits . . .', q.v.; undated (1964?) edn M. A. Makkī (Tetuan).

Ibn al-Ḳaṭṭānī (n.d.) *Kitāb al-Tashbīhāt min ash'ār ahl al-Andalus.*

Ibn Khaldūn, Walī al-Dīn 'Abd al-Raḥmān b. Muḥammad (14th cent.) *al-Muḳaddima*; 1858 ed. E. Quatremère, 3 vols (Paris: Duprat); 1863–8 French transl. W. M. de Slane, *Les Prolégomènes d'Ibn Khaldoun*, 3 vols (Paris: Imprimerie nationale); 1934–8 reprint (Paris: Geuthner); 1958 Eng. transl. F. Rosenthal, 3 vols (New York: Pantheon; Bollinger Series, 43); 1967–8 French transl. V. Monteil, *Discours sur l'histoire universelle*, 3 vols (Beirut: Commission internationale pour la traduction des chefs d'oeuvre); 1975 partial French transl. in J. Cuoq (q.v.), pp. 328–63.

Ibn Khaldūn . . . (14th cent.) *Kitāb al-'Ibār wa-diwan al-mubtada wa 'l-Khabar* ('Universal History'); 1868 edn, 7 vols (Būlāḳ); 1852–6, partial French transl. W. M. de Slane, *Histoire des Berbères et des dynasties musulmanes de l'Afrique septentrionale*, 4 vols (Algiers: Imprimerie du gouvernement); 1925–6 reprint (Paris: Geuthner); 1956–9, complete French transl., 7 vols (Beirut: Commission internationale pour la traduction des chefs d'oeuvre); 1975 partial French transl. in J. Cuoq (q.v.), pp. 328–63.

Ibn al-Khaṭīb (1361–71) *Iḥāṭa fī ta'rīkh Gharnāṭa* ('History of Granada'); 1901–2 partial edn (Cairo); 1975 partial French transl. in J. Cuoq (q.v.), pp. 324–6.

Ibn Khayr al-Ishbīlī (12th cent.) *Fahrasat mā rawāhu 'an shuyūkhi-hi min al-dawāwīn al-muṣannafa fī durūb al- 'ilm wa-anwā' al-ma'ārif*; 1963 edn (Cairo).

Ibn Ḳunfudh, Abu 'l-'Abbās Aḥmad b. Ḥasan (8th/9th cent.) *al-Fārisiyyah fī mabādi' al-dawla al Ḥafṣīyah*; 1968 ed. M. Nayfar, 'A. Turkī (Tunis).

Ibn Maḍā', Aḥmad b. 'Abd al Raḥmān (12th cent.) *Kitāb al-Radd'ala 'l-nuḥāt*; 1947 ed. S. Daif (Cairo).

Ibn Madjid al-Dīn Aḥmad (1490) *Kitāb al-Fawā'id fī uṣūl al-bahr wa 'l-Ḳawā'id*; 1971 ed. and Eng. transl. G. R. Tibbetts, *Arab navigation in the Indian Ocean before the coming of the Portuguese* (London: RASGBI, Publications of the Oriental translation fund, n.s. 42).

Ibn al-Mukhtār: see Ka'ti, Maḥmūd.

Ibn Rushd (Abu 'l-Walīd Muḥammad b. Aḥmad b. Muḥammad b. Rushd, also known as Averroes) (before 1169) *Kitāb al-Kulliyāt*; 1939 Spanish transl., *Libro de la generalidades* (Larache: Artes gráficas Bosca).

Ibn Rushd (1169–78) *Talkhīs* (short or 'middle' commentaries on Aristotle); 1977 English ed. and transl. C. E. Butterworth, *Averroes' three short commentaries on Aristotle's 'Topics', 'Rhetoric' and 'Poetics'* (Albany: State University of New York Press).

Ibn Rushd (*c.* 1174–8) *Faṣl al-maḳal*; 1959 ed. G. F. Hourani (Leiden: Brill); 1972 edn (Cairo); 1948 French transl. L. Gauthier (Algiers).

Ibn Rushd (1179) *Kashf al-manāhidj al-adilla*; 1859 edn; 1859 German transl. of the *Kashf* and the *Faṣl al-maḳal*, M. J. Müller, *Philosophie und Theologie von Averroës*; 1921 Eng. trans. M. Jamil-ur-Rehman, *Philosophy and Theology of Averroës* (Baroda: Widgery).

Ibn Rushd (*c.* 1180) *Tahāfut al-Tahāfut*; 1930 French transl. M. Bouyges (Beirut: Imprimerie catholique); 1954, 1969, Eng. transl. S. van den Bergh, *The incoherence of the incoherence* (London: Luzac).

Ibn Rushd (after 1180) *Tafsīr* ('Great commentaries' on Aristotle's *Metaphysics*); 1953 Latin edn, *Commentarium magnum in Aristotelis 'de Anima Libros'* (Cambridge, Mass.: Medieval Academy of America).

Ibn Ṣāḥib al-Ṣalāt, Abū Marwān 'Abd al-Malik b. Muḥammad al-Badjī (12th cent.) *al-Mann bi 'l-imāma 'ala 'l-musta-d'afīn bi-an dja 'alahum Allāh al-a'imma wa-dja'alahum al-wārithīn*; 1964 ed. 'Abd al-Hādī al-Tāzī (Beirut).

Ibn Sa'īd, Abu 'l-Ḥasan 'Alī b. Mūsā, al-Maghribī (1243) *Kitāb al-Mughrib fī ḥula 'l-Maghrib*; 1953 ed. Z. M. Hasan, R. Dauf and S. Kashif (Cairo).

Ibn Sa'īd, al Maghribī (13th cent.) *Mukhtaṣar Djughrāfiyā*, sometimes called *Kitāb basṭ al-arḍ fī tūlihā wa 'l-ard*; 1970 ed. I. al-'Arabī (Beirut); partial French transl. in J. M. Cuoq (q.v.), pp. 201–19.

Ibn Taghrībirdī: see Abu 'l-Maḥāsin b. Taghrībirdī

Ibn Ṭufayl, Abū Bakr Muḥammad b. 'Abd al-Malik ... (*c.* 1169) *Risālat Ḥayy b. Yakẓān fī asrār al-hikma al-mushrikiyya*; 1671 Latin transl. E. Pocock, *Philosophus utodidactus* (Oxford: H. Half); 1905 Eng. transl. S. Ockley, *The improvement of human reason* (Cairo: El-Maaref Printing Office); 1910 (4th edn) Eng. transl. P. Brönnle (London: Murray); 1972 Eng. transl. L. G. Goodman, *Ibn Tufayl's Hayy ibn Yaqzan: a philosophical tale* (New York: Twayne).

Ibn Tūmart (12th cent.) *Kitāb A'azz mā yutlab*; 1903 ed. and French transl. R. Luciani, with preface by I. Goldziher (q.v.), *Le Livre de Mohammed Ibn Toumert* (Algiers: Fontana).

Idris, H. R. (1961) 'Commerce maritime et hirad en Berbérie orientale d'après un recueil inédit de *fatwās* medievales', *JESHO*, **4**, 3, pp. 235–9.

Idris, H. R. (1962) *La Berbérie orientale sous les Zirides: 10e–12e siècles*, 2 vols (Paris: Maisonneuve; Publication de l'Institut d'études orientales de la faculté des lettres et sciences de l'Université d'Alger, 12).

Idris, H. R. (1970–4) 'Le mariage en Occident musulman: analyse de fatwās médiévales, extraites du Mi'yar d'al Wancharichi', *SI*, **32**, pp. 157–67, and ROMM, **12**, pp. 45–64; **17**, pp. 71–105.

Idris, H. R. (1973a) 'Contributions à l'étude de la vie économique musulmane médiévale. Glanes de données chiffrées', *ROMM*, **15–16**, (Mélanges le Tourneau, 2) pp. 75–87.

Idris, H. R. (1973b) 'Des prémices de la symbiose arabo-berbère', in *Actes du premier congrès d'études des cultures méditerranéennes, 1972* (Algiers: SNED), pp. 382–93.

Idris, H. R. (1974) 'Les tributaires en occident musulman médiéval d'après le Mi'yar d'Al-Wansarisi', in *Mémorial Anouar Abdel-Malek*, (Brussels), pp. 172–96.

al-Idrīsī, Abū 'Abd Allāh (1154) *Kitāb Nuzhat al-mushtāḳ fī 'khtirāḳ al-āfāḳ* (also known as the 'Book of Roger' after its royal patron, Roger II of Sicily); 1866 partial edn and French transl. R. Dozy and M. J. de Goeje, *Description de l'Afrique et l'Espagne* (Leiden: Brill); 1970ff., complete edn in progress, ed. E. Cerulli *et al.*, *Opus geographicum, sive Liber ad eorem delectationem qui terras peragrare studeant* (Rome: Instituto Italiano per il Medio e l'Estremo Oriente); 1836–40, French transl. P. A. Jaubert, *Géographie d'Edrisi*, 3 vols (Paris: Imprimerie royale); 1975 partial French transl. in J. Cuoq (q.v.), pp. 126–65.

al-Ifrānī, Abū 'Abd Allāh Muḥammad, known as al-Saghīr (before 1745) *Nuzhat al-ḥādī bi-akhbār mulūk al-Ḳarn al- ḥādī*; 1888, 1889, ed. and French transl. O. Houdas, *Histoire de la dynastie saadienne au Maroc (1151–1670)*, 2 vols (Paris: Leroux; Publications de l'Ecole des langues orientales vivantes, série 3, 2–3).

Iglauer, E. (1973) *Goldewinnung und Goldhandel im Raum von Simbabwe in der portugiesischen Zeit von 1497–1840* (Vienna: Institut für Völkerkunde, Universität).
Ikime, O. (ed.) (1980) *Groundwork of Nigerian history* (Ibadan: Heinemann).
Imamuddin, S. M. (1966) *Some aspects of the socio-economic and cultural history of Muslim Spain, 711–1492 AD* (Leiden: Brill).
'Inān, Muḥammad 'Abd Allāh (1964) *'Asr al-Murābitin*, 2 vols (Cairo).
Innes, G. (ed.) (1974) *Sunjata; three Mandinka versions* (London: SOAS).
Inskeep, R. R. (1978) *The peopling of Southern Africa* (Cape Town: Philip; London: Global Book Resources); 1979 (New York: Barnes and Noble).
International Geographical Union, Commission on early maps (1964–) *Monumenta cartographica vetustioris aevi, AD 1200–1500*, eds R. Almagia and Maral Destombes (Amsterdam: Israel; Imago Mundi, supplement 4).
al-Ishbīlī: see Ibn Khayr al-Ish bīlī
Ishumi, A. G. M. (1971) 'The kingdom of Kiziba', *CHM*, **13**, 4, pp. 714–35.
Itandala, B. (1978) 'Ilembo, Nkanda and the girls: establishing a chronology of the Babinza', in J. B. Webster (ed.), *Chronology, migration and drought in interlacustrine Africa* (Dalhousie: Dalhousie University Press), pp. 145–72.
Izard, M. (1965–) *Traditions historiques des villages du Yatenga* (Paris: CNRS; Recherches voltaïques, 1–).
Izard, M. (1970) *Introduction à l'histoire des royaumes mossi*, 2 vols (Paris: CNRS; Recherches voltaïques, 12–13).
Izard, M. (1971) 'Les Yarsés et le commerce dans le Yatenga précolonial', in C. Meillassoux (ed.), *The development of indigenous trade and markets in West Africa* (*L'Evolution du commerce africain depuis le 19e siècle en Afrique de l'ouest*) *Studies presented at the 10th International African Seminar, 1969* (London: IAI), pp. 214–19.
Izard, M. (1973a) 'La lance et les guenilles', *L'Homme*, **13**, 1–2, pp. 139–49.
Izard, M. (1973b) 'Remarques sur le vocabulaire politique mossi', *L'Homme*, **13**, 1–2, pp. 193–230.

Jackson, K. A. (1972) 'An ethnohistorical study of the oral tradition of the Akamba of Kenya' (doctoral dissertation, University of California).
Jadin, L. (1966) 'L'Afrique et Rome depuis les découvertes jusqu'au 18e siècle', in *Acts of the 12th International Congress of Historical Sciences* (Vienna: Berger Verlag; Louvain: Nauwaelerts), pp. 33–70.
Jarniat, L. (1968) *Contribution à l'étude de l'hippopotame nain, subfossile de Madagascar* (*craniologie*) (Tananarive).
Jeffreys, M. D. W. (1953a) 'The Arabs discover America before Columbus', *Muslim Digest*, **4**, 2, pp. 18–26.
Jeffreys, M. D. W. (1953b) 'Precolombian maize in Africa', *Nature*, **172**, 4386, pp. 965–6.
Jeffreys, M. D. W. (1953c) 'Precolombian negroes in America', *Scientia*, **88**, 7–8, pp. 202–12.
Jeffreys, M. D. W. (1957) 'Origins of the Portuguese word Zaburro as their name for maize', *BIFAN*, B, **19**, 2, pp. 111–36.
Jeffreys, M. D. W. (1963a) 'How ancient is West African maize?', *Africa*-(L), **33**, pp. 116–18.
Jeffreys, M. D. W. (1963b) 'Milho Zaburro-Milho de Guinée = Maize', *Garcia da Orta*, **11**, 2, pp. 213–26.
Jeffreys, M. D. W. (1964) 'Congo Maza = Portuguese Maize?', *Ethnos*, **29**, 3–4, pp. 191–207.
Jeffreys, M. D. W. (1969) 'Precolombian maize north of the old world equator', *CEA*, **9**, 35, pp. 146–9.
Jeffreys, M. D. W. (1971) 'Maize and the Mande myth', *CA*, **12**, 3, pp. 291–320.
Jobson, R. (17th cent.) *The Golden Trade*; 1932 edn (London).
Johnson, M. (1970) 'The cowrie currencies in West Africa', *JAH*, **2**, 1, pp. 17–49; 3, pp. 331–53.
Johnson, S. (1921) *The history of the Yoruba from the earliest times to the beginning of the British protectorate* (London: Routledge; Lagos: CMS Bookshop).
Julien, C. A. (1961) *Histoire de l'Afrique du nord, Tunisie, Algérie, Maroc.* (Paris: Payot) 2nd edn.

K. W. (1935–7) 'Abakama ba Bunyoro-Kitara', *UJ*, **3**, 2, pp. 155–60; **4**, 1, pp. 75–83; **5**, 1, pp. 53–68.
Kabuga, C. E. S. (1963) 'The genealogy of Kabaka Kintu and the early Bakabaka of Buganda', *UJ*, **27**, 2, pp. 205–16.
Kagame, A. (1951) *La poésie dynastique au Rwanda* (Brussels: IRCB; Mémoires de l'Académie royale des sciences d'outre-mer, classe des sciences morales et politiques, **22**, 1).
Kagame, A. (1952a) *Le code des institutions politiques du Rwanda précolonial* (Brussels: IRCB; Mémoires de l'Académie royale des sciences d'outre-mer, classe des sciences morales et politiques, mémoires in octavo, **26**, 1).

Kagame, A. (1952b) *La Divine Pastorale* (Brussels: Editions du Marais).

Kagame, A. (1954) *Les organisations socio-familiales de l'ancien Ruanda* (Brussels: IRCB; Mémoires de l'Académie royale des sciences d'outre-mer, classe des sciences morales et politiques, 38, 3).

Kagame, A. (1955) 'La structure de quinze clans du Rwanda', *AL*, **18**, pp. 103–17.

Kagame, A. (1959) *La notion de génération appliquée à la généalogie dynastique et à l'histoire du Rwanda des 10e–11e siècles à nos jours* (Brussels: IRCB; Mémoires de l'Académie royale des sciences d'outre-mer, classe des sciences morales et politiques, n.s. **9**, 5).

Kagame, A. (1961) *L'histoire des armées bovines dans l'ancien Rwanda* (Brussels: IRCB; Mémoires de l'Académie royale des sciences d'outre-mer, classe des sciences morales et politiques, n.s. 28, 4).

Kagame, A. (1963) *Les milices du Rwanda précolonial* (Brussels: IRCB; Mémoires de l'Académie royale des sciences d'outre-mer, classe des sciences morales et politiques, n.s. **28**, 3).

Kaggwa, A. (1905) *Ekitabo ky 'ekika kya nsenene* (*The history of the grasshopper clan*) (Mengo, Uganda: A. K. Press).

Kaggwa, A. (1971) *The kings of Buganda*, transl. M. S. M. Kiwanuka (Nairobi: EAPH).

Kake, I. B. (ed.) (1977) *Histoire générale de l'Afrique*, 12 vols (Vol. 2: *L'Ere des grands empires*) (Paris: ABC).

Kake, I. B. (1980) *Les armées traditionnelles de l'Afrique* (Paris/Libreville: Lion).

Kake, I. B. (1981) 'Les Portugais et le Gabu: XVe, XIXe siècles', in 'Colloque international sur les traditions orales du Gabu (unpublished communication).

Kalck, P. (1959) *Réalités oubanguiennes* (Paris: Berger-Levrault).

Kalck, P. (1974) *Histoire de la République centrafricaine; des origines préhistoriques à nos jours* (Paris: Berger-Levrault).

al-Ḳalḳashandī, Aḥmad (before 1418) *Ṣubḥ al-a'shā fī ṣinā'at al-inshā'*; 1913–19 ed. Dār al-Kutūb, 14 vols (Cairo); 1975 partial French transl. in J. M. Cuoq (q.v.), pp. 369–80.

Kano Chronicle: see Palmer, H. R. (1909)

Kanyamunyu, P. K. (1951) 'The tradition of the coming of the Abalisa clan in Buhwezu, Ankole', *UJ*, **15**, 2, pp. 191–2.

Karpinski, R. (1968) 'Considérations sur les échanges de caractère local et extérieur de la Sénégambie dans la deuxième moitié du 15e siècle et du début du 16e siècle', *AB*, **8**, pp. 65–86.

Karugire, S. R. (1971) *A history of the kingdom of Nkore in Western Uganda to 1896* (Oxford: Clarendon Press).

Kasanga, F. (1956) *Tantaran 'ny Antemoro-Anakara teto Imerina tamin 'ny Andron 'Andrianampoinimerina sy Ilaidama* (Tananarive/Antananarivo).

Kasanga, F. (1963) *Fifindra-monina. Ny Antemoro-anakara voasoratra tamin'ny taona 1506.* (Tananarive: Iarivo).

Katate, A. G. and Kamugungunu L. (1953) *Abagabe b' Ankole* (*History of the kings of Ankole, Books 1–2*), 2 vols (Kampala: Eagle Press); 1967 edn (Nairobi: East Africa Literature Bureau).

Ka'ti, Maḥmūd b. al-Ḥadjdj al-Mutawakkil (before 1593), completed (1654–5) by grandson, called Ibn al-Mukhtār by N. Levtzion (1971c, q.v.), who attributes whole work to him, *Ta'rīkh al-fattāsh*; 1913–14 (revised 1964) ed. and French transl. O. Houdas and M. Delafosse (Paris: Publications de l'Ecole des langues orientales vivantes, 5e série, 10); 1981 Unesco reprint of 1913–14 edn and transl. (Paris: Maisonneuve; Librairie d'Amérique et d'Orient).

Katoke, I. K. (1971) 'Karagwe; a pre-colonial state', *CHM*, **13**, 5, pp. 515–41.

Katoke, I. K. (1975) *The Karagwe kingdom: a history of the Abanyambo of Northwestern Tanzania* c. *1400–1915* (Nairobi: EAPH).

al-Ḳaṭṭān: see Ibn al-Ḳaṭṭān

Kawada, J. (1979) *Génèse et évolution du système politique des Mosi méridionaux: Haute-Volta* (Tokyo: Asia Africa gengo bunla kenkyûzyo).

Keech, S. and McIntosh, R. J. (1980) 'Jenne-Jeno: ancient African city', *Times*, 1 September, p. 18.

Kent, R. K. (1969) 'Alfred Grandidier et le mythe des fondateurs d'états malgaches d'origine asiatique', *BM*, 277–8, pp. 603–20.

Kent, R. K. (1970) *Early kingdoms in Madagascar: 1500–1700* (New York: Rinehart and Winston).

Kilhefner, D. W. (1967) 'The Christian kingdoms of the Sudan: 500–1500', *The Africanist*, 1, 1, pp. 1–13.

Kilwa Chronicle, in G. S. P. Freeman-Grenville (1962a), 34–49.

Kimambo, I. N. (1969) *A political history of the Pare of Tanzania*, c. *1500–1900* (Nairobi: EAPH).

Kirkman, J. S. (154a) *The Arab city of Gedi: excavations at the great mosque, architecture and finds* (London: OUP).

Kirkman, J. S. (1954b) *Men and monuments on the East African coast* (London: Lutterworth).

Kirkman, J. S. (1957) 'Historical archaeology in Kenya: 1948–1956', *AJ*, **37**, pp. 16–18.

Kirkman, J. S. (1959) 'The excavations at Ras Mkumbuu on the islands of Pemba', *TNR*, **53**, pp. 161–78.
Kirkman, J. S. (1960) *The tomb of the dated inscription at Gedi* (London: Royal Anthropological Institute; occasional papers, 14).
Kirkman, J. S. (1963) *Gedi: the palace* (The Hague: Mouton).
Kirkman, J. S. (1967) 'Les Importations de céramiques sur la côte du Kenya', *Taloha*, **2**, pp. 1–10.
Kiwanuka, M. S. M. S. (1971) *A history of Buganda: from the foundation of the kingdom of 1900* (London: Longman); 1972 edn (New York: Barnes and Noble).
Ki-Zerbo, J. (1972) *Histoire de l'Afrique noire d'hier à demain* (Paris: Hatier) 2nd edn.
Klapwijk, M. (1974) 'A preliminary report on pottery from north-eastern Transvaal, South Africa', *SAAB*, **29**, pp. 19–23.
Kodjo, N. G. (1971) 'Ishaq II et la fin de l'empire Songhai' (doctoral dissertation, University of Paris).
Köhler, O. (1958) 'Zur Territorial-Geschichte des Nizerbogens', *BA*, **61**, 2, pp. 229–61.
Köhler, O. (1963) 'Observations on the central Khoisan language group', *JAL*, **2**, 3, pp. 227–34.
Köhler, O. (1975) 'Geschichte und Probleme der Gliederung der Sprachen Afrikas', in H. Baumann (ed.), *Die Völker Afrikas und ihre traditionellen Kulturen* (Wiesbaden: Steiner; Studien zur Kulturkunde, 34), pp. 305–37.
Kolmodin, J. (1912–14) 'Traditions de Tsazzaga et Hazzega: textes tigrana', *Aeo*, **5**, 5, pts 1–3.
Krieger, K. (1959) *Geschichte von Zamfara, Sokoto-Provinz Nord-Nigeria* (Berlin: Reimer).
Kuper, A. (1975) 'The social structure of the Sotho speaking people of Southern Africa', *Africa-(L)* **45**, 1, pp. 139–49.

Labarun Hausawa da Makwabtansu: see East, R. M. (1933)
Labatut, F. and Raharinarivonirina, R. (1969) *Madagascar: étude historique* (Paris: Nathan).
Labib, S. Y. (1965) *Handelsgeschichte Ägyptens im Spätmittelalter, 1171–1517* (Wiesbaden: Steiner).
Laburthe-Tolra, P. (1977) *Minlaaba: histoire et société traditionnelle chez les Béti du sud Cameroun*, 3 vols (Lille: University of Lille II; Paris: Champion).
Lacoste, Y. (1966) *Ibn Khaldoun: naissance de l'histoire, passé du Tiers-Monde* (Paris: Maspéro).
Lambert (Captain) (1907) 'Le Pays mossi et sa population: étude historique, économique et géographique suivie d'un essai d'ethnographie comparée' (Dakar: Archives du Sénégal, unpublished monograph).
Lampen, G. D. (1950) 'History of Darfur', *SNR*, **31**, pp. 177–209.
Landerouin, M. A. (1909) 'Notice historique', in M. Tilho (ed.), *Documents scientifiques de la mission Tilho* (Paris: Imprimerie nationale), Vol. 2, pp. 341–417.
Lang, K. (1923–4) 'Arabische Lehnwörter in der Kanuri Sprache', *Anthropos*, **18–19**, pp. 1063–74.
Lange, D. (1977a) *Le Dīwān des sultans du (Kanem)-Bornu: chronologie et histoire d'un royaume africain de la fin du 10e siècle jusqu'à 1808* (Wiesbaden: Steiner; Studien zur Kulturkunde, 42).
Lange, D. (1977b) 'Al-Qasaba et d'autres villes de la route centrale du Sahara', *Paideuma*, **23**, pp. 19–40.
Lange, D. (1978) 'Progrès de l'Islam et changement politique du Kanem du 11e siècle au 13e siècle', *JAH*, **19**, 4, pp. 495–513.
Lange, D. (1979a) 'Les Lieux de sépulture des rois sefuwa (Kanem-Bornu): textes écrits et traditions orales', *Paideuma*, **25**, pp. 145–57.
Lange, D. (1979b) 'Un texte de Maqrizi sur "les races du Soudan"', *AI*, **15**, pp. 187–209.
Lange, D. (1980) 'La Région du lac Tchad d'apres la geographie d'Ibn Said: texte et cartes', *AI*, **16**, pp. 149–81.
Lange, D. (1982) 'L' Eviction des Sefuwa du Kanem et l'origine des Butlala', *JAH*, **23**, 3, pp. 315–32.
Lange, D. (forthcoming) 'The Chad region as a crossroads', in M. El Fasi (ed.), *General History of Africa* (London: Heinemann; Paris: Unesco; Berkeley: University of California Press), Vol. III, Chap. 15.
Lange, D. and Berthoud, S. (1972) 'L'intérieur de l'Afrique occidentale d'après G. L. Anania', *CHM*, **14**, 2, pp. 299–351.
Langworthy, H. W. (1972) *Zambia before 1890: aspects of pre-colonial history* (London: Longman).
Lanham, L. W. (1964) 'The proliferation and extension of Bantu phonemic systems influenced by Bushman and Hottentot', in *Proceedings of the ninth International Congress of Linguists, 1962* (Paris/The Hague: Mouton), pp. 382–9.
Lanning, E. C. (1966) 'Excavations at Mubende Hill', *UJ*, **30**, 2, pp. 153–64.
Lapidus, I. M. (1967) *Muslim cities in the later Middle Ages* (Cambridge, Mass.: Harvard University Press).
Lapidus, I. M. (1972) 'Ayyubid religious policy and the development of the law schools in Cairo', in

Colloque international sur l'histoire du Caire, 1969 (Cairo: General Egyptian Book Organization), pp. 279–86.

Larochette, J. A. (1958) 'Les Langues du groupe Moru-Mangbetu', *Ko*, **24**, 3, pp. 118–35.

la Roncière, C. de (1919) 'Une Histoire du Bornou au 17e siècle', *RHCF*, **7**, 3, pp. 78–88.

la Roncière, C. de (1924–7) *La Découverte de l' Afrique au Moyen Age, cartographes et explorateurs*, 3 vols (Cairo: Mémoires de la Société royale de géographie d'Egypte, 5, 6, 13).

la Roncière, C. de (1967) 'Portulans et planisphères conservés à la Bibliothéque nationale: la succession dans les écoles cartographiques', *RHES*, **45**, 1, pp. 7–14.

la Roncière, M. de (1967) 'Les Cartes marines de l'époque des grandes decouvertes', *RHES*, **45**, 1, pp. 15–22.

Laroui, A. (1970) *L'Histoire du Maghreb: un essai de synthèse*, 2 vols (Paris: Maspero); 1977 Eng. transl. R. Manheim, *The History of the Maghrib: an interpretative essay* (Princeton: Princeton University Press).

Latham, J. D. (1972) 'Arabic into medieval Latin', *JSS*, **17**, pp. 30–67.

Lavergne de Tressan, M. de (1953) *Inventaire linguistique de l'Afrique occidentale française et du Togo* (Dakar: Mémoire de L'IFAN, 30); 1972 reprint (Amsterdam: Swets and Zeitlinger).

Lavers, J. (1971) 'Islam in the Bornu caliphate: a survey', *Odu*, **5**, pp. 27–53.

Law, R. C. C. (1973) 'The heritage of Oduduwa: traditional history and political propaganda among the Yoruba', *JAH*, **14**, 2, pp. 207–22.

Lebeuf, A. M. D. (1969) *Les Principautés kotoko: essai sur le caractère sacré de l'autorité* (Paris: CNRS).

Lebeuf, J. P. and Mason Detourbet, A. (1950) *La Civilisation du Tchad* (Paris: Payot).

Le Bourdiec, F. (1974) 'La Riziculture à Madagascar: les hommes et les paysages' (doctoral dissertation, University of Aix-Marseille).

Legassick, M. (1969) 'The Sotho-Twana peoples before 1800', in L. M. Thompson (ed.) *African societies in Southern Africa* (London: Heinemann), pp. 86–125.

Le Moal, G. (1963) 'Commentaire des cartes ethniques', in G. Brasseur (ed.), *Cartes ethno-démographiques de l' Afrique occidentale française* (Dakar: IFAN), pp. 9–21.

Leo Africanus (1550) 'Descrittione dell 'Africa', in G. B. Ramusio, *Navigationi e viaggi* (Venice), Vol. 1; 1956 French transl. A. Epaulard, *Description de l'Afrique* (Paris: Maisonneuve).

Lepionka, L. (1977) 'Excavations at Tautswemogala', *BNR*, **9**, pp. 1–16.

Le Rouvreur, A. (1962) *Sahéliens et Sahariens du Tchad* (Paris: Berger-Levrault).

Leroy, J. (1964) 'La Peinture chrétienne d'Ethiopie antérieure à l'influence occidentale', in K. Wessel (ed.), *Christendum am Nil* (Recklinghausen: A. Bongers), pp. 61–78.

Lesourd, M. (1960) 'Notes sur les Nawakhid, navigateurs de la Mer Rouge', *BIFAN*, B. **22**, 1–2, pp. 346–55.

Le Tourneau, R. (1949) *Fès avant le protectorat: étude économique et sociale d'une ville de l'Occident musulman* (Casablanca: SMLE).

Le Tourneau, R. (1961) *Fez in the age of the Marinides* (Oklahoma: Oklahoma University Press).

Le Tourneau, R. (1969) *The Almohad movement in North Africa in the twelfth and thirteenth centuries* (Princeton: Princeton University Press).

Le Tourneau, R. (1970) 'Sur la disparition de la doctrine almohade', *SI*, **32** pp. 193–201.

Levaud, R. and Nelli, R. (eds) (1960) *Les troubadours* (Paris: Desclée de Brouwer).

Lévi-Provençal, E. (1925) 'Six fragments inédits d'une chronique anonyme du début des Almohades', in *Mélanges René Basset: études nord-africaines et orientales* (Paris: Geuthner; Publications de l'Institut des hautes études marocaines, 10–11), Vol. 2, pp. 335–93.

Lévi-Provençal, E. (1928a) *Documents inedits d'histoire almohade* (Paris: Geuthner)

Lévi-Provençal, E. (1928b) 'Ibn Tumart et Abd al-Mumin: le "Fakih du Sus" et le "flambeau des Almohades"', in *Mémorial Henri Basset: nouvelles études nord-africaines et orientales* (Paris: Geuthner; Publications de l'Institut des hautes études marocaines, 17–18), Vol. 2, pp. 21–37.

Lévi-Provençal, E. (1930) 'Notes d'histoire almohade', *Hespéris*, **10**, pp. 49–90.

Lévi-Provençal, E. (1941a) *Majmu rasail muwahhidiyah: trente-sept lettres officielles almohades* (Rabat: Publications de l'Institut des hautes études marocaines, 10).

Lévi-Provençal, E. (1941b) 'Un Recueil de lettres almohades: analyse et commentaire historique', *Hespéris*, **28**, pp. 21–69.

Lévi-Provençal, E. (1948) *Islam d'Occident: études d'histoire médiévale* (Paris: Maisonneuve).

Levtzion, N. (1963) 'The thirteenth- and fourteenth-century kings of Mali', *JAH*, **4**, 3, pp. 341–53.

Levtzion, N. (1968) *Muslims and chiefs in West Africa: a study of Islam in the Middle Volta Basin in the pre-colonial period* (Oxford: Clarendon Press).

Levtzion, N. (1971a) 'The early states of the western Sudan to 1500', in J. F. A. Ajayi and M. Crowder (eds), *History of West Africa* (London: Longman), Vol. 1, pp. 120–257.

Levtzion, N. (1971b) 'Maḥmūd Ka'ti fut-il l'auteur du Ta'rīkh al-Fattāsh?, *BIFAN*, B, **33**, 4, pp. 665–74.
Levtzion, N. (1971c) 'A seventeenth century chronicle by Ibn al-Mukhtār: a critical study of Ta'rīkh al-Fattāsh', *BSOAS*, **34**, 3, pp. 571–93.
Levtzion, N. (1973) *Ancient Ghana and Mali* (London: Methuen; Studies in African history, 7).
Levtzion, N. (1977) 'The western Maghrib and Sudan', in R. Oliver (ed.), *Cambridge History of Africa* (Cambridge: CUP), Vol. 3, pp. 331–414.
Lewicki, T. (1964) 'Traits d'histoire du commerce trans-saharien: marchands et missionnaires ibadites au Soudan occidental et central au cours des 8e–20e siècles', *EP*, **8**, pp. 291–311.
Lewicki, T. (1966) 'A propos de la génèse de *Nuzhat al-Mūstāq fi-Htirāq al-āfāq* d'al-Idrisi', *SM*, **1**, pp. 41–55.
Lewicki, T. (1967) 'Les Ecrivains arabes du Moyen Age au sujet des pierres précieuses et des pierres fines en territoire africain et leur exploitation', *AB*, **7**, pp. 49–68.
Lewicki, T. (1971) 'The Ibadites in Arabia and Africa', *CHM*, **13**, 1, pp. 51–81.
Lewicki, T. (1974) *Arabic external sources for the history of Africa to the south of Sahara* (London: Curzon Press), 2nd edn.
Lewis, B. (1970) 'The central Islamic lands', in P. M. Holt (ed.), *The Cambridge History of Islam* (Cambridge: CUP), Vol. 2, pp. 175–230.
Lezine, A. (1971) *Deux villes d'Ifriqiya: Sousse, Tunis: études d'archéologie, d'urbanisme, de démographie* (Paris: Geuthner; Bibliothèque d'études islamiques), 2.
Lhote, H. (1955, 1956) 'Contribution à l'étude des Touareg soudanais', *BIFAN*, B, **17**, 3–4, pp. 334–470; **18**, 3–4, pp. 391–407.
Libro del conoscimiento de todos los reynos, tierras, senorios que son por el mundo (n.d.); 1877 ed. J. Jimenes de la Espada (Madrid: Fortanet); 1912 Eng. transl., *Book of the knowledge of all the kingdoms, lands and lordships* (London: Hakluyt Society).
Linschoten, J. H. van (1885) *The voyage to the East Indies*, 2 vols (London: Hakluyt Society).
Livingstone, F. B. (1962) 'Anthropological implications of sickle-cell gene distribution in West Africa', in A. Montagu (ed.), *Culture and the evolution of man* (New York: OUP), pp. 271–99.
Lo Jung-Pang (1955) 'The emergence of China as a sea power during the late Sung and early Yuan periods', *FEQ*, **14**, 4, pp. 489–503.
Lo Jung-Pang (1957) 'China as a sea power: 1127–1368' (doctoral dissertation, University of California).
Lombard, M. (1972) *Espaces et réseaux au haut Moyen Age* (Paris: Mouton).
Lombard, J. (1973) 'La Royauté sakalava: formation, développement et effrandrement du 17e au 20e siècle: essai d'analyse d'un système politique' (unpublished).
Lonis, R. (1978) 'Les conditions de navigation sur la côte occidentale de l'Afrique dans l'antiquité: le problème du retour', in *Colloque: Afrique noire et monde méditerranéen dans l'antiquité* (Dakar: NEA).
Lopes, D. (1591): see Pigafetta, F. and Lopes, D.
Lopez, R. S. (1974) *La révolution commerciale dans l'Europe médiévale* (Paris: Aubier-Montaigne).
Lovejoy, P. E. (1973), 'The Wangara impact on Kano', *KS*.
Lovejoy, P. E. (1978) 'The role of the Wangara in the economic transformation of the central Sudan in the fifteenth and sixteenth centuries', *JAH*, **19**, 2, pp. 173–93.
Lubogo, Y. K. (1960) *A history of the Basoga* (Nairobi: East Africa Literature Bureau).
Lucas, S. A. (1968) 'Baluba et Aruund: étude comparative des structures socio-politiques, 2 vols (doctoral dissertation, University of Paris).
Lukas, J. (1939) 'The linguistic research between Nile and Lake Chad', *Africa*–(L), **12**, 1, pp. 335–49.
Lwamgira, F. X. (1949) *Amakuru ga Kiziba*; 1969 Eng. transl., E. R. Kamuhangire, *The history of Kiziba and its kings* (Kampala: Makerere University College).
Ly-Tall, M. (1972) 'Quelques remarques sur le *Ta'rikh el-Fettach*', *BIFAN*, B, **34**, 3, pp. 471–93.
Ly–Tall, M. (1977) *Contribution à l'histoire de l'empire du Mali, (13e–16e siècles): limites, principales provinces, institutions politiques* (Dakar: NEA).
Ly-Tall, M. (1981) 'Quelques précisions sur les relations entre l'empire du Mali et du Gabu', in *Colloque international sur les traditions orales du Gabu, 1980* (*Ethiopiques*, numéro spécial, October 1981), pp. 124–8.

McCall, D. F. (1968) 'Kisra, Chosroes, Christ', *AHS*, **1**, 2, pp. 255–77.
MacGaffey, W. (1970) 'The religious commissions of the Bakongo', *MAN*, **5**, 1, pp. 27–38.
McIntosh, R. J. (1980): see Keech, S. and McIntosh, R. J.
McIntosh, R. J. and McIntosh, S. K. (1981) 'The inland Niger delta before the empire of Mali: evidence from Jenne-Jeno', *JAH*, **22**, 1, pp. 1–22.

MacMichael, H. A. (1920) 'The Tungur-Fur of Dar Furnung', *SNR*, **3**, 1, pp. 24–72.
MacMichael, H. A. (1922) *A history of the Arabs in the Sudan, and some account of the people who preceded them and of the tribes inhabiting Darfūr*, 2 vols (London: CUP).
MacMichael, H. A. (1967) *The tribes of northern and central Kordofan* (London: Cass).
al-Madani, A. T. (1972) *Harb al-thalathmi' a sanat bayna al-Djaza'ir wa Isbaniyya 1492–1792* (Algiers).
Magalhães Godinho, V. de: see Godinho, V. de Magalhães
Maggs, T. M. O'C. (1976a) *Iron Age communities of the southern Highveld* (Pietermaritzburg: Council of the Natal Museum; Occasional publication, 2).
Maggs, T. M. O'C. (1976b) 'Iron Age patterns and Sotho history of the southern Highveld: South Africa', *WA*, **7**, 3, pp. 318–32.
al-Maghīlī, Muḥammad b. 'Abd al-Karīm (*c.* 1490), untitled treatise written for Askiya Muḥammad of Gao; 1932 Eng. transl. T. H. Baldwin, *The obligations of princes: an essay of Moslem kingship* (Beirut: Imprimerie catholique); 1975 partial French transl. in J. Cuoq (q.v.), pp. 398–432.
Mahefamanana, M. (1965) *Ali-Tawarath sy Madagasikara 1495–1548* (Tananarive: Imp. Iarivo).
Mahjoubi, A. (1966) 'Nouveau témoignage épigraphique sur la communauté chrétienne de Kairouan au 11e siècle', *Africa* (Tunis), pp. 85–96.
Maḥmūd Ka'ti: see Ka'ti, Maḥmūd
Mainga, M. (1973) *Bulozi under the Luyana kings: political evolution and state formation in pre-colonial Zambia* (London: Longman).
al-Makkarī, Abu 'l-'Abbās Aḥmad b. Muḥammad (17th cent.) *Nafḥ al-Ṭīb min Ghuṣn al-Andalūs al-Ratīb . . .*; 1949 edn, 10 vols (Cairo); 1840, 1843 Eng. transl. P. de Gayangos, *The history of the Mohammedan dynasties in Spain*, 2 vols (London: Oriental translation fund of Great Britain and Ireland); 1855, 1861, French transl. R. Dozy *et al.*, *Annalectes sur l'histoire et la littérature des arabes d'espagne*, 2 vols (Leiden: Brill).
al-Makrīzī, Abu 'l-'Abbās Aḥmad b. 'Alī (before 1442) MS (a) 'al-Khbar an adjnas al-Sudan' (MSS, Arabic 1744, folio 194v–195r) (Paris: Bibliothèque Nationale).
al-Makrīzī, Abu 'l-'Abbās Aḥmad b. 'Alī (before 1442) MS (b) 'al-Khbar an adjnas al-Sudan' (MSS, Cod. Or 372a, folio 339v–340r) Leiden: Rijksuniversität Bibliothek); 1820 ed. and Latin transl. H. A. Hamaker, *Specimen catalogi codicum Mss. orientalium bibliothecae Academiae lugduno-batavae* (Leiden: Luchtmans); 1979 French transl. D. Lange, 'Un texte de Makrīzī sur les "races du Soudan"', *Annales islamologiques*, **15**, pp. 187–209.
al-Makrīzī, Abu 'l–'Abbās Aḥmad b. 'Alī (before 1442) *Macrizi historia regum islamiticorum in Abyssinia*, 1790 ed. and Latin transl. F. T. Rinck (Leiden: Luchtmans).
al-Makrīzī, Abu 'l-'Abbās Aḥmad b. 'Alī (before 1442) *al-Ilmām bi akhbar man bi-arḍ al-Ḥabasha min mulūk al-Islam* 1895 edn (Cairo).
al-Makrīzī, Abu 'l-'Abbās Aḥmad b. 'Alī (before 1442) *Kitāb al-Sulūk li-ma 'rifa duwal al-mulūk*; 1934, 1956 edn (Cairo).
al-Makrīzī, Abu 'l-'Abbās Aḥmad b. 'Alī (before 1442) *al-Dhahab al-masbūk fī dhikr man ḥadjdja . . .*; 1955 edn (Cairo); 1975 partial French transl., *Les Pèlerinages des sultans du Takrūr* in J. M. Cuoq (q.v.), pp. 390–3.
Mâle, E. (1923) 'Les Influences arabes dans l'art roman', *RDM*, ser. 13, **18**, pp. 311–43.
Mālik b. Anas (8th cent.) *Kitāb al-Muwaṭṭa'*; 1962, 1967, edn with commentary, *Muwaṭṭa' 'l-Imām Mālik* (Cairo).
Malowist, M. (1966) 'Le Commerce d'or et d'esclaves au Soudan occidental', *AB*, **4**, pp. 49–72.
Malowist, M. (1969a) 'Les Débuts au système de plantations dans la période des grandes découvertes dans l'ile de St Thomas', *AB*, **10**, pp. 9–30.
Malowist, M. (1969b) *Europa a Afryka Zachodina w dobie wczesnej ekspansji kolonialnej* (Warsaw: Panstwowe Wydawnictwo Naukowe).
Malowist, M. (1970) 'Quelques observations sur le commerce de l'or dans le monde occidental au Moyen-Age', *AESC*, **25**, pp. 1630–6.
Mané, M. (1978) 'Contribution à l'histoire du Kaabu, des origines au 19e siècle', *BIFAN*, B, **40**, 1, pp. 87–159.
Mané, M. (1981) 'Les origines et la formation du Kaabu,' in *Colloque international sur les traditions orales du Gabu, 1980* (*Ethiopiques*, numéro spécial, October 1981), pp. 93–104.
Manessy, G. (1963) 'Rapport sur les langues voltaïques', in *Actes du 2e Colloque international de linguistique négro-africaine, Dakar, 1962*, pp. 239–66 (no further details available).
Manoukian, M. (1951) *Tribes of Northern Territories of the Gold Coast* (London: IAI; Ethnographic survey of Africa: Western Africa), p. 5.
Maquet, J. J. P. (1961) *The premise of inequality in Ruanda: a study of political relations in a Central African Kingdom* (London: OUP for IAI).
Marc, L. F. (1909) *Le Pays mossi* (Paris: Larose).

Marçais, G. (1913) *Les Arabes en Berbérie du 11e au 14e siècle* (Constantine/Paris: Leroux).
Marçais, G. (1950) *Tlemcen* (Paris: Renouard; Les Villes d'art célèbres).
Marçais, G. (1954) *Architecture musulmane d'Occident: Tunisie, Algérie, Maroc* (Paris: Arts et Métiers Graphiques).
Marees, P. de (1602) Dutch edn; 1605 French transl., *Description et récit historique du riche royaume d'or de Guinée* ... (Amsterdam: Claessen); 1605 abridged Eng. Transl., *Description and historical declaration of the golden kingdom of Guinea.*
Maret, P. de (1977) 'Sanga: new excavations, mode data and some related problems', *JAH*, **18**, 3, pp. 321–37
Maret, P. de and Msuka, F. (1977) 'History of Bantu metallurgy: some linguistic aspects', *Africana Linguistica*, **4**, pp. 43–66.
Maret, P. de, van Noten, F. and Cahen, D. (1977) 'Radiocarbon dates from West Central Africa: a synthesis', *JAH*, **18**, 4, pp. 481–505.
Marks, S. (1969) 'The traditions of the natal Nguni: a second look at the work of A. T. Bryant', in L. M. Thompson, *African societies in Southern Africa* (London: Heinemann), pp. 126–44.
Mármol Carvajal, L. del (1667) *L'Afrique de Marmol*, tr. N. Perrot, 3 vols (Paris: Billaine).
Marquart, J. (1913) *Die Benin-Sammlung des Reichsmuseums für Völkerkunde in Leiden* (Leiden: Brill; Veröffentlichungen des Reichsmuseums für Völkerkunde in Leiden, Ser. 2, 7).
al-Marrākushī: see: Ibn 'Idhārī al-Marrākushī
Martin, B. G. (1969) 'Kanem, Bornu and the Fezzan: notes on the political history of a trade route', *JAH*, **10**, 1, pp. 15–27.
Martin, P. (1972) *The external trade of the Loango coast, 1576–1870: the effects of changing commercial relations on the Vili kingdom of Loango* (Oxford: Clarendon Press).
Martini, R. (13th cent.) *Pugio fidei adversus Mauros et Judaeos*; 1687 edn (Leipzig, Frankfurt); 1872 (Paris: Sciaparelli); 1968 edn (Farnborough: Gregg).
Martini, R. (13th cent.) 'Vocabulista in arabico', MSS (Florence: Biblioteca Riccardiana).
Mashafa Senkesar (1928) *The book of the saints of the Ethiopian Church*, Eng. transl. E. A. Wallis Budge, 4 vols (London: CUP).
Mas Latrie, L. de (1866) *Traités de paix et de commerce et documents divers concernant les relations des chrétiens avec les Arabes de l'Afrique septentrionale au Moyen Age* (Paris: Plon).
Mas Latrie, L. de (1886) *Relations et commerce de l'Afrique septentrionale ou Maghreb avec les nations chrétiennes* (Paris: Firmin-Didot).
Mason, M. D. (1970–1) 'The Nupe kingdom in the nineteenth century: a political history' (doctoral dissertation, Birmingham University).
Mason, R. (1962) *Prehistory of the Transvaal, a record of human activity* (Johannesburg: Witwatersrand University).
Mason, R. J. (1973) 'Early Iron Age settlements of Southern Africa', *SAJS*, **69**, pp. 324–6.
Massignon, L. (1906) *Le Maroc dans les premières années du 16e siècle: tableau géographique d'après Leon l'Africain* (Alger: Jourdan).
al-Mas'ūdī, Abu 'l-Ḥassan 'Alī b. al-Ḥusayn b. 'Alī (10th cent.) *Murūdj al-dhahab*; 1861–77 ed. and French transl. C. Barbier de Meynard and J. Pavet de Courteille, *Les Prairies d'or*, 9 vols (Paris: Imprimerie impériale); 1962–71, French transl. C. Pellat, *Les Prairies d'or* (Paris: Société asiatique); partial French transl. in J. Cuoq (q. v.), pp. 59–62.
Mathew, G. (1951) 'Islamic merchant cities of East Africa', *Times*, 26th June, p. 5.
Mathew, G. (1953) 'Recent discoveries in East African archaeology', *Antiquity*, **27**, 108, pp. 212–18.
Mathew, G. (1956) 'Chinese porcelain in East Africa and on the coast of south Arabia', *OA*, n.s., **2**, 2, pp. 50–5.
Mathew, G. (1958) 'The East Coast cultures', *South Africa*, **2**, pp. 59–62.
Matiyela (1979) 'Port St John's Iron Age sites', *NAk*, **14**, pp. 51 ff.
Matveiev, V. V. (1971) 'Zaniatiia vostochnykh bantu (zindzhei v X–XIII vv.: Les métiers des Zendjs est-africains pendant les 10e–12e siècles', in *Africana Etnografiia, istoriia, izzyki narodov Afriki*) (Leningrad; Akademiia nauk SSSR. Trudy Instituta etnografii im. N. N. Miklukho-Maklaia, n.s., **96**; Afrikanskii etnograficheskii sbornik, **8**).
Matveiev, V. V. and Kubbel, L. E. (1965) *Arabskie istochniki X–XII vekov*. Podgotovka tekstov i perevody V. V. Matveieva i L. E. Kubbelia (Moscow: Nauka; Drevnie i srednevekovye istochniki po etnografii i istorii narodov Afriki iuzhnee Sakhary, 2).
Mauny, R. (1948) 'L'Afrique occidentale d'après les auteurs arabes anciens', *NA*, **6**, 40, p. 6.
Mauny, R. (1949) 'L'expédition marocaine d'Ouadane (Mauritanie), vers 1543–1544', *BIFAN*, B, **11**, pp. 129–40.
Mauny, R. (1950) 'Les Prétendues Navigations dieppoises à la côte occidentale d'Afrique au 14e siècle', *BIFAN*, B, **12**, pp. 122–34.

Mauny, R. (1957) 'Etat actuel de nos connaissances sur la préhistoire et l'archéologie de la Haute-Volta', *NA*, **73**, pp. 16–24.
Mauny, R. (1960) *Les Navigations médiévales sur les côtes sahariennes antérieures à la découverte portugaise, 1434* (Lisbon: Centro de estudos históricos ultramarinos).
Mauny, R. (1961) *Tableau géographique de l'Ouest africain au Moyen Age d'après les sources écrites, la tradition orale et l'archéologie* (Dakar: IFAN; Mémoires, 61).
Mauny, R. (1963) 'Poteries engobées et peintes de tradition nilotique de la région de Koro Toro (Tchad)', *BIFAN*, B, **25**, 1–2, pp. 39–46.
Mauny, R. (1965) 'Navigations arabes anonymes aux Canaries au 12e siècle', *NA*, **106**, p. 61.
Mauny, R. (1971) 'Hypothèses concernant les relations pré-colombiennes entre l'Afrique et l'Amérique', *AEA*, **17**, pp. 369–84.
Mayers, W. F. (1874–6) 'Chinese explorations of the Indian Ocean during the fifteenth century', *China Review*, **3**, 2, pp. 219–331; **4**, pp. 61–7, 173–90.
M'Baye, E. H. R. (1972) 'Un Aperçu de l'Islam ou: réponses d' al-Magili aux questions, posées par Askia El-Hadj Muhammad, empereur de Gâo', *BIFAN*, B, **34**, 1–2, pp. 237–67.
Médeiros, F. de (1973) 'Recherches sur l'image des noirs dans l'occident médiéval, 13–15e siècles' (doctoral dissertation, University of Paris).
Méditerranée et Océan Indien (1970) *Travaux du sixième colloque international d'histoire maritime*, Venice, 1962 (Paris: SEVPEN).
Meek, C. K. (1925) *The northern tribes of Nigeria: an ethnological account of the northern provinces of Nigeria together with a report on the 1921 decennial census*, 2 vols (London: OUP).
Meek, C. K. (1931a) *A Sudanese kingdom: an ethnographical study of the Jukun-speaking peoples of Nigeria* (London: Kegan Paul, Trench, Trubner).
Meek, C. K. (1931b) *Tribal studies in northern Nigeria*, 2 vols (London: Kegan Paul, Trench, Trubner).
Meillassoux, C. (ed.) (1971) *The development of indigenous trade and markets in West Africa: studies presented at the 10th International African Seminar, 1969* (London: IAI).
Meillassoux, C. (ed.) (1975) *Esclavage en Afrique précoloniale* (Paris: Maspero).
Meillassoux, C., Doucouré, L. and Simagha, D. (eds) (1967) *Légende de la dispersion des Kusa (épopee soninké)* (Dakar: IFAN; Initiations et études africaines, 22).
Menéndez Pidal, R. (1941) *Poesía árabe y poesía europea* (Buenos Aires: Espasa-Calpe Argentina).
Merad, A. (1957) '"Abd al-Mu'min à la conquête de l'Afrique du nord, 1130–1163', *AIEOA*, **15**, pp. 109–63.
Merad, A. (1960–1) 'Origine et voies du réformisme en Islam', *AIEOA*, **17–19**, pp. 359–402.
Merad, A. (1962) *AIEOA*, **20**, 2, pp. 419 ff.
Meyerhof, M. (1935) 'Esquisse d'histoire de la pharmacologie et botanique chez les musulmans d'Espagne', *al-Andalus*, **3**, pp. 1–41.
Michalowski, K. (1965) 'La Nubie chrétienne', *AB*, **3**, pp. 9–26.
Michalowski, K. (1967) *Faras, die Kathedrale aus dem Wüstensand* (Zürich: Benzinger).
Mieli, A. (1966) *La Science arabe et son rôle dans l'évolution scientifique mondiale* (Leiden: Brill).
Miers, S. and Kopytoff, I. (eds) (1977) *Slavery in Africa: historical and anthropological perspectives* (Madison: University of Wisconsin Press).
Mille, A. (1970) *Contribution à l'étude des villages fortifiés de l'Imérina ancien*, 2 vols (Tananarive: Musée d'art et d'archéologie; Travaux et documents, 2–3).
Mille, A. (1971) 'Anciens horizons d'Ankatso', *Taloha*, **4**, pp. 117–26.
Miller, J. C. (1972a) 'The Imbangala and the chronology of early central African history', *JAH*, **13**, 4, pp. 549–74.
Miller, J. C. (1972b) 'Kings and kinsmen: the Imbangala impact on the Mbundu of Angola' (doctoral dissertation, University of Wisconsin).
Miller, J. C. (1972c) 'A note on Kasanze and the Portuguese', *CJAS*, **6**, 1, pp. 43–6.
Miller, J. C. (1973) 'Requiem for the Jaga', *CEA*, **49**, pp. 121–49.
Miller, J. C. (1976) *Kings and Kinsmen: early Mbundu states in Angola* (Oxford: Clarendon Press).
Miller, K. (1926–31) *Mappae Arabicae; arabische Welt- und Länderkarten des 9–13. Jahrhunderts in arabischer Ursschrift*, 6 vols (Stuttgart).
Millot, C. (1912) 'Les Ruines de Mahilaka', *BAM*, **10**, pp. 283–8.
Miquel, A. (1967–75) *La Géographie humaine du monde musulman jusqu'au milieu du 11e siècle* (Paris: Mouton; Civilisations et Sociétés, 7, 37).
Miracle, M. P. (1963) 'Interpretation of evidence on the introduction of maize into West Africa', *Africa*-(L), **33**, pp. 132–5.
Miracle, M. P. (1965) 'The introduction and spread of maize in Africa', *JAH*, **6**, 1, pp. 39–55.
Mischlich, A. (1903) 'Beiträge zur Geschichte der Haussastaaten', *MSOS*: Afrikanische Studien, **6**, pp. 137–242.

Misiugin, V. M. (1966) 'Suakhiliiskaia khronika srednevekovnogo gosudarstva Pate: La Chronique swahili de l'état médiéval du Paté', in *Africana. Kul'tura i iazyki narodov Afriki* (Moscow: Akademiia nauk SSSR. Trudy Instituta etnograffii im. N. N. Miklukho-Maklaia. n.s., **90**, Afrikanskii etnograficheskii sbornik, **6**), pp. 52–83.

Misiugin, V. M. (1971) 'Zamechaniia k starosuakhiliiskoi pis'mennosti: Notes sur l'écriture ancienne Souahéli', in: *Africana. Etnografiia, istoriia, iazyki narodov Afriki* (Leningrad: Akademiia nauk SSSR. Trudy Instituta etnograffii im. N. N. Miklukho-Maklaia. n.s. **96**; Afrikanskii etnograficheskii sbornik, **8**), pp. 100–15.

Misiugin, V. M. (1972) 'K voprosu o proiskhozhdenii moreplavaniia: sudostroeniia v indiiskom okeane: Contribution à la question de l'origine de la navigation et de la construction navale dans l'Océan Indien', in *Soobshchenie ob issledovanii protoindiiskikh tekstov* (Moscow: Akademiia nauk SSSR. Trudy Instituta etnografii im. N. N. Miklukho-Maklaia).

Mollat, M. (1972) '"Le Passage" de Saint Louis à Tunis: sa place dans l'histoire des croisades', *RHES*, **50**, 3, pp. 289–303.

Mollat, M. (1980) 'Historical contacts of Africa and Madagascar with south and south-east Asia: the role of the Indian ocean' in Unesco (1980a), q.v., pp. 45–60.

Monchicourt, C. (1939) *Etudes kairouanaises: Kairouan et les Chabbia, 1450–1592* (Tunis).

Mones, H. (1962), 'Le Malékisme et l'échec des Fatimides en Ifrikya', in: *Etudes d'orientalisme dédiées à la mémoire d'E. Lévi-Provençal*, 2 vols (Paris: Maisonneuve et Larose).

Monlaü, J. (1964) *Les Etats barbaresques* (Paris: PUF; Que sais-je 1097).

Monneret de Villard, U. (1938) *Storia della Nubia cristiana* (Rome; Pontificium Institutum Orientalium Studiorum Orientalia christiana analecta, 118).

Monneret de Villard, U. (1944) *Lo studio dell'Islam in Europa nel 12 e nel 13 secolo* (Vatican City: Biblioteca Vaticana; Studi e testi, 110).

Montagne, R. (1930) *Les Berbères et le makhzen dans le sud du Maroc: essai sur la transformation politique des Berbères sédentaires (groupe chleuh)* (Paris: Alcan).

Monteil, C. (1929) 'Les Empires du Mali: étude d'histoire et de sociologie soudanaise', *BCEHSAOF*, **12**, 3–4, pp. 291–444; 1968 edn, *Les Empires du Mali* (Paris: Maisonneuve et Larose).

Monteil, C. (1951) 'Problèmes du Soudan occidental: Juifs et Judaisés', *Hespéris*, **38**, pp. 265–98.

Monteil, V. (1964) *L'Islam noir* (Paris: Seuil).

Monteil, V. (1966) *Esquisses sénégalaises: Wâlo, Kayor, Dyolof, Mourides, un visionnaire* (Dakar: IFAN; Initiations et études africaines, 21).

Monteil, V. (1968) 'Al-Bakri (Cordoue, 1068). Routier de l'Afrique blanche et noire du nord-ouest', *BIFAN*, B, **30**, 1, pp. 39–116.

Monteiro, A. (1970) 'Vestiges archéologiques du cap Delgado et de Quisiva: (Mozambique)', *Taloha*, pp. 155–64.

Moorsel, H. van (1968) *Atlas de préhistoire de la plaine de Kinshasa* (Kinshasa: University of Lovanium).

Morris, H. F. (1962) *A history of Ankole* (Nairobi: East African Literature Bureau).

Mufaḍḍal b. Abī 'l-Faḍā'il (Mufazzal) (14th cent.) 1973–4 French transl. E. Blochet, *Histoire des sultans mamelouks* (Turnhout: Brepols; Patrologia orientalis, **12**, 3; **14**, 3; **20**, 1).

Muḥammad al-Uḳbani al-Tilimsānī (n.d.) *Tuḥfat al-nāzir*; 1967 ed. A. Chenoufi, 'Un Traité de ḥisba', *BEO*, **19**, pp. 133–344.

Muḥammad b. Khalīl, Ibn Ghalbūn (n.d.) *Ta'rīkh Tarābulus al-Gharb*; 1930 edn (Cairo); 1970 ed. Mahmad Naji (Benghazi).

Muḥammad Bello, M. (n.d.) *Infāḳ al-Maysūr*; 1922 ed. and transl. E. J. Arnett, *The rise of the Sokoto Fulani* (Kano: Emirate Printing Department).

Munthe, L. (1977) 'La Tradition écrite arabo-malgache: un aperçu sur les manuscrits existants', *BSOAS*, **40**, 1, pp. 96–109.

Murdock, G. P. (1959) *Africa: its peoples and their culture history* (New York: McGraw-Hill).

Musa, I. U. A. (1969) 'Tanẓīmāt al-muwaḥḥidīn wa-nuzumhum fī 'l Maghrib', *Abhath*, **33**, 1.4, pp. 53–89 (dissertation, American University of Beirut).

Mworoha, E. (1977) *Peuples et rois de l'Afrique des lacs au 19e siècle: le Burundi et les royaumes voisins* (Abidjan: NEA).

Nachtigal, G. (1879, 1881, 1889) *Sahara und Sudan: Ergebnisse sechsjahriger Reisen in Afrika*, Vols 1 and 2 (Berlin: Weidmann), Vol. 3 (Leipzig: Brockhaus); 1967 reprint (Graz: Akademie Drüker); 1971, 1974 (in progress) Eng. transl. A. G. B. and H. J. Fisher (London).

Nadel, S. F. (1942) *A black Byzantium: the kingdom of Nupe in Nigeria* (London/New York: OUP for the Institute of African Languages and Cultures).

al-Naqar, U. A. (1971) 'The historical background to "the Sudan Road"', in Y. F. Hasan (ed.), *Sudan in Africa* (Khartoum: Khartoum University Press), pp. 98–108.
Ndoricimpa, L., *et al.* (1981) 'Technologie et économie du sel végétal au Burundi', in *La Civilisation ancienne des peuples des grands lacs; colloque de Bujumbura* (Paris: Karthala, Centre de civilisation burundaise), pp. 408–16.
Nelli, R. (ed.) (1960) *Les Troubadours* (Paris: Desclée de Brouwer).
Neufville, R. de and Houghton, A. A. (1965) 'A description of Ain Farah and of Wara', *Kush*, **13**, pp. 195–204.
Nganwa, K. K. (1948) *Abakozire eby'okutangaza omuri Ankole* ... (Nairobi: Eagle Press).
Ngcongco, L. (1980) 'Problems of Southern African historiography', in Unesco (1980b), q.v.
Niane, D. T. (1960; 2nd edn 1971) *Soundjata ou l'épopée mandingue* (Paris: Présence africaine).
Niane, D. T. (1975) *Recherches sur l'empire du Mali au Moyen Age*, followed by *Mise en place des populations de la Haute-Guinée* (Paris: Présence africaine).
Nicolas, G. (1969) 'Fondements magico-religieux du pouvoir au sein de la principauté hausa du Gobir', *JSA*, **39**, 2, pp. 199–231.
Nicolas, G. (1979) 'La question du Gobir', Paper presented to the Zaria Seminar on the history of central Sudan before 1804.
Niven, C. R. (1957) 'Nigeria: past and present', *AA*, **56**, 225, pp. 265–74.
Noten, F. van (1968) *The Uelian: a culture with a neolithic aspect, Uele Basin (N.E. Congo Republic): an archaeological study* (Tervuren: Annales du musée royal de l'Afrique centrale, série in octavo: sciences humaines, 64).
Noten, F. van (1972) 'La plus ancienne sculpture sur bois de l'Afrique centrale', *A–T*, **18**, 3–4, pp. 133–6.
Nougarède, M. P. (1964) 'Qualités nautiques des voies arabes', in *Océan Indien et Méditerranée; actes du sixième colloque international d'histoire maritime Lourenço Marques, 1962* (Paris: SEVPEN), pp. 95–122.
Nurse, D. (1974) 'A linguistic sketch of the north-east Bantu languages with particular reference to Chaga history', (doctoral dissertation, University of Dar es Salaam).
Nurse, D. (**1979**) *Classification of the Chaga dialects: languages and history on Kilimanjaro, the Taita Hills, and the Pare Mountains* (Hamburg: Buske).
Nurse, D. and Phillipson, D. W. (1974) 'The north-eastern Bantu languages of Tanzania and Kenya: a classification' (University of Dar es Salaam).
Nyakatura, J. (1936–7) 'Abakama ba Bunyoro-Kitara', *UJ*, **3**, 1, pp. 155–60; **4**, 1, pp. 75–83; **5**, 2, pp. 53–69.
Nyakatura, J. (1947) *Abakama ba Bunyoro Kitara* (St Justin, P.Q., Canada: White Fathers Society); 1973 edn and transl., *Abakama ba Bunyoro-Kitara: The Kings of Bunyoro-Kitara* (Garden City: Anchor Press).

L'Occidente e l'Islam nell'alto medievo (1965) 2 vols (Spoleto: Centro Italiano di Studi sull'Alto Medievo).
O'Fahey, R. S. (1974) 'The Sudan papers of the Rev. Dr A. J. Arkell', *SNR*, **55**, pp. 172–4.
O'Fahey, R. S. (1977) 'The office of Qadi in Darfur: a preliminary inquiry', *BSOAS*, **40**, 1, pp. 110–24.
Ogot, B. A. (1967) *A history of the southern Luo*, Vol. 1: *Migration and settlement, 1500–1900* (Nairobi: EAPH).
Ogot, B. A. and Kieran, J. A., (eds) (1968) *Zamani: a survey of East African history* (Nairobi: EAPH).
Olbrechts, F. M. (1941) *Bijdrage tot de kennis van de chronologie der afrikaansche plastiek* (Brussels: Van Campenhout; Mémoires de l'Académie royale des sciences d'outre-mer, classe des sciences morales et politiques, **10**, 2).
Olderogge, D. A. (1960) *Zapadnyi Sudan v piatnadtsatykh deviatnadtsatykh vv* (The western Sudan in the sixteenth-nineteenth centuries) (Moscow: Nauk).
Oliver, R. (1953) 'A question about the Bachwezi', *UJ*, **17**, 2, pp. 135–7.
Oliver, R. (1955) 'The traditional histories of Ankole, Buganda and Bunyoro', *JRAI*, **85**, 1–2, pp. 111–18.
Oliver, R. (1959) 'Ancient capital sites of Ankole', *UJ*, **23**, 1, pp. 51–63.
Oliver, R. (1962) 'Reflections on the sources of evidence for the precolonial history of East Africa', in *The historian in tropical Africa* (London/Ibadan/Accra: OUP for IAI), pp. 305–21.
Oliver, R. (1966) 'The problem of the Bantu expansion', *JAH*, **7**, 3, pp. 361–76.
Oliver, R. and Mathew, G. (eds) (1963–76) *History of East Africa*, 3 vols (Oxford: Clarendon Press).
Ottenberg, S. (1961) 'Present state of Igbo studies', *JHSN*, **2**, 2, pp. 211–30.

Ottino, P. (1974a) 'La Hiérarchie sociale et l'alliance dans le royaume de Matacassi des 16e et 17e siècles', *Tantara*, 1, pp. 52–105.
Ottino, P. (1974b) *Madagascar, les Comores et le sud-ouest de l'Océan indien: projet d'enseignement et de recherches* (Antananarivo: Centre d'anthropologie culturelle et sociale).
Ottino, P. (1975) *Le Moyen Age de l'Océan indien et le peuplement de Madagascar* (Ile de la Réunion).
Ozanne, P. (1969) 'Atmospheric radiocarbon', *WAAN*, **11**, pp. 9–11.

Pacheco Pereira, D. (1505–6) *Esmeraldo de situ orbis*; 1905 ed. A. Epiphanio da Silva Dias (Lisbon: Typ. Universal); 1937 ed. and Eng. transl. G. H. T. Kimble (London: Hakluyt Society); 1954 ed. D. Peres (Lisbon: Typ. Universal); 1956 French transl. R. Mauny (Bissau: Publicações do Centro de estudos da Guiné portuguêsa, 19).
Paden, J. N. (1973) *Religion and political culture in Kano* (Berkeley: University of California Press).
Pageard, R. (1962a) 'Contribution critique à la chronologie historique de l'ouest africain, suivie d'une traduction des "tables chronologiques" de Barth', *JSA*, **32**, 1, pp. 91–117.
Pageard, R. (1962b) 'Réflexions sur l'histoire des Mossi', *L'Homme*, **2**, 1, pp. 111–15.
Pageard, R. (1963) 'Recherches sur les Nioniossé', *EV*, **4**, pp. 5–71.
Pagès, A. (1933) *Au Ruanda, sur les bords du lac Kivu (Congo belge). Un royaume hamite au centre de l'Afrique* (Brussels: Memoires de l'Académie royale des sciences d'outre-mer, classes des sciences morales et politiques, 1).
Palmer, H. R. (ed.) (1909) 'The Kano Chronicle', *JAI*, **38**, pp. 58–98; reprinted in H. R. Palmer, (1928), q.v., Vol. 3, pp. 97–132.
Palmer, H. R. (1914, 1915) 'An early Fulani conception of Islam', *JAS*, **13**, pp. 407–14; **15**, pp. 53–9, 185–92.
Palmer, H. R. (1927) 'History of Katsina', *JAS*, **26**, pp. 216–36.
Palmer, H. R. (1928) *Sudanese memoirs: being mainly translations of a number of Arabic manuscripts relating to the central and western Sudan*, 3 vols (Lagos: Government Printer); 1967 edn (London: Cass).
Palmer, H. R. (ed.) (1932): see Ibn Furṭūwa, Aḥmad
Palmer, H. R. (1936) *The Bornu, Sahara and Sudan* (London: Murray).
Pannetier, J. (1974) 'Archéologie des pays Antambahoaka et Antaimoro', *Taloha*, **6**, pp. 53–71.
Papadopoulos, T. (1966) *Africanabyzantina: Byzantine influences on Negro-Sudanese cultures* (Athens: Grapheion Demosieymaton Akademias Athenon; Pragmateiai tēs Akademias Athenon, 27).
Pardo, A. W. (1971) 'The Songhay empire under Sonni Ali and Askia Muhammade: a study in comparison and contrasts', in D. F. McCall and N. R. Bennett (eds), *Aspects of West African Islam* (Boston: African Studies Center, Boston University, Papers on Africa, 5), pp. 41–59.
Paul, A. (1955) 'Aidhab: a medieval Red Sea port', *SNR*, **36**, pp. 64–70.
Paulme, D. (1956–7) 'L'Afrique noire jusqu'au 14e siècle', *CHM*, **3**, 2, pp. 277–301; 3, pp. 561–81.
Pauwels, M. (1967) 'Le Bushiru et son Muhinza ou roitelet Hutu', *AL*, **31**, pp. 205–322.
Pearce, S. and Posnansky, M. (1963) 'The re-excavation of Nzongezi rock shelter, Ankole', *UJ*, **27**, 1, pp. 85–94.
Peires, J. B. (1973) *Chronology of the Cape Nguri till 1900* (Madison: University of Wisconsin Press).
Pelliot, P. (1933) 'Les Grands Voyages maritimes chinois', T'oung Pao, **30**, pp. 237–452.
Penn, A. E. D. (1931) 'The ruins of Zamkor', *SNR*, **14**, pp. 179–84.
Peres, D. (1960) *Historia dos descobrimentos portuguêses*, 2nd edn (Coimbra: Ediçào do autor).
Perez-Embid, F. (1969) 'Navegacion y commercio en el puerto de Sevilla en la Baja Edad Media', in *Les routes de l'Atlantique: travaux du 9e colloque international d'histoire maritime* (Paris: SEVPEN), pp. 43–96.
Perrot, C. (1974) 'Ano Asema: mythe et histoire', *JAH*, **15**, 2, pp. 199–222.
Perruchon, J. (1889) 'Histoire des guerres d'Amda Seyou, roi d'Ethiopie', *JA*, série 8, **14**, pp. 271–493.
Perruchon, J. (1893) 'Notes pour l'histoire d'Ethiopie: lettre adressée par le roi d'Ethiopie au roi Georges de Nubie sous le patriarcat de Philothée (981–1002 ou 3)', *RS*, **1**, pp. 71–6.
Perruchon, J. (1894) 'Histoire d'Eskender, d'Amda-Seyou II et de Na'od, rois d'Ethiopie', *JA*, serie 9 3, pp. 319–84.
Person, Y. (1961) 'Les Kissi et leurs statuettes de pierre dans le cadre de l'histoire ouest africaine', *BIFAN*, B, **23**, 1, pp. 1–59.
Person, Y. (1962) 'Le Moyen Niger au 15e siècle d'après les documents européens', *NA*, **78**, pp. 45–57.
Person, Y. (1968) *Samori; une révolution dyula*, 3 vols (Dakar: IFAN; Mémoire, 80 ...).
Person, Y. (1970) chapter in H. J. Deschamps (ed.), *Histoire générale de l'Afrique noire* (Paris: PUF), Vol. 1.

Person, Y. (1971) 'Ethnic movement and acculturation in Upper Guinea since the fifteenth century', *AHS*, **4**, 3, pp. 669–89.
Phillipson, D. W. (1968) 'The Early Iron Age in Zambia: regional variants and some tentative conclusions', *JAH*, **9**, 2, pp. 191–212.
Phillipson, D. W. (1974) 'Iron Age history and archaeology in Zambia', *JAH*, **15**, 1, pp. 1–25.
Phillipson, D. W. (1977) *The later prehistory of Eastern and Southern Africa* (London: Heinemann).
Pigafetta, F. and Lopes, D. (1591); 1881 Eng. transl. M. Hutchinson, *A report of the kingdom of Congo and the surrounding countries* (London: Murray), 1970 reprint (London: Cass); 1963, rev edn 1965, French transl. W. Bal, *Description du royaume de Congo* (Léopoldville/Kinshasa: University of Lovanium; Publication du Centre d'études des littératures romanes d'inspiration africaine, 4).
Poirier, C (1954) 'Terre d'Islam en mer malgache: (îlot Nosy Langany ou Nosy Manja)', *BAM*, no. spécial du cinquantenaire, pp. 71–116.
Polet, J. (1974) 'Feuilles d'enceinte à la Séguié', in Bonduku Seminar Papers, q.v.
Polet, J. (1976) 'Sondages archéologiques en pays éothilé: Assoco-Monobaha, Belibete et Anyanwa', *Godo-Godo*, **2**, pp. 111–39.
Polo, Marco (1955) *Description du monde* (Paris: Klincksieck).
Portères, R. (1955) 'L'Introduction du maïs en Afrique', *JATBA*, **2**, 5–6, pp. 221–31.
Posac Mon, C. (1959) 'Relaciones entre Genova y Ceuta durante el siglo XII', *Tamuda*, pp. 159–68.
Posnansky, M. (1966) 'Kingship, archaeology and historical myth', *UJ*, **30**, 1, pp. 1–12.
Posnansky, M. (1968) 'The excavation of an Ankole capital site at Bweyorere', *UJ*, **32**, 2, pp. 165–82.
Posnansky, M. (1971) 'East Africa and the Nile valley in early times', in Y. F. Hasan (ed.), *Sudan in Africa* (Khartoum: Khartoum University Press), pp. 51–61.
Posnansky, M. (1974) 'Archaeology and Akan civilisation', in Bonduku Seminar Papers, q.v.
Posnansky, M. (1975a) 'Archaeology, technology and Akan civilization', *JAS*, **3**, pp. 24–38.
Posnansky, M. (1975b) 'Redressing the balance: new perspectives in West African archaeology', *Sankofa*, **1**, 1, pp. 9–19.
Poulle, E. (1969) *Les Conditions de la navigation astronomique au 15e siècle* (Coimbra: Junta de investigações do Ultramar; Agrupamento de estudos de cartografia antiga: serie separata, 27).
Premier colloque international de Bamako (1975) Actes du colloque, *L'Empire du Mali, histoire et tradition orale* (Paris: Fondation SCOA pour la recherche scientifique en Afrique noire, Projet Boucle du Niger).
Princeps, J. (ed.) (1834–9) 'Extracts from the Mohi't, that is the Ocean, a Turkish work on navigation in the Indian seas', transl. J. von Hammer, *JRASB*, 1834, pp. 545–53; 1836, pp. 441–68; 1837, pp. 505–12; 1838, pp. 767–80; 1839, pp. 823–30.
Prins, A. H. J. (1961) *The Swahili speaking peoples of Zanzibar and the East African coast: Arabs, Shirazi and Swahili* (London: IAI; Ethnographic survey of Africa, East Central Africa, pt 12).
Prins, G. (1980) *The hidden hippopotamus: reappraisal in African history: the early colonial experience in western Zambia* (Cambridge: CUP).
Prost, A. (1953) 'Notes sur l'origine des Mossi', *BIFAN*, B, **15**, 2, pp. 1933–8.

Q: for Arabic names sometimes spelt with Q, see under Ḳ
Quatremère, E. M. (1811) *Mémoires géographiques et historiques sur l'Egypte et sur les contrées voisines*, 2 vols (Paris: Schoell).

Rabi, H. M. (1972) *The financial system of Egypt AH 564–741/*AD *1169–1341* (London: OUP; London Oriental Studies, 25).
Raffenel, A. (1846) *Voyage dans l'Afrique occidentale exécuté en 1843–1844*, 2 vols (Paris: Bertrand).
Raffenel, A. (1856) *Nouveau voyage dans le pay des nègres*, 2 vols (Paris: N. Chaix).
Rainihifina, J. (1975) *Lovantsaina*, 2 vols (Fianarantsoa: Ambozontany).
Rainitovo (1930) *Tantaran 'ny Malagasy manontolo* (Tananarive: Paoli).
Raison, J. P. (1972), 'Utilisation du sol et organisation de l'espace en Imérina ancienne', in *Etudes de géographie tropicale offertes à Pierre Gourou* (Paris/The Hague: Mouton), pp. 407–26.
Raison, J. P. and Vérin, P. (1968) 'Le site des subfossiles de Taolambiby, sud-ouest de Madagascar, doit-il être attribué à une intervention humaine?' *AUM*, 7, pp. 133–42.
Ralaimihoatra, G. (1969) 'Le Peuplement de l'Imérina', *BLPHGAM*, **1**, pp. 39–45.
Ralaimihoatra, G. (1971) 'Eléments de la connaissance des protomalgaches', *BAM*, **49**, 1, pp. 29–33.
Ramiandrasoa, F. (1968) 'Tradition orale et histoire: les Vazimba, le culte des ancêtres en Imérina du 16e au 19e siècle' (doctoral dissertation, University of Paris).
Ramiandrasoa, F. (1971) *Atlas historique du peuplement de Madagascar* (Antananarivo: University of Madagascar).

Ramilison, E. (1951–2) *Ny Loharanon 'ny Andriana manjaka teto Imerina*, 2 vols (Tananarive).
Ramon Marti: see Martini, R.
Randall-MacIver, D. and Mace, A. C. (1902) *El Amrah and Abydos*, pts 1–2 (London/Boston: Egypt Exploration Fund).
Randles, W. G. L. (1968) *L'Ancien Royaume du Congo, des origines à la fin du 19e siècle* (Paris: Mouton; Civilisations et sociétés, 14).
Randles, W. G. L. (1975) *L'Empire du Monomotapa du 15e au 19e siècle* (Paris: Mouton; Civilisations et sociétés, 46).
Ratsimbazafimahefa, P. (1971) *Le Fisakana: archéologie et couches culturelles.* (Tananarive: Musée d'art et d'archéologie de l'Université de Madagascar; Travaux et documents, 9).
Rattray, R. S. (1913) *Hausa folklore: customs and proverbs*, 2 vols (London: OUP); 1969 edn (New York: Negro University Press).
Rattray, R. S. (1929) *Ashanti law and constitution* (Oxford: Clarendon Press).
Rattray, R. S. (1932) *Tribes of the Ashanti hinterland* (Oxford: Clarendon Press), 2 vols.
Rau, V. (1967) 'Alfari mercanti in Portogallo dal 14 al 16 secolo: Economia e storia', *RISES*, pp. 447–56.
Rau, V. (1975) 'Notes sur la traite portugaise à la fin du 15e siècle et le florentin Bartolomeo di Domenico Marchioni', in *Miscellanea offerts à Charles Verlinden à l'occasion de ses trente ans de professorat* (Ghent), pp. 535–43.
Ravoajanahary, C. (1980) 'The settlement of Madagascar: two approaches', in Unesco (1980a), q.v., pp. 83–94.
Recueil de littérature mandingue (1980) (Paris: Agence de coopération culturelle et technique).
Redhouse, J. W. (1862) 'History of the journal of the events ... during seven expeditions ... against the tribes of Bulala', *JRAS*, **19**, pp. 43–123, 199–259.
Redmayne, A. (1968) 'The Hehe', in A. Roberts (ed.), *Tanzania before 1900* (Nairobi, EAPH), pp. 37–58.
Reefe, T. Q. (1975) *A history of the Luba empire to 1895* (doctoral dissertation, Berkeley University).
Reefe, T. Q. (1977) 'Traditions of genesis and the Luba diaspora', *HAJM*, **4**, pp. 183–206.
Reefe, T. Q. (1981) *The rainbow and the kings; a history of the Luba empire to 1891* (Berkeley: University Press).
Renan, E. (1866, 1925) *Averroes et l'averroisme: essai historique* (Paris: Calmann-Levy).
Rennie, J. K. (1972) 'The precolonial kingdom of Rwanda: a reinterpretation', *TJH*, **2**, 2, pp. 11–64.
Riad, M. (1960) 'The Jukun: an example of African migrations in the 16th century', *BIFAN*, B, **22**, 3, pp. 476–86.
Ribeiro, O. (1962) *Aspectos e problemas da expansão portuguesa* (Lisbon: Junta de investigações do Ultramar).
Richard, R. (1936) 'Le commerce de Berbérie et l'organisation économique de l'empire portugais aux 15e et 16e siècles', *AIEOA*, **2**, pp. 266–85.
Richard, R. (1955) *Etudes sur l'histoire des portugais au Maroc* (Coimbra).
Rigby, P. (1969) *Cattle and kinship among the Gogo: a semi-pastoral society of central Tanzania* (Ithaca: Cornell University Press).
Riley, C. L. (ed.) (1971) *Man across the sea: problems of pre-Colombian contacts* (Austin: University of Texas Press).
Robert, D., Robert, S. and Devisse, J. (1970) *Tegdaoust* (Paris: Arts et métiers graphiques).
Roberts, A. (1976) *A history of Zambia* (London: Heinemann).
Robineau, C. (1962) 'L'Islam aux Comores: une étude culturelle de l'île d'Anjouan', in P. Vérin (ed.), *Arabes et islamisés à Madagascar et dans l'Océan indien* (Tananarive: Revue de Madagascar), pp. 39–56.
Robson, J. A. (1959) 'The Catalan fleet and the Moorish sea power, 1337–1344', *EHR*, **74**, pp. 386–408.
Rockhill, W. W. (1915) 'Notes on the relations and trade of China with the eastern archipelago and the coast of the Indian Ocean during the fourteenth century, Ormuz, coast of Arabia and Africa', *T'oung Pao*, **15**, pp. 419–47; **16**, pp. 604–26.
Rodney, W. (1966) 'African slavery and other forms of social oppression on the Upper Guinea coast in the context of the Atlantic slave-trade', *JAH*, **7**, 3, pp. 431–43.
Rodney, W. (1970) *A history of Upper Guinea coast: 1545–1800* (Oxford: Clarendon Press).
Romains, J. (1963) *Donogoo* (Paris: Gallimard).
Romano, R., Tenenti, A. and Tucci, U. (1970) 'Venise et la route du Cap: 1499–1517', in *Méditerranée et Océan indien; actes du sixième colloque international d'histoire maritime* (Paris: SEVPEN), pp. 109–40.

Rombaka, J. P. (1957) *Tantaran-drazana Antaimoro-Anteony: Histoire d'Antemero Anteony* (Tananarive: Soarano).

Roncière, C. de la: see la Roncière, C. de

Rosenberger, B. (1964) 'Autour d'une grande mine d'argent du Moyen Age marocain: le Jebel Aouam', *H-T*, **5**, pp. 15–78.

Rosenberger, B. (1970) 'Les Vieilles Exploitations minières et les centres métallurgiques du Maroc: essai de carte historique', *RGM*, **17**, pp. 71–107; **18**, pp. 59–102.

Rouch, J. (1953) 'Contribution à l'histoire des Songhay', in G. Boyer, *Un Peuple de l'ouest soudanais: les Diawara* (Dakar: IFAN; Mémoires, 29). pp. 141–261.

Rouch, J. (1954) *Les Songhay* (Paris: PUF).

Rouch, J. (1960) *La religion et la magie des Songhay* (Paris: PUF).

Rudner, J. (1968) 'Strandloper pottery from South and South-West Africa', *ASAM*, **49**, 2, pp. 441–663.

Rudner, J. and Rudner, I. (1970) *The hunter and his art: a survey of rock art in southern Africa* (Cape Town: Struik).

Rwandusya, Z. (1972 and 1977) 'The origin and settlement of people in Bufimbira', in D. Denoon (ed.), *A history of Kigezi in South-West Uganda* (Kampala: National Trust, Adult Education Centre).

***Sa'ad, E.** (1979) paper in *KS*, **1**, 4, pp. 52–66.

al-Sa'dī 'Abd al-Raḥmān b. 'Abd Allāh (1656) *Ta'rīkh al-Sūdān*; 1898 ed. O. Houdas and E. Benoist, with 1900 French transl. O. Houdas, 2 vols (Paris: Leroux); 1964 rev. transl. (Paris: Maisonneuve et Larose).

Saidi, A. (1963) 'Contribution à l'histoire almohade: une première expérience d'unité maghrébine' (doctoral dissertation, University of Lyon).

al-Sakhāwī, Muḥammad b. 'Abd al-Raḥmān (15th cent.) *Kitāb al-tibr al-masbuk*; 1897 edn (Cairo).

al-Salāwī, Shihāb al-Dīn ... b. Ḥammād al-Nāṣirī (1894) *Kitāb al-Istikṣā li-Akhbār Duwal al-Maghrib al-akṣā*, 4 vols (Cairo); 1906–7 ed. and partial transl. E. Fumey (Paris: Leroux; Archives marocaines 9–10); 1923–5 ed. and French transl., 4 vols (Paris: Geuthner); 1954–6 ed. and French transl. *Histoire du Maroc*, 9 vols (Casablanca).

Salifou, A. (1971) *Le Damagaram, ou sultanat de Zinder au 19e siècle* (Niamey: Etudes nigériennes, 27, Centre nigérien de recherches en sciences humaines).

Salmon, M. G. (1904) 'Essai sur l'histoire politique du nord marocain', *AM*, **2**, pp. 1–99.

Sanneh, L. (1976) 'The origin of clericalism in West African Islam', *JAH*, **17**, 1, pp. 49–72.

Sarton, G. (1927–48) *Introduction to the history of science*, 3 vols (Baltimore: Carnegie Institute).

Sayous, A. E. (1929) *Le commerce des Européens à Tunis, depuis le 12e siècle jusqu'à la fin du 16e siècle* (Paris: Société d'éditions géographiques, maritimes et coloniales).

Schatzmiller, W. (1977) 'Etude d'historiographie mérinide: La Nafha al-nisriniyya et la Hawdat al-nisrin d'Ibn al-Ahmar', *Arabica*, **24**, 3, pp. 258–68.

Schaube, A. (1906) *Handelsgeschichte der romanischen Völker des Mittelmeergebiets bis zum Ende der Kreuzzüge* (Berlin: Oldenbourg).

Schefer, C. (ed.) (1892) *Le voyage d'outre-mer de Bertrandon de la Brocquière* (Paris: Leroux).

Schlüter, H. (1972) *Index libycus: bibliography of Libya, 1958–1969, with supplementary material 1915–1956* (Boston: Hall).

Schlüter, H. (1979) *Index libycus, bibliography of Libya 1970–1975, with supplementary material* (Boston: Hall).

Schofield, J. F. (1948) *Primitive pottery; an introduction to South African ceramics, prehistoric and protohistoric* (Cape Town: South African Archaeological Society, handbook series, 3).

Schoonraad, M. (ed.) (1971) *Rock paintings of South Africa* (South African Journal of Science, supplement 2).

Schwarz, E. H. L. (1938) 'The Chinese connections with Africa', *JRASB*, **5**, pp. 175–93.

Schweeger-Hefel, A.-M. and Staude, W. (1972) *Die Kurumba von Lurum: Monographie eines Volkes aus Obervolta (West-Afrika)* (Vienna: Schendl).

Scully, R. T. K. (1978a) 'Phalaborwa oral tradition' (doctoral dissertation, State University of New York, Binghamton).

Scully, R. T. K. (1978b) 'Report on South Africa', *NAk*, **13**, pp. 24–5.

Sergew Hable Selassie (1972) *Ancient and medieval Ethiopian history to 1270* (Addis Ababa: United Printers).

Serjeant, R. B. (1963) *The Portuguese off the South Arabian coast: Hadramī chronicles with Yemeni and European accounts of Dutch pirates off Mocha in the seventeenth century* (Oxford: Clarendon Press).

Serra Rafols, E. (n.d.) 'Los Mallorquinas en Canarias', *RHC*, **7**, 54, pp. 195–209.

Shaw, T. (1970) *Igbo-Ukwu: an account of archaeological discoveries in eastern Nigeria*, 2 vols (London: Faber and Faber for the Institute of African Studies, Ibadan).
Shaw, T. (1973) 'A note on trade and the Tsoede bronzes', *WAJA*, **3**, pp. 233–8.
Shaw, W. B. K. (1936) 'The ruins at Abu Sufyan', *SNR*, **19**, pp. 324–26.
Shinnie, P. L. (1965) 'New light on medieval Nubia', *JAH*, **6**, 3, pp. 263–73.
Shinnie, P. L. (ed.) (1971a) *The African Iron Age* (Oxford: Clarendon Press).
Shinnie, P. L. (1971b) 'The culture of medieval Nubia and its impact on Africa', in Y. F. Hasan (ed.), *Sudan in Africa* (Khartoum: Khartoum University Press), pp. 42–50.
Shinnie, P. L. and Chittick, H. N. (1961) *Ghazali: a monastery in the northern Sudan* (Khartoum: Sudan Antiquities Service, Occasional Papers, 5).
Shorter, A. (1968) 'The Kimbu', in A. Roberts (ed), *Tanzania before 1900* (Nairobi: EAPH), pp. 96–116.
Siré-Abbâs–Soh (1913) *Chroniques du Foûta sénégalais*, ed. M. Delafosse and H. Gaden (Paris: Leroux; Collection de la Revue du Monde Musulman).
Skinner, D. E. (1978) 'Mande settlement and the development of Islamic institutions in Sierra Leone', *IJAHS*, **11**, pp. 32–62.
Skinner, E. P. (1957) 'An analysis of the political organization of the Mosi people', *TNYAS*, **19**, 8, pp. 740–50.
Skinner, E. P. (1958) 'The Mosi and the traditional Sudanese history', *JNH*, **43**, 2, pp. 121–31.
Skinner, E. P. (1962) 'Trade and markets among the Mosi people', in P. Bohannan and G. Dalton (eds.); *Markets in Africa* (Evanston: Northwestern University Press), pp. 237–78.
Skinner, N. (1968) 'The origin of the name Hausa', *Africa*–(L), **38**, 3, pp. 253–7.
Slaoui (Slāwī): see al-Salāwī
Smith, H. F. C. (Abdullahi) (1961) 'A further adventure in the chronology of Katsina', *BHSN*, **6**, 1, pp. 5–7.
Smith, H. F. C. (Abdullahi) (1970a) 'Some considerations relating to the formation of states in Hausaland', *JHSN*, **5**, 3, pp. 329–46.
Smith, H. F. C. (Abdullahi) (1970b) 'Some notes on the history of Zazzau under the Hausa kings', in M. J. Mortimore (ed.), *Zaria and its region, a Nigerian savanna city and its environs* (Zaria: Ahmadu Bello University, Department of Geography, occasional paper 4), pp. 82–101.
Smith, H. F. C. (Abdullahi) (1971) 'The early states of central Sudan', in J. F. A. Ajayi and M. Crowder (eds), *History of West Africa* (London: Longman), Vol. 1, pp. 158–201.
Smith, H. F. C. (Abdullahi) (1979) 'The contemporary significance of the academic ideals of the Sokoto Jihad', in Y. B. Usman (ed.) (1979a), q.v., pp. 242–60.
Smith, M. G. (1959) 'The Hausa system of social status', *Africa*–(L) **29**, 3, pp. 239–52.
Smith, M. G. (1960) *Government in Zazzau, 1800–1950* (London: OUP for IAI).
Smith, M. G. (1964a) 'The beginnings of Hausa society', in *The Historian in Tropical Africa* (London: OUP for IAI), pp. 348 ff.
Smith, M. G. (1964b) 'Historical and cultural conditions of political corruption among the Hausa', *CSSH*, **6**, 2, pp. 164–94.
Snellow, I. (1964) 'Die Stellung der Slaven in der Hausa-Gesellschaft', *MIO*, **10**, 1, pp. 85–102.
Soh, S. A.: see Siré-Abbâs-Soh
Southall, A. W. (1954) 'Alur tradition and its historical significance', *UJ*, **18**, pp. 137–65.
Stanley of Alderley Lord: see Alvares, F. (1881)
Staude, W. (1961) 'La légende royale de Kouroumba', *JSA*, **31**, 2. pp. 209–59.
Steenberghen, F. van (1946) *Aristote en Occident* ... (Louvain: Institut supérieur de philosophie).
Steiger, A. (1941): see Alfonso X, el Sabio
Stewart, J. M. (1966) 'Akan history: some linguistic evidence', *GNQ*, **9**, pp. 54–7.
Storbeck, F. (1914) *Die Berichte der arabischen Geographen des Mittelalters über Östafrika* (Berlin, Humboldt University, Mitteilungen des Seminars für orientalische Sprachen, **18**, 2).
Stow, G. W. (1905) *The native races of South Africa: a history of the intrusion of the Hottentots and Bantu* (London: Sonnenschein; New York: Macmillan).
Strandes, J. (1899) *Die Portugiesenzeit von Deutsch- und Englisch Östafrika* (Berlin: Reimer); 1961 Eng. transl. J. F. Wallwork, *The Portuguese period in East Africa* (Nairobi: East African Literature Bureau).
Strong, S. A. (1895) 'History of Kilwa, from an Arabic manuscript', *JRAS*, **14**, pp. 385–430.
Sulzmann, E. (1959) 'Die Bokope Herrschaft der Bolia', *ARSP*, **15**, 3, pp. 389–417.
Summers, R. (1960) 'Environment and culture in Southern Rhodesia', *PAPS*. **104**, 3, pp. 266–92.
Summers, R. (1963) *Zimbabwe, a Rhodesian mystery* (Johannesburg/New York: Nelson).
Summers, R. (1969) 'Ancient mining in Rhodesia', *MNMMR*, **3**.
Suter, H. (1900) *Die Mathematiker und Astronomen der Araber und ihre Werke* (Leipzig: Teubner).
Sutton, J. E. G. (1972) 'New radiocarbon dates for Eastern and Southern Africa', *JAH*, **13**, 1, pp. 1–24.

Sutton, J. E. G. (1976, 1977) 'Iron working around Zaria', *Zaria Archaeological papers*, no 8, and 'Addendum to No 8' (Zaria).
Sutton, J. E. G. (1979) 'Towards a less orthodox history of Hausaland', *JAH*, **20**, 2, pp. 179–201.
Sutton, J. E. G. and Roberts, A. D. (1968) 'Uvinza and its salt industry', *Azania*, 3, pp. 45–86.
Sykes, J. (1959) 'The eclippe at Buharwe', *UJ*, **23**, 1, pp. 44–50.
Sylla, Djiri (1975) Paper presented at *Premier Colloque international de Bamako* (Paris: Fondation SCOA pour la recherche scientifique en Afrique noire).
Szolc, P. (1977) 'Die Konsequenzen der Islamisierung in Kordofan: Bemerkungen und Beobachtungen zum religiösen Wandel', *Am*, **10**, 1, pp. 51–67.

Talbi, M. (1954) 'Quelques données sur la vie en Occident musulman d'après un traité de *hisba* du 15e siècle', *Arabica*, **1**, 3, pp. 294–306.
Talbi, M. (1966) *L'Emirat aghlabide 184/296–800/909* (Paris: Maisonneuve).
Talbi, M. (1973) 'Ibn Khaldun et l'histoire', in *Actas del secundo coloquio hispanico-tunecino de estudios historicos* (Madrid: Instituto hispanico-arabe de cultura), pp. 63–90.
Tamakloe, E. F. (1931) *A brief history of the Dagbamba people* (Accra: Government Printer).
Tamrat, T. (1972a) *Church and state in Ethiopia: 1270–1527* (Oxford: Clarendon Press).
Tamrat, T. (1972b) 'A short note on the traditions of pagan resistance to the Ethiopian church, fourteenth and fifteenth centuries', *JES*, **10**, 1, pp. 137–50.
Tamrat, T. (1974) 'Problems of royal succession in fifteenth century Ethiopia', in *Quarto congresso internazionale di studi etiopici* (Rome: Accademia nazionale dei Lincei), pp. 526–33.
Tanghe, B. (1929) *De Ngbandi: geschiedkundige bijdragen* (Bruges: Walleyn).
Ta'rīkh al-fattāsh: see Ka'ti, Maḥmūd
Ta'rīkh al-Sūdān: see al-Sa'dī
Tauxier, L. (1917) *Le noir du Yatenga; Mossis, Nioniossés, Samos, Yarsés, Silmi-Mossis, Peuls* (Paris: Larose).
Tauxier, L. (1921) *Le noir de Bondoukou; Bondoukous, Koulangos-Dyoulas, Abrons* (Paris: Larose).
Tauxier, L. (1924) *Nouvelles notes sur le Mossi et le Gourounsi* (Paris: Larose).
Tauxier, L. (1932) *Religion, moeurs et coutumes des Agnis de la Côte-d'Ivoire* (*Indenie et Sanwi*) (Paris: Geuthner).
Taylor, B. K. (1962) *The western lacustrine Bantu* (London: OUP for IAI; Ethnographic survey of Africa, East Central Africa, pt. 13).
Teixeira da Mota, A. (1950) *Topónimos de origem portuguêsa na costa ocidental de Africa desde o Cabo Bojador ao Cabo de Santa Caterina* (Bissau: Publicações do centro de estudos da Guiné portuguêsa, 14).
Teixeira da Mota, A. (1954) *Guiné portuguêsa*, 2 vols (Lisbon: Agência geral do Ultramar).
Teixeira da Mota, A. (1958) 'L'Art de naviguer en Méditerranée du 14e au 16e siècle et la navigation astronomique dans les océans', in *Le Navire et l'économie maritime du Moyen Age au 18e siècle, principalement en Méditerranée: Travaux du 2e colloque international d'histoire maritime, Paris, 1957* (Paris, SEVPEN), pp. 127–54.
Teixeira da Mota, A. (1963) *Méthodes de navigation et cartographie nautique dans l'Océan Indien avant le 16e siècle* (Lisbon: Junta de Investigações do Ultramar; Agrupamento de estudos de cartografia antiga, secção de Lisboa, serie separata, 5).
Teixeira da Mota, A. (1969) 'Un document nouveau pour l'histoire des Peul au Sénégal pendant les 15e et 16e siècles', *BCGP*, 96, pp. 781–860.
Teixeira da Mota, A. (1970) *Fulas e Beafadas no Rio Grande no seculo XV: achegas para a ethno-historia da Africa ocidental* (Coimbra: Junta de investigações do Ultramar; Agrupamento de estudos de cartografia antiga, serie separata, 60).
Teixeira da Mota, A. (1978) *Some aspects of Portuguese colonisation and sea trade in West Africa in the fifteenth and sixteenth centuries* (Bloomington: Indiana University African Studies Program).
Teixeira da Mota, A. (1981) 'Entrees d'esclaves noirs à Valence (1445–1482): le remplacement de la voie saharienne par la voie atlantique', in *Le Sol, la parole et l'écrit: 2,000 ans d'histoire africaine: mélanges en hommage à Raymond Mauny*, 2 vols (Paris: Société française d'histoire d'outre-mer), pp. 579–94.
Les Tellem et les Dogon Mali (1973) (Catalogue de l'exposition du 9 Juin au 23 Août 1973, Galerie Numaga).
Temple, O. S. M. (1922) *Notes on the tribes, provinces, emirates and states of the northern provinces of Nigeria*, (Lagos: CMS Bookshop; Exeter: J. Townsend); 1967 reprint (London: Cass).
Terrasse, H. (1949–50) *Histoire du Maroc des origines à l'établissment du protectorat français*, 2 vols (Casablanca: Atlantides).
Terrasse, H. (1958) *Islam d'Espagne; une rencontre de l'Orient et de l'Occident* (Paris: Plon).

Thoden, R. (1973) *Abū 'l-Hasan 'Alī: Merinidenpolitik zwischen Nordafrika und Spanien in den Jahren 710–752, 1310–1351* (Freiburg: Schwarz; Islamische Untersuchungen, 21).
Thompson, L. (ed.) (1969) *African societies in southern Africa: historical studies* (London: Heinemann; New York: Praeger).
Thurstan Shaw: see Shaw, T.
Tibbetts, G. R. (1961) 'Arab navigation in the Red Sea', *GJ*, **127**, 3, pp. 322–34.
Tibbetts, G. R. (1969) *The navigational theory of the Arabs in the fifteenth and sixteenth centuries* (Coimbra: Junta de Investigaçoẽs do Ultramar; Agrupamento de estudos de cartografia antigua, serie separata, 36).
Tibbetts, G. R. (ed.) (1971) *Arab navigation in the Indian Ocean before the coming of the Portuguese* (London: RASGBI; Oriental translation fund, n.s. 42).
al-Tīdjānī (14th cent.) *Riḥla*; partial French transl. A. Rousseau, 'Voyage du Scheikh el-Tidjani dans la régence de Tunis, pendant les années 706, 707 et 708 de l'hégire (1306–1307),' *JA*, serie **4**, pp. 57–208; série **5**, 1, pp. 102–68, 354–424.
Tiendrebeogo, Y. (1964) *Histoire et coutumes royales des Mossi de Ouagadougou* (Ouagadougou: Naba).
Tolmacheva, M. A. (1969) 'Vostochnoe poberezh'e Afriki v arabskoi geograficheskoi literature', in *Strany i narody Vostoka* (Moscow: Nauka; Strany i narody Afriki. Akademiia nauk SSSR. Vostochnaia komissiia geograficheskogo obshchsteva SSSR, 9), pp. 268–96.
Tonnoir, R. (1970) *Giribuma: contribution à l'histoire et à la petite histoire du Congo équatorial* (Tervuren: Musée royal de l'Afrique centrale; Archives d'ethnographie, 14).
Toussaint, A. (1961) *Histoire de l'Océan indien* (Paris: PUF; Peuples et civilisations d'outre-mer, 4).
Toussaint, A. (1972) *Histoire des îles mascareignes* (Paris: Berger-Levrault).
Tremearne, A. J. N. (1913) *Hausa superstitions and customs: an introduction to the folklore and the folk* (London: Bale and Daniels).
Triaud, J. L. (1973) *Islam et sociétés soudanaises au Moyen Age: étude historique* (Paris: Collège de France; Recherches voltaïques, 16).
Trimingham, J. S. (1949) *Islam in the Sudan* (London: OUP).
Trimingham, J. S. (1962) *A history of Islam in West Africa* (London: OUP).
Trimingham, J. S. (1964) *Islam in East Africa* (Oxford: Clarendon Press).
Tubiana, M. J. (1964) *Survivances préislamiques en pays zaghawa* (Paris: Institut d'ethnologie; Travaux et mémoires, 67).
Turaiev, B. (ed.) (1906) *Vitae sanctorum Indigenarum: l: Acta S. Eustathii* (Corpus scriptorum christianorum orientalium, 32: Scriptores aethiopici, 15, Paris).

al-'Umarī, Ibn Faḍl Allāh (14th cent.) *al-Ta'rif bi 'l-muṣṭalaḥ al-sharīf*; 1894 edn (Cairo).
al-'Umarī, Ibn Faḍl Allāh (14th cent.) *Masālik al-abṣār fī Mamālik al-amṣar*; 1924 edn (Cairo); 1927 transl., Gaudefroy-Demombynes, *L'Afrique moins l'Egypte* (Paris: Geuthner; Bibliothèque des géographes arabes, 2).
al-'Umarī, Ibn Faḍl Allāh (14th cent.), 1975 French transl. in J. M. Cuoq (q.v.), pp. 254–89.
Unesco (1980a) *Historical relations across the Indian Ocean: proceedings of the meeting of experts, 1974* (Paris: Unesco; International Scientific Committee for the Drafting of a General History of Africa, 3).
Unesco (1980b) *The Historiography of Southern Africa: proceedings of the meeting of experts, 1977* (Paris: Unesco; International Scientific Committee for the Drafting of a General History of Africa, 4).
Urvoy, Y. (1949) *Histoire de l'empire de Bornou* (Dakar: IFAN; Mémoires, 7; Paris: Larose); 1968 edn (Amsterdam: Swets and Zeitlinger).
Usman, Y. B. (1972) 'Some aspects of the external relations of Katsina before 1804', *Savanna*, 1, 2, pp. 175–97.
Usman, Y. B. (ed.) (1979a) *Studies in the history of the Sokoto caliphate: the Sokoto seminar papers* (Zaria: Ahmadu Bello University, Department of History for the Sokoto Caliphate Bureau).
Usman, Y. B. (1979b) 'The transformation of political communities: some notes on a significant dimension of the Sokoto Jihad', in Y. B. Usman (ed.) (1979a), q.v., pp. 34–58.

Valette, J. (ed.) (1964) *Madagascar vers 1750 d'après un manuscrit anonyme* (Tananarive: Imp. nationale).
Van Der Merwe, N. J. and Scully, R. T. K. (1971–2) 'The Phalaborwa story: archaeological and ethnographic investigation of a South African Iron Age group', *WA*, **3**, 3, pp. 178–96.
Van Sertima, I. (1976) *They came before Columbus* (New York: Random Press).
Vansina, J. (1960) *L'évolution du royaume Rwanda des origines à 1900* (Brussels: Mémoires de l'Académie des sciences d'outre-mer, classe des sciences morales et politiques, n.s. **26**, 2).
Vansina, J. (1966a) *Introduction à l'ethnographie du Congo* (Kinshasa: University Lovanium; Brussels: Centre de recherches et d'information socio-politiques).

Vansina, J. (1966b) *Kingdoms of the savanna* (Madison: University of Wisconsin Press).
Vansina, J. (1966c) 'More on the invasions of Kongo and Angola by the Jaga and the Lunda', *JAH*, 7, 3, pp. 421–9.
Vansina, J. (1969) 'The bells of kings', *JAH*, **10**, 2, pp. 187–97.
Vansina, J. (1971) 'Inner Africa', in A. A. Boahen, *et al.* (eds), *The horizon history of Africa* (New York: Heritage Printing), pp. 260–303.
Vansina, J. (1973) *The Tio kingdom of the Middle Congo, 1880–1892* (Oxford: OUP for the International African Institute).
Vansina, J. (1974) 'Probing the past of the lower Kwilu peoples (Zaire)', *Paideuma*, **19**, pp. 332–64.
Vansina, J. (1978) *The children of Woot: a history of the Kuba peoples* (Madison: University of Wisconsin Press).
Vedder, H. (1938) Eng. transl. (from German), *South-West Africa in early times: being the story of South-West Africa up to the date of Maharero's death in 1890* (London); 1966 reprint (New York: Barnes and Noble).
Velgus, V. (1969) 'Issledovanie nekotorykh spornykh voprosov istorii morekhodstva v Indiiskom okeane: Etudes de quelques points controversés dans l'histoire de la navigation dans l'Océan indien', in *Africana. Etnografiia, istoriia, lingvistika* (Leningrad: Akademiia nauk SSSR. Trudy Instituta etnograffii im. N. N. Miklukho-Maklaia, n.s., **93**, Afrikanskii etnografskii sbornik, 7), pp. 127–76.
Verhulpen, E. (1936) *Baluba et balubaises du Katanga* (Anvers: Edition de l'avenir belge).
Vérin, P. (1967a) 'Les antiquités de l'île d'Anjouan', *BAM*, **45**, 1, pp. 69–80.
Vérin, P. (ed.) (1967b) *Arabes et islamisés à Madagascar et dans l'Océan indien* (Tananarive: Revue de Madagascar).
Vérin, P. (1972) *Histoire du nord-ouest de Madagascar*, *Taloha*, **5**, (numéro special).
Vérin, P. (1975) *Les échelles anciennes du commerce sur les côtes de Madagascar*, 2 vols (Lille: University of Lille).
Vérin, P. (1980) 'Cultural influences and the contribution of Africa to the settlement of Madagascar', in Unesco (1980a) q.v., pp. 95–116.
Vérin, P., Kottack, C. P. and Gorlin, P. (1966) 'The glotto-chronology of Malagasy speech communities', *OL*, **8**, pp. 26–83.
Verlinden, C. (1955a) *L'Esclavage dans l'Europe médiévale*, Vol. 1, *Péninsule ibérique, France* (Bruges: de Tempel).
Verlinden, C. (1955b) 'Navigations, marchands et colons italiens au service de la découverte et de la colonisation portugaise sous Henri le Navigateur', *MA*, **44**, 4, pp. 467–98.
Verlinden, C. (1961) 'Les Découvertes portugaises et la collaboration italienne d'Alphonse IV à Alphonse V', in *Actas do congresso internacional de historia dos descobrimentos*, 6 vols (Lisbon), Vol. 3, pp. 593–610.
Verlinden, C. (1962) 'La Crête, débouché et plaque tournante de la traite des esclaves aux 14e et 15e siècles', in *Studi in onore di Amintore Fanfani*, (Milan: Giuffrè).
Verlinden, C. (1966a) 'Esclavage noir en France méridionale et courants de traite en Afrique', *Annales du Midi*, **128**, pp. 335–443.
Verlinden, C. (1966b) 'Les Gênois dans la marine portugaise avant 1385', *SHG*, **41**.
Verlinden, C. (1967) 'Les Débuts de la traite portugaise en Afrique: 1433–1448', in *Miscellanea medievalia in memoriam Jan Frederick Niermeyer* (Groningen: Wolters), pp. 365–77.
Verlinden, C. (1977) *L'Esclavage dans l'Europe médiévale*, Vol. 2, *Italie, colonie italienne du Levant, Levant latin, empire byzantin* (Bruges: de Tempel).
Verly, R. (1977) 'Le Roi divin chez les Ovimbundu et les Kimbudu de l'Angola', *Zaire*, **9**, 7, pp. 675–703.
Vernet, J. (1958) 'La Carta magrebina', *BRAH*, **142**, 2, pp. 495–533.
Vernier, E. and Millot, J. (1971) *Archéologie malgache: comptoirs musulmans* (Paris: Musée national d'histoire naturelle, catalogue du Musée de l'homme, série F, Madagascar, 1).
Viagem de Lisboa à ilha de S. Tomé, escrita por um piloto português (1940), transl. S. F. de Mendo Trigoso (Biblioteca das grandes viagens, 2, Lisbon: Portugalia Editora).
Vianes, S. and Deschamps. H. J. (1959) *Les Malgaches du Sud-Est: Antemoro, Antesaka, Antambahoaka, peuples de Faragangana* (Paris: PUF).
Vidal, J. (1924) 'La Légende officielle de Soundiata, fondateur de l'empire mandingue', *BCEHSAOF*, **2**, pp. 317–28.
Vidal, P. (1969) *La civilisation mégalithique de Bouar: prospection et fouilles 1962–1966* (Paris: Firmin Didot, Recherches oubanguiennes, 1).
Vidal, P. and David, N. (1977) 'La civilisation mégalithique de Bouar', *NAk*, **2**, pp. 3–4.
Vilar, P. (1974) *Or et monnaie dans l'histoire, 1450–1920* (Paris: Flammarion).

Vinnicombe, P. (1976) *People of the eland: rock paintings of the Drakensberg Bushmen as a reflection of their life and thought* (Natal: University of Natal Press).
Vogel, J. O. (1971) *Kamangoza: an introduction to the Iron Age cultures of the Victoria Falls region* (London/New York: OUP for the National Museum of Zambia, Zambia Museum papers, 2).
Vogt, J. L. (1973) 'The Lisbon slaves house and African trade: 1486–1521', *PAPS*, **107**, 1, pp. 1–16.
Voll, J. O. (1978) *Historical dictionary of the Sudan* (Metuchen: Scarecrow Press; African Historical Dictionary 17).

Wannyn, R. L. (1961) *L'Art ancien du métal au Bas-Congo* (Champles: Editions du Vieux Planquesaule).
Wansbrough, J. (1968) 'The decolonization of North African history', *JAH*, **9**, 4, pp. 643–50.
al-Wansharīsī, Aḥmad ibn Yaḥyā (15th cent.) *Kitāb al-mi'yār*; 1896–8 edn (12 vols) Fez; 1908–9, French transl. E. Amar, *La Pierre de touche des fetwas* (*Kitāb al-mi'yār*) (Paris: Leroux; Archives marocaines, 12–13).
Watson, A. M. (1967) 'Back to gold and silver', *ECHR*, **20**, pp. 1–67.
Watt, W. M. (1972) *The influence of Islam on medieval Europe* (Edinburgh: Edinburgh University Press; Islamic survey, 9).
Wauters, G. (1949) *L'Esotérie des noirs dévoilée* (Brussels: Editions européennes).
al-Wazīr, al-Andalusī: see Abū 'Abd Allah Muḥammad al-Wazīr al-Andalusī
Webster, J. B. (1978) *A history of Uganda before 1900* (Nairobi).
Werner, A. (1914–15) 'A Swahili history of Pate', *JAS*, **14**, pp. 148–61, 278–97, 392–413.
Westermann, D. (1952) *Geschichte Afrikas: Staatenbildungen südlich der Sahara* (Köln: Greven Verlag).
Westermann, D. (1957): see Baumann, H.
Westermann, D. and Bryan, M. A. (1970) *Languages of West Africa* (Folkestone: Dawsons; Handbook of African languages, pt 2).
Westphal, E. O. (1963) 'The linguistic prehistory of Southern Africa: Bush, Kwadi, Hottentot and Bantu linguistic relationships', *Africa*–(L), **33**, pp. 237–65.
Weydert, J. (1938) *Les Balubas chez eux: étude ethnographique* (Luxembourg: Heffingen).
Wheatley, P. (1954) '*The land of Zanj: exegetical notes on Chinese knowledge of East Africa prior to* AD 1500', in R. W. Steel (ed.) *Geographers and the tropics: Liverpool essays* (London: Longman), pp. 139–88.
Wheatley, P. (1959) 'Geographical notes on some commodities involved in maritime trade', *JMBRAS*, **32**, pp. 111–12.
Wheeler, A. (1971) 'Kitagwenda: a Babito kingdom in southern Toro' (Kampala: Makerere Seminar Paper, 4).
Wiener, L. (1920–2) *Africa and the discovery of America*, 3 vols (Philadelphia: Innes).
Wiet, G. (1937) 'L'Egypte arabe, de la conquête arabe à la conquête ottomane, 647–1517 de l'ère chrétienne', in G. Hanotaux (ed.), *Histoire de la nation égyptienne* (Paris: Société de l'histoire nationale), Vol. 4.
Wiet, G. (1951–2) 'Les roitelets de Dhalak', *BIE*, **34**, pp. 89–95.
Willcox, A. R. (1971) 'Domestic cattle in Africa and a rock art mystery', in *Rock paintings of southern Africa* (*SAJS*, special issue, 2), pp. 44–8.
Willcox, A. R. (1975) 'Pre-Colombian intercourse between the old world and the new: consideration from Africa', *SAAB*, **30**, pp. 19–28.
Willett, F. (1962) 'The introduction of maize into West Africa; an assessment of recent evidence', *Africa*–(L), **32**, 1, pp. 1–13.
Willett, F. (1967) *Ife in the history of West African sculpture* (London: Thames and Hudson; New York: McGraw-Hill).
Wilson, A. (1972) 'Long distance trade and the Luba Lomani empire', *JAH*, **13**, 4, pp. 575–89.
Wilson, M. (1959a) *Communal rituals of the Nyakyusa* (London: OUP for IAI).
Wilson, M. (1959b) 'The early history of the Transkei and Ciskei', *AS*, **18**, 4, pp. 167–79.
Wilson, M. (1969a) 'Changes in social structure in Southern Africa: the relevance of kinship studies to the historian', in L. Thompson (ed.), *African societies in southern Africa* (London: Heinemann), pp. 71–85.
Wilson, M. (1969b) 'The Nguni People', in M. Wilson and L. Thompson (eds), 1969, 1971 (q.v.), Vol. 1.
Wilson, M. (1969c) 'The Sotho, Venda and Tsonga' in M. Wilson and L. Thompson (eds), 1969, 1971 (q.v.), Vol. 1, pp. 131–86.
Wilson, M. and Thompson, L. (eds) (1969, 1971) *The Oxford history of South Africa*, 2 vols (Oxford: Clarendon Press).
Withers-Gill, J. (1924) 'The Moshi tribes: a short history' (Accra: Legon University).

Witte, C. M. de (1956) 'Une ambassade éthiopienne à Rome en 1450', *OCP*, **22**, 3–4, pp. 286–98.
Wolde-Mariam, N. (1970) *An Atlas of Africa*, Addis Ababa.
Wondji, C. (1974) 'Conclusion', in *Bonduku Seminar Papers* (q.v.)
Wright, T. (1977) 'Observation sur l'évolution de la céramique en Imérina centrale', in *Colloque de l'Académie malgache.*
Wright, T. and Kus, S. (1977) 'Archéologie régionale et organisation sociale ancienne de l'Imérina central', in *Colloque de 'l'Académie malgache.*
Wright, W. (ed.) (1877) *Catalogue of the Ethiopic manuscripts in the British Museum acquired since the year 1847* (London: British Museum Department of Oriental Printed Books and Manuscripts).
Wrigley, C. (1958) 'Some thoughts on the Bachwezi', *UJ*, **22**, 1, pp. 11–21.
Wrigley, c. (1959) 'Kimera', *UJ*, **33**, 1, pp. 38–43.
Wrigley, C. (1973) 'The story of Rukidi', *Africa*–(L), **43**, 3, pp. 219–31.
Wrigley, C. (1974) 'Myths of the savanna', *JAH*, **15**, 1, pp. 131–5.
Wylie, K. C. (1977) *The political kingdoms of the Temne: Temne government in Sierra Leone, 1825–1910* (London/New York: Africana Publications).

Yaḥyā b. Abi Bakr, Abū Zakariyyā' (1878) *Chronique d'Abou Zakaria*, transl. E. Masqueray (Algiers: Allaud).
al-Ya'ḳūbī Aḥmad b. Abī Ya'ḳūb (9th cent.) *Kitāb al-Buldān*; 1870–94 ed. M. J. de Goeje, in *Bibliotheca geographorum Arabicorum* (Leiden: E. J. Brill); 1937 ed. and transl. G. Wiet, *Les Pays* (Cairo: Publications de l'Institut français d'archéologie orientale: textes et traductions d'auteurs orientaux, 1).
Yāḳūt b. 'Abd Allāh al-Ḥamawī (13th cent.) *Mu'djam al-Buldān*; 1866–73 ed. J. F. Wüstenfeld, *Jacut's geographisches Wörterbuch*, 6 vols (Leipzig: Brockhaus), **5**, pp. 75–6, 302–699.
Yoder, J. C. (1977) 'A people on the edge of empires: a history of the Kanyok of central Zaïre' (doctoral dissertation, Northwestern University).
Young, M. W. (1966) 'The divine kingship of the Jukun: a re-evaluation of some theories', *Africa*–(L), **36**, 2, pp. 135–53.
Yūsuf Kamāl (1926–51) *Monumenta cartographica Africae et Aegypti*, 5 vols (Cairo).
Yver, G. (1903) *Le commerce et les marchands dans l'Italie méridionale au 13e et au 14e siècle* (Paris: Fontemoing).

Zahan, D. (1961) 'Pour une histoire des Mossi du Yatenga', *L'Homme*, **1**, 2, pp. 5–22.
Zanzibar and the East African coast: Arabs, Shirazi and Swahili (London: IAI; Ethnographic survey of Africa, East Central Africa, pt 12).
al-Zarkashī, Muḥammad b. Ibrāhīm (1872) *Ta'rīkh al-dawlatayn* (Tunis); 1895 French transl. E. Fagnan, *Chronique des Almohades et des Hafçides* (Constantine: Braham).
Zeltner, J. C. (1970) 'Histoire des Arabes sur les rives du lac Tchad', *AUA*, F, **3**, 2, pp. 109–237.
Zouber, M. (1977) *Ahmad Baba de Tombouctou, 1556–1627: sa vie, son oeuvre* (Paris: Maisonneuve et Larose; Publications du département d'islamologie de l'Université de Paris-Sorbonne, 3).
Zunon Gnobo, J. (1976) 'Le rôle des femmes dans le commerce pré-colonial à Daloa', *Gogo-Godo*, **2**, pp. 79–105.
Zurara, G. E. de (1896, 1899) *Cronica dos feitos de Guiné*; *The chronicle of the discovery and conquest of Guinea*, ed. and Eng. transl. C. R. Beazley and E. Prestage, 2 vols (London: Hakluyt Society); 1949 edn. *Cronica dos feitos de Guiné* (Lisbon: Divisao de publicações et biblioteca, agencia geral das colonias); 1960 French transl. L. Bourdon, *Gomes Eanes de Zuraga, Chronique de Guinée* (Dakar: IFAN; Mémoires, 1).